Web Services & SOA

Visit the *Web Services & SOA: Principles and Technology*, Second Edition, Companion Website at **www.pearsoned.co.uk/papazoglou** to find:

- Links to useful sites on the web

Web Services & SOA: Principles and Technology

Second Edition

Michael P. Papazoglou

European Research Institute in Service Science, Tilburg University, The Netherlands

Harlow, England • London • New York • Boston • San Francisco • Toronto • Sydney • Auckland • Singapore • Hong Kong
Tokyo • Seoul • Taipei • New Delhi • Cape Town • São Paulo • Mexico City • Madrid • Amsterdam • Munich • Paris • Milan

Pearson Education Limited
Edinburgh Gate
Harlow
Essex CM20 2JE
England

and Associated Companies throughout the world

Visit us on the World Wide Web at:
www.pearson.com/uk

First published 2008
Second edition published 2012

ISBN 978-0-273-73216-7

British Library Cataloguing-in-Publication Data
A catalogue record for this book is available from the British Library

Library of Congress Cataloging-in-Publication Data
A catalog record for this book is available from the Library of Congress

ARP Impression 98

Typeset in 10/12 Times by 71
Printed in Great Britain by Ashford Colour Press Ltd

This book is dedicated to Marion without whose support, continuous encouragement and infinite patience this book would have been impossible.

Brief Contents

Contents

Part II Enabling infrastructure 57

Chapter 2: Distributed computing infrastructure 59

Chapter 3: Brief overview of XML 93

Chapter 12: Service policies 501

Part VII Service semantics and business protocols 535

Chapter 13: Semantics and Web services 537

Supporting resources

Visit **www.pearsoned.co.uk/papazoglou** to find valuable online resources

Companion Website for students

- Links to useful sites on the web

For instructors

- Complete, downloadable Solutions Manual
- PowerPoint slides that can be downloaded and used for presentations

For more information please contact your local Pearson Education sales representative or visit **www.pearsoned.co.uk/papazoglou**.

Preface

Web services have emerged as the next generation of Web based technology for exchanging information over the Internet and, as part of the service oriented computing paradigm, promise to revolutionise the process of developing and deploying distributed software applications. Service Oriented Architecture (SOA) and Web services hold the promise of moving to the concept of accessing, programming, and integrating application services that are encapsulated within old and new applications.

An important economic benefit of the Web service computing paradigm is that it enables application developers to grow application portfolios more quickly by creating composite application solutions that use internally existing organisational software assets, which they combine with external components possibly residing in remote networks. This represents a fundamental change to the socio-economic fabric of the software developer community that improves the effectiveness and productivity in software development activities and enables enterprises to bring new products and services to the market more rapidly.

The visionary promise of Web service and SOA technologies is a world of cooperating services where application components are assembled rather quickly and with ease into end-to-end services that can be loosely coupled to create business processes and flexible SOA applications that span organisations and computing platforms. It is therefore expected that Web service technologies will increasingly help shape modern society as a whole, especially in vital areas such as business, health, education, manufacturing and government services.

With every new technology, such as Web services, there is still a lot of groundwork to be put in place. In fact, today, developing complex Web service applications is still an increasingly complex undertaking. However, once the groundwork and infrastructure are in place then things will be easier. Applying Web service technologies will then be a matter of exposing and reusing core business functionality and combining processes in unanticipated ways to create value-added propositions. This will then lead to reduced complexity and costs, increased flexibility, and improving operational efficiency. For all these reasons, it is expected that the Web service computing paradigm will exhibit a steeper adoption curve, as it solves expensive and intractable business and technology problems, and will infiltrate more of the applications portfolio than previous application technologies.

One of the ramifications of the growth of Web services and SOA is the increase in the number of professions where an understanding of Web services and SOA technologies is essential for success. This has led to a proportionate increase in the number of people – who come from a variety of academic and professional backgrounds – wanting to understand the concepts, principles and technologies underpinning Web services. Therefore, the purpose of this book is to address this phenomenon by providing a comprehensive and systematic coverage and treatment of the concepts, foundations, issues and technologies in Web services and SOA. Its objective is to pave the way for understanding the directions in which the field is currently developing and is likely to develop in the future.

What's new in the second edition

The technology underlying Web service systems and Service Oriented Architectures is changing so rapidly that I have made a large number of changes and additions to the material of the first edition. The second edition of the book has been revised to improve readability and clarity, to update coverage of existing material, remove redundancy and to include new material.

Perhaps, the most significant updates to the second edition are the introduction of Chapter 15 on SOA modelling, the introduction of Chapter 18 on Cloud Computing and the addition of a comprehensive case study.

- Chapter 15 concentrates on SOA based modelling and uses the popular Business Process Modeling Notation (BPMN), which is rapidly becoming an industry standard, to illustrate how to model services and business processes. This chapter not only helps better explain key concepts found in the chapter on Business Processes but also helps connect them with that of the SOA design and methodology.
- Chapter 18 focuses on Cloud Computing, an important technology that has been gaining increasing attention from organisations of all sizes as a way to obtain secure access to advanced technology that is not necessarily owned or hosted by the user. This chapter is designed to provide a basic understanding of cloud technology, relate it to services technology and help identify the strengths and weaknesses associated with different cloud computing models.
- Another important addition to the second edition is the introduction of a detailed real life case study with numerous examples, which are referenced throughout the entire book and used to enhance readers' understanding and add insight to the theoretical exposure and explanation of the concepts. In this book I adopt a progressive disclosure approach as I follow the case study continuously and add to it the layers of Web service and SOA technologies and standards. Detailed coding solutions can be found in the book's companion Web site.

Other significant changes in the second edition are as follows.

- Much of the text has been rewritten to improve clarity and reader comprehension.
- Many of the figures and illustrations have been revised to improve clarity.
- New figures and illustrations have been added as warranted by revisions of, or additions to, existing text.
- Superfluous or obsolete content has been removed.

- Several additional examples have been added in almost every chapter to explain the text concepts better.
- All chapters have been revised and improved and chapter previews have been added.
- Chapter 1 has been revised and improved.
- Chapter 5 has been restructured, rewritten and slightly condensed to improve readability and understanding.
- Chapter 7 has been condensed and simplified.
- Chapter 9 has been largely rewritten, simplified and brought up-to-date by introducing the new standard Business Process Execution Language (BPEL) v2.0. It now includes several examples in BPMN, which are eventually mapped to BPEL.
- Chapter 12 has been condensed and now includes more examples.
- A new Chapter 15 has been added to describe SOA modelling and includes several modelling examples in BPMN.
- Chapter 16 (Chapter 15 in previous edition) has been largely rewritten and extended to include examples in BPMN and reflect improvements in the SOA development lifecycle.
- The old Chapter 17 on Grid and Mobile Computing has been replaced by Chapter 18, which covers recent advances in Cloud Computing and relates this important technology to the concept of software services.

As with the previous edition, emphasis is placed on demonstrating how Web service technology can be used to address demanding business problems and develop solutions that achieve integration and information delivery between business-to-business SOA applications involving fairly complex service interactions. For this reason I stress SOAP/WSD/BPEL-based Web services rather than RESTful service technology, which is also treated briefly in this book for the sake of completeness.

Distinguishing features

The material in this book spans an immense and diverse spectrum of the literature, in origin and in character. It strives to present the Web services and SOA literature in a form that is easily readable and allows the reader to see through the complexity of Web service technologies. Readers will learn about the distinct concepts, technologies, protocols and standards in one part of the architecture, while seeing the big picture of how all parts fit together in the Web services and SOA landscape. Unlike many excellent books about Web service standards and programming books, this book is neither about Web service standards nor about Web service programming techniques. It is rather about teaching readers the concepts and principles underlying Web services and SOA, and the technologies and methodologies that make them happen.

This book is unique in terms of its coverage, approach, and treatment of its subject matter. More specifically, this book:

1. provides an extensive treatment and a solid foundation for understanding what Web services and SOA are;
2. places emphasis on acquiring deep knowledge, insight and understanding of the *concepts, principles, mechanisms and methodologies* underpinning Web services and SOA, *not on programming or implementation*;
3. provides sufficient depth for readers to have a basic understanding of each of the technologies that underlie the Web services and SOA paradigm and where each fits in the Web service landscape;
4. explains how SOA and Web services are introduced in organisations, in particular how they are designed, deployed, and used;
5. introduces key standards necessary for Web service development at a level where they are understandable by the lay reader;
6. helps readers learn through action, by walking them through sample code that illustrates how real life problems can be solved using SOA and Web service implementation techniques and best practices.

Another important characteristic of this book is that it tries to make Web services understandable to readers who do not necessarily have a strong technical background, while still providing substance comprehensive enough to challenge experienced readers. The book is written with this mix of readership in mind by concentrating on the theoretical and technical underpinnings of Web services and connecting them to Web standards and novel developments.

To ensure thorough understanding of the material presented in this book, a large number of **graphical illustrations** and abundant **real-world examples** are used as a means to gaining greater insight, understanding and confidence in the material that is presented herein.

How this book is organised

The book is divided into 10 parts. This has been done to group topics and assist readers and instructors. The order of the book is such that when the readers read the book sequentially, the introductory parts and chapters largely precede the more advanced topics that build on them. The book parts and their respective chapters are as follows:

Case study

This edition is more problem solving and project oriented than the earlier edition. The running example in the first edition has been replaced with a comprehensive case study that allows readers and students to experiment with the concepts and technologies covered in this book, thereby helping them to gain an improved understanding and make text concepts more intuitive and meaningful. This is a scenario based case study that follows a progressive disclosure technique, 'ramping up' the reader from simple to more complex topics and solutions. It serves as a means to illustrate and clarify the concepts covered and to test the individual's progressive understanding of the material covered in this book.

Throughout the book simple concepts and enabling technologies are introduced first and, as the book progresses, new concepts are elaborated, using examples relating to the case study. In this way, readers can grasp the core concepts on which SOA and Web services rely.

Part I: Basics (Chapter 1)

This part includes only Chapter 1 and serves to introduce foundation material and the concept of Web services to the reader.

Chapter 1 introduces the concept of Web services and presents several examples of SOA and Web service development and use. It compares Web service applications to traditional Web based application development and concludes with a discussion about the types and features of Web services.

Part II: Enabling infrastructure (Chapters 2 and 3)

This part serves to provide a general overview of Web service computing and introduces support concepts and technologies.

Chapter 2 is an introductory chapter that examines the types of systems and technologies that fall under the umbrella terms *enterprise application integration* and *cross-enterprise computing*, which are key enabling technologies that enable the development of distributed applications for Web services.

Chapter 3 deals with XML, which is used as an enabling technology that makes it possible for business document forms and messages to be comprehensible and interoperable. XML is one of the key ingredients that will accelerate the reality of a network economy and new business models for e-Business applications.

Part III: Core functionality and standards (Chapters 4, 5 and 6)

This part serves to cover core Web service technologies and standards. It provides a comprehensive treatment of the Web service architecture, Web service standards, and technologies for representing, registering and discovering Web services. This part gives a solid basis for the rest of the book.

Chapter 4 provides a comprehensive introduction to the Simple Object Access Protocol (SOAP). This includes overviews of the SOAP specification and SOAP data structures, and explains by means of examples how SOAP is used to provide a consistent serialisation format and general protocol for Web services.

Chapter 5 gives an in depth coverage of the Web Services Description Language (WSDL) and explains how WSDL is key to making Web services the enabling technology for developing loosely coupled Web applications. It includes an overview of the WSDL specification and data structures, as well as WSDL examples.

Chapter 6 provides a comprehensive coverage of the Universal Description, Discovery and Integration (UDDI) framework. This includes an overview of the UDDI data model and numerous examples for publishing business data on UDDI and discovering UDDI based information. It also explains in some detail how Web services represented in WSDL can be accommodated in UDDI and can be discovered by Web service enabled applications.

Part IV: Event notification and Service Oriented Architectures (Chapters 7 and 8)

This part serves to introduce Service Oriented Architectures (SOAs) and the concepts of event processing and notification on which these rely.

Chapter 7 introduces the concept of the notification pattern for SOAs, whereby an information providing service sends messages to one or more interested receivers. In this pattern the message frequently carries information about an event that has occurred, rather than a request that some specific action should occur.

Chapter 8 introduces SOAs and explains their general characteristics and functionality. It presents the Enterprise Service Bus, which offers a whole range of functions designed to offer a manageable standards based IT backbone connecting heterogeneous components and systems.

Part V: Service composition and transactions (Chapters 9 and 10)

This part serves to introduce the concepts of business processes and Web service transactions that rely on them. Business processes are used to create assemblies of services that cross organisational boundaries, Business processes may also exhibit advanced transactional properties.

Chapter 9 explains how core workflow technologies can be used to combine and orchestrate Web services in order to develop SOA applications across different enterprises and computing platforms.

Chapter 10 introduces the concept of Web service transactions and discusses its unique features and requirements for supporting cross-enterprise computing applications composed of Web services.

Part VI: SOA security and policies (Chapters 11 and 12)

This part serves to introduce security mechanisms as well as the use of policies that govern SOA based applications.

Chapter 11 introduces the concept of security for Web services and explains the different security mechanisms and protocols used for developing Web service based applications. This chapter also looks at authentication and authorisation protocols that can be used in conjunction with these applications.

Chapter 12 introduces the concept of service policies that are used for communicating such information as security requirements, supported features, preferred ways of invoking the service and so on, among Web services. It also explains how to create and describe contracts, agreements and guarantees from offers between a service provider and a service client for Web service applications.

Part VII: Service semantics and business protocols (Chapters 13 and 14)

This part serves to introduce the problems of semantic interoperability and how metadata, standard vocabularies and semantic taxonomies help alleviate these problems.

Chapter 13 discusses the problems of enabling disparate systems to understand the information that is being shared appropriately, which relates to the logical aspect of using and sharing data and business processes based on their intended meaning. The chapter also introduces the Resource Description Framework (RDF), the World Wide Web Consortium's official format for describing metadata, which is used to supplant WSDL constructs to facilitate an understanding of the business domain underlying Web services.

Chapter 14 discusses semantic problems when attempting to integrate business processes that span organisations, and presents business protocols, specifications and concepts for business process integration and interoperability that are especially relevant to Web services.

Part VIII: SOA modelling, design and development (Chapters 15 and 16)

This part provides insights on how to model, design and develop enterprise scale and cross-enterprise SOA based applications and the requirements driving the development of these applications.

Chapter 15 introduces SOA modelling techniques and focuses on the Business Process Modeling Notation (BPMN), and presents sample business process models in BPMN that are explored to illustrate the main concepts and notational innovations necessary to deliver sound SOA applications.

Chapter 16 introduces a methodology for designing cross-enterprise computing applications using Web services. This chapter explains that Web services are not just an approach to complex business solving using abstract interfaces and modular pieces of software functionality. It includes several design guidelines, such as various forms of coupling and cohesion, organisational guidelines and policies, and specialised modelling techniques.

Part IX: Service management (Chapter 17)

This part contains one chapter that explores various Web service management approaches and their underlying architectural concepts.

Chapter 17 describes service management techniques and mechanisms that enable enterprises to monitor and measure service levels for processes that are distributed and federated. Such functionality helps to diagnose and combat problems as they occur, so as to ensure that the Web services supporting a given business task are performing in accordance with service level objectives.

Part X: Emerging trends (Chapter 18)

This part contains one chapter that describes emerging trends and developments in the field of services.

Chapter 18 concentrates on the topic of Cloud Computing. It introduces the characteristics, deployment and delivery models and architectural features of Cloud Computing, and examines the consanguinity between SOA, Web services and cloud services.

Logical organisation and paths through the text

There is sufficient material in this book for at least two one-semester courses. An entire term basic course can be built around the first three parts of the book, followed by either Part IV or Part V, or even elements of both, depending on the interests of the instructor and students. I would also strongly advise instructors to use Part VIII as a component of an introductory course to Web services. The logical organisation of the book, along with suggested paths through it for an introductory course, is shown in Figure P.1.

A more advanced course (or second level course on Web services) could skim through Parts I, III, IV, and V, and be followed by Parts VI, VII, VIII and IX. By organising the book in this way, I have attempted to provide an instructor with a number of teaching options. The logical organisation of the book, along with suggested paths through it for an advanced course, is shown in Figure P.2.

Intended readership

This book targets a broad audience with a detailed coverage of the major issues, topics and technologies underlying Web services. The book is intended both as a textbook and a reference book.

The style has been tailored to bring out the key points and reach those who feel intimidated by the jargon, bewildering plethora of standards and programming techniques in the

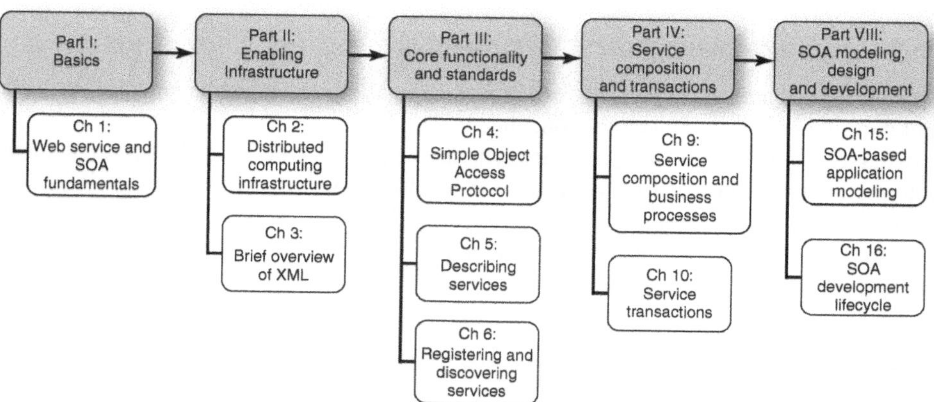

Figure P.1 Suggested paths for an introductory course

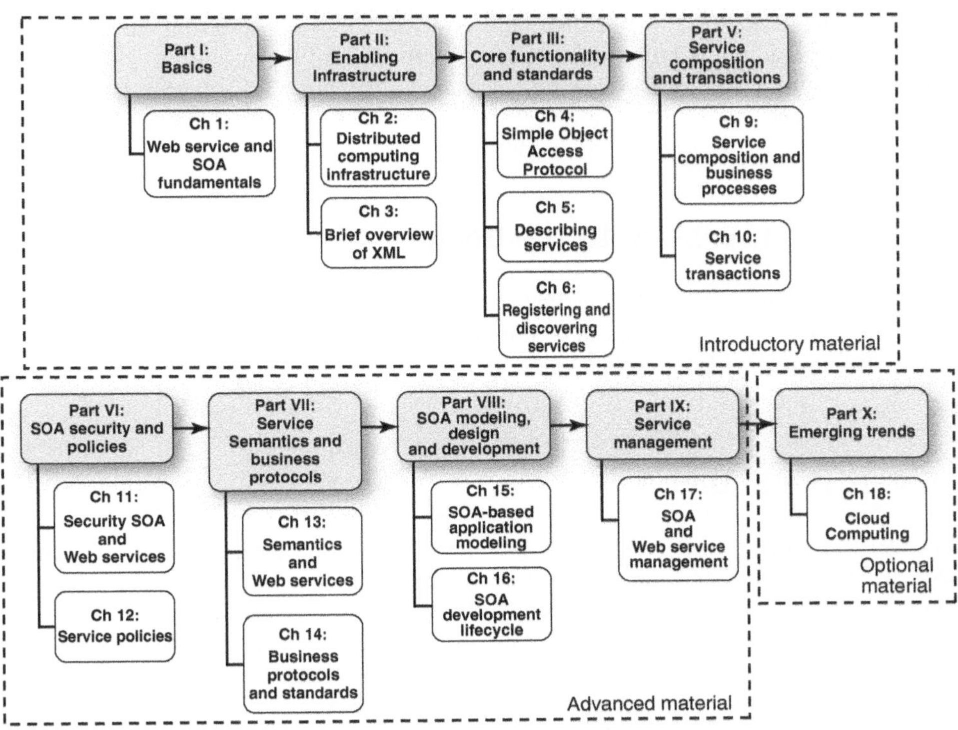

Figure P.2 Suggested paths for advanced course

current Web services literature. More specifically, the book is aimed at advanced undergraduate/postgraduate students, researchers, professionals such as IT planners, software architects, software analysts, designers, developers, software engineers and programmers; and, in general, individuals who wish to develop a deep understanding of the concepts, technologies, scope and extent of Web services, and wish to learn how to apply them to complex applications such as e-Business problems. Equally it is aimed at business strategists, business process engineers and business architects. More significantly, my hope is for the book to also reach business minded individuals, especially the new breed of professionals and students that is emerging as the dividing lines between business requirements and IT grow increasingly blurred. Many of the issues and problems raised in this book are directly related to the design of software solutions for business applications.

The reader will learn several aspects of Web services and enterprise computing in depth and will understand how these are applied in the context of business-to-business commerce. For the advanced student, I provide a comprehensive and in depth treatment of the concepts, issues, standards and technical underpinnings of Web services, thereby enabling them to acquire important skills in understanding how complex distributed systems and applications work and how they can be developed. For the practitioner, I show how to use Web service technology effectively to solve real life problems and offer approaches to reasoning and designing complex distributed systems and applications on the basis of the Web service paradigm. To achieve its stated objectives, the book makes heavy use of illustrations, examples and realistic business scenarios. The book seldom mentions specific platforms or vendors.

Companion Website to the book

Supplementary material, including PowerPoint slides, solutions to exercises and additional publications and sources, can be found at the book's dedicated website: www.pearsoned.co.uk/papazoglou.

About the author

Michael P. Papazoglou is a Professor at Tilburg University, where he is the Executive Director of the European Research Institute in Service Science and the Scientific Director of the European Network of Excellence in Software Services and Systems (S-Cube). He is also an honorary professor at the University of Trento in Italy, and professorial fellow at the Universities Lyon 1 (France), Univ. of New South Wales (Australia) and Universidad Rey Juan Carlos, Madrid (Spain). Prior to this he was full Professor and head of the School of Information Systems at the Queensland Univ. of Technology (QUT) in Brisbane Australia (1991-1996).

Professor Papazoglou is well known for developing fundamental concepts and techniques in Web services. His research interests lie in the areas of service oriented computing, Web services, large scale data sharing, business processes and federated and distributed information systems. He made pioneering contributions in these areas. He has published 22 books (monographs/edited books/international conference proceedings), and well over 250 journal and conference papers. He has an H-index of 38 and over 8,500 citations to his work. His research was, and in many cases still is, funded by the European Commission, the Australian Research Council, the Japanese Society for the Promotion of Science and Departments of Science and Technology in Europe and Australia.

He is frequently invited to give keynote talks and tutorials on service computing in international conferences in several countries in Europe, N. America, Asia and Oceania. He is a golden core member and a distinguished visitor of the Institute of Electrical & Electronics Engineers (IEEE) Computer Science section.

Foreword to second edition

It is with great pleasure that I write the foreword to this exceptional volume on Web services & Service-Oriented Architectures (SOA). This revised and expanded second edition is timely, because today there is much discussion of XaaS or "Everything as a Service" - Infrastructure, Platform, Software, Organizations, and more. As one of the co-founders and major proponents of the emerging area of study known as Service Science, Management, Engineering, and Design (SSME+D), which embraces this notion of "everything with capabilities as a service," I am especially aware of the need to build this new area on a strong practical foundation. This book provides just such a foundation for software engineers, application developers, and enterprise architects.

Before discussing some of the exciting and comprehensive details of the book, it is important to reflect on the growing importance of Web services as an emerging computing paradigm with enormous economic significance. As more and more of both the mundane and the sophisticated capabilities in business and society are implemented as software components and become accessible as Web services residing in "the cloud," dramatic reductions in development costs and development times become feasible. We are already seeing a proliferation of apps on smart phones from Apple, Google, and others, and this is an accelerating trend still in its early stages. We are also seeing the rise of "smarter software systems" such as IBM's Watson Jeopardy! super-computer with advanced natural language processing capabilities allowing it to outscore the best human players in the world across a wide range of human knowledge. In addition, McKinsey and others have described "big data and analytics" as a megatrend impacting all industries. Furthermore, as businesses, governments, and non-profits re-conceptualize their enterprise operations in terms of Service Oriented Architectures, they will be well positioned for continuous efficiency improvements as well as capability expansions, what IBM calls a Smarter Planet. The "double win" opportunity to both improved productivity and quality of service is feasible for the first time enabled by this emerging computing paradigm.

However, before these benefits can be realized, a next generation of professionals must master the fundamentals of service computing. Chapter 1 provides the needed definitions and characteristics of Web services and Service Oriented Architectures, and grounds the reader in the understanding of customer(requestor)-provider interactions, which is fundamental. Also, the message-centric architectural style of SOAP/WSDL-based Web services (the primary focus of the book) is contrasted with the resource-centric REST architectural style. Both architectural styles are likely to continue to evolve as Web services standards organizations strive "to improve the performance, effectiveness, and enterprise readiness of Web services." Chapter 2 provides the necessary grounding in Internet protocols (TCP/IP), and more broadly distributed computing and Java Messaging Service (JMS). Chapter 3 introduces XML, XML document structure, and re-use of XML schemas. Chapter 4 dives deep into SOAP and messaging, contrasting SOAP with conventional distributed object communication protocols, such as CORBA, DCOM, Java/RMI. Chapter 5 introduces WSDL, and the importance of service description language to describe the mechanics of interactions, and the essential of a high-level "contract" to govern interactions between requestor and provider entities. Chapter 6 begins to outline the need for service registries and UDDI for service discovery. Chapter 7 lays the groundwork for more detailed event-processing discussion by first introducing WS-Addressing and notification services.

A next generation of business leaders might also benefit from awareness of this book. Chapter 8 begins the detailed discussion of SOA and Enterprise Service Bus. The challenge of building distributed software systems that can automate business processes that cross enterprise boundaries requires a consistent architectural style be adopted by multiple organizations. Chapter 9 dives deep into BPEL and business process descriptions and choreography. Chapter 10 continues the discussion of essential business concepts introducing transactions, transaction processing, and WS-Coordination model. Chapter 11 deals with another critical business reality, namely security, and Chapter 12 provides the generalization to service policies. Chapter 13 provides an overview of RDF, metadata, ontologies, and points the way to smarter Web services in the future. Chapter 14 returns to business vertical and industry specific protocols and conventions, including ebXML and RossetaNet. Chapters 15, 16, and 17 address service modeling, design, and management, rounding out the set of core competency areas that business practitioners should know. Throughout, the book provides numerous case studies and comprehensive references to related literature.

Stepping back again, as the service sectors of national economies continue to grow, and businesses, even traditional manufacturers, experience "servitization" and witness the growth of service component of annual revenue, we are entering what Berkeley political scientist John Zysman (2006) calls "The 4th Service Transformation: The Algorithmic Revolution." Essentially, software systems will become more and more capable, including speech and image understanding, and other capabilities heretofore only possible by humans. The Algorithmic Revolution will fuel further growth of national service sectors and business service revenue. In fact, coming full circle, the service computing paradigm described in this book represents essentially the "productization" of many traditional, directly human-provided service capabilities. Economist Brian Arthur (2011) calls this "The Second Economy" which in a few decades may easily surpass the traditional physical economy in size. What is in fact happening is both an increasing depth and breadth of access to service capabilities by individuals (via their smart phones and social media) and institutions/organizations (via public and private clouds). Professionals from all sectors and industries will be impacted by the Algorithmic Revolution and service computing paradigm, and therefore would benefit from a better understanding of Web services and SOA as described herein.

In conclusion, I offer my sincere congratulations to Michael P. Papazoglou of the European Research Institute in Service Science (Tilburg University, The Netherlands) for a job exceptionally well done. Those who master the contents of this book will be able to build the future better.

References

Zysman, J. (2006). The 4th Service Transformation: The Algorithmic Revolution. *Communications of the Association for Computing Machinery* (Special Issue on Services Sciences, Editors Spohrer & Riecken).

Arthur, W. Brian (2011). The Second Economy. *McKinsey Quarterly.*

Dr. James C. Spohrer
Innovation Champion and
Director, IBM University Programs World-Wide
San Jose, CA
October 2011

Our world has been changing rapidly and irreversibly thanks to a new breed of hardware and software that has revolutionized personal, professional and corporate living. In turn, our changing world is imposing new challenges for Software Engineering that go beyond what can be accommodated by conventional concepts, tools and techniques. Today, software systems have to be designed as open architectures that can evolve at run-time to better fulfill their requirements, or deal with new ones. The components that comprise these architectures may be autonomous and heterogeneous, but still need to be composed dynamically into a coherent system. Service orientation promises to address these challenges by offering a new computing paradigm founded on the concept of service and service-oriented architecture. The paradigm is supported by a host of satellite concepts, standards and technologies that together accommodate openness, heterogeneity and autonomy.

The second edition of this book comes at an opportune time. Service orientation has matured in the past decade to the point that it now impacts software practice. Today the field commands attention in communities of research and practice through a number of high-quality international conferences and journals and prominent presence in the most prestigious Software Engineering conferences. Most importantly perhaps, Service orientation now boasts a presence in Computer Science and Information Technology curricula around the world.

The book stands out as a university textbook, having been written in the best traditions of scholarly writing and sound educational practices, whereby complex concepts are made easy to grasp and use. It untangles the labyrinth of web service standards that constitute a substantial entrance barrier for the uninitiated. At the same time, it covers the full lifecycle of services, paying attention to critical design aspects, such as quality-of-service and other non-functional requirements. Last, but not least, the book offers a glimpse into the emerging technology of Cloud Computing and the impact this may have on services and service-oriented architectures.

This is an excellent textbook for the university student taking a course on Service-Oriented Computing, but also a valuable reference point for the practitioner or researcher who wants to enter and enjoy the world of services and the technologies that are making it possible.

John Mylopoulos

Distinguished Professor, University of Trento

Trento, Italy

September 20, 2011

Foreword to first edition

Software technology is currently undergoing a significant change. This change is centered on the concept of a *service*. From an abstract point of view, a service is a piece of well defined functionality that is available at some network endpoint and is accessible via various transport protocols and serialisation formats. The functionalities provided by services cover a vast spectrum, reaching from low level features like offering storage capabilities, over simple application functions like changing a customer address, to complex business processes like hiring a new employee.

Another fundamental aspect of a service is its *always on* behaviour: a potential client simply uses the service without having to take care about its construction or destruction, like in case of using functions via object technology. In this sense, a service is comparable with water or power: opening a tap without any water flowing out can be considered a severe error situation, i.e. water is considered to be an *always on* service. And, like water being provided by a utility, providing functionality via services may be seen as another kind of utility.

A new kind of middleware has evolved that supports dealing with services in such a way. Requesting a function using this middleware is simple: based on the specification of the functionality needed by a client, this middleware automatically determines a service that will perform the corresponding request. All the idiosyncrasies of discovering and selecting an appropriate service, using the proper transport protocol to get to the service, using the proper format to exchange data with the service, or understanding the concrete implementation behind the service are completely hidden from the client. In that sense, service technology is *virtualisation technology*, abstracting collections of potentially very different implementations of a particular piece of functionality into a single service.

Thus, the concept of a service introduces a new compute paradigm called *service oriented computing (SOC)*. This paradigm assumes that complete systems are built based on services. A new architectural style called *Service Oriented Architecture (SOA)* defines the actors participating in a service oriented computing environment, defines their relationships and shows their interactions to achieve complete systems. The ingredients of such a system are typically distributed and run in heterogeneous environments; thus, standards are needed to allow interoperability. The stack of standards that has been built over the last few years to support SOA in an interoperable manner is called the *Web service stack* (*WS**) of specifications.

If you think that this is too complex to understand: rest easy, and read this unique book – it expertly weaves all of the above topics together and explains in a lucid and comprehensive manner how it all works. It explains the fundamental concepts and techniques from various areas of computer science and software technology, which are applied in the domain of Service Oriented Architecture. It describes the concrete usage and rendering of these concepts and techniques in actual standard specifications from the Web service stack. It outlines the complete lifecycle of developing service based systems. It explains in detail how non-functional aspects like security, reliability or transactionality are covered in this environment. It works out how service environments can be managed – being on premise or even outsourced. And it shows how business processes are realised in service environments.

A whole spectrum of communities will benefit from reading this book: students will get an in depth introduction into the complex subject domain; researchers not familiar with the domain will get enough information to understand the underpinnings of service oriented computing and how it relates to established domains in computer science; software architects will be able to assess the impact of services on their company's IT environment; developers will get a clear picture of how the various Web service technologies relate and about the lifecycle of service oriented applications; business oriented IT users will get enough information to understand the potentials of services in their domain.

All users will definitely benefit from the clear structure of each of the chapters of the book: each chapter starts with a section about its learning objectives, highlighting the key concepts covered. The main body of each chapter closes with a set of review questions that can be used by the reader for a quick self test. A set of exercises, which can be used to deepen the understanding of the subjects covered, closes each chapter.

Once you start reading this book you will be hooked and it will be difficult to stop reading it. This book is an *un-putdownable read*. I thoroughly enjoyed reading this book and I highly recommend it. I believe that many more readers will experience the same feeling.

Frank Leymann
Former IBM Distinguished Engineer and Past Member, IBM Academy of Technology
Professor of Computer Science and Director
Institute of Architecture of Application Systems
University of Stuttgart, Germany
February 2007

Acknowledgements

Writing this book was quite a challenge in many ways but something that I aspired to for a long time. It was a daunting exercise that took the better part of three years to complete. In the process I did extensive research, used a huge number of sources, and had discussions with numerous individuals and experts in the field who made invaluable suggestions. This has broadened my scientific horizons and knowledge, inspired many ideas found in this book, and led to a more comprehensive treatment of its subject matter.

My intention was to write a book that is authoritative, and synthesises diverse views in the WS and SOA literature, and help define a common academic field. A large number of leading scholars in the field were contacted and assisted me by providing their comments and views. I relish this opportunity to thank them.

I would especially like to thank the following people who gave their time unstintingly to review substantial portions of the book, provided me with feedback and comments or gave valuable recommendations on how to improve the final manuscript: Marco Aiello of the University of Groningen, Athman Bouguettaya of RMIT, Melbourne, Fabio Casati of Trento University, Paco Curbera of IBM TJ Watson Research Labs, Vincenzo d'Andrea of Trento University, Asit Dan of IBM TJ Watson Research Labs, Andrzej Goscinski of Deakin University, Bernd Kraemer of the University of Hagen, Frank Leymann of Stuttgart University, Maurizio Marchese of Trento University, Monica Martin of Sun Microsystems, Tiziana Margaria of the University of Potsdam, John Mylopoulos of the University of Toronto, Anne Ngu of Texas State University, Barbara Pernici of the Polytechnic University of Milan, Robert Steele of the University of Sydney, Farouk Toumani of Blaise Pascal University, and Olaf Zimmerman of IBM, Zurich.

I also wish to thank the anonymous reviewers of the first edition of this book, whose comments and suggestions significantly improved the second edition.

I am also heavily indebted to the following scholars for reviewing chapters in the manuscript at various stages and for all of their helpful suggestions, feedback and insight: Gregory Antoniou of the University of Crete, who reviewed Chapter 13; Dave Chappell of Sonic Software, who reviewed Chapter 8; Jean Jacques Dubray of Attachmate and editor of OASIS ebXML, who reviewed Chapter 1; George Feuerlicht of Sydney University of Technology, who reviewed Chapter 16; Rania Khalaf of IBM TJ Watson Research Labs, who reviewed Chapter 9; Heather Kreger of IBM TJ Watson Research Labs, who reviewed Chapter 17; Francesco Lelli of Tilburg University, who reviewed Chapter 18; Heiko Ludwig of IBM TJ Watson Research Labs, who reviewed Chapter 12; Yehai Taher of Tilburg University, who reviewed Chapter 9; Willem Jan van den Heuvel of Tilburg University, who reviewed Chapters 8 and 16; and Andrea Zisman of City University in London, who reviewed Chapters 5 and 6.

Special thanks also go to my doctorate students Vassilios Andrikopoulos, Amal Elgammal, Benedikt Kratz, Michele Mancioppi at Tilburg University who helped me by providing tips and solutions for several of the exercises in this book. My sincere thanks go to Dinh Khoa Nguyen and several of my graduate students for the implementation and testing of the automotive case study.

Finally, I wish to thank Rufus Curnow of Pearson for his continuous encouragement, perseverance and especially patience with me, and for giving me invaluable advice and assistance. I also wish to thank Patrick Bond, who was involved in the last stages of this book, and the various staff members of the Pearson team, who did an excellent job of editing and producing the book; Ken Brown, copyeditor and Gowri Vasanthkumar – Project Manager, Laserwords, India.

Michael P. Papazoglou

Publisher's acknowledgements

We are grateful to the following for permission to reproduce copyright material:

Figures

Figures 2.4, 2.7, 2.14 and 2.16: From *e-Business: Organizational and Technical Foundations*, John Wiley & Sons (Papazoglou, M.P. and Ribbers, P.M.A. 2006); Figure 5.7: from *Database Systems: An Application-Orientated Approach*, 2nd edition, Addison Wesley (Kifer, M., Bernstein, A. and Lewis, P.M., 2005) reprinted by permission of Pearson Education, Inc., Upper Saddle River, NJ; Figures 9.16 and 9.17: From *Building Web Services with Java*, SAMS Publishing (Graham, S., Boubez, T., Daniels, G., Davis, D., Nakamura, Y., Neyama, R. and Simeonov, S., 2005) reprinted by permission of Pearson Education, Inc., Upper Saddle River, NJ; Figure 10.12: From *Java Transaction Processing*, Prentice Hall (Little, M., Maron, J. and Pavlik, G., 2004) reprinted by permission of Pearson Education, Inc., Upper Saddle River, NJ; Figures 11.12 and 11.13: From *Core Security Patterns: Best Practices and Strategies for J2EE, Web Services and Identity Management*, Prentice Hall (Steel, C., Nagappan, R. and Lai, R., 2006) reprinted by permission of Pearson Education, Inc., Upper Saddle River, NJ; Figure 11.23: from *J2EE Platform Web Services*, Prentice Hall (Lai, R., 2004) reprinted by permission of Pearson Education, Inc., Upper Saddle River, NJ.

In some instances we have been unable to trace the owners of copyright material and we would appreciate any information that would enable us to do so.

Comprehensive case study

Case study preview

The objective of this chapter is to provide a comprehensive case study based on the production of Original Equipment (OE) automotive parts used in the assembly of a new motor vehicle. This case study demonstrates how a number of small projects need to be applied in sequence and how gradually to develop a Service Oriented Architecture (SOA) solution for effectively processing activities in OE automotive supply chains.

A.1 Overview of case study

The majority of examples in this book revolve around a company called AVERS (Advanced automotiVE paRtS), a hypothetical manufacturer of speciality automotive parts. The parts AVERS produces include power train components, electrical equipment and steering and braking systems, to name a few.

Due to the diversity of the automotive parts manufacturing industry, there is a wide variety of processes and materials embodied in the finished parts, such as those AVERS makes. Car makers once made many of these parts in-house, but now mostly procure them from independent producers such as AVERS. As a diversified supplier of automotive parts, AVERS provides its customers, e.g. automotive parts dealers and car assemblers, with a global, single point sourcing capability and automotive parts and systems tailored to meet their specific needs.

A.2 Background: Automotive supply chain

The manufacture of motor vehicles requires vast quantities of materials, such as steel, rubber, plastics, glass and other basic materials. The automotive supply chain touches nearly every other industry, including steel, plastics, textiles, electronics and more.

AVERS embraces different business units including sales, logistics and manufacturing, and collaborates with partners like suppliers, distributors, banks, transportation carriers, etc. In particular, it works with a number of second tier suppliers via an extended dealership chain that usually sends records of customer details, orders, sales figures and stock positions to AVERS.

Today's car manufacturers adopt a global perspective in their operations. Cars are primarily sourced out to produce various sub-assemblies in a multitude of disparate locations around the world. This means a vehicle production plant is an active assembly point, where skilled workers and robotic systems bring together all of the necessary components to create a final product on a *just-in-time* basis.

Central to the car assembly process is the concept of the automotive supply chain. As we shall see in Section 14.1, a supply chain essentially has three main parts: *supply*, *manufacturing*, and *distribution*.

- The supply side concentrates on how, from where, and when raw materials are procured and supplied to manufacturing.
- Manufacturing converts these raw materials to finished products.
- Distribution ensures that these finished products reach the final customers through a network of distributors, warehouses, and retailers.

Over time, the automotive supply chain has evolved from a model in which most parts were built by the primary auto manufacturer, to a highly functional segmented model in which Original Equipment Manufacturers (OEMs) provide finished parts for automotive assembly lines. Figure A.1 shows a simple automotive supply chain involving interacting processes across organisation boundaries.

The case study is a fairly complex project that examines the production of Original Equipment (OE) automotive components to be used in the assembly of a new motor vehicle (e.g. automobile, light truck or truck).

Suppliers of OE parts are organised on three levels. First tier suppliers manufacture and supply finished components (e.g. the fuel pump) directly to the vehicle manufacturer. Second tier suppliers produce some of the simpler individual parts that would be included in a component manufactured by a first tier supplier (e.g. the housing of the fuel pump), and the third tier suppliers would mostly supply raw materials (e.g. the steel and plastic to make the fuel pump).

The growing system complexity, either at an OEM or first tier supplier is inducing the new type of supplier that does not supply physical products, but rather services, particularly in design and engineering [Veloso 2002]. An important service role that emerges from these relationships is that of an aggregator and intermediator. The Internet and software service technologies now enable firms to perform the electronic mediation of supply relationships, either on a one-to-one basis, or by aggregating demand for particular automotive goods or services.

A.3 Case study objectives

The intent of the case study is to help demonstrate how AVERS can develop an SOA based solution that captures automotive parts related information more quickly, helps analyse trends in their business to establish how each supplier and dealership is and, in general, to streamline and control its supply chain more effectively and efficiently.

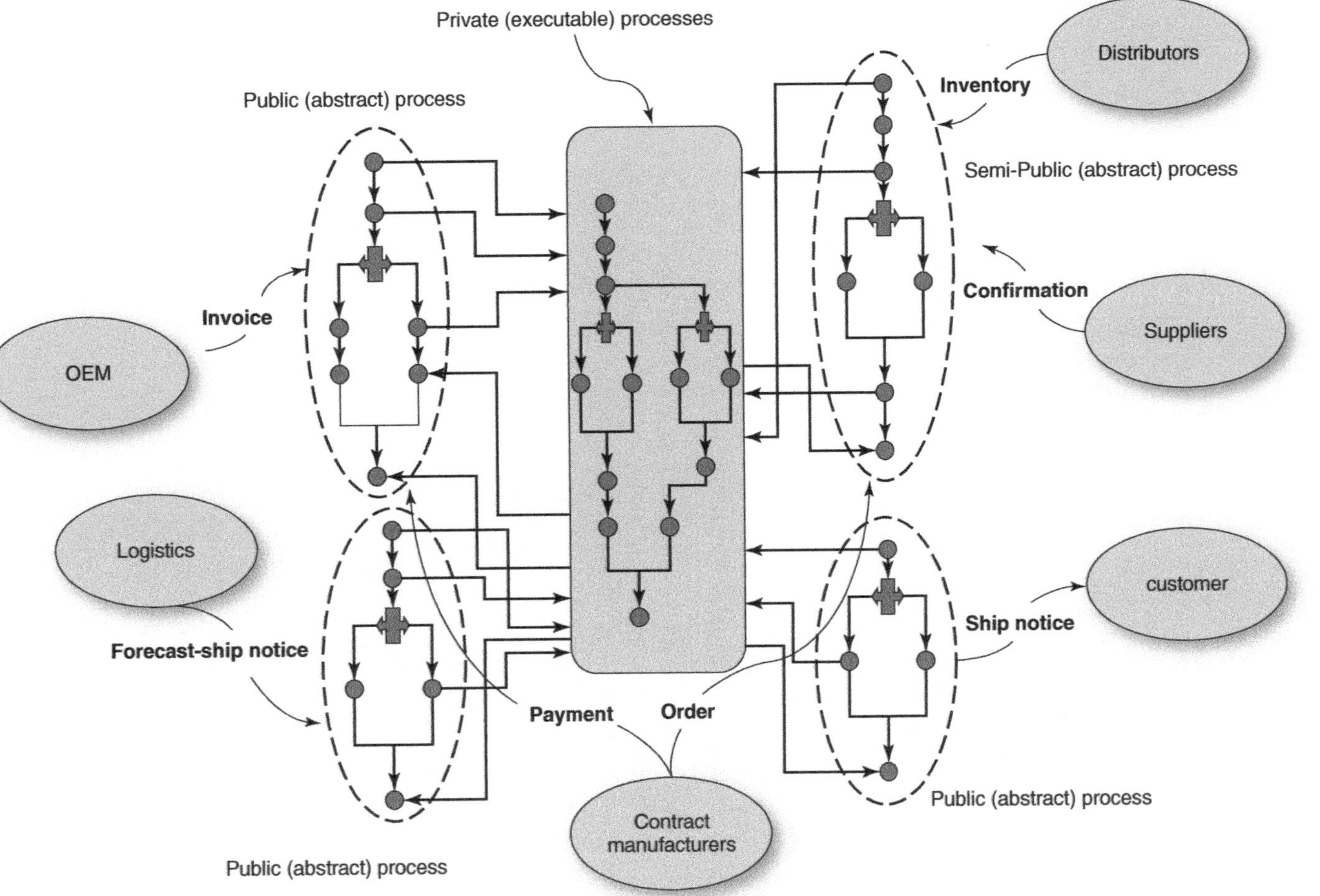

Figure A.1 Simple automotive supply chain

The final objective will be to provide the AVERS supply chain with visibility into end-to-end business processes and to help it increase profit margins and lower costs wherever they may exist.

A.3.1 The current situation

Currently, customer, financial, business process and inventory data is captured in a traditional Enterprise Resource Planning (ERP) system that integrates internal and external management information from the various business units of AVERS. However, the data and information contained in the systems is entered and updated manually, which is time consuming, slow and prone to error. Furthermore, the current implementation does not manage production planning nor inventory levels, suffers from poor performance and unreliability, and does not provide the level of detail or accuracy required. Due to the ERP system's proprietary nature, it also cannot be easily extended to include the Customer Relationship Management (CRM) tools for managing the company's interactions with customers and sales prospects as AVERS requires. The lack of integration and coordination between the ERP and CRM systems is causing information delays and discrepancies in management information, such as sales, operations, future forecasts and inventories. As a result of these problems, there is a negative impact on supply chain processes such as manufacturing, logistics and billing.

A.3.2 The desired SOA solution

The solution to this case study is built using an SOA based approach that resolves the current deficiencies, with an end-to-end business process solution to manage purchase orders submitted by customers, e.g. car dealers, to a specific OE supplier such as AVERS.

The SOA solution presented in the book's Companion Website (see Section A5), covers the entire course of the OE production process – i.e., from when a distributor orders vehicle parts through production to shipment and, finally, delivery. The central goal of using an SOA approach is to provide all stakeholders with complete visibility of an order's progress. An SOA approach can also help update distributors' systems to facilitate their dispatch planning and the electronic transfer of orders and acknowledgements, can help communicate the daily progress of production plans and dispatch status updates to the distributor.

The Order Management Solution (OMS) presented requires cross-functional integration within AVERS and across the network of second tier suppliers and distributors that comprise its whole supply chain. The OMS needs to collect the information generated by disparate systems, e.g. ERP, CRM and in-house inventory management solutions, etc, to produce a common format for data transfer and unify disparate processes into one consistent order process flow across all business units, product lines and trading partners.

The order management solution will be crafted in such a way so as to interlace the Web service principles and concepts covered in this book.

A.3.2.1 Processing steps in the SOA solution

The OMS scenario is triggered when a customer submits a purchase order. Upon receiving a purchase order from a client, several tasks are performed at the OE supplier's site: the credit worthiness of the customer is checked, the product inventory is consulted to determine whether or not an ordered part is available, a shipper is selected, the production and final shipment to the dealers of the part(s) is scheduled, the final price for the order is calculated and the customer's account is billed. AVERS responds with either acceptance or rejection that is based on a number of criteria, including the availability of the part(s) and the credit history of the customer.

To achieve a robust SOA solution the following (simplified) processing steps are introduced in the OMS:

1. The purchase order received from the (customer) is registered with the date of receipt and a newly assigned, internal order identification number, which is used to keep track of the order within the OMS.
2. AVERS verifies whether the order contains sufficient information for processing, including the necessary customer data, the list of ordered items and the price that the customer has already been quoted.
   (a) If the order verification fails, then an order cancellation is sent back to the customer.
   (b) Otherwise, an order confirmation will be sent to the customer and the order is passed for further processing.
3. During the next step, the AVERS CRM checks whether the order comes from a long-term customer, which could be a *preferred* or *standard* retailer, or simply from an incidental customer. The OMS then performs a credit check. If the credit check fails the purchase order is rejected, otherwise the order is passed for further processing.
4. The purchase order is annotated with customer profile details and all ordered items purchased from a single customer are consolidated on a single purchase order.
5. A bill is created.
6. The inventory is checked against the appropriate quantities required by the purchase order. If there is insufficient stock of the parts required, an inventory replenishment process can be initiated to move stock from centralised warehouses to subsidiary warehouses.
7. The inventory results are then sent to a logistics service provider to determine delivery dates, shipment, loading, timing, and routing data–possibly offering multiple shipping options. The logistics provider is responsible for routing the shipment from the warehouses to the customer, which may include many shipment routes.
8. Shipment details are then relayed to AVERS for approval. When a shipment schedule is available, the final price for the order is calculated, including shipment charges, and the OMS notifies the customer by sending the customer an updated invoice.
9. Finally, arrangements for payment are made at the customer's site.

While some of the above processing steps can proceed concurrently, there are synchronisation dependencies between these tasks. For instance, the customer's creditworthiness must be ascertained first before accepting the order, the shipping price is required to finalise the price calculation, and the shipping date is required for the complete fulfilment schedule. When these tasks are completed successfully, invoice processing can proceed and the invoice will be sent to the customer.

A.4 SOA work plan stages

To realise the OMS, the work it requires will be divided into four sequential stages until the complete solution is built. The stages of the OMS workplan are described below.

A.4.1 Modelling the Service Oriented Architecture

The first stage in the workplan is to model the entire OMS scenario using a standard graphical notation for analysing, expressing and visualising business processes, business process operations and data flows. The OMS model should describe the interaction between sub-processes of the AVERS business units and those of the external stakeholders, i.e. customers/retailers, logistics providers and financial institutions, etc.

For this purpose we can first use the design techniques from Section 16.12 to design the appropriate types of services and processes for the OMS. Then we can employ the Business Process Modelling Notation (BPMN) introduced in Section 15.4 for capturing the elements of business processes and business process interactions in the automotive SOA development project.

A.4.2 Specifying design patterns in the XML Schema

During this stage, all simple and complex canonical data types and message structures in the OMS will be specified using the XML Schema. This will include data and messages such as orders, shipment and delivery notices, payment requests, customers, receivables and sales data.

The objective is to design XML Schema document patterns that can be then used as a basis to develop service interfaces, service message exchanges and service orchestrations. The XML Schemas will be designed with the following characteristics in mind:

- Potential for reuse within a single service interface.
- Potential for reuse across services and service interfaces.
- Potential for future service modification or enhancement and later extension of the service interface.
- Service interface simplicity, modularity and maintainability.

A.4.3 Describing services in WSDL

During this stage the service interface definitions within the OMS will be developed according to information provided in Chapter 5, using the XML Schema types developed in the previous project stage.

Each business unit may have one or more service interface definitions (hence one or more WSDLs) since it may expose one or many software functions as services. Each service interface definition will contain:

- One (or more) PortType(s) that expose a set of (one or more) service operations.
- Each service operation may follow one of the following interaction patterns: *one-way-request* (asynchronous invocation) or *two-way request-response* (synchronous invocation).

A.4.4 Service orchestration in BPEL

During this final project stage, Business Process Execution Language (BPEL) processes for all participants in the OMS will be developed according to information provided in Chapter 9, using the WSDL service descriptions developed in the preceding project stage.

The BPEL service orchestration created will demonstrate how the services developed in the previous project stage can be composed to support the entire supply chain–from when a distributor orders a vehicle part through to production and shipment. It will also capture all OMS processing steps introduced in Section A.3.2.1.

A.5 Solution

For a detailed solution to the AVERS Original Equipment automotive parts project that covers all the SOA workplan stages, visit the book's Companion Website at www.pearsoned.co.uk/papazoglou.

PART I

Basics

CHAPTER 1

Web service and SOA fundamentals

Learning objectives

The term Web services describes a distributed technology that enables disparate applications running on different machines to exchange messages and integrate with one another without requiring additional, proprietary third party software or hardware.

Web services are self-describing and self-contained network available software modules that perform concrete tasks and are deployed easily because they are based on common industry standards and existing technology, such as XML and HTTP. They reduce application interface costs, and provide a universal mechanism for integrating business processes within an enterprise and, ultimately, among multiple organisations.

After completing this chapter you will understand the following key concepts:

- The nature, broad characteristics and types of Web services.
- The difference between Web services and the application service provider model and Web-based applications.
- The concepts of tight and loose coupling.
- The concepts of stateful and stateless services.
- The notion of the Service Oriented Architecture and its main building blocks.
- The Web services technology stack and how Web service standards help develop distributed applications.
- Functional versus non-functional service characteristics and the notion of quality of service.

Chapter preview

This chapter presents an overview of Web service technologies and the notion of Service Oriented Architecture. A definition of Web services is given at the outset of the chapter and is related to the concept of software as a service. The chapter then goes on to cover the different types and characteristics of Web services. Following this, we introduce the concept of Service Oriented Architecture and its main components, as well as the concept of Quality of Service and its implications for SOA based applications. The chapter concludes with a comparison between Web service, REST and component technologies, as well as a summary of the impacts and shortcoming of Web services.

Emphasis as always in this book is placed on business-to-business interactions involving relatively complex services.

1.1 Introduction

Service oriented computing is an emerging computing paradigm that utilises services as the constructs to support the development of rapid, low cost composition of distributed applications. Services are self-contained modules – deployed over standard middleware platforms – that can be described, published, located, orchestrated and programmed using XML based technologies over a network. Any piece of code, and any application component deployed on a system, can be transformed into a network available service.

Software services (or simply 'services') reflect a *service-oriented* approach to programming, based on the idea of describing available computational resources, e.g. application programs and information system components, as services that can be delivered through a standard and well defined interface. Services perform functions that can range from answering simple requests to executing business processes requiring peer-to-peer relationships between service consumers and providers. Services are most often built in a way that is independent of the context in which they are used. This means that the service provider and consumers are loosely coupled. Service based applications can be developed by discovering, invoking and composing network available services, rather than building new applications from scratch.

Service-oriented computing represents the fusion of several technologies, including distributed systems, software engineering, information systems, computer languages, Web based computing, and XML technologies, rather than being a new technology. This technology is expected to have an impact on all aspects of software construction at least as wide as that of object oriented programming.

The premise for the foundation of service oriented computing is that an application can no longer be thought of as a single process running within a single organisation. The value of an application is actually no longer measured by its functional capabilities but rather by its ability to integrate with its surrounding environment [Papazoglou 2003]. This means that services can help integrate applications that were not written with the intent to be integrated with other applications and define architectures and techniques to build new functionality leveraging existing application functionality. A new breed of applications can therefore be developed solely on the basis of collections of interacting services offering well defined interfaces to their potential users. These applications possess the ability to integrate with other service based applications and are often referred to as *composite applications*.

Service orientation enables loosely coupled relationships between applications of transacting partners. At the middleware level, the concept of loose coupling requires that the *service-oriented* approach be independent of specific technologies or operating systems. The service oriented model does not even mandate any kind of predetermined agreements before the use of an offered service is allowed.

The service oriented model allows for a clear distinction to be made between three types of software organisations:

- *service providers* (organisations that provide the service implementations, supply their service descriptions and provide related technical and business support);
- *service clients* (end user or consumer organisations that use some service);
- *service aggregators* (organisations that consolidate multiple services into a new, single orchestrated service offering that is commonly known as a business process).

Since services may be offered by different enterprises and communicate over the Internet, they provide an effective distributed computing medium for both intra- and cross-enterprise application integration and collaboration. Clients of services can be other solutions or applications within an enterprise or clients outside the enterprise, whether these are external applications, processes or customers/users. This distinction between service providers and consumers is independent of the relationship between consumer and provider, which can be either client/server or peer-to-peer.

For the service oriented computing paradigm to exist, we must find ways for services to be technology neutral, loosely coupled and support location transparency.

- To be *technology neutral*, services must be invoked through standardised lowest common denominator technologies that are available to almost all IT environments. This implies that the invocation mechanisms (protocols, descriptions and discovery mechanisms) should comply with widely accepted standards.
- To be *loosely coupled*, services must not require knowledge or any internal structures or conventions (context) at the client or service side.
- Finally, to *support location transparency*, services should have their definitions and location information stored in a public repository such as the Universal Description and Discovery and Integration Repository (see Chapter 6) and be accessible by a variety of clients that can locate and invoke them irrespective of their location.

A major advantage of services is that they may be implemented on a single machine or on a large number and variety of devices, and be distributed on a local area network or more widely across several wide area networks (including mobile and *ad hoc* networks).

A particularly interesting case is when the services use the Internet (as the communication medium) and open, Internet based standards. This results in the concept of Web services, which share the characteristics of more general services but they require special consideration as a result of using a public, insecure, low fidelity mechanism, such as the Internet, for distributed service interactions.

1.1.1 What are Web services?

A *Web service* is a self-describing, self-contained software module available via a network, such as the Internet, which completes tasks, solves problems or conducts transactions on behalf of a user or application. Web services constitute a distributed computer infrastructure made up of many different interacting application modules trying to communicate over private or public networks, including the Internet and the Web, to form virtually a single logical system.

A Web service can be:

- a self-contained business task, such as a funds withdrawal or funds deposit service;
- a fully fledged business process, such as automated bill inquiry handling;
- an application, such as a life insurance application or demand forecasts and stock replenishment;
- a service enabled resource, such as access to a particular back end database containing patient medical records.

Web services can vary in function from simple requests (e.g. credit checking and authorisation, pricing enquiries, inventory status checking or a weather report) to complete business applications that access and combine information from multiple sources, such as an insurance brokering system, an insurance liability computation, an automated travel planner or a package tracking system.

Web services address the problems of rigid implementations of predefined relationships and isolated services scattered across the Internet. The long term goal of Web service technology is to enable distributed applications that can be dynamically assembled according to changing business needs, and customised based on device (such as personal computers, workstations, laptops, WAP enabled cellular phones or personal digital assistants), network (such as cable, UMTS, XDSL, Bluetooth, etc.) and user access, while enabling wide utilisation of any given piece of business logic wherever it is needed. Once a Web service is deployed, other applications and Web services can discover and invoke it.

A more appropriate and complete definition of Web services is given in Section 1.4 after readers have familiarised themselves with the concept of *software-as-a-service (SaaS)* and understood the differences between Web services and Web based applications.

1.1.2 Typical Web service scenarios

Web service efforts focus on reusing existing applications (including legacy code) to facilitate integration with other applications, often motivated by the desire for new forms of sharing of services across lines of business or between business partners.

Example 1.1: An insurance liability service

To better understand the mission of Web service technology, consider, as an example, an insurance company that decides to offer an *on line-quoting* Web service to its customers. Rather than developing the entire application from scratch, this enterprise looks to supplement its home grown applications with modules that perform industry standard functions. Therefore, it may seamlessly link up with the Web service of another enterprise that, for instance, specialises in insurance liability computations. The insurance liability Web service may present a quote form to the customer to collect customer information based on the type of desired insurance. Subsequently, the Web service would present the customer with a quote including a premium estimate. If the customer selected to buy that particular insurance policy, the system would take the customer's payment information and run it through a payment Web service offered by yet another company (service provider). This payment Web service would ultimately return billing information to the customer and to the originating company.

Enterprise applications, such as the insurance quoting Web service in Example 1.1, are among the most likely candidate applications that can benefit from the use of Web service technologies. Enterprise applications cover a wide spectrum of Web service scenarios, including interactions between the departments within an organisation as well as interactions between business partners.

Enterprises can typically use a single Web service to accomplish a specific business task, such as billing or inventory control, or they may compose several Web services together to create a distributed enterprise application such as customised ordering, customer support, procurement and logistical support. These enterprise application scenarios require both the reuse and integration of existing back end systems within an enterprise, which are the target of enterprise application integration (or EAI), see Section 2.10. More sophisticated enterprise applications may focus on business-to-business, or cross-enterprise interactions involving transacting business partners over the Internet (also covered in Section 2.10), which is typical of the way in which large companies procure, manufacture, sell and distribute products [Papazoglou 2006].

1.2 The concept of software as service (SaaS)

As terminology is often used very loosely today, it is easy to confuse someone by describing a 'service' as a Web service when it is in fact not. Consequently, it is useful to examine the concept of *software-as-a-service* on which Web service technology builds and then compare Web services to Web server based functionality.

The concept of *software-as-a-service* is revolutionary and appeared first with the applications service provider software model. Application service providers (ASPs) are companies that package software and infrastructure elements together with business and professional services to create a complete solution that they present to the end customer as a service on a subscription basis. Software offered using an ASP model is also sometimes called *on-demand software* or *software as a service* (SaaS).

A typical ASP is a third party (service organisation) that owns, deploys, hosts and manages access to packaged software applications at a centrally managed facility for multiple customers across a network, offering application availability and security. The ASP owns, operates and maintains the servers that support the software, while applications are delivered over networks on a subscription or rental basis, and end users access these applications remotely through a Web browser using HTML or by special purpose thin client software provided by the vendor. In essence, ASPs were a way for companies to outsource some or even all aspects of their IT needs.

The basic idea behind an ASP is to bill customers on a *per-use* basis or *rent* applications to subscribers on a monthly/annual fee. An ASP hosts the entire application and the customer has little opportunity to customise it beyond setting up tables, or perhaps the final appearance of the user interface (such as adding company logos). The client relies on the provider to provide essential business functions, therefore limiting their control of that function and instead relying on the provider. This means that integration with the client's non-ASP systems may also prove problematic. Access to the application for the client is provided simply via browsing and manually initiated purchases, and transactions occur by downloading reports. This activity can take place by means of a browser. Overall this is not a very flexible solution, but it does offer considerable benefits in terms of deployment provided that the customer is willing to accept the application *as is*.

By providing a centrally hosted Internet application, the ASP takes primary responsibility for managing the software application on its infrastructure, using the Internet as the conduit between each customer and the primary software application. What this means for a customer is that the ASP maintains the application, the associated infrastructure and the customer's data, and ensures that the systems and data are available whenever needed.

An alternative to this approach is where the ASP is providing a software module that is downloaded to the customer's site on demand – this is for situations where the software does not work in a client/server fashion or can be operated remotely via a browser. This software module might be deleted at the end of the session, or may remain on the customer's machine until replaced by a new version, or the contract for using it expires.

Although the ASP model introduced the concept of *software-as-a-service* first, it suffered from several inherent limitations such as the inability to develop highly interactive applications, inability to provide complete customisable applications and inability to integrate applications. This resulted in monolithic architectures, highly fragile, customer specific, non-reusable integration of applications based on tight coupling principles.

The Web services paradigm allows the *software-as-a-service* concept to expand naturally to include the delivery of complex business processes and transactions as a service. Perceiving the relative benefits of Web service technology, many ASPs are modifying their technical infrastructures and business models to be more akin to those of Web service providers. The use of Web services provides a more flexible solution for ASPs. The core of the application – the business and data components – remains on the ASP's machines, but is now accessed programmatically via Web service interfaces. The customers can now build their own custom business processes and user interfaces, and are also free to select from a wide variety of Web services that are available over the network to satisfy their needs.

1.3 Web services versus Web based applications

To fully understand the purpose and characteristics of Web services it is essential that we understand their difference from general purpose, Web based applications. When comparing Web services to Web based applications we may distinguish four key differences [Aldrich 2002]:

1. Web services act as resources to other applications that can request and initiate those Web services, with or without human intervention. This means that Web services can call on other Web services to outsource parts of a complex transaction to those other Web services. This provides a high degree of flexibility and adaptability not available in today's Web based applications.
2. A Web service knows what functions it can perform and what inputs it requires to produce its outputs, and can describe this to potential users and to other Web services. A Web service can also describe its non-functional properties: for instance, the cost of invoking the service, the geographical areas the Web service covers, security measures involved in using the Web service, performance characteristics, contact information and more (see Section 1.9). This advanced functionality is not present in general purpose, Web based applications.
3. Web services are more visible and manageable than Web based applications. The state of a Web service can be monitored and managed at any time by using external application management systems. Despite the fact that a Web service may not run on an in-house (local) system or may be written in an unfamiliar programming language, it still can be used by local applications, which may detect its state (active or available) and manage the status of its outcome.
4. Web services may be brokered or auctioned. If several Web services perform the same task, then several applications may place bids for the opportunity to use the requested service. A broker can base its choice on the attributes of the competing Web services (cost, speed, degree of security).

1.4 A more complete definition of Web services

In the previous sections we have provided you with enough information to understand the origin of Web services and their main differences from Web based applications. In this section we shall consider a more in depth description of the key operational characteristics of Web services.

We have seen that Web services form the building blocks for creating distributed applications in that they can be published to, and accessed over, the Internet and corporate intranets. To achieve this, they rely on a set of open Internet standards that allow developers to implement distributed applications that join together possible existing software modules from systems in diverse organisational departments or from different enterprises. For example, an application that tracks the inventory level of parts within a car assembly supply chain can provide a useful service that answers queries about the inventory level in an inventory control application.

Another characteristic of Web services, and one that makes the primary candidates for Service Oriented Architecture, which we shall examine in Section 1.7, is that Web services can discover and communicate with other Web services and trigger them to fulfill or outsource part of a higher-level transaction by using a published directory of their capabilities.

The modularity and flexibility of Web services make them ideal for business-to-business application integration [Papazoglou 2006]. Perhaps, one of the most useful features of a Web service is that it can be combined with other services to perform any kind of useful (business related) task. Web services possess the ability to engage other services in a common computation in order to complete a concrete task, conduct a business transaction or solve a complex problem. For example, an inventory Web service can be accessed together with other related Web services by a business partner's warehouse management or reverse logistics application, or can be part of a new distributed application that is developed from scratch and implements an extended materials management solution.

At this stage a more complete definition of a Web service can be given. A Web service is a platform independent, loosely coupled, self-contained, programmable Web enabled application that can be described, published, discovered, composed and configured using XML artifacts (open standards) for the purpose of developing distributed interoperable applications.

In the following we shall examine the above definition more closely and deconstruct its meaning:

> *Web services are loosely coupled software modules:* Web service interfaces, protocols and registry services enable applications to work cooperatively together using the principle of loose coupling. To achieve this requirement, the service interface is defined in a neutral manner that is independent of the underlying platform, the operating system and the programming language the service is implemented in. In this way, services, built on a variety of such systems, can interact with each other in a uniform and universal manner (see also Section 1.5.4).
>
> *Web services encapsulate discrete functionality:* A Web service is a self-contained software module that performs a single well defined task. The module describes its own interface characteristics, i.e. the operations available, the parameters, data typing and the access protocols, in such a way that other software modules can determine what it does, how to invoke its functionality and what result to expect in return.
>
> *Web services can be accessed programmatically:* A Web service provides programmable access and this allows embedding of Web services into remotely located applications. Web services operate at the code level. They are called by, and exchange data with, other software modules and applications. However, Web services can certainly be incorporated into software applications designed for human interaction.

Web services can be dynamically found and included in applications: Unlike existing interface mechanisms, Web services can be assembled to serve a particular function, solve a specific problem or deliver a particular solution to a customer.

Web services are described in terms of a standard description language: the Web Services Description Language or WSDL is primarily used to describe functional service characteristics. Functional characteristics include operational characteristics that define the overall behaviour of the service. Non-functional characteristics mainly describe quality characteristics of the hosting environment (refer to Sections 1.5.2 and 1.9) and are described as appropriate WSDL extensions (refer to Chapter 12 on Web service policies).

Web services are distributed over the Internet: Web services make use of existing, ubiquitous transport Internet protocols like HTTP. By relying on the same, well understood transport mechanism as Web content, Web services leverage existing infrastructure and can comply with current corporate firewall policies.

1.5 Characteristics of Web services

This section introduces the most important characteristics of Web services, such as simple and complex Web services, stateful and stateless services, service granularity, loose coupling, synchronous and asynchronous services and so on.

1.5.1 Types of Web service

Topologically, Web services can come in two flavours as shown in Figure 1.1: Simple or informational and complex services. Informational Web services support only simple request/response operations and always wait for a request; they process it and respond. Complex Web services implement some form of coordination between inbound and outbound operations. Each of these two models exhibits several important characteristics and is in turn subdivided in more specialised subcategories.

1.5.1.1 Simple or informational services

Informational services are services of relatively simple nature. They either provide programmatic access to content, interacting with an end user by means of simple request/response sequences, or alternatively may expose back end business applications to other applications. For instance, they may expose function calls, typically written in programming languages such as Java/EJB, Visual Basic or C++. The exposed programmatic simple services perform a request/response type of business task as shown in Figure 1.1. Applications access their function calls by executing a Web service through a standard programmatic interface specified in the Web Services Description Language or WSDL (see Chapter 5).

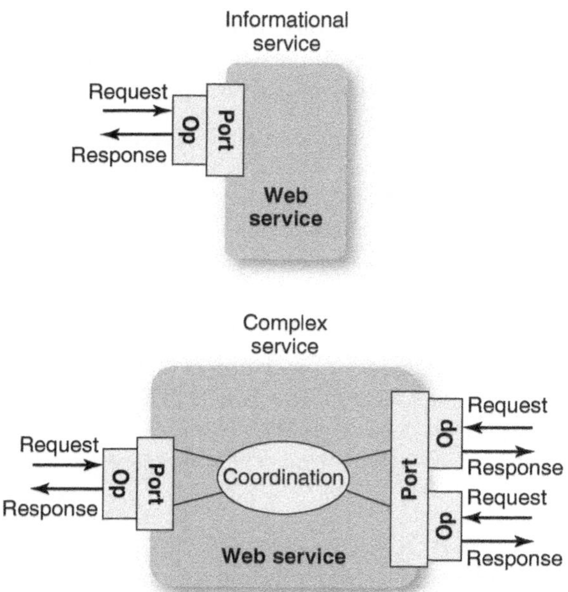

Figure 1.1 High-level view of informational and complex services

Informational services can be subdivided into three subcategories according to the business problems they solve:

1. Pure content services, which provide programmatic access to content such as weather report information, simple financial information, stock quote information, design information, news items and so on.

2. Simple trading services, which are more complicated forms of informational services that can provide a seamless aggregation of information across disparate existing systems and information sources, including back end systems, giving programmatic access to a business information system so that the requester can make informed decisions. Such service requests may have complicated realisations. Consider, for example, *pure* business services, such as logistic services, where automated services are the actual front ends to fairly complex physical organisational information systems.

3. Simple syndication services, which are value-added information Web services that purport to *plug into* commerce sites of various types, such as *e-marketplaces*, or *sell-sites*. Generally speaking, these services are offered by a third party and run the whole range from commerce enabling services, such as logistics, payment, fulfilment, and tracking services, to other value-added commerce services, such as rating services. Typical examples of syndicated services might include reservation services on a travel site or *rate quote* services on an insurance site.

Informational services can be viewed as *atomic* (discrete or singular) in nature, in that they perform a complete unit of work that leaves its underlying data stores in a consistent state. They are not transactional in nature (although their back end realisations may be). An informational service does not keep any memory of what happens to it between requests. In that respect this type of service is known as a stateless Web service (refer to Section 1.5.3 for a definition of this term).

Informational and simple trading services require support by three Web services standards for:

1. communication (Simple Object Access Protocol);
2. service description (Web Service Description Language);
3. service publication and discovery (Universal Description, Discovery, and Integration infrastructure).

These are described in Chapters 4, 5, and Chapter 6 of this book.

1.5.1.2 Complex services (business processes)

Enterprises can use an atomic (discrete or singular) service to accomplish a specific business task, such as billing or credit checking. However, for enterprises to obtain the full benefit of Web services, business process and transactional like Web service functionality is required that is well beyond that found in informational Web services.

When enterprises need to create a business process, such as customised ordering, customer support, procurement and logistical support, they need to compose several services together. Such a composite service is also known as a complex Web service. *Complex* (or *composite*) services typically involve the assembly and invocation of many pre-existing services, possibly found in diverse enterprises, to complete a multi-step business interaction that requires coordination. This is depicted in Figure 1.1.

Example 1.2: A simple supply chain application

To understand better the behaviour of a complex service, consider a supply chain application, such as the one depicted in Figure A.1, which involves order taking, stocking orders, sourcing, inventory control, financials and logistics. Numerous document exchanges will occur in this process, including requests for quotes, returned quotes, purchase order requests, purchase order confirmations, delivery information and so on. Long running activities and asynchronous messaging will also occur, and business *conversation* and even negotiations may occur before the final agreements are reached. This functionality is a typical characteristic of business processes, which are a type of complex Web service and will be covered in Chapter 9.

Complex Web services can in turn be categorised according to the way that they compose simple services, which are commonly known as the *constituent services* (of a complex service). Some complex Web services compose simple services that exhibit programmatic behaviour, whereas others compose services that exhibit mainly interactive behaviour where input has to be supplied by the user. This makes it natural to distinguish between the following two types of complex Web services:

1. *Complex services that compose programmatic Web services:* The clients of these Web services can assemble them to build complex services. An example, typical of a simple service exhibiting programmatic behaviour, could be an inventory checking service that comprises part of an inventory management process.
2. *Complex services that compose interactive Web services:* These services expose the functionality of a Web application's presentation (browser) layer. They frequently expose a multi-step Web application behaviour that combines a Web server, an application server and underlying database systems, and typically deliver the application directly to a browser and eventually to a human user for interaction. Clients of these Web services can incorporate interactive business processes into their Web applications, presenting integrated (aggregated) applications from external service providers. Obviously interactive services can be combined with programmatic services, thus delivering business processes that combine typical business logic functionality with Web browser interactivity.

Complex services exhibit coarse grained functionality and are stateful. A stateful Web service maintains some state between different operation invocations issued by the same or different Web service clients (see Section 1.5.3).

The complex Web services standards are still evolving and are converging on the communication protocol (Simple Object Access Protocol), WSDL, Universal Description, Discovery, and Integration infrastructure, WS-MetaDataExchange (which allows service endpoints to provide metadata information to requesters and support the bootstrapping of Web service interactions) and the Web service Business Process Execution Language or BPEL.

1.5.2 Functional and non-functional properties

Services are described in terms of a description language. A service description has two major interrelated components: its functional and non-functional characteristics.

- The *functional description* of a service is the operational characteristics that define the overall behaviour of the service, i.e. details of how the service is invoked, the location where it is invoked and so on. This description focuses on operational details regarding the syntax of messages and how to configure the network protocols to deliver messages.
- The *non-functional description* of a service concentrates on service quality attributes, such as service metering and cost, performance metrics, e.g. response time or accuracy, security attributes, authorisation, authentication, (transactional) integrity, reliability, scalability and availability. Non-functional descriptions force the service requester's run time environment to include, for instance, SOAP headers that specify non-functional requirements that may influence which service provider a service requester may choose. An example of this may be a security policy statement (refer to Chapter 12 for details regarding service security policies).

Functional properties of services are examined in Chapter 5, while non-functional ones are examined in Section 1.9 of this chapter and in Chapter 12 as part of service policies.

1.5.3 State properties

Services could be stateless or stateful. If services can be invoked repeatedly without having to maintain context or state they are called *stateless*, while services that may require their context to be preserved from one invocation to the next are called *stateful*. The service access protocol is always connectionless. A *connectionless protocol* means that the protocol has no concept of a job or a session and does not make any assumptions about eventual delivery (see Section 2.1.1.2).

A Web service in its simplest form, e.g. an informational weather report service, does not keep any '*memory*' of what happens to it between requests. Such informational Web services are therefore known to be stateless. The concept of statelessness means that, each time a consumer interacts with a Web service, an action is performed. After the results of the service invocation have been returned the action is finished. There is no assumption that subsequent invocations are associated with prior ones.

In contrast to a stateless Web service, a stateful Web service maintains some state between different operation invocations issued by the same or different Web service clients. If a particular '*session*' or '*conversation*' involves composite Web services then transient data between operation invocations is stateful. A message sent to a Web service stateful instance would be interpreted in relation to that instance specific state.

Typically, business processes specify stateful interactions involving the exchange of messages between partners, where the state of a business process includes the messages that are exchanged as well as intermediate data used in business logic and in composing messages sent to partners.

Example 1.3: A stateful order management service

Consider the order management application in our case study, where an automotive company might offer a service that begins an interaction by accepting a purchase order from customers through an input message and then returns an acknowledgement to the customer if the order can be fulfilled. The application might later send further messages to the customer, such as shipping notices and invoices. This type of functionality implies that the supplier's business process must *remember* the state of each customer purchase order interaction separately from other similar interactions. This is necessary when a customer has many purchase processes open with the same supplier that are executed simultaneously.

1.5.4 Loose coupling

Web services interact with one another dynamically and use Internet standard technologies, making it possible to build bridges between systems that otherwise would require extensive development efforts. The term coupling indicates the degree of dependency any two systems have on each other.

In a *tightly coupled message exchange* applications need to know how their partner applications behave. They also need to know intimate details of how their partner requires to be communicated with – the number of methods it exposes and the details of the parameters that each method accepts, and the type of results it returns. In addition, tightly coupled applications need to know the location of the applications with which they work (and this implies a certain *security* guarantee).

A key design pattern in tightly coupled environments is synchronous interactions. Tight coupling requires that the interfaces between the different components of an application are tightly interrelated in function and form, thus making them brittle when any form of change or replacement is required to parts or the whole application. It is often quite difficult and cumbersome to build tightly coupled applications because, when the number of applications and services increases, the number of interfaces that need to be created and maintained quickly becomes unwieldy.

As opposed to tight coupling principles that require agreement and shared context between communicating systems as well as sensitivity to change, loose coupling allows systems to connect and interact more freely (possibly across the Internet). In a *loosely coupled message exchange*, applications need not know or care how their partner applications behave or are implemented. The benefit of a loosely coupled system lies in its agility and the ability to survive evolutionary changes in the structure and implementation of the internals of each service, which make up the whole application. Systems that are loosely coupled in time have an asynchronous or event driven model rather than a synchronous model of interaction (see Section 2.5). Loose coupling of applications provides a level of flexibility and interoperability that cannot be matched using traditional approaches to building highly integrated, cross-platform, program-to-program communications environments.

With the Web service approach, the binding from a service requester to a service provider is loosely coupled. This means that the service requester has no knowledge of the technical details of the provider's implementation, such as the programming language, deployment platform and so forth. The service requester typically invokes operations by way of messages – a request message and the response – rather than through the use of application programming interfaces.

Table 1.1 summarises the differences between loose and tight coupling. In particular, it contrasts the two approaches with respect to mode of communication, messaging style, underlying platforms, binding protocols and overall approach to distributed computing.

Table 1.1 Tight versus loose coupling

	Tight coupling	*Loose coupling*
Method of communication	Synchronous	Asynchronous
Messaging style	RPC-style	Document-style
Message path	Hard coded	Routed
Underlying platform	Homogeneous	Heterogeneous
Binding protocol	Static	Dynamic – late binding
Overall objective	Re use	Re use, flexibility, broad applicability

1.5.5 Service granularity

Web services may vary in function from simple requests to complex systems that access and combine information from multiple sources. Even simple service requests may have complicated realisations. Simple services are discrete in nature, exhibit normally a request/reply mode of operation, and are of fine granularity. In contrast, complex services are coarse grained. For instance, the `SubmitPurchaseOrder` process in our case study involves interactions with other services and possibly end users in a single or multiple sessions. Coarse grained communication implies larger and richer data structures, i.e. those supported by XML schema, and enables looser coupling, which in turn enables asynchronous communication where the information exchange is the minimum required to complete the task.

More on this important topic can be found in Chapter 16 and Section 16.12.1.1 where we explain how service granularity affects the design of services.

1.5.6 Service synchronicity

When talking about services, we may distinguish between two methods of communication or programming styles: synchronous or remote procedure call (RPC) style versus asynchronous or message (document) style (see also Sections 2.5 and 2.6):

> *Synchronous services:* Clients of synchronous services express their request as a method call with a set of arguments, which returns a response containing a return value. This implies that, when a client sends a request message, it expects a response message before continuing with its computation. This makes the whole invocation an all-or-nothing proposition. If one operation is unable to complete for any reason, all other dependent operations will fail. This requires a tightly coupled model of communication between the client and service provider as shown in Table 1.1. RPC-style Web services are normally used when an application exhibits the following characteristics:
>
> - The client invoking the service requires an immediate response.
> - The client and service work in a back and forth conversational way.
>
> Examples of typical simple synchronous services with an RPC style include: returning the current price for a given stock; providing the current weather conditions in a particular location; or checking the credit rating of a potential trading partner prior to the completion of a business transaction.
>
> *Asynchronous services:* Asynchronous services are document style or message driven services. When a client invokes a message style service, the client typically sends it an entire document, such as a purchase order, rather than a discrete set of parameters. The service accepts the entire document; it processes it and may or may not return a result message. A client that invokes an asynchronous service does not need to wait for a response before it continues with the remainder of its application. The response from the service, if any, can appear hours or even days later.

Asynchronous interactions (messaging) are a key design pattern in loosely coupled environments. Messaging enables a loosely coupled environment in which an application does not need to know the intimate details of how to reach and interface with other applications. This allows a communication operation between any two processes to be a self-contained, standalone unit of work. Document style Web services are normally used when an application exhibits the following characteristics:

- The client does not require (or expect) an immediate response.
- The service is document oriented. This means that the client typically sends an entire document, e.g. a purchase order, rather discrete parameters.

Example 1.4: Typical document-style services

Examples of common, document style Web services include processing a purchase order, responding to a request for a quote order from a customer, or responding to an order placement by a particular customer. In all these cases, the client sends an entire document, such as a purchase order, to the Web service and assumes that the Web service is processing it in some way, but the client does not require an immediate answer.

1.5.7 Well-definedness

The service interaction must be well defined. The Web service allows by means of WSDL applications to describe to other applications the rules for interfacing and interacting. WSDL provides a uniform mechanism for describing abstract service interfaces and specific protocol bindings that support the service. As such it is a widely supported way of describing the details required by a service requester for binding to a service provider. The service descriptions focus on how operations interact with a service, how messages invoke operations, details of constructing such messages and details of where to send messages for processing, i.e. determining service access points.

WSDL does not include any technology details of the implementation of a Web service. The service requester neither knows nor cares whether the service is implemented in a programming language such as Java, C#, C and so forth. These issues are described further in Section 1.6 where we distinguish between the service interface and service implementation sections of a service definition.

1.5.8 Service usage context

In addition to the types and characteristics of Web services we mentioned above, it also useful to divide services into different categories based on the Web service requester's perspective. Here, we may distinguish between replaceable and mission critical services.

> A *replaceable Web service* is a service provided by several providers, and replacing one provider with another does not affect application functionality as long as the service interfaces are identical. The productivity is not impacted severely if the

service is unavailable for a short period of time as another provider (and service) may be chosen. A discrete (enumerated) discovery process, involving several alternative possibilities, may be pursued here.

A *mission-critical Web service* is a service possibly provided by a single specific provider, which if replaced compromises severely the functionality of an entire application. If the service were unavailable for a period of time it would drastically reduce the productivity of the application. This type of service would typically hold some critical business data and be integrated at the process level.

Example 1.5: A replaceable car rental service

A typical example of a replaceable service is a car rental service. Here we may pursue different car rental agencies, e.g. Avis, Hertz, Budget, and choose the first service response that arrives and satisfies our needs. This type of service is usually well integrated with the consumer processes (e.g. rent-a-car activity) and does not exchange any critical business data.

1.6 Service interface and implementation

One important aspect of services is that they make a sharp distinction between an interface and implementation part.

- The *service interface* part defines service functionality visible to the external world and provides the means to access this functionality. It is common practice that the service describes its own interface characteristics, i.e. the operations available, the parameters, data typing and the access protocols, in such a way that other software modules can determine what it does, how to invoke its functionality and what result to expect in return. In this regard, services are contractible software modules as they provide publicly available descriptions of the interface characteristics used to access the service so that potential clients can bind to it. The service client uses the service's interface description to bind to the service provider and invoke its functionality. This type of black box encapsulation imposed by services finds its roots in the principles of modularity in software engineering.
- The *service implementation* part realises a specific service interface whose implementation details are hidden from the users of the service. Different service providers using any programming language of their choice may implement the same interface. One service implementation might provide the functionality itself directly, while another service implementation might use a combination of other service implementations to provide the same functionality.

It is important to distinguish between a service interface and a service implementation because in many cases the organisations that provide service interfaces are not the same as the organisations that implement the services. A service interface is a concept that should be specified with an application or the user of the service in mind. The service realisation for this specific service interface, i.e. the service content, may be provided by a software package, e.g. an enterprise resource planning (ERP) package, a special purpose built component, a commercial off-the-shelf application, or a legacy application that represents a consistent chunk of business logic.

Component technology is normally used to implement (realise) the service functionality. A component is an independent, encapsulated part of a system, which is simple enough to implement a well defined set of responsibilities and has well defined limits to its functionality. In summary, we are dealing with two largely complementary elements: the service interface and its corresponding implementation component that realises the Web service implementation.

To a service client it is irrelevant whether the service implementation is provided by a fine grained suite of components, or a single monolithic system such as ERP. However, it is important that the developer who implements the service still thinks about the granularity of implementation so that they can optimise its performance, possibly by changing parts of the implementation with the minimum amount of disruption to other components, applications and services (see Chapter 16 which deals with service design and development concerns).

To cater for service composition into business processes we need to introduce the concept of the service orchestration interface, in addition to the concept of an interface. The *service orchestration* (or *assembly*) *interface* explicitly describes all the interfaces that a client of a composite service expects.

The service orchestration interface serves as a means to define how a composite service interface can be specified by means of imported service constituent interfaces. In this sense the service orchestration interface has a mission identical to a composition meta-model that provides a description of how the Web service interfaces interact with each other and how to define a new Web service interface (or `<PortType>`, see Section 5.2.3) as a collection (assembly) of existing interfaces (viz. imported `<PortType>`s of its service constituents). The concept of a service orchestration interface is shown in Figure 1.2, where it defines the encapsulation boundary of a service. This is the only way to design services reliably by importing and combining (orchestrating) service interfaces without knowledge of their implementations.

As service development requires that we deal with multiple imported service interfaces it is useful to introduce at this stage the concept of a provided and a requested service interface.

- A *provided service interface* describes the composite service (business process) that a provider offers to its clients and is the only interface viewed by a client application.
- A *required interface*, on the other hand, specifies the operations that a service provider needs to perform to fulfill its obligations to its clients.

Figure 1.2 shows how an orchestrated service may be assembled by reusing constituent services as parts in an assembly of services by wiring together their required and provided interfaces. A service can have any number of provided and required interfaces, provided interfaces show operations that a specific service provides for other services to use. Required interfaces show operations that a specific service uses in other services. This

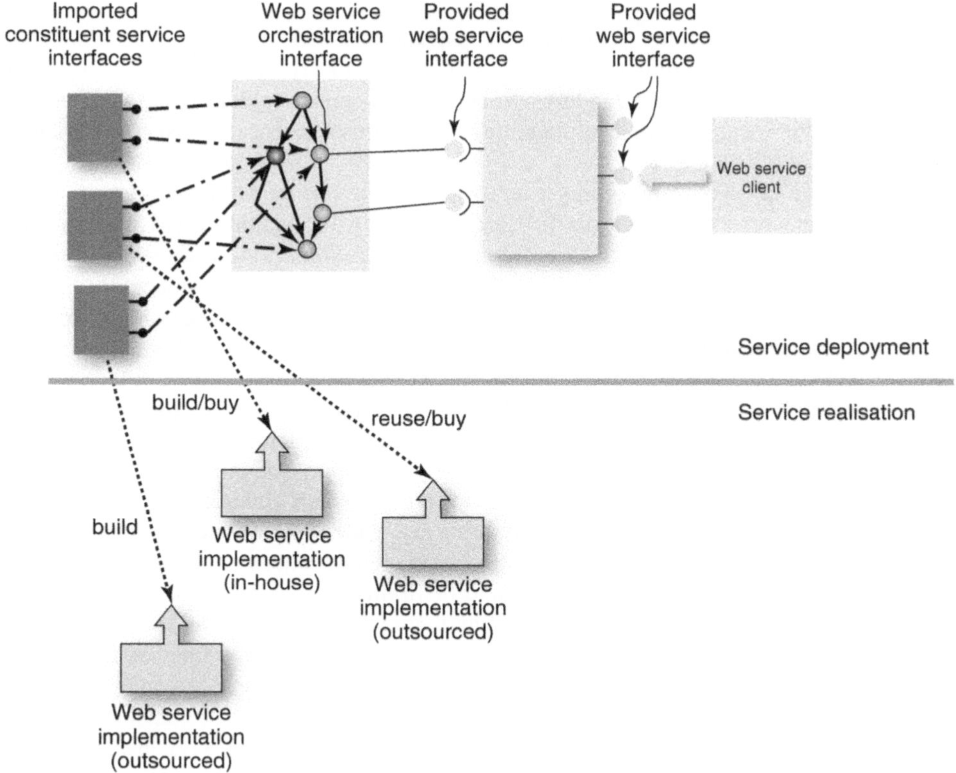

Figure 1.2 Service interfaces and service realisations

idea is depicted in Figure 1.2 which also illustrates dependencies between required and provided interfaces.

Finally, Figure 1.2 distinguishes between two broad aspects of services: *service deployment* and *service realisation*. Service deployment is connected to the interfaces that a service exposes, rolls out the service to all its participants and makes it ready for execution (see Section 16.6). Service realisation involves constructing the service by choosing from an increasing diversity of different implementation options (see Section 16.13). Service implementation may be mixed in various combinations including: in-house service design and implementation, purchasing/leasing/paying for services, outsourcing service design and implementation and using wrappers and/or adapters (see Section 2.8.1) for service enabling, reusable legacy functionality.

1.7 The Service Oriented Architecture

Web services hold the promise of moving beyond the simple exchange of information – the dominating mechanism for application integration today – to the concept of accessing, programming and integrating application services that encapsulate existing and new application functionality. This means organisations will be able not only to move information from application to application, but also to create complex customisable composite applications, leveraging any number of back end and older (legacy) technology systems found in local or remote applications. Key to this concept is the Service Oriented Architecture (or SOA).

SOA is a logical way of designing a software system to provide services to either end user applications or to other services distributed in a network, via published and discoverable interfaces. To achieve this, SOA reorganises a portfolio of previously siloed software applications and support infrastructure in an organisation into an interconnected collection of easily usable services. Each of these services is discoverable and accessible through a standard interface and messaging protocol. Once all the elements of an SOA are in place, existing and future applications can access the SOA based services as necessary. This architectural approach is particularly applicable when multiple applications, running on varied technologies and platforms, need to interoperate with each other.

The essential goal of an SOA is to enable general purpose interoperability among existing technologies and extensibility to future purposes and architectures. SOA lowers interoperability hurdles by converting monolithic and static systems into modular and flexible components, which it represents as services that can be requested through an industry standard protocol. Much of SOA's power and flexibility derives from its ability to leverage standards based functional services, calling them when needed on an individual basis, or aggregating them to create composite applications or multi-stage business processes. The building block services might employ pre-existing software components that are reused, and can also be updated or replaced without affecting the functionality or integrity of other independent services. Simply put, an SOA is an architectural style, inspired by the service oriented approach to computing, for enabling extensible interoperability.

SOA as a design philosophy is independent of any specific technology, e.g. Web services or J2EE. Although the concept of SOA is often discussed in conjunction with Web services, these two terms are not synonymous. In fact SOA can be implemented without the use of Web services, e.g. using Java, C# or J2EE. However, Web services should be seen as a primary example of a message delivery model that makes it much easier to deploy an SOA.

1.7.1 Roles of interaction in the SOA

The main building blocks of an SOA are threefold and they are determined on the basis of three primary roles that can be undertaken by these architectural modules. These are the service provider, the service registry and the service requester (client). Providers are software agents that provide the service. Providers are responsible for publishing a description of the service(s) they provide on a services registry. Clients are software agents that request the use and execution of a service. Agents can be simultaneously both service clients and providers. Clients must be able to find the description(s) of the services they require and must be able to bind to them. To achieve this functionality SOA builds on today's Web services baseline specifications of SOAP, WSDL, UDDI, and the Business Process Execution Language for Web services that are going to be examined in Chapters 4, 5, 6, and 9.

1.7.1.1 Web service provider

The first important role that can be discerned in SOA is that of the Web service provider. From a business perspective the Web service provider is the organisation that owns the Web service and implements either internally or externally the business logic that underlies the service. From an architectural perspective this is the platform that hosts and controls access to the service.

The Web service provider is responsible for publishing the Web services it provides in a service registry hosted by a service discovery agency. This involves describing the business, and technical information of the Web service, and registering that information with the Web services registry in the format prescribed by the discovery agency.

1.7.1.2 Web service requester

The next major role in SOA is that of the Web service requester (or client). From a business perspective, this is the enterprise that requires certain functions to be satisfied. From an architectural perspective, this is the application that is looking for, and subsequently invoking, the service.

The Web service requester searches the service registry for the desired Web services. This effectively means discovering the Web service description in a registry provided by a discovery agency and using the information in the description to bind to the service.

1.7.1.3 Web service registry

The last important role that can be distinguished in SOA is that of the Web service registry, which is a searchable directory where service descriptions can be published and searched. Service requesters find service descriptions in the registry and obtain binding technical and other information for services. This information is sufficient for the service requester to contact, or bind to, the service provider and thus make use of the services it provides.

The Web service discovery agency is responsible for providing the infrastructure required to enable the three SOA operations described in the following section.

1.7.2 SOA operations

For an application to take advantage of service interactions between the three roles in an SOA, three primary operations must take place. These are *publication* of the service descriptions, *finding* the service descriptions, and *binding* or invocation of services based on their service description. These three basic operations can occur singly or iteratively.

A logical view of the SOA is given in Figure 1.3. This figure illustrates the relationship between the SOA roles and operations. First, the Web services provider publishes its Web service(s) with the discovery agency. Next, the Web services client searches for desired Web services using the registry of the discovery agency. Finally, the Web services client invokes (binds to) the Web services provided by the Web services provider using the information obtained from the discovery agency. The SOA operations are described briefly below.

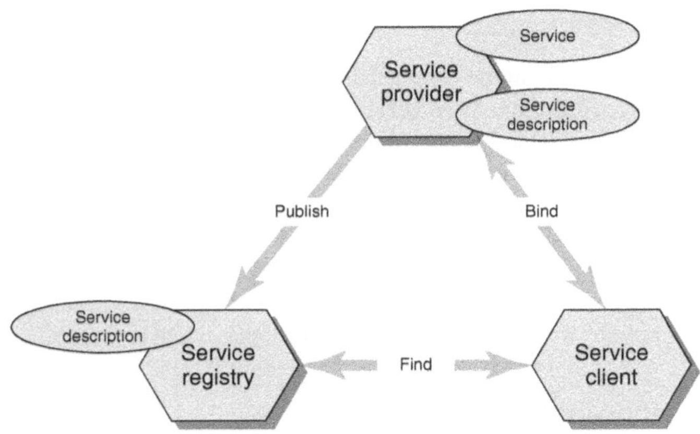

Figure 1.3 Web service roles and operations in an SOA

1.7.2.1 The publish operation

Publishing a Web service so that other users or applications can find it actually consists of two equally important operations. The first operation is describing the Web service itself; the other is the actual registration of the Web service.

The first requirement for publishing Web services with the service registry is for a service provider to properly describe them in WSDL. As we shall see in Chapter 6, three basic categories of information, necessary for proper description of a Web service, can be discerned:

- *business information:* information regarding the Web service provider or the implementer of the service;
- *general service information:* information about the nature of the Web service;
- *technical service information:* information about implementation details and the invocation methods for the Web service.

The next step in publishing a Web service is registration. *Registration* deals with storing the three basic categories of descriptive information about a service in the Web service registry. For Web service requesters to be able to find a Web service this service description information needs to be registered with at least one discovery agency.

1.7.2.2 The find operation

In a similar fashion to publishing, finding Web services is also a twofold operation. Finding the desired Web services consists of first discovering the services in the registry of the discovery agency that publishes the service and then selecting the desired Web service(s) from the search results.

Discovering Web services involves querying the registry of the discovery agency for Web services matching the needs of a Web services requester. A query consists of search criteria, such as type of service, preferred price range, what products are associated with this service, with which categories in company and product taxonomies this Web service is associated as well as other technical service characteristics (see Chapter 6). A query is executed against the Web service information in the registry that was entered by the Web services provider. The find operation can be involved in two different instances by the requester. It can either be specified statically (at design time) to retrieve a service's interface description for program development or dynamically (at run time) to retrieve a service's binding and location description for invocation.

Selection deals with deciding which Web service to invoke from the set of Web services the discovery process returned. Two possible methods of selection exist: manual and automatic selection. Manual selection implies that the Web services requester selects the desired Web service directly from the returned set of Web services after manual inspection. The other possibility is automatic selection of the best candidate between potentially matching Web services. A special client application program provided by the Web services registry can achieve this. In this case the Web services requester has to specify preferences to enable the application to infer which Web service the Web services requester is most likely to wish to invoke.

1.7.2.3 The bind operation

The final SOA operation, and perhaps the most important one, is the actual invocation of the Web services. During the binding operation the service requester invokes or initiates an interaction at run time using the binding details in the service description to locate and contract to the service. The technical information entered in the registry by the Web services provider is used here.

Two different possibilities exist for the service invocation. The first possibility is direct invocation of the Web service by the Web services requester who uses the technical information included in the description of the service. The second possibility is mediation by the discovery agency when invoking the Web service. In this case all communication between the Web service requester and the Web service provider goes through the Web service registry of the discovery agency.

Example 1.6: SOA view of composing a purchase order service

To exemplify the use of SOA for composing complex services, let us consider again the example of a business process that implements the processing of a purchase order submitted by a manufacturing company such as AVERS in our case study. Here, we assume that a car manufacturer has built a business based on providing specialty and custom fabricated car components on a spot and contract basis. Its role is in the middle of the supply chain – between commodity suppliers supplying luxury leather interiors, modern engines and running gear and the assembly and manufacturing plants who install a variety of parts to complete the vehicle. This requires that the manufacturing company manages relationships with multiple business partners and even acts as an intermediary between its suppliers and customers.

The purchase order process can be developed in terms of interacting Web services involving purchase orders, credit checks, automated billing, stock updates and shipping

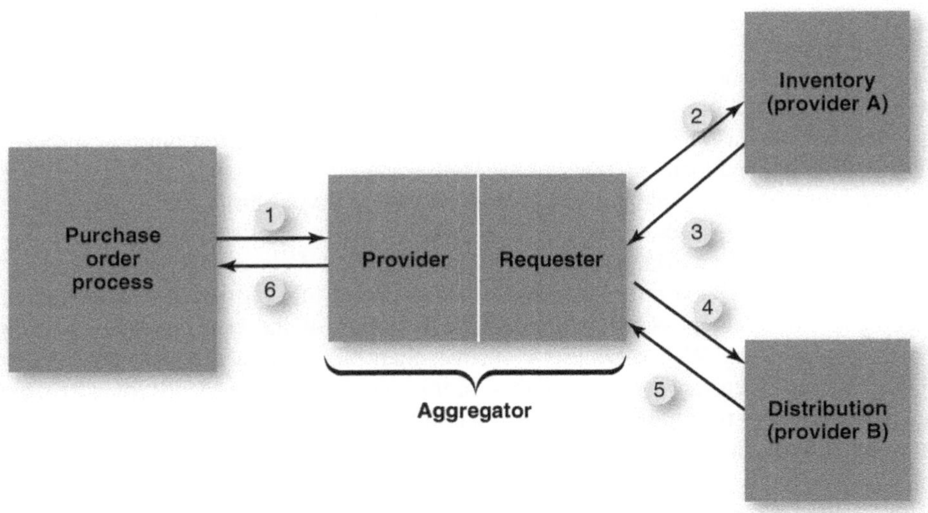

Figure 1.4 SOA: composite service example

originating from various service providers. To simplify things we assume that the purchase order process employs a relatively simple composite service that is provided by a commodity supplier that composes two separate relatively simple services, namely an inventory and a distribution service. The SOA representation of this type of aggregate (composite) service is illustrated in Figure 1.4.

To address the requirements of composite Web services, Figure 1.4 involves a hierarchical service provision scheme whereby a requester (client) sends a request to an aggregator, a system that offers a composite Web service for an application such as order management (Step 1). The aggregator (parts supplier), which is just another service provider, receives the initial request and decomposes it into two parts, one involving an inventory check service and a distribution service request. The aggregator thus acts as a Web services requester and forwards the order request to the inventory (Step 2) service provider. This service provider determines whether or not the ordered parts are available in the product inventory and sends its response to the aggregator (Step 3). If all is well, the aggregator selects a distributor, which schedules the shipment for the order (Steps 4 and 5). Finally, the aggregator reverts to its role as service provider and calculates the final price for the order, bills the customer and relays its final response to the client process (Step 6).

1.7.3 SOA entry points

Organisations that use SOAs may distinguish between the following three distinct SOA entry points on the basis of their business requirements and priorities:

> *Implementing enterprise service orchestrations:* This small scale SOA model can work well with a limited number as a foundation with a limited number of

consumers and services that are well known to an organisation. It primarily focuses on a typical implementation within a department, or between a small number of departments and enterprise assets, and comprises two steps.

1. First, transforming enterprise assets and applications into an SOA enabled implementation. This can start by service enabling existing individual applications or creating new applications using Web services technology. This can begin by specifying a Web service interface into an individual application or application element (including legacy systems).
2. The next step after this basic Web service implementation is implementing service orchestrations out of the service enabled assets or newly created service applications. This step involves integrating multiple services into a process that accomplishes a particular business task. This step supports a range of integration types, including integrating interdepartmental applications, interdepartmental data, business processes, and heterogeneous systems.

Service enabling the entire enterprise: The next stage in the SOA entry point hierarchy is when an enterprise seeks to provide a set of common services based on SOA components that can be used across the entire organisation. Enterprise wide service integration is achieved on the basis of commonly accepted standards. This results in achieving service consistency across departmental boundaries and is a precursor to integrating an organisation with its partners and suppliers. Consistency is an important factor for this configuration as it provides both a uniform view to the enterprise and its customers as well as ensuring compliance with statutory or business policy requirements.

Implementing extended enterprise end-to-end business processes: The term end-to-end business process signifies that a succession of automated business processes and information systems in different enterprises (which are typically involved in inter-company business transactions) are successfully integrated. The aim is to provide seamless interoperation and interactive links between all the relevant members in an extended enterprise – ranging from product designers, suppliers, trading partners and logistics providers to end customers. At this stage an organisation moves into the highest strategic level of SOA implementation. Deployment of services becomes ubiquitous, and federated services collaborate across enterprise boundaries to create complex products and services. Individual services in this extended enterprise may originate from many providers, irrespective of company specific systems or applications.

In this book we shall focus on the latter two SOA entry points: service enabling the enterprise and end-to-end collaborative business processes.

1.7.4 Layers in an SOA

One problem when implementing an SOA at the enterprise level or implementing a cross-enterprise collaborative SOA is how to manage the SOA model, how to categorise the elements in this model and how to organise them in such a way that the different stakeholders reviewing the model can understand it. To surmount complexity, it is often convenient to

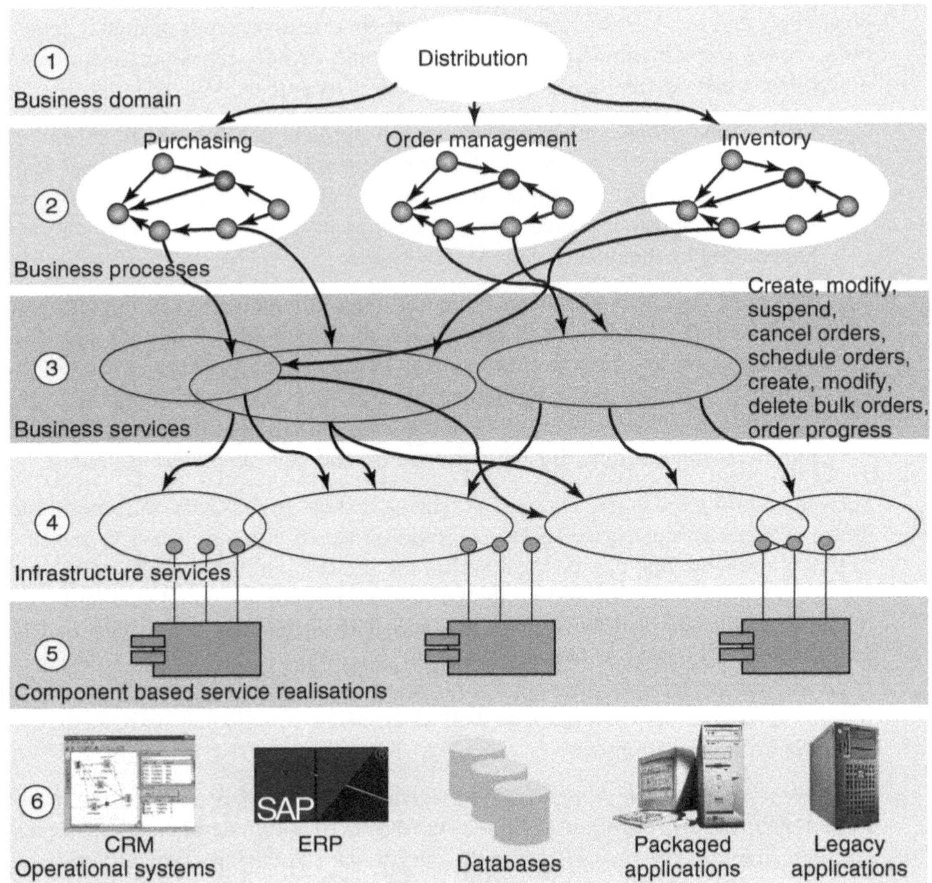

Figure 1.5 Layers in an SOA

think of the SOA as comprising a number of distinct layers of abstraction that emphasise service interfaces, service realisations and compositions of services into higher level business processes. This requires that a stratified approach to SOA be pursued.

The principle of SOA layering is illustrated in Figure 1.5. In this figure an SOA is shown to comprise six distinct layers: domains, business processes, business services, infrastructure services, service realisations and operational systems. Each of the SOA layers describes a logical separation of concerns by defining a set of common enterprise elements. Note that in Figure 1.5 each layer, starting from the bottom SOA layer, passes basic functionality at the request of the layer above it, without unavailing all details of the layer, and in turn requests more basic functionality of the layer below it (if present). The adjacent higher layer then extends this functionality to accomplish its objectives.

The logical flow employed in the layered SOA development model may focus on a *top down development* approach, which emphasizes how business processes are decomposed into a collection of business services and how these services are implemented in terms of pre-existing enterprise assets. Other variations include a *bottom up development* (where emphasis is placed on enterprise information systems) and the more common *meet-in-the-middle development* approach. The bottom up approach emphasises how existing enterprise assets are transformed into business services and how business services are in turn composed into business processes. All these Web service development options are part of the Web service design and development methodology that we introduce in Chapter 16.

In the following we shall analyse the layered SOA development model starting with a downward flow from the top.

1.7.4.1 Business domain

The topmost layer (Layer 1) is formed on the basis of the observation that all business processes in an enterprise target a particular business domain. A *business domain* is a functional domain comprising a set of current and future business processes that share common capabilities and functionality and can work with each other to accomplish a higher level business objective, such as loans, insurance, banking, finance, manufacturing, human resources and so on. In this way, an enterprise can be partitioned into a set of disjointed domains.

In our manufacturing case study, we assume that a hypothetical automotive assembly company (AVERS) is partitioned into four associated domains, namely distribution, finance, manufacturing and human resources, which can be linked together to provide a complete financial and operational view of this specific enterprise. We shall concentrate on distribution as an example of a business domain in this section.

1.7.4.2 Business processes

SOA views an enterprise from the perspective of processes, such as order management, and perceives an enterprise as a complete set of well defined, core business processes. This is reflected in Layer 2 in the SOA model, the business process layer in Figure 1.5. This layer is formed by subdividing a business domain, such as distribution, into a small number of *core business processes*, such as purchasing, order management and inventory, which are made entirely standard for use throughout the enterprise. This process decomposition is illustrated in Figure 1.5. In Figure 1.5 we assume that the domain decomposition results in three well defined relatively coarse processes. This is largely a design issue because having a large number of fine grained processes leads to tremendous overhead and inefficiency (refer to Section 16.8, which describes process design criteria). Clearly, having a small collection of coarser grained processes that are usable in multiple scenarios is a better option.

Now let us concentrate on the order management process in Layer 2, which is central to the AVERS case study, and deconstruct its meaning and functionality. This process typically performs order volume analysis, margin analysis, sales forecasting and demand forecasting across any region, product or period. It can also provide summary and transaction detail data on order fulfilments and shipment according to item, sales representative, customer, warehouse, order type, payment term and period. Furthermore, it can track order quantities, payments, margins on past and upcoming shipments and cancellations for each order. In an SOA we may think of such a business process as consisting of people, business services and the interfaces between the business services.

1.7.4.3 Business services

The order management process in Figure 1.5 is shown to be divided into several generic business activities, which essentially represent fine grained simple services for creating, modifying, suspending, cancelling, querying orders and scheduling order activities. The idea is to decompose a process into increasingly smaller sub-processes until the process cannot be decomposed any further. The resulting sub-processes become candidate discrete business services for subsequent implementation and are called *business services*. The more processes that an enterprise decomposes in this way the more commonality across these sub-processes can be achieved. In this way, an enterprise has the chance of building an appropriate set of reusable business services.

Business services exhibit a fine level granularity and simply automate specific atomic business tasks that are part of the order management process. Business services in the order management process are shown to create and track orders for a product, a service or a resource, and capture customer selected service details. They can also create, modify and delete bulk orders and order activities, and inform customers of the progress of an order and its order activities. A common data vocabulary is used to describe this kind of information so that various business services (that may belong to different organisations) can interpret messages unambiguously, communicate with each other, and be easily orchestrated and used together under the order management process. This topic is addressed in Chapters 13 and 14, which presents mechanisms for the semantic enrichment and standardisation of service descriptions.

The business service interfaces in Layer 3 are exported as service descriptions using a service description language, such as WSDL (see Chapter 5). These service descriptions can be implemented by a number of service providers, each offering various choices of qualities of service based on technical requirements in the areas of availability, performance, scalability and security.

1.7.4.4 Utility services

During the exercise of defining business services it also important to take existing utility logic, ingrained in code, and expose it as services which themselves become candidate services that specify not the overall business process, but rather the mechanism for implementing the process. This exercise should thus yield two categories of services: business services that, as we already explained, are reusable across multiple processes, and a collection of fine grained *utility* (or commodity) *services* (not shown in Figure 1.5). The latter provide value to, and are shared by, business services across the organisation. Examples of utility services include services implementing calculations, algorithms, directory management services and so on.

1.7.4.5 Infrastructure services

An SOA requires the provision of infrastructure services to implement business services and processes. Infrastructure services are subdivided into technical utility services, access services, management and monitoring services, as well as interaction services. All types of infrastructure services are considered as an integral part of the Enterprise Service Bus, which is the technical infrastructure and implementation backbone that enables standards based integration in an SOA environment (see Chapter 8).

Technical utility services in Layer 4 are coarse grained services that provide the technical infrastructure enabling the development, delivery, maintenance and provisioning of atomic business services (in Layer 3) and their integration into processes (in Layer 2) as well as capabilities that maintain QoS such as security, performance, and availability. They also include mechanisms that seamlessly interlink services that span enterprises.

Access services are dedicated to transforming data and integrating legacy applications and functions into the SOA environment. This includes the wrapping and service enablement of legacy functions. In the distributed computing systems literature access services are commonly known as adapters (see Section 2.8.1). In the layered SOA model, access services are distinctly responsible for rendering these adapters as services so that they can help transform elements of legacy assets and enterprise application systems into atomic business services and business processes.

Management services manage resources both within and across system boundaries, gather information about managed systems and managed resource status and performance, and offer specific management tasks such as root cause failure analysis, reporting and capacity planning. *Monitoring services* monitor the health of SOA applications, giving insights into the health of systems and networks, and into the status and behaviour patterns of applications, thus making them more suitable for mission critical computing environments. Management and monitoring services rely on emerging standards such as WS-Management, which are covered in Chapter 17.

Finally, *interaction services* support the interaction between applications and end users. Interactions with the external world are not limited to just interactions with humans. In some cases, interaction logic needs to orchestrate the interface to vehicles, sensors, radio frequency identification (RFID) technology devices, environmental control systems, process control equipment and so on.

1.7.4.6 Component services

The two lowest layers in Figure 1.5 are Layer 5 and 6. Layer 5 is the component realisation layer that is used for implementing services out of pre-existing applications and systems found in the operational systems layer (Layer 6).

Layer 5 uses component technology to implement (realise) the required service functionality. Component realisations are invoked by the technical services in Layer 4 to create the content of and construct business services. For instance, they can use transformation facilities and programming facilities for orchestrating business services and building applications and systems based on SOA. This procedure is explained further in Section 16.13.2, where we described the Service Component Architecture which is part of the SOA construction phase.

Component technology is the preferred technology for service implementations (see Section 1.11 for a comparison between Web services and component technologies). Because components are autonomous units of functionality they provide natural demarcation of implementation work. Component implementation is discussed in Section 16.13.2.

1.7.4.7 IT assets – operational systems

Finally, the implementation of a business service will often consist of an entire assembly of application and middleware functionality, potentially integrated across different application origins. Such functionality is provided by operational systems in Layer 6. The operational systems in this layer are used by components to implement business services and processes.

Layer 6 in Figure 1.5 is shown to contain existing enterprise systems or applications, including Customer Relationship Management (CRM) and Enterprise Resource Planning (ERP) systems and applications, legacy applications, database systems and applications, other packaged applications and so on. These systems are usually known as enterprise information systems (see Section 2.10). This explains how an SOA can leverage existing systems and integrate them using a service oriented style of integration.

1.8 The Web service technology stack

The goal of Web service technology is to allow applications to work together over standard Internet protocols, without direct human intervention. By doing so, we can automate many business operations, creating new functional efficiencies and new, more ffective ways of doing business. The minimum infrastructure required by the Web services paradigm is purposefully low to help ensure that Web services can be implemented on, and accessed from, any platform using any technology and programming language.

By intent, Web services are not implemented in a monolithic manner, but rather represent a collection of several related technologies. The more generally accepted definition for Web services leans on a stack of specific, complementary standards, which are illustrated in Figure 1.6. The development of open and accepted standards is a key strength of

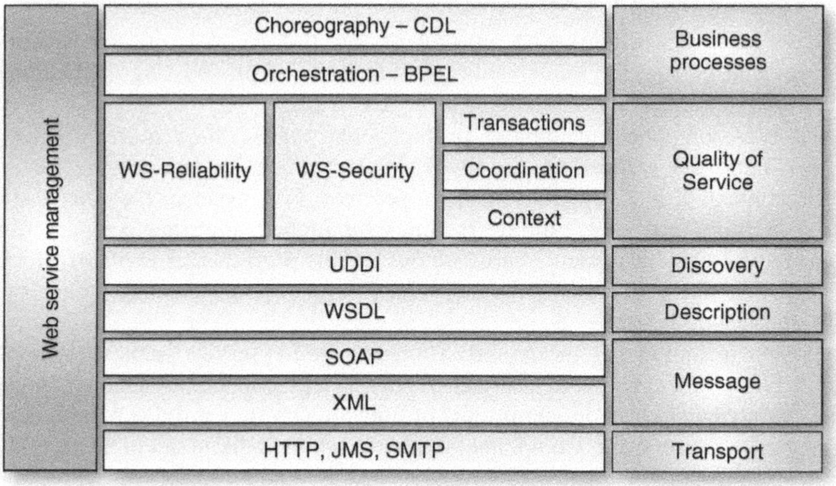

Figure 1.6 The Web service technology stack

the coalitions that have been developing the Web services infrastructure. At the same time, as can be seen in Figure 1.6, these efforts have resulted in the proliferation of a dizzying number of emerging standards and acronyms. In order to simply things and help readers understand the multitude of Web services, we provide a classification scheme for the most important standards in the Web service technology stack. We introduce this classification scheme briefly below.

1.8.1 Enabling technology standards

Web services build on ubiquitous Internet connectivity and infrastructure to ensure nearly universal reach and support although not specifically tied to any particular transport protocol. For instance, at the transport level Web services take advantage of HTTP, the same connection protocol used by Web servers and browsers. Another enabling technology is the Extensible Markup Language (XML). XML is a widely accepted format for all exchanging data and its corresponding semantics. Web services use XML as the fundamental building block for nearly every other layer in the Web services stack. We cover XML briefly in Chapter 3.

1.8.2 Core service standards

The core Web service standards comprise baseline standards for message transportation, service description and publication, which are briefly described below.

Communication protocol: The Simple Object Access Protocol or SOAP is a simple XML-based messaging protocol on which Web services rely to exchange information among themselves. This protocol implements a request/response model for communication between interacting Web services, and uses HTTP to penetrate firewalls, which are usually configured to accept HTTP and FTP service requests. We cover SOAP in some detail in Chapter 4.

Service description: Web services can be used effectively when a Web service and its client rely on standard ways to specify data and operations, to represent Web service contracts and to understand the capabilities that a Web service provides. To achieve this, the functional characteristics of a Web service are first described using a Web Services Description Language. WSDL defines the XML grammar for describing services as collections of communicating endpoints capable of exchanging messages. We cover WSDL in some detail in Chapter 5.

Service publication: Web service publication is achieved using the Universal Description, Discovery and Integration (UDDI) registry. This is a public directory that provides publication of on line services and facilitates eventual discovery of Web services. Companies can publish WSDL specifications for services they provide and other enterprises can access those services using the description in WSDL using the UDDI. In this way, independent applications can advertise the presence of business processes or tasks that can be utilised by other remote applications and systems. We cover UDDI in some detail in Chapter 6.

1.8.3 Service composition and collaboration standards

These include the following standards:

- *Service composition:* This family of standards describes the execution logic of Web service based applications by defining their control flows (such as conditional, sequential, parallel, and exceptional execution) and prescribing the rules for consistently managing their unobservable business data. In this way, enterprises can describe complex processes that span multiple organisations – such as order processing, lead management and claims handling – and execute the same business processes in systems from other vendors. The Business Process Execution Language (BPEL), which we cover in Chapter 9, is the *de facto* standard that can achieve service composition for Web services [Alves 2007].
- *Service collaboration:* This standard describes cross-enterprise collaborations of Web service participants by defining their common observable behaviour, where synchronised information exchanges occur through their shared contact points, when commonly defined ordering rules are satisfied. The Web Services Choreography Description Language (WS-CDL) [Kavantzas 2004], which we also cover in Chapter 9, supports service collaboration.
- *Coordination/transaction standards:* The WS-Coordination and WS-Transaction initiatives complement BPEL to provide mechanisms for defining specific standard protocols for use by transaction processing systems, workflow systems, or other applications that wish to coordinate multiple Web services. These three specifications work in tandem to address the business workflow issues implicated in connecting and executing a number of Web services that may run on disparate platforms across organisations involved in e-Business scenarios. We cover WS-Coordination and WS-Transaction in some detail in Chapter 10.
- *Value-added standards:* Additional elements that support complex business interactions must still be implemented before Web services can automate truly critical business processes. Value-added service standards include mechanisms for security and authentication, authorisation, trust, privacy, secure conversations, contract management and so on. We cover value-added service standards such as WS-Security, WS-Policy, and WS-Management in Chapters 11, 12, and 17 respectively.

1.9 Quality of service (QoS)

A significant requirement for an SOA based application is to operate in such a way that it functions reliably and delivers a consistent service at a variety of levels. This requires not only focusing on the functional properties of services but also concentrating on describing the environment hosting the Web service, i.e. describing the non-functional capabilities of services. Each service hosting environment may offer various choices of Quality of Service based on technical requirements regarding demands for around the clock levels of service availability, performance and scalability, security and privacy policies and so on, all of which must be described.

QoS refers to the ability of the Web service to respond to expected invocations and to perform them at the level commensurate with the mutual expectations of both its provider and its customers. Several quality factors that reflect customer expectations, such as constant service availability, connectivity and high responsiveness, become key to keeping a business competitive and viable as they can have a serious impact upon service provision. QoS thus becomes an important criterion that determines the service usability and utility, both of which influence the popularity of a particular Web service. In other words, it comprises an important selling and differentiating point between Web services providers.

Delivering QoS on the Internet is a critical and significant challenge because of its dynamic and unpredictable nature. Applications with very different characteristics and requirements compete for all kinds of network resources. Changes in traffic patterns, securing mission critical business transactions, and the effects of infrastructure failures, low performance of Web protocols and reliability issues over the Web create a need for Internet QoS standards. Often, unresolved QoS issues cause critical applications to suffer from unacceptable levels of performance degradation.

Traditionally, QoS is measured by the degree to which applications, systems, networks and all other elements of the IT infrastructure support availability of services at a required level of performance under all access and load conditions. While traditional QoS metrics apply, the characteristics of Web service environments bring both greater availability of applications and increased complexity in terms of accessing and managing service, and thus impose specific and intense demands on organisations, which QoS must address.

QoS can be viewed in the Web service context as providing assurance on a set of quantitative characteristics. These can be defined on the basis of important functional and non-functional service quality properties that include implementation and deployment issues, as well as other important service characteristics such as service metering and cost, performance metrics (e.g. response time), security requirements, (transactional) integrity, reliability, scalability and availability. These characteristics are necessary requirements to understand the overall behaviour of a service so that other applications and services can bind to it and execute it as part of a business process.

1.9.1 QoS requirements for Web services

The key elements for supporting QoS in a Web service environment are summarised in what follows and were inspired by [Mani 2002]:

1. *Availability:* Availability is the absence of service downtimes. Availability represents the probability that a service is available. Larger values mean that the service is always ready to use, while smaller values indicate unpredictability over whether the service will be available at a particular time. Also associated with availability is time-to-repair (TTR), which represents the time it takes to repair a service that has failed.

2. *Accessibility:* Accessibility represents the degree with which a Web service request is served. It may be expressed as a probability measure denoting the success rate or chance of a successful service instantiation at a point in time. A high degree of

accessibility means that a service is available for a large number of clients and that clients can use the service relatively easily.

3. *Conformance to standards:* Describes the compliance of a Web service with standards. Strict adherence to correct versions of standards (e.g. BPEL v 2.0) by service providers is necessary for proper invocation of Web services by service requesters. In addition, service providers must stick to thße standards outlined in Service Level Agreements (SLA) between service requesters and providers.
4. *Integrity:* Describes the degree with which a Web service performs its tasks according to its WSDL description as well as conformance with SLA. A higher degree of integrity means that the functionality of a service is closer to its WSDL description or SLA.
5. *Performance:* Performance is measured in terms of two factors: throughput and latency. *Throughput* represents the number of Web service requests served during a given time period. *Latency* represents the length of time between sending a request and receiving the response. Higher throughput and lower latency values represent good performance of a Web service. When measuring the transaction/request volumes handled by a Web service it is important to consider whether these come in a steady flow or burst around particular events, like the open or close of the business day or seasonal rushes.
6. *Reliability:* Reliability represents the ability of a service to function correctly and consistently, and provide the same service quality despite system or network failures. The reliability of a Web service is usually expressed in terms of the number of transactional failures per month or year.
7. *Scalability:* Scalability refers to the ability consistently to serve the requests despite variations in the volume of requests. High accessibility of Web services can be achieved by building highly scalable systems.
8. *Security:* Security involves aspects such as authentication, authorisation, message integrity, and confidentiality (see Chapter 11). Security has added importance because Web service invocation occurs over the Internet. The amount of security that a particular Web service requires is described in its accompanying SLA, and service providers must maintain this level of security.
9. *Transactionality:* There are several cases where Web services require transactional behaviour and context propagation (see Chapter 10). The fact that a particular Web service requires transactional behaviour is described in its accompanying SLA, and service providers must maintain this property.

1.9.2 Service level agreements (SLAs)

As organisations depend on business units, partners and external service providers to furnish them with services, they rely on the use of SLAs to ensure that the chosen service provider delivers a guaranteed level of service quality. An SLA is a formal agreement (contract) between a provider and client, formalising the details of a Web service (contents, price, delivery process, acceptance and quality criteria, penalties and so on, usually in measurable terms) in a way that meets the mutual understandings and expectations of both the service provider and the service requester.

An SLA is basically a QoS guarantee typically backed up by *charge-back* and other mechanisms designed to compensate users of services and to influence organisations to fulfil SLA commitments. Understanding business requirements, expected usage patterns and system capabilities can go a long way towards ensuring successful deployments. An SLA is an important and widely used instrument in the maintenance of service provision relationships as both service providers and clients alike utilise it.

An SLA may contain the following parts [Jin 2002]:

1. *Purpose:* This field describes the reasons behind the creation of the SLA.
2. *Parties:* This field describes the parties involved in the SLA and their respective roles, e.g. service provider and service consumer (client).
3. *Validity period:* This field defines the period of time that the SLA will cover. This is delimited by start time and end time of the agreement term.
4. *Scope:* This field defines the services covered in the agreement.
5. *Restrictions:* This field defines the necessary steps to be taken for the requested service levels to be provided.
6. *Service level objectives:* This field defines the levels of service that both the service customers and the service providers agree on, and usually includes a set of service level indicators, like availability, performance and reliability. Each of these aspects of the service level will have a target level to achieve.
7. *Penalties:* This field defines what sanctions should apply in case the service provider underperforms and is unable to meet the objectives specified in the SLA.
8. *Optional services:* This field specifies any services that are not normally required by the user, but might be required in case of an exception.
9. *Exclusion terms:* These specify what is not covered in the SLA.
10. *Administration:* This field describes the processes and the measurable objectives in an SLA and defines the organisational authority for overseeing them.

SLAs can be either static or dynamic in nature. A *static SLA* is an SLA that generally remains unchanged for multiple service time intervals. Service time intervals may be calendar months for a business process that is subject to an SLA, or may be a transaction or any other measurable and relevant period of time for other processes. They are used for assessment of the QoS and are agreed between a service provider and service client. A *dynamic SLA* is an SLA that generally changes from service period to service period, to accommodate changes in provision of service.

To enter into a Web service SLA, specific QoS metrics, evaluated over a time interval to a set of defined objectives, should be employed. Measurement of QoS levels in an SLA will ultimately involve tracing Web services through multi-domain (geographical, technological, application and supplier) infrastructures. In a typical scenario, each Web service may interact with multiple Web services, switching between the roles of being a service provider in some interactions to being a consumer in other interactions. Each of these interactions could potentially be governed by an SLA. The metrics imposed by SLAs should correlate with the overall objectives of the services being provided. Thus an important function that an SLA accomplishes is addressing QoS at the source. This refers to the level of service that a particular service provides [Mani 2002].

To address QoS and SLA Web service concerns, the evolving Web service suite of standards supports a standard policy framework that makes it possible for developers to express the policies of services, and for Web services to understand policies and enforce them at run time. The Web Services Framework (WS-Policy) [Vedamuthu 2007a] assists this undertaking by providing building blocks that may be used in conjunction with other Web service and application specific protocols to assist in expressing, exchanging and processing the policies governing the interactions between Web service endpoints (see Chapter 12).

1.10 Web service interoperability

Details of Web service specifications, implementations and best practices are gradually becoming established. Given the potential to have many necessary interrelated specifications at various versions and schedules of development, it becomes a very difficult task to determine which products support which levels of the Web service specifications. In many situations, there are versions of products that implement the specifications in ways that are different enough to prevent their implementations from being fully interoperable. This requires that individual enterprises provide individual interpretations of how their specifications are to be used. This has resulted in many Web service applications that were isolated and could serve only a limited community, and certainly defies the purpose of Web service interoperability. Web service interoperability needs, among other things, to address the problem of ambiguity among the interpretation of standards that have been agreed upon, and insufficient understanding of the interaction among the various specifications.

The Web Services Interoperability Organization (WS-I) addresses web service interoperability concerns. WS-I (www.ws-i.org) is an open, industry consortium chartered to promote Web service interoperability amongst the stack of web service specifications. This organisation works across the industry and standards organisations to respond to developer needs by providing guidance, best practices and resources for developing Web service solutions that are interoperable. WS-I does not define standards for web services; rather, it creates guidelines and tests for interoperability.

WS-I brands versions of a Web service specification as interoperable profiles. Interoperable profiles identify target Web service technologies and provide clarifications on their usage both individually and in conjunction. *WS-I profiles* contain a list of named and versioned Web service specifications, together with a set of implementation and interoperability guidelines recommending how the specifications should be used to develop interoperable Web services. Profiles make it easier to discuss Web service interoperability at a level of granularity that makes sense for developers, users and executives making investment decisions about Web services and Web service products.

Basic Profile 1.0 includes implementation guidelines on using core Web service specifications together to develop interoperable Web services, and concentrates on conventions around messaging, description and discovery. Those specifications include SOAP 1.1, WSDL 1.1, UDDI 2.0, XML 1.0, and XML Schema. Version 1.0 of the profile is intended to provide a common framework for implementing interoperable solutions while giving customers a common reference point for purchasing decisions. Meanwhile WS-I has also developed Basic Profile v 1.1, which extends v 1.0, and v 2.0 was also published in November 2010. Basic Profile v 2.0 uses SOAP 1.2, UDDI 3 and WS-Addressing.

Among the key deliverables of WS-I are testing tools, which developers can use to test conformance of their Web services with the test assertions that represent the interoperability guidelines of established WS-I profiles. The process used to develop these profiles, interoperability guidelines, test assertions and testing tools generates other related resources useful to developers. The tools that have been developed monitor the interactions with a Web service, record those interactions, and analyse them to detect implementation errors.

1.11 Web services versus components

Web services are primarily developed to provide a standard framework for distributed applications to communicate with each other in a way that promotes understanding, reuse, development and integration of independently developed applications. As distributed components share the same concerns at first, it may seem that Web services and components are simply different flavours of the same type of distributed computing. However, when compared to conventional distributed component software, which is traditionally used to develop tightly coupled solutions, Web services are not an attempt to define a new component model but rather a functional distributed service specification that can be layered over any existing component model, language or execution environment.

The primary requirement for an integration solution, as advocated by both Web services and components, is to support neutrality along various dimensions, by establishing an abstraction layer (implemented either as Web services or as components) that hides the specifics of the endpoint implementations. The integration solution should be neutral to platforms, languages, application component models, transaction models, security models, transport protocols, invocation mechanisms, data formats, endpoint availability models and so on. The challenges for achieving this endeavour can be naturally grouped under four dimensions: type of coupling between the endpoints, types of interfaces, types of invocation, and finally, type of brokering. In the following, we shall use these dimensions to serve as the set of criteria for a brief comparison between Web services and distributed components.

1. *Type of coupling between endpoints:* Distributed components rely on tightly coupled interactions that typically involve invocation of multiple, fine grained APIs (Application Programming Interfaces). Such tightly coupled interactions largely depend upon a general acceptance of the component model on which the application is designed. This forces the use of a homogeneous infrastructure on both

the client and service machines and thus distributed component platforms cannot interoperate easily. For example, CORBA requires all applications to conform to IDL (Interface Description Language), and use of an Object Request Broker; and Java Remote Method Invocation requires the communicating entities to be written using Java. While implementations that are tightly coupled to specific component technologies are perfectly acceptable in a controlled environment, they become impractical and do not scale on the Web. As the set of participants in an integrated business process changes, and as technology changes over time, it becomes increasingly difficult to guarantee a single, unified infrastructure among all participants.

In contrast to components, Web services do not bind to each other using application specific interfaces. Instead, they make use of abstract message definitions to mediate their binding with respect to each other. Web services focus on the message definitions, or processing of events, as opposed to method signatures. This supports general purpose message definitions, such that the application code can independently handle the complexity of processing specific message instances, which makes the interfaces reusable. By focusing solely on messages, Web services are completely language, platform and object model agnostic.

2. *Type of interface:* Components expose fine grained object level interfaces to applications. With the distributed component approach, the sender makes many assumptions about the recipient regarding how the application will be activated, the kinds of interfaces that are called and their signatures. In contrast, messaging systems as used by Web services form the contract at the wire format level. The only assumption the requester makes is that the recipient will be able to understand the message being sent. The requester makes no assumptions about what will happen once the message is received, nor does it make any assumptions about what might occur between the sender and the receiver.

   With the Web service approach, application level interfaces are coarse grained interfaces that describe services that are useful at the business level. For instance, with a Web service approach an inventory service would expose the inventory replenishment service and associated parameters. Unlike a component-based approach it would not expose the inventory object and all its interfaces, or the replenishment object and its interfaces, which are of no interest to a business application.

3. *Type of invocation:* Components focus on locating services by name – for instance, CORBA uses naming contexts. In contrast to this, Web services introduce the concept of service capability. Service capability describes the classification, functionality and conditions under which a particular service can be published, discovered and invoked. For example, we may be able to find the categories of services that a number of businesses may offer, e.g. manufacturing or logistics services, and choose the most appropriate one on the basis of pricing and QoS – including technical parameters such as response times, load balancing and so on.

4. *Type of binding:* Component frameworks rely on pre-defined interfaces to invoke remote objects: the code that uses the service understands the message formats

of the target service. In contrast, services rely on a quite different service binding paradigm. They rely on two types of binding: static and dynamic binding. With static binding the application knows the details of the collaborating service, as this has been determined during the design time. With dynamic binding the application knows how to ask a service broker for the precise collaborating service.

Other important differences between these two technologies include the wide use of open standards by Web services, which components lack, and advanced service composition functionality provided by Web service technologies [Papazoglou 2011].

In conclusion, while distributed component technologies provide excellent support in integrating disparate endpoints, they do not inherently (or at least not easily) support building business process management solutions. It is difficult to create the technical agreement and coordination needed to build a distributed object system that spans enterprises.

Because Web services provide a rich integration environment, they can build intra- and cross-enterprise business process management solutions. Web services are best suited for implementing shared business tasks between enterprises. They could, however, also be used for enterprise application integration purposes (see Section 2.10).

1.12 RESTful services

REpresentational State Transfer (REST) is an architectural style for distributed hypermedia systems such as the World Wide Web. In this architectural style Web services are viewed as resources and can be uniquely identified by their URLs. The key characteristic of a RESTful Web service is the explicit use of HTTP methods to denote the invocation of different operations [Richardson 2007].

REST is a resource-centric approach (rather than message-centric like SOAP). Clients navigate between Web resources identified by Uniform Resource Identifier (URI) and invoke a set of standard actions or methods (as defined in the core HTTP command set) on these resources. The HTTP commands with REST are similar to CRUD (Create, Read, Update and Delete) activities.

REST-style architectures consist of clients and servers. Clients initiate requests to servers; servers process requests and return appropriate responses. Requests and responses are built around the transfer of representations of resources. A resource can be essentially any coherent and meaningful concept that may be addressed. A representation of a resource is typically a document that captures the current or intended state of a resource.

REST also defines the notion of state as being transferred from one participant to another. For instance, state could be transferred from the requester of an HTML page to the server. Everything required to complete the interaction is provided in the request, and the result is exposed in the response. At any particular time, a client can either be in transition between application states or '*at rest*' A client in a rest state is able to interact with its user, but creates no load and consumes no per-client storage on the servers or on the network.

The emergence of the RESTful style of Web services was a reaction to the more heavyweight SOAP based standards. RESTful Web services are a simple, clean and proven architectural style, which does not require a significant set of complex standards. In RESTful Web services, the emphasis is on simple point-to-point communication over HTTP using plain old XML (POX). POX is completely compatible with XML Schema. However, many POX users shun XML Schema to avoid the poor or inconsistent quality of XML Schema-to-Java tools. REST is very lightweight, and relies upon the HTTP standard to perform its work. It is a very flexible style when the user needs to get a useful Web service up and running quickly. If you do not need a strict API definition, then REST is the way to go.

The major advantages of REST services are:

- They are highly reusable across platforms (e.g. Java, .NET, PHP, etc.) since they rely on basic HTTP protocols.
- They rely on human readable documentation that defines requests URIs and responses.
- They use basic XML instead of the complex SOAP/XML and are easily consumable.

In recent years a battle of sorts has been raging in service developer circles between proponents of two main Web service architecture styles: Simple Object Access Protocol (SOAP) on the one hand and REpresentional State Transfer (REST) on the other. We will not go into the details of this debate, but will rather present the rationale for choosing between one of these styles depending on the application in hand. Here, we distinguish between two broad types of Web service applications:

Web services for human consumption: By humans consuming Web services, we mean a programmer that develops some code to use a Web service. The common example of this is a developer from a Website using the Google Maps, Twitter or Facebook API to integrate with their site. Even in the business world, when a developer needs to write a piece of code to connect two APIs together, REST is the best option. The REST style of Web services is easier to work with and usually results in much cleaner code.

For the above reasons, REST based Web services are increasingly being used for business-to-consumer and browser based interactions. REST is also the preferred option for integration with back end enterprise services. In comparison to SOAP-based Web services, the programming model is simpler and the use of plain old XML instead of SOAP reduces the serialisation and deserialisation complexity, as well as the need for additional third party libraries for the same.

Web services for machine consumption: In this space the objective is to allow machines to interpret the Web Services (or other technologies) and allow the user just to map from service to service. The user needs to know nothing about the transport or how the service functions are handled by the middleware infrastructure. This type of approach is typically used in the business world and not on the Web. The advantage with this style is that application requests and responses can be very well structured. For this type of business-to-business, strictly defined specifications in WSDL and BPEL provide a valuable tool to the middleware infrastructure that needs to interpret it. The downside is that this approach relies on SOAP/XML, and is very verbose. However, this approach is not meant to be for human consumption and is advantageous if two parties need to have a strict service contract (say for inter-bank communication).

In this textbook we shall concentrate on SOAP/WSDL based Web services, as our main objective is to demonstrate how Web service technology can be used to address demanding business problems and develop solutions that achieve integration and information delivery between business-to-business SOA applications.

1.13 Impact and shortcomings of Web services

In this chapter we have explained the nature and characteristics of Web services and have focused on the positive aspects of their use. However, despite the great promise that Web services hold for improving efficiency and broadening application portfolios, there is still a lot of work that needs to be done to augment the Web service paradigm in order to enable Web service applications to be run in production, mission critical computing environments using formal standards.

This section first describes the impact of Web services for business applications and then goes on to identify the primary concerns of making Web services a robust, reliable, secure, and manageable technology, capable of being used in the challenging, mission critical, industrial strength environments of the future.

The true potential for Web service technologies lies in supporting business functions by addressing recurring business problems and changing market demands. Coupled with a well designed SOA, Web services technology enables enterprises effectively to achieve reuse of business functionality and reduce time to market of new applications. Consequently, Web services are widely viewed by enterprises as a means to extend existing investments in information repositories, applications and business processes, both within organisations and across extended value chains.

The most appealing characteristic of Web services is that they are evolving to embrace the convergence of e-Business, Enterprise Application Integration (EAI), traditional middleware and the Web. Web services are not a replacement for traditional middleware, but when used in combination with middleware and EAI techniques, Web services provide a simplified and standards based approach to integration. To this effect Web services offer:

- A standard way to expose legacy application functionality as a set of reusable self-contained, self-describing services that can interoperate with other services in a well behaved, manageable way.
- A standard, easy and flexible way to help overcome application integration issues that leads to rapid application assembly out of tested, trusted, interoperable modules that implement application functionality.
- A standard way to develop and/or assemble Internet native applications for both the internal and the extended enterprise by using internally or externally created

services as building blocks that can be assembled in whole sections into fully fledged applications.

- A common facade for cross-enterprise specific systems, making it easier to create the SLAs needed for business-to-business integration.

As the business requirements that drive Web services become ever more complex, Web service technologies require additional capabilities to handle demanding situations that severely test the most obvious current shortcomings of Web services. These include performance issues, lack of appropriate support for sophisticated transaction management, lack of expressing business semantics and, especially, achieving widespread agreement and harmonisation on a wide range of existing and emerging standards. Going without these capabilities can expose a company to risks and degrade the value of its Web services. We shall examine these Web service shortcomings in turn in what follows.

A much maligned problem with Web services lies in sharing and employing data between different flavours of Web service software. This includes simple tasks, such as sending a video clip from a handheld computer to a desktop, and major jobs, such as exchanging large documents among several collaborators, which can severely impact performance. A major part of the problem is that Web service applications are based on XML, which takes a lot of bandwidth and significantly slows down applications when binary data – such as a picture – is encoded in XML format and transferred across the network. Recently, Web service standards organisations have been making strides to improve the performance, effectiveness and enterprise readiness of Web services.

Today, Web service transactional standards, e.g. WS-Transaction, which we shall examine in Chapter 10, are still rather immature. Therefore, Web services that provide transactional services should be carefully considered, designed and implemented. When building service based transactional solutions, it is important to keep a sharp eye on maintaining interoperability, reducing complexity of client integration, and utilizing the *right* type of standards – those that are accepted industry wide. Designing reliable and secure business transactions and advanced applications by creating and deploying proprietary extensions is quite possible. However, developing such *ad hoc* solutions is time consuming and expensive, and enterprises must resolve these solutions separately with each partner or customer. This approach obviously encroaches upon a central value area of Web services – cross-organisational interoperability. Thus there is a clear need to provide advanced transactional capabilities, required by more sophisticated Web services, on a broader basis to unleash the full power and promise of Web service development.

In contrast to business transactions, progress has been achieved in the area of security where WS-Security describes how to use the existing W3C security specifications, XML Signature and XML Encryption, to ensure the integrity and confidentiality of SOAP messages. Together, these specifications form the bottom layer of comprehensive modular security architecture for XML Web services. Future security specifications will build on these basic capabilities to provide mechanisms for credential exchange, trust management, revocation and other higher level capabilities.

With SOAs in place, applications can be built quickly to provide a collection of applications and processes that function as a unified and clearly understandable unit. However, alignment is not possible when business processes, using diverse business terminologies, try to communicate with each other across organisational boundaries, and, more importantly, when there is lack of commonly accepted and understood processes and commonly accepted business protocols that drive the business process exchanges and interactions. In an SOA it becomes imperative for the service requesters and providers to communicate meaningfully with each other, notwithstanding the heterogeneous nature of the underlying information structures, business processes and artifacts. This requirement is known as semantic interoperability and will be examined in Chapters 13 and 14.

The good news is that a prime formalism in the Semantic Web, the Resource Description Format (RDF), which is a formal specification for describing and exchanging metadata, has successfully penetrated various business domains with highly practical applications in knowledge management, knowledge engineering, production support, and large scale database applications. As we shall see in Chapter 13, RDF is the basis for interoperability among diverse metadata, and is considered the cornerstone of Semantic Web efforts.

One of the most serious pitfalls that hinder wide acceptance of Web services is the existence of many different standards that are either overlapping or conflicting. There are no fewer than four organisations – Liberty Alliance, Oasis, W3C and WS-I – that are vying to preside over the process, each with different goals, each with differing degrees of power and influence. It is these standards bodies that make Web services function. But in addition to that there are also vendor coalitions that also provide specifications. A vendor coalition actually develops a lot of the Web service specifications initially. They work on it for some period of time until they feel that it is reasonably mature and then they generally submit it to a standards body for standardisation. The trend is that competing vendor coalitions are usually proposing Web service specifications – some proprietary, some not – with unclear patent and licensing implications for software companies.

Today there is an overwhelming number of existing and emerging standards. Trying to understand how the different standards, some of which are still in flux, must interact to fulfil the Web services vision is in itself a daunting task. Unless these standards mature enough to the degree that they are harmonised and can act together, the long term viability of Web service applications being used in mission critical production computing environments will be severely tested.

1.14 Summary

Web services are a distinct family of automated services that use the Internet (as the communication medium) and open Internet based standards. A Web service is a service available via a network such as the Internet that completes tasks, solves problems, or conducts transactions on behalf of a user or application.

- Web services are used for composing applications based on the principle of loose coupling by discovering and invoking network available services – rather than building new applications – or by invoking available applications to accomplish some task.
- Key to the concept of Web services is the Service Oriented Architecture. SOA is a logical way of designing a software system to provide services to either end user

applications or to other services distributed in a network, via published and discoverable interfaces.

- Coupled with a well designed SOA, Web service technology enables enterprises effectively to achieve reuse of business functionality and reduce time to market of new applications.

Review questions

- What are Web services?
- How do Web services differ from application service providers and Web based applications?
- Name and briefly describe each of the types of Web service.
- What are stateful and stateless services? Give examples.
- What is service granularity? Give examples of typical fine grained and coarse grained services.
- How do synchronous services differ from asynchronous services?
- What is loose coupling and how does it compare to tight coupling? Give examples of technologies that use tight and loose coupling.
- Define and describe the significance of a Service Oriented Architecture.
- List and describe the roles and operations in an SOA.
- List some benefits of an SOA.
- What are the main layers in an SOA and what is their purpose?
- What is the Web service technology stack?
- What is quality of service and why is it important for Web services? What is the role of a Service Level Agreement?
- List some of the benefits and some of the pitfalls of Web services.

Exercises

1.1. Mention a few typical examples that make use of Web services to solve complex business applications. Explain how these differ from conventional business solutions that use paper, fax and e-mail exchanges.

1.2. Develop an application that comprises a number of atomic Web services that are composed to create complex services (business processes). Explain whether the business processes that you designed are stateless or stateful. Justify your answer. Compare the granularity level of simple and complex services. What do you observe?

1.3. Consider a consumer electronics company that manufactures customisable personal computers and devices. This company delivers to its customers new versions of products on a very frequent basis, say every six months. For example, the personal computer that a customer may buy today is a different product version to that the same customer might have bought six months ago. Typically there is constant reconfiguration of components, delivering new or specialised functionality using existing interfaces on the motherboard. Develop an SOA solution so that customers of this company may make frequent changes to very limited areas of their computer configuration to upgrade its functionality in a highly manageable and controllable fashion. Explain your design choices and describe the services that you are going to introduce to the SOA solution.

1.4. The purchasing process in the distribution domain in Figure 1.5 provides purchase order details (quantity, unit price and extended price) according to purchase order, vendor, buyer, authoriser, inventory item, any chart of accounts combination and non-invoiced receipts. In this way purchasing departments are able to research purchases made through blanket orders, planned orders and standard purchase orders, and can also analyse vendor performance, lead time based on the promised-by date and the need-by date. The process can also help analyse goods received and invoice received, and shipped item costs for distribution to charged accounts. Decompose this standard business process into a number of appropriate services and indicate how these services interact with each other.

1.5. The distribution inventory process in the distribution domain in Figure 1.6 helps track the amount of inventory on hand and expected arrival of items, and monitors the movement of physical inventory. It also helps analyse inventory transactions through various accounts, warehouses and sub-inventories as well as tracking inventory on hand, by warehouse, across the organisation at any time. Inventory items can be monitored by arrival date, per geographic location ensuring correct inventory levels are met. In this way slow moving inventory and obsolete inventories can be quickly identified, allowing the department managers to reduce the cost of the inventory. Decompose this standard business process into a number of appropriate services and indicate how these services interact with each other.

1.6. Explain which of the services in the inventory business process are synchronous and which are asynchronous.

PART II

Enabling infrastructure

CHAPTER 2

Distributed computing infrastructure

Learning objectives

New developments in distributed computing technologies in areas such as inter-process communication and remote methods invocation, distributed naming, security mechanisms, data replication and distributed transactions, in conjunction with the advent of XML technologies, led to the current dominant paradigm of Web services.

This chapter acts as a launching pad to discuss a number of key distributed technologies that are pertinent to Web services. In particular, it introduces the material that is necessary to understand more advanced concepts that use the services technical infrastructure.

After completing this chapter you will understand the following key concepts:

- Internet protocols.
- Synchronous and asynchronous forms of communication.
- Publish/subscribe messaging and event processing mechanisms.
- Message oriented middleware and integration brokers.
- Transaction monitors.
- Enterprise application and e-Business integration technologies and architectures.

Chapter preview

Service Oriented Architectures have become the blueprint infrastructure for service based designs, providing highly flexible, loosely coupled systems and applications. This chapter presents foundational topics required for implementing SOAs on the basis of distributed computing.

We begin first by examining the nature of distributed computing and Internet protocols as used by Web services. We then focus on middleware infrastructures, inter-process communication principles and present synchronous and asynchronous forms of middleware that are in conjunction with Web services and SOA implementations. Subsequently, we cover such topics as request/reply messaging and message oriented middleware. We conclude by examining the concepts of Enterprise Application and e-Business Integration.

2.1 Distributed computing and Internet protocols

A distributed system is characterised as a collection of (probably heterogeneous) networked computers, which communicate and coordinate their actions by passing messages. Distribution is transparent to the user so that the system appears as a single integrated facility. A distributed system has numerous operational components (computational elements, such as servers and other processors, or applications), which are distributed over various interconnected computer systems. Components are autonomous, as they posses full control over their parts at all times. In addition, there is no central control in the sense that a single computing component assumes control over all the other components in a distributed system. Distributed systems usually use some kind of client-server organisation. A computer system that hosts some component of a distributed system is referred to as a host.

Distributed components are typically heterogeneous, as they are written in different programming languages and may operate under different operating systems and diverse hardware platforms. The sharing of resources is the main motivation for constructing distributed systems. As a consequence of component autonomy, distributed systems execute applications concurrently and applications are often multi-threaded. They may create a new thread whenever they start to perform a service for a user or another application. In this way the application is not blocked while it is executing a service and is available to respond to further service requests.

One important characteristic of a distributed system is that processes are not executed on a single processor but rather span a number of processors. This requires that inter-process communication mechanisms be introduced to manage interaction between processes executing on different machines. Another important characteristic of a distributed system is that it can fail in many ways [Coulouris 2001]. For example, the failure of a computer, or an unexpected application crash, is not immediately detected by other components with which the failed computer communicates. Each component in a distributed system can fail independently, leaving others still running.

Distributed computing has evolved significantly over the past decades in self-contained and distinct stages. For example, inter-process communication and remote invocation techniques, distributed naming, security mechanisms, distributed filing systems, data replication, distributed transaction mechanisms and so forth were introduced over the past two decades. Each stage introduced new architectural modes and new sets of protocols.

In this section we shall present a number of key distributed computing protocols that are relevant to Web service technologies.

2.1.1 Internet protocols

To enable data to be transmitted across the Internet typical distributed platforms, such as J2EE, rely on the support of Internet protocols. Internet protocols are essentially methods of data transport across the Internet. They define, in general, the standards by which the different components in a distributed system communicate with each other and with remote components. Internet protocols, just like other conventional protocols, define the format and the order of messages exchanged between two or more communication entities, as well as the actions taken on the transmission and/or receipt of a message or event [Kurose 2003].

The most prominent of the Internet protocols is the Transport Control Protocol over Internet Protocol (or TCP/IP).

- The Internet Protocol (IP), the basic protocol of the Internet, enables the unreliable delivery of individual packets from one host to another. IP makes no guarantees as to whether the packet will be delivered, how long it will take, or if multiple packets will arrive in the order they were sent.
- The Transport Control Protocol (TCP) adds the notions of connection and reliability. These two protocols provide for the reliable delivery of streams of data from one host to another across communication networks, and the Internet in particular.

To be able to identify a host within an interconnected network, each host is assigned an address, called an IP address. Internet protocol addresses, or IP addresses, uniquely identify every network or host on the Internet. The IP address consists of two parts: a network identifier and a host identifier. The *network identifier* part of the IP address identifies the network within the Internet. It is assigned by a central authority and is unique throughout the Internet. The authority for assigning the *host identifier* part of the IP address resides with the organisation that controls the network identified by the network number.

Before we examine the TCP/IP model closer we shall first summarise the layers of the ISO Open Systems Interconnection (OSI) model. Knowing the OSI layer at which the TCP/IP model operates is one of the keys to understanding the different layers of the TCP/IP model.

2.1.1.1 The Open Systems Interconnection reference model

A *reference model* is a conceptual blueprint of how communications should take place. It addresses all the processes required for effective communication and divides these processes into logical groupings called layers. When a communication system is designed in this manner, it is known as *layered architecture*.

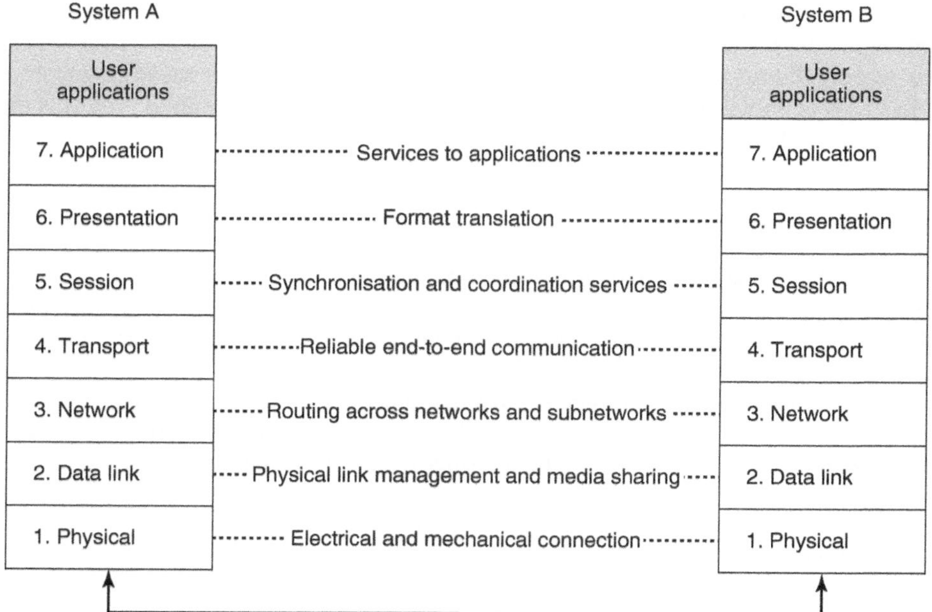

Figure 2.1 The ISO/OSI reference model

The Open Systems Interconnection (OSI) reference model is an abstract description of the digital communications between application processes running in distinct systems distributed over a network. The OSI model employs a hierarchical structure of seven layers as shown in Figure 2.1. Each layer in this figure performs value-added service at the request of the adjacent higher layer and, in turn, requests more basic services from the adjacent lower layer. The OSI layers are as follows:

Physical layer (or Layer 1): This is the lowest of seven hierarchical layers in the ISO/OSI reference model and specifies the electrical, mechanical, procedural and functional requirements for activating, maintaining and deactivating a physical link between end systems.

Data link layer (or Layer 2): This layer provides the means to transfer data between network entities and to detect and possibly correct errors that may occur in the physical layer. The data link layer provides the physical transmission of the data and handles error notification, network topology and flow control. *Flow control* is vitally important at this layer as it is provides a method by which devices communicate their status to each other. The data link layer formats the messages into pieces, called *data frames*, and adds a customised header containing the hardware destination and source address.

Network layer (or Layer 3): This layer responds to service requests from the transport layer (its immediate higher level layer) and issues service requests to the data link layer. The network layer provides the functional and procedural means of transferring variable length data sequences from a source to a destination via one or more networks. This layer performs network routing, flow control, segmentation/de segmentation and error control functions.

Transport layer (or Layer 4): This layer responds to service requests from the session layer (its immediate higher level layer) and issues service requests to the network layer. The purpose of the transport layer is to provide transparent transfer of data between end users, thus relieving the upper layers from any concern with providing reliable and cost effective data transfer. Data integrity is ensured at the transport layer by maintaining flow control and by allowing users to request reliable data transport between systems.

Session layer (or Layer 5): This layer provides the mechanism for managing the dialogue between end user application processes. The session layer is responsible for setting up, managing, and then tearing down sessions between presentation layer entities. This layer coordinates communication between systems, and serves to organise their communication by offering three different modes: simplex, half duplex and full duplex. It also establishes check-pointing, termination and restart procedures.

Presentation layer (or Layer 6): This layer presents data to the application layer and is responsible for data translation and code formatting. Tasks like data compression, decompression, encryption and decryption are associated with this layer.

Application layer (or Layer 7): This is the highest layer in the ISO/OSI reference model that gives an application program access to the OSI network. This layer interfaces directly to, and performs common application services required by, the application programs and also issues requests to the presentation layer. The common application services provide syntactic conversion between associated application processes.

Layers 1 through 4 deal with the communication, flow control, routing and error handling needed to transport data end-to-end across the network. Below the transport layer, there can be many different types of physical network – for example, an X.25 packet-switched data network (PSDN) or a local area network (LAN). Layers 5 through 7 deal with the coordination of applications across the network and the way that information is presented to the applications. A wide range of application programs, providing various types of end user services, can be supported by a common transport layer implementation.

2.1.1.2 The TCP/IP network protocol

The TCP/IP is a layered protocol that relies on a protocol stack to achieve its operational purpose [Moss 1997]. The protocol stack is a hierarchical arrangement of all predefined protocols necessary to complete a single transfer of data between two computing systems.

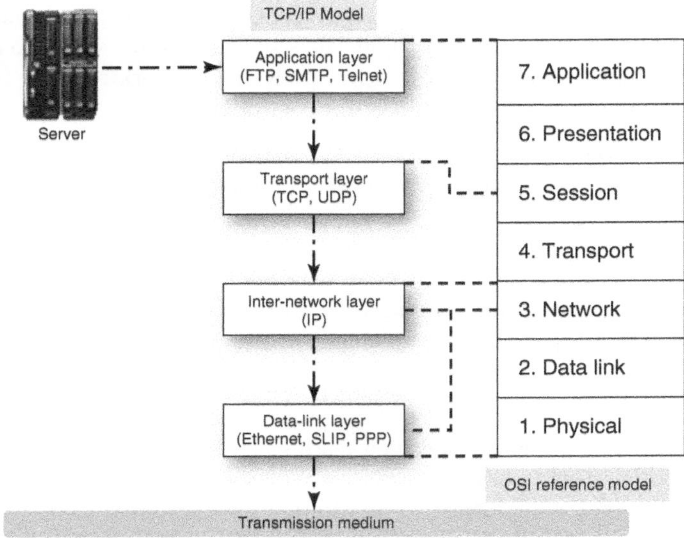

Figure 2.2 The TCP/IP stack in relation to the ISO reference model

The TCP/IP stack is shown in Figure 2.2 in association with the various layers of the ISO/OSI model. This figure shows that each level of the TCP/IP stack builds on the services provided by the layer below it. Layers communicate with those above and below via concise interfaces. Intercommunication requirements are handled at the lowest level within the stack. The lowest level protocol is concerned purely with sending and receiving data using specific network hardware. At the top are protocols designed specifically for tasks like transferring files or delivering e-mail. In between are protocol levels concerned mainly with routing and reliability.

Note that there is no standard TCP/IP model, and some sources include an additional physical layer at the bottom of the stack. Figure 2.2, however, illustrates that TCP/IP is a four layer protocol [Moss 1997], [Rodriguez 2001], where the physical connection standards are included as part of the data link layer. The TCP/IP stack comprises the following layers:

Data link layer: The data link layer, or link layer, is the lowermost layer and provides the interface to the actual network hardware. This interface may or may not provide reliable delivery, and may be packet or stream oriented. In fact, TCP/IP does not specify any protocol at this level but can use almost any network interface available, which illustrates the flexibility of the IP layer.

Internetwork layer: The internetwork layer is responsible for routing *datagrams* – a term which basically means *blocks of data* – from one host to another. The internetwork layer provides the *virtual network* image of an Internet as this layer shields the higher levels from the physical network architecture below it. IP is the most important protocol in this layer and is the bedrock protocol of TCP/IP. Every message and every piece of data sent over any TCP/IP network is sent as an IP packet. IP provides a routing function that delivers transmitted messages to their destination.

IP is a connectionless protocol that does not assume reliability from lower layers. A *connectionless protocol* means that the protocol has no concept of a job or a session and does not make any assumptions about eventual delivery. Each packet is treated as an entity in itself. IP simply routes packets, one at a time, to the next location on the delivery route and is also unconcerned with whether a packet reaches its eventual destination, or whether packets arrive in the original order. There is no information in a packet to identify it as part of a sequence or as belonging to a particular job. IP does not provide reliability, flow control or error recovery. These functions must be provided at a higher level.

Transport layer: The transport layer provides end-to-end data transfer by delivering data between the client and server sides of an application. Multiple applications can be supported simultaneously. The most used transport layer protocol is the TCP, which provides connection oriented reliable data delivery, duplicate data suppression, congestion control and flow control.

TCP is the transport layer protocol used by most Internet applications, like Telnet, the File Transfer Protocol (FTP) and HTTP. It is a *connection oriented protocol*. The connection oriented reliable service guarantees that the data transmitted from a sender to a receiver will eventually be delivered to the receiver in order and in its entirety. This means that two hosts – one a client, the other a server – must establish a connection before any data can be transferred between them. Once a connection has been made, data can be sent. TCP is a *sliding window protocol*, so there is no need to wait for one segment to be acknowledged before another can be sent. Acknowledgements are sent only if required immediately, or after a certain interval has elapsed. This makes TCP an efficient protocol for bulk data transfers. TCP provides reliability. An application that uses TCP knows that the data it sends is received at the other end, and that it is received correctly.

Application layer: The application layer is responsible for supporting network applications. The program that uses TCP/IP for communication provides the application layer. An application is a user process cooperating with another process usually on a different host (there is also a benefit to application communication within a single host). Examples of applications include Telnet, FTP and the Simple Mail Transfer Protocol (SMTP). Port numbers and sockets define the interface between the application and transport layers.

TCP/IP programs are usually initiated over the Internet and most of them are client-server oriented. When each connection request is received, the server program communicates with the requesting client machine. To facilitate this process, each application (FTP or Telnet, for example) is assigned a unique address, called a *port*. The application in question is bound to that particular port and, when any connection request is made to this port, the corresponding application is launched. Table 2.1 shows some of the most common ports and the applications that are typically bound to them.

Table 2.1 Common ports and their corresponding applications

Application	*Port*
File Transfer Protocol (FTP)	21
Telnet	23
Simple Mail Transfer (SMTP)	25
HyperText Transfer Protocol (HTTP)	80
Network News Transfer Protocol (NNTP)	119

2.2 Middleware

Middleware is connectivity software that is designed to help manage the complexity and heterogeneity inherent in distributed systems by building a bridge between different systems, thereby enabling communication and transfer of data. Middleware could be defined as a layer of enabling software services that allow application elements to interoperate across network links, despite differences in underlying communication protocols, system architectures, operating systems, databases and other application services.

The role of middleware is to ease the task of designing, programming and managing distributed applications by providing a simple, consistent and integrated distributed programming environment. Essentially, middleware is a distributed *platform* that lives above the operating system and abstracts over the complexity and heterogeneity of the underlying distributed environment with its multitude of network technologies, machine architectures, operating systems and programming languages.

Middleware services provide a more functional set of Application Programming Interfaces (APIs) than the operating system and network services to allow an application to:

- locate applications transparently across the network, thereby providing interaction with another or service;
- shield software developers from low level, tedious and error prone platform details, such as socket level network programming;
- provide a consistent set of higher level network oriented abstractions that are much closer to application requirements in order to simplify the development of distributed systems;
- leverage previous developments and reuse them, rather than rebuild them for each usage;
- provide a wide array of services such as reliability, availability, authentication and security that are necessary for applications to operate effectively in a distributed environment;
- scale up in capacity without losing function.

Modern middleware products mask heterogeneity of networks and hardware, operating systems and programming languages. They also permit heterogeneity at the application

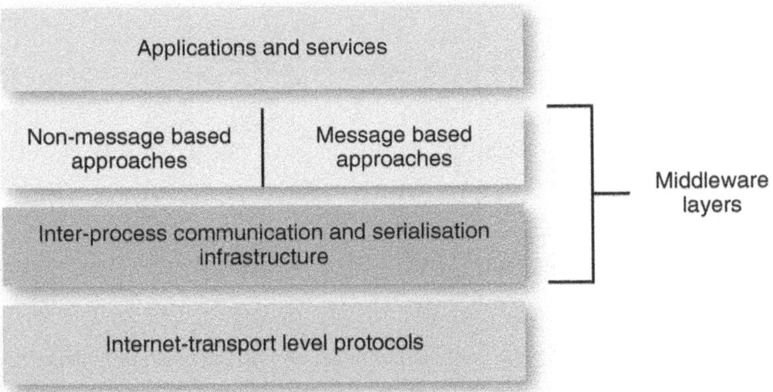

Figure 2.3 Middleware layers

level by allowing the various elements of the distributed application to be written in any suitable language. Finally, programming support offered by the middleware platform can provide transparency with respect to distribution in one or more of the following dimensions: location, concurrency, replication and failure. This means that applications can interoperate irrespective of whether they are located in diverse geographical locations, whether operations execute concurrently, or whether data is replicated in multiple locations.

Figure 2.3 shows that the middleware layers are interposed between applications and Internet transport protocols. The figure shows that the middleware abstraction comprises three layers. The bottom layer is concerned with the characteristics of protocols for communicating between processes in a distributed system and how the data objects, e.g. a sales order, and data structures used in application programs can be translated into a suitable form for sending messages over a communications network, taking into account that different computers may rely on heterogeneous representations for simple data items. The adjacent higher layer is concerned with inter-process communication mechanisms, while the layer above that is concerned with non-message and message based forms of middleware. Non-message based forms of middleware provide synchronous communication mechanisms designed to support client-server communication. Message based forms of middleware provide asynchronous messaging and event notification mechanisms to exchange messages or react to events over electronic networks.

Before delving into the middleware layers depicted in Figure 2.3, we shall first describe the characteristics of client-server architectures, as these are the most prevalent structure for Internet applications and central to the material that follows.

2.3 The client-server model

Client-server computing is a widely applied form of distributed processing. The client-server architecture is one of the common solutions to the conundrum of how to handle

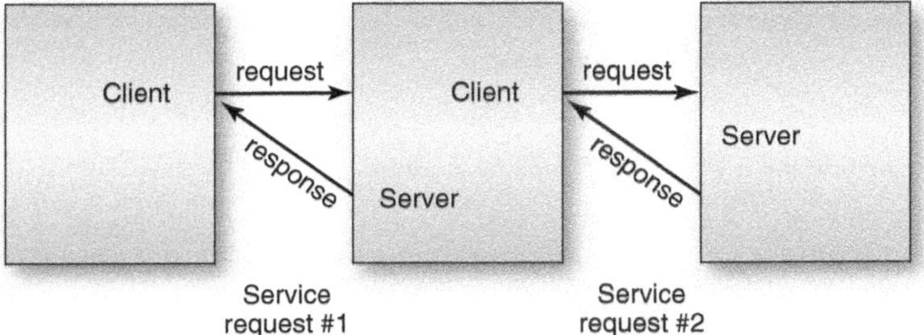

Figure 2.4 Client-server architecture
(*Source*: From M. P. Papazoglou and P. M. A. Ribbers, *e-Business: Organizational and Technical Foundations*, J. Wiley & Sons, 2006. Reproduced with permission.)

the need for both centralised data control and widespread data accessibility. In short, a client-server architecture, as shown in Figure 2.4, is a computational architecture in which processing and storage tasks are divided between two classes of network members, clients and servers.

Client-server involves client processes (service consumers) requesting service from server processes (service providers). Servers may, in turn, be clients of other servers. For instance, a Web server is often a client of a local file server (or database server) that manages the files (storage structures) in which Web pages are stored. In general, client-server computing does not emphasise hardware distinctions; it rather focuses on the applications themselves. The same device may function as both client and server. For example, there is no reason why a Web server – which contains large amounts of memory and disk space – cannot function as both client and server when local browser sessions are run there.

The client-server model is the most prevalent structure for Internet applications. The Web, e-mail, file transfer, Telnet applications, newsgroups and many other popular Internet based applications adopt the client-server model. Since a client program typically runs on one computer and the server program runs on another computer, client-server Internet applications are, by definition, distributed applications. The client program and the server program interact with each other by sending each other messages over the Internet.

In a client-server architecture the client machine runs software and applications that are stored locally. Some of the applications may be stored and executed on the server, but most of them are on the client. The server also provides the data for the application. In a client-server architecture, the client actually has two tasks. It makes requests to servers and is also responsible for the user interface. For example, Web browser software, which is a client process, not only requests documents from Web servers but must also display those documents for the user to make requests.

The term *thin client* is used to differentiate the client used in Web based applications from the client in traditional client-server architectures, which stores large parts of the application locally. This architecture has the characteristic that it does not download the code of applications into the client's computer. Instead, it executes them on a powerful computer server.

2.4 Inter-process communication

Processes on two different end systems (with potentially different operating systems) communicate with each other by exchanging messages across a computer network. Figure 2.3 indicates that the middleware API to Internet transport level protocols, such as UDP, provides a message passing abstraction – the simplest form of inter-process communication. This enables the sending process to transmit a single message to a receiving process.

2.4.1 Messaging

Distributed systems and applications communicate by exchanging messages. Messaging is a technology that enables high speed, asynchronous, program-to-program communication with reliable delivery. Programs communicate by sending packets of data called messages to each other. The concept of a message is a well defined, data driven text format – containing the business message and a network routing header – that can be sent between two or more applications. A message typically comprises three basic elements: a header, its properties and a message payload or body, which are briefly described below.

1. The *message header* is used by both the messaging system and the application developer to provide information about message characteristics, e.g. the destination of a message, the message type, the message expiration time and so forth.
2. The *properties of a message* contain a set of application defined name/value pairs. These properties are essentially parts of the message body that get promoted to a special section of the message so that clients can apply filtering to the message or specialized routers [Chappell 2004].
3. The *message body* carries the actual *payload* of the message. The format of the message payload can vary across messaging implementations. Most common formats are plain text, a raw stream of bytes for holding any type of binary data, or a special XML message type that allows the message payload to be accessed using any number of common XML parsing technologies.

The message can be interpreted simply as data, as the description of a command to be invoked on the receiver, or as the description of an event that occurred in the sender. The business data usually contains information about a business transaction, such as a sales order, payment processing, or shipping and tracking.

The simplest form of messaging is a request/reply message, whereby the sender sends a message and may pickup a reply from the message recipient (if there is one) at a later time. Message passing between a pair of processes is supported by two message communication operations: send and receive, defined in terms of destinations and messages [Coulouris 2001]. In order for one process to communicate with another, one process sends a message to a destination and another process at the destination receives the message. This activity involves the communication of data from the sending process to the receiving process and may involve the synchronisation of the two processes. A receiving process receives the messages and may respond by sending messages back. Distributed applications have application layer protocols that define the format and orders of the messages exchanged between processes, as well as the actions taken on the transmission or receipt of a message.

The data stored in application programs in distributed systems is normally represented as data structures (for instance, a series of interlinked objects in Java), whereas the messages exchanged between interacting processes consist of byte sequences. Irrespective of the form of communication used, the data structures must be flattened (converted to a sequence of bytes) before transmission and rebuilt on arrival. To enable two or more heterogeneous computers to exchange data values, the principle of marshalling is used.

Marshalling is the process of taking an object or any other form of structured data item and breaking it up so that it can be transmitted as a stream of bytes over a communications network in such a way that the original object or data structure can be reconstructed easily on the receiving end. Marshalling comprises the transformation of structured data items and primitive values into an agreed standard form of representation for transmission across the network.

Unmarshalling is the process of converting the assembled stream of bytes on arrival to produce an equivalent object or form of structured data at the destination point. Unmarshalling comprises the generation of primitive values from their external data representation and the reconstruction of the same (equivalent) data structures at the receiving end.

Java and XML use the terms *serialisation* and *deserialisation* to denote the process of marshalling and unmarshalling, respectively. In this book we shall use the terms serialisation and marshalling interchangeably.

2.4.2 Message destinations and sockets

In Section 2.1.1 we explained that in the case of Internet protocols, messages are sent to ports. For inter-process communication, processes may use multiple ports from which to receive messages. Servers usually publicise their port numbers for use by clients, and processes use multiple ports from which to receive messages. Any process that knows the identifier of a port can send a message to it.

During inter-process communication messages are sent to (Internet address, local port) pairs. A local port is a message destination within a computer, specified as an identifier. There is a serious drawback with this approach in a case where the client uses a fixed address to a service, in that the service must always run on the same computer for its address to remain valid. This can be avoided either if client applications refer to services by name or use a name server to translate names into server locations at run time, or by having the operating system provide location independent identifiers for messages allowing service relocation [Coulouris 2001].

Many applications involve two processes in different hosts, communicating with each other over a network. These two processes communicate with each other by exchanging (sending and receiving) messages. A process sends messages into, and receives messages from, the network through its socket. A process' socket could be thought of as the entry point to the process. Inter-process communication consists of transmitting a message between a client and a socket in another process, as illustrated in Figure 2.5. Once the message arrives at its destination, it passes through the receiving process' socket and the receiving process then acts on the message. Figure 2.5 illustrates that, for a particular

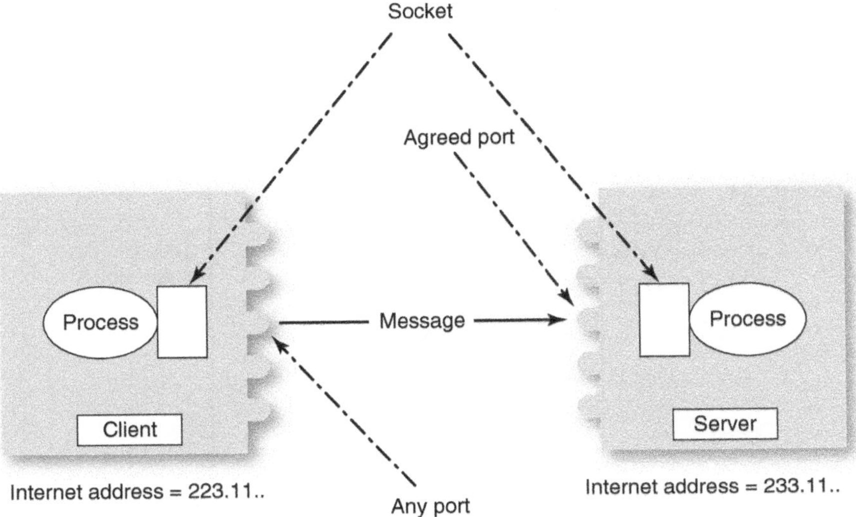

Figure 2.5 Ports and sockets

process to receive messages, its socket must be bound to a local port and must refer to the Internet address of the computer on which it is hosted.

2.4.3 Forms of message communication

While there are different types of messaging middleware, they all can support one, or sometimes two, basic modes of message communication. These modes are: *synchronous* or time dependent and *asynchronous* or time independent.

The defining characteristic of a synchronous form of execution is that message communication is synchronised between two communicating application systems, which must both be up and running, and that execution flow at the client's side is interrupted to execute the call. Both the sending and the receiving application must be ready to communicate with each other at all times. A sending application initiates a request (sends a message) to a receiving application. The sending application then blocks its processing until it receives a response from the receiving application. The receiving application continues its processing after it receives the response. Figure 2.6 shows this form of synchronous request/response mode of communication. Synchronous communication is exemplified by remote procedure calls (also discussed in Section 2.5).

When using asynchronous messaging, the caller employs a *send and forget* approach that allows it to continue to execute after it sends the message. With asynchronous communication, an application sends (requester or sender) a request to another while it continues its own processing activities. The sending application does not have to wait for the receiving application to complete and for its reply to come back. Instead it can continue processing other requests. Unlike the synchronous mode, both application systems

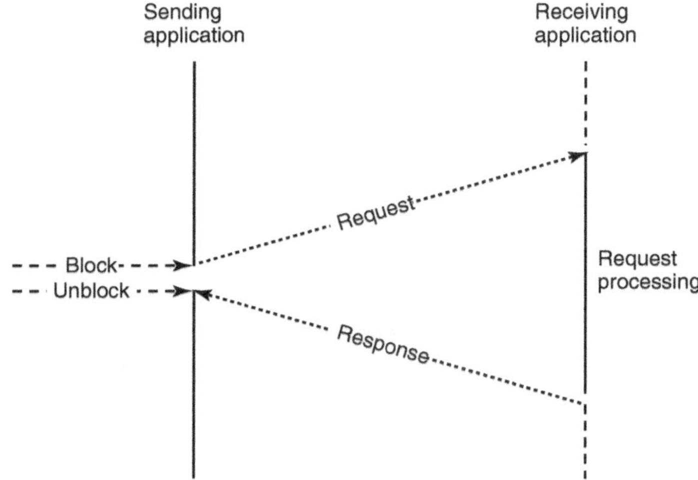

Figure 2.6 Synchronous messaging

(sender and receiver) do not have to be active at the same time for processing to occur. Asynchronous messaging is usually implemented by some queuing mechanism. Two types of message queues exist: these are store and forward and publish/subscribe and are described in Section 2.6.

In choosing a type of communication infrastructure, it is important to consider the trade-offs between loosely and tightly coupled interfaces, and asynchronous versus synchronous modes of interaction. We shall examine these modes of communication in some detail in the following two sections.

2.5 Synchronous forms of middleware

Programming models for synchronous forms of middleware are composed of cooperating programs running in several interacting distributed processes. Such programs need to be able to invoke operations synchronously in other processes, which frequently run in different computing systems.

The most familiar approaches to non-message-based forms of middleware are typified by the remote procedure call (RPC) and the remote method invocation (RMI). We shall concern ourselves with examining these two approaches in this section.

2.5.1 Remote procedure calls (RPC)

RPC is a basic mechanism for inter-program communication. In effect, RPC is the middleware mechanism used to invoke a procedure that is located on a remote system, and the results are returned. With this type of middleware the application elements

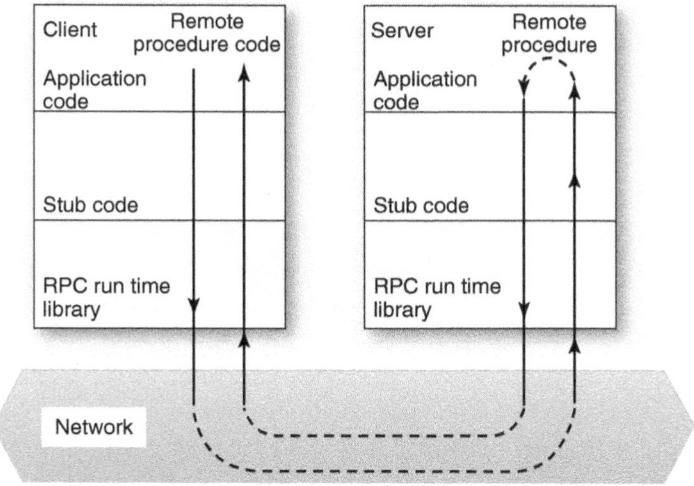

Figure 2.7 RPC communication
(*Source:* From M. P. Papazoglou and P. M. A. Ribbers, *e-Business: Organizational and Technical Foundations*, J. Wiley & Sons, 2006. Reproduced with permission.)

communicate with each other synchronously, meaning that they use a request/wait-for-reply model of communication. By design, the RPC programming style mimics the serial thread of execution that a *normal* non-distributed application would use, where each statement is executed in sequence. The RPC mechanism is the simplest way to implement client-server applications because it keeps the details of network communications out of the application code.

Figure 2.7 shows the relationship between application code and the RPC mechanism during an RPC. In RPC style programming, an object and its methods are *remoted* such that the invocation of the method can happen across a network separation. In client application code, an RPC looks like a local procedure call, because it is actually a call to a local proxy known as a *client stub* (a surrogate code that supports RPCs). The client stub mimics the interface of the remote object and its methods. It essentially behaves like a local procedure to the client, but instead of executing the call, it marshalls the procedure identifier and the arguments into a request message, which it sends via its communication module to the server. The client stub communicates with a *server stub* using the RPC run time library, which is a set of procedures that support all RPC applications. A server stub is like a *skeleton* method in that it unmarshalls the arguments in the request message, calls the corresponding service procedure, and marshalls the return results for the reply message. The server stub communicates its output to the client stub, again by using the RPC run time library. Finally, the client stub returns to the client application code.

Figure 2.8 illustrates that RPC style programming leads to *tight coupling* of interfaces and applications. In an RPC environment each application needs to know the intimate details of the interface of every other application – the number of methods it exposes and the details of each method signature it exposes. This figure clearly shows that the

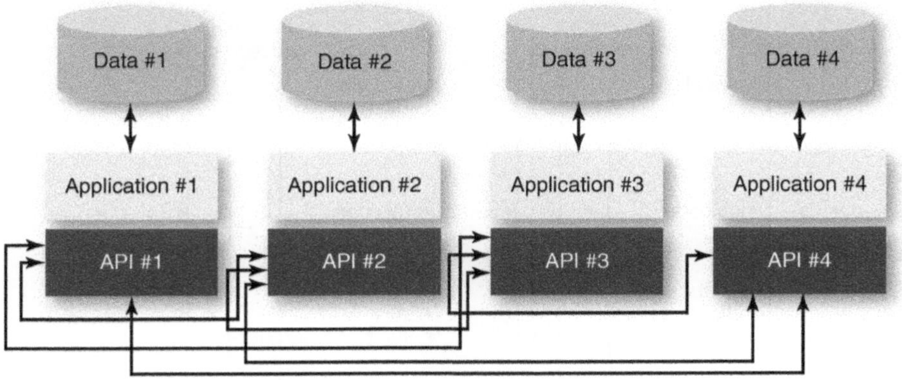

Figure 2.8 Tightly coupled RPC point-to-point integrations

synchronised nature of RPC tightly couples the client to the server. The client cannot proceed – it is blocked – until the server responds, and the client fails if the server fails or is unable to complete.

RPCs work well for smaller, simple applications where communication is primarily point-to-point (rather than one system to many) and do not scale well to large, mission critical applications. Scalability is in fact a serious drawback with RPC technology as it leaves many crucial details to the discretion of a programmer, including handling network and system failures, handling multiple connections and synchronisation between processes. When performing a synchronous operation across multiple processes, the success of one RPC call depends on the success of all downstream RPC style calls that are part of the same synchronous request/response cycle. This makes the invocation a whole-or-nothing proposition. If one operation is unable to complete for any reason, all other dependent operations will fail with it, as shown in Figure 2.8.

RPC style programming has had reasonable adoption in the industry for a number of years. However, due to their synchronous nature, RPCs are not a good choice to use as the building blocks for enterprise wide applications where high performance and high reliability are needed.

2.5.2 Remote method invocation

Traditional RPC systems are language neutral, and therefore cannot provide functionality that is not available on all possible target platforms. The Java RMI provides a simple and direct model for distributed computation with Java objects on the basis of the RPC mechanism.

The Java RMI establishes inter-object communication. If the particular method happens to be on a remote machine, Java provides the capability to make the RMI appear to the programmer to be the same as if the method is on the local machine. Thus, Java makes RMI transparent to the user. RMI applications comprise two separate programs: a server and a client. RMI provides the mechanism by which the server and the client communicate and pass information back and forth.

2.6 Asynchronous forms of middleware

As we already noted in the previous section, in an environment where multiple applications and Web services need to interact with each other it is not practical to expect that each application knows the signature characteristics of every other application's methods. Instead, the intricacies of the service interface should not necessarily be known to all interacting applications.

Asynchronous communication promotes a loosely coupled environment in which an application does not need to know the intimate details of how to reach and interface with other applications. Each participant in a multi-step business process flow need only be concerned with ensuring that it can send a message to the messaging system. This is illustrated in Figure 2.9.

Asynchronous communication is exemplified by the two approaches to messaging store and forward and publish/subscribe. We shall examine these two asynchronous processing mechanisms as well as another interesting approach to messaging known as event processing.

2.6.1 Store and forward messaging

With the store and forward queuing mechanism, messages are placed on a virtual channel called a *message queue* by a sending application and are retrieved by the receiving application as needed. Messages are exchanged through a queue, which is the destination to which senders send messages and a source from which receivers receive messages. The queue is a container that can keep hold of a message until the recipient collects it. The message queue is independent of both the sender and receiver applications and acts as a buffer between the communicating applications. In this form of communication, two applications can be senders and receivers relative to the message queue. This is shown in Figure 2.10.

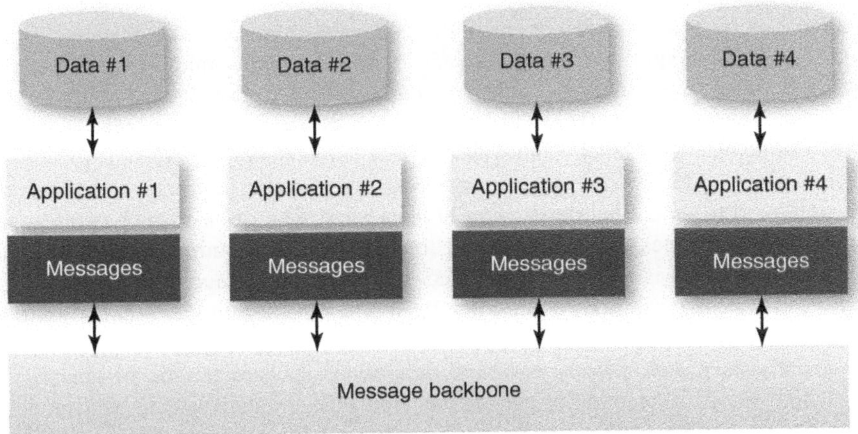

Figure 2.9 Loose coupling of asynchronous interfaces

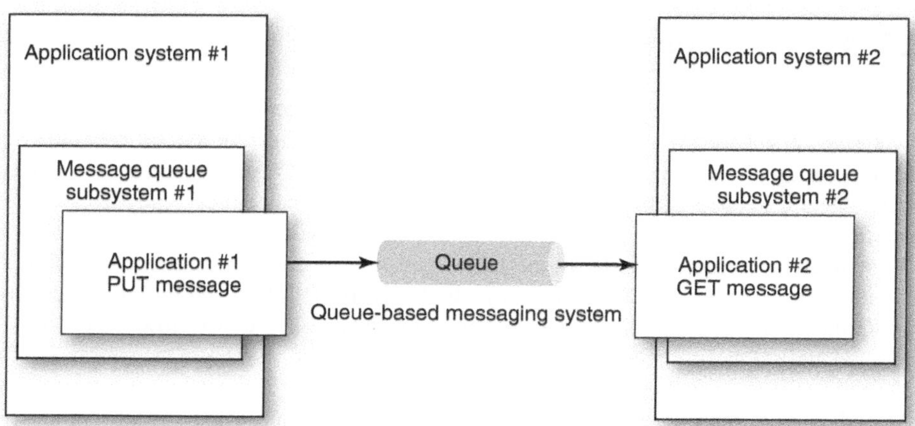

Figure 2.10 Store and forward messaging

Figure 2.10 shows an example of a common messaging scenario from the application's point of view. Messages are placed on a message queue by an application and reviewed by another application (Application system #2 in Figure 2.10). The implication in this diagram is that the physical location of the queue is not known to either application. Similarly, the physical details of the host platform are not known either. All that is required is that an application is in some way registered or connected to the message queue subsystem. This provides a useful form of abstraction that enables physical implementations to be changed on either platform, without affecting the rest of the implementation. Asynchronous communication with the store and forward queuing mechanism allows work to be performed whenever applications are ready. Message queuing provides a highly reliable, although not always timely, means of ensuring that application operations are completed.

The store and forward queuing mechanism is typical of a many-to-one messaging paradigm where multiple applications can send messages to a single application. The same application can be sender, receiver, or both sender and receiver. The message delivery semantics include several *message delivery options*, which range from *exactly-once delivery* to *at-least-once delivery* and to *at-most-once delivery*. It is critical for many applications to ensure guaranteed delivery of a message to its final destination and elimination of duplicates. This level of message service delivery is referred to as *exactly-once message delivery*. The *at-least-once message delivery* mode guarantees that messages will be delivered to their final destination at least once. The *at-most-once delivery* mode guarantees that messages will be delivered to their final destination at most once. This latter mode of delivery is a less stringent QoS setting on a message, as it implies that the messaging system is permitted to occasionally lose a message in the event of hardware, software or network breakdown.

The exactly-once guarantee of message delivery is a characteristic of message reliability, which we shall examine as part of the Web services standards in Section 8.4.2 in conjunction with reliable messaging, and is accomplished in part by the store and forward queuing mechanism.

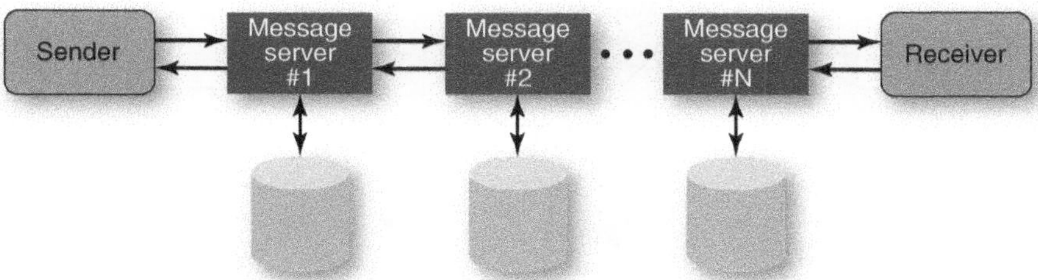

Figure 2.11 Store and forward involving multiple chained message servers

In many applications there is an additional requirement that the concept of store and forward is capable of being repeated across multiple message servers that are chained together. This leads to the configuration illustrated in Figure 2.11 where each message server uses the principle of store and forward and message acknowledgements to get the message to the next server in the chain of interconnected message servers. A *message acknowledgement* is a mechanism that allows the messaging system to monitor the progress of a message so that it knows when the message was successfully produced and consumed. With this kind of knowledge, message oriented middleware systems can manage the distribution of messages to their destinations and guarantee their delivery.

2.6.2 Publish/subscribe messaging

Another form of reliable messaging is publish/subscribe messaging. This mode of messaging is a slightly more scalable form of messaging when compared to the store and forward mechanism. With this type of asynchronous communication the application that produces information publishes it and all other applications that need this type of information subscribe to it. Messages containing the new information are placed in a queue for each subscriber by the publishing application. Each application in this scheme may have a dual role: it may act as a publisher or subscriber of different types of information.

The publish/subscribe messaging works as follows. Suppose that a publisher application publishes messages on a specific topic, such as sending out new product prices or new product descriptions to retailers. Multiple subscribing applications can subscribe to this topic and receive the messages published by the publishing application. Figure 2.12 shows message publishers publishing messages by sending them to topics and all the message subscribers, who had registered to the topic for messages, receiving them as soon as the publisher makes them available. This figure describes how the publish/subscribe semantics work:

1. Publishers publish messages to specific topics.
2. A message server keeps track of all the messages, and all its currently active and durable subscribers (subscribers who specifically expressed interest in the topic). The message server provides a secure environment for the messaging system by handling authorisation and authentication.

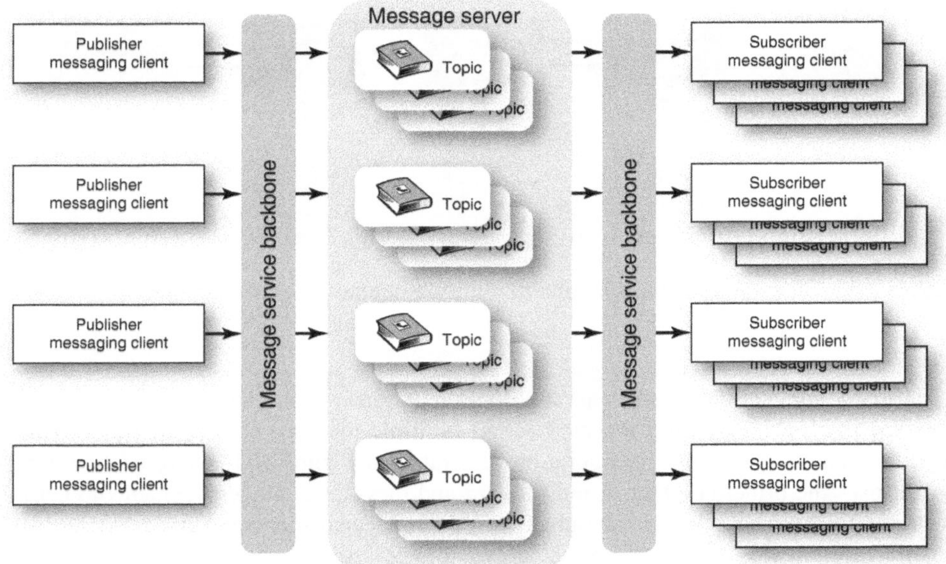

Figure 2.12 Publish/subscribe messaging

3. As soon as messages are published on a specific topic, they are distributed to all of its subscribers. Durable subscribers, who were not connected at the time of message delivery, can retrieve the messages if they come up within a specified time.

The message server takes the responsibility for delivering the published messages to the subscribing applications based on the subscribed topic. Every message has an expiration time that specifies the maximum amount of time that it can live from the time of its publication in a topic.

All subscribers have a message event listener that takes delivery of the message from the topic and delivers it to the messaging client application for further processing. Subscribers can also filter the messages that they receive by qualifying their subscriptions with a message selector. Message selectors evaluate message headers and properties (not their bodies) with the provided filter expression strings.

The subscription list can be easily modified, on-the-fly, providing a highly flexible communications system that can run on different systems and networks. The publish/subscribe messaging mode usually includes the ability to transform messages, acting as an interpreter, which enables applications that were not designed to work together to do so.

In general, asynchronous communication is often the preferred solution for Enterprise Application Integration (EAI) and cross-enterprise computing, especially when applications want to transfer data between internal enterprise information systems, e.g. databases and Enterprise Resource Planning (ERP) packages, or between their systems and those of their partners. In these cases the reply from clients may not be important, or, if it is, its contents are not. For example, when sending a group of new product prices out to the enterprise information systems of retail partners, the publisher of those messages is not expecting an answer. It simply wants to be certain that the partners have received the information.

2.6.3 Event driven processing mechanisms

The familiar one-to-one request/reply interaction pattern that is commonly used in client-server systems is inadequate for systems that must react to events representing changes in the environment, information of interest or process status, which are particularly well suited for distributed environments without central control. Applications such as process support systems and workflow management systems are best constructed using event middleware, realising the control flow and inter-task dependencies by event driven task managers.

The actual data, e.g. attributes of business events, contained within messages, referred to as *content* (or sometimes message body or payload), are typically invisible to the transport mechanism and, therefore, are not considered when performing addressing or routing operations.

In traditional network addressing and routing mechanisms, the flow of information between a message producer and a message consumer can be seen as the result of producers directing messages to selected consumers, given their use of explicit destination specifications and explicit identity attributes. A rather different approach is to expose the content to the network transport mechanism so that it can influence the addressing and routing of messages. In the extreme, no information other than the content is used; a network that takes this approach is said to use a *content-based addressing* and routing scheme [Carzaniga 2000].

Unlike the flow of information in traditional network addressing and routing mechanisms, the content based addressing and routing mechanism implicitly emerges from the circumstantial interplay between expressions of interest and any messages that are generated. The content based scheme is usually based on the processing of incoming events. Under this approach, message producers will generate messages, but with no particular destinations intended. The destinations are determined by clients expressing interest in the delivery of messages satisfying some arbitrary predicates on the content, independent of the producers of the messages.

The asynchrony, heterogeneity, and inherent loose coupling that characterise modern applications in a wide area network promote event interaction as a natural design abstraction for a growing class of software systems. Such systems are based on a technical infrastructure known as an *event notification* service [Rosenblum 1997].

An event notification service complements other general purpose middleware services, such as point-to-point and multicast communication mechanisms, by offering a many-to-many communication and integration facility. Clients in an event notification scheme are of two kinds: *objects of interest*, which are the producers of notifications, and *interested parties*, which are the consumers of notifications. It is noteworthy that a client can act as both an object of interest and an interested party. An event notification service typically realises the publish/subscribe asynchronous messaging scheme that we described earlier in this section.

An event notification service performs a *selection process* to determine which of the published notifications are of interest to which of its clients, routing and delivering notifications only to those clients that are interested. In addition to serving clients' interests, the selection process also can be used by the event notification service to optimise communication within the network. The information that drives the selection process originates with clients. More specifically, the event notification service may be directed to apply a *filter* to the contents of event notifications on behalf of a client, such that it will deliver only notifications that contain certain specified data values. The selection process may also be asked to look for *patterns* of multiple events, such that it will deliver only sets of notifications associated with that pattern of event occurrences (where each individual event occurrence is matched by a filter) [Carzaniga 2001]. At its most generic, a pattern might correlate events according to any compound relationship. For example, a customer might be interested in receiving price change notifications for a certain product if specific suppliers of the product introduce a change in the price of this product simultaneously.

In order to achieve scalability in a wide area network, the event notification service by necessity must be implemented as a distributed network of servers. It is the responsibility of the event notification service to route each notification through the network of servers to all subscribers that registered matching subscriptions, and to keep track of the identity of the subscriber that registered each subscription.

The event notification scheme is particularly appealing for developing service based applications, (see also Section 7.2 on Web services notification). The fact that notifications are delivered based on their content rather than on an explicit destination address adds a level of indirection that provides a great deal of flexibility and expressive power to clients of the service. However, this may complicate the final implementation of the service. Furthermore, the behaviour of subscribers is dynamic, since they add and remove subscriptions. Yet this dynamism is transparent to publishers of notifications, since they simply generate content irrespective of its eventual recipients.

2.7 Request/reply messaging

Most of the asynchronous messaging mechanisms that we have examined so far follow the *fire-and-forget* messaging principle. This means that the sending application can conduct its work as usual once a message was asynchronously sent. As already explained, the sending application assumes that the message will arrive safely at its destination at some point in time. This mode of asynchronous messaging does not necessarily preclude the necessity to perform request/reply operations.

On many occasions applications require that request/reply messaging operations be performed. Here, we can distinguish between two types of request/reply messaging operations: *synchronous request/reply messaging* and *asynchronous request/reply messaging*. Synchronous request/reply messaging is often necessary when trying to integrate with a Web service client that blocks and waits for a synchronous response to return to it. In the asynchronous version of request/reply messaging, the requester (sender) expects the reply to arrive at a later time and continue its work unaffected.

Figure 2.13 illustrates a simple request/reply asynchronous messaging configuration. Observe that, in this figure, message delivery channels are not bi-directional. To perform a request/reply operation the sender must use two channels: one for the request and one for the reply. The request message needs to contain reference to the receiver's endpoint, along with a correlation identifier that is needed to correlate the request with the response message. The requester needs to poll a reply channel for the reply message.

Both request/reply messaging modes can be layered on top of message oriented middleware. Some message oriented middleware systems can further automate this process by managing the contents of the request/reply message.

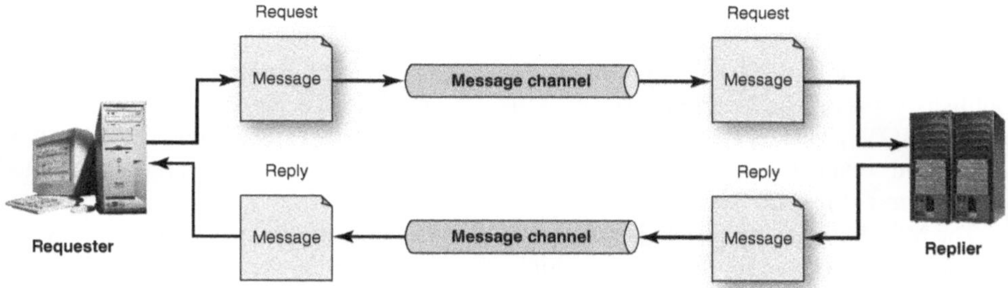

Figure 2.13 Asynchronous request/reply messaging

Request/reply messaging is a useful mechanism for Web services and we shall be referring to it later in this book (Section 8.4.2) in the context of reliable messaging and associated Web service standards.

2.8 Message oriented middleware

Message oriented middleware (MOM) is an infrastructure that involves the passing of data between applications using a common communication channel that carries self-contained messages. In an MOM-based communication environment, messages are usually sent and received asynchronously. Using message-based communications, applications are abstractly decoupled as senders and receivers are not aware of each other. Instead they send and receive messages from the messaging system and it is the responsibility of the messaging system, namely the MOM, to forward the messages to their intended destination.

MOM is interposed between the client and the server part of the client-server architecture and handles asynchronous calls between clients and servers, see Figure 2.14. When an event occurs, the client application hands off to the messaging middleware application

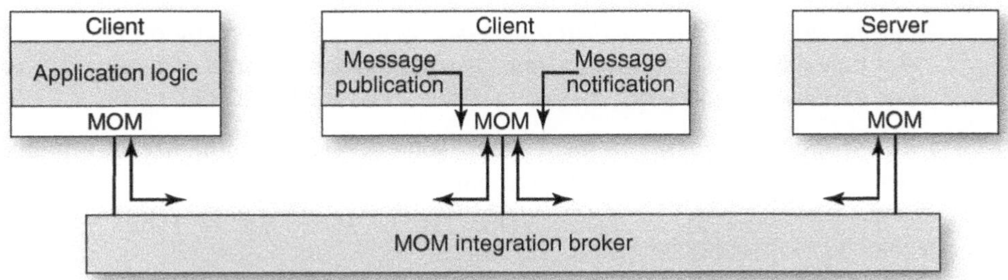

Figure 2.14 Message-oriented middleware (MOM)
(*Source*: From M. P. Papazoglou and P. M. A. Ribbers, *e-Business: Organizational and Technical Foundations*, J. Wiley & Sons, 2006. Reproduced with permission.)

the responsibility of notifying a server that some action needs to be taken. Messages containing requests for action can trigger other messages to be fired. Normally when an event occurs, a notification is required. The natural form of communication here is to publish events to which various listeners (clients) subscribe. To support this asynchronous model, MOM products typically use message queues to store calls temporarily and allow clients and servers to run at different times. Messages in the queue can consist of formatted data, requests for action, or both.

The MOM messaging system is responsible for managing the connection points between messaging clients, and for managing multiple channels of communication between the connection points. A message (or integration) broker usually implements the messaging system as shown in Figure 2.14 and discussed in Section 2.8.1.

MOM products, in general, cover more than just passing information. They usually include services for translating data, security, broadcasting data to multiple programs, error recovery, locating resources on the network, cost routing, prioritisation of messages and requests, and extensive debugging facilities. As opposed to RPC and ORB (Object Request Broker) products, MOM does not assume that a reliable transport layer exists. MOM tries to handle all problems that may surface when the transport layer is unreliable.

Modern MOM technologies typically possess features that can be used as a springboard for developing Web service technologies, including:

- Message multi-cast supporting event driven processing, i.e. the publish/subscribe model.
- Reliability and serialisation of messages, thus guaranteeing message delivery in the appropriate order.
- Subject based (textual) names and attributes to abstract from the physical names and addresses that are interpreted and implemented by the network.
- Support for multiple communication protocols such as store and forward, request/reply and publish/subscribe.
- Support for transactional boundaries.

In summary, there are several features that make the MOM particularly appealing when integrating applications. These include – but are not limited to – the following:

Transparent cooperation of heterogeneous systems: The integration broker provides transformation software to transform application data running under diverse programming environments, operating systems and hardware platforms.

Prioritisation of requests: In many cases, some services need higher priority than others. All messages in a MOM environment may have priority attached to them. When a message is delivered to a client process, it is added to the client's message queue in prioritised order.

Automatic message buffering and flow control: A distributed application often will need to read messages from diverse applications and programs. To support this undertaking each application can have message queues that transparently buffer the messages when there are variable traffic rates, providing automatic flow control. This method of communication increases performance and greatly simplifies development.

Persistent messaging: This brings reliability and ensures that messages are guaranteed to be delivered at most once to their subscribers.

Flexibility and reliability: This is achieved because an application does not need an immediate answer. It can send its messages whenever it decides, independently of the recipient's availability. Senders and recipients are independent, and thus unattached, and reliability is achieved because a persistent message is never lost.

Load balancing: The asynchronous nature of MOM provides flexibility for load balancing. Load balancing is achieved as messages can be forwarded from a relatively busy application system to a less busy one. Dynamic load balancing can be designed into a MOM environment using selected algorithms including *least busy* and *round robin*. This results in a cost effective use of network facilities. With this configuration, a low bandwidth system may still attain acceptable performance, whereas it would have collapsed in a synchronous messaging environment.

Scalability and optimal use of resources: When process volumes increase, MOM brokers employ dynamic routing and multiplexing techniques. *Dynamic routing* allows clients and servers that are not preprogrammed to communicate as the MOM automatically connects the requester to the necessary service. In addition, in case of a server breakdown, the MOM platform can dispatch a message to another backup server. *Multiplexing* is a function offered by MOM brokers that enables several applications to share a message queue. Processing volumes of several hundreds of messages per second on a local network are quite typical.

MOM has demonstrated an ability to deliver the benefits of asynchronous messaging for applications and process-to-process interoperability, distributed transaction processing (such as banking, brokerage and airline reservations), distributed enterprise workflow (such as process manufacturing and insurance claim processing), real-time automation (such as utility and process control), and systems management (such as distributed backup and software distribution) among others.

A nice feature of many MOM implementations is that they can switch between synchronous and asynchronous communication mode. Although MOM is, in principle, an asynchronous peer-to-peer protocol, some implementations can handle synchronous message passing too.

2.8.1 Integration brokers

Before leaving the subject of MOM, it is useful to complement our discussion with a short description of integration brokers. An *integration broker* is an application-to-application middleware service that is capable of one-to-many, many-to-one, and many-to-many message distribution.

When a business event takes place, the application will publish the message(s) corresponding to that event. An integration broker is a software hub that records and manages the contracts between publishers and subscribers of messages. The integration broker allows multiple applications to implement a published service, with the broker providing application integration. An integration broker is a high performance communication module and supports large volumes of messages. Several hundreds of messages per second are quite typical of integration brokers.

In addition to its publish/subscribe functions, an integration broker consists of components that provide the following functions: message transformation, business rules processing, routing services, directory/naming services, adapter services, repository services, and events and alerts. We shall examine these components of an integration broker briefly in turn.

Message transformation: The integration broker transforms application specific messages into commonly understood messages, e.g. between different XML schemas using eXtensible Stylesheet Language Transformations (see Section 3.5.2). To achieve transformation the integration broker uses transformation rules defined by an application developer. The message transformation functionality *understands* the format of all messages transmitted among applications. Using this knowledge, the broker can translate between schemas by restructuring the data of these messages. In this way, receiving applications can make sense of received messages.

Business rule processing: A *business rule* is a precise statement that describes, constrains and controls the structure, operations and strategies of an enterprise [BRCommunity 2005]. Business rules can express pricing and billing policies, quality of service, process flow – where they describe routing decisions, actor assignment policies, etc. – regulations and so on. The business rules processing functionality is usually implemented as a rule processing engine within the broker. The integration broker allows the application of business rules to messages, so that new application logic can reside within the integration broker.

Routing services: The routing functionality takes care of the flow control of messages. It identifies the origin of the message and routes it to the appropriate target application. It also uses the message transformation functionality, since messages usually have to be translated for a receiving application to understand its content. The business rules engine may also be involved to determine under which conditions the message can be sent to the recipient.

Directory services: The directory services functionality is needed, since integration brokers function in a distributed environment and need a way to locate and use network resources. Applications using the integration broker are able to find other applications or hardware on the network.

Adapter services: The integration broker deploys communications middleware and associated protocols of various types as applicable to the particular application target. Many integration brokers use adapters as layers between the broker and a large enterprise's back end information systems to convert the data formats and application semantics from the source application to the target application. Adapters provide the integration broker with both data and process access to disparate applications within an enterprise.

The widespread adoption of standards, such as J2EE and XML, has laid the foundation for a standardised approach to the development of adapters. Perhaps the most significant of these standards for application integration is the J2EE Connector Architecture (CA), which defines a standardised approach for the development of adapters connecting the J2EE platform to heterogeneous enterprise information systems [Sharma 2001].

Repository services: These are implemented by using a repository holding extensive information on target and source applications. The repository keeps track of input/output to the applications, its data elements, interrelationships between applications, and all the metadata from the other subsystems of the broker like the rule processing component. When repositories are used in conjunction with adapters they enable the integration broker to understand the source and target applications and interact with them by relying on metadata about the source and target applications.

Event and alter services: Messages passing through the integration broker may trigger events or alerts based on specified conditions. Such conditions may be used for tracking business processes that move outside given parameters, and create a new message, run a special purpose application, or send an alert, in response.

2.8.2 The Java Message Service (JMS)

Until recently, MOM products required use of their own proprietary programmatic interfaces. This meant that all applications needed to be recorded to adapt to a middleware package. This changed when Java launched the Java Message Service (JMS), a framework that specified a set of programming interfaces by which Java programs could access MOM software.

JMS is a vendor agnostic API for enterprise messaging that can be used with many different MOM vendors. JMS acts as a wrapper around different messaging products, allowing developers to focus on actual application development and integration, rather on the particulars of each other's APIs. Application developers use the same API to access many different systems. JMS is not a messaging system itself. It is an abstraction of the interfaces and classes needed by messaging clients when communicating with different messaging systems. JMS not only provides a Java API for connectivity to MOM systems, but also supports messaging as a first class Java distributed computing paradigm on an equal footing with RPC [Monson-Haefel 2001].

JMS based communication is a potential solution in any distributed computing scenario that needs to pass data either synchronously or asynchronously between application elements. A common application for JMS involves interfacing Enterprise Java Beans (EJBs) with legacy applications and sending legacy related data between the two. JMS provides the two principal models of MOM messaging: point-to-point queuing and publish/subscribe.

The JMS messaging point-to-point model allows JMS clients to send and receive messages both asynchronously and synchronously via queues. In the JMS publish/subscribe messaging model, publishers send messages to a named topic, and subscribers receive all messages sent to this topic. There may be multiple message listeners subscribed to each topic and an application can be both sender and receiver.

JMS supports different message sending configurations, including: one-to-one messages, one-to-many messages, and many-to-many messages. One-to-one messages allow one message to be sent from one publisher (sender) to one subscriber (receiver).

One-to-many messages allow one message to be sent from one publisher to numerous subscribers. Many-to-many messages allow many messages to be sent from many publishers to numerous subscribers.

JMS supports two types of message delivery: *reliable message delivery* and *guaranteed message delivery*. With *reliable message delivery*, the messaging server will deliver a message to its subscribing client as long as there are no application or network failures. Delivery would fail if some disruption were to occur. This characteristic is known as *at-most-once delivery*. With *guaranteed message delivery*, the message server will deliver a message even if there are application or network failures.

In addition to this basic messaging functionality, JMS works with other Java technologies, such as the Java Transactions API, to provide features like distributed transaction support. There exist some typical middleware issues that are not specified in the JMS standard including: administration and monitoring, load balancing, fault tolerance, error and advisory notification, routing methodologies, wire protocols and security.

2.9 Transaction oriented middleware

Transaction oriented middleware encompasses transaction processing monitors, which coordinate information movement and method sharing between many different resources. Although transaction management for Web services is covered in depth in Chapter 10, we shall briefly examine transaction monitors as part of middleware for reasons of completeness.

Transaction processing (TP) monitor technology provides the distributed client-server environment with the capacity to efficiently and reliably develop, execute and manage transaction applications. TP monitors enable building on line TP by coordinating and monitoring the efforts of separate applications. TP monitors reside between front end applications and back end applications and databases to manage operations on transactional data. They manage processes and orchestrate applications by breaking complex applications into a set of transactions. The transaction is the mechanism that binds the client to one or more servers and is the fundamental unit of recovery, consistency and concurrency in a client-server system.

TP monitors were invented to run applications that serve large numbers of clients. By interjecting themselves between clients and servers, TP monitors can manage transactions, route them across systems, load balance their execution and restart them after failures. Under the control of a TP monitor, a transaction can be managed from its point of origin – typically on a client – across one or more servers and back to the originating client. When a transaction ends, all parties involved agree that it either succeeded or failed. Transaction models define when a transaction starts, when it ends, and what the appropriate units of recovery are in case of failure. A TP monitor can manage transactional resources on a single server or across multiple servers, and it can cooperate with other TP monitors in federated arrangements.

TP can adversely affect application performance because the processing of a transaction is synchronous, from the point of view of the transaction's requester. The requester must wait until all the processing of the transaction has completed before it can proceed with further computations. Moreover, during the processing of a transaction all the resources used by it are locked until the transaction completes. No other application can use these resources during the execution of a transaction.

2.10 Enterprise application and e-Business integration

Until a few years ago, traditional enterprise architectures grouped the classical bureaucratic organisation model into functional compartments, like sales, manufacturing and procurement. The results of this architectural approach were multi-functional businesses that were effectively being run in silos where mission-critical data was *locked* within disparate information systems. For many years, the solution to the siloed enterprise architecture was to integrate disparate systems by building point-to-point bridges between them. Point-to-point integration is an architectural approach where applications are linked through hand coded, custom built connectivity systems and data is interchanged directly between any two systems. The approach is generally to *build an interface* for each and every connection between information systems. This tactical approach has enormous limitations, as with each new connection point-to-point solutions become unyielding, unmanageable and unproductive. This situation is, of course, exacerbated when we start building interfaces between disparate systems belonging to distinct organisations.

2.10.1 Enterprise application integration

One of the key enabling technologies that has emerged to help organisations eliminate islands of data and automation, and to integrate diverse custom and package applications (including legacy), is enterprise application integration. The objective of *Enterprise Application Integration* (EAI) is to transform an organisation's internal applications into a cohesive corporate framework. To achieve this, EAI enables applications throughout the enterprise to communicate and integrate seamlessly in the form of business processes.

The internal applications in an enterprise that EAI attempts to integrate are called enterprise information systems (EIS). An EIS encompasses the business processes and IT assets used within enterprises and delivers the information infrastructure internal to an enterprise [Sharma 2001]. An EIS exposes a set of services to its users at differing levels of abstraction – including data level, function level, business object or process level. Many different applications and systems qualify collectively as EIS:

- *Custom applications* that have been developed by an enterprise to meet specific business needs and are developed using different programming languages, such as C, C++ or Java.
- *Legacy systems and database applications* that manage mission critical data to the business processes within an enterprise. Database and legacy systems may support core business tasks such as taking and processing orders, initiating production and delivery, generating invoices, crediting payments, distribution, inventory management, and related revenue generating, cost saving and accounting tasks. Legacy systems are the subject of Section 16.13.1.

- *Enterprise Resource Planning systems:* These are management information systems that provide a unified, organisation wide view of business processes and associated information by integrating and automating many of the business practices associated with the operations or production aspects of a company. They typically include manufacturing, logistics, distribution, inventory, shipping, invoicing and accounting. ERP systems are often called *back-office* systems, indicating that customers and the general public are not directly involved.
- *Customer Relationship Management (CRM) systems*: These provide functionality that supports the process of creating relationships with customers through the introduction of reliable service automated processes, personal information gathering and processing, and self-service throughout the supplying company to create value for the customer. CRM systems achieve their functionality by accessing and analysing data from disparate databases within the enterprise, drawing heavily on data already available in ERP systems. CRM systems are known as *front-office* systems that help the enterprise deal directly with its customers.
- *TP systems and applications*: These coordinate data movement between various data repositories.

EAI solutions combine a fast, robust communications backbone with integration broker technology, business process workflow, business process management (BPM) facilities and tools that provide for explicit management of cross-functional business processes (see Section 8.5.5.4), and application specific adapters – along with complete end-to-end application control and management – to create an environment that enables new business processes for competitive advantage [Papazoglou 2006].

Figure 2.15 shows a typical EAI solution integrating various EIS. In the EAI architecture, integration brokers focus on the message and process flow and are responsible for brokering messages exchanged between two or more applications, providing the ability to transform, store and route messages, and also to apply business rules and respond to events.

EAI solutions normally use application servers to connect an enterprise with the outside world. An application server is a natural point for application integration as it provides a platform for development, deployment and management of Web based, transactional, secure, distributed and scalable enterprise applications (see also Section 8.5.5.2). Application servers can be used in tandem with integration brokers, whereby the integration broker functions as a service provider to the application server by providing data access, transformations and content based routing.

2.10.2 e-Business integration

e-Business (or business-to-business) integration solutions grow on the back of successful internal EAI solutions and provide the capability to link together disparate processes between trading partners. e-Business integration makes systems internal to an enterprise able to interact with those of customers, suppliers, and partners. For instance, e-Business integration solutions focus on supply chain integration by providing seamless interoperability between multiple systems, e.g. manufacturing, inventory management and warehousing, logistics and billing, across the integrated supply chain. Interoperability in a supply chain is

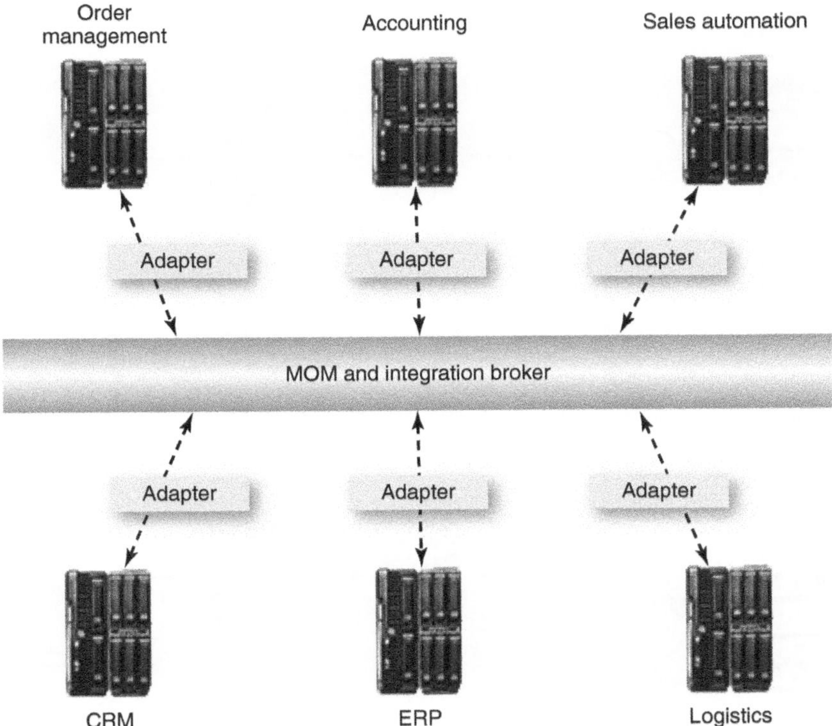

Figure 2.15 Typical EAI solution

necessary to gather useful business information, such as consumption forecasts and trends, to improve visibility into these systems, thereby seamlessly integrating and coordinating cross-functional and cross-firm business processes in the supply chain.

Sharing business logic between applications is an important factor when attempting to integrate applications that originate from different enterprises. Application servers provide a flexible platform for integrating business applications, not only because they provide a platform for development, deployment and management of Web based business applications, but also because they can be interconnected using either synchronous or asynchronous communication methods. The ability to interconnect application servers is a key requirement for integrating e-Business applications. Application servers coordinate the sequence of complex integration steps with support for checkpoints and transaction boundaries.

Figure 2.16 illustrates how application servers interlink business applications across partners by accommodating business and integration logic. Figure 2.16 also illustrates that business process integration introduces an additional independent coordination layer that provides a non-invasive fit into the existing application server architectures. Rather than being primarily focused on integrating physical entities, such as data or business components, the business process integration layer involves the integration of logical entities represented as business process elements. The application server thus encapsulates the process logic of application integration in its business process

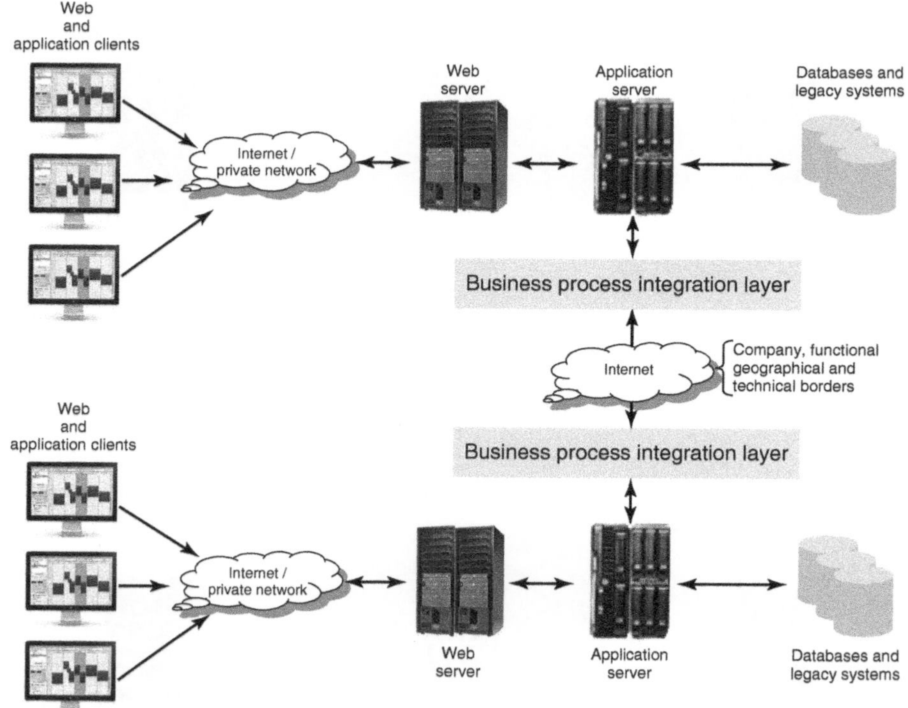

Figure 2.16 Typical e-Business integration solution
(*Source*: From M. P. Papazoglou and P. M. A. Ribbers, *e-Business: Organizational and Technical Foundations*, J. Wiley & Sons, 2006. Reproduced with permission.)

integration layer. This moves integration logic out of the applications codifying the logic, including the sequencing of events and dataflow, and ensuring transaction integrity for transactions that span multiple organisations.

2.11 Summary of learning objectives

SOA applications and Web service technologies build upon distributed systems that comprise collections of (probably heterogeneous) networked computers that communicate and coordinate their actions by passing messages.

- Web services also rely on Internet protocols to enable data to be transmitted across the Internet so that the different components in a distributed system can communicate with each other and with remote components.
- Other key enabling technologies that facilitate the development of distributed applications for Web services include remote procedure calls, message based

middleware, event processing mechanisms, message oriented middleware, and integration brokers.

- The asynchronous nature of Message Oriented Middleware makes it most appropriate for event driven Web service applications.
- A particular type of MOM with appealing properties for Web service applications is an integration broker. In the Web service, world integration brokers can be used as the software hub that records and manages the contracts between publishers and subscribers of messages.

Review questions

- Why is a service description necessary for representing Web services?
- What are Internet protocols?
- Describe the two types of message communication. What are their main differences?
- What are remote procedure calls and what is remote method invocation?
- What are the most popular forms of asynchronous messaging?
- List and describe the characteristics of publish/subscribe messaging and event driven processing. How are they related to each other?
- What is point-to-point queuing and how does it differ from publish/subscribe messaging?
- List and describe the role and features of message oriented middleware.
- List some benefits of message-oriented middleware.
- What is an integration broker and how is it used in MOM solutions?
- Define and describe the concept of enterprise application integration.
- Define and describe the concept of e-Business integration.
- What are enterprise information systems and what problems do they cause if they are not appropriately integrated?

Exercises

2.1. Write a Java program that:

- Takes a host address and checks whether a connection is available on port 80. If the connection is available the application sends an HTTP request echoing on the reply.
- Acts as a server listening on port 8888 and echoes any request it receives.

2.2. Implement a simple store and forward queuing system such as the one shown in Figure 2.10, where a J2EE application client sends several messages to a queue. The messages that are sent to the queue are asynchronously received by a server, which processes them.

2.3. Implement a distributed application that distributes computations among many clients. The clients are located on different machines and they connect themselves to a single server in a network using sockets. A single task is to be divided into many jobs, which may be assigned to different clients at different times.

2.4. Write a Java Web application to implement a simple e-commerce application that represents a shopping cart in an on line bookstore. Clients may add a book to the cart, remove a book, or retrieve the cart's contents. For information on how to develop such Web applications on the J2EE platform readers are referred to https://blueprints.dev.java.net/petstore/.

2.5. Develop a simple publish/subscribe messaging stock ticker application. A stock ticker works by continuously presenting all the trades that occur in a stock exchange, providing the name of the company, the number of shares traded and the price of the trade. A stock ticker application can be seen as one that sends an event to a topic for every trade that occurs in a stock exchange to many traders. Traders receive only the desired events from selected companies' trades by subscribing to the appropriate topic and specifying the desired companies. In this case, the message selector is the company name or symbol. Every participant (trader) in a stock trading session uses this stock trading program to join a specific stock (topic), and deliver and receive messages to and from the producer of this topic.

2.6. Topic based bulletin board systems consist of a set of newsgroups, which are classified according to subject (e.g. wine, cooking, holiday resorts, clothing, etc.). Users can send messages to these newsgroups or read messages from them. Bulletin board systems usually have one or more central servers, which store messages, and many clients, which make requests to servers for reading or sending messages. Implement a distributed architecture for a bulletin board system that does not rely on a central server. Your implementation should rely on a peer-to-peer architecture where peers can send to or read messages from other peers. It is recommended that you use JXTA technology (http://www.jxta.org/) to solve this problem. JXTA is a set of open protocols that allow connected devices on the network, ranging from cell phones and wireless PDAs to PCs and servers, to communicate and collaborate in a peer-to-peer manner. JXTA peers create a virtual network where any peer can interact with other peers and resources directly even when peers and resources are on different network transports.

CHAPTER 3

Brief overview of XML

Learning objectives

All Web service technologies are based on XML and the XML Schema Definition Language, which make possible precise machine interpretation of data and fine tune the entire process of information exchange between organisations and heterogeneous computing infrastructures. It is important that you have a good understanding of XML, XML namespaces, and the W3C Schema Language so that you can understand fundamental Web service technologies such as SOAP, WSDL, UDDI, and BPEL.

This chapter provides a brief overview of XML to help you understand the material that follows in this book. After completing this chapter you will understand the following key concepts:

- XML document structure.
- XML namespaces.
- Defining schemas.
- Reusing schemas by deriving complex type extensions and polymorphic types.
- Reusing schemas by importing and including schemas.
- Document navigation and the XML Path Language.
- Document transformation and the eXtensible Stylesheet Language Transform.

For more details about XML and XML schemas, in particular, we refer interested readers to the following books: [Walmsley 2002], [Skonnard 2002], [Valentine 2002].

Chapter preview

This chapter introduces the Extensible Markup Language, which is used for describing and delivering Web service messages over the Web. We present the structure and elements in XML documents and explain the use of XML Schema Definition Language that bestows a type system for XML processing environments, providing numerous examples. Following this we explain how XML can be used to derive complex types and how XML documents can be reused and extended. Finally, we describe how XML documents can be navigated and how XML data can be transformed in a different format.

3.1 XML document structure

Extensible Markup Language (XML) is a language used for the description and delivery of marked up electronic text over the Web. The two important characteristics of XML which distinguish it from other markup languages are:

1. The notion of a *document type*. XML documents are regarded as having types. XML's constituent parts and their structure formally define the type of a document.
2. Its concept of *portability* to ensure that documents are portable between different computing environments. All XML documents, whatever language or writing system they employ, use the same underlying character encoding scheme.

An XML document is composed of named containers and their contained data values. Typically, these containers are represented as declarations, elements and attributes.

- A *declaration* declares the version of XML used to define the document.
- An XML comprises a set of elements. *Element* is the technical term used in XML for a textual unit, which is viewed as a structural component. Element containers may be defined to hold data, other elements, both data and other elements, or nothing at all.
- An *attribute* specifies a single property for an element using a name/value pair.

An XML document is also known as an instance or *XML document instance*. This signifies the fact that an XML document instance represents one possible set of data for a particular markup language.

Example 3.1: Sample XML document instance

The example in Listing 3.1 typifies an XML document instance. This example shows billing information associated with a purchase order issued by a car parts manufacturer. We assume that this company has built a business based on providing speciality and custom fabricated car components on a spot and contract basis.

```
<?xml version="1.0" encoding="UTF-8"?>
<BillingInformation>
    <Name> Auto Parts & Car Accessories </Name>
    <BillingDate> 2008-09-15 </BillingDate>
    <Address>
      <Street> 158 Edward st. </Street>
      <City> Brisbane </City>
      <State> QLD </State>
      <PostalCode> 4000 </PostalCode>
    </Address>
</BillingInformation>
```

Listing 3.1 Example of an XML document instance

In the following we shall examine the XML named containers more closely.

3.1.1 XML declaration

The first few characters of an XML document must make up an XML declaration. The XML processing software uses the declaration to determine how to deal with the subsequent XML content. A typical XML declaration begins with a *prologue* that typically contains a declaration of conformity to version 1.0 of the XML standard and to the UTF-8 encoding standard: `<?xml version="1.0" encoding="UTF-8"?>`. This is shown in Figure 3.1.

3.1.2 XML elements

An element is a fundamental data container of an XML message. This means that an element can be declared to contain a data value, another element, a combination of a data value and another element, or it may remain empty. The content of an element can be character data, other nested elements, or a combination of both.

XML enforces a structural hierarchy of elements. The topmost element of the XML document is a single element known as the *root element*. As with any hierarchy there is a single *root* element to any XML encoded artifact. Elements contained in other elements are referred to as *nested elements*. The containing element is the parent element and the nested element is called the child element. This is illustrated in Figure 3.1, where a `Purchase Order` element is shown to contain a `Customer` element, which in turn contains `Name`, `BillingAddress` and `ShippingAddress` elements.

The data values contained within a document are known as the *content* of the document. When descriptive names have been applied to the elements and attributes that contain the data values, the content of the document becomes intuitive and self-explanatory to a person. This denotes the *self-describing* property of XML [Bean 2003].

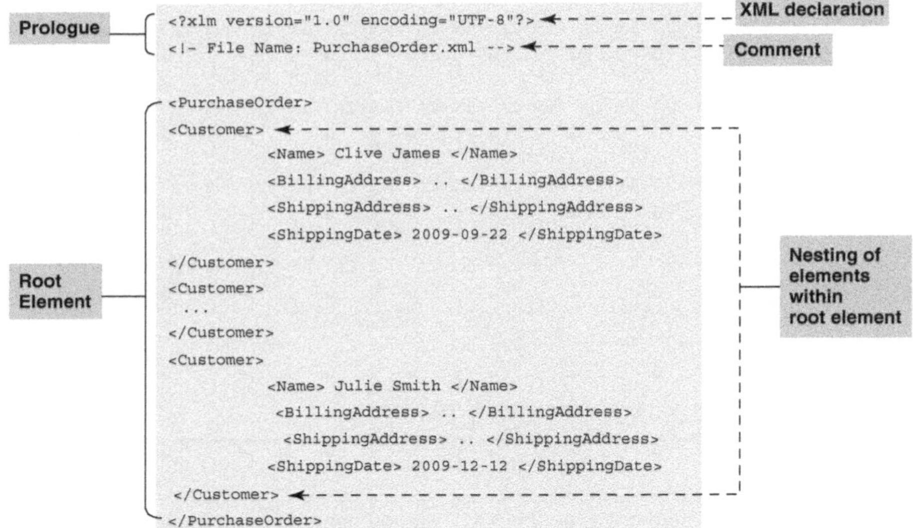

Figure 3.1 Layout of typical XML document

Different types of elements are given different names, but XML provides no way of expressing the meaning of a particular type of element, other than its relationship to other element types. For instance, all one can say about an element such as `<BillingAddress>` in Figure 3.1 is that instances of it may occur within elements of type `<Customer>`, and that it may be decomposed into elements of type `<StreetName>` and `<StreetNumber>`.

3.1.3 XML attributes

Another way of putting data into an XML document is by adding attributes to start tags. *Attributes* are used to better specify the content of an element on which they appear by adding information about a defined element. An attribute specification is a name–value pair that is associated with an element.

Each attribute is a name–value pair where the value must be in either single or double quotes. Unlike elements, attributes cannot be nested. They must also always be declared in the start tag of an element.

Example 3.2: Sample XML attribute declaration

Listing 3.2 is an example of an element declaration using an attribute (shaded) to specify the type of a particular customer as being a manufacturer.

```
<?xml version="1.0" encoding="UTF-8"?>
<BillingInformation customer-type="manufacturer">
    <Name> Auto Parts  & Car Accessories </Name>
    <BillingDate> 2002-09-15 </BillingDate>
    <Address>
      <Street> 158 Edward st. </Street>
      <City> Brisbane </City>
      <State> QLD </State>
      <PostalCode> 4000 </PostalCode>
    </Address>
</BillingInformation>
```

Listing 3.2 Example of attribute use for Listing 3.1

3.2 XML namespaces

XML allows designers to choose their own names and, as a consequence, it is possible that name clashes occur when two or more document designers choose the same tag names for their elements. XML *namespaces* provide a way to distinguish between elements that use the same local name but are in fact different, thus avoiding name clashes. For instance, a namespace can identify whether an address is a postal address, an e-mail address or an IP address. Tag names within a namespace must be unique.

To understand the need for namespaces consider the example in Listing 3.3. This listing illustrates an example of an XML document containing address information without an associated namespace.

Example 3.3: XML document without an associated namespace

```
<?xml version="1.0" encoding="UTF-8"?>
    <Address>
      <Street> 158 Edward st. </Street>
      <City> Brisbane </City>
      <State> QLD </State>
      <PostalCode> 4000 </PostalCode>
    </Address>
```

Listing 3.3 XML example with no associated namespace

Now, if we compare the instance of the Address markup in Listing 3.3 against the `BillingInformation` markup in Listing 3.2, we observe that both markups contain references to Address elements. In fact, the Address markup has its own schema in XML Schema Definition Language. It is desirable that every time that address information is used in an XML document that the `Address` declaration is reused and is thus validated against the `Address` markup schema. This means that the `Address` element in Listing 3.2 should conform to the Address markup, while the rest of the elements in this listing conform to the `BillingInformation` markup. We achieve this in XML by means of namespaces.

Namespaces in XML provide a facility for associating the elements and/or attributes in all or part of a document with a particular schema. All namespace declarations have a scope, i.e. all the elements to which they apply. A namespace declaration is in scope for the element on which it is declared and of that element's children. The namespace name and the local name of the element together form a globally unique name known as a *qualified name* [Skonnard 2002]. A qualified name is often referred to as *QName* and consists of a prefix and the local name separated by a colon.

A namespace declaration in XML is indicated by a Uniform Resource Identifier (URI), which denotes the namespace name. The Uniform Resource Identifier is the basis for identifying resources in WWW. A URI consists of a string of characters that uniquely identifies a resource. The URI provides the capability for an element name to be unique, such that it does not conflict with any other element names.

The W3C uses the broader term URI to describe network resources rather than the familiar but narrower term Uniform Resource Locator (URL). URI is all inclusive, referring to Internet resource addressing strings that use any of the present or future addressing schemes. URIs include URLs, which use traditional addressing schemes such as HTTP and FTP, and Uniform Resource Names (URNs). URNs are another form of URI that provide persistence as well as location independence. URNs address Internet resources in a location independent manner and unlike URLs they are stable over time.

The URI may be mapped to a prefix that may then be used in front of tag and attribute names, separated by a colon. In order to reference a namespace, an application developer needs to first declare one by creating a namespace declaration using the form: `xmlns:<Namespace Prefix> = <someURI>`.

Example 3.4: XML document without an associated namespace

When the prefix is attached to local names of elements and attributes, the elements and attributes then become associated with the correct namespace. An illustrative example can be found in Listing 3.4. As the most common URI is a URL, we use URLs as namespace names in our example (always assuming that they are unique identifiers). The two URLs used in this example serve as namespaces for the `BillingInformation` and `Address` elements, respectively. These URLs are simply used for identification and scoping purposes and it is, of course, not necessary that they point to any actual resources or documents.

```
<?xml version="1.0" encoding="UTF-8"?>
<BillingInformation customer-type="manufacturer"
     xmlns="http://www.auto-parts.com/BillingInfo">
    <Name> Auto Parts  & Car Accessories </Name>
    <Address xmlns="http://www.auto-parts.com/Address">
      <Street> 158 Edward st. </Street>
      <City> Brisbane </City>
      <State> QLD </State>
      <PostalCode> 4000 </PostalCode>
    </Address>
    <BillingDate> 2002-09-15 </BillingDate>
</BillingInformation>
```

Listing 3.4 An XML example using namespaces

The `xmlns` declarations in Listing 3.4 are the default namespaces for their associated element and all of its declarations. The scope of a default element applies only to the element itself and all of its descendants. This means that the declaration `xmlns="http://www.auto-parts.com/Address"` applies only to elements nested within the element `Address`. Similarly, the declaration `xmlns="http://www.auto-parts.com/BillingInfo"` applies to all elements declared within `BillingInformation` but not to `Address` elements as they define their own default namespace.

Example 3.5: XML document using qualified names

Using default namespaces can get messy when elements are interleaved or when different markup languages are used in the same document. To avoid this problem, XML defines a shorthand notation for associating elements and attributes with namespaces. Listing 3.5 illustrates.

```
<?xml version="1.0" encoding="UTF-8"?>
<bi:BillingInformation customer-type="manufacturer"
     xmlns:bi="www.auto-parts.com/BillingInfo"
     xmlns:addr="http://www.auto-parts.com/Address">

    <bi:Name> Auto Parts  & Car Accessories </bi:Name>
    <addr:Address>
      <addr:Street> 158 Edward st. </addr:Street>
      <addr:City> Brisbane </addr:City>
      <addr:State> QLD </addr:State>
      <addr:PostalCode> 4000 </addr:PostalCode>
    </addr:Address>
    <bi:BillingDate> 2002-09-15 </bi:BillingDate>
</bi:BillingInformation>
```

Listing 3.5 Using qualified names in XML

The example in Listing 3.5 illustrates the use of QNames to disambiguate and scope XML documents. As already explained earlier, QNames comprise two parts: the XML namespace and the local name. For instance, the QName of an element like City is composed of the `"http://www.auto_parts.com/Addr"` namespace and the local name `City`.

The use of valid documents can greatly improve the quality of document processes. Valid XML documents allow users to take advantage of content management, enterprise integration, and all other kinds of business processes that require the exchange of meaningful and constrained XML documents.

3.3 Defining structure in XML documents

A way to define XML tags and structure is with schemas. Schemas provide much needed capabilities for expressing XML documents. They provide support for metadata characteristics such as structural relationships, cardinality, valid values and data types. Each type of schema acts as a method of describing data characteristics and applying rules and constraints to a referencing XML document [Bean 2003]. The term *schema* when used in XML refers to a document that defines the content of, and structure of, a class of, XML documents.

3.3.1 The XML Schema Definition Language

The XML Schema Definition Language (XSD) as proposed by W3C provides a type system for XML processing environments. XSD provides a granular method for describing the content of an XML document and provides extensive capabilities in the areas of data types, customisation, and reuse [Bean 2003].

XSD provides a very powerful and flexible way in which to validate XML documents. It includes facilities for declaring elements and attributes, reusing elements from other schemas, defining complex element definitions, and for defining restrictions for even the simplest of data types. This gives the XML schema developer explicit control over specifying a valid construction for an XML document. For instance, a document definition can specify the data type of the contents of an element, the range of values for elements, the minimum as well as maximum number of times an element may occur, annotations to schemas and much more.

An XML schema is made up of *schema components*. These are building blocks that make up the abstract data model of the schema. Element and attribute declarations, complex and simple type definitions and notifications are all examples of schema components. Schema components can be used to assess the validity of well formed element and attribute information items and furthermore may specify augmentations to those items and their descendants.

XML schema components include the following [Valentine 2002]:

- data types that embrace both simple and complex/composite and extensible data types;
- element type and attribute declarations;
- constraints;
- relationships that express associations between elements;
- namespaces and import/include options to support modularity, as they make it possible to include reusable structures, containers and custom data types through externally managed XML schemas.

3.3.2 The XML schema document

Schemas are more powerful when validating an XML document because of their ability to clarify data types stored within the XML document. Because schemas can more clearly define the types of data that are to be contained in an XML document, they allow for a closer check on the accuracy of XML documents.

Example 3.6: XML schema for a purchase order

Listing 3.6 illustrates an XML schema for a sample purchase order for the fictitious car part manufacturer AVERS in our case study.

Listing 3.6 depicts a purchase order for various items. This document allows a customer to receive the shipment of the goods at its manufacturing plant and billing information to be sent to the customer's headquarters. This document also contains specific information about the products ordered, such as how much each product costs, how many were ordered and so on. The root element of an XML schema document, such as the purchase order schema, is always the `schema element`. Nested within the schema element are element and type declarations. For instance, the purchase order schema consists of a schema element and a variety of sub-elements, most notably element `complexType` and `simpleType` that determine the appearance of elements and their content in instance documents. These components are explained in the following sections.

The schema element assigns the XML schema namespace (`"http://www.w3.org/2001/XMLSchema"`) as the default namespace. This schema is the standard schema namespace defined by the XML schema specification and all XML schema elements must belong to this namespace. The schema element also defines the `targetNamespace` attribute, which declares the XML namespace of all new types explicitly created within this schema. The schema element is shown to assign the prefix `PO` to the `targetNamespace` attribute. By assigning a target namespace for a schema, we indicate that an XML document, whose elements are declared as belonging to the namespace of a given schema, should be validated against the XML schema. Therefore, the `PO targetNamespace` can be used within document instances so that they can conform to the purchase order schema.

```
<?xml version="1.0" encoding="UTF-8"?>
<xsd:schema
  xmlns:xsd="http://www.w3.org/2001/XMLSchema"
  xmlns:PO="http://www.auto-parts.com/PurchaseOrder"
  targetNamespace="http://www.auto-parts.com/PurchaseOrder">

  <!-- Purchase Order schema for AVERS -->
  <xsd:element name="PurchaseOrder" type="PO:PurchaseOrderType"/>

  <xsd:complexType name="PurchaseOrderType">
    <xsd:all>
      <xsd:element name="ShippingInformation" type="PO:Customer"
           minOccurs="1" maxOccurs="1"/>

      <xsd:element name="BillingInformation" type="PO:Customer"
           minOccurs="1" maxOccurs="1"/>
      <xsd:element name="Order" type="PO:OrderType" minOccurs="1"
                                                     maxOccurs="1"/>
    </xsd:all>
  </xsd:complexType>

  <xsd:complexType name="Customer">
    <xsd:sequence>
      <xsd:element name="Name" minOccurs="1" maxOccurs="1">
        <xsd:simpleType>
          <xsd:restriction base="xsd:string"/>
        </xsd:simpleType>
      </xsd:element>
      <xsd:element name="Address" type="PO:AddressType" minOccurs= "1"
                                                          maxOccurs="1"/>
        <xsd:choice>
        <xsd:element name="BillingDate"  type=" xsd:date "/>
        <xsd:element name="ShippingDate" type=" xsd:date "/>
      </xsd:choice>
    </xsd:sequence>
  </xsd:complexType>

  <xsd:complexType name="AddressType">
    <xsd:sequence>
      <xsd:element name="Street"       type="xsd:string"/>
      <xsd:element name="City"         type="xsd:string"/>
      <xsd:element name="State"        type="xsd:string"/>
      <xsd:element name="PostalCode "  type="xsd:decimal"/>
    <xsd:sequence>
  </xsd:complexType>

  <xsd:complexType name="OrderType">
    <xsd:sequence>
      <xsd:element name="Product" type="PO:ProductType"
                         minOccurs= "1" maxOccurs="unbounded"/>
    </xsd:sequence>
    <xsd:attribute name="Total">
```

```
      <xsd:simpleType>
        <xsd:restriction base="xsd:decimal">
          <xsd:fractionDigits value="2"/>
        </xsd:restriction>
      </xsd:simpleType>
    </xsd:attribute>
    <xsd:attribute name="ItemsSold" type="xsd:positiveInteger"/>
  </xsd:complexType>

  <xsd:complexType name="ProductType">
    <xsd:attribute name="Name" type="xsd:string"/>
    <xsd:attribute name="Price">
      <xsd:simpleType>
        <xsd:restriction base="xsd:decimal">
          <xsd:fractionDigits value="2"/>
        </xsd:restriction>
      </xsd:simpleType>
    </xsd:attribute>
    <xsd:attribute name="Quantity" type="xsd:positiveInteger"/>
  </xsd:complexType>
</xsd:schema>
```

Listing 3.6 A sample purchase order schema

We shall explain the elements, attributes, and compositions in the purchase order schema later in this section.

Example 3.7: Instance document for the purchase order schema

As the purpose of a schema is to define a class of XML documents, the term instance document is often used to describe an XML document that conforms to a particular schema. Listing 3.7 illustrates an instance document that conforms to the schema in Listing 3.6.

The remainder of this section is devoted to understanding the XML schema for the XML document shown in Listing 3.6.

3.3.3 Schema type definitions and declarations

The XSD differentiates between:

- *complex types*, which define their content in terms of elements that may consist of further elements and attributes;
- *simple types*, which define their content in terms of elements and attributes that can contain only data.

```
<?xml version="1.0" encoding="UTF-8"?>

xmlns:xsd="http://www.w3.org/2001/XMLSchema"

  targetNamespace=" ">

<PO:PurchaseOrder
 xmlns:PO="http://www.auto-parts.com/PurchaseOrder"
 xmlns:xsi="http://www.w3.org/2001/XMLSchema-instance"
 xsi:schemaLocation=" http://www.auto-parts.com/
 purchaseOrder.xsd">

  <ShippingInformation>
    <Name> Auto Parts  & Car Accessories </Name>
    <Address>
      <Street> 459 Wickham st. </Street>
      <City> Fortitude Valley </City>
      <State> QLD </State>
      <PostalCode> 4006 </PostalCode>
    </Address>
     <ShippingDate> 2010-09-20 </ShippingDate>
  </ShippingInformation>

  <BillingInformation>
    <Name> Auto Parts  & Car Accessories </Name>
    <Address>
      <Street> 158 Edward st. </Street>
      <City> Brisbane </City>
      <State> QLD </State>
      <PostalCode> 4000 </PostalCode>
    </Address>
    <BillingDate> 2010-09-15 </BillingDate>
  </BillingInformation>

  <Order Total="32000.00" ItemsSold="200">
    <Product Name="Catalytic Converter="240.00"
     Quantity="100"/>
    <Product Name="Drive Axle" Price="80.00"
     Quantity="100"/>
  </Order>
</PO:PurchaseOrder>
```

Listing 3.7 An XML instance document conforming to the schema in Listing 3.6

The XSD also introduces a sharp distinction between:

- *definitions* that create new types (both simple and complex);
- *declarations* that enable elements and attributes with specific names and types (both simple and complex) to appear in document instances.

To *declare* an element or attribute in a schema means to allow an element or attribute with a specified name, type and other features to appear in a particular context within a conforming XML document.

3.3.3.1 Element declarations

Elements are the primary ingredients of an XML schema and can be declared using the `<xsd:element>` construct from the XSD. The element declaration defines the element name, content model, and allowable attributes and data types for each element type. W3C XML schemas provide extensive data type support, including numerous built in and derived data types that can be applied as constraints to any elements or attribute. The `<xsd:element>` element either denotes an element declaration, defining a named element and associating that element with a type, or is a reference to such a declaration [Skonnard 2002]. Elements may also contain attributes. Some elements may also be defined intentionally to remain empty.

The location at which an element is defined determines its availability within the schema. The element declarations that appear as immediate descendants of the `<xsd:element>` element are known as *global element declarations* and can be referenced from anywhere within the schema document or from other schemas. For example, the `PurchaseOrderType` in Listing 3.6 is defined globally and in fact constitutes the root element in this schema. Global element declarations describe elements that are always part of the target namespace of the schema. Element declarations that appear as part of *complex type definitions* either directly or indirectly – through a group reference – are known as local element declarations. In Listing 3.6 local element declarations include elements such as `Customer` and `ProductType`.

A construct that declares an element content may use *compositors* to aggregate existing types into a structure. In this way, one can define, and constrain the behaviour of child elements. A compositor specifies the sequence and selective occurrence of the containers defined within a complex type or group. There are three types of compositors that can be used within XML schemas. These are `sequence`, `choice`, `all`, and combinations of these.

- The `sequence` construct requires that the sequence of individual elements defined within a complex type or group must be followed by the corresponding XML document (content model).
- The construct `choice` requires that the document designer make a choice between a number of defined options in a complex type or group.
- Finally, the construct `all` requires that all the elements contained in a complex type or group may appear once or not at all, and may appear in any order.

3.3.3.2 Attribute declarations

Attributes in an XML document are contained by elements. XML attributes cannot be nested and do not exhibit cardinality or multiplicity. To indicate that a complex element has an attribute, we use the `<attribute>` element of the XSD. For instance, from Listing 3.6 we observe that, when declaring an attribute (such as `Total`), we must specify its type. This type must be one of the simple types: `boolean`, `byte`, `date`, `dateTime`, `decimal`, `double`, `duration`, `float`, `integer`, `language`, `long`, `short`, `string`, `time`, `token`, etc. This example shows that an attribute may be defined based on `simpleType` elements.

3.3.4 Simple types

Most programming languages only allow developers to arrange the various built in types into a structured type of some sort, but do not allow them to define new simple types that have user defined value spaces. XML Schema is different in this regard because it allows users to define their own custom simple types, whose value spaces are subsets of the pre-defined built in types. In XML creating a `simpleType` element with one of the supported data types as a base, and adding constraining facets to it, can define custom data types.

Listing 3.6 indicates that the values of the simple element `Name` in `Customer` are restricted to only string values. Moreover, this listing specifies that each of the simple attributes `Name`, `BillingDate`, and `ShippingDate` must appear exactly once as a child of the `Customer` element. This is indicated by the presence of the occurrence constraint attributes `minOccurs` and `maxOccurs`, which specify that the minimum and maximum number of times these elements may appear is set to one. By the same token, Listing 3.6 indicates that simple attribute types like `Total` and `Price` are restricted to decimal values only, with two digits allowed to the right of the decimal point.

3.3.5 Complex types

The `complexType` element is used to define structured types. An element is considered to be a complex type if it contains child elements and/or attributes. Complex type definitions appear as children of an `xsd:schema` element and can be referenced from elsewhere in the schema and from other schemas. Complex types typically contain a set of element declarations, element references, and attribute declarations.

To declare a `complexType` element, a schema developer must define the type of the element using the `xsd:complexType` element and include within it a compositor model that describes all permissible child elements, the arrangement of these elements and rules for their occurrences.

An example of a complex type in Listing 3.6 is `PurchaseOrderType`. This particular element contains three child elements – `ShippingInformation`, `BillingInformation` and `Order` – as well as the attribute `Total`. The use of the `maxOccurs` and `minOccurs` attributes on the element declarations, with a value of one for these attributes, indicates that the element declarations specify that they must occur only once within the `PurchaseOrderType` element.

Notice the use of the `xsd:sequence` and `xsd:choice` composition elements in Listing 3.6 that defines `Customer` as a complex type element. The `xsd:sequence` element is used to indicate when a group of elements or attributes is declared within an xsd:sequence schema element; they must appear in the exact order listed. This is the case with the Name and Address elements in the complex type Customer.

The <xsd:choice> element is used to indicate when a group of elements or attributes is declared within an <xsd:choice> schema element. Any one, but not all, of the child elements may appear in the context of the parent element. This is the case with the BillingDate and ShippingDate attributes in the complex type Customer.

3.4 Reuse of XML schemas

One of the most challenging problems facing XML designers is how to design structures that can be reused. There are many benefits to designing XML schemas using reusable components. These benefits lead directly to shorter development cycles, reducing application development costs, simpler maintenance of code, as well as promoting the use of enterprise data standards. XML schema reuse is central to theses activities and is highlighted in this section.

3.4.1 Deriving complex types

XML Schema allows the derivation of a complex type from an already existing simple or complex type. Complex types are derived from other types either by extension or by restriction [Walmsley 2002]. *Extension* allows for adding additional descendants and/or attributes to an existing (base) type. *Restriction* restricts the value contents of a type. The values of the new type are a subset of those for the base type.

3.4.1.1 Complex type extensions

Adding attributes may extend complex types but one cannot modify or remove existing attributes. When defining a complex content extension the XML processor handles the extensions by appending the new content model after the base type's content model, as if they were together in a sequence compositor construct.

Example 3.8: Extending an address complex type

Listing 3.8 illustrates how to extend a complex type such as Address (which includes number, street, and city) to create an AustralianAddress. The City element in the listing is optional and this is indicated by the value of zero for the attribute minOccurs. The base type Address in Listing 3.8 can be used to create other derived types, such as EuropeanAddress or USAddress as well.

```
<?xml version="1.0" encoding="UTF-8"?>

<xsd:schema
  xmlns:xsd="http://www.w3.org/2001/XMLSchema"
  xmlns:PO="http://www.auto-parts.com/PurchaseOrder"
  targetNamespace="http://www.auto-parts.com/PurchaseOrder">

      <xsd:complexType name="Address">
          <xsd:sequence>
              <xsd:element name="Number" type="xsd:decimal"/>
              <xsd:element name="Street" type="xsd:string"/>
              <xsd:element name="City" type="xsd:string" minOccurs="0"/>
          </xsd:sequence>
      </xsd:complexType>

      <xsd:complexType name="AustralianAddress">
          <xsd:complexContent>
              <xsd:extension base="PO:Address">
                    <xsd:sequence>
                    <xsd:element name="State" type="xsd:string"/>
                    <xsd:element name="PostalCode" type="xsd:decimal"/>
                    <xsd:element name="Country" type="xsd:string"/>
                    </xsd:sequence>
              </xsd:extension>
          </xsd:complexContent>
      </xsd:complexType>
</xsd:schema>
```

Listing 3.8 Extending XML complex types

3.4.1.2 Complex type restrictions

Complex types may be restricted by eliminating or restricting attributes, and subsetting content models. When restriction is used, instances of the derived type will always be valid for the base type as well.

Example 3.9: Restring the address complex type

As an example of restricting complex types, consider the case where a developer needs to create an additional type, named `AustralianPostalAddress`, from the `AustralianAddress` type that omits the `City` element. This is shown in Listing 3.9. If the state and postal code are included in an Australian address it is not necessary to include the city as well.

```
<!-- Uses the data type declarations from Listing 3.8 -->
 <xsd:complexType name="AustralianPostalAddress">
    <xsd:complexContent>
       <xsd:restriction base="PO:AustralianAddress">
          <xsd:sequence>
             <xsd:element name="Number" type="xsd:decimal"/>
             <xsd:element name="Street" type="xsd:string"/>
             <xsd:element name="City" type="xsd:string" minOccurs="0"
                                                        maxOccurs="0"/>
             <xsd:element name="State" type="xsd:string"/>
             <xsd:element name="PostalCode" type="xsd:decimal"/>
             <xsd:element name="Country" type="xsd:string"/>
          </xsd:sequence>
       </xsd:restriction>
    </xsd:complexContent>
 </xsd:complexType>
```

Listing 3.9 Defining complex types by restriction

The purpose of the complex content restrictions is to allow designers to restrict the content model and/or attributes of a complex type. Listing 3.9 shows how the restriction element achieves this purpose. In this example, the derived type `AustralianPostalAddress` contains the `Number`, `Street`, `State`, `PostalCode`, and `Country` elements but omits the `City` element. It is omitted as the value of both attributes `minOccurs` and `maxOccurs` is set to zero.

3.4.1.3 Polymorphism

One of the attractive features of XML Schema is that derived types can be used polymorphically with elements of the base type. This means that a designer can use a derived type in an instance document in place of a base type specified in the schema.

Example 3.10: Defining variants of the purchase order type

Listing 3.10 defines a variant of the `PurchaseOrder` type introduced in Listing 3.6 to use the base type `Address` for its `billingAddress` and `shippingAddress` elements.

Since XML Schema supports polymorphism, an instance document can now use any type derived from base type `Address` for its `billingAddress` and `shippingAddress` elements. Listing 3.11 illustrates that the `PurchaseOrder` type uses the derived `AustralianAddress` type as its `billingAddress` and the derived `AustralianPostalAddress` type as its `shippingAddress` elements.

```
<!-- Uses the data type declarations from Listing 3.8 -->

  <xsd:complexType name="PurchaseOrder">
    <xsd:sequence>
      <xsd:element name="Name" minOccurs="1" maxOccurs="1">
        <xsd:simpleType>
          <xsd:restriction base="xsd:string"/>
        </xsd:simpleType>
      </xsd:element>
      <xsd:element name="shippingAddress" type="PO:Address"
                                     minOccurs= "1" maxOccurs="1"/>
      <xsd:element name="billingAddress" type="PO:Address"
                                     minOccurs= "1" maxOccurs="1"/>
        <xsd:choice minOccurs="1" maxOccurs="1">
            <xsd:element name="BillingDate"  type="xsd:date"/>
            <xsd:element name="ShippingDate" type="xsd:date"/>
        </xsd:choice>
    </xsd:sequence>
  </xsd:complexType>
```

Listing 3.10 Defining types polymorphically

```
<!-- Uses type declarations from Listing 3.10 -->

<?xml version="1.0" encoding="UTF-8"?>
<PO:PurchaseOrder xmlns:PO="www.auto-parts.com/PurchaseOrder">

    <Name> Auto Parts  & Car Accessories </Name>
    <shippingAddress xsi:type="PO:AustralianAddress">
      <Number> 459 </Number>
      <Street> Wickham st. </Street>
      <City> Fortitude Valley </City>
      <State> QLD </State>
      <PostalCode> 4006 </PostalCode>
      <Country> Australia </country>
    </shippingAddress>

    <billingAddress xsi:type=="PO:AustralianAddress">
      <Number> 158 </Number>
      <Street> Edward st. </Street>
      <State> QLD </State>
      <PostalCode> 4000 </PostalCode>
      <Country> Australia </Country>
    </billingAddress>
     <BillingDate> 2010-09-15 </BillingDate>
</PO:PurchaseOrder>
```

Listing 3.11 Using polymorphism in an XML schema instance

3.4.2 Importing and including schemas

W3C XML schemas provide extensive capabilities in the area of cross-domain reuse. Leveraging W3C XML schemas for cross-domain reuse implies that a schema (or sub-schema) can represent a repeatable pattern, and it can be used in different contexts and by different applications. This allows an XML Schema (or parts thereof) to be referenced and its content to be reused by other XML Schemas. This approach allows developers to reuse schema components and each other's schemas and therefore reduces the complexity of developing schemas, while easing development, testing and maintainability.

Combining schemas in the XSD can be achieved by using the `include` and the `import` elements. Through the use of these two elements, we can effectively *inherit* attributes and elements from referenced schemas.

3.4.2.1 Including schemas

The XML Schema `include` element allows for modularisation of schema documents by including other schema documents in a schema document that has the same target namespace. The `include` syntax enables global components that are defined in other schemas to act as extensions to the including file's namespace. To support the components that are added into the namespace, an included schema must be either in the same or no namespace. This option is useful when a schema becomes large and difficult to manage. In this case it is desirable to partition the schema into separate sub-schemas (modules), which we can eventually combine by using the include element.

Example 3.11: Including complex types in the purchase order document

In the following we shall exemplify the use of the XML Schema `include` element by illustrating how to include additional complex types in the XML definition for a purchase order. This will be done in two steps.

The declaration in Listing 3.12 illustrates that the `Customer` type has been placed in its own schema document, which has the same target namespace as the purchase order schema depicted in Listing 3.6. We also assume that the same applies for the `ProductType` type, which has been placed in its own schema document and has the same target namespace as the purchase order schema (shaded in the listing).

Now these two sub-schemas can be combined (included) in the context of the purchase order schema using the include element. This is illustrated in Listing 3.13, where the two include statements are shaded.

Notice that in Listing 3.13 we do not need to specify the namespaces for the two included schemas, as these are expected to match the namespace of the purchase order schema.

```
<?xml version="1.0" encoding="UTF-8"?>
<xsd:schema
  xmlns:xsd="http://www.w3.org/2001/XMLSchema"
  xmlns:PO=="http://www.auto-parts.com/PurchaseOrder"
  targetNamespace="http://www.auto-parts.com/PurchaseOrder">

  <xsd:complexType name="Customer">
      <xsd:sequence>
        <xsd:element name="Name" minOccurs="1" maxOccurs="1">
          <xsd:simpleType>
            <xsd:restriction base="xsd:string"/>
          </xsd:simpleType>
        </xsd:element>
        <xsd:element name="Address" type="PO:AddressType"
                                    minOccurs= "1" maxOccurs="1"/>
          <xsd:choice minOccurs="1" maxOccurs="1">
          <xsd:element name="BillingDate"  type="xsd:date"/>
          <xsd:element name="ShippingDate" type="xsd:date"/>
        </xsd:choice>
      </xsd:sequence>
  </xsd:complexType>
</xsd:schema>
```

Listing 3.12 Sample customer sub-schema

3.4.2.2 Importing schemas

The `import` element is used when we wish to use Schema definitions from a different XML namespace. This is due the fact that W3C XML Schema does not allow a single Schema file to contain definitions for more than a single namespace. An `import` element is used to instruct the XML parser that it should refer to components from other namespaces. The `import` element differs from the `include` element in two important ways [Walmsley 2002]:

1. The `include` element can only be used within the same namespace, while the `import` element is used across namespaces.
2. The purpose of the `include` element is specifically to introduce other schema documents, while the purpose of the `import` element is to record dependency on another namespace, not necessarily another schema document. The `import` mechanism enables designers to combine schemas to create a larger, more complex schema. It is very useful in cases where some parts of a schema, such as address types, are reusable and need their namespace and schema.

```
<?xml version="1.0" encoding="UTF-8"?>
<xsd:schema xmlns:xsd="http://www.w3.org/2001/XMLSchema"
 xmlns:PO=" http://www.auto-parts.com/PurchaseOrder"
 targetNamespace="http://www.auto-parts.com/PurchaseOrder">

  <xsd:include
    schemaLocation="http:// www.auto-parts.com/customerType.xsd"/>

  <xsd:include
    schemaLocation="http:// www.auto-parts.com/productType.xsd"/>

  <xsd:element name="PurchaseOrder" type="PO:PurchaseOrderType"/>

  <xsd:complexType name="PurchaseOrderType">
    <xsd:all>
      <xsd:element name="ShippingInformation" type="PO:Customer"
                                 minOccurs="1" maxOccurs="1"/>
      <xsd:element name="BillingInformation" type="PO:Customer"
                                 minOccurs="1" maxOccurs="1"/>
      <xsd:element name="Order" type="PO:OrderType" minOccurs= "1"
                                               maxOccurs="1"/>
    </xsd:all>
  </xsd:complexType>

  <xsd:complexType name="AddressType">
    <xsd:sequence>
      <xsd:element name="Street"          type="xsd:string"/>
      <xsd:element name="City"            type="xsd:string"/>
      <xsd:element name="State"           type="xsd:string"/>
      <xsd:element name="PostalCode "     type="xsd:decimal"/>
    <xsd:sequence>
  </xsd:complexType>

  <xsd:complexType name="OrderType">
    <xsd:sequence>
      <xsd:element name="Product" type="PO:ProductType"
                       minOccurs= "1" maxOccurs="unbounded"/>
    </xsd:sequence>
    <xsd:attribute name="Total">
      <xsd:simpleType>
        <xsd:restriction base="xsd:decimal">
          <xsd:fractionDigits value="2"/>
        </xsd:restriction>
      </xsd:simpleType>
    </xsd:attribute>
    <xsd:attribute name="ItemsSold" type="xsd:positiveInteger"/>
  </xsd:complexType>
</xsd:schema>
```

Listing 3.13 Using the `include` statement in the purchase order schema

Example 3.12: Importing address types in the purchase order document

Listing 3.14 defines a separate schema and namespace for all types related to addresses in the purchase order example. This schema defines a complete address markup language for purchase orders that contains all address related elements such as the

```
<?xml version="1.0" encoding="UTF-8"?>

<xsd:schema xmlns:xsd="http://www.w3.org/2001/XMLSchema"
 xmlns:addr=http://www.auto-parts.com/NewAddress
 targetNamespace="http://www.auto-parts.com/NewAddress">
 <xsd:import namespace="http://www.auto-parts.com/Address"
             schemaLocation="addressType.xsd"/>

  <xsd:complexType name="AddressType" abstract="true">
    <xsd:sequence>
      <xsd:element name="Number"  type="xsd:decimal"/>
      <xsd:element name="Street"  type="xsd:string"/>
      <xsd:element name="City"    type="xsd:string" minOccurs="0"/>
    <xsd:sequence>
  </xsd:complexType>

  <xsd:complexType name="AustralianAddress">
    <xsd:complexContent>
      <xsd:extension base="addr:AddressType">
        <xsd:sequence>
           <xsd:element name="State"          type="xsd:string"/>
           <xsd:element name="PostalCode "    type="xsd:decimal"/>
           <xsd:element name="Country"        type="xsd:string"/>
        <xsd:sequence>
      </xsd:extension>
    </xsd:complexContent>
  </xsd:complextype>

  <xsd:complexType name="AustralianPostalAddress">
    < xsd:complexContent>
      <xsd:restriction base="addr:Austtralian Address">
        <xsd:sequence>
           <xsd:element name="Number"         type="xsd:decimal"/>
           <xsd:element name="Street"         type="xsd:string"/>
           <xsd:element name="State"          type="xsd:string"/>
           <xsd:element name="PostalCode "    type="xsd:decimal">
           <xsd:element name="Country"        type="xsd:string"/>
        </xsd:sequence>
      </xsd:restriction>
    </xsd:complexContent>
  </xsd:complextype>
</xsd:schema>
```

Listing 3.14 The address markup schema

```
<?xml version="1.0" encoding="UTF-8"?>
<xsd:schema xmlns:xsd="http://www.w3.org/2001/XMLSchema">
 targetNamespace=http://www.auto-parts.com/PurchaseOrder
 xmlns:PO="http://www.auto-parts.com/PurchaseOrder"
 xmlns:addr="http:// www.auto-parts.com/Address">

  <xsd:include
    schemaLocation="http:// www.auto-parts.com/productType.xsd"/>

  <xsd:import namespace="http:// www.auto-parts.com/Address"
    schemaLocation="http:// www.auto-parts.com/addressType.xsd"/>

  <xsd:element name="PurchaseOrder" type="PO:PurchaseOrderType"/>

  <xsd:complexType name="PurchaseOrderType">
    <xsd:all>
      <xsd:element name="ShippingInformation" type="PO:Customer"
                                   minOccurs="1" maxOccurs="1"/>
      <xsd:element name="BillingInformation" type="PO:Customer"
                                   minOccurs="1" maxOccurs="1"/>
      <xsd:element name="Order" type="OrderType" minOccurs= "1"
                                             maxOccurs="1"/>
    </xsd:all>
  </xsd:complexType>

  <xsd:complexType name="Customer">
    <xsd:sequence>
      <xsd:element name="Name" minOccurs="1" maxOccurs="1">
        <xsd:simpleType>
          <xsd:restriction base="xsd:string"/>
        </xsd:simpleType>
      </xsd:element>
      <xsd:element name="Address" type="addr:AddressType"
                                 minOccurs= "1" maxOccurs="1"/>
      <xsd:choice minOccurs="1" maxOccurs="1">
           <xsd:element name="BillingDate"  type="xsd:date"/>
           <xsd:element name="ShippingDate" type="xsd:date"/>
      </xsd:choice>
    </xsd:sequence>
  </xsd:complexType>

  <xsd:complexType name="OrderType">
    <xsd:sequence>
      <xsd:element name="Product" type="PO:ProductType"
                                 maxOccurs="unbounded"/>
    </xsd:sequence>
    <xsd:attribute name="Total">
      <xsd:simpleType>
        <xsd:restriction base="xsd:decimal">
            <xsd:fractionDigits value="2"/>
        </xsd:restriction>
      </xsd:simpleType>
    </xsd:attribute>
    <xsd:attribute name="ItemsSold" type="xsd:positiveInteger"/>
  </xsd:complexType>
</xsd:schema>
```

Listing 3.15 A purchase order schema using the `import` and `include` statements together

AddressType, AustralianAddress, EuropeanAddress, USAddress, AustralianPostalAddress, EuropeanPostalAddress, and so on. The namespace attribute for the address markup schema is "http://www.auto-parts.com"/Address",which is a distinct and separate namespace from that of the purchase order elements.

As the purchase order example depends on the AddressType type, we shall need to import the address markup schema into the purchase order schema as illustrated in Listing 3.15.

Listing 3.15 shows the use of both the import and the include elements. These appear together at the top level of the purchase order schema definition document. In particular, the listing illustrates that the import statement references the namespace and location of the schema document that contains the address markup language for purchase orders. The imported namespace needs to be assigned a prefix before we can use it. In this case it is assigned the prefix addr. In this way, the declaration of the Address element in the complex type Customer is able to reference the AddressType type by using this prefix.

For conciseness we included the definition of the complex type Customer as part of the purchase order schema, instead of defining it in a separate sub-schema document as we did in Listing 3.12.

3.5 Document navigation and transformation

In contrast to languages such as HTML, XML is primarily used to describe and contain data. Although the most obvious and effective use of XML is to describe data, other technologies such as the eXtensible Stylesheet Language Transform (XSLT) can also be used to format or transform XML content for presentation to users. The XSLT process transforms an XML structure into presentation technology such as HTML or into any other required forms and structures. XML transactions that are targeted for direct viewing by individuals will generally require an applied style sheet transformation by means of XSLT.

XSLT intensively uses the XML Path Language or XPath (defined as a separate specification at the W3C) to address and locate sections of XML documents [Gardner 2002]. XPath is a standard for creating expressions that can be used to find specific pieces of information within an XML document.

3.5.1 The XML Path Language

The XPath data model views a document as a tree of nodes. Nodes correspond to document components, such as elements and attributes. It is very common to think of XML documents as trees comprising roots, branches and leaves. This is quite natural as trees are hierarchical in nature, just as XML documents are.

XPath uses genealogical taxonomy to describe the hierarchical makeup of an XML document, referring to children, descendants, parents and ancestors [Goldfarb 2001]. The parent is the element that contains the element under discussion, while an element's list of ancestors includes its parent as the entire set of nodes preceding its parent in a directed path leading from this element up to the root. A list of descendants includes the children of an element in a direct path from this element all the way down to leaf nodes.

The topmost node in XPath is known as the *root* or *document root*. The root is not an element. It is rather a logical construct that holds together the entire XML document. The root element is the single element from which all other elements in the XML document instance are children or descendants. The root element is itself the child of the root. The root element is also known as the *document element*, because it is the first element in a document and it contains all other elements in the document.

Figure 3.2 exemplifies the previous points as it shows an abridged version of the logical (XPath tree) structure for the instance document defined in Listing 3.7. Note that the root element in this figure is Purchase Order. Attributes and namespaces are associated directly with nodes (see dashed lines) and are not represented as children of an element. The document order of nodes is based on the tree hierarchy of the XML instance. Element nodes are ordered prior to their children (to which they are connected via solid lines), so the first element node would be the document element, followed by its descendants. Children nodes of a given element (as in conventional tree structures) are processed prior to sibling nodes. Finally, attributes and namespace attachments of a given element are ordered prior to the children of the element.

Example 3.13: Sample XPath query for purchase orders

The code in Listing 3.7 provides a good baseline sample XML structure that we can use for defining XPath examples. Listing 3.16 illustrates a sample XPath expression and the resulting node set.

```
XPath Query#1: /PurchaseOrder/Order[2]/child::*
Resulting Node Set#1:
=====================
    <Product Name="Catalytic Converter" Price="240.00"
    Quantity="1"/>
```

Listing 3.16 Sample XPath query and resulting node set

The XPath query in Listing 3.16 consists of three location steps, the first one being `PurchaseOrder`. The second location step is `Order[2]`, which specifies the second Order element within the `PurchaseOrder`. Finally, the third location step is `child::*`, which selects all child elements of the second Order element. It is important to understand that each location step has a different context node. For the first location step (`PurchaseOrder`), the current context node is the root of the XML document. The context for the second location step (`Order[2]`) is the node `PurchaseOrder`, while the context for the third location step is the second `Order` node (not shown in Figure 3.2).

More information on XPath and as well as sample XPath queries can be found in books such as [Gardner 2002], [Schmelzer 2002].

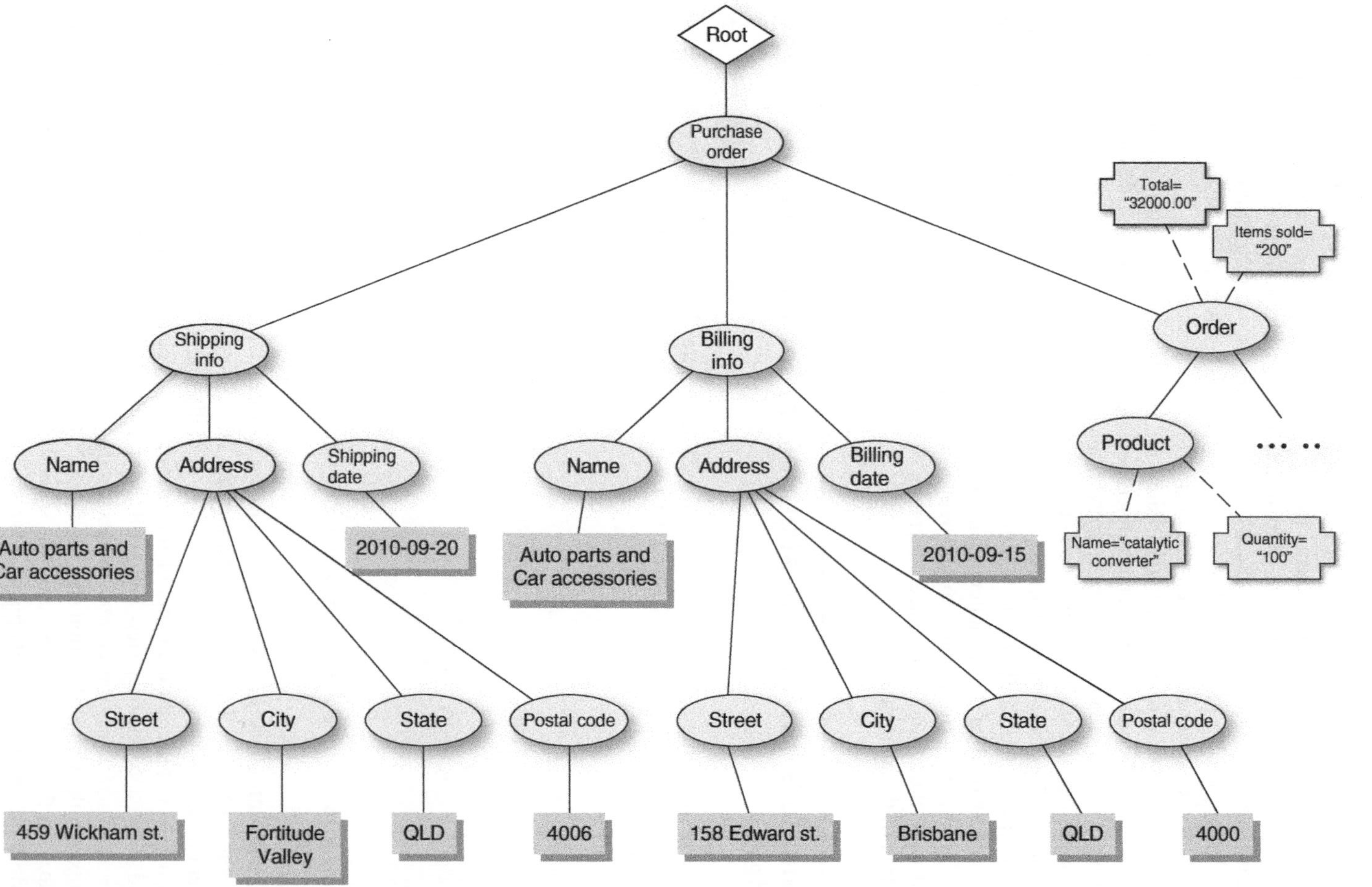

Figure 3.2 XPath tree model for the instance document in Listing 3.7

3.5.2 Using XSLT to transform documents

To perform document transformation, a document developer usually needs to supply a style sheet, which is written in XSLT. The *style sheet* specifies how the XML data will be displayed. XSLT uses the formatting instructions in the style sheet to perform the transformation. The converted document can be another XML document or a document in another format, such as HTML, that can be displayed on a browser. Formatting languages, such as XSLT, can access only the elements of a document that are defined by the document structure, e.g. XML schema.

An XSLT style sheet or script contains instructions that inform the transformation processor of how to process a source document to produce a target document. This makes XSLT transformations very useful for business applications. Consider, for example, XML documents generated and used internally by an enterprise that may need to be transformed into an equivalent format that customers or service providers of this enterprise are more familiar with. This can help to easily transfer information to and from an enterprise's partners.

Figure 3.3 shows an example of such a transformation. This figure shows an XML fragment which represents the billing element of a purchase order message. As shown in this

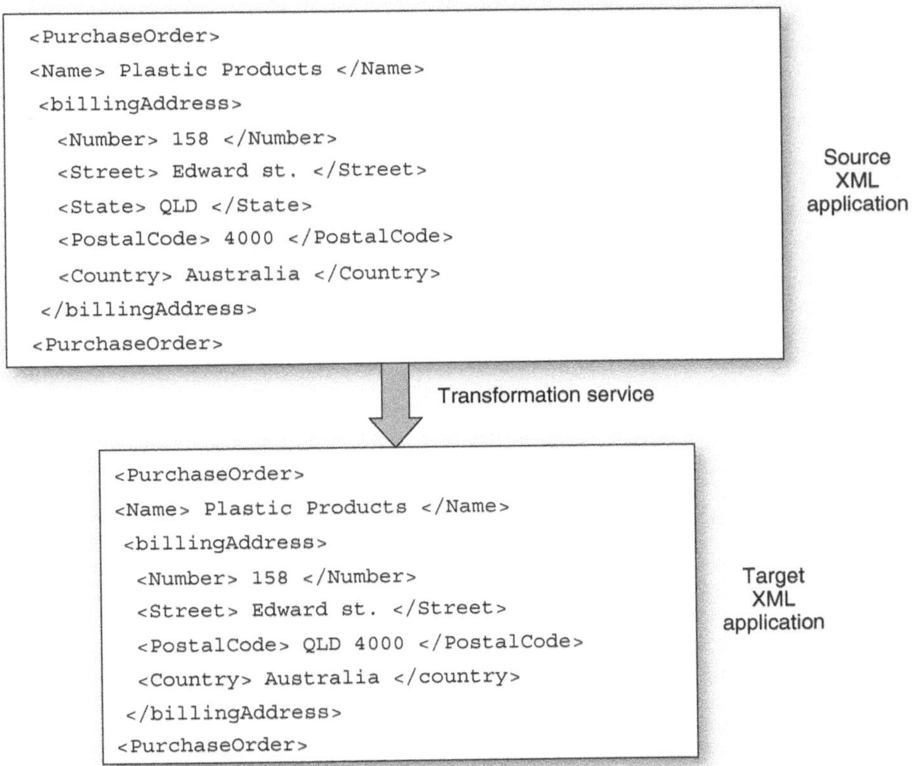

Figure 3.3 Using XSLT to transform business-related information

message, the source XML application uses separate elements to represent street numbers, street addresses, states, postal codes and countries. The target application is shown to use a slightly different format to represent postal codes, as it uses seven characters to represent postal codes by combining state information with conventional four digit postal codes.

More information on XSLT and transformations, as well as examples, can be found in books such as [Gardner 2002], [Tennison 2001].

3.6 Summary of learning objectives

XML is an extensible markup language used for the description and delivery of marked up electronic text over the Web. Important characteristics of XML are its emphasis on descriptive rather than prescriptive (or procedural) markup, its document type concept, its extensibility and its portability.

An important aspect of XML is its notion of a document type. XML documents are regarded as having types. Its constituent parts and their structure formally define the type of a document.

- XML Schema describes the elements and attributes that may be contained in a schema conforming document and the ways that the elements may be arranged within a document structure.
- Schemas are powerful when validating an XML document because of their ability to clarify data types stored within the XML document.

XML can be perceived as a dynamic trading language that enables diverse applications to exchange information flexibly and cost effectively. The ability of XML to model complex data structures, combined with the additional ability of XML Schema to reuse and refine the data model of other schema architectures, enables reuse and extension of components, reduces the development cycle and promotes interoperability. It is precisely the suite of technologies that are grouped under XML that had profound influence on the development of Web service technologies and provide the fundamental building blocks for Web services and Service Oriented Architectures.

Review questions

- What are the two important features of XML that distinguish it from other markup languages?
- What are XML elements and what are XML attributes? Give examples of both.
- Describe URIs and XML namespaces using examples.
- What is the purpose of the XML Schema Definition Language?
- List and describe the main XML schema components.

- What are simple and what are complex XML types?
- How do you achieve reusability in XML?
- Give an example of a derived complex type.
- Define and describe the concept of polymorphism in XML.
- What is the purpose of the include and import elements in the XML Schema Definition Language? How do they differ?
- What is the purpose of the XPath data model? Describe how it views an XML document.
- How can XSLT help with document transformation?

Exercises

3.1. Define a simple purchase order schema for a hypothetical online grocery. Each purchase order should contain various items. The schema should allow one customer to receive the shipment of the goods and an entirely different individual, e.g. spouse, to pay for the purchase. This document should include a method of payment that allows customers to pay by credit card, direct debit, check, etc., and should also contain specific information about the products ordered, such as how much each product cost, how many items were ordered and so on.

3.2. Extend the purchase order schema in the previous exercise to describe the case of an on line grocery that sells products to its customers by accepting only credit cards as a payment medium. This simple order processing transaction should contain basic customer, order and product type information, as well as different methods of delivery, and a single method of payment, which includes fields for credit card number, expiration date and payment amount. Show how this purchase order schema can import schema elements that you developed for Exercise 3.1.

3.3. Define a schema for a simple clearing-house application that deals with credit card processing and (PIN-based) debit card processing for its customers who are electronic merchants. In order to process a credit card a merchant will need to have a valid merchant account with the clearing-house. A merchant account is a commercial bank account established by contractual agreement between a merchant and the clearing-house and enables a merchant that provides shopping facilities to accept credit card payments from its customers. A merchant account is required to authorise transactions. A typical response for a credit card is authorised, declined, or cancelled. When the clearing-house processes credit card sales it returns a transaction identifier (TransID) only when a credit card sale is authorised. If the merchant needs to credit or void a transaction, the TransID of the original credit card sale will be required. For simplicity assume that one credit is allowed per sale and that a credit amount cannot exceed the original sale amount. The application should be able to process a number of payments in a single transmission as a batch transaction.

3.4. Define a schema for a flight availability request application that requests flight availability for a city pair on a specific date for a specific number and type of passengers. Optional request information can include: time or time window, connecting cities, client preferences, e.g. airlines, flight types, etc. The request can be narrowed to request availability for a specific airline, specific flight, or specific booking class on a specific flight.

3.5. Define a schema for handling simple requests for the reservation of rental vehicles. The schema should assume that the customer has already decided to use a specific rental branch. It should then define all the information that is needed when requesting information about a vehicle rental. The schema should include information such as rate codes, rate type, promotional descriptions and so on, as well as rate information that had been supplied in a previous availability response, along with any discount number or promotional codes that may affect the rate. For instance, the customer may have a frequent renter number that should be associated with the reservation. Typically rates are offered as either leisure rates or corporate rates. The schema should also define the rental period, as well as information on a distance associated with a particular rate, e.g. limited or unlimited miles per rental period, and customer preferences regarding the type of vehicle and special equipment that can be included with the reservation of a rental vehicle.

3.6. Define a simple hotel availability request schema that provides the ability to search for hotel products available for booking by specific criteria that may include: dates, date ranges, price range, room types, regular and qualifying rates, and/or services and amenities. A request can also be made for a non-room product, such as banquets and meeting rooms. An availability request should be made with the intent ultimately to book a reservation for an event or for a room stay. The schema should allow a request for *static* property data published by the hotel that includes information about the hotel facilities, amenities, services, etc., as well as *dynamic* (e.g. rate oriented) data. For example, a hotel may have an AAA rate, a corporate rate (which it does not offer all the time), or may specify a negotiated code as a result of a negotiated rate, which affects the availability and price of the rate.

PART III

Core functionality and standards

CHAPTER 4

SOAP: Simple Object Access Protocol

Learning objectives

Conventional distributed object communication protocols, such as CORBA, DCOM, Java/RMI, and other application-to-application communication protocols for server-to-server communications, present severe weaknesses for client-to-server communications, especially notable when the client machines are scattered across the Internet. Such protocols have a symmetrical requirement, which necessitates that both ends of the communication link be implemented under the same distributed object model and require the deployment of libraries developed in common. To address such limitations the Simple Object Access Protocol (SOAP), was developed. SOAP facilitates interoperability among a wide range of programs and platforms, making existing applications accessible to a broader range of users.

This chapter introduces SOAP v1.2, describes its main characteristics and the structure of SOAP messages, and concentrates on the following topics:

- The use of SOAP as a messaging protocol.
- How SOAP promotes interoperability.
- The structure of SOAP messages.
- RPC and document style messages.
- Error handling in SOAP.
- The use of HTTP as transport protocol with SOAP.
- Advantages and limitations of SOAP.

Chapter preview

In this chapter we examine distributed computing inter-application protocols and introduce the Simple Object Access Protocol, which is an XML based protocol used in conjunction with Web services. We first motivate the use of SOAP and then go on to explain how it relates to transport protocols such as HTTP. Following this we introduce the structure and elements of SOAP messages and explain how the SOAP communication model is used to invoke Web services. We conclude this section by itemising the advantages and disadvantages of SOAP.

4.1 Inter-application communication and wire protocols

In the world of Web services, it is possible for enterprises to leverage mainstream application development tools and Internet application servers to bring about inter-application communication. This undertaking can only take place successfully if proprietary systems running on heterogeneous infrastructures are overcome.

To address the problem of overcoming proprietary systems running on heterogeneous infrastructures, Web services rely on SOAP. This is an XML based communication protocol for exchanging messages between computers regardless of their operating systems, programming environment or object model framework. SOAP provides the definition of XML based information which can be used for exchanging structured and typed information between peers in a decentralised, distributed environment. The primary application of SOAP is inter-application communication, e.g. e-Business integration.

SOAP codifies the use of XML as an encoding scheme for request and response parameters using HTTP as a means for transport. In particular, a SOAP message is simply an HTTP request and response that complies with the SOAP encoding rules. A SOAP endpoint is simply an HTTP-based URL that identifies a target for method invocation.

SOAP provides a wire protocol, in that it specifies how service related messages are structured when exchanged across the Internet. It can be defined as a simple messaging framework for exchanging structured and typed information back and forth between disparate systems in a distributed environment, such as the Internet or even a LAN (Local Area Network), enabling remote method invocation [Cauldwell 2001]. The term lightweight wire protocol means that SOAP possesses only two fundamental properties. It can send and receive HTTP (or other) transport protocol packets, and process XML messages [Scribner 2000].

One distinction that many people find confusing is the difference between the wire protocol (format) and the transport protocol. Whereas the *wire protocol* specifies the form or shape of the data to be exchanged between disparate applications, and eventually systems, the term *transport protocol* signifies the method by which that data is transferred from system to system. The transport protocol is responsible for taking its payload from its point of origin to its destination.

4.1.1 SOAP as a wire representation

SOAP makes use of *openly available* technologies that, when combined, specify a wire protocol. SOAP commonly uses HTTP to transport XML encoded serialised method argument data from system to system. This serialised argument data is used on the remote end to execute a client's method call on that system, rather than on a local system. If HTTP is used as a SOAP transport protocol, then SOAP processing is very much aligned with the Internet, which specifies a stateless programming model.

Wire protocols, such as SOAP, are designed to meet specific design criteria, including [Scribner 2002] compactness, protocol efficiency, coupling, scalability and interoperability:

> *Compactness* refers to how terse a network package becomes while conveying the same information. Small degree of compactness is usually best.
>
> *Protocol efficiency* is directly related to compactness. Efficiency is rated by examining the overhead required to send the payload. The more overhead required, the less efficient the protocol is.
>
> *Coupling* is the rate at which the client application needs to adapt to changes. Loosely coupled protocols are quite flexible and can easily adapt to changes, while tightly coupled protocols require significant modifications to both the server and existing clients.
>
> *Scalability* addresses the ability of a protocol to work with a large number of potential recipients. Some protocols are limited to a few hundreds of clients, while others can easily handle millions.
>
> *Interoperability* refers to the ability of the protocol to work with a variety of computing platforms. For instance, general purpose protocols enable clients to send information to a variety of systems.

Protocols, including XML and SOAP, generally lie on a continuum of these characteristics. No single protocol achieves all these properties. For instance, XML and SOAP are both loosely coupled and interoperable. This adversely affects compactness and efficiency. Both XML and SOAP as document based protocols are rather verbose and this makes them rather inefficient. The SOAP commonly uses HTTP and is therefore very scalable in its native form.

The following sections will concentrate on the description and characteristics of SOAP 1.2.

4.2 SOAP as a messaging protocol

The goal of SOAP is to diffuse the barriers of heterogeneity that separate distributed computing platforms. SOAP achieves this by following the same recipe as other successful Web protocols: simplicity, flexibility, firewall friendliness, platform neutrality and XML messaging based (text based). SOAP is simply an attempt to codify the usage of existing

Internet technologies to standardise distributed communications over the Web, rather than being a new technological advancement.

SOAP has a clear purpose: exchanging data over networks. Specifically, it concerns itself with encapsulating and encoding XML data and defining the rules for transmitting and receiving that data [Monson-Haefel 2004]. SOAP describes how a message is formatted but it does not specify how it is delivered. The message must be embedded in a transport level protocol to achieve this purpose. Although SOAP may use different protocols, such as HTTP, FTP, SMTP or RMI, to transport messages, locate the remote system and initiate communications, its natural transport protocol is HTTP.

In short, SOAP is a network application protocol that is used to transfer messages between service instances described by WSDL interfaces. This is illustrated in Figure 4.1, which depicts that SOAP messages use different protocols such as HTTP to transport messages and locate the remote systems associated with interacting Web services. The SOAP message, shown in Figure 4.1, becomes the body of an HTTP message and is sent to its destination. At the next layer in the protocol hierarchy illustrated in Figure 4.1, the HTTP message becomes data in a TCP stream sent over a connection. At the other end (destination) an HTTP listener passes the body of the HTTP message on to a SOAP processor that understands the syntax of SOAP messages and is capable of processing the message it receives. We elaborate further on this below.

SOAP is fundamentally a stateless, one way message exchange paradigm, but applications can create more complex interaction patterns (e.g. request/response, request/multiple responses, etc.) by combining such one-way exchanges with features provided by an underlying protocol and/or application specific information.

SOAP does not itself define any application semantics, such as a programming model or implementation specific semantics. Rather it defines a simple mechanism that provides a modular packaging model and encoding mechanisms for encoding data within modules. This allows SOAP to be used in a large variety of systems ranging from messaging systems to RPC. It also does not concern itself with such issues as the routing of SOAP messages, reliable data transfer, firewall traversal and so on. However, SOAP provides the framework by which application specific information may be conveyed in an extensible manner. Also, SOAP provides a full description of the required actions taken by a SOAP node on receiving a SOAP message.

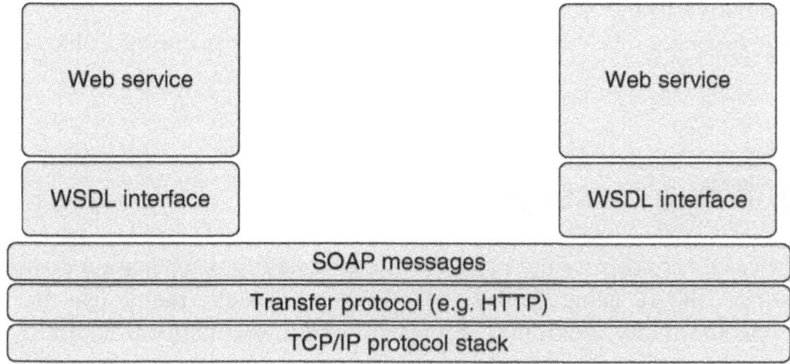

Figure 4.1 The Web services communication and messaging network

SOAP plays the role of a connecting mechanism between two conversing endpoints. A SOAP endpoint is simply an HTTP based URL that identifies a target for a method invocation. It is the goal of SOAP to allow for flexible binding. For example, a particular Web service might provide two bindings. A client may submit a SOAP request using either HTTP or as an e-mail using SMTP. It is important to realise that the type of the binding used does not affect the design of the SOAP message format.

For simple Web services, SOAP specifies a structure for a single message exchange. However, in many cases where business processes or complex Web services are involved there is a need to exchange multiple messages. Usually, this may be achieved using a conversational mode that has no fixed pattern. The decision as to who sends a message, or when to send the next message, may be determined by examining the body SOAP messages exchanged. This is due to the fact that the SOAP body carries the XML documents exchanged between interacting Web services. In other cases, there might be a predetermined pattern such as a request/response pattern, which is the simplest and most natural pattern for procedure like invocations. This pattern is commonly known as RPC style SOAP. We shall discuss the SOAP communication modes in Section 4.4 after we examine the structure of a SOAP message.

SOAP codifies the use of XML as an encoding scheme for request and response parameters, typically using HTTP as a transport protocol, to reach any destination in the Internet without needing any additional wrapping or encoding. In particular, a SOAP method is simply an HTTP request and response that complies with the SOAP encoding rules, while a SOAP endpoint is simply an HTTP based URL that identifies a target for method invocation. SOAP does not require that a specific object be tied to a given endpoint. Rather, it is up to the implementer to decide how to map the object endpoint identifier on to a provider side object.

In its most recent version (SOAP version 1.2 [Mitra 2007]), SOAP adds clear rules for supporting transport protocols like SMTP or FTP, making it a global exchange protocol. In addition, SOAP introduces the concept of intermediaries (stops between a SOAP call and the endpoint that do not affect the contents of the message, useful for information routing). This notion of endpoint means a SOAP message can send a piece of information all the way along a chain of intermediaries to a final recipient. The information concerning the various intermediaries, and the data dedicated to them, is found in the header of the SOAP message. The information in the body of the SOAP message is destined for the message end user.

Distributed application processing with SOAP can be achieved in terms of the basic steps illustrated in Figure 4.2 and outlined below.

1. A service client creates a SOAP message as a result of a request to invoke a desired Web service operation hosted by a remote service provider. The XML code in the body of the SOAP request is the location where the method request and its arguments are placed. The service requester forwards the SOAP message together with the provider's URI (typically over HTTP) to the network infrastructure.

2. The network infrastructure delivers the message to the message provider's SOAP run time system (e.g. a SOAP server). The SOAP server is simply special code that listens for SOAP messages and acts as a distributor and interpreter of SOAP documents.

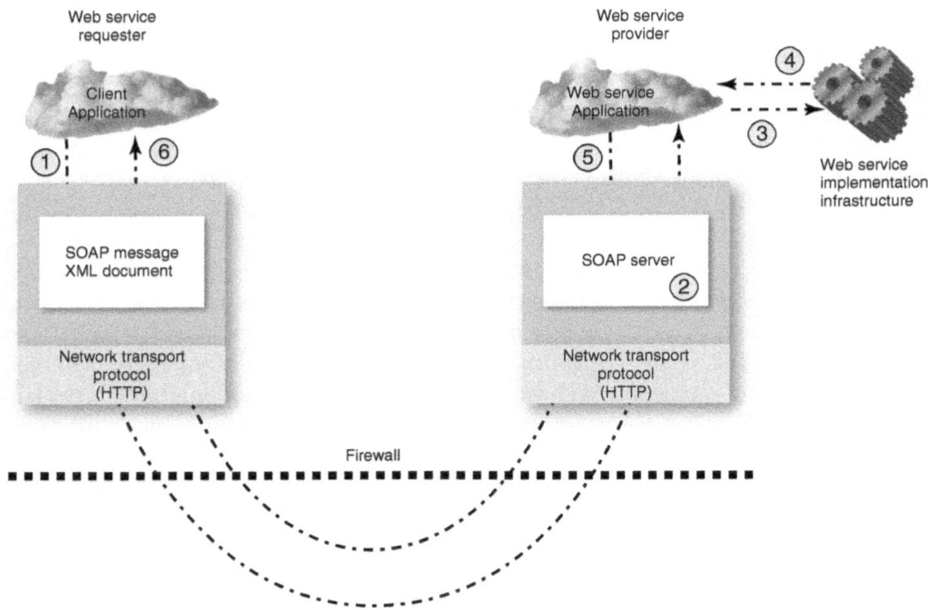

Figure 4.2 Distributed messaging using SOAP

3. The SOAP server routes the request message to the service provider's Web service implementation code. The SOAP server ensures that documents received over an HTTP SOAP connection are converted from XML to programming language specific objects required by the application implementing the Web services at the provider's site. This conversion is governed by the encoding scheme found within the SOAP message envelope. In doing so the SOAP server also ensures that the parameters included in the SOAP document are passed to the appropriate methods in the Web service implementation infrastructure.

4. The Web service is responsible for processing the request and formulating a response as a SOAP message. The response SOAP message is presented to the SOAP run time system at the provider's site with the service requester's URI as its destination.

5. The SOAP server forwards the SOAP message response to the service requester over the network.

6. The response message is received by the network infrastructure on the service requester's node. The message is routed through the SOAP infrastructure, potentially converting the XML response into objects understood by the source (service requester's) application.

Web services can use *one-way messaging* or *request/response messaging*. In the former, SOAP messages travel in only one direction, from a sender to a receiver. In the latter, a SOAP message travels from the sender to the receiver, which is expected to

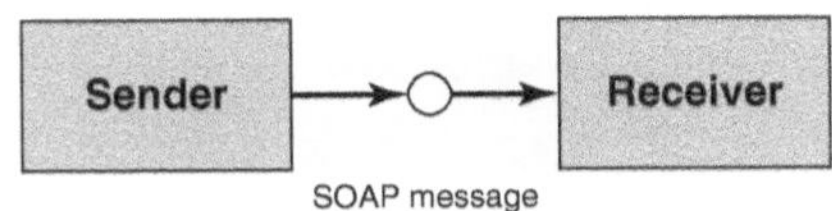

Figure 4.3 One-way messaging

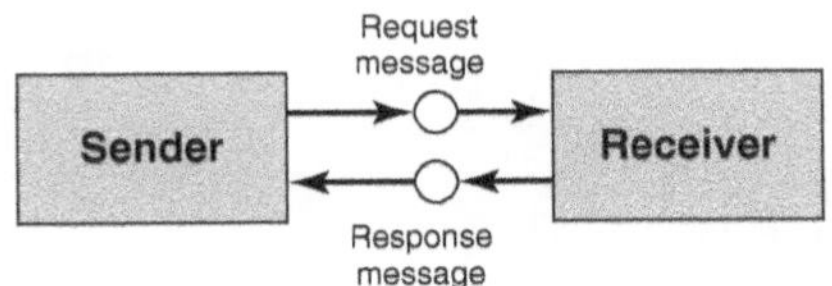

Figure 4.4 Request/response messaging exchange pattern

send a reply back to the sender. SOAP allows for any number of message exchange patterns, of which request/response is just one. Other examples include solicit/response (the reverse of request/response), notifications and long running peer-to-peer conversations. Figure 4.3 illustrates a simple one-way message where the sender does not receive a response. The receiver could, however, send a response back to the sender as illustrated in Figure 4.4.

4.3 Structure of a SOAP message

The current SOAP specification v1.2 describes how the data types defined in associated XML schemas are serialised over HTTP or other transport protocols [Gudgin 2003]. Both the provider and requester of SOAP messages must have access to the same XML schemas in order to exchange information correctly. The schemas are normally posted on the Internet, and may be downloaded by any party in an exchange of messages.

A SOAP message contains a payload and every SOAP message is essentially an XML document. A pictorial representation of the SOAP message structure is shown in Figure 4.5. In this figure it is shown that a SOAP message consists of an `<Envelope>` element containing an optional `<Header>` and a mandatory `<Body>` element [Gudgin 2003]. The contents of these elements are application defined and not a part of the SOAP specifications, although the latter do have something to say about how such elements must be handled.

We shall examine the elements of the SOAP message in some detail below, giving several examples of its use.

4.3.1 SOAP envelope

The SOAP envelope serves to wrap any XML document interchange and provide a mechanism to augment the payload with additional information that is required to route it to its ultimate destination.

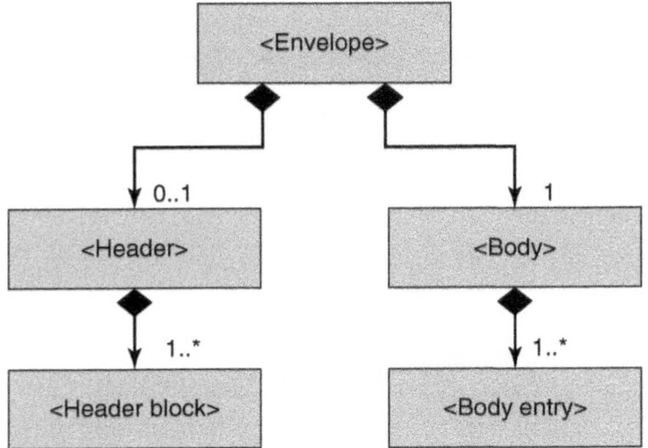

Figure 4.5 The SOAP message containment structure described in UML

The SOAP envelope is the single root of every SOAP message and must be present for the message to be SOAP compliant. The `<Envelope>` element defines a framework for describing what is in a message and how to process it.

Listing 4.1 shows the structure of a SOAP message. This listing shows that in SOAP the `<Envelope>` element is the root element, which may contain an optional `<Header>` section and a mandatory `<Body>` section. If a `<Header>` element is used, it must be the immediate child of the `<Envelope>` element, and precede the `<Body>` element. The `<Body>` element is shown to delimit the application specific data. A SOAP message may have an XML declaration, which states the version of XML used and the encoding format, as shown in the snippet in Listing 4.1.

```
<env:Envelope
      xmlns:env="http://www.w3.org/2003/05/soap-envelope">
      <env:Header> <!-- optional -->
            <!-- header blocks go here ... -->
      </env:Header>
      <env:Body>
            <!-- payload or Fault element goes here ... -->
      </env:Body>
</env:Envelope>
```

Listing 4.1 Structure of SOAP message

All elements of the SOAP envelope are defined using W3C XML Schema. In SOAP, namespaces are declared as usual with the `xmlns` keyword. To actually identify the envelope tag as belonging to the SOAP namespace, it must contain the reference to the SOAP envelope namespace URI. The URI where the envelope schema is located for the

SOAP v1.2 specification (used throughout this chapter) is "http://www.w3.org/2003/05/soap-envelope". The expression env is used as the namespace qualifier referring to this URI. The expression env namespace qualifier in Listing 4.1 is shown to include not only the <Envelope> element but also the <Header> and <Body> sections. This rule ensures that all conforming messages are using exactly the same namespace and XML schema, and therefore the same processing rules.

SOAP defines a data model that can be used to represent arbitrary data structures, e.g. integers, arrays and records, and then it specifies the rules for transforming the instances of this model into serialised ASCII strings that are contained in SOAP messages. It is up to the client and service provider to map an instance of a data type, specified in the client's or provider's representation language, into an instance of the model. The term client in this context is associated with the initial sender of a request message. A SOAP envelope can specify a set of encoding rules serialising the application defined XML data over the network. Both the provider and requester must agree on the encoding rules (typically by downloading the same XML schema that defines them).

Encoding style is simply a set of rules that describe how data can be expressed (serialised to XML) between two communicating parties' systems. To allow two or more communicating parties that agree on a specific encoding style for XML messages to express that agreement in the SOAP messages, they can use the global encodingStyle attribute.

In order to allow for added flexibility SOAP allows applications to define their own encoding style. For example, if two applications use an array as argument in a SOAP message, one application may serialise the array as a sequence of rows using one set of tags, while another may serialise the array as a sequence of columns using a different set of tags. The set of rules that is used must be identified using the encodingStyle attribute. For more information on the encodingStyle attribute refer to Section 4.4.

Example 4.1: SOAP envelope

The SOAP specification allows the envelope tag to contain any number of additional, custom attributes. However, each of these custom attributes must be namespace qualified. This means that a custom prefix must be associated with the custom attribute's namespace URI through an xmlns declaration and that prefix must be used for the custom attribute. This is illustrated in Listing 4.2, which is a brief example of the SOAP <Envelope> element syntax.

```
<env:Envelope
      xmlns:env="http://www.w3.org/2003/05/soap-envelope"
      env:encodingStyle="http://schemas.xmlsoap.org/soap/encoding/">
                ...
</env:Envelope>
```

Listing 4.2 Example of a SOAP envelope

4.3.2 SOAP header

A SOAP <Header> element contains blocks of information relevant to how the message is to be processed. The <Header> may contain information about where the document shall be sent, where it originated, and may even carry digital signatures. This type of information must be separated from the SOAP <Body> that is mandatory and contains the SOAP payload (the XML document).

The purpose of the <Header> is to encapsulate extensions to the message format without having to couple them to the payload or to modify the fundamental structure of SOAP. This allows specification of additional features and functionality, such as security, transactions, object references, billing, QoS attributes and many others, which can be added over time to SOAP messages without breaking the specification. For example, the header information can be used to supply authentication credentials to a Web service. Rather than requiring every single method call on the Web service to ask for user name and password, this information can be included in the SOAP <Header>. Moreover, SOAP can be used with a variety of messaging systems (asynchronous, synchronous, RPC, one way and others), which can be combined in non-traditional ways.

The SOAP <Header> provides a mechanism for providing further detailed information describing the payload being carried by the SOAP <Body>. When a <Header> is included in a SOAP message it must be the first child element of the SOAP <Envelope> element. The schema for the optional SOAP header element allows for an unlimited number of child elements to be placed within the header. The immediate child elements of the <Header> element are called *header blocks*, and represent a logical grouping of data that can individually be targeted at SOAP nodes that might be encountered in the path of a message from a sender to an ultimate receiver. Each header block in the <Header> element should have its own namespace. This is a particularly important issue, since namespaces help SOAP applications identify header blocks and process them separately.

A variety of standard header blocks, which deal with topics such as security, transactions and other service characteristics, are in development by organisations such as W3C and OASIS. Each of the proposed standards defines its own namespaces and XML schemas, as well as processing requirements.

Example 4.2: Transactional integrity for the payment of orders

Listing 4.3 shows an example of a <Header> element involving two header blocks. The first block presumably deals with the transactional integrity rules associated with the payment of orders. The second header block includes a notarization service to associate a token with a particular purchase order, as a third party guarantee that the purchase order was dispatched and contained the particular items that were ordered. In this way each header block provides different extensibility options by encapsulating extensions to the SOAP message format.

```
<env:Envelope
      xmlns:env="http://www.w3.org/2003/05/soap-envelope">
            ...
      <env:Header>
            <tx:transaction-id
                  xmlns:tx="http://www.transaction.com/transaction"
                        env:mustUnderstand="true">
                              512
            </tx:transaction-id>
            <notary:token xmlns:notary="http://www.notarization-
                                          services.com/token"
                  env:mustUnderstand="true">
                        GRAAL-5YF3
            </notary:token>
      </env:Header>
            ...
</env:Envelope>
```

Listing 4.3 Example of a SOAP header

Namespaces enable a SOAP receiver to handle different versions of a SOAP message, without impairing backward compatibility or requiring different Web service endpoints for each version of a particular SOAP message. Differences in a particular version of a header block, for example, can affect how a receiver processes messages, so identifying the header block version by its namespace enables a receiver to switch processing models, or to reject messages if it does not support the specified version. This modularity enables different parts of a SOAP message to be processed independently of other parts and to evolve separately. For instance, the version of the SOAP `<Envelope>` or `<Header>` blocks may change over time, while the structure of the application specific contents in the `<Body>` element remains the same. Similarly, the application specific contents may change while the version of the SOAP message and the header blocks do not.

The modularity of SOAP messaging enables developers to use different code libraries to process different parts of a SOAP message, as shown in Figure 4.6, which is based on [Monson-Haefel 2004]. This figure shows the structure of a SOAP message and the code modules that are used to process each of its parts. The code modules in grey boxes are associated with namespaces used in the current SOAP message, while the code modules in white boxes represent alternatives. These alternatives are associated with different namespaces, used to process alternative versions of the SOAP message.

The SOAP `<Header>` element also provides for extensibility. SOAP *extensibility* refers to the fact that additional information required for a particular service, such as security requirements that the requester be authenticated before a method is invoked or that a method must have transactional properties, can be added to SOAP. This can be accomplished without changing the body of the message that contains the information meant to

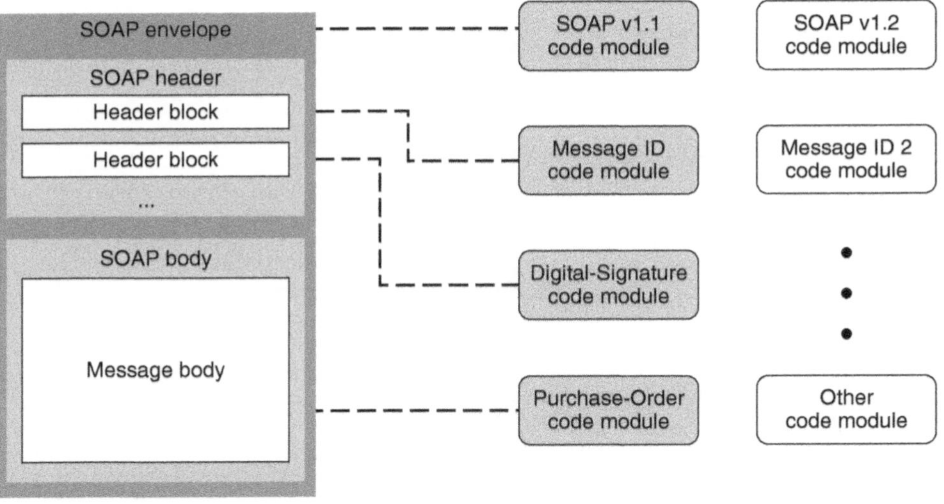

Figure 4.6 Using different code libraries to process parts of a SOAP message

be for the intended receiver of the message, i.e. the invocation information. This is also illustrated in Figure 4.6 where a `<Header>` element can contain a header block specifying a digital signature extension.

4.3.2.1 SOAP intermediaries

SOAP headers have been designed in anticipation of various uses for SOAP, many of which will involve the participation of other SOAP processing nodes – called *SOAP intermediaries* – along a message's path from an initial SOAP sender (point of origin) to an ultimate SOAP receiver (final destination). The route taken by an SOAP message, including all intermediaries it passes through, is called the *SOAP message path.*

A SOAP message travels along the message path from a sender to a receiver. All SOAP messages start with the initial sender, which creates the SOAP message, and end with the ultimate receiver. As a SOAP message travels along the message path, its header blocks may be intercepted and processed by any number of SOAP intermediaries along the way. Headers may be inspected, inserted, deleted or forwarded by SOAP nodes encountered along a SOAP message path. The applications along the message path (the initial sender, intermediaries and ultimate receiver) are commonly referred to as *SOAP nodes*. Three key use cases define the need for SOAP intermediaries: crossing trust domains, ensuring scalability and providing value-added services along the message path.

Figure 4.7 illustrates the message path for validating a purchase order SOAP message that is generated by a customer. In this figure the purchasing service node validates that the purchase order was indeed sent to it by a particular customer. This intermediary

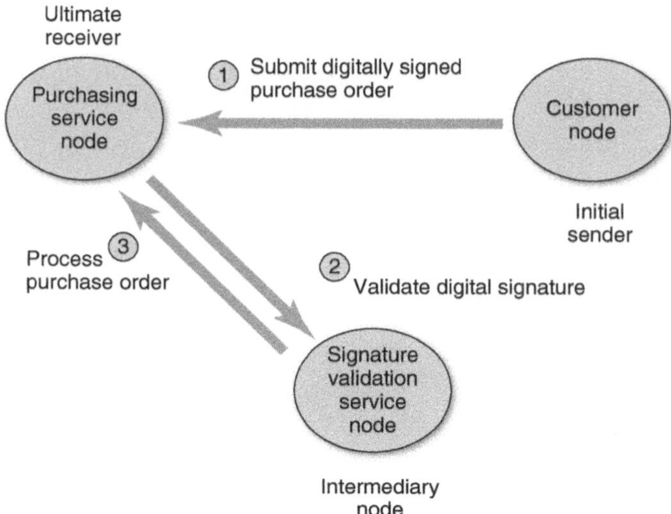

Figure 4.7 The SOAP message path for validating a purchase order

service verifies that the customer's digital signature header block embedded in the SOAP message is actually valid. The SOAP message is automatically routed to the intermediary node (signature verification service), which extracts the digital signature from the SOAP message, validates it, and adds a new hear block telling the purchasing service whether the digital signature is valid.

Example 4.3: Header block containing order data

To illustrate how nodes in a message path process a header we use Listing 4.4. In Listing 4.4, the `<Header>` element contains two header blocks, each of which is defined in its own XML namespace and which represents some aspect pertaining to the overall processing of the body of the SOAP message.

Listing 4.4 specifies that the next SOAP intermediary that is encountered in the message path must process the header block's purchase order and customer. The fact that the header block's purchase order and customer are targeted by the next SOAP node encountered en route is indicated by the presence of the attribute `env:role` with the value `"http://www.w3.org/2003/05/soap-envelope/role/next"`, which is a role that all SOAP nodes must be willing to play. This indicates the fact that while processing a message, a SOAP node may be willing to assume one or more *roles* to influence how SOAP header blocks and the `<Body>` are processed. Roles are given unique names (in the form of URIs) so they can be identified during processing.

```
<env:Envelope
  xmlns:env="http://www.w3.org/2003/05/soap-envelope">
   <env:Header>
      <m:order
           xmlns:m="http://www.auto-parts.com/purchase-order"
           env:role="http://www.w3.org/2003/05/soap-envelope/role/next"
           env:mustUnderstand="true">
         <m:order-no >uuid:0411a2daa</m:order-no>
         <m:date>2004-11-8</m:date>
      </m:order>
      <n:customer xmlns:n="http://www.auto-parts.com/customers"
              env:role="http://www.w3.org/2003/05/soap-envelope/role/next"
              env:mustUnderstand="true">
              <n:name> Marvin Sanders </n:name>
      </n:customer >
    </env:Header>
    <env:Body>
      <-- Payload element goes here -->
    </env:Body>
</env:Envelope>
```

Listing 4.4 Example of a header block with message routing

When a SOAP node receives a message for processing, it must first determine what roles it will assume. It may inspect the SOAP message to help make this determination. SOAP defines the (optional) `env:role` attribute that may be present in a header block, which identifies the role played by the intended target of that header block. A SOAP node is required to process a header block if it assumes the role identified by the value of the URI. How a SOAP node assumes a particular role is not a part of the SOAP specifications. The `env:role` attribute in Listing 4.4 is used in combination with the XML namespaces to determine which code module will process a particular header block.

After a SOAP node has correctly identified the header blocks (and possibly the body) targeted at itself using the `env:role` attribute, the additional attribute, `env:mustUnderstand`, in the header elements determines further processing actions that have to be taken. The presence of a `mustUnderstand` attribute with value *true* indicates that the node(s) processing the header must absolutely process these header blocks in a manner consistent with their specifications, or else not process the message at all and report a fault. For instance in Listing 4.3, the header indicates that a message is part of an ongoing (hypothetical) transaction, which uses the `mustUnderstand` attribute to require the provider to support transactions if the client wants to use them. If the provider (the recipient of the message) does not support transactions, the receipt of this message will raise an error.

4.3.3 SOAP body

The SOAP <Body> element is the mandatory element within the SOAP <Envelope>, which implies that this is where the application specific XML data (payload), being exchanged in the message, is placed. The <Body> element must be present and must be an immediate child of the envelope. It may contain an arbitrary number of child elements, called body entries, but it may also be empty. All body entries that are immediate children of the <Body> element must be namespace qualified.

The <Body> element contains either the application specific data or a fault message. A SOAP message may carry either application specific data or a fault, but not both.

Application specific data is the information that is exchanged with a Web service. It can be arbitrary XML data or parameters to a method call. The SOAP <Body> is where the method call information and its related arguments are encoded. It is where the responses to a method call is placed, and where error information can be stored. The <Body> element has one distinguished root element, which is either the request or the response object.

A fault message is used only when an error occurs. The receiving node that discovers a problem, such as a processing error or a message that is improperly structured, sends it back to the sender just before it in the message path. Examples involving the <Body> element are given in the following section.

4.4 SOAP communication model

The Web services communication model describes how to invoke Web services and relies on SOAP. The SOAP communication model is defined by its encoding and its communication style. The SOAP encoding style conveys information about how the contents of a particular element in the header blocks, or the <Body> element of a SOAP message, are encoded. We briefly described the SOAP encoding style in Section 4.3.1 in conjunction with SOAP headers.

SOAP supports two possible communication styles:

- RPC;
- document (or message).

In the following we shall examine the two SOAP communication styles in some detail.

4.4.1 RPC style Web services

An RPC style Web service appears as a remote object to a client application. The interaction between a client and an RPC style Web service centers around a service specific interface. Clients express their request as a method call with a set of arguments, which returns a response containing a return value. These are represented as sets of XML elements embedded within a SOAP message as shown in Figure 4.8.

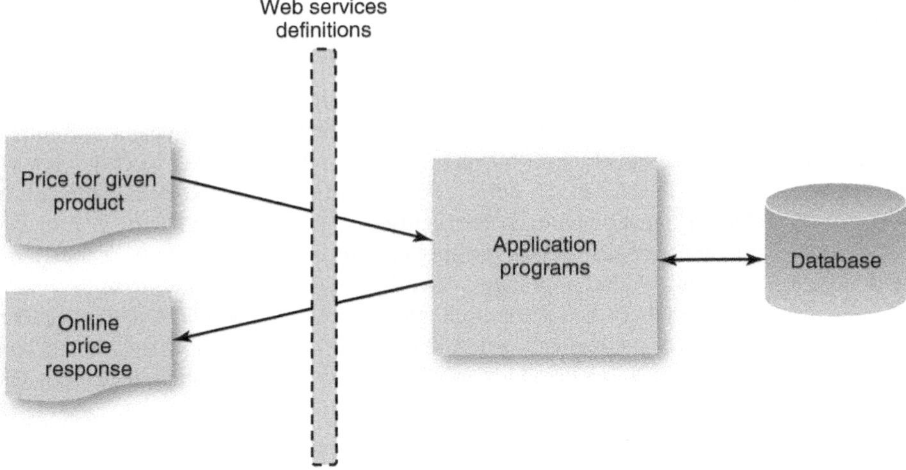

Figure 4.8 RPC style Web service for calculating the price of a given product

RPC style supports automatic serialisation/deserialisation of messages, permitting developers to express a request as a method call with a set of parameters, which returns a response containing a return value. Because of this type of bilateral communication between the client and Web service, RPC style Web services require a tightly coupled (synchronous) model of communication between the client and service provider.

The RPC/Literal messaging enables SOAP messages to issue method calls with parameters and return values. RPC/Literal messaging is used to expose traditional components as Web services, such as a servlet, a stateless session bean, a Java RMI object, a CORBA object or a DCOM component [Monson-Haefel 2004]. These components do not explicitly exchange XML data: rather, they have methods with parameters and return values.

The rules for packaging an RPC/Literal request in a SOAP envelope are quite simple:

- A URI identifying the transport address for the call is required.
- An RPC request message contains the method name and the input parameters of the call. The method call is always formatted as a single structure with each in or in–out parameter modelled as a field in that structure.
- The names and the physical order of the parameters must correspond to the names and physical order of the parameters in the method being invoked.
- An RPC response message contains the return value and any output parameters (or a fault). Method responses are similar to method calls in that the structure of the response is modelled as a single structure with a field for each parameter in the method signature.

Example 4.4: Price quote service in SOAP

Listing 4.5 is an example of a SOAP <Body> specification. It illustrates a price quote service that requests the product price be associated with a specific car accessory. As shown from this listing, the SOAP <Body> element contains the actual method call (as its first child element). The namespace identifies the URI of the target object. In addition, the method call requires the method name (GetProductPrice) and the parameters (product-id).

```
<env:Envelope
 xmlns:SOAP="http://www.w3.org/2003/05/soap-envelope"
 xmlns:m="http:// www.auto-parts.com//product-prices">
    <env:Header>
        <tx:Transaction-id
             xmlns:t="http://www.transaction.com/transactions"
             env:mustUnderstand='1'>
                  512
        </tx:Transaction-id>
    </env:Header>
    <env:Body>
        <m:GetProductPrice>
           <product-id> 450R6OP </product-id>
        </m:GetProductPrice>
    </env:Body>
</env:Envelope>
```

Listing 4.5 Example of an RPC-style SOAP body

Once a SOAP message containing a call body (a method element and arguments in the <Body> element) has been sent, it is reasonable to expect that a response message will ensue.

Example 4.5: Responding with product prices

The response message will contain a <Body> element that includes the results of the remote method call. The response message corresponding to the price quote request made in Listing 4.5 could look like the response in Listing 4.6.

A useful feature of the HTTP binding when RPC style messages are transmitted is that it provides a way automatically to associate the request with the corresponding response.

```
<env:Envelope
 xmlns:SOAP="http://www.w3.org/2003/05/soap-envelope"
 xmlns:m="http://www.auto-parts.com/product-prices">
    <env:Header>
       <--! - Optional context information -->
    </env:Header>
    <env:Body>
       <m:GetProductPriceResponse>
          <product-price> 134.32 </product-price>
       </m:GetProductPriceResponse>
    </env:Body>
</env:Envelope>
```

Listing 4.6 Example of a SOAP RPC response message

This feature is important for applications where a client communicates with multiple providers. In this case an application may have several outstanding requests and it is necessary to correlate an arriving response with its corresponding request.

4.4.2 Document (message) style Web services

SOAP provides no means for encoding source and destination information into the envelope. It is up to the individual client of SOAP to decide where and how the information is to be transmitted. Typically, sending non-coded XML content in the body is known as *document-style* SOAP, as it focuses on the message as an XML document rather than an abstract data model that happens to be encoded into XML.

Document style Web services are message driven. When a client invokes a message style Web service, the client typically sends it an entire document, such as a purchase order, rather than a discrete set of parameters, see Figure 4.9. The Web service is sent an entire document, which it processes; however, it may or may not return a response message. This style is thus asynchronous in that the client invoking the Web service can continue with its computation without waiting for a response. The response from the Web service, if any, may appear at any time later.

Unlike the RPC style, the document style does not support automatic serialisation/deserialisation of messages. Rather it assumes that the contents of the SOAP message are well formed XML documents. For instance, a set of XML elements that describes a purchase order, embedded within a SOAP message, is considered an XML document fragment.

In the Document/Literal mode of messaging, a SOAP `<Body>` element contains an XML document fragment, a well formed XML element that contains arbitrary application data that belongs to an XML schema and namespace, separate from that of the SOAP message. The `<Body>` element reflects no explicit XML structure. The SOAP run time environment accepts the SOAP `<Body>` element as it stands and hands it over to the application it is destined for unchanged. There may or may not be a response associated with this message.

Example 4.6: Purchase order for car products

Listing 4.7 shows a purchase order SOAP message ordering two hundred catalytic converters of a certain type on behalf of a car parts company. This application data upload scenario is not very well suited for an RPC like request, such as the one shown in Listing 4.6. Instead, the application aims to transfer the application data in one piece to a service provider for further processing. Under this scenario a document style SOAP message carrying the entire application data as part of one concise, self-contained XML document (called purchase order) is the proffered option.

```
<env:Envelope
 xmlns:SOAP="http://www.w3.org/2003/05/soap-envelope">
    <env:Header>
      <tx:Transaction-id
          xmlns:t="http://www.transaction.com/transactions"
          env:mustUnderstand='1'>
             512
    </env:Header>
    <env:Body>
      <po:PurchaseOrder orderDate="2009-12-20"
          xmlns:m="www.auto-parts.com/PurchaseOrder">
          <po:from>
            <po:accountName> Nifty Cars Inc. </po:accountName>
            <po:accountNumber> PSC-0343-02 </po:accountNumber>
          </po:from>
          <po:to>
            <po:supplierName> Auto Parts & Car Accessories
                                            </po:supplierName>
            <po:supplierAddress> Yara Valley Melbourne
                                            </po:supplierAddress>
          </po:to>
          <po:product>
            <po:product-name> Catalytic Converter </po:product-name>
            <po:product-model> GTTX-100 </po:product-model>
            <po:quantity> 200 </po:quantity>
          </po:product>
      </po:PurchaseOrder >
    </env:Body>
</env:Envelope>
```

Listing 4.7 Example of a document-style SOAP body

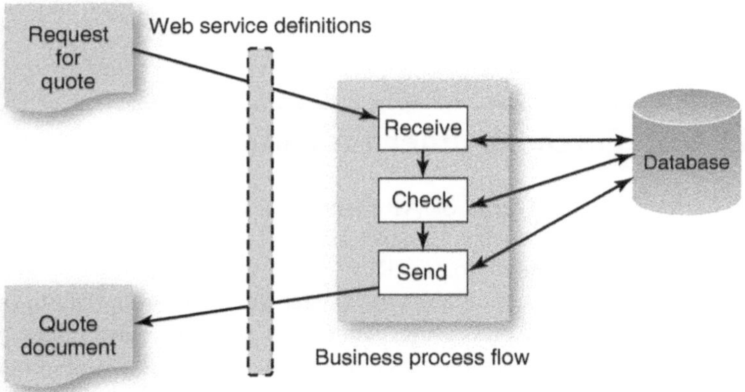

Figure 4.9 Processing a request for a price quote

4.5 Error handling in SOAP

SOAP provides a model for handling situations when faults arise in the processing of a message. The SOAP `<Body>` element has another distinguishing role in that it is the place where fault information is placed. The SOAP fault model requires that all SOAP specific and application specific faults be reported using a special purpose element called `env:Fault`.

Example 4.7: Signalling an invalid a purchase order

Listing 4.8 shows a SOAP message returned in response to the RPC request in Listing 4.5 that indicates a failure to process the RPC. The `env:Fault` element in this listing is shown to be carried within the `<Body>` element. The `env:Fault` element contains two mandatory sub-elements, `env:Code` and `env:Reason`, and (optionally) application specific information in the `env:Detail` sub-element.

In Listing 4.8, the `env:Value` element contains a number of standardised fault codes (values) in the form of XML qualified names (`QNames`) each of which identifies the kind of error that occurred. The value `env:Sender` indicates that the sender of the message incorrectly formed the message (syntax error) or the message was lacking information (missing parameters or authentication information). In addition, the `env:Subcode` element indicates that an InvalidPurchaseOrder error defined by the namespace `"www.auto-parts.com/product-prices"` is the cause of the failure to process the request. The `env:Reason` sub-element contains a human readable description that gives an account of the fault situation. Finally, the `env:Detail` element, when present, is a place where application specific error information can be placed. This error information is not likely to be generally understood by all SOAP nodes, only nodes aware of the specific application that generated the error information.

```
<env:Envelope
 xmlns:SOAP="http://www.w3.org/2003/05/soap-envelope"
 xmlns:m="http:// www.auto-parts.com/product-prices">
    <env:Header>
        <tx:Transaction-id
             xmlns:t="http://www.transaction.com/transactions"
             env:mustUnderstand='1'>
                512
        </tx:Transaction-id>
    </env:Header>
    <env:Body>
        <env:Fault>
            <env:Code>
                <env:Value>env:Sender</env:Value>
                <env:Subcode>
                    <env:Value> m:InvalidPurchaseOrder </env:Value>
                </env:Subcode>
            </env:Code>
            <env:Reason>
                <env:Text xml:lang="en-UK"> Specified product
                 did not exist </env:Text>
            </env:Reason>
            <env:Detail>
              <err:myFaultDetails
                  xmlns:err="http://www.auto-parts.com /
                  faults">
                <err:message> Product number contains invalid
                 characters
                </err:message>
                <err:errorcode> 129 </err:errorcode>
              </err:myFaultDetails>
            </env:Detail>
        </env:Fault>
    </env:Body>
</env:Envelope>
```

Listing 4.8 Example of a fault SOAP message

4.6 Advantages and disadvantages of SOAP

As with any other protocol, several aspects of using SOAP can be seen as advantages, whereas other aspects can be seen as limitations. The primary advantages of SOAP are summarised as follows:

- *Simplicity:* SOAP is simple as it based on XML, which is highly structured and easy to parse.

- *Portability:* SOAP is portable without any dependencies on the underlying platform, like byte-ordering issues or machine-word widths. Today, XML parsers exist for virtually any platform from mainframes to *write watch size* devices.
- *Firewall friendly:* Posting data over HTTP means not only that the delivery mechanism is widely available but also that SOAP is able to get past firewalls that pose problems for other methods.
- *Use of open standards:* SOAP uses the open standard of XML to format the data, which makes it easily extendable and well supported.
- *Interoperability:* SOAP is built on open, rather than vendor specific, technologies and facilitates true distributed interoperability and loosely coupled applications. Because SOAP is a wire protocol based on XML and HTTP, it is possibly the most widely interoperable protocol to date and can be used to describe message exchanges between autonomous technical environments and highly diverse enterprise applications.
- *Acceptance:* SOAP is a widely accepted standard in the message communication domain.
- *Resilience to changes:* Changes to the SOAP infrastructure will likely not affect applications using the protocol, unless significant serialisation changes are made to the SOAP specification.

There are, however, several aspects of SOAP that can be considered as disadvantages. These include [Scribner 2000] the following:

- SOAP was initially tied to HTTP and this mandated a request/response architecture that was not appropriate for all situations. HTTP is a relatively slow protocol and, of course, the performance of SOAP suffered. The latest version of the SOAP specification loosens this requirement.
- SOAP is stateless. The stateless nature of SOAP requires that the requesting application must reintroduce itself to other applications when more connections are required as if it had never been connected before. Maintaining the state of a connection is desirable when multiple Web services interact in the context of business processes and transactions.
- SOAP serialises by value and does not support serialisation by reference. Serialisation by value requires that multiple copies of an object will, over time, contain state information that is not synchronised with other dislocated copies of the same object. This means that currently it is not possible for SOAP to refer or point to some external data source (in the form of an object reference).

4.7 Summary of learning objectives

SOAP is a lightweight protocol for exchange of information in a decentralised, distributed environment.

- It defines a simple and extensible XML messaging framework that can be used over multiple protocols with a variety of different programming models.
- SOAP messages are effectively service requests sent to some endpoint on a network, which may be implemented in any number of ways and may be running on any platform.

SOAP is fundamentally a stateless, one-way message exchange paradigm, but applications can create more complex interaction patterns, e.g. request/response, request/multiple responses, etc. It provides the framework by which application specific information may be conveyed in an extensible manner and a full description of the required actions taken by a SOAP node on receiving a SOAP message.

SOAP consists of the following three parts:

1. An envelope, which provides a mechanism to augment the payload with additional information that is required to route it to its ultimate destination.
2. A header that contains all processing hints that are relevant for the endpoints or intermediate transport points, and provides an extension hook for specifying security, transactional and other conventions.
3. A body element that carries the application specific XML data being exchanged.

Review questions

- What are wire protocols and what is the purpose of SOAP?
- What does a stateless one-way exchange protocol do?
- Describe how SOAP processes distributed applications.
- Describe how SOAP works with WSDL.
- What are the two most popular forms of messaging used with SOAP?
- List and describe the elements in a SOAP message.
- How is modularity achieved with SOAP?
- Give an example of a SOAP intermediary and explain how it functions.

- Describe the two SOAP communication models.
- How is HTTP used with SOAP?
- How does SOAP achieve interoperability?
- Describe how SOAP achieves serialisation.

Exercises

4.1. Write a simple SOAP program that returns information about commercial flights from the XML Schema of Exercise 3.4.

4.2. Write a simple SOAP program that charges the credit card of a traveller that made a reservation for a particular trip.

4.3. Write a simple SOAP program that returns the value of a particular stock ticker symbol.

4.4. Assume that you have written a simple Java method that checks the status of an order you have placed with the following signature checkOrderStatus(String OrderNumber, String companyID) that can be invoked with the following arguments: ("ZRA56782C", "Mega Electronics Ltd."). Write a simple method embedded within a SOAP message that achieves the same result.

4.5. Write a SOAP message that declines charging the credit card of a client in Exercise 4.2 due to an invalid card number.

4.6. Write a simple SOAP program that:

(a) Uses an RPC style message to check the inventory for a particular product. The message should accept two arguments: the product identifier and the number of products to be shipped.

(b) Converts the SOAP RPC style message into an equivalent SOAP document style message.

CHAPTER 5

Describing Web services

Learning objectives

A service description language is an XML encoded artifact that describes the mechanics of interacting with a particular Web service. It essentially specifies a *contract* that governs the interaction between requester and provider parties – and not information that is relevant only to one party or the other, such as internal implementation details.

This chapter concentrates on describing the Web Services Description Language, an XML dialect for describing Web services. In this chapter we focus on WSDL version 1.1, which is broadly implemented and has found wide acceptance and support from many vendors. Another important reason for this decision is that the Business Process Execution Language, BPEL, which we describe in Chapter 9, is based on WSDL version 1.1.

After completing this chapter you will understand the following key concepts:

- Why a Web service description language is needed.
- The nature of a service interface and contract.
- The Web Services Description Language.
- The difference between a Web service interface definition and a Web service implementation.
- Defining Web service interfaces and implementations in WSDL.
- The WSDL message exchange conventions.
- How WSDL accommodates non-functional service characteristics.

Chapter preview

Service definition is an integral part of designing and developing SOA based applications. In this chapter we look at this important element of services and explain why it plays a pivotal role for SOAs. Following this, we concentrate on describing the elements of the Web Services Description Language (WSDL), an XML based language that provides a model for describing Web services. We place particular emphasis on the distinction between the abstract and concrete parts of WSDL enabled service specifications. Finally, we discuss briefly what facilities are used to describe the non-functional service aspects of services. This topic will concern us again in Chapter 12 where we describe service policies.

5.1 Why is a service description needed?

To develop service based applications and business processes, which comprise service assemblies, Web services need to be described in a consistent manner. In this way, they can be published by service providers, discovered by service clients and developers, and assembled in a manageable hierarchy of composite services that are orchestrated to deliver value-added service solutions and composite application assemblies. However, in order to accomplish this, consumers must determine the precise XML interface of a Web service along with other miscellaneous message details *a priori*. In the Web services world, XML Schema can partially fill this need as it allows developers to describe the structure of XML messages understood by Web services. However, XML Schema alone cannot describe important additional details involved in communicating with a Web service, such as service functional and non-functional characteristics or service policies.

Service description is a key to making the SOA loosely coupled and reducing the amount of required common understanding, custom programming, and integration between the service provider and the service requester's applications. *Service description* is a machine understandable specification describing the structure, operational characteristics and non-functional properties of a Web service. It also specifies the wire format and transport protocol that the Web service uses to expose this functionality and the payload data using a type system.

When the service description is combined with the underlying SOAP infrastructure, it sufficiently isolates all technical details, such as machine and implementation language specific elements, from the service requester's application and the service provider's Web service. In particular, it does not mandate any specific implementation decisions on the service requester side, provided that the contract specified in a standard service description language is abided by. Later in the book we shall discover that service description may also include metadata, behavioural properties and descriptions of policies (see Chapters 13 and 16).

5.2 WSDL: Web Services Description Language

Web Services Description Language (WSDL) is an XML based specification language that has become the *de facto* language for describing the public interface of a Web service (or the contract that a service exposes to its clients). WSDL recognises the need for rich type systems for describing message formats, and supports the XML Schema specification (XSD) as its canonical type system. In this way, it provides the means to group messages into operations and operations into interfaces. WSDL supports extensibility to specify some technology specific binding. This allows enhancements in the area of network and message protocols without having to revise the base WSDL specification.

At present, WSDL version 1.1 is broadly implemented and supported by industry. WSDL version 2.0 was recently defined as a recommendation of the World Wide Web Consortium. While there are declarative and syntactical differences between these two WSDL specifications, their overall purpose is identical. That is, WSDL serves as the overall service description and overall service interface contract. In this chapter we shall focus on WSDL 1.1, as it is broadly implemented and has found wide acceptance and support from many vendors. Another important reason for this decision is that the Business Process Execution Language (BPEL), which we describe in Chapter 9, is based on WSDL 1.1. Throughout this book we shall refer to WSDL 1.1 simply as WSDL.

In summary, a WSDL document uses the following elements in the definition of services:

- *Types.* A container for data type definitions using some type system (such as XSD).
- *Message.* An abstract, typed definition of the data being communicated.
- *Operation.* An abstract description of an action supported by the service.
- *Port Type.* An abstract set of operations supported by one or more endpoints.
- *Binding.* A concrete protocol and data format specification for a particular port type.
- *Port.* A single endpoint defined as a combination of a binding and a network address.
- *Service.* A collection of related endpoints.

5.2.1 The service interface and implementation

Essentially, WSDL is used to describe precisely three things:

1. *What a service does,* that is the operations the service provides.
2. *Where it resides,* that is the details of the protocol specific address, e.g. a URL.
3. *How to invoke it,* that is the details of the data formats and protocols necessary to access the service's operations.

In general terms, WSDL provides a mechanism by which service providers can describe the basic format of Web requests over different protocols (e.g. SOAP) or encoding (e.g. Multipurpose Internet Messaging Extensions or MIME). It also allows most of the WSDL elements to be extended with elements from other namespaces. WSDL makes it easy to reap the benefits of SOAP by providing a way for Web service providers and users of such services to work together easily. Although WSDL has been designed such that it can express bindings to protocols other than SOAP, our main concern in this chapter is WSDL as it relates to SOAP over HTTP.

Although a Web service description in WSDL is written exclusively from th e point of view of the Web service (viz. the service provider that publishes that service), it is inherently intended to constrain both the service provider and the service requester that make use of that service. This implies that WSDL represents a service contract between the service requester and the service provider, in much the same way that an interface in an object oriented programming language, e.g. Java, represents a contract between client code and the actual object itself. The prime difference is that WSDL is platform and language independent and is used primarily (but not exclusively) to describe SOAP enabled services.

The partitioning into a distinct service interface and service implementation sections, as described above, enables each part to be defined separately and independently of the other, and be reused by other matching parts.

- The *service interface definition* (abstract service description), which describes the general Web service interface structure in a language and platform independent manner. This helps define a set of services that several diverse Web sites can implement. The abstract service description section contains all the operations supported by the service, the operation parameters and abstract data types, which are all part of the abstract definition of the Web service interface.
- The *service implementation* (concrete endpoint), which binds the abstract interface to a concrete network address, to a specific protocol, and to concrete data structures. This section describes the concrete details of how the abstract interface maps to messages on the wire, i.e. defines site specific matters such as serialisation.

This separation enables each part to be defined separately and independently and be reused by other matching parts.

The service interface definition, together with the service implementation definition, make up a complete WSDL specification of the service. The combination of these two parts contains sufficient information to describe to the service requester how to invoke and interact with the Web service at a provider's site.

For SOA and Web services, the service interactions and the requisite responsibilities are defined in the service interface and, more specifically, by a set of service interface artifacts. The WSDL specification describes a service as a combination of type references, ports, operations and bindings. When combined with XML Schema for its types, WSDL can be thought of as the overall service interface and contract. It is through this service description that the service provider can communicate all the specifications for invoking a particular Web service to the service requester.

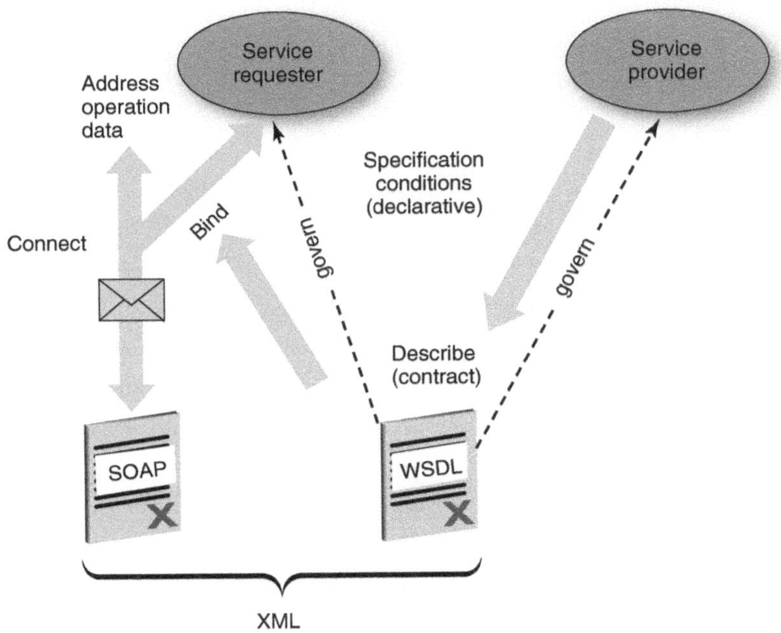

Figure 5.1 WSDL service description and contract

Figure 5.1 illustrates how a WSDL service description is used as a means of communication between service providers and requesters by specifying the operational characteristics, binding details and specific URIs available for invoking a service. This figure shows that the Web service description is concerned only with information that both the service requester and provider must agree upon and is specified in the service contract, which governs the interaction between both parties.

In WSDL, the abstract definition of endpoints and messages is separated from their concrete network deployment or data format bindings. In WSDL the data being exchanged between the endpoints is specified as part of *messages* and every kind of processing activity allowed at an endpoint is considered as an *operation*. Collections of permissible operations at an endpoint are grouped together into *port types*. This allows the reuse of abstract definitions which contain messages, operations and port types.

Service clients interact with a Web service by invoking its operations. Related operations are grouped into the interfaces of the Web service. Clients must know not only the interfaces of a Web service and the operations it contains, but also what communication protocol to use for sending messages to the service.

The concrete protocol and data format specifications for a particular port type constitute a reusable *binding*. A binding specifies the concrete details of what is transferred on the wire by out lining how to map abstract messages on to a particular network level communication protocol. It also influences the way abstract messages are encoded on the wire by specifying the style of service, e.g. asynchronous or synchronous messaging to process

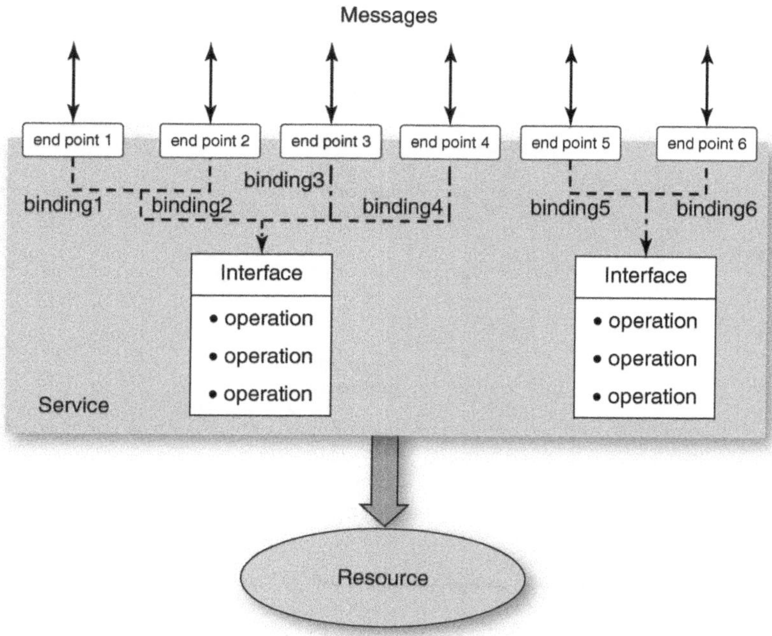

Figure 5.2 Web service endpoints

requests, and the encoding mechanism used. A service can support multiple bindings for a given interface but each binding should be accessible at a unique address identified by a URI commonly referred to as a *service endpoint*. This situation is illustrated in Figure 5.2. Finally, a *port* is defined by associating a network address with a reusable binding and a collection of ports define a *service*.

When the service interface is represented as a collection of operations defined in WSDL it does not indicate the order of execution of these operations. This is the responsibility of BPEL managed orchestration, which represents a service interface as an assembly of artifacts rather than a single monolithic fine grained artifact (as is the case with WSDL). BPEL, which we shall examine in Chapter 9, is used to orchestrate a set of subordinate, relatively fine grained (simple) services described in WSDL and XML Schema into a single coarse grained (composite) service.

In the remainder of this section we shall concentrate on describing the WSDL elements starting from elements that part of its interface definition followed by elements in its concrete section.

5.2.2 WSDL definition element

Figure 5.3 is used to illustrate the relationship between the WSDL interface definition and concrete description data structures employing UML. This figure illustrates that all the parts of the abstract and concrete sections of WSDL are housed within a root element called

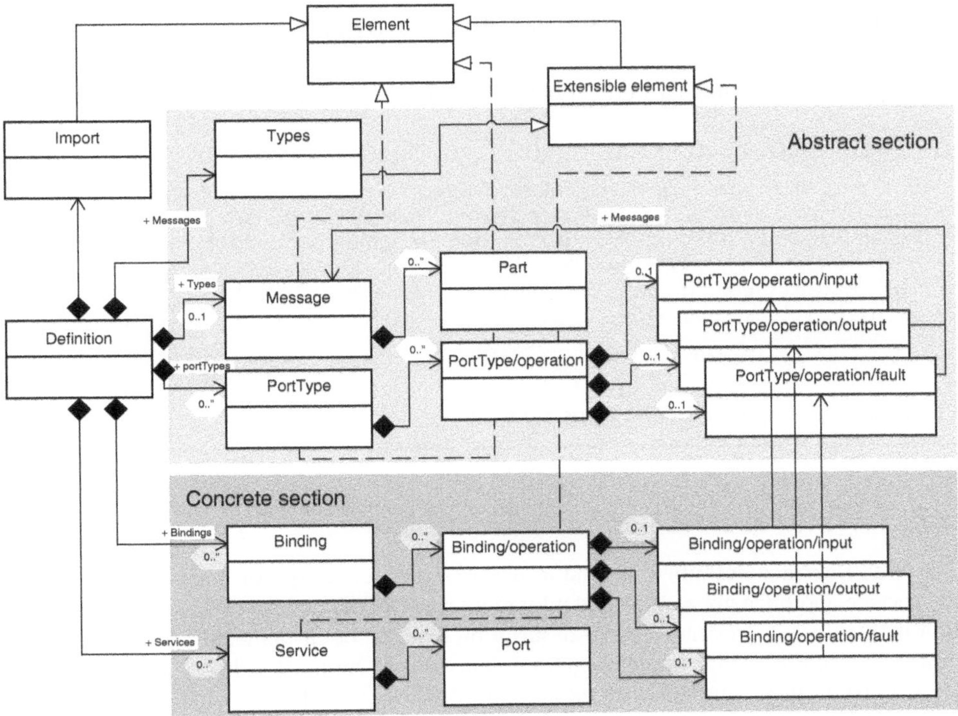

Figure 5.3 WSDL syntax, abstract and concrete sections

the `<definitions>` element. This element is in fact the root element in every WSDL specification. It encapsulates the entire WSDL document and provides it with its name.

The first attribute in the `<definitions>` element is `name`, which is used to name the entire WSDL document. The `<definitions>` element also declares an attribute called `targetNamespace`, which identifies the logical namespace for elements defined within the WSDL document and characterises the service. This element is usually chosen to be unique to the individual service (a URL set to the name of the original WSDL file). This helps clients differentiate between Web services and prevents name clashes when importing other WSDL files.

The `<definitions>` element can establish a range of namespace prefixes. This is the purpose of the `xmlns:tns` (sometimes referred to as *this namespace*) attribute. This attribute is set to the value of `targetNamespace` and is used to qualify (scope) properties of this service definition.

Among the namespace declarations of the `<definitions>` element is one for the namespace of the WSDL XML schema `"http://schemas.xmlsoap.org/wsdl/"`. Declaring the WSDL namespace as the default namespace avoids having to qualify every WSDL element explicitly with a prefix. The namespace definitions `xmlns:soap` and `xmln:xsd` are used for specifying SOAP binding specific information as well as XSD data types, respectively. Finally, the `xmlns:types` definition encapsulates schema definitions of all types using XML XSD.

Example 5.1: WSDL definition of a purchase order

Listing 5.1 illustrates the definition element of a purchase order service.

```
<wsdl:definitions name="PurchaseOrderService"
 targetNamespace="http://www.auto-parts.com/PurchaseService/wsdl"
 xmlns:tns="http://www.auto-parts.com/PurchaseService/wsdl"
 xmlns:xsd="http://www.w3.org/2001/XMLSchema"
 xmlns:soap="http://schemas.xmlsoap.org/wsdl/soap/"
 xmlns:wsdl="http://schemas.xmlsoap.org/wsdl/">
```

Listing 5.1 Example of a definitions element

5.2.3 WSDL abstract service description

The Web interface definition is used to describe a specific type of interface provided by the service and does not carry any deployment specific details. A service interface definition is therefore an abstract service description that can be instantiated and referenced by multiple concrete service implementations. This allows common industry standard service types to be defined and implemented by multiple service implementers.

The Web service public interface contains operational information relating to a Web service including:

- data type information for messages;
- all publicly available operations, their purpose and function;
- all message protocols supported by the Web service in order to engage the operations;
- any constraints that govern the invocation of operations.

In a WSDL the abstract definition of the Web service interface is specified using the `<types>`, `<message>`, `<part>`, `<portType>`, and `<operation>` elements as shown in Figure 5.3. The `<portType>` element is essentially an abstract interface (analogous to a Java interface definition) that combines `<operation>` and `<message>` definitions as shown in Figure 5.3 and described in Table 5.1. Each `<message>` definition describes the payloads of outgoing and incoming messages, i.e. messages that are sent or received by a Web service. Messages consist of `<part>` elements, each of which represents an instance of a particular type (typed parameter). Each `<operation>` element is declared by a `<portType>` element and contains a number of `<message>` definitions describing its input and output parameters as well as any faults.

The elements described in Table 5.1 constitute the programmatic interface of a Web service that a client will typically interface within its code. This set of operational information is roughly analogous to a contract that is designed to oversee the service operations and behaviour. Ensuring that service clients understand and comply with the expectations

Table 5.1 The WSDL abstract level elements

Types	Defines the data that the Web service uses in its messages through an XML schema definition.
Message	Defines the messages used by the service, each message referring to a data type.
Part	Represents either incoming or outgoing operation parameter data.
Operation	Represents a particular interaction (a Web service function) with the service and is used to describe the input, output and exception messages that are possible during that interaction.
Port Type	Defines the service interface with an abstract set of operations.

of the service contract is central to the usability of a service. WSDL is vital in that respect as it is the sole means to describe the details of the overall interface exposed by a Web service and, therefore, constitutes the instrument to accessing a Web service.

In the following we shall provide a brief summary of the elements in the WSDL abstract interface shown in Table 5.1.

5.2.3.1 The types element

WSDL adopts as its basic type system the W3C XML Schema built in types. WSDL provides a specific element for the purpose of defining types for messages. For this purpose the WSDL `<types>` element serves as a container that contains all abstract data types that define a Web service interface.

The WSDL `<types>` element is used to contain XML schemas or external references to XML schemas that describe the data type definitions used within the WSDL document. The WSDL `<types>` element refers to an XSD `simpleType` or `complexType` using a `QName`. This element helps define all data types that are described by the built in primitive data types that XML Schema Definition defines and allows developers to either use them directly or build complex data types based on those primitive ones before using them in messages. This is why developers need to define their own namespace when referring to complex data types.

Example 5.2: Definition of a purchase order using complex types

Listing 5.2 illustrates three complex types that have been defined in the WSDL `<types>` section: `CustomerInfo`, `POType` and `InvoiceType`. These three complex types are assigned the `xmlns:tns` namespace by the `targetNamespace` attribute. The elements `<sequence>` and `<all>` are standard XSD elements. The construct `<sequence>` requires that the content model follows the element sequence defined, while the construct `<all>` denotes that all the elements that are declared in the `<complexType>` statement must appear in an instance document.

```
<wsdl:types>
    <xsd:schema
        targetNamespace=
            "http://www.auto-parts.com/PurchaseService/wsdl"
        <xsd:complexType name="CustomerInfoType">
            <xsd:sequence>
                <xsd:element name="CusNamer" type="xsd:string"/>
                <xsd:element name="CusAddress" type="xsd:string"/>
            </xsd:sequence>
        </xsd:complexType>
        <xsd:complexType name="POType">
            <xsd:sequence>
                <xsd:element name="PONumber" type="integer"/>
                <xsd:element name="PODate" type="string"/>
            </xsd:sequence>
        </xsd:complexType>
        <xsd:complexType name="InvoiceType">
            <xsd:all>
                <xsd:element name="InvPrice" type="float"/>
                <xsd:element name="InvDate" type="string"/>
            </xsd:all>
        </xsd:complexType>
    </xsd:schema>
</wsdl:types>
```

Listing 5.2 Type element declarations for a sample purchase order service

5.2.3.2 The message element

In WSDL operation messages are represented by a <message> element that describes the payload of outgoing and incoming messages. The <message> element corresponds to a single piece of information moving between the invoker and a Web service. Consequently, a regular round trip method call is modelled as two messages, one for the request and one for the response.

Messages in WSDL are abstract collections of typed information cast upon one or more logical units used to communicate information between services. A <message> element can contain one or more input or output parameters that belong to an operation. Each <part> element defines one such parameter. It provides a name/value set, along with an associated data type.

A message can consist of one or more <part> elements with each part representing an instance of a particular type (typed parameter). When WSDL describes a software module, each <part> element maps to an argument of a method call. The <part>s of a message (message payload) use XML Schema built in types, complex types or elements that are defined in the WSD document's <types> construct or defined in external WSDL elements that are linked by the <import> element. In addition, the message element can describe contents of SOAP header blocks and fault detail elements [Monson-Haefel 2004].

Example 5.3: Definition of input parameters for a purchase order

The code snippet in Listing 5.3 illustrates that the message called POMessage (when associated with the <portType> element PurchaseOrderPortType) describes the input parameters of the service while the message InvMessage represents the return (output) parameters.

```
<!-- message elements that describe input and output parameters
     for the PurchaseOrderService -->
<!--input message -->
<wsdl:message name="POMessage">
        <wsdl:part name="PurchaseOrder" type="tns:POType"/>
        <wsdl:part name="CustomerInfo" type="tns:CustomerInfoType"/>
</wsdl:message>
<! -- output message -->
<wsdl:message name="InvMessage">
        <wsdl:part name="Invoice" type="tns:InvoiceType"/>
</wsdl:message>
```

Listing 5.3 Message declarations for a sample purchase order service

The input message POMessage in the above code snippet is shown to contain two <part> elements, PurchaseOrder and CustomerInfo, which refer to the complex types POType and CustomerInfoType (both defined in Listing 5.2), respectively. POType consists of PONumber and PODate elements.

A message is defined depending on which mode of messaging is used, i.e. RPC-style or document style messaging. When *RPC style messaging* is used, <message> elements describe the payloads of the SOAP request and reply messages. If RPC style messaging is used, messages commonly have more than one part. This is, for example, shown in the code snippet above where the input message POMessage contains the two <part> elements PurchaseOrder and CustomerInfo.

Example 5.4: Definition of a document style message for a purchase order

The following code snippet defines a document style message where the <message> element definition refers to a top level element in the <types> definition section. The code snippet (Listing 5.4) shows that the PurchaseOrder service now defines one document style <message> element using a PurchaseOrder <types> element.

```
<!-- message element that describes input and output parameters -->
<wsdl:message name="POMessage">
        <wsdl:part name="PurchaseOrder" element="tns:PurchaseOrder"/>
</wsdl:message>
```

In *document style messaging* a message part may declare an <element> instead of a <type> attribute. WSDL allows a message part to declare either an <element> or a <type> attribute, but not both. A document style <message> element commonly uses one-way messaging where there is no reply message. Document style messaging exchanges XML document fragments and refers to their top level (global) elements. In document style messaging the <input> is the XML document fragment sent to the Web service, and the <output> is the XML document fragment sent back to the client.

5.2.3.3 The `operation` and `portType` elements

In WSDL, a typical operation element consists of a group of related input and output messages. The execution of an operation requires the transmission or exchange of these messages between the service requester and the service provider.

Operations in WSDL are the equivalent of method signatures in programming languages. They represent the various methods being exposed by the service. An operation defines a method on a Web service, including the name of the method and the input and output parameters. Each <operation> element is composed of, at most, one <input> or one <output> element and any number of <fault> elements. In WSDL the <input> and <output> elements, and the order in which they are organised, establishes message exchange patterns (or MEPs) between a Web service and its clients. The four MEPs that are used to define the data exchange of WSDL operations are described in Section 5.2.5.

The central element externalising a service interface description in WSDL is the <portType> element. A WSDL <portType> element may have one or more <operation> elements, each of which defines an RPC style or document style Web service method. A <portType> element is considered as simply a logical grouping of operations that describe the interface of a Web service and define its methods. A <portType> element describes the kinds of operation that a Web service supports – the messaging mode and payloads – without specifying the Internet protocol or physical address used. A WSDL <portType> and its associated <operation> elements are analogous to a Java interface and its method declarations.

A <portType> element is used to bind the collection of logical operations to an actual transport protocol such as SOAP, thus providing the linkage between the abstract and concrete portions of a WSDL document. In WSDL the <portType> element is implemented by the <binding> and <service> elements, which dictate the Internet protocols, encoding schemas and an Internet address used by the Web service implementation.

A WSDL definition can contain zero or more <portType> definitions. Typically, most WSDL documents contain a single <portType>. This convention separates out different Web service interface definitions into different documents. This granularity allows each business process to have separate binding definitions, providing for reuse, significant implementation flexibility for different security, reliability, transport mechanism and so on [Cauldwell 2001].

Example 5.5: Definition of a `portType` for purchase order

The WSDL example in Listing 5.4 defines a Web service that contains a single `<portType>` named `PurchaseOrderPortType` that supports a single `<operation>`, which is called `SendPurchase`.

```
<wsdl:portType name="PurchaseOrderPortType">
      <wsdl:operation name="SendPurchase">
            <wsdl:input message="tns:POMessage"/>
            <wsdl:output message="tns:InvMessage"/>
      </wsdl:operation>
</wsdl:portType>
```

Listing 5.4 `PortType` and operation declarations for a sample purchase order service

5.2.3.4 Example of an abstract service definition in WSDL

In the following we shall specify the WSDL definition of a simple service WSDL interface definition describing a purchase order service.

Example 5.6: Definition of an abstract purchase order service

Listing 5.5 shows that `purchase order` service takes a purchase order number, a date, and customer details as input and returns an associated invoice document. The service contains a single `<portType>` named `PurchaseOrderPortType` that supports a single `<operation>`, which is called `SendPurchase`.

The example in Listing 5.5 assumes that the service is deployed using SOAP v1.1 as its encoding style, and is bound to HTTP. In Listing 5.5, the `<portType>` PurchaseOrderPortType `<operation>` element is an RPC style operation that declares the message POMessage as its `<input>` and the message Inv(oice)Message as its `<output>` message. The `<input>` message represents the payload sent to the Web service, and the `<output>` message represents the payload sent to the client. In Listing 5.5, the `<operation>` element `SendPurchase` will be called using the message `POMessage` and will return its results using the message Inv(oice)Message.

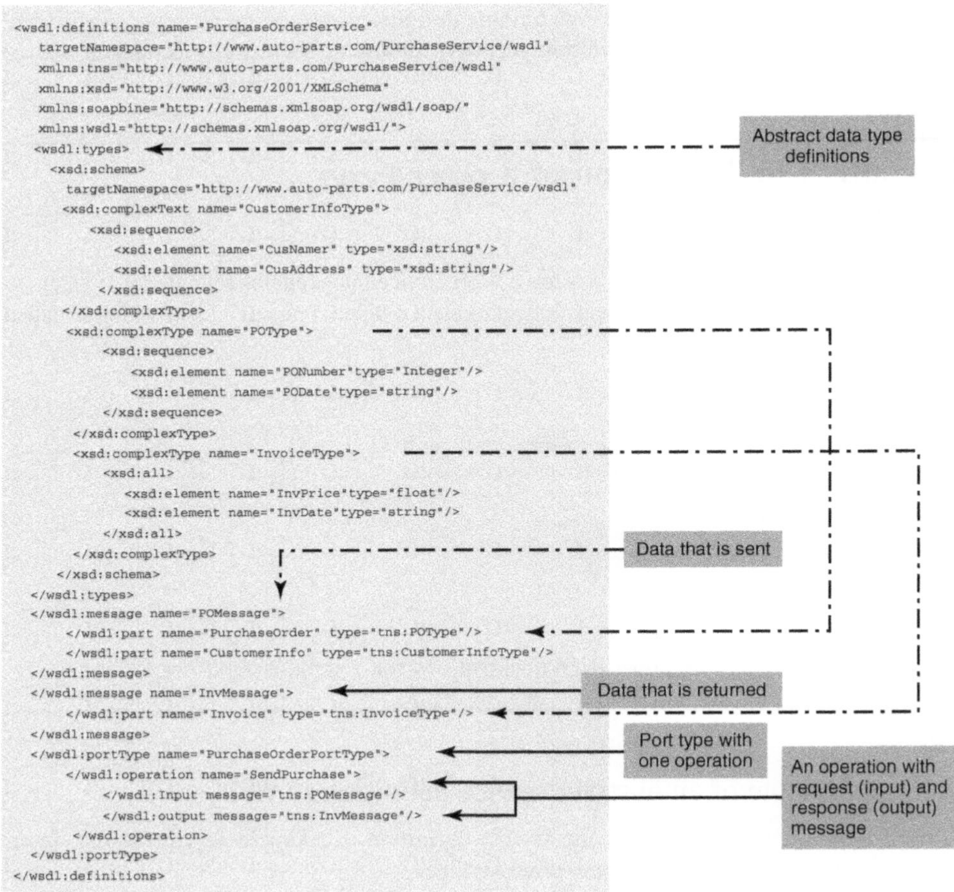

```
<wsdl:definitions name="PurchaseOrderService"
   targetNamespace="http://www.auto-parts.com/PurchaseService/wsdl"
   xmlns:tns="http://www.auto-parts.com/PurchaseService/wsdl"
   xmlns:xsd="http://www.w3.org/2001/XMLSchema"
   xmlns:soapbine="http://schemas.xmlsoap.org/wsdl/soap/"
   xmlns:wsdl="http://schemas.xmlsoap.org/wsdl/">
  <wsdl:types>
    <xsd:schema>
      targetNamespace="http://www.auto-parts.com/PurchaseService/wsdl"
      <xsd:complexText name="CustomerInfoType">
         <xsd:sequence>
            <xsd:element name="CusNamer" type="xsd:string"/>
            <xsd:element name="CusAddress" type="xsd:string"/>
         </xsd:sequence>
      </xsd:complexType>
      <xsd:complexType name="POType">
          <xsd:sequence>
             <xsd:element name="PONumber"type="Integer"/>
             <xsd:element name="PODate"type="string"/>
          </xsd:sequence>
       </xsd:complexType>
       <xsd:complexType name="InvoiceType">
          <xsd:all>
             <xsd:element name="InvPrice"type="float"/>
             <xsd:element name="InvDate"type="string"/>
          </xsd:all>
       </xsd:complexType>
    </xsd:schema>
  </wsdl:types>
  </wsdl:message name="POMessage">
      </wsdl:part name="PurchaseOrder" type="tns:POType"/>
      </wsdl:part name="CustomerInfo" type="tns:CustomerInfoType"/>
  </wsdl:message>
  </wsdl:message name="InvMessage">
      </wsdl:part name="Invoice" type="tns:InvoiceType"/>
  </wsdl:message>
  </wsdl:portType name="PurchaseOrderPortType">
      </wsdl:operation name="SendPurchase">
          </wsdl:Input message="tns:POMessage"/>
          </wsdl:output message="tns:InvMessage"/>
       </wsdl:operation>
  </wsdl:portType>
</wsdl:definitions>
```


Listing 5.5 Sample abstract service definition in WSDL

The dashed arrows at the right hand side of the WSDL definition in Listing 5.5 link the input message `POType` definition with its associated incoming parameter data and the output message `InvoiceType` with its associated outgoing parameter data. The input and output message elements of an operation link the services method, `SendPurchase`, in the case of Listing 5.5, to SOAP messages that will provide the transport for input parameters and output results.

5.2.4 WSDL concrete service description – implementation

In the previous section we explained how to define WSDL operations and messages in an abstract manner without worrying about the details of implementation. In fact, the purpose of WSDL is to specify a Web service abstractly and then to define how the WSDL developer will reach the implementation of these services. The concrete or implementation

Table 5.2 The WSDL concrete level elements

Binding	Defines a concrete protocol and data format specification for a particular port type and specifies binding of each operation in the portTypes section.
Service	A collection of related endpoints at which the Web service can be accessed, each consisting of a set of port elements each of which references a binding element.
Port	Associates between a binding and the network address at which it can be found. It contains endpoint data, including physical address and protocol information.

level of a service specifies how the abstract definition of a service is implemented and is the topic of the present subsection.

Table 5.2 summarises the service implementation part of WSDL and shows that it contains the elements `<binding>`, `<port>`, and `<service>`. This part of WDL describes how a particular service interface is implemented by a given service provider. The service implementation describes where the service is located or, more precisely, to which network address the message must be sent in order to invoke the Web service. Because of the modularity of WDL definitions, an abstract description can be offered to different clients via multiple implementations, possibly residing in different locations.

Figure 5.4 employs the constructs introduced in the previous discussion by illustrating how the various WSDL elements can be involved in a client – service interaction. This figure shows one client invoking a Web service by means of SOAP over HTTP and another client invoking the same service by means of HTTP.

Figure 5.4 depicts a single service that contains multiple ports. This figure shows that a service may contain more than one port, which are bound to binding elements which, in turn are associated with a `<portType>`. Service providers all have different bindings and/or addresses.

Recall that the Web service implementation elements are also shown in Figure 5.3 (together with abstract level elements).

5.2.4.1 The binding element

The central element of the implementation description is the `<binding>` element. The `<binding>` element specifies how the client and Web service should exchange messages. In WSDL a `<binding>` element maps an abstract `<portType>` to a set of concrete protocols such as SOAP and HTTP, message styles (RPC or document), and encoding styles (literal or SOAP encoded) protocol and message format information to operations. The structure of the `<wsdl:binding>` element (henceforth referred to as `<binding>` element) resembles that of the `<portType>` element. In fact, the operation construct that resides within the binding block resembles its counterpart in the interface section. This is no coincidence, as the binding must map an abstract port type description to a concrete implementation.

For example, if a message is to be sent using SOAP over HTTP, the binding describes how the message parts are mapped to elements in the SOAP `<Body>` and `<Header>` and

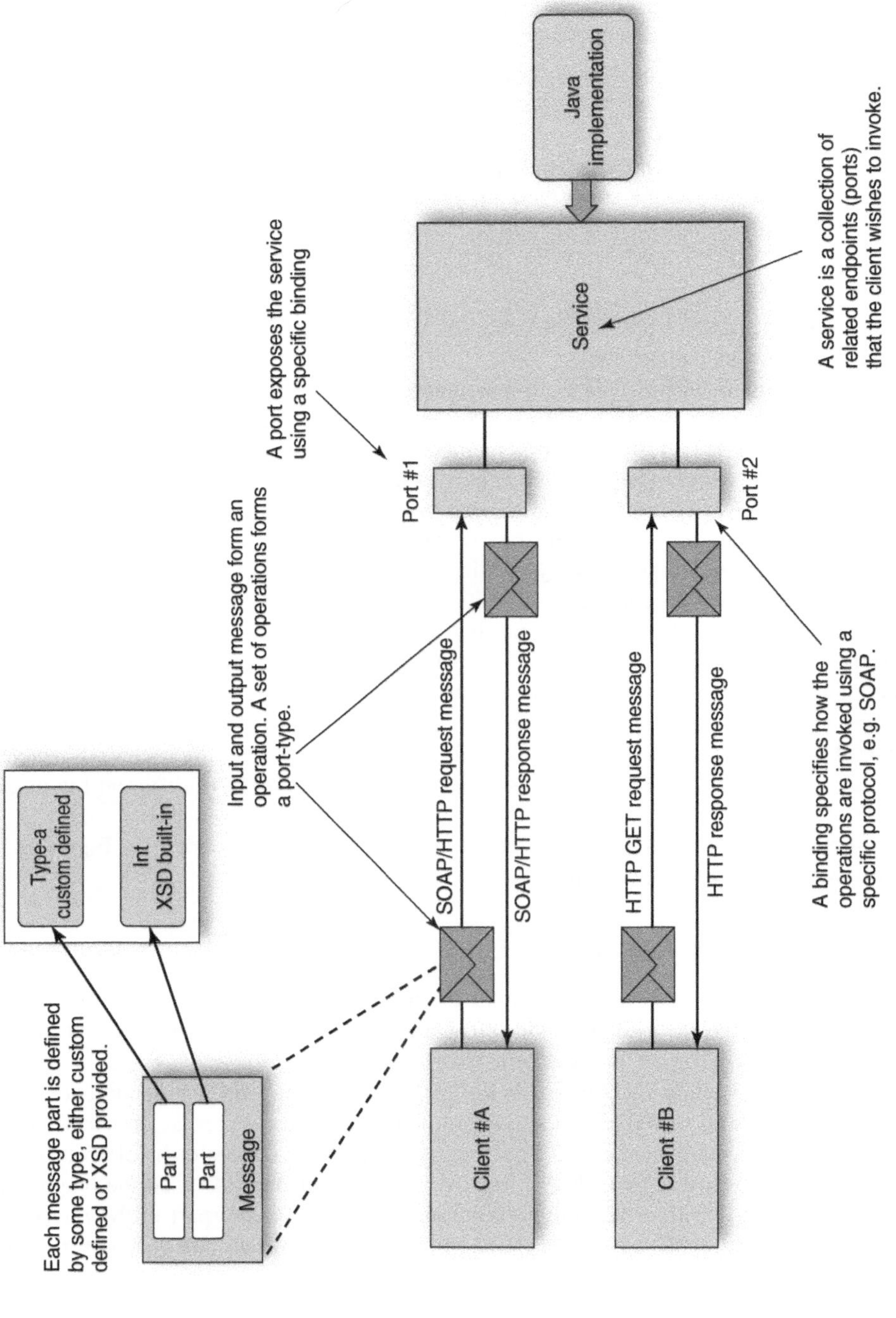

Figure 5.4 Elements of concrete WSDL as part of requester–service interaction

what the values of the corresponding attributes are. Notice that each type of protocol, e.g. MIME, SOAP or HTTP GET or POST, has its own set of protocol specific elements and its own namespace.

Example 5.7: Binding element for the purchase order service

```
<wsdl:binding name="PurchaseOrderSOAPBinding"
              type="tns:PurchaseOrderPortType">

     <!-- leverage off soapbind:binding synchronous style -->
     <soap:binding style="rpc"
                   transport="http://schemas.xmlsoap.org/soap/http/"/>

     <wsdl:operation name="SendPurchase">

       <!-- bind to SOAP now -->
       <soap:operation
             soapAction="http://www.auto-parts.com/
                            PurchaseService/wsdl/SendPurchase"
             style="rpc"/>

        <!-- specify that the messages in wsdl:operation use SOAP -->
        <wsdl:input>
            <soap:body  use="literal"
              namespace=
               "http://www.auto-parts.com /PurchaseService/wsdl"/>
        </wsdl:input>

        <wsdl:output>
           <soap:body  use="literal"
             namespace=
               "http://www.auto-parts.com /PurchaseService/wsdl"/>
        </wsdl:output>
     </wsdl:operation>
</wsdl:binding>
```

Listing 5.6 Binding declaration for a sample purchase order service

Let us have a look at a binding element corresponding the portType definition in Listing 5.4. This is depicted in Listing 5.6. So far we have dealt with abstract descriptions of service interfaces, operations and messages. Now we are getting concrete by describing the transport protocol for the message exchange, the data format and give information about transport and coding of the messages. In our example, we are using SOAP as transport protocol.

The <type> attribute in Listing 5.6 identifies which <portType> element this binding describes. The <binding> element declared in Listing 5.6 is actually composed of two different namespaces. On the one hand, there are elements that are members of the WSDL 1.1 namespace, which is declared in Listing 5.5. On the other hand, the soap:binding, soap:operation and soap:body elements are SOAP specific elements that are members of the namespace for the SOAP–WSDL binding "http://schemas.xmlsoap.org/wsdl/soap/" that is also declared in Listing 5.5.

The <soap:binding> (not to be confused with the WSDL <wsdl:binding> element) and <soap:body> elements are to express the SOAP specific details of the Web service. More specifically, in Listing 5.6 the purpose of the <soap:binding> is to signify that the messaging style is RPC (via the soap:operation construct and the style attribute which defines the type of default operations within this binding). It also indicates that the lower level transport service that this binding will use is HTTP (specified via the transport attribute), and the SOAP format is going to be used as a binding and transport service. This declaration applies to the entire binding.

It is important to understand that the sub-elements of the <binding> element (<operation>, <input> and <output>) in Listing 5.6 map directly to the corresponding children of the <portType> element in Listing 5.5.

In Listing 5.6 the <soap:operation> element is used to link the binding of a specific operation, e.g. SendPurchase, together with the mapping of its input and output messages from the abstract service interface description (see Listing 5.5) to a specific SOAP implementation. The data types of these messages that are abstractly described by means of XSD in the service interface description should be SOAP encoded for the transfer.

The <soap:body> element enables applications to specify the details of the input and output messages and enable the mapping from the abstract WSDL description to the concrete protocol description. In particular, the <soap:body> element specifies the SOAP encoding style and the namespace associated with the specific service (PurchaseOrderService in our case). In Listing 5.6 the <soap:body> construct specifies that both the input and output messages are literally encoded.

Several bindings may represent various implementations of the same <portType> element. If a service supports more than one protocol, then the WSDL <portType> element should include a <binding> for each protocol it supports. For a given <portType> element, a <binding> element can describe how to invoke operations using a single messaging/transport protocol, e.g. SOAP over HTTP, SOAP over SMTP or a simple HTTP POST operation, or any other valid combination of networking and messaging protocol standards. It must be noted that a binding does not contain any programming language or service implementation specific details. How a service is implemented is an issue completely external to WSDL.

5.2.4.2 The service and port elements

After a binding definition is specified, we need to assign it a physical network address so that clients can locate it. This is the purpose of the WSDL <service> and <port> elements.

The <service> element binds the Web service to a specific network addressable location. A <service> is modelled as a collection of related WSDL <port> elements at which a service is made available. The <service> element takes the bindings that were

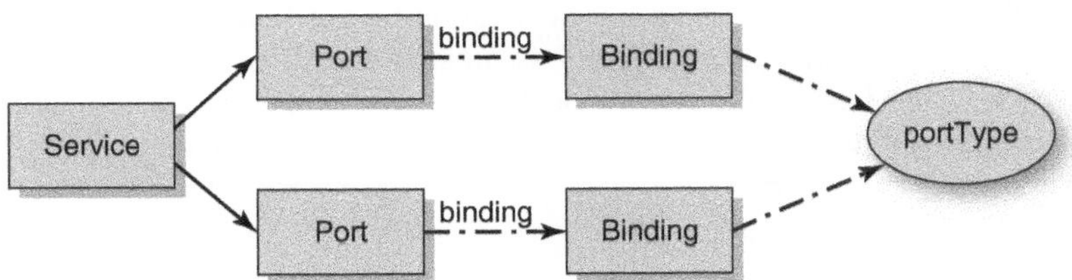

Figure 5.5 Connecting the service interface with the service implementation

declared previously and ties them to one or more <port> elements, each of which represents a physical location for a Web service (often called an endpoint).

In WSDL a <port> element defines the location at which the operations of a specific <portType> using a particular transport protocol can be invoked. A <port> associates an endpoint (for instance a network address location or URL) with a specific WSDL <binding> element to denote the physical endpoint that service requesters must use to connect to the service. Since the <binding> specifies a <portType>, the <port> element effectively ties the <portType> to an address.

Figure 5.5 illustrates the fact that a single service contains multiple ports that all use the same <portType>. This implies that there could be multiple service implementations for the same service interface provided by different service providers. These all have different bindings and/or addresses. For instance, a standard <portType> for order management may be provided by a particular vertical industry. Different manufacturers may then provide different order management services that implement the same <portType>. All these implementations should provided the semantically equivalent behavior. Alternatively, a service implemented by a particular provider may contain several <port>s for the same <portType>, each of which is provided by a different <binding>. This allows a service requester to choose the most convenient way to communicate with the service provider that implements the service.

Example 5.8: Service and port elements for the purchase order service

```
<wsdl:service name="PurchaseOrderService">
    <wsdl:port name="PurchaseOrderSOAPPort"
             binding="tns:PurchaseOrderSOAPBinding">
       <!-- give the binding a network endpoint address or URI
            of service -->
      <soapbind:address
       location=
        "http:// www.auto-parts.com:8080/PurchaseOrderService"/>
    </wsdl:port>
</wsdl:service>
```

Listing 5.7 Service and port declaration for a sample purchase order service

Listing 5.7 illustrates the service and port declaration for the binding in Listing 5.6. The `<soap:address>` attribute in Listing 5.7 is another SOAP extension to WSDL that is used to signify the URI of the service or the network endpoint. This element simply assigns an Internet address to a SOAP binding via its location attribute.

5.2.4.3 Example of a concrete service definition in WSDL

This sub-section provides examples of how to define a concrete service for the abstract service depicted in Listing 5.5 and how to connect an abstract with a concrete service.

Example 5.9: Definition of a concrete purchase order service

Listing 5.8 provides a complete WSDL definition of a concrete service that combines the binding and service declaration examples given in Listings 5.5 and 5.6. The binding element in Listing 5.8 contains a single operation `SendPurchase`, which maps each of the abstract input, output and fault elements of operation `SendPurchase` from the `PurchaseOrderPortType` in Listing 5.5 to its SOAP on-the-wire format. In this way, the `PurchaseOrderService` Web service can be accessed.

As already explained, the `<soap:operation>` in Listing 5.8 specifies the messaging style (RPC or document) for a specific operation. The `SOAPAction` attribute of the `<soap:operation>` is used to specify the HTTP `SOAPAction` header, which in turn can be used by SOAP servers as an indication of the action that should be taken by the receipt of a message at run time. This usually captures the name of a method to invoke in a service implementation. The purpose of this is to achieve interoperability between client and service provider applications. The SOAP client will read the SOAP structure from the WSDL file and coordinate with a SOAP server on the other end.

The code in Listing 5.8 illustrates how the input and output messages of the `<operation> SendPurchase` appear in the parts of the SOAP message. The `<input>` and `<output>` elements for the `<operation> SendPurchase` specify exactly how the input and output messages of this operation should appear in the SOAP message. Both input and output contain a `<soap:body>` element with the value of its namespace corresponding to the name of the service that is deployed on the SOAP server. In RPC style messages, the namespace attribute must be specified with a valid URI, which can be the same as the `targetNamespace` attribute of the WSDL document.

The code in Listing 5.8 specifies that the entire POMessage message from the `<portType>` declaration for the SendPurchase operation is declared to be abstract. This is indicated by the `use="literal"` attribute. This means that the XML code defining the input message and its parts is in fact abstract, and the real, concrete representation of the data is to be derived. The purpose of the `use` attribute within the `<soap:body>` element enables applications to specify how the parts of the message are defined. The *literal* encoding indicates that the resulting SOAP message contains data formatted exactly as specified in the abstract WSDL definitions. Consequently, the data type that the message part references will be serialised according to its exact representation in the type definition section, i.e. according to the XML schema.

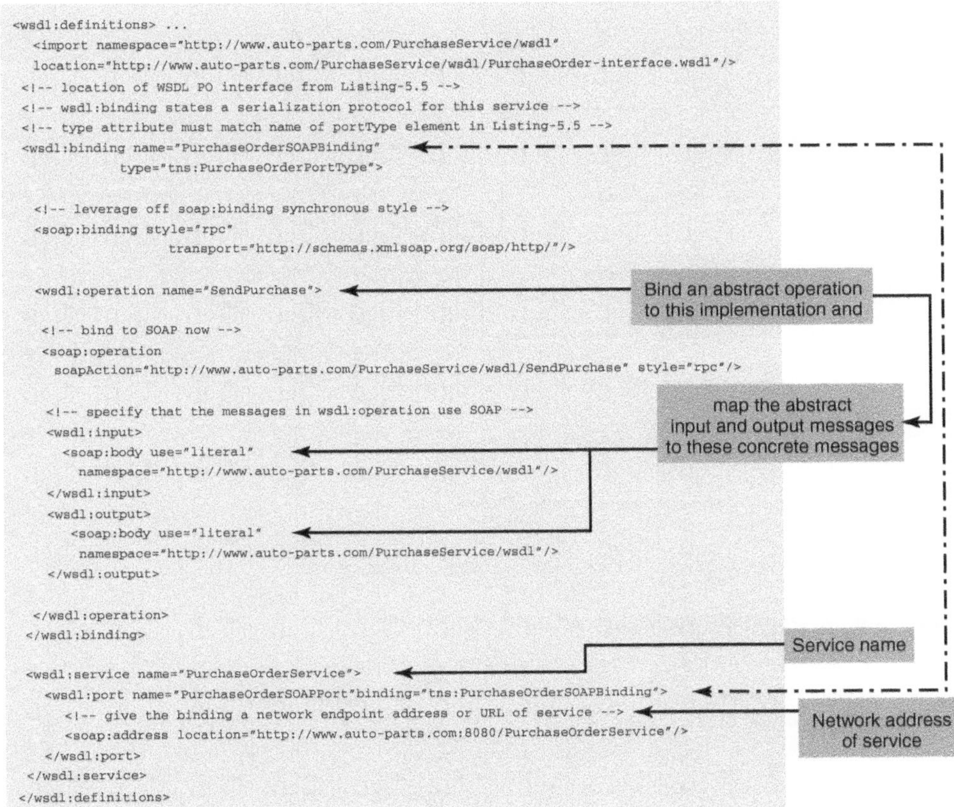

```
<wsdl:definitions> ...
  <import namespace="http://www.auto-parts.com/PurchaseService/wsdl"
  location="http://www.auto-parts.com/PurchaseService/wsdl/PurchaseOrder-interface.wsdl"/>
 <!-- location of WSDL PO interface from Listing-5.5 -->
 <!-- wsdl:binding states a serialization protocol for this service -->
 <!-- type attribute must match name of portType element in Listing-5.5 -->
 <wsdl:binding name="PurchaseOrderSOAPBinding"
          type="tns:PurchaseOrderPortType">

   <!-- leverage off soap:binding synchronous style -->
   <soap:binding style="rpc"
              transport="http://schemas.xmlsoap.org/soap/http/"/>

   <wsdl:operation name="SendPurchase">

    <!-- bind to SOAP now -->
    <soap:operation
     soapAction="http://www.auto-parts.com/PurchaseService/wsdl/SendPurchase" style="rpc"/>

    <!-- specify that the messages in wsdl:operation use SOAP -->
    <wsdl:input>
      <soap:body use="literal"
       namespace="http://www.auto-parts.com/PurchaseService/wsdl"/>
    </wsdl:input>
    <wsdl:output>
       <soap:body use="literal"
       namespace="http://www.auto-parts.com/PurchaseService/wsdl"/>
    </wsdl:output>

   </wsdl:operation>
 </wsdl:binding>

 <wsdl:service name="PurchaseOrderService">
   <wsdl:port name="PurchaseOrderSOAPPort"binding="tns:PurchaseOrderSOAPBinding">
     <!-- give the binding a network endpoint address or URL of service -->
     <soap:address location="http://www.auto-parts.com:8080/PurchaseOrderService"/>
   </wsdl:port>
 </wsdl:service>
</wsdl:definitions>
```


Listing 5.8 Sample concrete service definition for the abstract service in Listing 5.5

Finally, Listing 5.8 shows that the binding `PurchaseOrderSOAPBinding` links the `<portType>` element named `PurchaseOrderPortType` (refer to Listing 5.5) to the `<port>` element named `PurchaseOrderSOAPPort`. This connection can be seen by following the dashed arrow in Listing 5.8. The listing contains only one Web service, namely the `PurchaseOrderService`, thus only the `<port>` element named `PurchaseOrderSOAPPort` is used to reveal the service location.

Example 5.10: Connecting the abstract and concrete parts of purchase order

To improve understanding, Figure 5.6 illustrates how the abstract and concrete level constructs can be associated to each other. This figure shows how the SendPurchase `<operation>` defined in the `PurchaseOrderPortType` `<portType>` element and its message parts (e.g. purchase order) are mapped to an RPC style SOAP message.

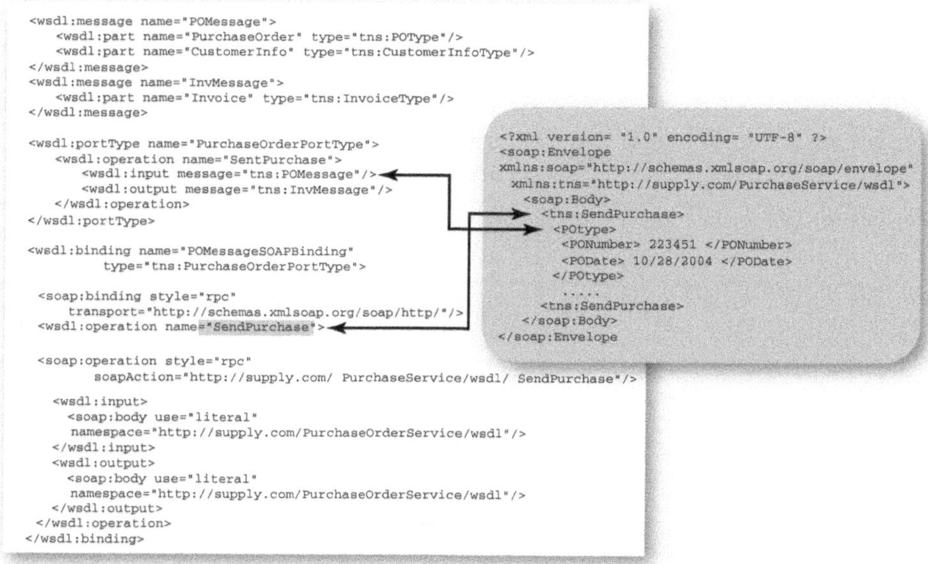

```
<wsdl:message name="POMessage">
   <wsdl:part name="PurchaseOrder" type="tns:POType"/>
   <wsdl:part name="CustomerInfo" type="tns:CustomerInfoType"/>
</wsdl:message>
<wsdl:message name="InvMessage">
   <wsdl:part name="Invoice" type="tns:InvoiceType"/>
</wsdl:message>

<wsdl:portType name="PurchaseOrderPortType">
   <wsdl:operation name="SentPurchase">
      <wsdl:input message="tns:POMessage"/>
      <wsdl:output message="tns:InvMessage"/>
   </wsdl:operation>
</wsdl:portType>

<wsdl:binding name="POMessageSOAPBinding"
      type="tns:PurchaseOrderPortType">

 <soap:binding style="rpc"
    transport="http://schemas.xmlsoap.org/soap/http/"/>
 <wsdl:operation name="SendPurchase">

 <soap:operation style="rpc"
       soapAction="http://supply.com/ PurchaseService/wsdl/ SendPurchase"/>

   <wsdl:input>
     <soap:body use="literal"
     namespace="http://supply.com/PurchaseOrderService/wsdl"/>
   </wsdl:input>
   <wsdl:output>
     <soap:body use="literal"
     namespace="http://supply.com/PurchaseOrderService/wsdl"/>
   </wsdl:output>
 </wsdl:operation>
</wsdl:binding>
```

```
<?xml version= "1.0" encoding= "UTF-8" ?>
<soap:Envelope
xmlns:soap="http://schemas.xmlsoap.org/soap/envelope"
  xmlns:tns="http://supply.com/PurchaseService/wsdl">
   <soap:Body>
     <tns:SendPurchase>
      <POtype>
       <PONumber> 223451 </PONumber>
       <PODate> 10/28/2004 </PODate>
      </POtype>
      .....
     <tns:SendPurchase>
   </soap:Body>
</soap:Envelope
```

Figure 5.6 Mapping between abstract and concrete levels

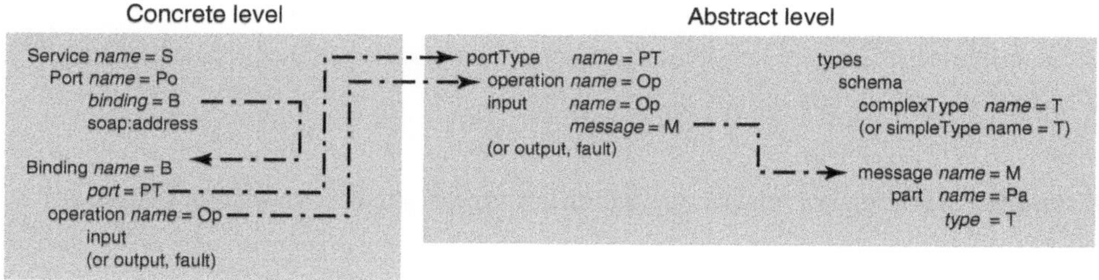

Figure 5.7 Connecting the abstract and concrete levels of a Web service (*Source:* M. Kifer, A. Bernstein and P. M. Lewis, *Database Systems: An Application-Oriented Approach*, Second Edition, Addison Wesley, 2005. Reproduced with permission.)

Finally, Figure 5.7 represents an overview of how the concrete and abstract levels of WSDL are connected. The indented items in this figure denote information represented by child elements. In Figure 5.7 attributes are italicised to distinguish them from elements.

5.2.5 Message exchange patterns

Each operation defined by WSDL can have an input and/or an output. The WSDL operations correspond to the incoming and outgoing versions of two basic operation types:

an incoming single message passing operation and its outgoing counterpart (*one-way* and *notification* operations), and the incoming and outgoing versions of a synchronous two-way message exchange (*request/response* and *solicit/response*). These operations represent the most common interaction arrangements for Web services and establish specific message exchange patterns (MEPs) between a Web service and its clients. A *message exchange pattern* is defined as the possible order of the input and/or output elements supported by a given operation.

The Web service message exchange patterns are shown in Figure 5.8 and summarised in Table 5.3. For reasons of brevity we only provide sample code listings of the two most popular message exchange patterns: one-way and request/response.

It should be noted that any combination of incoming and outgoing operations can be included in a single WSDL interface. As a result, the four types of MEPs presented in

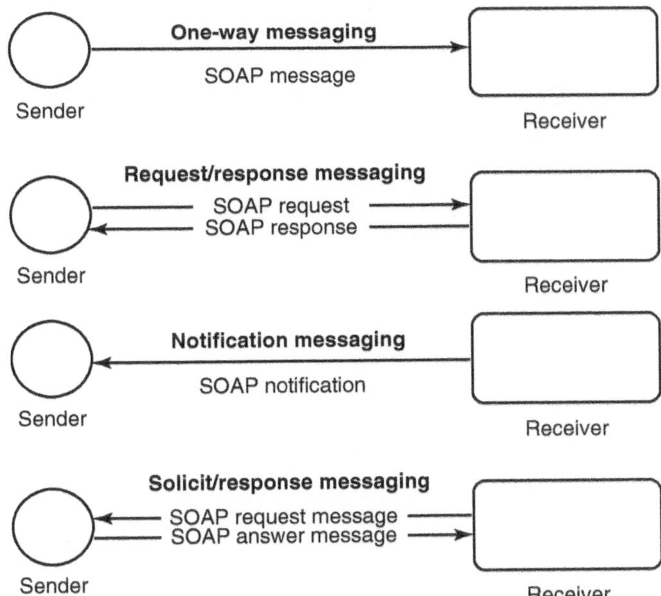

Figure 5.8 WSDL message exchange patterns

Table 5.3 Summary of WSDL message exchange patterns

Type	*Definition*
One-way	The operation can receive a message but will not return a response
Request-response	The operation can receive a request and will return a response
Notification	The operation can send a message but will not wait for a response
Solicit-response	The operation can send a request and will wait for a response

Table 5.3 provide support for both push and pull interaction models at the interface level. The inclusion of outgoing operations in WSDL is motivated by the need to support loosely coupled peer-to-peer interactions between services.

5.2.5.1 One-way

A one-way operation is an operation in which the service endpoint receives a message, but does not return a response. An example of a one-way operation might be an operation representing the submission of an order to a purchasing system. Once the order is sent, no immediate response is expected. This message exchange pattern is typically thought of as asynchronous messaging. A one-way message defines only an input message. It requires no output message and no fault.

If an <operation> element is declared with a single <input> element but no <output> element, it defines a one-way operation.

Example 5.11: Definition of a one-way operation for the purchase order service

The following snippet illustrates the SubmitPurchaseOrder <portType> that defines a one-way operation and has been adapted from [Monson-Haefel 2004]:

```
<!-- portType element describes the abstract interface of a Web
    service -->
<wsdl:portType name="SubmitPurchaseOrder_PortType">
     <wsdl:operation name="SubmitPurchaseOrder">
          <wsdl:input name="order"
               message="tns:SubmitPurchaseOrder_Message"/>
     </wsdl:operation>
</wsdl:portType>
```

5.2.5.2 Request/response

A request/response operation is an operation in which the service endpoint receives a message and returns a message or fault in response. In the request/response message exchange pattern a client requests that some action is taken by the service provider. If an <operation> element is declared with a single <input> element followed by a single <output> element, it then defines a request/response operation. By listing the <input> tag first, the <operation> indicates that the Web service receives a message that is sent by the client. Listing the <output> tag second indicates that the Web service should respond to the message.

Example 5.12: Definition of a request/response operation for the purchase order service

The following code snippet taken from Listing 5.5, which illustrates the SendPurchase operation is an example of the request/response messaging pattern.

```
<!-- portType element describes the abstract interface of a Web
     service -->
<wsdl:portType name="PurchaseOrder_PortType">
     <wsdl:operation name="SendPurchase">
          <wsdl:input message="tns:POMessage"/>
          <wsdl:output message="tns:InvMessage"/>
     </wsdl:operation>
</wsdl:portType>
```

The `SendPurchase` operation receives as input a message containing a purchase order (order number and date) and customer details and responds with a message containing an invoice. In an RPC environment this is equivalent to a procedure call, which takes a list of input arguments and returns a value.

5.2.5.3 Notification

A notification operation is an operation in which the service endpoint sends a message to a client, but it does not expect to receive a response. This type of messaging is used by services that need to notify clients of events. A Web service that uses the notification messaging pattern follows the push model of distributed computing. The assumption is that the client (subscriber) has registered with the Web service to receive messages (notifications) about an event.

Notification is when a `<portType>` element contains an `<output>` tag but no `<input>` message definitions. An example of this could be a service model in which events are reported to the service and where the endpoint periodically reports its status. No response is required in this case, as most likely the status data is assembled and logged and not acted upon immediately.

5.2.5.4 Solicit/response

A solicit/response operation is an operation in which the service endpoint sends a message and expects to receive an answering message in response. This is the opposite of the request/response operation since the service endpoint is initiating the operation (soliciting the client), rather than responding to a request. With this type of messaging the `<portType>` element first declares an `<output>` tag and then an `<input>` message definition – exactly the reverse of a request/response operation. An example of this operation might be a service that sends out order status to a client and receives back a receipt.

5.3 Non-functional service descriptions

From what we have seen so far, one can understand that WSDL specifies the syntactic signature for a service but does not specify any non-functional service aspects. However, in Section 1.9 we argued that non-functional characteristics are an integral part of any Web service. The Web service platform should be capable of supporting a multitude of different types of application with different QoS requirements. In fact, programmers and applications need to be able to understand the QoS characteristics of Web services to be able to develop applications that invoke Web services and interact with them. Thus, the non-functional characteristics of a Web service should be described too.

QoS enabled Web services require a separate language to describe non-functional characteristics of Web services. Currently, the most widely used approach to describing non-functional Web service characteristics is through the Web service policy framework, which we shall examine in Chapter 12.

The Web service policy framework provides an additional description layer for services and offers a declarative policy language for expressing and programming policies. By employing this policy language, characteristics of the hosting environment can be described including security characteristics (including authentication and authorisation) at the provider's endpoint, transactional behaviour, the levels of QoS and quality of protection offered by the provider, privacy policies observed by the provider and application specific service options, or capabilities and constraints specific to a particular service domain.

WS-PolicyAttachment accomplishes this objective (see Section 12.4.4). It offers a flexible way of associating policy expressions with existing and future Web service artifacts. For instance, WS-PolicyAttachment addresses the requirements for associating Web service policy with a policy subject such as a WSDL `<portType>` or `<message>` and can even attach policies to UDDI entities.

5.4 WSDL 1.1 versus WSDL 2.0

Currently, the World Wide Web Consortium is busy standardising WSDL. Although WSDL 1.1, which we use throughout this book, is the *de facto* standard, WSDL 2.0 is the version of WSDL that the W3C is currently standardising. WSDL 2.0 is a simpler and more usable language than WSDL 1.1. It provides several improvements over WSDL 1.1, including language clarifications and simplifications, support for interoperation, and making it easier for developers to understand and describe services.

The WSDL 1.1 message element was mainly intended to serve as the bridge between message and RPC centric communication. It can be used to describe a document type message based on just one part element, or it can support RPC type (parameter driven) messages based on multiple parts. However, its expressive power for RPC is limited. For example, it cannot describe a variable number of input parameters or a choice of responses. WSDL 2.0 addresses this gap by removing support for the message element altogether. It simply allows an operation to reference a type directly, using the XML schema type system in the types element. In addition, the WSDL 2.0 language introduces some noticeable differences to the document structure of a WSDL definition, namely:

- The `definitions` element is renamed to `description`.
- The `portType` element is renamed to `interface`. Support for interface inheritance is achieved by using the `<extends>` attribute in the interface element. The `<extends>` attribute allows multiple `<interface>` declarations to be aggregated together and further extended to produce a completely new `<interface>` element.
- The `port` element is renamed to `endpoint`.

5.5 Summary of learning objectives

A service description language is an XML based language that describes the mechanics of interacting with a particular Web service and is inherently intended to constrain both the service provider and all requesters who make use of that service.

- The Web Services Description Language is an XML based specification schema providing a standard service representation language used to describe the details of the public interface exposed by a Web service.
- The public interface of a service can include operational information such as all publicly available operations, data type information for messages, binding information about the specific transport protocol to be used, and address information.
- The service implementation describes how a particular service interface is implemented by a given service provider and describes where the service is located.

Review questions

- Why is a service description necessary for representing Web services?
- What is the purpose of the Web Services Description Language? How does WSDL achieve its objective?
- Define and describe the Web service interface.
- Define and describe the Web service implementation.
- How do the Web service interface and implementation relate to each other?

- Describe the parts of the Web services `<portType>` element.
- Describe the parts of the Web services `<wsdl:binding>` element.
- How can you define RPC and document style Web services in WSDL?
- Can a single service contain multiple ports? What is the implication?
- How does a one-way operation differ from a request/response operation?
- How does a notification operation differ from a solicit/response operation?
- How can you use WSDL to create client stubs?

Exercises

5.1. Define a simple stock trading Web service in WSDL that requests the stock price associated with a specified stock ticker symbol. This exercise is similar to Exercise 4.3.

5.2. Define a simple insurance claim Web service in WSDL using both RPC/literal and document bindings.

5.3. Define a simple Web service in WSDL that returns flight information regarding flights of a particular flight operator, see Exercise 3.4.

5.4. Define a simple Web service in WSDL that uses the car rental reservation schema in Exercise 3.5 to reserve vehicles on the basis of a customer request.

5.5. Define a WSDL interface on the basis of the card processing schema that you defined in Exercise 3.3. Typical operations should be *CreditCardSale* for credit card debit authorisation, *DebitCardSale* for debit card debit authorisation, *CancelCreditCardSale* for cancelling a credit card sale, *CheckCardDebitStatus* for determining the current status of a credit card sale, *CreditCardUserDetails* for getting the details of a credit card user and so on.

5.6. Develop a simple inventory checking service. The inventory service should check the availability of an item. Based on this check, the inventory service should respond either that the purchase order could be fulfilled or by issuing a fault stating that the order cannot be completed.

CHAPTER 6

Registering and discovering services

Learning objectives

Service registration and discovery are two core functions of the service oriented architecture approach. In SOA based applications a service registry is necessary to keep track of what services an organisation has to offer and the characteristics of those services. To address the challenges of service registration and discovery, the Universal Description, Discovery, and Integration (UDDI) standard was created.

In this chapter we describe the role of service registries and the service discovery process for Web services. After reading this chapter you will understand the following key concepts:

- The use of UDDI v3.0 as a standard registry.
- The UDDI data structures and their relationship to WSDL documents.
- The UDDI to WSDL mapping model.
- The UDDI APIs.
- How the UDI APIs are used to publish Web services in UDDI and enquire about Web services contained in the UDDI.
- Different UDDI usage models and variants.

Chapter preview

At the core of the SOA is the need to be able to manage services as first order deliverables. This makes service discovery an essential element of SOA based applications and the key to communication between the service provider and consumer.

In this chapter we concentrate on the role of service registries and service discovery. We then introduce the Universal Description, Discovery and Integration specification, which defiines a universal method for enterprises to discover dynamically and invoke Web services. We describe its data structures, APIs, connection to WSDL, and practices for querying UDDI resident service data.

6.1 The role of service registries

One important measure of SOA application effectiveness is evidenced by the simplicity in which services are discovered and reused to resolve new SOA servicing requirements. The proliferation of new services that are the same as, or closely similar to, those that already exist leads to unnecessary, uncontrolled service duplication, unnecessary work and loss of productivity. Therefore, prior to designing new services developers are encouraged to seek out existing services to discover whether they might resolve their service requirements. Insufficient knowledge of available services is a potential failure of SOA and service design.

To enable businesses to discover each other's services, and learn what kinds of service capabilities their potential trading partners have, requires the creation of a service registry architecture that enables enterprises to:

- discover each other;
- defiine how they interact over the Internet;
- share information and services in a registry that will more rapidly accelerate the global adoption of joint SOA based applications.

As we have already noted in Section 1.7.2.1, publishing a Web service in a service registry so that other applications can find it entails two equally important operations: describing and registering the service. Publication of a service requires proper description of a Web service in terms of business, service and technical information. Registration deals with persistently storing the service descriptions in a services registry.

Service registries are all about visibility and control. At the simplest level, a service registry keeps track of what services an organisation has and characteristics of those services. A *document-based service registry* enables its clients to publish information by storing XML based service documents, such as business profiles or technical specifications (including WSDL descriptions of the service), in the registry. The registry is completely oblivious to the content of the service documents themselves. When these descriptive documents are submitted to the registry, service providers must also provide descriptive information about each document in the form of service metadata.

As we shall see in Section 13.2, *metadata* is one of the key elements of any registry solution because it is used to describe the structure of information held in the disparate systems and processes. This may range from the structure of XML schemas, interface defiinitions or endpoints in locations across the network, to the detailed description of an entire process (e.g. a process that sets up a new customer account or processes a customer initiated order).

In summary, an advanced registry offers several appealing characteristics:

- It maximises Web service reuse and encourages broad usage by all potential users in an SOA solution.
- It creates a management and governance structure to grow and sustain a successful SOA implementation.
- It contains all the metadata about Web services and their associated objects. It also contains information about service providers, consumers and their relationships.
- It provides general and special purpose interfaces that address the needs of providers, consumers, administrators and operators.
- It ensures that the evolving SOA can handle the growing number of services and service consumers and quickly adapt to changing business requirements.

In this chapter we shall examine the Universal Description, Discovery and Integration (UDDI) version 3.0, a platform independent, XML-based registry as a mechanism to register and locate Web service applications. Although UDDI has not been widely adopted in the way its designers had hoped, it is commonly found inside a company where it might be used dynamically to bind client systems to implementations. It can, therefore, form a sound basis for understanding how service registries operate and illustrate how Web services can be published and retrieved using standard APIs.

6.2 Service discovery

Service discovery is an important element of an SOA. *Service discovery* is the process of locating service providers, and retrieving service descriptions that have been previously published. Service discovery involves locating and interrogating service defiinitions, which is a preliminary step for accessing a service. It is through the service locating process that service clients learn that a particular service exists and find it.

Interrogating services involves querying the service registry for the services that match the needs of a service requester. A query consists of search criteria such as the type of the desired service, preferred price and maximum number of returned results, and is executed against service information published by the service provider. After the discovery process is complete, the service developer or client application should know the exact location of a Web service (a URI for the selected service), its capabilities and how to interface with it. *Service selection* involves deciding on what Web service to invoke from the set of Web services the discovery process returned.

There are two basic types of service discovery [Graham 2004]:

- *static service discovery,* which occurs at design time;
- *dynamic service discovery,* which occurs at run time.

With static discovery, the service implementation details, such as the network location and network protocol to use, are bound at design time and service retrieval is performed on a service registry. A human designer usually examines the results of the retrieval operation, and the service description returned by the retrieval operation is incorporated into the application logic.

With dynamic discovery, the service implementation details, such as the network location and network protocol to use, are left unbound at design time so that they can be determined at run time. In this case, the service requester has to specify preferences to enable the application to infer which Web service(s) the requester is most likely to want to invoke. The application issues a retrieval operation at run-time against the service registry to locate one or more service implementation defiinitions that match the service interface defiinition used by the application. Based on application logic, QoS considerations such as best price, performance, security certificates and so on, the application chooses the most appropriate service, binds to it and invokes it.

6.3 Universal Description, Discovery and Integration (UDDI)

To address the challenges of service registration and discovery, the Universal Description, Discovery, and Integration specification was created. UDDI is an open industry initiative, sponsored by the Organization for the Advancement of Structured Information Standards (OASIS), enabling businesses to publish service listings and discover each other and define how the services or software applications interact over the Internet.

UDDI is designed for use by developer tools and applications that use Web service standards such as SOAP/XML and WSDL. UDDI provides a global, platform independent, open framework, making it easier to publish an enterprise's preferred means of conducting business, find trading partners, and interoperate with these trading partners over the Internet. It enables service providers to describe their services and business processes in a global, open environment on the Internet, thus extending their reach. It also enables service clients to discover information about enterprises offering Web services; find descriptions of the Web services these enterprises provide; and, finally, find technical information about Web service interfaces and defiinitions.

The core concept of the UDDI initiative is the UDDI business registration, an XML document used to describe a business entity and its Web services. Conceptually, the information provided in a UDDI business registration consists of three interrelated components:

- White pages, which include address, contact and other key points of an organisation.
- Yellow pages, which include a taxonomy classification of information according to industry norms based on standard industry taxonomies.

- Green pages, which include the technical capabilities and information about services that are exposed by the business, including references to specifications for Web services and pointers to various file and URL based discovery mechanisms.

Typical applications of a service registry such as UDDI, include:

- Publishing or finding Web services (within an organisation or across organisational boundaries) that meet arbitrary functional or QoS criteria.
- Determining the security and transport protocols supported by a given Web service.
- Insulating applications (and providing fail-over) from failures or changes in invoked services.

Using a UDDI registry, enterprises can discover the existence of potential trading partners and basic information about them (through white pages), find companies in specific industry classifications (through yellow pages), and uncover the kind of Web services offered to interact with the enterprises (through green pages). The information that is stored in the UDDI registry allows applications and developers to determine who the business entity represents, what they do, where the services they provide can be found and how they can be accessed.

The UDDI usage model involves service providers, standard bodies and industry consortia publishing the descriptions of available services. It is illustrated in Figure 6.1.

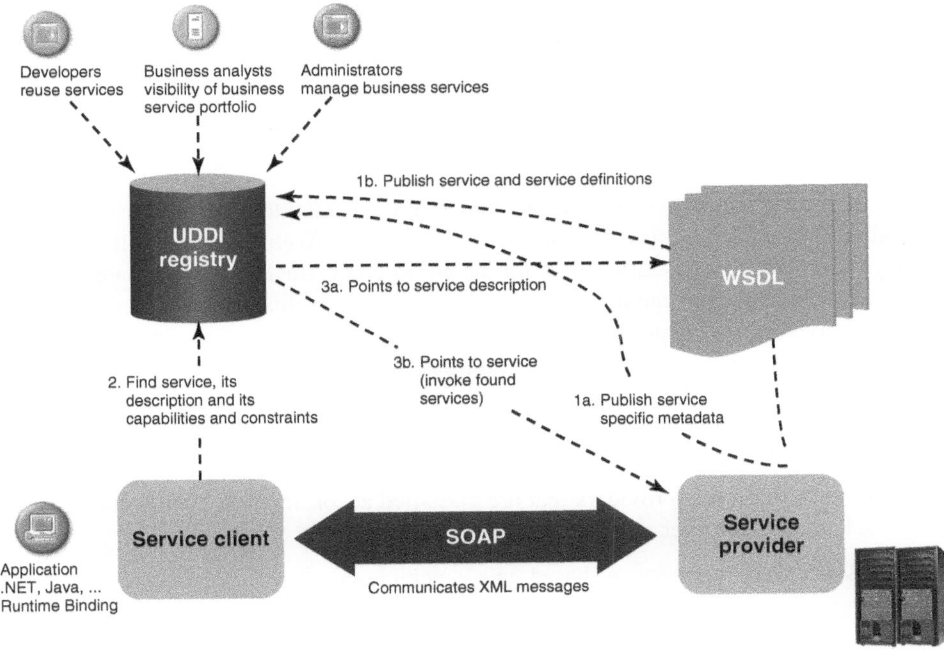

Figure 6.1 The UDDI usage model

Once the descriptions of available services have been published, service providers implement and deploy Web services conforming to these type defiinitions. Prospective clients can then query the UDDI registry based on various criteria such as the name of the business, product classification categories, or even services that implement a given service type defiinition. These clients can then get the details of the service type defiinition from the location specified. Finally, the clients can invoke the Web service because they have the service endpoint, and also the details on how to exchange messages with it.

As UDDI uses SOAP as its transport layer, enterprises can interact with UDDI both at design time and at run time through SOAP based XML API calls in order to discover technical data about an enterprise's services. In this way enterprises can link up with service providers and invoke and use their services.

UDDI has been designed in a highly normalised fashion, not bound to any technology. An entry in the UDDI registry can contain any type of resource, e.g. a J2EE or CORBA interface, independently of whether the resource is XML based or not. The point is that, while UDDI itself uses XML to represent the data it stores, it allows for other kinds of technology to be registered.

One key difference between a UDDI registry and other registries and directories is that UDDI provides a mechanism to categorise businesses and services using taxonomies. For example, service providers can use a taxonomy to indicate that a service implements a specific domain standard, or that it provides services to a specific geographic area [Bean 2010]. Such taxonomies make it easier for consumers to find services that match their specific requirements.

An organisation may set up multiple private UDDI registries in-house to support intranet and e-Business operations by connecting departments in an organisation. In addition, a business may use UDDI registries set up by its customers and business partners. Once a Web service has been developed and deployed it is important that it is published in a public UDDI registry so that potential clients and service developers can discover it.

6.3.1 The UDDI data structures

A UDDI registry, either for use in the public domain or behind the firewall (private), offers a standard mechanism to classify, catalogue, and manage Web services, so that they can be discovered and consumed. Whether for the purpose of e-Business or alternate purposes, businesses and providers can use UDDI to represent information about Web services in a standard way such that queries can then be issued to a UDDI registry – at design time or run time. Queries address the following scenarios [Clement 2004]:

- Find Web service implementations that are based on a common abstract interface defiinition.
- Find Web service providers that are classified according to a known classification scheme or identifier system.
- Issue a search for services based on a general keyword.

- Determine the security and transport protocols supported by a given Web service.
- Store the technical information about a Web service and then update that information at run time.

UDDI defiines a data structure standard for representing company and service description information. The data model used by the UDDI registries is defiined in an XML schema. XML was chosen because it offers a platform neutral view of data and because it allows hierarchical relationships to be described in a natural way. The UDDI v 3.0 defiines a number of types of information that provide the white/yellow/green page functions. These are [OASIS 2004]:

1. *businessService:* A description of a service's business function.
2. *businessEntity:* Information about the organisation that published the service.
3. *bindingTemplate:* The service's technical details, including a reference to the service's programmatic interface or API.
4. *tModel:* Information about technical specifications for services, including various attributes such as taxonomy, transports, digital signatures, etc.
5. *publisherAssertion:* Relationships among entities in the registry.
6. *subscription:* Standing requests to track changes to a list of entities.

Figure 6.2 provides a high level view of the UDDI data structures, while the relationship between the UDDI data structures expressed in UML is shown in Figure 6.3.

The diagram in Figure 6.2 shows the relationships between the various UDDI structures, their substructures and attributes. The core UDDI XML schema specifies information about the business entity, e.g. a company, that offers the service (`<businessEntity>`),

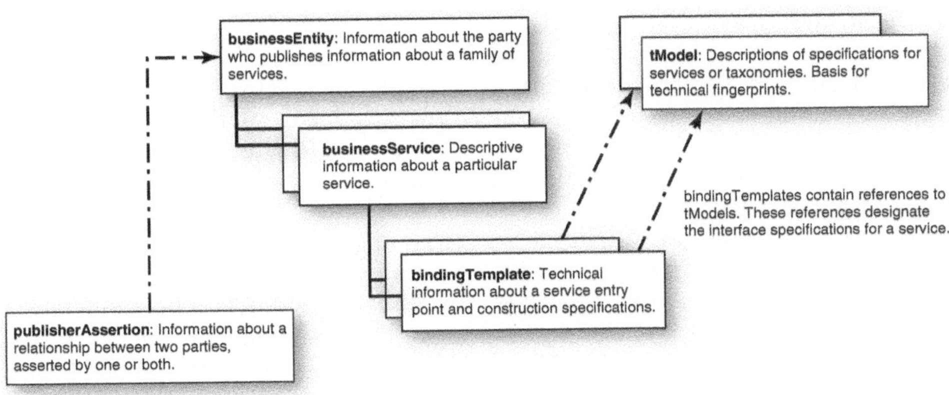

Figure 6.2 Overview of the UDDI data structures

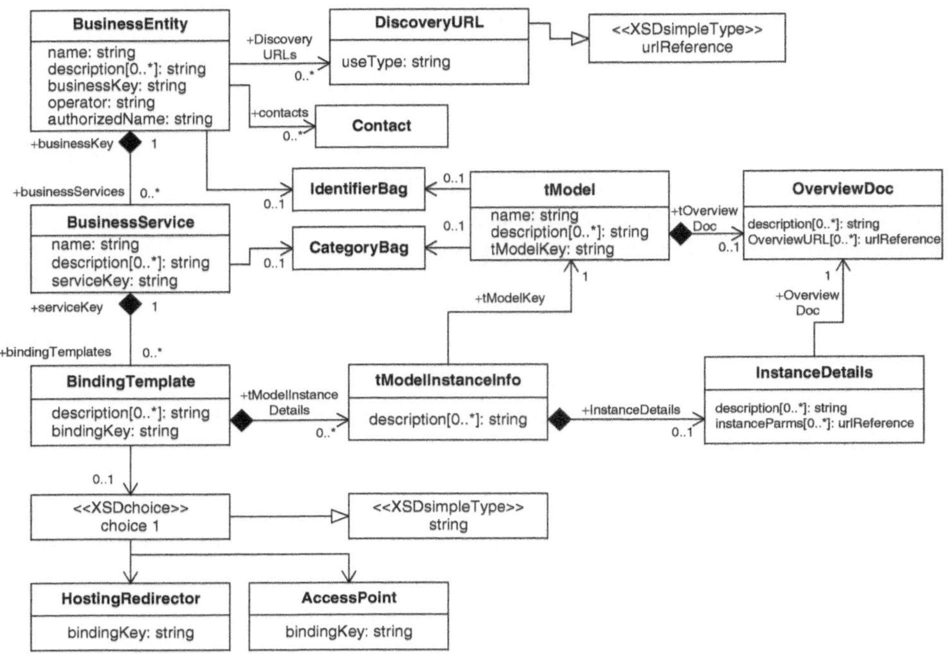

Figure 6.3 Relationships between the UDDI data structures expressed in UML

which describes the services exposed by the business (called <businessService>), and captures the binding information (<bindingTemplate>) required to use the service. The (<bindingTemplate>) captures the service endpoint address, and associates the service with the technical models (<tModel>s) that represent its technical specifications. A service implementation registration represents a service offered by a specific service provider.

Each <businessService> can be accessed in one or more ways. For example, a retailer might expose an order entry service accessible as a SOAP based Web service, a regular Web form, or even a fax number. To convey all the ways a service is exposed, each service is bound to one or more <tModel>s via a binding template. Each of these four core UDDI structures has, for identification purposes, a unique key called a universal unique identifier (UUID).

Figure 6.3 shows that there also exists a hierarchical relationship among the UDDI data structures. A business publishes a business entity containing, among other things, one or more business services. A business service has descriptive information about a service that a business provides, and can have one or more binding templates. The binding template has information on how to access a service entry point. It also has references to <tModel>s (using <tModel> keys) that point to the specification or interface defiinitions for a service. The interface defiinitions are usually in the form of WSDL defiinitions. The relationship between <tModel>s and <bindingTemplate>s is many-to-many. Accordingly, <tModel>s are not unique to <bindingTemplate>s. These UDDI core elements and their relationships are explained in some detail in the remainder of this section.

6.3.1.1 Service provider information

Partners and potential clients of an enterprise's services that need to be able to locate information about the services provided would normally have, as a starting point, a small set of facts about the service provider. They will know, for example, either its business name or perhaps some key identifiers, as well as optional categorisation and contact information (white pages). Service provider information is recorded by the data structures depicted in UML in Figure 6.4 and outlined below.

The business entity element and business key attribute. The XML elements for supporting publishing and discovering information about a business – the UDDI Business Registration – are contained in an element named <businessEntity>. This XML element serves as the top level structure and contains *white page* information about a particular business unit (service provider). The <businessEntity> structure can be used to model any businesses and providers within UDDI. It contains descriptive information about the business or provider and about the services it offers. This would include information such as names and descriptions in multiple languages, contact information and classification information.

All other non-business or provider elements related to the organisation that a <businessEntity> entity represents, such as service descriptions and technical information, are either contained in this entity or referred to by elements nested within it. For instance, each <businessService> contained within a <businessEntity> structure describes a logical service offered by the business or organisation. Similarly, each <bindingTemplate> contained within a given <businessEntity> provides the technical description of a Web service that belongs to the logical service that is described by the <businessService>.

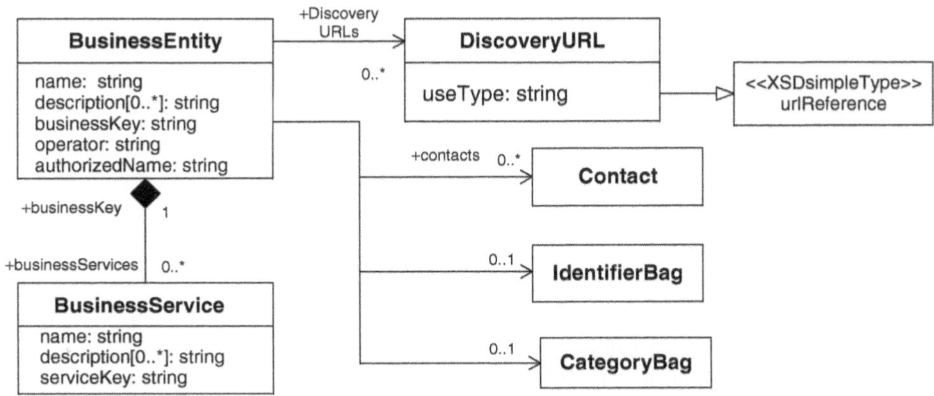

Figure 6.4 The <businessEntity> data structure expressed in UML

Example 6.1: An automotive manufacturing business entity

Listing 6.1 provides an example of a <businessEntity> data structure. This listing illustrates the attributes and elements in a <businessEntity>.

```
<businessEntity businessKey="d2300-3aff-.."
                xmlns = "urn:uddi-org:api_v3">
<name xml: lang="en"> Automotive Equipment Manufacturing Inc. </name>
<description xml: lang="en">
   Automotive Equipment, Accessories and Supplies for European firms
</description>
<contacts>
   <contact useType="Sales Contact">
      <description xml: lang="en"> Sales Representative </ description>
      <personName> Reginald Murphy </personName>
      <email useType="primary"> joe.murphy@automeq.com </email>
      <address useType="http">
         <addressLine> http://www.medeq.com/sales/ </addressLine>
      </address>
   </contact>
</contacts>
<businessServices>
   <!-- Business service information goes here -->
</businessServices>
<identifierBag>
   <!-- DUNS Number identifier System -->
   <keyedReference keyName="DUNS Number" keyValue="..." tModelKey="..."/>
</identifierBag>
<categoryBag>
   <!—North American Industry Classification System (NAICS) -->
   <keyedReference
         keyName="Automotive parts distribution" keyValue="..."
tModelKey="...">

    ......
</categoryBag>
</businessEntity>
```

Listing 6.1 Example of a <businessEntity> structure

The element <businessEntity> in Listing 6.1 is shown to contain a <businessKey> element, which is a unique business identifier for that <businessEntity>. The value of this attribute is a UUID, which the UDDI registry generates automatically and assigns to the <businessEntity> when it is first created. Entities like <businessService>, <bindingTemplate>, and <tModel> also contain UUID keys. A prospective partner (client) can search the UDDI on the basis of one or more of the <businessEntity> attributes in Listing 6.1 and locate matching enterprises.

The discovery URLs element. This is an optional element and contains the URLs that point to alternate Web addressable (via HTTP GET) discovery documents.

An example of a <discoveryURL>, generated by a UDDI node that is accessible at www.medeq.com and rendered by the publisher of the <businessEntity> that is identified by the hypothetical <businessKey> attribute uddi:medeq.com:registry:sales:55, is:

```
<discoveryURL useType="businessEntity">
   http://www.medeq.com?businessKey=uddi:example.com:registry:sales:55
</discoveryURL>
```

The name element. The name element contains the common name of the organisation that a business entity represents. A <businessEntity> may contain more than one name. Multiple names are useful in order to specify both the legal name and a known abbreviation of a <businessEntity>. In Listing 6.1 the attribute xml:lang="en" signifies that the company's name is specified in English.

The description element. This element is a short narrative description for the business. A <businessEntity> can contain several descriptions, e.g. in different languages.

The contacts element. As shown in Listing 6.1 this element is an optional list of contact information for the organisation. The contact structure records contact information for a person or a job role within the <businessEntity> so that someone who finds the information can make human contact for any purpose.

The business services element. This is an additional optional list containing information describing logical families of the business services that this business entity provides. This simple container holds one or more <businessService> entities, each of which represents a Web service implementation. The <businessService> data structure is covered in some detail in the following section.

The identifier bag element. In addition to the descriptive information, the UDDI registry provides information about enterprises and their services. It also provides formal identifiers for business entities. The UDDI specification requires that UDDI products support several identifier systems, including two industry standards, the Dunn and Bradstreet's Data Universal System Number Identification System (DUNS) and the Thomas Register Supplier Identifier Code system. These systems are useful for looking up companies in the UDDI registry and provide unique supplier identification digits.

The <identifierBag> is an optional list of name–value pairs that can act as alternative identifiers for the company: for example, the US tax code and business identifiers such as DUNS. A company may have multiple identifiers in this field. An <identifierBag> structure is modelled as a list of "tModelKey/keyName/keyValue". Each such triplet is called a keyed reference. An <identifierBag> is a list of one or more <keyedReference> structures, each representing a single identification.

Example 6.2: Identifying a company by its DUNS number

Identifying SAP AG by its by its Dun & Bradstreet D-U-N-S number, using the corresponding <tModelKey> element within a public UDDI Business Registry (UBR), is accomplished as follows:

```
<identifierBag>
    <keyedReference
        tModelKey="uddi:uddi.org:ubr:identifier:dnb.com:d-u-n-s"
        keyName="SAP AG"
        keyValue="31-626-8655" />
</identifierBag>
```

The category bag element. An important part of UDDI is providing a foundation and best practices that help provide semantic content to Web services contained in a registry. To achieve this, UDDI allows users to defiine multiple taxonomies that can be used in a registry by using the <categoryBag> element.

A <categoryBag> element is similar to the <identifierBag>. This element is a list of one or more <keyedReference> structures that tag the business entity with specific classification information, e.g. industry, product or geographic codes. This could be in the form of industry taxonomy classifiers, e.g. the Universal Standard Products and Services Classification (UNSPC), which is an open, global coding system for classifying products and services, or geographic classifiers, or the North American Industry Classification System (NAICS), which likewise defiines codes for business and product categories.

6.3.1.2 Representing business service information

The top-level entity <businessEntity> declares an element called a <businessService>, which contains descriptive *yellow pages* information about a company – names, descriptions and classification information – outlining the purpose of the individual Web services found within it. More specifically, each <businessService> data structure provides the ability to assemble a set of services under a common rubric by representing a logical service classification about a family of Web services offered by a company and contains descriptive information in business terms.

The <businessService> structure is a descriptive container that is used to group a series of Web services related to either a business process or category of services. It is used to reveal service related information, such as the name of a Web service aggregate, a description of the Web service or categorisation details. Examples of business processes that would include related Web service information include purchasing services, shipping

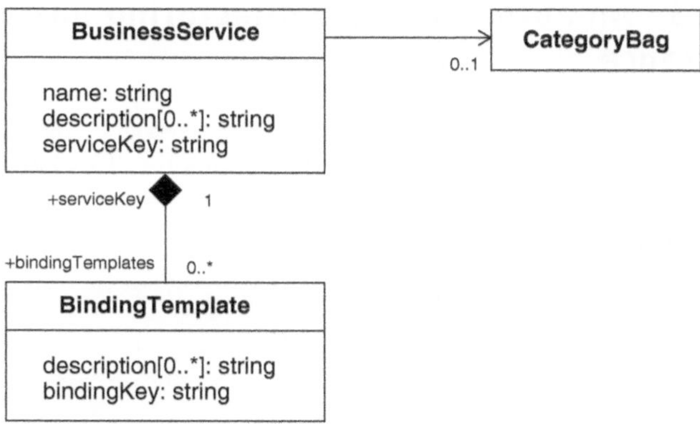

Figure 6.5 The <businessService> data structure expressed in UML

services and other high level business processes. Such <businessService> information sets as these can each be further categorised, allowing Web service descriptions to be segmented along combinations of industry, product and service, or geographic category boundaries. For example, a <businessService> structure could contain a set of purchase order Web services (submission, confirmation, and notification) that is provided by a business.

Figure 6.5 illustrates the <businessService> data structure expressed in UML. This figure reveals that a <businessService> element may contain one or more <bindingTemplate> entities. The relationship between a <businessService> and <bindingTemplate> entity is similar to the relationship between a WSDL <service> and the WSDL <port> elements. A <bindingTemplate> describes a Web service endpoint and represents the *technical fingerprint* of a Web service [Monson-Haefel 2004]. This means that it lists all <tModel> types that describe a Web service, which uniquely identify the technical specifications of a Web service.

A given <businessService> entity is uniquely identified by its service key. To this end, the <businessKey> attribute uniquely identifies the <businessEntity>, which is the provider of the <businessService>. The <categoryBag> element contained in a <businessService> data structure is the same type that is used in the <businessEntity> structure. This element contains a list of business categories where each describes a specific business aspect of the <businessService> (e.g. industry, product category or geographic region). A given <businessService> contains a <bindingTemplate> element, which is a list of technical descriptions for the Web services provided. More information on binding templates is given in the following sub-section.

A prospective partner can search the UDDI to locate businesses which service a particular industry or product category, or which are located within a specific geographic region.

Example 6.3: An automotive manufacturing business service instance

The example in Listing 6.2 shows a sample <businessService> instance in the UDDI registry corresponding to the company modelled in Listing 6.1. This information was not shown in Listing 6.1. As can be seen in the listing, <businessService> contains the service name, description and classification information (<categoryBag> element).

```
<businessServices>
   <businessService serviceKey=" ">
      <name>
      Search the Automotive Equipment Manufacturing parts Registry
      </name>
         <description lang="en">

            Get to the Automotive Equipment Manufacturing parts Registry
         </description>
         <bindingTemplates>
            <bindingTemplate bindingKey="..">
               <description lang="en">
                  Use your Web Browser to search the parts registry
               </description>
               <accessPoint URLType="http">
                  http://www.automeq.com/b2b/actions/search.jsp
               </accessPoint>

               <tModelInstanceDetails>
                  <tModelInstanceInfo
                      tModelKey="uddi:.."/>
               <tModelInstanceDetails>
            </bindingTemplate>
         </bindingTemplates>
   </businessService>
</businessServices>
```

Listing 6.2 Example of a <businessService> structure

6.3.1.3 Representing technical service information

Technical descriptions of Web services – the *green pages* data – reside within the <bindingTemplate> elements listed in a <businessService>. These structures provide support for determining a technical endpoint or optionally support remotely hosted services, as well as a lightweight facility for describing unique technical characteristics of a given implementation.

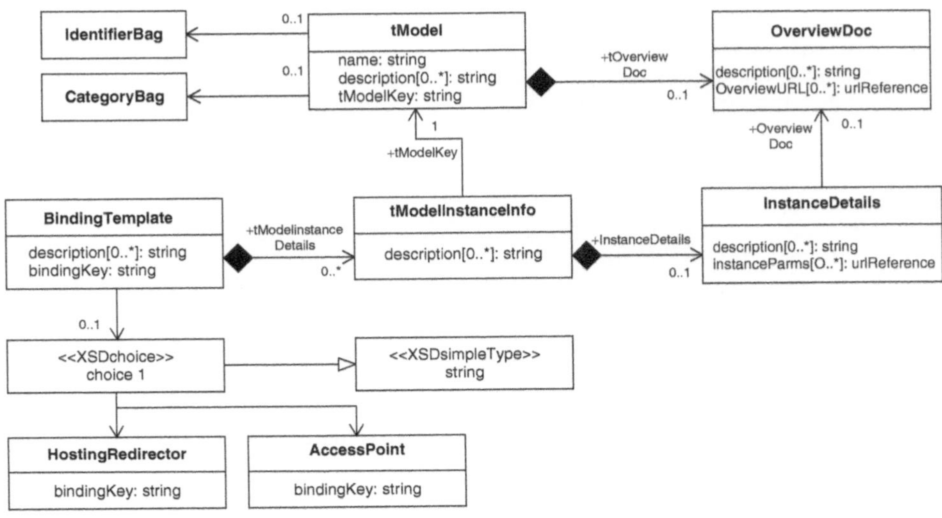

Figure 6.6 The `<bindingTemplate>` and `<tModel>` structures

Support for technology, and application specific parameters and settings, is also provided. This information is relevant for application programs and clients that need to connect to, and t hen communicate and invoke a remote Web service.

Figure 6.6 shows that each `<businessService>` may potentially contain multiple `<bindingTemplate>` structures, each of which describes a Web service. All access information required to invoke a service is described in the information element named `<bindingTemplate>`. Each `<bindingTemplate>` structure represents an individual Web service. In contrast with the `<businessService>` and `<businessEntity>` structures, which are oriented toward auxiliary information about providers and services, a `<bindingTemplate>` provides the technical information needed by applications to bind (map the name of a service to its WSDL description) and interact with the Web service being described. It must contain either the access point for a given service or an indirection mechanism that will lead one to the access point. More precisely, each `<bindingTemplate>` represents a different Web service `<port>` or `<binding>`.

Example 6.4: Reference details for automotive manufacturing business service

Listing 6.3 shows the `<bindingTemplate>` structure that corresponds to the `<businessService>` structure in Listing 6.2. The `<bindingTemplate>` in this listing provides references to details about data formats and requirements of the trading partners.

```
<bindingTemplate bindingKey="..">
   <description lang="en">
      Use your Web Browser to search the parts registry
   </description>
   <accessPoint URLType="http">
      http://www.automeq.com/b2b/actions/search.jsp
   </accessPoint>
   <tModelInstanceDetails>
       <tModelInstanceInfo
          tModelKey="uddi:.."/>
   <tModelInstanceDetails>
</bindingTemplate>
```

Listing 6.3 An example of a <bindingTemplate> structure

When a <bindingTemplate> structure is defiined, the designer may declare a single <accessPoint> element to provide the exact electronic address of a Web service. Valid access point values can include the URL, e-mail, or even a phone number. The <accessPoint> has a <URLType> attribute to facilitate searching for entry points associated with a particular type of service. An example could be a purchase order service that provides three types of entry points: one for HTTP, one for SMTP and one for fax ordering.

It is not always enough simply to know where to contact a particular Web service. For instance, if we know that a service provider provides a Web service that accepts purchase orders, knowing the URL for that service is not enough. There is a clear requirement to understand the technical details regarding a service, such as what format the purchase order should be sent in, which protocols are appropriate, what security is required, and what form of response will result after sending the purchase order. This objective is met by using the UDDI element <tModel>. Technical Models, or <tModel>s for short, are used in UDDI to represent unique technical concepts or constructs. They provide a structure that allows re use and, thus, standardisation within a software framework.

A <tModel> provides green page information describing the technical details of a service. In particular a <tModel> contains (within the <overviewDoc> element) a pointer to a file that could contain the WSDL description of the service. These technical details are supplied in the specification of the service, which we described in Section 5.2.

To understand the relationship between a binding template and a technology model, which both provide technical service data, we need to realize that a <businessService>

structure can support several business protocols or specifications (XML vocabularies, EDI standards, RosettaNet Partner Interface Processes, and so on) each having a separate <bindingTemplate>. The <bindingTemplate> can reference each such protocol or specification with a specific <tModel>.

When describing how a Web service is to interact with its clients, the primary role that a <tModel> plays is to provide a technical specification. For instance, in the case of a purchase order, the Web service that accepts a purchase order exhibits a set of well defined behaviours if the proper document format is sent to the proper address in the right way. A UDDI registration for this service would consist of an entry for the business partner <businessEntity>, a logical service entry that describes the purchasing service <businessService>, and a <bindingTemplate> entry that describes the purchase order service by listing its URL and a reference to a <tModel> that is used to provide information about the service's interface and its technical specification.

In the purchase order example, the <tModel> reference (<tModelKey>) found in its <binding-Template> is a pointer to information about the specifics of this purchase order Web service that contain such information as software settings that the service provider's system needs in order to connect and exchange data. The designers of the purchase order specifications can thus establish a unique technical identity within a UDDI registry by registering information about the specification in a <tModel>. In this way the <tModel> becomes a technical fingerprint that is unique to a given specification. This refers to any technical specifications such as service types, bindings and wire protocols, or prearranged agreements on how to conduct business.

It is important that taxonomies are used when publishing data in a UDDI registry. To facilitate the discovery of businesses, services, bindings or service types, the <tModel> defines an abstract namespace reference that is used to identify or classify business entities, business services, and even <tModel>s. A namespace <tModel> represents a scoping domain. For example, the Universal Standard Products and Services Classification (UNSPSC), a set of categorisation codes representing product and service categories, could be used to specify a product and service offering of a particular business in a more formalised way. Several UDDI compliant service registry products also provide the ability to reference and relate <tModel>s in the form of a hierarchy. One registry <tModel> can refer to other <tModel>s, and so forth [Bean2010].

Example 6.5: Classifying products and services

Figure 6.7 shows that a <tModel> for a given *Subject Area* may refer to subordinate <tModel>s for *Products, Locations, Parties, Events* and *Financial instruments.* This taxonomy may be extended as the inventory of reusable and discoverable Web service increases.

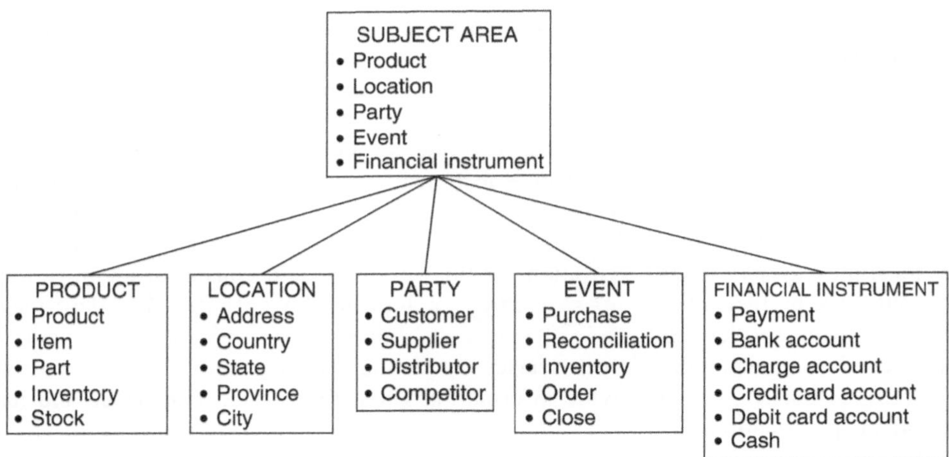

Figure 6.7 Example of <tModel> hierarchy

The <tModel> data structure expressed in UML is illustrated in Figure 6.6. As shown in this figure, a given <tModel> structure is uniquely identified by its <tModelKey> attribute. The <description> element is a short narrative description for this technical model, which may appear multiple times for different languages. As already explained earlier, the <overviewDoc> element is a reference to remote instructions or descriptions related to the <tModel> element. The <overviewURL> element in the <overviewDoc> element can be any valid URL, but the convention is to use a URL that points to a file, e.g. a WSDL defiinition of a service. Other elements in the <tModel> data structure were described in Section 6.3.1.1.

Example 6.6: Technical model for a RosettaNet request quote process

Finally, Listing 6.4 shows a sample <tModel> entry in the UDDI registry for a RosettaNet Partner Interface Process (PIP) for enabling trading partners to request and provide quotes. RosettaNet defines a set of standards for IT, an electronic component, and a semiconductor manufacturing supply chain (see Section 14.3). RosettaNet PIPs define business processes between trading partners.

Listing 6.4 refers to the PIP 3A1 *Request Quote* which, enables a buyer to request a product quote from a provider, and a provider to respond with either a quote or a referral. As can be seen from Listing 6.4, the specification is not stored in the UDDI registry; instead the <tModel> has a URL <overviewURL> element that points to where it can be found.

```
<tModel  tModelKey="...">

  <name> RosettaNet-Org </name>
  <description xml:lang="en">
      Supports a process for trading partners to request and provide quotes
  </description >

  <overviewDoc>
    <description xml:lang="en">
        This compressed file contains the specification in a word
        document, the html guidelines document, and the XML schemas.
    </description>
    <overviewURL>
         http://www.rosettanet.org/rosettanet/Doc/0/
                        K96RPDQA97A1311M0304UQ4J39/3A1_RequestQuote.zip
    </overviewURL>
  </overviewDoc>

  <categoryBag>
      <keyedReference  keyName=" Trading quote request and provision"
                       keyValue=" 80101704"  tModelKey="..."/>
  </categoryBag>
</tModel>
```

Listing 6.4 Example of a sample <tModel> entry

UDDI, just like WSDL, draws a sharp distinction between abstraction and implementation. In fact, as we have already seen, a <tModel> fulfils the role of providing technical fingerprints, abstract types of metadata and interfaces. An example might be a specification that outlines wire protocols and interchange formats. These can, for instance, be found in the RosettaNet PIPs, the Open Applications Group Integration Specification, various EDI efforts and so on.

6.3.1.4 Best practices for storing technical service information

Published *best practices* for using a UDDI registry to store technical information about WSDL services recommend that a <bindingTemplate> contains two different <tModelKey> attributes that point to two different <tModel>s for a specific Web service [Kifer 2005]. One <tModel> entry points to a file containing the WSDL description of the <portType> of the service while the other points to file containing the WSDL description of its <binding>.

One reason for this recommendation for having two different <tModel>s for a specific Web service is that the <portType> of the service might be shared by many businesses providing the same service. For instance, there might be a standard order management service having a generic <portType> available to the entire electronics manufacturing sector. Many individual enterprises within this sector may provide the same service, each with their own binding. The <bindingTemplate>s of each of these enterprises would then point to the same <tModel> <portType> and to different <tModel>s for their individual <binding>s. This means that all manufacturing enterprise order management services are semantically equivalent but are implemented differently.

Another reason for having two different <tModel>s for a specific Web service is that a single provider may wish to provide the same <portType> with different <binding>s for a particular service.

6.3.1.5 The publisher assertion structure

A single <businessEntity> does not effectively represent many enterprises, since their description and, hence, their discovery is likely to be diverse. For instance, large multinational organisations have many divisions and departments that may need to create their own UDDI entries for Web services they offer, but still want to be recognised as part of a larger organisation. As a consequence, several <businessEntity> structures can be published, representing individual divisions or subsidiaries of an organisation. This objective can be achieved using a <publisherAssertion> structure. To eliminate the possibility that one publisher claims a relationship to another that is not reciprocated, both publishers must publish identical assertions for the relationship to become visible.

Example 6.7: Defining relationships between business entities

A <publisherAssertion> structure defines relationships between pairs of <businessEntity> structures. Two (or more) related enterprises may use the <publisherAssertion> structure to publish assertions of business relationships, which are mutually acceptable to both parties. A <publisherAssertion> entity may be digitally signed using XML digital signatures.

```
<publsiherAssertion>
     <fromKey> FE565 ... <\fromKey>
     <toKey> A237B   ...  <\toKey>
     <keyedReference  tModelKey="uuid:807A  .. "/>
                      keyName="subsidiary"

                      keyValue="parent-child">
     </ keyedReference >
</publsiherAssertion>
```

Listing 6.5 Example of a sample <publisherAssertion> entry

Listing 6.5 shows a <publisherAssertion> entity expressing the relationship between a fictitious corporation and one of its divisions. In this listing, the <fromKey> and <toKey> constructs contain the business keys of two related companies. The <tModelKey> attribute in the <keyedReference> element refers to the type of relationship, e.g. business partners, holding company or franchise, which represents the relationship between these organisations. UDDI has defined a canonical <tModel> for such business relationship types. This allows for three valid <keyeValue>s in this canonical <tModel>: parent–child (for organisational hierarchies such as holding company/subsidiary), peer-to-peer (for companies on an equal footing such as business partners or departments in a company), and identity (for indicating that the two business entities represent the same company).

6.3.2 Mapping WSDL to UDDI

Due to the fact that both UDDI and WSDL schema have been architected to delineate clearly between interface and implementation, these two constructs will work quite complementarily together.

The primary focus in this section is on how to map WSDL service description into a UDDI registry, which is required by existing Web service tools and run time environments. The WSDL to UDDI mapping model is designed to help users find services that implement standard defiinitions. The mapping model describes how WSDL <portType> and <binding> element can be associated with <tModel>s. How the <port>s of WSDL become UDDI <bindingTemplate>s and how each WSDL service is registered as a <businessService>.

In this section we use the term WSDL interface file to denote a WSDL document that contains the <types>, <message>, <portType> elements, and the term *WSDL binding file* to denote a WSDL document that contains the <binding> element. The term WSDL implementation file denotes a WSDL document that contains the <service> and <port> elements. The WSDL implementation file imports the interface and binding file, while the binding file imports the interface file.

A complete WSDL service description is a combination of a service interface, service binding and a service implementation document. Since the service interface and service binding represent a reusable defiinition of a service, they are both published in a UDDI registry as a <tModel>. A service interface is published first as a <tModel> before the service implementation is published as a <businessService>. By decoupling a WSDL specification and registering it in UDDI, we can populate UDDI with standard interfaces that have multiple implementations. An overview of this mapping is given in Figure 6.8. We summarise this process in two major steps: publication of service interfaces and service implementations.

6.3.2.1 Publishing service interfaces and service bindings

When trying to publish a service, the first step is to create the service interface definition, which includes service interfaces and protocol bindings, both publicly available.

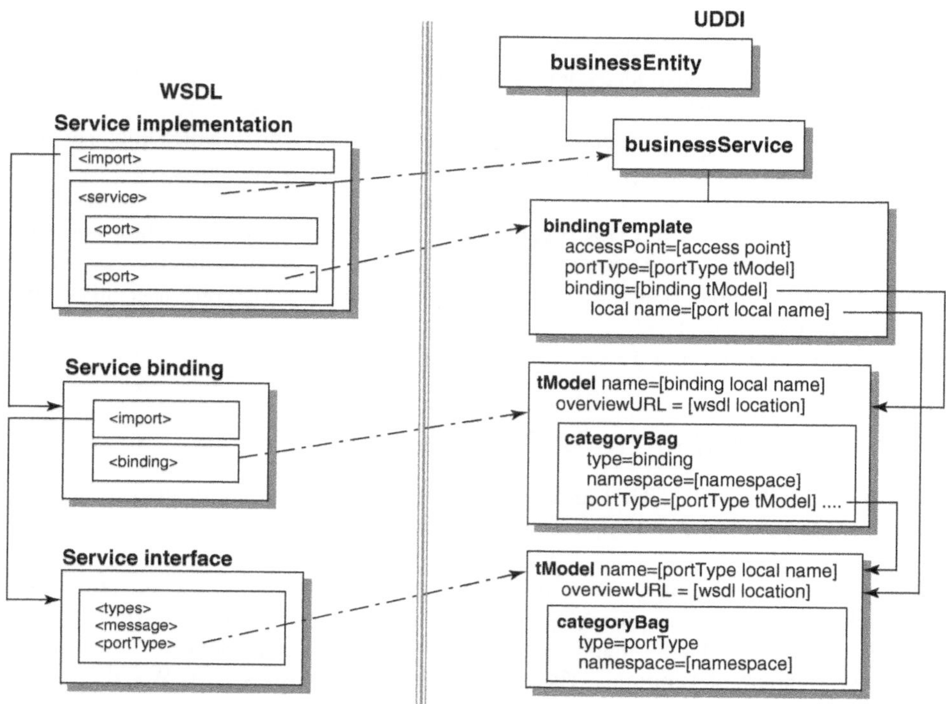

Figure 6.8 Mapping WSDL to UDDI schemas

Any Web service registered with UDDI must be associated with a <tModel>. This <tModel> describes the abstract interface, i.e. a set of operations, exposed by a specific Web service. As WSDL allows a <portType> and a <binding> to have the same name, a <keyedReference> is used to differentiate two <tModel>s, one of which relates to a <portType> and the other to a <binding> [Colgrave 2004], Colgrave 2003a].

Figure 6.8 illustrates that a WSDL <portType> is represented by a UDDI <tModel>. This <tModel> is categorized as a WSDL <portType tModel> to distinguish it from any other type of <portType>. In this <tModel> only meta-data is stored about a <portType>. As the detailed information in the <portType> relating to messages, operations, and so on is not duplicated in UDDI the <portType tModel> must refer to the WSDL document in which the <portType> is defined. In this way, application development tools that wish to generate a programming language interface from the <portType>, or systems that wish to validate requests against the defiinition of the <portType>, can retrieve the WSDL document.

Listing 6.6 contains the UDDI <portType tModel> corresponding to the Web service interface defiinition illustrated in Listing 5.5. The WSDL binding entity maps to a <tModel>. The <tModel> name is the same as the WSDL binding local name in Listing 5.5. The <tModel> contains a <categoryBag> that specifies the WSDL namespace and supplies a pointer to the <portType tModel>.

```
<tModel tModelKey="uuid:e8cf1163...">
   <name>
      PurchaseOrderPortType
   </name>

   <overviewDoc>
      <!-- WSDL service interface definition -->
      <overviewURL>
         http://www.auto-parts.com:8080/PurchaseOrderService.wsdl
      <overviewURL>
   <overviewDoc>
   <categoryBag>
     <keyedReference
        tModelKey="uuid:d01987d1..."
        keyName="portType namespace"

        keyValue=
        "http://www.auto-parts.com/PurchaseService/wsdl"/>
     <keyedReference
        tModelKey="uuid:6e090afa..."
        keyName="WSDL type"
        keyValue="portType"/>
   </categoryBag>
</tModel>
```

Listing 6.6 UDDI <tModel> created from WSDL <portType> element

Registering a Web service as a <tModel> provides flexible design patterns for applications using Web services. For example, there might be a standard interface for Web services that provide purchase orders. Assuming that many providers may create Web services that implement this standard interface, clients can search the UDDI registry for a list of these companies and select the most suitable one based on such criteria as cost or response time. Furthermore, if a client uses the purchase order service from a preferred service provider and finds out that for some reason the service is unavailable, then the client's application can dynamically query the UDDI for another company that implements the same interface, i.e. that has the same <tModel>, and use that service instead.

6.3.2.2 Publishing service implementations

A WSDL service is represented by a UDDI <businessService> element and the WSDL port entity maps to a <bindingTemplate>. If the WSDL service represents a Web service interface for an existing service, there may be an existing UDDI <businessService> element that is relevant. In this case, the WSDL information can be added to that existing service. If there is no suitable existing service then a new UDDI <businessService> can be created.

The information contained in the new <businessService> references the industry implemented standards and provides additional deployment details such as:

- The <businessService> name is generated from the service name in the WSDL service implementation document.
- A <bindingTemplate> is created for each service access endpoint. The network address of the <soap:address> extension element in the service implementation is encoded in the <accessPoint> element (refer to Listing 6.3).
- One <tModelInstanceInfo> is created in the <bindingTemplate> for each <tModel> that is relevant to the service endpoint being described.

A WSDL <port> is represented by a UDDI <bindingTemplate>. The containment relationship between a WSDL service and its ports is exactly mirrored by the containment relationship between a UDDI <businessService> and its <bindingTemplate>s.

Example 6.8: Implementation model for a purchase order service

Listing 6.7 gives the <businessService> structure for the service implementation found in Listing 5.8. The service registered in Listing 6.7 shows its compliance by referring to the <portType> <tModelKey> of the purchase order service in Listing 6.6 (uuid:e8cf1163...) in the <tModelInstanceDetails> structure. It also refers to the <binding> <tModelKey> of the purchase order service (uuid:49662926-f4a...), which is not given. Listing 6.7 also includes the <accessPoint> element, which refers to the endpoint of the service or the location where it can be accessed. This corresponds to the network address of the service specified in the WSDL <service> element, and in particular the <location> attribute value of the SOAP <address> extensibility in Listing 5.8.

Figure 6.9 gives an overview of the mapping from the WSDL service interface and service implementation defiinitions to the appropriate UDDI entries. This figure gives a high level view of how the listing in the WSDL service interface (Listing 5.5) and service implementation (Listing 5.8) are associated with UDDI schema entries such as the <tModel> in Listing 6.6 and <businessService> and <bindingTemplate> in Listing 6.7.

```
<businessService
      serviceKey="102b114a..."
      businessKey="1e65ea29...">
   <name> Purchase Order Service </name>
   <bindingTemplates>
      <bindingTemplate
            bindingKey="f793c521..."
            serviceKey="102b114a...">
         <accessPoint URLType="http">
            http://www.auto-parts.com:8080/PurchaseOrderService
         </accessPoint>
         <tModelInstanceDetails>
            <tModelInstanceInfo
               tModelKey="uuid:49662926-f4a...">
               <description xml:lang="en">
                  The wsdl:binding that this wsdl:port implements.
                  The instanceParms specifies the port local name.
               </description>
               <instanceDetails>

                  <instanceParms> PurchaseOrderPort </instanceParms>
               </instanceDetails>
            </tModelInstanceInfo>
            <tModelInstanceInfo
               tModelKey="uuid:e8cf1163...">
               <description xml:lang="en">
                  The wsdl:portType that this wsdl:port implements.
              </description>
            </tModelInstanceInfo>
         </tModelInstanceDetails>

      </bindingTemplate>
   </bindingTemplates>
   <categoryBag>
      <keyedReference
         tModelKey="uuid:6e090afa..."
         keyName="WSDL type"
         keyValue="service" />
      <keyedReference
         tModelKey="uuid:d01987d1..."
         keyName="service namespace"

         keyValue=
           "http://www.auto-parts.com /PurchaseService/wsdl"/>
      <keyedReference
         tModelKey="uuid:2ec65201... "
         keyName="service local name"
         keyValue="PurchaseOrderService"/>
   </categoryBag>
</businessService>
```

Listing 6.7 UDDI <businessService> created from WSDL service implementation

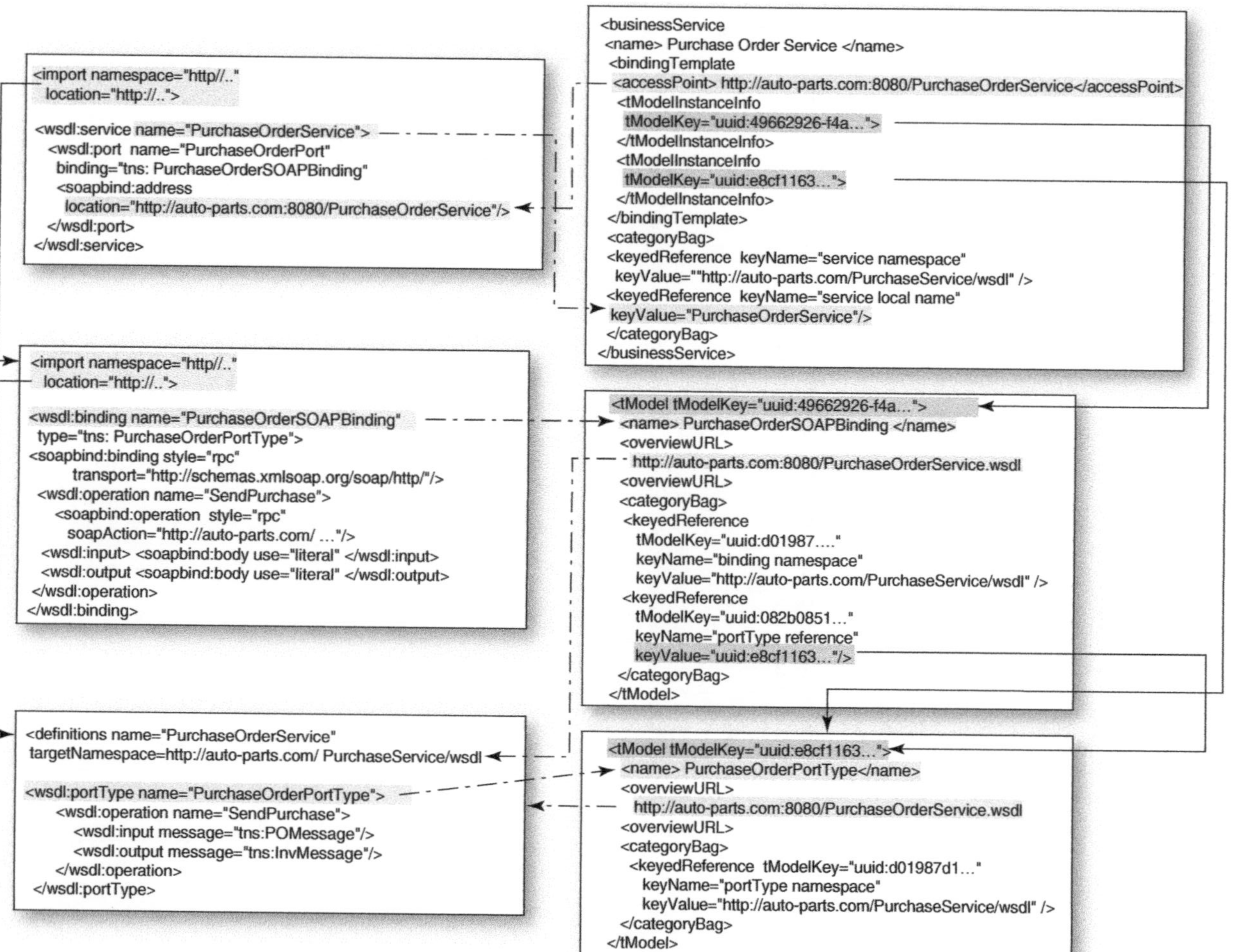

Figure 6.9 Overview of WSDL to UDDI mapping

6.3.2.3 Summary of the WSDL to UDDI mapping model

This section summarises the WSDL to UDDI mapping model. In particular, Tables 6.1 to 6.4 summarise the mapping of WSDL artifacts to the UDDI data structures `<tModel>`, `<businessService>`, and `<bindingTemplate>` according to the UDDI Technical Note [Colgrave 2004].

Table 6.1 shows that a `wsdl:portType` must be mapped to `uddi:tModel` categorised as a `<portType>`. The minimum information that must be captured about a `wsdl:portType` is its entity type, its local name, its namespace, and the location of the WSDL document that defiines the `<portType>` [Colgrave 2004]. Capturing the entity type enables users to search for `<tModel>`s that represent `<portType>` artifacts. Capturing the local name, namespace and WSDL location enables users to locate the definition of the specified `portType` artifact.

Table 6.2 shows that a `wsdl:binding` must be modeled as a `uddi:tModel` categorised as a `<binding>`. The minimum information that must be captured about a binding is its entity type, its local name, its namespace, the location of the WSDL document that defiines the binding, the `<portType>` that it implements, its protocol and, optionally, the transport information [Colgrave 2004]. Capturing the entity type enables users to search for `<tModel>`s that represent binding artifacts. The link to the `<portType>` enables users to search for bindings that implement a particular `<portType>`.

Table 6.3 shows that a `wsdl:service` must be modeled as a `uddi:businessService`. An existing `<businessService>` may be used or a new `<businessService>`

Table 6.1 Summary of mapping of wsdl:portType to uddi:tModel

WSDL	*UDDI*
portType	tModel (categorized as portType)
Local name of portType	TModel name
Namespace of portType	keyedReference in categoryBag
Location of WSDL document	overviewURL

Table 6.2 Summary of mapping of wsdl:binding to uddi:tModel

WSDL	*UDDI*
Binding	tModel (categorised as binding and wsdlSpec)
Local name of binding	tModel name
Namespace of binding	keyedReference in categoryBag
Location of WSDL document	OverviewURL
portType binding relates to	keyedReference in categoryBag
protocol from binding extension	keyedReference in categoryBag
transport from binding extension (if there is one)	keyedReference in categoryBag

Table 6.3 Summary of mapping of wsdl:service to uddi:businessService

WSDL	*UDDI*
Service	businessService (categorised as service)
Namespace of service	keyedReference in categoryBag
Local name of service	keyedReference in categoryBag; optionally also the name of the service.

Table 6.4 Summary of mapping of wsdl:port to uddi:bindingTemplate

WSDL	*UDDI*
Port	Bindingtemplate
Namespace	Captured in keyedReference of the containing businessService
Local name of port	InstanceParms of the tModelInstanceInfo relating to the tModel for the binding
Binding implemented by port	tModelInstanceInfo with tModelKey of the tModel corresponding to the binding
portType implemented by port	tModelInstanceInfo with tModelKey of the tModel corresponding to the portType

is created. Only one `wsdl:service` can be modelled by an individual `uddi:businessService`.

The minimum information that must be captured about a `wsdl:service` is its entity type, its local name, its namespace and the list of ports that it supports [Colgrave 2004]. Capturing the entity type enables users to search for services that are described by a WSDL defiinition. The list of ports provides access to the technical information required to consume the service.

Finally, the `<bindingTemplate>` element of the `<businessService>` must model the ports of the `<wsdl:service>`, as shown in Table 6.4. A `<wsdl:port>` must be modelled as a `<uddi:bindingTemplate>`. The minimum information that must be captured about a port is the binding that it implements, the `<portType>` that it implements and its local name. By capturing the binding, users can search for services that implement a specific binding. By capturing the `<portType>`, users can search for services that implement a particular `<portType>` without necessarily knowing the specific binding implemented by the service.

6.3.3 The UDDI API

Organisations and providers can use UDDI to represent information about Web services in a standard way such that queries can then be issued against a UDDI registry – at design time or run time. UDDI uses SOAP as its transport layer and this enables enterprises to interact with UDDI registries through SOAP based XML API calls in order to discover technical data about an enterprise's services.

The UDDI API is an interface that accepts XML messages wrapped in SOAP envelopes. All UDDI interactions use a request/response model, in which each message requesting a service from a UDDI registry generates some kind of response. The UDDI specifications allow two types of exchanges with UDDI registered sites: enquiries and publishing.

- The *publishing API* is used to add, update and delete data about a service in a UDDI registry.
- The *inquiry API* is used for searching a UDDI registry for information about a service based on the different classification schemes.

These inquiry and publishing functions represent the core data management tools of a UDDI registry and are described in the remainder of this section. The UDDI registry also includes optional APIs that deal with security, custody transfer and subscription APIs, which are outside the scope of this chapter. Details about these APIs can be found in [Clement 2004].

6.3.3.1 Publishing API

The publishing interface can be used by enterprises to store and update information contained in a UDDI registry. UDDI sites use publishing functions to manage the information provided to requesters. The publishing API essentially allows applications to save and delete the five UDDI data structures `<businessEntity>`, `<businessService>`, `<bindingTemplate>`, `<tModel>`, and `<publisherAssertion>` described earlier in this chapter. These calls are used by service providers and enterprises to publish and un publish information about themselves and their services in the UDDI registry. These API calls require authenticated access to the registry, unlike the inquiry API [Cauldwell 2001].

The publishing API supports four kinds of operations:

1. *Authorisation:* The authorisation operations allow a client to authenticate itself, obtain an authorisation token, and terminate a session and its authentication token. There are two authorisation operations: `get_authtoken`, which logs a client into the registry, and `discard_authtoken`, which terminates a session and logs a client out of a registry. To start a publishing session with a UDDI operator, a client must first establish an HTTPS connection with a UDDI operator and then send it a `get_authtoken` message containing its login credentials. When a client finishes accessing the UDDI publishing endpoint, it terminates its session by sending a `discard_authtoken` operation that instructs the registry to invalidate the authentication token.
2. *Save:* The save operations allow a client to add or update the primary UDDI data structures. Each of the primary UDDI data structures has a corresponding save operation except for `<publisherAssertion>`, which has special add and set operations that add and update one or more `<publisherAssertion>` entries.

3. *Delete:* The delete operations allow a client to remove information from the UDDI. Each of the primary UDDI data structures has a corresponding delete operation.
4. *Get:* The get operations allow a client to view <publisherAssertion>s. The get operations allow for obtaining summary data about data structures published by a client.

6.3.3.2 Inquiry API

Requesters can obtain information from a UDDI registry using its inquiry interface. Inquiries enable trading organisations to find businesses, services or bindings (technical characteristics) meeting certain criteria. The corresponding <businessEntity>, <businessService> or <bindingTemplate> information matching the search criteria is then returned.

The UDDI inquiry API has two usage patterns: browse and drill down. These are described briefly below.

Browse: this UDDI usage pattern allows developers to get a list of all entries (find API calls) satisfying broad criteria to find the entries, services or technical characteristics, and then use the drill down pattern (get API calls) to get the more specific features. For example, a find_business call could be first issued to locate all businesses in a specific category area, and then a get_BusinessDetail call could be used to get additional information about a specific business. The browse pattern allows for searching the UDDI registry for data structures that match some criteria. The browse pattern uses the following five operations:

1. *find_business:* This operation helps locate one or more <businessEntity> entries that match the search criteria. The search criteria are expressed in terms of categories, identifiers, <tModel>s or <discoveryURL>s. The search can be performed on the partial name of the business, the business identifiers, the category/classification identifiers or the technical fingerprints of the services. The operation returns a lightweight list of <business-Entity> listings, including their keys, names, descriptions and <businessService> names and keys.
2. *find_relatedBusinesses:* This operation is used to locate information about <businessEntity> registrations that are related to a business entity. This operation returns a lightweight list of all the businesses that have visible <publisherAsertion> relationships with a specified organisation. The search can be modified to list a subset of all related businesses, according to <keyedReference> elements.
3. *find_service:* This operation returns a lightweight list of business service entries that match the search criteria, which are expressed in terms of given categories, <tModel> keys, or both.
4. *find_binding:* This operation is used to locate specific bindings within a registered business service and returns the <bindingTemplate> entries whose

<tModel>s match the search criteria. The binding templates have information on invoking services.

5. *find_tModel:* This operation returns a list of <tModel>s that match the names, identifiers or categories listed in the request message. This operation returns a lightweight list of <tModel> keys.

Drill down: This UDDI usage pattern allows specific data structures to be requested by their unique identifiers. A drill down or get operation can return one or many of the same types of data structure, depending on how many unique identifiers are supplied in the request message.

The drill down pattern uses the following five operations:

1. *get_Business:* This operation details requests one or more <businessEntity> data structures by their unique business keys. This operation returns the complete <businessEntity> object for one or more business entities.
2. *get_BusinessDetailExt:* This operation is identical to the operation get_BusinessDetail, but returns extra attributes in case the source registry is not an operator node.
3. *get_serviceDetail:* This operation requests one or more <businessService> data structures by their unique service keys. The operation returns the complete <businessService> object for a given business service.
4. *get_bindingDetail:* This operation requests one or more <bindingTemplate> data structures by their unique binding keys. It returns the run time binding information (<bindingTemplate> structure) used for invoking methods against a business service.
5. *get_tModelDetail:* This operation requests one or more <tModel> data structures by their unique <tModel> keys. It returns <tModel> details.

6.3.4 Querying the UDDI model

The ability to programmatically query UDDI at run time allows UDDI to act as an infrastructure to build reliable, robust SOA based applications. In this section we shall display how to query the UDDI registry in order to discover information relating to businesses and their offered services. The sample queries described in this section are based on the inquiry API and can be issued at design/build time or at run time, depending on the type of application being developed. These queries are issued against the listings found in Section 6.3.1 and are largely based on similar sample queries found in [Colgrave 2003b], and [Colgrave 2004].

6.3.4.1 Retrieving information about businesses

In this subsection we shall focus on queries that retrieve information about businesses.

Example 6.9: Finding a business entity by name

```
<find_business xmlns="urn:uddi-org:api_v3">
   <name xml: lang="en"> Automotive Equipment Manufacturing Inc. </name>
   <name xml: lang="en"> Manufacturing Goods Co. </name>

</find_business>
```

Query 6.1 Finding business entities by name

Query 6.1 performs an OR search (default case) for businesses matching the names specified in the query predicate. Query 6.1 returns the business entity with name Automotive Equipment Manufacturing Inc. and `businesKey="d2300-3aff..."` found in Listing 6.1.

Example 6.10: Finding a business entity by key

```
<find_business xmlns="urn:uddi-org:api_v3">

<categoryBag>
   <!—North American Industry Classification System (NAICS) -->
   <keyedReference

            keyName="Automotive parts distribution"
            keyValue="..."
            tModelKey="..."/>
    ......
</categoryBag>
</find_business>
```

Query 6.2 Finding `<businessEntity>` entries by category

Query 6.2 returns a list of businesses with matching `<keyedReference>` values. Only those `<businessEntity>` entries that declare the `<keyedReference>` values involved in the `<categoryBag>` in the query will yield a match. Query 6.2 returns the business entity with `businesKey="d2300-3aff..."` found in Listing 6.1.

6.3.4.2 Retrieving technical service information

In the remainder of this section we shall concentrate mainly on issuing queries involving <tModel>s to retrieve technical information regarding services that are the point of interest. Recall from the previous section that all WSDL service interfaces are published in a UDDI registry as a <tModel> (see Figure 6.6). Each of these <tModel>s is categorised to identify it as a WSDL service description. WSDL service interface descriptions can be found using the UDDI inquiry API.

The UDDI find_tModel message is used to retrieve <tModel>s that have been categorised. This message will return a list of <tModel> keys. Using the drill down get_tModelDetail message, applications and developers can then retrieve a specific service interface description. This message could, for instance, return a <tModel> such as the one given in Listing 6. Additional <keyedReference>s can be added to the <categoryBag> to limit the set of <tModel>s that are returned in response to the find_tModel message. After a <tModel> has been retrieved, the overview URL can be used to retrieve the contents of a WSDL service interface document [Brittenham 2001a].

Example 6.11: Finding a technical for a purchase order service

```
<find_tModel xmlns="urn:uddi-org:api_v3">
   <name> PurchaseOrderPortType </name>
   <categoryBag>
      <keyedReference
         tModelKey="uuid:d01987d1..."
         keyName="portType namespace"
         keyValue="http://www.auto-parts.com/PurchaseOrderService/wsdl"/>

      <keyedReference
         tModelKey="uuid:6e090afa..."
         keyName="WSDL type"
         keyValue="portType"/>
   </categoryBag>
</tModel>
```

Query 6.3 Finding the <tModel> for <portType> name

Query 6.3 is a simple query that finds the <portType Model> for PurchaseOrderPortType in the namespace "http://auto-parts.com/PurchaseService/wsdl". This query should return the tModelKey="uuid:e8cf1163..." found in Listing 6.6.

```
<find_tModel xmlns="urn:uddi-org:api_v3">
   <categoryBag>

      <keyedReference
         tModelKey="uuid:6e090afa..."
         keyName="WSDL type"
         keyValue="binding" />
      <keyedReference
         tModelKey="uuid:082b0851... "
         keyName="portType reference"
         keyValue="uuid:e8cf1..." />
   </categoryBag>
</tModel>
```

Query 6.4 Find all `<binding tModel>` for PurchaseOrderPortType

Query 6.4 finds all `<binding tModel>` for a `PurchaseOrderPortType` that has a corresponding `<portType tModel>` with a key of `tModelKey="uuid:082b0851..."`, regardless of the protocol and/or transport specified in the binding. This query returns the `tModelKey="uuid:49662926-f4a..."`. If a particular protocol and/or transport is required, then extra `<keyedReference>`s involving a messaging protocol, such as SOAP, and/or transfer protocol, such as HTTP, can be added to the predicate of the previous query as necessary.

More information about the UDDI APIs can be found in references such as [Brittenham 2001a], [Colgrave 2003b], [Colgrave 2004], and [Clement 2004].

6.3.5 Service registry usage model and deployment variants

A service registry usage model is concerned with helping ensure that global registry information is always available and readily accessible to all of its users. A service registry usage model envisages at least three different business information provider roles such as:

- *Registry operators:* These refer to the organisations that host and operate a public registry, such as the UDDI Business Registry, which is considered as a cornerstone of Web services architecture because it enables businesses to register and discover Web services via the Internet. The operator nodes manage and maintain the directory information, and cater for replication of business information and other directory related functions. These operators provide a Web interface to the UDDI registry for browsing, publishing and un publishing business information.
- *Standards bodies and industry consortia:* These publish descriptions in the form of technical service type defiinitions. These defiinitions (`<tModel>`s in the case of UDDI) do not contain the actual service defiinitions; instead they contain a URL that points to the location where the service descriptions are stored.

- *Service providers:* Commonly implement Web services conforming to service type defiinitions such as those supported by UDDI. They publish information about their business and services in a service registry. The published data also contains the endpoint of the Web services offered by these enterprises.

From the discussion until now, several patterns emerge for potential use of a service registry. Based on the kind of information stored in the registry, such as UDDI, it can be used simply to get contact information for a business entity (*white pages* style information) or to understand the interaction pattern of a service and communicate with it (*green pages* style information). These service registry deployment patterns can be classified into several categories as follows:

- *Private service registry:* A private registry is an internal registry that resides behind a firewall and is isolated from the public network. Access to both administrative features and registry data is restricted. Data is not shared with other registries. This type of registry enables developers to publish and test internal SOA based applications in a secure, private environment. This is by far the most commonly used deployment model for UDDI today.
- *Public service registry:* In contrast to a private registry, a public service registry is a collection of peer directories that contain information about businesses and services. From an end user's perspective, a public registry appears to be a service in a cloud (see Chapter 18). Although administrative functions may be secured, access to the registry data itself is essentially open and public. Data may be shared or transferred among other registries, and content may or may not be moderated. The public registry helps locate services that are registered at one of its peer nodes and facilitates the discovery of published Web services. Data is replicated at each of the registries on a regular basis. This ensures consistency in service description formats and makes it easy to track changes as they occur.

In addition to these two standard deployment variants we may also distinguish the following service registry deployment possibilities:

- *Affiliated registry:* A registry deployed within a controlled environment, but with limited access by authorised clients. Administrative features may be delegated to trusted parties. Data may be shared with other registries in a controlled manner. This variant is typical of a trading partner network (or service market place), which is a local community of service providers and requesters organised in vertical markets and gathering around portals. A standards body, or a consortium of organisations that participate and compete in the industry can host this private service node. The entries in this private UDDI relate to a particular industry or narrow range of related industries. This gives rise to the idea of a Web services discovery agency (or service broker) that is the organisation (acting as a third trusted party) whose primary activities focus on hosting the registry, publishing and promoting Web services.
- *Portal registry:* This type of deployment is on an enterprise's firewall and could be a private UDDI node that contains only metadata related to the enterprise's Web

services. External users of the portal would be allowed to invoke find operations on the registry; however, a publish operation would be restricted to services internal to the portal. The portal UDDI gives a company ultimate control over how the metadata describing its Web services is used. For example, an enterprise can restrict access. It can also monitor and manage the number of lookups being made against its data and potentially get information about who the interested parties are.

- *Internal division registry:* This is a private registry variant that allows applications in different departments of the organisation to publish and discover services, and is useful to develop segregated registries corresponding to diverse divisions that are parts of large organisations. The major distinction of this variant is the potential for an administrative domain that can be formed according to specific standards (e.g. a fixed set of `<tModel>`s can be used).

The service registry deployment patterns listed above can be combined and result in a variety of distributed service registry topologies. The possibilities have expanded from a stand alone, single registry approach to include hierarchical, peer based, delegated and others. In short, the structure of a service registry (or registries) can now reflect the realities and relationships of the underlying business processes that it supports.

Managing multiple versions of registry entries presents a challenge, but it is a critical aspect of managing this sort of distributed infrastructure. Standards such as UDDI provide guidance to help facilitate the maintenance and mapping of UDDI based keys and records across registries. However, it is up to the registry operators and software developers to design and implement a wide range of business policies and constructs on top of the basic UDI infrastructure to facilitate the consistency of registry entries and records.

6.4 Summary of learning objectives

One of the most important elements of SOA application efficacy is the ease with which services are discovered and reused to resolve new servicing requirements. Lack of knowledge or poor descriptions of available services is a potential failure of SOA applications. Service registration and discovery mechanisms and tools have been developed to this effect.

The most prominent approach to service registration and discovery is the Universal Description, Discovery and Integration specification, which provides a platform independent way of describing services, discovering businesses, and integrating business services using the Internet. Conceptually, the information provided in a UDDI consists of three interrelated components:

- *white pages* that include address, contact, and other key points of contact;
- *yellow pages* that provide information according to industrial classifications based on standard industry taxonomies;
- *green pages* that describe the technical capabilities and information about services, which are exposed by the business, and may include references to specifications for Web services.

Standard inquiry and publishing operations form the core data management mechanisms that operate on the UDDI data structures and provide detailed business or technical service information to its users.

Review questions

- What are service registries and what is service discovery?
- What is the UDDI and what are its major characteristics?
- What are operator nodes?
- Describe the UDDI data structures and their interrelationships in UML.
- What is a `<businessEntity>` and what are its major sub-elements?
- Which data structure in UDDI is used to describe Web service access information?
- What is a `<tModel>` and how does it describe technical service information?
- How does UDDI differentiate between service interface and service implementation?
- What is the purpose of a WSDL to UDDI mapping model?
- Describe the concept of a UDDI API for registering and finding service information.
- Describe how the UDDI model can be queried.
- Explain why it is useful to have various UDDI deployment variants. Briefly describe two important private UDDI variants.

Exercises

6.1. Give an example of a `<businessEntity>` and a `<tModel>`.

6.2. Give an example of a `<businessService>` associated with the `<businessEntity>` you specified in Exercise 6.1. Additionally, give an example of a `<bindingTemplate>` associated with this `<businessService>`.

6.3. Write a query that finds all the implementations of the `PurchaseOrderPortType` in Listing 6.6. This query should use the APIs `find_service` and `find_binding`.

6.4. If we wish to query `<businessService>`s in their own right, as opposed to querying them as part of querying `<bindingTemplate>`s, then it is possible to use any combination of the service's WSDL related information (the service name, its namespace, and the fact that the `<businessService>` corresponds to a WSDL service) and generic UDDI information, primarily categorisations of the service. Write a query that finds the `<businessService>` for `PurchaseOrderService` in the namespace `"http://auto-parts.com/PurchaseService/wsdl"` in Listing 6.6.

6.5. Consider Listings 5.7 and 5.8, which fully describe a purchase order service. Show how these WSDL documents can be decomposed into two `<tModel>`s (one for the `<portType>` and one for the binding) and one `<businessService>` with one `<bindingTemplate>`.

6.6. Write queries to find the `<portType>` `<tModel>` and all bindings for the `PurchaseOrderPortType`.

PART IV

Event notification and Service Oriented Architectures

CHAPTER 7

Service addressing and notification

Learning objectives

Event driven SOA implementations rely on event processing and notification. This form of processing introduces a notification pattern for SOAs whereby an information-providing service sends messages to one or more interested parties and the message frequently carries information about an event that has occurred. Event notification unifies the principles and concepts of SOA with those of event based programming.

In this chapter we describe critical components of the Web services notification infrastructure such as handling stateful resources, transport neutral mechanisms for addressing Web services and messages and using topic based publish/subscribe mechanisms. After completing this chapter you will understand the following key concepts:

- The concept of an endpoint reference.
- Mechanisms for routing messages and addressing Web services.
- Event processing and notification mechanisms for Web services.
- The WS-Notification family of specifications.
- Peer-to-peer notifications and topic based notification patterns.

The material presented in this chapter is used to lay the groundwork for more advanced material that relates to event driven SOAs and the Enterprises Service Bus (see Chapter 8).

Chapter preview

Event processing plays a vital role in SOA as it enhances it to cover event driven and hybrid applications involving events and services.

This chapter presents the foundational topics of event processing and notification that bring about SOA implementations and form the spine of the Enterprise Service Bus. We begin by explaining how Web services in an SOA are referenced and subsequently introduce the WS-Addressing standard that provides transport neutral mechanisms to address Web services and messages. Following this, we introduce the WS-Notification standard and explain how SOA implementations manage event subscribers and topics, how they handle filer expressions, and broker notifications.

7.1 Referencing and addressing Web services

Web services need to provide transport neutral mechanisms to address Web services and messages that go beyond the classical WSDL Request-Response interaction pattern in which the service endpoint receives a message and returns a message or fault in response. As we already explained in Chapter 5, normally Web services are invoked by the service endpoint information that is provided by WSDL. For instance, a WSDL service port has a location address, which identifies the endpoint.

In an SOA world, producers and consumers are loosely coupled with each other through virtual channels, called publish and subscribe channels or point-to-point channels (see Section 2.6.2). With SOA applications the producer does not need to know which applications are receiving a message and the consumer does not need to know which applications are sending the data. In SOA a service endpoint is suitable in most cases for referencing Web services, with the exception of stateful Web services and cases that add more dynamic information to the service address. This includes instance information, policy, complex binding, asynchronous behaviour and so on. Like these, stateful services and dynamic interactions require a client or run time system uniquely to identify a service at run time, based on run time information. This binding specific information could include a unique identifier.

The challenge is to design the model in such a way that it adheres to industry standards and complies with the rules of SOA and, at the same time, provides transport neutral mechanisms to address Web services and messages. One such mechanism is the use of Enterprise Service Bus (see Chapter 8) as a service transport and routing channel, and the use of Web service standards (WS-Addressing and WS-Base Notification) as carriers of message information.

This chapter continues where Chapters 4 and 5 broke off, by explaining how SOAP messages and services defined in WSDL can be expanded by employing flexible addressing mechanisms that are provided by the WS-Addressing specification.

7.1.1 WS-Addressing

SOAP does not provide any feature to identify endpoints; and normal endpoints like message destination, fault destination and message intermediary are delegated to the transport layer. To close this gap, WS-Addressing provides transport neutral mechanisms that allow Web services to communicate addressing information [Bosworth 2004]. The main purpose of WS-Addressing is to incorporate message addressing information into Web service messages. Combining WS-Addressing with SOAP makes it a real message oriented specification.

WS-Addressing provides a uniform addressing method for SOAP messages travelling over synchronous and/or asynchronous transports. Additionally, it provides addressing features to help Web service developers build applications around a variety of messaging patterns beyond the typical exchange of requests and responses.

WS-Addressing defines how message headers direct messages to a service, provides an XML format for exchanging endpoint references, and defines mechanisms to direct replies or faults to a specific location. It also enables messaging systems to support message transmission through networks that include processing nodes, such as endpoint managers, firewalls and gateways in a transport neutral manner.

The WS-Addressing standard designates that addressing and action information, normally embedded in communication transport headers, should be placed within the SOAP envelope. In accordance with this, WS-Addressing provides a set of standardised SOAP headers that support [Bosworth 2004]:

- Message functionality that is used to identify, route, deliver and correlate messages.
- Complex synchronous and asynchronous messaging conventions.
- Communication with and between clients and stateful service instances.

To achieve its purposes WS-Addressing defines two constructs [Bosworh 2004]:

1. endpoint references;
2. message addressing properties.

These convey information that is typically provided by transport protocols and messaging systems in an interoperable manner. Endpoint references and message addressing properties normalise this kind of information into a uniform format that can be processed independently of transport or application. We describe briefly endpoint references and message addressing property constructs below.

7.1.1.1 Endpoint references

The WS-Addressing standard defines a schema for a portable address construct known as an endpoint reference. An *endpoint reference* provides an address, not an identity, where a Web service can be contacted and invoked. A Web service endpoint reference is the equivalent of an XML representation of a Web service pointer. The address construct is a URI that is used to provide the logical address of an endpoint, and appears in the header block of every SOAP message targeted at that endpoint.

Endpoint references must contain the address of a service along with metadata descriptions, such as service name, port name, port type and WS-Policy statements that describe the requirements, capabilities and preferences of the service. Such properties allow discovery of contract details and policies.

Endpoint references are designed to support the following usage scenarios:

- *Dynamic addressing:* End point reference parameters can be used dynamically to generate and customise service endpoint descriptions.
- *Service instance routing:* End point reference parameters can be used to identify specific service instances that are created as the result of stateful interactions.
- *State messaging:* End point reference parameters can be used to hold and express state information that has specific meaning to a Web service.

In WS-Addressing the term end point reference denotes any XML message element of the type `<wsa:EndpointReferenceType>`.

7.1.1.2 Message addressing properties

WS-Addressing defines a set of message addressing properties that collectively augment a message with the following abstract properties to support one-way, request-response, and other interaction patterns. These provide references for the endpoints involved in an interaction. Message addressing properties essentially allow developers to add processing and delivery instructions into the SOAP message itself.

The WS-Addressing message addressing properties are:

- *destination:* Contains an Internationalized Resource Identifier (IRI) representing the address of the intended receiver of this message.
- *source endpoint:* Reference to the endpoint from which the message originated.
- *reply endpoint:* An endpoint reference for the intended receiver for replies to this message.
- *fault endpoint:* An endpoint reference for the intended message recipient to communicate faults related to processing this message.
- *action:* Contains an IRI that uniquely identifies the overall intent implied by this message.
- *message id:* An absolute IRI that uniquely identifies a message. It can be used for various purposes including tracking and correlation with other messages.
- *relationship:* A pair of values that indicate how this message relates to another message.
- *reference parameters*: Is used to add details that will be used to extend an address with parameters.

The Internationalized Resource Identifier, used in the message addressing properties above, is a means to identify Internet resources using non-ASCII characters that cannot be present in URLs. The WS-Addressing headers are introduced in the following example.

Example 7.1: Specifying message address properties

The sample code in Listing 7.1 illustrates a message containing message addressing properties serialised as header blocks in a SOAP 1.2 message. More specifically, it demonstrates the use of these WS-Addressing mechanisms in a SOAP 1.2 message being sent from the site `http://myclient.com/business/someClient` to the site `http://www.auto-parts.com/purchasing`.

```
<Soap:Envelope xmlns:Soap="http://www.w3.org/2003/05/soap-envelope"
               xmlns:wsa="http://www.w3.org/2005/08/addressing">
    <Soap:Header>
        <wsa:MessageID>
            uuid:SomeUniqueMessageIdString
        </wsa:MessageID>
        <wsa:ReplyTo>
          <!-- End point reference for intended receiver
                                          of message reply -->
           <wsa:Address>
             http://myclient.com/business/someClient
           </wsa:Address>
        </wsa:ReplyTo>
        <!-- End point reference for ultimate receiver of message -->
        <wsa:To> http://www.auto-parts.com/purchasing </wsa:To>
        <wsa:Action> http://www.auto-pars.com/SubmitPO </wsa:Action>
    </Soap:Header>
    <Soap:Body>
         <!-- The message body of the SOAP request appears here -->
         <SubmitPO> ... </SubmitPO>
    </Soap:Body>
</Soap:Envelope>
```

Listing 7.1 A typical SOAP message using WS-Addressing

In Listing 7.1, the lines included in the SOAP header first specify the identifier for this message, and the endpoint to which replies to this message should be sent as an endpoint reference. The message addressing property construct `<wsa:MessageID>` specifies an IRI that uniquely identifies a message; the construct `<wsa:From>` specifies the endpoint where the message originated from; while the construct `<wsa:To>` specifies the address of the intended receiver of this message.

The construct `<wsa:ReplyTo>` specifies an endpoint reference that identifies the intended receiver for replies to this message. If a reply is expected, a message must contain a `<wsa:ReplyTo>` header. The sender must use the contents of the `<wsa:ReplyTo>` header to formulate the reply message. If the `<wsa:ReplyTo>` header is absent, the contents of the `<wsa:From>` header may be used to formulate a message to the source. This property may be absent if the message has no meaningful reply.

The last two statements in the SOAP header specify the address URI of the ultimate receiver of this message and a <wsa:Action> element, which is an identifier that uniquely (and opaquely) identifies the action semantics implied by this message, e.g. the submission of a purchase order.

Example 7.2: Identifying a car manufacturer that provides purchase services

The example in Listing 7.2 shows a sample WS-Addressing endpoint reference that identifies a car manufacturer that provides purchase services with discount prices available for premium customers. The example uses the construct <wsaw:InterfaceName> to reference a WSDL <PortType> named PurchaseOrderPortType, which is described in Listing 5.5, and is located at the endpoint IRI "http://www.auto-parts.com/PurchaseService/wsdl". The metadata section of an endpoint reference can contain a reference to a WSDL specification, can include embedded WSDL statements, or both.

```
<wsa:EndpointReference
   xmlns:wsa="http://www.w3.org/2005/08/addressing"
   xmlns:wsaw="http://www.w3.org/2006/05/addressing/wsdl"
   xmlns:wsp="http://www.w3.org/ns/ws-policy"
   xmlns:tns="http://www.auto-parts.com/PurchaseService/wsdl">
   <wsa:Address> http://auto-parts.com/PurchaseService/wsdl
   </wsa:Address>
   <wsa:Metadata>
       <wsaw:InterfaceName>
          tns:PurchaseOrderPortType
      </wsaw:InterfaceName>
      <wsaw:ServiceName>
          tns:PurchaseOrderService
      </wsa:ServiceName>
   </wsa:Metadata>
   <wsa:ReferenceProperties>
       <tns:CustomerServiceLevel> Premium </tns:CustomerServiceLevel>
   </wsa:ReferenceProperties>
   <wsp:Policy>
       <!-- policy statement omitted for brevity -->
   </wsp:Policy>
</wsa:EndpointReference>
```

Listing 7.2 Specifying an endpoint reference

The listing also shows that policies may be included in an endpoint to facilitate easier processing by the consuming application. This is achieved by using the <wsp:Policy> element in Listing 7.2, which describes the behaviour, requirements and non-functional capabilities of the endpoint according to the WS-Policy specification, see Chapter 12.

The WS-Addressing `<EndpointReference>` in Listing 7.2 includes a `<ReferenceProperties>` child element that indicates that a reference may contain a number of individual properties, which are required to identify the entity or resource being conveyed. For instance, the reference property in Listing 7.2 indicates that the purchase order comes from a version of the service that provides purchase services with discount prices available for premium customers.

Two endpoint references that share the same IRI, but specify different reference property values, represent two different services. Reference properties are used to dispatch a request to the appropriate service. For example, an application might deploy two different versions of a service and have requests specify a target version in their reference parameters. One service version may target basic service level customers while the other could target premium service level customers.

As we have seen from Example 7.2, although WS-Addressing is independent of the other Web service specifications, it can be used in conjunction with them. This particular example shows how WS-Addressing can be used to embed WSDL or WS-Policy references with an endpoint reference. Figure 7.1 illustrates how WS-addressing relates to other Web services standards including WS-Notification that we cover in the next section.

7.2 Web Services Notification

In Chapter 2 we observed that publish-and-subscribe processing is at the heart of the functionality embodied in event driven architectures and message oriented middleware. Event driven processing and notification is especially important for the event driven SOA model (see Chapter 8) where Web services interact with each other through the exchange of asynchronous messages.

Event driven processing and notification introduces a pattern known as the *notification pattern* for SOA implementations. In the notification pattern (sometimes also referred to as the event pattern), an information providing service sends one-way messages to one or

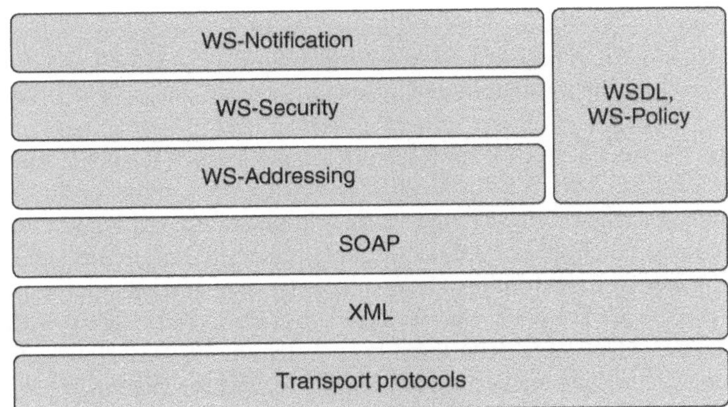

Figure 7.1 Relationship between WS-Addressing and other Web service standards

more interested receivers. It is possible that more than one consuming service is registered to consume the same information. In addition, the information providing (distributing) service may send any number of messages to each registered consuming service as the application may require. In this pattern the message frequently carries information about an event that has occurred, rather than a request that some specific action should occur. Another requirement is that message receivers are registered prior to receiving the notifications. Service registration may be initiated either by the consuming services themselves, or by a third party. Registration may be preconfigured or may happen dynamically.

The OASIS Web Services Notification is a family of related specifications that define a standard Web service approach to notification using a topic based publish/subscribe pattern. The WS-Notification specification defines standard message exchanges to be implemented by service providers that wish to participate in notifications and standard message exchanges – allowing publication of messages from entities that are not themselves service providers. The basic approach taken is to define mechanisms and interfaces that allow clients to subscribe to topics of interest. WS-Notification is intended to work together with various Web service standards, including WS-Policy and WS-ReliableMessaging.

The WS-Notification family of OASIS standards provides support for both brokered as well as peer-to-peer publish/subscribe notification and proposes three normative specifications: WS-BaseNotification, WS-Topics, and WS-BrokeredNotification. We shall examine these three OASIS standards in succession in the remainder of this chapter.

7.2.1 Peer-to-peer notification

The WS-BaseNotification specification is a standard that defines the standard interfaces of notification consumers and producers [Graham 2006]. This specification includes standard message exchanges to be implemented by service providers that wish to act in these two roles, along with operational requirements expected of them. With this specification, notification producers have to expose a subscribe operation that notification consumers can use to request a subscription. Consumers, in turn, have to expose a notify operation that producers can use to deliver the notification.

The configuration where a `NotificationConsumer` is subscribed directly to the `NotificationProducer` is referred to as the peer-to-peer, direct, or *point-to-point notification pattern*. There are other variations of the notification pattern, where the NotificationConsumer is subscribed to an intermediary `NotificationBroker` service. These are covered by the WS-BrokeredNotification specification, which we examine in Section 7.2.5.

The WS-BaseNotification is the base specification on which the other WS-Notification specifications depend. The WS-BaseNotification describes three basic roles that are required to allow a subscriber to register interest in receiving notification messages from a notification producer [Graham 2006]. These roles are: notification producer, notification consumer, publisher and a subscriber. It also includes standard message exchanges to be implemented by service providers that wish to act in these roles, along with operational requirements expected of them. The three basic roles in WS-BaseNotification and their message interaction patterns are depicted in Figure 7.2 and are examined below.

A *notification producer* is a Web service that is responsible for managing the actual process of notification. The notification producer is responsible for maintaining a list

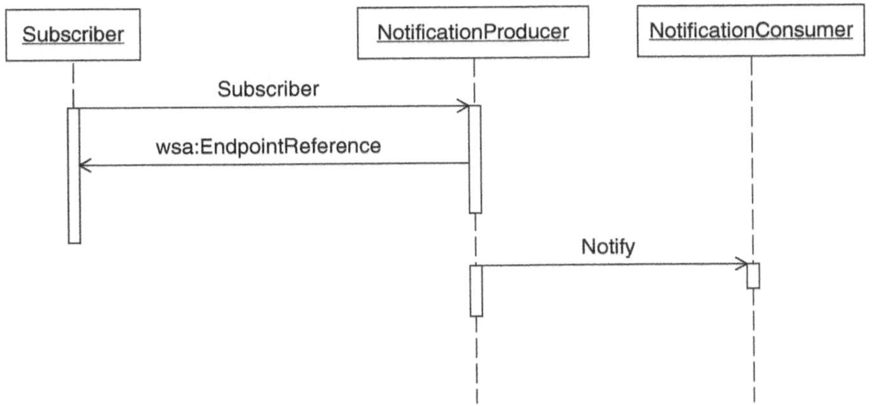

Figure 7.2 Base message exchange pattern

of interested receivers and arranging for notification messages to be delivered to those receivers. This may involve a matching step, which compares each notification message against the interests expressed by the individual receivers (notification consumers). A notification producer performs two functions: it produces notifications and handles notification subscriptions.

As shown in Figure 7.2, a notification producer accepts incoming subscribe requests where each subscribe request identifies one or more topics of interest and a reference to a notification consumer. If the notification producer is willing to accept this request, it creates a new subscription and adds it to its list of active subscriptions. The notification producer is then in a position where it can start delivering notification messages to the relevant notification consumer.

A *notification consumer* is a Web service that is the counterpart of a notification producer and receives notification messages from a notification producer. A notification can concern anything: a change in the value of a resource property, e.g. a change of status of a purchase order, a time based event, such as payment expiry, some other internal change in the state of the notification producer, or some other *situation* within the environment.

A *publisher,* which could be a notification producer that acts under this role, is an entity that creates notification messages, based upon situation(s) that it is capable of detecting and translating into notification message artifacts. The publisher selects the appropriate type of notification message and constructs a notification message instance containing information relevant to a particular situation. If the notification producer does not act as publisher, it is referred to as a *notification broker* and does not actually create notification messages, but instead manages the notification process on behalf of one or more publishers, see Section 7.2.5.

A *situation* identifies an object of interest reacting to an event. Situations in WS-Notification relate to changes of state, e.g. the purchase order changing status from pending to invoiced; time based events, e.g. expiry of a timer; or system resource related events, e.g. server breakdown. For instance, we can detect situations related to a purchase order and generate related notification messages. What is important to the notification pattern is that information relating to a particular situation can be communicated to interested services.

WS-Notification uses the term *notification* to refer to the one-way message that conveys information about a particular situation to other services. The sender of a notification message could choose to format this information in whatever way it sees fit and use a different representation for each occurrence of each situation. Notification messages include the topic associated with the message, the dialect used to specify the topic, and an optional endpoint reference to the producer. Notification messages serve as a general notification–delivery approach because they can contain any type of application specific notification message.

A single `notify` message can contain multiple notification messages, which are essential to bundle up raw messages with notification specific information, thus supporting a form of efficient batch notification delivery. The `notify` message allows the notification producer to supply additional WS-Notification defined information (such as the topic) in addition to the application specific notification message content. The notification producer maintains a list of subscriptions.

A *topic* is the concept used to categorise notifications and their related notification message schemas. Topics are used as part of the matching process that determines which (if any) subscribing notification consumers should receive a notification message. When the notification producer has a notification to distribute, it matches the notification against the interest registered in each subscription known to it. If it identifies a match, it issues the notification to the notification consumer associated with that subscription.

A *subscription* is an entity that represents the relationship between a notification consumer and a notification producer. It records the fact that the notification producer is interested in some, or even all, of the notifications that a notification producer can provide, and can contain filter expressions, policies and context information. Each notification producer holds a list of active subscriptions, and when it has a notification to perform it matches this notification against the interest registered in each subscription in its list. If it identifies a match, it performs the notification to the notification consumer associated with that subscription. In essence, a subscription represents the relationship between a notification consumer, a notification producer, a topic, and various other optional filter expressions, policies and context information.

Finally, a *subscriber* is an entity (often a Web service) that acts as a service requester, sending the subscribe request message to a notification producer, see Figure 7.2. This results in creating a subscription resource. Note that a subscriber may be a different entity than the notification consumer that actually receives the notification messages. For example, the Web service that places a purchase order request (by invoking a `SendPurchase` operation on the `PurchaseOrderPortType`) might subscribe for changes in the status of the purchase order. Alternatively, it may indicate that a separate inventory management system is the notification consumer.

To create a subscription, a subscriber must send specific information to a notification producer. This information includes a consumer endpoint reference to which the producer can send notification messages; a topic expression, which identifies the topics the consumer is interested in; and a dialect for that expression. The response to a subscription request is an endpoint reference that includes an identifier for the newly created subscription, as well as an address for a subscription manager service, which can manage the subscription (when contacted).

Figure 7.3 illustrates the WS-BaseNotification entities that we described above. The figure shows a subscriber making a subscribe request to a notification producer on behalf

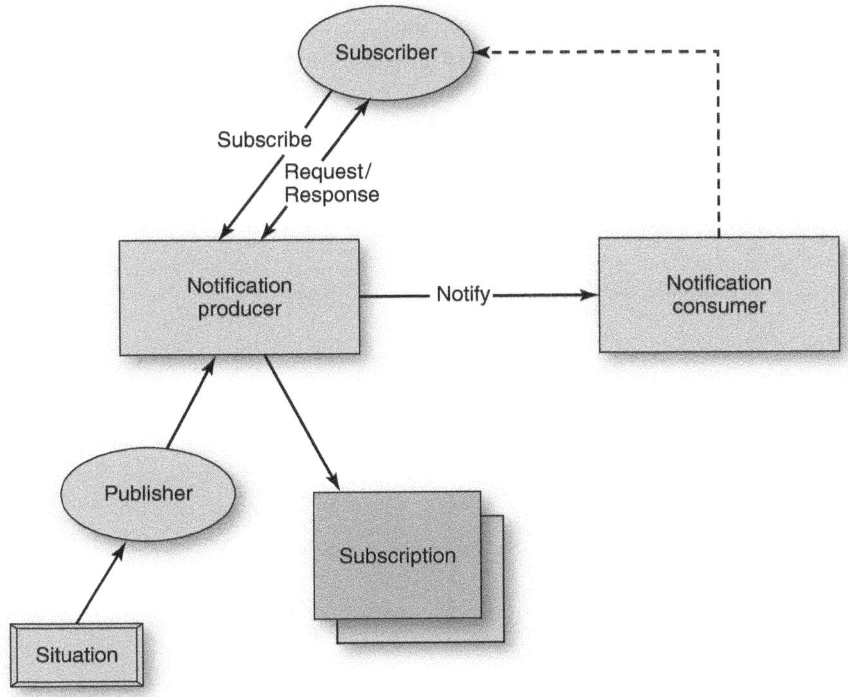

Figure 7.3 WS-BaseNotification entities

of a notification consumer (shown via the dashed lines). As a result of this request, the notification producer adds a subscription to its list of subscriptions and sends a response to the subscriber. Each subscription entry records the identity of the notification consumer, along with other properties of the subscription such as the termination time of the subscription and any filter expressions associated with it. As soon as the publisher detects a situation (e.g. expiry date of an invoice has been exceeded), then the notification producer sends a notification to the notification consumer.

7.2.2 WS-BaseNotification interfaces

The main contribution of WS-BaseNotification is twofold: to define the notification producer interface (supported by applications that accept notification subscriptions and send notification messages) and the notification consumer interface (supported by applications that subscribe to notification messages). These are briefly summarised in the following.

7.2.2.1 The notification consumer interface

WS-Notification allows a notification producer to send a notification message to a notification consumer in either one of two ways. The notification producer may simply send the raw notification message, i.e. the application specific content, to the notification consumer. Alternatively, the notification producer may send the notification message data using the notify operation. This operation implies that the notification consumer can receive a wide range of notification messages without having to explicitly provide support for each one in its WSDL.

Example 7.3: Notification message using SOAP

Listing 7.3 is an example of a notify message using SOAP.

```
<Saop:Envelope
   xmlns:Soap="http://www.w3.org/2003/05/soap-envelope"
   xmlns:wsnt="http://docs.oasis-open.org/wsn/b-2"
   xmlns:wsa="http://www.w3.org/2005/08/addressing">
  <Soap:Header>
    <wsa:Action>
         http://docs.oasis-open.org/wsn/bw-2/NotificationConsumer/Notify
    </wsa:Action>
    <wsa:To s12:mustUnderstand="1">
        http://www.consumer.org/ConsumerEndpoint
    </wsa:To>
    <ncex:NCResourceId>
       uuid: ... ...
    </ncex:NCResourceId>
  </Soap:Header>
  <Soap:Body>
    <wsnt:Notify>
      <wsnt:NotificationMessage>
        <wsnt:Topic
            dialect=
             "http://docs.oasis-open.org/wsn/t-1/TopicExpression/Simple">
              npex:SomeTopic
        </wsnt:Topic>
        <wsnt:ProducerReference>
             xmlns:npex="http://www.producer.org/RefProp">
          <wsa:Address>
             http://www.example.org/NotificationProducer
           </wsa:Address>
        </wsnt:ProducerReference>
        <wsnt:Message>
            <npex:NotifyContent>exampleNotifyContent</npex:NotifyContent>
        </wsnt:Message>
      <wsnt:NotificationMessage>
    </wsnt:Notify>
  </Soap:Body>
</Soap:Envelope>
```

Listing 7.3 Use of the notify message in conjunction with SOAP

7.2.2.2 The notification producer interface

A subscriber registers interest in receiving notification messages on one or more topics by issuing a subscribe message (operation). The subscriber sends a message to a notification producer in order to register the interest of a notification consumer for notification messages related to one or more topics.

The notification producer interface supports message exchanges that allow the notification producer to advertise its support for one or more topics, and allow a subscriber to create subscriptions or to control the delivery of notification messages by the notification producer.

To allow a newly subscribed notification consumer to get the last notification message that other notification consumers have received, a `GetCurrentMessage` message can be sent to the notification producer. In response to a `GetCurrentMessage` message, the notification producer may return the last notification message published to a given topic.

7.2.2.3 The subscription manager interface

When a notification producer accepts a subscription request, it returns an endpoint reference in its response to this request as a reference to the subscription. The Web service, whose address is carried in the endpoint reference, is in fact a subscription manager, which is a service that allows a service requester to query, delete or renew subscriptions [Niblett 2005]. The Subscription Manager provides this query capability by supporting a number of resource properties that return, for example, the subscription's filter expressions, the consumer endpoint reference, and the scheduled termination time. There are two styles of Subscription Manager interface: base and pausable.

The basic behaviour of a Subscription Manager is to renew the duration of a subscription resource and terminate a subscription. To modify the current lifetime of a subscription, a requester sends a `Renew` request message to the Subscription Manager. A `Renew` request message may contain the service requester's suggestion for change in expiration, or termination time of a subscription resource. There are two forms of this temporal component, absolute time and duration. If the Subscription Manager successfully processes the `Renew request` message, it must respond with a `Renew response` message.

```
<s:Envelope ... >
  <s:Header>
   <wsa:Action>
     http://docs.oasis-open.org/wsn/bw-2/SubscriptionManager/RenewRequest
   </wsa:Action>
   ...
  </s:Header>
  <s:Body>
   <wsnt:Renew>
     <wsnt:TerminationTime>P1D</wsnt:TerminationTime>
   </wsnt:Renew>
  </s:Body>
</s:Envelope>
```

Listing 7.4 Sample `Renew request` message

```
<s:Envelope ... >
  <s:Header>
    <wsa:Action>
      http://docs.oasis-open.org/wsn/bw-2/SubscriptionManager/RenewResponse
    </wsa:Action>
    ...
  </s:Header>
  <s:Body>
    <wsnt:RenewResponse>
      <wsnt:TerminationTime>
        2010-12-26T00:00:00.00000Z
      </wsnt:TerminationTime>
    </wsnt:RenewResponse>
  </s:Body>
</s:Envelope>
```

Listing 7.5 Sample `Renew response` message

Listings 7.4 and 7.5 present examples of a `Renew request` and a `Renew response` message using SOAP.

7.2.3 Filter expressions

Filter expressions serve to indicate the kind of notification that the consumer is interested in, by restricting the messages to be sent to a subscriber on a subscription. Filtering occurs on a per subscription basis. This means that a given notification producer may have several active subscriptions, each with different filter expressions. Moreover, a notification consumer can be the target of multiple subscriptions, each involving different filter expressions.

WS-BaseNotification defines three basic kinds of filter expression. The three kinds of filter expression defined by WS-BaseNotification are [Graham 2006]:

1. *Message filters:* A message filter is a Boolean expression evaluated over the content of a notification message. A message filter excludes all messages, which do not evaluate to true. An example of a message filter is when an inventory service requires automatic replenishment for products that fall below a certain threshold.

2. *Topic filters:* As we shall see in the next section, topics provide a convenient way of categorising kinds of notification. A topic filter excludes all notifications that do not correspond to the specified topic or list of topics.

3. *Notification producer state filters:* These filters involve expressions on the basis of some state of the notification producer itself, which is not carried in message exchanges, and which the subscriber needs to know about.

Developers are free to augment this set with filter expressions defined outside the standard.

7.2.4 Notification topics

Applications that use notifications, typically declare their interest in receiving notification messages that fulfil certain criteria, e.g. having particular content, and it is this expression of interest that is used to route messages through the network to notification consumers.

WS-Notification supports specific topics that help consumers receive only those notification messages of specific interest. The WS-Topics specification defines the features required to allow applications to work with topic oriented notification systems [Vambenepe 2006]. In particular, it defines a mechanism to organise and categorise items of interest for subscriptions known as *topics.* These constructs are used in conjunction with the notification mechanisms defined in WS-BaseNotification.

A topic is a category of notification message (see Section 7.2.1 for a proper definition of the term topic). When a subscriber creates a subscription, it associates the subscription with one or more topics to indicate which kinds of notification it is interested in. A subscriber does this by supplying a topic filter, rather than a filter specified in terms of the message body. This allows more flexibility, as topic filters are not tied to notification messages. The topic name does not have to appear in the message itself and more than one message type can be associated with a given topic.

In addition to detecting situations and creating notification messages, the notification producer is responsible for matching notifications against the list of subscriptions, and for sending the notification messages to each appropriately subscribed consumer. When the notification producer has a notification to perform, it matches this notification against subscriber interest registered in topics in its topic list. When the producer identifies a match it performs the notification to the notification consumer who subscribed with that topic [Vambenepe 2006]. This organisation allows the notification producer to declare the types of situations for which it produces notification messages. In this way, it allows a requester to understand what topics and information it can subscribe for.

7.2.4.1 Topic trees and spaces

A collection of related topics is used to organise and categorise a set of notification messages. Topics are organised hierarchically into a *topic tree* that provides a convenient means by which subscribers can reason about notifications of interest [Vambenepe 2006]. Each topic tree contains a *root topic.* This hierarchical topic structure allows subscribers to subscribe against multiple topics. For example, a subscriber can subscribe against an entire topic tree or a subset of the topics in a topic tree. This reduces the number of subscription requests that a subscriber needs to issue if it is interested in a large subtree. It also means that a subscriber can receive notification messages related to descendant topics without having to be specifically aware of their existence.

Topics are arranged within *topic spaces,* which use XML namespaces to avoid topic definition clashes. A topic space is a collection (forest) of topic trees. The topic space contains additional metadata describing how its member topics can be modelled as an XML document. All root topics must have unique names within their topic space. A topic space associates topic trees with a namespace in such a way that each topic tree can be uniquely identified by the name of the root of its topic tree. Child topics can only be referred to relative to their ancestor root topic using a path based topic expression dialect.

A topic space is not tied to a particular notification producer. It contains an abstract set of topic definitions, which can be used by many different notification producers. It is also possible for a given notification producer to support topics from several different topic spaces. A notification producer can support an entire topic tree, or just a subset of the topics in that topic tree. The list of topics supported by the notification producer may change over time, by supporting additional topics from a topic space not previously supported or by supporting extension topics to a (new or already supported) topic space.

Example 7.4: Topic trees describing payment methods and company orders

As an example of a sample topic space that contains two hierarchically organised topic trees, consider the diagram depicted in Figure 7.4. This figure describes a topic space named `"http://auto-parts.com/topicsSpace/order-mgt-example/"`. The topic space uses WS-Notification to specify two root topics, one describing payment methods while the other represents company orders. As part of a payment application, one can model a payment method that is the root topic of all topics related to payment. There might be several sub-categories of the payment method, including paying by credit card, by cheque, or direct transfer order. These subtopics are organised as descendants of the payment method root topic in Figure 7.4.

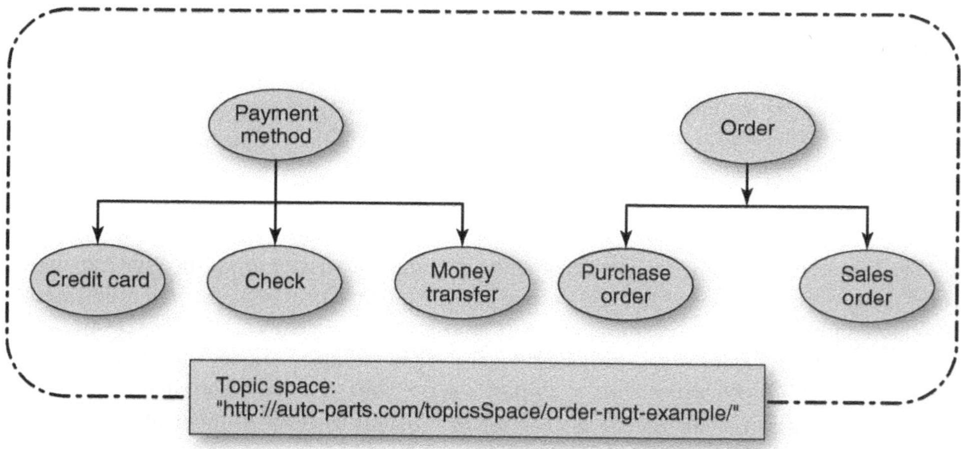

Figure 7.4 Sample topic space

7.2.4.2 The WS-Topics specification

The WS-Notification specifications allow the use of the WS-Topics specification as a way to organise and categorise a set of notifications. WS-Topics is a Web service specification that works as part of the WS-Notification specification family, providing a convenient means to define and address topics (event notifications) to which Web service consumers can subscribe, as well as organising them into complex structures allowing hierarchies (topic trees) and synonyms (topic aliasing).

The WS-Topics XML Schema contains element and type definitions used to create `Topic Namespace` documents. A `Topic Namespace` document is associated with a single `Topic Namespace` and contains the names of topics in that `Topic Namespace` along with their metadata.

Example 7.5: Specifying a money transfer topic space

The code snippet in Listing 7.6 illustrates how a topic space can be specified using the WS-Topics XML model. This listing illustrates that an optional name can be assigned to each topic space element for documentation purposes. Each topic may contain a `messageTypes` attribute that defines the types of notification message that may be used in conjunction with the topic. The purpose of this attribute is to scope the contents of notification messages associated with the topic [Vambenepe 2006]. For example, in the case of a money transfer payment, the listing indicates that all notification messages associated with the money transfer topic are `MoneyTransferNotification` conformant messages. The `messageTypes` attribute thus contains information helpful to design the appropriate selector expressions to filter messages on a subscribe request. Each topic may also contain an optional attribute, called final, whose default value is *false*. If the value is *true* it indicates that the notification producer cannot dynamically add any further child topics to this topic.

```
<?xml version="1.0" encoding="UTF-8"?>
<wstop: TopicNamespace name="TopicSpaceOrderMgt-Example"
   targetNamespace="auto-supply.com/topicsSpace/orderMgt-example"
   xmlns:tns="http://auto-parts.com/topicsSpace/orderMgt-example"
   xmlns:wstop="http://docs.oasis-open.org/wsn/t-1">
   <wstop:topic name="PaymentMethod">
      <wstop:topic name="CreditCard"
             messageTypes="tns:CreditCardPaymentNotification"/>
      <wstop:topic name="Check"
             messageTypes="tns:CheckPaymentNotification"/>
      <wstop:topic name="MoneyTransfer"
             messageTypes="tns:MoneyTransferNotification" final="false">
   </wstop:topic>

   <wstop:topic name="Order">
      <wstop:topic name="PurchaseOrder"
             messageTypes="tns:m1" ... />
      <wstop:topic name="SalesOrder"
             messageTypes="tns:m2" ... />
         ... ... ...
   </wstop:topic>
</wstop:topicSpace>
```

Listing 7.6 Sample WS-Topics topics space definition

A important feature of the WS-Topics specification is that it supports several *topic expressions,* which are used to identify topics in subscribe and notify messages, as well as to indicate the topics that notification producers support. The WS-Topics standard specifies several topic expressions, ranging from a simple approach that refers only to root topics within a given topic space to an approach that uses Xpath like expressions to refer to topics. The three topic expression dialects that can be used as subscription expressions in WS-Topic are as follows:

1. *Simple topic expressions:* These are defined in terms of a simple topic expression language for use by resources that are constrained entities in the WS-Notification system that deal only with simple topic spaces.
2. *Concrete topic path expressions:* These are used to identify exactly one topic within a topic space by employing a path notation. Concrete path expressions employ a simple path language that is similar to file paths in hierarchical directory structures.
3. *Full topic path expressions:* The full topic expression dialect builds on the concrete topic dialect by adding wildcard characters and logical operations. Full topic path expressions are made up of XPath expressions, which are evaluated over a document whose nodes are made up of the topics in the topic space and where topics include their child topics as contained XML elements.

More information as well as examples of WS-Topic expressions can be found in [Vambenepe 2006].

7.2.5 Brokered notification

The kind of direct connection approach, adopted by the peer-to-peer notification (or direct) pattern, is useful in closed systems in which producer and consumer applications know each other and are unaffected by the coupling introduced by direct connections between notification producers and consumers. However, most event based systems (see, for instance, the event driven Enterprise Service Bus in Section 8.5) seek to completely decouple notification producers and consumers. To achieve this, the WS-BrokeredNotification specification was created [Chappell 2006]. This specification introduces an additional role, called a notification broker, as an intermediary, which allows the publisher/subscribers to be decoupled, and thus provides greater scalability.

A notification broker is an intermediary Web service that is designed to provide scalable notification handling that decouples notification consumers from publishers. Notification brokers operate as intermediaries between producer and consumer applications, such that producers and consumers each know about the broker but do not know about each other. A notification broker takes on the role of both notification producer and notification consumer (as defined in WS-BaseNotification), and its interactions with other notification producers and notification consumers are largely defined by the WS-Base Notification specification.

The notification broker, as defined by WS-BrokeredNotification, is an extension of the capabilities offered by a basic notification producer. These extensions include [Graham 2006]:

- Relieving a publisher from having to implement message exchanges associated with a notification producer. The notification broker takes on the duties of a subscription manager (managing subscriptions) and notification producer (distributing notification messages) on behalf of the publisher.
- Reducing the number of inter-service connections and references, in cases where there exist many publishers and many notification consumers.
- Acting as a finder service to facilitate potential publishers and subscribers effectively to find each other.
- Providing anonymous notification, so that publishers and notification consumers need not be aware of each other's identity.

The notification broker on the incoming side fulfills the notification consumer interface, while on the outgoing side it fulfils the notification producer interface. To a notification producer, the broker appears as a consumer but, to a consumer, it appears as a producer.

An implementation of a notification broker may provide an additional added value function that is beyond the scope of the WS-BrokeredNotification specification. For example, WS-Notification features and composable features of related standards, which provide facilities such as logging notification messages for auditing purposes, or using facilities such as authentication, message persistence, message integrity, message encryption, delivery guarantees and so on, are offloaded to a broker. This brokered implementation has one additional benefit, namely that publishers need never know anything about any of the subscribers. The complete decoupling of subscribers from publishers, along with the centralised subscription and topic management, provides enterprises with more control and allows more accurate measures of performance against SLAs.

The diagram depicted in Figure 7.5 illustrates a possible sequence of brokered message exchanges. In the brokered case, the sequence of message exchanges between a subscriber and the notification broker is the same as the sequence of message exchanges between a subscriber and notification producer in the non-brokered case in Figure 7.2. The only difference is that, instead of interacting directly with the ultimate notification consumers, publishers interact with the notification broker using a sequence of message exchanges supported by the notification broker. This is implemented as follows:

- The publisher publishes a notification message to the notification broker, using the notify message.
- Subsequently, the notification broker delivers the notification messages to any notification consumer identified by subscriptions that match the publication.

Because the publish function is implemented by sending the notify message, a notification broker appears to the publisher as any other notification consumer. This

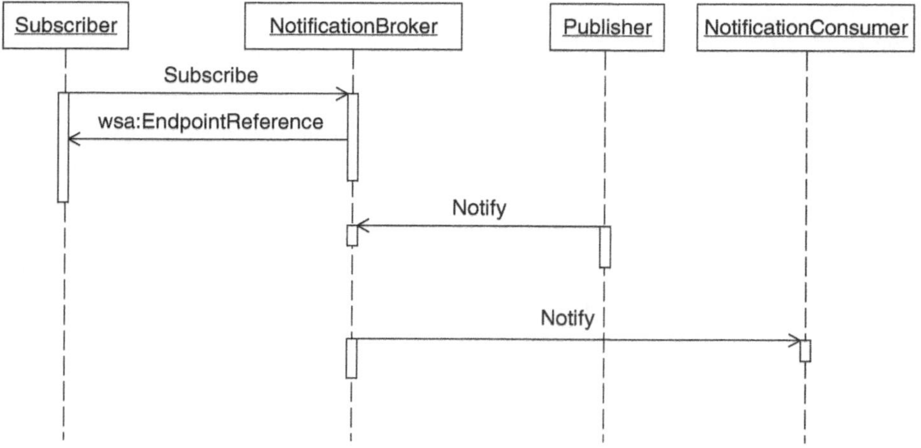

Figure 7.5 Brokered message exchange patterns

allows notification brokers to be inserted into the message flow (for instance, for auditing purposes) without the publisher needing to change the way it sends its notification messages.

As a final remark, the WS-Notification family of standards currently outlines only the push delivery mode for notifications, which is based on a fully fledged publish/subscribe model. The push model is one in which notifications are pushed to the consumer. An advantage of the push model is that notifications are routed to the consumer as soon as they are available. WS-Notification also incorporates support for delegated delivery of notifications, where an intermediary, the broker, can push notifications to the consumer.

7.3 Summary of learning objectives

Describing business activities as a series of events is a critical requirement for most SOAs, as it pulls attention away from the fundamental architectural goal of building a centralised SOA management model. Instead, it treats event handling capabilities as part of a full featured SOA — along with numerous other capabilities, such as policy based processing, multichannel coordination, reliable messaging filtered message delivery, and more. Dealing with such concerns requires the following approach, which was covered in this chapter:

- A standard addressing mechanism to enable intermediate message handling, message forwarding, and multiple message transports in a single message path.
- A standard Web services approach to notification using a topic based publish/subscribe pattern.

- A standard Web service scheme to define and address event notifications (topics) to which Web service consumers can subscribe, as well as organising these into complex structures allowing hierarchies (topic trees) in subscribe request messages and other important parts of an SOA based application.

Review questions

- Describe the problem of addressing with stateful Web services.
- What type of usage scenarios are endpoint references designed to support?
- What is Web service addressing and what is a Web service endpoint reference?
- What is the purpose of the notification pattern for SOA implementations?
- What are the three basic roles that are required to allow a subscriber to register interest in receiving notification messages from a notification producer?
- What is the purpose of WS-BaseNotification and what kind of notifications does it support?
- What is the meaning of the term situation for WS-Notification?
- What are notification topics?
- Describe the three topic expression dialects that can be used with the WS-Topic standard.
- What is WS-BrokeredNotication and how does it relate to WS-BaseNotification?

Exercises

7.1. Assume that, when an insurance claim is submitted from an insurance agent to an insurance company, message routing and delivery information, such as endpoint addresses, must be provided. Use WS-Addressing headers in SOAP messages with reference properties and parameters to achieve this purpose.

7.2. In a domestic application, autonomous devices may interact asynchronously using WS-Notification publish/subscribe mechanisms. The events could be, for instance, topic based, representing critical factors such as fire, gas presence, and the health status of an inhabitant. Write a program to manage a simple WS-Notification topic namespace like the one illustrated in the example below. The program must be able to parse the XML file, recognise its tree structure, and show it to the user in a meaningful way. Moreover, the program should allow the user to modify the tree (adding, renaming or removing nodes as required). All the events the publisher can generate are specified in the topic namespace below.

```
<?xml version="1.0" encoding="UTF-8"?>

<wstop:TopicNamespace name="Event"
  targetNamespace="http://publisher.domotic.com/topicnamespace.xml"
  xmlns:wstop="xmlns:wstop="http://docs.oasis-open.org/wsn/t-1">
      <wstop:topic name="Alarm events">
            <wstop:topic name="Fire presence"/>
            <wstop:topic name="Gas presence"/>
      </wstop:topic>
      <wstop:topic name="Health events">
            <wstop:topic name="Arm dislocation"/>
            <wstop:topic name="Irregular heartbeat"/>
      </wstop:topic>
</wstop:topicSpace>
```

7.3. Extend Exercise 7.2 by adding the possibility to read and store incoming WS-Notification subscription messages to specific topics. You can store the subscription in an XML file similar to the topic namespace that will look like the following code snippet:

```
<?xml version="1.0" encoding="UTF-8"?>

<wstop:topicSpace name="Event"
targetNamespace="http://publisher.domotic.com/topicnamespace.xml"
xmlns:domPub="http://publisher.domotic.com/xmlnamespace.xml"
xmlns:wstop="xmlns:wstop="http://docs.oasis-open.org/wsn/t-1">
    <wstop:topic name="Alarm events">
          <wstop:topic name="Fire presence"/>
          <wstop:topic name="Gas presence"/>
    </wstop:topic>
    <wstop:topic name="Health events">
          <wstop:topic name="Arm dislocation"/>
          <wstop:topic name="Irregular heartbeat"/>
          <domPub:Address name="simpleSubscriber:1234"/>
    </wstop:topic>
</wstop:topicSpace>
```

To do that, you also need a simple WS-Notification subscriber able to send a SOAP message as follows:

```
<s12:Envelope xmlns:s12="http://www.w3.org/2003/05/soap-envelope"
 xmlns:wsa="http://www.w3.org/2005/08/addressing">
 xmlns:wsnt="http://docs.oasis-open.org/wsn/b-2"
 xmlns:domPub="http://publisher.domotic.com/xmlnamespace.xml">
 <s12:Header/>
    <s12:Body>
          <wsnt:Subscribe>
                <wsnt:ConsumerReference>
                      <wsa:Address>
                           simpleSubscriber:1234
                      </wsa:Address>
                </wsnt:ConsumerReference>
                <wsnt:UseNotify>
                   true
                </wsnt:UseNotify>
                <wsnt:TopicExpression
                  dialect=http://publisher.domotic.com/topicdialect.ebnf>
                  domPub:Event/Health events
                </wsnt:TopicExpression>
          </wsnt:Subscribe>
    </s12:Body>
</s12:Envelope>
```

7.4. Extend exercises 7.2 and 7.3 to implement a simple WS-Notification event broker, able to receive *notify* messages and forward them to registered subscribers. To do that you also need a simple WS-NotificationPublisher able to send SOAP messages such as follows:

```
<s12:Envelope xmlns:s12="http://www.w3.org/2003/05/soap-envelope"
 xmlns:wsa="http://www.w3.org/2005/08/addressing">
 xmlns:wsnt="http://docs.oasis-open.org/wsn/b-2 "
 xmlns:domBro="http://broker.domotic.com/xmlnamespace.xml">
    <s12:Header/>
    <s12:Body>
          <wsnt:Notify>
                <wsnt:NotificationMessage>
                      <wsnt:Topic dialect="+dialect+">
                         domBro:Event/Health events/Arm Dislocation
                      </wsnt:Topic>
                      <wsnt:Message>
                       Arm dislocation detected!
                      </wsnt:Message>
                </wsnt:NotificationMessage>
          </wsnt:Notify>
    </s12:Body>
</s12:Envelope>
```

7.5. Figure 7.6 shows an insurance claims topic tree. Descendant topics of the root topic insurance claim include property, health and casualty claims. Use the WS-Topics notation to represent the insurance claim topic tree in Figure 7.6.

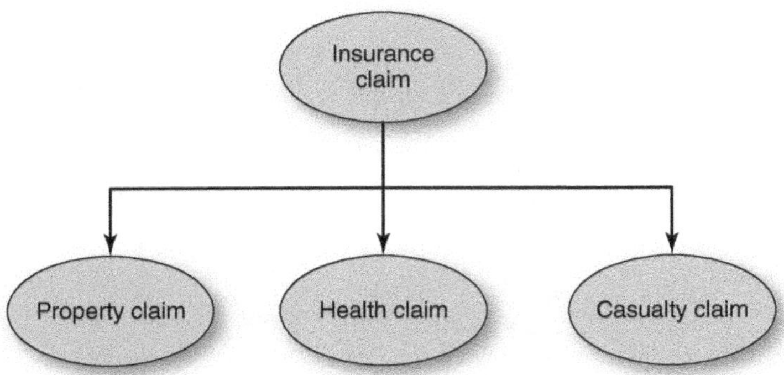

Figure 7.6 Sample insurance claims topic tree

CHAPTER 8

Service Oriented Architectures

Learning objectives

Much of SOA's power derives from its ability to leverage standards based functional services, calling them when needed on an individual basis, or aggregating them to create composite applications or multi-stage business processes. SOA is focused on creating a design style, technology and process framework that will allow enterprises to develop, interconnect, and maintain applications and services efficiently and cost effectively. In this chapter we describe architectural approaches and implementation technologies that unify the principles and concepts of SOA with those of event based programming.

After completing this chapter you will understand the following key concepts:

- The concept of software architecture.
- The purpose of reliable messaging.
- The structure of WS-ReliableMessaging.
- The meaning of event driven computing for SOA applications.
- The Enterprise Service Bus integration infrastructure for SOA applications.
- Connectivity, integration and scalability issues in the context of the Enterprise Service Bus.

Chapter preview

As organisations adopt SOA and Web services, these application frameworks pose new infrastructure challenges regarding messaging middleware that connects, mediates, secures and manages interactions among distributed services and applications. The purpose of this chapter is to introduce the Enterprise Service Bus, which addresses SOA implementation issues and surmounts service interoperability problems.

In this chapter, we first revisit the concepts behind SOAs and then study the features of reliable messaging, as it constitutes a backbone for message exchange in ESBs. We then explain the event driven nature of an ESB, examine the key capabilities and the integration styles of an ESB, as well as the various modules that comprise an ESB. We conclude this chapter by introducing the notion of an extended SOA.

This chapter not only introduces the infrastructure underlying robust SOA implementations but also serves as a foundation to inter-connect Chapters 4, 5, 6 and 7 with succeeding chapters Chapter 9, 10, 11, 12, 16 and 17.

8.1 What is software architecture?

The art of building distributed software systems involves fitting together resources and systems from diverse organisations, as well as developing implementation code. For example, when automating business processes that cross enterprise boundaries, these will traverse diverse systems in various organisations, leveraging shared resources such as Web servers, business logic components, security systems and back end enterprise information systems, such as databases and/or ERP systems. In this environment, partners must not only agree on a core set of interfaces and standards, but also agree on how to use those interfaces and standards. Central to such considerations is the concept of software architecture.

Software architecture of a computing system involves the description of the structures from which systems are built (software components), the externally visible properties of those components, their interrelationships as well as principles and guidelines governing their design and evolution over time [Shaw 1996], [Bass 2003]. Externally visible properties are assumptions other components can make of a specific component, such as its provided interfaces and services, performance characteristics, fault handling, shared resource usage and so on.

More precisely, software architecture is the high level structure of a software system – including distributed and service oriented systems – that is commonly specified in terms of functional components and interactions/interconnections among those components. Components are identified and assigned responsibilities that client components interact with through *contracted* interfaces [Soni 1995]. Component interconnections specify communication and control mechanisms, and support all component interactions needed to accomplish system behaviour.

Software architecture forms the backbone for building successful software intensive systems; it represents a capitalised investment in the form of an abstract reusable model that can be transferred from one system to the next. Important properties of software architecture include [Bass 2003]:

- It is at a high enough level of abstraction that the system can be viewed as a whole and yet it must provide enough information to form a basis for analysis, decision making, and hence risk reduction.
- The structure must support the functionality required of the system. Thus, the dynamic behaviour of the system must be taken into account when designing the architecture.
- It must conform to the system qualities (captured in SLAs or non-functional requirements). These likely include performance, security, interoperability and reliability requirements associated with current functionality, as well as flexibility or extensibility requirements associated with accommodating future functionality at a reasonable cost of change. As system qualities may conflict, trade-offs are an essential part of designing architecture. These trade-offs need to be made among alternative solutions and must take into account the relative priorities of the system qualities.
- At the architectural level, all implementation details are hidden.

It is important to understand that architectural decisions directly impact on system qualities, and often a decision in favour of one quality has an impact on another. It is also important to remember that the benefits of the most applicable architecture design can be eliminated by poor implementation.

In this chapter we briefly examine the nature and implications of two essential elements of a software architecture, namely system quality requirements and architectural concerns. Recall that we first discussed system quality requirements in Section 1.9; however, we re-examine them in this section to improve reader understanding. Service development techniques that concentrate on functional requirements of SOAs are presented in Chapter 16.

8.1.1 System quality attributes

While the design of software systems concentrates on satisfying the functional requirements for a system, the design of the software architecture for systems concentrates on the non-functional or quality requirements of systems. Quality requirements of systems are described in terms of quality attributes, which are those system properties over and above the functionality of the system that determine the technical qualities of the system. System quality attributes describe how well behavioural or structural aspects of a system are accomplished. System qualities are judged by some externally observable/measurable property of the system behaviour and not its internal implementation. These may be judged by the user in terms of some characteristic that the user values or is concerned about.

System qualities can be categorised into four parts: run time quality attributes, development quality attributes, business quality attributes and architecture quality attributes, as described below.

- *Run time quality attributes* include: usability (ease of use, learnability, memorability, etc); configurability and supportability; correctness, reliability, availability;

technical system requirements such as performance (throughput, response time, transit delay, latency, etc); safety properties such as security and fault tolerance; and operational scalability, including support for increased user involvement, additional system nodes and higher transaction volumes.

- *Development time quality attributes* influence the effort and cost associated with software development as well as support for future changes or uses (maintenance, enhancement or reuse). Examples of development time quality requirements include: maintainability; extensibility – ability to add (unspecified) future functionality; evolvability – support for new capabilities or ability to exploit new technologies; composability – ability to compose systems from plug-and-play components; and reusability – ability to (re)use in future systems.
- *Business qualities* are non-software system qualities that influence other quality attributes and include cost, marketability, and software architecture appropriateness for the organisation.
- Finally, *architecture qualities* include quality attributes specific to the architecture itself, such as conceptual integrity and architectural correctness.

To understand the impact of system qualities, such as for instance development time qualities, consider the client–server architectural pattern. This pattern describes collaboration between the providers and users of a set of services by separating one collection of responsibilities (the client's) from another (the server's). The consequence of this separation is enhanced modifiability and upgradeability. Modifying the implementation of the services or modifying the number of servers providing services is invisible to the clients. Moreover, the addition of new clients has no effect on the server. On the downside is the fact that, although this separation of computations might improve reliability, increased network traffic might increase the vulnerability to certain types of security attacks. Therefore, special attention needs to be paid to security considerations.

8.1.2 Common architectural concerns

A distinctive characteristic of architectural decisions is that they need to be made from a broad scoped or technical system perspective. This is due to the fact that architectural decisions impact on, if not the entire system, at least different parts of the system. A broad scoped perspective is required to take this impact into account, and to make the necessary trade-offs across the system. Key concerns that need to be addressed by (distributed) software architectures, include but are not limited to [Malan 2002], [Bass 2003]:

- *Meta-architecture:* This is a set of architectural vision and style principles, key communication and control mechanisms, and concepts, which results in high level decisions that will strongly influence the integrity and structure of the system. The meta-architecture, through style, patterns of composition or interaction, principles and philosophy, rules certain structural choices out and guides selection decisions and trade-offs among others.
- *Architectural patterns:* Over time, software developers distinguish patterns in the way that systems are structured, and as these patterns become widespread they

become dominant designs. Patterns allow the architect to start with a problem and a vision for the solution, and then find a pattern that fits that vision. Subsequently, the architect can further define the additional functional pieces that the application will need to succeed. For instance, well tested patterns such as client–server, three-tier, and multi-tier (layered) architectures have become prevalent within the IT industry. Architectural patterns are gradually emerging also in an SOA to address system decomposition concerns and how to achieve system properties [Chappell 2004], [Endrei 2004].

- *Architectural views:* Software architectures are best envisioned in terms of a number of complementary views or models. In particular, structural views help document and communicate the architecture in terms of the components and their relationships, and are useful in assessing architectural qualities like extensibility. Behavioural views are useful in thinking through how the components interact to accomplish their assigned responsibilities and evaluating the impact of what-if scenarios on the architecture. Behavioural models are especially useful in assessing run time qualities such as performance and security. Execution views help in evaluating physical distribution options and documenting and communicating decisions.
- *System decomposition principles and good interface design:* These identify the high level components of the system and the relationships among them. Their purpose is to direct attention at an appropriate decomposition of the system without delving into unnecessary details. Subsequently, externally visible properties of the components are made precise and unambiguous through well defined interfaces and component specifications and key architectural mechanisms are detailed. Concerns such as whether the components fit together and whether the congruence of structural pieces achieves the necessary degree of system integrity and consistency are important decisions and need to be factored into architectural decisions.
- *Key architectural design principles:* These include abstraction, separation of concerns, postponing decisions and simplicity, and related techniques such as interface hiding and encapsulation.

Such architectural concerns play a fundamental role in the success of SOA based applications. The first architectural concern relates mainly to system functional and quality requirements and is addressed in this chapter, while the remaining concerns relate to design principles and characteristics of SOAs, which are addressed in Chapter 16.

8.2 SOA revisited

As we have learned in Section 1.7, SOA is a meta-architectural style that supports loosely coupled services to enable enterprise flexibility in an interoperable, technology agnostic manner. To this end, SOA is focused on creating a design style, technology and process framework that will allow enterprises to develop, interconnect, and maintain applications and services efficiently and cost effectively. While this objective is not new, SOA seeks to eclipse previous efforts such as modular programming, code reuse, and object-oriented software development techniques.

SOA represents a significant advance in the *abstracted development* of software applications. An SOA provides a set of guidelines, principles and techniques by which business processes, information, and enterprise assets can be effectively (re-)organised and (re-) deployed to support and enable strategic plans and productivity levels that are required by competitive business environments.

A well constructed SOA can empower a business environment with a flexible infrastructure and processing environment by provisioning independent, reusable, automated business processes (which it deploys as services). It also provides a robust architectural backbone for leveraging these services.

An SOA is based on the combination of, and interaction between, business services, associated with messages, and governed by policies (see Chapter 12). In this way, new business processes and alliances can be routinely mapped to business services that can be used, modified, built or orchestrated. In an SOA, business aligned services are well defined, self-contained (elementary) business process steps, such as *create invoice*, *customer lookup*, or *bill customer*, and are independent of the state or context of other services. These business aligned services are used as the basis for constructing flexible and dynamically reconfigurable end-to-end business processes. This concept will be explained further in Chapter 16.

Another important characteristic of an SOA is that business aligned services are implemented with standard ways to invoke them and are *loosely coupled*, in that they can be invoked without the caller needing to understand anything about the technology choice or location of the service provider. In this respect, a service such as *bill customer* can be invoked from any other business application that simply requires customer information.

A (business) service in SOA is an exposed piece of functionality with three essential properties. An SOA based service is a self-contained (i.e. the service maintains its own state) and platform independent (i.e. the interface contract to the service is platform independent) service that can be dynamically located and invoked. Services in an SOA exhibit the following characteristics [Channabasavaiah 2003]:

1. All functions in an SOA are defined as services. Services used in composite applications in an SOA may be brand new service implementations, they may be fragments of old applications that were adapted and wrapped, or they may be combinations of the above.

2. All services are independent of each other. A service operation is perceived as opaque by external services. Service opaqueness guarantees that external components neither know nor care how services perform their function. They merely anticipate that they return the expected result. The technology and location of the application providing the desired functionality are hidden behind the service interface.

3. Service interfaces are invokable. This means that, at the architectural level, it is irrelevant whether services are local (within a specific system) or remote (external to the immediate system), what interconnect scheme or protocol is used to effect the invocation, or what infrastructure components are required to make the connection. The service may be within the same application or in a different address space on an entirely different system.

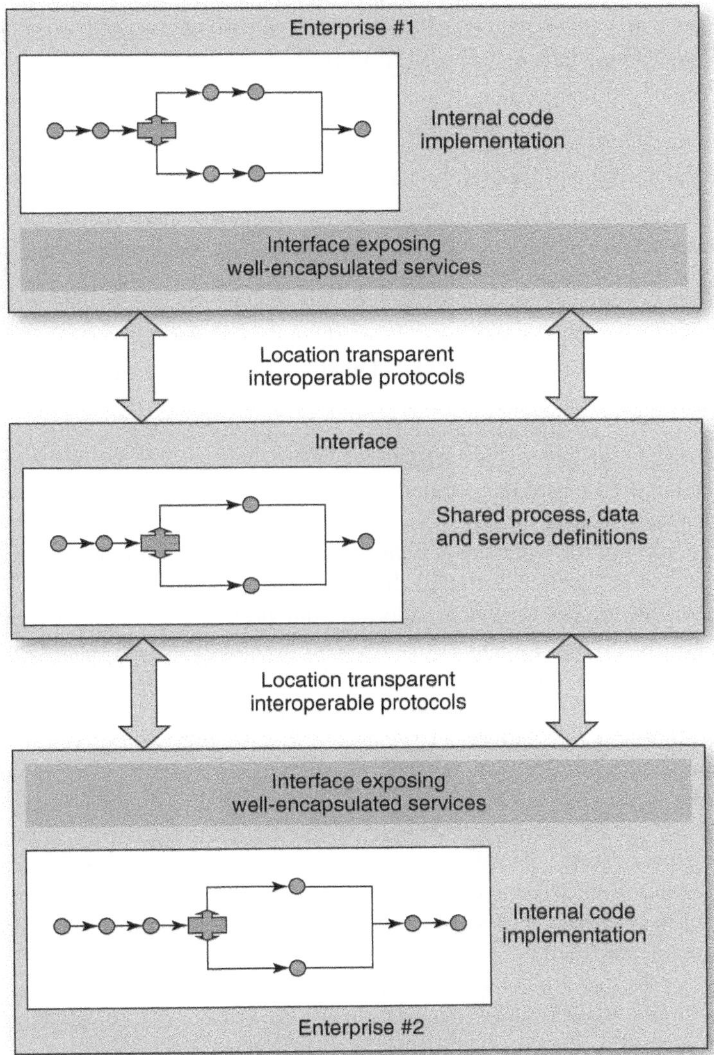

Figure 8.1 Intercommunicating services in an SOA source: [Channabasavaiah 2003]

Figure 8.1 illustrates how a business process uses well defined service interfaces from two diverse enterprises, which it composes to create and encapsulate a reusable business function while hiding its implementation details.

Although SOAs can be implemented using different technologies, such as established middleware technologies like J2EE, CORBA and JMS, Web services are the preferred environment for realising the SOA promise of maximum service sharing, reuse and interoperability. A Web services SOA realisation reduces application complexity by employing encapsulation principles, and minimises the requirements for shared understanding by a clear definition of interfaces. Additionally, Web services enable integration of legacy applications. A topic that will concern us in Section 16.13.1.

8.3 Service roles in an SOA

SOAs and Web service solutions include two well known key roles: a service requester (client) and service provider, which communicate via service requests. Service requests are messages formatted according to SOAP (see Figure 8.2). In Chapter 4 we explained that SOAP is by nature a platform neutral and vendor neutral standard. However, SOA does not necessarily require the use of SOAP. Other technologies, such as Representational State Transfer (REST), can be used to implement an SOA solution that implements simple applications. REST is an alternative to SOAP and other Web service specifications such as WSDL or BPEL. The basis of the REST style is that it allows defining the resources for an application and then it uses the standard HTTP methods to perform the state changes to those resources (see Section 1.12).

A *service container* provides deployment and a run time support environment that makes a Web service highly distributed. In particular, a service container is the physical manifestation of the abstract service endpoint, and provides the implementation of the service interface. It allows applications to monitor and manage supported components as well as the service(s) that monitor and manage the components. It also provides facilities for lifecycle management such as startup, shutdown and resource cleanup. A Web service container is similar to a J2EE container [Anagol-Subbaro 2005] and serves as an interface between business services and low level infrastructure services. A service container can host multiple services, even if they are not part of the same distributed process.

While SOA services are visible to the service client, their underlying component implementations are transparent. The service consumer does not have to be concerned with the implementation or realisation of the service, as long as it supports the required functionality and QoS. This represents the *client view* of SOA. For the service provider, the design of components, their service exposure and management reflect key architecture and design decisions that enable services in SOA. The *provider view* offers a perspective on how to design the realisation of the component that offers the services its architectural decisions and designs.

The process of a service requester having to directly communicate with a service provider exposes service requesters to the potential complexity of negotiating and reserving

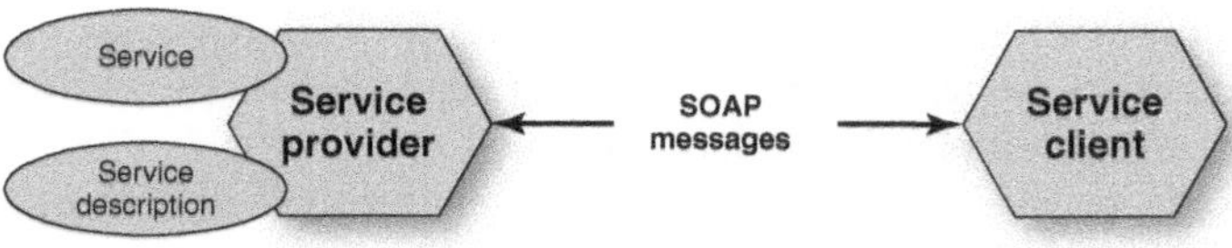

Figure 8.2 Service client and service provider roles

services between different service providers. An alternative approach is for an organisation to provide this combined functionality direct to the service requester. This service role could be described as a *service aggregator*. The service aggregator (see also Section 1.7.3) performs a dual role. First, it acts as an application service provider as it constructs a complete *service* solution, by creating composite, higher level services, which it provides to a service client. Service aggregators can accomplish this composition using specialised choreography languages like BPEL (which we describe in Section 9.7). Second, it acts as a service requester as it may need to request and reserve services from other service providers. This process is shown in Figure 8.3.

SOA technologies such as UDDI, and security and privacy standards such as SAML and WS-Trust, introduce a third role called a *service broker* [Colan 2004]. Service brokers (also known as certification authorities, see Section 11.3) are trusted parties that force service providers to adhere to information practices that comply with privacy laws and regulations, or, in the absence of such laws, industry best practices. The service broker is able to add value to its registry of application service providers by providing additional information about its services. This may include differences about the reliability, trustworthiness, quality of the service, SLAs, and possible compensation routes, to name but a few.

Figure 8.4 shows a classical Web service SOA diagram, where a service broker serves as an intermediary that is interposed between service requesters and service providers. The classical Web services SOA that we illustrated in Figure 1.4 falls under this category with the service registry (UDDI operator) being a specialised instance of a service broker. Under this configuration the UDDI registry serves as a broker where the service providers publish the definitions of the services they offer using WSDL, and where the service requesters find information about the available services.

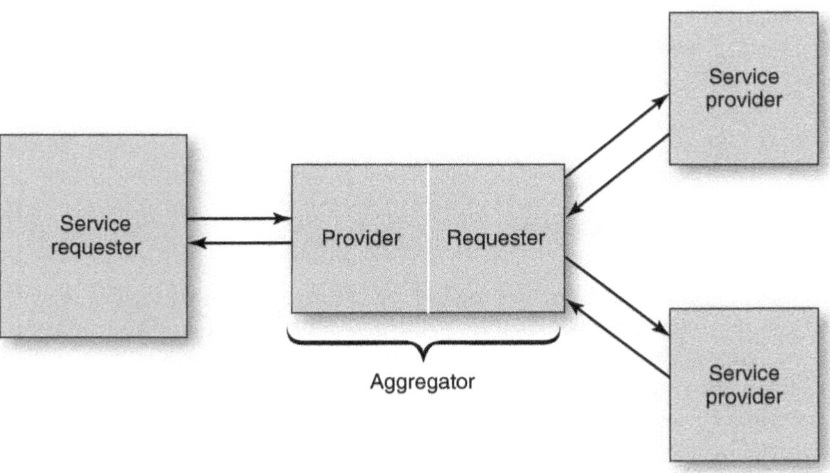

Figure 8.3 The role of service aggregator

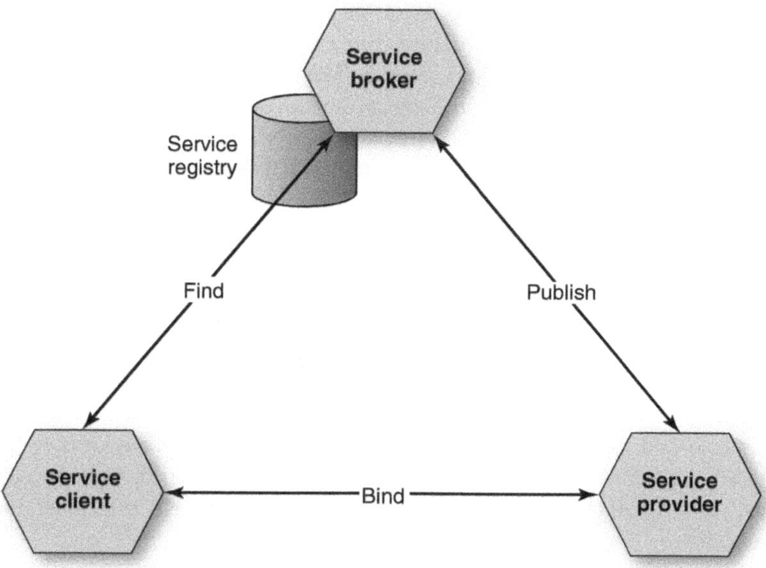

Figure 8.4 Service brokering

SOA implementations are based around messages exchanged between services, where SOAP messages were chosen as the recommended intercommunication mechanism, and services are defined as network addressable entities that send and receive messages. To support SOA applications effectively, SOAP requires a protocol that allows its messages to be reliably delivered between distributed applications in the presence of software component, system or network failures. For this reason, we examine in the following section the concept of reliable messaging, along with the WS-ReliableMessaging standard that is used in conjunction with other Web Services specifications, e.g. SOAP and WSDL, and application specific protocols, to build a complete messaging solution.

8.4 Reliable messaging

The core SOAP specification does not provide reliability mechanisms addressing complex message routing requirements. Therefore, there is a clear need for more robust SOAP based messaging specifications to guarantee that messages are being received by their intended recipients; and that message addressing remains consistent despite the fact that messages might be routed to Web services implemented on different platforms, e.g. .NET or J2EE, using heterogeneous messaging transport protocols. Reliable messaging becomes one of the first problems that need to be addressed for Web services to become a truly accomplished technology for robust SOA implementations.

8.4.1 Definition and scope of reliable messaging

Reliability at the level of messages is often referred to as *reliable messaging*. Reliable messaging for Web services is the execution of a transport agnostic, SOAP based protocol providing QoS in the reliable delivery of messages. Reliable messaging is a problem that has plagued Internet application development since its inception. The Internet is, by its very nature, unreliable. In particular, the protocols used to connect senders and receivers were not designed to support reliable messaging constructs, such as message identifiers and acknowledgements (see Section 2.6). When specifying reliable messaging features there are three aspects that must be addressed equally. We need to:

1. Make certain that both the sender and recipient of a message know whether or not a message was actually sent and received, and that the message received is the same as the one sent.
2. Ensure that the message was sent once, and only once, to the intended recipient.
3. Guarantee that the received messages are in the same order as they were sent.

With Web services, messaging reliability guarantees an agreed upon quality of delivery in spite of network, software and hardware failures. It allows message senders and receivers to overcome the unreliability of the Internet/intranet environment, and otherwise guarantees some awareness of failure conditions.

Currently, reliable messaging in the world of Web services is supported by the WS-ReliableMessaging standard [Davis 2009]. This standard is an example of a specification for an acknowledgement infrastructure that leverages the SOAP extensibility model and defines protocols that are independent of the underlying transport layer. In the following, we shall concentrate on describing WS-ReliableMessaging, which is a natural companion of other Web service standards that we examined in the preceding chapter, such as WS-Addressing and WS-Notification.

8.4.2 WS-ReliableMessaging

The WS-ReliableMessaging standard has been developed to provide a framework for interoperability between different reliable transport infrastructures [Davis 2009]. More specifically, the WS-ReliableMessaging protocol determines invariants maintained by the reliable messaging endpoints and the directives used to track and manage the delivery of a sequence of messages. It provides an interoperable protocol that a reliable messaging source and reliable messaging destination use to provide the application source and the application destination with a guarantee that a message that is sent will be delivered.

The WS-ReliableMessaging protocol depends upon other Web service specifications for the identification of service endpoint addresses and policies. When WS-ReliableMessaging is used in conjunction with WS-Addressing (see Section 7.1.1) it enables transport neutral, bi-directional, synchronous, asynchronous and stateful service interactions across networks that include the likes of endpoint managers, firewalls and gateways.

The WS-ReliableMessaging model is illustrated in Figure 8.5, where it is shown that implementation of the WS-ReliableMessaging model is distributed across the initial

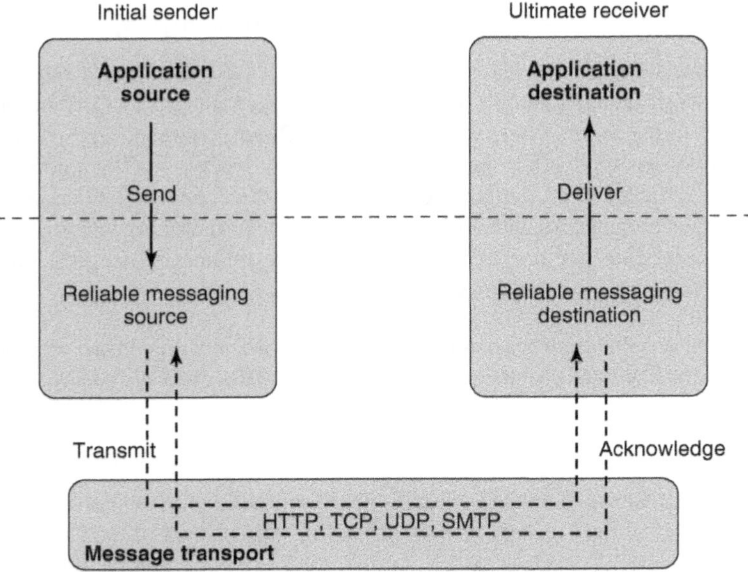

Figure 8.5 Reliable messaging model

sender and ultimate receiver (service). This figure also illustrates that there might be multiple receivers interposed between the initial message sender and the ultimate receiver. The message is transmitted using the reliable messaging protocol. First, both interacting endpoints establish preconditions for message exchange. Subsequently, the sender formats the message to the transport protocol agreed. The messaging handler of the receiver then forwards the message to the appropriate recipient. Finally, the messaging handler in the receiver transforms the message into a form that is suitable for use for the receiver application. While reliable messaging actions, e.g. retransmission of a message due to transport loss, are handled transparently by the messaging infrastructure, other end-to-end characteristics, such as in-order delivery, require that both the messaging infrastructure and the receiver application collaborate.

WS-ReliableMessaging distinguishes two important traits:

- The reliability protocol between message handlers, which they implement using the same notions of sequence of messages within which each message is identified by a sequence number, and using a resending mechanism combined with a notion of acknowledgement.
- The reliability QoS contract, which provides a delivery assurance and QoS delivery guarantees to the communicating parties.

In WS-ReliableMessaging the guarantee for delivery is specified as a delivery assurance. Endpoints that implement the WS-ReliableMessaging protocol provide delivery assurances for the delivery of messages sent from the initial sender to the ultimate receiver. It is the responsibility of the reliable messaging source and reliable messaging destination to fulfill the delivery assurances, or raise an error. There are four basic delivery assurances that endpoints provide and are supported by WS-ReliableMessaging. These are [Davis 2009]:

- *AtLeastOnce delivery:* This feature guarantees that every message sent will be delivered, or an error will be raised on at least one endpoint. Some messages may be delivered more than once.
- *AtMostOnce delivery:* This feature guarantees that every message will be delivered at most once without duplication, or an error will be raised on at least one endpoint. It is possible that some messages in a sequence may not be delivered.
- *ExactlyOnce delivery:* This feature guarantees that every message sent will be delivered without duplication, or an error will be raised on at least one endpoint. This delivery assurance is the logical AND of the two prior delivery assurances.
- *InOrder delivery:* This feature enforces the delivery of a sequence of messages at the destination, in the same order as the submission order by the sending application. This delivery assurance says nothing about duplications or omissions.

WS-ReliableMessaging takes advantage of the algorithms used in reliable messaging and transaction protocols to provide a flexible acknowledgement scheme in which receivers can efficiently convey the range of messages that have (and have not) been received. WS-ReliableMessaging also provides an efficient ordering mechanism to ensure that receivers can process messages in the same order in which they were sent, even in the face of reordering due to retransmissions or multi-path routing.

WS-ReliableMessaging was designed to comply with the existing Web service infrastructure. In particular, WS-ReliableMessaging is layered on top of existing application protocols and interfaces described in WSDL and XML Schema. The WS-ReliableMessaging specification integrates with and complements the WS-Security [Nadalin 2006], WS-Policy [Vendamuthu 2007a], and other Web service specifications. Combined, these allow for a broad range of reliable, secure messaging options.

8.4.2.1 Structure of WS-ReliableMessaging

Reliable message delivery does not require an explicit coordinator. When using WS-ReliableMessaging, the participants must recognise the protocol based on the information sent in SOAP message headers. A message sequence can be established either by the initiator/sender or the Web service, and often by both when establishing a duplex association. WS-ReliableMessaging is developed around the following three core elements:

- *Sequences:* The WS-ReliableMessaging specification models a message exchange between two endpoints always as a sequence, irrespective of whether only one or an entire sequence of messages transmitted as a group are exchanged. When the initiator attempts to establish a sequence, the service is informed of this request by the inclusion of a WS-ReliableMessaging `<Sequence>` header block in the request.
- *Message numbers:* An ascending sequence number identifies individual messages in a sequence. This numbering scheme makes it simple to detect missing or duplicate messages, and simplifies acknowledgement generation and processing.

- *Acknowledgements:* An acknowledgement is an indication that a message was successfully transferred to its destination.

WS-ReliableMessaging leverages the ability of WS-Addressing to allow messages to be sent asynchronously in either direction in several ways [Davis 2009]. Rather than send an acknowledgement message for every message received, WS-ReliableMessaging allows the destination cumulatively to acknowledge every message it has received in a single, compact control element. This control element can be sent in its own message or included with a subsequent application message that is sent back to the source (e.g. a response message in a request/reply conversation).

Example 8.1: Specifying a reliable message transfer

The ReliableMessaging protocol uses a `<Sequence>` header block to track and manage the reliable transfer of messages. The ReliableMessaging source must include a `<Sequence>` header block in all messages for which reliable transfer is required. The ReliableMessaging source must identify `<Sequence>`s with unique `<Identifier>` elements. In addition, it must assign each message within a `<Sequence>` a `<MessageNumber>` element.

Listing 8.1 is an example of a message containing the `<Sequence>` element. The message in the example is the third in sequence and is identified by some URI, indicated by the mandatory `<Identifier>` and `<MessageNumber>` elements.

```
<Soap:Envelope
  xmlns:Soap="http://www.w3.org/2003/05/soap-envelope"
  xmlns:wsrm="http://docs.oasis-open.org/ws-rx/wsrm/200702"
  xmlns:wsa="http://www.w3.org/2005/08/addressing">
  <Soap:Header>
      ...
    <wsrm:Sequence>
       <wsrm:Identifier> xs:anyURI </wsrm:Identifier>
          ...
       <wsrm:MessageNumber> 3 </wsrm:MessageNumber>
          ...
    </wsrm:Sequence>

  </Soap:Header>
  <Soap:Body>
     <GetOrder xmlns="http://supply.com/orderservice"
        ...
     </GetOrder>
  </Soap:Body>
</Soap>
```

Listing 8.1 Sample sequence element in WS-ReliableMessaging

Example 8.2: Acknowledging a message sequence

WS-ReliableMessaging proposes the use of a `<SequenceAcknowledgement>` header element, which is used to return a receipt acknowledgement for one or more messages in a given sequence, either in an arbitrary response message or in a response created exclusively to return the acknowledgement.

Listing 8.2 is an example of a message containing the `<SequenceAcknowledgement>` element. As shown in this listing, an acknowledgement uses a number of `<AcknowledgementRange>` elements to indicate that the range of messages in the sequence being acknowledged is not contiguous. The example in the listing specifies that while messages number 1, 2, and 4 have been received, message number 3 in the sequence has not been received by the reliable messaging destination.

```
<Soap:Envelope
  xmlns:Soap="http://www.w3.org/2003/05/soap-envelope"
  xmlns:wsrm="http://docs.oasis-open.org/ws-rx/wsrm/200702"
  xmlns:wsa="http://www.w3.org/2005/08/addressing">
<Soap:Header>
     ...
   <wsrm:SequenceAcknowledgement>
      <wsrm:Identifier>  http://supply.com/abc </wsrm:Identifier>
      <wsrm:AcknowledgementRange Upper="2" Lower="1"/>
      <wsrm:AcknowledgementRange Upper="4" Lower="4"/>
      <wsrm:Nack> 3 </wsrm:Nack>
   </wsrm:SequenceAcknowledgement>
   <Soap:Body>
     ...
   </Soap:Body>
</Soap:Envelope>
```

Listing 8.2 Sample acknowledgement element in WS-ReliableMessaging

8.5 The Enterprise Service Bus

As the number of mission critical business processes and service components used in SOA applications increases, organisations realise only a flexible and scalable shared service infrastructure will allow them to meet the demanding service levels required to compete in today's business environment. This infrastructure must support both the established Web services technologies and standards, and provide a set of capabilities in the form of messaging middleware that comes equipped with the secure interoperability and message transport functionality necessary for integrating applications and services to enable an SOA.

A dedicated SOA infrastructure, at the most basic level, should involve provision of the capabilities to route and deliver service requests to the correct service provider and the ability to compose services. The infrastructure should enable service interfaces to be specified according to SOA principles. The requirements to provide an appropriately capable and manageable infrastructure for Web services and SOA coalesce into the concept of the Enterprise Service Bus, which is the main subject of this chapter.

8.5.1 The role of an Enterprise Service Bus

The requirements to provide an appropriately capable and manageable integration infrastructure for Web services and SOA are combined together under the concept of an Enterprise Service Bus (ESB). The *Enterprise Service Bus* is an open standards based message backbone designed to enable the implementation, deployment and management of SOA based solutions, with a focus on assembling, deploying and managing distributed Service Oriented Architectures.

An ESB is a set of infrastructure capabilities implemented by middleware technology that enable an SOA, and alleviate disparity problems between applications running on heterogeneous platforms and using diverse data formats. The ESB is designed to provide interoperability between larger grained applications and other components via standards based adapters and interfaces. The bus functions as both transport and transformation facilitator to allow distribution of these services over disparate systems and computing environments.

An ESB is about configuring applications rather than coding and hardwiring applications together. It is a dedicated service infrastructure that provides plug-and-play enterprise functionality. It is ultimately responsible for the proper control, flow, and even translations of all messages between services, using any number of possible messaging protocols. It establishes proper control of messaging, as well as applying the needs of security, policy, reliability and accounting, in an SOA architecture.

The two key ideas behind the ESB approach are to loosely couple the systems taking part in the integration and break up the integration logic into distinct, easily manageable pieces. The ESB itself can be a single engine or even a federated system consisting of several peer and sub-peer ESBs, all working together to enable efficient messaging and mediation in the SOA system. Conceptually, it has evolved from the store-and-forward mechanism found in earlier distributed computing concepts, such as the message queues, message oriented middleware and distributed transactional computing that we examined in Chapter 2.

An ESB acts as a mediator between service consumers and service providers. It decouples the service consumer from the service provider, providing services to resolve differences in protocol and format. It shrinks the number of interfaces and improves the reusability of interface components to cut cycle time from design to deployment. Connections are made to the ESB rather than directly between the communicating service consumers and service providers. An ESB achieves decoupling of the consumer's view of a service from the implementation of a service, which enables service virtualisation and brings a number of advantages, which are summarised below. It:

- reduces the number, size and complexity of interfaces;
- reduces the impact of changes that are made to the format and location of services, both in terms of impact to the applications and in terms of system management;

- enables integration between disparate resources;
- allows substitution of one service provider for another without the service consumer being aware of the change or without needing to alter the architecture to support the substitution.

The above ESB features make it possible for previously isolated software systems, such as ERP, CRM, supply chain management, financial and legacy systems, to become SOA enabled and integrated more effectively than when relying on custom, point-to-point coding or proprietary EAI technology. Today, ESBs are already being put to use in a variety of industries, including financial services, insurance, manufacturing, retail, telecommunications, food and so on.

The ESB is aware of the applications and services it supports, and uses content based routing facilities to make informed decisions about how to communicate with them. In essence the ESB provides docking stations for hosting applications and services that can be assembled and orchestrated and are available for use by any other service on the bus. Once a service is deployed into a service container it becomes an integral part of the ESB and can be used by any application or service connected to it. The service container hosts, manages, dynamically deploys services and binds them to external resources, e.g. data sources, enterprise and multi-platform applications, such as the ones shown in Figure 8.6.

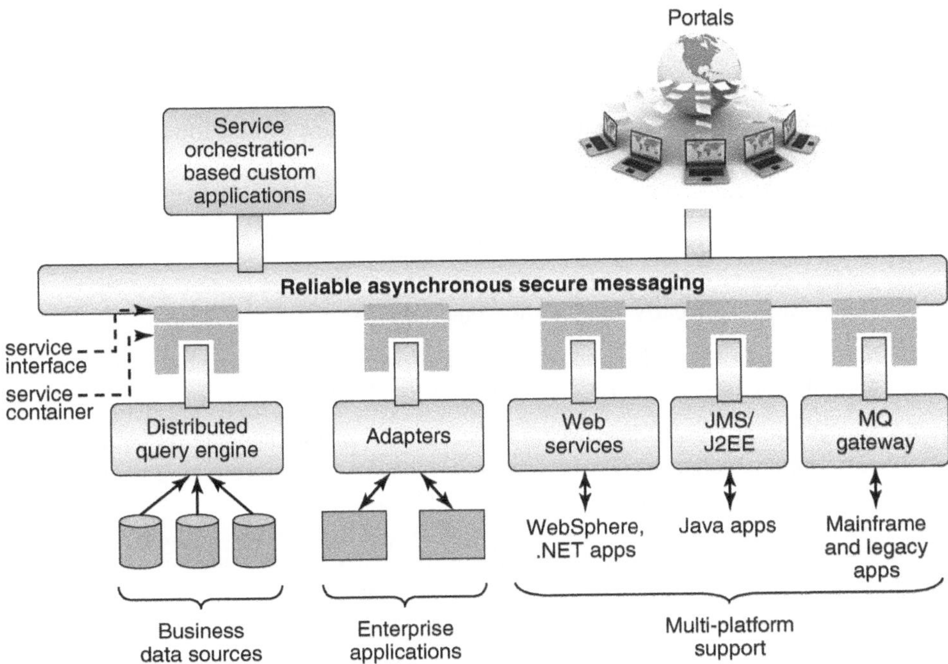

Figure 8.6 ESB connecting diverse applications and technologies

In an ESB, new or existing distributed applications are exposed as Web services and can be accessed via an ESB portal. An *ESB portal* is a user facing visual aggregation point of a variety of resources that draws content from a variety of different systems and presents this content and associated functionality on a browser as a single screen. For example, an ESB sales application portal may contain sales information, calendars of special events, e.g. sales discounts, sales forecasting and so on.

Figure 8.6 also shows that the ESB integrates back end applications such as a J2EE application using JMS, a .NET application using a C# client, an MQ application that interfaces with legacy applications, as well as external applications and data sources to the portal. In general, resources in the ESB are modelled as services that offer one or more business operations. Technologies like J2EE Connector Architecture (JCA) may also be used to create services by integrating packaged applications (like ERP systems), which would then be exposed as Web services (see Section 8.5.5.2).

An ESB enables the more efficient value added integration of a number of different application components, by positioning them behind a service oriented facade and by applying Web service technology to the problem. For instance, in Figure 8.6 a distributed query engine, which is normally based on XQuery or SQL, enables the creation of business data services, e.g. sales order data or available product sets, by providing uniform access to a variety of disparate business data sources or organisation repositories.

Endpoints in the ESB depicted in Figure 8.6 provide abstractions of physical destination and connection information (like TCP/IP host name and port number). In addition, they facilitate asynchronous and highly reliable communication between service containers using reliable messaging conventions (see Section 8.4).

To build and deploy successfully a distributed SOA on an ESB formation, there are five design/deployment and management aspects that need to be addressed first:

1. *Service analysis and design:* A service development methodology should be used to enable service oriented development and the reuse of existing applications and resources.

2. *Service enablement:* The service development methodology should determine which discrete application elements need to be exposed as services.

3. *Service orchestration:* Distributed services need to be configured and orchestrated in a unified and clearly defined distributed process.

4. *Service deployment:* Emphasis should also be placed on the production environment that addresses security, reliability and scalability concerns.

5. *Service management:* Services must be audited, maintained and reconfigured, and corresponding changes in processes must be made without rewriting the services or underlying application.

The first four concerns will be addressed in Chapter 16, which examines service design and development methodologies, and the fifth in Chapter 17, which focuses on service management technology and mechanisms. In this chapter we assume that services in an

ESB are well designed according to the principle of a service development methodology and can be managed appropriately by a service management framework.

8.5.2 The event driven nature of SOA

An SOA requires an additional fundamental technology beyond the services aspect to realise its full potential: event driven computing. Ultimately, the primary objective of most SOA implementations is to automate as much processing as necessary and to provide critical and actionable information to human users when they are required to interact with a business process. This requires the ESB infrastructure itself to recognise meaningful events and respond to them appropriately. The response could be either by automatically initiating new services and business processes or by notifying users of business events of interest, putting the events into topical context and, often, suggesting the best courses of action. In the enterprise context business events, such as a customer order, the arrival of a shipment at a loading dock, or the payment of a bill and so forth, affect the normal course of a business process and can occur in any order at any point in time. Consequently, applications that use orchestrated processes that exchange messages need to communicate with each other using a broad capability known as an event driven SOA.

An *event driven SOA* is an architectural approach to distributed computing, where events trigger asynchronous messages that are then sent between independent software components which need not have any information about each other, by abstracting away from the details of underlying service connectivity and protocols. An event driven SOA provides a more lightweight, straightforward set of technologies to build and maintain the service abstraction for client applications [Bloomberg 2004].

In an ESB enabled, event driven SOA, applications and services are treated as abstract service endpoints, which can readily respond to asynchronous events [Chappell 2005]. To achieve a more loosely coupled lightweight arrangement, an event driven SOA requires that two participants in an event (server and client) be decoupled. With fully decoupled exchanges the two participants in an event need not have any knowledge about each other before engaging in a business transaction. This means that there is no need for a service contract in WSDL that explicates the behaviour of a server to the client. The only relationship is indirect, through the ESB, to which clients and servers are subscribed as subscribers and publishers of events. To achieve its functionality, the ESB must support both the established Web service technologies such as SOAP, WSDL and BPEL, as well as standards like WS-ReliableMessaging and WS-Notification (see Chapter 7).

Despite the notion of decoupling in event driven SOA, recipients of events require metadata about those events. In such situations, recipients of events still have some information about those events. For instance, the publishers of the events often organise them on the basis of some (topical) taxonomy or, alternatively, provide details about the event, including its size, format, etc., which is a form of metadata. Such metadata describes published events that consumers can subscribe to, the interfaces that service clients and providers exhibit as well as the messages they exchange, and even the agreed format and context of this metadata, without falling into the formal service contracts themselves.

Example 8.3: An event based distributed procurement process

To orchestrate effectively the behaviour of services in a distributed process, the ESB infrastructure includes a distributed processing framework and XML based Web services. To exemplify these features, we use a simplified distributed procurement business process, which we will configure and deploy using an ESB.

In the distributed procurement business process an automated inventory system initiates a replenishment signal and thereby triggers an automated procurement process flow. During this procurement process flow a series of logical steps need to be performed:

- First, the sourcing service queries the enterprise's supplier reference database to determine the list of possible suppliers, which could be prioritised on the basis of existing contracts and supplier metrics.
- A supplier is then chosen based on some criterion and the purchase order is automatically generated in an ERP purchasing module and is sent to the vendor of choice.
- Finally, this vendor uses an invoicing service to bill the customer.

In this example we assume that the inventory is out of stock and the replenishment message is routed to a supplier order service.

The services that are part of the simplified distributed procurement business process can be seen in use in Figure 8.7. Although this figure shows only a single supplier order service as part of the inventory, in reality a plethora of supplier services may exist. The supplier order service, which executes a remote Web service at a chosen supplier to fulfil the order, is assumed to generate its output in an XML message format that is not understood by the purchase order service.

To avoid heterogeneity problems, the message from the supplier order service leverages the ESB's transformation service to convert the XML into a format that is acceptable by the purchase order service. This figure also shows that JCA is used within the ESB to allow legacy applications, such as a credit check service, to be placed on to the ESB through JCA resource adapters.

Once services, which are part of the distributed procurement business process depicted in Figure 8.7, have been chained together, it is necessary to provide a way to manage and reconfigure them to react to changes in business processes.

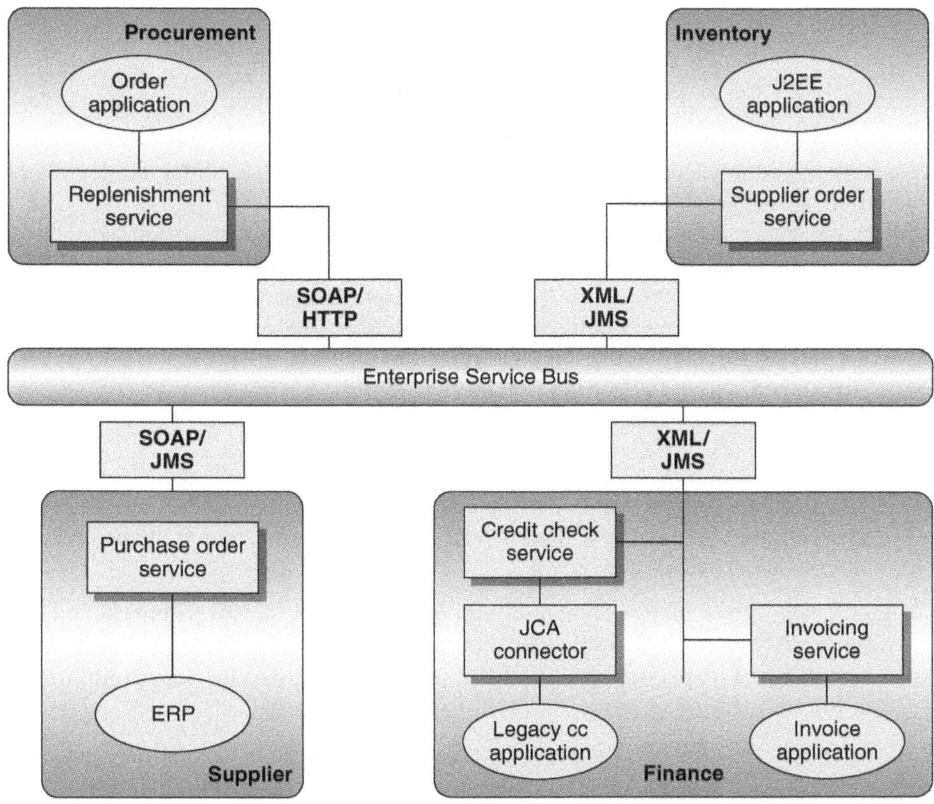

Figure 8.7 ESB example connecting remote interacting services

---

The ESB is a federated environment that can be managed from any point. Ideally, this could be achieved through a sophisticated graphical business process management tool that can be used to configure, deploy and manage services and endpoints. This allows the free movement and reconfiguration of services without requiring rewriting or modifying the services themselves.

In the remainder of this chapter and throughout the rest of this book we shall make no distinction between SOAs and event driven SOAs (unless necessary) and shall henceforth use the generic term SOA to refer to both terms.

8.5.3 Key capabilities of an ESB

Enabling an application for SOA involves the creation of service interfaces to existing or new functions, either directly or through the use of adapters. At the most basic level, this involves provision of the capabilities to route and deliver secure service requests to the correct service provider. However, it is also vital that the infrastructure supports the substitution of one service implementation by another with no effect on the clients of that service. This requires not only that the service interfaces be specified according to SOA principles, but also that the infrastructure allows client code to invoke services irrespective of the service location and the communication protocol involved. Such service routing and substitution are among the many capabilities of the ESB.

Although there is no formal industry standard that defines what the common functional components of an ESB are, at least we can find a set of commonalities across the different ESB products. The most typical ESB functional requirements have also been discussed by several authors including [Robinson 2004], [Candadai 2004], [Channabasavaiah 2003] and [Chappell 2004]. The following list summarises most of the important findings. It should be noted that not all of the capabilities described below are offered by current commercial ESB systems today.

Communication infrastructure: To enable the various service interaction protocols that maybe required, the ESB implements support for multiple communication abstractions, such as event driven publish-and-subscribe, synchronous and asynchronous invocation, and others.

Dynamic connectivity: Dynamic connectivity is the ability to connect to Web services dynamically without using a separate static API or proxy for each service. The dynamic connectivity API is the same regardless of the service implementation protocol (Web services, JMS, EJB/RMI, etc.).

Reliable messaging: Reliable messaging can be primarily used to ensure guaranteed delivery of these messages to their destination and for handling events. This capability is crucial for responding to clients in an asynchronous manner and for a successful ESB implementation.

Topic and content based routing: The ESB should be equipped with routing mechanisms to facilitate not only topic based routing, but also more sophisticated content based routing. Topic based routing assumes that messages can be grouped into fixed, topical classes, so that subscribers can explicate interest in a topic and, as a consequence, receive messages associated to that topic. Content based routing, on the other hand, allows subscriptions on constraints of actual properties of business events (see Section 2.6.3).

Content based routing logic rules are usually expressed in XPath or a scripting language, such as JavaScript. For example, if a manufacturer provides a wide variety of products to its customers, only some of which are made in-house, depending on the product ordered it might be necessary to route the message directly to an external supplier, or route it internally to be processed by a warehouse fulfillment service. Content based ESB capabilities could be supported by standards such as WS-Notification, see Section 7.2.

Transformation and mapping: The ESB plays a major role in transforming between differing data formats and messaging models, whether between basic

XML formats and Web services messages, or between different XML formats (e.g. transforming an industry standard XML message to a proprietary or custom XML format). A major source of value in an ESB is that it shields any individual component from any knowledge of the implementation details of any other component. The ESB connectivity and translation infrastructure is discussed in Section 8.5.6.

Service enablement: Service enablement includes the ability to access already existing resources such as legacy systems – technically obsolete, mission critical elements of an organisation's infrastructure – and include them in an SOA implementation. Tactically, legacy assets must be leveraged, service enabled and integrated with modern service technologies and applications. This issue is the subject of Section 16.13.1.

Endpoint discovery with multiple QoS capabilities: The ESB should be capable of supporting various QoSs and allow clients to discover the best service instance with which to interact, based on QoS properties. Such capabilities should be controlled by declarative policies associated with the services involved, using a policy standard such as the WS-PolicyFramework.

Service orchestration and long running processes: The ESB should provide the ability to support business process composition and long running processes – services that tend to run for long duration, exchanging message (conversation) as they progress. To this end an ESB can implement processes that aggregate smaller services into larger services, which may also require transaction management. A typical example of a long running process is an on line reservation system, which interacts with the user as well as various service providers (airline ticketing, insurance claims, credit applications, etc.).

Transaction management: ESBs that behave like service brokers for synchronous invocation may also need to support conventional, tightly coupled transactions with support for distributed units of work. Because standards for SOA transactions are still immature, this is still an evolving area of capability for ESBs, with capabilities of the products varying widely. Chapters 9 and 10 discuss business processes, long running services, and transactions.

Security: The ESB can enforce security policies regarding service usage. The ESB needs both to provide a security model to service consumers and to integrate with the (potentially varied) security models of service providers. Both point-to-point (e.g. SSL encryption) and end-to-end security capabilities, e.g. federated authentication, validation of service requests, authorisation, etc, are required. To address these intricate security requirements the ESB must rely on WS-Security and other security related standards for Web services that are treated in Sections 11.5 and 11.6.

Integration: To support SOA in a heterogeneous environment, the ESB needs to integrate with a variety of systems that do not directly support service style interactions. These may include legacy systems, packaged applications or other EAI technologies. When assessing the integration requirements for ESB, several types or styles of integration must be considered, e.g. process versus data integration.

Management and monitoring: In an SOA environment, applications cross system and organisational boundaries, they overlap, and they can change over time. Managing these applications is a serious challenge. Examples include dynamic load balancing, fail-over when primary systems go down, achieving topological or geographic affinity between the client and the service instance, and so on. Monitoring enables human operators to investigate problems, find root causes, and take action to correct the issues they discover. As we shall explain in Chapter 16, of particular significance is the ability of service management and monitoring to spot problems and exceptions in business processes and move towards resolving them as soon as they occur.

Scalability: With a widely distributed SOA, there will be the need to scale some of the services or the entire infrastructure to meet integration demands. For example, transformation services are typically very resource intensive and may require multiple instances across two or more computing nodes. At the same time, it is necessary to create an infrastructure that can support the large nodes present in a global service network. A decentralised architecture enables independent scalability of individual services, as well as the communications infrastructure itself. Scalability is discussed further in Section 8.5.7.

Support for the service life cycle: Service life cycle management tracks services and their related artifacts through their whole life cycle, from design, development, reuse and integration, to deployment and management, to optimisation. The topic of service life cycle is discussed in detail in Chapter 16.

Table 8.1 summarises the most typical ESB functional capabilities described above, along with their related standards.

As the core ESB integration capabilities in the above list are central in understanding the material that follows, and essential to understanding service oriented integration issues, we shall revisit them in the following section.

8.5.4 ESB integration styles

One salient characteristic of the ESB architectural integration style is that it is technology agnostic (it encompasses more than one particular set of technologies) and can reuse functionality in existing applications to support new application development. There is a series of important technical requirements that need to be addressed by a service oriented integration solution in the context of an ESB, which we examine below.

8.5.4.1 Integration at the presentation tier

Integration at the presentation tier is concerned with how the complete set of applications and services, which a given user accesses, are fabricating a highly distributed yet unified

Table 8.1 ESB functional areas and related standards

Functional area	*Capabilities*	*Relevant standards*
Connectivity	- Transport - Guaranteed delivery - Routing	- SOAP - WS-ReliableMessaging - WS-Addressing
Content based routing Event notification	- Content based routing - Topic based routing - Business event notification	- XPath - WS-Topic - WS-Notification
Transformation	- Protocol transformation - Message transformation - Data transformation	- XSLT - WS-Addressing - WS-ReourceFrameowrk
Service enablement	- Wrapping - Transformation - Access to legacy resources	- WSDL - BPEL
Service Orchestration	- Process description - Process execution - Long running processes	- BPEL
Transaction Management	- Transactional services - Coordination	- WS-Transaction - WS-Coordination
Security	- Authentication - Authorization - Access rights - Encryption	- WS-Security - WS-SecurePolicy - SAML - XCML
Discovery with multiple Q	- Run time service discovery using multiple QoS capabilities & policies	- WS-PolicyFramework
Management and Monitoring	- Monitoring QoS - Enforcing SLAs - Controlling tasks - Managing resource life-cycles	WS-DistrbutedManagement WS-Policy

portal framework that provides a usable, efficient, uniform and consistent presentation tier. In this way the ESB can provide one face to the users with unified information delivery, while allowing underlying applications to remain distributed. The two complementary industry standards in the portal space that can assist with these efforts are:

- JSR 168 [JCP 2003]: This is an industry standard that defines a standard way to develop portlets. It allows portlets to be interoperable across portal vendors. For example, portlets developed for Oracle 10g WebLogic Portal can be interoperable with IBM Portal. This allows organisations to have a lower dependency on the portal product vendor.

- WSRP (Web Service for Remote Portals) [Thompson 2008]: This is an industry standard that allows remote portlets to be developed and consumed in a standard manner and facilitates federated portals. WSRP combines the power of Web services and portal technologies and is fast becoming the major enabling technology for distributed portals in an enterprise.

JSR 168 complements WSRP by dealing with local rather than distributed portlets. A portal page may have certain local portlets, which are JSR 168 compliant, and some remote, distributed portlets that are executed in a remote container. As depicted in Figure 8.6, a portlet may be an ESB service. This allows the portlet developer to view the entire universe of back end systems in a normalised fashion through the ESB.

8.5.4.2 Application connectivity

Application connectivity is an integration style concerned with all types of connectivity that the ESB integration layer must support. At one level, this means things such as synchronous and asynchronous communications, routing, transformation, high speed distribution of data, gateways and protocol converters. On another level, application connectivity also relates to the virtualisation of input and output, or sources and sinks. It requires that inputs are received and passed to applications in the ESB in a source neutral way. Special purpose front end device and protocol handlers should make that possible.

For connectivity, an ESB can utilize J2EE components, such as the Java Message Service for MOM connectivity, and JCA for connecting to application adapters. An ESB can also integrate easily with applications built with .NET, C#, C++, and C. An ESB can integrate easily with any application that supports SOAP and Web services. It allows these different kinds of application to connect together by supporting notification features, such as those embodied in WS-Notification (which we examined in Section 7.2). For example, a notification message might be published by a JMS application and received by a notification consumer, as defined by WS-Notification.

The ESB can also mediate between request/response SOA and event oriented SOA services, by managing a set of topic spaces in its registry and by providing an implementation of one or more distributed notification brokers as defined by WS-Notification. The ESB administrator can configure one or more WS-Notification style notification brokers to be used by WS-Notification publishers or subscribers.

Application connectivity has to deal with several types of integration, which have some form of incarnation within any enterprise, even though in some cases they might be simplified or not clearly defined. It is important to note that all the following integration styles must be considered when embarking on an ESB implementation.

- *Application integration:* The main concern of application integration is building and evolving an integration backbone capability that enables fast assembly and disassembly of various platform and component technologies.

- *Business process integration:* Process integration is concerned with the development of automated processes that map to, and provide solutions for, business processes, integration of existing applications into processes, and integrating processes with other processes. For process integration needs, technologies such as BPEL can be used, See section 9.7.
- *Business data integration:* Data integration is the process of providing consistent access to business data in the enterprise, by all the applications that require it, in whatever form they need it, without being restricted by the format, source or location of the data. This requirement, when implemented, might involve adapters and transformation facilities, aggregation services to merge and reconcile disparate data, e.g. merging two customer profiles, and validation to ensure data consistency, e.g. minimum income should be equal to or exceed a certain threshold. Business data should be transformed irrespective of the formats under which it exists, the operating system that manages it, and the location where it is stored. Access to distributed business data is provided by a distributed query engine, such as the one shown in Figure 8.6.

One of the requirements for the application development environment must be that it takes into account all the styles and levels of integration that could be implemented within the enterprise, and provides for their development and deployment.

8.5.5 Modules of an ESB

Depending on the SOA entry point pursued (see Section 1.7.3) there are alternative ways to implement an ESB. The ESB itself can be a single centralised service, or even a distributed system consisting of peer and sub-peer ESBs – in the form of an ESB federation – all working in tandem to keep SOA applications operational.

In small scale SOA implementations of integration solutions, e.g. implementing small scale SOA orchestrations (see Section 1.7.3), the physical ESB infrastructure is likely to be a centralised ESB topology. A *centralised ESB topology* is concentrated on a single cluster, or hub, of servers. This solution is reminiscent of hub-and-spoke middleware topologies, which simply carries out one integration process on the central node. The central node is a central point of control responsible for integration/translation activities, maintaining routing information, service naming and so forth. The most popular hub-and-spoke EAI solution for the inter-enterprise arena is integration brokering (see Section 2.8.1 and Section 8.5.5.1). However, as already noted, hub-and-spoke solutions can quickly become a point of contention for large scale implementations.

In circumstances where the organisational or geographically dispersed units need to act independently from one another, the infrastructure may become more physically distributed while retaining at least logically the central control over configuration. This calls for a federated hub solution. The *federated ESB topology* is depicted in Figure 8.8, where it is shown to allow different enterprises, such as manufacturers, suppliers and customers, to plug together their integration domains into a larger federated integration network. This topology allows for local message traffic, integration components

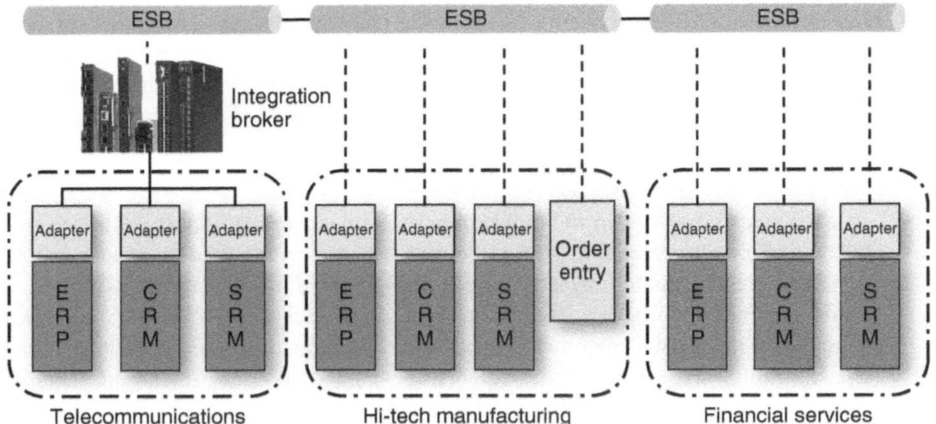

Figure 8.8 Distributed ESB allowing geographically dispersed organisations to ooperate

and adapters to be locally installed, configured, secured and managed, while allowing for a single integrated transaction and security model. The ESB reuses and integrates information and functionality found in typical enterprise systems such as Enterprise Resource Planning (ERP), Customer (CRM) and Supplier Relationship Management (SRM) systems. In this figure a federated ESB solution is used to form a virtual network of trading partners across industries and services, able to take advantage of the wider range of options and partnering models.

Irrespective of its implementation topology, the main aim of the ESB is to provide virtualisation of the enterprise resources, allowing the business logic of the enterprise to be developed and managed independently of the infrastructure, network and provision of business services. Implementing an ESB requires an integrated set of middleware facilities that support the following interrelated architectural styles [Endrei 2004]:

- Service Oriented Architectures, where distributed applications are composed of granular reusable services with well defined, published and standards compliant interfaces.
- Message driven architectures, where applications send messages through the ESB to receiving applications.
- Event driven architectures, where applications generate and consume messages independently of one another.

The physical deployment of the ESB depends on candidate technologies, e.g. specialised MOM, integration brokers, application servers, etc. The use and combination of different candidate ESB technologies results in a variety of ESB patterns, each having its own requirements and constraints in connection with its physical deployment.

Some ESB configurations might be suited to very widespread distribution to support integration over large geographical areas, while others might be more suited to deployment in localised clusters to support high availability and scalability. Matching the requirements for physical distribution to the capabilities of candidate technologies is an important aspect of ESB design. Also important is the ability incrementally to extend the initial deployment to reflect evolving requirements, to integrate additional systems, or to extend the geographical reach of the ESB infrastructure [Robinson 2004]. These middleware solutions that support the physical deployment of an ESB are discussed in the following sections.

8.5.5.1 Integration brokers

To integrate disparate business applications one must concentrate on the characteristics and functions of integration brokers, which we covered as part of the introduction to the distributing infrastructure in Section 2.8.1. Figure 8.9 presents a high level view of the typical architecture for implementing an integration broker.

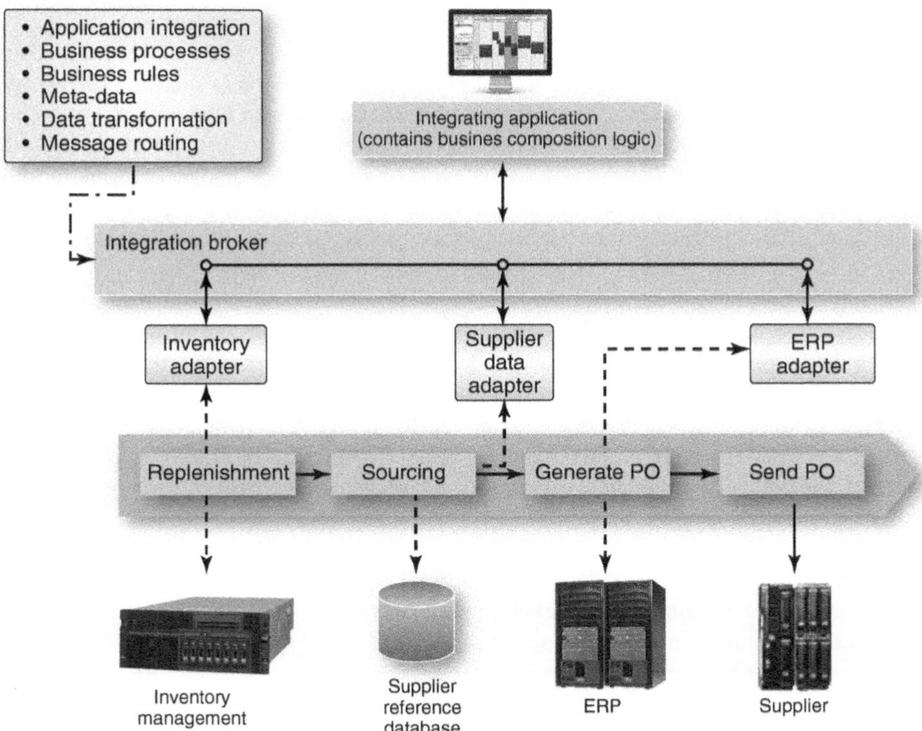

Figure 8.9 Integration broker integrating disparate back end systems

Example 8.4: Using an integration broker to implement the procurement process

Figure 8.9 illustrates the use of an integration broker to integrate functions and information from a variety of back-end EISs. To illustrate effectively the behaviour of the integration broker, we use the simplified distributed procurement process we examined earlier in conjunction with Example 8.3. Figure 8.9 shows that when an automated inventory system triggers a replenishment signal, an automated procurement process flow is triggered and, first, the enterprise's supplier reference database is queried to determine the list of possible suppliers, which could be prioritised on the basis of existing contracts and supplier metrics. A supplier is then chosen and the purchase order is automatically generated in the ERP purchasing module and is sent to the vendor of choice.

Figure 8.9 illustrates that the integration broker is the system centerpiece. The integration broker facilitates information movement between two or more resources (source and target applications), shown by means of solid lines in Figure 8.9, and accounts for differences in application semantics and heterogeneous platforms. The various existing (or component) EIS, such as CRM, ERP systems, transaction processing monitors, legacy systems and so on, in Figure 8.9 are connected to the integration broker by means of resource adapters. The dashed lines in this figure mark this type of connection.

A *resource adapter* is used to provide access to a specific EIS and enable non invasive application integration in a loosely coupled configuration. Adapters map the differences between two distinct interfaces: the integration broker interface and the native interface of the source or target application. Adapters hide the complexities of that interface from the end user or even the developer, using the integration broker. For instance, an integration broker vendor may have adapters for several different source and target applications (such as packaged ERP applications), or adapters for certain types of databases (such as Oracle, Sybase or DB2), or even adapters for specific brands of middleware.

The integration broker architecture presents several advantages given that integration brokers try to reduce the application integration effort by providing pre-built functionality common to many integration scenarios. In an ESB, the functionality of an integration broker, such as messaging and connectivity, application adapters, data transformation engine and routing of messages, is spread out across a highly distributed architecture that allows selective deployment and independent scalability of each of those pieces. This is an important difference from the classic integration broker model where these capabilities are localised to a central monolithic server.

In many situations it is essential that newly developed ESB solutions be bridged to existing integration broker installations. In this scenario, the ESB utilises an integration broker to support new application development. Section 8.5.7 explains this approach in some detail in conjunction with ESB scalability.

8.5.5.2 Application servers

Another critical middleware module used in connection with ESBs is an application server. An *application server* is a natural point for application integration, as it provides a platform for development, deployment and management of Web based, transactional, secure, distributed and scalable enterprise applications.

Application servers offer an integrated development environment for developing and deploying distributed Web and non Web based applications and services. This makes application servers ideal for portal based ESB development. Unlike an integration broker, an application server does not integrate back end systems directly but rather expects the integration broker to function as a service provider, providing data access, transformations and content based routing.

Example 8.5: Using an application server for a wholesale process

Figure 8.10 illustrates the use of an application server for a wholesale application that brings together ERP capabilities with customer interfaces to open up possibilities for sales and distribution. In this figure the adapter/component wrapper modules are responsible for providing a layer of abstraction between the application server and the component EIS, e.g. ERP, CRM applications. This layer allows for EIS component communications as if the component EIS were executed within the application server environment itself. Execution in this type of architecture occurs among component wrappers within the application server. The component wrappers in this figure facilitate point integration of component EIS by wrapping legacy systems and applications, and other back end resources such as databases, ERP, CRM and SRM, so that they can express data and messages in the standard internal format expected by the application server. The application server is oblivious to the fact that these components are only the external facade of existing EIS that do the real processing activities.

Application servers are principally J2EE based and include support for JMS, the Java 2 Connector Architecture (JCA), and Web services.

Application servers can plug into an ESB using established conventions such as JMS, see Section 2.8.2. For application server implementations, JMS provides access to business logic distributed among heterogeneous systems. Having a message based interface enables point-to-point and publish/subscribe mechanisms, guaranteed information delivery, and interoperability between heterogeneous platforms.

JCA is a technology that can be used to address the hardships of integrating applications in an ESB environment. JCA is a standardised method for integrating disparate applications in J2EE application architectures. When JCA is used in an ESB implementation, the ESB could provide a JCA container that allows packaged or legacy applications to be plugged into the ESB through JCA resource adapters. For instance, a process order servic e uses JCA to talk to a J2EE application that internally fulfils incoming orders.

In conclusion, just like the case of integration broker solutions, the centralised nature of the application-server-centric model of integrating applications, can quickly become a point of contention and introduce severe performance problems for large scale integration projects.

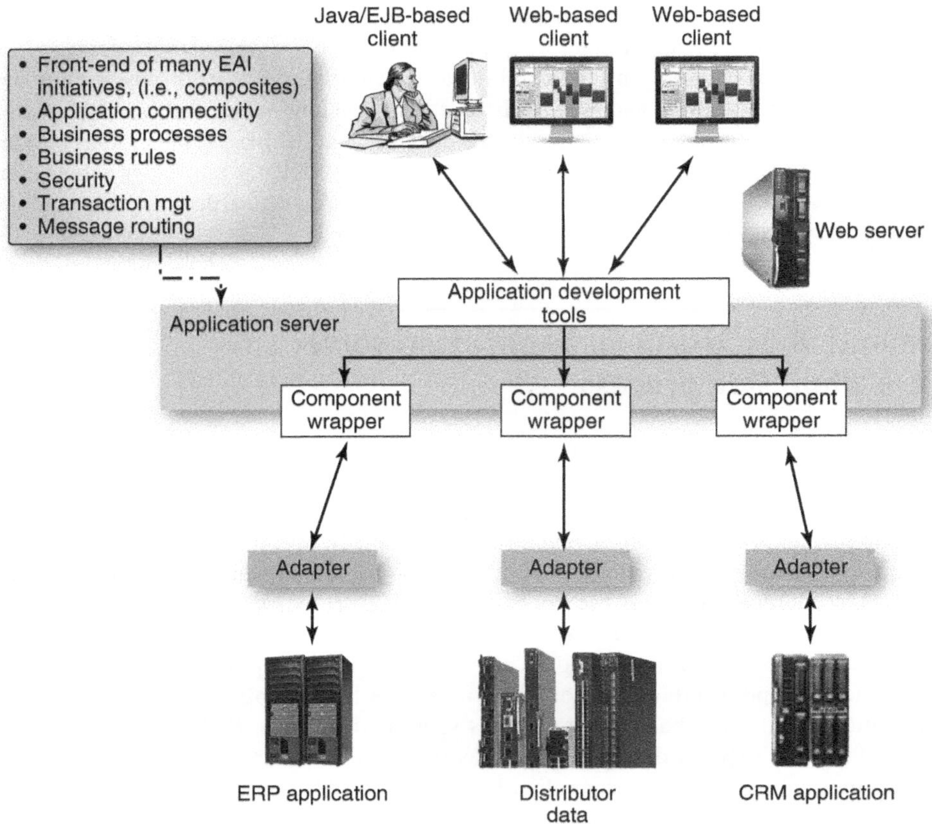

Figure 8.10 Application server providing a platform for the development of Web based applications

---

8.5.5.3 ESB wrappers

In the previous section we explained the need to employ wrappers to encapsulate legacy and/or package functionality. The functions of wrappers are, in general, not very well understood outside the EAI community. Moreover, as in the Web services literature there seems to be a lot of confusion regarding the concept of wrappers and adapters, it is useful to clarify their meaning and intended purpose.

A *wrapper* is nothing but an abstract software module that provides a service implemented by legacy software that can be used to hide existing system dependencies. A wrapper can provide a standard interface on one side, while on the other it interfaces with existing application code in a way that is particular to the existing application code. The wrapper combines the existing application functionality that it wraps with other necessary service functionality and represents it in the form of a virtual component that is accessed via a standard service interface by any other service in an ESB.

When a legacy business process is wrapped, its realisation comprises code to access an adapter that invokes the legacy system. This is shown in Figure 8.10. An adapter, unlike a wrapper, does not contain presentation or business logic functions. As implied in the integration broker configuration in Figure 8.9, an adapter is rather a software module interposed between two software systems in order to convert between their different technical and programmatic representations and perceptions of their interfaces. Resource adapters translate the applications' messages to and from a common set of standards – standard data formats and standard communication protocols (see also Section 2.8.1).

8.5.5.4 Business Process Management

Today, enterprises are striving to become electronically connected to their customers, suppliers and partners. To achieve this, they are integrating a wide range of discrete business processes across application boundaries of all kinds. When integrating on such a scale, enterprises need a greater latitude of functionality to overcome multiple challenges arising from the existence of proprietary interfaces, diverse standards, and approaches targeting the technical, data, automated business process, process analysis, and visualisation levels. Such challenges are addressed by Business Process Management (BPM) technology. In this section we shall only provide a short overview of BPM functionality in the context of ESB implementations. BPM is driven primarily by the common desire to integrate supply chains, as well as internal enterprise functions, without the need for even more custom software development.

BPM is the term used to describe the new technology that provides end-to-end visibility and control over all parts of a long lived, multi-step information request or transaction/process that spans multiple applications and human actors in one or more enterprises. It also provides the ability to monitor both the state of any single process instance and all process instances in an aggregate, using real time metrics that translate actual process activity into key performance indicators.

BPM software solutions provide workflow related business processes, process analysis and visualisation techniques in an ESB setting. In particular, BPM allows the separation of business processes from the underlying integration code. When sophisticated process definitions are called for in an ESB, a process orchestration engine – that supports BPEL or some other process definition language – may be layered onto the ESB. The process orchestration may support long running stateful processes. Process orchestration can be combined with stateless, itinerary based routing to create an SOA that solves complex integration problems. For more details about BPM technology, readers are referred to Section 9.3 where we examine BPM in conjunction with business processes.

8.5.5.5 ESB transport level choices

Finally, before we close this section, it is important to understand the transport level protocol choices that can be used in conjunction with an ESB.

Web services in the ESB can communicate using SOAP messages over a variety of protocols. Each protocol effectively provides a service bus connecting multiple endpoints. Currently, the most common service bus transport layer implementations include SOAP/HTTP(S) and SOAP/JMS [Keen 2004].

The SOAP over HTTP service bus is the most familiar way to send requests and responses between service requesters and providers. Use of an ESB enables the service requester to communicate using HTTP and permits the service provider to receive the request using HTTP or a different transport mechanism. Many ESB implementation providers have an HTTP service bus in addition to at least one other protocol. Any of these protocols can be used for ESB interactions and often are chosen based on service-level requirements.

As already noted, JMS provides a conventional way to create, send and receive enterprise messages. While it does not quite provide the level of interoperability based on the wide adoption that the HTTP ESB can boast, the SOAP/JMS ESB brings advantages in terms of QoS. A SOAP/JMS based ESB can provide asynchronous and reliable messaging to a Web service invocation.

8.5.6 ESB connectivity and translation infrastructure

For the most part, business applications in an enterprise are not designed to communicate with other applications. There is often an impedance mismatch between the technologies used within internal systems and with external trading partner systems. In order to seamlessly integrate these disparate applications, there must be a way in which a request for information in one format can easily be transformed into a format expected by the called exposed to non-J2EE clients such as .NET applications and other clients. In doing so, a Web service may have to integrate with other instances of EIS in an organisation. In such scenarios, how the application exchanges information with the ESB depends on the application accessibility options.

There are three alternative ways an application can exchange information with the ESB [Keen 2004]:

1. *Application provided Web service interface:* Some applications and legacy application servers have adopted the open standards philosophy and have included a Web service interface. WSDL defines the interface to communicate directly with the application business logic. Where possible, taking a direct approach is always preferred.

2. *Non-Web service interface:* The application does not expose business logic via Web services. An application specific adapter can be supplied to provide a basic intermediary between the application API and the ESB.

3. *Service wrapper as interface to adapter:* In some cases the adapter may not supply the correct protocol (JMS, for example) that the ESB expects. In this case, the adapter would be Web service enabled.

Example 8.6: Using Web services and adapters in a complex integration scenario

As complementary technologies in an ESB implementation, (resource) adapters and Web services can work together to implement complex integration scenarios. This is illustrated in Figure 8.11, which shows that adapters can take on the role of data translation and synchronisation services.

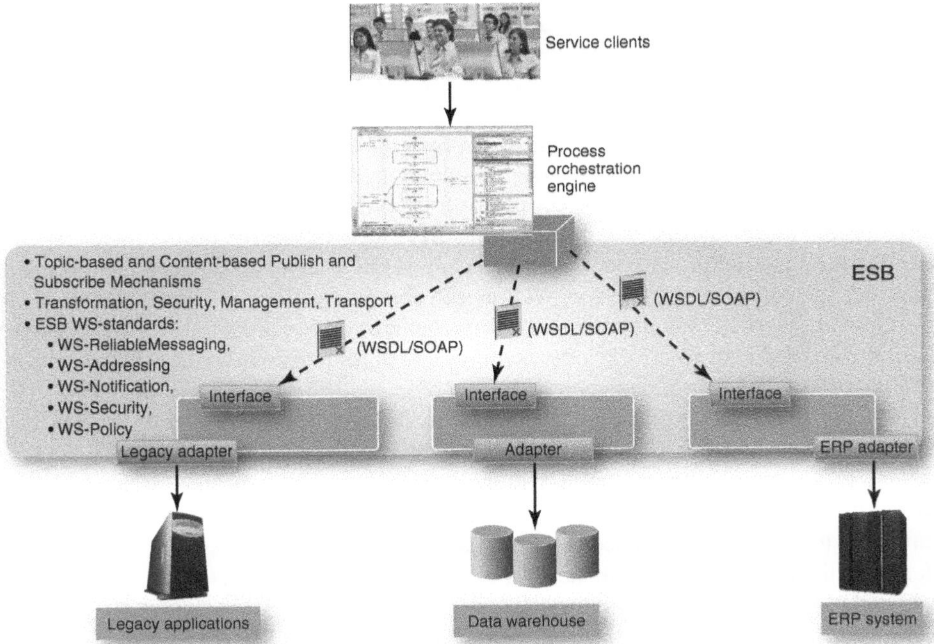

Figure 8.11 Combining Web services with resource adapters

In the scenario illustrated in Figure 8.11, Web services are an ideal mechanism for implementing a universally accessible application function (service) that may need to integrate with other applications using a process orchestration engine. An event to which a Web service reacts could be a user initiated request, e.g. a purchase order or an on line bill payment. User events can naturally be generated by applications, such as an order management application requiring a customer status check from an accounting system. On the other hand, a state change in a data object can be an activity, like the addition of a new customer record in the customer service application or an update to the customer's billing address. These state changes trigger an adapter to add the new customer record or update the customer record in all other applications that keep their own copies of customer data.

Another potential integration pattern in which Web services and resource adapters are required to collaborate is when business processed are integrated, as shown in Figure 8.11. Applications that use business processes will have to expose required functionality. Obviously, Web services are ideal for this purpose. When the applications need to integrate with other EIS to fulfil their part in the business process, they can employ resource adapters.

8.5.7 ESB scalability concerns

Scalability is a particularly important issue for any automated business integration solution. The fact that the ESB uses asynchronous communications, message itineraries, message and process definitions, allows different parts of the ESB to operate independently of each other. The use of asynchronous communications, message itineraries, message and process definitions allow different parts of the ESB to operate independently of one another. This results in a decentralised model providing complete flexibility in scaling any aspect of the integration network. Such a decentralised architecture enables independent scalability of individual services, as well as the communications infrastructure itself. In the following we shall examine the scalability concerns and options for an effective SOA solution. We shall start first by briefly examining the problems with typical EAI solutions and shall proceed by examining centralised and federated ESB configurations.

The ESB approach comes in stark contrast to the approach followed by typical EAI solutions, which rely on integration broker technologies to handle scalability. These EAI solutions use a centralised hub-and-spoke model, i.e. they handle changes in load and configuration by increasing broker capacity or by adding integration brokers in a centralised location. A centralised rules engine for the routing of messages, such as those offered by the typical hub-and-spoke EAI broker approach, can quickly become a bottleneck, and also a single point of failure.

Figure 8.12 illustrates how the integration broker functionality is incorporated in the ESB to address scalability and load balancing concerns. When the capacity of a single broker is reached, brokers can be combined into clusters. These may act as a single virtual broker to handle increased demand from users and applications. The ESB's use of integration brokers and broker clusters increases scalability, by allowing brokers to communicate and dynamically distribute load on the bus. For example, in the event that an increase in the use of the inventory services has overloaded the capacity of their host machine(s), new machines and new brokers can be added to handle the load without the need to change any of the services themselves, and without requiring any additional development or administration changes to the messaging system. The distributed functional pieces are able to work together as one logical piece with a single, globally accessible namespace for locating and invoking services.

The service integration pattern in Figure 8.12 uses a *centralised ESB* solution. The benefits of this type of integration pattern are that it breaks a fairly complex process into multiple smaller, manageable pieces. Unfortunately, this integration pattern is clearly not scalable as it creates an unmanageable number of small, segregated standalone pieces of

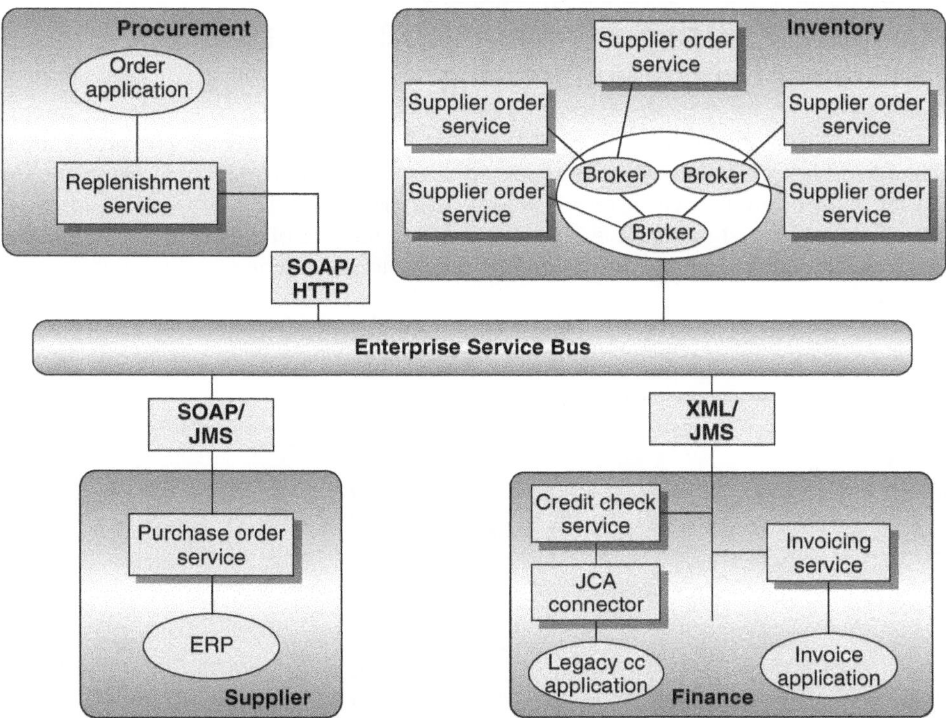

Figure 8.12 Scaling services in the ESB
(*Source*: adapted from [Chappell 2004])

integration logic that implement simple business rules. This ability to centralise functionalities, such as message routing, transformation, and workflows in a centralised ESB solution, is probably useful for lightweight SOA implementations but quite unrealistic in medium to large enterprise environments.

If large scale SOA applications (see Section 1.7.3) run on distributed locations and, as business processes span organisational boundaries, a central ESB deployment will not suffice. Enterprises need to move to a more flexible integration pattern in which the SOA functionality is partitioned across multiple lightweight physical ESBs that are grouped as a federated entity.

An *ESB federation,* as already noted in Section 8.5.5, allows different ESB products to be employed in different autonomous domains, based on lines of business, functional or governance areas, e.g. distribution and logistics, inventory and warehousing, manufacturing, etc., allowing an optimal match between domain requirements and product capabilities. In such situations a centralised ESB very often is one of the fundamental causes of failed SOA initiatives. Federated ESBs form a single, logical ESB infrastructure that enables sharing of data, applications, resources and skills that can ultimately reduce integration costs and complexity.

Example 8.7: Using a federated ESB for distributed procurement and manufacturing

Figure 8.13 exemplifies the concept of federated ESBs in a distributed procurement and manufacturing application, where products are completed after receipt of a customer order and are built or configured in response to a customer order. This example is an extension of that examined in Figure 8.12, as it involves a number of collaborating companies, e.g. manufacturers, suppliers, logistics providers, etc, in a series of distributed supply chain activities.

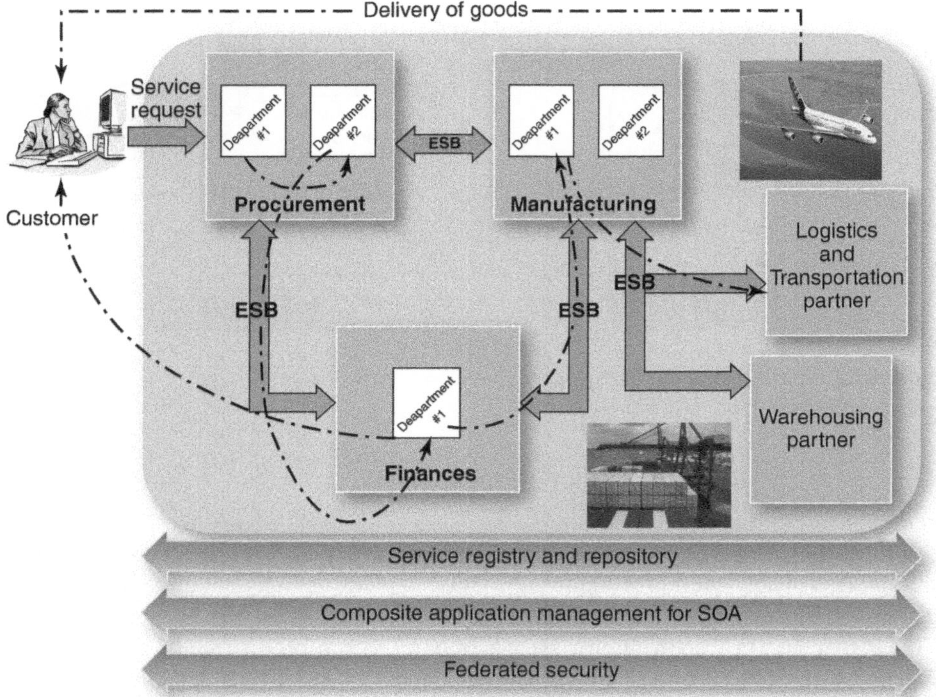

Figure 8.13 The federated ESB approach

Activities in this distributed procurement example range from selection, procurement and physical movement of sourced products (e.g. raw materials, fabricated components, subassemblies or required ingredients) from a stocking location (e.g. stockroom, a location on the production floor or a supplier) to a specific point of use and production. It also includes the movement of finished packaged products into warehouses and their shipment per the associated customer order.

Figure 8.13 shows that, to address the scalability requirements of large scale SOA applications, the service infrastructure is portioned into separate ESB that can be scaled and configured separately. For instance, in this integration pattern, we can have a specific ESB infrastructure to host the procurement or manufacturing process activities, while another ESB is in charge of the financial transaction processing or logistics and distribution.

Enterprise service governance, security, and registry management become important considerations in a federated approach. The federated ESB approach in Figure 8.13 is shown to centralise certain services, such as security, a common service registry and repository or endpoint configuration. These do not impose any scalability limitation on the SOA infrastructure. An individual ESB domain may be chosen to establish an access and control point for a collection of services, e.g. security or registry, in that domain. Such a separation of service buses may provide independence for each application portfolio and yet enable access to shared resources when appropriate.

8.6 The extended SOA

When we look at the capabilities of the ESB we realize that it offers a wide range of service functionality at various levels. At the lower level it offers a functionality typical of service containers, including communication and connectivity capabilities. At a higher (middle) level it offers long running processes, unconventional transaction support and service orchestration capabilities. It also provides service management and monitoring capabilities that transcend both the middle and lower levels. Therefore, it becomes obvious that there is a clear necessity to be able to streamline and structure related service functionality to tackle efficiently the functional requirements of complex SOA applications that make use of the ESB. Such overarching concerns are addressed by the extended SOA (xSOA).

The xSOA [Papazoglou 2003], [Papazoglou 2005] is an attempt to provide a layered service based architecture that appropriately extends conventional SOAs. The architectural layers in the xSOA, which are depicted in Figure 8.14, describe a logical separation of functionality in such a way that each layer defines a set of constructs, roles and responsibilities, and leans on constructs of its preceding layer to accomplish its mission. The logical separation of functionality is based on the need to separate basic service capabilities provided by the conventional SOA (e.g. building relatively simple service based applications) from more advanced service functionality needed for composing services, and the need to distinguish between the functionality for composing services from that for the management of services. The overall objective of these functional layers is to provide facilities for ensuring consistency across the organisation, high availability of services, security of non-public services and information, orchestration of multiple services as part of mission critical composite applications – all essential requirements for business strength SOAs.

As illustrated in Figure 8.14, xSOA offers three functional planes: the foundation, the composition, and the management and monitoring. The lowermost plane in the xSOA

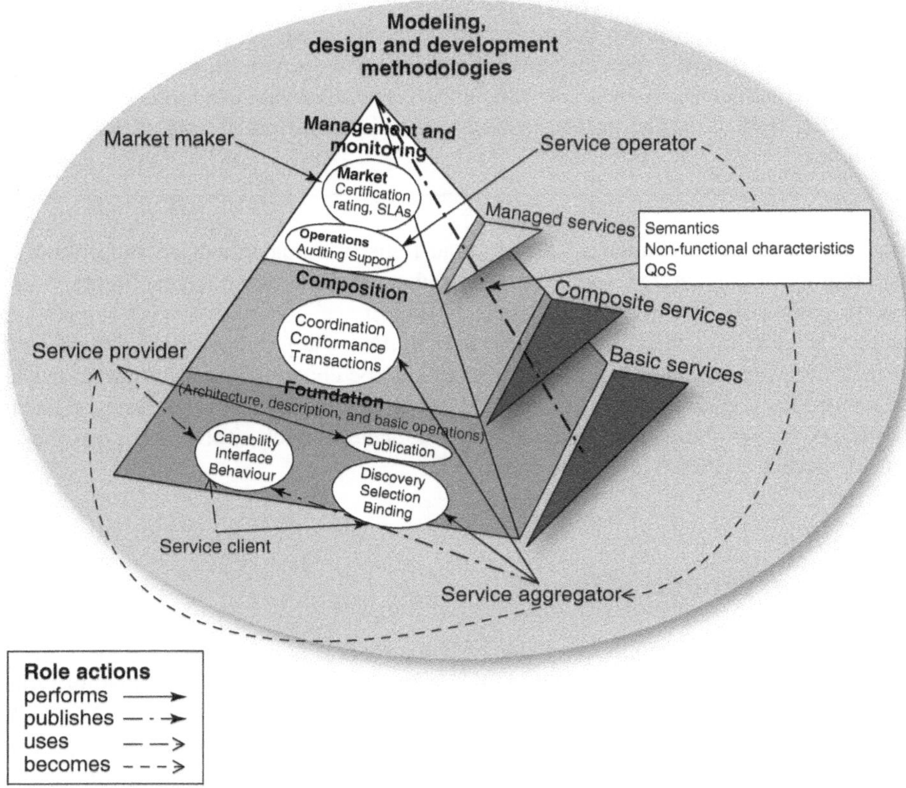

Figure 8.14 The extended SOA (xSOA)

is the foundation plane, which supports Web services communication primitives and utilises the basic service middleware for describing, publishing, discovering and executing services, which are widely accepted and implemented quite uniformly. Higher level planes are layered on top of the foundation plane and extend it with business process functionality, and the management and monitoring of Web service processes and applications. The perpendicular axis in Figure 8.14 designates service characteristics that cut across all three planes. These include service semantics, non-functional service properties, and QoS. The xSOA is shown to support a variety of roles. In addition to the classical roles of service client and provider, it also supports the roles of service aggregator, service operator and market maker. In the following we shall focus briefly on the characteristics of the individual xSOA planes.

The service foundation plane offers the baseline functionality found in the classical concept of SOA as we know it, and as illustrated in Figure 8.4. This plane provides a service oriented middleware backbone that realises the run time SOA infrastructure that connects heterogeneous components and systems, provides a variety of communication protocols over a variety of networks. This backbone infrastructure allows definition of the classical SOA functions involving communication, and the description, publishing, finding and binding of services. Five sets of standards implement the service foundations plane. These are SOAP, WSDL, UDDI, WS-Notification, and WS-MetaDataExchange (see Chapter 13).

The following plane in Figure 8.14 is the service composition plane. This encompasses roles and functionality that are necessary for the aggregation of multiple (possibly singular) services into a single composite service. Resulting composite services may be used as discrete services in further service compositions or may be offered as complete applications/solutions to service clients. Service aggregators accomplish this task. The role actions in Figure 8.14 indicate that service aggregators can become service providers by publishing the service descriptions of the composite service they create. Service aggregators develop specifications and/or code that permit the composite service to perform functions that are based on features such as metadata descriptions, standard terminology and reference models (see Chapters 13 and 14); service coordination to control the execution of the composite services (i.e. processes), and Web service transactions (see Chapters 9 and 10); as well as policy enforcement (see Chapter 12).

Currently, standards such as BPEL and WS-CDL are used at the level of the service composition plane in xSOA and enable the creation of large service collaborations that allow companies to conduct business in an automated fashion. Managing the health of loosely coupled applications in an SOA is therefore an absolute requirement. This brings us to the top most plane in xSOA, namely service management and monitoring.

A consistent management and monitoring infrastructure is essential for production quality Web services and applications, and is provided by the management and monitoring plane in xSOA. This requires that a critical characteristic be realised, namely that services be managed and monitored. Service management encompasses the control and monitoring of SOA based applications throughout their lifecycle. This counters such situations as the failure or change of a single application component that may bring down other interdependent components, the addition of new applications or components that can overload existing components, or unexpected degradation or failure of seemingly unrelated systems. Service management spans a large number of activities that range from installation and configuration to collecting metrics and tuning to ensure responsive service execution and to efficiently manage service operations. Because of its importance, service management is treated in a dedicated chapter (Chapter 17).

A critical trend that is emerging with the introduction of SOA and Web services is the rise in service mediated interaction involving a large number customers, suppliers, regulators, financial institutions, and literally every outside party involved in an enterprise's operations. This trend is expected to trigger *open service marketplaces* (also known as service based trading communities) whose purpose is to create opportunities for buyers and sellers to meet and conduct business electronically, or aggregate service supply/demand by offering added value business services and grouping buying power. Service marketplaces typically support integrated value networks by providing to their members a unified view of products and services standard business terminology and naming conventions, standard business data formats, services and processes to enable enterprises to transact business over the Internet. In addition, service market places are expected to offer a comprehensive range of services supporting trade, e.g. business transaction negotiation and facilitation, financial settlement, enforcement of SLAs, etc. This kind of functionality introduces a new role, that of a *market maker,* which is the entity that supports and maintains an open service market.

Finally, a quintessential requirement for developing advanced applications according to the xSOA planes is the use of an SOA lifecycle methodology. A service development methodology starts with analysing and modelling the business environment, including key performance indicators of business goals and objectives, translating that model into service design, deploying that service system, and managing and monitoring that deployment. These and related topics are the province of Chapter 16.

8.7 Summary of learning objectives

Service Oriented Architectures and technologies must employ a reliable messaging backbone so that organisations can use Web services for the deployment in industrial strength business applications.

- The WS-ReliableMessaging standard is at the heart of service oriented computing architectural approaches and serves as the enabling feature for addressing the requirements of loosely coupled, reliable distributed computing and SOA applications.

SOA enabling technologies and architectural approaches serve as the springboard for business integration projects and deliver a flexible environment that enables Web services and SOA application integration to be put in place productively, effectively and in a staged manner.

- Of particular interest is the Enterprise Service Bus, which is a Web services middleware infrastructure that provides a whole range of functions designed to offer a manageable, standards based, messaging oriented middleware functionality connecting heterogeneous components and systems.
- Combining Web services standards with an ESB infrastructure can potentially deliver the broadest connectivity between systems. It can leverage existing infrastructure for universal service delivery and easily extend it to federated ESB and service federation models.

Review questions

- What are system quality attributes and how do they relate to software architectures?
- Briefly describe the common architectural constraints and explain how they relate to the SOA.

- What is reliable messaging and why is it important for SOA based applications?
- Briefly describe the WS-ReliableMessaging model.
- How does WS-ReliableMessaging relate to SOA?
- What is the purpose of an event driven SOA?
- How can an event driven SOA be realised by an Enterprise Service Bus?
- Briefly describe the key capabilities of an Enterprise Service Bus.
- Which are the most common Web service standards used by an Enterprise Service Bus solution?
- Briefly describe the integration styles employed in an ESB solution.
- How are integration brokers and application servers used in an ESB solution?
- How is scalability achieved in an ESB solution? Explain the differences between a centralised and a federated ESB solution.

Exercises

8.1. Assume that the purchase order service allows its clients to make bulk order submissions under the condition that bulk orders are submitted as part of the same sequence and that WS-ReliableMessaging is used to perform the submissions. Encode an SOAP header using WS-ReliableMessaging to address this problem. Use the code snippet in Listing 8.1 to help you develop your solution.

8.2. An organisation that produces goods, and relies on the services of carriers to distribute them to its customers, wishes to develop an SOA solution that enables it to integrate its systems with those of carriers, suppliers and customers. As the organisation tends to do business with a variety of carriers, it requires that a single interface be provided to those carriers. Moreover, the organisation requires that the integration solution should offer functionality that would help it to manage visibility of orders as they move outbound in its distribution chain to its customers. The use of open standards is preferred as the organisation has no direct control over the technologies used by its partners. Develop an SOA compliant architecture based on a Web services broker required to provide secure, manageable access from external parties to those applications.

8.3. The solution for the previous exercise should be modified so that the service interactions between the transacting enterprises should combine at some level to form business processes and workflow solutions. These processes should be explicitly modelled and executed using an appropriate business process execution language in compliance with appropriate open standards.

8.4. Broadly speaking, business process integration may result in several business integration patterns whose aim is to manage and support business automation and integration across distributed enterprises [Papazoglou 2006]. The business process integration patterns include: the integrated enterprise, the brokered enterprise, and the federated enterprise integration patterns. Selecting the most appropriate business process pattern for an organisation depends on the business needs, structure, and business priorities of an enterprise.

The integrated business pattern is about ensuring that end-to-end business processes are managed and monitored in a complete fashion across and within all business units. Business processes are viewed across the entire enterprise, where activities span organisational units and are carried out by separate business sections that have a responsibility for them. This business integration pattern assumes that workflow and integration process may cross-organisational units and are managed by a group within the enterprise. This group is also responsible for setting policies on toolset selection and on message standards. The integrated enterprise business pattern is most suitable for small enterprises or larger enterprises where a common standard integration toolset is imposed.

Design an ESB solution for a large enterprise employing the integrated enterprise business pattern. In this enterprise, end-to-end business process flows occur between departmental units and the activities carried out in the various departments can be treated as organisational activities within business units (which may contain one or more departments). Business units simply identify the responsibility to carry out organisational activities. This implies that business unit boundaries have no impact on the business process flow. In the ESB solution an external partner is responsible for carrying out the logistics and distribution processes, such as warehousing, distribution and management inventory. The logistical workflow should be seamlessly integrated into the end-to-end business processes of the enterprise and is dependent on the exchange and processing of consignment notes, goods advice invoices and other business documents.

8.5. The brokered enterprise business pattern is about ensuring that processes are managed and monitored across all business units by means of a broker business unit. This is a distributed business enterprise scheme, where business units are fairly autonomous but use the business broker to manage communication and interoperation. The individual business units still own the processes provided, but must maintain standards for both messages and inter-business unit processing, and must register the services they provide and the processes supporting them with the broker unit registry. With this scheme all requests are handled by the broker unit, so a service client is not aware of which organisational unit provides the business process handling the service. The brokered enterprise pattern is applicable to organisations where the individual organisation units want to maintain their autonomy but benefit from the advantages of a hub style service management and a common messaging infrastructure. Design an ESB solution for a large enterprise employing the brokered enterprise business pattern.

8.6. The federated enterprise business pattern is driven by the expectation that individual business units in a large enterprise, or an integrated value chain, are completely autonomous and are expected to cooperate when there is a need for it. As there is no overall business management and monitoring, business processes are not viewed end-to-end and each unit is responsible for providing and maintaining standard interfaces so that it can cooperate with other such units. Common standards for messaging and for describing the services provided are introduced with each business unit managing its own service repository. The federated enterprise pattern is applicable to organisations where the individual organisation units want to maintain their autonomy but benefit from the advantages of coop erating with other business units in the organisation and the use of a common messaging infrastructure and cooperation standards. Design an ESB solution for a large enterprise employing the federated enterprise business pattern.

PART V

Service composition and transactions

CHAPTER 9

Service composition and business processes

Learning objectives

To create business processes, Web services need to be composed. Service composition refers to the aggregation of Web services. Various Web service composition languages and technologies have emerged to provide the mechanisms for describing how individual Web services can be composed to create reliable and dependable business process based solutions with the appropriate level of complexity.

In this chapter we introduce workflow and business process technologies and explain how they can support linking together applications comprising Web services. After reading this chapter you will understand the following key concepts:

- Business processes and workflow systems.
- How business processes can be integrated and managed.
- The main ingredients of a business process solution, such as flow modelling, and composition of Web services.
- The concepts of process orchestration and process choreography.
- The main constructs of the Web Services Business Process Execution Language v2.0.
- A high level view of the Web services Choreography Description Language.

Chapter preview

SOA is not just the architecture of services seen from a technology perspective, but the policies, practices and frameworks by which we ensure the right services are provided and consumed. Processes are the core component of the SOA approach.

In this chapter we introduce the characteristics and workflow origins of business processes and explain how business processes can be composed of services. Following this we focus on patterns of Web service interaction and present the concepts of service orchestration and choreography, which are geared towards achieving long term solutions for business connectivity. Finally, we delve into the service orchestration standard Business Process Execution Language for Web Services (BPEL) version 2.0 and use several examples to explain its main features. This standard is designed to reduce the inherent complexity of connecting Web services together.

9.1 Business processes and their management

The SOA approach focuses on organisational efforts on the use of fewer, reusable applications that can be easily integrated and repurposed. This focus helps to integrate disparate applications, and assemble services rapidly into new, composite applications. Since a true SOA plan requires that services be created that are independent of each other, it is imperative that there be a mechanism in place to enable these services to be linked together. This mechanism is the concept of business process, which lies at the heart of SOA.

Before discussing business processes it is useful to understand the concept of a process. A *process* is an ordering of activities with a beginning and an end; it has inputs (in terms of resources, materials and information) and a specified output (the results it produces). We may thus define a process as any sequence of steps that is initiated by an event, transforms information, materials or commitments, and produces an output [Harmon 2003a].

A *business process* is a process in which a set of logically related tasks is performed to achieve a well defined business objective. A (business) process view implies a horizontal view of a business organisation and looks at processes as sets of interdependent activities designed and structured to produce a specific output for a customer or a market. A business process defines the results to be achieved, the context of the activities, the relationships between the activities, and the interactions with other processes and resources. A business process may receive events that alter the state of the process and the sequence of activities. It may produce events for input to other applications or processes. It may also invoke applications to perform computational functions, and it may post assignments to human work lists to request actions by human actors.

Each enterprise has unique characteristics that are embedded in its business processes. Most enterprises perform a similar set of repeatable routine activities that may include the development of manufacturing products and services, bringing these products and services to market, and satisfying the customers who purchase them. Automated business processes can perform such activities. We may view an *automated business process* as a precisely orchestrated sequence of activities systematically directed towards performing a certain business task and bringing it to completion. The subject of this book is automated business processes. Examples of typical automated business processes in manufacturing firms include, among other things, new product development (which cuts across research and development, marketing and manufacturing), customer order fulfilment (which combines sales, manufacturing, warehousing, transportation and billing), and financial asset management.

At run time, a business process definition may have multiple *instantiations,* each operating independently of the other, where each instantiation may have multiple activities that are concurrently active. A process instance is a defined thread of activity that is being enacted (managed) by a workflow engine. In general, instances of a process, its current state, and the history of its actions will be visible at run time and is expressed in terms of the business process definition. In this way, process users can determine the status of business activities, and business specialists can monitor the activity and identify potential improvements to the business process definition.

The possibility to design, structure, measure processes, and determine their contribution to customer value makes them an important starting point for business improvement and innovation initiatives. Business processes can be measured, and different performance measures applied, like cost, quality, time and customer satisfaction.

9.1.1 Characteristics of business processes

A business process is typically associated with operational objectives and business relationships, e.g. requisition and payment of a product, or a billing and collections management process. A business process may be wholly contained within a single organisational unit or may span different organisations, such as in a customer–supplier relationship. Typical examples of processes that cross organisational boundaries are purchasing and sales processes, which are jointly set up by buying and selling organisations.

Every process has a client and is initiated by a client request. The client may be external, like the final customer for whom a service or product is produced, or internal, like another process for which the output of the process under consideration forms an input. Not every process is directly triggered by a customer order. It is possible that a process is triggered by a standard procedure (event). For example, salary payments are triggered by a specific date in the month.

Business processes are characterised by the activities they perform, the decisions they make, and the results they deliver.

Every business process implies computation: a series of *activities* (processing steps) leading to some form of transformation of data or products for which the process exists. An activity is an element that performs a specific function within a process. Activities can be as simple as sending or receiving a message, or as complex as coordinating the execution of other processes and activities. An activity may invoke another business process in the same or a different business system domain. Transformations may be executed manually or in an automated way. A *transformation* will encompass multiple processing steps. For example, the process *authorising invoices* will encompass the steps *checking whether the invoice has not yet been paid, checking the agreed purchasing conditions, checking the receiving report, checking calculations,* and *checking name, address, and bank account of the creditor.* If, and only if, all the checkpoints are correct, the invoice will be registered in the accounts payable administration. In general, a business process may encompass a series of complex activities some of which run on back end systems, such as a credit check, automated billing, a purchase order, stock updates and shipping, or even such mundane activities as sending a document and filling a form. Activities will inevitably vary greatly from one company to another and from one business analysis effort to another.

Typically, a workflow application is associated with business processes and their activities. This is irrespective of whether the issue is the management of a logistics chain, supply chain planning, or simply the exchange of documents between trading partners, or any other kind of business process centered application.

Processes have *decision points.* Decisions have to be made with regard to routing and allocation of processing capacity. In a highly predictable and standardised environment, the trajectory in the process of a client request will be established in advance in a standard way. Only if the process is complex, and if the conditions of the process are not predictable, will routing decisions have to be made on the spot. In general, the client request will be split into a category that is highly proceduralised (and therefore automated) and a category that is complex and uncertain. Here human experts will be needed and manual processing is a key element of the process.

Finally, every process *delivers a product,* like a mortgage or an authorised invoice. The extent to which the end product of a process can be specified in advance and can be standardised impacts on the way that processes and their work flows can be structured and automated.

To summarise this discussion, a real business process may exhibit the following features and behaviour:

- It may contain defined conditions triggering its initiation in each new instance (e.g. the arrival of a claim) and defined outputs at its completion.
- It may involve formal or relatively informal interactions between participants.
- It has a duration that may vary widely.
- It may contain a series of automated activities and/or manual activities. Activities may be large and complex, involving the flow of materials, information, and business commitments.
- It may exhibit a very dynamic nature, so it can respond to demands from customers and to changing market conditions.
- It may be widely distributed and customised across boundaries within and between organisations, often spanning multiple applications with very different technology platforms.
- It is can be long running – a single instance of a process, such as order to cash, may run for months or even years.

9.2 Workflows

Workflows are closely related to business processes. A workflow system *automates* a business process, in whole or in part, during which documents, information or tasks are passed from one participant to another for action, according to a set of procedural rules [WfMC 1999]. Workflows are based on document lifecycles and forms based information processing, so generally they support well defined, static, *clerical* processes. They provide transparency, since business processes are clearly articulated in the software, and they are agile because they produce definitions that are fast to deploy and change.

We may define a *workflow* as the sequence of processing steps (execution of business operations, tasks and transactions), during which information and physical objects are passed from one processing step to another. Workflow is a concept that links together technologies and tools able to automatically route events and tasks with programs or users.

Process oriented workflows are used to automate processes whose structure is well defined and stable over time, which often coordinate subprocesses executed by machines and which only require minor user involvement (often only in specific cases). A sales management process or a loan request is an example of a well defined process. Certain process oriented workflows may have transactional properties.

The process oriented workflow is made up of tasks that follow routes, with checkpoints, e.g. *check customer creditworthiness.* Such business process rules govern the overall processing of activities, including the routing of requests, the assignment or distribution of requests to designated roles, the passing of workflow data from activity to activity, and the dependencies and relationships between business process activities.

A workflow involves activities, decision points, routes, rules and roles. These are briefly described below.

> Just like a process, a workflow normally comprises a number of logical steps, each of which is known as an *activity.* An activity is a set of actions that are guided by the workflow. As Figure 9.1 illustrates, an activity may involve manual interaction with a user or workflow participant, or might be executed using diverse resources such as application programs or databases. A *work item* or data set is created, and is processed and changed in stages at a number of processing or decision points (steps in Figure 9.1) to meet specific business goals.
>
> A workflow can depict various aspects of a business process, including automated and manual activities, decision points and business rules, parallel and sequential work routes, and how to manage exceptions to the normal business process.
>
> A workflow can have logical *decision points* that determine which branch of the flow a work item may take in the event of alternative paths. Every alternative path within the flow is identified and controlled through a bounded set of logical decision points. An instantiation of a workflow to support a work item includes all possible paths from beginning to end.

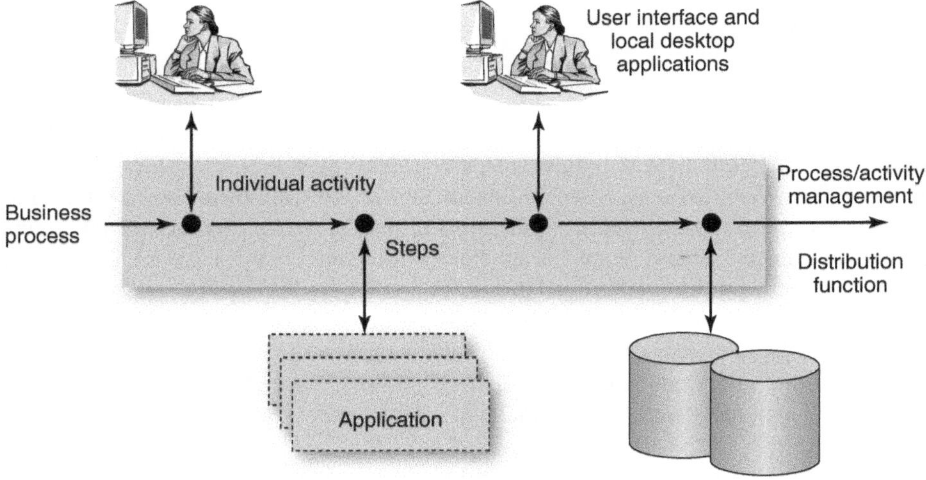

Figure 9.1 The workflow management coalition diagram of process flow across applications

Workflow technology enables developers to describe full intra- or inter-organisational business processes with dependencies, sequencing selections and iteration. It effectively enables the developers to describe the complex rules for processing in a business process, such as merging, selection based on field content, time based delivery of messages and so on. To achieve these objectives, workflows are predicated upon the notion of pre-specified routing paths.

A segment of a process instance under enactment by a workflow management system, in which several activities are executed in sequence under a single thread of execution, is called *sequential routing.* A segment of a process instance under enactment by a workflow management system, where two or more activity instances are executing in parallel within the workflow, giving rise to multiple threads of control, is called *parallel routing.* Parallel routing normally commences with an AND-Split (or split) and concludes with an AND-Join (or join or rendezvous) point.

A *split point* is a synchronisation point within the workflow where a single thread of control splits into two or more threads that are executed in parallel within the workflow, allowing multiple activities to be executed simultaneously.

A *join point* in the workflow is a synchronisation point where two or more parallel executing activities converge into a single common thread of control. No split or join points occur during sequential routing.

Workflow routing includes two more synchronisation points: OR-Split (or conditional routing) and OR-Join (or asynchronous join), which can be employed by both sequential and parallel routing constructs. A point within the workflow, where a single thread of control makes a decision as to which branch to take when having to select between multiple alternative workflow branches, is known as *condition routing.*

Finally, a point within the workflow where two or more alternative activity(ies) workflow branches re converge to form a single common activity as the next step within the workflow is known *asynchronous join.* It must be noted that, as no parallel activity execution has occurred at the join point, no synchronisation is required.

Within a workflow, business rules in each decision point determine how workflow related data is to be processed, routed, tracked and controlled. *Business rules* are core business policies that capture the nature of an enterprise's business model and define the conditions that must be met in order to move to the next stage of the workflow. Business rules are represented as compact statements about an aspect of the business that can be expressed within an application, and as such they determine the route to be followed [vonHalle 2002], [Ross 2003].

Example 9.1: Business rules in transportation applications

As an example of business rules, consider their use in a transportation process as part of the AVERS case study. Transportation applications typically involve freight billing, rating and cost calculation, and require deep knowledge of the moving industry, the standards that govern it, the services contracts, and the tariff documents that provide written industry guidance for moving services performance and pricing. Business rules for such applications may include policies on how shipments that contain hazardous materials should be transported, that cargo shipments will be billed on a per pound basis, that port handling rates include loading or unloading cargo from the truck/train by the stevedores but not onward movement (inland transportation) of the cargo, and so on. Business rules can represent among other things typical transportation business situations, including:

- escalation, e.g. freight billing, rating and cost calculation always requires a supervisor for approval;
- managing exceptions, e.g. all delivery services are paid upon arrival except for expedited delivery services which must be prepaid;
- progression assurance, e.g. make sure that this shipment is transported within three days or as specified in the customer's service-level agreement.

Roles in a workflow define the function of the people or programs involved in the workflow. A *role* is a mechanism within a workflow that associates participants to a collection of workflow activity(ies). The role defines the context in which the user participates in a particular process or activity. The role often embraces organisational concepts such as structure and relationships, responsibility or authority, but may also refer to other attributes such as skill, location, value data, time or date, etc.

The definition, creation and management of the execution of workflows are achieved by a *workflow management system,* which may run on one or more workflow engines. A workflow management system (WMS) is capable of interpreting the process and activity definitions, interacting with workflow participants, and, where required, invoking the

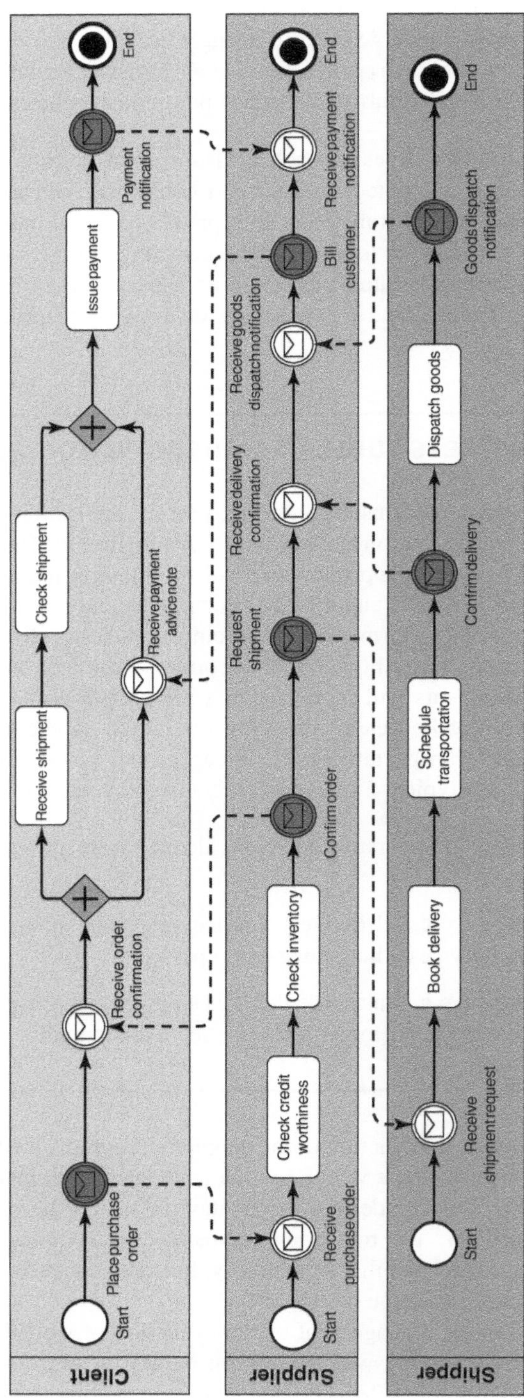

Figure 9.2 Order management application flow diagram in BPMN

use of software enabled tools and applications, see Figure 9.1. Most WMS integrate with other systems used by an enterprise, such as document management systems, databases, e-mail systems, office automation products, geographic information systems, production applications and so on. This integration provides structure to a process that employs a number of otherwise independent systems. It can also provide methods, e.g. a project folder for organising documents and data from diverse sources.

Example 9.2: Simplified order management workflow

Figure 9.2 illustrates a simplified version of an order management workflow as part of the AVERS case study. This involves an order management process (at a supplier side), a shipping and a billing business process. The workflow application is modelled using Business Process Modeling Notation (BPMN), which we shall examine in Section 15.4. Here, it suffices to say that BPMN allows business process modellers and developers to create a business process diagram, which represents the activities of the business process and the flow controls that define the order in which they are performed. In addition, BPMN is also to be able to generate execution definitions for the Web Services Business Process Execution Language (or simply BPEL) that is used to implement the business processes (see Section 15.4).

Steps in Figure 9.2 contain process-to-process coordination and communication. In the example in Figure 9.2, three roles are involved: a client, a supplier and a shipper. The order management application describes how a product is sent from a supplier to a client via a shipper. Several activities are executed at the supplier's site, such as checking the creditworthiness of the customer, determining whether or not an ordered part is available in the product inventory (not modelled in this figure), calculating the final price for the order and billing the customer, selecting a shipper, and scheduling the shipment for the order. An instance of this process is actually dispatching a product(s) to a specific customer. The instance of a process comprises activity instances that include the actual work and data items that are passed to a workflow participant – the client, supplier and shipper roles – within this activity for action, or to another process for action. For instance, in the order management application, a specific shipping company may receive all shipment related documents for a specific product from a specific supplier and may be asked to come up with a specific shipment date and shipping price for the proposed shipment.

Modern workflow technology tries to connect cross enterprise systems together by employing business process management functionality. This issue is discussed in some length in the following section.

9.3 Business process management

Business processes are the defining elements of a particular organisation in that they control and describe precisely how business is conducted both internally and externally. It is the entire supply chain, not a single enterprise, which delivers the products or services and makes enterprises competitive and successful. Consequently, both internal and cross enterprise integration initiatives must be managed and deployed in a systematic and coherent fashion.

Business process integration can be described as the ability to define a commonly accepted business process model that specifies the sequence, hierarchy, events, execution logic and data movement between systems residing in the same enterprise and systems residing in multiple interconnected enterprises (respectively named EAI and e-Business integration in Section 2.10). BPI is an integration solution that provides enterprises with end-to-end visibility and control over the contributing parts of a multi-step business process, which may include people, customers, partners, applications and databases. For instance, this might include all the steps in an order management, inventory management or fulfilment process, and their underlying Enterprise Information Systems (see Section 2.10).

BPI solutions allow enterprises to take advantage of information systems that are already in place, by automating and managing the business processes that span these systems. With BPI, enterprises can preserve major investments in legacy systems, thereby avoiding the expense of having to write additional code to replicate existing functionality. The business processes that are linked together are typically defined in terms of workflow activities.

Figure 9.3 illustrates a typical application of a business process integration workflow involving the order management application in Figure 9.2. This typical SOA application is shown to span multiple functional areas within an enterprise, and even between enterprises. The figure shows how activities specified at the business process flow level map to corresponding Enterprise Information System activities at the data flow level. Data flows (message exchanges) at the EIS implementation level are represented as dashed lines.

The extension of BPI with management aspects is commonly referred to as Business Process Management (BPM) [Weske 2007]. BPM, as part of an ESB solution, emphasises the management aspect of automating processes to achieve maximum ongoing flexibility with minimum development cost and time, see Section 8.5.5.4. BPM provides a modelling tool to visually construct, analyse and execute cross organisational business processes.

BPM is a commitment to expressing, understanding, representing and managing a business (or the portion of business to which it is applied) in terms of a collection of business processes that are responsive to a business environment of internal or external events [McGoveran 2004], [Jeston 2008]. The BPM framework comprises five main building blocks that represent the concepts, methods and techniques that collectively contribute to BPM technology. The BPM building blocks are:

1. *Business process modelling, simulation analysis, and design:* Process models are needed to help business managers and analysts understand actual processes and enable them, by visualisation and simulation, to propose improvements. Business process modelling tools, such as BPMN, provide a shared environment for the capture, simulation analysis and design of business processes by business analysts, managers and developers. Process models are simulated and analysed prior to being designed and implemented.
2. *Business process integration:* This item involves connecting the process elements so that they can seamlessly exchange information to achieve business goals.

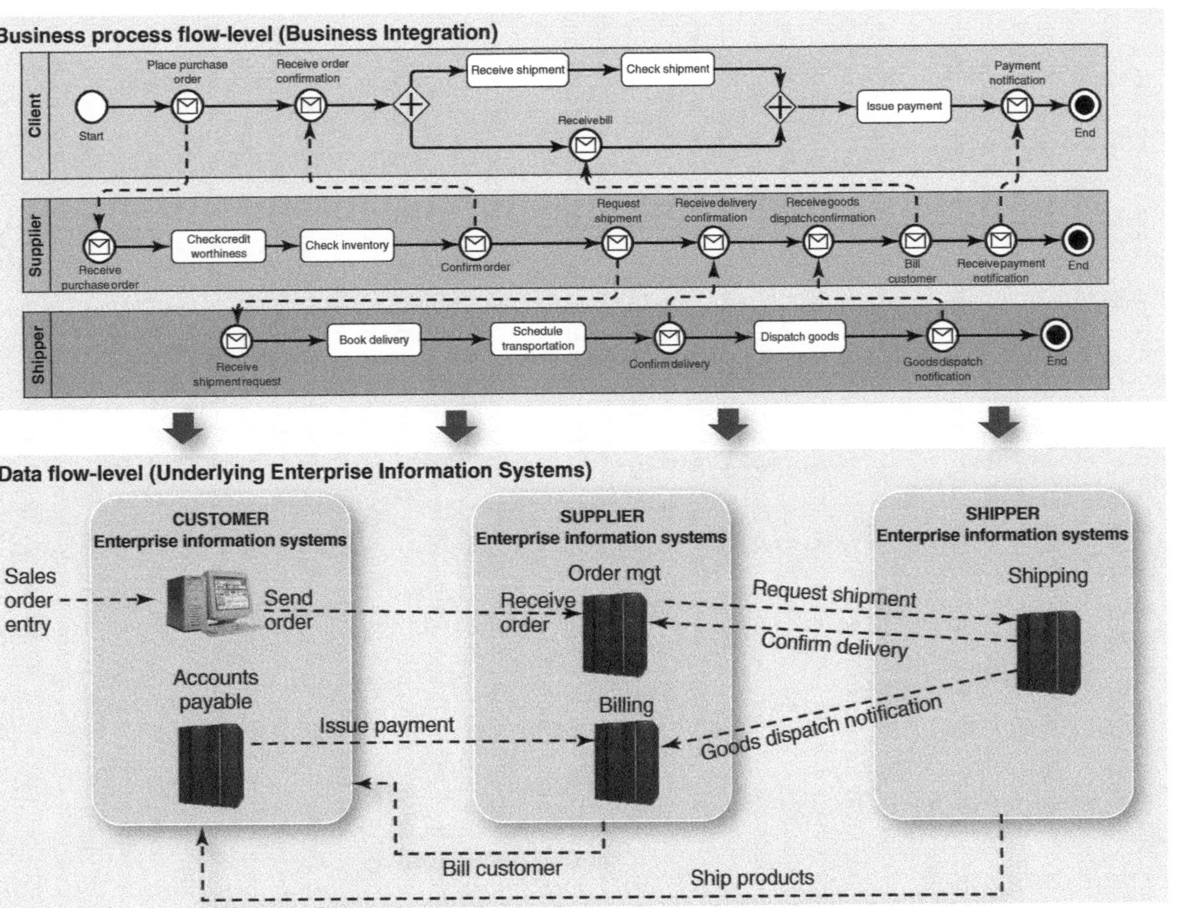

Figure 9.3 Example of a BPI workflow with underling information system implementation

For applications this means using APIs and messaging to interconnect disparate EIS found in various enterprises.

3. *Business process deployment and execution:* Business process deployment means rolling out new processes to all clients, including other enterprises, applications and processes. This involves publishing a process model to a process engine that actually automates the process allocating the integrated process to system resources, delegating human tasks to employees, and enforcing business rules. Once business processes have been deployed, the BPM execution environment navigates through the process models to proactively move forward their instances of execution. In doing so, the execution environment orchestrates the instances and coordinates the human work items, rules based automation, and system-to-system integration activities.
4. *Business process monitoring and interactive dashboards:* This involves providing graphical administrative tools that illustrate processes that are in progress, processes that are completed, and integrate business metrics and key performance indicators with process descriptions. Audit trails and process history/reporting information is automatically maintained and available for further use. Analytical tools guide business process improvement and deployment while graphical reports can be also produced to check the status of all running and finished processes. These tools include facilities to query the state of live business processes and to intervene to resolve exceptions if required. For example, they can check for processes awaiting further inputs in order to complete execution, such as a process waiting for new inventory to come in. This process can then be observed and appropriately monitored.
5. *Business process measurement and optimisation:* Process management ensures that, if a process is out of bounds or service level agreements are not being met, then it is adjusted and optimised by reconfiguring resources or modifying business rules dynamically. The ability to capture the definition of familiar business metrics and relate them to computational measurements is an essential part of BPM [McGoveran2004]. Business metrics are defined in terms of *Key Performance Indicators* (KPIs). For example, a KPI (metric) expected time to completion of a business transaction is of immense interest to the business analysts and management. Similarly, mean queue times, mean activity service times and most probable path to completion are too technical and too detailed for business analysts and management, however, they are essential for IT developers. Optimisation means process improvement, which should be an ongoing activity. Business process optimisation involves optimising process flows of all sizes, crossing any application, company boundary and connects process design and process maintenance. For example, the BPM system should detect bottlenecks, deadlocks and other inconsistencies in processes across the whole extended enterprise; and should easily act on or change processes in real time to minimise inefficiencies. Ideally, this should be done by the BPM system itself in an automatic manner.

Although BPM technology shares the same space with workflow, its focus is on the business user, and provides more sophisticated management and analysis capabilities.

BPM tools place considerable emphasis on management and business functions. This fact accentuates the business applicability of BPM, instead of a technological solution, which is the case with workflow systems. With a BPM tool the business user is able to manage all the process of a certain type, e.g. claim processes, and should be able to study them from historical or current data; produce costs, or other business measurements; and produce, on the basis of these measurements, business charts or reports. In addition, the business user should also be able to analyse and compare the data or business measurements based on the different types of claim. This type of functionality is typically not provided by workflow systems. Nowadays BPM and workflow technologies are converging.

Finally, it is worth emphasising the relatedness between BPM and SOA. BPM is a natural complement to SOA, and a mechanism through which an organisation can apply SOA to high value business challenges. The objective is effectively to align technical initiatives with the strategic goals of the business user at every level within the organisation, and between organizations, to achieve a comprehensive approach to real business transformation.

Both SOA and BPM can each be pursued without the other, but the two approaches in concert offer reciprocal benefits. Layering BPM on top of a solid SOA allows actions within business processes to be exposed via automated services. With BPM orchestration, the exposure of key business events and information to users at the appropriate times, and in the appropriate contexts, adds tremendous business value that might not otherwise be achieved with a SOA not making use of BPM. In addition, BPM helps deliver control over business processes, fostering standardisation across a company or an end-to-end process chain, and compliance with regulations, policies and best practices. It also enables some services required by the business process to be outsourced to trading partners, and opens up brand new business models in which the enterprise's own business processes can be exposed as services to new customers, both internal and external.

9.4 Cross-enterprise business processes

In previous chapters we observed that Web services provide standard and interoperable means of integrating loosely coupled Web based components that expose well defined interfaces, while abstracting the implementation and platform specific details. Core Web service standards, such as SOAP, WSDL and UDDI, provide a solid foundation to accomplish this. These specifications primarily enable development of simple Web service applications that can conduct simple interactions. However, the ultimate goal of Web service technology is to enable and automate service composition by assembling services that were created to be independent of each other.

Building enterprise solution(s) typically requires the ability to compose distributed existing Web services. These composite services can be, in turn, recursively composed with other services into higher process level solutions, and so on. Therefore, the ability to explicitly describe the relationships between the composite (complex services) and their *service constituents* is essential for SOA based applications. In fact, this recursive composition of services is one of the most important features of SOA, allowing it rapidly to build new solutions based on the existing services. In this way, collaborative business processes can be realised as integrative Web service solutions. For example, an SOA order management application can be developed by combining elementary services such as handling orders; checking the creditworthiness of the customer; determining whether an ordered part is available in the inventory; calculating the final price and billing the customer; selecting a shipper; and scheduling the production and shipment for the order.

We use the term *service composability* to describe independent service specifications that can be combined to provide powerful business process capabilities. Service composition combines services following a certain composition pattern to achieve a business goal, solve a problem, or provide new service functions. The definition of composite services requires coordinating the flow of control and information between the component services. Business logic can be seen as the ingredient that sequences, coordinates and manages interactions among services. Mechanisms for Web services composability draw heavily on business process modelling and workflow processing languages.

When processes span enterprise boundaries, loose coupling based on precise external protocols is required, because the parties involved do not share application and workflow implementation technologies, and will not allow external control over the use of their back end applications. Such business interaction protocols are by necessity message centric. *Message centric protocols* specify the flow of messages representing business activities between interacting business processes and trading partners, without requiring any specific implementation mechanism.

A trio of standards tackles the problem of traditional workflows as stated above and enables composing and orchestrating loosely coupled Web services. These specifications are: the Web Services Business Process Execution Language [Alves 2007], WS-Coordination (WS-C), and WS-AtomicTransaction [Little 2009], and WS-Activity [Freund 2009]. These three specifications work together to form the bedrock for reliably orchestrating SOA based applications, providing process management functionality and execution, transactional integrity and generic coordination facilities.

As already discussed earlier in this book, BPEL is a workflow like definition language that describes sophisticated business processes that can orchestrate Web services. WS-Coordination and WS-Transaction complement BPEL to provide mechanisms for defining specific standard protocols for use by transaction processing systems, workflow systems, or other applications that wish to coordinate multiple Web services.

We shall examine BPEL in a subsequent section of this chapter, while we shall concentrate on the transactional aspects of Web services and cover WS-Coordination and WS-Transaction (among other coordination and transaction protocols) in Chapter 10.

9.5 Service composition model

This section explains the elements of service composition using BPMN graphs. BPMN will be used thought out this section to model and represent the concepts, constructs, semantics and relationships that are inherent in Web service composition. The purpose of using BPMN graphs in this section is to make it easier for readers to understand the concepts and mechanisms that are introduced later in this chapter as part of BPEL.

Example 9.3: More detailed order management process

To illustrate the various aspects of service composition we shall consider a variant of the AVERS order management case study that we introduced earlier in this book as a basis for illustrating the steps involved in a process oriented workflow. Figure 9.4 is a more detailed model of the order management process that appears in Figure 9.2. In particular, it includes constructs that are necessary for service composition that will be described throughout this section.

Recall that activities in the order management process include receiving the purchase order, checking customer creditworthiness, allocating inventory, shipping products, billing, and making sure that the payment is received. Some of these processes may execute for long periods of time, while others may execute in milliseconds.

9.5.1 Process flow modelling

Flow models are used for the specification of complex service interactions. A *flow model* describes a usage pattern of a collection of available services, so that the composition of those services provides the functionality needed to achieve a certain business objective [Leymann 2000]. The flow model describes how activities (implemented as Web service operations) are combined, specifies the order in which these steps are executed, the decision points where steps may or may not have to be performed, and the passing of data items between the steps involved.

Figure 9.4 illustrates the key ingredients for the description of a flow model, which are:

- activities;
- events that trigger activities;
- the specification of the control flow describing the sequencing of these activities;
- decision points;
- the specification of the associated data flow describing the passing of data between them.

We shall examine these five concepts in succession in what follows.

Figure 9.4 consists of a series of activities that are executed in a certain order. As already explained earlier in this book, an activity is an element that performs a specific function as a single step within a process. Activities are normally implemented as operations of Web services. Activities are represented as nodes in a directed acyclic graph (DAG) describing process flows. This means that loops are not allowed within the control structure of a flow. The figure also shows how data items are passed between activities. These comprise the edges in the graph. For instance, client details are passed to the activity that checks customer creditworthiness.

An event signifies the occurrence of an important incident that happens during the course of a business process. Events affect the flow of the process and usually have a cause (trigger) or an impact (result). An event in BPMN is represented by a circle with open

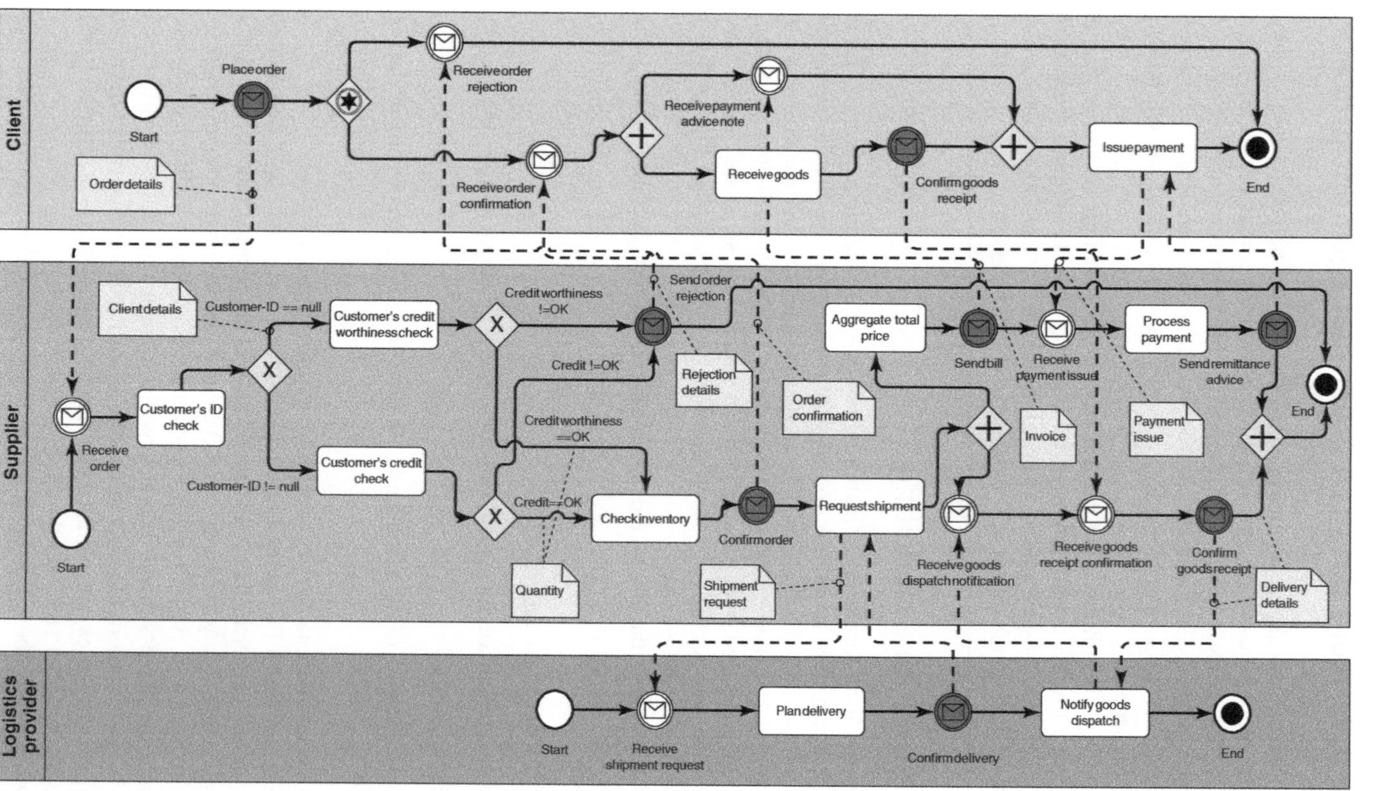

Figure 9.4 Sample order management application revisited

centres to allow internal markers to differentiate different triggers or results. In Figure 9.4 there are three types of events, based on when they affect the flow: start, intermediate and end events. There are also two kinds of intermediate message events: one kind responsible for reception of messages and one kind responsible for sending messages. When used to receive a message the event marker will be unfilled (white). When used for sending messages to a participant, the event marker will be filled (dark). For example, Figure 9.4 illustrates when an activity such as `CheckCreditWorthiness` is used to evaluate the financial condition of a customer, if it fails a `SendOrderRejection` event is triggered and is sent to the client.

Activities in Figure 9.4 are interconnected by means of *control links.* A control link is a directed edge that prescribes the order in which activities will have to be performed. A control link is a sequencing relationship between two activities A_1 and A_2 that prescribes the order of their execution, e.g. A_1 must precede A_2. The need for executing two activities in a certain order follows from logical dependencies between them. The endpoints of the set of all control links that leave a given activity A represent the possible successor activities A_1, A_2, ..., A_n of the activity A.

A control link points from its source activity to its target activity; that is, from an activity to its (or one of its) potential successor activities. Next, such an edge is *guarded* by a transition condition that determines the actual flow of control. Transition conditions determine which of the activities A_1, A_2, ... , A_n need to be performed in a business process. A *transition condition* is a predicate expression that is associated with a control link [Leymann 2000]. The formal parameters of this expression can refer to messages that have been produced by some of the activities that preceded the source of the control link in the flow. When an activity A completes, it is succeeded by those control links that originate from this activity whose transition conditions evaluate to true. This set of activities is referred to as *actual successor activities* of A in contrast to the full set $\{A_1, A_2, ..., A_n\}$ of *potential successor activities* of the activity A. As an example, consider again the case of the activity `CheckCreditWorthiness`. After execution of this activity, either activity `SendOrderRejection` or `CheckInventory` is chosen. The chosen activity is the actual successor activity to `CheckCreditWorthiness` whereas both these activities are in its potential successor activity set. At most, one control link between two different activities is allowed and the resulting directed graph must be acyclic as pointed out earlier in this section.

Example 9.4: Transition conditions for the order management process

Figure 9.5 is fragment of the BPMN representation in Figure 9.4, which explicitly illustrates transition conditions and control links for the order management process. This figure shows that there exist transition conditions, i.e. decision points such as determining the credit history of an existing customer, which are evaluated at run time. Depending on the evaluation, control moves from activity such as `CustomerCreditCheck` to either raising an event `SendOrderRejection` (link-4 or link-6) or to a follow up activity `CheckInventory` (link-5). Evaluation depends on determining the extent of credit of

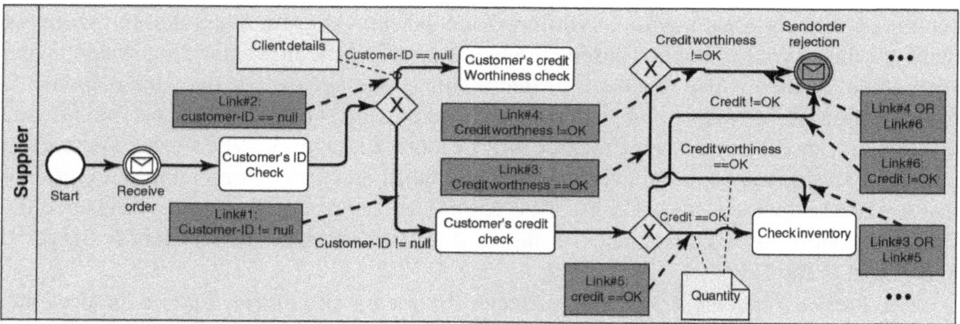

Figure 9.5 Transition conditions and control links for process flow model in Figure 9.4

a specific customer and the particular products to be offered to this customer who has already a trading relationship with the supplier. For reasons of simplicity it is assumed that, if a customer has already a client identification number, then this customer is trustworthy.

Finally, the flow model's data flow part specifies how the result message of a given activity is consumed by one (or more) of its successor activities. A data link specifies that its source activity passes some data item(s) to its target activity(ies). A data link can be specified only if the target of the data link is reachable from the source of the data link through a path of (directed) control links. The data flow has to be superimposed on the control flow. This makes certain that error prone situations are avoided. For example, in Figure 9.5 activity `CheckCreditWorthiness` is shown to receive both order and client data and is shown to pass quantity data to the activity `CheckInventory`.

9.5.2 Composing Web services

In the previous section we introduced the basic ingredients of a service composition model without concentrating on the actual realisations of the flow activities. In this section we shall concentrate on the composition of flows that perform the coordination of Web services, which implement also the individual activities in a process flow. The aim is to provide readers with enough intuition regarding the characteristics of service compositions so that they can understand much easier the material that comes in Section 9.7.

Service providers are the units that participate in service compositions in a service flow model. Service providers represent the functionality that a flow model requires from business partners in a business process. A service provider presents a public interface in the form of a set of WSDL `<portTypes>` that gives a formal representation of the service or services that each service provider must offer in order to participate in the flow model. This defines essentially the ways in which this service provider can interact with other providers. A service composition consists of a set of interconnected and coordinated services provided by diverse service providers offered in the form of a business process. Compatibility of operations is required between interacting service providers for the service composition to be successful. For instance, a solicit/response operation defined by one service provider requires a matching request/response operation to be provided by another service provider.

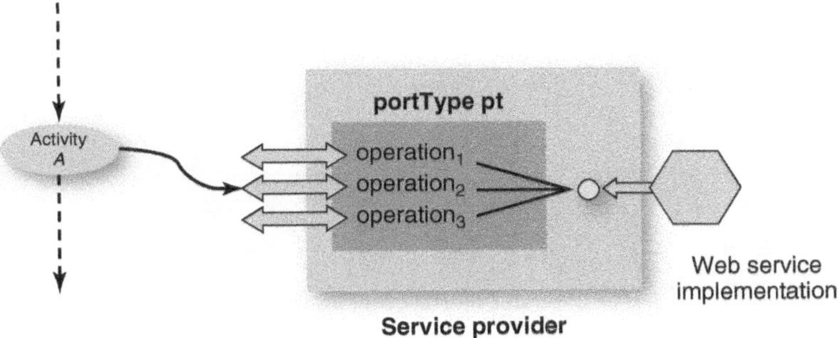

Figure 9.6 Service providers and port types

One goal of service composition is to enable discrete Web services as implementations of activities of business processes. For this purpose, an activity may refer to an operation of the service provider type's port type that defines the external interface of the flow model to specify which kind of service is required at run time to perform the business task represented by an activity. For example, Figure 9.6 shows a flow in which an activity called *A* is implemented by a service that realises operation $operation_2$ of a `<portType> pt` at run time, when navigation encounters *A*, a concrete port is chosen that provides an implementation of port type *pt* and operation $operation_2$. A corresponding binding is used to actually invoke this implementation.

Binding service providers to actual business partners, who offer the required services, can happen either statically or dynamically. When the binding is static we simply locate the actual business partner, who acts as a specific service provider, by means of a direct reference to a WSDL service that provides the required operations. The specific WSDL service, to which we bind statically, implements the interface defined by the service provider of the required type. Alternatively, one can bind to a service provider dynamically by looking up the UDDI directory according to some specified criteria, e.g. performance, price, etc., to find a suitable service provider of the required type. Subsequently, the most suitable service is chosen (according to some QoS criterion) and bound. This is explained in Section 9.7 where we explore the nature of BPEL compositions.

Example 9.5: Composing services for the order management process

Reverting now to service composition for our order management application. Figure 9.7 illustrates how supplier `<portType>`s are linked to a client and logistics provider to create a composite service. The figure shows how multiple services like credit check, inventory, payment and shipment are connected together in a single business process called `PurchaseOrderManagement` residing at the supplier side.

The purpose of Figure 9.7 is to show how a set of interconnected and coordinated service operations and message exchanges form a service composition. This figure illustrates visible (public) message exchanges on behalf of each of the parties involved in the service composition. The composite service represents a single point of access to the set

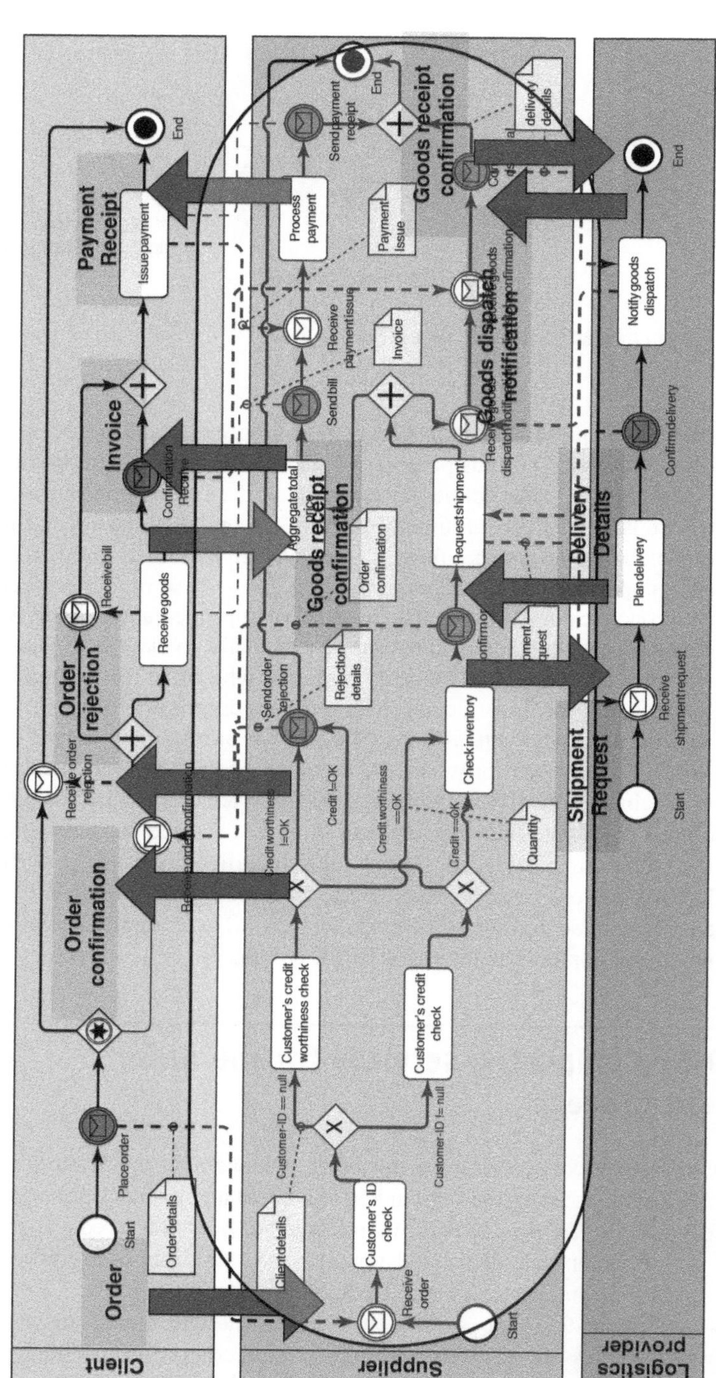

Figure 9.7 Composing services in the order management application flow model in Figure 9.4

of underlying services. This single point of access provides a simple way of enforcing service coordination of constituent service invocations and related messages that produce concrete results across three participants (roles). The access to constituent services is provided by message exchanges and input/output parameter correspondences. For instance, it is shown that when interconnecting the inventory and shipment services their message exchanges must be mutually understood and that their input and output parameters should match each other. This means that the `<operation> RequestShipment` of the inventory service sends an output message called `ShipmentRequest` to the `<operation> PlanDelivery` of the shipment service of a logistics provider. This message is then caught as an input message by the `<operation> PlanDelivery` of the shipment service, which in its turn returns an output message `DeliveryDetails` to the inventory service. Interaction between the other constituent services of the composite service `PurchaseOrderManagement` follows a similar course.

The example in Figure 9.7 highlights that when two constituent services are composed to create a composite service such as `PurchaseOrderManagement` the messages that the constituent services invoke must be mutually understood and their input/output message parameter `<type>`s at the WSDL-level must be compatible (i.e. they must match each other).

In this section we focused our attention on functional service composition. Non-functional composition, e.g. service composition at the performance or security level, is still an important aspect of service composition, which is still (with the exception of simple cases) very much an open research problem.

Now that you have familiarized yourselves with the commonest concepts and constructs of workflow systems and service composition, it is relatively easy to understand the concepts and constructs found in Web service composition languages, which will concern us in the remainder of this chapter. We shall first concentrate on the concepts of service orchestration and choreography, which relate to different aspects of service composition.

9.6 Service orchestration and choreography

Models for SOA interactions typically require specifying sequences of peer-to-peer message exchanges between a collection of Web services, both synchronous and asynchronous, within stateful, possibly long running, interactions involving two or more parties. Such interactions necessitate that business processes be described in terms of a business protocol (or abstract business model), which precisely specifies the mutually visible (public) message exchange behaviour of each of the parties involved in the protocol without revealing their internal (private) implementation. It also requires describing the actual behaviour of participants involved in a business interaction.

In the previous section, we used terms such as *service composition* to describe the composition of services in a process flow. To describe the composition of processes that span multiple participants, with message exchanges moving in different direction according to business protocols, the terms orchestration and choreography are normally used. Orchestration and choreography are both attempts to control the course of service compositions and message flows but on a different scale. There is an important distinction between Web service orchestration and choreography that we shall explain below.

9.6.1 Service orchestration

Orchestration describes how services can interact with each other at the message level, including the business logic and execution order of the interactions from the perspective and under control of a specific participant. The intention is to build a flow of control around (or orchestrate) the interactions of this specific participant with all its given partners. For instance, Figure 9.8 assumes an orchestration stance when describing the case of the process flow depicted in Figure 9.7 where the business process flow is seen from the vantage point of a supplier.

With orchestration, service interactions of a central business process are always controlled from the perspective of the participant that drives this specific process. In addition, this process coordinates the execution of the different operations on the Web services it composes. The constituent services are not aware that they are involved in the course of a composition, and that they are part of a higher level business process. Only the central coordinator of the orchestration knows this fact. What this means is that orchestration represents an executable process to be executed by an orchestration engine in a single place. As Figure 9.8 indicates, only the central coordinator of the orchestration is aware of this composition procedure, so the orchestration is centralised with explicit definitions of operations and the order of invocation of services. Figure 9.8 also illustrates sample public message exchanges from the vantage point of a supplier who acts as an orchestrator of services. Orchestrations describe what an overall process appears to do without specifying how any of it is implemented. Private activities are meant to implement internal requirements and are not visible to the partners.

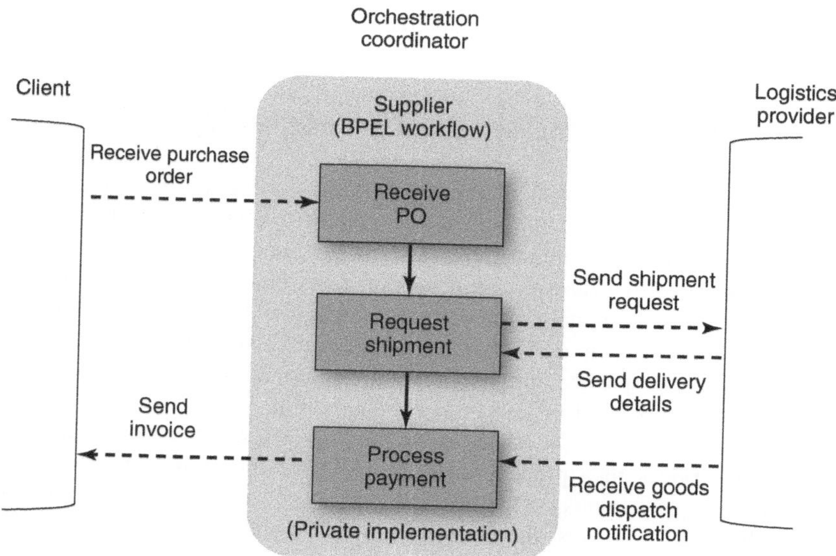

Figure 9.8 An example of orchestration from the supplier perspective

9.6.2 Service choreography

Choreography refers to a description of the global message exchange protocol, i.e. globally visible message exchanges, which governs how services interact between two or more participants. Unlike an orchestration choreography this does not imply a centralised control mechanism. Rather, each service involved in the choreography knows exactly when to execute its operations and whom to interact with. It assumes that control is equally shared between interacting participants, where each party involved in the choreography is perfectly aware of the business process, operations to execute, messages to exchange, and the order of message exchanges.

Choreography is more collaborative in nature than orchestration. It is described from the perspectives of all parties (common view), and, in essence, defines the shared state of the interactions between participants in a business process. This common view can be used to determine specific deployment implementations for each individual entity. Significantly, this means that choreography in essence represents a description of how to distribute control between the collaborating participants, using no single execution engine to achieve this type of collaboration. Figure 9.9 shows a simplified version of the purchase

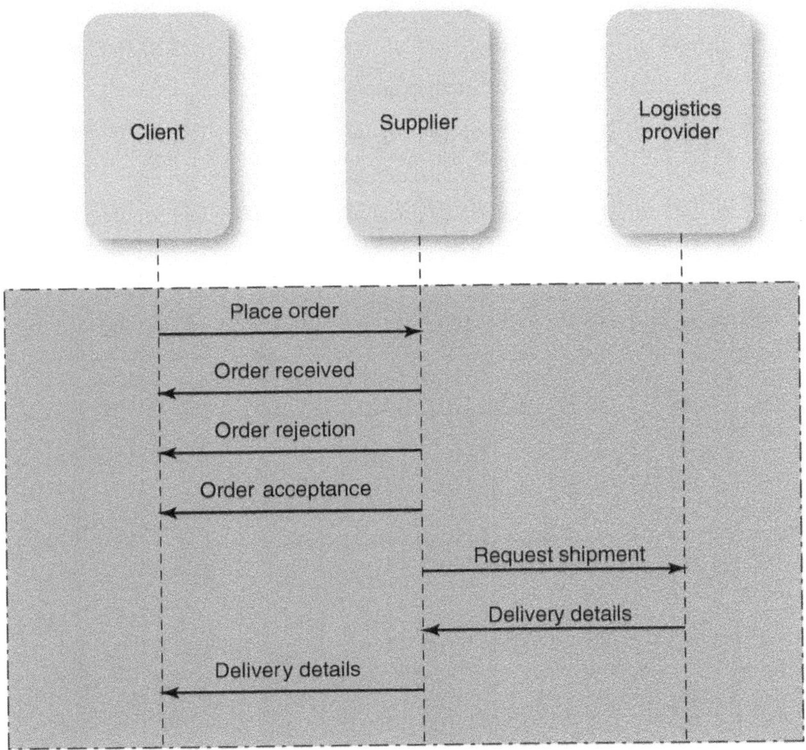

Figure 9.9 A simplified view of a choreography involving three participants.

order management process (composite service) from a choreography perspective involving an observable (global) public exchange of messages. The rectangle surrounded by dashed lines signifies the observable public exchange of messages in the choreography.

The dominant service orchestration language is the Web Services Business Process Execution Language, while the Web Services Choreography Language (WS-CDL) is the leading choreography language. Although these two XML based languages feature a similar flow oriented design style, only BPEL is meant to have an actual run time platform (the BPEL execution engine).

WS-CDL is not an *executable business process description language* or an implementation language. WS-CDL is essentially an XML based protocol language for expressing global collaboration protocols for composite Web services. The global WS-CDL specification is then realised by a combination of the execution engines of the business process languages that host the services in this global specification. Figure 9.10 illustrates the connection between a WS-CDL global specification and two BPEL processes.

In the following section we shall first concentrate on the BPEL, which is the standard industry specification that is designed specifically for Web services based orchestration, and subsequently we shall summarise important elements of WS-CDL.

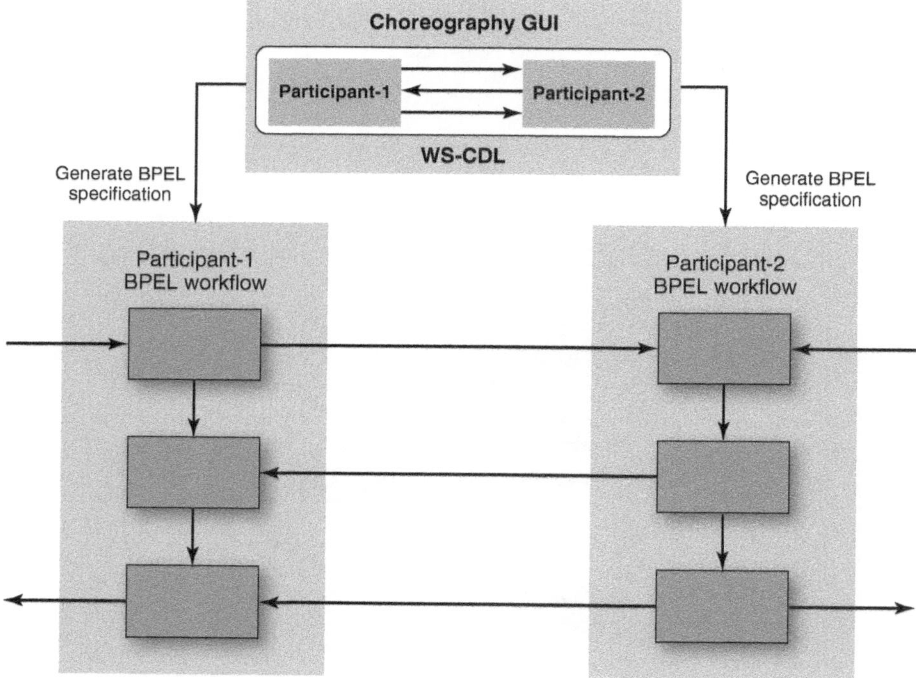

Figure 9.10 Realising a WS-CDL choreography in terms of two BPEL orchestrations

9.7 WS-BPEL: the Business Process Execution Language

Web service orchestration specifications pick up things from where WSDL ends. WSDL essentially permits definition of the static interface of a Web service. The interaction model of a WSDL `<portType>` is stateless and static without any correlation of interactions at the level of the interface defined. Additionally, WSDL describes interfaces from the perspective of a service (provider) and hence it is geared towards a client–server model of interaction. Collaborative process models typically involve both client–server and peer-to-peer types of interactions with long running and stateful conversations involving two or more parties, which WSDL is not equipped to deliver. Consequently, the Web services orchestration specifications use WSDL as a basis and extend its functionality.

WS-BPEL v2.0 (or simply BPEL) has emerged as the standard to define and manage business process activities and business interaction protocols comprising collaborating Web services. This is an XML based flow language for the formal specification of business processes and business interaction protocols. By doing so, it extends the Web services interaction model and enables it to support complex business processes and transactions. Enterprises can describe complex processes that include multiple organisations – such as order processing, inventory management and claims handling – and execute the same business processes in systems from other vendors.

BPEL v2.0 as a service composition (orchestration) language provides several features to facilitate the modelling and execution of business processes based on Web services. Its main features include:

- modelling business process collaboration (through `<partnerLink>`s);
- modelling the execution control of business processes (through the use of a self contained block and transition structured language that support representation of directed graphs);
- separation of abstract definition from concrete binding (static and dynamic selection of partner services via endpoint references);
- data manipulation;
- repetitive execution activities using the `<while>`, `<repeat until>`, and `<for each>` constructs;
- representation of participants' roles and role relationships (through `<partner-LinkType>`s);
- parallel execution of processes (through `<flow>`) and spawning off and synchronising processes (through `<pick>` and `<receive>` activities);
- service composability (structured activities can be nested and combined arbitrarily);
- advanced message operations through a join style correlation set to enable multiple instance process scenarios and collaboration;
- compensation support (through fault handlers and compensation);

- context support (through the <scope> mechanism);
- event and fault handling (through the use of event and fault handlers).

BPEL v2.0 can also be extended to provide other important composition language properties, such as support for Web service policies, and security and reliable messaging requirements.

In this section we summarise the most prominent BPEL v2.0 features and constructs. BPEL v2.0 utilises several XML specifications: WSDL 1.1, XML Schema 1.0, XPath 1.0 and XSLT 1.0. It also works with the BPMN 1.1 specifications. Some familiarity with them is helpful for understanding BPEL. Our intention is to provide a sound understanding of BPEL concepts and features and not to present a detailed tutorial of BPEL and its constructs. More information about this language can be found in [Alves 2007] and [Barreto 2007].

9.7.1 The structure of a BPEL process

A BPEL process is a flow chart like expression, specifying process steps and entry points into the process that is layered on top of WSDL, with WSDL defining the specific operations allowed and BPEL defining how the operations can be sequenced. The role of BPEL is to define a new Web service by composing a set of existing services through a process integration type mechanism with control language constructs. The entry points correspond to external WSDL clients invoking either input-only (request) or input/output (request/response) operations on the interface of the composite BPEL service. Recall that Figure 1.6 illustrates how BPEL is related to WSDL and other Web service standards.

At the core of the BPEL process model lies the notion of peer-to-peer interaction between services described in WSDL. Both the process and its Web service partners are modelled in WSDL. BPEL uses WSDL to specify activities that should take place in a business process and describes the Web services provided by the business process. A BPEL process leverages WSDL in the following three ways:

1. Every BPEL process is exposed as a Web service using WSDL to its consumers. WSDL describes the public entry and exit points for the process. A BPEL process represents all partners and partner interactions in terms of abstract WSDL interfaces.
2. WSDL data types are used within a BPEL process to describe the information that passes between requests.
3. WSDL might be used to reference external services required by a business process.

BPEL provides a mechanism for creating implementation and platform independent compositions of services woven strictly from the abstract interfaces provided in the WSDL definitions. The definition of a BPEL business process also follows the WSDL convention of strict separation between the abstract service interface and service implementation. In particular, a BPEL process represents parties and interactions between these parties in terms of abstract WSDL interfaces (by means of <portType>s and <operation>s),

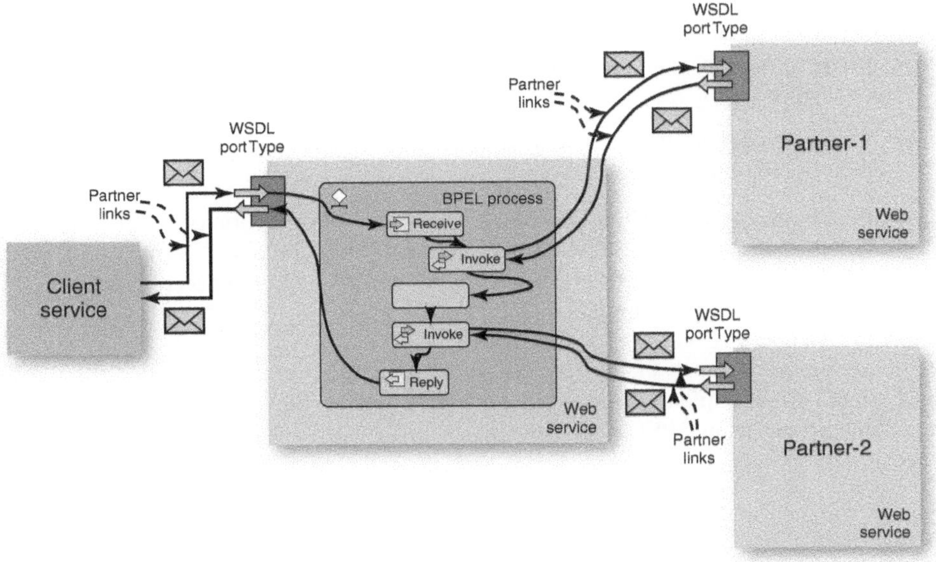

Figure 9.11 The BPEL, WSDL interaction model

while no references are made to the actual services (binding and address information) used by a process instance. Both the interacting process as well as its counterparts are modelled in the form of WSDL services. This is shown in Figure 9.11.

Actual implementations of the services themselves may be dynamically bound to the partners of a BPEL composition, without affecting the composition's definition. Business processes specified in BPEL are fully executable portable scripts that can be interpreted by business process engines in BPEL-conformant environments.

BPEL distinguishes five main sections: the *message flow,* the *control flow,* the *data flow,* the *process orchestration,* and the *fault, termination* and *exception handling* sections. These sections are shown in Listing 9.1. This listing shows that a BPEL process definition is written as an XML document using the `<process>` root element.

- The *message flow* section of BPEL is handled by basic activities that include invoking an operation on some Web service, waiting for a process operation to be invoked by some external client, and generating the response of an input/output operation. Sequencing and repetitive execution (loop) activities complement the basic activities and are known as structured activities.
- The *control flow* section of BPEL is a hybrid model principally based on block structured definitions with the ability to define selective state transition control flow definitions for synchronisation purposes. The *data flow* section of BPEL comprises variables that provide the means for holding messages that constitute the state of a business process. The messages held are often those that have been

received from partners or are to be sent to partners. Variables can also hold data that are needed for holding a state related to the process and never exchanged with partners. Variables are scoped and the name of a variable should be unique within its own scope.

- The *process orchestration* section of BPEL uses partner links to establish peer-to-peer partner relationships.
- Finally, the *fault, termination* and *exception handling* section of BPEL deals with errors that might occur when services are being invoked, termination logic, handling of compensations of units of work and dealing with exceptions during the course of a BPEL computation.

We shall summarise each of the five BPEL sections, giving examples in BPEL where appropriate, in subsequent sections after we first define the concepts of abstract and executable processes in BPEL.

```
<process name = PurchaseOrderManagement>
  <!--  Roles played by actual process participants at endpoints of an
        interaction -->
  <partnerLinks> ... </partnerLinks>

  <!- Data used by the process -->
  <variables> ... </variables>

  <!- Activities that the process performs -->
   (activities)*

  <!- Supports asynchronous interactions -->
  <correlationSets> ... </correlationSets>


  <!- Code  that is executed when an action is "undone" -->
  <compensationHandler> ... </compensationHandler>

  <!- Handling of concurrent events, handlers are invoked when a
      corresponding event occurs -->
  <eventHandler> ... </eventHandler>

  <!- Exception handling: Alternate execution path to deal with faulty
     situations -->
  <faultHandler> ... </faultHandler>

  <!- Controls forced termination -->
  <terminationHandler> ... </terminationHandler>

</process>
```

Listing 9.1 Structure of a BPEL process

9.7.2 Abstract and executable BPEL processes

Although the BPEL name suggests that this is a language for specifying executable business processes, the language supports two levels of process description: abstract and executable business processes. BPEL provides the same language constructs to define both abstract and executable processes.

9.7.2.1 Abstract BPEL processes

An *abstract process* in BPEL specifies the external message exchange between Web services and does not contain any internal details of the business process. Abstract business processes are partially specified processes that are not intended for execution. An abstract process may hide some of the required concrete operational details. This type of process is typically used to model the public message interaction (business protocol) between two Web services without exposing the internal business logic of these services and, therefore, is not executable.

There are two good reasons to separate the public aspects of business process behaviour from internal or private aspects. One is that businesses obviously do not want to reveal all their internal decision making and data management to their business partners. The other is that, even where this is not the case, separating public from private process provides the freedom to change private aspects of the process implementation without affecting the observable behaviour. Observable behaviour must clearly be described in a platform independent manner and captures behavioural aspects that may have cross enterprise business significance.

Figure 9.12 illustrates a simplified view of the purchase order management abstract process. In this figure the customer (client) and the supplier have two distinct roles, each with its own port types and operations. The structure of their relationship at the interface level is typically modelled as a publicly visible exchange of messages.

9.7.2.2 Executable BPEL processes

In contrast to an abstract process, an *executable process* defines both the external message exchange and the complete internal details of the business logic, is executable by BPEL engines and follows the orchestration paradigm. It contains all the actual detailed interactions and behaviour of participants in the overall business process flow, essentially modelling a private workflow. An executable process contains all the details of the process, including a full description of the process state and how it is processed. We can think of an abstract business process as the projection of an executable process. When we define an executable process in BPEL, we actually define a new Web service that is the composition of existing services. The most common scenario in BPEL is to use abstract processes as a template to define executable processes.

All the constructs of executable processes are made available to abstract processes; consequently, executable and abstract WS-BPEL processes share the same expressive power. In addition to the features available in executable processes, abstract processes provide two mechanisms for hiding operational details [Alves 2007]: (1) the use of explicit opaque tokens and (2) omission. Although a particular abstract process definition

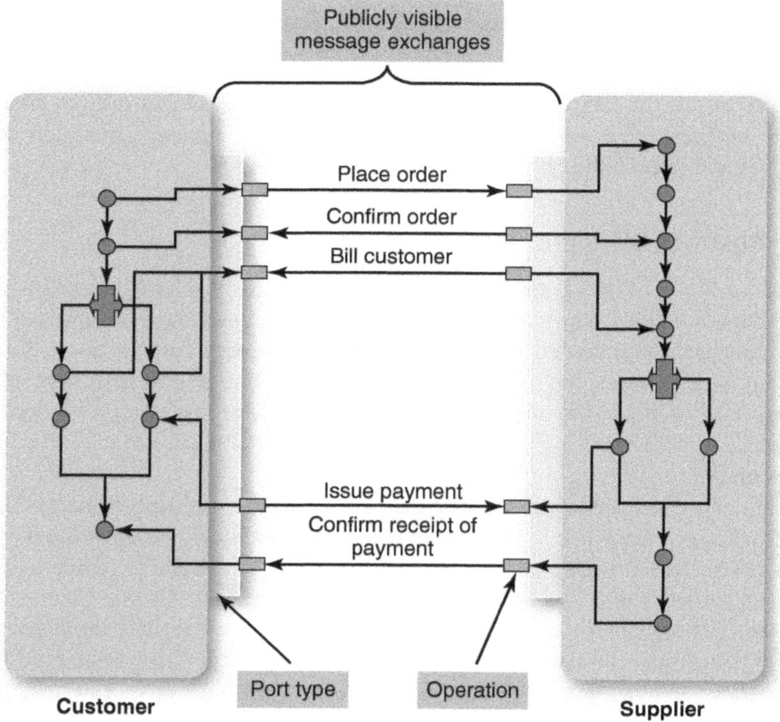

Figure 9.12 Simplified purchase order management abstract process

might contain complete information that would render it executable, its abstract status states that any concrete realisations of it are permitted to perform additional processing steps that are not relevant to the audience to which it has been given.

9.7.2.3 Differences between abstract and executable processes

There are two main differences between abstract and executable processes.

1. Abstract processes are modelled as business protocols in BPEL. A business protocol specifies the public interaction of business partners via publicly visible message exchanges and their potential sequence, i.e. the order in which messages between partners are exchanged in order to achieve a concrete business objective. Abstract processes define the behaviour that each party is expected to perform within the overall business process. The details of what else happens internally to realise these protocols are not important and are thus ignored. Unlike executable business processes, business protocols are not executable and hide the internal (private) details of a process flow. For instance, the types of products that are ordered by an order management process are not protocol relevant. However, the protocol might be sensitive to the method of payment, as the sequence of messages exchanged may depend on the mode of payment.

2. The abstract process approach to data handling reflects the level of abstraction required to identify protocol relevant data that can be embedded in messages. Abstract processes rely on language extensions consisting of *opaque tokens* that are used as explicit placeholders for missing details. An opaque activity is an explicit placeholder for exactly one executable BPEL activity, and any activities that could be nested within that activity. Opaque data is usually related to back end EIS. Opaque data affects the business protocol only by creating non-determinism because the manner in which it affects decisions is opaque. In contrast, transparent data affects the public business protocol in a direct way. The computation in the executable process is thus replaced by an opaque assignment in the corresponding abstract process. For instance, in the case of a purchase order business protocol the supplier may provide a service that receives a purchase order and responds with either acceptance or rejection of the process based on a number of criteria, such as availability of the goods, the creditworthiness of the buyer, etc. The decision process is opaque, while the result of the decision is reflected as behaviour alternatives exhibited by the external business protocol. In other words, the protocol acts as a *switch* within the behaviour of the supplier's service, while the selection of the decision branch taken in the process flow is implemented internally.

9.7.3 Message flow in BPEL

BPEL comprises basic and structured activities. *Basic activities* are the simplest form of interaction with a service, while *structured activities* are used in conjunction with control flow and are described in the succeeding section.

Basic activities are not sequenced and comprise individual steps to interact with a service, manipulate the exchange data, or handle exceptions encountered during execution. For example, basic activities would handle receiving or replying to message requests as well as invoking external services. The typical scenario is that there is a message received into the BPEL process. The process may then invoke a series of external services to gather additional data, and then respond to the requester in some fashion. BPEL activities such as `<receive>`, `<reply>`, and `<invoke>` all represent basic activities that allow a business process to exchange messages with the services it composes. These are described below; other basic activities include exception handling mechanisms and state management activities, which are covered later in this section.

The message flow section of BPEL deals with the sending and the receiving of messages so that a process (Web service) instance can communicate with other Web services. The message flow section of BPEL is handled by basic activities that include waiting for an input-only process operation to be invoked by some external client (`<receive>`), invoking an operation on some related Web service (`<invoke>`), and generating the response of an input/output operation (`<reply>`). As a language for composing Web services, BPEL processes interact by making invocations to other services and receiving invocations from clients. The former is done using the `<invoke>` activity, and the latter using the `<receive>` and `<reply>` activities. A business process provides services to its partners and communicates with them by means of the `<receive>` and `<reply>` activities. These three constructs are briefly described below.

BPEL calls other service partners. A partner is a Web service that a process invokes and/or any client that invokes a process. It is essentially a mapping to a WSDL <portType> description of a physical partner's Web service. This was shown in Figure 9.11.

A BPEL process interacts with each partner using a <partnerLink> construct. Partner links are channels along which peer-to-peer conversations with partners take place. A <partnerLink> element reflects the fact that such a link is a conversational interface by defining the roles played by each of the services in the conversation and specifying the <portType> provided by each service to receive messages within the context of the conversation. Each <role> specifies exactly one WSDL <portType>. This is illustrated in Figure 9.13. Each of the <invoke>, <receive>, and <reply> activities in the message flow section of BPEL specifies the <partnerLink> – <portType> operation and the variables that it relates to. For more details on <partnerLink>s refer to Section 9.7.6, which describes the concept of service orchestration in BPEL.

To invoke a Web service a process uses the <invoke> activity. This construct allows the business process to invoke either a synchronous (request/response) or an asynchronous (one-way) operation on a <portType> offered by a partner Web service. The <invoke> construct calls the partner Web service identified by the <partnerLink> attribute and its respective WSDL <portType> and operation. In addition to the <portType>, partner, and operation, the <invoke> element specifies input and output variables for the input and output of the operation being invoked. A synchronous Web service requires both input and output variables to be passed in. In the case of asynchronous operation invocations, only an input variable is required.

Whereas an <invoke> activity allows a process to call an operation of a partner's Web service, the <receive> activity allows the business process to wait for a matching message to arrive from a partner client service. It also specifies a variable (or a set of variables) that holds the requested data that will be received from the partner. Just like the <invoke> activity, <receive> uses <partnerLink>, WSDL <portType> and <operation> to identify the service it expects a specific partner to invoke. The arguments passed in by

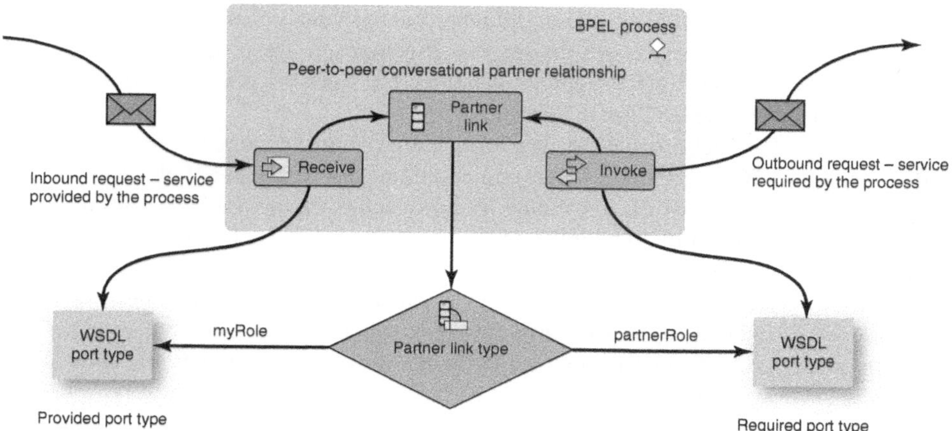

Figure 9.13 BPEL partner links

the caller are bound to a specified variable. In this way, <receive> explicitly marks the place in the business process logic where an inbound request message is accepted. In this way a partner triggers the execution of a process by calling its services.

In BPEL a process usually starts with a <receive> or <pick> activity, implying that a process must begin by being called as a service of a particular type. Therefore, the <receive> activity is a process activity on to which a WSDL operation maps. Another use of the <receive> activity (as well as the <pick> activity, which is described in the next section) is to create a *process instance*. The creation of a process instance in WS-BPEL is always implicit. An activity that receives messages (i.e. the <receive> activity) can be annotated to indicate that the occurrence of that activity causes a new instance of the business process to be created. This is done by setting the createInstance attribute of such an activity to *yes*. When a message is received by the <receive> activity, an instance of the business process is created if it does not already exist. A <receive> activity is used to receive a message that has been sent either synchronously or asynchronously. Listing 9.2 shows the use of the <invoke> and the <receive> activity in a process.

```
<process name= ... >

  <sequence>
    <!-- Wait for the incoming request to start the process -->
    <receive ... />

    <!-- Invoke a set of related activities in sequence -->
    <invoke ... />
    <invoke ... />
    <invoke ... />
      ...
  </sequence>

</process>
```

Listing 9.2 Messages in a BPEL process.

The <reply> construct allows the business process to send a message in reply to a message that was received through a <receive> activity. A <reply> activity is the place where a response is conveyed to the Web service client. The combination of a <receive> and a <reply> forms a synchronous request/response operation on the WSDL <portType> for the process. The effect is that of a single Web service call in which the <receive> activity accepts the input and the <reply> passes back the output, while the process may perform arbitrary computations in between. The <reply> activity must match the <partnerLink>, <portType>, and operation attributes of <receive> activity, while its variable attribute specifies the output. An asynchronous process does not use the <reply> activity. If such an activity needs to send a reply to the client, it then uses the <invoke> activity to call an operation on the client's <portType>. In this case an output variable is not necessary.

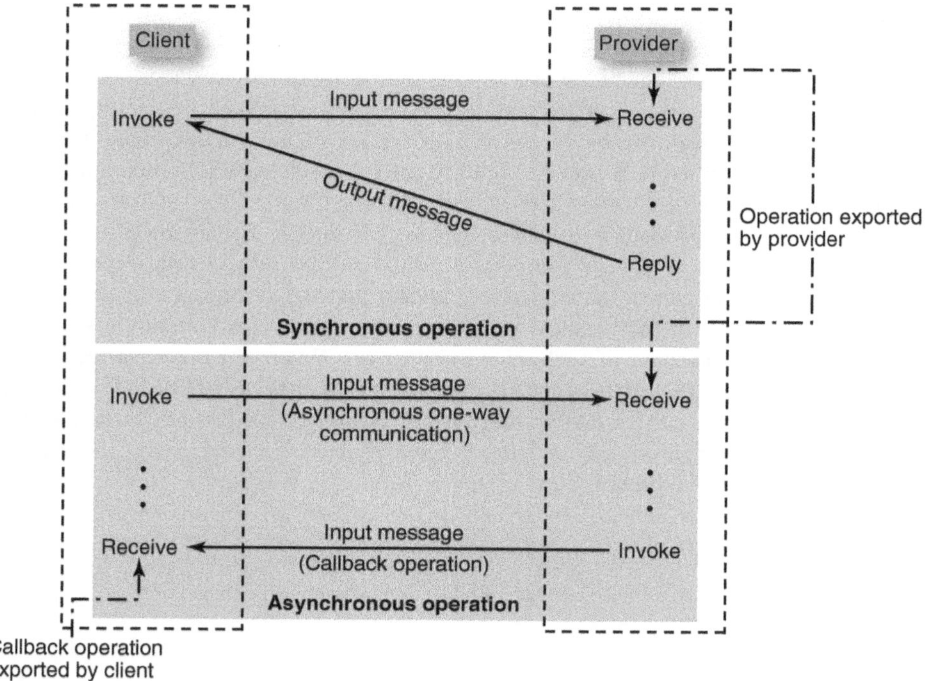

Figure 9.14 Synchronous and asynchronous modes of communication in BPEL

Figure 9.14 depicts how the <invoke> activity can invoke both synchronous and asynchronous types of activity in BPEL. The figure shows the synchronous (request/response) and asynchronous (one-way) modes of communication, which involve the <receive>, <reply>, and <invoke> activities. This figure indicates that the provider's asynchronous response (if it is forthcoming) in the asynchronous mode of communication is referred to as callback. However, it must be noted that it is not required that an asynchronous process returns a response.

Multiple <reply> activities may be defined in the process to answer a partner's call. However, only one matching <reply> may become active at any one time. Matching of the appropriate <reply> activity is done at run time, when the process looks for such an activity that is ready to run and has the same <portType>, <operation> and <partnerLink> as the <receive>.

9.7.4 Control flow in BPEL

A fundamental part of a BPEL specification is the definition of the activities and the sequence of steps required to make up a given process. This is where structured activities are employed to define selective state transition control flow definitions for synchronisation purposes. The control flow part of BPEL includes the ability to define an ordered sequence of activities (<sequence>), to have activities run in parallel

(<flow>), have branching activities (<switch>), to define iterations (<while>), and to execute one of several alternative paths (non-deterministic choice) based on external events (<pick>).

One may think of structured activities as the underlying programming logic for BPEL. Structured activities describe how a business process can be created by organising the basic activities it performs into structures. The structured BPEL activities are described below.

9.7.4.1 Sequencing activities

The <sequence> activity contains one or more activities that are executed absolutely sequentially. The activities are executed in the order in which they appear within the <sequence> element. When the final activity in the <sequence> has completed, the <sequence> activity itself is complete.

9.7.4.2 Parallelising activities

Parallelising activities that have no dependencies can be accomplished by enclosing the activities that are to run in parallel within a <flow> construct. This construct provides concurrency and synchronisation and also the ability to define guarded links. A <flow> activity allows definition of sets of activities (including other flow activities) that are connected via a <links> construct. The <links> construct is used to express synchronisation dependencies between nested child activities within a <flow> construct, providing among other things the potential for parallel execution of parts of the flow. Every link declared within a <flow> activity must have exactly one activity within the flow as its <source> and exactly one activity within the flow as its <target>. A <flow> activity in BPEL may create a set of concurrent activities directly nested within it. It also enables synchronisation dependencies to be expressed between activities that are nested directly or indirectly within it. When a <flow> activity is started, all the activities in it are ready to run unless they have incoming links that have not yet been evaluated.

Activities within <flow> start concurrently as soon as the <flow> activity is started. The <flow> activity completes when all nested activities complete. At the beginning of the execution of a <flow> activity, all links are inactive and only those activities that have no dependencies can execute. A <link> construct may be associated with a transition condition, which is a predicate expression that is evaluated over values in the different data variables in a process. A transition condition is specified using an optional element called `transitionCondition`, which may be part of a <source> element. As already explained in Section 9.5.1, a transition condition is associated with each control link and evaluated at the completion of an activity that is the source of a link. Once execution of activities completes, each activity evaluates its transition condition to determine the status of its outgoing links, which were inactive prior to the completion of this activity.

Once all incoming links to an activity are in force (they have been assigned a true or false state as a result of the evaluation of their respective transition conditions, see Figure 9.5), the join condition of this activity is evaluated. A `joinCondition` is a Boolean expression associated with each activity that is a target of a link. A join condition decides whether the activity should execute based on the value of the transition conditions of the links (paths) that point at it. This condition evaluates every one of the incoming links (there can be more than one and each one must have a Boolean value in order to continue), and decides whether or not the activity will be executed. For instance, a join condition may specify that a process may expect that either all of its incoming paths have completed successfully or just a single path needs to be successful before proceeding with the execution of a specific activity in the flow.

9.7.4.3 Branching activities

The `<switch>` activity functions much like the switch construct that occurs in many traditional programming languages, e.g. C or Java. There is an ordered list of one or more conditional branches, defined by `<case>` elements, followed by an optional `<otherwise>` element. Each `<case>` branch specifies a Boolean XPath expression, and the expressions are evaluated in the order in which they appear. The `<switch>` activity allows branches in a workflow to be navigated. Navigation is conducted on the basis of conditions defined in `<case>` elements. In the case that these conditions are not satisfied, a specific branch can be specified. The switch activity finishes when the activity of the selected branch completes.

Activities are iterated by nesting them within a `<while>`, a `<repeatUntil>` or a `<forEach>` activity. The `<while>` activity in BPEL evaluates a condition defined in an XPath expression and, if that condition evaluates to true, another iteration of its enclosed children activities is executed. This means that the body of a `<while>` activity might not be executed at all (if the entering condition does not evaluate to true). In contrast, the `<repeatUntil>` activity has the difference that the body of the activity is performed at least once, since the condition is evaluated at the end of each iteration. The third activity in the group of repetitive activities is the `<forEach>` activity. In its default behaviour, the `<forEach>` activity iterates sequentially *N* times over a given set of activities.

The `<pick>` activity is akin to an asynchronous event driven `<switch>` activity and contains a set of event handlers [Duftler 2002]. A `<pick>` activity is a set of branches of the form event/activity, and exactly one of the branches will be selected based on the occurrence of the event associated with it before any others. After the `<pick>` activity has accepted an event for handling, all other events are ignored. Possible events include the arrival of some message in the form of the invocation of an inbound one-way or request/response operation, or an *alarm* based on a timer. The event handlers include alarm handlers, which specify an event duration (time relative from now) or deadline (fixed future time), and message handlers (`onMessage`), which wait for messages from a particular partner, `<portType>`, and operation triplet. A `<pick>` activity completes when one of its branches is triggered by the occurrence of its associated event and the corresponding activity completes.

Each `<pick>` activity may contain at least one message handler (`onMessage` event). The `onMessage` events dictate when an activity becomes active, i.e. when a matching message is received. Only the first event handler to receive its event will run, and the `<pick>` activity will complete once that handler's activity completes. The message handlers are able to create a process instance in the same way as a `<receive>` activity. In this way a `<pick>` activity can provide the entry point into a process and acts very much like a `<receive>` activity. The key difference is that a `<pick>` activity can initiate a process based on a number of messages, rather than the single message that the <receive> activity supports.

In BPEL, choices are made depending on conditions and conditional branches are defined with the <if> activity. The <if> activity can have several <elseif> branches and one <else> branch.

9.7.4.4 Scoping activities

Finally, it is customary to associate scoping activities with structured activities in BPEL. Scopes provide a way to divide a complex business process into hierarchically organised parts, called scopes. Scopes provide behavioural contexts for activities. A <scope> activity is a means of explicitly packaging activities (or sets of activities gathered under a common structured activity, such as <sequence> or <flow>) together and providing an activity context such that the activities packaged within a scope can share common fault handling and compensation handling methods. In addition to fault and compensation handlers, scopes provide a way to declare variables that are visible within the scope. Scopes have their own local variables, and partner links, and they also define local correlation sets, event handlers, termination handler and message exchanges. Isolated scopes provide control of concurrent access to shared resources.

9.7.5 Data flow in BPEL

Business processes in BPEL specify stateful interactions involving the exchange of messages between partners. The state of a business process includes the content of the messages that are exchanged, as well as intermediate data used in business logic and in composing messages sent to partners. To maintain the state of a business process, state variables, which are called <variable>s, are used in BPEL. In addition, state data can be extracted and combined by means of data expressions to control the behaviour of processes. Finally, state update requires a notion of assignment. BPEL provides these features for XML data types and WSDL message types that constitute the data flow section of BPEL.

In BPEL, data <variable>s specify the business context of a particular process. These are collections of WSDL messages, which represent data that is important for the correct execution of the business process, e.g. for routing decisions to be made or for constructing messages that need to be sent to partners. Data <variable>s are used to manage the persistence of data across Web service requests. These provide the means for holding message content that constitute altogether the state of a business process. The messages held are often those that have been received from partners or are to be sent to partners. Data <variable>s can also hold data that are needed for a holding state related to the process and never exchanged with partners. Figure 9.15 shows the use of BPEL data variables.

Variables may exchange specific data elements via the use of <assign> statements. The <assign> statement is used to copy data messages (messages, parts of messages and service references) between variables. A BPEL variable is a typed data structure that stores messages associated with a workflow instance in order to facilitate stateful interactions

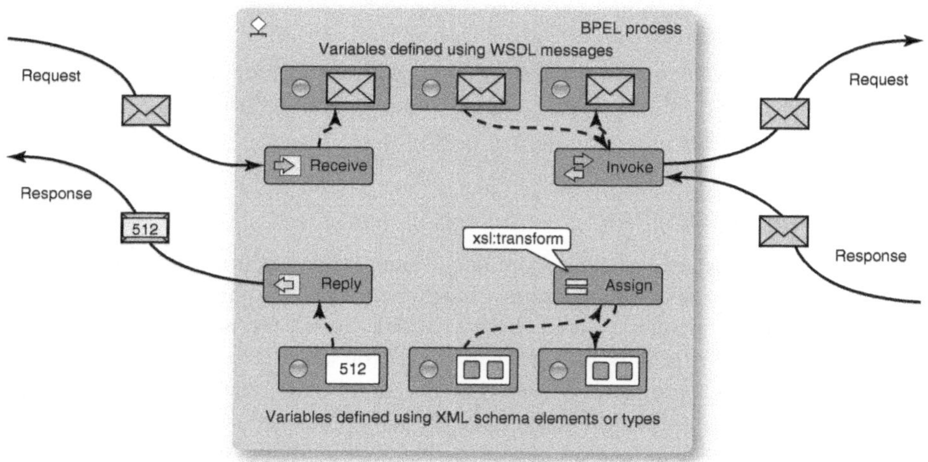

Figure 9.15 The use of variables in BPEL

among Web services. In a workflow, the state of the application is simply a function of the messages that have been exchanged and these can be stored in variables. Variables begin their lives initialised and are populated over time by the arrival of messages or computations that are being executed. An `<assign>` activity follows one of several paths depending on what is being assigned. In all assignment activity forms, type compatibility between the source and the destination of the assignment must be maintained. Therefore, valid assignments can only occur where both the `<from>` (source) and `<to>` (destination) reference variables hold the same message types, or where both endpoints of an assignment are the same. The `<assign>` statement allows not only data manipulation, but also dynamic binding to different service implementations.

9.7.6 Service composition in BPEL

In BPEL, business processes from one enterprise must be able to interact through Web service interfaces with the processes of other enterprises. This requires the ability to model a partner process. WSDL already describes the functionality of a service provided by a partner, at both the abstract and concrete levels. The relationship of a business process to a partner is typically peer-to-peer, requiring a two-way dependency at the service level [Alves 2007]. In other words, a partner represents both a consumer of a service provided by the business process and a provider of a service to the business process. This is especially the case when the interactions are based on asynchronous messaging rather than on remote procedure calls. BPEL provides also a mechanism for capturing the roles undertaken by business partners in a Web services based workflow through *partner linking,* and *endpoint references.*

The services that a business process composes (and interacts with) are modelled as <partnerLink>s in WS-BPEL. More specifically, BPEL uses <partnerLink>s to establish peer-to-peer partner relationships by specifying the roles of each party and the (abstract) interface that each provides. <partnerLink>s are the most abstract form of relation supported in BPEL and specify the shape of a relationship with a partner by defining the message and <portType>s used in the service interactions in both directions between any two partners, i.e. the operations provided or invoked by a business process. The actual partner service may be dynamically determined within the process.

Each <partnerLink> is characterized by a <partnerLinkType>. The <partnerLinkType> element is used to describe the communication (or conversational) relationship between a BPEL process and the involved parties, which include the Web services that the BPEL process invokes and the client that invokes the BPEL process. Each <partnerLink> defines the type of role played by each of the services in the conversation and specifies the <portType> provided by each service to receive messages within the context of the conversation. More than one partner can be characterised by the same <partnerLinkType>. For example, a certain procurement process might use more than one vendor for its transactions, but might use the same <partnerLinkType> for all° vendors. A BPEL partner is defined to play a role from a given <partnerLinkType>. The role element of the <partnerLinkType> points to exactly one WSDL <portType>, where one partner provides a one-way or request/response operation that is consumed by the other partner.

It is important to understand that <partnerLinkType>s are actually not part of the BPEL process specification document. This is due to the fact that <partnerLinkType> belongs to the service and not the process specification. They can therefore be placed within the WSDL document that describes the partner Web service of a BPEL process using the WSDL extensibility mechanisms.

A <partnerLinkType> in BPEL describes a requirement on the port types supported by two services that interact, but it does not identify the services themselves. Many pairs of services might satisfy the requirements described in a <partnerLinkType> specification. To achieve this objective, the services with which a business process interacts are modeled as <partnerLink>s in BPEL.

Finally, BPEL defines the notion of endpoint reference to represent the static or dynamic data required to address a message. Endpoint references are defined as given in WS-Addressing. We shall start the description of the BPEL process orchestration section by first describing <partnerLinkType> elements.

9.7.6.1 Synchronous operations

The <partnerLink> element can specify a single role, which is usually the case with synchronous request/response operations. A synchronous BPEL process is one that returns the results of processing back to the client immediately. The client is blocked until the results are returned. The WSDL interface for this process will have a request/response type endpoint as shown in Figure 9.14.

Example 9.6: Synchronous credit check operation

The synchronous type of process typically follows the following logic and syntax pattern:

```
<process>
   <receive partnerLink="CreditChecking" portType="CustomerCreditCheckPT"
    operation="initiate-customer-credit-check" variable="creditCheckVar">

   ..... perform processing .....

   <reply partnerLink="CreditChecking" portType="CustomerCreditCheckPT"
    operation="initiate-customer-credit-check"
    variable="creditCheckResponseVar">
</process>
```

For a BPEL process containing synchronous operations, there is a single role for each <partnerLinkType> because the operation is only invoked in a single direction. In this case, the BPEL process has to wait for completion of the operation and gets a response only after the operation is completed. If a <partnerLinkType> specifies only one role, one service in the relationship must implement a WSDL <portType>. In the following code snippet a *customerCreditCheck* service defines a <partnerLinkType> with a single role *creditChecker.* The role *creditChecker* refers to an initiate credit check WSDL operation through a <portType> called *customerCreditCheckPT.*

```
<partnerLinkType name="Customer-CreditCheckPLT">
    <role name="creditChecker"
               portType="tns:customerCreditCheckPT">
    </role>
</partnerLinkType>
```

The *initiate customer credit check* operation (shown in Example 9.7) defines an input to be sent to a service provider, and expects either a reply or a fault. Here, the service that implements the *creditChecker* role must implement the WSDL <portType> *customer-CreditCheckPT.*

9.7.6.2 Asynchronous operations

A better alternative is to define asynchronous BPEL processes, especially for long running applications. Asynchronous BPEL processes can be used in a scenario where it may take a long time to compute the results. When using an asynchronous BPEL process, the client need not block the call. Instead, the client implements a callback interface and, once the results are available, the BPEL process simply makes a callback invocation on the client.

One scenario where an asynchronous BPEL process can be used is if the underlying Web services to be orchestrated are asynchronous. This means that the client invokes the process and, when it completes, it performs a callback to the client. This has the following implications:

- For a BPEL process to be able to perform a callback operation to the client, the client must be a service and must be able to implement a specific WSDL `<portType>`.
- For asynchronous callback operations, two roles need to be specified by the `<partnerLinkType>` of the client. The first role describes the invocation of the operation by the client. The second role describes the invocation of a callback operation. If a `<partnerLinkType>` element specifies two roles, each of the two services that participate in the relationship must implement one role.
- Finally, the BPEL process will not `<reply>` to the client. Rather it will `<invoke>` the call back operation.

Example 9.7: Asynchronous credit check operation

The asynchronous type of process typically follows the following logic and syntax pattern:

```
<process>
   <receive partnerLink="CreditChecking" portType="Customer-CreditCheckPT"
    operation=" initiate-customer-credit-check" variable="creditCheckVar">

    ....... Perform time-consuming processing .....

    <!--Perform an invocation on the client to return the results -->
    <invoke partnerLink="CreditChecking" portType="CreditCheck-CallBackPT"
     operation="credit-check-response"
     inputVariable="creditCheckResponseVar">
</process>
```

In the following code snippet a *customerCreditCheck* service defines the two roles *creditRequester* and *creditChecker:*

```
<partnerLinkType name="Customer-CreditCheckPLT">
        <role name="creditRequester"
                    portType="tns:CreditCheck-CallbackPT">
        </role>
        <role name="creditChecker"
                    portType="tns:CustomerCreditCheckPT">
        </role>
</partnerLinkType>
```

For each partner service involved in a process, a <partnerLinkType> element identifies the WSDL <portType> elements referenced by <partnerLink> elements within the process definition. Here, the service that implements the *creditRequester* role must also implement the WSDL <portType> *creditCheckCallbackPT*, while the service that implements the *creditChecker* role must implement the WSDL <portType> *customerCreditCheckPT*.

Figure 9.16 exemplifies the asynchronous BPEL mode of communication. More specifically, this figure shows the relationship between partner links, partner link types, and associated port types for a purchase order and associated customer credit check process. As usual, partner links are used for operations provided or consumed by a service.

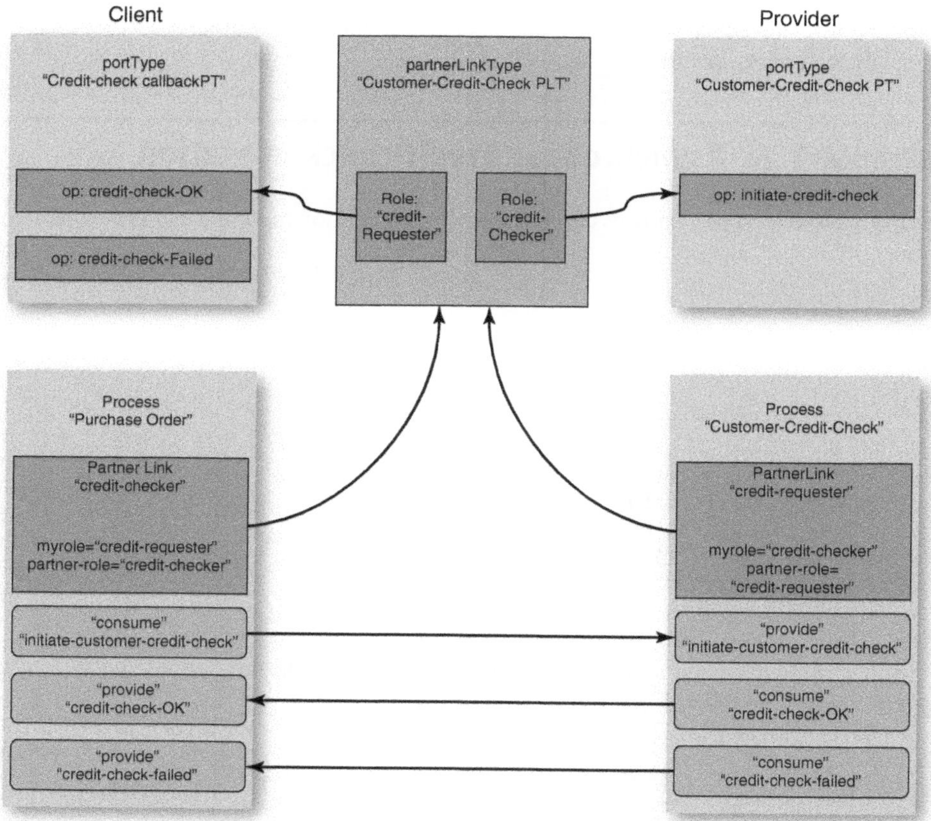

Figure 9.16 Partner links and associated link types
(*Source:* S. Graham, T. Boubez, G. Daniels, D. Davis, Y. Nakamura, R. Neyama, S. Simeonov, *Building Web Services with Java, Second Edition*, SAMS Publishing, 2005. Reproduced with permission.)

9.7.6.3 Binding options

BPEL allows business processes to become adaptive and portable by decoupling business logic from available service endpoints. Before operations on a partner's service can be invoked via a <partnerLink>, the binding and communication data for the partner service must be available. When a process needs to execute, each <partnerLink> must be bound to a concrete endpoint.

Four binding schemes are possible in BPEL [Weerawarana 2005]:

1. A process might be bound statically at design time to known endpoints.
2. A process can also be bound statically at deployment time by specifying a set of endpoints into which the process is deployed. This scheme is useful if instances of a particular process deployment must use the same endpoints.
3. Because in BPEL partners are likely to be stateful, the service endpoint information needs to be extended with instance specific information. This requires that actual partner services be selected and assigned dynamically. In BPEL the endpoint references implicitly present in <partnerLink>s can be selected, extracted and assigned dynamically in one of two ways. First, by using lookups for evaluating criteria attached to a <partnerLink> that might include QoS policies, transactional capabilities or functional requirements.
4. Second, by means of using passed in endpoints that are copied from variables previously assigned, not by the process itself but by either a response to an invocation (as a result of an <invoke> activity) or a request from a partner (as an input to a <receive> activity).

Figure 9.17 illustrates the binding of the two roles of a <partnerLink>, as depicted in Figure 9.16, to Web service endpoints. This binding is shown from the point of view of the purchase order process. For the credit requester role, the WSDL port contains the address where the operations of the process are provided. For the credit checker role, the WSDL port contains the address of the Web service provided by the business partner of the purchase order process.

9.7.7 Service correlation in BPEL

Business processes typically follow a stateful approach. A BPEL service can concurrently execute multiple BPEL processes and, for each process, multiple process instances. Each time the service creates a process instance it needs a way of keeping that instance (and its data) separate from other process instances (and their data). The service must also make sure that messages intended for one process instance do not mistakenly get dispatched to another process instance. This is the case if an appropriate transfer mechanism such as WS-Addressing is used. If, however, a lightweight transport mechanism is used or many partners are interacting, an explicit (manual) mechanism needs to be used to identify instances. In such cases, we need to use specific business data such as customer id numbers, product codes, order numbers and so on. Maintaining the relationship between a

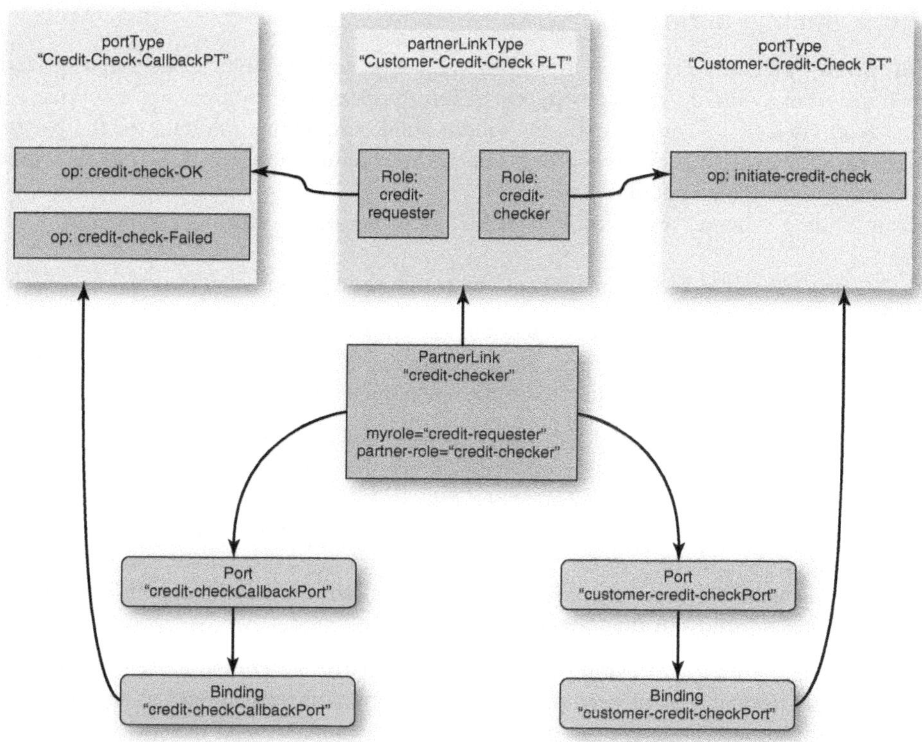

Figure 9.17 Binding a partner link to Web service endpoints
(*Source:* S. Graham, T. Boubez, G. Daniels, D. Davis, Y. Nakamura, R. Neyama, S. Simeonov, Building Web Services with Java, Second Edition, SAMS Publishing, 2005. Reproduced with permission.)

message and its corresponding process instance is called *correlation.* A message is said to be correlated with respect to a process instance.

Message correlation is the BPEL mechanism that allows multiple processes to participate in stateful conversations while maintaining references to specific process instances. Loosely speaking, a message correlation is the record that the process supplier uses to keep track of multiple partners in the same business process. Message correlation determines to which particular conversation a message belongs, i.e. in BPEL's case this is the task of locating/instantiating a process instance. Correlation can be used, for instance, to match returning or known customers to long running, multi-party business processes that may be running concurrently.

Message correlation occurs when one service calls another service asynchronously and passes *correlation tokens.* For example, a customer identification number might be used as a correlation token to identify an individual customer in a long running, multi-party business process relating to a specific purchase order. This is shown in Figure 9.18. In a correlation, the property name, e.g. customer-id, order-number, invoice-number,

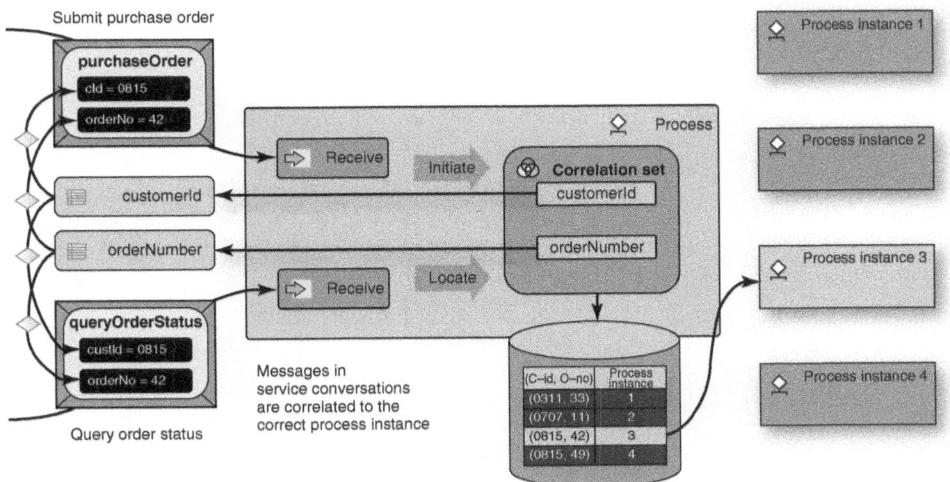

Figure 9.18 Example of message correlation connecting customers to specific purchase orders

vendor-id and so on, must have global significance to be of any use. BPEL uses the notion of *property* to represent and identify data elements exchanged within a message that have particular significance. A set of correlation tokens is defined as a set of properties shared by all messages in the correlated group. Such a set of properties is called a *correlation set.*

Using correlation sets, BPEL enables a business process engine to create new instances of a process for handling inbound requests, or to route inbound requests to existing process instances based on the values of message properties within the requests.

A *correlation set* declares the correlation tokens that are used by the BPEL compliant infrastructure to build process instance routing. A correlation set can be used with all types of activities that deal with sent or received messages. As `<receive>` and `<pick>` activities provide the entry points into a process, correlation sets often appear on them to enable message-to-instance routing. A correlation set declares the correlation tokens that are used by the BPEL compliant infrastructure to build instance routing. A correlation set is basically a set of properties such that all messages, having the same values as all the properties in the set, are part of the same interaction and are thus handled by the same instance. This implies that a correlation set identifies a particular process instance among a set of many process instances of that specific process. In general, a correlation set in conjunction with a `<port>` uniquely identifies a process instance among all process instances at a host machine. Correlation sets are particularly useful in supporting asynchronous service operations.

Correlation sets are declared within scopes (see Section 9.7.4.4 for a definition of the `<scope>` element) and are associated with them in a manner that is analogous to variable declarations. Each correlation set is declared within a scope and is said to belong to that scope. Correlation sets may belong to the global process scope or may also belong to other, non-global scopes.

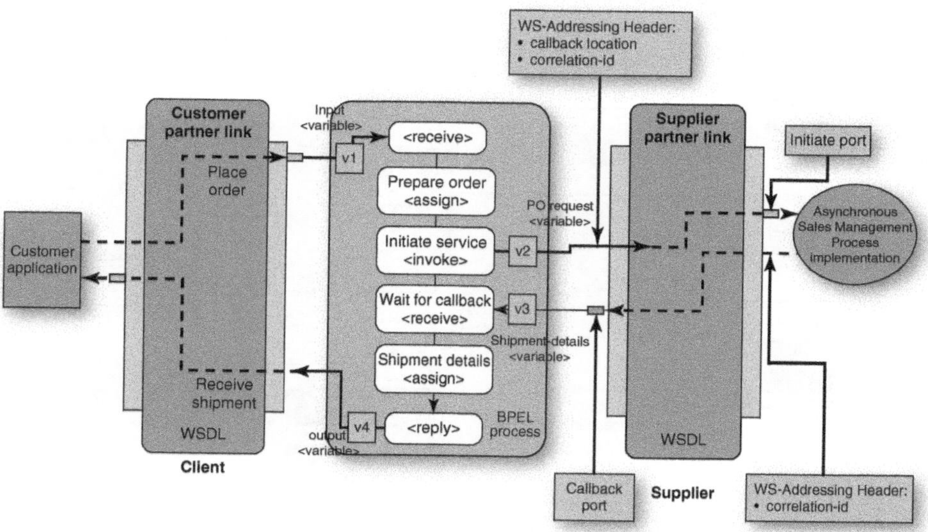

Figure 9.19 Asynchronous BPEL process corresponding to the abstract process in Figure 9.12

In multi-party business protocols, the partner starting a message exchange and creating the property values of the properties in the correlation set that tags the conversation is called the *initiator* of the exchange. All other partners are *followers* of the message exchange. Each participant process in a correlated message exchange acts either as the initiator or as a follower of the exchange. The initiator process sends the first message (as part of an operation invocation) that starts the conversation. The followers bind their correlation sets in the conversation by receiving an incoming message that provides the values of the properties in the correlation set. Both initiator and followers must mark the first activity in their respective groups as the activity that binds the correlation set.

Finally Figure 9.19 illustrates a simplified version of an asynchronous purchase order process developed on the basis of the abstract process in Figure 9.12. This figure illustrates the use of BPEL mechanisms including message and control flow constructs, `<partnerLinkType>`s, endpoint references – defined in WS-Addressing – as well as message correlation by means of identifiers.

9.7.8 Fault handling and compensation in BPEL

Given that communication between Web services is handled over Internet connections, which may or may not be reliable, faults may occur. To handle such faults or faults, due to logical errors and execution errors, BPEL employs faulting handling facilities.

The BPEL `<faultHandlers>` section contains structures defining the activities that must be performed in response to faults resulting from the invocation of services. In BPEL, all faults, whether internal or resulting from a service invocation, are identified by a qualified name. In particular, each WSDL fault is identified in BPEL by a qualified name formed by the target namespace of the WSDL document in which the relevant `<portType>` and fault are defined, and the name of the fault. Certain operations can return faults, as defined in their WSDL definitions.

In BPEL the `<scope>` element not only provides a way to divide a complex process into hierarchically organised parts but also allows *defining fault handlers* for different sets of activities. Fault handling in a business process can be thought of as a mode switch from the normal processing in a scope. The optional fault handlers attached to a scope provide a way to define a set of custom fault handling activities, syntactically defined as `<catch>` activities. Each `<catch>` activity is defined to intercept a specific kind of fault.

Each fault handler of a scope can initiate the reversal of the results of a previous activity by invoking a *compensation handler*. Compensation is used when application specific activities need to reverse the effects of a previous activity, which was carried out as part of a larger unit of work that is being abandoned when a two-phase commit protocol (see Section 10.3.1.1) is not used. BPEL provides a compensation protocol that has the ability to define fault handling and compensation in an application specific manner, resulting in long running (business) transactions. The compensation handler can be invoked by using the `<compensate>` activity, which names the `<scope>` element for which the compensation is to be performed; that is, the scope whose compensation handler is to be invoked. A compensation handler for a scope is available for invocation only when the scope completes normally.

9.7.9 Event handling in BPEL

A business process normally reacts to certain events. A BPEL process usually waits for an incoming message and reacts to it by means of the `<receive>` activity. This incoming message becomes the event that sets the entire process in motion. Using the `<receive>` activity we can initiate a process based on a single message at a time. Often, however, we may need to wait for more than one message, of which only one will occur. BPEL provides the means to deal with such situations, as well as the concurrent processing of asynchronous events through the notion of event handlers. This comes in addition to the `<receive>` and `<pick>` activities in its control structure that we examined earlier in this chapter.

An *event handler* enables the scope to react to events, or the expiration of timers, at any point during the execution of a scope. `<eventHandlers>` can deal with two kinds of events, namely *message events* and *alarm events*. A message event is triggered by incoming messages through operation invocation on `<portType>`s. A message event implements a request/response or one-way operation that a business process implements. An alarm event is time related and is triggered whenever a specified time is reached or expires.

The `<eventHandlers>` are similar to a `<pick>` activity insofar as they contain a number of `<onMessage>` or `<onAlarm>` activities. However, unlike a `<pick>` activity that specifies that a business process must wait for events to occur, event handlers can be executed concurrently with the process if the corresponding events occur. This allows concurrent processing within a single scope where previously concurrent *threads* of control were not permitted.

9.7.10 A comprehensive example in BPEL

To demonstrate how business processes are specified in BPEL, we shall use a version of the purchase order management supplier side process shown in Figure 9.4. In this example, we show a customer placing a purchase order and a supplier who tries to fulfil the customer's order. In this version, the supplier communicates with credit service, billing service, inventory and shipping service to fulfil the client's wishes. Once an invoice is generated, it is then sent back to the client. We shall begin developing this example by concentrating on the process orchestration section of BPEL. In this section several BPEL details are skipped in the interest of brevity and simplicity.

9.7.10.1 Process orchestration

When defining a business process in BPEL we are effectively creating a new Web service that combines existing elementary Web services. A BPEL process represents parties and interactions between these parties in terms of abstract WSDL interfaces (by means of `<portType>`s and `<operation>`s). The WSDL specification for this new composite Web service defines the relationships between this and other Web services (also defined in WSDL). The WSDL specification for the process specifies the port types it exposes to its clients, as well as operations, messages, partner link types and properties of interest to the process. This is shown in Figure 9.11. As already noted earlier in this chapter, relationships between the process and partner Web services (e.g. credit, check, inventory, billing, etc.) are achieved by means of the `<partnerLinkType>` construct. Every BPEL process must have at least one partner link.

Example 9.8: Orchestrating a purchase order management process

Figure 9.20 illustrates a `<partnerLink>` that is associated with a `<partnerLinkType>` element and indicates which role the process will play and which role the partner is expected to play. The example shows how a customer placing an order is connected to a supplier provided, purchase order management process. Each role specifies exactly one WSDL `<portType>` that must be implemented by the service implementing that role.

Listing 9.3 illustrates some of the `<partnerLink>`s and `<partnerLinkType>`s used in the example. Each `<partnerLinkType>` element in turn defines the dependencies between the services and the WSDL `<portType>`s associated with each role for this element. Listing 9.3 illustrates these connections too. For instance, Listing 9.3 shows that the WSDL `<portType>` *POManagementPT* of the supplier process is associated with a request initiated by the client. The supplier *PurchaseOrderMangement* process will also have a reference to the *CreditCheck* provider for requesting a credit service for the client and receiving a credit check response. This communication occurs by means of the two port types *CustomerCreditCheckPT* and *CreditCheck-CallBackPT* (mentioned in Section 9.7.5 but not shown in Listing 9.3).

In Listing 9.3 the *PurchaseOrderManagement* process excerpt is defined from the perspective of the purchase order supplier (i.e. the BPEL process itself). When the customer

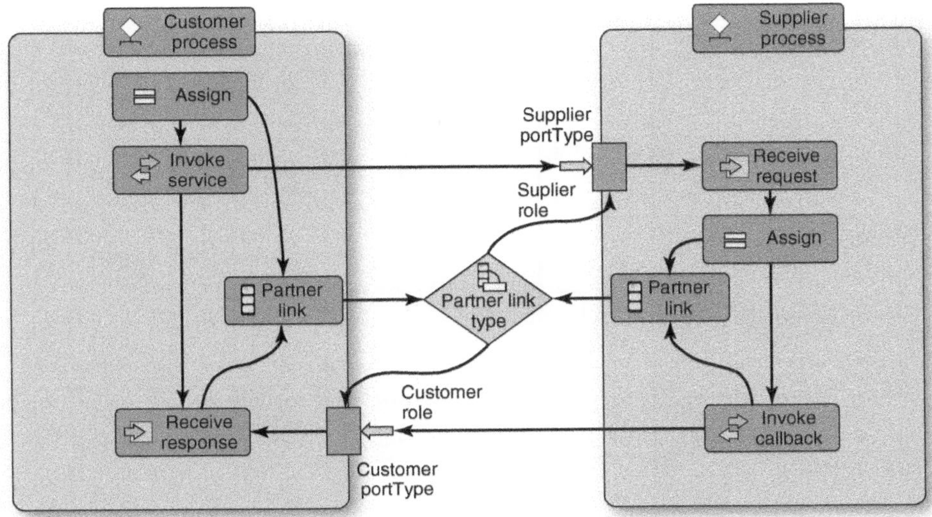

Figure 9.20 BPEL portrayal of place order service and purchase order management processes

(client) interacts with the supplier, the customer role is the purchase order requester while the supplier is the purchase order manager. From this listing we can observe that a BPEL process is divided into two distinct parts: the <partnerLinkType> declarations (with associated WSDL files, which describe the interactions between the BPEL process and the outside world) and the core BPEL process itself (supplier process), which describes the process to be executed at runtime.

At this point the previous code fragments specify the types of service an application is interacting with (through <partnerLinkType> element declarations) and the roles of the enterprises that are going to provide the necessary functionality for achieving this (through <partnerLink> declarations). The next thing is to declare the data flow between the customer and supplier processes.

9.7.10.2 Data flow

Recall from Section 9.7.5, BPEL processes manage the flow of data between partners represented by their service interfaces by employing variables. Variables are used to hold the state of the process and the data exchanged between processes. In particular, the <variable>s section of BPEL defines the data variables used by the process, providing their definitions in terms of WSDL message types and XML schema elements. Variables provide the means for holding messages that constitute a part of the state of a business process.

The <messageType>, <type>, or <element> attributes are used to specify the type of a variable. Attribute <messageType> refers to a WSDL message type definition. Attribute <type> refers to an XML schema simple or complex type. Attribute <element> refers to an XML schema element.

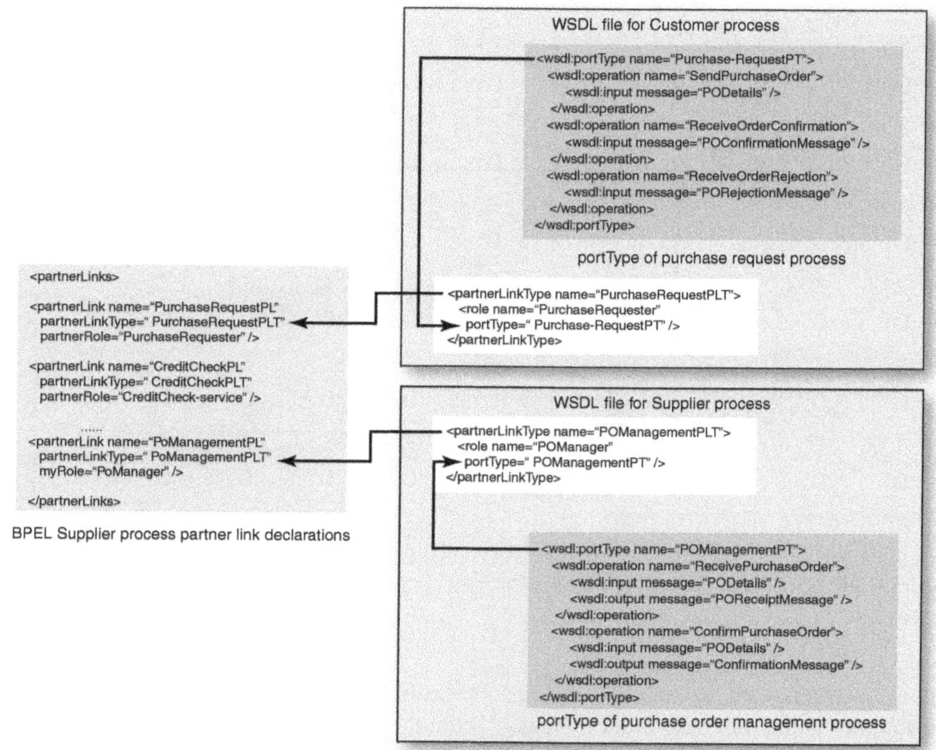

Listing 9.3 Definition of partner links, roles and connection of WSDL files to a BPEL process

---

Example 9.9: Storing customer details in the purchase order management process

The example in Listing 9.4 shows a purchase order management business process that stores a *CustomerDetailsMessage* in a *CustomerDetails* variable. The connection between this WSDL message and the variable is shown in the lower part of Listing 9.4.

Using `<assign>` and `<copy>`, data can be copied and manipulated between variables. The `<assign>` element is used to copy data (messages, parts of messages and service references) between variables, while `<copy>` supports XPath queries to sub-select data expressions. A typical example of an assignment is where (parts of) the contents of one message are copied to another. For instance, as shown in Listing 9.4, the *OrderID* of an *OrderRequestMessage* in the supplier process could be assigned to the invoice part of a message that will be sent to a customer.

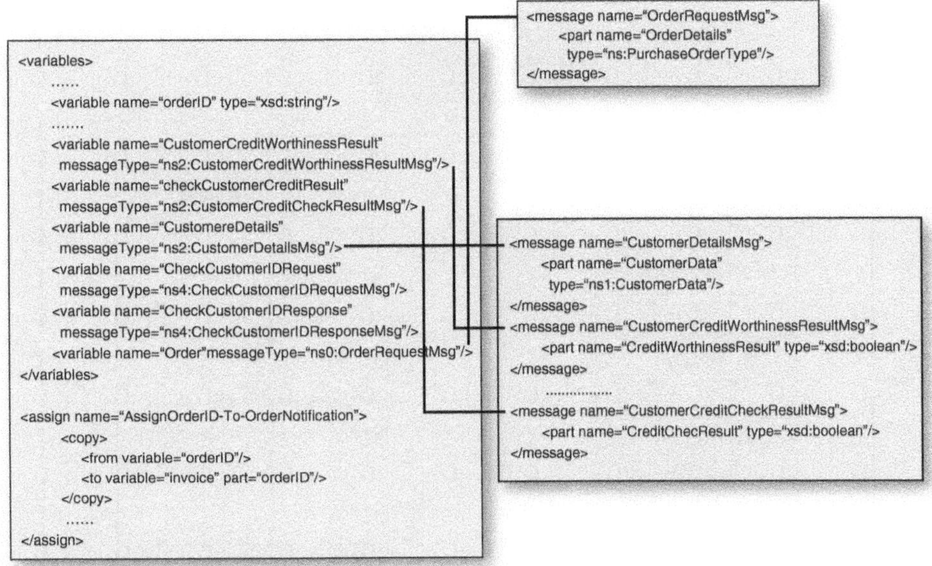

Listing 9.4 BPEL supplier process variables

Subsequently, we need to specify the process steps, which is the topic of the following subsection.

9.7.10.3 Process steps and control flow

At this stage we are ready to code the main process body. This is the key part of a BPEL application, which contains the definition of the basic sequence of steps required to handle a request. The main process body is where basic and structured activities come into play. It contains only one top level activity. Usually, this is a `<sequence>` that allows us to define several activities that will be performed sequentially. Within the sequence, we first specify the input message that initiates the business process. We do this with the `<receive>` construct, which waits for the matching message. In our case, this is the request for a purchase order submitted by a customer. Within the `<receive>` construct, we do not specify the message directly. Rather, we specify the partner link, the port type, the operation name and, optionally, the variable that holds the received message for consequent operations.

The process flow in the BPMN diagram in Figure 9.4 is shown to comprise an initial request from a customer asking for a purchase order, followed by an invocation of credit check service and inventory check service, shipment and payment service executed in sequence, assuming that the credit and inventory checks have succeeded; and ultimately a

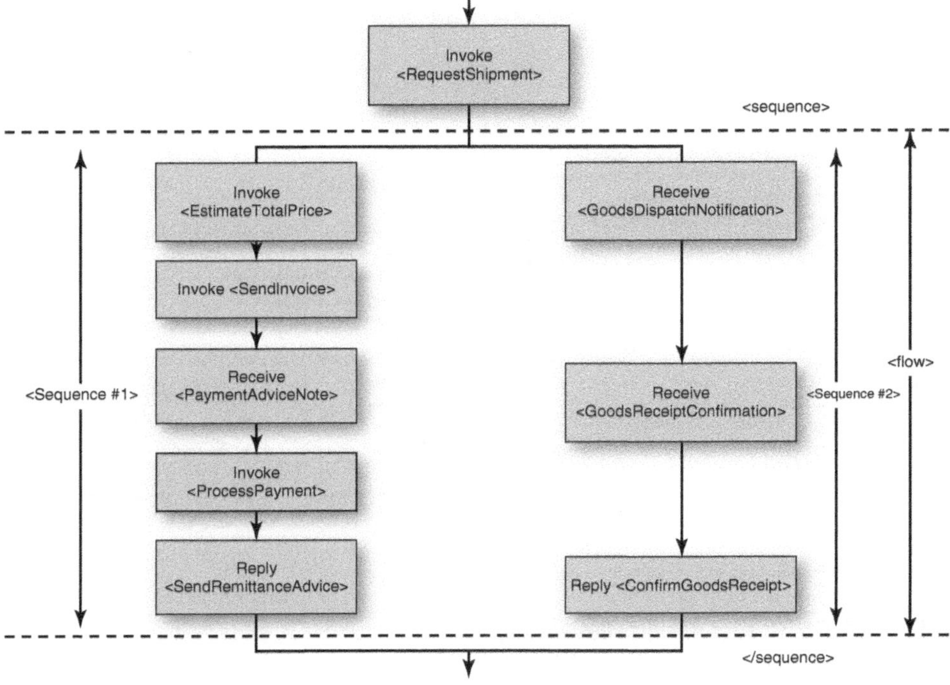

Figure 9.21 Sequencing and flow activities corresponding to Figure 9.4

response to the customer from the supplier sending an invoice. The only part of the supplier process in Figure 9.4 that involves parallel activities is that which aggregates prices and that which receives a goods dispatch notification from a logistics service. We will focus on the shipment and payment part of the purchase order management process, which we represent pictorially in Figure 9.21.

Example 9.10: Sequencing flow activities in a shipment and payment process

Listing 9.5 defines the constructs necessary to implement the sequencing and flow activities in the shipment and payment process. In Listing 9.5 the structure of the main processing section is defined by the outer `<sequence>` element, which states that the activities contained inside it are performed in order. The shipment request is received and then processed inside a `<flow>` section that enables concurrent behaviour by issuing parallel `<invoke>` activities. There are two sets of sequential activities that are embedded in different `<sequence>` statements. One set of sequential activities correspond to the activities that estimate total prices for the order and reply by sending a remittance advice to the customer, while the other set of activities receives a goods dispatch notification from a shipping service.

```
<process>
  .....
 <sequence name="outer-sequence">
    .....
  <invoke name="RequestShipment" partnerLink="LogisticsServicePL"
    operation="ProcessShipmentRequest"
    portType="LogisticsProviderServicePT" inputVariable="shipmentRequest"
    outputVariable="shipmentResponse"/>
      .....
  </invoke>
  <flow>
   <sequence name="sequence#1">

    <!-- estimate total price & taxes for ordered goods -->
    <invoke name="EstimateTotalPrice" partnerLink="PricingServicePL"
     operation="EstimateTotalPrice" portType="PricingServicePT"
     inputVariable="TotalPriceRequest"
     outputVariable="TotalPriceResponse"/>
      .....
    </invoke>

    <!-- send invoice to customer -->
    <invoke name="SendInvoice" partnerLink="CustomerPL"
     operation="ReceiveBill" portType="PurchaeRequestPT"
     inputVariable="invoice">
       .....
    </invoke>

    <!-- receive payment advice note from customer -->
    <receive name="ReceivePaymentAdviceNote"
     partnerLink="PaymentProcessingPL" operation="ProcessPayment"
     portType="PaymentProcessingPT" createInstance="no" variable="...">
       .....
    </receive>

    <!-- now process payment with financial institute -->
    <invoke name="ProcessPayment" partnerLink="FinancialServicePL"
     operation="ProcessPayment" portType="FinancialServicePT"
     inputVariable="ProcessPaymentRequest"
     outputVariable="ProcessPaymentResponse"/>
       .....
     </invoke>

     <!-- send payment receipt to customer -->
     <reply name="SendPaymentReceipt" partnerLink="PaymentProcessingPL"
      operation="ProcessPayment" portType="PaymentProcessingPT"
      variable="paymentReceipt">
        .....
     </reply>
    </sequence>
    .....
```

```
    <sequence name="sequence#2">
     <!-- receive goods dispatch notice from logistics provider -->
     <receive name="ReceiveGoodsDispatchNotification"
      partnerLink="GoodsDispatchNotificationPL"
      operation="ProcessGoodsDispatchNotification"
      portType="GoodsDispatchNotificationPT" createInstance="no"
      variable="...">
       .....
     </receive>

     <!-- receive goods receipt confirmation from customer -->
     <receive name="ReceiveGoodsReceiptConfirmation"
      partnerLink="GoodsReceiptNotificationPL"
      operation="ProcessGoodsReceiptNotification"
      portType="GoodsReceiptNotificationPT" createInstance="no"
      variable="...">
       .....
     </receive>
     <!-- send response to logistics provider service -->
     <reply name="ConfirmGoodsArrival"
      partnerLink="GoodsDispatchNotificationPL"
      operation="ProcessGoodDispatchNotification"
      portType="GoodsDispatchNotificationPT" variable="..." >
       .....
     </reply>
    </sequence>
   </flow>
     .....
  </sequence>
 </process>
```

Listing 9.5 BPEL process flow for the shipment and payment process

In Listing 9.5 the <invoke> activities are used to call Web services offered by the supplier via <partnerLink>s. Requests are sent by clients, i.e. callers, of the BPEL *PurchaseOrderManagement* process via the <receive> activity. Finally, results are returned to clients of the BPEL *PurchaseOrderManagement* process via the <reply> activity. Notice the use of the <createInstance> attribute in the <receive> activities. This attribute is used to instantiate a business process in BPEL. Its default value is "no" as shown in Listing 9.5. Normal convention is to annotate the initial <receive> activity with a <createInstance>="yes" attribute. This has already occurred earlier in Listing 9.5.

9.7.10.4 Declaring message correlations

The final part of this BPEL example for the purchase order management process concentrates on correlation sets. Recall that BPEL provides the concept of correlation sets for situations where WS-Addressing is not appropriate or available.

Example 9.11: Message correlation in order management process

Figure 9.22 shows a graphical representation of a correlation. In this figure we consider the example of order management application where a customer sends a purchase order to a seller. Moreover, we assume that the customer and seller have a stable business relationship and are statically configured to send documents related to purchasing interactions to the URLs associated with the relevant WSDL service ports.

In particular, Figure 9.22 shows that there exists a unique purchase order identifier for each purchase order forwarded by a customer and received by a supplier, a unique customer number for the customer and a unique number for each corresponding invoice created by the supplier. A customer may start a correlated exchange with a supplier by sending a purchase order and using an Order_id in the purchase order document as the correlation token. The supplier uses this Order_id in the PO confirmation. The supplier may later send an invoice document that carries both the Order_id, to correlate it with the original purchase order, and an invoice number. In this way future payment related messages may carry only the invoice number as the correlation token. The invoice message thus carries two separate correlation tokens and participates in two overlapping correlated exchanges. The scope of correlation is not, in general, the entire interaction specified by a service, but may span a part of the service behaviour.

WS-BPEL addresses correlation scenarios by providing a declarative mechanism to specify correlated groups of operations within a process instance. A set of correlation

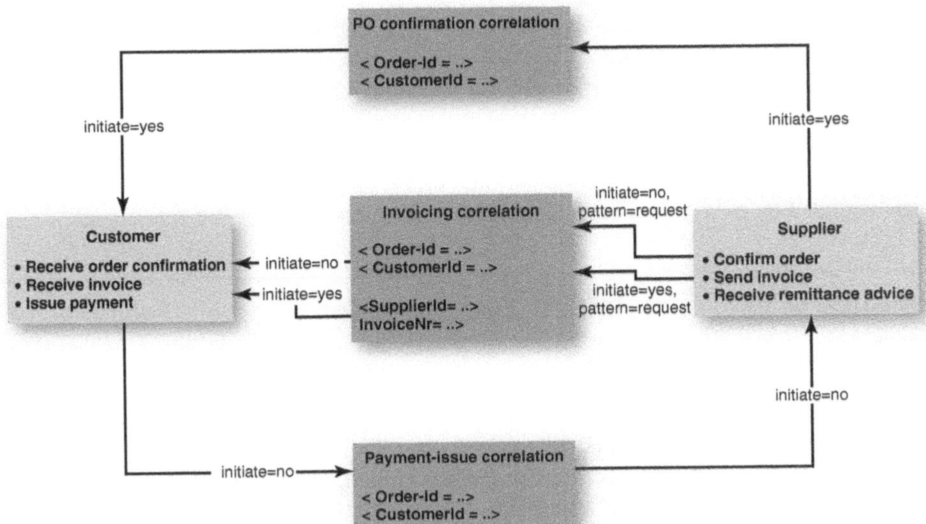

Figure 9.22 Correlation property sets for the BPEL Purchase Order Management process

tokens is defined as a set of properties shared by all messages in the correlated group. Such a set of properties is called a correlation set (see Section 9.7.7).

A <correlationSet> can be declared within a process or scope element in a manner that is analogous to a variable declaration. The name of a <correlationSet> must be unique among the names of all <correlationSet> defined within the same immediately enclosing scope. A <correlationSet> resembles a late bound constant rather than a variable. The binding of values to a <correlationSet> is triggered by a specially marked send or receive message operation. A <correlationSet> can be initiated only once during the lifetime of the scope to which it belongs. After a correlation set is initiated, the values of the properties for a correlation set must be identical for all the messages in all the operations that carry the correlation set and occur within the corresponding scope until its completion.

To specify which data is used for correlation, *message properties* are employed to associate relevant data with names that have greater significance than simple data types. Message properties are usually parts of messages, usually embedded in the relevant <part> element in a message. To associate a property to a specific element of a message, BPEL provides *property aliases.* With the help of property aliases we can map property to a specific element (or attribute) in a chosen message part. We can then use this property name as an alias to refer to this message part. This is particularly useful for abstract business processes where message exchange descriptions are used.

Example 9.12: Properties and property aliases in order management process

Listing 9.6 illustrates how properties and property aliases are used in the context of Figure 22. In particular it shows how properties and property aliases can be specified for correlation tokens, such as Order_Id, Customer_Id, Invoice_Nr and so on. The figure also illustrates how global properties such as Supplier_id, Order_Id, etc, are used to map properties between an inbound WSDL file for a supplier and a corresponding imported outbound WSDL file for a customer. A WSDL specification is named as inbound when a Web service receives an input message from a client. The outbound WSDL specification is characterised by the transmission of a message from the Web service to a client.

Example 9.13: Correlation sets in order management process

Listing 9.7 illustrates how correlation sets can be used to specify the constructs graphically depicted in Figure 9.22. This figure shows the BPEL specification used in conjunction with the inbound WSDL specification for suppliers. Listing 9.7 shows that correlation set specifications can be used in <invoke>, <receive>, and <reply> activities (the latter is not shown in this figure). In the case of <invoke>, when the operation invoked is a request/response operation, a pattern attribute on the <correlation> specification is used to indicate whether the correlation applies to the outbound message (*request*), the inbound message (*response*), or both (*request-response*). The listing also shows that

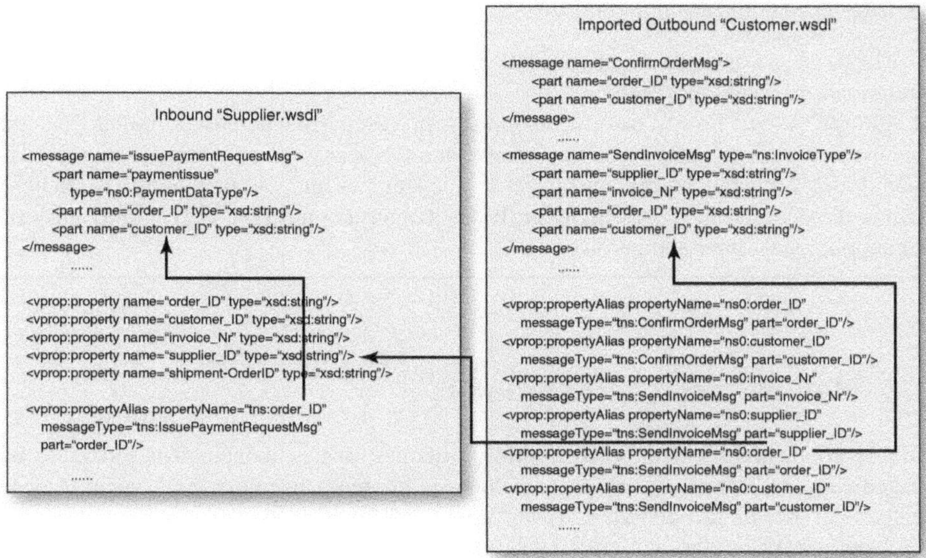

Listing 9.6 Mapping properties to messages

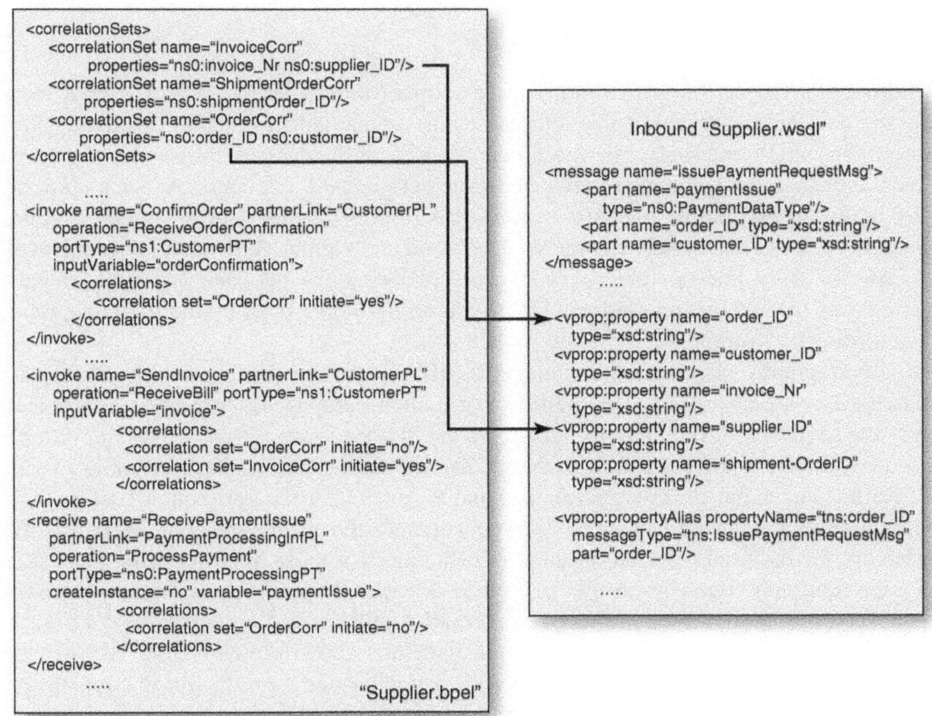

Listing 9.7 Specifying correlation sets in BPEL for the process in Figure 22

the `<initiate>` attribute on a correlation specification is used to indicate whether the correlation set is being initiated.

Listing 9.7 shows how to use correlation sets in a scenario where the supplier first confirms the receipt of an order, sends an invoice and receives payment from a customer. The figure shows that when an invoice is sent by the supplier and received by the customer it contains the correlation tokens Supplier_Id, Customer_id, and Invoice_Nr to identify the right supplier, customer and invoice.

9.8 Web service choreography

Business applications that involve multiple organisations or independent processes are engaged in a collaborative fashion to achieve a common business goal, such as order management. For the collaboration to work successfully, long lived, peer-to-peer message interchanges between the participating services, i.e. choreographies, within or across the trusted domains of an organisation must be performed. The primary goals of a choreography definition are: to verify at run time that all message interchanges are proceeding according to plan, and to guarantee that changes in the implementations of services are still in compliance with the message interchange definition.

9.8.1 Choreography description

A choreography description is a multi-party contract that describes from a global viewpoint the external observable behaviour across multiple clients (which are generally Web services) in which external observable behaviour is defined as the presence or absence of messages that are exchanged between a Web service and its clients. As such choreography is not an executable business process description language, or an implementation language, such as Java or C#, it is rather monitored and validated (or invalidated). Its role is to specify truly interoperable peer-to-peer collaborations between any type of party regardless of the supporting platform or programming model used by the implementation of the hosting environment.

A choreography description language (CDL) is the means by which multi-party collaborations are described. The main use of a choreography description is to precisely define the sequence of interactions between a set of cooperating Web services in order to promote a common understanding between participants and to make it possible to validate conformance, ensure interoperability, and to generate code skeletons [Austin 2004]. A choreography description can be used to generate the necessary code skeletons that implement the required external observable behaviour for those Web services. For example, a choreography description that is used to describe the multi-party contract between a manufacturing company, a number of potential suppliers, and a number of distributors might be used by any potential participant to generate a code skeleton for a Web service that can be guaranteed to be interoperable with that particular manufacturing company.

Recall that Figure 9.10 illustrates how a business choreography language relates to the business process languages layer. Figure 9.10 illustrates that a GUI and a toolset are used to specify interactions between a customer and supplier to generate a specification in terms of Web Services-CDL (see next section). This WS-CDL representation can then be used to generate a BPEL workflow template for both the customer and supplier, reflecting the nature of their business agreement.

9.8.2 Web Services Choreography Description Language (WS-CDL)

The Web Services Choreography Description Language is an XML specification for representing the choreography of collaborating services. With WS-CDL we can specify the peer-to-peer collaboration of Web services regardless of the supporting platform or programming model used by the implementation of the hosting environment. We can define a specification containing a *global* definition of sets of rules that describe how, and in which order, different services should interact. Such specification provides a flexible systemic view of collaborating processes.

WS-CDL is purely for specifying *abstract business processes,* independent of platform and programming languages that are used to implement the Web service participation. In the WS-CDL specification, choreography definitions can involve two (binary) or more (multi-party) participants. WS-CDL is positioned as a complementary language to BPEL (and other business process languages). While BPEL focuses on the specification of the behaviour of a specific party (organisation), WSDL focuses on the description of global message interchanges between a number of interacting parties. WS-CDL provides the global model needed by BPEL processes to ensure that the behaviour of endpoints is consistent across all cooperating services. WS-CDL, like BPEL, is a specification language, which does not contain any business semantics (e.g. resources, commitments, agreements and so on).

A choreography definition in WS-CDL is always defined abstractly between *roles,* which are later bound to *participants.* Roles are related to each other via *relationships.* A relationship is always between exactly two roles. A participant may implement any number of non-opposite roles in the choreography. Roles in WS-CDL are somewhat similar to `<partnerLink>`s in BPEL. WS-CDL choreography specifications are used to generate public interfaces, e.g. specified in abstract BPEL processes. WS-CDL specifications are also useful at run time as they are used to verify the execution of message exchanges between interacting parties.

Choreographies are composed of activities. The main activity is called an *interaction* and is the basic building block of a choreography, which results in the exchange of messages between participants and possible synchronisation of their states and the actual values of the exchanged information. Interactions specify the unit of message exchange between roles. An interaction corresponds to the invocation of a Web service operation on a role. Consequently, an interaction is defined as a request with zero or more responses. Interactions can involve ordering activities (*sequence, parallel, choice*) or can compose another choreography in the parent choreography. Choreography definitions may be data driven, i.e. the data contained in the messages impacts the ordering of interactions. Data is modeled as *variables,* which may be associated to message content, a channel, or the state of roles involved in the choreography. *Tokens* are aliases that may represent parts of a variable. Tokens in WS-CDL relate to the concept of properties in a BPEL correlation set, which we described in the previous section.

A WS-CDL document is simply a set of definitions. The WS-CDL definitions are named constructs that can be referenced. There is a *package* element at the root, and individual choreography definitions inside it. A WS-CDL package contains a set of one or more choreographies and a set of one or more collaboration type definitions. The WS-CDL package construct allows aggregation of a set of choreography definitions.

Example 9.14: Customer supplier choreography

The example in Listing 9.8 shows a sample choreography specified in WS-CDL. The `<package>` element is shown to contain exactly one top level `<choreography>`, which is explicitly marked as the root `<choreography>`. This root choreography can be initiated and is shown to involve one interaction. The interaction happens from role customer to role supplier on the channel *supplier-channel* as a request/response message exchange. In this listing the message *purchaseOrder* is sent from a customer to a supplier as a request message while the message *purchaseOrderAck* is sent from a supplier to a customer as a response message.

The `<variable>` consumer channel is populated at a supplier at the end of the request using the `<record>` element. The element `<record>` is used to create/change one or more states at both the roles at the ends of the `<interaction>`. For example, the PurchaseOrder message contains the channel of the `<role>` *manufacturer* when sent to the `<role>` *supplier*. This can be copied into the appropriate state variable of the *supplier* within the `<record>` element. When align is set to *true* for the `<interaction>`, it also means that the manufacturer knows that the supplier now has the address of the

```
<package name="CustomerSupplierChoreography" version="1.0"
    <informationType name="purchaseOrderType"
                     type="pons:PurchaseOrderMsg"/>
    <informationType name="purchaseOrderAckType"
                     type="pons:PurchaseOrderAckMsg"/>
    <token name="purchaseOrderID" informationType="tns:intType"/>
    <token name="supplierRef" informationType="tns:uriType"/>    ......
    <role name="Customer">
         <behavior name="CustomerForSupplier"
                   interface="cns:CustomerSupplierPT"/>
         <behavior name="CustomerForWarehouse"
                   interface="cns:SupplierWarehousePT"/>
    </role>
    <role name="Supplier">
         <behavior name="supplierForCustomer"
                   interface="rns:CustomerSupplierPT"/>
    </role>
```

```
    <relationship name="CustomerSupplierRelationship">
          <role type="tns:Customer" behavior=" CustomerForSupplier"/>
          <role type="tns:Supplier" behavior="supplierForCustomer"/>
    </relationship>
    <channelType name="CustomerChannel">
          <role type="tns:Customer"/>
          <reference>
              <token type="tns:CustomerRef"/>
          </reference>
          <identity>
             <token type="tns:purchaseOrderID"/>
          </identity>
    </channelType>    ......
    <choreography name=" CustomerSupplierChoreo" root="true">
       <relationship type="tns:CustomerSupplierRelationship"/>
       <variableDefinitions>
       <variable name="purchaseOrder"
                 informationType="tns:purchaseOrderType"/> ......
       <variable name="supplier-channel"
                 channelType="tns:SsupplierChannel"/>
          ......
       <interaction channelVariable="tns:supplier-channel"
                    operation="handlePurchaseOrder"
                    align="true"initiateChoreography="true">
          <participate relationship="tns:CustomerSupplierRelationship"
                       fromRole="tns:Customer" toRole="tns:Supplier"/>
          <exchange messageContentType="tns:purchaseOrderType"
                    action="request">
              <use variable="cdl:getVariable(tns:purchaseOrder,
                   tns:Customer)"/>
              <populate variable="cdl:getVariable(tns:purchaseOrder,
                        tns:Supplier )"/>
          </exchange>
          <exchange messageContentType="purchaseOrderAckType"
                    action="respond">
              <use variable="cdl:getVariable(tns:purchaseOrderAck,
                   tns:Supplier)"/>
             <populate variable="cdl:getVariable(tns:purchaseOrderAck,
                       tns:Customer)"/>
          </exchange>
          <record role="tns: Supplier "action="request">
              <source variable="cdl:getVariable(tns:purchaseOrder,
                      PO/Customer Ref, tns: Supplier)"/>
              <target variable="cdl:getVariable(tns:Customer-channel,
                      tns:Supplier )"/>
          </record>
       </interaction>
    </choreography>
</package>
```

Listing 9.8 Sample choreography in WS-CDL

manufacturer. The `<source>` and the `<target>` elements within the `<record>` element represent the `<variable>` names related to the `<role>` element that is specified in the role attribute of the `<record>` element.

In Listing 9.9 the `<interaction>` activity happens on the supplier channel which has a `<token>` *purchaseOrderID* used as an identity of the channel. This identity element is used to identify the business process of the supplier. The request message *purchaseOrder* contains the identity of the supplier business process, while the response message *purchaseOrderAck* contains the identity of the manufacturer business process.

WS-CDL represents an important new layer of the Web services stack that complements BPEL. The W3C Web Services Choreography Working Group, was closed in July 2009 leaving WS-CDL as a candidate recommendation. At this stage it is difficult to picture exactly what the future of WS-CDL will be as it has not gained much industry support so far.

9.9 Summary of learning objectives

To specify how individual Web services can be composed to create reliable and dependable business process based solutions with the appropriate level of complexity, various Web service composition languages have emerged. Service composition languages span service orchestration and service choreography.

- Service orchestration describes how Web services can interact with each other at the message level from the perspective and under control of a single endpoint.
- Service choreography is typically associated with peer-to-peer collaborations of Web service participants by defining from a global viewpoint their common and complementary observable behaviour.

Two complementary languages target Service orchestration and choreography.

- The Business Process Execution Language for Web Services has emerged as the standard to define and manage business process activities and business interaction protocols comprising collaborating Web services from an orchestration point of view.
- The Web Services Choreography Description Language is an XML specification targeted at describing the global view of observable behaviour of message exchanges of all Web service participants that are involved in a business collaboration.

Review questions

- Briefly describe the major characteristics of automated business processes.
- List and describe the main components of a workflow system.

- Give an example of a workflow application using UML.
- What is business process integration and how does it differ from business process management?
- Describe the purpose of cross enterprise business processes and their relationship to workflow systems.
- What is the purpose of a service composition meta-model?
- What is a flow model and what are control links and transition conditions?
- How are Web services composed?
- What are Web service orchestration and choreography languages? How do they differ from each other?
- List and describe the main components of BPEL.
- How does BPEL orchestrate Web services?
- What is the purpose of WS-CDL and how can it work with BPEL?

Exercises

9.1. Further develop the sample BPEL process in Section 9.7.10 to include credit check and billing service providers.

9.2. Develop an abstract BPEL process for a simplified shipping service. This service handles the shipment of orders, which are composed of a number of items. The shipping service should offer two options, one for shipments where the items are shipped all together, and one for partial shipments where the items are shipped in groups until the order is fulfilled.

9.3. Extend the BPEL process in Exercise 9.1 to offer an inventory check service, consumed by the BPEL process that provisions the purchase order service. When the purchase order service provider receives the client request, the following events should occur:

(a) The purchase order service provider assigns the price and the current date of the request, and invokes the inventory service to check inventory status.

(b) The inventory service checks the availability of an item and reports to the purchase order service provider.

(c) Based on the result from the inventory service, the purchase order service provider responds either by fulfilling the purchase order or by issuing a fault stating that the order cannot be completed.

Develop your solution by assuming the service client and inventory check service provider use exclusively synchronous operations.

9.4. In your solution for the previous exercise, replace all synchronous operations with asynchronous operations that achieve the same results.

9.5. Develop a simple BPEL process for travel booking. This process should be partially based on Exercises 5.3, 5.4, and 5.5 and involve interactions with partners such as flight, hotel and car reservation services, as well as a simple credit checking service.

9.6. Use BPEL to develop a simple application involving a credit card holder and an electronic merchant. The card holder sends a message containing the order instructions and payment details to the merchant. The merchant then initiates a payment authorisation request at its bank to determine whether or not the purchase request contains valid information about the buyer's account and financial status. If authorisation of payment is successful then the merchant receives a payment approval response and dispatches the ordered goods to the purchaser.

CHAPTER 10

Service transactions

Learning objectives

In situations where business processes need to drive their collaboration to achieve a shared business objective between collaborating Web services, transactional support may be needed. This kind of support is required in order to orchestrate loosely coupled services into cohesive units of work and guarantee consistent delivery of critical data and reliable execution. However, classical transaction models are far too constraining for SOA based applications as these rely on long lived activities and services that are disjointed in both time and location.

In this chapter we focus on the features, requirements of, and architectural support for transactional Web services. This chapter will help you gain a thorough understanding of the following key concepts:

- Transaction support for both centralised and distributed systems.
- Distributed transaction architectures.
- Concurrency control and coordination mechanisms for distributed transactions.
- Closed and open nested transactions.
- Transactional workflows.
- Properties and models of transactional Web services.
- Transactional Web service standards and frameworks that work with other Web services standards, such as BPEL, WS-Policy and WS-Security.

Chapter preview

This chapter begins with a definition and discussion of the concept of business level transactions for centralised and distributed systems and its importance for distributed applications. We then consider nested transactions and transactional workflows as they are the foundations of every transactional Web service solution. Following this, we introduce the concept and main characteristics of transactional approaches for Web services. This discussion concludes with the introduction of the WS-Coordination and WS-Transaction standards and explanations as to how they can be used in the context of SOA based applications that exhibit transactional nature.

10.1 What is a transaction?

Transaction processing systems are widely used by enterprises to support mission critical applications. These applications need to store and update data reliably, provide concurrent access to data by large numbers of users, while maintaining data integrity despite failures of individual system components. Given the complexity of contemporary business requirements, transaction processing occupies one of the most complex and important segments of business level distributed applications.

A *transaction* is a series of operations performed as a single unit of work that either completely succeeds, or fails with all partially completed work being undone. By tying a set of related operations together in a transaction, one can ensure the consistency and reliability of the system despite any errors that occur. All operations in a transaction must complete successfully in order to make the transaction successful.

A transaction has a beginning and an end that specify its boundary within which it can span processes and machines. Application programs must be able to start and end transactions, and must also be able to indicate whether data changes are to be made permanent or discarded. Indicating transaction boundaries for an application program is called *transaction demarcation.*

An *atomic transaction* is a computation consisting of a collection of operations that take place indivisibly in the presence of both failures and concurrent computations. That is, either all of the operations prevail or none of them prevails, and other programs executing concurrently cannot modify or observe intermediate states of the computation. A transaction ends when one of two things happen:

- either the transaction is committed by the application; or
- the transaction fails and is rolled back (e.g. due to inadequate resources or data consistency violations).

If the transaction successfully commits, changes associated with that specific transaction are written to persistent storage and made visible to new transactions. If the transaction fails and is rolled back, all changes made by it will be discarded. The net result will be as if the transaction never happened at all.

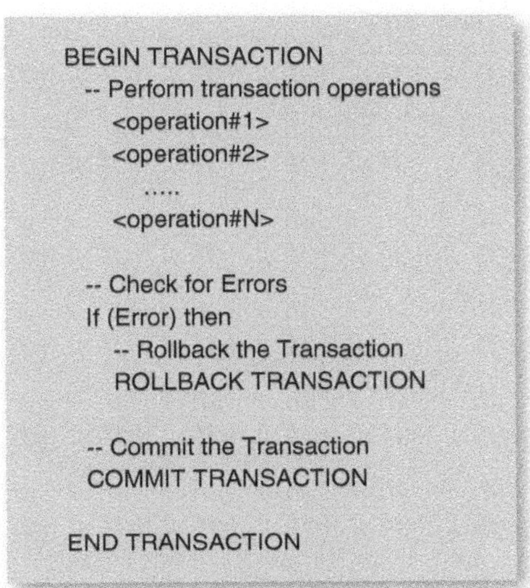

BEGIN TRANSACTION
-- Perform transaction operations
<operation#1>
<operation#2>
.....
<operation#N>
-- Check for Errors
If (Error) then
-- Rollback the Transaction
ROLLBACK TRANSACTION
-- Commit the Transaction
COMMIT TRANSACTION
END TRANSACTION

Figure 10.1 Structure of a transaction

In the pseudo-code shown in Figure 10.1, the `begin transaction` statement begins a new transaction. A transaction can end either by committing changes to the database using the `commit transaction` statement or by undoing all the changes if any error occurs using the `rollback transaction` statement. Operations are of two types: operations that read from the database and operations that update (write) some data items in the database.

Figure 10.2 illustrates a state transition diagram for a transaction. In this diagram a transaction is shown to transit through the following states:

- *Active:* This state indicates that the transaction is performing some work (operations). A transaction enters this state immediately after it starts execution.
- *Partially committed:* A transaction that has executed its final (`end transaction`) statement. At this stage, recovery protocols need to be tested to ensure that a system failure will not result in an inability to record the changes of the transaction permanently. In case this check is successful, any updates can be safely recorded and the transaction can move to the `committed` state. If any of these checks fail then the transaction transits to the `failed` state.
- *Committed:* A transaction that has performed all of its work successfully and terminated is said to have committed by making its changes permanent in persistent storage.
- *Failed:* A transaction that was initially in active state but cannot be committed.
- *Aborted:* A transaction that does not execute successfully and rolls back all of the work it has performed. This can happen either due to a recovery check failure or if the transaction is aborted during its active state.

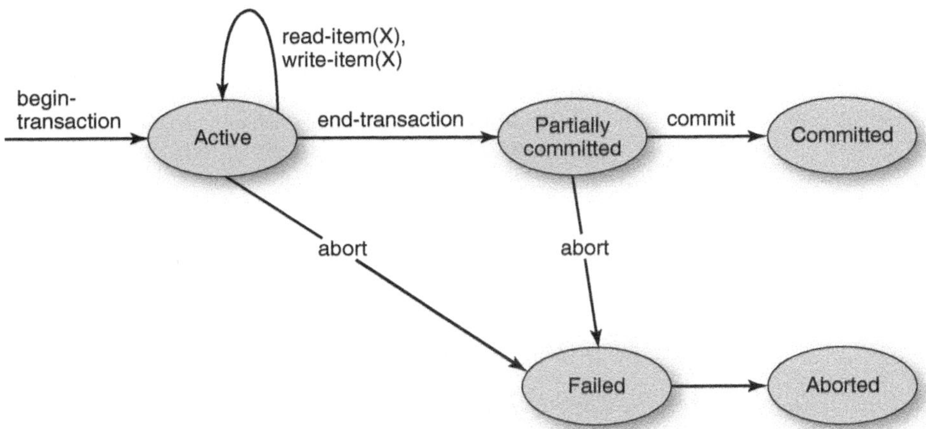

Figure 10.2 Transaction states

10.1.1 Properties of transactions

To maintain consistency across resources within a transaction boundary, a transaction must exhibit ACID properties, namely Atomicity, Consistency, Isolation and Durability.

Atomicity: means that a transaction is an indivisible unit of work. Either all of the operations of a transaction are applied to the application state, or none of them is applied. If the transaction cannot complete successfully, it will roll back to the state before the beginning of the transaction.

Consistency: means that the transaction must correctly transition data from one consistent state to another, preserving the integrity of data. This means that any integrity constraints implicit in the application are not violated by the transaction. In practice, the notion of consistency is application specific. For example, in an accounting application, consistency would include the integrity constraint that the sum of all asset accounts equals the sum of all liability accounts.

Isolation: When multiple transactions execute concurrently, one transaction may want to read or write the same data another transaction has changed but not committed. Until the latter transaction commits, the changes it has made should be treated as transient state, because it could roll back these changes. Isolation requires that several concurrent transactions produce the same results in the data as those same transactions if they were executed sequentially in some (unspecified) order. Isolation guarantees that the execution of concurrent transactions is controlled and coordinated since they are accessing a shared database and may potentially interfere with one another. Concurrent transactions are executed in a manner that gives the illusion that each transaction is executing in isolation while in reality it may work concurrently with other transactions on the same database items. Isolation is generally implemented using a locking mechanism.

Durability: means that committed updates are made permanent. Failures that occur after a commit cause no loss of data. Durability also implies that data for all committed transactions can be recovered after a system or media failure.

Atomic transactions are useful for activities that manipulate data, transform data from one or more sources to one or more targets, or coordinate multiple transaction participants. The all-or-nothing (atomicity) guarantee ensures that all data changes and messages exchanged in the context of the transaction retain their consistency, regardless of how many steps are required in order to complete the transaction.

10.1.2 Concurrency control mechanisms

When transactions execute concurrently, for instance in financial or commercial applications where there is a need for multiple applications to access the same database at the same time, they may interfere with each other and cause the database to become inconsistent. This may happen despite the fact that the transactions preserve individually the consistency of the database.

When two or more transactions are executing concurrently, their database *operations interleave*. This means that operations from one transaction may execute in between operations from another transaction and thus interfere with them. This interleaving can cause serious problems by corrupting the consistency of data, thereby leading the database to an inconsistent state. The objective of concurrency control is to combat this interference and thereby avoid any potential errors.

Concurrency control is a method for the management of contention for data resources. This mechanism is used to ensure that database transactions are executed in a safe manner (i.e. without loss of data). Concurrency control is especially applicable to relational databases and database management systems, which must ensure that transactions are executed safely and that they follow the ACID rules described earlier. The database management system must be able to ensure that only serialisable, recoverable schedules are allowed, and that no actions of committed transactions are lost while undoing aborted transactions.

10.1.2.1 Transaction serialisability

A *serialisable schedule* is a schedule S of some set of concurrently executing transactions that is the equivalent (or has the same effects) of some (serial) schedule S_{ser} that executes the transactions of that set sequentially. Informally speaking, what is required is that in both schedules the values returned by the corresponding read operations are the same and updates to each data item occur in the same order. This means that if the read operations return the same values in S and S_{ser} the computations of the transactions will be identical in both schedules and consequently the transactions will write the same values back to the database. Given that the write operations occur in the same order in both schedules, S will have the same effect as (and therefore is equivalent to) S_{ser}.

Serial equivalence, when applied to a transaction, means that when a number of transactions are applied concurrently the effect of these transactions will be the same as if they were applied sequentially (or one after the other). This, in effect, provides a hard requirement for the transaction server that ensures that effects of such inconsistent updates do not occur. Typical problems here include the dirty read, the lost update problem, the inconsistent update, and the cascading abort problems [Ullman 1988].

10.1.2.2 Two-phase locking

Traditionally, concurrency mechanisms for database systems can be managed by means of locking. When a concurrency control mechanism uses locks, transactions must request and release locks in addition to reading and writing data items. At the most fundamental level, locks can be classified into (in an increasingly restrictive order) shared, update and exclusive locks. A *shared* (or read) *lock* signifies that another transaction can take an update or another shared lock on the same piece of data. Shared locks are used when data is read. If a transaction locks a piece of data with an *exclusive* (write) lock, it signifies its intention to write this data item and no other transaction may take a lock on the same item. Some database systems provide an update lock, which can be used by transactions that initially want to read a data item but later may want to update it. An *update lock* allows a transaction to read but not write a data item and indicates that the lock is likely to be upgraded later to a write lock. An update lock ensures that another transaction can take only a shared lock on the same data item.

To achieve transaction consistency the following two general rules must apply [Garcia-Molina 2002]:

1. A transaction can only read or write a data item if it previously requested a lock on that item and has not yet released that lock.
2. If a transaction locks a data item it must later unlock that data item.

Most concurrency control mechanisms in commercial systems implement serialisability using a strict *two-phase locking* protocol [Eswaran 1976]. This protocol uses locks associated with items in the database and requires that a transaction acquires the appropriate lock (read or write) before it accesses a specific data item in the database for either reading or writing.

Once a transaction needs to read (or write) a data item, it must be granted a read (or write) lock (as the case may be) on this data item before it can perform this operation. The locks on a transaction can be released only after the transaction has committed/aborted. This version has the disadvantage that some locks may be maintained longer than they are needed. However, it eliminates all kinds of anomalies. Proofs of the fact that a concurrency control mechanism, which uses a strict two-phase locking protocol, produces only serialisable schedules can be found in [Ullman 1988].

10.1.2.3 Transaction isolation

Transaction isolation levels are achieved by taking locks on the data items that they access until the transaction completes. There are two general mechanisms for managing concurrency control by taking locks: pessimistic and optimistic. These two modes are necessitated by the fact that, when a transaction accesses data, its intention to change (or not change) the data may not be readily apparent.

A concurrency control scheme is considered *pessimistic* when it locks a given data resource early in the data access transaction – to prevent more than one application from updating the database simultaneously – and does not release it until the transaction is closed (see Section 10.3.1.2).

A concurrency control scheme is considered *optimistic* when it is based on the assumption that database transactions mostly do not conflict with other transactions, and that allows this scheme to be as permissive as possible in allowing transactions to execute. Under optimistic concurrency control locks are not obtained, thus allowing for maximum concurrency in reading, and a read is performed immediately before a write to ensure that the data item in question has not changed in the interim. There are three phases in the optimistic concurrency control scheme: a read phase, a validation phase and a write phase.

- In the *read phase* the required data items are read from the database and write operations are performed on local copies of these items.
- During the *validation phase* a check for serialisability is performed.
- When a transaction commits, the database checks if the transaction could possibly have conflicted with any other concurrent transaction. If there is a possibility of conflict, the transaction aborts and is restarted. Otherwise, the transaction commits and the data items modified by the transaction are written into the database (*write phase*).

If there are few conflicts, validation can be done efficiently, and leads to better performance than other concurrency control methods. Unfortunately, if there are many conflicts, the cost of repeatedly restarting transactions impacts performance significantly.

The objective of optimistic concurrency is to minimise the time over which a given resource would be unavailable for use by other transactions. This is especially important with long running transactions (for more detail, see Section 10.4), which under a pessimistic scheme would lock up a resource for unacceptably long periods of time.

10.2 Distributed transactions

In today's complex distributed environments, transactions are fundamental to many distributed operations. Consider, for example, the guaranteed delivery and ordering of a series of messages exchanged between two distributed application components. In this scenario, the message exchange should take place within an atomic execution sequence.

Atomic transactions greatly simplify the coding of distributed applications. These are mechanisms for building reliable distributed systems in the presence of failures. As we already explained, they provide two important properties: recoverability and serialisability. Recoverability implies that actions in a transaction exhibit an *all-or-nothing* behaviour: an action either executes to completion, in which case it commits, or has no effect on the persistent state of a database, in which case it aborts. Serialisability implies that the actual effect of executing transactions concurrently is equivalent to the effect of executing these actions in some serial order. Recoverability thus protects from failures, while serialisability allows reasoning about concurrency by considering the effect of each action separately.

Typically, transaction semantics are provided by some underlying system infrastructure (usually in the form of products such as Transaction Processing Monitors [Gray 1993]). This infrastructure deals with failures, and performs the necessary recovery actions to guarantee the property of atomicity. Applications programming is therefore greatly simplified since the programmer does not have to deal with a multitude of possible failure scenarios.

A *distributed transaction* bundles multiple operations in which at least two network hosts are involved. Distributed transactions can span heterogeneous transaction aware data resources, and may include a wide range of activities such as retrieving data from an SQL Server database, reading messages from a message queue server, and writing to other databases. A distributed transaction is simply a transaction that accesses and updates data on two or more networked resources, and therefore must be coordinated among those resources.

Distributed transaction processing provides the necessary mechanism to combine multiple software components into a cooperating unit that can maintain shared data, potentially spanning multiple physical processors or locations, or both. This enables construction of applications that manipulate data consistently, using multiple products that can easily be scaled by adding additional hardware and software components. Programming of distributed transactions is simplified by distributed transaction management software, such as TP Monitors, that coordinates commit and abort behaviour and recovery across several data resources.

10.2.1 Distributed transaction architectures

The components involved in the distributed transaction processing model that are relevant to our discussion are: the application program, the application server, the resource manager, the resource adapter and the transaction manager. These are shown in Figure 10.3.

The simplest form of distributed transaction processing involves only the application program, a resource manager and an application server. The application program implements the desired function of the end user enterprise, e.g. an order processing application. Each application program specifies a sequence of operations that involves shared resources, such as databases. An application program defines the start and end of transactions, accesses to resources within transaction boundaries, and normally makes the decision whether to commit or roll back each transaction.

A *resource manager* provides and manages access to shared resources. These may be accessed using services that the resource manager provides. Examples for the resource manager are database management systems, a file access method such as X/Open ISAM, and a print server. To simplify the discussion, we concentrate in this section only on examples involving relational databases systems. The resource manager could thus be a relational database management system (RDBMS), such as Oracle or SQL Server. All of the actual database management is handled by this component.

A *resource adapter* (see also Section 2.8.1) is a software component that allows application components to access and interact with the underlying resource manager of a specific resource, e.g. a relational database. Because a resource adapter is specific to its resource manager, typically there is a different resource adapter for each type of database or enterprise information system, such as an enterprise resource planning or legacy system (managing transactions, external functionality and data). The resource adapter is the component that is the communications channel, or request translator, between the *outside world,* in this case a transactional application, and the resource manager.

Transactions that are managed internal to a resource manager are called *local transactions.* If a single resource manager participates in a transaction, the application server usually lets the resource manager coordinate the transaction internally. The application program (client) sends a request for data to the resource adapter via an application server. Application servers handle the bulk of application operations and initiate transactions on behalf of clients. The application server handles *house-keeping* activities such as the network connections, protocol negotiation, and other advanced functionality such as transaction management, security, database connection pooling and so on. The resource adapter then translates the request and sends it across the network to the RDBMS. The RDBMS returns the data to the resource adapter, which then translates the result to

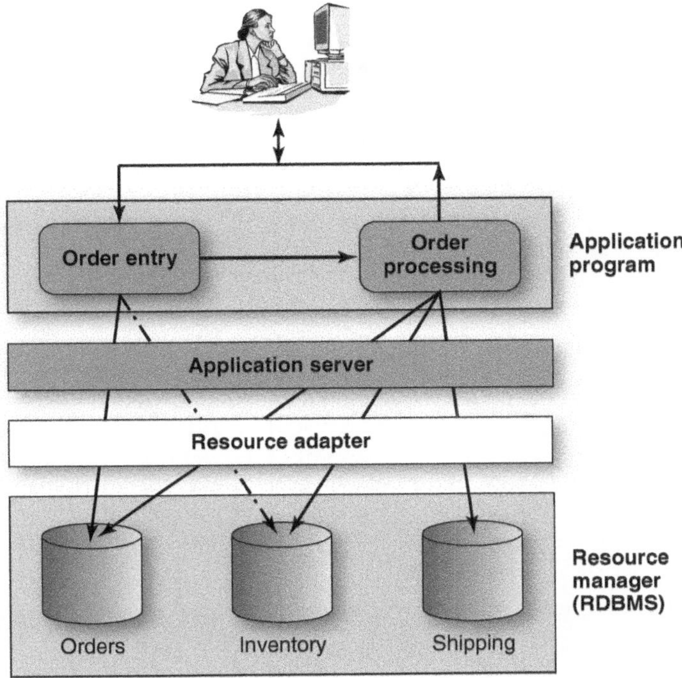

Figure 10.3 Transaction architecture involving only local transactions

the application. This situation is illustrated in Figure 10.4, where an application issues transactional requests (such as order entry and order processing) against three relational databases (orders, inventory and shipping) that are housed on a single server and are managed within the confines of a single resource manager. Solid arrows indicate activities that both read and write from the database while dashed arrows denote a read operation.

The above example illustrates a single, local transaction and describes four components involved in a distributed transaction model. An additional fifth component, the transaction manager, comes into consideration only when transactions are to be distributed. The *transaction manager* is the intermediary between the clients and/or application server and the distributed transaction functionality.

A transaction manager works with applications and application servers to provide services to control the scope and duration of distributed transactions. A transaction manager also helps coordinate the completion of distributed transactions across multiple transactional resource managers (e.g. DBMS), provides support for transaction synchronisation and recovery, and coordinates the decision to start distributed transactions and commit them or roll them back. This ensures atomic transaction completion. A transaction manager may provide the ability to communicate with other transaction manager instances. In order to satisfy a client's dependence on a guarantee for an atomic sequence of operations, a transaction manager is responsible for creating and managing a distributed transaction that encompasses all operations against the implied resources. The transaction manager accesses each resource, e.g. a relational database system, through the respective resource manager. This situation is illustrated in Figure 10.5.

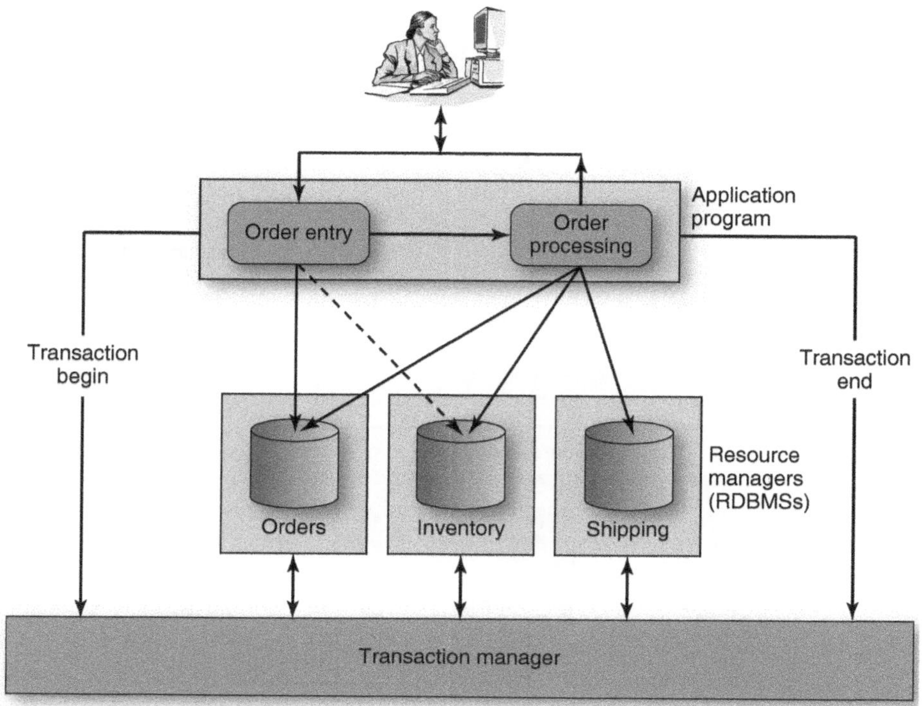

Figure 10.4 Distributed transaction architecture

In this environment resource managers provide two sets of interfaces: one set for the application components to get connections and perform operations on the data, and the other set for the transaction manager to participate in the two-phase commit and recovery protocol (see Section 10.2.2). In addition, the resource manager may, directly or indirectly, register resources with the transaction manager so that the transaction manager can keep track of all the resources participating in a transaction. This process is known as *resource enlistment.* The transaction manager uses this information to coordinate transactional work performed by the resource managers and to drive the two-phase commit and recovery protocol.

When two or more transaction managers cooperate within a distributed transaction, the transaction manager that works on behalf of the application program making the request is designated the superior transaction manager and is referred to as the *root transaction coordinator,* or simply root coordinator. Any transaction manager that is subsequently enlisted or created for an existing transaction (e.g. as the result of interposition, see Section 10.4.4) becomes a subordinate in the process. Such a coordinator is referred to as a *subordinate transaction coordinator,* or simply subordinate coordinator, and by registering a resource becomes a *transaction participant.* Recoverable servers are always transaction participants.

The principle behind the superior–subordinate transaction manager relationship is that the superior system drives all the systems subordinate to it using the two-phase commit protocol. Each transaction manager can have many transaction managers subordinate to it but can have at most one superior, See Figure 10.5. These superior and subordinate relationships form a tree of relationships called the transaction's commit tree. The root

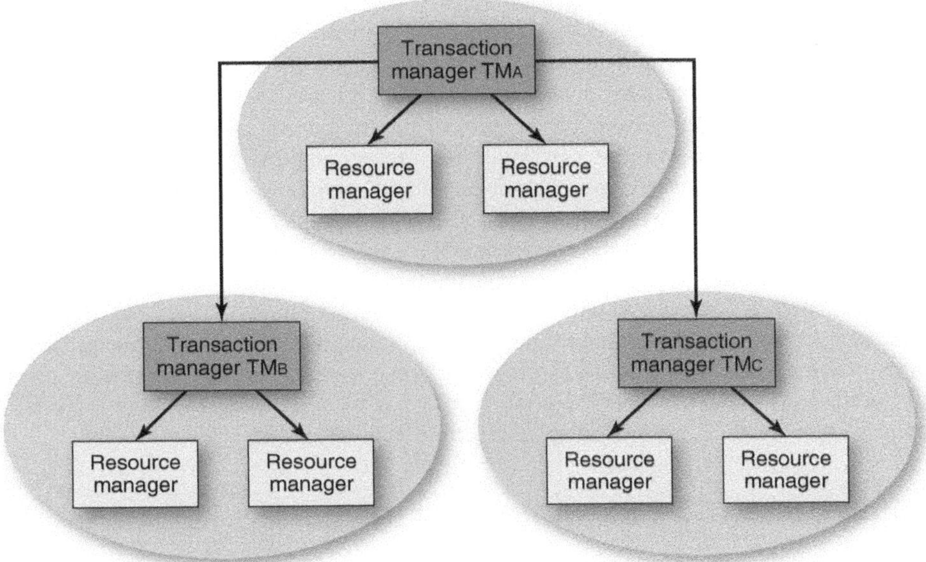

Figure 10.5 Collaborating transaction managers

transaction coordinator of the commit tree acts as the *global commit coordinator* for the entire distributed transaction. There are no fixed limits as to how many subordinate coordinators a single superior can have, or as to how many levels of intermediates there are between the root coordinator and the bottommost leaf subordinate. The actual creation of the tree depends on the behaviour and requirements of the application.

The enlisted resource managers are also members of this commit tree. They usually have a subordinate relationship to their local transaction manager. The superior and subordinate relationships are relevant only for a particular transaction. That is, a particular transaction manager can be the superior to another on a particular transaction while the roles may be reversed for a different transaction.

When a distributed transaction commits or aborts, the prepare, commit and abort messages flow outwards on the commit tree. Any node of the tree can unilaterally abort a transaction at any time before it agrees to the prepare request sent to it in the first phase. After a node has prepared, it remains prepared and in doubt until its commit coordinator instructs it to commit or abort the transaction. The global commit coordinator makes the decision to either commit or abort the entire transaction and is never in doubt.

System or communication failures can leave transactions in doubt for extended periods of time. While a transaction is in doubt, the resources modified by the transaction remain locked and unavailable to others. These situations require manual intervention and normally rely on the use of an administrative tool to resolve transactions that remain in doubt.

A typical transactional application begins a transaction by the client application issuing a request to a transaction manager to initiate a transaction. In response, the transaction manager starts a transaction and associates it with the calling transaction branch. A transaction branch is associated with a request to each resource manager involved in the distributed transaction. Although the final commit/rollback decision treats the distributed transaction as a single logical unit, there can be many transaction branches (threads) involved. For instance, transactional requests to different RDBMS result in an equal number of transaction branches.

Since multiple application components and resources participate in a transaction, it is necessary for the transaction manager to establish and maintain the state of the transaction as it occurs. This is usually done in the form of the transaction context. The *transaction context* covers all the operations performed on transactional resources during a transaction, associates the transactional operations with resources, and provides information about the components invoking these operations. Conceptually, a transaction context is a data structure that contains a unique transaction identifier, a timeout value, and the reference to the transaction manager that controls the transaction scope. A transaction manager associates a transaction context with the currently executing thread. Therefore, during the course of a transaction, all the threads participating in the transaction share the transaction context and are associated with the same transaction context dividing a transaction's work into parallel tasks, if possible. The context also has to be passed from one transaction manager to another if a transaction spans multiple transaction managers.

10.2.2 Two-phase commit protocol

In order to respect transaction atomicity, each transaction branch in a distributed transaction topology must be committed or rolled back by its local resource manager. The transaction manager controls the boundaries of the transaction and is responsible for the final decision as to whether or not the total transaction should commit or roll back. This decision is made in two phases and the protocol that governs them is widely known as the *two-phase commit protocol* (2PC).

The 2PC is a method of coordinating a single transaction across two or more resource managers. It guarantees data integrity by ensuring that transactional updates are committed in all of the participating databases, or are fully rolled back out of all the databases, reverting to the state prior to the start of the transaction. In other words, either all the participating databases are updated, or none of them is updated. In the 2PC we assume that the transaction coordinator of one site, called the *coordinator,* plays a special role in deciding whether the entire distributed transaction can commit. The coordinator is normally associated with the site at which the distributed transaction originates.

10.2.2.1 Phase I: preparation

The first phase of the 2PC contains the following two steps:

1. As an initial step of the 2PC, the coordinator for distributed transaction *T* decides when to attempt to commit this transaction. In order to achieve this, it first polls all of the resource managers (RDBMS) involved in the distributed transaction *T* by issuing a prepare message `<prepare T>` to see if each resource manager is ready to commit. The *prepare message* notifies each resource manager to prepare for the commitment of the transaction. The resource manager of each site receiving the message `<prepare T>` decides whether to commit its component of *T* or veto the transaction commit operation. If a resource manager cannot commit, it responds negatively and aborts its particular part of the transaction so that data is not altered. A site can delay if its transactional component has not completed its activity but must eventually respond to the `<prepare T>` message.

2. If a site decides to commit its component, it enters a state called the *pre-committed state.* During this state the resource manager performs all actions necessary to ascertain that this portion of *T* will not have to abort, even in the presence of a system failure. The resource manager of this site then forwards the message `<ready T>` to the coordinator. If the resource manager of this site decides to abort its portion of *T* it then forwards the message `<donot commit T>` to the coordinator. It must be noted that, once a site is in the pre-committed state, it cannot abort its portion of *T* without an explicit directive by the coordinator.

10.2.2.2 Phase II: commitment/abortion

In the second phase (commitment/abortion), the coordinator determines the fate of the transaction. If all resource managers have voted to commit their portion of transaction T (by sending `<ready T>`) the coordinator commits the whole transaction by sending a `<commit T>` message to all resource coordinators involved in the transaction. Subsequently, the coordinator returns the results to the application program.

If any of the resource managers have responded negatively by sending the message `<donot commit T>` then the coordinator sends an `<abort T>` message to all resource managers involved in the transaction. This effectively rolls back the entire transaction. In case a resource manager in the transaction has not responded with either a `<commit T>` or `<donot commit T>` message, the coordinator will assume that this site has responded with a `<donot commit T>` message after a suitable timeout period.

The 2PC is illustrated in Figure 10.6. This figure shows the sequence of events during a two-phase commit operation involving two RDBMS. The process begins with a call by the

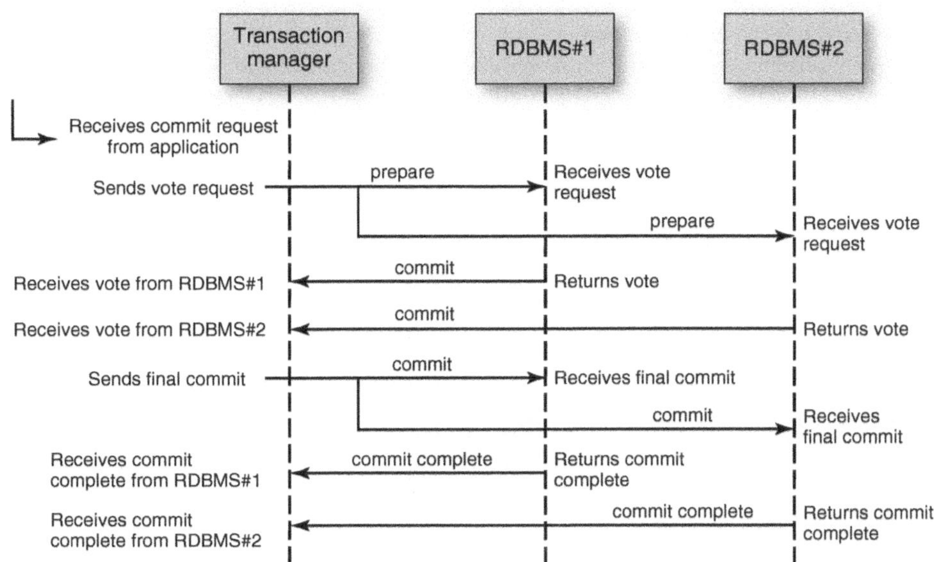

Figure 10.6 The 2PC for distributed transactions

application to commit the transaction. Once the application issues the commit request, the transaction manager prepares all the resources (in this case RDBMS 1 and RDBMS 2) for a commit operation (by conducting a voting). The resource managers respond (in this case they both voted to commit). Subsequently, the resource manager analyses the votes it has received and, based on whether all resources are ready for a commit or not, issues a commit or rollback request to all the resources. In Figure 10.6 a commit operation is issued to both resource managers.

10.3 Nested transactions

Distributed transactions have evolved from the need to integrate transactions from different servers into a single transaction unit. This is due to the fact that, over the years, enterprises have developed a number of dedicated applications and transaction processing systems to automate business functions, such as billing, inventory control, payroll and so on. These systems were developed in many cases independently under different hardware platforms and DBMS.

Transaction managers can provide transactional support for applications using different implementation models. The most common is the transaction model that we described in Section 10.1, which is the classical transaction model that involves a database on a single server and has no internal structure, and is commonly referred to as a *flat transaction.* A transaction manager that follows the flat transaction model does not allow transactions to be nested within other transactions. Figure 10.7 illustrates a flat transaction accessing data items (through their respective resource managers) in three different servers S_1, S_2, and S_3. In a flat transaction model, the only way correctly to control the scope of transactions that span multiple transaction services is to reach an agreement beforehand on how these services will be combined for a business activity, and to apply appropriate transaction policies for the services by agreement.

As the requirements for automation increase, enterprises face the necessity to construct new transaction applications by composing already existing transactional systems. Hence the need for developing distributed transactions as modules, which may be composed

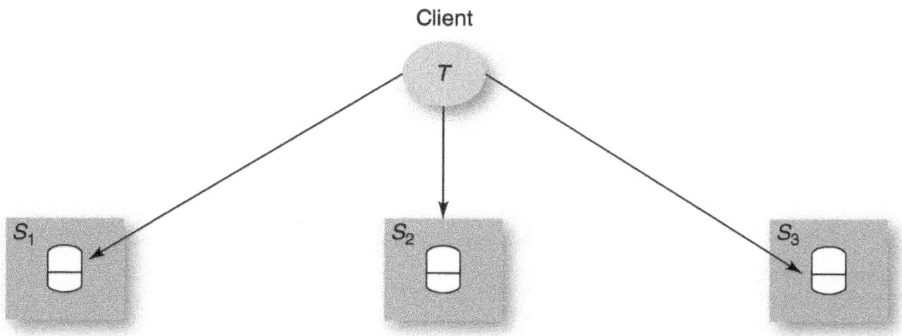

Figure 10.7 Example of a flat transaction

freely from existing transactions exported from several servers. With distributed transactions the transaction server controls the function of each exported (local) transaction. Any commit/abort decisions are controlled by the local transactions separately. This rules out transaction designers from explicitly controlling the structure of distributed transactions. As a result of this type of bottom up approach, transactions may not reflect a clean functional decomposition of the application [Kifer 2005].

Nested transactions evolved from the requirement to allow transaction designers to design complex, functionally decomposable transactions from the top down. A nested transaction model allows transaction services to be built independently and later combined into applications. Each service can determine the scope of its transaction boundaries. The application or service that orchestrates the combination of services controls the scope of the top level transaction. A sub-transaction in this model is a transaction that is started within another transaction. It occurs when a new transaction is started on a session that is already inside the scope of an existing transaction. This new sub-transaction is said to be nested within (or below the level of) the existing (parent) transaction. *Nested transactions* allow an application to create a transaction that is embedded in an existing transaction. The existing transaction is called the *parent of the sub-transaction;* the sub-transaction is called a *child* of the parent transaction. Multiple sub-transactions can be embedded in the same parent transaction. The children of one parent are called *siblings.*

The *ancestors of a transaction* are the parents of the sub-transaction and (recursively) the parents of its ancestors. The descendants of a transaction are the children of the transaction and (recursively) the children of its descendants. Figure 10.8 illustrates that a top level transaction is one with no parent. A top level transaction and all of its descendants are called a *transaction family.* A sub-transaction is similar to a top level transaction in that the changes made on behalf of a sub-transaction are either committed in their entirety or rolled back. However, when a sub-transaction is committed, the changes remain

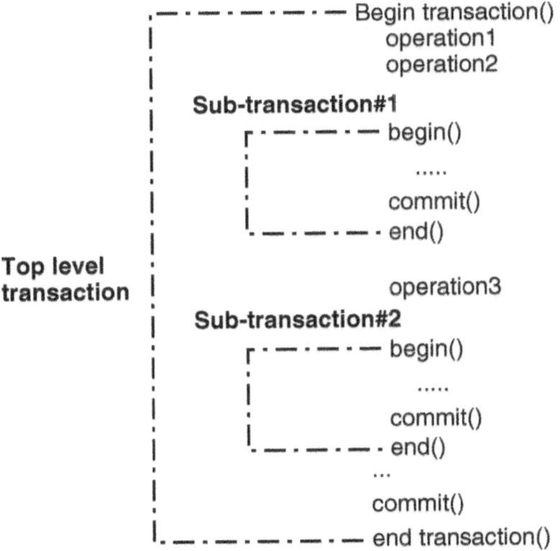

Figure 10.8 Structure of a nested transaction

contingent upon commitment of all of the transaction's ancestors. Nesting can occur to an arbitrary depth; the resulting structure can be described using a transaction tree.

Like distributed transactions, sub-transactions have recoverability and serialisability properties and control their commit/abort decision. However, the handling of this decision is quite different. Instead of the all-or-nothing approach of the distributed transaction model, individual sub-transactions in a transaction tree can fail independently from their parents without aborting the entire transaction. Changes made within the sub-transaction are invisible to its parent transaction until the sub-transaction is committed. This provides a kind of checkpointing mechanism. *Checkpointing* guarantees that the work accomplished by a parent transaction prior to starting a child will not be lost if the child aborts. In Figure 10.8 the complete operation will be committed into the database only when the outermost `commit()` is called. The inner `commit()` methods do not control operation completion.

A number of models have been proposed for nested transactions. These fall under two broad categories: closed versus open transaction models, which we examine in the following two sub-sections.

10.3.1 The closed nested transaction model

The closed nested model due to Moss [Moss 1985] views a top level transaction and all of its sub-transactions as a transaction tree. This distributed transaction model is shown in Figure 10.9. The nodes of the tree represent transactions, and the edges illustrate the

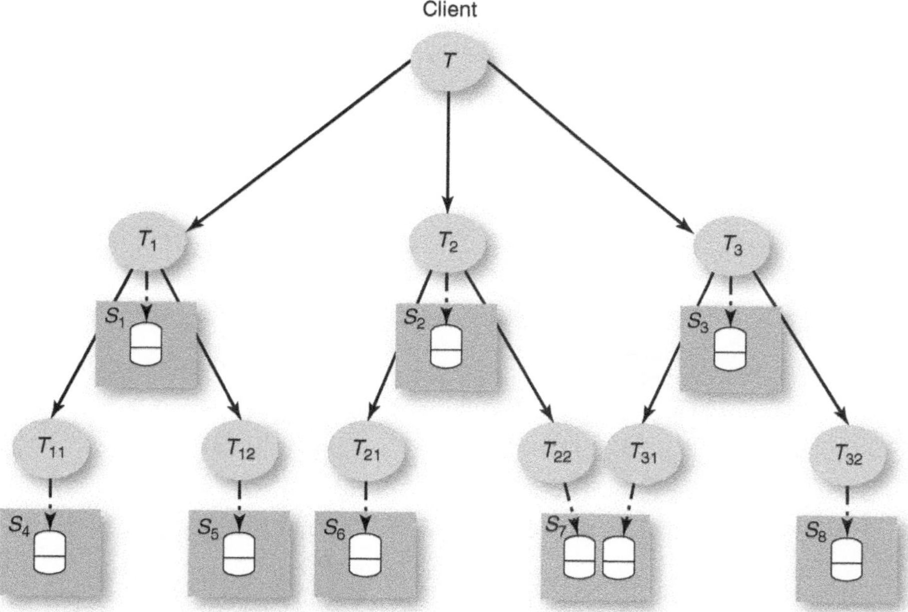

Figure 10.9 The nested transaction model

parent/child relationships between the related transactions. The terms parent, child, ancestor, descendant and siblings have their usual meanings. In this nested transaction model, the top level transaction can spawn sub-transactions down to any depth of nesting.

Figure 10.9 shows a client top level transaction T that spawns three sub-transactions T_1, T_2 and T_3. Sub-transactions T_1, T_2 and T_3 access data objects at servers S_1, S_2 and S_3, respectively. Sub-transactions at the same level such as T_1, T_2 and T_3 can run concurrently on different servers. Sub-transactions such as T_{11}, T_{12}, T_{21}, T_{22}, etc., that have no children are called *leaves*. Not all leaves need be at the same level. The six sub-transactions at the leaf level in Figure 10.9 can also run concurrently.

The semantics of the nested transaction model can be summarized as follows:

1. A parent can create children sequentially so that one child finishes before the next one starts. Alternatively, the parent can specify that some of its children can run concurrently. The transaction tree structure in Figure 10.9 does not distinguish between children that run concurrently or sequentially. A parent node does not execute concurrently with its children. It waits until all children in the same level are complete and then resumes execution. It may then decide to spawn additional children.

2. A sub-transaction and all of its descendants appear to execute as a single isolated unit with respect to its concurrent siblings. For instance if T_1 and T_2 run concurrently, T_2 views the sub-tree T_1, T_{11}, T_{12} as a single isolated transaction and does not observe its internal structure or interfere with its execution. The same applies for T_2 and the sub-tree T_2. T_{21} and T_{22}. Siblings are thus serialisable and the effect of their concurrent execution is the same as if they had executed sequentially in some serial order.

3. Sub-transactions are atomic. Each sub-transaction can commit or abort independently. The commitment and the durability of the effects of sub-transactions are dependent on the commitment of its parent. A sub-transaction commits and is made durable when all of its ancestors (including the top level transaction) commit. At this point the entire nested transaction is said to have committed. If an ancestor aborts then all of its descendants are aborted.

4. If a sub-transaction aborts, its operations have no effect. Control is returned to its parent, which may take appropriate action. In this way, an aborted sub-transaction may have an impact on the state of the database, as it may influence its parent to alter its execution path. This situation can be contrasted with flat transactions where an aborted transaction cannot alter the transaction path of the transaction coordinator.

5. A sub-transaction is not necessarily consistent. However, the nested transaction is consistent as a whole.

10.3.1.1 The two-phase commit protocol for nested transactions

The two-phase commit protocol (2PC) for nested transactions is similar to that of distributed transactions. The only difference is that a server involved in a sub-transaction makes either a decision to abort or a provisional decision to commit a transaction. A provisional commit is not the same as being prepared. It is simply a local decision to perform a *shadow write* (a write that updates a temporary copy of the actual data).

In the 2PC for nested transactions, a client starts a set of nested transactions by opening a top-level transaction (using an `openTransaction()` operation). This operation returns a transaction identifier for the top-level transaction. The client starts a sub-transaction by invoking an `openSub-transaction()` operation, whose argument specifies its parent transaction via its transaction identifier. The new sub-transaction automatically joins the parent transaction, and a transaction identifier by the sub-transaction is returned [Coulouris 2001]. The identifier of a sub-transaction is constructed in such a way that the transaction identifier of its parent can always be recognised from the sub-transaction identifier. Sub-transaction identifiers are globally unique. The transaction manager (coordinator) of a transaction provides an operation to open a sub-transaction, together with an operation enabling the coordinator of a sub-transaction, to enquire about the status of its parent, i.e. whether it has yet committed or aborted.

The client makes a set of nested transactions come to completion by invoking the `closeTransaction()` or `abortTransaction()` on the coordinator of the top level transaction. Meanwhile, each of the sub-transactions carries out its operations. When they are finished, the server managing a sub-transaction records information as to whether the sub-transaction committed provisionally or aborted. Note that, as already explained, if a parent of a sub-transaction aborts then the sub-transaction will be forced to abort. A real commit operation occurs only when all descendants of a transaction have had their status examined. The sub-transactions will wait until the entire transaction that contains them is committed. Because sub-transactions adhere to the semantics of transactions they can be aborted without causing the parent transaction to abort. The parent transaction may contain code that handles the abortion of any of its sub-transactions. For instance, the parent transaction of an aborted transaction may decide to forward a new sub-transaction to a server holding replicated data.

When a top level transaction completes, its coordinator carries out a 2PC. The only reason for a participant sub-transaction being unable to complete is if it has crashed since it completed its provisional commit. A coordinator of each parent transaction has a list of all of its descendant sub-transactions. When a sub-transaction commits provisionally it reports its status and the status of its descendants to its parent. The top level transaction eventually receives a list of all the sub-transactions in the tree, together with the status of each of them. Descendants of aborted sub-transactions are omitted from this list.

The top-level transaction plays the role of *coordinator* in the 2PC. The *participants list* consists of the coordinators (transaction mangers) of all sub-transactions in the tree that have provisionally committed but have no aborted ancestors. At this stage, the business logic in the application program determines whether the top level transaction can commit whatever is left in the tree in spite of aborted sub-transactions. The coordinator will then ask the participants to vote on the outcome of the transaction. If they vote to commit, then they must prepare their transactions by saving their transaction context in permanent storage. This context is recorded as belonging to the top level transaction of which it will eventually form a part.

The second phase of the 2PC is the same as that for the non-nested case. The coordinator collects the votes and then informs the participants as to the outcome. When it is complete, coordinator and participants will have committed or aborted their respective transactions.

Example 10.1: Two-phase commit protocol for nested transactions

Figure 10.10 clarifies the 2PC for nested transactions. This figure shows a top level transaction that contains three further sub-transactions that correspond to the sub-transactions T_1, T_2 and T_3 in Figure 10.9. Sub-transactions T_1, T_2 and T_3 access data objects at servers S_1, S_2 and S_3, respectively. This figure shows the status of each sub-transaction at a point in time, with each transaction being labeled with either provisional commit or abort. In Figure 10.10 the decision as to whether transaction T can commit is based on whether T_1 and T_3 can commit by virtue of transaction T_2 having aborted. Each sub-transaction of these transactions has also either provisionally committed or aborted. For example, T_{11} has aborted while T_{12} has provisionally committed. The fate of T_{12} depends on that of its parent T_1 and eventually on the recommendation of the top-level transaction. T_2 has aborted, thus the whole sub-tree T_2, T_{21} and T_{22} must abort despite the fact that T_{21} has provisionally committed. The sub-tree T_3, T_{31} and T_{32} could also commit depending on the top-level transaction. Assume that T decides to commit in spite of the fact that T_2 has aborted.

The information held by each coordinator in the example shown in Figure 10.10 is given in Table 10.1. Note that sub-transactions T_{22} and T_{31} share a coordinator, as they both run at server S_7. Sub-transactions T_{21} and T_{22} are called *orphans,* as their parent T_2 has aborted. When aborting, a transaction does not pass any information about its descendants to its parent. Therefore, T_2 has not passed any information about T_{21} and T_{22} to the top-level transaction T. A provisionally committed sub-transaction of an aborted transaction must abort irrespective of whether the top transaction decides to commit or not. In

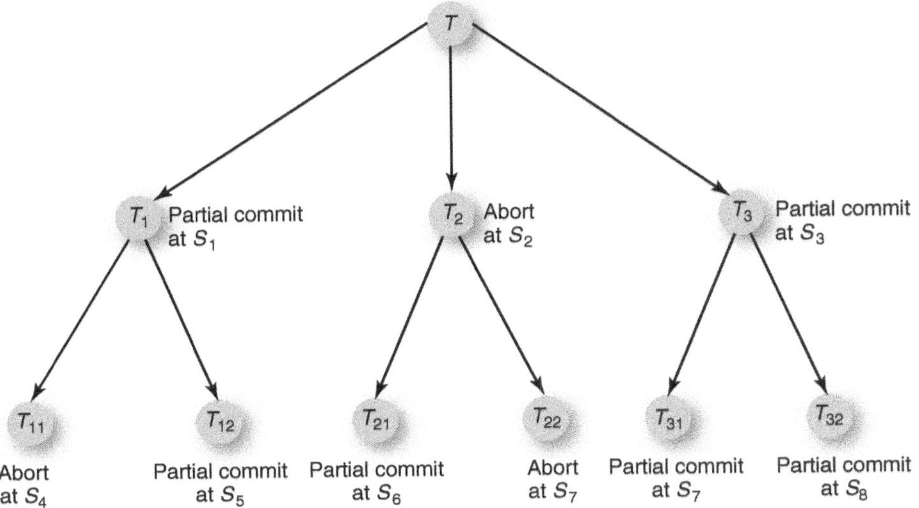

Figure 10.10 Example of the two-phase commit tree for the example in Figure 10.9

Table 10.1 Information held by coordinators of nested transactions

Coordinator of transaction	*Child transactions*	*Participant*	*Provisional commit list*	*Abort list*
T	T_1, T_2, T_3	Yes	T_1, T_{12}, T_3, T_{31}, T_{32}	T_{11}, T_2
T_1	T_{11}, T_{12}	Yes	T_1, T_{12}	T_{11}
T_2	T_{21}, T_{22}	No (aborted)		T_2, T_{22}
T_3	T_{31}, T_{32}	Yes	T_{31}, T_{32}	
T_{11}		No (aborted)		T_{11}
T_{12}		Yes	T_{12}	
T_{21}		No (parent aborted)	T_{21}	
T_{22}, T_{31}		T_{31} but no T_{22}	T_{31}	T_{22}
T_{32}		T_{32}	T_{32}	

Figure 10.9, the coordinators of T, T_1, T_{12}, T_3, T_{31} and T_{32} are participants and will eventually be asked to vote on the outcome during the 2PC.

10.3.1.2 Concurrency control

In the closed nested paradigm locks are acquired as in two-phase locking, but additional policies are needed to determine the behaviour of sub-transactions with respect to each other. More precisely, several sub-transactions of a top level transaction may execute concurrently and request conflicting database applications. This requires that additional rules be enforced regarding how sub-transactions of a single (nested) transaction are granted locks.

The closed nested transaction is governed by the following rules [Kifer 2005]:

1. Each transaction must be in its entirety isolated and thus serialisable with respect to other nested transactions.
2. A parent sub-transaction never executes concurrently with its children.
3. Each child sub-transaction (including all its descendants) must be isolated and hence serialisable with respect to each sibling (together with all of its descendants).

The rules for locking for a nested transaction implement the previous steps and are as follows [Gray 1993]:

1. If a sub-transaction T_i of a nested transaction T requires a read lock on a shared data item then the lock is granted, provided that no other nested transaction holds a write lock on that item and any sub-transactions of T that are holders of a write lock on the same data item are all ancestors of T_i (and thus not executing).

2. If a sub-transaction T_i of a nested transaction T requires a write lock on a shared data item then the lock is granted, provided that no other nested transaction holds a read or write lock on that item and any sub-transactions of T that are holders of a read or write lock on the same data item are all ancestors of T_i (and thus not executing).

3. All locks obtained by a sub-transaction are held until this sub-transaction aborts or commits. As soon as a sub-transaction finishes, any locks that it obtained and which its parent does not hold are passed on to it. Only then can a sibling inherit these locks whenever it needs access to the same data. Without this feature, children of the same parent could potentially block each other. When a sub-transaction aborts, any locks that it obtained, and which are not held by its parent, are released.

To summarise the previous discussion regarding the nested transaction model, ACID properties apply only to top level transactions. Sub-transactions appear atomic to other transactions and may commit and abort independently. Aborting a sub-transaction does not affect the outcome of the transactions not belonging to the sub-transaction's hierarchy, and hence sub-transactions act as firewalls, shielding the outside world from internal failures. The concurrency control scheme introduced by the closed nested transaction model guarantees isolated execution for sub-transactions and that the schedules of concurrent nested transactions are serialisable.

10.3.2 The open nested transaction model

Business processes are found across a broad spectrum of industries and may involve transactional services like finance, logistics and transportation. Typically, such processes perform transactions upon goods, instruments and services, such as product delivery, trade settlement and service provisioning. Typical workflow based business applications rely on collaborative activities that result in complex interactions between business processes that often create critical interdependencies of transactional nature, e.g. trade clearing and settlement, shipment of consigned goods and so on. In addition, they often require the ability to define complex processes by nesting simpler ones within each other. This in turn requires the support of nested transactions for the transactional execution of such nested processes. Such applications must coordinate their update operations to create a consistent outcome across collaborating/transacting parties. However, classical (ACID) transactions, and even nested transaction models based on the ACID transactions, are too constraining for the applications that include activities/services that are disjoint in both time and location.

The traditional transaction model, which provides ACID guarantees for each transaction, is ideal for applications that are synchronous and involve small numbers of parties: a customer debiting a bank account, a customer ordering goods, a traveler reserving a plane seat, or a stock trader completing a buy transaction. These applications are typically simple in nature and have a relatively short duration.

The closed nested transaction model is incapable of handling process based applications, because it adheres strictly to the classical serialisability paradigm to control network wide transaction management and provide full isolation at the global level. Business processes usually involve *long-running transactions,* i.e. transactions that could take hours, days, weeks, and even years to complete, which cannot be implemented with the traditional 2PC. This is due to the fact that the 2PC requires the locking of transactional resources over the lifespan of any transaction. The failure atomicity requirement of the closed nested transaction model dictates that all work must be rolled back in the event of failures. This requirement is unsuitable for long lived transactions due to the fact that much work might have been done and will be lost in the event of a failure. In addition, long lived transactions typically access many data items during the course of their execution. Due to the isolation requirement of the traditional transaction model, these data items cannot be released until the transaction commits. As long lived transactions run for extended periods of time they can cause short transactions to wait excessively long (as they remain locked) to access data items accessed by long lived transactions. This increases the possibility of denial-of-service attacks and results in non-functional systems. It is a clear requirement that the isolation property (which controls locking) be relaxed in such applications.

For these reasons, several extensions to the conventional closed nested transaction model – collectively referred to as *open nesting* – have been proposed to increase transaction concurrency and throughput, by relaxing the atomicity and isolation properties of the traditional transaction model [Elmagarmid 1992]. Open nested models usually involve a mix of coordinated transactions that can be automatically rolled back with the 2PC, and extended transactions that require the explicit definition of compensated transactions, which are invoked when the extended transaction cannot be committed due to a system failure.

Most open nested transactions are based on a variation of the saga model [Garcia-Molina 1987]. Saga is a transaction model introduced to adequately serve the requirements of long lived transactions. A saga consists of a set of independent sub-transactions $T_1, T_2, T_3 \ldots, T_n$ (called *component transactions*). Each sub-transaction is a conventional (short duration) transaction that maintains the ACID properties and can interleave with any other transaction. Sub-transactions use conventional concurrency control mechanisms, such as locking. The sub-transactions $T_1, T_2, T_3 \ldots, T_n$ execute serially in a predefined order and may interleave arbitrarily with sub-transactions of other sagas.

Sagas are organised in a graph [Garcia-Molina 2002] that comprises nodes that are either sub-transactions or the special `abort` and `complete` nodes. Arcs in the graph link pairs of nodes. The special `abort` and `complete` nodes are *terminal nodes,* with no arcs leaving them. The node at which a saga starts is called the `start` node. Those paths that lead to the `abort` node represent sequences of sub-transactions that cause the overall transaction to be rolled back. These sequences of sub-transactions should leave the state of the database unchanged. Paths to the `complete` node represent successful sequences of sub-transactions. The effects of such sub-transactions become permanent.

Each sub-transaction T_i in a saga has an associated compensating transaction CT_i. *Compensating transactions* semantically undo the effects of their respective sub-transaction. Compensation is the logic for reversing the effects of a failed transaction. Compensation is the act of making amends when something has gone wrong or when plans are changed. If a sub-transaction aborts, then the entire saga aborts by executing the compensating transactions in reverse order to the order of the commitment of the relevant sub-transactions.

Since the component transactions of a saga may arbitrarily interleave with the component transactions of other sagas, consistency is compromised. Furthermore, once a component transaction completes execution, it is allowed to commit and release its partial results to other transactions, thereby relaxing the isolation property. Despite all this, sagas preserve both the atomicity and durability properties.

Example 10.2: Transactional workflow for order processing

Figure 10.11 illustrates a simplified transactional workflow version of the order processing example used earlier in this book, whereby products can be scheduled for production if there are insufficient quantities in a warehouse to fulfill an order. The transactional

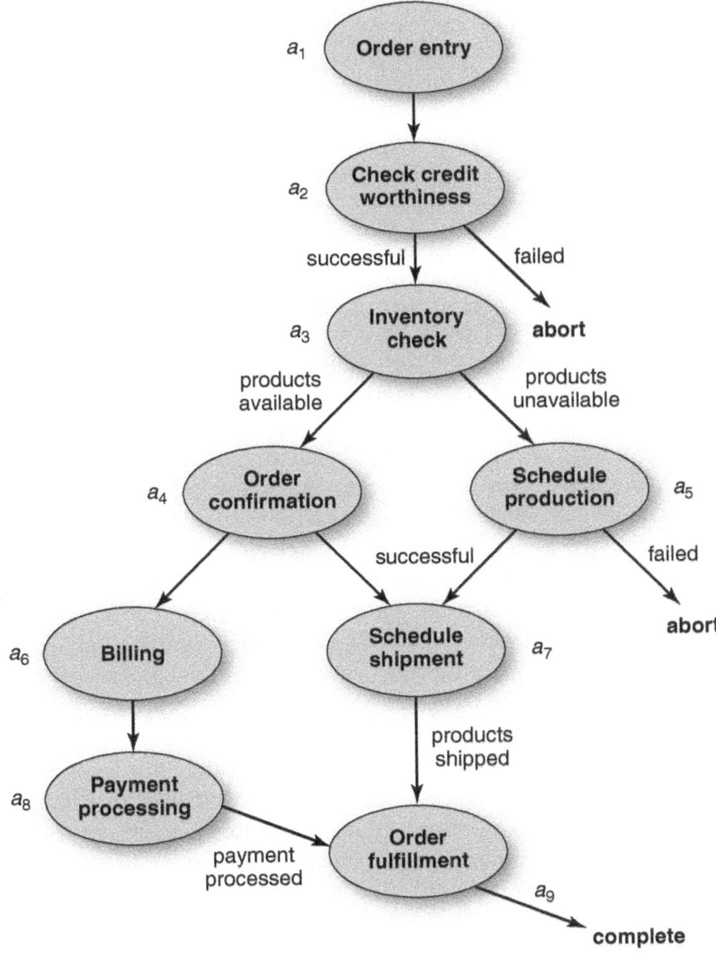

Figure 10.11 Simplified transactional workflow graph for the order processing application

workflow indicates that once the customer has been billed and shipment has been made, the order is fulfiled and the workflow can complete. The workflow in Figure 10.11 comprises a set of interrelated activities. An activity is a unit of (distributed) work that may or may not be transactional. During its lifetime an activity may have transactional and non-transactional periods. An activity is created, made to execute, and then completed. The result of a completed activity is its outcome, which can be used to determine subsequent flow of control to other activities. Activities can run over long periods of time and can thus be suspended and then resumed later.

The paths in the graph of Figure 10.11 that lead to the abort node comprise the activities a_1, a_2, and a_1, a_2 , a_3, a_5 . The path in the graph of Figure 10.11 that leads to the complete node comprises the activities a_1, a_2, a_3, a_4, a_5, a_6, a_7, a_8 and a_9. To understand how a compensating transaction works, consider the activities a_7 (schedule shipment) and a_9 (order fulfilment). Activity a_9 (order fulfilment) assumes that if an order was shipped it was also successfully sent. However, in case the transportation has not arrived, due to a breakdown, strike, etc., then a_7 (schedule shipment) needs to be cancelled (by issuing a compensating activity to undo the effects of the activity schedule shipment). In this case the business logic in the application may automatically reissue a new schedule shipment activity so that the goods can arrive at their destination safely. In fact, this is the assumption with the workflow scenario depicted in Figure 10.11.

10.3.2.1 Transactional workflows

Several variants of sagas have been proposed in literature. One variant requires serial execution of sub-transactions, while other variants allow concurrent execution of sub-transactions. Other variants adopt a forward recovery policy where the remaining sub-transactions are executed in the event of a sub-transaction aborting, while other variants adopt a backward recovery policy of executing the compensating transactions of all the already committed transactions (see the following section). One interesting variant of open nested transactions is a transactional workflow.

The term *transactional workflow* is used to emphasise the relevance of transactional properties for collaborative workflows. *Collaborative workflows* implement public (visible) processes that transcend functional units within an enterprise or cross enterprise boundaries. Strictly speaking, a collaborative workflow is a public workflow only if the workflow has not been customised to execute private processes. For the sake of simplicity, the terms collaborative workflow and transactional workflow are considered interchangeable in this book.

Transactional workflow systems provide scripting facilities for expressing the composition of an activity (or a business process) and offer a flexible way of building application specific open nested transactions. A transactional workflow manages processes – such as order fulfillment, new product introduction, and cross enterprise, supply chain management – that span separate functional units in an enterprise and that integrate their activities with those of other organisations. A transactional workflow involves coordinated execution of activities (or processes) which can have logical decision points that determine which branch of the flow a work item may take at run time in the event of alternate paths. Every alternate path within the flow is identified and controlled through a bounded set of logical decision points. Business rules in each decision point determine how workflow related data is to be processed, routed, tracked and controlled. The same workflow definition yields different instantiated multiple times and may be traversed in different ways if the flow contains decision points.

The coordination requirements are expressed by control flow dependencies that specify an invariant controlling the execution of each activity. These invariants in an activity are based on the execution states of other activities within the transactional workflow, i.e. whether they are active, committed or aborted; response parameters of other activities; and on external variables, such as time properties.

For instance, assume that the invariant (business rule) that governs the execution of activity a_3 (inventory check) in Figure 10.11 is a workflow variable (Boolean) – response parameter of activity a_2 (check creditworthiness) – that states that a particular customer is creditworthy. A *workflow variable* is typically used to store application specific information required by the workflow at run time. Variables are created and assigned values largely to control the logical path through a *workflow instance*. Likewise, the invariant for execution of activity a_7 (schedule shipment) is that either of the activities a_4 (order confirmation) or a_5 (schedule production) has completed successfully.

Processes in transactional workflows must be adapted to specific circumstances, such as inventory outages or negative responses to new products. For instance, sagas do not support executing processes to abort an order after the order has been delivered to the customer. In addition, sagas assume that there is always a semantically equivalent compensation transaction that undoes the effects of a sub-transaction. This may not always be true. In some cases compensating transactions may not be able to guarantee complete backward recovery. Consider a cancelled order entry workflow transaction (see Figure 10.11), which may issue a compensating activity (performing backward recovery) by returning goods to the supplier. This activity will still incur shipping and restocking costs, for the supplier may decide to charge the customer a cancellation fee. For such transactional requirements, existing open nested transaction models, e.g. sagas, often do not provide adequate support. A transactional workflow may require varying isolation levels within its internal structure. This means that the isolation requirements between some activities in a transactional workflow may differ from others.

Not all activities in a transactional workflow need to occur for the transactional workflow to commit. Some activities may be optional while other activities may have alternatives defined. Also, not all activities need to be compensated for a transactional workflow to abort. In addition, the same activity, if used in different workflows, may have different compensation transactions. Finally, the aborting of a transactional workflow may require the execution of complex business processes. Compensating transactions are so fundamental to automating business processes that BPEL includes an explicit declarative mechanism to embed them for failed Web service activities, see Section 9.7.8.

10.3.2.2 Recovery mechanisms

The open nested transaction model relaxes the classical isolation requirement of ACID transactions. There are two possible modes of recovery for open nested transactions: backward recovery and forward recovery.

Backward recovery is used in case the transaction aborts to guarantee that the encompassing transaction will return to the consistent state that existed before execution of the aborted transaction. This includes the contexts of its children, if any. To achieve this outcome the transaction initiates some compensating activity that will cancel the effects of the failed transaction. An open nested transaction may not be able to guarantee complete backward recovery in all cases because it may include activities with non-reversible side effects. For this reason, the transactional workflow must define the appropriate business logic to perform backward recovery as already explained. Note that not all activities of transactional workflows are transactional. Obviously, non-transactional activities do not require atomic properties and hence compensating transactions. For instance, there is no need to compensate activities such as sending quotes to a customer, calculating quotes, or receiving a purchase order from a customer.

Forward recovery is a guarantee that in the event of system failure, the transaction state can be restored to a consistent state and its execution can resume and continue reliably past the point of failure. Forward recovery assumes that the resource manager of each sub-transaction durably maintains the state and results produced by it. With forward recovery a sub-transaction is allowed to continue its execution taking into account that the transaction failed. Compensating activities are used wherever the execution of an activity cannot be rolled back (such as when an order is shipped).

Compensation is the logic for implementing recovery and reversing the effects of a completed activity or transaction. Compensation activities, which may perform forward or backward recovery, are typically application specific.

The relation between recovery and compensation is as follows [Arkin 2002]:

- Forward recovery happens before the transaction completes in order for it to proceed towards completion.
- Backward recovery happens while the transaction aborts in order to cancel the effects of the transaction.
- Compensation occurs after the transaction completes in order to reverse the effects of the completed transaction.
- During backward recovery, a parent transaction will compensate for any descendant sub-transactions that it performed by using the compensate activity.
- A (sub-)transaction can specify its compensation logic as part of its definition, if that logic depends on the activities that the transaction performs. The logic is invoked when applicable using the compensate activity for that particular transaction. The logic that compensates for the transaction after its completion is defined separately from the logic that performs backward recovery in order to abort the transaction.

The separation between the compensation logic of a transaction and the activities that invoke the compensation as part of a larger context allows for different activities, performed in different contexts or flows, to compensate the same transaction using the same logic.

10.4 Web service transactions

The Web service vision is often understood as being about building integration bridges that span independent enterprises and their systems by linking the elements of business together into a cohesive whole. Cross enterprise service applications are distributed applications that appropriately fuse together business functionality and business logic from disparate client applications to provide a range of automated processes such as procurement and order management, forecasting and replenishment, demand and capacity planning, production scheduling, shipping/integrated logistics and so on. This approach aggregates several back end technology components into high level, business oriented services and allows easier migration from legacy applications to new solutions.

One key requirement, in making cross enterprise business process automation happen, is the ability to describe the collaboration aspects of the business processes, such as commitments and exchange of monetary resources, in a standard form that can be consumed by tools for business process implementation and monitoring. Business collaboration requires transactional support in order to guarantee consistent and reliable execution. Collaborating business processes span everything from short lived, real time transactional systems to long lived, extended collaborations. This creates demanding requirements for transactional integrity, resilience and scalability in the extended enterprise.

The push towards sophisticated business applications makes reliable, consistent, and recoverable composition of back end services more important, as inconsistencies and failures become quickly visible to the entire value chain. A Web service solution must, therefore, be able to support the advanced transaction management solutions that we described in the preceding sections.

Traditional transactions depend upon tightly coupled (synchronous) protocols, and thus are often not well suited to more loosely coupled Web service based applications, although they are likely to be used in some of the constituent technologies. As we already explained in this chapter, strict ACIDity and isolation, in particular, are not appropriate to a loosely coupled world of autonomous trading partners, where security and inventory control issues prevent hard locking of local resources that is impractical in the business world.

A Web services environment requires more relaxed forms of transactions – those that do not strictly have to abide by the ACID properties – such as collaborations, workflow, real time processing and so on. In the loosely coupled environment represented by Web services, long running applications will require support for coordination, recovery and compensation, because processors may fail, processes may be cancelled, and services may be moved or withdrawn. Another important requirement is that Web service transactions must span multiple transaction models and protocols native to the underlying infrastructure on to which the Web services are mapped. Finally, there is a need to group Web services into applications that require some form of correlation, but do not necessarily require transactional behaviour.

In this section we shall look at how the concepts of traditional and open nested transactions are coalescing with those of Web services and examine the general characteristics and behaviour of Web service transactions. Subsequently, we shall concentrate on two standard specifications designed to support Web service transactions. These are WS-Coordination, and WS-Transaction.

10.4.1 Characteristics of Web service transactions

Web service transactions are a new generation of transaction management that builds out from core transactional technology, particularly from distributed coordinated transactions, open nested transactions, transactional workflows, and different forms of recovery. A Web service transaction is a consistent change in the state of the business that is driven by a well defined business function. At the end of a Web service transaction the state of transacting parties must be aligned, i.e. they must have the same understanding of the outcome of the message interchange throughout the duration of the Web service transaction. A Web service transaction in its simplest form could represent an order of some goods from some company. The completion of an order results in a consistent change in the state of the affected business: the back end order database is updated and a document copy of the purchase order is filed.

More complex Web service transactions may involve activities such as payment processing, shipping and tracking, determining new product offerings, granting/extending credit, managing market risk, product engineering and so on. Such complex Web service transactions are usually driven by interdependent transactional workflows, which must interlock at points to achieve a mutually desired outcome. This synchronisation is one part of a wider business coordination protocol (such as WS-Coordination which we shall examine later in this chapter) that defines the public, agreed interactions between interacting business parties.

An important requirement for Web service transactions is that they provide a mechanism for maintaining transactional behaviour and a transactional coordination context at a higher level of abstraction (on top of SOAP messages) capable of expressing the real nature and imperfect determinism of business processes (which are designed to cope with innumerable variations and with incremental and partial successes). This is shown in Figure 10.12, which depicts a high level view of a Web service transaction architecture.

The Web service transaction architecture depicted in Figure 10.12 is based on the notion of a transaction coordinator, transaction participants and transaction contexts [Little 2004]. As this figure illustrates, the application client interacts with a Web service transaction coordinator in a similar manner to conventional distributed transaction systems. Specific details of how a client and a transaction coordinator interact depend on the transaction protocol used, e.g. WS-Business Activity v1.1. Context information in this architecture is as usual propagated between clients and services to provide a flow of application context information between interacting distributed systems. This may happen using SOAP header information as the figure indicates.

Whenever transactional services are required, the Web service transactional infrastructure (bottom part in the figure) is responsible for propagating the context to the requested service. When a service that has transactional properties receives an application invocation that also carries a transaction context with it, it registers a participant with the transaction referenced in the context. The transactional service, e.g. an inventory control system, must ultimately (through its container) handle concurrent accesses by different clients and guarantee transactional consistency and the integrity of critical data, e.g. ordered product quantities.

Once a participant is registered then the transaction coordinator controls its work as shown in Figure 10.12. Web service transaction participants are also similar to participants in conventional distributed database systems. All interactions between a transaction coordinator and participant take place according to the specifics of the transactional protocol under which the service is invoked.

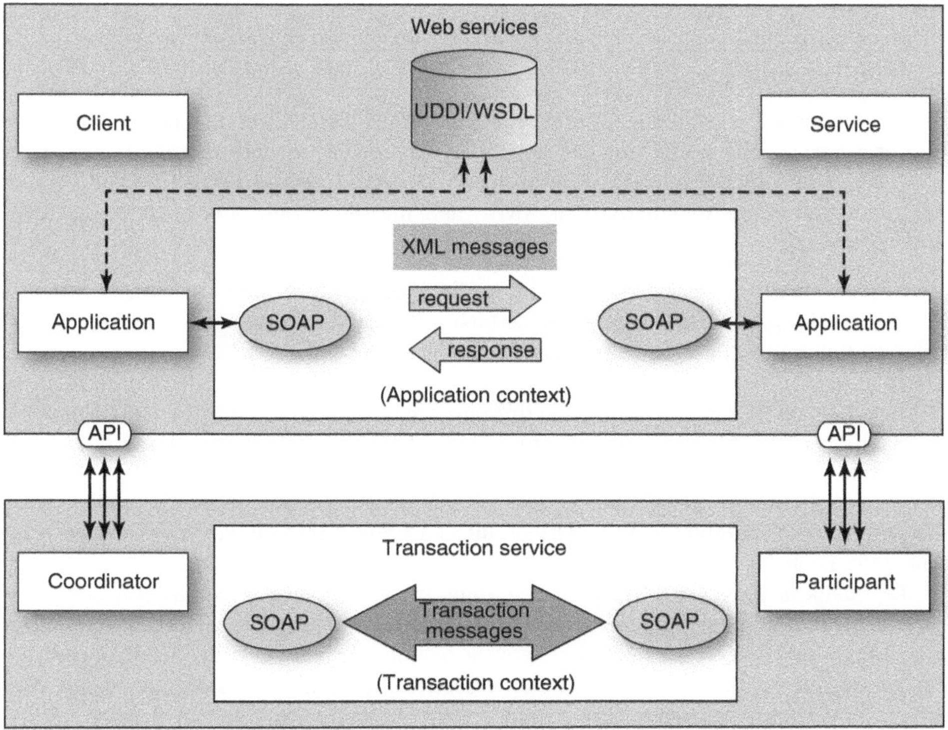

Figure 10.12 Web service transaction architecture
(Source: M. Little, J. Maron, G. Pavlik, *Java Transaction Processing,* Prentice Hall, 2004. Reproduced with permission.)

10.4.2 Operational characteristics of Web service transactions

Every Web service transaction generates multiple business processes, such as credit checks, automated billing, purchase orders, stock updates and shipping on the back end systems of the enterprises involved. The challenge is how to integrate operational systems and enterprise data with the Web applications, to enable customers, partners and suppliers to transact directly with an enterprise's corporate systems, such as inventory, accounting and purchasing. Performance of these business related tasks requires the infusion of transactional properties on to the Web service paradigm. Web service transactions that attempt to incorporate business level decisions with the transactional infrastructure exhibit the following characteristics:

- They normally represent a function that is critical to the business, e.g. supply chain management.

- They can involve more than two parties (organisations) and multiple resources operated independently by each party, such as business applications, databases and ERP systems.
- They define communication protocol bindings that target the domain of Web services, while preserving the ability to carry Web service transaction messages also over other communication protocols. Protocol message structure and content constraints are schematised in XML, and message content is encoded in XML instances.
- They should be based on a formal trading partner agreement, expressed in terms of business protocols such as RosettaNet, Partner Interface Processes, or ebXML Collaboration Protocol Agreements, see Chapter 14.

When a business function is invoked through a Web service as part of a larger business process, the overall transactional behaviour associated with that business process depends on the transactional capabilities of the Web service. Rather than having to compose ever more complex end-to-end offerings, application developers choose those elements that are most appropriate, combining the transactional and non-transactional Web service fragments into a cohesive service.

Like business processes, Web service transactions are structured around activities. An activity is a general purpose computation carried out as a set of scoped operations on a collection of Web services that require a mutually agreed outcome. Cooperating Web services are called participants in a transactional unit of work. Participants are Web services that share a common transaction context. As already noted in Section 10.2.1, transaction context is a data structure containing information pertinent to the shared purpose of the participants, such as the identification of a shared resource, collection of results, common security information, or pointer to the last known stable state of a business process.

Web service transactions comprise two different types of transactional activities: atomic actions (or short lived transactions) and long duration activities, which we examine in the following.

10.4.2.1 Atomic actions

Atomic actions are small-scale interactions made up of services that all agree to enforce a common outcome (commit or abort) of the entire transaction. The atomic action guarantees that all participants will see the same consistent outcome in which all participants complete, otherwise they will be reversed into their original state. In case of a success, all services make the results of their operation durable (i.e. they commit). In case of a failure, all services undo (compensate or roll back) operations that they invoked during the course of the transaction.

The atomic action does not necessarily follow the ACID properties. It may, in fact, relax isolation and durability depending on the coordination protocol applied, e.g. volatile or durable 2PC. The atomic action could be nested (closed nesting model) and gives an all-or-nothing guarantee to the group of atomic activities that are executed as part of the transaction. In summary, an atomic action is considered as an independent, coordinated, transactional short duration unit of work (atomic unit of work) performed by a participant of a Web service transaction.

Example 10.3: Specifying atomic actions

To understand the nature of atomic actions we revert to the AVERS case study again. Assume that a client application (application initiator in Figure 10.13) decides to invoke one or more operations from a particular service such as `order confirmation`, or `inventory check`. It is highly likely for the client application to expect these operations to succeed or fail as a unit. We can thus view the set of operations used by the client in each Web service as constituting an atomic unit of work (namely, atomic action). An atomic transaction is the simplest unit of work and behaves like existing X/Open XA-compliant, two-phase commit transactions. An atomic action must either fully commit or fully roll back. Within an atomic action, the operations exposed by a single transactional Web service and the internal processes of the service, e.g. support processes, would usually make up a single atomic action. Atomic actions frequently appear when the business model represents one of the core business processes, e.g. order entry of an enterprise. Non-atomic Web service activities usually support the service atoms and are frequently found within ancillary processes, e.g. travel expense accounts.

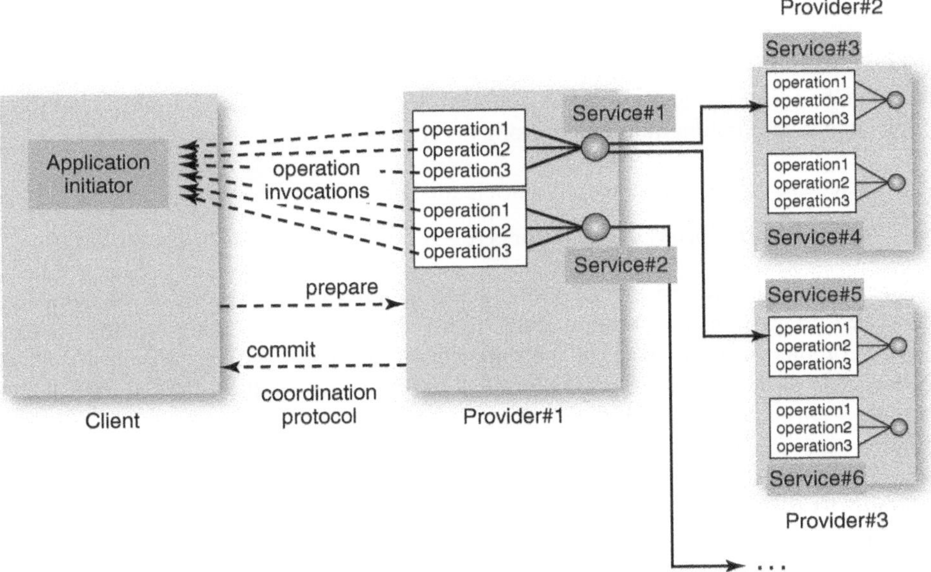

Figure 10.13 Web service transactions and applications

Figure 10.13 illustrates that atomic actions use a 2PC (with presumed abort) whereby a coordinating process is required to manage the coordination protocol messages, e.g. `prepare`, `commit`, `cancel`, that are sent to the participating services within a given atomic transaction. This coordinating process might be implemented within the application itself, or, more likely, it will be a specialised Web service [Webber 2001]. Once the actual work involving the consumed Web services in an atomic action has finished, the client application (service client) can begin the two-phase commit coordination of those Web services. The client (transaction initiator) is expected to control all aspects of the 2PC, i.e. prepare phase and confirm phase. The rationale behind allowing the client to govern when prepare and confirm calls are made on the atomic transaction is to permit maximum flexibility within the protocol. Allowing the client to decide upon timings implicitly permits reservation style business processes to be carried out with ease. For instance, this can apply to an order reservation system, where the prepare phase of the 2PC reserves a number of products, and the confirm phase actually buys the reserved products.

10.4.2.2 Long duration transactions

Recall that business processes are long running, e.g. a single instance of a process such as order to cash may run for months, and very dynamic, thus responding to demands from customers and to changing market conditions. Accordingly, business processes are usually large and complex, involving the flow of materials, information and business commitments. Long duration activities are aggregations of several atomic actions and may exhibit the characteristics and behaviour of open nested transactions and transactional workflows, and area characteristic of many business processes.

With Web services *long duration activity* aggregates atomic actions with conventional business logic functions into a cohesive Web service transaction. The initiator of a Web service transaction (typically a client application) can manipulate the embedded atomic actions in a long duration transaction. Long duration activities are non-atomic, they allow:

- selective confirm (commit) of participants; or
- cancelling (rollback) of participants (even if they are capable of committing).

Atomic activities can be part of a long duration activity. The actions of the embedded short lived transactions are committed and made visible before the long running business activity completes. In the event of the long running business activity failing, the effects of such short lived (atomic) transactions need to be compensated for. The atomic actions forming a particular long duration business activity do not necessarily need to have a common outcome. Under application control (business logic), some of these may be performed (confirmed), while others may fail or raise exceptions such as timeouts or failure.

Figure 10.14 illustrates the concept of transactional nesting for long duration as well as atomic activities. Because long duration activities can be nested, there exists a certain parent–child relationship not only between long duration activities (in Figure 10.14 activity A_2 is nested within activity A_1) but also between long duration activities and atomic actions (in the same figure, atomic actions a_3, a_4, and a_6 are nested within activity A_2 and atomic actions a_1, a_2 , a_5, and a_7 are nested within activity A_1). A client application can dictate whether an atomic activity within the long duration activity succeeds or fails, even if the service is capable of succeeding.

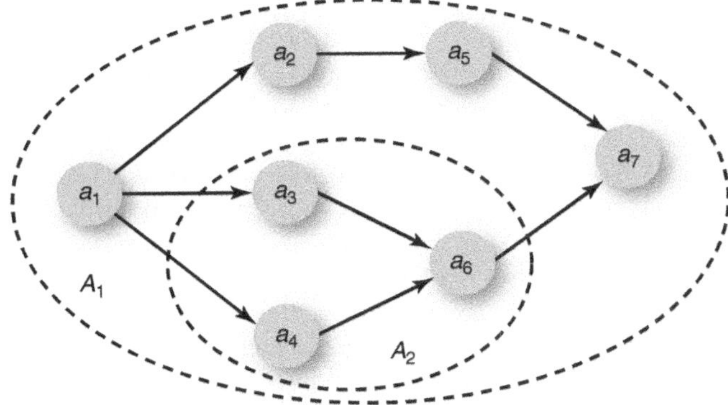

Figure 10.14 Atomic activities, long-duration activities, and nesting

Example 10.4: Specifying a long running business activity

To exemplify a long duration business activity, consider a slight variation of the order processing scenario where a manufacturer asks one of its suppliers to provide it with a valuable and fragile piece of equipment. Now consider that one atomic action arranges for the purchase of this product, while a second arranges for its insurance, and a third one for its transportation. If the client application is not risk averse (due to excessive costs), then, even if the insurance operation (atomic action) votes to cancel, the client might still confirm the Web service transaction and get the item shipped uninsured. Most likely, however, the client application would probably retry to obtain insurance for the item. In this case the Web services infrastructure comes into play, and the client would opt for another insurer via, for instance, the UDDI service infrastructure. Once the client discovers a new insurer, it can try again to complete the long duration business activity with all the necessary atomic actions voting to confirm on the basis of the particular coordination protocol used.

Splitting a long duration activity into atomic actions introduces flexibility because not all individual atomic actions need to lock resources at the same time. In addition, in case a failure occurs at one atomic action level, the overall long duration activity can still continue using an alternate path either to compensate already done tasks or to do other tasks (e.g. trying out a different insurer or using a safer transportation medium in case the preferred insurer is too expensive).

One of the major problems with long running activities is that their underlying Web service implementations are located remotely and hosted by third parties (service providers in Figure 10.13). This means that there is an increased risk of failure during their application. To cater for this threat a long duration activity may decide selectively to cancel atomic transactions and create new ones during its lifetime. Thus, the membership of long duration activity is established dynamically by the business logic part of a client application. For instance, a transaction composition service (invoked by the client application) may take interim *polls* to discover whether atomic activities are ready or have been cancelled, or it may decide to withdraw its participants because of a timeout.

10.4.3 Consensus groups and interposition

In a Web service transaction, consensus about the outcome of specific tasks among the participants is of high importance. This is true in particular because of the monetary value often involved in service transactions. To share consensus, participants are grouped into *consensus groups* in which participants are structured so that they see the same outcome (i.e. consensus of opinion). Another term for consensus groups is transaction scope. A *transaction scope* is a business task consisting of a general purpose computation carried out as a bounded set of operations on a collection of Web services that require a mutually agreed outcome. Different participants of a Web service transaction can be part of different consensus groups, so that participants in one group can observe a different outcome than participants in other groups. Every consensus group can have a particular level of atomicity. These characteristics distinguish Web service transactions from traditional transactions. Another distinction from traditional transactions is the fact that a participant of a consensus group can also leave the consensus group before the transaction is terminated.

Related to the consensus groups is the notion of nesting. Consensus groups containing tasks or lower level activities (children) that are required to perform a higher level activity (parent) can be regarded as child scopes. Child scopes can complete independently of a parent. The parent may, however, have some ultimate control of the child scopes. Child scopes may terminate bottom up, but the parent scope may have ultimate control over them. So, for example, a nested scope (child scope) may think it has terminated, when in fact the parent scope will eventually complete and tell the child what to do.

Next to the flexible consensus groups and nesting, another important notion for Web service transactions is the concept of interposition of subordinate coordinators. Recall from Section 10.2.1 that the first coordinator created for a specific top level transaction (root coordinator) is responsible for driving the 2PC. Any coordinator that is subsequently created for an existing transaction (e.g. as the result of interposition) becomes a subordinate in the process. The root coordinator initiates the 2PC and participants respond to the operations that implement the protocol. A coordinator in Web service transactions can take the responsibility for notifying the participants of the outcome, making the outcomes of the participants persistent, and managing the transaction context. A coordinator becomes a participant when it registers itself with another coordinator for the purpose of representing a set of other, typically local, participants. When a coordinator represents a set of local participants, this is known as *interposition.* This technique allows a proxy to handle the functions of a coordinator in the importing domain (server) and is generally used to increase performance (when the number of participants increases beyond a certain threshold) and security in a Web service transaction. Interposed coordinators act as subordinate coordinators. An interposed coordinator registers as a participant in the transaction.

Example 10.5: Transaction interposition

The relationships between coordinators in the transaction form a tree as shown in Figure 10.15. The root coordinator is responsible for completing the Web service transaction (top level transaction). A coordinator is not concerned with what the participant implementation is. One participant may interact with a database to commit a transaction (e.g. participants of enterprises 1 and 5 in Figure 10.15), another may just as readily be responsible for forwarding the

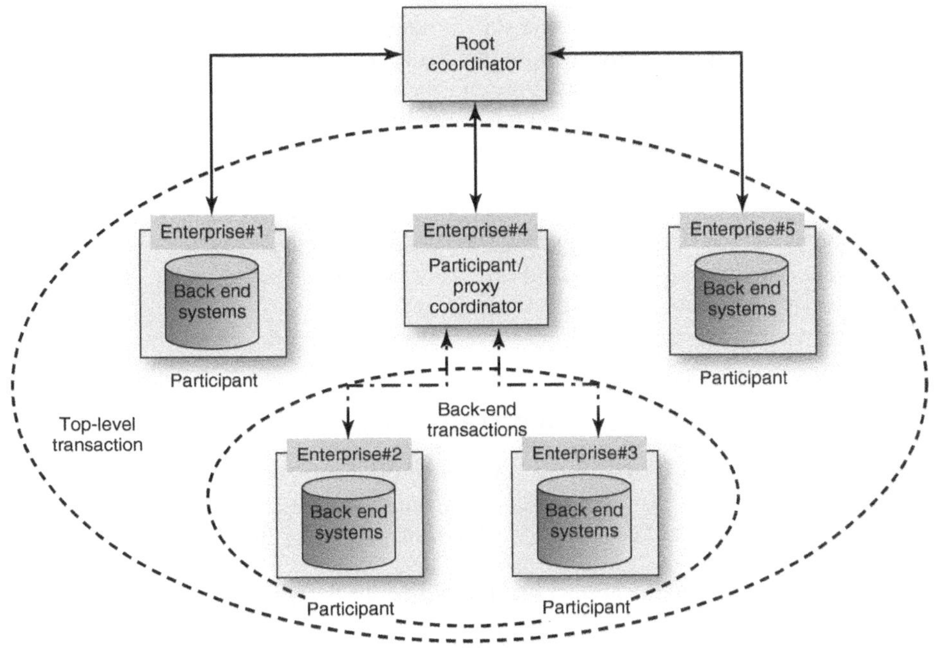

Figure 10.15 Transaction interposition

(root) coordinators' messages to a number of back end systems, essentially acting as a coordinator itself as shown (participant at Enterprise 4). In this case, the participant is acting like a proxy for the coordinator (the root coordinator). In the example of Figure 10.15 the proxy coordinator (participant at Enterprise 4) is responsible for interacting with two participants (Enterprises 2 and 3) when it receives an invocation from the root coordinator and collates their responses (along with its own) for the root coordinator. As far as the root coordinator is concerned, the interposed (child) coordinator is a participant that obeys the parent's transaction protocol (typically two-phase). However, each child coordinator will be tailored to the domain in which it operates and the protocol(s) that domain uses.

An interposed participant (i.e. a subordinate coordinator) forwards information from its own participants to the next higher level (superior) coordinator, receives decisions from a higher level coordinator and forwards these to its participants. It cannot make decisions on its own. Such an interposed actor does not manage but just coordinates transactions, e.g. across processes or machines. In interposition, participants of a subordinate coordinator cannot complete autonomously, but must be instructed by their coordinator. If a participant exits, the subordinate coordinator cannot do anything about that, and cannot make other decisions based on this fact.

This last point is a crucial difference between the principles of interposition and nesting (parent–child scopes). With nesting, applications have the control to properly manage scopes because of the parent–child relationship. If a parent completes its work and sees what the child has done, it can react to that by compensating, accepting its descendant's work, terminating the child, or start invoking other services (e.g. if the child exited). This means that there is full control by the parent.

Interposition of subordinate coordinators assists in achieving interoperability because the interposed coordinator can also translate a neutral outcome protocol into a platform specific protocol. This is illustrated in Figure 10.15 where the proxy coordinator shields the internal business process infrastructure in Enterprises 2 and 3 from the root coordinator. Not only does the interposed domain (Enterprises 2 and 3) require the use of a different context when communicating with services within the domain, but also each domain may use different protocols to those outside the domain. The subordinate coordinator may then act as a translator from protocols outside the domain to protocols used within the domain. The main benefit of adding transaction based protocols is that the participants and the coordinator negotiate a set of agreed actions or behaviours based on the outcome, such as rollback, compensation, three-phase commit, etc.

10.4.4 States of Web service transactions

Each Web service transaction instance transitions through a number of states in a similar fashion to transition states for conventional transactions (see Figure 10.2). These are depicted in Figure 10.16 and described in what follows [Arkin 2002]:

- *Active:* The transaction is active and performs the activities stated in its transaction context.
- *Preparing to complete:* The transaction has performed all the activities in its activity set and is now preparing to complete. This may involve additional work such as making data changes persistent, performing two-phase commit, and coordinating nested Web service transaction completion (i.e. context completion).
- *Completed:* The transaction has performed all the work required in order to complete successfully.
- *Preparing to abort:* The transaction has failed to complete successfully and is now preparing to abort. This may involve additional work such as reversing data by running compensating transactions, communicating the outcome to transaction participants (for atomic transactions only), and coordinating nested Web service transaction abortion.
- *Aborted:* The transaction has failed to complete successfully and has performed all the work required to abort.
- *Preparing to compensate:* The transaction is now executing activities within its own compensation activity set.
- *Compensated:* The transaction has performed successfully all the work within its own compensation activity set.

A transaction instance always starts in the active state and transitions to preparing to complete and completion state, if all its work is performed successfully (see Figure 10.16). A transaction will transition to preparing to abort and aborted if an exception is raised, e.g. timeout, or fault occurs, or one of its parents raises an exception, or the transaction cannot complete successfully. The transaction then performs

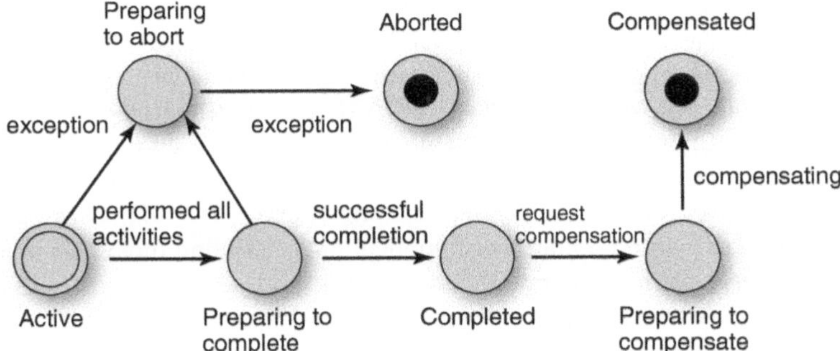

Figure 10.16 Transition diagram for Web service transaction instance states

all the work required, in particular the activities that were related to the exception and need completion.

It is possible to compensate for a transaction once it is in the complete state (see Figure 10.16). The initial attempt to compensate a Web service transaction will transition it to the compensating state. The transaction will then perform all of the activities in its compensation activity set before moving to the compensated state. Note that in Figure 10.16 only the aborted and compensated states are terminal states.

At this point you have sufficient knowledge to understand the workings of the current breed of transactional Web service standards that are used in advanced business applications. In the remainder of this chapter we shall first concentrate on examples of coordination protocols, and a transaction model as provided by the WS-Coordination and WS-Transaction specifications. The WS-Coordination and WS-Transaction initiatives complement BPEL to provide mechanisms for defining specific standard protocols for use by transaction processing systems, workflow systems, or other applications that wish to coordinate multiple Web services. We shall revisit business protocols in Chapter 14 where we explain several standard protocols that are able to express transactional behaviour at a high abstraction level.

10.5 Web service coordination

A business process may involve a number of Web services working together to provide a common solution. Each service needs to be able to coordinate its activities with those of the other services for the process to succeed. Such applications often take some time to complete due to business latencies, network latencies, and waiting for users to interact with the application.

Coordination refers to the act of organising a number of independent entities to achieve a specific goal. Coordination is necessary to ensure correct behaviour when more than one transactional resource is involved in a Web service transaction. This is because transaction managers in the individual resources need to be coordinated correctly to perform a commit or rollback. Typically, coordination is the act of one entity (known as the coordinator) disseminating information to a number of participants for some domain specific reason, e.g. reaching consensus on a decision like a distributed transaction protocol, or simply to guarantee that all participants obtain a specific message, as occurs in a reliable multicast environment [Webber 2003a]. When parties are being coordinated, information known as the coordination context is propagated to tie together operations that are logically part of the same activity.

The WS-Coordination specification is an OASIS standard that can be viewed as the facility to organise a number of independent applications into a coordinated activity and, as such, it describes an extensible framework for supporting a variety of protocols that coordinate the actions of distributed applications [Feingold 2007]. Such coordination protocols are used to support a number of applications, including those that need to reach consistent agreement on the outcome of distributed activities.

WS-Coordination coordinates operations in a process that spans interoperable Web services and enables participants to reach consistent agreement on the outcome of distributed activities. This framework enables participants to reach consistent agreement on the outcome of distributed activities and distributed transactions. The coordination protocols that can be defined in this framework can accommodate a wide variety of activities, including protocols for simple short lived operations, and protocols for complex long lived business activities. For example, WS-AtomicTransaction [Little 2009] and WS-BusinessActivity [Freund 2009] specifications, which are part of the WS-Transaction specification that we cover later in this chapter, use and build upon this specification. The set of coordination types is open ended. New types can be defined by an implementation, as long as each service participating in the joint work has common understanding of the required behaviour.

10.5.1 The WS-Coordination model

The WS-Coordination specification provides for extensibility along two dimensions. It allows for the publication of new coordination protocols and the selection of a specific protocol from a coordination type and the definition of extension elements that can be added to protocols and message flows. The WS-Coordination specification describes a framework for a coordination service (or coordinator) that aggregates three component services:

- An *activation service* that enables an application to create a coordination instance and its associated context.
- A *registration service* that enables an application to register for coordination protocols that coordinate the execution of distributed operations in a Web service environment.
- A *protocol service* that implements the coordination type and specific set of coordination protocols that are used to carry out a coordination activity. The protocol service may typically support the two coordination types atomic transaction and business activity, which are defined as part of WS-Transaction, as we shall explain later in this chapter. Each of these types defines a set of its own coordination protocols, which represent a set of coordination rules that are imposed on activities under the control of the specific coordination type, e.g. durable or volatile 2PC for atomic activities.

Another important element for the coordination of activities is the entity that drives the coordination protocol through to its completion. This entity is usually a client (application) that controls the application as a whole and that is not defined in the coordination framework. The three WS-Coordination component services and their interrelationships are illustrated in Figure 10.17.

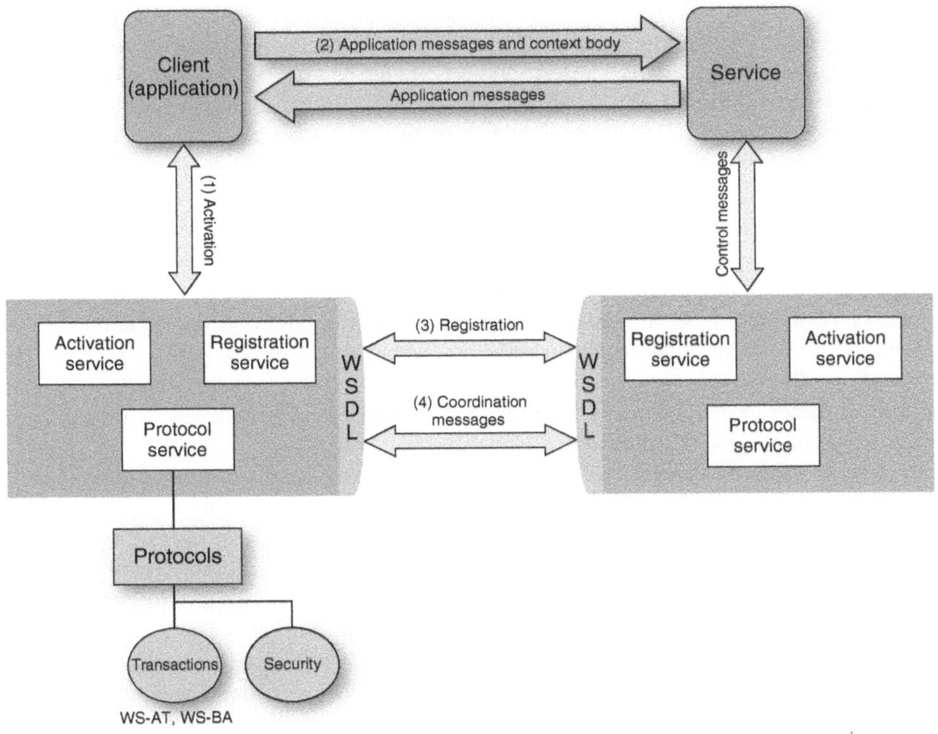

Figure 10.17 Overview of WS-Coordination architecture

To initiate a joint piece of work, an application first contacts the target activation service to create an activity, which is identified by a coordination context. The *coordination context* is a SOAP header block that uniquely identifies the joint piece of work that needs to be undertaken by means of an activity identifier. The context contains the necessary information to register into the activity, specifying the coordination behaviour that the application will follow.

When a request is received at one of the endpoints, unless the request is for creating a new activity, in which case a new coordinator is created, it is simply passed on to the coordinator responsible for the activity concerned. The respective coordinator then handles the requested operations. A *coordinator* is an entity that is responsible for keeping track of transactions and the various Web services involved in each one. For instance, if a purchase order service needs to make several Web service calls to some of its suppliers to order products, the coordinator is then responsible for keeping track of which suppliers were called and the overall status of a transaction. A coordinator normally exposes transaction related operations.

The *coordination service* maintains a central repository of all active coordinators. When a new request arrives at any of the endpoints, the activity identifier is used to look up the coordinator coordinating the particular activity to dispatch the request. To facilitate this process, the coordination service uses an activity identifier as a reference property (see Section 7.1.1 on WS-Addressing) at all of its endpoints.

Registration is a key operation in the coordination framework, as it allows the tying up of all the different Web services that desire to coordinate to perform a joint unit of work. The *registration service* is responsible for the registration of new participants (i.e. the registration of Web services) with the coordinator, and the selection of the coordination protocol. This enables the participants to receive the context and protocol messages of the coordinator during the application's lifetime. This last responsibility is provided by the coordination service. This service ensures that the registered Web services are driven through to completion by using the selected protocol.

The protocol defines the behaviour and the operations that are required for the completion of an activity. When creating the coordinator, one of the supported protocol types is chosen by the instantiating application. Later, when the coordination context is propagated to other applications, the other applications choose the coordination protocol supported by that coordination type to participate in the transaction. The activation and registration endpoints are defined by the WS-Coordination specification. All other endpoints are defined by coordination type specific protocols such as WS-AtomicTransaction and WS-BusinessActivity. The purpose of these *protocol services* is to facilitate communication between participants and the coordination service based on specific coordination protocols.

Finally, the role of a *transaction terminator* is generally played by the client application. The client application will, at an appropriate point, ask the coordinator to perform its particular coordination function with any registered participants in order to drive the protocol through to its completion [Webber 2003a]. Upon completion, the client application may be informed of an outcome for an activity. This may vary from simple succeeded/failed notification through to complex structured data detailing the activity's status.

Figure 10.18 illustrates the coordination service and its constituent components as well as the relationship between WS-Coordination and WS-Transaction. The figure indicates that the coordination type used is WS-AtomicTransaction (which defines operations such as prepare, commit and rollback) and the coordination protocol used is durable 2PC

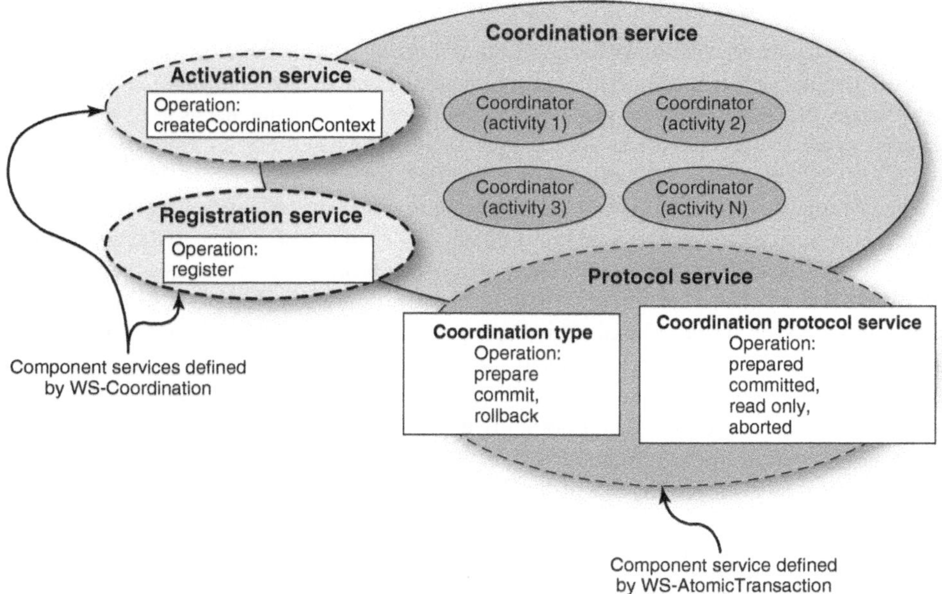

Figure 10.18 Coordination service and its constituent component services

(which defines oper ations such as prepared, aborted, committed and read-only). In addition, the figure shows that at any given time the number of active coordinators resident in the coordination service is equal to the number of activities coordinated by the service. This is due to the fact that, as new activities are created and existing activities are terminated, coordinators also get created and destroyed.

10.5.2 Typical message exchange between two applications

In this section we present an example showing a typical message exchange between two Web services that employ WS-Coordination. The example is taken from [Feingold 2007] and assumes that the two Web services (Applications 1 and 2) will create their own coordinators (Coordinators A and B) to interact with each other.

Figure 10.19 illustrates how two application services (called Application 1 and Application 2) with their own coordinators (Coordinator A and Coordinator B) interact as the activity propagates between them. The sequence of message exchanges in this example is as follows:

1. $Application_1$ calls the `CreateCoordinationContext` operation on $Coordinator_A$ to begin a new transaction and specifies the coordination type, say *CT* that governs this transaction. The application receives the coordination context ($CC_{a)}$ that contains the acitivity identifier A_1, the coordination type *CT*, and an endpoint reference to the registration service RS_a of $Coordinator_A$.

2. $Application_1$ sends and application message containing the coordination context CC_a as a SOAP header to $Application_2$. This acts as an invitation to $Application_2$ to participate in the activity using one of the coordination protocols for the coordination type in $CC_{a.}$ The service that receives this invitation can either register to participate or not.

3. $Application_2$ creates its own coordinator instead of using the coordinator sent by $Application_1$. $Application_2$ calls the `CreateCoordinationContext` operation on $Coordinator_B$ with the coordination context in CC_a that it received from $Application_1$. $Coordinator_B$ creates its own coordinator context CC_{b}. This new coordinator context CC_b contains the same activity identifier and coordination type as CC_a but has its own registration service RS_{b}.

4. $Application_2$ determines the coordination protocol supported by the coordination type *CT* and registers for a coordination protocol *CP* at $Coordinator_B$, thereby exchanging endpoint references for $Application_2$ and the protocol instance CP_{b}. All messages on protocol *CP* can now be exchanged between $Application_2$ and $Coordinator_B$.

5. The registration of $Application_2$ with $Coordinator_B$ triggers another registration. It causes $Coordinator_B$ to forward the registration on to registration service RS_a of $Coordinator_A$ exchanging port references for the protocol instances CP_b and CP_a. Enrollment and protocols selection allow the Web services involved in the two applications to establish the traditional roles of transaction coordinator and participants. Following this, all messages on protocol CP can be exchanged between the coordinator and participant and hence between the two applications.

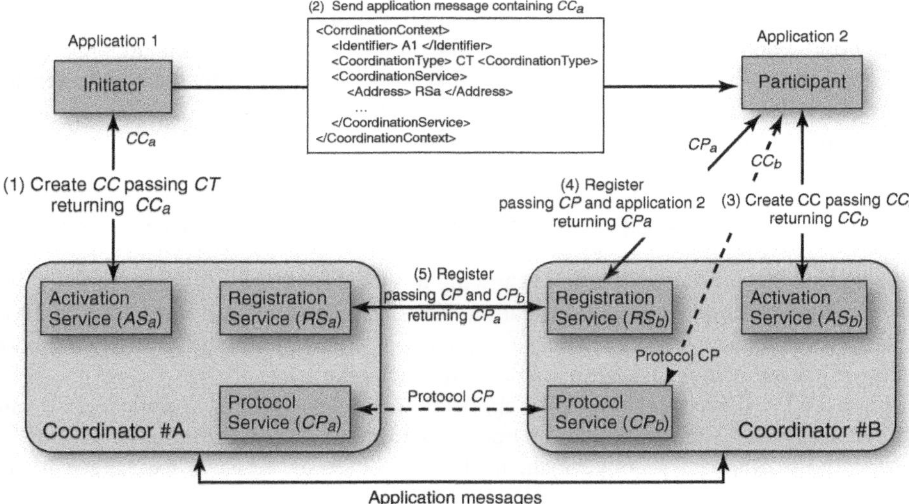

Figure 10.19 Two interacting applications using WS-Coordination with their own coordinator

In the following three subsections we shall explain how to specify coordination contexts and the activation and registration WS-Coordination component services.

10.5.3 Coordination context

`CoordinationContext` is a distinct context type that is defined to pass coordination information to the participants involved in a Web service transaction. In WS-Coordination context information is critical to coordination since it contains the information necessary for services to participate in the coordination protocol. The coordination context provides the mechanism to share processing information between interacting Web services and to bind all constituent Web services of an application together into a single coordinated application. To propagate an activity to another Web service the initiating client must send a coordination context. The coordination context is sent as part of the application message itself and can be generally exchanged by using the header in SOAP messages.

For each newly created transaction, the activation service returns a coordination context that contains a global identifier, an expiry field, the address (WS-Address) of a registration service, and a coordination protocol. In WS-Coordination the context contains a unique global identifier in the form of a URI. This identifier indicates which transaction the Web service call is for. To enable the enrolment of new participants, the context contains the location, or endpoint address, of the coordinator (registration service) where parties receiving a context can register participants into the protocol. The context also contains a time stamp (expiration) field, which indicates for how long the context should be considered valid. Finally, the context contains protocol specific information (`CoordinationType`) about the actual coordination protocol supported by the coordinator, such as WS-Transaction that describes specific completion processing behaviour.

Example 10.6: Sample CoordinationContext supporting a transaction service

Listing 10.1 is an example of a `CoordinationContext` supporting an atomic transaction service.

```
<?xml version="1.0" encoding="utf-8"?>
<soap:Envelope xmlns:soap="http://www.w3.org/2001/12/soap-envelope"
     <soap:Header>
          . . .
          <wscoor:CoordinationContext
               xmlns:wsu="http://schemas.xmlsoap.org/ws/2002/07/utility"
               xmlns:wsa="http://www.w3.org/2005/08/addressing"
               xmlns:wscoor="http://docs.oasis-open.org/ws-tx/wscoor/2006/06">
               <wcoor:Expires> 2012 </wscoor:Expires>
               <wscoor:Identifier>
                     http://supply.com/trans345
               </wscoor:Identifier>
               <wscoor:CoordinationType>
                   http://schemas.xmlsoap.org/ws/2004/10/wsat
               </wscoor:CoordinationType>
               <wscoor:RegistrationService>
                    <wsa:Address>
                      http://example.com/mycoordinationservice/registration
                    </wsa:Address>
                      . . .
               </wscoor:RegistrationService>
               . . .
          </wscoor:CoordinationContext>
          . . .
     </soap:Header>
```

Listing 10.1 Sample coordination context

10.5.4 Activation service

When an application wants to start a new transaction, it asks the coordinator to create a new context. It does so by invoking the `CreateCoordinationContext` operation of the coordinator activation service, passing the coordination type, its own port type reference (for the coordinator to send back the response), the port type reference of the activation service and other information. The coordinator in return calls the CreateCoordinationContextResponse operation of the requester, passing back the requester endpoint reference, the coordination context created in response to the CreateCoordinationContext operation call and other information.

Example 10.7: CoordinationContext request and response

Listing 10.2 is an example of a simple CreateCoordinationContext request message. This operation has only one actual parameter, which defines the type of transaction in use. Here we assume that the requesting application (purchase order service in our case) has asked the coordinator to create a new coordination context, which will subsequently be returned to the requester (purchase order service).

```
<?xml version="1.0" encoding="utf-8"?>
<soap:Envelope xmlns:soap="http://www.w3.org/2001/12/soap-envelope"
    <soap:Header>
        . . .
    </soap:Header>
      <soap:Body>
        <wscoor:CreateCoordinationContext
            xmlns:wsa="http://schemas.xmlsoap.org/ws/2005/08/addressing"
            xmlns:wscoor="http://docs.oasis-open.org/ws-tx/wscoor/2006/06">
          <wcoor:Expires> 2012 </wscoor:Expires>
          <wscoor:CoordinationType>
              http://schemas.xmlsoap.org/ws/2004/10/wsat
          </wscoor:CoordinationType>
        </wscoor:CoordinationContext>
        . . .
    </soap:Body>
</soap:envelope>
```

Listing 10.2 Creation of an activation service

Listing 10.3 is an example of a returning the CoordinationContext that was the created response to the above request message. As part of the newly created coordination context, the registration service endpoint reference of the coordinator is also returned.

The response in Listing 10.3 contains a context with a unique identifier, an expiry time, and the transaction that was passed to the request. The remaining element RegistrationService contains a reference pointer to the coordinator's registration service. This is an endpoint reference as defined by the WS-Addressing specification. This service is the one that each participant in the transaction would invoke to notify the coordinator that it is in the scope of the transaction (see the following section). For example, a purchase order service may contact several supplier services; those services will use the above address to register with the coordinator. In this way, the coordinator knows which suppliers to contact if they need to take some action on behalf of the transaction, e.g. prepare, commit, or rollback.

```
<?xml version="1.0" encoding="utf-8"?>
<soap:Envelope xmlns:soap="http://www.w3.org/2001/12/soap-envelope"
    <soap:Header>
        . . .
    </soap:Header>
      <soap:Body>
        <wscoor:CreateCoordinationContextResponse>
         <wscoor:CoordinationContext>
              <wscoor:Identifier>
                 http://supply.com/trans345
              </wscoor:Identifier>
              <wcoor:Expires> 2012 </wscoor:Expires>
              <wscoor:CoordinationType>
               http://schemas.xmlsoap.org/ws/2004/10/wsat
              </wscoor:CoordinationType>
              <wscoor:RegistrationService>
                <wsa:Address>
                  http://coordinator.com/registration
                </wsa:Address>
                  . . .
              </wscoor:RegistrationService>
             . . .
         </wscoor:CoordinationContext>
      </wscoor:CreateCoordinationContextResponse>
    </soap:Body>
</soap:envelope>
```

Listing 10.3 Response message to activation service in Listing 10.2

10.5.5 Registration service

Once a coordinator has been instantiated and a corresponding context created by the activation service, a registration service is then created and exposed. This service allows participants to register to receive protocol messages associated with a particular coordinator. Like the activation service, the registration service requires port type references on both the coordinator side for the request and the requester side for the response. This allows the coordinator and requester to exchange messages.

Example 10.8: Registering a purchase order and a supplier service

In the following example we assume that both a purchase order and a supplier service wish to both register with a coordinator to participate in a joint transaction. This situation is shown in Listing 10.4. Listing 10.5 shows the coordinator response after receiving the request for registration.

If the purchase order service wishes to invoke an operation such as `checkInventory()` on one of its suppliers then the entire coordination context is passed as a SOAP header to denote to the coordinator which transaction the supplier service is likely to register for. When the supplier service receives the message, it then examines the information

```
<?xml version="1.0" encoding="utf-8"?>
<soap:Envelope>
 <soap:Header>
  <wscoor:CoordinationContext soap:mustUnderstand="1">
          <wscoor:Identifier>
             http://supply.com/trans345
          </wscoor:Identifier>
          <wcoor:Expires> 2012 </wscoor:Expires>
          <wscoor:CoordinationType>
            http://schemas.xmlsoap.org/ws/2004/10/wsat
          </wscoor:CoordinationType>
          <wscoor:RegistrationService>
            <wsa:Address>
               http://coordinator.com/registration
            </wsa:Address>
                 . . .
          </wscoor:RegistrationService>
            . . .
   </wscoor:CoordinationContext>
 </soap:Header>
 <soap:body>
  <wscoor:Register>
   <wscoor:ProtocolIdentifier>
      http://schemas.xmlsoap.org/ws/2004/10/wsat#Durable2PC
   </wscoor:ProtocolIdentifier>
   <wscoor:ParticipantProtocolService>
       <wsa:Address>
          http://supplier.com/DurableParticipant
       </wsa:Address>
     . . .
   </wscoor:ParticipantProtocolService>
  </wscoor:Register>
 </soap:body>
</soap:Envelope>
```

Listing 10.4 Creating a registration service

in the context to decide whether it can participate in the transaction under the coordination type specified there.

For a requester, supplier service in our case, to register itself to the coordinator, the requester uses the registration service reference returned by the coordinator in response to the creation of a context. The requester then calls the Register operation of the coordinator registration service, passing the coordinator registration service endpoint reference, endpoint reference of itself (`PartcipantProtocolService`) to allow the coordinator to invoke transactional operations on this participant and send back transaction status information, URI of the coordination protocol selected for registration (`ProtocolIdentifier`), and other information. In this example the coordination protocol selected is Atomic and follows the two-phase commit protocol (`wsat#Durable2PC`).

In response to the registration request shown above, the coordinator calls in return the `RegisterResponse` operation on the requester. This operation returns the address the coordinator wants the registered participant to use for the coordination protocol (`CoordinatorProtocolService`), as shown in Listing 10.5. At this stage both the

```
<?xml version="1.0" encoding="utf-8"?>
<soap:Envelope>
 <soap:Header>
  <wscoor:CoordinationContext soap:mustUnderstand="1">
         <wscoor:Identifier>
            http://supply.com/trans345
         </wscoor:Identifier>
         <wcoor:Expires> 2012 </wscoor:Expires>
         <wscoor:CoordinationType>
           http://schemas.xmlsoap.org/ws/2004/10/wsat
         </wscoor:CoordinationType>
         <wscoor:RegistrationService>
           <wsa:Address>
              http://coordinator.com/registration
           </wsa:Address>
              . . .
         </wscoor:RegistrationService>
           . . .
   </wscoor:CoordinationContext>
 </soap:Header>
 <soap:body>
  <wscoor:RegisterResponse>
   <wscoor:CoordinatorProtocolService>
       <wsa:Address>
          http://coordinator.com/coordinator-service
       </wsa:Address>
   </wscoor:CoordinatorProtocolService>
  </wscoor:RegisterResponse>
 </soap:body>
</soap:Envelope>
```

Listing 10.5 Coordinator response to a registration request in Listing 10.4

coordinator and the requester have each other's endpoint reference and can exchange protocol messages. When a participant is registered with a coordinator through the registration service, it receives messages that the coordinator sends. These could be, for instance, prepare to complete and complete messages, if a two-phase protocol is used as in the case of Listing 10.5.

As seen above, WS-Coordination defines two core operations (`CreateCoordinationContext` and `Register`). However, the coordination service can be extended with additional transaction specific operations. WS-Coordination also supports the concept of interposition. Registered participants at a coordinator can also be a coordinator, enabling interposition and creating a tree of sub-coordinators. WS-Coordination does this by making it an integral part of the protocol. The context messages therefore (can) also contain information about other participants and about recovery information.

As already noted previously, the WS-Coordination specification does not define a protocol for terminating a coordination protocol instance. It requires for this purpose transaction (or coordination) types. We shall explain in the section that follows the two basic transaction types that are typically used in conjunction with WS-Coordination. These are: WS-AtomicTransaction and WS-BusinessActivity.

10.6 Web service transaction types

The two transaction (coordination protocol) types that can be executed within the WS-Coordination framework are: atomic transaction and business activity. These two transaction types are supplied by the OASIS standards WS-AtomicTransaction [Little 2009] (for specifying atomic transactions) and WS-BusinessActivity [Freund 2009] (for specifying long duration transactions.) Developers can use either or both of these coordination types when building applications that require consistent agreement on the outcome of distributed activities.

Atomic transactions are suggested for transactions that are short lived atomic units of work within a trust domain, while business activities are suggested for transactions that are long lived units of work comprising activities of potentially different trust domains. Each transaction type may employ a number of transaction coordination protocols, e.g. two-phase commit (durable and volatile), participant completion and coordination completion. Various participants may choose to register for one or more of these protocols. Based on the transaction coordination protocol that a participant registers for, a well defined number and type of message becomes available to the participant for exchanging with the coordinator.

We shall examine these two transaction types, their elements and functionality in turn starting with WS-AtomicTransaction.

10.6.1 Atomic transaction

Atomic transactions compare to the traditional distributed database transaction model (short lived atomic transactions). They also provide simple agreement coordination protocols for closely coupled systems that desire all-or-nothing outcomes.

WS-AtomicTransaction is usually confined to individual organisations where a client needs to consolidate operations across various internal applications. The Atomic Transaction coordination context is a `CoordinationContext` type with the coordination type defined as in the previous section, where messages that propagate a coordination context must use an Atomic Transaction coordination context. The WS-AtomicTransaction maps to existing ACID transaction standards and offers three kinds of transaction coordination protocols for atomic transactions, which we shall examine in the following section.

Example 10.9: A simple atomic transaction for transferring funds

The code snippet in the example of Listing 10.6 illustrates how to leverage WS-Policy to define an AtomicTransaction policy assertion that enables a Web service to describe transactional capabilities for its operations. Here we assume that the transaction involves a transactional operation that transfers funds. Unnecessary code details are omitted for reasons of brevity and simplicity.

```
<wsdl:definitions
    targetNamespace="bank.example.com"
    xmlns:tns="bank.example.com"
    xmlns:wsdl="http://schemas.xmlsoap.org/wsdl/"
    xmlns:wsp="http://schemas.xmlsoap.org/ws/2004/09/policy"
    xmlns:wsat="http://docs.oasis-open.org/ws-tx/wsat/2006/06"
    xmlns:wsu="http://docs.oasis-open.org/wss/2004/01/
              oasis-200401-wss-wssecurity-utility-1.0.xsd">
  <wsp:Policy wsu:Id="TransactedPolicy">
    <wsat:ATAssertion wsp:optional="true"/>
          <!-- omitted assertions -->
  </wsp:Policy>
    ... ... ... ...
  <wsdl:binding name="BankBinding" type="tns:BankPortType">
      ... ... ... ...
    <wsdl:operation name="TransferFunds">
      <wsp:PolicyReference URI="#TransactedPolicy"
                            wsdl:required="true"/>

      ... ... ... ...
    </wsdl:operation>
  </wsdl:binding>
</wsdl:definitions>
```

Listing 10.6 Using Atomic Transaction

In Listing 10.6, the AtomicTransaction policy assertion is provided by a Web service defined in WSDL to enforce the transactional processing of messages associated on the particular operation to which the policy assertion applies. The policy expression

<wsp:Policy> in Listing 10.6 includes an AtomicTransaction policy assertion with the identifier TransactedPolicy to indicate that the AtomicTransaction type could be used. The <wsp:PolicyReference> construct in this listing indicates that this policy applies to the WSDL binding defined in the code snippet. It specifies that the messages of the TransferFunds operation could exhibit AtomicTransaction behaviour.

10.6.1.1 Completion protocol

This protocol is used by the application that controls the atomic transaction. The Completion protocol is used by an application to tell the coordinator to either try to commit or abort an Atomic Transaction. After the transaction has completed, a status is returned to the application.

When an application starts an atomic transaction, it establishes a coordinator that supports the WS-AtomicTransaction protocol. The application registers for this protocol and instructs the coordinator to commit or to abort the transaction after all the necessary application work has been done. The sequence of actions during this protocol is illustrated in Figure 10.20 where solid arcs signify coordinator generated actions and dashed arcs signify participant generated actions. The state transition diagram assumes that a coordinator will receive either a commit or rollback message from a participant. In this way, the application can detect whether the desired outcome is successful or not.

10.6.1.2 Durable Two-Phase Commit (2PC) protocol

This protocol is the same as the traditional 2PC used to ensure atomicity between participants. This protocol is based on the classic two-phase commit with presumed abort technique, where the default behaviour in the absence of a successful outcome is to roll

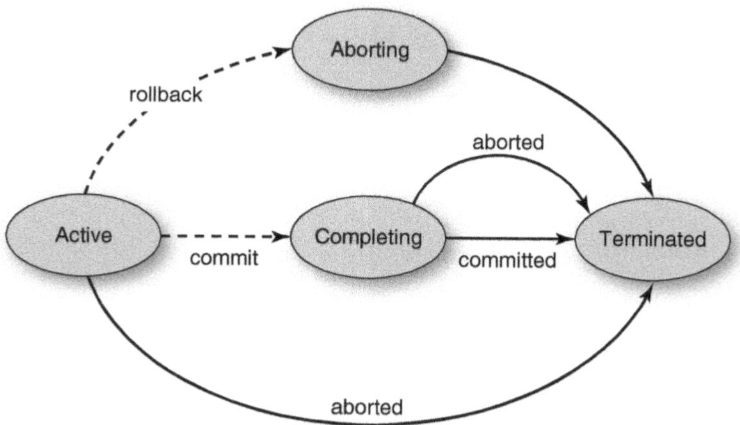

Figure 10.20 Sequence of actions of the completion protocol

back all actions in an activity. The durable 2PC is used to coordinate a group of participants that all need to reach the same decision, either a commit or an abort. After receiving a commit notification in the completion protocol, the root coordinator begins the prepare phase (phase 1) for durable 2PC participants. All participants registered for this protocol must respond with prepared or aborted notification. During the second (commit) phase, in case the coordinator has received a prepared response from the participants, it indicates a successful outcome by sending a commit notification to all registered participants. All participants then return a committed acknowledgement. Alternatively, if the coordinator has received an aborted response from one or more of the participants, it indicates a failed outcome by sending a rollback notification to all remaining participants. The participants then return aborted to acknowledge the result.

Figure 10.21 illustrates the state transitions of an Atomic Transaction with a durable phase commit protocol, and the message exchanges between coordinator and participant. As usual, solid lines indicate the coordinator generated messages, whereas dashed lines indicate the participant messages.

10.6.1.3 Volatile Two-Phase Commit (2PC) protocol

Accessing durable data storage for the duration of a transaction, as already explained, leads to hard locking of local resources and performance bottlenecks. Alternatively, operating on cached copies of data can significantly improve performance. However, volatile data on which a transaction has worked will eventually have to be written back to back end enterprise information systems such as databases, or ERP systems – where the state being managed by the applications ultimately resides – prior to this transaction committing. Supporting this requires additional coordination infrastructure. For example, to enable flushing of their updated cached state to the back end servers, participants need to be notified before 2PC begins. In the WS-AtomicTransaction specification, this is achieved by volatile 2PC.

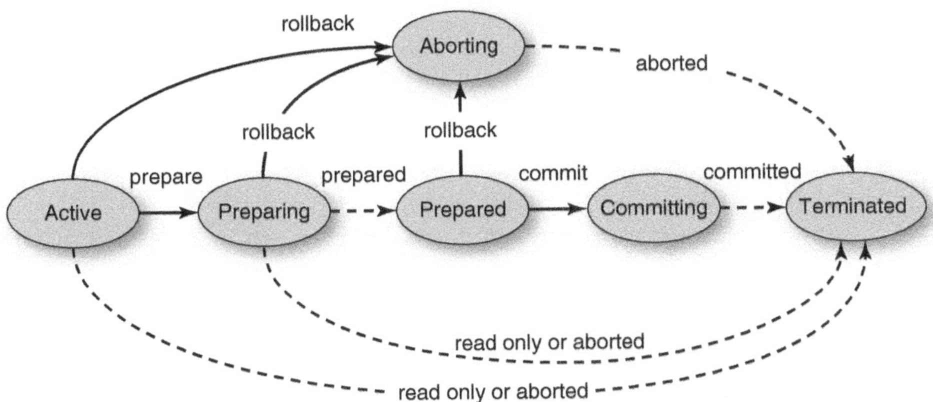

Figure 10.21 Durable two-phase commit state transitions

The volatile 2PC protocol is a variant of the 2PC protocol with many similarities to the durable 2PC with only some subtle exceptions. During phase 1, the coordinator sends a prepare message to those participants which have registered for volatile 2PC first, before sending this message to those participants registered for durable 2PC. Only when all volatile 2PC participants have voted *prepared* are prepare messages sent to participants registered for durable 2PC. During phase 2, the coordinator indicates the successful outcome, sending a commit notification to both volatile and durable participants.

Example 10.10: Succesful commit scenario with diverse coordination protocols

Figure 10.22 illustrates the sequencing of the messages at commit, for the scenario of a successful commit where three participants are involved, one for each of the above coordination protocols (completion, volatile 2PC, durable 2PC):

1. When all of the work has completed, the completion participant (i.e. the application) initiates the commit process by trying to commit. To achieve this it sends a commit message to the coordinator (step 1). The coordinator initiates the prepare phase on the volatile 2PC participant by sending it a prepare message (step 2).

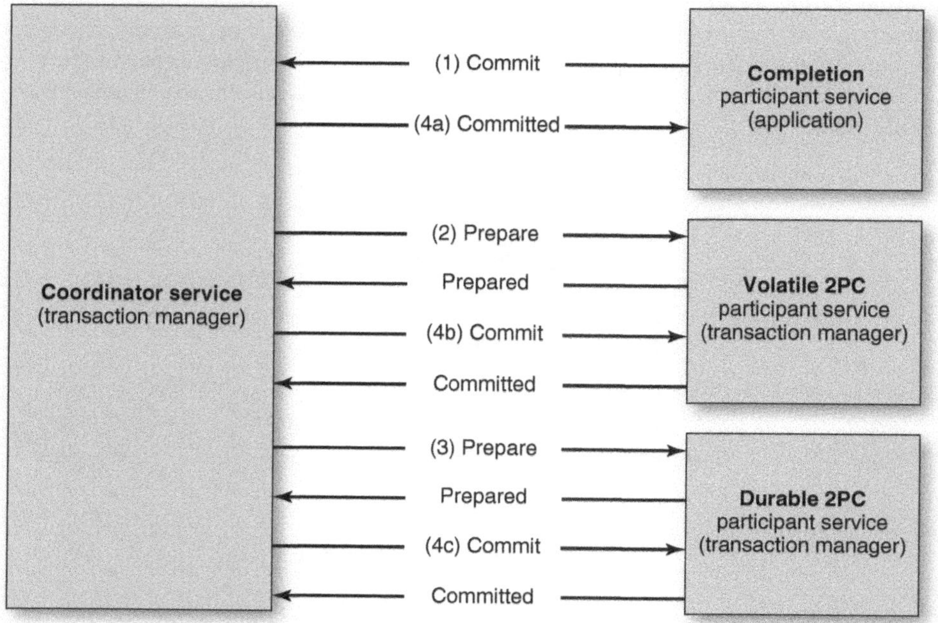

Figure 10.22 Successful commit scenario for an Atomic Transaction

Each volatile 2PC participant signals that it has successfully finished preparing by sending a prepared message.

2. The coordinator initiates the prepare phase on the volatile 2PC participant by sending a prepare message. Each volatile 2PC participant signals that it has successfully finished preparing by sending a prepared message.
3. When all prepared messages have been received from volatile 2PC participants, the root coordinator initiates the prepare phase on the durable 2PC participant by sending a prepare message (step 3). Each durable 2PC participant signals that it has successfully finished preparing by sending a prepared message.
4. When all prepared messages have been received from durable 2PC participants, the root coordinator decides to commit, sends the committed message to the completion participant (step 4a), and also sends the commit message to both the volatile 2PC and durable 2PC participants (steps 4b and 4c). It must be noted that there are no ordering constraints among messages 4a, 4b, and 4c.

In concluding the presentation of this particular coordination protocol, it is worth mentioning that the WS-AtomicTransaction protocol is superior to existing coordination protocols for traditional atomic transactions. It promotes interoperability as it is SOAP based, thus enabling its use by participants that have been developed on different platforms. It can also work together with other standards such as WS-Addressing, WS-Security and WS-Policy to express policy assertions and provide secure end-to-end operations in arbitrary network topologies [Little 2009].

10.6.2 Business activity

The WS-BusinessActivity coordination type supports transactional coordination of potentially long duration activities [Freund 2009]. These differ from atomic transactions, in that they take much longer to complete and do not require resources to be held for long periods of time. This allows many clients to reserve the same product for a specific period of time while eventually only one may obtain it (if it is the final item in the inventory). It also avoids denials of service that occur when resources are locked indefinitely. To minimise the latency of access by other potential users of the resources used by a business activity, the results of interim operations need to be realised prior to completing the overall activity. They also require that business logic be applied to handle exceptions. Participants are viewed as business tasks (scopes) that are children of the business activity for which they register. Participants may decide to leave a business activity (e.g. to delegate processing to other services), or a participant may declare its outcome before being solicited to do so.

Business activity does not maintain the full ACID transaction properties for maximum flexibility. This allows business activities to query multiple participants in order to finally select the most appropriate one and cancel the other ones. It also allows that results of completed tasks (e.g. transactions) within a business activity can be seen prior to the completion of the business activity, thereby relaxing isolation. These tasks are, in fact, tentative and, in case there is need for them to be compensated, business logic is required to make that possible.

Example 10.11: Sending a purchase order to multiple supplier services

As an example of a business activity involving multiple services, consider a manufacturer (client) service that sends a purchase order to multiple supplier services. The manufacturer service picks one of the quotes according to its standard selection criteria and instructs the other suppliers to cancel. In this case, the WS-BusinessActivity coordination protocol adds a standard structure to the application, but at the same time allows arbitrary application logic to handle the coordination. In another example, a manufacturer may issue a purchase order process, which may contain various activities that have to complete successfully but may run simultaneously (at least to some extent), such as credit checks, inventory controls, billing and shipment. The combination of WS-BusinessActivity, WS-AtomicTransaction and WS-Coordination makes sure that these tasks succeed or fail as a unit.

10.6.2.1 Business activity characteristics

Coordination protocols based on Business Activity provide added flexibility as they exhibit the following appealing characteristics:

- A business activity can be partitioned in scopes, with a scope being defined as a collection of a bounded set of operations that need to be executed on a collection of Web services that require a mutually agreed outcome to finish a task. A hierarchy of scopes can be created to finish a business activity. Nesting of scopes allows for various options. For instance, the parent can select which of its children to include in the outcome protocol thus making non-atomic results possible. Nested scopes allow:

  a business application to select which child tasks are included in the overall outcome processing. For example, a business application might solicit an estimate from a number of suppliers and choose a quote or bid based on lowest cost.

  a business application to catch an exception thrown by a child task, apply an exception handler, and continue processing even if something goes wrong. When a child completes its work, it may be associated with a compensation that is registered with the parent activity.

- A business activity defines a consensus group that allows the relaxation of atomicity based on business level decisions. Additionally, parents can catch exceptions thrown by their children's scope, apply an exception handler and continue doing processing. The state of the business activity is durably saved between steps in order to reach a desired goal, even if exceptions occur.
- The business activity coordination protocols allow a participant task within a business activity to specify its outcome directly without waiting for solicitation.
- The business activity coordination protocols allow participants in a coordinated business activity to perform *tentative* operations as a normal part of the activity. The

result of such tentative operations may become visible before the activity is complete and may require business logic to run in the event that the operation needs to be compensated. Such a feature is critical when the joint work of a business activity requires many operations performed by independent services over a long period of time.

The participants of a business activity can be coordinated in an all-or-nothing fashion by the coordinator. The coordinator in a business activity is not as restricted as the coordinator in an atomic transaction. What the behaviour of the coordinator will be is determined by the application driving the activity. A participant, after registering in the business activity, is allowed to leave the activity at any point in time during the transaction. This is opposite to how an atomic transaction handles its participants. Any participant once registered in an atomic transaction coordination type must confirm with the other participants but, if it chooses to cancel, it forces other participants also to cancel the task.

As with atomic transactions, WS-BusinessActivity defines two coordination protocols: Business Agreement with Participant Completion and Business Agreement with Coordinator Completion, which we examine in the forthcoming subsections. However, unlike the WS-AtomicTransaction protocol that is driven from the coordinator down to participants, this protocol is driven much more from the participants upwards.

10.6.2.2 Business agreement with participant completion protocol

The state diagram in Figure 10.23 illustrates the state transitions of a WS-BusinessActivity with Participant Completion protocol and the message exchanges between coordinator and participant. The states in Figure 10.23 reflect the view an individual participant or

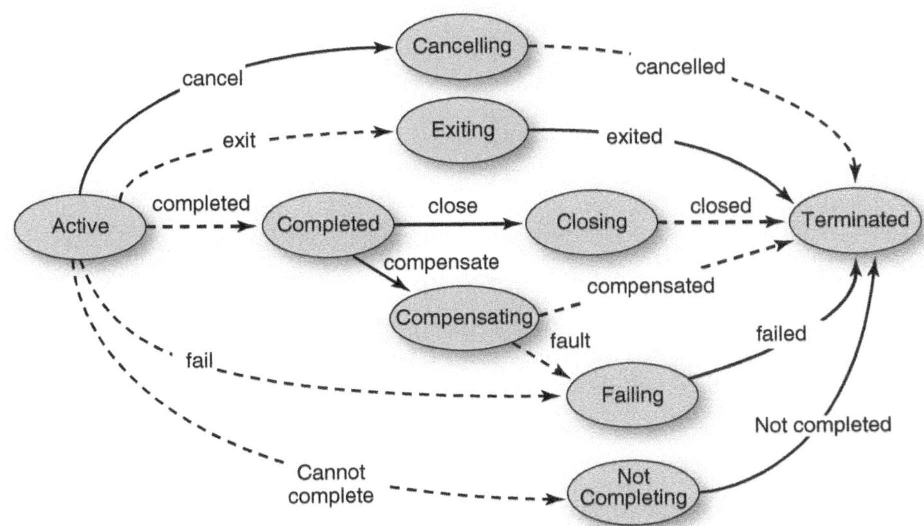

Figure 10.23 State transitions for business agreement with participant completion protocol

coordinator has of its state in the protocol at a given point in time. As usual, solid lines indicate the coordinator generated messages, whereas dashed lines indicate the participant messages.

With this protocol, a participant (child) activity is initially created in the active state. If the participant task finishes and wishes to be involved in the business activity further, then it must be in a position to compensate for the work it has performed. In this case, it sends a completed message to the coordinator and waits to receive the final outcome of the business activity from the coordinator. This outcome will be either a close message, meaning the business activity has completed successfully, or a compensate message indicating that the coordinator activity requires that the participant reverses the effects of its work. Alternatively, if a participant activity finishes the work it was created to do and decides it no longer needs to participate within the scope of the WS-BusinessActivity, then the participant can unilaterally send an exited message to the coordinator, which is equivalent to the participant resigning from the Web service transaction.

10.6.2.3 Business agreement with coordinator completion protocol

This protocol is identical to the Business Agreement with Participant Completion protocol with the exception that the participant cannot unilaterally decide to end its participation in the business activity, even if it can be compensated. Rather the participant task relies on the coordinator to inform it when it has received all requests for it to perform work. To accomplish this, the coordinator sends the complete message to the participant. The participant then acts in a similar fashion as it does in the Business Agreement with Participant Completion protocol.

Example 10.12: Order processing service asking for quotes from multiple supplier services

Figure 10.24 clarifies several of the points discussed above. This figure illustrates an order processing application in which a manufacturer service asks for quotes from three supplier services under the Business Agreement with Participant Completion protocol and chooses the best deal.

The steps in the Business Agreement with Participant Completion protocol interaction can be described as follows:

1. The manufacturer service (`coordinator`) sends each seller a `PurchaseOrder` message with a `CoordinationContext` header for this business activity. These messages can all be sent simultaneously.
2. All three suppliers (participants) register for the Business Agreement with Participant Completion protocol.
3. From this point onwards, each of the three suppliers has different flows, such as:
   a. Supplier 1 cannot make a quote. It notifies the manufacturer service using the coordination protocol `Fail` notification message.

b. Suppliers 2 and 3 can make a quote. They each notify the manufacturer service, using the coordination protocol `Completed` notification message along with price information.

4. After looking at the quotes from both suppliers, the manufacturer chooses Supplier 2. It then notifies:

   a. Supplier 2 with the coordination protocol `Close` message (to indicate success).

   b. Supplier 3 with the coordination protocol `Compensate` message.

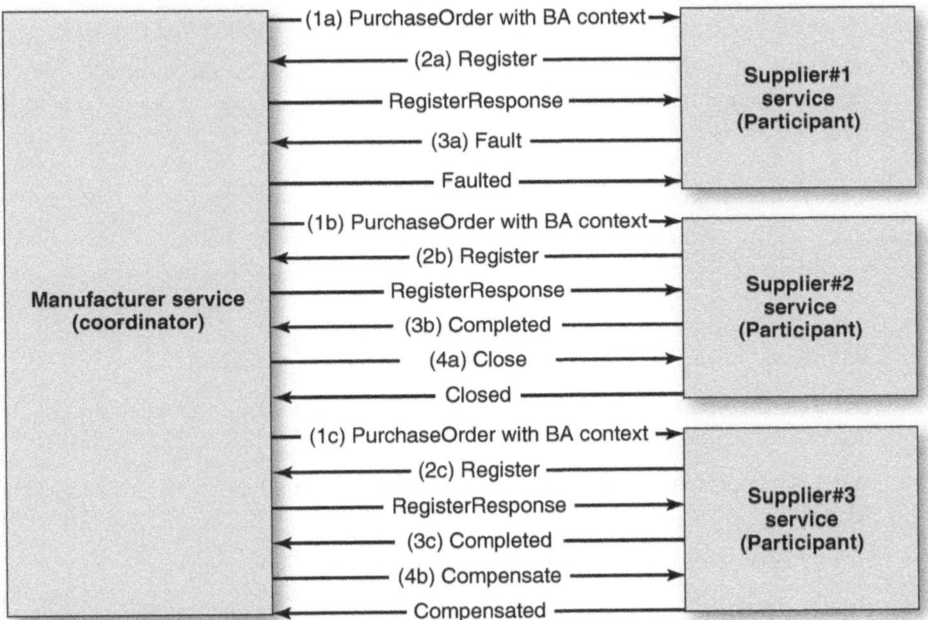

Figure 10.24 Business Activity protocol for order processing

10.7 Summary of learning objectives

The concept of a Web service transaction is central to SOA based applications, as it defines a shared view of messages exchanged between Web services from multiple organisations for the purpose of completing a business process. Web service transactions retain the driving ambition of consistency but also provide the ability to relax the classical isolation requirement of ACID transactions. To achieve their objective, Web service transactions comprise two different types of transactional activities:

- atomic actions (or short-lived transactions);
- flexible long duration activities.

At present a trio of standard specifications are designed to support Web service transactions. These are WS-Coordination, WS-AtomicTransaction and WS-BusinessActivity. These transaction specifications encompass a Web service transaction model and coordination protocols, and support two types of transaction protocols in which:

- short-lived atomic transactions and simple agreement coordination protocols are provided for closely coupled systems that desire all-or-nothing outcomes;
- transactional coordination is provided for potentially long duration activities so that they take much longer to complete and do not require resources to be held for long periods of time.

Review questions

- What is a transaction and what are its major properties? What are distributed transactions and how do they differ from centralised transactions?
- Describe the main building blocks of a distributed transaction architecture involving local and global transactions.
- What is a coordinator and what are subordinate coordinators and (transaction) participants?
- Briefly describe the two-phase commit protocol. What is its purpose?
- Briefly describe the concept of closed nested transactions and the two-phase commit protocol for nested transactions.
- What are open nested transactions and what are long running activities?
- Compare closed nested with open nested transactions.
- Why are long running activities important for Web service transactions? Describe the two types of Web service transactions and discuss their relative merits.
- What is interposition and why is it important for Web services?
- What are the main component services of WS-Coordination and how does it relate to the WS-AtomicTransaction and WS-BusinesActivity standards?
- Describe the two types of Web service coordination/transaction protocols.
- Why are Business Activities required for a transactional SOA based application? What do they provide in excess of atomic transactions?

Exercises

10.1. Develop a simple sequence diagram illustrating the WS-Coordination flow for an application involving a purchase order service that forwards orders for products and needs to make several Web service calls to some of its suppliers to order products, and a coordinator service that acts as both activation and registration service on behalf of WS-Coordination. Assume that the purchase order service invokes an operation called `checkInventory()` to accomplish its task.

10.2. Develop a simple sequence diagram illustrating the WS-Coordination flow for an application involving a sales service that receives orders for products and wishes to query an inventory service that provides inventory information from a warehouse about the availability of products, a shipping service that schedules shipments, and a coordinator service that acts as both activation and registration service on behalf of WS-Coordination.

10.3. Modify the solution to Exercise 10.2 to include durable 2PC. If all the products are available the activity should commit, otherwise the entire activity should roll back. Again draw a sequence diagram and use message exchanges defined in specifications, such as WS-Coordination and WS-AtomicTransaction, to show how message s are exchanged (excluding faults) between the initiator and participant.

10.4. Replace the WS-AtomicTransaction protocol by a WS-BusinessActivity protocol. The solution should include a purchase order service (acting on behalf of a customer), a coordination service associated with the purchase order service and, finally, a sales service (acting on behalf of a supplier). Assume that the buyer wants to buy three specific products and wants to know if the supplier can provide all these three products. If the supplier has no problem supplying all three products, the distributor will confirm the order. If there are problems with delivery of any of the three products, the buyer would like to reconsider the entire purchase activity. For example, the buyer may want to contact some other supplier to ask about the availability of the three items and may eventually buy only one product from the supplier in question. To solve this exercise you should take into account that the WS-BusinessActivity is nested. This means that the overall purchase activity can be considered as a parent activity, while there can be a number of child activities for this activity, where each child represents the purchase of a single product. Notice that each child activity may further consist of one or more WS-AtomicTransactions. Demonstrate the actual exchange of messages that accomplishes this activity using WS-Coordination and WS-BusinessActivity messages.

10.5. Extend the solution to Exercise 10.1 by assuming that the application uses durable 2PC and involves one initiator (purchase order) and a single participant (supplier). Again draw a sequence diagram and use message exchanges defined in specifications, such as WS-Coordination and WS-AtomicTransaction, to show how messages are exchanged (excluding faults) between the initiator and participant.

10.6. Extend the solution to Exercise 10.3 assuming that there is a rollback initiated by the participant (supplier service).

PART VI

SOA security and policies

CHAPTER 11

Securing SOA and Web services

Learning objectives

With SOA applications security becomes a major concern as Web services use the insecure Internet for mission critical transactions. Ensuring the integrity, confidentiality and security of Web services through the application of a comprehensive security model is therefore critical, for both organisations and their customers.

In this chapter we shall describe a comprehensive security model for Web services. This security model relies on the integration of currently available security mechanisms with the security requirements of SOA applications, which require a unified technological (secure messaging) and business (policy and trust) approach.

After completing this chapter you will understand the following key concepts:

- Common security threats for Web services and countermeasures.
- Network and application level security mechanisms.
- Architectural approaches to security.
- XML security services and standards such as XML Encryption, XML Signature, and SAML.
- Use cases for Web services security.
- Use of WS-Security to develop SOA based solutions.
- The family of WS-Security standards.

Chapter preview

SOA applications, because of their nature (loosely coupled connections) and their use of open access, add a new dimension to the traditional security landscape. This chapter provides a thorough understanding of security techniques appropriate for use in SOA applications without assuming any prior familiarity with security topics. We shall first provide a brief overview of network level security and then take a close look at application security mechanisms, as these are the core elements of Web service security. Following this, we shall explain how to implement and architect security in enterprises that use SOA, by examining standards such as XML Encryption, XML Signature, SAML and XACML. Finally, we shall concentrate on WS-Security, security policies and explain how to manage trust and federated identities in SOAs.

11.1 SOA and Web service security considerations

A major characteristic of services in SOA is that they are designed to be combined with each other in unanticipated ways. The current deployment of Web service technology is a promising early initiative in this direction. However, before SOAs can support mission critical, long lived Web service transactions, serious security requirements must be addressed. Enterprises that undertake Web service integration initiatives must place additional reliance on electronic means for protecting and safeguarding business critical information, transactions and communications.

In the physical world enterprises rely on conventional security measures to protect and safeguard confidential corporate information. Traditional enterprise security has focused almost entirely on keeping intruders out, by using tools such as firewalls and content filters. Firewalls act as a secure interface between a private, trusted enterprise network and external untrusted networks. A firewall can be used to control access to and from the enterprise network and uses content filters to permit/deny packet flow on the basis of the origin and destination of the packet's addresses and ports. This includes access to resources such as application services and specific hosts. When properly configured, to implement a judicious security policy, firewalls can protect an enterprise network from intrusion and compromise.

Traditionally, distributed computing security was modelled by islands of security, which describe systems and users on isolated networks or sub-networks. The network acts as an island, with its own perimeter security, but users within the network were considered to be trusted, whereas users outside the network were considered as untrusted. As a result of this, until recently enterprises have controlled and managed access to resources by building authorisation and authentication into every application that transcended enterprise boundaries. This piecemeal approach is not only time consuming but also error prone, and expensive to build and maintain. Eventually, this technique becomes unsustainable as an enterprise's e-Business portfolio grows, and as on line interactions between enterprises become more complex.

The *trusted* versus *untrusted* dichotomy breaks down in an SOA model, because applications can access *spontaneously* services located on systems across one or more enterprises. In an interface driven environment, application functionality is much more exposed compared to traditional, stove-piped applications. The concept of trusted groups no longer has meaning. Instead, enterprises must institute policies that apply to their entire enterprise network (including participants invited from outside), and administer that security in a tiered or hierarchical fashion [Bloomberg 2004]. What we require is a comprehensive Web service security solution that is easily managed and satisfies a demanding set of application and developer security requirements; and provides capabilities such as performance, speed of deployment and scalability, as well as the flexibility to accommodate evolving technologies such as wireless services.

Web service integration initiatives are forcing enterprises to move away from private communication networks to open public networks, such as the Internet, where they need to open their private network applications and information assets to customers, suppliers and business partners. This means letting customers and business partners into the private enterprise network, essentially through the firewall, but in a selective and controlled manner, so that they access only applications permitted to them. As a result, existing network infrastructures, e.g. routers, firewalls and load balancers, that operate at the network layer rather than at the application layer, are entirely unable to provide the application layer security that Web services require. This means a careful migration from network level to application level security is required to be able to protect business critical information, transactions and communication with a large number of trading partners, customers and suppliers, exchanged over insecure networks such as the Internet.

Web service security involves the complex interaction of multiple computer environments, communication protocols, policies and procedures. These must all be considered when implementing a coherent, consistent approach to Web service security. Web service security marks a departure from traditional security, as it poses new security requirements in connection with access (authentication, authorisation), confidentiality, non-repudiation, and integrity of information. These are the issues that will be of concern to us throughout this chapter. However, before we introduce and explain these topics it is important to understand what kind of security threats Web services face.

11.1.1 Security threats for Web services

The objective of Web services is to expose standardised interfaces to new and existing applications to allow the construction of applications and business processes that span organisational networks. Service aggregation makes it easy to create new value added services, e.g. an application that enables resellers to check the availability and pricing of a manufacturer's products, place orders, and track order status on line. Unfortunately, it also introduces a new set of security risks – as no previous technology has created this level of exposure to critical business applications. One major concern is that Web services are designed to penetrate firewalls, evading their usefulness at the application layer. Web services are designed to go through network firewalls, e.g. through port 80, and provide only rudimentary content inspection.

Application level security is required to protect against XML and Web service related security threats. While network firewalls continue to be absolutely essential to provide IP based access control and network level protection, a service (or XML) firewall is required to protect Web services. To achieve this, service firewalls must understand who the requesters are, what information is being requested, and what specific services are being requested. In addition, they must be able to intercept incoming XML traffic and take policy based actions based on the content of that traffic. This type of functionality is a prerequisite to providing the necessary security to protect Web services and SOA environments.

An additional security concern is that Web services are standardised and self describing. Given that Web service interfaces are standardised, they can be attacked in consistent ways. Intruders can more easily gain access to a standardised interface than a proprietary interface, since more is known about the standardised interface. Furthermore, SOAP messages provide information and structure for each message. A packaged application, for instance, may have a large number of critical operations exposed, all accessible through port 80. In addition, attackers have more information available to them. Since WSDL specifications and UDDI entries are self describing, they can provide detailed information that enables an intruder to gain entry to mission critical applications. WSDL documents provide significant information about each Web service, including where the service is located, how to access it, what kind of information to send to it, and what type of information a developer should expect to receive. This provides significant information to a potential intruder inappropriately to access the service. Again this points to a migration from network level security to application level security.

The fact that SOA based applications must operate at the application layer of the OSI stack poses a challenge, because all data specific network traffic appears to be the same to lower level devices. Current network and transport security layer solutions use conventional mechanisms such as firewalls, routers, proxies, load balancing, restricting access to known IP addresses, and use of Secure Socket Layer to secure Web transactions independent of the programming of Web service applications. However, such solutions are inadequate as they are simply network aware. Instead, they must be able to be XML application aware.

Application level security plays a pivotal role in Web service applications and involves inspecting the content of the network traffic, making authentication and authorisation decisions for that content, as well as verifying the individual parts of XML transactions and performing activities as security policies dictate. Application layer security also addresses confidentiality and privacy – using encryption to protect messages, guarantee message integrity, and provide audit functionality. In essence, Web service security presents many similarities to application security with distributed technologies and is based on an understanding of the:

- resources being managed and protected by an application;
- vulnerabilities relevant to the application's base technology;
- vulnerabilities relevant to the application's specific logic; and
- techniques that can be used to mitigate these risks.

To address Web service security concerns the WS-I Basic Security Profile [McIntosh 2007] has identified several security threats and challenges for Web services, as well as countermeasures (technologies and protocols) used to mitigate each threat. Below, we group the threats identified by the WS-I Basic Security Profile into four broad categories to illustrate some of the most frequent security concerns that come up with Web services:

- *Unauthorized access:* Information within the message is viewable by unintended and unauthorised participants, e.g. an authorised party obtains a credit card number.
- *Unauthorized alteration of messages:* These threats affect message integrity, whereby an attacker may modify parts (or the whole) message. Inserting, removing, or otherwise modifying information, created by the originator of the information and mistaken by the receiver as being the originator's intention, can alter message information. For example, an attacker may delete part of a message, or modify part of a message, or insert extra information into a message. This broad category may include: attachment alteration, replay attacks (signed messages are intercepted and sent back to a targeted site), session hijacking, forged claims and falsified messages.
- *Man in the middle:* In this kind of assault it is possible for an attacker to compromise a SOAP intermediary and then intercept messages between the Web service requester and the ultimate receiver. The original parties will think that they are communicating with each other. The attacker may just have access to the messages or may modify them. Threats known as *routing detours* comprise also a form of a *man-in-the-middle* attack which compromises routing information. Routing information (whether in the HTTP headers or in WS-Routing headers) can be modified en route to direct sensitive messages to an outside location. Traces of the routing can be removed from the message so that the receiving application does not realise that a routing detour has occurred.
- *Denial-of-service attacks:* Here the objective is to render target systems inaccessible by legitimate users. A flood of plain messages, or messages with large numbers of encrypted elements or signed elements, may cause system resources to be tied up and service levels to be affected. This can cause severe disruption to a system.

All the above security threats point out that securing open, loosely coupled systems requires a sophisticated security approach to support distributed clients (applications) and systems that may have different policies and possibly different security mechanisms. At the same time, because Web services have a high degree of interaction with varied clients, it is important to keep security measures from being overly intrusive and maintain the ease of use of a service.

A service needs to promote its interoperability features and make its security requirements and policies known to its clients. As a result, to ensure the appropriate security to the network of Web services a fundamental requirement is to be able to operate on the security context of applications that invoke services. *Security context* is a set of information regarding the use of services on behalf of an application (or user), including the rules and policies that apply to the application, as well as information about the business process or transaction that the application is currently participating in. When the application is separated from the service, that context is lost.

11.1.2 Security countermeasures

Although not all Web service threats can be eliminated, there are many circumstances where exposure can be reduced to an acceptable level through the use of application security. Application security applies to networked (distributed) applications and platforms, such as J2EE, and contains six basic requirements, expressed in terms of the messages exchanged between parties [Pilz 2003]. Such messages include any kind of communication between the sender (the party who wishes to access a network accessible application) and the recipient (the application itself). The six requirements for application level security include authentication, authorisation, message integrity, confidentiality, operational defense and non-repudiation. These countermeasures are addressed in Section 11.3, where we discuss application level solutions for networked applications and distributed platforms, and in Section 11.6 where we describe application level solutions for Web service based SOA applications.

In the next section we take a closer look at a variety of technology based solutions that address network level security concerns.

11.2 Network level security mechanisms

Network level security refers to the protection of the process by which data items are communicated from a network to an end system [Ford 1997]. In particular, this topic excludes any coverage of what happens within the end system – both client and server systems. Network level security incorporates embedded encryption functionality within network devices or operating systems, utilising Internet Protocol Security (IPSec). Network level solutions are usually designed to terminate the secure connections at the corporate firewall. Enterprises employing network level security solutions usually rely on two main technologies to protect their networks: firewalls and vulnerability assessment.

11.2.1 Firewalls

A *firewall* is a network security infrastructure placed between networks to logically separate and protect the privacy and integrity of business communications across these networks, and to safeguard against malicious use. Firewalls are built between an organisation's internal network and the Internet backbone and help define the network perimeter where an enterprise meets the Internet.

Firewalls examine message traffic coming into and leaving an organisation and block all access to local networks except authorised messages. They identify incoming traffic by name, IP address, application and so on. This information is checked against the access rules that have been programmed into the firewall system. Because firewalls determine what traffic is allowed to pass into an enterprise from the Internet, they are the essential first line of defence against intruders. A firewall that is a perfect brick wall admits no outside traffic and ensures perfect security for an enterprise. This is, however, hardly practical for Web applications because it isolates the company from its customers and partners. Instead, firewalls can be used to block unwanted protocols by blocking the TCP ports that they use, while leaving Web ports, i.e. ports 80 and 443 for SSL, open for Web browsing purposes. This has the effect of bypassing firewalls without compromising security, as firewalls continue to guard against lower layers of communication. Thus only authorised traffic, as defined by the local security policy, will be allowed to pass a firewall, while any unauthorised communication between the internal and the external network is prevented.

Functions typically provided by a firewall include [Ford 1997]:

- Limiting the set of applications for which traffic can enter the internal network from the Internet, and limiting the internal addresses to which traffic for different applications can go.
- Authenticating the sources of incoming traffic.
- Limiting the ability of internal enterprise networks and systems to establish connections to the external Internet, on the basis of the application used and other relevant information.
- Acting as a security gateway and encrypting and/or integrity checking all traffic over the Internet backbone to or from some other security gateway. Such a continuation is known as a virtual private network (VPN). VPNs allow organisations to use their corporate networks and the Internet as a wide area network to achieve secure connectivity with their branches, suppliers, customers and remote users.

11.2.1.1 Firewall architectures

The level of protection that any firewall is able to provide, in securing a private network when connected to the Internet, is directly related to the architecture(s) chosen for the firewall. Firewall architectures rely on information generated by protocols that function at various layers of the OSI model, see Section 2.1.1.1. The higher up in the OSI layer at which a firewall architecture examines IP packets, the greater the level of protection the architecture provides, as more information is available upon which to base security related decisions.

There are three general classes of firewall architectures: packet filtering, circuit and application proxies and stateful inspection. We shall examine these in turn.

IP packet filtering. Packet filtering firewalls are the oldest firewall architectures. A filtering firewall works at the network level (see Figure 11.1). This type of firewall employs a filtering process by examining individual IP packets. As packets arrive they are filtered by their type, source address, destination address and port information (contained in each IP packet).

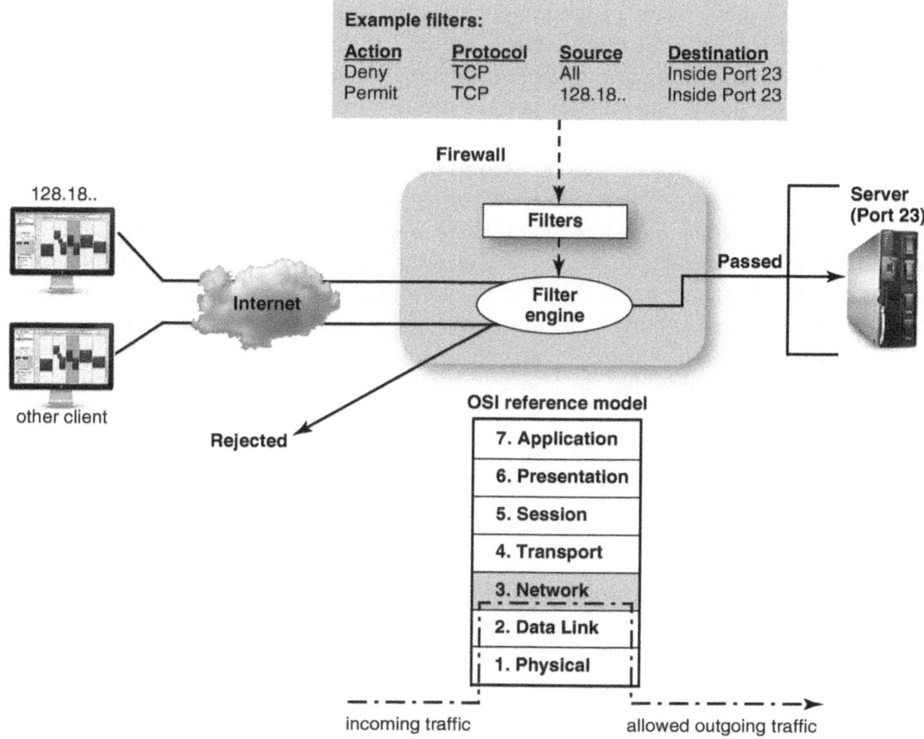

Figure 11.1 Packet filtering firewall

There are two types of packet filtering firewalls: static and stateful. A *static packet filter firewall* examines data in the IP header and the TCP header and compares this information against pre-specified packet filtering (access) rules that dictate whether the filtering firewall should deny or permit packets to pass the firewall. IP header information allows specifying packet filtering rules that deny or permit packets to and from a specific IP address, or range of IP addresses, as illustrated in Figure 11.1.

TCP header information allows the specification of service specific rules, i.e. allow or deny packets to or from ports related to specific services. For example, with a static packet filter the network administrator may write rules that allow certain services, such as HTTP from any IP address, to view the Web pages on a protected Web server, while blocking other IP addresses from using the HTTP service and viewing the Web pages. The *stateful packet filter firewall* is the next step in the evolution of the static packet filter. This type of firewall inspects packets in isolation (as its static counterpart does), as it maintains state information on connections, and tracks open, valid connections without reprocessing the access rule set; and can implement complex policies. The typical stateful packet filter is aware of the difference between a new and an established connection. As checks for new versus established connections are performed at the kernel level, substantial performance increase over a static packet filter is observed.

IP filtering is performed usually by a process within the operating system kernel of a router for performance purposes. If multiple firewalls are used, the first may mark certain packets for more exhaustive examination by a later firewall, allowing only *clean* packets to proceed. For example, a network administrator could configure a packet filter firewall to disallow FTP traffic between two networks, while allowing HTTP and SMTP traffic between the two, further refining the granularity of control on protected traffic between sites.

The main advantages of packet filter firewalls are that they are fairly easy to implement and they are transparent to the end users, unlike some of the other firewall methods. However, even though packet filters can be easy to implement, they can prove difficult to configure properly, particularly if a large number of rules have to be generated to handle a wide variety of application traffic and users. One of the main deficiencies is that packet filters are based on IP addresses, not authenticated user identification. Packet filtering also provides little defence against man-in-the-middle attacks and no defence against forged IP addresses. Additional limitations include lack of packet payload awareness, lack of state awareness, and susceptibility to application layer attacks.

Circuit level gateway. The circuit level gateway (circuit proxy) is an extension of a packet filter that performs basic packet filter operations and then adds verification of proper handshaking and verification of the legitimacy of the sequence numbers used in establishing the connection. This firewall enables users to utilise a proxy to communicate with secure systems, hiding valuable data and servers from potential attackers.

The proxy accepts a connection from the other side and, if the connection is permitted, makes a second connection to the destination host on the other side. The client attempting the connection is never directly connected to the destination. Because proxies can act on different types of traffic or packets from different applications, a proxy firewall (or proxy server, as it is often called) is usually designed to use proxy agents, in which an agent is programmed to handle one specific type of transfer, e.g. TCP traffic or FTP traffic. The more types of traffic that need to pass through the proxy, the more proxy agents need to be loaded and running on the proxy server.

Circuit level gateways focus on the TCP/IP layers, using the network IP connection as a proxy. As shown in Figure 11.2 the circuit level gateway operates at the session layer (OSI Layer 5). The circuit level gateway applies security mechanisms when a TCP or User Datagram Protocol (UDP) connection is established. In particular, it examines and validates TCP and UDP sessions before opening a connection, or circuit, through the firewall. Outbound connections are passed based on policy, and inbound connections are blocked. Management control is based primarily on port addresses. A circuit proxy is typically installed between an enterprise's network router and the Internet, communicating with the Internet on behalf of the enterprise network. Real network addresses can be hidden because only the address of the proxy is transmitted on the Internet.

Once a circuit level gateway establishes a connection, any application can run across that connection because a circuit level gateway filters packets only at the session and network layers of the OSI model. A circuit level gateway cannot examine the application data content of the packets it relays between a trusted network and an untrusted network. This can make the circuit proxy more efficient than an application proxy, which examines application data, but may compromise security. Another serious drawback of the circuit proxy is the lack of application protocol checking. For example, if two cooperating users

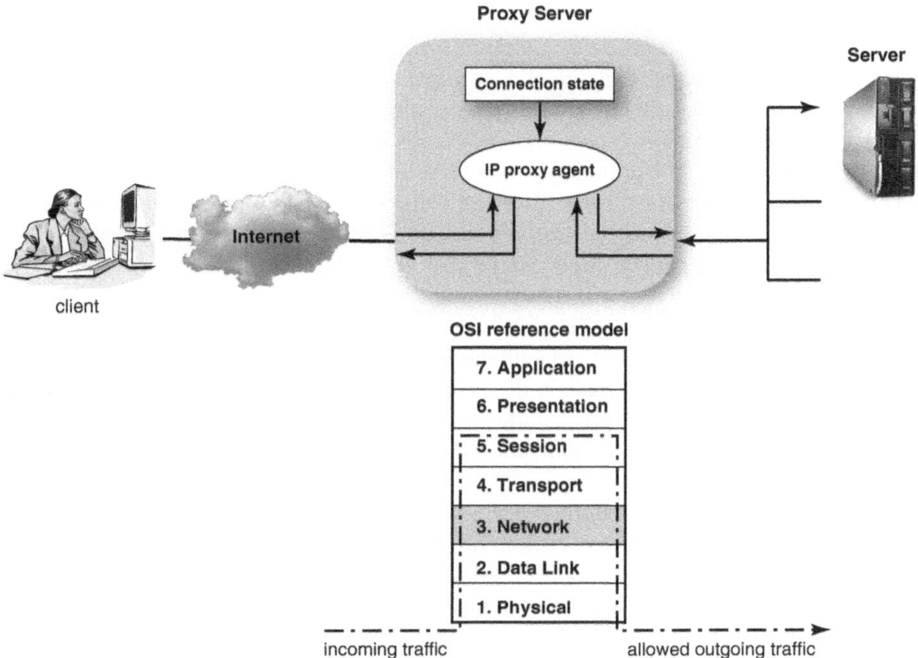

Figure 11.2 Circuit level gateway

use an approved port number to run an unapproved application, a circuit relay will not detect the violation. Finally, circuit proxies are slower than packet filters because they must reconstruct the IP header to each packet to its correct destination.

Application level gateway. Packet filters and circuit gateways look exclusively at some of the lower layers of the OSI model. Better, more secure firewalls can be designed if they examine all layers of the OSI model simultaneously. This principle led to the creation of application level gateways.

Application specific proxies check each packet that passes through the gateway, verifying the contents of the packet up through the application layer (Layer 7) of the OSI model. These proxies can filter on particular information or specific individual commands in the application protocols that the proxies are designed to copy, forward and filter.

Like a circuit level gateway, an application level gateway intercepts incoming and outgoing packets, runs proxies that copy and forward information across the gateway, and functions as a proxy server, preventing any direct connection between a trusted server or client and an untrusted host. The proxies that an application level gateway runs (Figure 11.3) often differ in two important ways from the circuit level gateway: the proxies are application specific and examine the entire packet and can filter packets at the application layer of the OSI model.

The application level gateway runs proxies that examine and filter individual packets, rather than simply copying them and recklessly forwarding them across the gateway.

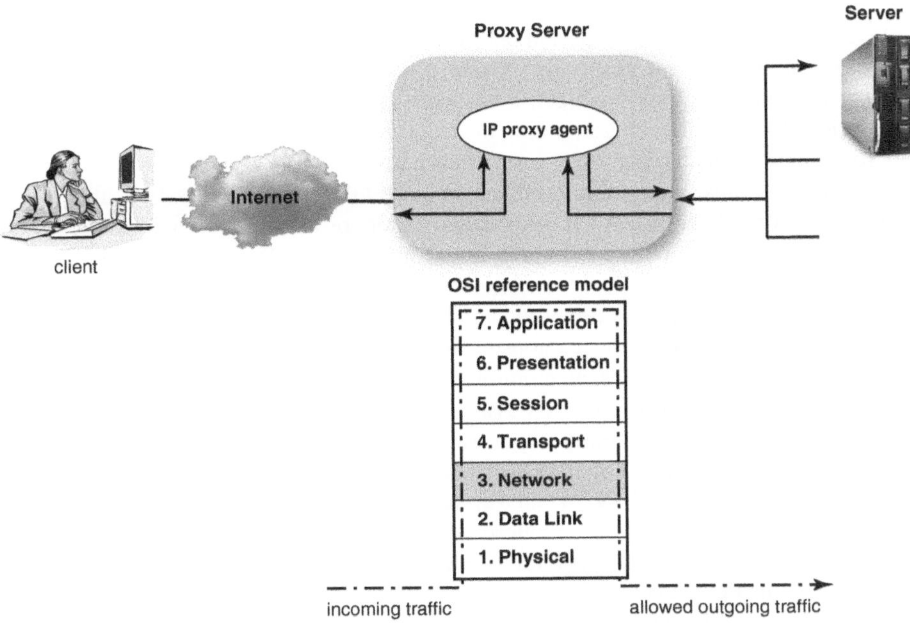

Figure 11.3 Application level proxy server

Unlike the circuit gateway, the application level gateway accepts only packets generated by services that they are designed to copy, forward and filter. For example, only an HTTP proxy can copy, forward and filter HTTP traffic. If a network relies only on an application level gateway, incoming and outgoing packets cannot access services for which there exists no proxy. All other services would be blocked.

Because application proxies operate as one-to-one proxies for a specific application, a proxy agent needs to be installed for every IP Service (HTTP/HTML, FTP, SMTP and so on) to which an enterprise wants to control access. This leads to two of the disadvantages of application proxies: a lag usually exists between the introduction of new IP services and the availability of appropriate proxy agents; and the application proxy requires more processing of the packets, leading to lower performance.

One important differentiating feature of application proxies is their capability to identify users and applications. This identification can enable more secure user authentication, because digital certificates or other secure token based methods can be used for identifying and authenticating use.

11.2.2 Intrusion detection systems and vulnerability assessment

One possible technology for network protection is *Intrusion Detection Systems* (abbreviated as IDS). An IDS is a defence system that detects and responds to hostile activities targeted at computing and networking resources. IDS tools are capable of distinguishing between insider attacks, originating from inside the organisation (coming from its own employees or customers), and external ones (attacks and the threat posed by hackers). One key feature of IDS is their ability to provide a view of unusual activity and issue alerts notifying administrators and/or block a suspected connection. With an IDS solution, an organisation discovers hacking attempts or actual break-ins by analysing its networks or hosts for inappropriate data or other anomalous activity.

IDS solutions raise alerts that an attack may be taking place. However, this is inadequate for SOA applications. What is needed is a more proactive approach that determines susceptibility to attacks before networks are compromised. This is provided by *vulnerability assessment.*

Vulnerability assessment is a methodical approach to identifying and prioritising vulnerabilities, enabling enterprises to non-intrusively test their networks from the *hacker's perspective.* Vulnerability assessment automatically identifies vulnerabilities and network misconfigurations. It identifies rogue devices, including wireless and VPN access points; detects and prioritises vulnerability exposures; validates firewall and IDS configurations; and provides remedies for known vulnerabilities. Vulnerability assessment works hand in hand with firewalls and IDS. When vulnerability assessment and IDS are combined, vulnerability assessment enables an enterprise to identify and close obvious holes so that the IDS produces a manageable volume of alerts. Vulnerability assessment also works in conjunction with firewalls continuously and seamlessly to monitor for vulnerabilities that may have inadvertently been introduced by firewall policy changes.

11.2.3 Securing network communications

Automated business processes and transactions using Web applications must flow over the public Internet. They, therefore, involve a large number of routers and servers through which the transaction packets flow. This situation is very different from a private network where dedicated communication lines are established between communicating parties. On unsecured networks, such as TCP/IP, there is a concern for both the sender and the receiver about the security of messages exchanged over the network. A number of technologies are available to protect the security of Internet communications, the most basic of which is message encryption.

Cryptography enables the user to encrypt and decrypt messages, allowing only authorised persons to read them. Both processes require a key, to transform the original text (called *plain text*) into a coded message (called *cipher text*) and back. *Encryption* is a process where the plain text is placed into a codified algorithm with an encryption key to transform the plain text into cipher text. The encryption key is used in the algorithmic formula to scramble the information in question in such a way that it could not easily be descrambled without knowledge of the secret encryption key. *Decryption,* on the other hand, is the reverse of encryption with the cipher text as input and the plain text as output. The function involves both an algorithm and a decryption key.

The security functions enabled by cryptography address four dimensions of the application level security requirements: authentication, confidentiality, message integrity and non-repudiation. There are currently three main cryptographic techniques that are used to protect the security of Internet communications and which we examine in this section. These are symmetric encryption or secret-key cryptography, asymmetric encryption or public-key cryptography, digital certificates and signatures, and are described briefly in the following.

11.2.3.1 Symmetric encryption

Symmetric-key encryption, also called *shared-key encryption* or *secret-key cryptography,* uses a single key that both the sender and recipient possess. This is shown in Figure 11.4. The term symmetric refers to the fact that the same key is used for both encryption and decryption. This key is called a *secret key* (also referred to as a symmetric or shared key).

Symmetric-key encryption is an efficient method for encrypting large amounts of data. Many algorithms exist for symmetric-key encryption, but all have the same purpose – the reversible transformation of plain text into cipher text. Cipher text is scrambled using an encryption key and is meaningless to anyone who does not have the decryption key. Deciphering is accomplished by retracing the key's algorithms in reverse order. Because symmetric key cryptography uses the same key for both encryption and decryption, the security of this process depends on no unauthorised person obtaining the symmetric key.

The advantage of symmetric encryption is that it is easily and quickly implemented. If the key is to be used only a few times, it works very effectively because there are only a limited number of previous messages with which to compare a new cipher text. The disadvantage is that every pair or group of users needs its own key – otherwise everyone

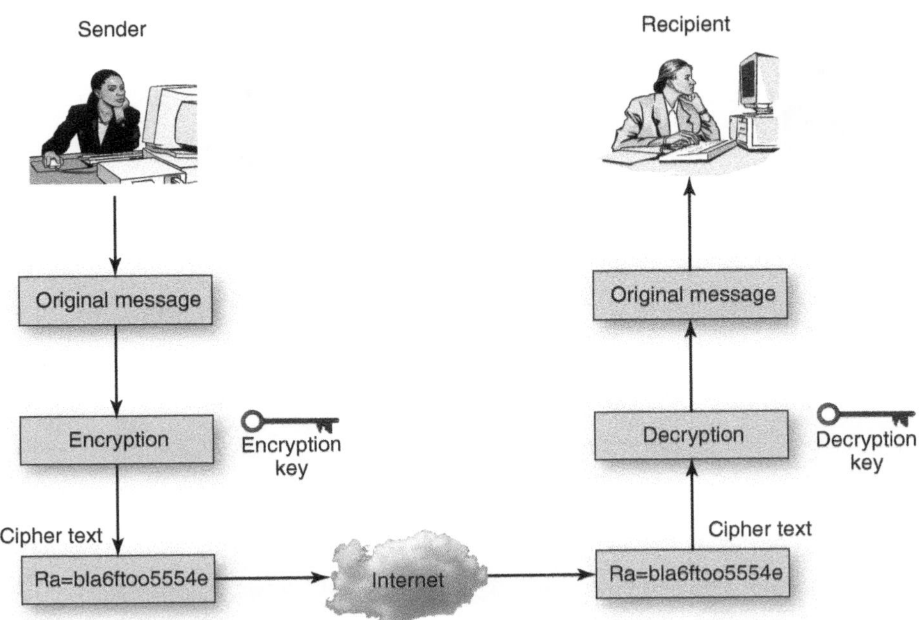

Figure 11.4 Symmetric-key cryptography

can read along – which results in a large number of keys. And if one key is lost or made public, all other keys must be replaced as well. Of the security requirements, symmetric encryption ensures confidentiality only: nobody but the sender and the receiver can read the message.

11.2.3.2 Asymmetric encryption

In order to overcome the disadvantages of symmetric encryption, a different cryptographic system, which involves the use of different keys for encryption and decryption, has been devised. This type of encryption is called *asymmetric encryption* or *public-key cryptography*. The most widely used public-key algorithm, especially for data sent over the Internet, is the Rivest–Shamir–Adleman (RSA) cryptographic algorithm.

In contrast to symmetric encryption, the primary characteristic of asymmetric encryption (public-key cryptography) is the fact that, instead of one key, both the sender and the receiver need two keys, one of which is public and the other private. These two keys share a specific property in that when one of these keys (public-key) is used to perform encryption, only the other key (private) is able to decrypt the data. These two keys are created during the same process and are known as a *key pair*. All keys are mathematically related to one another, so that data encrypted with one key can be decrypted using the other. This allows applications that are not possible with symmetric-key encryption.

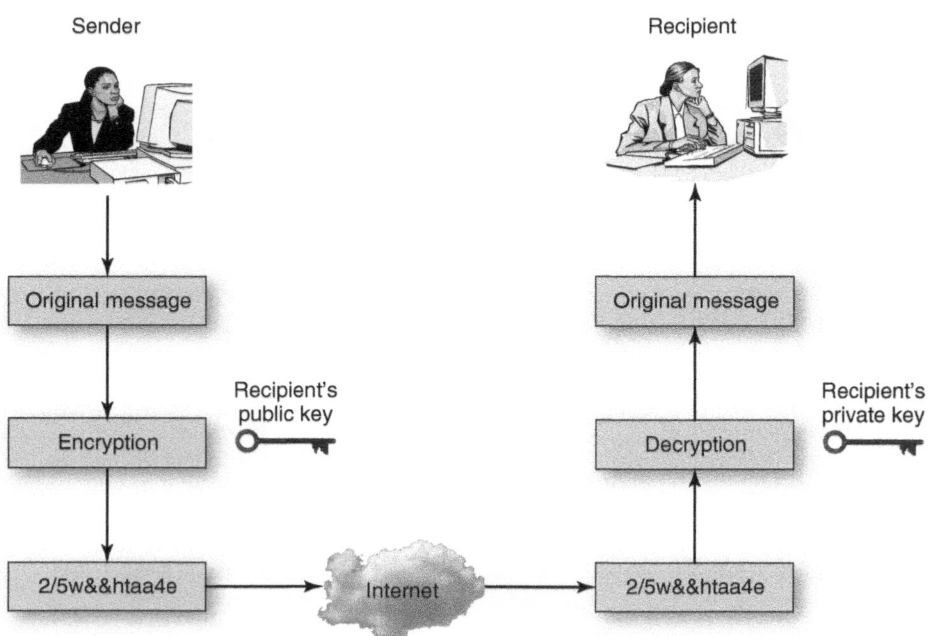

Figure 11.5 Asymmetric-key cryptography

Figure 11.5 illustrates a message encrypted with a public-key. Once a message is encrypted using the public-key, it is sent over the Internet and can be decrypted only with its matching private key. The private key is a secret key that only the recipient keeps. Both keys are different, and the key used for encrypting messages cannot be used for decrypting the same message. The public-key can be passed openly between the parties or published in a public repository, but the related private key remains private. Thus with the asymmetric encryption scheme both confidentiality and the receiver's authenticity are guaranteed. However, this scheme does not achieve accountability or non-repudiation and does not guarantee the sender's authenticity, since anybody can use the receiver's public-key.

To overcome the issue of accountability, digital signing can be used in conjunction with the public-key encryption scheme to provide confidentiality, integrity and non-repudiation. Figure 11.6 illustrates how digital signing and encryption work together. This figure illustrates that the sender creates a *secret* message that encrypts (signs) using the sender's own private key. The sender further encrypts (signs) the message using the recipient's public-key and the message is sent to the recipient over the Internet. On the other side, the recipient first decrypts the message using the recipient's own private key and then decrypts it further using the sender's public-key. Finally, the recipient receives the original message sent by the sender.

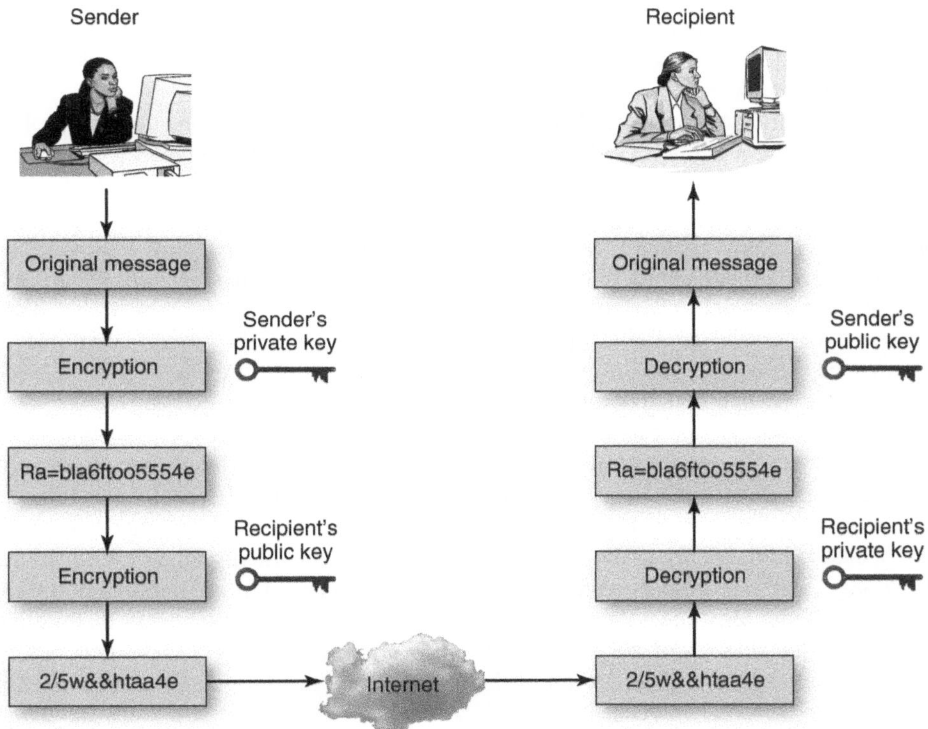

Figure 11.6 Asymmetric key cryptography using digital signing and public-key encryption

Asymmetric cryptography suffers from performance. The digital signature algorithm (DSA) [Kaufman 1995] is a technique used to address such concerns. The DSA is a public-key cryptosystem used only to calculate digital signatures (and not for data encryption). The DSA is optimised for speed of generating a signature, anticipating its use on low power microprocessors such as those on smart cards.

11.2.3.3 Digital certificates and signatures

Public-key encryption gives rise to another kind of encryption that is absolutely necessary for business-to-business interactions: digital certificates and signatures.

A *digital certificate* is a document that uniquely identifies a party (person or organisation) that owns the certificate, the time period for which the certificate is valid, the organisation that issued the certificate, and a digital signature that verifies the issuing organisation's identity. Digital certificates are exchanged during the set up of communication links to verify that the trading partner on the other end of the wire is the intended recipient of a message transmission and to prove the sender's identity. A digital certificate is issued by a *certification authority* and binds an entity's identification to its public key. This intermediary guarantees that the key belongs to the party identified, and announces this by signing and publishing the file containing the key owner's personal specifics and public key. This digital certificate is then sent along with the encrypted message. The certification authority's signature ensures the authenticity, integrity, and incontrovertibility of the certificate as well as the accuracy of the public-key. In order to prevent a massive spread of certificates, the Internet Engineering Task Force (IETF) is developing standards for them.

Digital certificates are interlinked with digital signatures, which can solve the problem of authenticating a public-key. *Digital signatures* guarantee that the enterprise or person represented in the digital certificate sent the message. A digital signature is a block of data created by applying a cryptographic signing algorithm to some data using the signer's private key. Digital signatures may be used to authenticate the source of a message and to assure message recipients that no one has tampered with a message since the time it was sent by the signer. These are attached to the message body to identify the sender. The receiver verifies the digital signature by decrypting it with the sender's public key to retrieve the message. In this way authentication mechanisms ensure that only the intended parties can exchange sensitive information.

Digital signatures use asymmetric encryption techniques whereby two different keys are generally used, one for creating a digital signature or transforming data into a seemingly unintelligible form, and another key for verifying a digital signature or returning the message to its original form. The keys for digital signatures are termed the *private key,* which is known only to the signer and is used to create the digital signature, and the *public-key,* which is ordinarily more widely known and is used to verify the digital signature. A recipient must have the corresponding public-key in order to verify that a digital signature is the signer's. If many people need to verify the signer's digital signatures, the public-key must be distributed to all of them, e.g. by publication in an on line repository or directory where they can easily obtain it. Although many people will know the public-key of a given signer and use it to verify that signer's signatures, they cannot discover that signer's private key and use it to forge digital signatures.

Use of digital signatures comprises two processes, one performed by the signer and the other by the receiver of the digital signature:

- *Digital signature creation* is the process of computing a code derived from, and unique to, both the signed message and a given private key.
- *Digital signature verification* is the process of checking the digital signature by reference to the original message and a public-key, and thereby determining whether the digital signature was created for that same message using the private key that corresponds to the referenced public-key.

A *hashing algorithm* is used in both creating and verifying a digital signature [Steel 2006]. Hashing algorithms enable the software for creating digital signatures to operate on smaller and predictable amounts of data, while still providing a strong evidentiary correlation to the original message content. A *digest* (hashing) *algorithm* creates a *message digest* of the message, which is a code usually much smaller than the original message but nevertheless unique to it. Digest algorithms consume (digest) data to calculate a hash value, called a message digest. The message digest depends upon the data as well as the digest algorithm. If the message changes, the hash result of the message will invariably be different. The digest value can be used to verify the integrity of a message; that is, to ensure that the data has not been altered while on its way from the sender to the receiver. The sender sends the message digest value with the message. On receipt of the message, the recipient repeats the digest calculation. If the message has been altered, the digest value will not match and the alteration will be detected. Public-key cryptography is typically used in conjunction with a hashing algorithm, such as Secure Hash Algorithm 1 (SHA-1) or Message Digest 5 (`http://rfc.net/rfc1321.html`), to provide integrity.

Figure 11.7 shows the creation of a digital signature. In order to sign a document or any other item of information, the signer first delimits the portion of the document that needs to be signed. The delimited text to be signed is termed the *message*. Subsequently, a hashing algorithm in the signer's side computes a message digest. Subsequently, the message digest

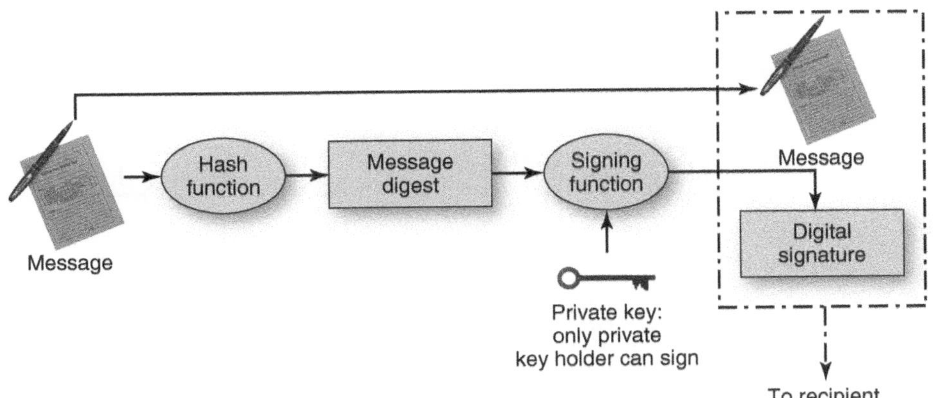

Figure 11.7 Creation of a digital signature

is encrypted using the digital signature by referring to the signer's private key. The resulting digital signature is thus unique to both the message and the private key used to create it.

Typically, a digital signature is attached to its message and stored or transmitted with its message. However, it may also be sent or stored as a separate data element, so long as it maintains a reliable association with its message. Since a digital signature is unique to its message, it is useless if wholly disassociated from its message.

Figure 11.8 depicts the verification process of a digital signature. This figure shows that the verification process is accomplished by computing a message digest of the original message by means of the same hashing algorithm used in creating the digital signature (which is agreed upon beforehand). The message digest is encrypted by the sender's private key. Subsequently, the message along with the message digest is sent to the recipient. The recipient uses the public-key to decrypt the digital signature and check whether the digital signature was created using the corresponding private key. The recipient then uses the same hashing algorithm to calculate its own message digest of the sender's plain text message. Subsequently, the recipient checks whether the newly computed message digest matches the message digest derived from the digital signature. If the signer's private key was used and the message digests are identical, then the digital signature as well as the original message are verified.

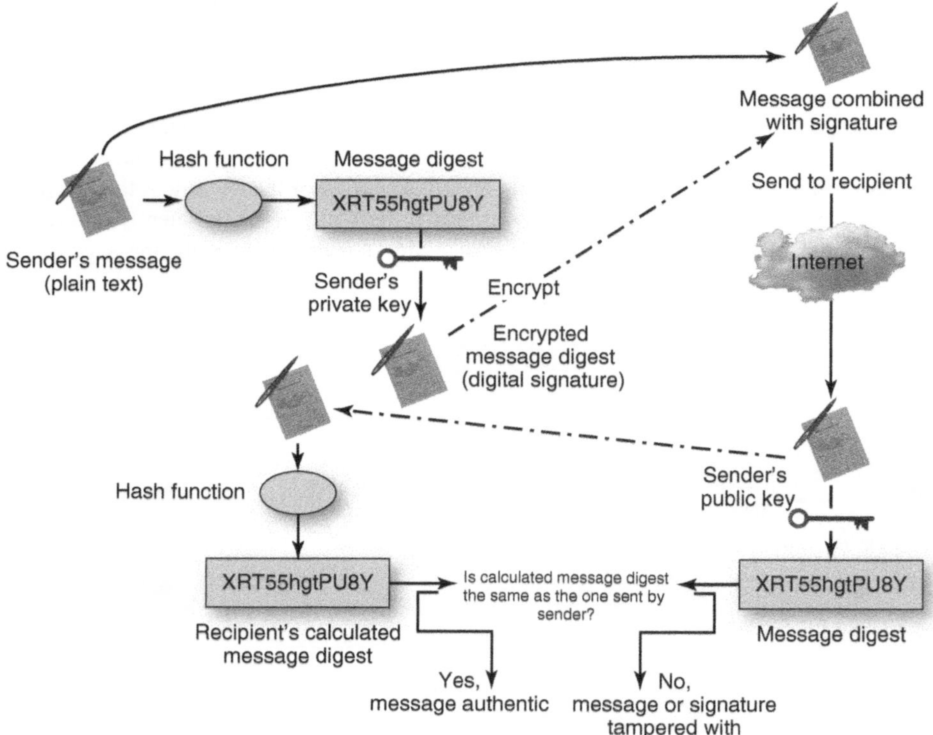

Figure 11.8 Verification of a digital signature

11.3 Application level security mechanisms

Several applications have intricate security requirements that cannot be met by network level security measures. The term application level security is used to refer to security safeguards that are built into a particular application and that operate independently of any network level security measures [Ford 1997].

When considering the application level security requirements, such as authentication, authorisation, message integrity, confidentiality and non-repudiation, that we addressed briefly in Section 11.1.2, it is important to understand that the fundamental need is for mechanisms and technologies used in any kind of communication between the sender and the recipient to be safe and secure. In the following we describe application level security mechanisms that are used in the context of distributed computing environments, such as J2EE (which we use as an example for application level security), while in Sections 11.4 and 11.5 we examine Web service related initiatives and solutions.

11.3.1 Authentication

In distributed computing environments, *authentication* is the mechanism through which clients and service providers prove to one another that they are acting on behalf of specific users or systems [Monzillo 2002], [Singh 2004]. A client usually presents an identifier and the service provider verifies the client's claimed identity. When the proof is bidirectional, it is referred to as *mutual authentication.* Authentication establishes the call identities and proves that the participants are authentic instances of these identities. For instance, authentication may verify that the identity of entities is provided by the use of public-key certificates and digital signature envelopes. Many authentication methods exist for distributed environments and e-Business applications, ranging from simple user names and passwords to stronger methods such as tokens and digital certificates.

Authentication in distributed environments is often achieved in two phases [Monzillo 2002]. First, an authentication context is established by performing a service independent authentication. The authentication context encapsulates the identity and is able to fabricate authenticators (proofs of identity). Subsequently, the authentication context is used to authenticate with other (called or calling) entities. The basis of authentication entails controlling access to the authentication context and thus the ability to authenticate as the associated identity. Most common policies and mechanisms for controlling access to an authentication context include the following:

- Once a client program performs an initial authentication, the processes that the client program starts inherits access to the authentication context.
- When a component is authenticated, access to the authentication context may be available to other related or trusted components, such as those that are part of the same application.

In a distributed environment, when a client program accesses a set of distributed components and resources, e.g. Java Server Pages (JSPs), Enterprise Java Beans (EJBs), databases, etc., the client must present its identity. Subsequently, a container component determines whether the client meets the criteria for access as specified by authorisation rules. A container is the run time environment in which an application runs that provides workload and performance management, resource management, security management, transaction management, deployment, configuration and administration capabilities (see Chapter 8 where we examine the Enterprise Service Bus). A container is synonymous with a J2EE application server. A J2EE application runs inside the container, which has specific responsibilities with respect to the application, e.g. it is interposed on all method calls and provides the standardised environment that supplies specific services to its underlying component. In many cases, processing a client's request to a component might require the component to make a chain of calls to access other components and resources and use an authentication context. Consequently, not only does the container enforce authentication and establish an identity when a client calls a component, but it also handles authentication when the component makes an initial chain of calls to these components and resources. The distributed platform allows the client identity, established with the authentication of the initial call, to be propagated along the chain of calls.

11.3.1.1 Protection domains

Distributed platforms allow entities to be grouped into special domains, called *protection domains,* where they can communicate with each other without requiring authentication [Monzillo 2002], [Singh 2004]. A protection domain is a logical boundary around a set of such entities that are assumed or known to trust each other. When one component interacts with others in the same protection domain, no constraint is placed on the identity that it can associate with its call. In a protection domain, authentication is required only for entities that cross the boundary of the protection domain. Interactions that remain within the protection domain do not require authentication.

In a distributed environment such as J2EE, to ensure that unproven or unauthenticated entities do not cross the protection domain boundary, a container provides an authentication boundary between external callers and the components it hosts. In general, it is the job of the container to provide bidirectional authentication functionality to enforce the protection domain boundaries of the deployed applications.

The container ensures that the identity of the call is authenticated before it enters the protection domain. For inbound calls, it is the container's responsibility to make an authentic representation of the caller identity available to the component in the form of a credential. An X.509 certificate and a Kerberos service ticket (see Section 11.3.6.3) are examples of credentials used in computing environments. An *X.509 certificate* is a digital container for the public-key part of a public/private (asymmetric) key pair. A certification authority that assents to the identity related to the public-key signs this digital certificate. For outbound calls, the container is responsible for establishing the identity of the calling component.

11.3.1.2 Web resource protection

In distributed environments, such as J2EE, available (exported) application business logic and Web connectivity to clients is provided by a dedicated tier known as the Web tier. The Web tier handles all application communication with Web clients, invoking business logic and transmitting data in response to incoming requests, and provides access to enterprise resources. Web tier resources available to a client may be protected or unprotected. Protected resources are mission critical resources, e.g. back end systems, which are distinguished by the presence of authorisation rules that restrict access to them to some subset of non-anonymous identities. To access a protected resource, a client must present a credential such that its identity can be evaluated against the resource authorisation policy.

With Web tier authentication, the developer specifies an authorisation constraint to designate those Web resources, e.g. HTML documents, Web components, image files, archives and so on, that need to be protected. When a client tries to access a protected Web tier resource, appropriate authentication mechanisms for the component or resource accessed are activated. For example, in the case of J2EE, Web containers support three authentication mechanisms [Singh 2004]: HTTP basic authentication, form based authentication, and HTTPS mutual authentication.

With *HHTP basic authentication* the Web server authenticates a principal using the user name and password obtained from the Web client. *Form based authentication* lets developers customise the authentication user interface presented by an HTTP browser. Like HTTP basic authentication, form based authentication is a relatively vulnerable authentication mechanism, since the content of the user dialogue is sent as plain text and the target server is not authenticated [Monzillo 2002]. Finally, with *HTTPS mutual authentication* both the client and the server use digital certificates to establish their identity, and authentication occurs over a channel protected by SSL.

Distributed environments also provide *single sign-on* among applications within a security policy domain boundary. Single sign on is a technique that allows a user to use a single password to access all network based resources that are available to them. In computer networks this is done by the use of so called tickets. On authentication, a user gets a ticket stating their identity and other security related information. While accessing resources on other servers than the one authenticated on, this ticket is used to state the user's identity. In this way the user does not have to authenticate multiple times at every server they use.

11.3.2 Authorisation

Authorisation mechanisms for distributed environments allow only authentic caller identities to access resources, such as hosts, files, Web pages, components and database entries, to name a few. Typical authorisation policies permit access to different resources for distinct collections of authenticated clients on the basis of roles, groups or privileges. Roles represent competencies, authorities, responsibilities or specific duty assignments, while groups are formed on the basis of organisational affiliation, e.g. division, department, laboratory, etc. Authorisation policies may also restrict access based on a global context (e.g. time of day), transactional context (e.g. no more than a certain number or amount of withdrawals per day) or data values. Since distributed platforms focus on permissions that state who can perform what function, authentication and identity need to be established before authorisation policies are enforced.

Once the supplied digital certificate or other credentials have authenticated a user's identity, the user's access privileges must be determined. Authorisation is meant to limit the actions or operations that authenticated parties are able to perform in a networked environment. The classical solution for restricting access (from either employees or trading partners) to sensitive information is by means of access control rules on a resource, such as a Web page or a component, and then evaluating the kind of access requested to determine if the requester has permission to access the resource. *Access control rules* can define any security policy expressible in a declarative form without a developer having to hard code the policy in an application. Essentially, access control refers to the process of ensuring that resources are not used in an unauthorised way. Access control may be applied in a distributed environment for protecting against unauthorised invocations of operations on resources in the context of a particular business process or application. None, read-only, add, edit or full control access rights can be assigned.

The most common approach to defining access control rules for distributed platforms is on the basis of permissions. Permissions focus on who can do what. They can be specified declaratively or programmatically.

With declarative authorisation, logical privileges called (security) roles are defined and are associated with components to specify privileges required for subjects (an entity, either human or computer, that has an identity in some security domain) and to be granted permission to access components, according to identity (established by authentication). Permissions indicate the ability to perform a certain operation according to functional role and/or data sensitivity, e.g. *create an order* or *approve an order,* on a component (resource). Security permissions written in this way are static, coarse grained and not very expressive. Callers are assigned logical privileges based on the values of their security attributes. When a security role is assigned to a security group in the operational environment, any caller whose security attributes indicate membership in the group is assigned the privilege represented by the role.

In addition to declaratively specified security roles, in many cases additional application logic needs to be associated with access control decisions. In such cases programmatic authorisation is used to associate application logic with the state of a resource, the parameters of a component invocation, or some other relevant information. Programmatic authorisation requires access to an application's source code in order to insert the appropriate checks. Programmatic security supports more fine grained authorisation than declarative security, but can restrict the reusability of a component. Assembling an application from several components that use programmatic security will be difficult or impossible if the programmed security model is not consistent between the components. An additional drawback to programmatic security occurs when the security policy changes. Every component must be revisited to verify and possibly update the security authorisation.

Mechanisms provided by the distributed platform can be used to control access to Web resources based on identity properties, such as the location and signer of the calling code, and the identity of the user of the calling code. Caller identity is usually established by selecting from the set of authentication contexts available to the calling code. In all cases, a credential is made available to the invoked component (that essentially protects a resource) [Monzillo 2002], [Singh 2004]. As an example, the container based authorisation mechanisms in J2EE require that a container serves as an authorisation boundary between the components it hosts and their callers. The authorisation boundary exists inside the container's authentication boundary, which identifies the user making the current request. In this way, authorisation is considered in the context of successful authentication. For inbound calls, the container compares security attributes from the caller's credential to the access control rules for the target component. If the rules are satisfied, the call is allowed. Otherwise, the call is rejected.

11.3.3 Integrity and confidentiality

In a distributed computing system, a significant amount of information is transmitted through networks in the form of messages. Message content is subject to three main types of attacks. Messages might be intercepted and modified for the purpose of changing the effects they have on their recipients. Messages might be captured and reused one or more times for the benefit of another party. An eavesdropper might monitor messages in an effort to capture information that would not otherwise be available. Using integrity and confidentiality mechanisms can minimise such attacks.

Message (data) integrity comprises two requirements. First, the data received must be the same as the data sent. In other words, data integrity systems must be able to guarantee that a message did not change in transit, either by mistake or on purpose. The second requirement for message integrity is that, at any time in the future, it will be possible to prove whether different copies of the same document are in fact identical.

Digital signatures can be used to verify if a message has been tampered with. A service requester can sign a document with the sender's private key and send it along with the payload of the message. The service provider can then verify the signature with the sender's public-key to see if any portion of the document has been compromised. Thus Web service applications can ensure data integrity when communicating with each other. For example, the XML Signature standard (see Section 11.5.1) provides a means for signing parts of XML documents, providing end-to-end data integrity across multiple systems.

Message integrity ensures that information that is being transmitted has not been altered. Secure transactions are the typical mechanism that guarantees that a message has not been modified while in transit. This is commonly known as *communication integrity* and is often accomplished through hashing algorithms and digitally signed digest codes.

Secure transactions should also guarantee confidentiality. *Confidentiality* refers to the ability to ensure that messages and data are available only to those who are authorised to view them. Confidentiality can be achieved by making sure the connection between the parties cannot be intercepted, e.g. by using encryption when the data is being sent across untrusted networks. Standard SSL encryption using HTTPS allows point-to-point data privacy between service requesters and service providers. However, in many cases, the service provider may not be the ultimate destination for the message. A service provider may act as a service requester, sending pieces of information to multiple services. In such situations, the XML encryption standard can be used in conjunction with Web services to permit encryption of portions of the message, allowing header and other information to be clear text while encrypting the sensitive payload. Sensitive information can then be left encrypted to the ultimate destination, allowing true end-to-end data privacy.

11.3.4 Non-repudiation

Non-repudiation is of critical importance for carrying out transactions over the Internet. Non-repudiation is a property achieved through cryptographic methods to prevent an individual or entity from denying having performed a particular action related to data. When transactions are performed, it is often a requirement to be able to prove that a particular action took place and that the transaction has been committed with valid credentials. This prevents trading partners from claiming that the transaction never occurred.

Digital signatures using digital certificates, e.g. PKI X.509 or Kerberos tickets, are key elements to providing non-repudiation. Digital signatures generated based on asymmetric cryptography have a non-repudiation property, in the sense that the person or organisation who created the signature cannot deny that they have done so. Non-repudiation usually combines the use of modification detection with digital signatures. When third party non-repudiation is required, digital receipts provide independent verification that specific transactions have occurred. Non-repudiation consists of cryptographic receipts that are created so that the author of a message cannot falsely deny sending a message. These tasks fall well within the premises of contract formation and enforcement. Tracking digitally signed messages using a tracking data repository provides an audit trail for guaranteeing non-repudiation. The receiver saves the digital signature together with the message in the repository for later reference, in case a dispute arises.

11.3.5 Auditing

Auditing is the practice of recording events, such as failed login attempts and denied requests to use a resource, that may indicate attempts to violate enterprise security. The value of auditing is not solely to determine whether security mechanisms are limiting access to a system. When security is breached, security relevant events are analysed to determine who has been allowed access to critical data. Knowing who has interacted with a system allows the determination of accountability for a breach of security.

In general, it should be possible for the deployer or system administrator to review the security constraints established for the platform and to associate an audit behaviour with each security constraint so that these can be analysed and audited. It is also prudent to audit all changes (resulting from deployment or subsequent administration) to the audit configuration, or the constraints being enforced by the platform. Audit records must be protected so that attackers cannot escape accountability for their actions by expunging incriminating records or changing their content.

11.3.6 Application level security protocols

Secure communications use a number of authentication and encryption protocols that employ encryption and authentication techniques to ensure secure sessions over the Internet. Traditionally, the Secure Sockets Layer (SSL), along with the de facto Transport Layer Security (TLS) and the Internet Protocol Security (IPSec), are some of the common ways of securing distributed application content over the Internet.

In this section we shall briefly examine some of the most commonly used protocols that address authentication, integrity and confidentiality concerns within open networks.

11.3.6.1 Secure sockets layer (SSL)

Application level integrated security requires that individual corporate business applications include functionality for achieving secure communications between a client and application server. SSL, used primarily with Web browsers, is the security protocol most commonly used in this approach. *Secure Sockets Layer* is an open standard Web protocol that provides server authentication, data encryption and message integrity over TCP/IP connections. SSL is widely used in Internet commerce, being implemented in almost all popular browsers and Web servers.

The purpose of SSL is to serve as an easily deployable, dedicated security protocol that offers full security for multiple applications, ensuring that communications between a client and application server remain private and allowing the client to identify the server and vice versa. This form of transport security results in creating a secure pipe between the two interacting servers. This is shown in Figure 11.9. Authentication occurs at the time the secure pipe is created, while confidentiality and integrity mechanisms are applied only while the message is in the secure pipe, as illustrated in Figure 11.9.

SSL offers a range of security services for client-server sessions including server and client authentication, data integrity and data confidentiality. SSL enabled clients and SSL enabled servers confirm each other's identities using digital certificates. SSL server authentication enables a client to confirm the identity of the server involved in any questioned transaction. This is accomplished in SSL using public-key cryptography techniques that verify that the server's certification is valid and issued by a trusted certification authority. Client authentication allows a server to confirm the identity of a client in the same manner as server authentication. SSL enabled server software can check that the client's certificate and public-key are valid and have been issued by a confidentiality authority listed in the server's list of trusted confidentiality authorities. SSL coordinates the process of encrypting and decrypting all information transmitted between a client and a server. Information transmitted via an encrypted SSL connection remains confidential and tamper free, ensuring that data received is unchanged and was not seen by others.

As SSL does not support certificate validation, certificate extensions are currently provided to facilitate certificate validation. Additionally, SSL extensions are also providing such features as monitoring, logging and access control authorisation, which are traditionally not supported by conventional SSL technology.

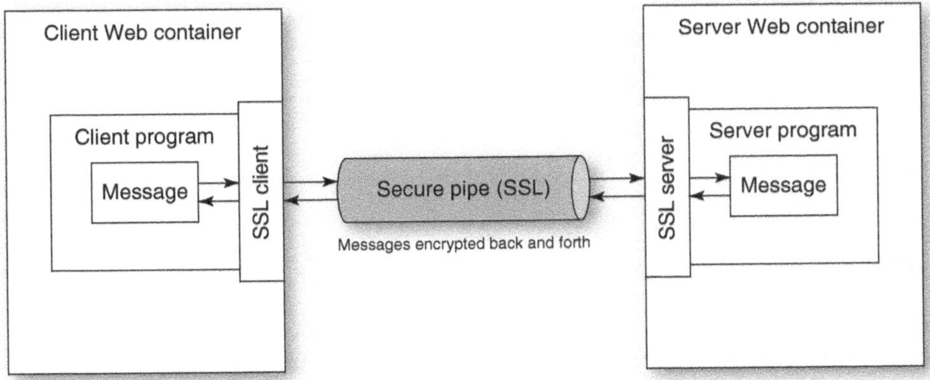

Figure 11.9 Transport security using SSL

11.3.6.2 Internet Protocol Security (IPSec)

IPSec is another network layer standard for transport security that may become important for distributed and e-Business applications. Like SSL/TLS, IPSec also provides secure sessions with host authentication, data integrity, and data confidentiality. However, these are point-to-point technologies. They create a secure tunnel through which data can pass [Mysore 2003]. For instance, SSL is a good solution for server-to-server security but it cannot adequately address the scenario where a message is routed via more than one server. In this case the recipient has to request credentials of the sender and the scalability of the system is compromised.

11.3.6.3 Kerberos

Kerberos was developed to provide a range of authentication and security facilities for computing networks, including single sign-on and use of public-key cryptography. The goal of Kerberos is to provide authentication in an insecure distributed environment. *Kerberos* is a third trusted party authentication protocol that deals with two kinds of security objects: a ticket and a session key. An authentication token (pieces of information used for authentication or authorisation that can be added to a SOAP header) called a *ticket* is issued by the Kerberos ticket granting service for presentation to a particular server, verifying that the client has recently been authenticated by Kerberos. Tickets include an expiry time and a newly generated session key for use by the client and the server. A *session key* is a secret key randomly generated by Kerberos and issued to a client for use when communicating with a particular server. Client processes must posses a ticket and a session key for each server that they use.

In a Web service security application, Kerberos provides a method for a Kerberos (third-party) server independently to verify trust with two parties (via an authentication service) and then to grant shared secret keys that these two parties can use as the basis for a secure interaction [Hall-Gailey 2004]. The Kerberos model performs centralised key management.

Figure 11.10 illustrates the ticket granting mechanism of Kerberos for a client accessing a Web service. In this scenario a key distribution center (KDC) maintains the principal's credentials. The KDC has a dual function:

- It first offers an authentication service that accepts the requester's credentials (typically login and password) from a client process.
- It subsequently sends back a credential called a ticket granting ticket (TGT) to the requester.

The TGT contains a temporary secret session key that can be persisted during the session to prevent having to use the permanent credentials. The TGT is encrypted so that only the legitimate principal who possesses the correct password is able to decrypt it and use it at a future time. When the client wishes to access a server application (in this case a particular Web service provided by a specific provider) using Kerberos, the client presents its TGT to the ticket granting service (TGS) part of the KDC. The TGS then returns a service (or session) ticket, which contains a secret session key, a client identifier and the

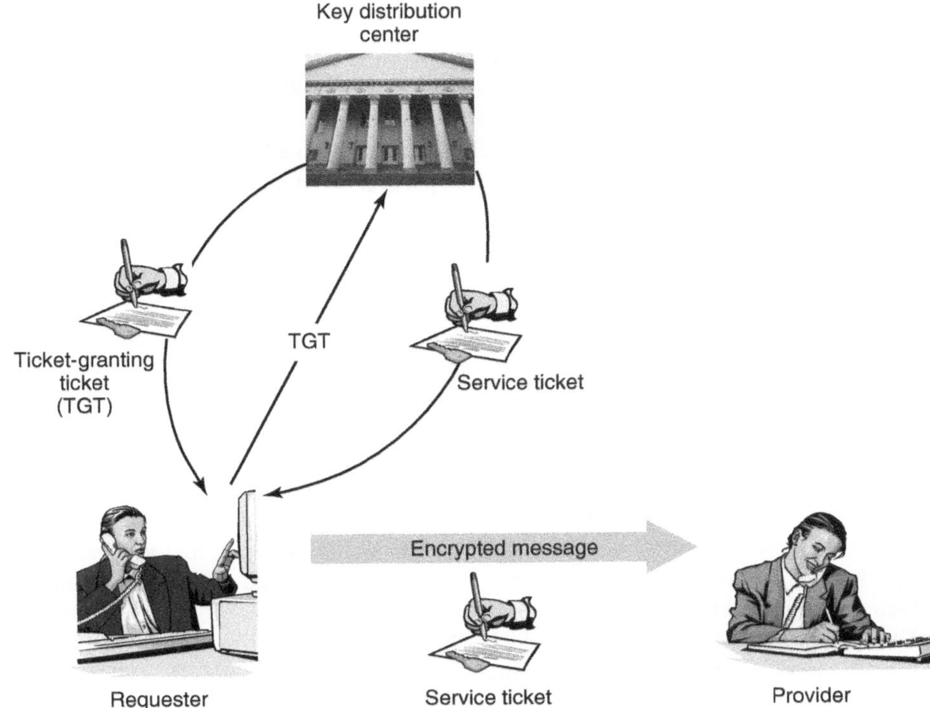

Figure 11.10 Kerberos ticket distribution

TGT expiration time. The client uses the session ticket to establish secure TCP/IP communication with the Web service application in question. The session ticket is protected by encrypting the requester's information with the provider's private key and is not exposed over the network. As a result, only the provider can authenticate the requester by decrypting the requester's identification. As long as the TGT is valid the requester can get various service tickets for different providers without identifying itself again. In this way, single sign-on is achieved.

11.3.7 Security infrastructures

To protect information assets, enterprises are expected to provide gatekeeping functions, such as data protection and network isolation, as well as facilitative functions, such as exposing enterprise data to outside applications, connecting users for extended collaboration, and enabling on-line transactions and communications. Security infrastructures are distributed infrastructures used as a sound foundation on which applications can communicate and exchange data securely. In the following we look at the two most prominent approaches in this field: the Public-key infrastructure and Directory services.

11.3.7.1 Public-key infrastructure

The foundation for providing application and network security in distributed multi-faceted environments is Public-key infrastructure (PKI) [VeriSign 2003]. A PKI is a foundation upon which other applications and network security components are built. PKI protects applications that demand the highest level of security, enabling on line banking and trading, SOA and Web service based business process automation, digital form signing, enterprise instant messaging and electronic commerce. In addition, it protects firewalls, VPNs, directories and enterprise applications. PKI becomes crucial when there is a risk of fraud, a risk of legal ramifications if a transaction is altered or disclosed, or when the confirmed identity of an individual or business entity is essential.

PKI refers to the technology, infrastructure and practices that support the implementation and operation of digital certificates and certification authorities that verify and authenticate the validity of parties involved in Internet transactions. In a broad sense PKI is an infrastructure of policies, servers and technologies that provide support for cryptographic solutions to critical security issues related to enterprise computing. PKI capabilities help create and manage asymmetric cryptographic keys or public/private keys required by automated business processes and e-Business applications. PKI uses a private key and a public-key to encrypt and decrypt confidential information and to generate and verify digital signatures. The main function of PKI is to distribute public-keys accurately and reliably to users and applications that need them.

The specific security functions for which a PKI can provide a foundation are confidentiality, integrity, non-repudiation and authentication, while it also ensures military grade physical security. PKI also integrates easily with all functions within an enterprise and with all sorts of internal and external enterprise applications, including legacy systems. In this way, PKI allows enterprises easily to create communities of trust with partners, customers and suppliers.

In practice, PKI refers to a system of digital certificates, certification authorities, and other registration authorities that verify and authenticate the validity of each party involved in an electronic transaction. A *public-key certificate* is a digitally signed statement that binds the value of a public-key to the identity of the subject (person, device or service) that holds the corresponding private key. Certification and registration authorities are two major PKI components that provide the necessary capabilities to establish, maintain and protect trusted relationships [Schlosser 1999].

The issuer and signer of the certificate are known as a *certification authority*. The entity being issued the certificate is the subject of the certificate. By signing the certificate, the certification authority attests that the private key associated with the public-key in the certificate is in the possession of the subject named in the certificate. The certification authority creates and signs digital certificates, maintains certificate revocation lists, makes certificates and revocation lists available, and provides an interface so that administrators can manage certificates. Certificates can be issued for a variety of functions, including Web user authentication, Web server authentication, secure e-mail using Secure/Multipurpose Internet Mail Extensions (S/MIME), IPSec, SSL/TLS and code signing.

Issuance of a certificate requires verification of the user's identity, usually accomplished by a *registration authority*. The registration authority evaluates the credentials and relevant evidence that an organisation requesting a certificate is indeed the organisation that it claims to be. A digitally signed message from the registration authority to the certification authority is required to authenticate the subscriber. One certification authority may operate several registration authorities.

Figure 11.11 illustrates one of the possible ways that a PKI can operate. A requester first generates a public/private key pair. The public-key is then placed into a certificate request signed with the requester's private key. The self signed certificate is sent to a registration authority, which verifies the identity of the subscriber. Once the identity of the requester is verified, the certificate is countersigned by the registration authority and sent to the certification authority. The certification authority verifies the registration authority's signature on the certificate request. It additionally verifies that this registration authority is entitled to make this request. Subsequently, the certification authority uses the public-key in the certificate request to create a public-key certificate with it, and signs the certificate. The certification authority may also take the certificate and place it in a directory so that any party wishing to communicate with the requester, or wishing to verify the requester's signature, can retrieve the requester's public-key. Finally, the certificate is returned to the requester who can forward it to a recipient. The recipient receives the digitally signed information from the requester and needs to use the PKI – in particular, the public-key certificate – to verify the requester's signature.

One of the most commonly cited PKIs is the PKI X.509 (PKIX) standard that defines the contents of public-key certificates on the basis of the X.509 certificate format with IETF protocols such as SSL, S/MIME and IPSec. PKI X.509 provides interoperability between digital certificates produced by different vendors.

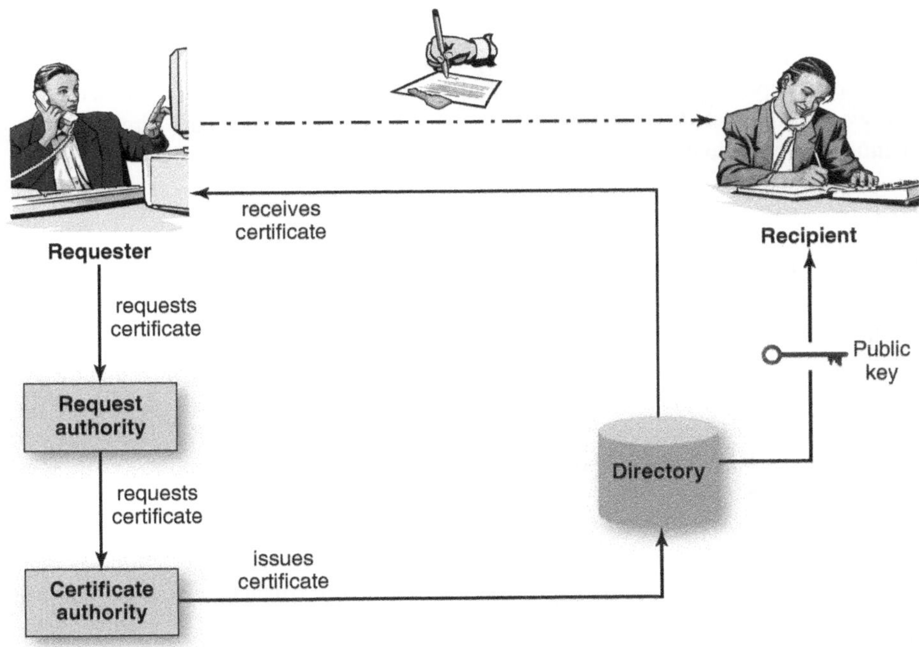

Figure 11.11 Public-key Infrastructure

11.3.7.2 Directory services

PKI application certificates are published in a public directory, which allows everyone who wishes to send someone an encrypted message to use the receiver's public-key that is given in the certificate. Third trusted parties, who serve as certification authorities, often manage directories, see Figure 11.11.

Directory services for application level security provide the ability to implement a security policy. As such they may be used to store authorisation information, such as group membership and access rights, support single sign-on and, in general, provide location information and other detailed information about network available resources and computing infrastructure. Where a PKI is deployed, a directory can be used to distribute certificates, for applications in which an end user certificate must be obtained before an encrypted message is sent, as well as certificate status information such as certificate revocation lists. The directory can also store private keys, when portability is required in environments where users do not use the same machine each day.

The most popular protocol for accessing the data in network directories is the Lightweight Directory Access Protocol (LDAP). LDAP uses the X.500 data model, which is a comprehensive directory architecture, designed under the auspices of ISO and other international standards organisations. In the X.500 model, the basic unit of data is a directory entry, which consists of one or more attribute–value pairs. LDAP operates over TCP/IP and, consequently, is considerably simpler to implement and deploy. The LDAP distributed architecture supports scalable directory services with server replication capabilities, ensuring that directory data is available when needed.

For security, LDAP supports both basic client authentication using a distinguished name and password and SSL services, which provide for mutual authentication between the client and the server and ensure confidentiality and integrity of queries and responses. To enable SSL, a server certificate is required. Certificate based client authentication, using, for example, client certificates issued through PKI, is also supported with appropriately configured LDAP directory servers. This restricts access to the directory to only authenticated individuals.

11.4 Security topologies

The classical security topology is based on the concept of a *demilitarized zone* (DMZ), which is a logical partition between two sets of firewalls. The assumption is that the infrastructure residing in the DMZ needs to be accessed directly and, therefore, is more likely to be compromised [Steel 2006]. The second firewall layer in a DMZ is used to protect against attackers, who have compromised servers, from gaining access to application servers and back end applications.

Security topologies define the security requirements of distributed application development in a DMZ environment in a way that addresses architectural capabilities, such as availability, scalability, reliability, manageability and performance. Two such topologies can be identified [Steel 2006]: *horizontally* and *vertically scaled security architectures.*

Figure 11.12 illustrates a horizontally scaled security architecture for a J2EE application that is partitioned as a Web tier (employing JSP/Servlets), application tier

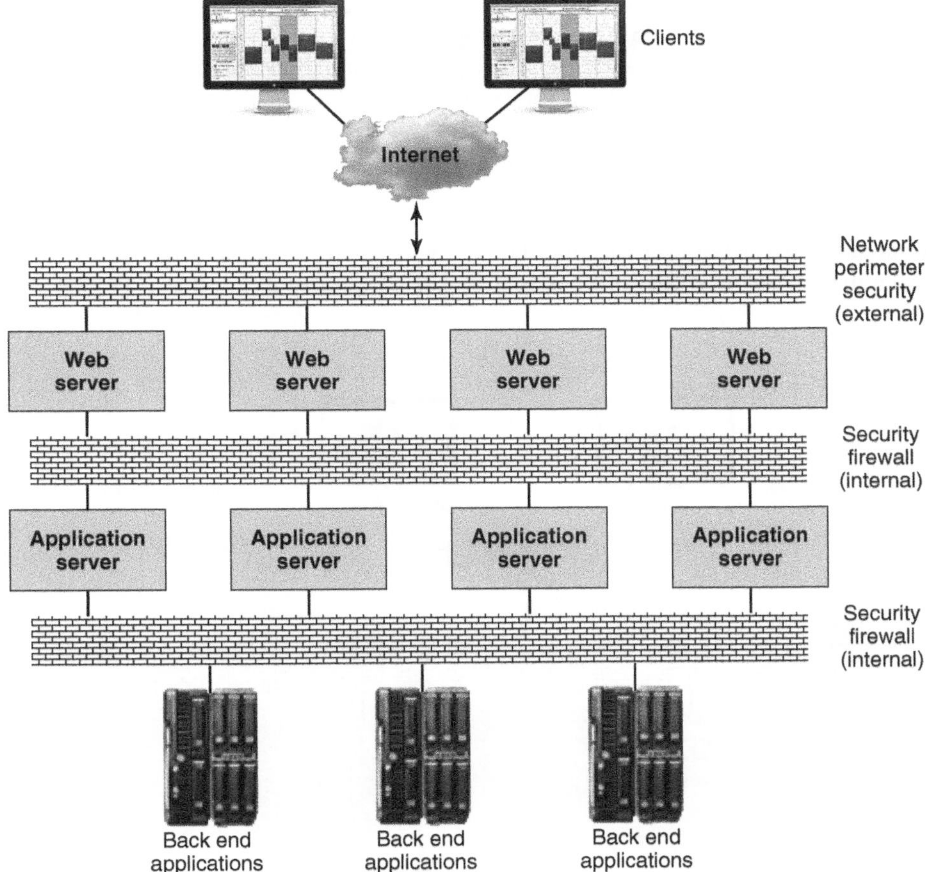

Figure 11.12 Horizontally scaled security architecture
(*Source*: C. Steel, R. Nagappan and R. Lai, *Core Security Patterns: Best Practices and Strategies for J2EE™, Web Services, and Identity Management*, Prentice Hall, 2006. Reproduced with permission.)

(employing EJB components), and back end resources. The horizontal scalability is achieved by using multiple instances of Web and application servers. The Web tier and the applications tier are separated by a firewall. This enhances security because the traffic between the Web and application servers is required to pass through the firewall. This architecture is not suitable for applications that have a relatively high degree of traffic between the Web tier and the back end resource tier.

To decouple the Web from back end resource applications, a Web server could be configured with a reverse proxy, which receives HTTP requests from a client on the incoming network side and opens a socket connection on the application server side to perform business application processing [Steel 2006]. This configuration targets environments with less stringent security requirements.

Figure 11.13 shows a vertically scaled security architecture for a J2EE application that is partitioned as a Web tier (employing JSP/Servlets), application tier (employing EJB components), and back end resources. Adding computing capacity, e.g. processors, memory, etc., achieves vertical scalability. This configuration can lead to an overall system failure if the server infrastructure fails. To avoid this, a high availability cluster can be introduced to provide resilience for both Web and application server infrastructure in the case of failure.

To decouple the Web from back end resource applications in a vertically scaled security architecture, a Web server could be configured with a reverse proxy that acts in a similar manner as in the case of a horizontally scaled security architecture.

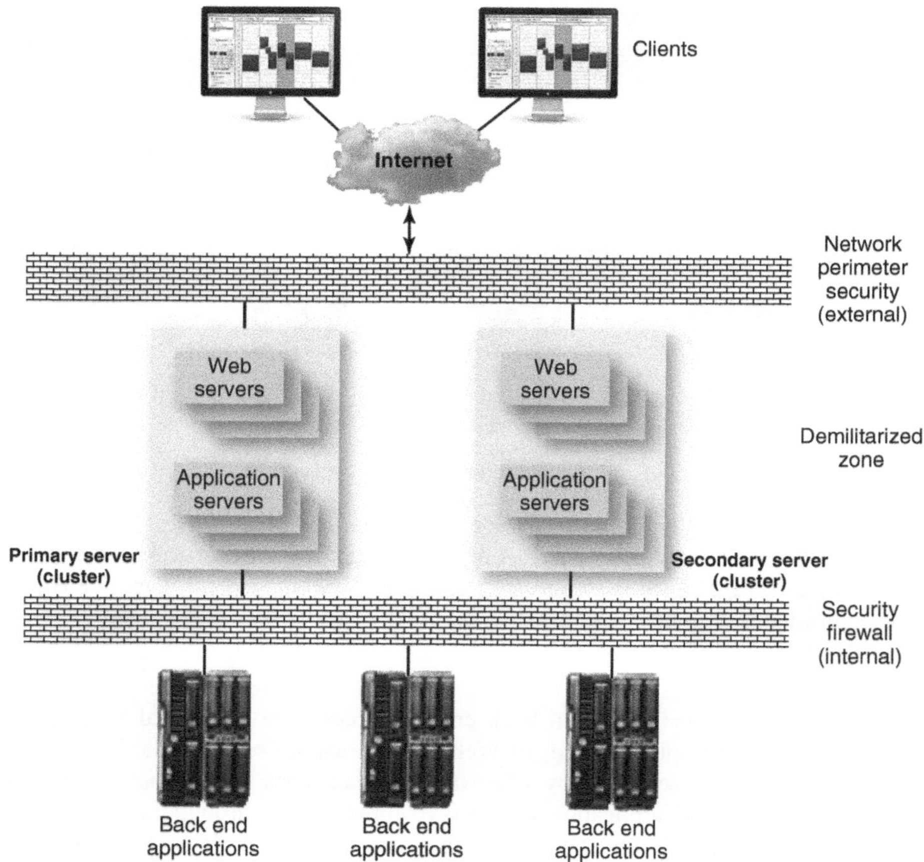

Figure 11.13 Vertically scaled security architecture
(*Source*: C. Steel, R. Nagappan and R. Lai, *Core Security Patterns: Best Practices and Strategies for J2EE™, Web Services, and Identity Management*, Prentice Hall, 2006. Reproduced with permission.)

11.5 XML security standards

XML and Web service based SOAs facilitate business integration within and across organisational boundaries. However, this benefit comes at a price: security systems themselves must also integrate. Without this security integration, security solutions remain at a per project level, with no central means of configuring, monitoring, analysing and controlling integration data flows. The implementation, management and monitoring of security policies across enterprise boundaries becomes increasingly vital to the success of integrated enterprises.

Web service technologies use XML based messages on Internet based protocols to interact with other applications. To achieve this, they rely on *XML Trust Services,* which is a suite of open XML specifications for application developers to make it easier to integrate a broad range of XML security services into integrated business applications over the Web.

The main technologies for XML Trust Services encompass:

- XML Signature for cryptographically authenticating data;
- XML Encryption for encrypting data;
- XML Key Management Specification (XKMS) for managing key registration and key authentication, Security Assertions Markup Language (SAML) for specifying entitlement and identity;
- XML Access Control Markup Language (XACML) for specifying fine grained data access rights.

This section explains how XML security solutions for integrated enterprises are an increasingly important element of SOA based applications.

11.5.1 XML Signature

When many parties author a single XML document then each of them needs to sign the part they have authored. This is not possible when using network level security. It is important to ensure the integrity of certain portions of the document, while leaving open the possibility of further changes and additions to the same document. The XML Signature specification forms the basis for securely exchanging an XML document and conducting business transactions. The objective of *XML Signature* is to ensure data integrity, message authentication and non-repudiation of services.

The XML Signature standard defines a schema for capturing the result of a digital signature operation applied to arbitrary (but often XML) data. XML Signature is applied to arbitrary digital content (data objects) via an indirection [Eastlake 2008]. Data objects are digested, the resulting value is placed in an element (with other information), which is then digested and cryptographically signed. XML Signature itself will generally indicate the location of the original signed object. XML Signature can sign more than one type of resource, e.g. character encoded data (HTML), binary encoded data (a JPG), XML encoded data, a specific section of an XML document, or external data referenced by an XPointer.

Generally, three types of signatures exist:

1. *Enveloping signatures,* where the signature envelops the entire document to be signed;
2. *Enveloped signatures,* where the XML signature is instead embedded within the document;
3. *Detached signatures,* where the XML document and signature reside independently and the document is usually referenced by an external URI. A detached signature means that the signed data is not in the signature element – it is elsewhere in the XML document or in some remote location.

XML Signatures are applied to arbitrary digital content (data objects) via an indirection. Data objects are digested, the resulting value is placed in an element (with other information) and that element is then digested and cryptographically signed. XML digital signatures are represented by the `<Signature>` element. Signature validation requires the data object that was signed to be accessible. XML Signature itself will generally indicate the location of the original signed object by referring to enveloping, enveloped, and detached signed objects.

Example 11.1: Using XML signature to digitally sign a request for a price quote

Listing 11.1 illustrates an XML signature example where the data object signed is a request for a price quote identified by the URI attribute of the first `<Reference>` element in Listing 11.1. This listing shows that an XML digital signature is represented by the `<Signature>` element. Information about the original data object that is signed is represented in the element via URIs. As shown in Listing 11.1, the XML signature specification does not address mechanisms for making statements or assertions. Instead, it defines what it means for something to be signed by an XML Signature.

In the case of an enveloping signature, the `<Signature>` element becomes the parent of the original data object. In the case of an enveloped signature, the `<Signature>` element becomes the child of the original data object. In the case of a detached signature, the `<Signature>` element could be a sibling of the original data object; alternatively the `<Signature>` element could carry a reference to an external data object. The code fragment in Listing 11.1 represents a detached signature because it is not part of the document being signed.

The `<Signature>` element enables applications to carry additional information along with the digest value and can also carry the key needed to validate the signature [Galbraith 2002]. This element contains among other things a `<SignedInfo>` element that provides information about the process that leads to an XML Signature and the data objects that are actually signed. It also contains a `<SignatureValue>` element that includes the actual value of the digital signature that is the encrypted digest of the `<SignedInfo>` element.

```
<?xml version="1.0" encoding="UTF-8"?>
<Signature xmlns="http://www.w3.org/2000/09/xmldsig#">
<SignedInfo Id="2ndDecemberNewsItem">
  <CanonicalizationMethod
    Algorithm="http://www.w3.org/TR/2001/REC-xml-c14n-20010315"/>
  <SignatureMethod
    Algorithm="http://www.w3.org/2000/09/xmldsig#dsa-sha1"/>
  <Reference URI="http://www.auto-parts.com/RFQ/2011/12_03_05.htm">
      <DigestMethod Algorithm="http://www.w3.org/2000/09/xmldsig#sha1"/>
      <DigestValue>j6lwx3rvEPO0vKtMup4NbeVu8nk=</DigestValue>
  </Reference>
  <Reference URI="#AMadeUpTimeStamp"
             Type="http://www.w3.org/2000/09/
             xmldsig#SignatureProperties">
     <DigestMethod Algorithm="http://www.w3.org/2000/09/xmldsig#sha1"/>
     <DigestValue>k3453rvEPO0vKtMup4NbeVu8nk=</DigestValue>
  </Reference>
   ... ...
</SignedInfo>
<SignatureValue>MC0E~LE=. . . </SignatureValue>
<KeyInfo>
  <X509Data>
     <X509SubjectName> <!— subject of certificate -->
       CN=Jim Fletcher, O=AVERS, Inc., C=USA
    </X509SubjectName>
    <X509Certificate> <!— signer of certificate -->
       MIID5jCCA0+gA...lVN
    </X509Certificate>
  </X509Data>
</KeyInfo>
<Object>
  <SignatureProperties>
    <SignatureProperty Id="AMadeUpTimeStamp"
      Target="#2ndDecemberNewsItem">
      <timestamp xmlns="http://www.ietf.org/rfcXXXX.txt">
        <date>2004122</date>
        <time>18:30</time>
      </timestamp>
    </SignatureProperty>
  </SignatureProperties>
</Object>
</Signature>
```

Listing 11.1 XML Signature example

Signature validation requires the data object that was signed to be accessible. Signature validation of `<SignedInfo>` consists of two mandatory processes:

- validation of the signature over `<SignedInfo>`;
- validation of each `<Reference>` digest within the `<SignedInfo>` element.

To validate the signature, the recipient decodes the message digest contained in the XML Signature element `<SignatureValue>` using the signatory's public-key. The recipient then compares it to the message digest obtained by following the instructions in the `<SignedInfo>` element.

The process of converting an XML document to canonical form is known as *canonicalization.* XML canonicalization is the use of an algorithm to generate the canonical form of an XML document, to ensure security in cases where XML is subject to surface representation changes or to processing that discards some information that is not essential to the data represented in the XML, e.g. entities or namespaces with prefixes. The first sub-element of the `<SignedInfo>` element, `<CanonicalizationMethod>`, is used to specify the canonicalization algorithm that is applied to its associated `<SignedInfo>` element before it is digested and produces the signature. The second sub-element, `<SignatureMethod>`, is the cryptographic algorithm that is used to convert the canonicalized `<SignedInfo>` into the `<SignatureValue>`.

In XML Signature, each referenced resource is specified through a `<Reference>` element, which identifies the data object via its URI attribute and carries the digest value of the data object. Each `<Reference>` element includes a `<DigestMethod>` element. This element specifies the digest algorithm applied to the data object to yield the digest value contained in a `<DigestValue>` element.

`<KeyInfo>` is an optional element that indicates the key to be used to validate the signature. Possible forms for identification include certificates, key names, and key agreement algorithms and information–we define only a few. In Listing 11.1 the keying information contains the X.509 certificate for the sender, which would include the public-key needed for signature verification.

The `<Object>` element in Listing 11.1 is an optional element used mostly in enveloping signatures where the data object is part of the signature element. The `<SignatureProperties>` element type in `<Object>` can contain additional information about the signature, e.g. date, time stamp, serial number of cryptographic hardware, and other application specific attributes.

XML Signature provides its own integrity for data. XML Signature is also important for authentication and non-repudiation; however, it does not provide these functions on its own. The WS-Security standard fulfils this role by describing how XML Signature can be used to bind a security token (a representation of security related information, see Section 11.6.3) to a SOAP message and, by extension, bind the identity of the signer to a SOAP message [O'Neill 2003].

More information about XML Signature, as well as examples of enveloping, enveloped and detached signatures specified in XML Signature, can be found in [Eastlake 2008], [Galbraith 2002] and [Siddiqui 2003a].

11.5.2 XML Encryption

The XML Signature initiative does not define any standard mechanism for encrypting XML entities, which is another important security characteristic to promote the trusted use of Web applications. This functionality is provided by the XML Encryption specification, a W3C effort, which supports encryption of all or part of an XML document.

The steps for XML Encryption include [Eastlake 2002]:

- Selecting the XML document to be encrypted (in whole or in part).
- Converting the XML document to be encrypted to a canonical form, if necessary.
- Encrypting the resulting canonical form using public-key encryption.
- Sending the encrypted XML document to the intended recipient.

Because XML Encryption is not locked into any specific encryption scheme, it requires that additional information be provided on encrypted content and key information. This is accomplished by the `<EncryptedData>` and `<EncryptedKey>` elements. The core element in XML Encryption syntax is the `<EncryptedData>` element, which, in conjunction with the `<EncryptedKey>` element, is used to transport encryption keys from the originator to a known recipient. Data to be encrypted can be arbitrary data, an XML document, an XML element, an XML element content, or a reference to a resource outside an XML document. The result of encrypting data is an XML encryption element that contains or references the cipher data. When an element or element content is encrypted, the `<EncryptedData>` element replaces the element or content in the encrypted version of the XML document. The `<EncryptedKey>` element provides information about the keys involved in the encryption.

Example 11.2: Using XML Encryption to encrypt payment data

Listing 11.2 depicts an XML Encryption example taken from [Eastlake 2002]. The first part in Listing 11.2 shows an XML markup representing fictitious payment data, which includes identification information as well as information appropriate to a payment method, e.g., credit card, money transfer, or electronic check.

The example in Listing 11.2 shows that John Smith is using his credit card with a limit of $5,000. The second part in this listing shows that it may be useful for intermediate agents to know that John Smith uses a credit card with a particular limit, but not the card's number, issuer and expiration date. In this case, the content (character data or children elements) of the credit card element is encrypted. The `<CipherData>` element is the element that contains the encrypted content. XML Encryption permits the encrypted content to be carried in two ways. If the encrypted content is carried in place, it is carried as content of the `<CipherValue>` element, which exists as a child of the `<CipherData>` element. This is shown in Listing 11.2. Alternatively, XML Encryption permits the encrypted content to be stored at an external location to be referenced by the `<CipherReference>` element, which is a child of the `<CipherData>` element.

An XML (Web services) firewall will receive the contents of Listing 11.2 (SOAP messages with encrypted elements) and translate the contents to a decrypted form before forwarding the decrypted SOAP message request to the SOAP server.

```
<?xml version="1.0"?>
<PaymentInfo xmlns='http://example.org/paymentv2'>
  <Name>John Smith</Name>
  <CreditCard Limit="5,000" Currency="USD">
    <Number>4019 2445 0277 5567</Number>
    <Issuer>Example Bank</Issuer>
    <Expiration>04/06</Expiration>
  </CreditCard>
</PaymentInfo>

-------------------------------------------------------------------

<?xml version="1.0"?>
<env:Envelope>
 <env:Body>
   <PaymentInfo xmlns="http://example.org/paymentv2">
     <Name> John Smith </Name>
     <CreditCard Limit="5,000" Currency="USD'">
       <EncryptedData xmlns="http://www.w3.org/2001/04/xmlenc#"
         Type="http://www.w3.org/2001/04/xmlenc#Content">
         <CipherData>
           <CipherValue> A23B45C56 </CipherValue>
         </CipherData>
       </EncryptedData>
     </CreditCard>
   </PaymentInfo>
 </env:Body>
</env:Envelope>
```

Listing 11.2 XML Encryption example

More information about XML Encryption, including a variety of examples, can be found in [Eastlake 2002], and [Galbraith 2002].

11.5.3 XML Key Management Specification (XKMS)

XKMS (http://www.w3.org/TR/xkms/) is an initiative used to simplify the integration of PKI and management of digital certificates with XML applications. The key objective behind XKMS is to enable the development of XML based trust (Web) services for the processing and the management of PKI based cryptographic keys [Galbraith 2002]. XKMS strives to remove the complexity of working with PKI, making it easier for XML based applications to incorporate security mechanisms into their context.

XKMS facilitates integration of authentication, digital signature and encryption services, such as certificate processing and revocation status checking, into applications without the constraints and complications associated with proprietary PKI software toolkits. Figure 11.14 shows how XML Signature and Encryption are related to XKMS. With XKMS, trust functions reside in servers accessible via easily programmed XML transactions.

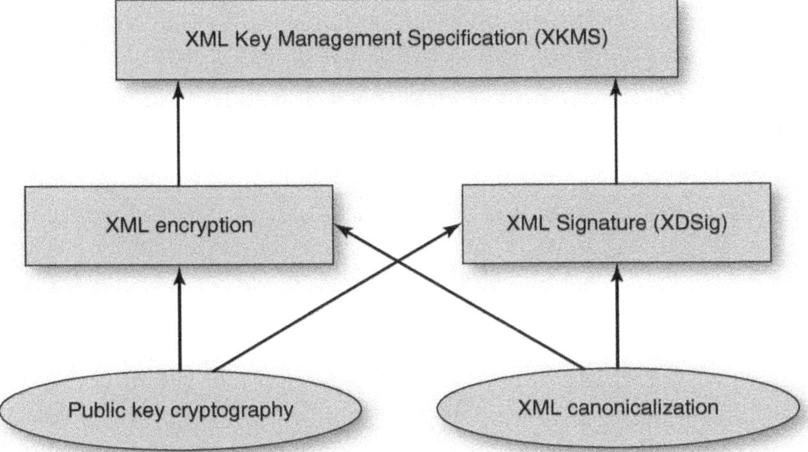

Figure 11.14 Basic blocks of the XML Trust framework

XKMS supports three major services: register service, locate service and validate service. The register service is used for registering key pairs for escrow services. Once the keys are registered the XKMS service manages the revocation, reissue and recovery of registered keys. The locate service is used to retrieve a public-key registered with the XKMS service. The validation service provides all the functionality offered by the locate service and, in addition, supports key validation.

Example 11.3: Sending and encrypted and signed message using XKMS

Figure 11.15 depicts an example showing the interactions that take place when a supplier sends a hypothetical encrypted and signed shipment message to a supplier company. The supplier is shown to no longer manage key information and instead consults the XKMS service for key processing activities. The process commences by both the supplier and shipper registering their key pairs with the XKMS trust service using the register service (Step 1). Subsequent to registering the keys, the supplier needs to encrypt the message to be sent to the supplier. For this purpose, the supplier sends a locate request (Step 2) to the XKMS server seeking the public key of the shipper. The server responds with the key, given that the shipper has already registered its key with the XKMS service. The supplier then uses this public key to encrypt the message, employs its private key to sign the message, and forwards it to the shipper (Step 3). On receipt of the message the shipper passes the XML Signature `<KeyInfo>` element contained in the signed message to the XKMS service for validation.

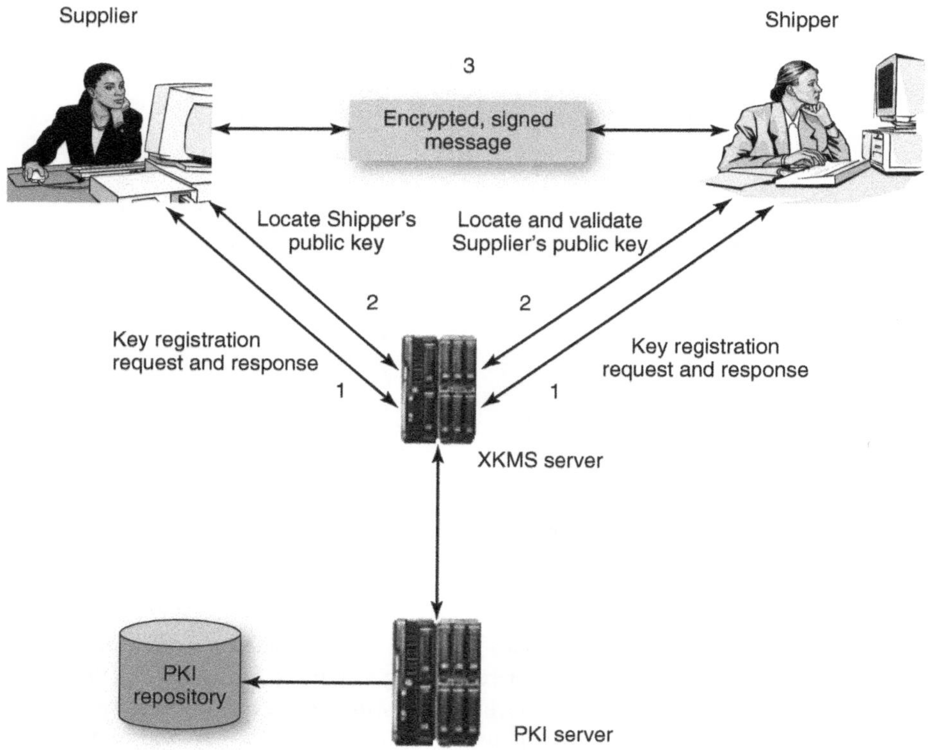

Figure 11.15 Example of using XKMS services

There are two verification stages for the signature:

1. Local verification that is carried out directly by the receiving application (shipper). During this stage the document is checked that it has been correctly signed and not been tampered with during transit. This phase comprises decoding the signature with the signatory's (supplier's) public-key and then comparing it to the footprint obtained locally.
2. Contacting the XKMS service and requesting information on the public-key transmitted. During this second stage the identity of the signatory (supplier) is made known and it is checked whether the key has been revoked (in case it was stolen) and valid (period of validity has not expired).

XKMS is made up of two major sub-parts: the XML Key Information Service Specification (X-KISS) and the XML Key Registration Service Specification (X-KRSS). The X-KISS protocol deals with public processing and validation, while the X-KRSS protocol deals with key pair registration.

11.5.3.1 XML Key Information Service Specification (X-KISS)

X-KISS defines protocols to support the processing, by a relying party, of key information associated with an XML digital signature, XML encrypted data, or other public-key usage in an XML aware application. Functions supported include locating required public-keys, given identifier information, and binding of such keys to identifier information. Applications that work in conjunction with X-KISS receive messages signed in compliance with XML Signature specifications.

X-KISS provides support for checks by means of two types of service: the locate service, which is used to find out the attached information from the data contained in the XML Signature specification key information element, and the validate service that makes sure that a key is valid.

11.5.3.2 XML Key Registration Service Specification (X-KRSS)

The goal of X-KRSS is to respond to the need for a complete, XML client focused key lifecycle management protocol. To achieve this X-KRSS defines an XML based protocol registration of public-key information. It allows an XML aware application to register its public-key pair and its associated binding information to an XKMS trust service provider.

X-KRSS supports the entire certificate lifecycle by means of the following services:

- *Key registration:* An XML application key pair holder registers its public-key with trusted infrastructure by means of a registration server. The public-key is sent to the registration server using a digitally signed request in KRSS that may optionally include name and attribute information, authentication information, and proof of possession of a private key.
- *Key revocation:* The revoke service handles the request to revoke a previously registered key binding, and any cryptographic credentials associated with it. A key binding may be revoked for different reasons, which all end up in the situation where the current key binding may not be considered trustworthy. The revoke service authenticates users who have lost control of their private key by allowing them to specify a special revocation identifier when the key binding is registered. The revocation request is authenticated using the corresponding revocation code.
- *Key recovery:* Because of the design of the encryption used in XML client encryption applications, it is statistically impossible to recover encrypted data when a private key, needed to decrypt the data, is lost. This mandates some form of key recovery provision. In X-KRSS, this function is not supported by standardised protocols but is rather built in. A recovery service in X-KRSS can only recover private keys if they have been previously escrowed. Use of the recovery service is accomplished by sending an authenticated request to the recovery service that, in return, sends back an encrypted private key if the requester is authenticated correctly.
- *Key reissuing:* Because of the need for periodically updating a key binding, X-KRSS provides a reissue service. The use of this service is very similar to the

use of the register service, with the exception of the request for the renewal of an existing key binding instead of generating a new one. After successful identification a renewed key pair is sent to the requester.

11.5.4 Security Assertions Markup Language (SAML)

One of the biggest challenges for XML based security applications is that of user authentication and single sign-on in a distributed environment across a number of disparate applications. Single sign-on in the case of Web services provides the ability to use multiple Web services, or a single Web service made up of multiple services, based on a single authentication.

XML based standard framework for describing and exchanging security related information, called assertions (declarations on facts about subjects), designed to facilitate the exchange of security information between different application components and trust domains [Ragouzis 2008]. It does so by inserting security information into assertions in XML form. These assertions convey information about an end user's authentication act, their authorisation to access a certain resource, or their attributes. SAML assertions may be bound to SOAP messages, to be sent to SAML aware Web services.

SAML enables disparate security systems to interoperate while allowing individual organisations to retain their own authentication systems. Instead of having an enterprise authenticate all incoming foreign individuals, or rely on central authentication registry for every partnership, SAML implementations provide an interoperable XML based security solution, whereby user information and corresponding authorisation information in the form of assertions can be exchanged by collaborating applications or services. To facilitate this undertaking, the SAML specification establishes assertion and protocol schemas for the structure of the documents that transport security. By defining how identity and access information is exchanged, SAML becomes the common language through which organisations can communicate without modifying their own internal security architectures.

The main components of SAML include the following [Cantor 2004]:

1. *Assertions:* SAML defines three kinds of assertions, which are declarations of one or more facts about a subject, e.g. a service requester. Authentication assertions require that the user prove their identity. Attribute assertions contain specific details about the user, such as their credit line or citizenship. Authorisation assertions state whether a client is allowed or denied a request and the scope of the client's privileges. Authorisation assertions permit or deny access to specific resources, such as files, devices, Web pages, databases and so on. For instance, authorisation assertions are typically a response to a request such as a *is the auto parts supplier AVERS allowed access to confidential Web page information about product design specs and blueprints?* All types of assertions include a common set of elements: the subject, which denotes who the assertion is identifying; the conditions, which denote conditions under which the assertion is valid; and an authentication statement, which denotes advice on how the assertion was made. Each assertion also includes information about the type of request made.

2. *Request/response protocol:* SAML defines a request/response protocol for obtaining assertions. An SAML request can either ask for a specific known assertion or make authentication, attribute and authorisation decision queries, with the SAML response providing back the requested assertions. The XML format for protocol messages and their allowable extensions is defined in an XML schema.
3. *Bindings:* This element details exactly how SAML request/response message exchanges should map into standard messaging or communication protocols. For instance, the SAML SOAP Binding defines how SAML protocol messages can be communicated within SOAP messages while the SAML URI Binding defines how SAML protocol messages can be communicated through URI resolution.
4. *Profiles:* These dictate how SAML assertions can be embedded or transported between communicating systems. Generally, a profile of SAML defines constraints and/or extensions in support of the usage of SAML for a particular application – the goal to enhance interoperability. For instance, the Web browser single sign-on profile specifies how SAML authentication assertions are communicated between an identity provider and service provider to enable single sign-on for a browser user. The Web user authenticates to the identity provider, which then produces an authentication assertion that, on being delivered to the service provider, allows it to establish a security context for the Web user.

Figure 11.16 illustrates the relationship between the SAML components. It also shows an SAML assertion being carried within an SAML response, which itself is embedded

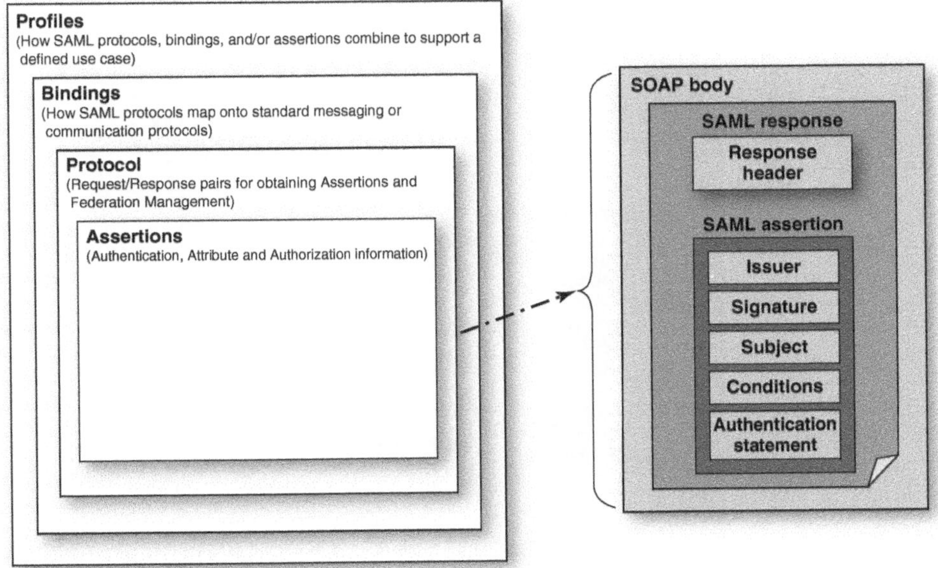

Figure 11.16 SAML components and assertion structure

within a SOAP Body. Note that an SAML response could contain multiple assertions, although it is more typical to have a single assertion within a response.

Using a protocol defined in SAML, clients can request assertions from SAML authorities and get a response from them in the form of SAML assertions related to these activities. Figure 11.17 illustrates the SAML model. In this model, the subject (client) may authenticate itself with up to three different SAML (authentication, attribute and authorisation) authorities by sending its credentials to them for validation. The subject then obtains assertion references, which it includes in a request for accessing a resource, such as a Web service. The subject forwards this information to a Policy Enforcement Point (PEP) module that protects this specific resource. The PEP uses the references to request the actual assertions (authentication decision) from the issuing authority or from a Policy Decision Point (PDP) module. The PEP and PDP modules are part of the XACML access control language that we shall examine in the following section. SAML and XACML are complementary standards that share basic concepts and definitions.

When a client attempts to access some target site, it will forward the SAML assertion from the SAML authentication authority. The target can then verify whether the assertion is from an authority that it trusts, and, if this is so, it can then use the SAML authentication assertion as an assurance that the principal has been authenticated. Subsequently, the target could then go to an SAML attribute authority to request an attribute assertion for the authenticated principal, passing along the authentication assertion. The returned

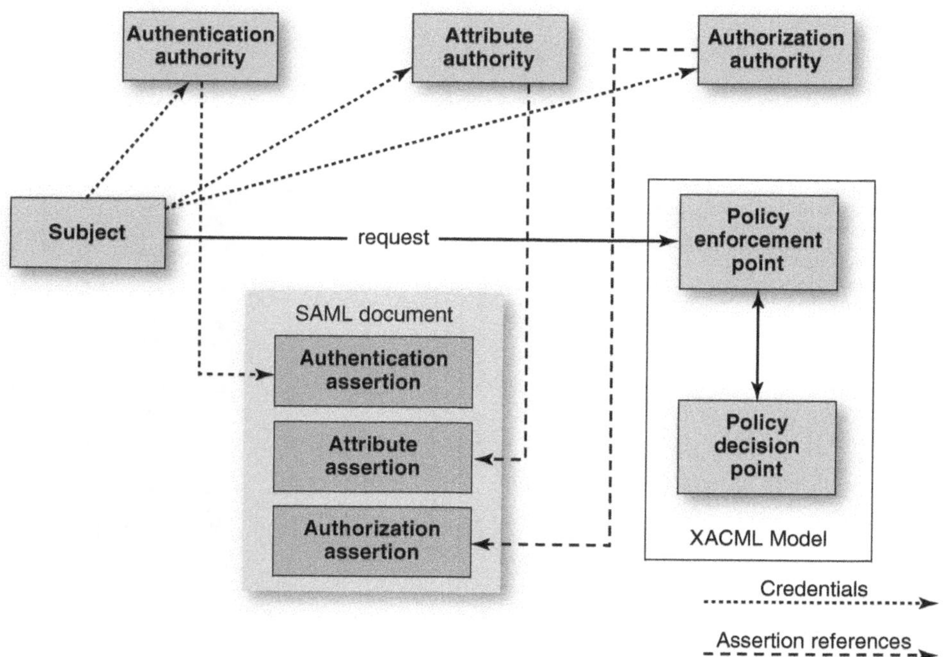

Figure 11.17 The SAML and XACML models

attribute assertion will contain the attributes for the principal, which will be guaranteed to be correct by the SAML attribute authority. Finally, the target may go to an authorisation service and, upon passing the attribute assertion, enquire whether the principal is permitted to perform an activity on a certain resource. The authorisation service could be a local service of the target company or an external SAML authorisation service. For instance, attribute assertion information may be used at a protected Web service in order to make an access control decision, e.g. *Only users who have authenticated to one of our trusted partners can access this Web service,* or *Only users with the attribute 'manager' can access this Web service,* etc. SAML authorities can use various sources of information, such as external policy stores and assertions that were received as input in requests, in creating their response.

Example 11.4: Using SAML to authenticate order messages

Listing 11.3 considers an order processing scenario involving an order message that needs to be forwarded from an order processing service to a shipment processing service and, finally, to a billing service. In the case of Listing 11.3, which contains only a single assertion, the order processing service is the subject of this assertion and the order processing service itself will eventually authorise the SOAP message to request shipment of the order by the shipment processing service.

Listing 11.3 packages an authentication statement in the format of an SAML assertion. Here, an authentication statement specifies the outcome of an act of authentication that took place in the past. We assume that an SAML authority authenticates a user and issues the security assertion. Listing 11.3 shows an assertion with a single authentication statement in the context of the order processing scenario. More specifically, the assertion in the listing states that the entity called name `"OrderProcService"` is the owner of a public key named `"OrderProcServiceKey"`. The asserting authority (some trusted party) has authenticated the `"OrderProcService"` using XML digital signatures. The basic information specifies a unique identifier used for the assertion identifier, date and time of issuance, and the time interval for which the assertion is valid.

The root `<Assertion>` element wraps three important sub-elements: a `<Conditions>` element, an `<AuthenticationStatement>` element, and a `<Signature>` element. The `<Conditions>` element specifies the time interval for which the assertion is valid. The `<AuthenticationStatement>` states the outcome (the final result) of an authentication process. The `<Signature>` element contains, as usual, XML digital signature tags.

In Listing 11.3 the subject that the authentication pertains to is `"Order-ProcService"`. The format of the subject could be chosen from a number of predefined formats provided in the SAML specification, including e-mail addresses and X.509 subject names, or alternatively could be custom defined. In Listing 11.3 the entity `"OrderProcService"` was originally authenticated using XML digital signatures (signified by `urn:ietf:rfc:3075`) at `"2004-07-19T17:02:0Z"`. Finally, the `<SubjectConfirmation>` element of an `<AuthenticationStatement>` specifies the relationship between the subject of an assertion and the author of the message that contains the assertion.

```
<saml:Assertion
  xmln's:saml="urn:oasis:names:tc:SAML:1.0:assertion"
  MajorVersion="1" MinorVersion="0"
  AssertionID="XraafaacDz6iXrUa"
  Issuer="www.some-trusted-party.com"
  IssueInstant="2004-07-19T17:02:00Z">
       <saml:Conditions
          NotBefore="2004-07-19T17:02:00Z"
          NotOnOrAfter="2004-07-19T17:10:00Z"/>
       <saml:AuthenticationStatement
          AuthenticationMethod="urn:ietf:rfc:3075"
          AuthenticationInstant="2004-07-19T17:02:00Z">
              <saml:Subject>
                  <saml:NameIdentifier
                     NameQualifier=http://www.some-trusted-party.com
                     Format="...">
                     uid="OrderProcService"
                  </saml:NameIdentifier>
                     <saml:SubjectConfirmation>
                     <saml:ConfirmationMethod>
                         urn:oasis:names:tc:SAML:1.0:cm:holder-of-key
                     </saml:ConfirmationMethod>
                       <ds:KeyInfo>
                          <ds:KeyName>OrderProcServiceKey</ds:KeyName>
                          <ds:KeyValue> ... </ds:KeyValue>
                       </ds:KeyInfo>
                  </saml:SubjectConfirmation>
              </saml:Subject>
       </saml:AuthenticationStatement>
</saml:Assertion>
```

Listing 11.3 Example of a SAML authentication assertion

Simply providing assertions from an asserting authority to a relying party may not be adequate for a secure system. To address this problem, SAML defines a number of security mechanisms that prevent or detect security attacks. The primary mechanism is for the relying party and asserting party to have a pre-existing trust relationship, typically involving PKI. While use of a PKI is not mandated, it is recommended, and use of particular mechanisms is described for each profile.

Although SAML defines mechanisms for user identification, authentication and authorisation, it does not address privacy policies. Rather, partner sites are responsible for developing mutual requirements for user authentication and data protection. SAML, however, defines the structure of the documents that transport security information among services. SAML enables single sign-on and end-to-end security for e-Business applications and Web services. Because the SAML standard is designed for the exchange of secure sign-on information between a user, or *relying party,* and multiple issuing parties, it allows issuing parties to use their own chosen methods of authentication, e.g. PKI, hash or password.

While SAML makes assertions about credentials, it does not actually authenticate or authorise users. This is achieved by an authentication server in conjunction with the LDAP directory (see Section 11.3.7.2). SAML links back to the actual authentication and makes its assertion based on the results of that event.

Several useful examples of the use of SAML, including how an application can request an SAML authority for the issuance of an SAML assertion as well as using SAML assertions in WS-Security applications, can be found in [Siddiqui 2003b].

11.5.5 XML Access Control Markup Language (XACML)

In the previous section we explained that SAML can only define how identity and access information is exchanged but does not specify how this information is used. This is the responsibility of the Access Control Markup Language (XACML), which is a declarative access control policy language implemented in XML, and a processing model. XACML is an extension of SAML that allows access control policies to be specified and also provides a processing model describing how to interpret these policies. The latest XACML version 2.0 was ratified by OASIS standards organization in 2005 [Moses 2005].

XACML is a general purpose access control policy language that uses the same definitions of subjects and actions as SAML and provides a syntax (defined in XML) for expressing the rules needed to define an organisation's security policies and managing authorisation decisions. XACML has two basic components [Proctor 2003]:

1. An access control policy language that lets developers specify the rules about who can do what and when. The access control policy language is used to describe general access control requirements, and has standard extension points for defining new functions, data types, combining logic and so on.
2. A request/response language that presents requests for access and describes the answers to those queries. The request/response language lets users form a query to ask whether or not a given action should be allowed, and interpret the result. The response always includes an answer about whether the request should be allowed using one of four values: permit, deny, indeterminate (an error occurred or some required value was missing, so a decision cannot be made), or not applicable (the request cannot be answered by this service).

In addition to providing request/response and policy languages, XACML also provides the other pieces of this relationship, i.e. finding a policy that applies to a given request and evaluating the request against that policy to come up with an affirmative or negative answer. XACML provides for fine grained control of activities (such as read, write, copy, delete) based on several criteria, including the following:

- Attributes of the user requesting access: Attributes are named values of known types that may include an issuer identifier or an issue date and time, e.g. *Only division managers and above can view this document.* A user's name, their security clearance, the document they want to access, and the time of day are all attribute values.

- The protocol over which the request is made: this may specify security protocols, e.g. *This data can be viewed only if it is accessed over secure HTTP.*
- The authentication mechanism used.

In a typical XACML usage (data flow) scenario, a subject, e.g. human user or Web service, may want to take some action on a particular resource. The subject submits its query to the Policy Enforcement Point entity that protects the resource, e.g. file system or Web server. The PEP forms a request (using the XACML request language) based on the attributes of the subject, action, resource and other relevant information. The PEP then forwards this request to a Policy Decision Point module, which examines the request, retrieves policies (written in the XACML policy language) that are applicable to this request, and determines whether access should be granted according to the XACML rules for evaluating policies. That answer (expressed in the XACML response language) is returned to the PEP, which can then allow or deny access to the requester. The PEP and PDP might both be contained within a single application, or might be distributed across several servers.

The complete policy, applicable to a particular decision request, may be composed of a number of individual rules or policies. For instance, in a personal privacy application, the owner of the personal information may define certain aspects of disclosure policy, whereas the enterprise that is the custodian of the information may define certain other aspects. In order to render an authorisation decision, it must be possible to combine the two separate policies to form the single policy applicable to the request.

The policy language model of XACML is shown in Figure 11.18. This figure shows that ach XACML policy document contains exactly one `<Policy>` or `<PolicySet>` root XML tag. The `<PolicySet>` element represents a single access control policy and contains a set of `<Policy>` or other `<PolicySet>` elements, as well as references to policies found in remote locations and a specified procedure for combining the results of their evaluation. It is the standard means for combining separate policies into a single combined policy. A policy can have any number of `<Rule>`s which contain the core logic of an XACML policy. `<Rule>`s are expressions describing conditions under which resource access requests are allowed or denied. `<Rule>`s comprise a `<Condition>`, which is a Boolean function, and have `<Effect>`s, which indicate the rule writer's intended consequence for a rule that is satisfied. The `<Rule>` element is not intended to form the basis of an authorisation decision by its own. It is intended to exist in isolation only within an XACML policy administration point, where it may form the basic unit of management, and be reused in multiple policies. An `<Obligation>` is an operation specified in a policy or policy set that should be performed in conjunction with enforcing an authorisation decision. An `<Obligation>` element is defined as an action that the PEP is obligated to perform before granting or denying access once the authorisation decision is complete. An example of an obligation would be the creation of a digitally signed record every time that a customer's financial records are accessed.

Given the fact that a `<Policy>` or `<PolicySet>` elements may contain multiple policies or rules, each of which may evaluate to different access control decisions, XACML needs some way of reconciling the decisions each makes. This is achieved through a collection of combining algorithms. Each algorithm represents a different way of combining multiple decisions into a single decision. There are `<PolicyCombiningAlgorithms>` (used by `<PolicySet>`) and `<RuleCombiningAlgorithms>` (used by `<Policy>`).

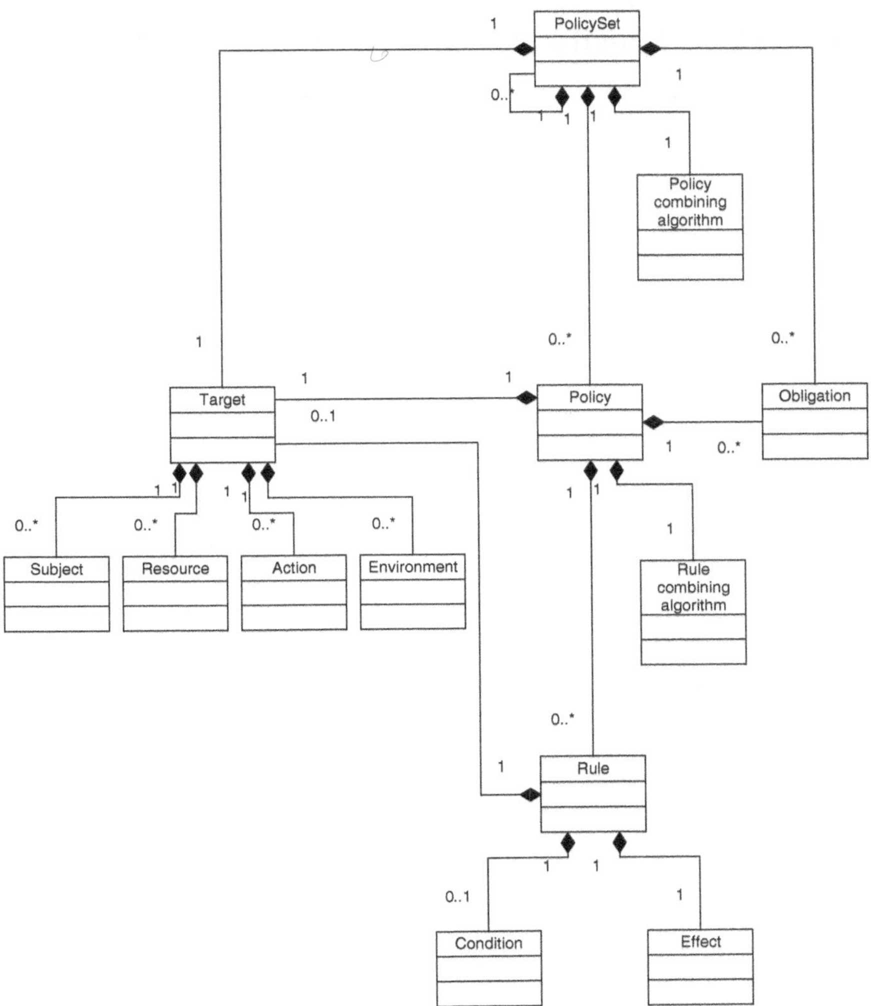

Figure 11.18 XACML policy language model

Part of what an XACML PDP does is find policies that apply to a given request. To this end, XACML provides a `<Target>` element. The `<Target>` of a policy statement is used by the PDP to determine where the policy is applicable for a particular request. The target specifies the subjects, resources and actions (such as read, write, copy, delete) of the policy. A `<Target>` is essentially a set of simplified conditions for the `<Subject>`, `<Resource>`, and `<Action>` sub-elements that must be met for a `<PolicySet>`, `<Policy>`, or `<Rule>` to apply to a given request. These use Boolean functions to compare values found in a request to those included in the `<Target>`. If all the conditions of a `<Target>` are met, then its associated `<PolicySet>`, `<Policy>`, or `<Rule>` applies to the request.

Example 11.5: Specifying a security policy in XACML

Listing 11.4 illustrates a simple policy from an automotive parts supplier (AVERS) stating that any subject with an e-mail address in the `auto-parts.com` domain can perform any action on any resource of this company.

```
<Policy PolicyId="identifier:example:SimplePolicy1"
        RuleCombiningAlgId="identifier:rule-combining-
          algorithm:deny-overrides">
   <Description>
     AVERS access control policy
   </Description>
   <Target>
      <Subjects><AnySubject/></Subjects>
      <Resources><AnyResource/></Resources>
      <Actions><AnyAction/></Actions>
   </Target>
   <Rule RuleId="identifier:example:SimpleRule1"
     Effect="Permit">
     <Target>
        <Subjects><Subject>
          <SubjectMatch
              MatchId="urn:oasis:names:tc:xacml:1.0:function:
                                                  rfc822Name-match">
             <AttributeValue
               DataType="http://www.w3.org/2001/XMLSchema#string">
               auto-parts.com
             </AttributeValue>
             <SubjectAttributeDesignator
                AttributeId="urn:oasis:names:tc:xacml:1.0:
                                                 subject:subject-id"
                DataType="urn:oasis:names:tc:xacml:1.0:
                                             data-type:rfc822Name"/>
          </SubjectMatch>
        </Subject></Subjects>
        <Resources><AnyResource/></Resources>
        <Actions><AnyAction/></Actions>
      </Target>
   </Rule>
</Policy>
```

Listing 11.4 Sample XACML policy

Rules can have an effect of either *permit* or *deny*. In the case shown in Listing 11.4, if the rule is satisfied, it will evaluate to permit, meaning that, as far as this rule is concerned, the requested access should be permitted. Finally, the rule `<Target>` section is similar to the target of a policy in that it describes the decision request to which this rule applies. The rule target is similar to the target of the policy itself, but with one important difference. The rule target states a specific value that the subject in the decision request must match. The `<SubjectMatch>` element specifies a matching function in the "`MatchId`" attribute, a literal value of `"auto-parts.com"` and a pointer to a specific subject attribute in the request context by means of the <SubjectAttributeDesignator> element. Only if the match returns *true* will this rule apply to a particular decision request.

In addition to defining a standard format for policy, XACML defines a standard way of expressing <Request>s and <Response>s. The <Request> and the <Response> elements provide a standard format for interacting with a PDP. A <Request> contains attributes that characterise the subject, resource, action or environment elements in which the access request is made. There can be multiple subjects, and each subject can have multiple attributes. In addition to attributes, the resource section allows the inclusion of the content of the requested resource, which can be considered in policy evaluation through XPath expressions. When a request is sent from a PEP to a PDP, that request is formed almost exclusively of attributes, which will be compared to attribute values in a policy in order to make the appropriate access decisions. A <Response> consists of one or more results, each of which represents the result of an evaluation. Typically, there will only be one result in a <Response>. Each result contains a decision (permit, deny, not applicable or indeterminate), some status information, e.g. why the evaluation failed, and optionally one or more <Obligation>s.

Example 11.6: An access request to execute a security policy

Listing 11.5 shows a hypothetical decision request that might be submitted to a PDP that executes the policy described in Listing 11.4. The access request that generates the

```
<Request>
 <Subject>
      <Attribute
               AttributeId="urn:oasis:names:tc:xacml:1.0:subject:
               subject-id"
       DataType="identifier:rfc822name">
        <AttributeValue>
            jsmith@auto-parts.com
        </AttributeValue>
      </Attribute>
  </Subject>
  <Resource>
      <Attribute AttributeId="identifier:resource:resource-uri"
                 DataType="xs:anyURI">
         <AttributeValue>
           http://auto-parts.com/tax-record/employee/JohnSmith
         </AttributeValue>
      </Attribute>
  </Resource>
  <Action>
      <Attribute AttributeId="identifier:example:action"
                 DataType="xs:string">
         <AttributeValue> read </AttributeValue>
      </Attribute>
  </Action>
</Request>
```

Listing 11.5 Sample XCML request

decision request may be stated as follows: John Smith, with e-mail name "jsmith@auto-parts.com", wants to read his tax record at AVERS. In the case of Listing 11.5, there is only one subject involved in the request and the subject has only one attribute: the subject's identity, expressed as an e-mail name.

The PDP processing this request context locates the policy in its policy repository. It compares the subject, resource, action and environment in the request context to the subjects, resources, actions and environments in the policy target.

Example 11.7: Responding to the access request

The sample response for the request in Listing 11.5 is given in Listing 11.6.

```
<Response>
    <Result>
        <Decision> Permit </Decision>
    </Result>
</Response>
```

Listing 11.6 Sample XCML response

11.6 Securing SOA and Web services

SOA based systems are often geographically and organisationally separated to provide services from disparate suppliers and technologies. This requires new types of security defence. As with all technological advances it is essential that the security implications of deployment are fully understood and assessed.

When designing robust SOA applications it is important to plough through a variety of standards, emerging specifications and products that can contribute features and functions for securing SOA based services. There exist a variety of standards and products that provide many options for SOA security, but this also makes security strategy development notably more complex. In this section we shall examine a number of complementary standards, which are coming together to achieve end-to-end SOA security. The important ones include WS-Security, WS-Trust, WS-SecurityPolicy and WS-Federation. We shall explain how these technologies are used in the context of SOA and Web service security and how they relate to the XML standards (XML Signature and XML Encryption, SAML and XACML) that we covered in previous sections. We shall first begin by explaining the technology implications and challenges of Web services security.

11.6.1 Web service application level security challenges

Web services rely on *message security,* which works by applying security technology to the message itself. Message security focuses on two critical security concerns:

- protecting message content from being disclosed to unauthorised individuals (confidentiality);
- preventing illegal modification of message content (integrity).

Message security also guarantees selectivity by securing portions of the message to different parties (authenticity) and flexibility as different security policies can be applied to request and responses independently [Rosenberg 2004]. An additional requirement is, of course, content access control. As today SSL, along with TLS, are used to provide transport level security for Web service applications, we shall first examine the shortcomings of SSL and then reflect on important application (message) level security challenges.

11.6.1.1 SSL shortcomings

One serious weakness in Web services lies in its use of HTTP. HTTP transport (the basic transport mechanism of the Internet) can tunnel through existing network firewalls and, using SOAP, establish communications with applications within an enterprise infrastructure. It, therefore, creates a major break in enterprise virus and hacking defences. Traditionally, SSL, TLS, VPNs, and IPSec are some of the common ways of securing content. For instance, SSL/TLS (see Section 11.3.6.1) offers several security features, including authentication, data integrity, and data confidentiality of messages in transit. SSL/TLS enables point-to-point secure sessions and can be used to secure communication from a transport level perspective. It provides rudimentary, point-to-point data privacy but not full security.

SSL/TLS is certainly sufficient to meet the straightforward requirement to secure interactions between Web browsers and Web servers that utilised the stateless HTTP connection protocol, but it cannot adequately address the scenario where a SOAP request is routed via more than one server. For situations where secure messages must pass from one intermediary to another, SSL/TLS is found lacking.

11.6.1.2 Message level security shortcomings

In the following we classify and summarise the most prominent message level security challenges for Web services.

> *Message processing intermediaries:* With Web service technologies SOAP is designed to support one or more intermediaries that can forward or reroute SOAP messages, based upon information either in the SOAP header or the HTTP header. This gives rise to the problem of message intermediaries in the context of Web services. To maximize the reach of Web services requires end-to-end and not just point-to-point security. Figure 11.19 highlights the differences between point-to-point and end-to-end security configurations. In the end-to-end security topology – where the security context is shared – the creator of the message may have written the payload, but intermediaries may inspect or rewrite the message afterwards. Therefore, there must be a way for the intermediary to read the part of the message that instructs it what to do, without compromising the confidential payload of the message. This process becomes even more compound when one considers long running orchestrated Web services involving multiple requests, responses and forks, and their ensuing security requirements. All of these scenarios

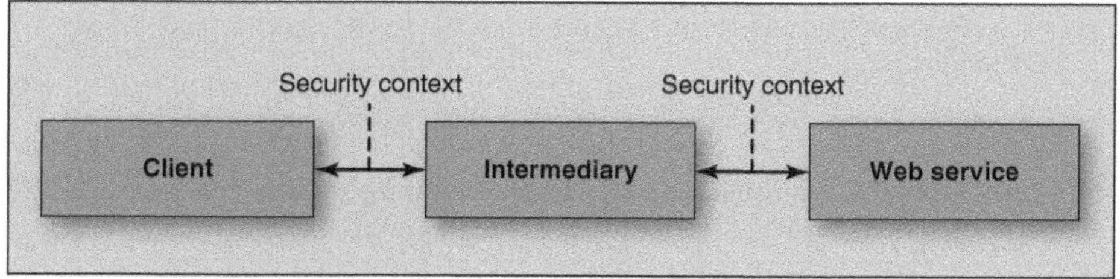

Point-to-point security configuration

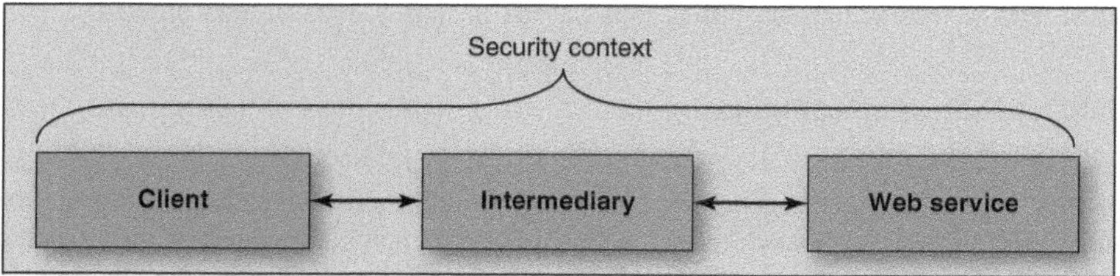

End-to-end security configuration

Figure 11.19 Point-to-point versus end-to-end security configuration

rely on an end-to-end security formation where message processing intermediaries can forward messages. When data is received and forwarded by an intermediary beyond the transport layer, both the integrity of data and any security information that flows with it may be lost. This forces any upstream message servers to rely on the security evaluations made by previous intermediaries and to completely trust their handling of the content of messages.

Types of security granularity: Web services require a high degree of granularity, i.e. different security requirements, for incoming and outgoing messages as well as waypoint visibility, i.e. partial visibility into the message. Web services need to maintain secure context and control it according to their security policies. The infrastructure securing Web services needs XML's granularity for encrypting or digitally signing select document portions and acting on rewritten individual headers. However, the problem is that SSL/TLS can be used for data privacy/encryption, signing/integrity, and for authentication/trust, but only provides transport level granularity for point-to-point communication and not granularity on encryption, such as encrypting sensitive information while exposing routing information in clear text. With SSL/TLS the security of each message is an all-or-nothing proposition: either the entire message is secure, or not. Therefore, whenever the security of particular parts of a message is important, for instance in cases where a Web service request might ask for several pieces of information that have different levels of confidentiality, SSL cannot cope.

Interoperability of security solutions: In addition to the transport level problems introduced due to the limitations of SSL, Web services face a variety of other application level security challenges when trying to enable two or more services, running under different security domains, to intercommunicate. For example, one Web service may use Kerberos tickets to authenticate clients, while another might only support client side SSL certificates. A question that arises is how can these services authenticate to each other? Similarly, as developers start writing enterprise grade, line-of-business applications, one problem that surfaces is that, when two or more Web services are running under different security domains, it is highly likely that each domain will maintain its own distinct *silo* of user profiles. Such issues require a security mechanism for providing a single point of sign-on and authentication, and a standardised way to obtain suitable security credentials to prove the authenticated identity.

The powerful and flexible security infrastructure that Web services require can only be developed by leveraging the transport mechanisms provided by SSL/TLS and extending them with advanced application layer security mechanisms to provide a comprehensive suite of Web services security capabilities that address problems at the message level. To address this challenge, several standards' bodies, including the W3C, OASIS, the Liberty Alliance and others, have proposed a number of security standards to solve problems related to authentication, role based access control (RBAC), messaging and data security. Their aim is to help strengthen Web service security. As a result, a number of standards, including XML Encryption, XML Signature, and SAML, are used in the context of a foundational security standard for Web services called WS-Security, ensuring the integrity, confidentiality and security of Web services. The remainder of this chapter explores the Web service security model, which we introduce in the following section.

11.6.2 Web service security roadmap

To address end-to-end security concerns and provide security foundations for Web Services, IBM and Microsoft have jointly written the Web services security roadmap as a means for developing a set of Web service security standard specifications and technologies. These are meant to describe a unifying approach for dealing with protection for messages exchanged in a Web services environment [WS-Roadmap 2002]. The proposed security framework and roadmap are sufficient to construct higher level key exchange, authentication, authorisation, auditing and trust mechanisms, while providing an integrating abstraction allowing systems and applications to build a bridge between diverse security systems and technologies. This security framework is shown in Figure 11.20 to comprise a foundational standard called WS-Security (which in turn is built on XML Signature, XML Encryption, SAML and various other security standards) followed by other standards that rely on it. These standards are briefly described below and will be studied later in this chapter.

- *WS-Security:* This set of SOAP extensions is focused on implementing message content integrity and confidentiality. The mechanisms specified by this standard can be used to accommodate a variety of security models and encryption technologies.
- *WS-SecurityPolicy:* WS-SecurityPolicy is an addendum to WS-Security and indicates the policy assertions for WS-Policy that apply to WS-Security. Security policy assertions in WS-SecurityPolicy specify the security requirements of Web services. These security requirements include the supported algorithms for encryption and digital signatures, privacy attributes, and how this information may be bound to a Web service.

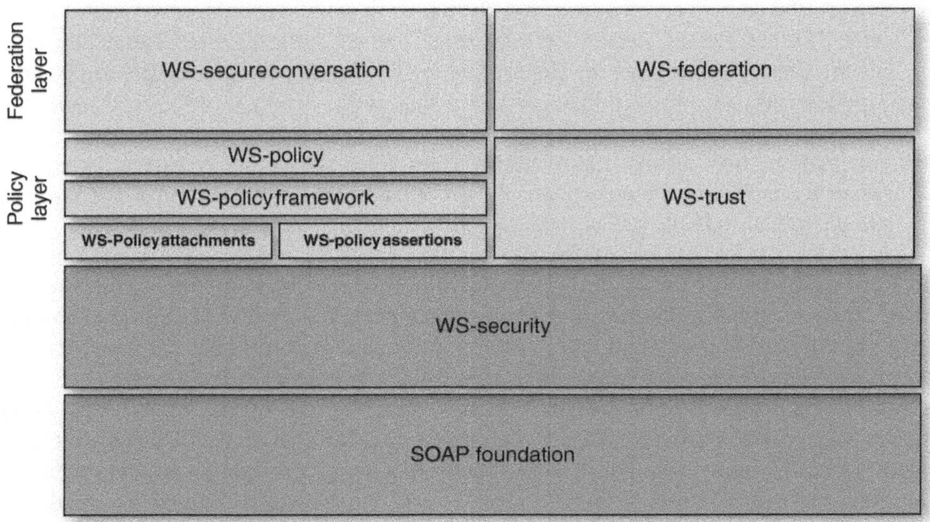

Figure 11.20 Web service security roadmap standards

- *WS-Trust:* This specification defines a series of XML based primitives for requesting and issuing security tokens, as well as for managing trust relationships.
- *WS-SecureConversation:* WS-SecureConversation defines extensions that build on WS-Security to provide secure communication.
- *WS-Federation:* WS-Federation defines mechanisms that are used to enable identity, attribute, authentication, and authorisation federation across different trust realms. This standard also includes privacy policies that are stated by organisations that deploy Web services and require the requester to indicate the restrictions it expects on the use and distribution of sensitive information contained in tokens it obtains. The WS-Federation standard also specifies several policy assertions to indicate support for services authorisation features.

In the security roadmap standards depicted in Figure 11.20, WS-Security serves as the foundation block (above that of SOAP) for a set of composable security building blocks that lean on it. This means that the various building block standards such as WS-Federation may be constructed using other security building blocks, including WS-Security, WS-Policy, WS-Trust, and WS-SecureConversation.

The standards in the security roadmap address distributed message based security in terms of three broad interrelated security concerns, namely interoperability, trust and integration, which are defined as follows:

- Interoperability in the context of security means that independent heterogeneous systems, which previously did not communicate, are able to work together and understand one another. This capability is especially important when communications between disparate systems are secure. The family of security standards that relate to secure interoperability include: WS-Security, WS-SecurePolicy and WS-SecureConversation.

- Trust for Web services security is also an important element that needs to be represented in relationships. It can be explicitly established or it may be presumed. The family of security standards that help promote trust include the WS-Trust standard.
- Integration in the world of Web services security stretches interoperability to address cross organisational integration, by extending and unifying (heterogeneous) system architectures across organisational borders so that existing services can be reused for new purposes. This means that identities, and the trust model under which services operate, need to be integrated. The family of security standards that relate to integration include: WS-Federation and WS-Authorization.

We shall first introduce a general Web service security model and then address the security roadmap specifications in turn, starting from the interoperability security standards, then moving on to trust standards, and ending with security integration standards.

11.6.3 Web service security model

In the context of Web services, applications need to be able to interoperate despite using their own security infrastructure and mechanisms, such as PKI or Kerberos. To facilitate this, the Web service roadmap specification has defined an abstract security model and architecture for this purpose [WS-Roadmap 2002]. This model is generic in the sense that is designed to fit many applications and is shown in Figure 11.21.

The Web services security model is defined in terms of generic protocols for exchanging generic (token) claims offered by service consumers and generic policy rules regarding such claims enforced by service providers. The advantage of this approach is that only such generic policy and token metadata need be generically exchanged across diverse administrative domains, leaving such domains free to use different concrete policy and token mechanisms, such as PKI, Active Directory and Kerberos.

Figure 11.21 illustrates that there are three parties involved in the security model for Web services. These are: the requester, the Web service, and the security token service (the darker shaded modules). The different security technologies in the Web services

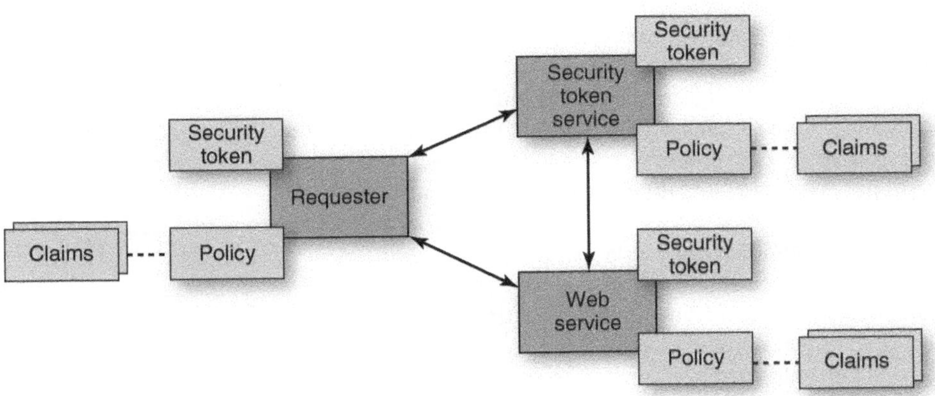

Figure 11.21 The general Web services security and trust model

security model are abstracted into interoperable formats that define a generic policy model, modularised into the following conceptual building blocks: policies, policy assertions, claims and security tokens. These are defined as follows:

- A *(security) policy* determines the security mechanisms that must be present in inbound SOAP messages and the security enhancements that need to be added to outgoing SOAP messages.
- As usual, *security policy assertions* specify the security requirements of their respective Web services and include the supported algorithms for encryption and digital signatures, privacy attributes, and how this information may be applied to a Web service.
- A *claim* is a statement about a subject (person, application or business entity) either by the subject or by a relying party that associates the subject with a property, such as identity of entitlements.
- A *security token* conveys claims as its statements. A security token can be thought of as data (added to a SOAP header), which expresses a claim about an end user or message originator, e.g. their identity, their entitlements and their authorisation to access a particular resource for a certain length of time. Examples include user name and password combinations, SSL client certificates, XRML licenses and Kerberos tickets.

In Figure 11.21 security tokens are used to provide an end-to-end security solution and must be shared, either directly or indirectly, between the parties involved in message exchanges. An authority can vouch for or endorse the claims in a security token by using its key to sign or encrypt the security token, thereby enabling the authentication of the claims in the token. An X.509 [Hallam-Baker 2004] certificate, claiming the binding between a principal's identity and public-key, is an example of a signed security token endorsed by the certification authority.

Security token acquisition can be done either directly, by explicitly requesting a token from an appropriate authority (as shown in Figure 11.21), or indirectly by delegating the acquisition to a trusted third party. For instance, to acquire a Kerberos ticket, an application needs to contact a Kerberos Key Distribution Center, while to acquire an X.509 certificate an application needs to contact a certification authority. The third party that issues a security token is referred to as a *security token service* in Figure 11.21. The role of the security token service is to link existing fragmented security islands into a federated security network through the exchange of diverse types of security tokens. The X.509 certification authority, the Kerberos Key Distribution Center, and the certification authority in PKI are good examples of security token services. The security token service does not simply issue and validate tokens, it also exchanges them. The key ability of a security token service as a brokering entity is its ability to exchange one type of token, e.g. X.509 certificate, for another, e.g. Kerberos ticket.

The security model for Web services in Figure 11.21 encompasses a trust model (illustrated by the solid lines interconnecting the heavy shaded modules). The *Web services trust model* defines trust as the characteristic that one entity is willing to rely upon a second entity to execute a set of actions and/or to make a number of assertions about a set of subjects and/or scopes. Trust relationships can be either direct or brokered. Direct trust is when a relying party accepts as true all (or some subset of) the claims in the token sent by the requester. In the case of brokered trust, a *trust proxy* (second party) is used to read the WS-Policy information and request the appropriate security tokens from an issuer of security tokens, thus vouching for a third party. Trust relationships are based on the exchange and brokering of security tokens and on the support of trust policies that have been established by the corresponding security authorities. WS-Security will be used to transfer the required security tokens making use of XML Signature and XML Encryption, which ensures message integrity and confidentiality.

When a requester wishes to invoke a Web service, it must produce claims such as its identity and privileges. On the other hand, each Web service has a security policy applied to it, which may, for instance, require the encryption and digital signing of messages and identification of the requester. Such Web service policies specify the security requirements to access the Web service. A Web service receives a message from a requester that possibly includes security tokens, and may have some protection applied to it using WS-Security mechanisms.

When an application is sending security claims, it will have to consider how to represent them in messages conveyed over SOAP and WS-Security. The Web service security model specifies all claims included in the security token that is attached to a request message [WS-Roadmap 2002]. For example, identity via a password or X.509v3 certificates are security claims. Therefore, they need to be represented as security tokens.

The general security messaging model – claims, policies and security tokens – subsumes and supports several more specific security models, including identity based security, access control lists, and capabilities based security [Rosenberg 2004]. It allows use of existing technologies such as passwords, X.509v3 certificates, Kerberos tickets and so on. This security model, in combination with WS-Security and WS-Policy primitives, provides sufficient support to construct higher level key exchanges, authentication, policy based access decisions, auditing and complex trust relationships.

11.6.4 WS-Security

WS-Security is an OASIS security standard specification, which proposes a standard set of SOAP extensions that can be used when building secure Web services to provide the ability to send security tokens as part of a message and implement message content integrity and confidentiality [Nadalin 2006]. This specification serves as a building block that can be used in conjunction with other Web service extensions and higher level application specific protocols to accommodate a wide variety of security models (including PKI, Kerberos and SSL) and security technologies.

WS-Security primarily describes how to secure SOAP messages with the use of XML signature and XML encryption. It defines how security tokens are contained in SOAP messages, and how XML security specifications are used to encrypt and sign these tokens, as well as how to sign and encrypt other parts of a SOAP message [Nadalin 2006]. The WS-Security model also caters to SOAP endpoints and intermediaries by supporting end-to-end security. Specifically, it defines scenarios where the integrity and confidentiality of SOAP messages is ensured while the messages traverse intermediaries, even when these intermediaries use security functionality themselves.

Before introducing the elements of WS-Security we shall introduce a simple and intuitive scenario, illustrating how the XML based security mechanisms described in Section 11.5 and WS-Security could be applied to protect a simplified order processing transaction involving a relatively simple business dialogue between a client, a seller, a credit rating company, a trusted third party and a shipment company. Following this we shall describe how Web service standards, based around WS-Security, help tackle the security challenges faced by enterprises seeking to implement an SOA or Web services based integration deployment. These two topics will help readers to improve understanding of the material that is related to WS-Security.

11.6.4.1 Use case for WS-Security

To achieve a sound security framework for SOA based applications, the interoperable protocols of the Web services security model that we described in the previous section need to define a generic process model that can be abstracted into the following basic four sub-processes:

1. Generate and distribute service security policies via Web service definitions, e.g. WSDL descriptions and service directories, such as UDDI.
2. Generate and distribute security tokens.
3. Present tokens in messages and service requests.
4. Verify whether presented tokens meet necessary security policies.

Verification activities confirm that the claims in a security token are sufficient to comply with the security policy and that a message conforms to the security policy. They are used to establish the identity of the claimant and verify that the issuers of the security tokens are trusted to issue the claims they have made. Only if these verification activities are performed successfully and the requester is authorised to perform the specific service operation requested can the Web service proceed with processing its actions.

Example 11.8: Order processing transaction scenario

To understand the above points we make use of the simplified AVERS order processing transaction scenario depicted in Figure 11.22. The scenario in Figure 11.22 assumes that a client creates a purchase order and sends the request to fulfill the order to a seller (Step 1). The Web service application at the seller's side begins the process of checking the requester's credit rating and verifying that the ordered parts are available in the product inventory, selecting a shipper and scheduling the shipment for the order, and billing the customer.

Before the order management service (at the seller's side) can interact with other Web services, it must be able to authenticate itself to those services. This will be accomplished by presenting a digital certificate that has been issued by a trusted third party. By providing an interface to a public-key management system, the XKMS server retrieves the order management company's digital certificate (Step 2 in Figure 11.22).

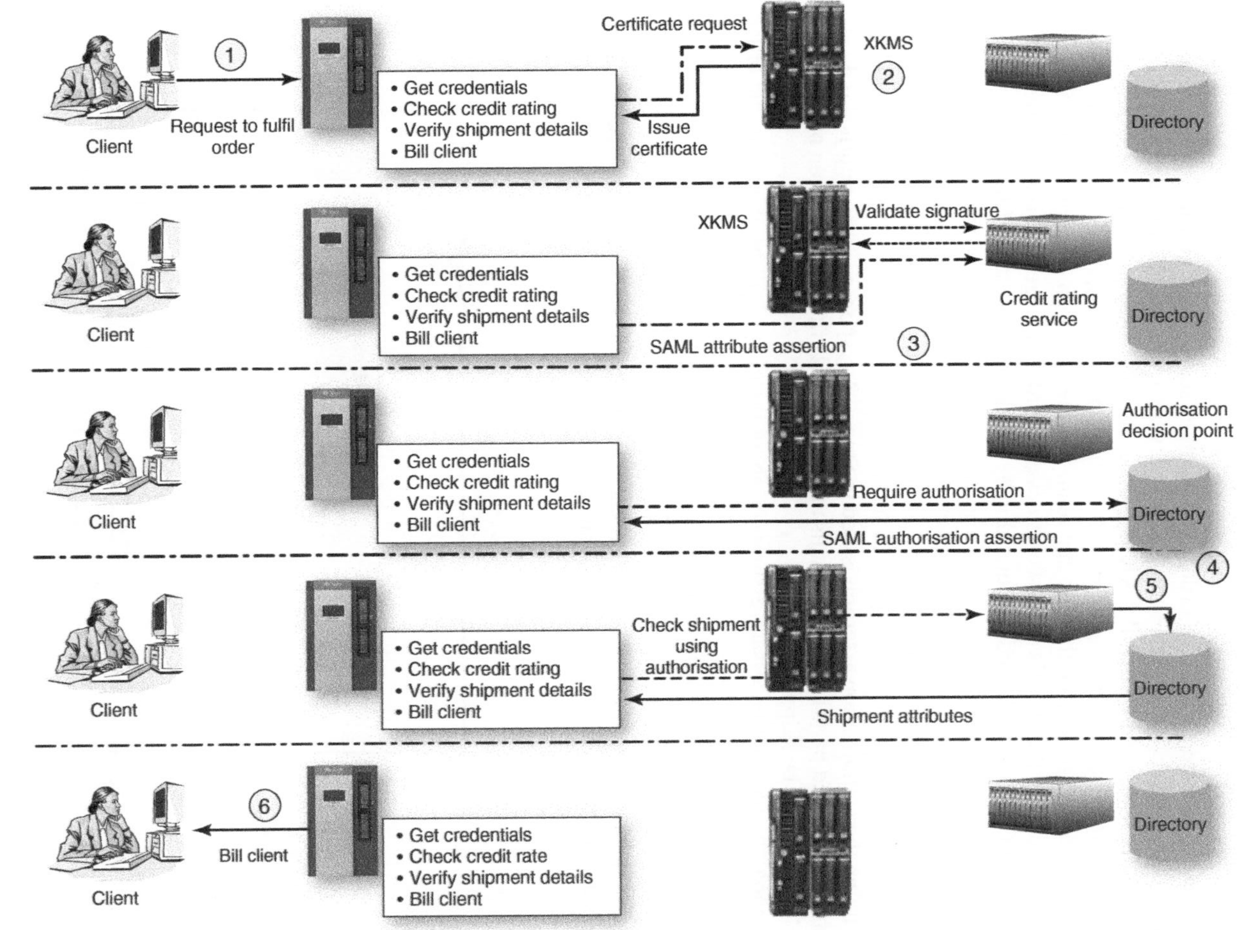

Figure 11.22 Scenario using XML security services

The seller submits a request to a credit rating company service to check the credit worthiness of the customer. The order management service (at the seller's side) knows that the credit rating service expects that requests will be digitally signed. This is stated by means of a WS-Policy assertion associated with the WSDL/UDDI description of the credit rating service. When the order management service submits its signed request, the credit rating service accesses the XKMS server to validate the requester's PKI credentials. Here, we assume that the XKMS server responds that the credentials are valid. The credit rating service then answers the order management application's request with an attribute assertion stating that the applicant has the appropriate credit rating (Step 3).

Having verified the client's creditworthiness, the order management service now needs to validate the details of the order in question by checking an inventory/shipment database maintained by a shipping agency. Before granting access, however, the shipping agency checks to verify that the seller has contracted to access this shipping service – and then returns an SAML authorisation assertion (Step 4). The order management application service submits an order shipment request to the shipping service, with a WS-Security header containing the authorisation assertion issued in Step 4. A response is then returned indicating that the ordered parts (shipment details in Figure 11.22) fit the description provided by the client and can be shipped (Step 5).

Having obtained the necessary assurances about the client and the shipment, the order management application issues a signed bill, billing for the order. XML-Signature and XML-Encryption ensure the integrity and confidentiality of this document.

The following section explains how an end-to-end interoperable Web service scenario, such as the one depicted in Figure 11.23, can be realised using a secure SOA implementation.

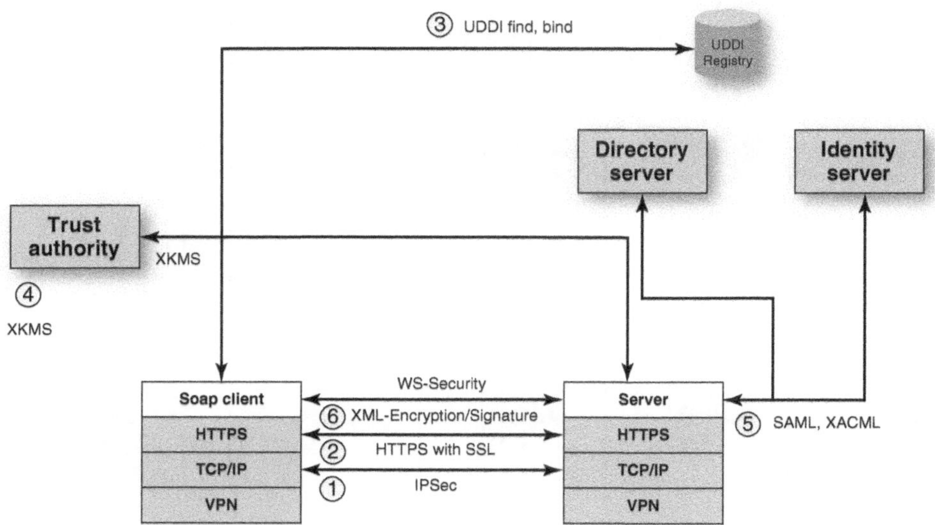

Figure 11.23 Conceptual architecture employing a Web service security solution (*Source*: [Lai 2004])

11.6.4.2 Integrating WS-Security in SOA applications

The benefits that can be realised from an integrated end-to-end, interoperable, Web service security framework are compelling enough that enterprises are using a mix of standardised protocols and leading edge specifications, including SSL for communication, WS-Security (including XML-Encryption and XML-Signature), SAML, and XACML in the context of an SOA based application.

A Web service call requires different layers of security to achieve end-to-end security connections in an SOA. Figure 11.23 illustrates a conceptual architecture employing an integrated Web service security infrastructure that can be used to implement a Web service security scenario, such as the one depicted in Figure 11.22. In the conceptual security architecture depicted in Figure 11.23 it is assumed that the service requester (a SOAP client initiating the purchase order request in Figure 11.22) is connected to a service provider via VPN over the Internet using IPSec to achieve secure connectivity (Step 1). This guarantees network layer security.

Transport security within the scope of this architecture is provided by means of HTTP (over SSL/TLS). We assume that each SOAP node has an associated HTTPS node and that SOAP messages between nodes are carried over HTTPS messages. The client also uses HTTPS to secure the connection between the client browser and the server at the provider's site using SSL certificates (Step 2). The use of HTTPS with SSL should safeguard the client session. Using a secure HTTPS connection, the client can browse various Web services (business processes) in a UDDI service registry, find the relevant business process, and retrieve the service endpoint URL (Step 3). This sequence refers to service discovery security.

Upon invoking the relevant business process, e.g. the purchase order process in Figure 11.22, the SOAP client needs to provide its credentials in order to authenticate itself for using the remote Web services in question. Here, we assume that the identity provider is part of a trusted authority that is managed by an external Liberty Alliance compliant identity provider. The identity provider then provides an authentication service using XKMS. The client's key is located from the trust authority via XKMS (Step 4). The service provider then provides a user identification and password to authenticate itself. Upon successful authentication, the identity provider enables single sign-on for the service client using SAML and XACML protocols (Step 5). This means that the service requester does not need to log in again to use other Web services. This sequence refers to the service negotiation security.

When the service requester invokes a Web service, the client side makes use of the public and private key infrastructure, using XKMS to encrypt the data content in the SOAP message using XML Encryption. The client may then generate a digital signature using XML Signature to attach to the SOAP envelope. As WS-Security leans on XML Encryption and XML Signature, it is used in this security architecture as the message level security to protect SOAP messages. In this way the service request and data content of the SOAP messages are secured by using the WS-Security standard (Step 6).

Due to reasons of simplicity, the conceptual architecture in Figure 11.23 involves only two interacting nodes. In reality, a Web service orchestration would entail a large number of interacting nodes (including many intermediaries). The scenario depicted in Figure 11.22, which involves credit rating, inventory, and shipping services, illustrates this point. In this scenario SOAP messages have to be routed over multiple *hops*. Each hop can only authenticate to the next, such that complete end-to-end authentication is unattainable. To establish a single security context among the message originator (client) and target Web services, message level security needs to be used. To pass security context with XML messages, existing directories with user or policy information in their XML gateways and security servers are used. By inserting end user credentials inside the message, it is possible for those credentials to be propagated along a chain of Web services or other intermediaries, so that eventually they can be conveyed to the target Web service. Any one of those intermediaries can verify the authenticity of the user's credentials, and can choose not to forward the message onwards for security reasons. For example, the message originator can insert an XML Signature into a SOAP message to ensure that any changes to the message contents will not go unnoticed by any intermediary that chooses to verify the signature.

11.6.4.3 Key WS-Security features

As we explained at the outset of this section, WS-Security describes enhancements to SOAP messaging to provide quality of protection through message integrity, message confidentiality and single message authentication. The purpose of WS-Security is not to invent new types of security, but instead to provide a common format to accommodate security in a SOAP message. WS-Security mechanisms can be used to accommodate a wide variety of security models and encryption technologies. It also provides a general purpose mechanism for associating security tokens with SOAP messages. It is interesting to note that no specific type of security token is required by WS-Security. It is designed to be extensible so it naturally supports multiple security token formats. For example, a client might provide proof of identity and proof that it has a particular business certification.

When securing SOAP messages, a variety of type of threats need to be considered, such as the message being modified or read by an adversary or an adversary sending messages to a service that, while well formed, lacks appropriate security claims to warrant processing. To cater for such threats, WS-Security provides a means to protect a message by encrypting and/or digitally signing a body, a header, or any combination of them (parts of them).

WS-Security utilises three core elements, which make up a SOAP security header:

- security tokens;
- XML Encryption;
- XML Signature.

Message integrity is provided by XML Signature [Eastlake 2008] in conjunction with security tokens to ensure that modifications to messages are detected. The integrity mechanisms are designed to support multiple signatures, potentially by multiple SOAP actors/roles, and to be extensible to support additional signature formats. Message confidentiality leverages XML Encryption [Eastlake 2002] in conjunction with security tokens to keep portions of a SOAP message confidential. The encryption mechanisms are designed to support additional encryption processes and operations by multiple SOAP actors/roles.

Figure 11.24 shows the WS-Security message structure and its core elements in relation to security tokens, XML Encryption and XML Signature. The figure shows that WS-Security specification encloses security tokens inside SOAP messages and describes how XML Signature and XML Encryption can be used for confidentiality and integrity of these tokens within the SOAP header.

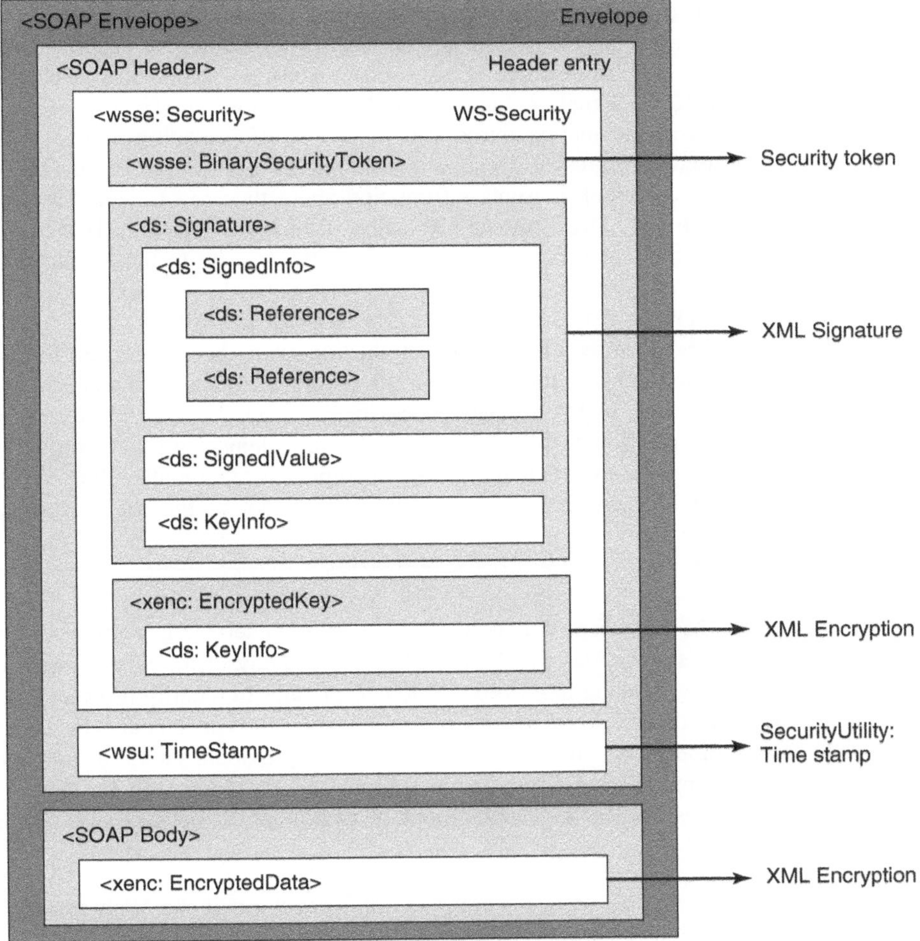

Figure 11.24 WS-Security elements and structure

Example 11.9: Using a WS-Security header to sign and encrypt messages

Listing 11.7 shows the basic WS-Security structure within a SOAP envelope. The most fundamental element that WS-Security defines is a `<Security>` element that resides inside the SOAP header. The `<Security>` header block provides a mechanism for attaching security related information targeted at a specific recipient in the form of a SOAP actor/role. This may be either the ultimate recipient of the message or an intermediary [Nadalin 2006]. Consequently, elements of this type may be present multiple times in a SOAP message. An active intermediary on the message path may add one or more new sub-elements to an existing `<Security>` header block if they are targeted for its SOAP node, or it may add one or more new headers for additional targets.

Listing 11.7 shows a security header that contains three children: a security token (`<UsernameToken>` is just an example of a security token), a `<Signature>` element which represents an XML-Signature, and an XML-Encryption `<ReferenceList>`. The `<UsernameToken>` element is introduced as a way of providing a user name, i.e. this element is used to represent a claimed identity. As well as enclosing security tokens, the security header block presents information about the use of XML Signature and SML Encryption in the SOAP message. Usually, if an XML signature is included, at a minimum it signs the whole or part of a SOAP body. A security header may also contain `<ReferenceList>` or `<EncryptedKey>` elements. A `<ReferenceList>` element contains a reference list to reference all the different `<EncryptedData>` elements. The `<EncryptedData>` element in conjunction with the `<EncryptedKey>` element is used to transport encryption keys from the originator to a known recipient (see Section 11.5.2). In this way, a WS-Security processor can read the security header and then decrypt all the data to which the `<EncryptedData>` element refers. Listing 11.7 also illustrates that often the SOAP body is also encrypted itself. Finally, the `wsu:Id` attribute in this listing is referenced by specifications that require the use of a global identifier.

Security Tokens in WS-Security. Authentication in the Web service environment usually involves credentials embedded in either the headers or body of the SOAP message. Standard Web technologies using passwords, X.509 certificates to identify browser based client identification, Kerberos tickets to authenticate clients and so on, can also be used to authenticate service requesters. Both service requesters and providers should be authenticated for sensitive communication.

WS-Security handles credential management in two ways. It defines two special elements:

- `<UsernameToken>` to pass the username and password if the Web service is using custom authentication;
- `<BinarySecurityToken>` to provide binary authentication tokens. The two classes designated in WS-Security are Kerberos tickets and X.509 Version3 certificates.

```
<?xml version="1.0" encoding="utf-8"?>
<env:Envelope
   xmlns:env="http://www.w3.org/2003/05/soap-envelope"
   xmlns:wsse=
   "http://docs.oasis-open.org/wss/2004/01/
                           oasis-200401-wsswssecurity-secext-1.0.xsd"
   xmlns:wsu=
   "http://docs.oasis-open.org/wss/2004/01/
                          oasis-200401-wsswssecurity-utility-1.0.xsd"
   xmlns:ds="http://www.w3.org/2000/09/xmldsig#"
   xmlns:xenc="http://www.w3.org/2001/04/xmlenc#">
 <env:Header>
  <wsse:Security>
    <!-- Security Token -->
    <wsse:UsernameToken>
       <wsse:Username> Zoe </wsse:Username>
    </wsse:UsernameToken >
    <!-- XML Signature -->
    <ds:Signature>
            ...
       <ds:Reference URI="#MsgBody">
            ...
    <ds:Signature>
    <!-- XML Encryption Reference List -->
    <xenc:ReferenceList>
    <xenc:DataReference URI="#bodyID">
    </xenc:ReferenceList>
  </wsse:Security>
 </env:Header>
 <env:Body>
  <!-- XML Encrypted Body -->
  <xenc: EncryptedData Id="bodyID" Type="content">
    <xenc:CipherData>
       <xenc:CipherValue>...</xenc:CipherValue>
    </xenc:CipherData>
  </xenc:EncryptedData>
 </env:Body>
</env:Envelope>
```

Listing 11.7 Structure of basic WS-Security Header

Example 11.10: Message flow involving security tokens

Figure 11.25 illustrates a typical message flow involving security tokens [Seely 2002].

1. Once a Web service client requests a security token to add to a SOAP message, a security token service returns the appropriate token (Step 1 in Figure 11.25). The tokens might be Kerberos, PKI, or a username/password validation service. Returned tokens may not be Web service based. For instance, a Kerberos service

ticket granting service might be accessed through the Kerberos protocols using operating system security functions.

2. Once the client gets the tokens it wants to use in the message, the client will embed those tokens within a SOAP message (Step 2).
3. Subsequently, the client should sign the message with private key that only they know (Step 3). SOAP messages must be signed or encrypted if authentication is important. It is not enough that a valid identity token is added to a message, as these tokens can be lifted from a valid message and added to messages used by attackers.
4. The receiver (Web service) is able to verify that the client sent the message if the signatures it generates for the message match the signatures contained in the message (Step 4). The receiver verifies the signature in a number of ways. For instance, if the client is using a <UsernameToken> for authentication, the receiver expects that the client sends a hashed password and signs the message using that password.
5. Finally the client is able to receive a response from the Web service (Step 5).

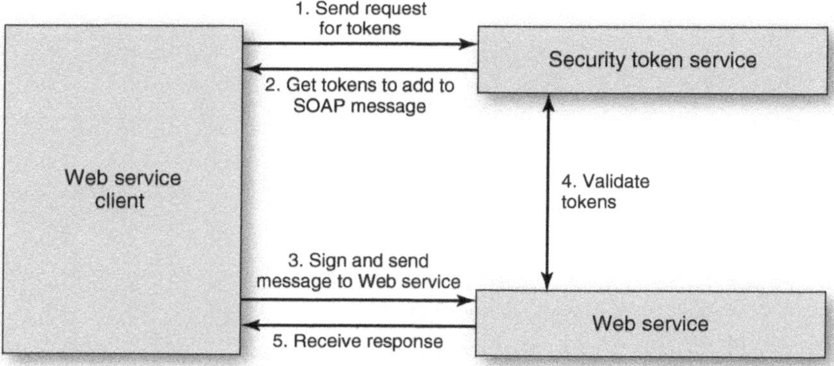

Figure 11.25 Typical message flow involving security tokens

Example 11.11: Embedding a security token in WS-Security

Binary security tokens (e.g. X.509 certificates and Kerberos tickets) or other non-XML formats require a special encoding format for inclusion. The <BinarySecurityToken> element is used to include a binary encoded security token. The code snippet in Listing 11.8 shows that an X.509v3 certificate is sent using the more general <BinarySecurityToken> element. The <BinarySecurityToken> element defines two attributes that are used to interpret it. The ValueType attribute indicates what the security token is, for example, an X.509v3 certificate. The EncodingType tells how the security token is encoded, for example Base64Binary.

```
<wsse:Security
 xmlns:wsse="http://schemas.xmlsoap.org/ws/2002/12/secext">
  <wsse:BinarySecurityToken
    ValueType="wsse:X509v3"
    EncodingType="wsse:Base64Binary">
    SSphfawHraPle ...
  </wsse:BinarySecurityToken>
</wsse:Security>
```

Listing 11.8 An X.509 certificate embedded in a <BinarySecurityToken>

As we have already seen WS-Security takes a flexible approach to conveying and authenticating identities. However, although two systems can both conform to WS-Security they might still be incapable of authenticating one another. One system might support only Kerberos, for instance, while the other allows only digital signature based authentication using X.509 certificates. Simply agreeing to use WS-Security is not enough; some agreement must also be in place about exactly what kinds of security tokens will be used.

Providing Confidentiality in WS-Security. The next major feature of WS-Security to cover is using XML Encryption to ensure confidentiality by providing a means to encrypt some or all of a SOAP message before it gets transmitted. Using the XML Encryption standard, WS-Security allows encrypting all or part of a SOAP message's header information, its body, and any attachments. WS-Security uses only three of the XML elements defined by this standard: <EncryptedData>, <EncryptedKey>, and <ReferenceList> (see Section 11.5.2) for encryption purposes.

Example 11.12: Using encrypted keys in WS-Security

Listing 11.9 is typical example of using encryption within WS-Security. This listing shows how a simple SOAP message might look if its sender chose to encrypt elements or element contents within a SOAP envelope with a symmetric (secret) key. In this example we have removed namespaces to ease reading.

In Listing 11.9 the <EncryptedKey> element uses a public key to encrypt a shared key, which is in turn used to encrypt the SOAP body. This technique is known as *key wrapping* or *digital enveloping* because the shared key is wrapped by the recipient's public-key [Rosenberg 2004]. The public key used to do the encryption is found within the <SecurityTokenReference> element in the <KeyInfo> block. The <SecurityTokenReference> element provides the means for referencing security tokens because not all tokens support a common reference pattern.

Providing Message Integrity in WS-Security. The next major feature of WS-Security to cover is using XML Signature to ensure message integrity. As explained in Section 11.5.1, XML Signature provides a detailed mechanism for digitally signing XML documents.

```
<env:Envelope>
 <env:Header>
  <wsse:Security>
    <wsse:EncryptedKey>
      <EncryptionMethod
        Algorithm="http://www.w3.org/2001/04/xmlenc#rsa-1_5"/>
        <ds:KeyInfo>
          <wsse:SecurityTokenReference>
            <ds:X509IssuerSerial>
              <ds:X509IssuerName>
                DC=ABC-Corp, DC=com
              </ds:X509IssuerName>
              <ds:X509SerialNumber>12345678</ds:X509SerialNumber>
            </ds:X509IssuerSerial>
          </wsse:SecurityTokenReference>
        </ds:KeyInfo>

      <!-- XML Encryption Reference List -->
      <xenc:ReferenceList>
      <xenc:DataReference URI="#EncryptedBody">
      </xenc:ReferenceList>
    </wsse:EncryptedKey>
  </wsse:Security>
 </env:Header>
 <env:Body>
  <!-- XML Encrypted Body -->
  <xenc: EncryptedData Id=" EncryptedBody" Type="content">
    <xenc:CipherData>
       <xenc:CipherValue>...</xenc:CipherValue>
    </xenc:CipherData>
  </xenc:EncryptedData>
 </env:Body>
</env:Envelope>
```

Listing 11.9 SOAP message with encrypted body

XML Signature is used within WS-Security for two main reasons [Rosenberg 2004]. The first is to verify a security token credential, such as an X509 certificate or SAML assertion; the other being *message integrity,* which verifies that the message has not been modified while in transit.

Example 11.13: Using XML Signature within WS-Security

Listing 11.10 shows the use of XML Signature within WS-Security. In this example we have omitted namespaces to ease readability. As usual a `<Signature>` element includes both the digital signature itself and information about how this signature was produced. A typical instance of `<Signature>` as used with SOAP will contain the `<SignedInfo>` and `<KeyInfo>` elements. The example in Listing 11.10 assumes that an order processing and a shipment service share a secret (symmetric) key, such as a password. Furthermore, it assumes that the order processing service can apply a digest algorithm to its password and arrive at a digest value. The order processing service can then use that digest as a symmetric key to encrypt or sign a message and send the message to the shipment service. The shipment service will use its knowledge of the shared key to repeat the digest calculation and use the digest value (as a key) for decryption and signature verification.

```
<?xml version="1.0" encoding="utf-8"?>
<env:Envelope>
 <env:Header>
  <wsse:Security>
   <wsse:UsernameToken wsu:Id="OrderProcServiceUsernameToken">
      <wsse:Username>ATrustedOrderProcService</wsse:Username>
      <wsse:Nonce>WS3Lhf6RpK...</wsse:Nonce>
      <wsu:Created>2004-09-17T09:00:00Z</wsu:Created>
   </wsse: UsernameToken>
   <ds:Signature xmlns:ds="http://www.w3.org/2000/09/xmldsig#">
    <ds:SignedInfo>
     <ds:CanonicalizationMethod
       Algorithm="http://www.w3.org/2001/10/xml-exc-c14N"/>
     <ds:SignatureMethod
       Algorithm="http://www.w3.org/2000/09/xmldsig#rsa-sha1"/>
     <ds:Reference URI="#Request4Shipment">
      <ds:DigestMethod
        Algorithm="http://www.w3.org/2000/09/xmldsig#sha1"/>
      <ds:DigestValue>
        aOb4Luuk...
      </ds:DigestValue>
     </ds:Reference>
    </ds:SignedInfo>
    <ds:SignatureValue>
      A9qqIrtE3xZ...
    </ds:SignatureValue>
    <ds:KeyInfo>
     <wsse:SecurityTokenReference>
      <wsse:Reference URI="#OrderProcServiceUsernameToken"/>
     </wsse:SecurityTokenReference>
    </ds:KeyInfo>
   </ds:Signature>
  </wsse:Security>
 </env:Header>
 <env:Body>
   <s:ShipOrder
    xmlns:s="http://www.auto-parts.com/shipping_service/"
    wsu:Id="Request4Shipment">
    <!-- Parameters passed with call -->
    <OrderNumber>PSC0622-X</OrderNumber>
      ... ... ...
   </s:ShipOrder>
 </env:Body>
</env:Envelope>
```

Listing 11.10 SOAP Message with digital signature

In WS-Security a SOAP header may contain more than one XML signatures, and these signatures can potentially overlap. For instance, in the AVERS order processing scenario an order message may need to pass through a number of intermediaries. First the message is directed to an order processing system, which inserts a header containing an order identifier and digitally signs it by putting an XML Signature into the security header. Following this the message is forwarded to a shipment processing system where a shipment identifier header is inserted and both the order and shipment identifier headers are digitally signed. Finally, when this message eventually arrives at a billing system, these XML signatures are validated prior to billing the customer.

Several examples of SOAP WS-Service requests, involving two actors using different types of security tokens as well as message exchanges involving two actors and a third trusted party, can be found in [Siddiqui 2003c].

11.6.5 Managing security policies

Whenever security mechanisms are being used between interacting Web services, some kind of security policy must also exist. These policies clarify the specific security requirements for a particular situation. With a Web service using WS-Security a service must describe its desired security policy. For instance, it may state that a signature is required on a particular XML element and that particular element must also be encrypted, and also state the digital signature algorithms that it expects and the encryption algorithms it supports for providing message integrity and confidentiality. The service may also state that it accepts Kerberos tickets for authentication, or X.509 certificates and digital signatures, and so on. Addressing these kinds of issues means defining security policies for Web services.

Policies are employed in several application domains, including security. The WS-Policy standard was developed to specify policy related expressions. This standard defines a general approach to specifying policies of all kinds and to associate them with particular services (see Chapter 12). To describe security conscious policies the WS-SecurityPolicy specification [Nadalin 2009a] is used. This specification is a domain specific language to represent policies for WS-Security. WS-Security Policy extends the WS-Policy standard to allow organisations initiating a SOAP exchange to discover what type of security tokens are understood at the target, in the same way that WSDL describes a target Web service. The WS-Policy standard and expressions are described in Section 12.4.1.

WS-SecurityPolicy defines XML elements that can be used to specify security related policies. These elements are referred to as assertions because they allow a Web service to specify its policies in an unambiguous way. Assertions allow a developer to specify the types of security tokens, signature formats, and encryption algorithms supported, required or rejected by a given subject. The assertions defined by WS-SecurityPolicy are summarized in Table 11.1.

Table 11.1 Security policy assertions defined by WS-SecurityPolicy

Policy assertion	*Description*
wsse:SecurityToken	Specifies a type of security token (defined by WS-Security).
wsse:Integrity	Specifies a signature format (defined by WS-Security).
wsse:Confidentiality	Specifies an encryption format (defined by WS-Security).
wsse:Visibility	Specifies portions of a message that must be able to be processed by an intermediary or endpoint.
wsse:SecurityHeader	Specifies how to use the `<Security>` header defined in WS-Security.
wsse:MessageAge	Specifies the acceptable time period before messages are declared *stale* and discarded.

Example 11.14: Using WS-SecurityPolicy

The WS-SecurityPolicy specification allows a single `<Policy>` element to contain policies about security tokens, integrity and confidentiality. A `<Policy>` element also has several other options regarding policies, including ways to specify relative preferences. For example, a Web service can define a `<SecurityToken>` that allows clients to authenticate using either Kerberos (see code snippet in Listing 11.11) or X.509 certificates, then indicate that it prefers Kerberos. By providing an unambiguous way for a Web service to state its security requirements, WS-SecurityPolicy facilitates Web services to make clear what clients must do to access that service.

```
<wsp:Policy
 xmlns:sp="http://docs.oasis-open.org/ws-sx/ws-securitypolicy/200702"
 xmlns:wsp="http://www.w3.org/ns/ws-policy"
   xmlns:wsse="  http://docs.oasis-open.org/wss/2004/01/oasis-200401-wss-
wssecurity-secext-1.0.xsd">
 <wsse:SecurityToken wsp:Usage="wsp:Required">
  <TokenType> wsse:Kerberosv5ST</TokenType>
 </wsse:SecurityToken>
</wsp:Policy>
```

Listing 11.11 Sample security policy.

More examples involving WS-SecurityPolicy can be found in Section 12.4 where we describe the WS-Policy language.

11.6.6 Managing secure sessions

When an application needs to exchange multiple SOAP messages with some other application, it is useful to create some kind of shared security context between the communicating applications. One common use of this shared context is to define a lifetime for an encryption key that will be used for the context's duration. For example, two communicating parties might want to create a symmetric key and then use it to encrypt the information they exchange over the lifetime of a particular security context. This allows contexts to be established and potentially more efficient keys or new key material to be exchanged, thereby increasing the overall performance and security of the subsequent exchanges. This section concentrates on defining WS-Security extensions to allow security context establishment and sharing, and session key derivation.

The WS-Security specification focuses on the message authentication model. This approach, while useful in many situations, is subject to several forms of attack, such as the possibility of a token substitution attack. In any situation where a digital signature is verified by reference to a token provided in the message, which specifies the key, it is possible for an unscrupulous producer to later claim that a different token, containing the same key, but different information was intended. The WS-SecureConversation standard introduces a security context and its usage. The context authentication model of WS-SecureConversation authenticates a series of messages, thereby addressing these shortcomings, but requires additional communications if authentication happens prior to normal application exchanges.

The WS-SecureConversation standard defines WS-Security extensions to allow security context establishment and sharing, and session key derivation [Nadalin 2009b]. A *security context* is an abstract concept that refers to an established authentication state and negotiated key(s) that may have additional security related properties. A security context is shared between two or more communicating parties for the lifetime of a session. The security context is defined as a new WS-Security token type that is obtained using a binding of the WS-Trust standard. The security context is represented on the wire as a new security token type called the security context token. A *security context token* (SCT) is a wire representation of that security context abstract concept, which allows a context to be named by a URI and used with WS-Security. Like SSL, WS-SecureConversation uses public (asymmetric) encryption to establish a shared secret key and from then on uses shared key (symmetric) encryption for efficiency.

A security context can be established in three different ways and Web services select the approach that is most appropriate to their needs.

1. A security token service may create a security context token and the initiating party has to obtain it to propagate it.
2. One of the communicating parties may create a security context token, which it may propagate to the other party.
3. The security context token may be created via a process of negotiation and exchanges. WS-Secure conversation defines a special binding for security context token requests WS-Trust operations.

Example 11.15: Negotiating the contents of security context tokens

The scenario in Listing 11.12 describes the situation where two parties need to negotiate about the contents of the security context token, such as a shared secret. In Listing 11.12 the <SecurityContextToken> specifies a security token that is associated with the message and points the security context (via the unique Id for this context). The next statement in Listing 11.12 specifies the digital signature. In this example, the signature is based on the security context (specifically the secret key associated with the context). The typical contents of the XML Digital Signature are not shown in this listing. Security contexts in this listing are referenced using the <SecurityTokenReference> element.

```
<?xml version="1.0" encoding="utf-8"?>
<Env:Envelope>
 <Env:Header>
     ...
  <wsse:Security>
     <wsc:SecurityContextToken wsu:Id="MyID">
        <wsc:Identifier> uuid:...</wsc:Identifier>
     </wsc:SecurityContextToken>
     <ds:Signature>
          ...
        <ds:KeyInfo>
           <wsse:SecurityTokenReference>
              <wsse:Reference URI="#MyID"/>
           </wsse:SecurityTokenReference>
        </ds:KeyInfo>
     </ds:Signature>
  </wsse:Security>
 </Env:Header>
 <Env:Body wsu:Id="MsgBody">
    <Shipment xmlns:tru="http://shipco.com/services/orderShipping">
       <Product Name="Injection Quantity="1" Weight= .../>
       <Product Name="Adjustable Worktable" Quantity="1" Weight= .../>
    </Shipment>
 </Env:Body>
</Env:Envelope>
```

Listing 11.12 Shared secret security context as part of WS-SecureConversation

11.6.7 Managing trust

While WS-Security and WS-SecurePolicy enable a service consumer and provider directly to interoperate in a secure and trusted manner, both assume that identical service token mechanisms are used at both endpoints. Furthermore, they assume that both endpoints are encompassed by a single *trust domain* (sphere of trust). For instance, both sites trust the same certificate authority. This means that these specifications alone are insufficient to define how to send a message from one trust domain, using one kind of key security technology, e.g. Kerberos, to a different trust domain using a different key technology, e.g. X.509 certificates.

The Web service security model defined in WS-Trust is based on a process in which a Web service can require that an incoming message prove a set of claims (e.g. name, key, permission, capability, etc.) [Nadalin 2009c]. If a message arrives without having the required proof of claims, the service should ignore or reject the message. A service can indicate its required claims and related information in its policy, as described by WS-Policy and WS-PolicyAttachment specifications.

Authentication of requests is based on a combination of optional network and transport provided security and information (claims) proven in the message. Requesters can authenticate recipients using network and transport provided security, claims proven in messages, and encryption of the request using a key known to the recipient.

The WS-Trust specification defines how security tokens are requested and obtained from security token services and how these services may broker trust and trust policies (refer to the Web services trust model described in Section 11.6.3 and Figure 11.21). WS-Trust proposes different models for obtaining tokens and brokering trust. These methods depend on whether the token issuance is based on explicit requests (token acquisition) or if it is external to a message flow (out-of-band and trust management). Using these extensions, SOA based applications can engage in secure communication designed to work with the general Web service framework, including WSDL service descriptions, UDDI `<businessServices>` and `<bindingTemplates>`, as well as SOAP messages. WS-Trust also employs conventional network and transport protection mechanisms, such as IPSec or TLS/SSL, to cater for different security requirements.

With WS-Trust a Web service requester can send messages that demonstrate its ability to prove a required set of claims, by associating security tokens with the messages and including signatures of the message that demonstrate proof of possession of (the contents of) the tokens. If the Web services requester does not have the necessary token(s) to prove the claim, it contacts an appropriate security token service to acquire the tokens. A service can indicate its required claims and related information in its policy, as described by WSPolicy and WS-SecurityPolicy specifications. Central to the WS-Trust is the Security Token Service (STS) model shown in Figure 11.26.

Figure 11.26 depicts the STS functioning in the role of an Identity Provider (IP). The primary function of an STS in this role is to issue identity tokens that contain claims about a security principal that correspond to the requester. A resource provider can also use an IP/STS to validate tokens it has received from requesters. In Figure 11.26 each arrow represents a possible communication path between participants. Each participant has its own policies, which combine to determine the security tokens and associated claims required to communicate along a particular path. The communication flow starts from the requester's perspective with the identification of a Web service, or resource provider, that the requester wishes to access. The requester queries the resource provider for its policies to determine its security requirements. Using WS-SecurityPolicy expressions the requester can check its own capabilities to determine whether it has a security token that meets the requirements to access the resource provider. If the requester does not have an acceptable

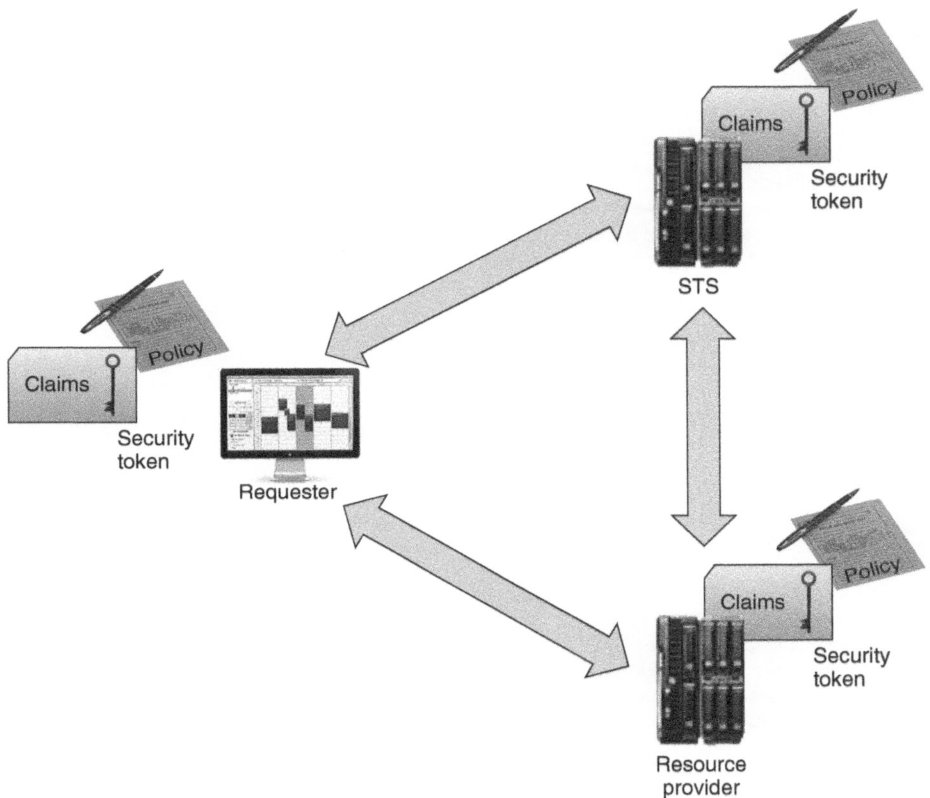

Figure 11.26 The WS-Trust Security Token Service model

token it might be able to request one from an appropriate STS that can be identified in the resource provider's policy. Each STS has its own associated policy and the requester can query the STS to determine the security requirements for requesting a particular type of token for use.

WS-Trust introduces protocol mechanisms independent of any particular application for requesting, issuing, renewing, cancelling and validating security tokens, which can be exchanged to authenticate principals and protect resources. The core of this protocol is the request-response message pair, Request Security Token (RST) and Request Security Token Response (RSTR).

Example 11.16: Request and response security token messages

The fragment in Listing 11.13 is a simple example of a Request Security Token message, illustrating the token type being requested (mySpecialToken) and the request type in the body of the message (Issue).

```
<s:Envelope>
  <s:Header>
    <wsa:Action>
      http://docs.oasis-open.org/ws-sx/ws-trust/200512/RST/Issue
    </wsa:Action>
    <wsse:Security>
            <xenc:ReferenceList>...</xenc:ReferenceList>
            <xenc:EncryptedData Id="encUsername">...</xenc:EncryptedData>
            <ds:Signature xmlns:ds="...">
              ...
             <ds:KeyInfo>
                <wsse:SecurityTokenReference>
                    <wsse:Reference URI="#myToken"/>
                </wsse:SecurityTokenReference>
             </ds:KeyInfo>
            </ds:Signature>
        </wsse:Security>
  </s:Header>
  <s:Body>
    <wst:RequestSecurityToken>
      <wst:TokenType>
        http://example.org/mySpecialToken
      </wst:TokenType>
      <wst:RequestType>
        http://docs.oasis-open.org/ws-sx/ws-trust/200512/Issue
      </wst:RequestType>
    </wst:RequestSecurityToken>
  </s:Body>
</s:Envelope>
```

Listing 11.13 Sample Request Security Token message

Other request types are possible, for example: cancel, renew and validate. WS-Trust is not limited to any particular token type. This example illustrates a custom token type being requested. In this example, a username token is used as the basis for the request as indicated by the use of that token to generate the signature. The username (and password) is encrypted for the recipient and a reference list element is added. The <ds:KeyInfo> element refers to a <wsse:UsernameToken> element that has been encrypted to protect the password. By remaining agnostic of the type of token being transmitted, WS-Trust enhances the interoperability of the basic protocol and allows migration of customer deployed products as the industry introduces new and improved security token formats.

This fragment in Listing 11.14 is an example Request Security Token Response message, illustrating a successful (and simple) issuance of the custom token from the previous RST example in Listing 11.13. Other responses are possible, including challenges that must be met before the requested token would be issued.

```
<s:Envelope>
  <s:Header>
    <wsa:Action>
      http://docs.oasis-open.org/ws-sx/ws-trust/200512/RSTR/Issue
    </wsa:Action>
    <!-- Other headers not shown for brevity -->
  </s:Header>
  <s:Body>
    <wst:RequestSecurityTokenResponseCollection>
      <wst:RequestSecurityTokenResponse>
        <wst:RequestedSecurityToken>
          <xyz:CustomToken xmlns:xyz="...">
            ...
          </xyz:CustomToken>
        </wst:RequestedSecurityToken>
      </wst:RequestSecurityTokenResponse>
    </wst:RequestSecurityTokenResponseCollection>
  </s:Body>
</s:Envelope>
```

Listing 11.14 Sample Request Security Token Response message

11.6.8 Managing federated identities

SOA is being used to support organisations in collaboration to create enterprise value networks, which span many organisations, systems, applications and business processes. This value network is made up of several constituents including an enterprise's customers, trading partners, suppliers, distributors and so on. Such arrangements result in federated systems that need to interoperate across organisational boundaries and interlink processes utilising different technologies, security approaches and programming environments. A crucial building block in the creation of collaborating enterprises is the provision of mechanisms to allow transparent access across security domains for users based on trust relationships that are established between the participating organisations.

A *federation* is a collection of security domains that have established a producer – consumer relationship for securely sharing resources. A resource provider in one domain can provide authorised access to a resource it manages, based on claims about a principal (such as identity or other distinguishing attributes) that are asserted by an Identity Provider or any Security Token Service in another domain. In a federation final access control decision is enforced strictly by the domain that controls a particular resource, while the federation can provide mechanisms that enable the decision to be based on the declaration (or brokering) of identity, attribute, authentication and authorisation assertions between domains. The choice of such mechanisms is dependent upon trust relationships between the domains.

The goal of federation is to allow security principal identities and attributes to be shared across trust boundaries according to established policies. The policies dictate, among other things, formats and options, as well as trusts and privacy/sharing requirements. A *federated identity* is a collection of agreements for the creation, maintenance, and use of identities and their attributes, as well as credentials and entitlements, plus a supporting infrastructure and standards that make user identity and entitlements portable across autonomous security domains within a federation. Federated identity infrastructure enables cross-boundary single sign-on, dynamic user provisioning and identity attribute sharing. Federated single sign-on allows users to sign on only once with a member in a federation and subsequently use various services in the federation without signing on again.

In this section we shall provide an overview of WS-Federation, a summary of federation services and of trust models.

11.6.8.1 Overview of WS-Federation

The WS-Federation specification is an evolving standard that defines a model and set of messages for brokering trust and the federation of identity and authentication information between participating Web services across different security domains [Goodner 2009]. A fundamental goal of WS-Federation is to simplify the development of federation services (e.g. authentication, authorisation, attribute and pseudonym services) through cross domain communication and management of these services by re-using the WS-Trust Security Token Service model and protocol. A variety of federation services can be developed as variations of the base Security Token Service. The main objectives of WS-Federation are to:

- Enable appropriate sharing of identity, authentication and authorisation data using different or like security mechanisms.
- Allow federation using different types of security tokens, trust topologies and existing security infrastructures, e.g. existing identity management infrastructures.
- Facilitate brokering of trust and security token exchange for both SOAP requesters and Web browsers using common underlying mechanisms and semantics.
- Express federation metadata to facilitate communication and interoperability between federation participants.

To achieve its objectives, the WS-Federation specification rests on a foundation of WS-Security and WS-Trust that contain the primitives necessary to define security tokens, trust topologies and security infrastructures indicating how trust relationships are to be managed. WS-Trust is the foundation for federation by defining a service model, the Security Token Service, and a protocol for requesting/issuing these security tokens, which are used by WS-Security and described by WS-SecurityPolicy. The Security Token Service, which may represent the principal's primary identity, a pseudonym, or the appropriate attributes, is presented to the service provider for authentication and authorisation. WS-Federation uses several security tokens as well as the mechanism for associating them with messages. The primitives defined in WS-Policy and WS-SecurityPolicy, along with extensions that are defined as part of the WS-Federation specification, are intended to support the definition of policies that identify what the supported and required components of a federation are by participating members, and what the choices are for communicating the policy information between federation participants.

In WS-Federation the process of exchanging security tokens is typically initiated by a requester authenticating to a Security Token Service (STS) / Identity Providers (IP) to obtain initial security tokens using mechanisms defined in WS-Trust. A Web service that conforms to the WS-Trust specification may act as its own STS.

11.6.8.2 Federation services

This sub-section examines core features of WS-Federation in some detail.

Federation metadata. Participation in a federation requires knowledge of metadata, such as policies and potentially even WSDL descriptions and XML schemas, for the services within the federation. Additionally, in many cases mechanisms are needed to identify the identity provider or security token services, and attribute/pseudonym services for the target, i.e. a Web service, of a given policy. Therefore, participants in a federation must publish and exchange configuration information in the form of federation metadata that allows them to identify common services, such as tokens or authorisation credentials, to other participants in the federation. For Web services, this information can be expressed as statements in federation metadata documents and may include supplying WS-Addressing endpoint references to the federation participants, as well as security policies, which list the security tokens and claims required to access those end points.

To facilitate an organisation to federate with its partners, an organisation must provide federation metadata. It is necessary to discover the metadata and policies of any participants within the federation with whom a requester wishes to communicate. This discovery process begins with the target service, i.e. the service to which the requester wishes to ultimately communicate. Given the metadata endpoint reference (MEPR) for the target service allows the requester to obtain all requirement metadata about the service (e.g. federation metadata, communication policies, WSDL, etc.).

WS-Federation defines a federation metadata model and associated document format. The federation metadata model describes how federation metadata about related services can be discovered and combined. Federation metadata can be represented as a document that contains metadata for an endpoint that exists in one or more federations, for one or more services, with one or more MEPRs per service. It can also refer to external metadata documents, and can be contained inside a service's WSDL description. The metadata defined by WS-Federation augments other service definitions, e.g. WSDL and WS-Policy, and is not a replacement for that type of information.

To obtain and supply federation metadata, WS-Federation builds on the foundations outlined in WS-MetadataExchange (see Section 13.6), which defines SOAP request–response message types that retrieve different types of metadata associated with a Web service endpoint. More specifically, the request–response pairs retrieve WS-Policy, WSDL and XML Schema information associated with an endpoint receiving a Web service message, or a given target name space. This information can in turn be used to determine the metadata, security tokens, claims and communication requirements that are needed to obtain access to a specific resource.

Authorisation services. An authorisation service may be implemented as a special type of Security Token Service that provides decision brokering services for participants in a federation. While the internal processing of authorisation enforcement is implementation specific, interoperability between services in a federation requires a common model for interacting with authorisation services. Extensions to RST/RSTR mechanisms, as defined in WS-Trust, may be used for communicating authorisation requests and decision outputs.

WS-Federation defines an authorisation model that meets these requirements. The protocol also defines two extensions for rich authorisation capabilities. The first of these extensions allows additional context about a token request to be passed to an STS in an RST request. The second extension builds on the claims dialect mechanism, defined in WS-Trust, to allow resource providers and requesters to indicate specific claims that are required to process requests. Different claim representations are used across different web service implementations to address different application requirements.

Authentication types. The WS-Trust specification defines the AuthenticationType parameter to indicate a type of authentication that is required (or performed) or an assurance level with respect to a particular security token request. To facilitate interoperability, WS-Federation has identified and defined a set of Universal Resource Identifiers (URIs) for specifying the common authentication types and assurance levels that can be used for the AuthenticationType parameter in RST and RSTR messages.

Attribute services. The participants in a federation may not always be able to establish a federation context for a principal using only the claims obtained from security tokens. For example, after a principal's original request has been authenticated a resource provider may determine that additional information is required to authorise access to advanced functionality. A service provider offers a solution to this common problem by providing the ability to exchange information about requesters that are not already included in security tokens or requests by means of an attribute service. An *attribute service* is a Web service that maintains information (attributes) about principals, any system entity or person, within a trust domain or federation that requesters may use to obtain this additional information (e.g. claims). WS-Federation defines a model for either party to access attribute services based upon the security token service concept and reliant on the token issuance protocol defined in WS-Trust.

Pseudonym services. A pseudonym service is a further specialisation of an attribute service, which provides alternate identity information for principals who are concerned about the risks of identity fraud. A *pseudonym service* is a Web service that maintains alternate identity information about principals within a trust domain or federation and provides a mapping mechanism, which can be used to facilitate the mapping of trusted identities across federations to protect privacy and identity. This is enabled transparently by optionally integrating the pseudonym service into the Security Token Service model. WS-Federation describes how a pseudonym service that is combined with a Security Token Service may map pseudonyms to issued tokens. This includes describing how the mapping may be automatically performed, based on the target service for the token. It also defines extensions to the WS-Trust RST/RSTR syntax for requesters manually to specify how pseudonyms should be mapped.

An attribute, pseudonym service combination is used to provide mechanisms for restricted sharing of principal information and principal identity mapping (when different identities are used at different resources).

11.6.8.3 Federated trust scenarios

Federations may exist within one or multiple administrative domains, span multiple security domains, and may be explicit (where requester knows federation is occurring) or implicit (where a federation is hidden, e.g. in a portal). The WS-Federation specification extends the WS-Security, WS-Trust and WS-Policy foundation by describing how these models are combined to enable richer trust realm mechanisms across and within federations. This section describes different trust topologies and how token exchange (or mapping) can be used to broker the trust for each scenario.

In the federation some level of information is shared between participants. The amount of information shared is governed by policy and often dictated by a contract. The goal of the federation model is to allow security principal identities and attributes to be shared across trust boundaries according to established policies. The policies dictate, among other things, formats and options, as well as trusts and privacy/sharing requirements. In the context of Web services the goal is to allow these identities and attributes to be brokered from identity and security token issuers to services and other relying parties without requiring user intervention (unless specified by the underlying policies). This process involves the sharing of federation metadata, which describes information about federated services, policies describing common communication requirements, and brokering of trust and tokens via security token exchange (issuances, validation, etc.). More specifically, the federation model extends the WS-Trust model to describe how identity providers act as security token services and how attributes and pseudonyms can be integrated into the token issuance mechanism to provide federated identity mapping mechanisms.

To establish a federation context for a principal, either the principal's identity is universally accepted (so that its association is *pre-established* across trust realms within a federation context), or it must be brokered into a trusted identity relevant to each trust realm within the federation context. WS-Federation can be used as sound base to develop different trust topologies and derive possible token issuance patterns, the most important of which are briefly described below.

> *Direct trust model:* in this trust model a trust relationship exists between the requester and its identity provider/security token service. The identity of the IP/STS is universally accepted and as a consequence it can directly issue tokens and provide a set of descriptions to other parties in the federation.
>
> *Indirect trust model:* In the indirect trust model, there is no direct trust relationship between the requester's security token service and the target service's security token service, but trust relationships that both security token services have with a third party security token service are leveraged in order to provide a security token to the requester that will work with the target service.
>
> *Brokered trust model:* In this trust model, trust is brokered through a third party IP/STS. This case requires the process of identity mapping – that is, the conversion

of a digital identity from one realm to a digital identity valid in another realm, possibly by a third trusted party (IP/STS) that trusts the starting realm and has the rights to speak for (make assertions to) the ending realm, or make assertions that the ending realm trusts. Identity mapping is typically implemented by an IP/STS when initially obtaining tokens for a service or when exchanging tokens at a service's IP/STS.

Example 11.17: A simple federated trust scenario

Figure 11.27 illustrates one possible way the WS-Trust/WS-Federation model may be applied to a simple federated direct trust model scenario. In this configuration a requester in one trust domain is allowed to interact with a resource (Web service) in a different trust domain using different security models. The example illustrates a possible combination of an IP and STS to access a service.

1. First a requester obtains an identity security token from its identity provider (Step 1).
2. It presents/proves this to the security token services for the desired resource (Step 2).
3. If successful and if trust exists and authorisation is approved, the security token returns an access token to the requester (Step 3).
4. The requester then uses the access token on request to the Web service (Step 4). That is, a token from one STS is exchanged for another at a second STS or possibly stamped or cross certified by a second STS.

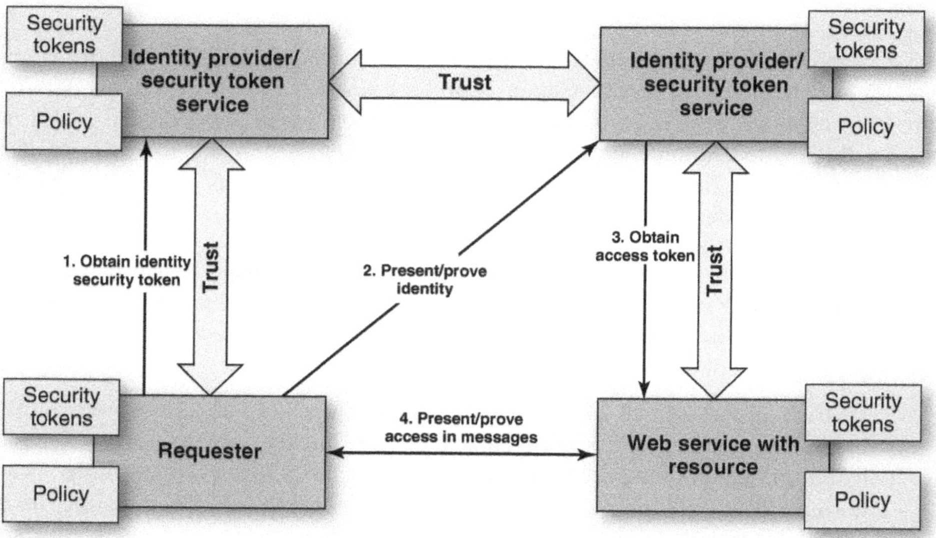

Figure 11.27 Simple federation scenario

Note that in the figure the trust of the requester to its IP/STS and the resource to its IP/STS are also illustrated.

Reference [Goodner 2009] provides more examples of WS-Federation trust models, detailed definitions of the XML document format for describing federations, as well as additional extensions to the WS-Trust specification in order to facilitate federations.

11.7 Summary of key points

The Web service security model is designed to allow mixing and matching of the specifications, enabling implementers to deploy only the specific parts they need. It allows Web service providers and requesters to develop solutions that meet the individual security requirements of their applications.

- WS-Security forms the foundation of the Web service security model.
- WS-Security provides the elements necessary to add message integrity and confidentiality to Web services, as well as a method of associating security tokens (for example, digital certificates and Kerberos tickets) to SOAP messages.
- It leverages the natural extensibility that is at the core of the Web service model and is build upon foundational technologies such as SOAP, WSDL, XML Digital Signatures, XML Encryption and SSL/TLS.

Other security related specifications address security policies, trust and federated identities, among other things.

Review questions

- What are the most common security threats for Web services?
- What are the most common countermeasures for Web service security threats?
- What is network level security and what is application level security?
- Briefly describe the most common firewall architectures.
- What are the most common techniques to protect the security of Internet communications?
- How do symmetric and asymmetric key cryptography differ?
- What are the most widely used application level security protocols?
- Briefly describe the XML security services and standards, XML Encryption, XML Signature, SAML and XACML.
- Explain how these XML standards are used in the context of Web services.

- What is the purpose of the Web service security and trust model?
- Briefly describe the components of WS-Security.
- How is message integrity and confidentiality achieved in the context of WS-Security?

Exercises

11.1. Develop a simple financial statement of a business customer in XML containing customer name, address, business account balance, and a credit card account where the outstanding balance should be charged. Use this financial statement to illustrate how an enveloped signature can be created in XML Signature.

11.2. Develop an enveloping and detached signature solution for the previous exercise.

11.3. Use a purchase order schema similar to the one defined in Chapter 3 Listing 3.6 to show how a customer can encrypt sensitive details of a purchase order, e.g. products and quantities ordered or credit card information.

11.4. Use XACML to define a simple service read request on behalf of a subject that has premium membership to access a security aware URL.

11.5. Define a WS based SOAP message that contains an X.509 certificate as a binary security token that is digitally signed and encrypted. The SOAP message body should contain an `<EncryptedData>` element to transport encryption keys from the originator to the recipient.

11.6. Define a SOAP message that appropriately combines the three principal WS-Security elements: integrity, confidentiality and credentials.

CHAPTER 12

Service policies

Learning objectives

Applications that compose Web services must not only fully understand the service's WSDL contract but also understand additional functional and non-functional service requirements, capabilities and preferences that allow a service to be fully described. Such features are collectively known as service policies and include authentication, authorisation, quality of service, quality of protection, reliable messaging, privacy, and application specific service options.

In this chapter we examine a comprehensive policy framework and language for Web services that use other Web service specifications such as WSDL, WS-Security, WS-ReliableMessaging, WS-Addressing and so forth. After completing this chapter you will understand the following key concepts:

- The nature of policies and their use in SOA based applications.
- Different types of policy including versioning, QoS and security policies.
- The WS-Policy framework.
- Merging and intersecting policies.
- Attaching policies to WSDL.
- Associating standalone policies with policy subjects.

Chapter preview

An important aspect of SOA is that they must provide a stable way of defining, managing and enforcing security policies. In this way, services can express QoS and other critical application requirements.

In this chapter, we concentrate on the topic of service policy, describe its main features and the key elements of a policy language, and evaluate different types of policy associated with services. Subsequently, we consider the WS-Policy standard, which relates to Web services in a variety of ways, e.g. through Web service security or attachment to parts of WSDL.

12.1 What are policies and why are they needed?

While the service description standard WSDL is designed to describe components of a Web service, such as exposed Web operations, data types, ports and SOAP message elements, it has proven less useful when it comes to describing choices, preferences, and other requirements not tied directly to the messaging interface itself.

For SOA applications it is important to be able to express the fact that a Web service must reject incoming SOAP requests that do not contain a certain type of security token or do not have the required signatures. It is equally important, of course, to communicate these requirements to clients that want to access the service. Information, such as how the Web service implements its interface and what it expects or provides to its requesters, is very important to prospective clients that wish to invoke this particular service. Additional information, such as what is expected or provided in a Web service hosting environment, whether the service exhibits transactional behaviour, whether its callers must sign and encrypt messages, what kind of security tokens the service is capable of processing and so on, is extremely important in order to understand the true requirements and capabilities of a service when trying to interact with it. To achieve the promise of a true SOA, it becomes important to express, exchange and process the conditions and requirements governing the interactions between Web service endpoints. These are the focal points of service policies that will concern us throughout this chapter.

12.1.1 Characteristics of service policies

To integrate successfully with a non-trivial Web service, one must not only fully understand the service's XML contract but also understand additional service characteristics, which relate to requirements (constraints), capabilities and preferences that allow the configuration of a service to be described. Such features are collectively known as *service policies*. Typical examples that service policies target include: security issues (including authentication and authorisation), transactional behaviour, QoS, quality of protection, reliable messaging, privacy, and application specific service options, or capabilities and constraints specific to a particular service domain.

Web service policies are consumable declarative expressions of policies required for interaction with a particular Web service. Policies describe in the form of *assertions* one or more characteristics that a service provider may instruct a client to follow. Policy assertions can range from simple expressions informing a client about the security tokens that a Web service is capable of processing (such as Kerberos tickets or X.509 certificates) to a set of rules evaluated in priority order that determine whether or not a client can interact with a service provider.

The desired objective is for the Web service endpoints (requester and provider) to communicate any requirements, agreements or expectations that affect either endpoint when providing a Web service. This includes policies that a Web service implementation declares to express regarding requirements on a hosting environment. This means that, among other things, policies can express SLAs, which are important for SOA based applications.

Service policies may affect different domains. *Domains* are contexts that apply to interacting services and are characterised by such factors as security, privacy, management, performance and traffic control, application priorities and so on. A set of requirements for Web service, i.e. a policy, needs to extend across many domains, such as, for instance, security, transaction and performance. Service policies allow single and cross domain applications to implement Web service solutions without having continuously to modify those applications to comply with changing corporate XML policies.

The scope of a policy is the subject to which a specific policy is bound and can range from concrete, low level artifacts, e.g. the security settings required for messages conforming to a specific input message definition that a Web service offers, to more abstract artifacts, e.g. the frequency with which messages need to be exchanged with a Web service so that a partner agreement can be fulfiled. For example, knowing that a service supports a Web service security standard such as WS-Security is not enough information to enable interaction with this specific service. The client needs to know if the service actually requires WS-Security, what kind of security tokens it is capable of processing (such as Username Token, Kerberos tickets or X.509 certificates), and which one it prefers. The client must also determine whether the service requires signed messages and what token type must be used for the digital signatures. And finally, the client must determine when to encrypt the messages, which algorithm to use, and how to exchange a shared key with the service. Trying to orchestrate with a service without understanding these details will inevitably lead to erroneous results.

Policies either can be used in a standalone fashion or are aggregated to perform more elaborate functions. *Standalone* policies are those that can be expressed in a simple statement. These normally include policy rules that represent Web service constraints and capabilities that have a simple character, in that they are either required/offered or not, e.g. the WS-Security protocol is offered by a certain Web service. *Aggregate policies* combine policy rules, to model either intricate interactions between service features or the combination of policies originating from diverse services that have complex interdependencies. For instance, they can parameterise and combine interdependent service features, e.g. a certain canonicalization algorithm needs to be used in combination with a certain security token type when digitally signing a message. While it is possible to use XML and WSDL extensibility to achieve some of these goals, it is preferable to provide a common framework to support Web service constraints and conditions. This framework should allow a clear articulation of the available options.

A *standard policy framework* is a common framework for the expression, exchange and processing of the policies governing the interactions between Web service endpoints. A policy framework provides an additional description layer for services and offers developers a declarative language for expressing and programming policies. To develop a common Web services policy framework, the Web service infrastructure is enhanced with policy specific extensions in order to understand policies and enforce them at run time [Skonnard 2003]. For example, a provider could write a policy stating that a given Web service requires Kerberos tokens, digital signatures and encryption. The infrastructure can then enforce these policy requirements without requiring a developer to develop any additional code. Clients use such policy information to reason about whether they can use the particular service under consideration.

12.1.2 Characteristics of a policy language

It is important for a Web service to rely on a declarative model to indicate, in a consistent and unambiguous manner, what the service is capable of supporting, including the types of protocol that it offers, as well as what requirements it places on its potential requesters. The service implementation should also be able to document requirements on a hosting environment, since much of the implementation of the Web service protocols and functions occurs in middleware and operating system functions supporting the service's implementation. Consequently, there must be a consistent way to describe the constraints/conditions derived from the environment hosting a particular Web service. This requirement points in the direction of a Web service policy language in order to express service related policies.

There are certain important requirements that a Web service policy language should meet:

1. It should provide expressive power, genericity, extensibility, flexibility and reusability features to describe a multitude of Web service policy aspects. These features of a policy language for Web services are briefly examined below.

2. It should be expressive enough to represent Web service constraints and capabilities at different levels of detail, addressing both policies that have a simple character as well as complex aggregated policies.

3. It should attain generic properties by striving to facilitate the definition of a set of common policies and aspects that are common across the various domains. In addition, the policy language should not change whenever new domain specific policy aspects need to be described. The policy language should support extensibility by allowing for a graceful migration that can facilitate the expression of complex domain specific policies.

4. It should describe both combinations of policies from different domains, e.g. support of a certain reliable messaging protocol in combination with WS-Security, and alternatives between policies from one domain, e.g. use of either X.509 or user name security tokens. The language also needs to provide mechanisms for referencing and including externally defined policies in order to allow reuse of well known policy patterns.

To cover the above requirements, WS-Policy [Vedamuthu 2007a] and WS-Policy-Attachment [Vedamuthu 2007b] have been developed. WS-Policy is a general purpose, extensible framework and model for expressing all types of domain specific policy models, including, transport level security and resource usage policy.

WS-Policy expresses requirements, preferences and capabilities in a Web service based environment as policies. Policy expressions allow for both simple declarative assertions as well as more sophisticated conditional assertions. WS-PolicyAttachment offers a flexible way of associating policy expressions with existing and future Web service artifacts. For instance, WS-PolicyAttachment addresses the requirements for associating Web service policy with Web service artifacts, such as WSDL artifacts and UDDI entities.

Before we concentrate on describing the characteristics of WS-Policy and WS-Policy-Attachment we shall first examine different types of policy and then explain the relation between service policies and other Web service standards.

12.2 Types of policy

We may group Web service policies in three broad categories: versioning policies, QoS policies and security policies. Although security is traditionally considered as part of QoS, it is convenient to think of security policies as a separate category, given the fact that the Web service security model suggests the use of WS-SecurityPolicy assertions to deal with the requirements of the Web service security domain.

12.2.1 Versioning policies

Once services are operational they usually undergo changes throughout their lifecycle. Service changes can impact some or even all of the clients of the given service. Service changes require that the service be designed (versioned) in such a way as to offer differentiated functionality, policies and QoS, which accommodate the different client requirements. With this approach, service operations can be added, removed or revised to reflect the different client requirements. *Service versioning* implies that the same service (or operation) can exist in the overall system in multiple guises while keeping exactly the same name. This usually leads to the necessity for SOA to support multiple service versions simultaneously. As an example, consider an Internet shopping Web service, which may have a special discount, offers for frequent as opposed to new customers. This means that although both frequent and new customers use the same purchase services, their status is detected and different pricing policies apply by invoking different operations for the same service. A *versioning policy* expresses the exact version of the service (operation) that is required for a particular invocation.

12.2.2 QoS policies

A *QoS policy* describes the non-functional service properties that collectively define a service. A QoS policy includes performance requirements, information regarding service reliability, scalability and availability, transactional requirements, change management and notification, and so on. It also includes factors relating to the Web service hosting environment. A QoS policy also describes technical service characteristics, including response times, tolerated system interruption thresholds, levels of message traffic, bandwidth requirements, dynamic rerouting for fail-over or load balancing, and so forth.

12.2.3 Security policies

Security policies indicate the security requirements and policies of a specific Web service. The Web service security policies describe security tokens, digital signatures and encryption. An example of a security policy is the requirement that a Web service may expect a requester to attach a security token when it sends a request to the Web service. For example, an SAML authorisation token, issued by a trusted authorisation authority, needs to be presented to access sensitive data. Another example is that a binary security token containing an X.509 certificate needs to be presented for signing purposes. Security policy is also used to indicate a required encryption format for interacting services. Security policies and assertions were treated in Section 11.6.5 as part of the WS-Security standards.

12.3 Service policy support standards

The developers of WS-Policy have gone to great lengths to make this standard a stand alone concept that can be associated with Web services in a variety of ways. For instance, specific parts of WSDL, such as operations or messages, may point to a policy. Another possibility is to have WS-Policy point to the set of the Web services that it covers. As policies are exchanged between trading parties involved in Web service interactions, one can discern three possible policy exchange mechanisms:

- Sending policies via SOAP messages as a SOAP header.
- Retrieving policies from a Web service registry, such as a UDDI.
- Retrieving policies from the Web service itself by means of protocols, such as WS-MetadataExchange (see Section 13.5).

These three policy exchange mechanisms are described below.

Sending policies via SOAP messages as a SOAP header: Sending policies via SOAP messages as a SOAP header is the simplest policy exchange mechanism that allows two interacting parties to understand each other's requirements. However, to support more accurate service discovery, WS-Policy proposes a framework that extends the description features already provided through WSDL. More refined service descriptions, qualified by specific Web service policies, support more accurate discovery of compatible services.

Retrieving policies from a Web service registry such as a UDDI: WS-Policy can be registered itself in UDDI (as tModels). It can also be associated with a UDDI business service (as key in a category bag). Such policies can be accessed via interaction with the UDDI. In a service registry (such as the UDDI registry), querying services described in WS-Policy facilitates the retrieval of services supporting desired/appropriate policies in conjunction with retrieving the correct service interface. For example, a query may request all services that support a Purchase Order WSDL interface (port type), use Kerberos for authentication purposes, and have an explicitly stated privacy policy. This allows a service requester to select a service provider on the basis of QoS offerings.

Retrieving policies from the Web service using the WS-MetadataExchange protocol: WS-Policy, as well as additional metadata relevant to the service interaction (such as XML Schema and WSDL descriptions), can be dynamically exchanged between interacting endpoints using the WS-MetadataExchange protocol (see Section 13.6). Using the WS-MetadataExchange protocol, service endpoints can exchange policies at run time to bootstrap their interaction with information about the settings and protocols that apply.

It is noteworthy that the exchanges of policies can support the customisation of each specific interaction based on a multitude of factors ranging from the identity of the interacting endpoint to any other aspect that characterises the context under which the interaction takes place. With this kind of flexibility, Web services can then be designed (versioned) to offer differentiated QoS, e.g. service precision, granularity, timeliness and scope, depending on the end customers that are targeted. Services can also be differentiated based on technical quality and QoS details, such as response time, performance bandwidth used, and reliability.

The core Web service policy standard is the WS-Policy framework, which we examine in the following section.

12.4 WS-Policy framework

The WS-Policy framework specification defines a common framework and language for services to annotate their interface definitions in order to describe their service assurance qualities and requirements. These can be described in the form of a machine readable expression containing combinations of individual assertions. The WS-Policy framework fits into the core Web service architecture since it is built on top of XML, XML Schema, WSDL and UDDI. The WS-Policy framework also allows for algorithms that determine which concrete policies to apply when the requester, provider and container support multiple service options.

The WS-Policy framework is a set of three interrelated specifications that together enable the seamless description and communication of Web service policies. These are:

1. The Web Services Policy (WS-Policy) specification, which provides a general purpose model and corresponding syntax to describe and communicate the policies of a Web service. WS-Policy defines a base set of constructs that can be used and extended by other Web service specifications to describe a broad range of service requirements, preferences and capabilities.

2. WS-PolicyAssertions, which indicate a set of common message policy assertions that can be specified within a policy.
3. The Web Services Policy Attachment (WS-PolicyAttachment) specification, which indicates three specific attachment mechanisms for using policy expressions with existing Web service technologies. More specifically, it defines how to associate policy expressions with WSDL type definitions and UDDI entities. It also defines how to associate implementation specific policy with all or part of a WSDL `<portType>` when exposed from a specific implementation.

Figure 12.1 shows how the WS-Policy specifications relate to other Web service standards, such WSDL and UDDI. Domain expressions in this figure identify policy subjects that are included in the policy scope, typically using URIs. *Domain expressions* are XML elements that describe the set of policy subjects. The three WS-Policy specifications also set the stage for WS-SecurityPolicy, which provides a set of WS-Security specific policies that is used to publish information about all aspects of WS-Security. WS-SecurityPolicy is described in Section 11.6.5 in this book.

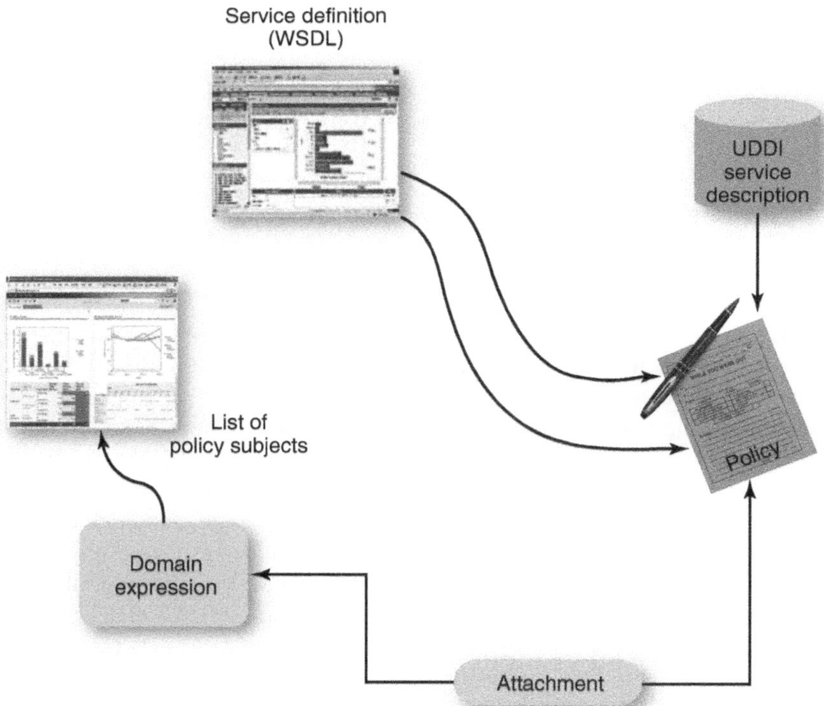

Figure 12.1 Connecting policies with other Web service standards

12.4.1 Overview of WS-Policy

WS-Policy provides a flexible and extensible XML based language for expressing the capabilities, requirements, and general functional or non-functional properties of Web services in a declarative manner. WS-Policy defines a framework and a model for the expression of these properties as policies. It enables a service to specify what it expects of callers and how it implements its interface. WS-Policy is critical to achieving interoperability at a higher level functional operation of the service. Security, transactions, reliable messaging and other specifications require concrete WS-Policy schemas. These allow services to describe the functional assurance that they expect from and provide to callers.

The WS-Policy abstract model defines a *policy* to be an XML expression that logically combines policy alternatives, where each policy alternative is a collection of policy assertions, see Figure 12.2. Assertions are constructs that specify concrete or abstract service characteristics, such as reliable messaging requirements, a required security authentication scheme or a desired QoS, which characterise an interaction between two Web services' endpoints. In a Web service environment assertions are used to convey such information to the service requester so that it can successfully invoke the provider's service. Satisfying assertions in the policy usually results in behaviour that reflects these conditions. In a

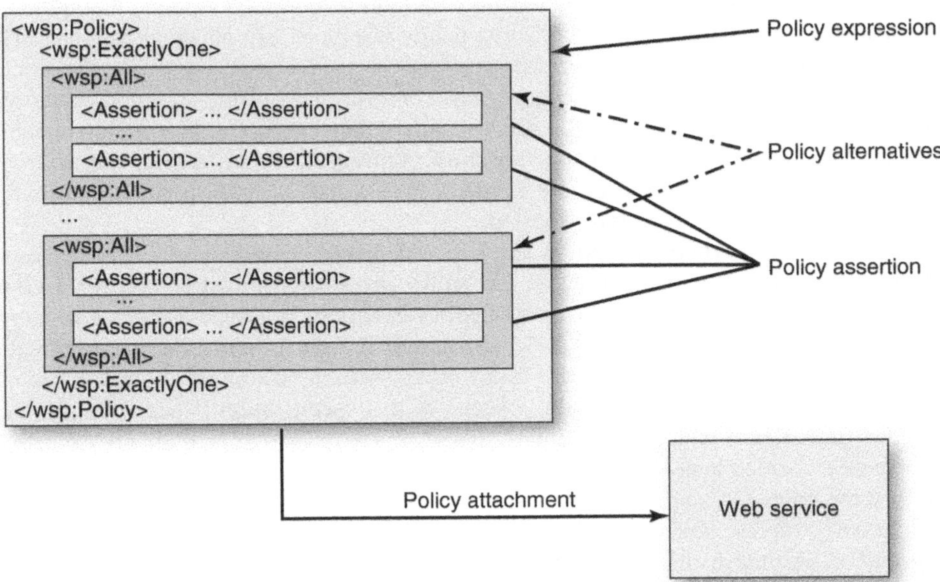

Figure 12.2 Pictorial representation of a WS-Policy statement and its elements

Web service interaction scenario, typically the provider of a Web service exposes a policy to convey conditions under which it provides the service. A requester may then use this policy to decide whether or not to use the service. WS-Policy defines three components: policy assertions, policy expressions and policy operations.

Policy assertions are the building blocks of policies. A *policy assertion* identifies a behaviour that is a requirement (or capability) of a policy subject [Vedamuthu 2007a]. Figure 12.2 gives a pictorial overview of WS-Policy and its elements. Each assertion in this figure describes an atomic aspect of the requirements of Web service. In particular, an assertion indicates domain specific (e.g. security, transactions) semantics that can be defined in a separate policy specification and targets an entity to which the policy expression is bound, or, in other words, the resource the policy describes, e.g. a Web service endpoint. Some policy assertions specify traditional requirements and capabilities that will ultimately manifest on the wire, e.g. authentication scheme or transport protocol selection. Other policy assertions have no wire manifestation yet are critical to proper service selection and usage, e.g. privacy policy, QoS characteristics. WS-Policy provides a single policy grammar to allow both kinds of assertions to be reasoned about in a consistent manner.

Policy assertions can come in many different forms and are inherently extensible. There are two additional specifications that define standard sets of policy assertions that can be used within a policy expression. The Web Services Policy Assertions Language (WS-PolicyAssertions) specification defines a set of general message assertions and the Web Services Security Policy Language (WS-SecurityPolicy) specification defines a set of common security related assertions.

WS-Policy defines a set of policy operators that enable us to construct different logical combinations of policy assertions to better describe complex policy requirements [Vedamuthu 2007a]. Policy operators group policy assertions into policy alternatives. The two most frequently used policy operators are `<All>` and `<ExactlyOne>`. The policy operator `<All>` signifies that a message must conform to all of the assertions or operations that are enclosed in the `<All>` element in a policy statement. The policy operator `<ExactlyOne>` signifies that a message must conform to exactly one of the assertion or operator elements enclosed in this element. To express complex policies compactly, policy operators may be recursively nested.

The WS-Policy syntax is used to describe acceptable combinations of assertions to form a complete set of instructions to the policy processing infrastructure, for a given Web service invocation. Each collection of policy assertions is termed a *policy alternative* [Vedamuthu 2007a], see Figure 12.2. An alternative with one or more assertions indicates behaviour characterised only by those assertions. Assertions within an alternative are not are applied to a subject are beyond the scope of this specification [Vedamuthu 2007a]. Another limitation is that although policy alternatives are meant to be mutually exclusive, it cannot be decided in general whether or not more than one alternative can be supported at the same time.

The XML representation of a Web service policy is commonly referred to as a *policy expression*. The mechanism for associating a policy expression with one or more policy subjects is referred to as a *policy attachment*.

Table 12.1 provides a quick reference to the policy terminology that we use throughout this section. The remainder of this section describes the concepts summarized in Table 12.1 in some detail.

Table 12.1 WS-Policy constructs and terminology

Term	*Definition*
Policy	An informal abstraction that is used to refer to the set of information that is being expressed as policy assertions.
Policy assertion	Represents an individual preference, requirement, capability or other property
Policy expression	An XML Infoset representation of one or more policy assertions.
Policy operator	Enables to construct different logical combinations of policy assertions.
Policy subject	An entity, e.g. an endpoint, object or resource, to which a policy expression can be bound.
Policy attachment	The mechanism for associating policy expressions with one or more subjects.

Example 12.1: Definition of a security policy using specific types of tokens

Listing 12.1 illustrates a security policy defined in WS-SecurityPolicy (see Section 11.6.5) using assertions. In particular, this listing represents a policy for authentication. The listing illustrates the use of the `<ExactlyOne>` policy operator. This listing represents two specific security policy assertions that indicate that two types of authentication are supported (Kerberos tokens or X.509 certificates). A valid interpretation of the policy in Listing 12.1 would be that an invocation of a Web service under this policy would need to contain one of the security token assertions specified.

```
<wsp:Policy
     xmlns:sp="http://docs.oasis-open.org/ws-sx/ws-securitypolicy/200702"
     xmlns:wsp="http://www.w3.org/ns/ws-policy">
<wsp:ExactlyOne>
    <wsse:SecurityToken>
       <wsse:TokenType>
         wsse:Kerberosv5TGT
       </wsse:TokenType>
    </wsse:SecurityToken>
    <wsse:SecurityToken>
       <wsse:TokenType>
         wsse:X509v3
       </wsse:TokenType>
    </wsse:SecurityToken>
  </wsp:ExactlyOne>
</wsp:Policy>
```

Listing 12.1 A sample WS Policy statement

Finally, a note of caution. Both WS-Policy and XACML use the term *policy* which can be very misleading at times. This overloaded use of the term policy sometimes may confuse readers who are new to these concepts. These two languages are designed for quite different purposes. XACML is a general purpose access control policy language that provides the syntax for managing authorisation decisions and is thus focused on the evaluation of access control policies by a Policy Decision Point module (see Section 11.5.5). In contrast to this, WS-Policy is defined for metadata descriptions of properties and capabilities of Web services and Web service endpoints.

12.4.1.1 Policy expressions

A policy expression is the XML representation of a policy. A policy expression is bound to a policy subject. A policy expression comprises three constructs:

1. policy operators;
2. an attribute to qualify an assertion;
3. a policy reference/inclusion mechanism.

WS-Policy provides a normative XML Schema definition that expresses the structure of a policy expression. The WS-Policy schema defines all of the constructs that may be used in a policy expression and it also includes definitions for WS-PolicyAssertions and WS-PolicyAttachment. These are briefly described below.

Normal form policies. To facilitate interoperability, the WS-Policy specification defines a *normal form* for policy expressions that is a straightforward representation of a policy, enumerating each of its alternatives that in turn enumerate each of their assertions. The normal form of policy is defined to simplify the manipulation and to clarify the understanding of policies.

```
<wsp:Policy ... >
   <wsp:ExactlyOne>
      [<wsp:All> [ <assertion ...>... </assertion>]* </wsp:All> ]*
   </wsp:ExactlyOne>
</wsp:Policy>
```

Listing 12.2 Syntax for normal policy form

The schema outline for the normal form of a policy expression is shown in Listing 12.2. In a normal form policy, each valid policy is contained within an `<All>` element, and all of the alternatives are contained under a single `<ExactlyOne>` operator. In effect each element within the `<ExactlyOne>` policy operator is a policy alternative, where each policy alternative is encapsulated within an <All> operator. The WS-Policy specification states that the normal form of a policy expression should be used where practical to simplify processing and improve interoperability. For instance, policies must be first described in a standardised normal form before policy aggregation operations can be applied.

Example 12.2: Definition of security policy alernatives

Listing 12.3 illustrates the normal form of the policy expression example introduced earlier in Listing 12.1. This listing expresses two alternatives in the policy. This is indicated by the <ExactlyOne> policy operator, which specifies that only one of its direct elements must be applicable. Each of these alternatives is shown to be wrapped in an <All> operator. The <All> operator means that all the assertions enclosed within this operator must be applicable. This means that if the first alternative is chosen, a Kerberos token type and the AES encryption algorithm must be employed. If conversely the second alternative is chosen, an X.509 certificate and the 3DES encryption algorithm must be employed.

```
<wsp:Policy>
  <wsp:ExactlyOne>
     <wsp:All>
       <wsse:SecurityToken>
         <wsse:TokenType>
           wsse:Kerberosv5TGT
         </wsse:TokenType>
       </wsse:SecurityToken>
       <wsse:Algorithm Type ="wsse:AlgSignature"
          URI="http://www.w3.org/2000/09/xmlenc#aes"/>
     </wsp:All>
     <wsp:All>
       <wsse:SecurityToken>
         <wsse:TokenType>
           wsse:X509v3
         </wsse:TokenType>
       </wsse:SecurityToken>
       <wsse:Algorithm Type ="wsse:AlgEncryption"
          URI="http://www.w3.org/2001/04/xmlenc#3des-cbc"/>
     </wsp:All>
  </wsp:ExactlyOne>
</wsp:Policy>
```

Listing 12.3 Normal form of policy in Listing 12.1

Policy identification. A policy expression can also itself be a Web resource and is hence identifiable by a URI.

Example 12.3: Associating a security policy with a specific URI

The example in Listing 12.4 illustrates how to associate a policy expression with a specific URI.

```
<wsp:Policy
      xml:base="http://www.auto-parts.com/policies"
      wsu:Id="SecurityTokens">
  <wsse:SecurityToken>
    <wsse:TokenType> wsse:Kerberosv5TGT </wsse:TokenType>
  </wsse:SecurityToken>
  <wsse:Integrity>
    <wsse:Algorithm Type="wsse:AlgSignature"
                    URI="http://www.w3.org/2000/09/xmldsig#rsa-sha1"/>
    </wsse:Integrity>
</wsp:Policy>
```

Listing 12.4 Associating a policy expression with a URI

Compact policy expressions. To express a policy in a more compact form while still using XML, this specification defines three constructs: optional assertions, recursively nested policy operators, and a policy reference/inclusion mechanism. Each sub-section below describes a construct and its equivalent normal form.

Optional policy assertions. To indicate the fact that a policy assertion is optional, the WS-Policy specification employs the `<Optional>` attribute. This attribute is a syntactic shortcut for expressing policy alternatives. If the `<Optional>` attribute defined in a policy is true, the expression of the assertion is semantically equivalent to the following construct:

```
<wsp:ExactlyOne>
  <wsp:All> <Assertion ...> ... </Assertion> </wsp:All>
</wsp:ExactlyOne>
```

The above code snippet indicates that two entries are created for each occurrence of the `<Optional>` attribute. One entry contains the assertion and the other specifies an empty policy. To represent these two entries, the `<ExactlyOne>` policy operator is used.

If the `<Optional>` attribute defined in the schema outline above is false, the expression of the assertion is semantically equivalent to the following construct:

```
<wsp:ExactlyOne>
   <wsp:All> <Assertion ...> ... </Assertion> </wsp:All>
</wsp:ExactlyOne>
```

Example 12.4: Defining an optional security policy

To exemplify the use of the <Optional> attribute consider the example in Listing 12.5, which indicates that the use of the X509 for a given service is optional.

```
<wsp:Policy>
 <wsse:SecurityToken wsp:Optional="true" >
   <wsse:TokenType>
     wsse:X509v3
   </wsse:TokenType>
 </wsse:SecurityToken>
</wsp:Policy>
```

Listing 12.5 Compact policy expression using the <optional> attribute

Policy assertion nesting. Any policy assertion may contain a policy expression. A nested policy expression is a policy expression that is a child element of another policy assertion element. A nested policy expression further qualifies the behaviour of its parent policy assertion. The schema outline for a nested policy expression is as follows:

```
<Assertion . . .>
   ...
   ( <wsp:Policy ...> ... </wsp:Policy> )?
   ...
</Assertion>
```

We shall use the WS-SecurityPolicy to illustrate the use of nested assertions. This is illustrated in Listing 12.6, which is an example of a transport security assertion.

Securing messages is a complex usage scenario. The WS-SecurityPolicy defines an <sp:TransportBinding> policy assertion to indicate the use of transport level security for protecting messages. Just indicating the use of transport level security for protecting messages is not sufficient. To interact successfully with a Web service, the consumer must know not only that transport level security is required, but also the transport token to use, the secure transport to use, the algorithm suite to use for performing cryptographic operations, etc. The <sp:TransportBinding> policy assertion can represent these dependent behaviours.

Example 12.5: Defining nested policies

In the example below, the child Policy element is a nested policy expression and further qualifies the behaviour of the <sp:TransportBinding> policy assertion. The <sp:TransportToken> is a nested policy assertion of the <sp:TransportBinding> policy assertion. The <sp:TransportToken> assertion requires the use of a specific transport token and further qualifies the behaviour of the <sp:TransportBinding> policy assertion, which already requires the use of transport level security for protecting messages. The <sp:AlgorithmSuite> is a nested policy assertion of the <sp:TransportBinding> policy assertion that requires the use of a specific algorithm and further qualifies the behaviour of the <sp:TransportBinding> policy assertion.

```
<sp:TransportBinding>
  <Policy>
    <sp:TransportToken>
      <Policy>
        <sp:HttpsToken>
          ...
        </sp:HttpsToken>
      </Policy>
    </sp:TransportToken>
    <sp:AlgorithmSuite>
      <Policy>
        <sp:Basic256Rsa15/>
      </Policy>
    </sp:AlgorithmSuite>
  </Policy>
</sp:TransportBinding>
```

Listing 12.6 Example of nested policies

If this security policy were attached to a Web service then clients that wish to invoke the Web service are forced to engage in transport level security as described in Listing 12.6.

Policy references. WS-Policy provides a mechanism for sharing policy assertions across different policy expressions through the <wsp:PolicyReference> element. This element references another policy expression and can be used wherever a policy assertion element is allowed inside a policy expression. The contents of the referenced policy expression conceptually replace the <wsp:PolicyReference> element and are wrapped in an <wsp:All> operator. A policy expression can be referenced by a URI, a digest of the referenced policy expression or by specifying the digest algorithm being used [Vedamuthu 2007a].

Example 12.6: Sharing a security policy

The example in Listing 12.7 illustrates how to share a policy (with an ID of tokens) across two other policies. The listing illustrates that the first policy expression is given an identifier (`"tokens"`) and specifies three different types of security tokens, while the second and third policy expressions are extended by including security token specifications, e.g. X509 and Kerberos. The second policy expression in Listing 12.7 specifies a signature format defined by WS-Security (see Section 11.6.4) and references the first policy element by URI indicating where the referenced element is placed within the document. Similarly, the third policy expression specifies an encryption format defined by WS-Security and references the first policy element also by URI indicating where the referenced element is placed within the document.

```
<wsp:Policy wsu:Id="tokens" xmlns:wsp="..." xmlns:wsse="...">
  <wsp:ExactlyOne wsp:Usage="Required">
     <wsse:SecurityToken>
       <wsse:TokenType> wsse:UsernameToken </wsse:TokenType>
     </wsse:SecurityToken>
     <wsse:SecurityToken>
       <wsse:TokenType>wsse:x509v3</wsse:TokenType>
     </wsse:SecurityToken>
     <wsse:SecurityToken>
       <wsse:TokenType>wsse:Kerberosv5ST</wsse:TokenType>
     </wsse:SecurityToken>
  </wsp:ExactlyOne>
</wsp:Policy>

<wsp:Policy wsu:Id="tokensWithSignature"
   xmlns:wsp="..." xmlns:wsse="...">
  <wsp:PolicyReference URI="#tokens" />
  <wsse:Integrity wsp:Usage="wsp:Required">
    ...
  </wsse:Integrity>
</wsp:Policy>

<wsp:Policy wsu:Id="tokensWithEncryption"
   xmlns:wsp="..." xmlns:wsse="...">
  <wsp:PolicyReference URI="#tokens" />
  <wsse:Confidentiality wsp:Usage="Required">
    ...
  </wsse:Confidentiality>
</wsp:Policy>
```

Listing 12.7 Referencing policies

12.4.2 Policy operators

The constructs that make up a policy, such as policy assertions and policy alternatives, have certain mathematical properties. In fact the policy operators <wsp:Policy>, <wsp:All> and <wsp:ExactlyOne> elements, which are used to group policy assertions into policy alternatives can be mixed to create fairly complex policy expressions. This section explains how the policy operator properties can affect policy structures that a services developer may craft.

The following simple algebraic properties apply when transforming a compact expression into a normal form expression using WS-Policy operators:

- Equivalence
- Associative
- Commutative
- Distributive
- Idempotent

These properties are explained below in turn using illustrative examples.

12.4.2.1 Equivalence property

The equivalence rule specifies that the <wsp:Policy> operator within a policy expression is equivalent to <wsp:All>. A collection of assertions in an <wsp:All> operator is equivalent to a policy alternative. For instance, the expression

```
<wsp:All>
   <!-- assertion A -->
   <!-- assertion B -->
</wsp:All>
```

is equivalent to:

```
<wsp:ExactlyOne>
  <wsp:All>
    <!-- assertion A -->
    <!-- assertion B -->
  </wsp:All>
</wsp:ExactlyOne>
```

12.4.2.2 Associative property

The associative rule specifies that the operators <wsp:ExactlyOne> and <wsp:All> are associative. This rule is often used for simplifying operator constructs by eliminating unnecessary nesting.

Example 12.7: Defining a security policy that requires specific policy assertions

Consider Listing 12.8, which describes a sample security policy that requires the inclusion of a certain security token as well as signing, encryption, timestamp, and username token policy assertions.

```
<wsp:Policy>
  <wsp:ExactlyOne>
    <wsp:All>
      <sp:SecurityToken>
        <sp:TokenType>sp:X509v3</sp:TokenType>
      </sp:SecurityToken>
      <wsp:ExactlyOne>
         <sp:UsernameToken />
         <sp:SignedParts />
         <sp:EncryptedParts>
            <sp:Body />
         </sp:EncryptedParts>
         <sp:TransportBinding>
            <sp:IncludeTimeStamp />
         </sp:TransportBinding>
       </wsp:ExactlyOne>
    </wsp:All>
  </wsp:ExactlyOne>
</wsp:Policy>
```

Listing 12.8 Sample security policy

The following listing is equivalent to the policy coded in Listing 12.8.

```
<wsp:Policy>
  <wsp:ExactlyOne>
    <wsp:All>
      <sp:SecurityToken>
        <sp:TokenType>sp:X509v3</sp:TokenType>
      </sp:SecurityToken>
      <sp:UsernameToken />
      <sp:SignedParts />
      <sp:EncryptedParts>
        <sp:Body />
      </sp:EncryptedParts>
      <sp:TransportBinding>
        <sp:IncludeTimeStamp />
      </sp:TransportBinding>
    </wsp:All>
  </wsp:ExactlyOne>
</wsp:Policy>
```

Listing 12.9 Security policy equivalent to the policy coded in Listing 12.8

In the following we shall revert to simpler expressions to illustrate the remaining policy operator properties.

12.4.2.3 Commutative property

The operators <wsp:ExactlyOne> and <wsp:All> are also commutative. This means that when two or more policy assertions are nested within either operator, their order does not matter. For example, the statement in the following listing, using the <wsp:All> operator

```
<wsp:All>
  <!-- assertion A -->
  <!-- assertion B -->
</wsp:All>
```

is equivalent to the following statement.

```
<wsp:All>
  <!-- assertion B -->
  <!-- assertion A -->
</wsp: All>
```

The same rationale applies to the <wsp:ExactlyOne> operator.

12.4.2.4 Distributive property

This rule is used for normalisation of policy expressions and states that the operator <wsp:All> is distributive over <wsp:ExactlyOne>. This rule is useful when specifying a set of alternatives at the top levels of an expression with further alternatives nested with the children elements. The following examples explain the use of this rule. The policy in the following listing

```
<wsp:All>
  <wsp:ExactlyOne>
    <!-- assertion A -->
    <!-- assertion B -->
  </wsp:ExactlyOne>
</wsp:All>
```

is equivalent to the following policy, which is formed by distributing the <wsp:All> over the <wsp:ExactlyOne> operators.

```
<wsp:ExactlyOne>
  <wsp:All>
    <!-- assertion A -->
  </wsp:All>
  <wsp:All>
    <!-- assertion B -->
  </wsp:All>
</wsp:ExactlyOne>
```

In a more complex example, the following policy expression

```
<wsp:All>
  <wsp:ExactlyOne>
    <!-- assertion A -->
    <!-- assertion B -->
  </wsp:ExactlyOne>
  <wsp:ExactlyOne>
    <!-- assertion C -->
    <!-- assertion D -->
  </wsp:ExactlyOne>
</wsp:All>
```

can be transformed to the equivalent policy expression by applying the algebraic property of distribution for set operations.

```
<wsp:ExactlyOne>
  <wsp:All>
    <!-- assertion A -->
    <!-- assertion C -->
  </wsp:All>
  <wsp:All>
    <!-- assertion A -->
    <!-- assertion D -->
  </wsp:All>
  <wsp:All>
    <!-- assertion B -->
    <!-- assertion C -->
  </wsp:All>
  <wsp:All>
    <!-- assertion B -->
    <!-- assertion D -->
  </wsp:All>
</wsp:ExactlyOne>
```

12.4.2.5 Idempotent rule

The term idempotent is used in mathematics to describe a function that produces the same result if it is applied to itself, i.e. $f(x) = f(f(x))$. Idempotency in WS-Policy means that nesting multiple occurrences of operators within each other is equivalent to a single occurrence. In other words, applying the same operator to itself multiple times yields the same result.

For example, the following expression using the idempotence property of the `<wsp:All>` operator

```
<wsp:All>
    <wsp:All>
        <!-- assertion A -->
        <!-- assertion B -->
    </wsp:All>
</wsp:All>
```

is equivalent to:

```
<wsp:All>
   <!-- assertion A -->
   <!-- assertion B -->
</wsp:All>
```

while the following expression using the idempotence property of the `<wsp:ExactlyOne>` operator

```
<wsp:ExactlyOne>
    <wsp:ExactlyOne>
       <!-- assertion A -->
       <!-- assertion B -->
    </wsp:ExactlyOne>
</wsp:ExactlyOne>
```

is equivalent to:

```
<wsp:ExactlyOne>
    <!-- assertion A -->
    <!-- assertion B -->
</wsp:ExactlyOne>
```

12.4.3 Combining and comparing policies

Stand alone policies can be aggregated into a more coarse grained policy to model situations in which services have intricate interdependencies. Policy combination is used to address the fragmented nature that policies have when they are first developed. Very often each element in the WSDL specification may have its own list of policies associated with it (see Section 12.4.4.1). Combining all these policies together to form a single merged policy (if compatible) is a necessary step in policy processing. In addition, combination policies may also need to be compared with each other to determine whether two Web services have common alternatives.

The first requirement for policies that need to be combined or compared is that they must be first normalised [Anderson 2007], [Vedamuthu 2007a]. Following this, policy compatibility must be determined prior to combining or comparing policies; otherwise policy combination will lead to erroneous results. Determining whether policy alternatives are compatible generally involves domain specific processing. This is due to the fact that the set of behaviours indicated by an aggregated policy alternative depends on the domain specific semantics of the assertion instances that comprise this aggregate policy. In particular, in the case of policy comparison, for two policy alternatives to be compatible they must have at least the same vocabulary. The vocabulary of a policy is the set of all assertions that appear in a policy statement. Every assertion that is declared within a policy is considered part of the policy's overall vocabulary. Domain independent algorithms can be employed to determine policy compatibility.

This section presents mechanisms for combining and intersecting policies on the basis of policy normalisation/compatibility criteria.

12.4.3.1 Merging policies

Policy merging is the process of combining sub-policies together to form a single policy. Merging is a commutative associative function. The merge operation occurs only when policies have first been converted to normal form. The alternatives from each sub-policy are combined to form the new merged alternative. The combination process follows a cross product pattern. One alternative is taken from each policy in turn until all permutations have been exhausted [Anderson 2007].

Example 12.8: Aggregating two existing security policies

Listings 12.10 and 12.11 illustrate two normalised stand alone security policies P_1, P_2 that can be merged to form an aggregate policy P_3.

Listing 12.12 shows the aggregate policy P_3 that is derived by merging policy P_1 with policy P_2. To derive the merged policy, each alternative from policy P_1 is combined with each alternative from policy P_2. The combination process is simply a matter of taking the cross product of alternatives (from normalised policies) and forming new alternatives as shown in Listing 12.12. Each of the policies P_1 and P_2 contains one policy alternative, so the resulting policy P_3 contains one policy alternative with all the policy assertions in both

```
<wsp:Policy
  xmlns:wsp="http://www.w3.org/ns/ws-policy"
  xmlns:sp="http://docs.oasis-open.org/ws-sx/ws-securitypolicy/200702">

  <wsp:ExactlyOne>
    <wsp:All>
      <sp:SecurityToken>
        <sp:TokenType> sp:X509v3 </sp:TokenType>
      </sp:SecurityToken>
      <sp:UsernameToken />
      <sp:EncryptedParts>
        <sp:Body />
      </sp:EncryptedParts>
      <sp:TransportBinding>
        <sp:IncludeTimeStamp />
      </sp:TransportBinding>
    </wsp:All>
  </wsp:ExactlyOne>
</wsp:Policy>
```

Listing 12.10 Source policy P_1

```
<wsp:Policy
  xmlns:wsp="http://schemas.xmlsoap.org/ws/2004/09/policy"
  xmlns:sp="http://schemas.xmlsoap.org/ws/2002/12/secext" >

  <wsp:ExactlyOne>
    <wsp:All>
      <sp:SecurityToken>
        <sp:TokenType>sp:X509v3</sp:TokenType>
      </sp:SecurityToken>
      <sp:SignedParts />
      <sp:EncryptedParts />
    </wsp:All>
  </wsp:ExactlyOne>
</wsp:Policy>
```

Listing 12.11 Source policy P_2

policy alternatives copied over to a new one. It is the responsibility of the policy framework and run time system to analyse and determine the meaning of any alternatives that yield duplicate assertions. It is also worth noting that there is the potential for rapid growth in the size of the merged policies if there are multiple choices in each source policy.

```
<wsp:Policy xmlns:wsp="http://schemas.xmlsoap.org/ws/2004/09/policy">
  <wsp:ExactlyOne>
    <wsp:All>
      <sp:SecurityToken
          xmlns:sp="http://schemas.xmlsoap.org/ws/2002/12/secext">
            <sp:TokenType> sp:X509v3 </sp:TokenType>
      </sp:SecurityToken>
      <sp:UsernameToken>
      </sp:UsernameToken>
      <sp:EncryptedParts>
        <sp:Body>
        </sp:Body>
      </sp:EncryptedParts>
      <sp:TransportBinding>
        <sp:IncludeTimeStamp>
        </sp:IncludeTimeStamp>
      </sp:TransportBinding>
      <sp:SecurityToken>
        <sp:TokenType>sp:X509v3</sp:TokenType>
      </sp:SecurityToken>
      <sp:SignedParts>
      </sp:SignedParts>
      <sp:EncryptedParts>
      </sp:EncryptedParts>
    </wsp:All>
  </wsp:ExactlyOne>
</wsp:Policy>
```

Listing 12.12 Merged policy P_3

12.4.3.2 Intersecting policies

Policy intersection is the process of comparing two Web service policies for common alternatives. Intersection is a commutative, associative function that takes two policies and returns a single policy. Policy intersection is an operation that takes place when two or more parties need to express a joint policy and want to limit its alternatives to those that are mutually compatible. For example, when a requester and a provider express requirements on a message exchange, intersection identifies compatible policy alternatives (if any) included in both requester and provider policies. The intersection of two policies gives zero or more alternatives on which both parties agree.

An intersection algorithm is defined in WS-Policy that approximates compatibility of policy assertions. Determining whether two policy assertions of the same type are compatible may involve domain specific knowledge (e.g., transactions, security, etc.) for determining assertion parameter compatibility [Vedamuthu 2007a]. The domain independent policy intersection algorithm in WS-Policy determines whether two policy assertions are compatible:

1. if they have the same type;
2. if either assertion contains a nested policy expression, the two assertions are compatible if they both have a nested policy expression and the alternative in the nested policy expression of one is compatible with the alternative in the nested policy expression of the other.

The intersection process then commences with both policies being expanded to normal form. The first phase of the intersection process requires that the normalised policies are now examined, one alternative at a time. The intention of the first phase is to eliminate those policy alternatives that are clearly different. This is accomplished by examining the vocabularies of the two alternatives. The vocabulary of an alternative is the QNames of the assertions in that alternative. If the vocabularies do not match, then the two alternatives are clearly different and can be discounted from the policy intersection. When two alternatives have a matching vocabulary they are combined to produce a single new valid alternative in the intersected policy. The process of combining alternatives from two policies is carried out in a cross product fashion. Each alternative from each policy is compared to every alternative from the other.

It is beyond the scope of the WS-Policy framework specification to define how combined alternatives in a policy intersection are to be interpreted. Domain knowledge is required to rationalise the newly combined alternatives into something meaningful to the underlying policy framework. For example, the WS-SecurityPolicy domain will be the only source of information as to whether two security assertions (one from a requester and one from a provider) contradict each other or are complementary refinements of each other.

Example 12.9: Intersecting two existing security policies

Listing 12.13 illustrates a normalised service provider policy that is to be compared (intersected) to another normalised service requester policy. Listing 12.13 contains the two policy alternatives A_1 and A_2. Alternative A_1 (Lines 03-10) contains two policy assertions. One indicates which elements should be signed (Lines 04-06); its type is `<sp:SignedElements>` (Line 04), and its parameters include an XPath expression for the content to be signed (Line 05). The other assertion (Lines 07-09) has a similar structure and indicates which elements should be encrypted. The second alternative A_2 (Lines 11-19) also contains two assertions, each with type (Line 12 and Line 16) and parameters (Lines 13-14 and Line 17). As this example illustrates, compatibility between two policy assertions is based on the assertion type used and delegates parameter processing to domain specific processing. The service requester policy is shown in Listing 12.14 also to contain the two policy alternatives A_3 and A_4.

Listing 12.15 shows that the policy intersection contains a single alternative that includes all of the assertions in (A_2) in the provider policy and all of the assertions in (A_3) in requester policy. This is due to the fact that there is only one alternative (A_2) in the

```
<wsp:Policy
  xmlns:sp="http://docs.oasis-open.org/ws-sx/ws-securitypolicy/200702"
  xmlns:wsp="http://www.w3.org/ns/ws-policy" >
  <!— Provider Policy -->
  <wsp:ExactlyOne>
    <wsp:All> <!-- Alternative A1 -->
      <sp:SignedElements>
        <sp:XPath>/S:Envelope/S:Body</sp:XPath>
      </sp:SignedElements>
      <sp:EncryptedElements>
        <sp:XPath>/S:Envelope/S:Body</sp:XPath>
      </sp:EncryptedElements>
    </wsp:All>
    <wsp:All> <!-- Alternative A2 -->
      <sp:SignedParts>
        <sp:Body />
        <sp:Header
           Namespace="http://www.w3.org/2005/08/addressing" />
      </sp:SignedParts>
      <sp:EncryptedParts>
        <sp:Body />
      </sp:EncryptedParts>
    </wsp:All>
  </wsp:ExactlyOne>
</wsp:Policy>
```

Listing 12.13 Service provider policy

```
<wsp:Policy
  xmlns:sp="http://docs.oasis-open.org/ws-sx/ws-securitypolicy/200702"
  xmlns:wsp="http://www.w3.org/ns/ws-policy" >
  <!—Requester Policy -->
  <wsp:ExactlyOne>
    <wsp:All> <!— Alternative A3 -->
      <sp:SignedParts />
      <sp:EncryptedParts>
        <sp:Body />
      </sp:EncryptedParts>
    </wsp:All>
    <wsp:All> <!— Alternative A4 -->
      <sp:SignedElements>
        <sp:XPath>/S:Envelope/S:Body</sp:XPath>
      </sp:SignedElements>
    </wsp:All>
  </wsp:ExactlyOne>
</wsp:Policy>
```

Listing 12.14 Service requester policy

```
<wsp:Policy
    xmlns:sp="http://docs.oasis-open.org/ws-sx/ws-securitypolicy/200702"
    xmlns:wsp="http://www.w3.org/ns/ws-policy" >
    <!-- Intersection of Provider and Requester policies -->
    <wsp:ExactlyOne>
      <wsp:All>
        <sp:SignedParts> <!- Alternative A2 -->
          <sp:Body />
          <sp:Header
             Namespace="http://www.w3.org/2005/08/addressing" />
        </sp:SignedParts>
        <sp:EncryptedParts>
          <sp:Body />
        </sp:EncryptedParts>
        <sp:SignedParts /> <!- Alternative A3 -->
        <sp:EncryptedParts>
          <sp:Body />
        </sp:EncryptedParts>
      </wsp:All>
    </wsp:ExactlyOne>
</wsp:Policy>
```

Listing 12.15 Intersected policy

provider policy that matches the assertion type of another alternative (A_3) in the requester policy.

Listing 12.15 includes now two assertions of the type `<sp:SignedParts>` and two assertions of the type `<sp:EncryptedParts>`, one from each of its input policies. In general, whether two assertions of the same type are compatible or their repetition is redundant depends on domain specific knowledge regarding the assertion type. Accordingly, one of the `<sp:EncryptedParts>` in the above example is redundant. Whether the two `<sp:SignedParts>` assertions are compatible or one of them is redundant depends also on the semantics defined for this particular assertion type.

12.4.4 Policy attachments

Policy specifications are not particularly useful if they cannot be associated with specific Web services. In this section we explore how policy expressions can be attached to different parts of a WSDL document and describe general purpose mechanisms for associating policies with one or more policy subjects.

The WS-PolicyAttachment specification [Vedamuthu 2007b] deals with the important issue of how to associate a particular policy with a specific Web service (subject). This specification defines how to reference policy expressions from XML elements, WSDL definitions and UDDI entities.Policies will often be associated with a particular policy subject using multiple policy attachments. This is shown in Figure 12.2. For example, there may be attachments at different points in a WSDL description that apply to a subject, and other attachments may be made by UDDI and other mechanisms. When multiple attachments are made, they must be combined to ascertain the effective policy for a particular policy subject. The term *effective policy* signifies the policy associated with a WSDL element. This is achieved by identifying which policy scopes a particular subject is under and combining the individual policies associated with these scopes, using the merge operation to form a merged policy.

A policy can be associated with a policy subject according to one of two strategies:

- Embed the policy as part of the subject's definition (e.g. within a WSDL document or pointed to from the WSDL document).
- Have a standalone policy residing externally to the subject's definition, which is then referenced from within the Web service or services (e.g. via WSDL definition documents) that it is associated with.

These two strategies are examined in the forthcoming two subsections.

12.4.4.1 WSDL policy attachments

It is often desirable to associate policies with the XML elements describing a subject. This allows description formats such as WSDL to be easily used with the WS-Policy framework.

Policies can be associated with several types of WSDL definitions, which serve as policy subjects. These are identified as the *service policy* subject, the *endpoint policy subject*, the *operation policy subject*, and the *message policy subject* as illustrated in Figure 12.3. This figure represents how the effective policies, with regard to WSDL, are calculated for each of these policy subjects. Subjects are nested due to the hierarchical nature of WSDL. In Figure 12.3, the dashed lines represent policy scopes implied by WSDL elements. When attaching a policy to a WSDL element, a policy scope is implied for that attachment. The policy scope only contains the policy subject associated with that element and not those associated with the children of that element. For example, assertions that describe behaviour regarding the manipulation of messages should only be contained within policies attached to WSDL message elements.

For a particular policy subject, the effective policy must merge the element policy of each element with a policy scope that contains the policy subject. For example, in Figure 12.3, for a particular input message to a deployed endpoint, there are four policy subjects involved, each with their own effective policy. There is an effective policy for the message, as well as an effective policy for the parent operation of that message, an effective policy for the deployed endpoint, and an effective policy for the service as a whole. All four effective policies are applicable in relation to that specific input message. This indicates that policies which are attached at a higher level in the WSDL hierarchy are inherited. Therefore, for example, a policy attached to a `<portType>` would be inherited by its `<operation>` and subsequently by its `<input>`, `<output>`, and `<fault>` message descendant elements.

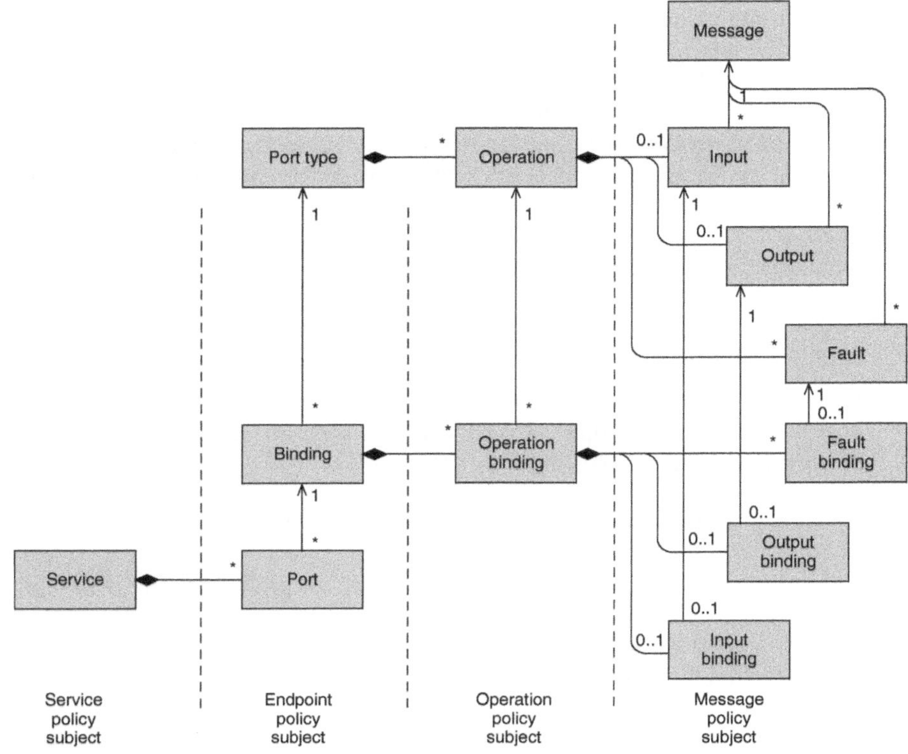

Figure 12.3 Effective policy and policy scopes in WSDL

WS-PolicyAttachment defines a global attribute, called wsp:PolicyURIs, which allows policy expressions to be attached to an arbitrary XML element. Alternatively it uses the <wsp:Policy> and the <wsp:PolicyReference> elements to point to policies that apply. The wsp:PolicyURIs attribute contains a list of one or more URIs while the <wsp:PolicyReference> element is equivalent to an include statement, in that it allows to attach the contents of one policy expression to another.

Example 12.10: Associating policies with WSDL elements

Listing 12.16 shows how to associate policies with WSDL elements describing a subject. In particular, this listing shows how the WS-PolicyAttachment <wsp:PolicyReference> attribute is used as part of a WSDL definition for a shipment order. For reasons of simplicity we have chosen to attach policies to an <operation> and not a <PortType> element. The WSDL inheritance properties discussed earlier would also apply to these elements.

Listing 12.16 illustrates two policies attached to a WSDL document: a reliable message and a secure message policy. The WS-RMPolicy assertion indicates that the WS-Reliable-Messaging must be used to ensure reliable message delivery [Davis 2009]. Specifically,

```
<?xml version="1.0"?>
<wsdl:definitions name="Shipment"
  targetNamespace="http://shipco.com/shipment/shipment/binding"
  xmlns:tns="http://shipco.com/shipment/shipment/binding"
  xmlns:ship="http://shipco.com/shipment"
  xmlns:wsdl=http://schemas.xmlsoap.org/wsdl/
  xmlns:wsrmp="http://docs.oasis-open.org/ws-rx/wsrmp/200702"
  xmlns:sp="http://docs.oasis-open.org/ws-sx/ws-securitypolicy/200702"
  xmlns:wsdl="http://schemas.xmlsoap.org/wsdl/"
  xmlns:wsoap12="http://schemas.xmlsoap.org/wsdl/soap12/"
  xmlns:wsp="http://www.w3.org/ns/ws-policy"
  xmlns:wsu="http://docs.oasis-open.org/wss/2004/01/oasis-200401-
wsswssecurity-utility-1.0.xsd" >

 <!— Policy that specifies that WS-ReliableMessaging protocol must be used
     when sending messages -->
 <wsp:Policy wsu:Id="RmPolicy" >
   <wsrmp:RMAssertion>
     <wsrmp:InactivityTimeout Milliseconds="600000" />
     <wsrmp:BaseRetransmissionInterval Milliseconds="3000" />
     <wsrmp:ExponentialBackoff />
     <wsrmp:AcknowledgementInterval Milliseconds="200" />
   </wsrmp:RMAssertion>
 </wsp:Policy>

 <wsp:Policy wsu:Id="SecureMessagePolicy" >
   <sp:SignedParts>
   <sp:Body />
   </sp:SignedParts>
   <sp:EncryptedParts>
   <sp:Body />
   </sp:EncryptedParts>

 <wsdl:import namespace="http://shipco.com/shipment/shipment"
    location="http://shipco.com/shipment/shipment.wsdl" />
 <wsdl:binding name="ShipmentQuoteSoapBinding" type="ship:Quote" >
    <wsoap12:binding style="document"
      transport="http://schemas.xmlsoap.org/soap/http" />
  <wsp:PolicyReference URI="#RmPolicy" wsdl:required="true" />
  <wsdl:operation name="GetShipmentPrice" >
     <wsoap12:operation
     soapAction="="http://shipco.com/shipment/Quote/GetShipmentPriceRequest"/>
     <wsdl:input>
       <wsoap12:body use="literal" />
       <wsp:PolicyReference URI="#SecureMessagePolicy" wsdl:required="true"/>
     </wsdl:input>
     <wsdl:output>
       <wsoap12:body use="literal" />
       <wsp:PolicyReference URI="#SecureMessagePolicy" wsdl:required="true"/>
     </wsdl:output>
  </wsdl:operation>
 </wsdl:binding>
</wsdl:definitions>
```

Listing 12.16 WSDL definition referencing policies

the WS-ReliableMessaging protocol determines invariants maintained by the reliable messaging endpoints and the directives used to track and manage the delivery of a sequence of messages. For service endpoints bound to the WSDL `"ShipmentQuoteSoapBinding"` the effective policy of the endpoint is found in Listing 12.16, while for the WSDL operation `"GetShipmentPrice"`, an additional message level effective policy is in effect for the input message. This policy can be found in Listing 12.17.

```
<wsp:Policy
   xmlns:sp="http://schemas.xmlsoap.org/ws/2005/07/securitypolicy"
   xmlns:wsp="http://schemas.xmlsoap.org/ws/2004/09/policy"
   xmlns:wsu="http://docs.oasis-open.org/wss/2004/01/oasis-200401-
wsswssecurity-utility-1.0.xsd"
   wsu:Id="SecureMessagePolicy" >
   <sp:SignedParts>
      <sp:Body />
   </sp:SignedParts>
   <sp:EncryptedParts>
      <sp:Body />
   </sp:EncryptedParts>
</wsp:Policy>
```

Listing 12.17 Effective policy for part of the WSDL operation definition in Listing 12.16

12.4.4.2 External policy attachments

The WS-Policy `<wsp:PolicyAttachment>` element allows stand alone policies to be associated with a policy subject independent of that subject's definition and/or representation. This element has three components: the policy scope of the attachment, the policy expressions being bound, and optional security information. The *policy scope* of the attachment is defined using one or more extensible domain expressions (see Figure 12.1) that identify policy subjects, typically using URIs.

To describe resources that a policy applies to the sub-element `<wsp:AppliesTo>` of `<wsp:PolicyAttachment>` is used. The `<wsp:PolicyAttachment>` sub-element specifies and/or refines the domain expression(s) that define the policy scope. When more than one domain expression is present, the policy scope contains the union of the policy subjects identified by each expression.

Example 12.11: Using external policy attachments

Listing 12.18 illustrates the use of the external policy attachment mechanism with an `<EndpointReference>` domain expression for a deployed endpoint as defined in WS-Addressing. In this example, the policy expression (policy assertions) found at the policy expression at http://www.example.com/policies#RmPolicy applies to all interactions with the endpoint at http://www.example.com/acct.

```
<wsp:PolicyAttachment
  <wsp:AppliesTo>
    <wsa:EndpointReference>
      <wsa:Address>http://www.example.com/acct</wsa:Address>
    </wsa:EndpointReference>
  </wsp:AppliesTo>
  <wsp:PolicyReference
    URI="http://www.example.com/policies#RmPolicy" />
</wsp:PolicyAttachment>
```

Listing 12.18 Sample external policy attachment

12.5 Summary of learning objectives

Web service applications must rely on a standard policy framework to describe and process polices and available policy options.

- This framework provides an additional description layer for services and offers developers a declarative language for expressing and programming policies.
- To cover these requirements, WS-Policy and WS-Policy Attachment have been developed.

WS-Policy is a general purpose, extensible framework and model for expressing all types of domain specific policy models, such as transport level security and resource usage policy.

- It expresses requirements, preferences and capabilities in a Web service based environment as policies.
- Policy expressions allow for both simple declarative assertions, as well as more sophisticated conditional assertions.

WS-PolicyAttachment offers a flexible way of associating policy expressions with existing and future Web service artifacts. For instance, WS-PolicyAttachment addresses the requirements for associating Web service policy with Web service artifacts, such as WSDL artifacts and UDDI entities.

Review questions

- What are policies and why are they important for Web service applications?
- What are the most common types of policies for Web services?

- How can policies be exchanged?
- What are the main components of WS-Policy Framework?
- What are policy assertions and what are policy alternatives? How are they related?
- Briefly describe the characteristics and role of normalised policies.
- How can policies be referenced?
- Briefly describe policy merging and policy intersection. What are the requirements for merging/intersection of policies?
- Explain how policies can be associated with subjects (Web services).
- Briefly explain what is the purpose of effective policies and policy scopes in WSDL.
- What is the purpose of a Web service agreement? How does an agreement differ from a policy?
- Briefly describe how agreements and templates are created in WS-Agreement.

Exercises

12.1. Use WS-Policy specification to develop a simple policy, ensuring that any request message must contain X.509 based security tokens as well as UsernameTokens, but both are optional.

12.2. Develop a policy that states that any requesting application must provide one of three kinds of security tokens: UsernameToken, Kerberos tickets or X509 certificates. The policy should also state its preference to let the requesting application know which types of token are preferred. The preference values should indicate that the preferred token type is x509, followed by Kerberos, followed by UsernameToken.

12.3. Modify the policy expression in the previous exercise to indicate that the subject requires UsernameToken, x509 or Kerberos security tokens and that the messages must also have all of the following characteristics: UTF-8 encoding, comply to SOAP 1.1, and must be digitally signed.

12.4. Develop an example of a policy expression that illustrates how two policies, which make use of wsp:PolicyReferences (that allows to associate a collection of policies to any policy subject), can share a common policy.

12.5. Convert the compact policy expression in Listing 12.5 which uses an `<Optional>` attribute to an equivalent normalised policy expression.

12.6. Modify the example in Listings 12.16 and 12.17 to show how the WS-Policy-Attachment can use `<message>` and `<part>` elements rather than an `<operation>` element.

PART VII

Service semantics and business protocols

CHAPTER 13

Semantics and Web services

Learning objectives

To develop robust SOA based integration scenarios, Web services must identify the intended meaning of information they share with interacting services. To achieve this objective, Web services must carry a variety of metadata, including descriptions of the kinds of parameters and data passed to and expected from other services, as well as the names of the processes they engage and operations they support, business rules, order of interactions and so on.

This chapter examines the use of metadata associated with Web services and focuses on a declarative metadata description language and mechanisms that discover and retrieve Web service related metadata. After completing this chapter you will understand the following key concepts:

- The semantic interoperability problem.
- The nature of metadata and its use in SOA based applications.
- XML based mechanisms for describing Web service metadata beyond WSDL and WS-Policy.
- The Resource Description Framework (RDF).
- Mechanisms for querying and retrieving Web service metadata.
- The WS-MetadataExchange Framework.

Chapter preview

Semantic interoperability is a significant architectural feature in an SOA because it enables service providers and consumers to exchange information that is mutually understood, and which can then be acted upon.

In this chapter, we investigate the use of semantics in conjunction with SOA based applications. First, we explain the importance of the semantic interoperability for SOA based applications and then introduce the concept of service metadata for locating services and understanding their intended purpose and meaning. Following this, we concentrate on the use of formal, machine processable definitions of metadata and a standard model for data interchange on the Web. Then we introduce the Resource Description Framework, which achieves these aims. Finally, we describe recent advances in the area of semantics for Web services.

13.1 The semantic interoperability problem

Web service enabled systems can communicate with each other via a platform independent messaging protocol. However, the underlying data (e.g. customer records) to which the service refers usually remain in a structure and nomenclature unique to the application (e.g. a customer relationship management application). This incompatibility can make extraordinarily difficult the assembly of composite applications that source data and business functionality from multiple enterprise systems and associated services. For instance, a CRM system using a certain dialect of XML will not necessarily understand the dialect of an order management system.

The challenges of enabling disparate systems to understand the information that is being shared relates to the logical aspect of using and sharing data and business processes, based on their intended meaning. For Web services to interact properly with each other as part of composite applications, which perform more complex functions by orchestrating numerous services and pieces of information, the requester and provider entities must agree on both the service description (WSDL definition) and the semantics that will govern the interaction between services. This is part of a broader problem known as the *semantic interoperability problem.* Semantic interoperability enables Web services to interact with each other despite their semantic nuances.

When an enterprise begins using an SOA to integrate processes across diverse functional areas, a clear requirement is that client services must convert their local definitions to the local definitions of the target services to be able to interoperate with each other. Addressing these semantic concerns involves discovering how information is used differently by each of the members in a trading partnership (or community), and how that information maps to the normative community view. Thus, a data level integration technique must focus on a complete picture that delivers more than data or messages. It needs to focus on conveying meaning to create fluency. Meaning, in a practical sense, is about metadata, business rules, and user supplied application context to facilitate robust information transformation between disparate systems and applications.

Example 13.1: Interpreting the term *order status*

To understand the semantic interoperability problem at the data level, consider the interpretation of the seemingly simple concept of *order status* as proposed in [Jaenicke 2004]. This concept is vital to the correct execution of many business processes within an enterprise or between collaborating enterprises. However, what are the true semantics of this term?

- Does it signify the status of issuing a request for a quote, or placing a purchase order?
- Perhaps *order status* refers to the manufacturing, shipping, delivery, return or payment status.
- Moreover, how does *order status* relate to the status of a credit check on the customer?
- What limitations should be placed on the order if the credit check reveals anomalies?

In practice, *order status* is probably all of these things as well as the inter-dependencies between them.

Applications in different functional areas of an enterprise (let alone diverse enterprises) will most likely have different interpretations of *order status* and different data repositories will store different order status values. Each database and application within a given area of responsibility, such as order management, manufacturing or shipping, uses a locally consistent definition of order status. However, the problem gets particularly acute when different target services, such as order management, manufacturing and shipping services, each with a different definition of order status, may need to exchange messages with each other.

The former example illustrates the semantic interoperability problem at the data level. However, the semantic interoperability problem can also be encountered at the business process level. A complete semantic solution requires that the semantic interoperability problem be addressed not only at the terminology level but also at the level that services are used and applied in the context of business scenarios, i.e. at the business process level. This implies that there must be agreement between a service requester and provider as to the implied processing of messages exchanged between interacting services that are part of a business process. For example, a purchase order Web service is expected – by the requester which places the order – to process the document containing the purchase order and respond with a quotation, as opposed to simply recording it for auditing purposes. This relates to semantic interoperability concerns at the business process level. As semantic interoperability at the business process level raises a multitude of interesting issues that require elaborate treatment, this important topic deserves special consideration. Therefore, it is not discussed any further in this chapter, but rather examined in depth in a dedicated companion chapter (Chapter 14) in this book where we examine business protocols. In the remainder of this chapter we shall concentrate exclusively on semantic interoperability issues that arise at the data level.

13.2 The role of metadata

Currently, most semantic interoperability issues are handled by using a common vocabulary of terms that each party must adhere to when communicating to a group of trading partners and/or developing custom coded, point-to-point bridges that translate one particular vocabulary to the group's vocabulary or to that of a trading partner. Typical semantic interoperability solutions at the data level exhibit the following three key characteristics:

1. *Semantic intermediation:* Semantic interoperability solutions use a common ontology as a mediation layer in order to abstract data terms, vocabularies and information into a shareable distributed model. This is analogous to creating a model driven enterprise, which uses core information models as a means to reflect enterprise data in whatever form is required.
2. *Semantic mapping:* Mapping to ontology preserves the native semantics of the data and eliminates the need for custom developed code. In semantic interoperability solutions, mapping accounts for much more than simple many-to-many data formatting rules or data syntax arbitrations. It is about how the semantics are captured, aligned and structured in relation to the data itself, thereby creating useful information out of semantically poor data descriptions.
3. *Context sensitivity:* The meaning of any data item is bound to a specific context. Consequently, any semantic interoperability solution must accommodate the fact that the same data item may mean different things from different semantic viewpoints. Typically, the business rules, context definitions and environmental metadata are captured and stored in metadata repositories so that they can be used during the semantic mapping process.

13.2.1 Organisation of metadata

The core element that is needed to support any semantic based interoperability solution is metadata. *Metadata* is data describing a data resource, such as schema data, business domain data, company related data and so on. Typical metadata includes schema based data type descriptions, descriptions of data relationships, relations, attributes, primary/foreign key constraints, and other database centric metadata. The descriptive information metadata allows users and systems to locate, evaluate, access and manage on line resources. To fully enable efficient communication and interoperation between systems, extending conventional metadata with human defined context and business rules is also desirable.

Metadata is organised into fields, where each field represents a characteristic of the data resource, for instance, a resource's title or summary abstract. Each field has a value and some fields may have multiple values. For example, the abstract field may have only a single value, a brief summary of the material, or the field may have multiple values, if the same abstract is provided in several languages. Following a metadata schema creates the actual metadata describing a resource. A *metadata schema* describes a particular set of metadata and the kinds of values that will be used to express the information. Each schema is designed to label a different kind of resource. The organisation of the metadata information reflects the manner in which metadata schemas are managed.

13.2.2 Types of metadata

The primary drive behind the creation of metadata has traditionally been the need for more effective search methods for locating resources over the Internet and understanding their intended purpose and meaning. Therefore, common metadata fields were used to describe the type of resource so that potential users and applications can discover it.

We can identify four typical types of metadata [Ahmed 2001]:

1. *Annotation based metadata:* This refers to side notes added to a document for a specific purpose. It could be used mainly to add side notes in a variety of literary and linguistic texts for on line research, teaching and preservation.
2. *Resource based metadata:* This kind of metadata is used to associate specific properties and their values with whatever the metadata is about: for example, a metadata record for a manufactured product, giving its name, serial number, weight, production date and so on. In XML applications, this type of metadata typically holds information about the properties of information resources, leading to the more appropriate name for this type of metadata.
3. *Subject based metadata:* This refers to data that represents subjects and their interrelationships. It also usually designates specific information resources as belonging to these subjects: for example, a subject index to a record of manufactured products in the form of an *index* Web page that gives collections of links to other documents, with the links organised using a list of subject areas.
4. *Structural mappings:* These resemble annotations and are used to cross reference documents in ways not foreseen by their original authors. Cross references may have specific meanings such as *see also, superseded by,* and so on. Structural mappings are also found in engineering product data where, for instance, an interface can be provided for a field engineer that interlinks a maintenance manual for a complex piece of equipment to supplementary data from its design documentation, and to a parts manual used for ordering spare parts.

In the following we shall focus only on resource based metadata. Readers who are interested in other aspects of metadata usage are referred to [Ahmed 2001].

13.2.3 Metadata and ontologies

It should be noted that the use of metadata alone is not a complete solution. Metadata has to be connected to an ontology. An *ontology* is a set of vocabulary definitions that express a community's consensus knowledge about a specific domain. This body of knowledge is meant to be stable over time and can be used to solve multiple problems [Gruber 1993]. Formal ontology definitions include a name of a particular concept, a set of relations to other concepts, and a natural language description that serves strictly as documentation. In business-to-business integration, an ontology can serve as the reference model of entities and interactions in some particular domain of application and knowledge, e.g. petrochemicals, financial transactions, transportation, retail, etc. The ontology provides meaning to data because it puts raw structured or unstructured data in the form of a structured conceptual specification.

Ontology driven tools are emerging to help companies to automate the translation and processing of information. Using these products, companies can leverage standard vocabularies, and add their own domain specific information classifications, to associate meaning with information expressed in XML. This means that more transformation and processing logic can be driven by business rules, and less of it has to be handled by opaque and hard to maintain program code.

The extensive use of metadata is an important part of the SOA approach. It fosters interoperability by requiring increased precision in the documentation of the services in an SOA application. In the SOA world, an ontology can serve as the basis to establish a common linguistic understanding of business terminology across individual organisations or even across an entire vertical industry. In this way, the meaning of Web services can be formally expressed through relation to an agreed upon set of business concepts and terms.

In the following sections we shall be concerned with the use of metadata in the context of SOA based applications and we shall first examine the nature of service metadata and then focus on standard approaches, such as the Resource Description Framework and WS-MetaDataExchange.

13.3 Service metadata

Once a provider implements a service and wishes to make it available for remote use, the first order of business is to describe that service. In addition to the WSDL definition of a service, other useful elements describing the service may be included. Metadata describing a service typically contains descriptions of the interfaces of a service – the kinds of data entities expected and the names of the operations supported – such as vendor identifier, narrative description of the service, Internet address for messages, format of request and response messages, and may also contain choreographic descriptions of the order of interactions.

Example 13.2: Aspects of service metadata

Metadata descriptions may range from simple identifiers, implying a mutually understood protocol, to a complete description of the vocabularies, expected behaviours, and so on. However, a valid use of a service is not equivalent to a permitted use of the service. For example, one may present a syntactically correct request to a service for ordering products from a preferred supplier. If that request is not accompanied by a suitable authentication, then the request is typically denied. Many security considerations and QoS considerations lie in this realm of agreement. Thus metadata for a service should also include QoS as well as policy descriptions (see Chapter 12). Service policy metadata describes the assertions that govern the intent on the part of a participant when a service is invoked. Policies apply to many aspects of services: to security, to privacy, manageability, QoS and so forth.

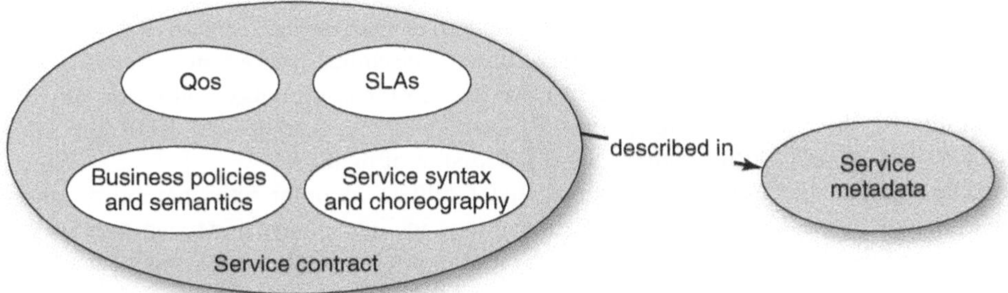

Figure 13.1 Service metadata

What transpires from this discussion is that a service should contain a set of metadata declaring all aspects of a service necessary for a service requester to understand all the externally inspectable aspects of a service. In general, service metadata should be able to describe service contracts that cover a wide range of aspects of services including:

- QoS agreements;
- interface, orchestration and choreography arrangements;
- SLAs;
- commercial agreements.

Figure 13.1 illustrates the various service aspects that require metadata support. These service aspects can be described in a simple declarative metadata description language such as the one offered by the Resource Description Framework [Brickley 2004].

13.4 Resource Description Framework

The Resource Description Framework (RDF) promises an architecture for Web based resource (including Web service) metadata and has been advanced as the primary enabling infrastructure of the Semantic Web activity in the W3C [Beckett 2004]. The Semantic Web activity is a W3C project whose goal is to enable a *cooperative* Web where machines and humans can exchange electronic content that has clear cut, unambiguous meaning. This vision is based on the automated sharing of metadata terms across Web applications.

At present the RDF Schema (RDFS) specification [Brickley 2004] offers the basis for a simple declaration of schemas. It provides a common data model and simple declarative language. RDF is an additional layer on top of XML that is intended to simplify the reuse of vocabulary terms across namespaces and is designed to support the reuse and exchange of vocabularies. Most RDF deployment to date has been experimental, though there are significant applications emerging in the world of e-commerce.

RDF is an infrastructure that enables the encoding, exchange and reuse of structured metadata. This infrastructure enables metadata interoperability through the design of mechanisms that support common conventions of semantics, syntax and structure. RDF does not stipulate semantics for each resource description community, but rather provides the ability for these communities to define metadata elements as needed. RDF uses XML as a common syntax for the exchange and processing of metadata.

RDF supports the use of conventions that facilitate modular interoperability among separate metadata element sets. These conventions include standard mechanisms for representing semantics that are grounded in a simple, yet expressive, data model discussed below. RDF additionally provides a means for publishing both human readable and machine processable vocabularies. Vocabularies are the set of properties, or metadata elements, defined by resource description communities.

This introduction to RDF begins by discussing the functionality of RDF and provides an overview of the model, schema and syntactic considerations.

13.4.1 The RDF data model

The main purpose of RDF is to provide a model for describing resources on the Web. The basic RDF data model consists of three fundamental concepts: resource, properties and statements.

Resources are the central concept of RDF and are used to describe individual objects of any kind, e.g. an entire Web page, a part of a Web page, or a whole collection of Web pages such as an entire Web site. A resource may also be an object that is not directly accessible via the Web, e.g. a printed book or a travel brochure. RDF defines a resource as any object that is uniquely identifiable by a URI [Brickley 2004], [Manola 2004], which can be a Web address or some other kind of unique identifier. Resources map conceptually to entities or parts of entities.

A *property* is used to express a specific aspect, characteristic, attribute or relation that is used to describe a resource. The properties associated with resources are identified by property types, which have corresponding values. In RDF, values may be atomic in nature (text strings, numbers, etc.) or other resources, which in turn may have their own properties. A collection of these properties that refers to the same resource is called a *description.* At the core of RDF is a syntax independent model for representing resources and their corresponding descriptions. Figure 13.2 illustrates a generic RDF description.

Finally, *statements* are composed of a specific resource, together with a named property and the value of that property for that resource. These three individual parts of a statement are called, respectively, the *subject,* the *predicate* and the *object.* These three parts (subject, predicate, object) are often referred to as a *triple.* A triple of the form *(x, P, y)* corresponds to the logical formula *P(x, y),* where the binary predicate *P* relates the subject *x* to the object *y.* This representation is used for translating RDF statements into a logical language ready to be processed automatically in conjunction with rules. The object of a statement (the property value) can be another resource or can be a literal – a resource (specified by a URI) or a simple string or other primitive data type defined by XML. In RDF terms, a literal may have content that is XML markup but is evaluated no further by the RDF processor.

To distinguish characteristics of the data model, the RDF Model and Syntax specification represents the relationships among resources, property types and values in a directed

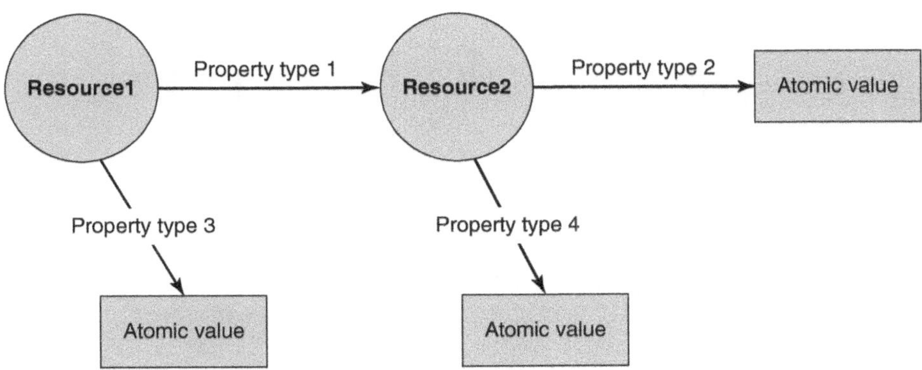

Figure 13.2 Generic RDF description

labeled graph. The arcs are directed from the resource (the subject of the statement) to the value (the object of the statement). This is shown in Figure 13.3.

Example 13.3: Requisitioning a consignment

The simple graph in Figure 13.3 shows the data model corresponding to the statement "Consignment_1 has as consignee John Smith." This statement has a single resource, "Consignment_1", a property type of consignee and a corresponding value of "John Smith". In this figure, resources are identified as nodes (ovals), property types are defined as directed label arcs, and string literal values are written in rectangles. In Figure 13.3, "Consignment_1" is the subject, "John Smith" is the object, and "has as consignee" is the predicate.

If additional descriptive information regarding the consignee were desired, e.g. the consignee's e-mail address and affiliation, an elaboration on the previous example would be required. In this case, descriptive information about `John Smith` is desired. As noted earlier in Example 13.3, before descriptive properties can be expressed about the person `John Smith`, there needs to be a unique identifiable resource representing him. Given the directed label graph notation in the previous example, the data model corresponding to this description is graphically represented as illustrated in Figure 13.4.

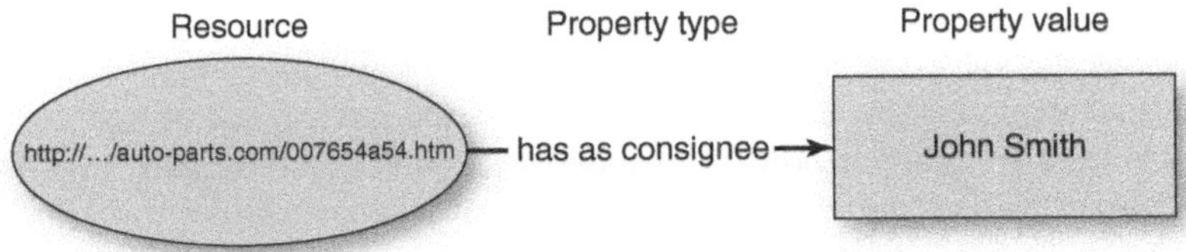

Figure 13.3 Three Simple graph based representation of RDF statement

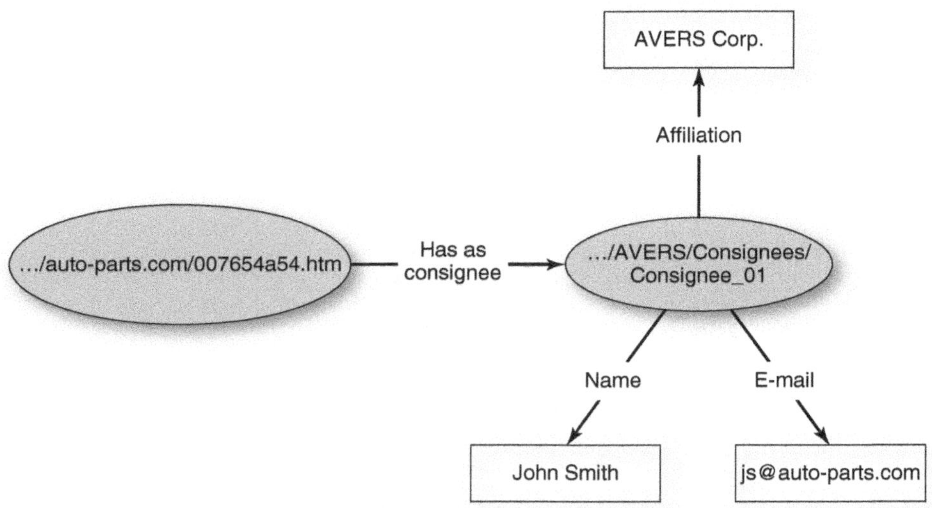

Figure 13.4 Graph based representation of RDF statement with more details

In Figure 13.4, the string `John Smith` is replaced by a uniquely identified resource denoted by `Consignee_01` with the associated property types of name, e-mail and affiliation. The use of unique identifiers for resources allows for the unambiguous association of properties. This is an important point, as the person John Smith may be the value of several different property types. John Smith may be the consignee of *Consignment_1,* but also may be the value of the CEO of AVERS pointing thus to the set of current employees that work in this company. The unambiguous identification of resources provides for the reuse of explicit, descriptive information.

The RDF model allows for the creation of resources at multiple levels. Concerning the representation of personal names, for example, the creation of a resource representing the consignee's name could have additionally been described using *first-name, middle-name,* and *surname* property types. Clearly, this iterative descriptive process could continue down many levels.

13.4.2 RDF syntax

In the previous section we explained how RDF models metadata by using graphs. In this section we shall examine how this information is actually represented in XML.

RDF defines a simple, yet powerful model for describing resources. A syntax representing this model is required to store instances of this model into machine readable files and to communicate these instances among applications. XML is this syntax. RDF imposes formal structure on XML to support the consistent representation of semantics.

Example 13.4: Specifying a consignee who requisitions a consignment

```
<rdf:RDF xmlns:rdf="http://www.w3.org/1999/02/22-rdf-syntax-ns#"
         xmlns:ex="http://auto-parts/staff/">
  <rdf:Description
        rdf:about="http://www.auto-parts.com/Consignees/007654a54.htm">
      <ex:has_consignee > John Smith </ex:has_consignee>
  </rdf:Description>
</rdf:RDF>
```

Listing 13.1 RDF/XML syntax corresponding to the graph in Figure 13.3

The basic ideas behind the RDF/XML syntax can be illustrated using the examples presented already. Listing 13.1 illustrates the RDF/XML syntax corresponding to the graph in Figure 13.3. The `<rdf:Description>` start tag in Listing 13.1 indicates the start of a description of a resource, and goes on to identify the resource the statement is about (the subject of the statement) using the `<rdf:>` attribute to specify the URI reference of the subject resource. Listing 13.1 declares a property element, with the `<QName>` `ex:has_consignee` as its tag, to represent the predicate and object of the statement. The content of this property element is the object of the statement, the plain literal `John Smith` (the value of the consignee property of the subject resource).

```
<rdf:RDF xmlns:rdf="http://www.w3.org/1999/02/22-rdf-syntax-ns#"
         xmlns:ex="http://auto-parts.com/staff/">
  <rdf:Description
     rdf:about="http://www.auto-parts.com/Conisgnees/007654a54.htm">
     <ex:has_consignee
       rdf:resource="http://www.auto-parts.com/Conisgnees/
       Consignees/Consignee_01">
    </rdf:Description>

  <rdf:Description
         rdf:about=
          "http://www.auto-parts.com/Conisgnees/Consignees/Consignee_01" >
     <ex:name> John Smith </ex:name>
     <ex:e-mail> js@auto-parts.com </ex:e-mail>
     <ex:affiliation> AVERS Corp. </ex:affiliation>
  </rdf:Description>
</rdf:RDF>
```

Listing 13.2 RDF/XML syntax corresponding to the graph in Figure 13.4

Listing 13.2 illustrates the RDF/XML syntax corresponding to the graph in Figure 13.4. In Listing 13.2 the element ex:has_consignee represents a property whose value is another resource, rather than a literal. The <rdf:resource> attribute indicates that the property element's value is another resource, identified by its URI reference.

```
<rdf:RDF xmlns:rdf="http://www.w3.org/1999/02/22-rdf-syntax-ns#"
        xmlns:ex="http://auto-parts.com/staff/">
  <rdf:Description
        rdf:about="http://www.auto-parts.com/Conisgnees/007654a54.htm">
     <ex:has_consignee>
        <rdf:Description
            rdf:about="http://www.auto-parts.com/Conisgnees/
              Consignees/Consignee_01">
           <ex:name> John Smith </ex:name>
           <ex:e-mail> js@auto-parts.com </ex:e-mail>
           <ex:affiliation> AVERS Corp. </ex:affiliation>
        </rdf:Description>
     </ex:has_consignee>
  </rdf:Description>
</rdf:RDF>
```

Listing 13.3 Code in Listing 13.2 using a nested <rdf:Description> element

RDF syntax also allows nesting of <rdf:Description> elements. Using this approach, the code in Listing 13.2 is transformed to the equivalent code in Listing 13.3.

Example 13.5: Specifying multiple consignees

Now consider Listing 13.4, which represents an RDF document (say Consignees.rdf) listing the various consignees who have requisitioned consignments on behalf of AVERS, along with some of their properties. We assume that this RDF document can be found at http://www.auto-parts.com/Conisgnees/Consignees.rdf.

Note that in Listing 13.4 the <rdf:Description> element has an <rdf:ID> attribute instead of an <rdf:about> attribute. The attribute <rdf:ID> specifies a fragment identifier, given by the value of the <rdf:ID> attribute (JohnSmith or

```
<rdf:RDF>
   <rdf:Description rdf:ID="John-Smith">
      <ex:name> John Smith </ex:name>
      <ex:e-mail> js@auto-parts.com </ex:e-mail>
      <ex:affiliation> AVERS Corp. </ex:affiliation>
   </rdf:Description>

   <rdf:Description rdf:ID="Frank-James">
      <ex:name> Frank James </ex:name>
      <ex:e-mail> fj@auto-parts.com </ex:e-mail>
      <ex:affiliation> AVERS Corp. </ex:affiliation>
   </rdf:Description>

   <rdf:Description rdf:ID="Jim-Fletcher">
      <ex:name> Jim Fletcher </ex:name>
      <ex:e-mail> jf@auto-parts.com </ex:e-mail>
      <ex:affiliation> AVERS Corp. </ex:affiliation>
   </rdf:Description>
</rdf:RDF>
```

Listing 13.4 RDF document listing various consignees

JimFletcher in this case) as an abbreviation of the complete URI reference of the resource being described.

Example 13.6: Refering to specific consignees

In RDF the attribute `<rdf:ID>` is somewhat similar to the ID attribute in XML and HTML, in that it defines a name that must be unique relative to the current base URI. Listing 13.5 shows how we can refer to the consignees who acted on behalf of AVERS and who are specified in Listing 13.4. This listing shows that a fragment identifier such as "John-Smith" or "Jim-Fletcher" will be interpreted relative to a base URI.

RDF can classify resources into different kinds or categories in a manner similar to the one used in object oriented programming language where objects can have different types or classes. RDF supports this concept by providing a predefined property, the attribute `<rdf:type>`. The `<rdf:type>` attribute allows us to indicate that a resource is of a particular class. This allows parsers that are able to process this information to glean more about the metadata [Ahmed 2001].

```
<rdf:RDF xmlns:rdf="http://www.w3.org/1999/02/22-rdf-syntax-ns#"
         xmlns:ex="http://auto-parts/staff/">
  <rdf:Description
       rdf:about="http://www.auto-parts.com/Conisgnees/007654a54.htm">
     <ex:has_consignee
         rdf:resource="http://www.auto-parts.com/Conisgnees/
         Consignees.rdf#John-Smith">
  </rdf:Description>

  <rdf:Description
       rdf:about="http://www.auto-parts.com/Conisgnees/007654a42.htm">
     <ex:has_consignee
         rdf:resource="http://www.auto-parts.com/Conisgnees/
         Consignees.rdf#Frank-James">
  </rdf:Description>

  <rdf:Description
       rdf:about="http://www.auto-parts.com/Conisgnees/007654a58.htm">
     <ex:has_consignee
         rdf:resource="http://www.auto-parts.com/Conisgnees/
         Consignees.rdf#Jim-Fletcher">
  </rdf:Description>
</rdf:RDF>
```

Listing 13.5 Referring to the consignees' document

Example 13.7: Refering to a standard resource

The purpose of this example is to illustrate that materials management operations and logistics, in the AVERS case study, will be performed according to the norms of the Global Materials Management Operations Guideline Logistics Evaluation (MMOG/LE) standard. This standard provides best practices that guide automotive manufacturers in assessing, improving and benchmarking materials management and logistics/consignment processes to increase plant efficiency and streamline process efficiency. Better delivery rating scores and savings on premium freight, obsolescence and administration are a few of the gains reported.

Listing 13.6 below specifies that the RDF resource being referred to in the listing is the Odette MMOG/LE standard document. This document is provided by the Organization for Data Exchange by Tele Transmission in Europe (ODETTE).

RDF uses the concept of typed element, which is an XML element where a resource that could otherwise be referred to by an `<rdf:type>` property is turned into a namespace qualified element. Listing 13.7 illustrates the use of an RDF typed element to represent the `<rdf:type>` statement in Listing 13.6. Notice that the `<rdf:Description>` element in Listing 13.6 is replaced by a `Global_MMOG` element.

```
<rdf:RDF xmlns:rdf="http://www.w3.org/1999/02/22-rdf-syntax-ns#"
         xmlns:ex="http://auto-parts.com/staff/">
  <rdf:Description
       rdf:about="http://www.auto-parts.com/Conisgnees/007654a54.htm">
       rdf:type="https://forum.odette.org/publications/executive-
                 summaries/logistics/Global_MMOG/">
     <ex:has_consignee
         rdf:resource="http://www.auto-parts.com/Conisgnees/
         Consignees.rdf#John-Smith">
     <ex:publisher
         rdf:resource="http://www.auto-parts.com/company_id/3423X0P">
  </rdf:Description>
</rdf:RDF>
```

Listing 13.6 Use of typed attributes in RDF

```
<rdf:RDF xmlns:rdf="http://www.w3.org/1999/02/22-rdf-syntax-ns#"
         xmlns:ex="http://auto-parts/staff/"
         xmlns:odette="https://forum.odette.org/publications/executive-
                         summaries/logistics/
  <odette:Global_MMOG
         rdf:about="http://www.auto-parts.com/Conisgnees/007654a54.htm">
     <ex:has_consignee
          rdf:resource=
         "http://www.auto-parts.com/Conisgnees/Consignees.rdf#John-Smith">
     <ex:publisher
          rdf:resource="http://www.auto-parts.com/company_id/3423X0P">
  </odette:Global_MMOG>
</rdf:RDF>
```

Listing 13.7 Using typed elements in RDF

In the previous discussion we dealt with, and described, the properties that the <rdf:Description> element may contain. We have consequently explained that RDF property elements can be expressed in three ways: string literals, resources and nested RDF statements. When specifying metadata, there is often a need to describe groups of resources. This is helpful when, for instance, we need to state that several consignees requisitioned a specific consignment, or to list the software modules in a package. RDF describes such groups of resources by means of containers. A container is a list, or collection, of resources. Resources in a container are called members. The members of a container may be resources (including blank nodes) or literals. RDF provides a container vocabulary consisting of three predefined types. These are: bag, sequence and alternative.

An RDF *bag* (a resource having type <rdf:Bag>) represents a group of resources or literals, possibly including duplicate members, where there is no significance in the order of the members. For example, a bag might be used to describe a group of part numbers in which the order of entry or processing of the part numbers does not matter.

An RDF *sequence* (a resource having type <rdf:Seq>) represents a group of resources or literals, possibly including duplicate members, where the order of the members is significant. For example, a sequence might be used to describe a group that must be maintained in alphabetical order.

An RDF *alternative* (a resource having type <rdf:Alt>) represents a group of resources or literals that are alternatives (typically for a single value of a property). For example, an alternative might be used to describe alternative language translations for the title of a book, or to describe a list of alternative Internet sites at which a resource might be found. An application using a property whose value is an <rdf:Alt> container should be aware that it can choose any one of the members of the group as appropriate.

Example 13.8: Multiple consignees for a specific car part

Listing 13.8 shows the RDF syntax for a bag that enables more than one consignee to be associated with a specific car part, such as a specific power seat. This example covers a shipment of like merchandise (viz. power seats) that were all imported during a specific time period and were consigned to various ultimate consignees in the same company. The syntax for an RDF bag is simply the enclosing element <rdf:Bag> followed by the list of resources in the bag. This listing also shows that RDF/XML provides the <rdf:li> element as a convenience element to identify members of the container, thus avoiding explicitly numbering each membership property.

```
<rdf:RDF xmlns:rdf="http://www.w3.org/1999/02/22-rdf-syntax-ns#"
         xmlns:ex="http:/auto-parts.com/staff/">

   <rdf:Description
       about="http://www.auto-parts.com/Seat/Power_Seat007654.htm">
      <ex:has_consignee>
        <rdf:Bag>
          <rdf:li
           rdf:resource="http://www.auto-parts.com/Conisgnees/
           Consignees/John-Smith">
          <rdf:li
           rdf:resource="http://www.auto-parts.com/Conisgnees/
           Consignees/Frank-James">
          <rdf:li
           rdf:resource="http://www.auto-parts.com/Conisgnees/
           Consignees/Jim-Fletcher">
        </rdf:Bag>
      </ex:has_consignee>
   </rdf:Description>
</rdf:RDF>
```

Listing 13.8 RDF/XML example for a bag of consignees

To describe RDF statements using RDF itself, for instance to record information about when statements were made, who made them, or other similar information, RDF relies on the concept of reification. RDF provides a built in vocabulary intended for describing RDF statements. A description of a statement using this vocabulary is called a reification of the statement. Reification enables statements to be quoted and have evaluations expressed about them, such as to agree or disagree with them, i.e. to assert whether they are true or false. The RDF reification vocabulary consists of the type `<rdf:Statement>`, and the properties `<rdf:subject>`, `<rdf:predicate>`, and `<rdf:object>`. Detailed examples of the use of the concept of reification in RDF can be found in [Ahmed 2001], [Manola 2004].

This section has served as a brief overview of the RDF syntax and functionality. More details on the RDF syntax as well as examples of its use can be found in [Ahmed 2001], [Beckett 2004], [Manola 2004].

13.4.3 RDF Schema

RDF Schema is used to declare vocabularies, the sets of semantic property types defined by a particular community [Beckett 2004]. RDF Schema defines the valid properties in a given RDF description, as well as any characteristics or restrictions of the property type values themselves. To understand a particular RDF Schema is to understand the semantics of each of the properties in that description. RDF Schemas are structured based on the RDF data model.

RDF Schema refers to the metadata entities it describes as classes. The XML namespace mechanism serves to identify RDF Schemas. A class in RDF Schema corresponds to the generic concept of a type or category, somewhat like the notion of a class in object oriented programming languages such as Java [Manola 2004]. RDF classes can be used to represent almost any category of a modelled entity, such as Web pages, people, document types, databases or abstract concepts. Classes are defined using the RDF Schema resources `<rdfs:Class>` and `<rdfs:Resource>`, and the properties `<rdf:type>` (see preceding section) and `<rdfs:subClassOf>`.

Example 13.9: Classifying cat seat parts

Suppose that AVERS wanted to use RDF to provide information about different kinds of car seat parts. Using RDF Schema, AVERS would first need a class to represent the category of entities that are car seats. This is depicted in Figure 13.5.

In RDF Schema, a class is any resource having an `<rdf:type>` property whose value is the resource `<rdfs:Class>`. Therefore the car seat class would be described by assigning the class a URI reference, say `ex:CarSeat` and describing that resource with an `<rdf:type>` property whose value is the resource `<rdfs:Class>` as shown by the solid line connecting ex:`CarSeat` to `<rdfs:Class>` in Figure 13.5.

Figure 13.5 also illustrates that there are several other classes such as `ex:ManualSeat`, `ex:HeatedSeat`, and `ex:PowerSeat` that are all specialisations of class `ex:CarSeat`.

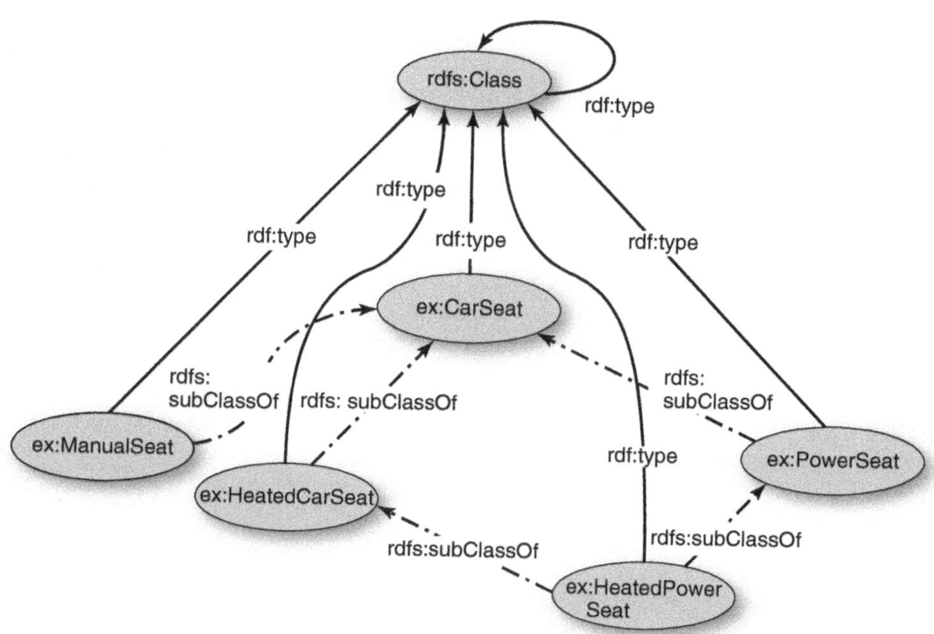

Figure 13.5 The CarSeat class hierarchy

Specialised classes can be described in the same way as class `ex:CarSeat`, by assigning a URI reference for each new class, and writing RDF statements describing these resources as classes. To indicate that these classes are also specialised classes of the class `ex:CarSeat`, the pre-defined `<dfs:subClassOf>` property is used to associate the specialised classes with the class `ex:CarSeat`. Dashed lines in Figure 13.5 denote this. Note that the resource `<rdfs:Class>` itself has an `<rdf:type>` of `<rdfs:Class>`. Moreover, RDF makes use of multiple inheritance to allow a resource to be an instance of more than one class, e.g. the class `ex:HeatedPowerSeat` in Figure 13.5. Listing 13.9 illustrates how the schema described in Figure 13.5 can be coded in RDF/XML.

The resources that belong to a class are called its instances. In the case of AVERS, it intends for the instances of this class to be resources that are car seats. The meaning of the `<rdfs:subClassOf>` relationship dictates that any instance of a class of the more specialised type, e.g. `ex:PowerSeat`, is also an instance of the class of the more general type with which it is associated, e.g. `ex:CarSeat`. Before explaining how instances for the classes defined in Listing 13.9 can be created, we shall first explain how we can define class properties.

In addition to describing specific classes, user communities also need to be able to describe specific properties that characterise those classes (such as the consignee and the type of a car seat). In RDF Schema, properties are described using the

```
<rdf:RDF
     xmlns:rdf="http://www.w3.org/1999/02/22-rdf-syntax-ns#"
     xmlns:rdfs="http://www.w3.org/2000/01/rdf-schema#"
     xml:base="http://http://www.auto-parts.com/schemas/CarSeats">

     <rdf:Description ID="CarSeat">
       <rdf:type resource="http://www.w3.org/2000/01/rdf-schema#Class"/>
     </rdf:Description>
     <rdf:Description ID="PowerSeat">
       <rdf:type resource="http://www.w3.org/2000/01/rdf-schema#Class"/>
              <rdfs:subClassOf rdf:resource="#CarSeat"/>
     </rdf:Description>
     <rdf:Description ID="HeatedSeat">
       <rdf:type resource="http://www.w3.org/2000/01/rdf-schema#Class"/>
              <rdfs:subClassOf rdf:resource="#CarSeat"/>
     </rdf:Description>
     <rdf:Description ID="ManualSeat">
       <rdf:type resource="http://www.w3.org/2000/01/rdf-schema#Class"/>
              <rdfs:subClassOf rdf:resource="#CarSeat"/>
     </rdf:Description>
     <rdf:Description ID="HeatedPowerSeat">
       <rdf:type resource="http://www.w3.org/2000/01/rdf-schema#Class"/>
              <rdfs:subClassOf rdf:resource="#PowerSeat"/>
              <rdfs:subClassOf rdf:resource="#HeatedSeat"/>
   </rdf:Description>
</rdf:RDF>
```

Listing 13.9 The car seat class hierarchy in RDF/XML

RDF class `<rdf:Property>`, and the RDF Schema properties `<rdfs:domain>`, `<rdfs:range>`, and `<rdfs:subPropertyOf>`.

All properties in RDF are described as instances of class `<rdf:Property>` where a URI identifies the resource which represents the property, and the `<rdf:type>` of the resource is `<rdf:Property>`. RDF Schema also provides a vocabulary for describing how properties and classes are intended to be used together in RDF data. Using the RDF Schema properties `<rdfs:domain>` and `<rdfs:range>` supply the most important information of this kind to further describe application specific properties [Manola 2004]. The `<rdfs:domain>` property is used to indicate that a particular property applies to a designated class. The `<rdfs:domain>` property constrains the classes of subjects (resources) for which this specific property is a valid predicate. For example, we may wish to indicate that the property `ex:Consignee` applies to instances of class `ex:CarSeat`. The `<rdfs:range>` property is used to indicate that the values of a particular property are instances of a designated class. The `<rdfs:range>` property constrains the classes of objects (resources) for which this particular property is a valid predicate. For example, we may indicate that a property such as `ex:Consignee` may have values that are instances of class `ex:Person`.

Example 13.10: More details for the car seat schema in Example 13.9

Listing 13.10 illustrates a more detailed specification of the car seat schema in Listing 13.9. For brevity this listing includes only simple properties for the car seat class.

```
<rdf:RDF
      xmlns:rdf="http://www.w3.org/1999/02/22-rdf-syntax-ns#"
      xmlns:rdfs="http://www.w3.org/2000/01/rdf-schema#"
      xml:base="http://http://www.auto-parts.com/schemas/CarSeats">

      <rdf:Class ID="CarSeat">

      <rdf:Class ID="PowerSeat">
          <rdfs:subClassOf rdf:resource="#CarSeat"/>
      </rdf:Class>

      <rdf:Class ID="HeatedSeat">
       <rdfs:subClassOf rdf:resource="#CarSeat"/>
      </rdf:Class>

      <rdf:Class ID="ManualSeat">
          <rdfs:subClassOf rdf:resource="#CarSeat"/>
      </rdf:Class>

      <rdf:Class ID="HeatedPowerSeat">
          <rdfs:subClassOf rdf:resource="#PowerSeat"/>
          <rdfs:subClassOf rdf:resource="#HeatedSeat"/>
      </rdf:Class>


      <rdfs:Class rdf:ID="Consignee"/>
      <rdfs:Class rdf:ID="CarManufacturer"/>
      <rdfs:Datatype rdf:about="&xsd;integer"/>

      <rdf:Property rdf:ID="hasConsignee">
        <rdfs:domain rdf:resource="#CarSeat"/>
        <rdfs:range rdf:resource="#Consignee"/>
      </rdf:Property>
           ... ... ...
      <rdf:Property rdf:ID="SeatCover">
         <rdfs:domain rdf:resource="#CarSeat"/>
         <rdfs:range rdf:resource="&xsd;integer"/>
      </rdf:Property>
</rdf:RDF>
```

Listing 13.10 CarSeat schema including properties

Properties for other classes in this listing can be defined in an analogous manner. Note that the schema in Listing 13.10 uses the RDF/XML typed node abbreviation for the definition of classes. This listing also introduces the classes ex:Consignee and ex:CarSeat. The ex:hasConsignee property applies to any ex:CarSeat and its corresponding value is of type ex:Consignee. Finally, the ex:SeatCover property also applies to instances of the class ex:CarSeat and its value is an <xsd:integer> giving the seat covers in a car seat.

Example 13.11: Creating instances for the car seat class in Example 13.10

We conclude this section by illustrating how we can create instances from a class defined in Listing 13.10. Listing 13.11 illustrates by describing an instance of the ex:CarSeat class defined in Listing 13.10, together with some hypothetical values for its properties.

```
<rdf:RDF
      xmlns:rdf="http://www.w3.org/1999/02/22-rdf-syntax-ns#"
      xmlns:rdfs="http://www.w3.org/2000/01/rdf-schema#"
      xml:ex= http://http://www.auto-parts.com/schemas/CarSeats#"
      xml:base="http://www.auto-parts.com/entities">

      <ex:CarSeat rdf:ID="JohnSimthsConsignment">
          <ex:hasConsignee
           rdf:resource="http://www.auto-parts.com/staffid/5583"/>
          <ex:PowerSeat rdf:datatype="&xsd;integer">007654</ex:PowerSeat>
          <ex:hasPublisher
               rdf:resource=
                 "http://www.auto-parts.com/manufacturerer-id/3423X0P"/>
     </ex:CarSeat>
</rdf:RDF
```

Listing 13.11 Instantiating the CarSeat class

As a final note, it is interesting to point out that conceptually RDF is very similar to WSDL, which is simply a collection of metadata about XML based services. It is therefore quite easy to build a bridge between these two specifications.

In a similar manner to the preceding section, this section has served only as a brief overview of the RDF Schema declarations. More information on RDF Schema, as well as examples of its use, including defining schema constraints, how RDF Schema differs from type systems of object oriented programming languages such as Java, and details of how statements can be validated using the RDF Schema, can be found in [Ahmed 2001], [Manola 2004].

13.5 Richer schema languages

The expressiveness of RDF and RDF Schema that we described in the previous sections is deliberately restricted. RDF is (roughly) limited to binary ground predicates, and RDF Schema is (again roughly) limited to a subclass hierarchy and a property hierarchy, with domain and range definitions of these properties. In particular, RDF Schema provides basic capabilities for describing RDF vocabularies, but additional capabilities are also possible, and can be useful. These capabilities may be provided through further development of RDF Schema, or in other languages based on RDF.

The Web Ontology Working Group (http://www.w3.org/2001/sw/WebOnt) identified a number of characteristic use cases for the Semantic Web, which would require much more expressiveness than RDF and RDF Schema.

Some of the richer schema capabilities that have been identified as useful (but that are not provided by RDF Schema) include [Manola 2004]:

- Cardinality constraints on properties, e.g. that a person has exactly one biological father and mother.
- Specifying that a given property (such as `ex:hasAncestor`) is transitive, e.g. that if `A ex:hasAncestor B`, and `B ex:hasAncestor C`, then `A ex:hasAncestor C`.
- Specifying that a given property is a unique identifier (or key) for instances of a particular class.
- Specifying that two different classes (having different URI references) actually represent the same class.
- Specifying that two different instances (having different URI references) actually represent the same individual.
- Specifying cardinality restrictions of a property that depend on the class of resource to which a property is applied, e.g. being able to say that for a soccer team the `ex:hasPlayers` property has 11 values, while for a basketball team the same property should have only 5 values.
- The ability to describe new classes in terms of combinations (e.g. unions and intersections) of other classes, or to say that two classes are disjoint (i.e. that no resource is an instance of both classes).

The capabilities mentioned above, in addition to other semantic constructs, are the targets of ontology languages such as the Ontology Working Language (OWL) [Antoniou 2008], [McGuiness 2004]. This ontology language is based on RDF and RDF Schema and provides all the additional capabilities mentioned above. The intent of languages such as OWL is to provide additional machine processable semantics for resources, to provide semantic foundations for situations involving dynamic discovery of businesses and services by relying on knowledge representation and reasoning techniques. Its intention is to make representations of resources more closely mirror the semantics of their intended business applications and real world counterparts. While such capabilities are not necessarily needed to build useful applications using RDF, the development of such languages is a very active subject of work as part of the development of the Semantic Web [Manola 2004].

Currently, there are several attempts to reinvent concepts found in the Semantic Web to provide semantics to Web services in the form WSDL extensions, thereby facilitating dynamic SOA based applications. Some of the attempts in this direction are OWL and Darpa Agent Markup Language (DAML) [DAML].

13.6 WS-MetadataExchange

To enable Web services to be self describing it is necessary to use expressive metadata to describe what other endpoints need to know to interact with them. For this purpose, the Web service architecture defines SOAP based access protocols for metadata described in the WS-MetadataExchange specification [Ballinger 2006].

WS-MetaDataExchange is a Web Service protocol specification, designed to work in conjunction with WS-Addressing, WSDL and WS-Policy to allow retrieval of metadata about a Web services endpoint. Using WS-Addressing, WS-MetadataExchange defines a bootstrap mechanism for metadata driven message exchange, supporting especially XML Schema, WSDL and WS-Policy. This enables the creation of an interaction protocol for discovering and retrieving Web service metadata from a specific address. WS-MetadataExchange is not simply a system of additional SOAP headers, but rather a definition of a complete messaging protocol to be carried out independently of, and prior to, any requester–provider interaction.

To bootstrap communication with Web services and to retrieve metadata, the WS-MetadataExchange specification defines two request/response interactions. Metadata retrieval is implemented by the metadata request operations "`Get Metadata`" and "`Get`". The operation "`Get Metadata`" is used by for general purpose metadata queries and is the only required operation for WS-MetadataExchange compliant endpoints. To retrieve the metadata of a service, a requester may send a "`Get Metadata`" request message to the service endpoint. When the type of metadata sought (known as dialect) is known, e.g. WSDL or WS-Policy, a requester may indicate that only that type should be returned. The contents of a response message can consist of the actual metadata definitions, address references to metadata definitions, or a combination of both. To retrieve a referenced metadata section (that is probably returned by a "`Get Metadata`" request message), a requester may send a "`Get`" request message to the metadata reference. Metadata reference endpoints are required to support a single operation with the sole purpose of returning a specific set of metadata definitions. Together these two request/response message pairs allow efficient, incremental retrieval of a Web service's metadata.

The interactions defined in WS-MetadataExchange are intended for the retrieval of metadata (i.e. service description information) only. They are not intended to provide a general purpose query or retrieval mechanism for other types of data associated with a service, such as state data, properties and attribute values, etc.

Example 13.12: Sample metadata request for a given service policy

Listing 13.12 illustrates a sample GetMetadata request for a specific WS-Policy. The <wsa:Action> element, which is part of the WS-Addressing specification, identifies that the action denoted by the message in Listing 13.12 is a GetMetadata request. As indicated in this listing, addressing may be included in the request and response messages, according to the usage and semantics defined in the WS-Addressing specification (see Section 7.1.1). The listing illustrates a pattern where the endpoint is identified by a <wsa:To> header block as well as an application specific header block (identified by <ex:MyRefProp>). As the message in the SOAP body indicates, this request is for the policy of the receiver; alternatively, it could include an identifier to request a policy within a given target namespace. If no dialect, e.g. WS-Policy, or identifier is specified in the SOAP body then the request is for all metadata available at the receiver's site.

```
<env:Envelope
    xmlns:wsa="http://www.w3.org/2005/08/addressing"
    xmlns:wsx="http://schemas.xmlsoap.org/ws/2004/09/mex" >
   <env:Header>
     <wsa:Action>
       http://schemas.xmlsoap.org/ws/2004/09/mex/GetMetadata/Request
     </wsa:Action>
     <wsa:MessageID>
       uuid:73d7edfc-5c3c-49b9-ba46-2480caee43e9
     </wsa:MessageID>
     <wsa:ReplyTo>
       <wsa:Address>http://client.example.com/MyEndpoint</wsa:Address>
     </wsa:ReplyTo>
     <wsa:To>http://server.example.org/YourEndpoint</wsa:To>
     <ex:MyRefProp xmlns:ex="http://server.example.org/refs">
          78f2dc229597b529b81c4bef76453c96
     </ex:MyRefProp>
   </env:Header>
   <env:Body>
     <wsx:GetMetadata>
       <wsx:Dialect>
          http://schemas.xmlsoap.org/ws/2004/09/policy
       </wsx:Dialect>
     </wsx:GetMetadata>
    </env:Body>
</env:Envelope>
```

Listing 13.12 Sample GetMetadata request message

Example 13.13: Sample metadata response for the policy in Example 13.12

Listing 13.13 illustrates a sample GetMetadata response to the GetMetadata request in Listing 13.12. The information that is returned in a GetMetadata response is included with a <wsx: Metadata> element. The children of this element are a variable number of <wsx: MetadaSection>s, each of which contains information about either one

```
env:Envelope
    xmlns:s12="http://www.w3.org/2003/05/soap-envelope"
    xmlns:wsa="http://www.w3.org/2005/08/addressing"
    xmlns:wsp="http://www.w3.org/ns/ws-policy"
    xmlns:wsx="http://schemas.xmlsoap.org/ws/2004/09/mex">
  <env:Header>
    <wsa:Action>
      http://schemas.xmlsoap.org/ws/2004/09/mex/GetMetadata/Response
    </wsa:Action>
    <wsa:RelatesTo>
      uuid:73d7edfc-5c3c-49b9-ba46-2480caee43e9
    </wsa:RelatesTo>
    <wsa:To>http://client.example.com/MyEndpoint</wsa:To>
  </env:Header>
  <env:Body>
   <wsx:Metadata>
    <wsx:MetadataSection
        Dialect="http://schemas.xmlsoap.org/ws/2004/09/policy">
     <wsp:Policy
       xmlns:wsse="http://schemas.xmlsoap.org/ws/2002/12/secext">
       <wsp:ExactlyOne>
         <wsse:SecurityToken>
            <wsse:TokenType>wsse:Kerberosv5TGT</wsse:TokenType>
         </wsse:SecurityToken>
         <wsse:SecurityToken>
            <wsse:TokenType>wsse:X509v3</wsse:TokenType>
         </wsse:SecurityToken>
       </wsp:ExactlyOne>
     </wsp:Policy>
    </wsx:MetadataSection>
   </wsx:Metadata>
  </env:Body>
</env:Envelope>
```

Listing 13.13 Sample GetMetadata response message

```
<env:Envelope
 xmlns:s12="http://www.w3.org/2003/05/soap-envelope"
    xmlns:wsa="http://www.w3.org/2005/08/addressing"
    xmlns:wsx="http://schemas.xmlsoap.org/ws/2004/09/mex">
   <env:Header>
     <wsa:Action>
       http://schemas.xmlsoap.org/ws/2004/09/mex/GetMetadata/Response
     </wsa:Action>
     <wsa:RelatesTo>
       uuid:a6e37bfb-f324-4e71-b33a-4f6d5c6027f4
     </wsa:RelatesTo>
     <wsa:To>http://client.example.com/MyEndpoint</wsa:To>
   </env:Header>
   <env:Body>
    <wsx:Metadata>
      <wsx:MetadataSection Dialect="http://schemas.xmlsoap.org/wsdl">
       <definitions name="PurchaseOrderService"
        targetNamespace="http://supply.com/PurchaseService/wsdl"
        xmlns:tns="http://supply.com/PurchaseService/wsdl"
        xmlns:xsd="http://www.w3.org/2001/XMLSchema"
        xmlns:wsdl="http://schemas.xmlsoap.org/wsdl/"
        xmlns:soapbind="http://schemas.xmlsoap.org/wsdl/soap/">
           .. ..
        <wsdl:portType name="PurchaseOrderPortType">
            <wsdl:operation name="SendPurchase">
                 <wsdl:input message="tns:POMessage"/>
                 <wsdl:output message="tns:InvMessage"/>
             </wsdl:operation>
        </wsdl:portType>
        <wsdl:service name="PurchaseOrderService">
           <wsdl:port
                name="PurchaseOrderPort"
                binding="tns: PurchaseOrderSOAPBinding">
               <soapbind:address
                 location="http://supply.com:8080/PurchaseOrderService"/>
           </wsdl:port>
        </wsdl:service>
       </definitions>
      </wsx:MetadataSection>
      <wsx:MetadataSection
         Dialect="http://www.w3.org/2001/XMLSchema"
         Identifier="urn:plastics_supply:schemas:sq">
       <wsx:MetadataReference>
        <wsa:Address>
           http://www.plastics_supply.com/schemas/sq
        </wsa:Address>
       </wsx:MetadataReference>
      </wsx:MetadataSection>
    </wsx:Metadata>
   </env:Body>
</env:Envelope>
```

Listing 13.14 Sample `Get Metadata` response message for retrieving all metadata

metadata definition or a set of related definitions of the same dialect, and describes a particular aspect of the endpoint behaviour. Each metadata section includes a <dialect> attribute to indicate the type of metadata it carries. The <wsa:Action> element now identifies that the action denoted by the message is a GetMetadata response to the message in Listing 13.12. This is identified by the <wsa:RelatesTo> element. Note that the code in Listing 13.13 contains a single metadata section. In particular the required dialect attribute specifies that the metadata in this section is of type, or dialect, WS-Policy. Finally, the <wsp:Policy> element contains the policy corresponding to the receiver of the GetMetadata request in Listing 13.12.

Now let us assume that a requester specifies a GetMetadata request for all metadata for a particular service by omitting to specify a dialect or identifier as part of the <wsx:GetMetadata> in Listing 13.11. A sample response to this request may be found in Listing 13.14.

Listing 13.14 indicates that this message is a response to a GetMetadata request, and in particular that it is a response to the request identified by the message identifier in our hypothetical request. It is interesting to note that the <wsx:Metadata> element in this listing contains two metadata sections. The first section contains a WSDL document that contains an element that describes the target service. Here, we assume that the target service is the purchase order processing service that we described in Section 5.2. Listing 13.14 also contains a second metadata section for an XML schema that is sent by reference using the <wsa:MetadataReference> element. The metadata requester may therefore fetch the metadata by issuing a Get operation against the specified endpoint.

Example 13.14: Sample metadata request for a service endpoint

To retrieve a referenced metadata section, a requester may send a Get request message to a metadata reference. Get fetches a one-time snapshot of the metadata, according to the metadata type (Dialect) and identifier specified in the metadata section.

```
<env:Envelope
    xmlns:s12="http://www.w3.org/2003/05/soap-envelope"
    xmlns:wsa="http://schemas.xmlsoap.org/ws/2004/08/addressing"
    xmlns:wsx="http://schemas.xmlsoap.org/ws/2004/09/mex">
  <env:Header>
    <wsa:Action>
      http://schemas.xmlsoap.org/ws/2004/09/mex/GetMetadata/Request
    </wsa:Action>
    <wsa:MessageID>
      uuid:3e3aac89-ba01-4568-80bf-273c2bc14d1c
    </wsa:MessageID>
    <wsa:ReplyTo>
      <wsa:Address>http://client.example.com/MyEndpoint</wsa:Address>
    </wsa:ReplyTo>
    <wsa:To>http://www.plastics_supply.com/schemas/sq</wsa:To>
  </env:Header>
  <env:Body/>
</env:Envelope>
```

Listing 13.15 Sample Get request message

Listing 13.15 illustrates a sample `Get` request message expressed against the endpoint specified in Listing 13.14. Listing 13.15 indicates that this is a `Get` request message and also that this is associated with the metadata included by reference in the second metadata section in Listing 13.14. A sample response to the request in Listing 13.15 is left as an exercise to the reader (see Exercise 13.4).

13.7 Summary of learning objectives

SOA based applications require a variety of metadata to be associated with services, such as descriptions of the interfaces of a service – the kinds of data entities expected and the names of the operations supported – Internet address for messages, format of request and response messages and so forth. Metadata for a service should also include QoS, as well as policy descriptions to describe security, privacy and other assertions that govern the intent on the part of a participant when a service is invoked.

The various service aspects that require metadata support can be described in a simple declarative metadata description language.

- The Resource Description Framework is an infrastructure that enables the encoding, exchange, and reuse of structured metadata and metadata interoperability.

It is also necessary that Web services metadata is discovered and retrieved from specific Internet addresses.

- WS-MetadataExchange standard defines how to query the network endpoint for WSDL definitions and associated policy information.

Review questions

- What is the problem of semantic interoperability and why is it important for Web services?
- What is the difference between data level and process level semantic interoperability?
- What are the main characteristics of data level semantic interoperability?
- What are the most typical types of metadata?
- What is the Resource Description Framework?
- Briefly describe the main elements of the RDF data model.
- What are containers and container vocabularies in RDF?
- What is the purpose of richer schema languages?

- What is the purpose of WS-MetadaExchange?
- What are the two request/response mechanisms for retrieving Web service metadata? How do they differ?
- What does a response to a metadata request typically consist of?
- How are endpoint references used in WS-MetadataExchange?

Exercises

13.1. Use RDF to develop a simple schema that describes different types of motor vehicles, such as passenger vehicles, trucks, buses, vans and minivans. All types are subclasses of the class motor vehicle, while minivans are also a subclass of vans. Encode the employment scenario in Figure 13.6 in RDF/XML.

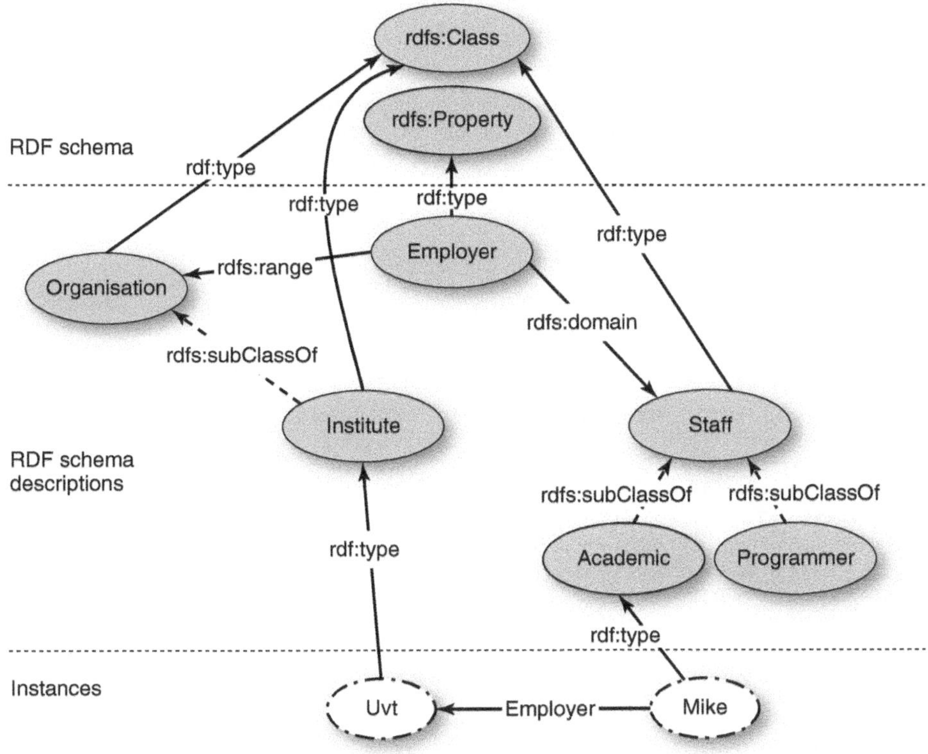

Figure 13.6 The employment hierarachy

13.2. Extend the solution to the previous exercise to describe members of staff in an academic institution. Members of staff are divided into academics, administrative staff and programmers. Common properties are first and last name, room number, telephone number and e-mail address. Academics have ranks, supervise projects and author papers, while programmers participate in projects and, finally, administrators manage projects.

13.3. Show a sample response to the WS-MetadataExchange request in Listing 13.15.

13.4. Assume that the procurement system of a manufacturer who needs to order plastics supplies from a supplier, before interacting with an order processing endpoint, needs to retrieve the endpoint's policy description using the operation "`GetMeta/Request`" in its `<wsa:action>` element. In this way it can verify that all requirements will be met when exchanging messages. Encode a WS-MetadataExchange request sent to endpoint enquiring about security policies. Show a response to this request indicating that the subject requires one of X.509 or Kerberos security tokens.

13.5. The sample request message of Listing 13.16 is a WS-Transfer "`Get`" request for the retrieval of a resource's representation [Alexander 2004]. In this case, the

```
<env:Envelope
    xmlns:wsa="http://schemas.xmlsoap.org/ws/2004/08/addressing"
    xmlns:wsx="http://schemas.xmlsoap.org/ws/2004/09/mex">
  <env:Header>
    <wsa:Action>
      http://schemas.xmlsoap.org/ws/2004/09/transfer/Get
    </wsa:Action>
    <wsa:MessageID>
      uuid:73d7edfc-5c3c-49b9-ba46-2480caee43e9
    </wsa:MessageID>
    <wsa:ReplyTo>
      <wsa:Address>http://client.example.com</wsa:Address>
    </wsa:ReplyTo>
    <wsa:To>http://supply.com/PurchaseService/metadata</wsa:To>
  </env:Header>
  <env:Body>
    <wsx:GetMetadata>
      <wsx:Dialect>
         http://schemas.xmlsoap.org/ws/2004/09/policy
      </wsx:Dialect>
    </wsx:GetMetadata>
   </env:Body>
</env:Envelope>
```

Listing 13.16 Sample "`Get`" request message

requested representation is the WS-MetadataExchange element about a Web service endpoint. Develop a sample response message to the request of Listing 13.16. In the response the content of the SOAP body should be a `<mex:Metadata>` element with metadata about the Web service endpoint containing three Metadata sections. The first metadata section should contain the WSDL of the Web service endpoint. The second metadata section should contain the location of the XML schemas used by the WSDL document. Finally, the third metadata section should contain the WS-Addressing endpoint reference of a resource, the representation of which is a WS-Policy. To solve this exercise you will need to refer to the WSDL Listings 5.5 and 5.8.

CHAPTER 14

Business protocols and standards

Learning objectives

Business standardisation is about interoperability of enterprise content and message exchange between business processes in different enterprises. Recognising the need for standardising these resources, there are significant efforts to provide additional capabilities to baseline XML and service based solutions in terms of naming and defining data. Such endeavours must be harnessed in conjunction with the drive of the emerging communities to establish a common understanding of business processes and data, which need to be transferred across existing and future platforms.

In this chapter, we introduce the concept of business standards and protocols. After completing this chapter you will understand the following key concepts:

- The supply chain business ecosystem.
- Interoperability problems at the business level.
- The concept of business protocols.
- The use of horisontal and vertical business standards for achieving interoperable business solutions.
- Examples of horizontal and vertical standard solutions for modern supply chains.
- The use of vertical industry standards based on XML initiatives.

Chapter preview

Business protocols and standards add business semantics to SOA so that interacting services can be understood by all parties involved in the design, provisioning, composition and utilisation of services.

In this chapter, we concern ourselves with the question of achieving business level interoperability for SOA based applications. We begin by introducing the topic of supply chain business ecosystems and explain how to relieve semantic problems at the business level. Following this, we introduce horizontal and vertical business standards that can be used to manage SOA based applications. Finally, we summarise critical business standardisation activities developed on the basis XML in different vertical industries.

14.1 The supply chain business ecosystem

In Chapter 2 we have introduced the concept of e-Business and explaned that it can be defined as the conduct of transactions by means of electronic communications networks (e.g. via the Internet and/or possibly private networks) end-to-end [Papazoglou 2006]. In fact, e-Business does not confine itself to supporting electronic buying and selling but encompasses the exchange of many kinds of information, including on line commercial transactions. The basic definition of e-Business today is the marriage of traditional supply chain management techniques with the Internet, Web technologies and the SOA based approach that helps bridge the business/IT gap.

e-Business covers business processes along the whole value chain: procurement and supply chain management, processing orders electronically, customer service and cooperation with business partners. e-Business applications make extensive use of Internet and Web service technologies throughout all the nodes in a supply chain operation. To achieve this, e-Business requires ensuring a seamless, consistent customer experience achieved by automating inter-organisational business processes that span across trading partners. Before we explain how XML and Web services facilitate the conduct of electronic business transactions, we first need to identify the business ecosystems that we are addressing in this chapter.

In e-Business settings, business activity traditionally concentrates within a well defined business ecosystem known as a supply chain. As we already explained in our case study at the outset of this book, a supply chain is a network of facilities and distribution options that performs the functions of procurement of materials; transformation of these materials into intermediate and finished products; and distribution of these finished products to customers. A supply chain essentially has three main parts:

- *Supply:* the supply side concentrates on how, from where and when raw materials are procured and supplied to manufacturing.
- *Manufacturing:* the manufacturing side converts these raw materials to finished products.
- *Distribution:* the distribution side ensures that these finished products reach the final customers through a network of distributors, warehouses and retailers.

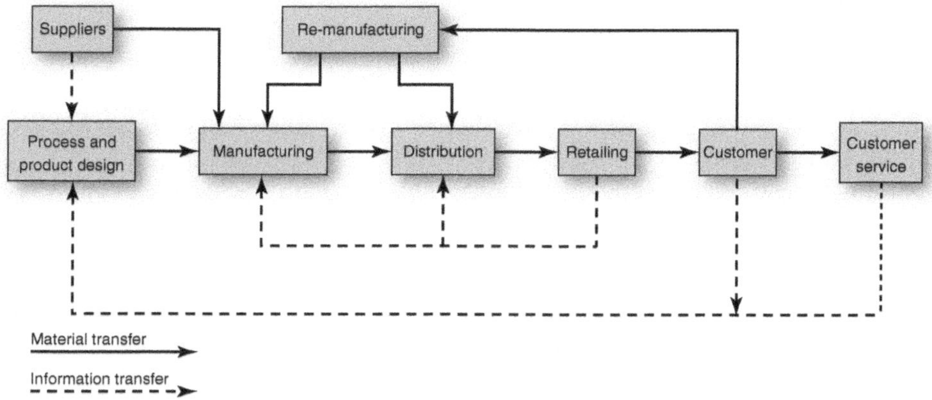

Figure 14.1 Physical product supply chain

The chain can be said to start with the suppliers of an enterprise and end with the customers of the customers of the enterprise. Figure 14.1 illustrates a typical supply chain for physical products. This figure shows that, while the physical transport and handling of goods constitute a flow made up of a straightforward series of activities, the corresponding information flow shows a more varied and complex pattern.

Supply chain management is a set of approaches used to integrate efficiently suppliers, manufacturers, warehouses and customers so that merchandise is produced and distributed at the right quantities, to the right locations and at the right time in order to minimise system wide costs while satisfying service level requirements. Successful supply chain management allows for an enterprise to anticipate demand and deliver the right product to the right place at the right time, at the lowest price to satisfy its customers.

At the highest level, supply chain management covers three key processes: planning, execution and performance measurement.

- *Planning* focuses on having the right product at the right place at the right time.
- *Execution* focuses on the physical movement of goods and services through the supply chain.
- *Performance measurement* keeps track of the health of the supply chain in order to make more informed decisions and respond to changing market conditions.

The common theme in all three is the need to optimise processes that extend beyond narrow functional areas, taking into account the needs of the customer.

Important issues in supply chain management include:

- *Network planning:* This item focuses on having the right product at the right place at the right time. It thus identifies the capacity of each warehouse to determine production requirements and inventory levels at the vendor's facility for each product, and develops transportation flows between these facilities to the warehouses.

Network capacity is planned in such a way as to minimise total production, inventory and transportation costs and satisfy service level requirements.

- *Inventory control:* This item determines where inventory is held (supplier, warehouse, retailer) and inventory quantities. It also determines the reasons why the inventory is held in such outlets. For instance, it considers whether the inventory held is due to uncertainty in production, distribution, or customer demand. If it is established that the inventory is held due to uncertainty in production, distribution, or customer demand, it then considers possibilities to reduce the uncertainty, thereby reducing the inventory.
- *Distribution strategies:* This item identifies relationships between suppliers and warehouse operators that specify delivery lead times, appointment processes and hours for receiving, and uses these relationships to optimise supply chain efficiency.
- *Supply chain integration and strategic partnering:* Information sharing and operational planning are keys to a successfully integrated supply chain. Supply chain integration and strategic partnering determines what type of information will be shared between partners, how it will be used, what level of integration is needed between partners, e.g. loose or tight coupling, and what type of partnerships can be implemented.
- *Product design:* This item encompasses effective product design and outlines techniques to simplify production and reduce inventory holdings at the vendor's facility. It places focus on the role that supply chain management plays in the implementation of product design to simplify production requirements and reduce lead time for inventory replenishment.
- *Customer value:* The measure of a company's performance to its customers based upon the entire range of products, services and intangibles that constitute the company's offerings. Its objective is to optimise supply chain management to fulfil the ultimate consumer needs and provide customer value.

The vision of e-Business concentrates on enterprises that will have access to a much broader range of trading partners to interact and collaborate, and will build supply networks that are far more responsive than the current suboptimal and sequential supply chains. Processes traditionally managed by single enterprises are beginning to spread out across multiple enterprises. Using novel technologies, such as SOA based solutions and business process management, traditional supply chains are transformed to adaptive supply chain networks that have the highest visibility, greatest velocity, and best ability to manage product demand and variability.

Special technical standards for e-Business that make extensive use of XML have recently emerged to facilitate the exchange of messages and combinations of processes between trading companies in a supply chain. The net effect is to change the linear and rather cumbersome structure of traditional supply chains into a flexible, SOA based Web of trading partners, encompassing also small to medium scale enterprises. Several of these initiatives will be discussed in this chapter including RosettaNet, aimed at establishing standard processes for the sharing of business information, and the application of XML in vertical industries.

Before we examine the XML based standards for e-Business we shall first concentrate on the semantic problems that appear when trying to integrate end-to-end business processes across companies and key partners in a supply chain.

14.2 Semantic problems at the business process level

In addition to the semantic interoperability problems on the data level (see Chapter 13), there exist semantic problems when attempting to integrate business processes that span organisations. At the process level, enterprises need a solution that can cohesively weave together business processes wherever they reside in or across the extended enterprise. The lack of agreement about how business processes are defined and managed can lead to serious problems, including serious process re-engineering, corresponding implementation efforts and organisational changes. These efforts are more about redesigning business processes than about making them easy to change and combine with those of customers, suppliers and business partners. Although interoperability within a supply chain is an important goal, interoperability between supply chains is equally important. An enterprise rarely interacts only within a single supply chain, but rather must connect with several supply chains as product offerings and business dictate.

The lack of effective solutions regarding custom coding, vocabulary and business process standards has led to limited success among serious e-Business projects. We may encounter three types of semantic problem with business process level e-Business:

1. Business terminology fluctuations (which are identical to the semantic problems that we examined for data level integration in Chapter 13).
2. Lack of commonly acceptable and understood processes.
3. Lack of commonly accepted business protocols.

We shall briefly discuss the latter two problems in the following as we have already discussed business terminology fluctuations in the preceding chapter.

The objective for process level integration is to provide a method for defining, automating and managing cross-application and cross-enterprise business processes. Before engaging in such a course of action, it is imperative that collaborating enterprises understand each other's business processes.

In many cases in vertical industries we can identify a standard shared set of business processes that have common accepted meaning. We can additionally identify *industry neutral business processes* that are generic in nature. The generic nature of these business processes enables one to reuse them within a specific context. The context essentially guides how the base set of business information must be adapted for use. On some occasions these shared business processes might require slight modifications to fulfil the requirements that are unique to the business process in a particular context.

Example 14.1: An e-Procurement business process with diverse meanings

Consider for example an e-procurement business process used in the European Union versus an e-Procurement business process used in the USA or some other part of the world. In such situations, it is important that trading partners identify not only such standard and common processes but also various components of a common business process specification that can be reused to create new business processes, e.g. the components for procurement, payment and shipping for a particular industry. Such core components are defined using identity items that are common across all businesses. Reuse of core components will typically occur at the business process, business collaboration, business transaction and business document model level. This enables users to define data that is meaningful to their businesses, while also maintaining interoperability with other business applications.

Implementing an effective SOA based solution for e-Business applications requires, in addition to the previous, that business processes be in a position to capture the information and exchange requirements. It is therefore essential that they identify the timing and order of interactions, as well as the purpose of each business collaboration and information exchange. This is the aim of a *business protocol,* which is associated with business processes and governs the exchange of business information and messages between trading partners across differing enterprise information systems, middleware platforms and organisations. A business protocol specifies the structure and semantics of business messages, how to process the messages, and how to route them to appropriate recipients. It may also specify the characteristics of messages related to persistence and reliability.

14.3 Business standards and protocols

Business standards typically manage the structure for defining form, fit and function of any product or service, regardless of the industry. They use specialised business and technical dictionaries to provide commonly used domain specific terminology and accepted values. In addition, they specify the structure, format and semantics of the business content of a message, as well as the message exchange requirements between trading partners. A common e-Business standard should provide the following functionality [Irani 2002]:

- Definition of common business processes that characterise business transactions, e.g. sending a purchase order.
- Definition of common data interchange formats, i.e. messages that are exchanged in the context of the above processes/transactions.
- Definition of a common terminology at the level of data items and messages seeking a way to bridge varying industry terminologies.

- Definition of a mechanism to describe an enterprise's profile, i.e. the enterprise's capabilities and the business transactions that an enterprise can perform, in such a way that it can be stored in a common repository accessible to all other organisations for querying.
- Definition of a mechanism that allows enterprises to negotiate on the business conditions before they commence transactions.
- Definition of a common transport mechanism for exchanging messages between enterprises.
- Definition of a security and reliability framework.

This functionality not only allows trading partners to integrate more easily with other partners to conduct business electronically, but also results in increased flexibility since an enterprise will have a larger number of potential trading partners to choose from.

Business protocols intend to make it much easier for enterprises to interact in e-Business transactions and process exchanges comprising aggregated Web services. This can happen as business protocols define the business intent of business transactions and processes, so that they can be easily understood and exchanged between transacting parties. A business protocol is bound to a business conversation definition and a delivery channel for a trading partner. It should also be able to specify collaboration or contractual agreements that exist between two trading partners and contain configuration information required for the partners to interoperate. A business protocol is indirectly bound to such a collaboration agreement through its associated conversation definition and associated trading partner delivery channel. A business protocol must minimally exhibit the following characteristics:

1. It invariably includes data dependent behaviour. For example, an order management protocol depends on data such as the number of line items in an order, the total value of an order, or a delivery by deadline. Defining business intent in these cases requires the use of conditional and timeout constructs.
2. It is able to specify exceptional conditions and their consequences, including recovery sequences.
3. It relies on the support of long running process interactions that include multiple, often nested units of work (see Section 10.4.3.2), each with its own data requirements. Business protocols frequently require cross partner coordination of the outcome (success or failure) of these units of work at various levels of granularity.

The lack of agreement on the terminology, grammar and dialogue that constitute e-Business processes demonstrates the need for standards. In response to these requirements, organisations have for quite some time started exploring the use of open XML based standards that help remove the formidable barriers associated with developing a common business process language and process methodology for Internet based collaboration, communication and commerce. Without any form of standardisation the flexibility of XML will become the biggest single obstacle to implementation within the e-Business domain. Flexibility must be managed in a manner that will enable reusability and facilitate harmonisation. Without this each non-standard XML dialect will not be able openly to and cost effectively communicate beyond the boundaries of its own implementation domain.

Vendors have begun to work together, facilitated by standards bodies and in unison with business experts to define meaningful business standards and protocols based on XML. Their aim was to define global (horizontal) and vertical business standards based on XML, based on the specificity of their domian.

- *Horizontal business standards,* like electronic Business XML (ebXML.org), are developed in depth for use within any vertical industry. Horizontal business standards do not apply to any particular industry specifically.
- On the other hand, *vertical business standards,* like RosettaNet (www.rosettanet.org) and business protocols such as the RosettaNet Partner Interface Processes (PIPs), enable the development of process centric e-Business applications within a specific vertical sector.

As Web services constitute the infrastructure for developing complex e-Business applications they can be used as an implementation vehicle for implementing business standards, such as, for instance, RosettaNet. In particular, asynchronous and stateful communication between Web services is critical to the development of e-Business applications and the facilitation of next generation business models. To this extent BPEL provides Web services with the necessary means to enable e-Business dialogues between peers and create asynchronous stateful interactions. Figure 14.2 illustrates the technology stack for supply chain networks in terms of business standards and protocols, and Web service technologies.

In parallel to the preceding standards initiatives, a flurry of distinct industry groups is working to develop their own domain specific, vertical XML standards. These efforts include the Automotive Industry Action Group, the Open Travel Alliance, the Association for Retail Technology Standards, Health Care and Medical Equipment, and the ACORD standards group for the insurance industry, to name but a few. Due to the relatively low barriers to entry, significant cost savings that come from reduced transaction costs and reduced processing costs, the automation of supply chains and increased productivity, such electronic marketplaces attract smaller companies that establish partnerships with them.

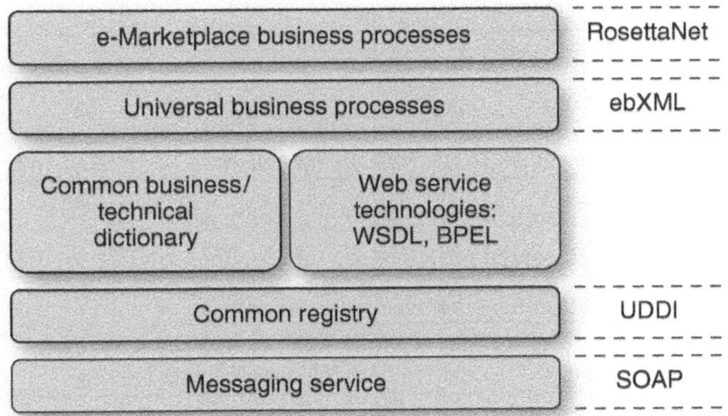

Figure 14.2 Business standards and Web service technologies

The industry initiatives that we shall briefly examine in the remainder of this chapter provide common business process definitions (promoting industry based standards through XML formats and defined APIs) and a standard terminology to combat semantic interoperability problems. For reasons of completeness, we shall start with Electronic Data Interchange, as this communications protocol forms the basis for extension for many current industry initiatives.

14.3.1 Electronic Data Interchange

The need for message exchange and interaction among companies and their trading partners did not originate with the Internet. In fact, it has its roots in technologies such as Electronic Data Interchange (EDI), which was first developed in the early 1980s. EDI is a broadly defined communications protocol for exchanging data and documents in a standard format. The development of EDI was motivated by the realisation that simple cross organisation business processes, such as purchasing, shipment tracking and inventory queries, were tremendously inefficient.

EDI is commonly defined as the application-to-application transfer of structured trading data or documents by agreed message standards between computing systems. With EDI, the standards define both the syntax for exchanging data and the business semantics. In operation, EDI is the interchange of these agreed messages between trading partners to ensure speed and certainty and better business practice in the supply chain. EDI is a fast and safe method of sending purchase orders, invoices, shipping notices, and other frequently used business data and documents between transacting partners.

Today EDI is viewed as a general enabling technology that provides for the exchange of critical business information between computer applications supporting a wide variety of business processes. A typical example is given in Figure 14.3, where a buyer and a

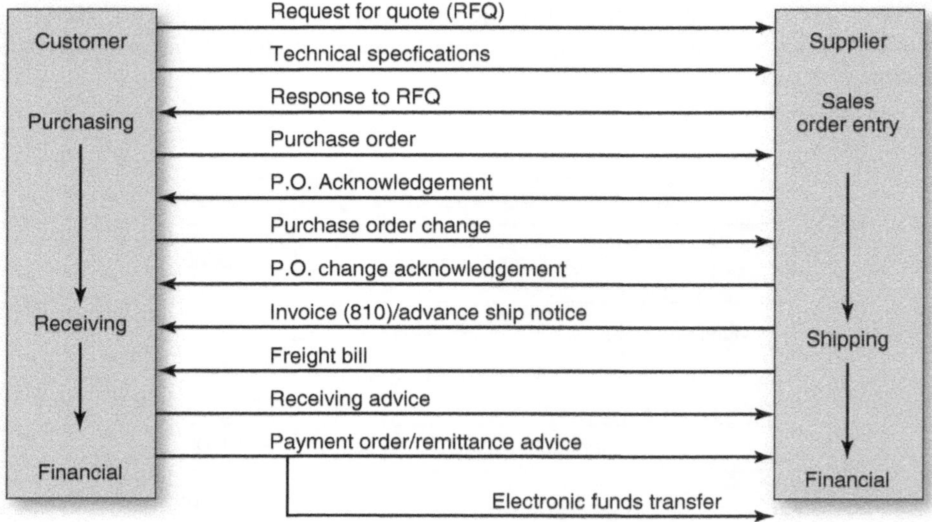

Figure 14.3 Typical EDI message exchange between interacting parties

supplier interact by exchanging standard EDI messages. This example illustrates that the two partner organisations need to agree on the exact formats of the documents exchanged between them.

The EDI standards provide definitions of common business documents. Without pre-defined, agreed standards EDI is of little value. By using standard messages, organisations can exchange information between many different trading partners and be sure of common understanding throughout the supply chain. EDI formats the structured trading information into a commonly recognised standard, published and maintained by a standards body such as ANSI X12 and UN/EDIFACT. The UN/EDIFACT standard (United Nations Electronic Data Interchange for Administration, Commerce, and Transport), which was extended beyond international trade, is the most important format.

Example 14.2: An EDIFACT purchase order

Figure 14.4 illustrates a sample EDIFACT order. This order specifies a specific purchase order number and orders 500 items of a particular product at a price of $2,500 per item. The order stipulates all 500 items should be delivered by a certain date. Descriptions of the segments that are used with EDIFACT orders can be found at the URL www.unece.org/trade/untdid/do4b/trmd/orders-c.htm.

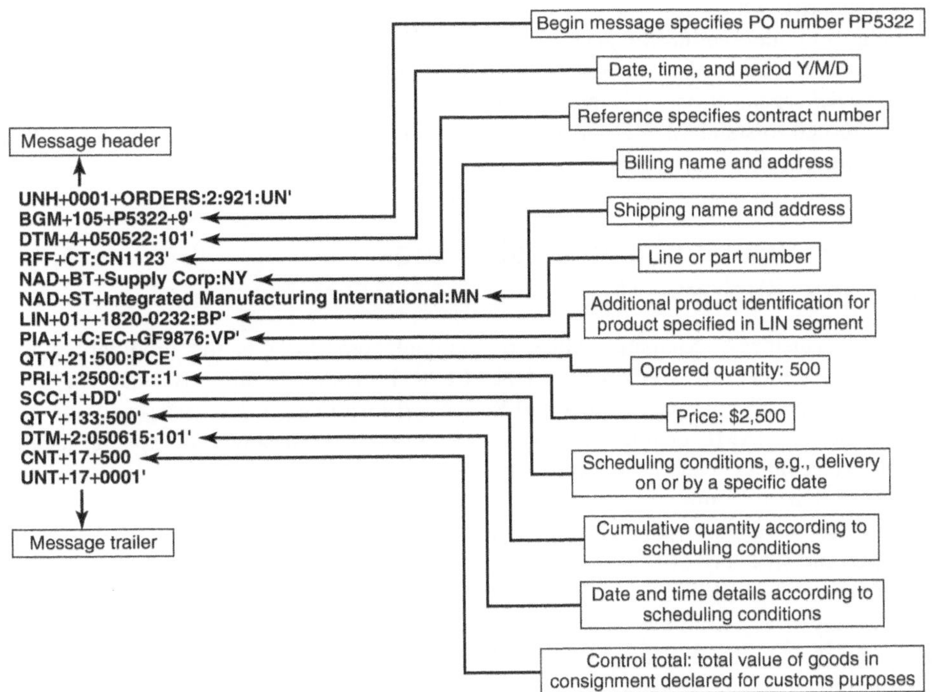

Figure 14.4 EDIFACT sample order

EDI has always been regarded as a specialised solution, optimised for *heavy* data volume performance between larger enterprises that have the resources to implement it. While traditional EDI had proved that feasibility and efficiencies are possible when using electronic business transactions, the limitations were found to be the cost of integration, deployment and maintenance to the smaller business partners. EDI supports direct bilateral communications between a small number of companies and does not permit the multilateral dynamic relationships of a true marketplace. It also does not scale easily to include new participants. It involves complex and costly mapping and re-engineering procedures each time a new partner enters the chain. It also involves tremendous operational costs and requires dedicated services, which apart from installation costs consume considerable repeat expenditure by way of maintenance. These facts have meant that EDI has become the preserve for large organisations and has only a meager adoption rate by SMEs (Small to Medium-sized Enterprises). Finally, another drawback of EDI is that it is not a means for *interactive* communication [Handfield 2002]. Each time a transaction is sent, it implies that a *decision* has been made, an order for a fixed amount placed, a forecast of future demand fixed, a lead time for delivery specified and so on. There is no means for the buying and supplying parties to reach a decision through joint, bilateral communication or negotiation. As a result of its drawbacks, EDI often cannot provide the agility enterprises need to respond to new business opportunities or integrate with their business partners.

The technical implications for e-Business information exchange technology are that it must be flexible, in a way that will accommodate the dynamic information requirements between disparate trading partners. An additional requirement is the ability to embrace open standards, which are essential to allow rapid establishment of business information exchange and interoperability. XML, by contrast to EDI, is ideally suited to these requirements, as it can be used to encode complex business information and transactions within and between organisations. It is therefore not surprising that several XML developers have already turned to standard EDI messages that map to XML to provide better descriptions and definitions of business operations.

14.3.2 Horizontal business standards: Electronic Business XML

Electronic Business eXtensible Markup Language (ebXML) is the modular suite of standards advanced by OASIS and UN/CEFACT (United Nations Center for Trade Facilitation and Electronic Business and Structured Information Standards) and approved as ISO 15000. ebXML enables enterprises of any size and in any geographical location to conduct business over the Internet. ebXML consists of a set of XML document type definitions that are common for business-to-business (ANSI X12 EDI) transactions across most industries. Its purpose is to preserve and extend the EDI infrastructure, by leveraging semantics and structure of EDI standards such as X12 and EDIFACT.

The vision of ebXML is to create a single global electronic marketplace where enterprises of any size, and in any geographical location, can meet and conduct business with each other through the exchange of XML based messages. To facilitate this, ebXML provides an infrastructure for data communication interoperability, a semantic framework for commercial interoperability, and a mechanism that allows enterprises to find, establish a relationship and conduct business with each other.

ebXML expresses in a common way several business concepts and constructs, e.g. descriptions of businesses, products and individuals, measurements, date, time, location, currencies, business classification codes and so on, which apply to all business domains and are across vendors. A complete business integration solution along the lines of ebXML requires: standardised tags (metadata), for each industry sector; a means for mapping between different metadata descriptions; and a means for processing XML documents, and invoking business applications and services provided by business processes and workflows.

14.3.2.1 The ebXML reference architecture

ebXML tackles the problem of providing a single global electronic marketplace for enterprises of sizes at two levels:

- At a high level, ebXML identified common cross-industry business processes that characterised business transactions, and defined a structure of those processes that enabled development of a business process specification schema (BPSS).
- At a more detailed level, ebXML defined core components with perhaps the most potential impact on e-Business applications. Core components address semantic interoperability at the level of individual data items, seeking a way to bridge the individual industry terminologies, much as ebXML business processes work at a high level.

It is convenient to think of ebXML in terms of its reference architecture that contains its architectural elements (components) and the systems analysis and development methodology. The latter is referred to as the process architecture and has the purpose to provide an analysis and development methodology for the reference architecture.

The ebXML reference architecture is composed of the following five major architectural components [Clark 2001]: messaging service, registry and repository, trading partner information, business process specification schema and core components. The lower level layers in this stack support lower level functionality, e.g. computer processing and message transport details or registry functions, required for the implementation of the higher level components.

Messaging service. This provides a standard way to exchange business messages between organisations. It provides for means to exchange a payload, which may or may not be an XML business document or traditional and encrypted payloads, over multiple communications services, e.g. SMTP or HTTP, reliably and securely. It also provides means to route a payload to the appropriate internal application once an organisation has received it.

The ebXML messaging service not only exchanges messages but also checks trading partner profiles to ensure that the exchanges conform to the business agreements and are being routed accordingly. It can also perform business rule checking services and interact with Web services based components that conform to the ebXML exchange requirements [Webber 2004].

Registry and repository. An ebXML compliant registry is a component that provides a set of services that enable the sharing of information between trading partners. An ebXML compliant registry is capable of representing a large range of data objects, including metadata, XML schemas, business process descriptions, ebXML core components, UML models, generic trading partner information and software components.

Examples of items in the registry might be XML schemas of business documents, definitions of library components for business process modelling, and trading partner agreements. The registry not only holds the ebXML base reference specifications, but also the business process and information meta-models developed by industry groups, SMEs and other organisations. These meta-models are XML structures that may utilise a classification system and are compatible with the registry and repository architecture requirements. In order to store the models they are converted from UML to XML.

Trading partner information. This item is known also as the Collaboration Protocol Profile (CPP) and Collaboration Protocol Agreement (CPA). The CPP/CPA defines the capabilities of a trading partner to perform a data interchange and how this data interchange agreement can be formed between two trading partners.

The CPP provides the definition (XML schema) of an XML document that specifies the details of how an organisation is able to conduct business electronically. The CPP is published to the ebXML registry and outlines supported technology binding details. The main purpose of the CPP is to ensure interoperability between trading partners relying on the ebXML framework from possibly disparate vendors.

Some of the message exchange details defined by the CPP include specifics, such as transport protocol mechanisms, message reliability mechanisms, transport security mechanisms, trust artifacts like X.509 certificates, and message level security policy information.

The CPA is a machine interpretable version of a trading partner agreement specifying both the technical and business related agreements. The CPA specifies the details of how two organisations have agreed to conduct business electronically and is formed by combining the CPPs of the two organisations.

Business process specification schema (BPSS). The BPSS is a relatively simple schema that provides a standard framework for public business process specification [Clark 2001]. It aims to support the specification of business transactions and their choreography into business collaborations. As such, it works with the ebXML CPP and CPA specifications to bridge the gap between business process modelling and the configuration of ebXML compliant software, e.g. an ebXML business service interface.

The BPSS provides the definition (in the form of an XML document) that describes how documents can be exchanged between trading organisations. While the CPP/CPA deals with the technical aspects of how to conduct business electronically, the BPSS deals with the actual business process. It identifies such objects as the overall business process, the roles, transactions, identification of the business documents used, document flow, legal aspects, security aspects, business level acknowledgements and status. A BPSS can be used by a software application to configure the business details of conducting business electronically with another organisation.

ebXML business processes define the ways in which trading partners engage each other, from the point of configuring their respective systems to actually do business. This is accomplished in such a way that business practices and interactions are represented both accurately and independently of any specific ways of implementing these transactions. Business process specifications are expressed as XML schemas or in UML.

The business transaction is a key concept in ebXML BPSS. The BPSS supports a long running business transaction model, based on proven e-Business transaction patterns used by standards such as RosettaNet. An ebXML *business transaction* represents business document flows between requesting and responding partners. In any ebXML business transaction there always is a requesting business document, and, optionally, a responding business document. Each business transaction request or response may require that a receipt acknowledgement be returned to the sender. For contract forming transactions, such as purchase order requests, an acceptance acknowledgement may need to be returned to the requester. Time constraints can be applied to the return of responses and acknowledgements.

Example 14.3: A simple business transaction to create a purchase order

Listing 14.1 defines a business transaction called `Create Order`. This transaction stipulates that, if a supplier accepts a purchase order from a customer, this acceptance is a binding legal agreement for the supplier to deliver the requested products or services to the customer at an agreed price and time, and for the customer to pay the supplier following delivery. The various messages and interactions sent between these external businesses constitute a binding contract between both parties. The BPSS specification of this transaction therefore includes the concepts of time periods for business response, plus non-repudiation: neither party can deny its legal obligations to the other party once the purchase order has been issued and accepted.

In Listing 14.1 the request message is specified as part of the `<RequestingBusinessActivity>` element, and the possible response messages are specified as part of the `<RespondingBusinessActivity>` element. A responding document envelope has a property `<isPositiveResponse>` that indicates the intent of the response from the respondent's perspective. This property is related to the business failure of a transaction.

```
<BusinessTransaction name="Create Order">
    <RequestingBusinessActivity name="SendOrder"
      isNonRepudiationRequired="true"
  timeToAcknowledgeReceipt="P2D"
      timeToAcknowledgeAcceptance="P3D">
    <DocumentEnvelope businessDocument="Purchase Order"/>
    </RequestingBusinessActivity>
    <RespondingBusinessActivity name="SendPOAcknowledgement"
    isNonRepudiationRequired="true"
       timeToAcknowledgeReceipt="P5D">
       <DocumentEnvelope isPositiveResponse="true"
       businessDocument="PO Acknowledgement"/>
     </RespondingBusinessActivity>
</BusinessTransaction>
```

Listing 14.1 Sample ebXML transaction

Ultimately, it is the responsibility of the requester to identify whether a transaction has been successful by looking at all its aspects (timeouts, signals and so on). To define the commercial and legal nature of this transaction, the `<RequestingBusinessActivity>` element requires non-repudiation with the properties `timeToAcknowledgeReceipt="P2D"` and `timeToAcknowledge-Acceptance="P3D"` (where "P2D" is a W3C Schema syntax standard that means Period=2 Days and P3D means Period=3 Days). These periods are all measured from the original sending of the request.

A BPSS business collaboration is essentially the specification of business transaction activities between the two partners, their associated document flow, and the choreography of these business transaction activities. BPSS describes public processes as collaborations between roles, with each role abstractly representing a trading partner. The business collaboration specifies all the business messages that are exchanged between two trading partners, their content, and their precise sequence and timing. All collaborations are composed of combinations of atomic transactions, each between two parties. There are two types of collaborations: binary collaborations and multi-party collaborations. Multi-party collaborations are decomposed to binary collaborations. The sequencing rules contained in a collaboration definition are not between messages but between business transaction activities.

Example 14.4: Fulfilling a business transaction

Listing 14.2 defines a binary collaboration called `"Product Fulfillment"`. This collaboration involves a buyer in the initiating role and a seller in the responding role. The collaboration involves two transactions, one creating an order (defined in Listing 14.1) and one defining notification of shipment. In this listing, the transactions are described by the `<BusinessTransactionActivity>` elements and their attributes. These two elements define the names of the two transactions as well as the authorised roles from the sender (from) and recipient (to). If necessary, additional transactions can be added to this binary collaboration to complete the entire data interchange between the buyer and the seller.

Core components. ebXML gives particular attention to business objects that appear in multiple domains, and calls the multiple reusable data items that cut across many industries *core components.* A core component captures information about a business concept, and relationships between that concept and other business concepts. It is a piece of basic business information that is designed to take into account commonality across industry business processes and can, therefore, be used to facilitate many different processes across different industry sectors. Some examples of core components are *date of purchase order, sales tax,* and *total amount.* A number of core components can be aggregated to form a building block used to support ebXML business transactions and business processes.

Figure 14.5 illustrates how the elements of the ebXML infrastructure may interact with each other. The CPA and CPP provide means to identify a business process specification

```
<BinaryCollaboration name="Product Fulfillment" timeToPerform="P5D">
  <Documentation>
   timeToPerform = Period: 5 days from start of transaction
  </Documentation>
  <InitiatingRole name="buyer"/>
  <RespondingRole name="seller"/>
  <!-- Transaction: buyer to create an order with seller -->
  <BusinessTransactionActivity name="Create Order"
      businessTransaction="Create Order"
      fromAuthorizedRole="buyer"
      toAuthorizedRole="seller"
      isLegallyBinding="true" />
  <!-- Transaction: buyer to notify seller in case of advance shipment -->
  <BusinessTransactionActivity name="Notify Shipment"
      businessTransaction="Notify of advance shipment"
      fromAuthorizedRole="buyer" toAuthorizedRole="seller"/>
</BinaryCollaboration>
```

Listing 14.2 Sample ebXML business collaboration

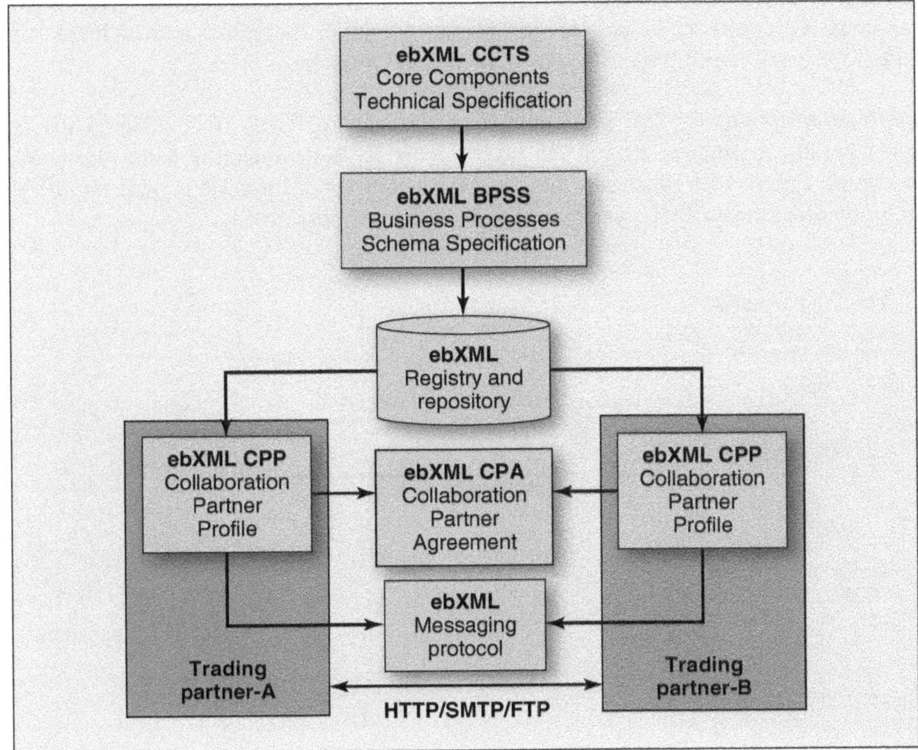

Figure 14.5 Elements of the ebXML infrastructure

governing how the parties do business and parameters for using the ebXML messaging service, but these are both optional and are not required. The BPSS may specify how services offered by the messaging service (such as signalling acknowledgements or requesting digital signatures) are used in the conduct of a business process. The BPSS document is incorporated with, or referenced by, the ebXML trading partner CPP and CPA. Each CPP declares its support for one or more roles within the BPSS, documented by UML use case diagrams. Within these CPP profiles and CPA agreements are added further technical parameters that result in a full specification of the run time by ebXML Business Service Interface software at each trading partner. The CPP, CPA and BPSS may be stored in an ebXML compliant registry.

The ebXML Message Service Specification provides the infrastructure for message/signal identification, typing and integrity, as well as placing any one message in sequence with respect to other messages in the choreography. In addition, all communications with the registry must use the ebXML messaging service. The messaging services may be used completely independently, although a message header may contain a reference to a CPA.

14.3.2.2 ebXML functional phases

Three functional phases are defined by the ebXML technical architecture [Clark 2001]: the implementation phase, discovery and retrieval phase, and run time phase. The first two phases of implementation and retrieval represent a handshake mechanism, while the final phase represents the actual units of business. Each of these phases, which are examined below, carries with it its own requirements and processes.

Implementation phase. The implementation phase of ebXML is considered the time when a trading partner is making an active decision to do business using the ebXML framework. Figure 14.6 illustrates that this phase consists of three steps: request information, implement the ebXML system and publish the business profile.

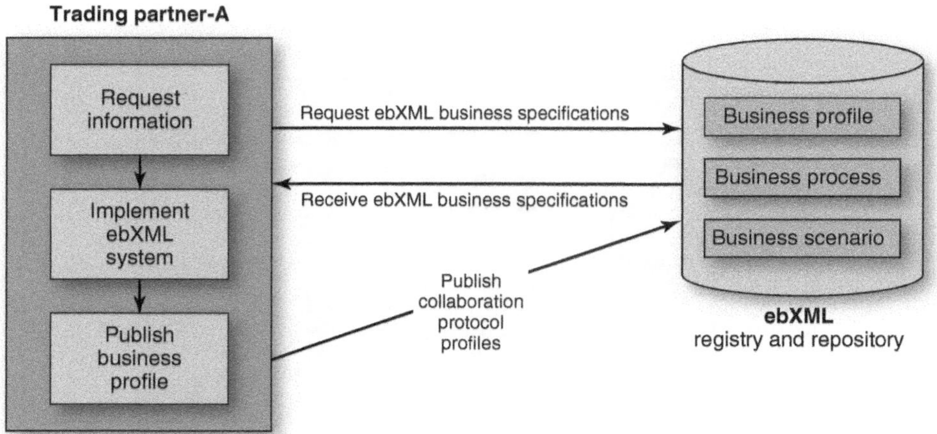

Figure 14.6 Implementation phase

The first step in the implementation phase is to request the ebXML specifications (business processes, business scenarios) and understand them. In this phase the trading partner will analyse its business processes in terms of the generalisations provided by the ebXML specification. Subsequently, the trading partner must decide which of its business processes it would implement in accordance with the ebXML specification. During this phase, an actual ebXML implementation must be produced, either built in-house from the core ebXML specifications or obtained from a third party vendor. The result of the implementation phase is a working ebXML framework, including a set of published business processes and interfaces. Once the system is built, organisations are ready to conduct business with each other. To achieve this, an organisation needs to publish its profile as a CPP to the ebXML repository for other organisations to discover it.

Discovery and retrieval phase. The discovery and retrieval phase of ebXML involves trading partners using the registry to discover business processes and interfaces published by other trading partners. Typically, the CPP for a specific partner or set of partners is exchanged at this time. The specific details denoted in the CPP are used as a basis for messages exchanged during the run time phase. Figure 14.7 shows two trading partners discovering each other's CPP documents. Figure 14.7 illustrates that each trading partner derives the CPA by performing an intersection between each of the partner's CPP instances. The CPA is a special business agreement tied to a specific transactional conversation and makes explicit requirements derived from the intersection of the various CPP instances published by each of the trading partners.

Run time phase. The last ebXML functional phase is the run time phase. This phase concerns itself with the conduct of actual business transactions and choreography of messages

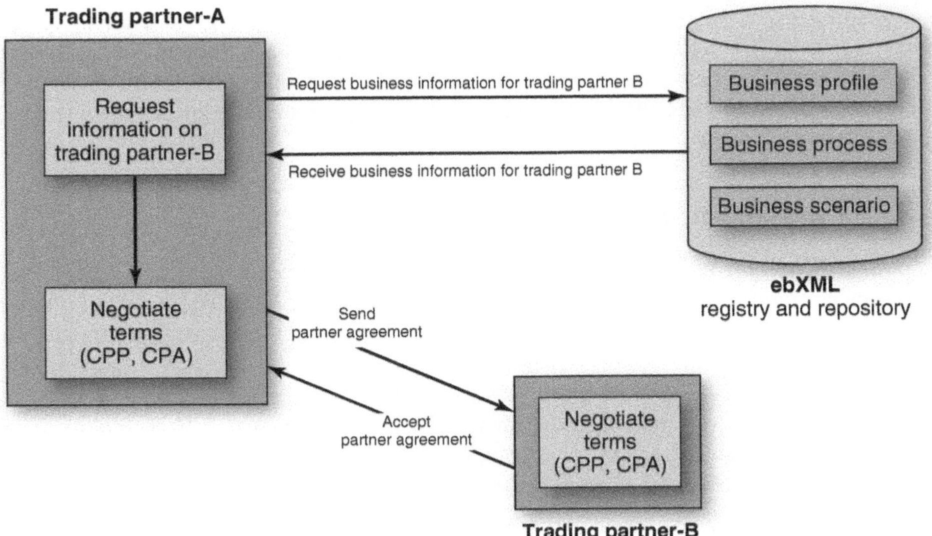

Figure 14.7 Discovery and retrieval phase

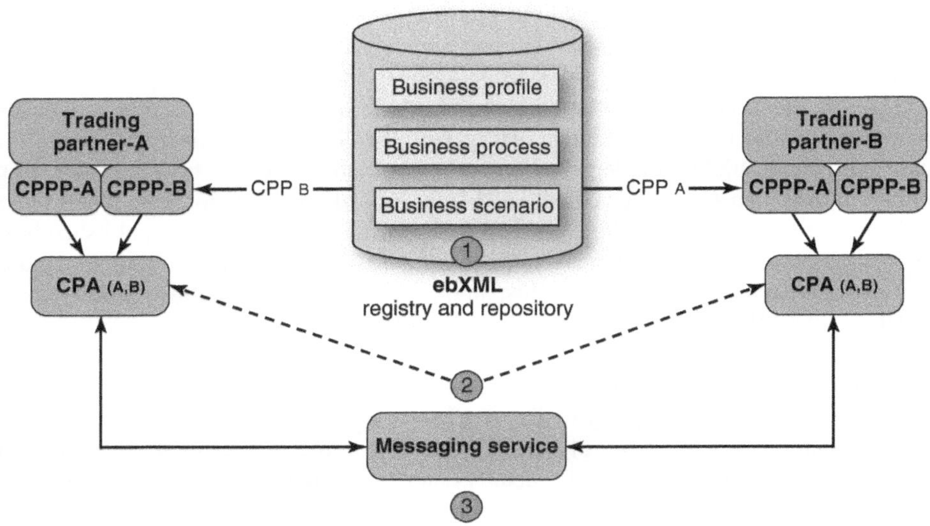

Figure 14.8 Run-time phase

exchanged between partners. From the previous phase, the CPP instances published by each participating trading partner are narrowed to form a CPA. Figure 14.7 shows that the CPA contains the negotiated terms and implementation contracts agreed by both trading partners. Before actual ebXML messages are exchanged, and before the transaction executes, the CPA instances should match on both ends of the transaction.

Figure 14.8 illustrates that the run time phase includes three simple steps. In Step 1 each trading partner is responsible for obtaining the necessary CPP document for the business partner it would like to engage. In most cases the CPP will be retrieved from an ebXML registry. In Step 2, each partner derives the CPA, which makes explicit the range of choices offered in the CPP. Finally, in Step 3, the partners can begin business transactions under the governance of the CPA.

14.3.2.3 ebXML and Web services

As both ebXML and Web services have their foundational roots in XML, they have many things in common. Their difference lies in the fact that ebXML provides a complete solution in the e-Business integration domain, while Web services are considered as an e-Business enabling technology.

ebXML addresses several of the layers in the Web service technology stack. At the core layers, the ebXML messaging specification provides secure, reliable communication on any transport, uses SOAP for packaging, and defines a rich set of metadata for carrying out e-Business transactions between trading partners [Patil 2003]. At the higher level layers, and in particular the description level, the ebXML collaboration protocol describes the trading partner's business services, the concrete binding where the service can be addressed and so on. BPSS also defines the collaboration aspects between processes and, thereby, how services are orchestrated. The collaboration protocol covers the business and service level agreements. Finally, at the publication and discovery level, the ebXML registry allows publication, sharing and discovery of different business artifacts, such as trading partner information, business process definitions and business document types.

When considering Web services as an implementation platform for ebXML, it is fairly easy to use WSDL to describe CPP. BPEL can also be used to implement the BPSS. It can be used to describe the overall business processes and then BPEL can be used to define components in the BPSS. Predefined BPEL components can be included into BPSS diagrams as nodes.

Business expectation of an SOA is that it represents a solution that is not end-to-end but is a solution that can be composed based on the needs of the business. OASIS has developed an advanced e-Business architecture that builds on ebXML and other Web service technology and is very much in line with this position. The OASIS Electronic Business Service-Oriented Architecture (ebSOA) Technical Committee (http://www.oasis-open.org/committees/) used ebXML Technical Architecture v1.04 as a starting point for describing an SOA, and practical implementation techniques that take into account work done in several standards development organisations including OASIS, the W3C, ISO, UN/CEFACT and others. The goal of the ebSOA specification is to describe a high level architecture blueprint and a set of accompanying patterns, which describe an infrastructure facilitating electronic business on a global scale in a secure, reliable and consistent manner.

14.3.3 Vertical business standards: RosettaNet

RosettaNet (www.rosettanet.org) is an independent, non-profit consortium of major IT, electronic component and semiconductor manufacturing companies dedicated to the collaborative development and rapid deployment of industry wide, open e-Business process standards. The supply chain standards of RosettaNet are meant to improve operational efficiencies by forming a common vertical e-Business language and aligning processes between supply chain partners on global high technology trading networks. Its standards serve the IT, electronic component and semiconductor manufacturing sectors. The approach of RosettaNet is based upon resolving real business issues in a consortium driven model.

14.3.3.1 The RosettaNet business architecture

The RosettaNet business architecture is based on identifying discrete segments of public business processes and then standardising the public business interaction processes involved within each of those segments. The segments themselves are broken into subprocesses until an event or document based interchange process is defined, called a partner interface process (or PIP).

RosettaNet PIPs define business processes between trading partners. PIPs are designed to fit into seven clusters of core business processes that represent the backbone of the trading network. PIPs apply to the following core industry processes: partner, product and service review; product information; order management; inventory management; marketing information management; service and support; and manufacturing. Each cluster is broken down into segments – cross-enterprise processes involving more than one type of trading partner. In truth, PIPs are specialised system-to-system XML based dialogues. Each PIP specification includes a business document with the vocabulary, and a business process with the choreography of the message dialogue.

Example 14.5: Managing purchase orders with RosettaNet

As an example of a PIP consider the PIP `"Manage Purchase Order"` (PIP3A4). A specification of this PIP is given in Figure 14.9. PIP3A4 is a key component for a large number of RosettaNet e-Business process standards and serves as a *building block* for a variety of other PIPs. This PIP supports a process for trading partners to issue and acknowledge purchase orders, and cancel and change them based on acknowledgement responses.

The PIP encompasses four complementary process segments supporting the entire chain of activities from purchase order creation to tracking and tracing, each of which is further decomposed into multiple individual processes. The provider's acknowledgement may also include related information about delivery expectations. When a provider acknowledges that the status of a purchase order product line item is *pending*, the provider may later use PIP3A7 `"Notify of Purchase Order Acknowledgment"` to notify the buyer when the product line item is either accepted or rejected. The process of issuing a purchase order typically occurs after checking for price and availability and requesting quotes. The process of issuing a purchase order may be followed by changing the purchase order, cancelling the purchase order, querying for purchase order status, and distributing purchase order status.

Example 14.6: Combining demand forecast and order management processes

Now consider how we can formulate an example of a general business model that combines demand forecast, forecast reply and order placement processes in RosettaNet. This is given in Figure 14.10. This figure shows that demand information is provided using PIP4A3 or 4A4. Moreover, there is also a case where PIP4A1 is used as strategic demand information over a long period of time. The combination of PIP3A4, 3A8, 3A7 and/or 3A9 is used for ordering processes, and PIP3C7 is used for account payable information. The RosettaNet site (www.rosettanet.org) provides more details about the usage of demand forecast (PIP4A3, 4A4) and ordering processes (PIP3A4, 3A8, 3A7, 3A9).

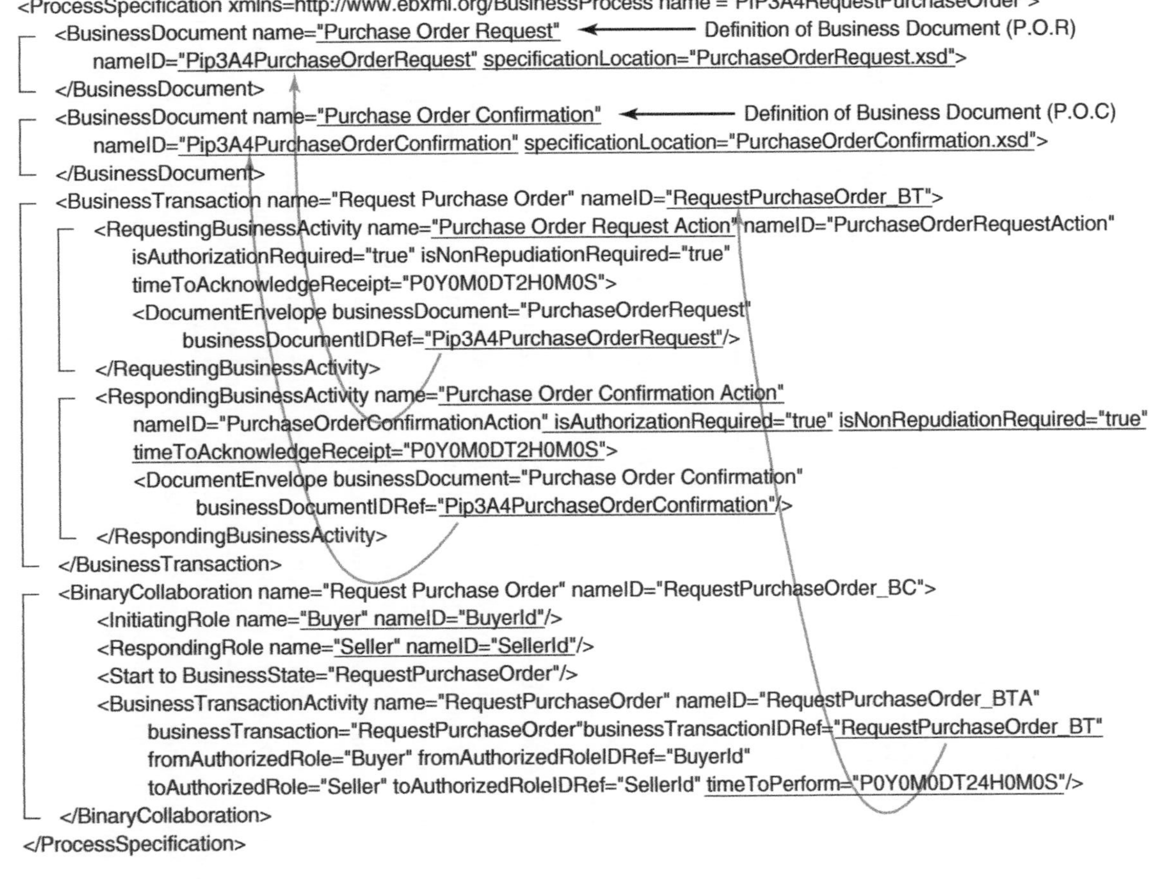

<ProcessSpecification xmlns=http://www.ebxml.org/BusinessProcess name ="PIP3A4RequestPurchaseOrder">
<BusinessDocument name="Purchase Order Request"
Definition of Business Document (P.O.R)
nameID="Pip3A4PurchaseOrderRequest" specificationLocation="PurchaseOrderRequest.xsd">
</BusinessDocument>
<BusinessDocument name="Purchase Order Confirmation"
Definition of Business Document (P.O.C)
nameID="Pip3A4PurchaseOrderConfirmation" specificationLocation="PurchaseOrderConfirmation.xsd">
</BusinessDocument>
<BusinessTransaction name="Request Purchase Order" nameID="RequestPurchaseOrder_BT">
<RequestingBusinessActivity name="Purchase Order Request Action" nameID="PurchaseOrderRequestAction"
isAuthorizationRequired="true" isNonRepudiationRequired="true"
timeToAcknowledgeReceipt="P0Y0M0DT2H0M0S">
<DocumentEnvelope businessDocument="PurchaseOrderRequest"
businessDocumentIDRef="Pip3A4PurchaseOrderRequest"/>
</RequestingBusinessActivity>
<RespondingBusinessActivity name="Purchase Order Confirmation Action"
nameID="PurchaseOrderConfirmationAction" isAuthorizationRequired="true" isNonRepudiationRequired="true"
timeToAcknowledgeReceipt="P0Y0M0DT2H0M0S">
<DocumentEnvelope businessDocument="Purchase Order Confirmation"
businessDocumentIDRef="Pip3A4PurchaseOrderConfirmation"/>
</RespondingBusinessActivity>
</BusinessTransaction>
<BinaryCollaboration name="Request Purchase Order" nameID="RequestPurchaseOrder_BC">
<InitiatingRole name="Buyer" nameID="BuyerId"/>
<RespondingRole name="Seller" nameID="SellerId"/>
<Start to BusinessState="RequestPurchaseOrder"/>
<BusinessTransactionActivity name="RequestPurchaseOrder" nameID="RequestPurchaseOrder_BTA"
businessTransaction="RequestPurchaseOrder"businessTransactionIDRef="RequestPurchaseOrder_BT"
fromAuthorizedRole="Buyer" fromAuthorizedRoleIDRef="BuyerId"
toAuthorizedRole="Seller" toAuthorizedRoleIDRef="SellerId" timeToPerform="P0Y0M0DT24H0M0S"/>
</BinaryCollaboration>
</ProcessSpecification>

Figure 14.9 Example of a RosettaNet business process "`Manage Purchase Order`" (PIP3A4)

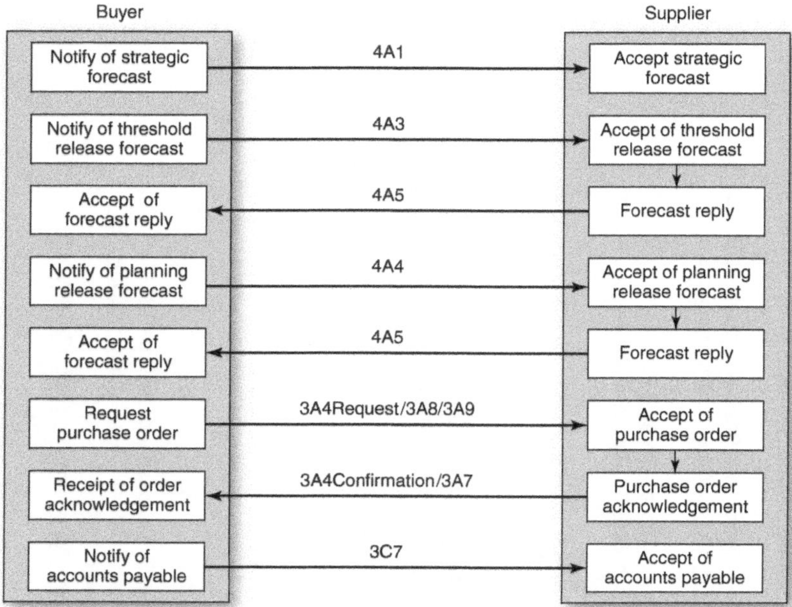

Figure 14.10 Combining demand forecast and order management processes (*Source*: [RosettaNet 2004])

14.3.3.2 The RosettaNet Implementation Framework

To support PIPs the RosettaNet architecture provides specifications for the RosettaNet Implementation Framework (RNIF) and business and technical dictionaries. The RNIF acts as the grammar and provides common exchange protocols, while PIPs form the dialogue. The RNIF together with the dictionary, which provides a common set of properties for business transactions and products, form the basis for the implementation of RosettaNet PIPs.

In addition to the RNIF, RosettaNet also provides business and technical dictionaries that contain properties for products and services, a common vocabulary for conducting e-Business as well as basic business roles, and elements that are required in fields of business documents or schemas that are necessary to support PIP exchanges. The RosettaNet Business Dictionary designates the properties for defining business transactions between trading partners. These are implemented as business data entities and fundamental business data entities in PIP message guidelines. The RosettaNet Technical Dictionary (RNTD) provides properties for defining products, services, partners and business transactions. The RNTD eliminates the need for partners to utilise separate dictionaries when implementing multiple PIPs and is not supply chain specific, allowing it to be used in a variety of supply chain applications.

14.3.3.3 RosettaNet and Web services

Again, as in the case of ebXML, both RosettaNet and Web services have the same foundational roots in XML and, consequently, have many things in common.

Web services can leverage RosettaNet in multiple ways to offer an even higher level of functionality for cross-enterprise supply chain communications. To cope with semantic problems, e-Business interactions require standardisation at an even higher level (standardised processes, messages, vocabulary and choreography) than what is currently offered by current Web service technology.

It is anticipated that Web services will initially take advantage of the standardisation provided by RosettaNet, e.g. business document formats developed by RosettaNet. In this way, Web services can permit e-Business interactions among multiple partners directly through their applications during the same standardised process, enabling commonly understood concepts such as production balancing between partners and suppliers within or across a supply chain. They will also permit activities, such as simultaneously sharing the same purchase order between the supplier, a financial organisation and a carrier, to validate all facets of completing an order at once, enabling each participant to work with its relevant portions of the interaction.

RosettaNet can also leverage Web service technology in several ways. Specifically, Web services, itself a standards based technology, could be incorporated as the underlying infrastructure to enable the deployment of RosettaNet compliant documents directly on to the Internet, in full accordance with the RosettaNet architecture. RosettaNet e-Business processes could then be advertised, discovered and accessed in the similar public settings as other services [RosettaNet 2003].

When considering Web services as an implementation platform for RosettaNet, it is fairly easy to model the PIP receipt and messages as WSDL operations [Masud 2003]. RosettaNet messages can be mapped to the types definitions of WSDL, while RosettaNet message definitions, including message names, can be mapped to the message definitions in WSDL. The actions in a RosettaNet PIP are mapped to operations in WSDL.

Choreography from the RosettaNet PIP is implemented in the choreography of the abstract and executable business process in BPEL. Exception messages from the RNIF are mapped to the exception handling mechanisms of BPEL. The `<partnerLink>` construct in BPEL can be used to implement PIP partner roles. The messaging layer from the RNIF provides methods for packing and unpacking messages and transporting them in a secure and reliable manner. BPEL and WSDL provide their own methods for encoding, transporting and securing messages. The workaround is to use best practices from RosettaNet in the Web service paradigm [Masud 2003].

BPEL and RosettaNet are ideally suited for use as a powerful combination, with BPEL as a language to define e-Business processes, and RosettaNet to create standardised industry e-Business processes. It is conceivable that RosettaNet can use BPEL as a standard e-Business process definition language to describe its e-Business processes.

14.4 Vertical industry standards

Today, trading exchanges are forming at a rapid pace and, as a result, several industry specific partnerships have been announced for just about every major manufacturing sector of the economy. Vertical industry standards hold the promise of cross-platform systems integration, consistent product and service descriptor semantics, and the formalisation and codification of best practices in any given industry. Their adoption is recognised to be a complicated interplay of market signals and individual evaluation by organisations, shaped by characteristics inherent to vertical standards as technology artifacts, as well as by community adoption behaviour exogenous to the standards.

Most vertical industry standards provide common business process definitions (promoting industry based standards through XML formats and defined APIs) and a standard terminology to combat semantic interoperability problems. This results in a universal foundation for conducting global electronic business, ensuring the integrity of fast, clean business transactions, guaranteeing common semantics and data integrity across the Internet, backed with the industry representation.

The objective of vertical standardisation efforts is to achieve relatively low barriers to entry, significant cost savings that come from reduced transaction costs and reduced processing costs, the automation of supply chains and increased productivity, so that they can attract companies of all sizes and establish partnerships with them.

The number of vertical industry organisations developing XML standard data formats and processes, which their members can use to interchange information, is potentially quite large. Many vertical industry standards groups are working on domain specific XML standards, including the automotive industry, insurance industry, real estate industry, healthcare, food industry and so forth.

In this section we shall describe four representative developments in industry wide collaboration and industry based standards that come from the aviation industry, automotive industry, retail grocery industry, travel industry and the insurance industry, and represent established organisations with considerable membership and traction. These are indicative of the efforts that are currently occurring also in numerous other industry domains.

14.4.1 XML standards for the aviation industry

Aeroxchange (www.aeroxchange.com) is an e-Business solutions provider and e-marketplace for the global aviation industry. Aeroxchange includes over 30 airlines, among them Air Canada, Air New Zealand, Cathay Pacific Airways, FedEx, Japan Airlines, KLM, Lufthansa, Northwest Airlines, Scandinavian Airlines, Singapore Airlines and others, and hundreds of suppliers, all dedicated to maximising efficiency across the complex aviation supply chain. Aeroxchange was founded to develop and implement next generation technology that creates value for all trading partners in the aviation supply chain. Aeroxchange's mission is to work with airlines, suppliers and partners to identify and develop supply chain solutions that drive efficiencies in the aviation industry.

Aeroxchange provides an open, neutral marketplace for commerce in the aviation supply chain. Aeroxchange is committed to reducing the inefficiencies in the current environment that are created by the different channels of communication between airlines and their suppliers, by consolidating EDI XML and Web based communications into a single hub, thus reducing the need for manual communication in the transaction lifecycle.

Aeroxchange provides e-negotiation services, e-procurement, and support services. E-negotiation services include a Web based negotiation tool, which supports Request for Quotation, Auction and Offer/Counter Offer, and services that extend customers' reach in repair, technical parts, commercial items, catering and airport services. Aeroxchange also provides an advanced repair service rich with features that create efficiencies for buyers and sellers throughout the service order lifecycle.

14.4.2 XML standards for the automotive industry

In the automotive distribution value chain the Standards for Technology in Automotive Retail or STAR (www.starstandard.org), a non-profit, automotive industry wide group, whose members are car dealers, manufacturers, retail system providers, and automotive related industry organisations. The goal of STAR is to use non-proprietary technology IT standards as a catalyst in fulfiling the business information needs of dealers and manufacturers while reducing the time and effort required to support related activities.

STAR is creating standards for the data elements and transmission format for communication among manufacturers, dealers and retail system providers. This organisation addresses the data interchange and electronic business requirements for distribution of automotive equipment. The aim of the STAR alliance is to define open, standard XML message formats for dealer to original equipment manufacturer communications for dealer to OEM business transactions such as parts order, sales lead and credit application. To define an open, standard architecture to support the delivery of messages between dealers and OEMs, and, in general, standardise the IT infrastructure at dealerships.

A major focus of STAR is to simplify business transaction processing as this means a more efficient retail automotive industry. To achieve this, STAR has developed a large number of automated tools for highly specific retail processes, such as parts locating, labour cost lookups, vehicle model codes and scheduling service appointments. These business processes are developed in a standard way and are made available to manufacturers, retailers and retail system providers.

14.4.3 XML standards for the travel industry

To harness the Internet along with established distribution channels, the travel industry also has common technical specifications for the electronic communication of information. The OpenTravel Alliance or OTA (www.opentravel.org) provides a community where companies in the electronic distribution supply chain work together to create an accepted structure for XML based messages, enabling suppliers and distributors to speak the same interoperability language, trading partner to trading partner.

OpenTravel is comprised of companies representing airlines, car rental firms, hotels, cruise lines, railways, leisure suppliers, service providers, tour operators, travel agencies, solutions providers, technology companies and distributors. OTA has specified a set of standard business processes and standard terminology for searching for availability and booking a reservation in the airline, hotel and car rental industry, as well as the purchase of travel insurance in conjunction with these services.

OTA specifications use structured data messages, including but not limited to the use of XML, to be exchanged over the Internet or other means of transport. OTA specifications also reference standards developed by the ISO, and the International Air Transport Association (IATA), which are used by the travel industry to provide standardised message structures and data for the travel industry. The OpenTravel specifications serve as a common language for travel related terminology and a mechanism for promoting the seamless exchange of information across all travel industry segments. OTA members are organisations that represent all segments of the travel industry, along with key technology and services suppliers.

14.4.4 XML standards for the insurance industry

The Association for Cooperative Operations Research and Development or ACORD (www.acord.org) is an insurance association that facilitates the development and use of standards for the insurance, reinsurance and related financial services industries. Affiliated with ACORD are hundreds of insurance and reinsurance companies, and thousands of agents and brokers, related financial service organisations, software providers and industry organisations. ACORD accomplishes its mission by remaining an objective, independent advocate for sharing information among diverse platforms and by pursuing standards based, straight through processing. Through these relationships, ACORD standards are being mapped and harmonised to other industry and cross-industry standards implemented in various countries and regions throughout the world.

ACORD's goal is to focus progressively on each link in the insurance value chain to respond to the industry's most pressing business needs. ACORD's participation in global cross-industry groups ensures standards interoperability between industries, and its joint initiatives and working groups seek to achieve interoperability within the insurance and financial services while also preventing duplication of standard setting efforts.

14.5 Summary of learning objectives

The objective of e-Business is to enable a wide range of trading partners to interact and collaborate and build supply responsive trading networks. Using flexible technologies such as Web services and business process management, and SOA as a design philosophy, traditional supply chains are gradually transformed to adaptive service based supply chain networks that have the ability to manage product demand and variability.

To achieve their objectives e-Business solutions and trading partner networks must employ:

- Versatile business protocols that capture the exchange of business information and message exchange requirements, identifying the timing, sequence and purpose of each business collaboration and information exchange.

An important requirement of e-Business solutions and trading partner networks is that they should both rely on horizontal or vertical industry standards according to the specificity of their domain.

- Horizontal standards describe basic levels of connectivity and are applicable across various industries. A classical example is ebXML, which describes specifications for messaging, registries and business processes that are reusable across several industries.
- By contrast, vertical standards, typified by RosettaNet, focus on data and business processes by developing common vocabularies, metadata, and processes that can be customised to the needs of very specific niches, and are designed to promote greater process and systems integration within a particular industry.

Review questions

- What is the purpose of a business ecosystem? What are its main building blocks?
- What are the most common semantic problems at the business process level?
- What kind of functionality should a common business standard/protocol provide to address these semantic problems?
- Briefly describe the functions and major characteristics of an EDI system.
- What are the major drawbacks of EDI with respect to e-Business?
- What is the purpose of RosettaNet and what are its major architectural elements?
- What is the purpose of partner interface processes in RosettaNet?
- How does the RosettaNet standard relate to Web services?
- What is the purpose of ebXML?
- What are the major architectural elements of the ebXML reference architecture?
- Describe the major characteristics of ebXML processes and transactions.
- What are the major differences between RosettaNet and ebXML?

Exercises

14.1. Use Figure 14.10 as a basis to develop a simple business model involving a number of RosettaNet PIPs in which a supplier develops replenishment plans for consignment inventory at the buyer's side. As in the case of Figure 14.10, demand information is provided using PIP4A3 or 4A4. Product receipt and inventory information is notified using PIP4B2 and PIP4C1, respectively, between consignment warehouses and suppliers. The other PIPs used in this solution are similar to those used in Figure 14.10. Visit the RosettaNet site (www.rosettanet.org) to find more about the definition and usage of these PIPs.

14.2. Modify the scenario in the previous exercise to develop a business model in which a purchase order recipient (supplier) supplies the required stock to a third party owned warehouse on the basis of demand information included in purchase orders. The buyer then retrieves the required stock from the warehouse and issues a receipt notification using PIP4B2 to report the status of a received shipment to the warehouse and the supplier.

14.3. Use RosettaNet PIPs to develop a general business model that describes an integrated logistics scenario involving a customer, suppliers and a logistics service provider. This simplified model consists of forecast notification, forecast acceptance, inventory reporting, shipment receipt, request and fulfil demand, consumption and invoice notification processes. To develop this scenario you need to use the PIPs described in the following. PIP4A2 `"Notify of Embedded Release Forecast"` supports a process in which a forecast owner sends forecast data to a forecast recipient. PIP4A5 `"Notify of Forecast Reply"` provides visibility of available forecasted product quantity between two trading partners. PIP4C1 `"Distribute Inventory Report"` supports a process in which an inventory information provider reports the status of the inventory to an inventory information user. PIP4B2 `"Notify of Shipment Receipt"` supports a process used by a consignee to report the status of a received shipment to another interested party, such as a shipper. PIP3B2 `"Notify of Advance Shipment"` allows a shipper to notify a receiver that a shipment has been assigned. This notification is often a part of the shipment process. PIP3C3 `"Notify of Invoice"` enables a provider to invoice another party, such as a buyer or financing processor, for goods or services performed.

14.4. The following exercises involve the encoding of ebXML business transactions:

(a) Encode a simple purchase order business transaction in ebXML with a requesting and responding business activity and an attached purchase order document.

(b) Encode a simple delivery notification business transaction in ebXML with a receipt and an acknowledgement for a purchase order. Another requirement is that this transaction should be performed within 3 days.

14.5. Encode a binary collaboration in ebXML regarding the fulfilment of a purchase order. The buyer should be the initiator of this binary collaboration and the seller should act as a responder. The binary collaboration could contain two simple transactions: a `create PO` transaction and a `notify shipment` transaction.

14.6. Encode a binary collaboration in ebXML involving the insurance of a given shipment. A client may request the insurance of a shipment; following this the insurer then creates a shipment contact, which is either accepted or rejected by the client.

PART VIII

SOA modelling, design and development

CHAPTER 15

SOA based application modelling

Learning objectives

The primary purpose of this chapter is to provide readers with an understanding of how they can model SOA applications comprising processes and process flows. We shall concentrate on SOA modelling techniques that help service developers express services and business processes in an SOA using a standard graphical notation. This notation gives modellers the ability to communicate modelling procedures in a standard manner. Moreover, we shall demonstrate how modelling fits into a SOA driven approach prior to coding applications and separate from considering the underlying service technology.

After completing this chapter you will understand the following key concepts:

- The concept of modeling software applications.
- Business process modeling techniques and notations.
- Business process reference models and their importance for SOA modeling.
- The Business Process Modelling Notation (BPMN).

Chapter preview

This chapter discusses the importance of modelling SOA based applications. We first introduce the principles of enterprise wide models and review standard process modelling techniques and methodologies. Subsequently, we delve into the concept of a reference model and explain how it helps describe common characteristics or general structures relevant to a domain. Further, we demonstrate how a reference model provides best practices to enable the describing of consistent process flows in a manner that addresses application needs. Finally, we present the Business Process Modeling Notation (BPMN) and sample business process models in BPMN to illustrate the fundamental concepts and notational innovations that are required to provide complete SOA solutions.

15.1 The art of modelling

Developers and analysts who build complex structures or systems create models of what they build before actually having them built. In a similar way, developing enterprise wide models prior to coding applications provides a conceptual *blueprint* that ensures that users and software developers have common understanding of the systems to be developed.

In this book, we use the term *model* to mean an abstract representation of the real world that reduces complexity and represents only the details necessary for a specific purpose. Loosely speaking, modelling constitutes the conceiving of software applications using an abstract form of representation before coding them. The art of modelling allows developers to consider alternatives, select the best option, work out details and achieve agreement before application developers start building an application.

Modelling the enterprise uses an organised systems approach. Generally, a functional system is defined as a set of elements characterised by interrelations and a common objective. Following a systems approach, modelling first requires the definition of the system boundaries, which answers the questions: what is considered to be internal to the system that has to be modelled? and what is considered as the external environment? Next the components of the system (the subsystems) and their interrelationships have to be determined. This is known as decomposition of the system. Decomposition reduces complexity and results in a workable overview (model) of the system. Interrelationships between subsystems may be physical, e.g. exchange of goods from one production unit to another, or informational, e.g. decisions or general information from one decision unit to another. Exchange of data between subsystems can be modelled as communication (exchange of messages). Also the relation between the focal system and its environment consists of physical and or information exchanges, which form either an input to the system or an output from the system to the environment.

The systems approach helps to move from higher to lower levels of analysis, which is necessary to develop a good understanding of the reality that is being modeled. Following two modelling principles reduces modelling complexity:

1. subsystems are considered as a black box;
2. modelling follows a top down pattern.

Treating subsystems as a black box helps to concentrate on relations between subsystems, and not to be confused by the internal specifics of each subsystem. Following the top down approach, once higher level subsystems and their relations have been identified, allows to further decompose each subsystem to lower levels of analysis.

Business process models follow the systems approach we described above and, as a consequence, they define how business processes are described. Business processes represent the artifacts of business exchanges and their definition enables an enterprise to express its business processes so that they are understandable within the enterprise itself, as well as by other enterprises (see Chapter 9 for more details).

Dependent on the type of activity and the industry in which business organisations operate they will differ or share specific characteristics. For example, a hospital viewed on an organisational level is different from a manufacturing company and differs from a financial institute. Viewed on a process level (or activity level) a buying or ordering process is typically present in almost any type of organisation, like manufacturing, trade or municipal organisations. Similarities between organisations can be used to improve the efficiency of the modelling activity by creating reference models. Reference models help with the modelling exercise as they are representations of particular types of organisation that help to decompose organisations into subsystems and can identify critical information systems.

Business models come in two main flavours:

- descriptive (or non-normative);
- normative.

Descriptive models are models where the real world is simply *described.* A descriptive model limits the types of object, relationships and properties to be identified and modelled, but does not limit the modeller in how to go about mapping these concepts to the domain of investigation. In short, the descriptive modeller can freely choose and name the objects perceived, their names and relationships and which properties to capture. As such, descriptive models offer a great deal of freedom and flexibility to the modeller. In contrast, a normative model restricts how the system being examined can be represented.

Normative models on the other hand force modellers to select from a pre-specified set of constructs and essentially map the perceived system into this pre-specified set. This substantially reduces flexibility and freedom (and variety) of models produced. However, it yields models that are rigorous, improves consistency and reduces representational complexity.

In addition to normative models, visual modelling becomes essential in the face of increasingly complex systems for business-to-business applications. As the complexity of a system increases, so does the importance of good modelling techniques. Several modelling techniques are based on *visual* (or graphical) *models,* allowing different stakeholders to represent and view the system from different angles and communicate their perspectives with each other. Visual models are frequently used in conjunction with normative models. Using a rigorous modelling language standard is one essential ingredient for the success of a modelling technique.

15.2 Business process modelling methodologies

A process-centric organisation is an organisation that is conceptualised as a set of business processes. A business process model is a powerful means for structuring and formatting enterprise related information. Process models are the cornerstones for the modelling and eventual development of business-to-business (or e-Business) SOA based applications. Such models can be used to define, among other things, standardised operating procedures, to analyse the structuring of value chains, to create a shared understanding of how a business functions, or even just to test assumptions.

Detailed business process models allow analysts and modellers to visualise, analyse and improve processes, so that workflow implementations are tested before design and implementation. Virtually all enterprises are using process modelling techniques before making actual investments in an SOA based application. A major advantage of a formalised business process model is the guarantee that processes will be executed in a repeatable, consistent and precise way. Errors are avoided and customers do not get frustrated. Every process instance follows the same rules of execution.

One immediate advantage of business process models is that they improve the visibility of the business rules in an SOA application. This makes it easier to adapt them to changing market conditions and a shared understanding of what functions are supported by the enterprise, and how these are supported. Business rules, as we already explained in Section 9.2, are precise statements that describe, constrain and control the structure, operations and strategies of an enterprise.

A *modelling methodology* sets out a procedure that should be followed to ensure consistent production and delivery of results on the basis of a specific model, such as a business process model. It specifies:

- activities to be performed;
- roles of participants;
- rules to be followed;
- techniques to be used;
- deliverables to be produced.

Its use is normally supported by the use of computer aided tools. A modelling methodology is used to enable application users and developer groups to adopt a common approach to specification of business application requirements and information, so that they can be shared within an enterprise and provided externally in a consistent manner.

The sheer diversity of SOA based applications shows that there is need to follow a series of meaningful steps to ensure consistent production and delivery of real technical implementations from high level problem descriptions. This methodology is independent of the middleware platform and tools used to develop cross-enterprise applications. The following items are useful tools when taking these steps:

1. A *reference architecture* or *standardised methodology* to organise cross-enterprise project activities needed to develop the process models (see, for example, the UN/CEFACT Modeling Methodology and the SCOR model in the following sections).

2. *Business protocols* to model the business information that is exchanged in cross-enterprise messaging, possibly on the basis of XML, e.g. RosettaNet (see Chapter 14).

3. A *modelling notation and language* precisely to model and represent the business processes that an application or system automates and the activities that are performed in these processes, (see the Business Process Modeling Notation in Section 15.4).

The above items guarantee consistency in modelling techniques and methodologies, which not only forces discipline on analysts and produces better analysis, but also produces analysis in a form that can be more easily validated by subject matter experts and used by software developers.

Modelling the enterprise offers a useful framework for documenting the organisation, providing the essential blueprints for the communication, interpretation and implementation throughout the organisation, while enabling the evolution to a service-centric IT environment. The use of industry and reference models can provide a useful starting point for a top down approach.

Process models are a core part of Business Process Modeling Notation (BPMN), see Section 15.4, and are generally shown in graphical form for defining or building a business process. The key elements of a process model are individual activities performed, the events that trigger actions, the ordering of activities, the business rules used to support decision making and execution flow, as well as exception handling and error handling mechanisms. Their objective is to help analysts faithfully represent actual processes and enable them to propose improvements. In the following we shall describe popular process modelling methodologies, reference models and notations that can be used in conjunction with SOA based application modelling.

In the following sections we shall first examine two standard modelling methodologies: the UMM modelling methodology and the Supply Chain Operations Reference Model (SCOR). Following this we shall focus on the Business Process Modeling Notation that is used to deliver BPEL process and SOA based application models.

15.2.1 The UN/CEFACT modelling methodology

A business environment may be large and complex. Any basic understanding of this environment begins with information and documentation provided by business experts. Business experts provide a categorisation and decomposition of the business environment into business areas, process areas and business processes. One such concerted effort for process-centric applications is the United Nations Centre for Trade Facilitation and Electronic Business (UN/CEFACT) Modeling Methodology (UMM) for business process and information modelling [UMM 2003].

The UMM is based on the Open EDI Reference Model, as defined by the ISO standard 14662 [ISO 1997]. This reference model outlines a different approach to EDI, based on business scenarios rather than the conventional EDI concept of individual transaction sets or messages. The business scenarios cover much of the interaction between companies and, as a result, the extended period and lengthy development cycle needed to establish an SOA relationship can be reduced significantly.

The process methodology used in UMM recognises that any software engineering or e-Business project passes through a series of general phases over the course of its liftime. These phases are:

- *Inception* where the project focuses on the requirement specification and determining the scope and vision of the overall project.
- *Elaboration* where the requirements are analysed in detail, further refined and expanded, and an architectural prototype is developed. This serves as a baseline for the overall system.
- *Construction* where software development and testing is performed.
- *Transition* where further testing and deployment of software occurs.

The view of such software engineering projects is a series of sequential steps, or workflows, moving from technology independent business process modelling to technology dependent deployment. A UMM workflow is a logical grouping in a software development process.

The inception and elaboration phases of the UMM concentrate on workflow prerequisites for understanding the business needs and producing business scenarios, business objects and business collaborations. These cover broad software engineering phases, such as requirements, analysis, design, implementation, testing and development. Each workflow produces a set of modelling artifacts, which, taken together, provide a description of the business case at various levels of detail and from various perspectives. The term artifact is a typical UML/UMM term that refers to any result produced in the software development project.

15.2.1.1 The UMM meta-model

UMM is an incremental business process and information model construction methodology that provides levels of specification granularity that are suitable for communicating the model to business practitioners, business application integrators and network application solution providers. UMM prescribes a specific way to perform business process and information modelling for electronic business.

The UMM meta-model underlies the business modelling, requirements and analysis. It specifies all of the items that must be produced from the analysis and describes their relationships. The UMM meta-model is a description of business semantics that allows trading partners to capture the details for a specific business scenario (e.g. a complex business process) using a consistent modelling methodology. This methodology is depicted in Figure 15.1.

In Figure 15.1 business process specification describes in detail how trading partners take on shared roles, relationships and responsibilities to facilitate interaction with other trading partners. The interaction between roles takes place as a choreographed set of business transactions. Each business transaction is expressed as an exchange of electronic business documents. The sequence of the exchange is determined by the *Business Process,* and by messaging and security considerations. Business documents are composed from reuseable business information objects, expressed in an appropriate format (e.g. XML,

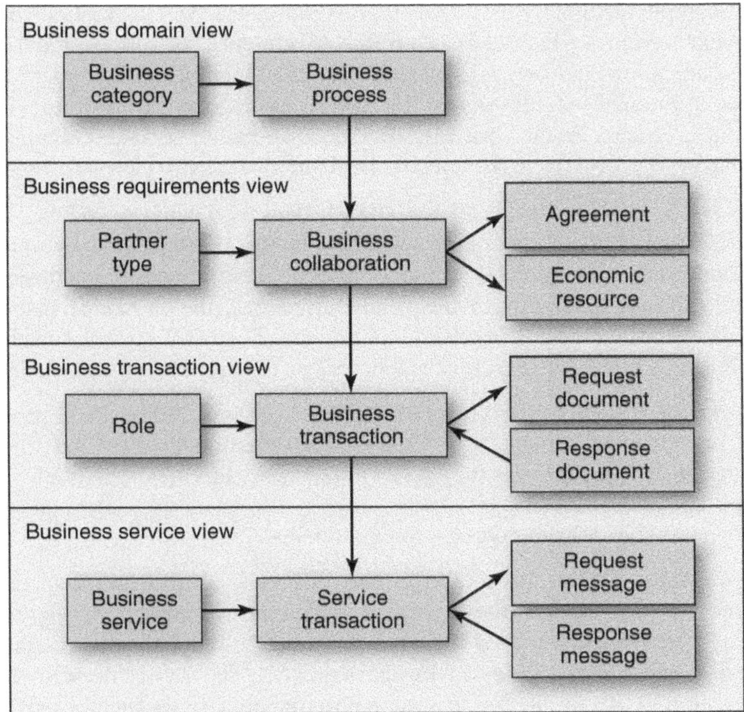

Figure 15.1 UMM meta-model

EDI, etc.). At a lower level, business processes can be composed of reuseable common business processes, and business information objects can be composed of reuseable core components. These common business processes and business information objects reside in a UMM Business Library.

The UMM meta-model supports a group of business process viewpoints that provide a set of semantics (vocabulary) for each viewpoint and forms the basis for specification of the semantics and artifacts that are required to facilitate business process and information integration and interoperability. The UMM meta-model structures modelling activities so that each business process and information model can be viewed from a number of perspectives. Each UMM meta-model view is shown in Figure 15.1 and is briefly described as follows [UMM 2003]:

> The *Business Domain View (BDV):* This view partitions a business domain into business areas, process areas and business processes. Its aim is to define an overall *frame of reference* for the business processes being identified and establish links with reusable, previously defined, process descriptions or terminology in the UMM libraries. The BDV is used consistently to define the business process area boundaries, and achieve business process interoperability with future trading partners also following the same business reference model for their operating practices. To achieve this, the BDV defines basic terms accepted by the given industry segment.

For example the Supply Chain Operations Reference (SCOR) model – discussed in the next section – which defines a frame of reference for supply chain, or the telecommunications industry's Enhanced Telecom Operations Map (eTOM) Business Process Framework, developed by the Tele-Management Forum. The eTOM Business Process Framework describes the most widely used and accepted standard for business processes in the telecommunications industry (www.tforum.org).

The *Business Requirements View (BRV):* This is a view of a business process model that captures the use case scenarios, inputs, outputs, constraints and system boundaries for commercial transactions and their interrelationships. This view defines the choreography of business transactions, the economic resources, economic events and agents involved in a process. The BRV concerns itself with how the business domain expert sees and describes the process to be modelled.

The *Business Transaction View (BTV):* This is a view of a business process model that captures the semantics of business information entities and their flow of exchange between roles as they perform business activities. This view is an elaboration on the business requirements view by the business analyst and is how the business analyst sees the process to be modelled.

The *Business Service View (BSV):* This is a view of an explicit specification of business process interactions according to the type of transaction, role, security and timing parameters, and their message (information) exchange as interactions necessary to execute and validate a business process. The set of interactions is derived from the BTV according to the system requirements. In essence, the BSV captures the syntax and semantics of business messages and their exchange between business services.

The above perspectives support a process-centric incremental construction methodology and provide levels of specification granularity that are suitable for communicating the model to business practitioners, business application integrators and network application solution providers.

15.2.1.2 The UMM worksheets

UMM uses business process and business information analysis worksheets as simple business process aids to capture business process and business information requirements. The worksheets and corresponding usage methodology are derived from the UMM. The worksheets can be extended for specific vertical industry needs, e.g. telecommunications, financials, etc.

Worksheets are the central element of UMM models, as they help collect and organise the information needed to produce the minimum UMM models for a particular work area corresponding to the first three UMM views, i.e. Business Domain View, Business Requirements View and Business Transaction View. Procedures within each of these work areas describe how to populate the worksheets [UMM 2003].

A high level overview of a UMM model and its associated worksheets is given in Figure 15.2.

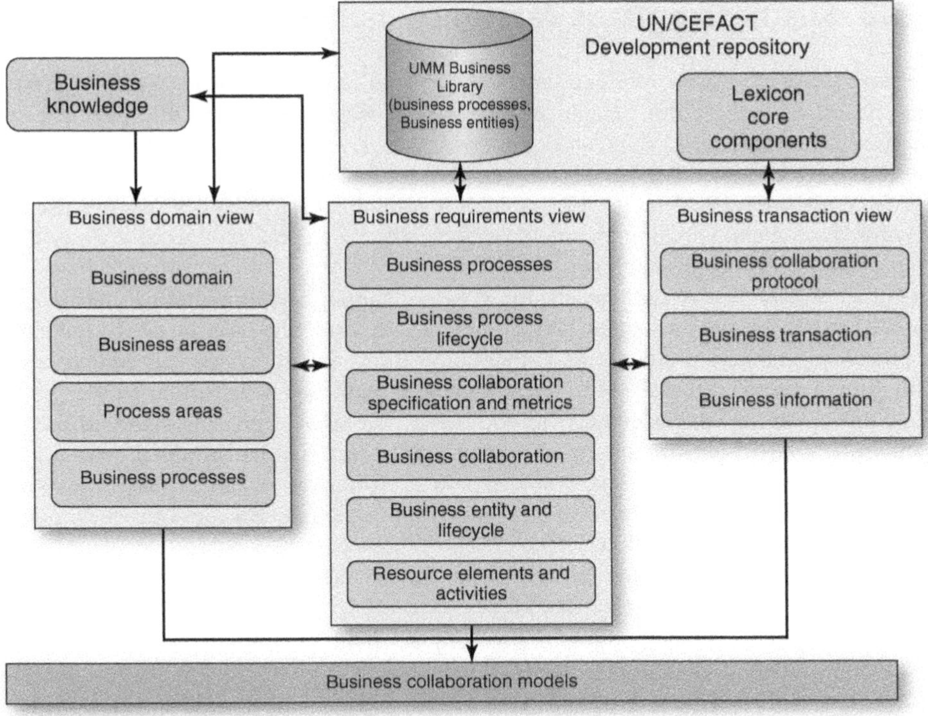

Figure 15.2 UMM models and worksheets

In this figure each UMM work area is composed of a set of procedures, which build on each other to define the minimum required UMM models for the first three UMM views. These procedures are based on use of the worksheets that are used to create UMM models. In the fourth UMM view, the Business Service View, models are not defined in the UMM User Guide as a work area. These are determined as a result of completing the procedures outlined in each of the preceding work areas.

Building a UMM compliant business model is a top down modelling activity, which starts off with a clear understanding of the specific domain of business activities within which the entire model exists. It de-emphasises the use of business documents and transactions to model this view, as that approach may capture only one part of the required model. Instead, emphasis is placed on the definition of business entities, their state management and state lifecycle identification to produce a model that encompasses all instances and can evolve as new business requirements emerge.

Using the UMM methodology and the UMM meta-model, the user may therefore create a complete business process and information model conforming to the UMM meta-model. As this model is syntax independent it can be easily implemented by Web services.

15.3 Business process reference models

The purpose of a process reference model is to fuse the well known concepts of business process re-engineering, benchmarking, process measurement and improvement into a unified cross-functional framework. A *process reference model* depicts the common characteristics or general structures that can be applied to numerous instances within a specific domain (vertical industry). As such it provides best practices that are used as basis for sharing and agreeing on core processes, allowing consistent process flows to be created that address application needs.

A process reference model may specify standard naming and terminology conventions, provide tested and proven standard core processes, describe the right level of granularity for processes, standard protocols, and other conventions that allow services and processes to interoperate on a large scale within a particular domain (see also Section 14.4).

A process reference model may, in addition to the above, provide standard metrics to measure process performance and management practices that produce best-in-class performance. Metrics are tightly connected to performance attributes, such as assets, cost, flexibility, reliability, performance and responsiveness. Business process models are process focused, which directs focus from systems to processes and concentrates on resolving problems rather than on combating symptoms. Using reference models can reduce the cost and time effort required for process modelling, design and representation.

In the following, we shall examine the Supply Chain Operations Reference (SCOR) model version 10 as it provides the means to evaluate, control, measure and improve existing supply chains from a business process perspective. SCOR highlights the functional requirements of best practices that have been identified.

15.3.1 The Supply chain operations reference model

The Supply Chain Operations Reference (SCOR) model embodies the approach proposed by the Supply Chain Council (www.supply-chain.org) who combined the expertise of supply chain professionals across a broad cross-section of industries to develop best-in-class business practices and design a specific methodology tailored to the analysis of supply chain processes [SCORv10].

SCOR is a business process methodology built by, and for, supply chain analysis and design, to link best practices, technology, benchmarks, standardised metrics and business processes in an effort to increase efficiencies in supply chain management operations. The SCOR model provides a unique framework that links business process, metrics, best practices and technology features into a unified structure to support communication among supply chain partners, and to improve the effectiveness of supply chain management and related supply chain improvement activities. The SCOR model is widely adapted to supply chain companies that seek standardised methods for representing business processes and process interactions, and easy communication with their partners.

SCOR enables companies to analyse and improve their supply chain operations, by helping them to communicate supply chain information across the enterprise and measure performance objectively. SCOR also assists enterprises with identifying supply chain performance gaps and improvement objectives, and influences the development of future supply chain management software. It also provides standard definitions of measures and procedures for calculating the metrics. The Model has been able successfully to describe and provide a basis for supply chain improvement for global projects, as well as site specific projects.

SCOR as a process reference model contains:

- standard descriptions of management practices;
- a framework of relationships among the standard processes;
- standard metrics to measure process performance;
- management practices that produce best in class performance;
- standard alignment to features and functionality.

The SCOR model has been developed to define all business activities associated with the supply chain. SCOR is flexible and configurable to the specific needs of an organisation, as the processes that are used to describe an organisation are dependant upon the role conducted in the network. The model spans all customer interactions, from order entry through paid invoice, all physical material transactions, from the supplier's supplier to the customer's customer, including field service logistics, and all market interactions, from the understanding of aggregate demand to the fulfilment of each order. SCOR does not attempt to describe every business process or activity. Specifically, the SCOR model does not address: sales and marketing (demand generation), product development, research and development, and several elements of post-delivery customer support.

SCOR contend that the core processes that are directly involved in the execution of a supply strategy could be made up of a combination of five primary management processes: *plan, source, make, deliver* and *return.* By describing supply chains using these process building blocks, the model can be used to describe very simple or very complex supply chains in a generic manner, using a common set of definitions. As a result, disparate industries can be linked to describe the depth and breadth of virtually any supply chain.

15.3.1.1 The SCOR primary management processes

As Figure 15.3 illustrates, the SCOR modelling approach starts with the assumption that any supply chain process can be represented as a combination of the five following basic processes [SCOR v10]. These are explained in some detail below.

Plan: this process targets Demand/Supply Planning and Management and its purpose is to balance demand and supply to best meet the sourcing, manufacturing and delivery requirements. In particular, the process:

- Balances resources with requirements and establishes/communicates plans for the whole supply chain, including Return, and the execution processes of Source, Make, and Deliver.

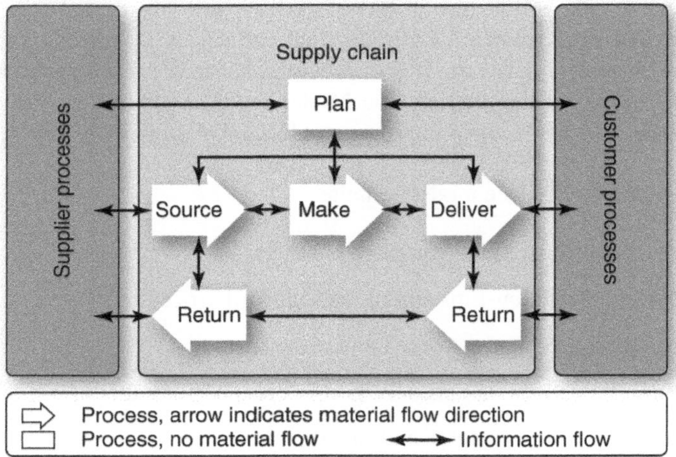

Figure 15.3 Elements of the SCOR model

- Manages business rules, supply chain performance, data collection, inventory, capital assets, transportation, planning configuration, regulatory requirements and compliance, and supply chain risk.
- Aligns the supply chain unit plan with the financial plan.

Source: this process targets Sourcing Stocked, Make-to-Order, and Engineer-to-Order Product and procures goods and services to meet planned or actual demand. The process:

- Schedules deliveries; receives, verifies, and transfers product; and authorises supplier payments.
- Identifies and selects supply sources when not predetermined, as for engineer-to-order product.
- Manages business rules, assesses supplier performance, and maintains data.
- Manages inventory, capital assets, incoming product, supplier network, import/export requirements, supplier agreements and supply chain source risk.

Make: this process targets Make-to-Stock, Make-to-Order, and Engineer-to-Order Production Execution to achieve its purpose it transforms these products to a finished state to meet planned or actual demand. The process:

- Schedules production activities, issue products, produces and tests, packages, stages products, and releases products to deliver.
- Finalises engineering for engineer-to-order products.
- Manages rules, performance, data, in-process products, equipment and facilities, transportation, production network, regulatory compliance for production, and supply chain make risks.

Deliver: this process targets Order, Warehouse, Transportation, and Installation Management for Stocked, Make-to-Order, and Engineer-to-Order Product. The process:

- Provides all order management steps from processing customer inquiries and quotes to routing shipments and selecting carriers, including warehouse management from receiving and picking product to load and ship product.
- Receives and verifies product at customer site and install, if necessary.
- Manages invoicing customer.
- Manages delivery business rules, performance, finished product inventories, capital assets, transportation, product life cycle, import/export requirements, and supply chain delivery risks.

Return: this process targets Return of Raw Materials and Receipt of Returns of Finished Goods. This process is associated with returning or receiving returned products for any reason. It extends into post-delivery customer support. Particularly, the process:

- Is associated with returning or receiving any returned defective or excess products from source.
- Manages return business rules, performance, data collection, return inventory, capital assets, transportation, network configuration, regulatory requirements and compliance.

SCOR processes exhibit the following characteristics [SCOR v10]. They:

- provide a balanced horizontal (cross-process) and vertical (hierarchical) view;
- are designed to be (re)-configurable;
- are used to represent many different configurations of a similar process;
- can aggregate a series of hierarchical process models.

15.3.1.2 SCOR levels of process detail

SCOR assigns three standard process levels within each major supply chain application to identify specific attributes of the five main processes described in the previous section. Figure 15.4 shows the three core SCOR levels, as well as two additional that may include company specific process extensions.

Level 1 is the highest level. This level describes supply chain processes at the most general level. It consists of the five key supply chain process types (Plan, Source, Make, Deliver and Return) and assumes that all supply chains are composed out of these five basic processes. In addition, performance targets are established.

Level 2 provides more definition of the five core process categories and defines the configuration level through which a company's operations strategy is implemented. Actually, Level 2 provides for variations in the Level 1 processes. A company's supply chain can be

configured-to-order at Level 2 from the core *process categories.* Companies implement their operations strategy through the configuration they choose for their supply chain. These are not in fact sub-processes, but variations in the way the processes can be implemented.

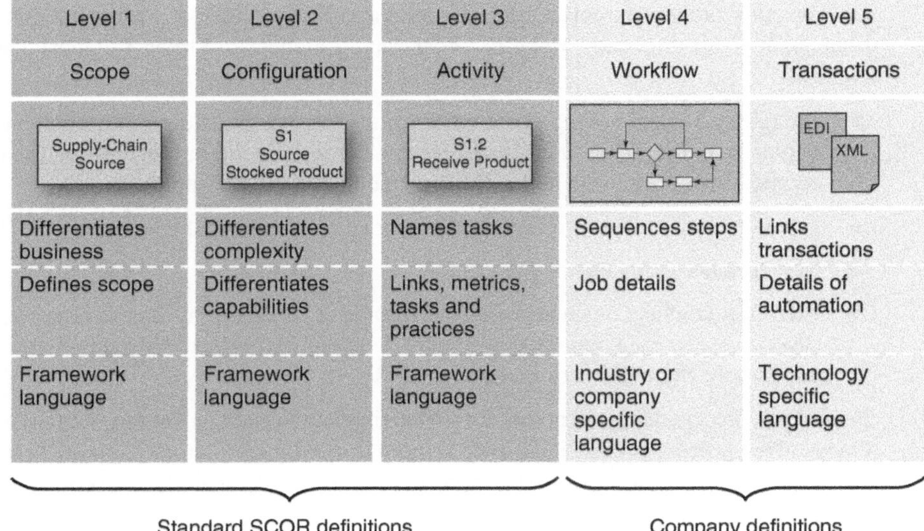

Figure 15.4 Standard SCOR and company definitions

Level 3 defines a company's ability to compete successfully in its chosen markets, and consists of:

- process element definitions;
- process element information inputs and outputs;
- process performance metrics, attributes and definitions;
- best practices definitions.

The SCOR model identifies an additional *Level 4* for processes, which are not in its scope, as a means of defining strategic, company specific supply chain processes and practices to achieve competitive advantage and to adapt to changing business conditions. Companies implement supply chain management practices that are unique to their organisations at this level. Level 4 and lower defines specific practices to achieve competitive advantage and to adapt to changing business conditions.

Figure 15.4 illustrates an extension of the standard SCOR definition that includes additional levels 4 and 5 with company (or vertical industry) specific components. As shown in this figure, Level 4 introduces company (or vertical industry) specific workflow constructs while Level 5 uses transactional constructs expressed in XML or EDI.

Example 15.1: SCOR supply chain comprising five levels

Figure 15.5 illustrates an example of a supply chain that follows the SCOR model and comprises five levels of processes. In this example, when implementing a process, an application developer first focuses on a delivery process (Level 1 process) and then may decide which of three (Level 2) variations of delivery process it is.

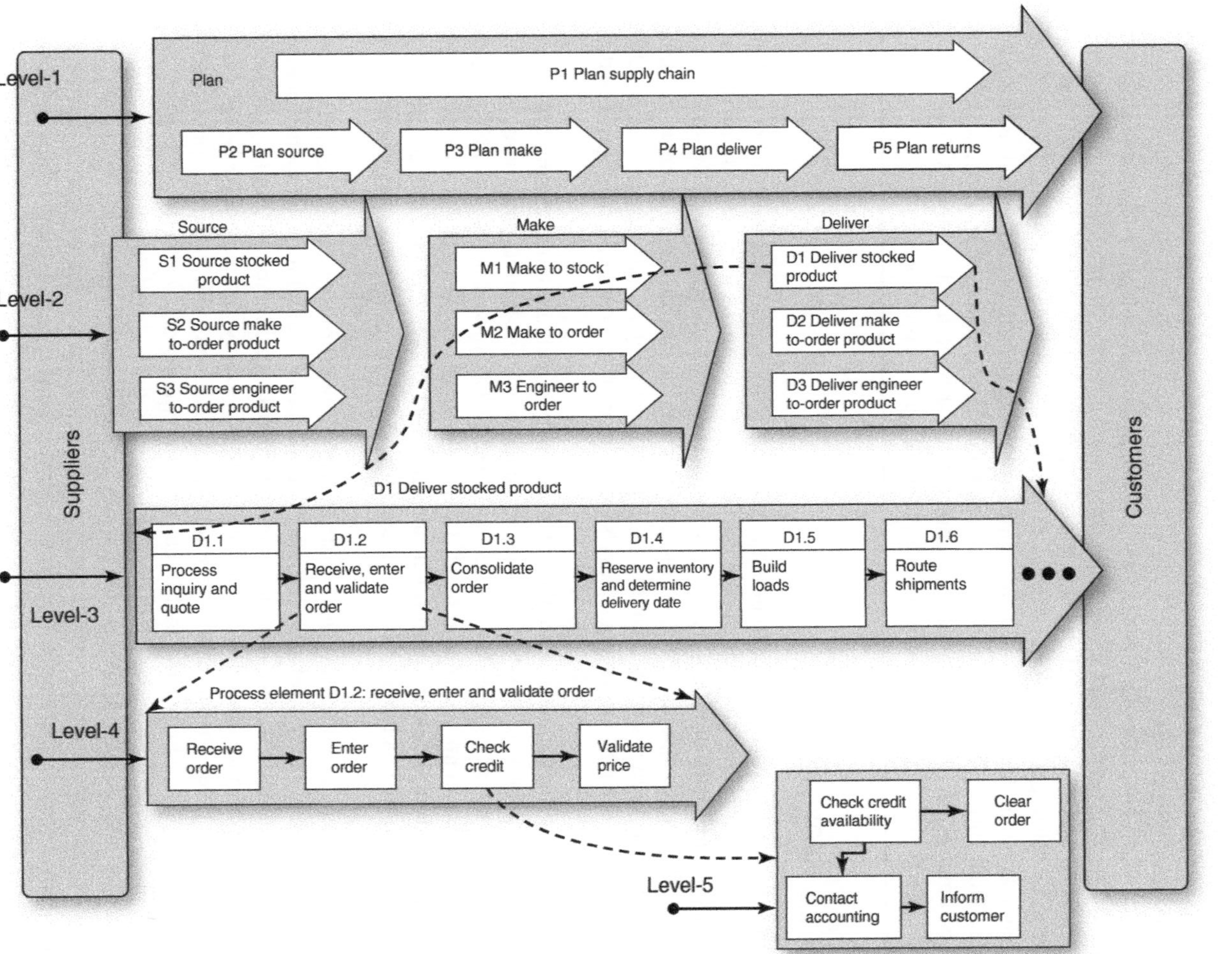

Figure 15.5 Implementation of a supply chain using SCOR processes at five levels

In the case of Level 1 Deliver process, the Level 2 variations are D1: Deliver Stocked Product, D2: Deliver Make-to-Order Product, or D3: Deliver Engineer-to-Order Product. Figure 15.5 shows all of the five basic SCOR Level 1 processes with current Level 2 variations for each Level 1 process. Each Level 2 process is further decomposed into a set of sub-processes or activities at Level 3 that define the basic sequence of steps involved in implementing the process.

Figure 15.5 shows that in this example the application developer is decomposing the Level 2 D1: Deliver Stocked Product process into a number of predefined SCOR sub-process such as D1.1, D1.2, D1.3, D1.4 and so on. The example further indicates that the application developer focuses on process D.1.2: Receive, Enter & Validate Order. This process will be implemented now using company specific practices and as such is not part of the SCOR model. The figure illustrates a possible implementation of process D.1.2 at Levels 4 and 5. As illustrated by this example, the first three levels of the SCOR framework serve as the foundation for the development of Level 4 processes.

15.3.1.3 SCOR metrics

SCOR provides standard metrics to measure process performance. The metrics are used in conjunction with performance attributes. SCOR metrics are used in conjunction with the performance attributes of reliability, responsiveness, agility, cost and assets. These performance attributes are characteristics of the supply chain that permit it to be analysed and evaluated against other supply chains with competing strategies. Like processes, SCOR metrics are classified into a number of levels but these do not necessarily correspond to the process levels.

The Level 1 strategic metrics are the calculations by which an implementing organisation can measure how successful they are in achieving their desired positioning within the competitive market space. Many metrics in the SCOR model are hierarchical – just as the process elements are hierarchical. Level 1 metrics are created from lower level calculations and are primary, high level measures that may cross multiple SCOR processes. Lower level calculations (Level 2 and 3 metrics) are generally associated with a narrower subset of processes.

Figure 15.6 is an example of Level 1 metrics. This figure shows that each metric is associated with exactly one out of five performance attributes (Reliability, Responsiveness, Flexibility Costs and Assets). The ten Level 1 metrics mentioned in Figure 15.6 are high level business measures that are of interest to the supply chain managers. It should be noted that a given metric can have multiple associations with processes on various levels depending on whether the metric calculation requires data carried by the process. Calculation of a metric may be dependent not only on the process data items but on the calculation of more detailed, lower level metrics as well.

Lower level calculations (Level 2 metrics) are generally associated with a narrower subset of processes. For example, *Delivery Performance* is calculated as the total number of products delivered on time and in full based on a commit date. Additionally, even lower level metrics (diagnostics) are used to diagnose variations in performance against plan. For example, an organisation may wish to examine the correlation between the request date and commit date. For example, consider the Level 2 metric *Delivery Performance* depends on finer grained metrics *Delivery Performance to Customer Commit Date* and

Level 1 metrics	Performance attributes				
	Customer-facing			Internal-facing	
	Reliability	Responsiveness	Flexibility	Costs	Assets
Perfect order fulfillment	X				
Order fulfillment cycle time		X			
Upside supply chain flexibility			X		
Upside supply chain adaptability			X		
Downside supply chain adaptability			X		
Supply chain management cost				X	
Cost of goods sold				X	
Cash-to-cash cycle time					X
Return on supply chain fixed assets					X
Return on working capital					X

Figure 15.6 SCOR Level 1 metrics

Delivery Performance to Customer Request Date). The SCOR model does not prescribe a method for rolling up the metrics.

Level 2 and 3 metrics associated with Level 1 metrics can be found in the SCOR 10.0 Metrics Hierarchy in the Metrics Chapter [SCOR v10].

Now you have an adequate background on the topics of modelling and modelling methodologies, so we can introduce the Business Process Modeling Notation, and demonstrate how to develop SOA application models.

15.4 Business Process Modeling Notation

In Chapter 9 we saw that BPEL provides a sound foundation for business process execution but is not a business process modelling language. Given the nature of BPEL, a complex business process could be organised in a block structured format that is handled very well by software developers or programmers, but is very hard to understand by the business analysts and managers tasked to develop, manage and monitor business processes.

From the preceding discussion, it is evident that business process modelling requires a notation that is readily understandable by all types of user. This includes the business analysts and modellers who create the initial drafts of the processes in an SOA based application, to the technical developers responsible for implementing the technology that will perform those processes, and, finally, business people who will manage and monitor those processes. A major improvement would be if the business process modelling activity would lead to the execution of the modelled business processes in some standard business process execution language such as, for example, BPEL. In this way, a standardised bridge can be created for the gap between the business process modelling and design, and process execution. These are precisely the primary goals of the Business Process Modeling Notation (BPMN) effort.

Business Process Modelling Notation is an attempt at a standards based business process modelling language that can unambiguously define business logic and information requirements to the extent that the resultant models are executable [OMG 2008]. The goal of BPMN is to provide a business process modelling notation that is readily usable by business analysts, modellers, technical developers and business people that manage and monitor these processes.

In essence, BPMN provides a standard visualisation mechanism for business processes defined in an execution optimised business process language. BPMN provides a rich set of semantics that provide a tool for capturing the complexity of an information rich SOA development project. This modelling notation contains notations and semantics for capturing workflows or sequences of activities, decision points and prerequisites, information transformation and flows, collaborations among multiple entities and actors. BPMN is a compelling choice for modelling and document SOA development projects for the following reasons:

- It is an intuitive and expressive process-centric visual notation, which has precise semantics.
- BPMN is supported with an internal model that enables the generation of executable Business Process Execution Language processes. It also maps to other process notations such as XPDL [WfMC 2008].
- Its event and temporal notation lends itself naturally to SOA's event driven design.

An important characteristic of BPMN is that it is not only a modelling notation but also provides a mapping that generates execution definitions in BPEL that can used to implement the modelled business processes. As such, BPMN positions itself as a bridge between modelling and execution, and between business analysts and systems developers and programmers that support the business.

The purpose of this chapter is to provide readers with a reasonable understanding of BPMN so that they are able to follow the notation and understand the BPMN examples given in Chapter 16, which deals with the design and development of SOA based applications.

In the following subsection we shall examine a number of essential BPMN constructs that process analysts and designers need to understand in order to create SOA based models.

15.4.1 BPMN constructs

BPMN specifies a single business process diagram, called the *Business Process Diagram* (BPD), which is a diagram designed for use by the people who design and manage business processes. BPD provides a summary of the BPMN graphical elements and their relationships. This diagram is easy to use and understand, offers the expressiveness to model complex business processes, and can be naturally mapped to business execution languages.

A business process diagram is defined as a series of events and activities connected by sequence flow, where the direction of the sequence flow arrowheads determines the order of the sequence. The purpose of this section is not to serve as an exhaustive description of BPMN. We shall rather examine the essential BPD constructs that readers need to understand in order to create BPMN processes. We shall therefore examine a series of graphical constructs that include events, activities, sequence and message flows, gateways and associations, which comprise a BPD. For a more detailed description of the BPMN language we refer readers to [OMG 2008], which focuses on the BPMN 1.1 notation and symbols used in this book.

Events: A basic BPMN process has a start event, one or more activities, and an end event. An event is the first basic element of BPMN. As usual an *event* signifies the occurrence of an important incident that happens during the course of a business process. Events affect the flow of the process and usually have a cause (trigger) or an impact (result). An event in BPMN is represented by a circle with open centers to allow internal markers to differentiate different triggers or results. There are three types of event, based on when they affect the flow: start, intermediate and end events. There are also two kinds of intermediate message events–one kind responsible for reception of messages (*catching*) and one kind responsible for sending messages (*throwing*). Start events can only react to (*catch*) a trigger while end events can only create (*throw*) a result. Intermediate events can catch or throw triggers.

Activities: An activity is the second basic element of BPMN. An *activity* is a generic term for work that a business process performs and is represented by a rounded corner rectangle. An activity can be atomic or non-atomic (compound). An atomic activity, also known as a task, performs a single action. A compound activity, also known as a process, has its own set of atomic or compound activities, as well as events, gateways and all other BPMN constructs. Processes can be nested and thus spawn children that are referred to as sub-processes. Finally, tasks are the lowest level processes, which cannot be further decomposed. A compensated activity is one that has special compensation logic attached to it to revert (undo) its effects. Processes are contained within a *pool* construct.

Gateways: A *gateway* is the third basic element used to determine traditional flow decisions, as well as the forking, merging and joining of paths and is represented by the familiar diamond shape.

Flow objects in BPMN (events, activities and gateways) are connected together in a diagram to create the basic skeletal structure of a business process. There are three types of connecting objects that provide this function: sequence flows, message flows and associations.

Sequence flow: A *sequence flow* is used to indicate the sequence in which activities will be performed in a business process. It is represented by a solid line with a solid arrowhead connecting source and target activities, events or gateways.

Message flow: A *message flow* is used to show the flow of messages between two separate process participants (business entities or business roles) that send and receive them, and is represented by a dashed line with an open arrowhead. In BPMN, two separate pools in a BPD will represent the two participants.

Associations: An *association* is used to associate data, text, and other artifacts with flow objects and is represented by a dotted line with a line arrowhead. Associations are used to show the inputs and outputs of activities. A directional association is often used with data objects to show that a data object is either an input to, or an output from, an activity.

15.4.2 Notation

The BPMN diagrams in Figures 15.7, 15.8 and 15.9 in the following subsection showcase the notational conventions of BPMN. The main conventions in these three figures are the following:

- Small rounded boxes are called activities.
- Circles containing an envelope symbol are inbound events. Events are asynchronous service operations that a process provides to its clients. A message arrives from a participant and triggers the event. When used to *catch* the message, then the event marker will be unfilled (white). Message intermediate events can be used for sending messages to a participant. When used to *throw* the message, the event marker will be filled (dark).
- Deferred choice, also known as an event pick, uses a diamond containing an inscribed star (known as an event based gateway) with arrows leading to a set of intermediate events.
- Workflow constructs, such as split and join patterns, are represented in BPMN by means of gateways, which represent common programming control structures as *if-then, switch, all* and *parallel execution.*
- The diamond containing an X symbol is an exclusive data gateway, which operates like an XOR split.
- The diamond containing a + symbol is a parallel gateway that provides a mechanism to synchronise parallel flow and to create parallel flow.

15.4.3 BPMN examples of use

In what follows, we shall illustrate various additional BPMN constructs that can help model SOA based applications using a number of examples based on the AVERS case study.

Example 15.2: Processing a CheckInventory activity

Figure 15.7 illustrates the processing of a *CheckInventory* activity. This example is based on a data based exclusive OR gateway, which uses an *if-then-else* and *switch* constructs with mutually exclusive properties as a control structure. In the split mode the exclusive OR gateway evaluates a separate condition for each of its outgoing paths and lets through the first one whose condition evaluates to true. All other paths are discarded. In the join mode the exclusive OR gateway lets through the first incoming path and ignores all others.

Figure 15.7 illustrates that a FinalizeOrder activity can be reached when either of the activities PlanForFutureDelivery or ClaimInventory completes successfully.

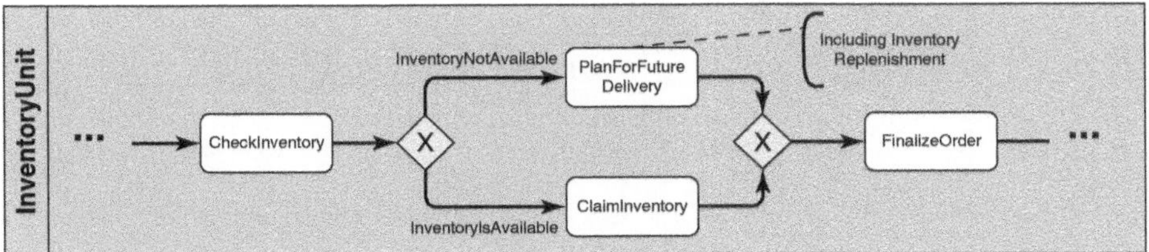

Figure 15.7 BPMN example of a data based exclusive OR gateway

Example 15.3: Confirming orders

The example in Figure 15.8 shows the process of order confirmation based on the concept of a deferred choice (event pick) gateway. This pattern represents a type of exclusive decision, where the intent is to wait for one of the process events to occur, execute its activities, and ignore all other remaining events.

In this example the gateway lets through the branch having the first triggered event, e.g. ReceiveOrderConfirmation and continues with the following event ReceiveShipmentArrivalDate. In this example the ReceiveOrderRejection event is ignored.

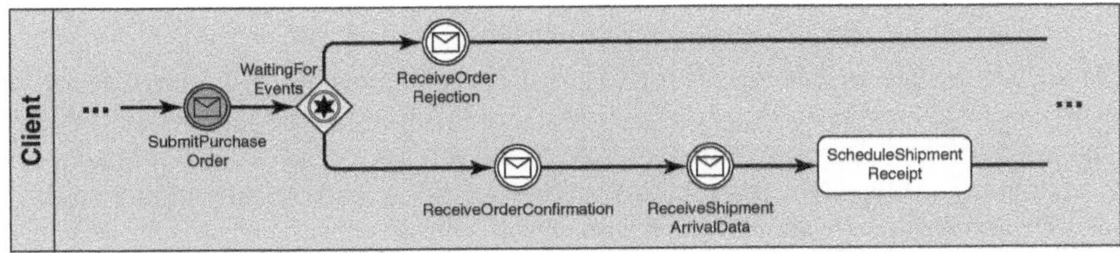

Figure 15.8 BPMN example of an event based exclusive OR gateway

Example 15.4: Reserving inventory and confirming orders

The example in Figure 15.9 shows the process of reserving inventory, scheduling release dates and order confirmation based on the concept of the parallel split pattern

The BPMN diagram in Figure 15.9 uses a gateway element to model split and join patterns, which represent common programming control structures such as *if-then, switch,*

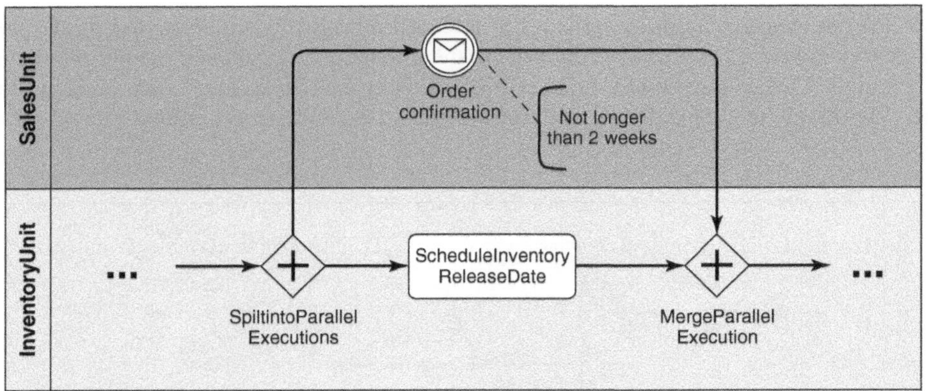

Figure 15.9 BPMN example of a parallel gateway

and *all*. In the split mode, it lets through each outgoing path. In the join mode, it blocks until each incoming path completes. This means that in this example ReserveInventory and ConfirmOrder are executed in parallel and only once both are complete is the order consolidated.

Flow objects and connectors can be used to specify BPMN process models at a high level of detail for documentation and communication purposes, as shown in Figure 15.8. Swimlanes are used as a mechanism to master complexity and organise activities into separate visual categories in order to illustrate different functional capabilities or responsibilities.

Example 15.5: Order processing involving logistics, inventory and sales

BPMN provides the swimlanes with two main constructs (pools and lanes), which are used to model and represent fairly complex services involving a number of actors involved in an inter-participant process. A pool represents the activities of a participant in a process, e.g. a company, while a lane represents a subdivision of the participant within a pool, e.g. often a department or division within a company.

Figure 15.10 shows two pools (supplier and client) and three lanes (logistics unit, inventory unit and sales unit) for a variant of the AVERS order processing application. Here, we assume that the supplier company is subdivided into three departments, logistics, inventory and sales. Message flow in the form of dashed lines is used to show inter-participant communication, i.e. from a client to a supplier and back. A pool also acts as a graphical container for partitioning a set of activities from other pools, usually in the context of e-Business applications.

Figure 15.10 illustrates that a lane is a sub-partition within a pool, for instance the logistics and inventory lanes within the supplier pool, which extends the entire length of the pool, either vertically or horizontally. Lanes are used to organise and categorise activities.

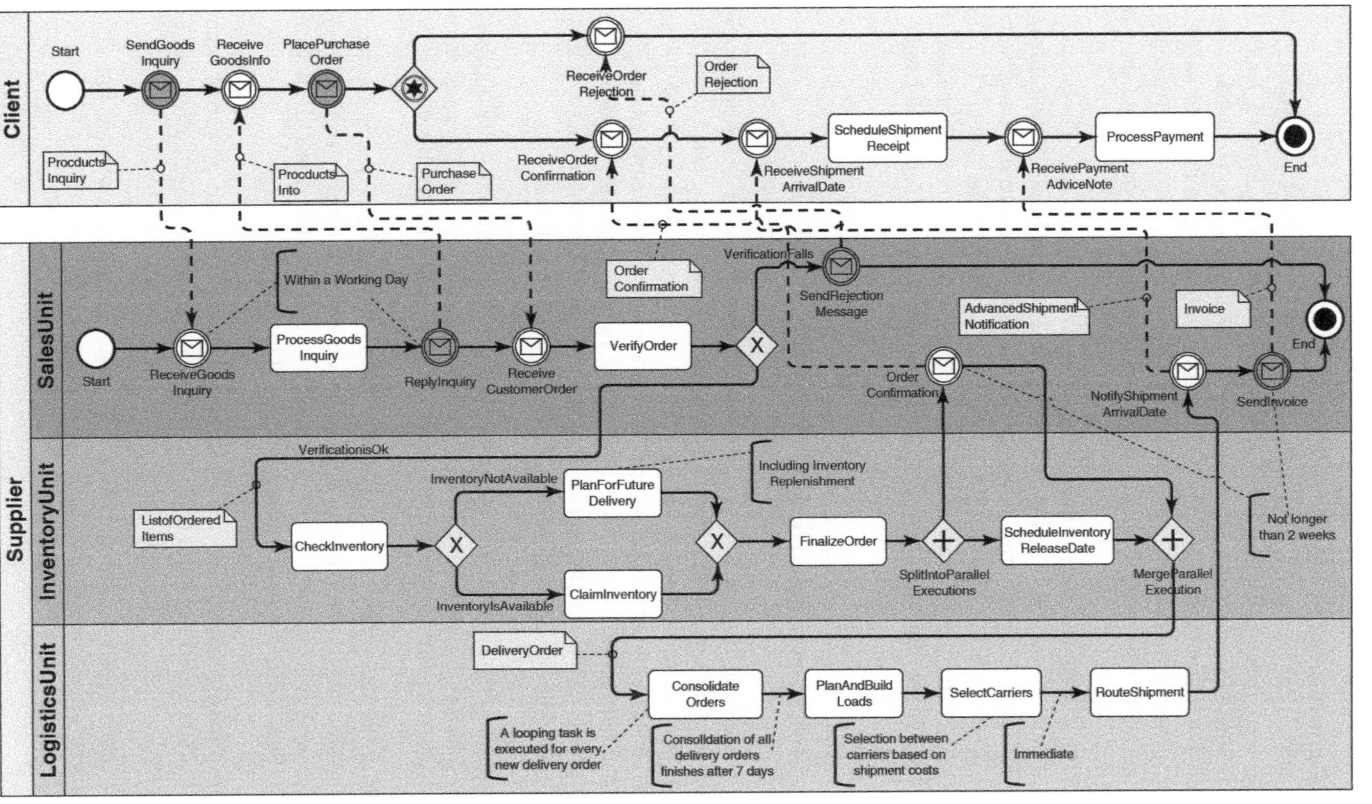

Figure 15.10 Comprehensive BPMN example including pools and lanes

In the application modelled in Figure 15.10 computation begins when the client sends a goods inquiry to the sales unit of the supplier. Computation ends when the client receives the invoice and processes payment.

It is noteworthy that Figure 15.10 depicts the most basic BPMN constructs. It contains data and event based exclusive OR gateways as shown in Figures 15.7 and 15.8. For instance, in the data based case when inventory is checked and is available it is then reserved, otherwise future delivery is planned and the order ends. In the data based case when an event *submit-purchase-order* occurs the process waits for one of the two catching events – *receive-order-rejection* or *receive-order-confirmation* – to occur and then shipment is scheduled.

Figure 15.10 also contains the use of parallel gateways that are employed in Figure 15.9. It also shows the use of activity looping in activity ConsolidateOrders, which displays a small looping indicator at the bottom centre of the activity. This activity uses a standard loop where the loop condition is evaluated before the activity, just like a *while* loop. This means that orders will be consolidated as long as they arrive. Finally, notice the use of data objects such as purchase orders, advanced shipment notices, delivery orders and so on.

15.5 Summary of learning objectives

The principal goal of business process models is to provide means of describing business processes in terms of business activities and collaborative behavior. Detailed business process models allow analysts to visualise, analyse and improve processes, so that SOA based applications are tested and improved before design and eventual implementation.

Process modelling is greatly assisted by process reference models as they provide detailed descriptions of the common characteristics or general process structures that can be applied to numerous instances within a specific application domain.

- The Supply Chain Operations Reference Model is a standardised, supply chain reference model designed specifically to enable companies to analyse and improve their supply chain process operations and measure performance objectively.

Business analysts and managers cannot use BPEL for business process modelling purposes, as it provides too many intricate technical details that are very hard for them to understand. The solution is to develop a graphical notation for describing SOA applications in the abstract, which is easy to understand at all levels.

- The Business Process Modeling Notation is an intuitive yet powerful notation that was developed for modelling business processes in accordance with SOA principles.
- BPMN can be used by users, business analysts and process owners but also by technical service architects and developers, alike.
- BPMN provides automatic transformation to executable BPEL code.

Review questions

- Explain what the terms modelling, modelling methodology, and business process modelling mean. Why is a modelling methodology important for SOA based applications?
- What is the purpose of a modelling notation?
- What is the United Nations Centre for Trade Facilitation and Electronic Business (UN/CEFACT) Modeling Methodology? What are the general phases that a process methodology used in UMM recognises that any software engineering or e-Business project must pass through over the course of time?
- Briefly describe the Supply Chain Operation Reference business process methodology. What are the five main processes that guide supply chain members using the SCOR methodology?
- Describe the five broad levels into which the SCOR methodology is divided. Why do business analysts need to differentiate between SCOR specific and company specific levels?
- What is the Business Process Modeling Notation and what are its goals? What are the main elements of BPMN and how can these assist in modelling business processes?

Exercises

15.1. Use the five levels of the SCOR methodology illustrated in Figure 15.5 to define core processes focused on inventory planning in geographies and on-order assignment of a hypothetical manufacturing company. The modelling solution should offer to customers of this manufacturer better flexibility and delivery responsiveness, with risks minimised by reducing cancellation windows and inventory exposure. To achieve this the modelling project should concentrate on two primary objectives. The first objective is to enable short lead time distribution options by implementing scalable processes and tools for managing geographic inventory levels through min-max control limits, daily review, scheduling replenishment shipments, and assigning customer orders to the best point of supply based on lead time and availability. The second objective is to improve the delivery planning and execution match between the semiconductor manufacturer and the transportation supplier's distribution network. This is intended to provide required delivery capability and reliability in meeting customer commitments by improving planning of throughput time and operating calendars, and by changing carrier contracts and execution to the delivery date requested by the customer.

15.2. Extend the solution to the previous assignment by introducing qualitative and quantitative measurements (metrics) that assist business analysts in determining the performance of the inventory planning application. Explain how this project can offer the manufacturer substantial benefits, including improved customer responsiveness and reliability, delivery performance, and factory agility focused on building the right product.

15.3. Use BPMN to model an SOA incident management application. The incident management application helps a customer relations team respond quickly and concisely to customer inquiries, ensuring that customers are taken care of. In this application we assume that a software manufacturer is triggered by a customer requesting help from their account manager because of a problem in a purchased product. First of all, an account manager should try to handle that request on their own and explain the solution to the customer, if possible. If not, the account manager will hand over the issue to a support agent, who will hand over to a software developer, if necessary. The software developer should figure out if the customer can fix the problem on their own or they need the developer's opinion. At the end the account manager will explain the solution to the customer.

15.4. Use BPMN to model an SOA automobile insurance claims processing application. This application starts by recording a claim and formulating a claim description. After the claim is evaluated, if it is accepted it is necessary to calculate the insurance sum awarded. If the insurance sum is fairly large then checking the customer's prior history with the insurance company is necessary. This action requires access to a customer relationship management system to ascertain the customer's trustworthiness. If this examination is unproblematic, then the insurance company asks a financial institution to transfer the funds that cover the estimated damage. Otherwise, compensation is not approved on the account of the customer's record and a compensation fee needs to be negotiated.

15.5. Use BPMN to model an SOA company loan processing application from an access right perspective. The application determines the level of risk for a loan and then, depending on the calculated risk, routes the loan request through a series of human tasks and/or automated processing. It assumes that, once a company loan request has been received, a credit broker first checks the customer's banking privileges status. If the privileges of the customer are not suspended for any reason, the credit broker accesses the customer information and checks if all loan conditions are met. Next, a loan threshold is calculated, and if the threshold amount is, say, less than \$1M, a processing clerk checks the credit worthiness of the customer. The processing clerk examines the credibility status of each client and automatically designates the status of each application. This status verdict is an approval or denial of the particular client's application. Next, the processing clerk initialises the loan form and approves the loan, if appropriate. If the threshold amount is exceeded, a supervisor should then perform the same activities instead of the processing clerk. Finally, a manager evaluates the loan risk, normally signs the loan form and sends the form to the customer to sign.

15.6. Use BPMN to model an SOA travel planning application that packages airline, hotel chain, travel agent, tour operator and car rental company offerings to create turnkey products. Users who want to book a travel package could use the booking system of an on line travel agency, and submit their travel specification to it. This system compares different airline offerings and chooses the airline ticket best suited to the travel specification (i.e. price range, departure date and time). It may then dynamically suggest a hotel and car rental for the same dates. Entertainment, dining and weather services can also be included in the package, if the travel specification calls for it. Tracking and adjusting travel plans due to unexpected events usually involves a lot of coordination work. For instance, in the case of a flight cancellation the airline booking service can automatically book a suitable replacement flight and the hotel and car rental service can be notified of a later arrival time. Subsequently, the hotel and car rental services automatically adjust the hotel and rental schedule, respectively. When all of these service interactions have been completed, and the new adjusted travel schedule is available, the traveller is notified by sending an updated itinerary.

CHAPTER 16

SOA development lifecycle

Learning objectives

SOA is not simply about deploying software. It also requires that organisations evaluate their business models, come up with service oriented analysis and design techniques, service deployment and support plans. Since SOA is based on open standards, and is frequently realised using Web services, a sound SOA development methodology is required for this purpose.

This chapter provides an overview of the methods and techniques that can be used in SOA based application development. The aim of this chapter is to examine an SOA development methodology and review the range of elements in this methodology. After reading this chapter you will gain an in depth understanding of the following key SOA design and development concepts:

- The nature of software development methodologies.
- Differences between conventional and service oriented development methodologies.
- Best practices for developing SOA based applications.
- Reference models for SOA development.
- Guiding principles of service oriented design and development.
- Phases in the SOA development lifecycle.
- SOA analysis and design techniques.
- SOA implementation techniques.
- SOA governance.

Chapter preview

This chapter, concentrates on the principles behind enabling SOA based applications – namely reducing the complexities involved in software development and defining processes as services that have well defined interfaces. It continues where the previous chapter left off by introducing software development activities and models. Subsequently, we describe the elements of, and the best practices for, SOA application development and present a reference model and principles for SOA based development. Finally, we elaborate on the SOA development lifecycle, its phases and the procedures used to oversee and control the adoption and implementation of an SOA in accordance with recognised principles, practices and regulations.

16.1 Unravelling the nature of SOA based applications

As we already noted in Section 1.7, SOA is an approach to architecting service-based applications that is specifically centreed on the concept of software services. SOA views services as a collection of independent mix-and-match entities (functions or typically business processes) that may reside on different machines (including geographically separated ones), and that are possibly under the control of different service providers. Services can be reused and abstracted from existing systems, built from scratch, or even leveraged from outside the enterprise.

In this chapter we shall use the generic term *service* to refer to both (Web) services and business processes. However, we shall make an exception and refer explicitly to atomic or discrete services when there is a need to emphasise the atomic nature of services. Similarly, we shall explicitly use the term *business process* when we wish to emphasise the assemblage of related services into a well defined business task.

When individual services are available as discrete building blocks that accomplish a well defined business task, such as order management, provisioning, billing, inventory control and the like, enterprises have the ability to use them or compose and group them differently to create new capabilities, such as customised ordering, customer support, procurement and logistical support processes. It is only when enterprises focus on the modelling, analysis, and specification of business processes for achieving their needs that the full potential of SOA is realised. True SOA development should impose a methodological process oriented thinking and an associated architected approach to designing and deploying services, some of which may cross-organisational boundaries.

Example 16.1: An SOA Sales Management application

Figure 16.1 exemplifies the points raised earlier by illustrating a sample SOA based application developed on the basis of our case study. This SOA application is referred to as *customised sales management* and will be used as a running example throughout this chapter. The purpose of this and every SOA based application is to be used as the instrument to reuse, compose and deliver services in order to address business priorities and integration

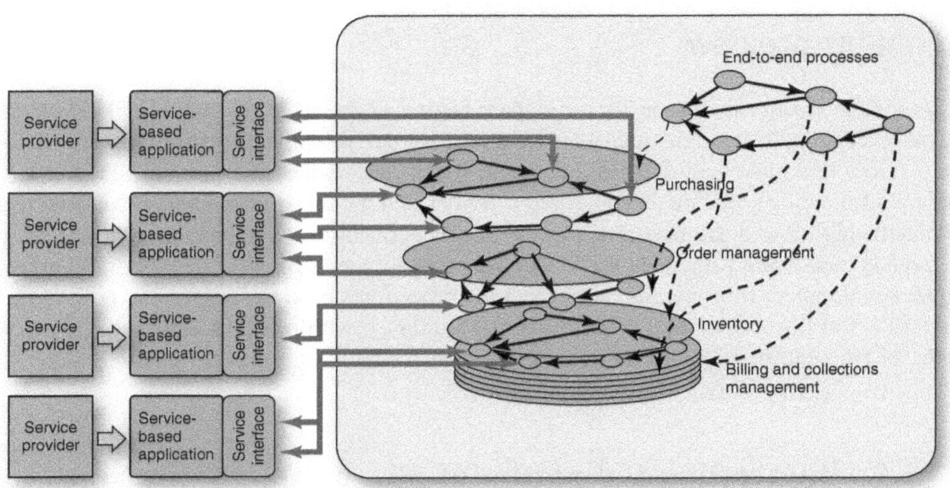

Figure 16.1 SOA based sales management application

needs. The SOA based customised sales management application in Figure 16.1 combines four automated independent business processes: Purchasing, Order Management, Inventory, Billing & Collections Management processes. These are arranged in a workflow to create a comprehensive SOA application. Here, we assume, as usual, that service providers supply the individual processes in the form of software services.

The `Order Management` business process in this application is responsible for accepting and issuing orders and deals with pre-order feasibility determination, credit authorisation, order issuance, order status and tracking, customer update on order activities and customer notification on order competition. It can also perform order volume analysis, margin analysis, sales forecasting and demand forecasting across any region, product or period. The `Purchasing` process in the same figure provides purchase order details (quantity, unit price and extended price) according to purchase order, vendor, buyer, authoriser, inventory item, any chart of accounts combination, and non-invoiced receipts. In this way, purchasing departments are able to research purchases made through blanket orders, planned orders and standard purchase orders, and can also analyse vendor performance, lead time based on the *promised-by* date, and the *need-by* date. The process can also help analyse goods received and invoice received, and *shipped item* costs for distribution to charged accounts. The Inventory process in this SOA based application helps track the amount of inventory on hand and expected arrival of items, and monitors the movement of physical inventory. It also helps analyse inventory transactions through various accounts, warehouses and sub-inventories, as well as tracking inventory on hand, by warehouse, across the organisation at any point in time. Finally, the `Billing & Collections Management` process encompasses creating and maintaining a customer's billing account, sending bills to customers, processing their payments, performing payment collections, and monitoring the status of the account balance.

Bolting together services offered by diverse service providers into service assemblies, and automating the flow of these services to provide end-to-end business processes, achieves the business value of creating a novel application, such as an automated sales management application depicted in Figure 16.1. The technology building blocks in an SOA based application such as this one are normally provided by services that have a published interface so that they can be discovered and can communicate with each other.

The maturing of Web service standards and technology provides a mechanism for SOA to be successfully deployed. In fact service composition, which is the cornerstone of SOA based applications, is vastly simplified by the use of standards that allow a common way for services to communicate effectively, so that an enterprise is able to free itself from the constrictions of having to manage business processes as defined by conventional software applications. This constitutes by no means a technology driven approach, as it is largely a matter of developing a conceptual architecture within which business problems can be defined, and solutions can be implemented in a coherent and repeatable way, exploiting reusable services.

16.2 Rationale for SOA based application development

The challenge of a successful SOA implementation – and the key to achieving business value – is to elevate service enablement beyond pure technology concerns and functions. Traditional software development approaches have created a *business/IT alignment gap*. SOA efforts that are purely focused on technology implementations – be it Web services or other software development technologies - without a clear focus on technology agnostic business processes are bound to fail. The reality is that an SOA has limited value unless it encompasses disparate applications and platforms, and, most importantly, it moves beyond technology implementations, and is orchestrated and controlled in the context of business processes. In addition to concentrating on technology agnostic processes, SOA should offer a better way of designing integrateable, reusable services rather than rebuilding from scratch to close this *business/IT alignment gap*.

The SOA focus on business processes can lead to the consolidation of services and the infrastructure through improved reuse of software assets, increased flexibility and alignment with business objectives gained from implementing business processes that are composed of services, and easier integration of new and legacy systems to create business processes. To achieve such requirements and address the serious SOA shortcomings, the internal architecture of an SOA needs to evolve into a multi-tier, service based system, often with a diversified technical implementation under the guidance of SOA design and development methodologies. This diversity is the result of a very broad spectrum of business and QoS requirements, e.g. performance or security, as well as different execution and reuse contexts, and calls for a sound services design and development methodology.

SOA design and development methodologies allow an organisation to avoid the pitfalls of deploying an uncontrolled maze of services and provide a solid foundation for service enablement of IT assets in an orderly fashion so that Web services can be efficiently used in SOA based business applications. As already noted in the previous section, without a service based development methodology, projects aiming at building SOA processes are doomed to be over time, violate quality criteria, incorporate designs that infringe basic principles (such as loose coupling), are hard or virtually impossible to manage, and are likely to result in systems that are notably intricate, time consuming and costly to maintain.

From the outset of developing an SOA solution, especially when service enabling the enterprise or implementing extended enterprise end-to-end business processes, (see Section 1.7.3) organisations face the challenge of:

- where to start;
- how to identify the services that are consumed by the most critical business processes in an organisation;
- how to decide which of these services are going to add immediate value;
- how to decide how these services can be assembled into useful business processes.

In addition, organisations have to decide how the services that they offer can be managed, reused, priced and metered. All these decisions can be a daunting proposition. Consequently, the main challenge in selecting and following an SOA development methodology is to provide sufficient principles and regulations to deliver the software quality required for business success, while avoiding steps that waste time, squander productivity and frustrate developers.

This chapter documents an SOA based development methodology and the key characteristics of successful SOA implementations. It presents a set of emerging best practices for organisations considering adopting an SOA based approach and also provides insight to the key issues and potential pitfalls that need to be addressed as an organisation considers implementing an SOA. In this chapter we deal only with key issues of the SOA based development methodology but not with complementary issues such as business re-engineering and legacy transformation techniques or service change management. Good sources for business re-engineering and legacy transformation techniques are [Ulrich 2002] and [van den Heuvel 2007], while for service change management are [Yu 2008] and [Papazoglou 2011].

16.3 Typical SOA development pitfalls

Today a dangerous *difficult-to-customise, one-size-fits-all* philosophy permeates SOA development leading to brittle implementations. In addition, traditional SOA software development concentrates on a kind of *big design upfront* where the prevailing belief is that it is possible to gather all of a developer's or customer's requirements upfront, prior to coding a software solution. So despite its promises SOA has so far failed to deliver promised benefits except in rare situations, leading yet again to a software development crisis. In fact, recent analyst studies confirm the impact of such complexity on SOA software quality. To summarise the above discussion, some of the most typical SOA development pitfalls can be summarised as follows:

1. It can end up with a large number of cluttered services with no sound service architecture and with no associated coherent development roadmap.

2. Services developed for one application are found not to be reusable by others.

3. Each service interface that is applied to an existing system may simply mimic its underlying data structures and function calls and is therefore inextricably tied to it. Consequently, the granularity of the service interface may not be right for the service it is applied to.

4. The lack of governance, overall aims, agreed upon principles, reference architecture models, standards and so on, can mean service solutions developed in one area are not reused in others, even when they could have been.

Gartner estimates that in modern SOA based applications, application code and poor engineering practices cause some 60% of the problems [Cappelli 2007]. There are various reasons why many SOA applications fail today but, largely, failures are the result of service application developers employing incorrect practices when carrying out their work [Natis 2007]. For instance, many enterprises in their use of SOA think that they can port existing software components to act as services just by creating wrappers and leaving the underlying component implementations untouched. Consequently, introducing a thin SOAP/WSDL/UDDI veneer atop existing applications or components that implement Web services is by now widely practised by the software industry. Yet, this is in no way sufficient to construct commercial strength enterprise applications. Unless the nature of the component makes it suitable for use as a Web service, and most are not, it takes serious thought and redesign effort properly to deliver component functionality through a Web service.

To summarise this discussion, we observe that a common denominator in incorrect SOA development practices is the lack of a rigorous SOA development methodology and associated coherent roadmap to discipline the course of reusing existing services, designing new services and composing new services from existing services to meet demands. This is of particular concern for SOA based applications that require to be designed and (re)-configured to reflect inter-organisational collaborations.

16.4 Software development lifecycle

SOA based development requires a well thought out strategy that considers the impact of SOA and services on technology and tools, organisational alignment, business methodology and processes. Successful service oriented development results in harmonising the business processes that make operations run smoothly in an enterprise through well orchestrated collaboration among the various participants in any given business process.

Software development lifecycle is the overall process of designing and developing software systems through a multi-step process, from investigation of initial requirements through analysis, design, implementation and maintenance. All software development projects can be managed better when they are segmented into a hierarchy of chunks, such as phases, stages, activities and steps. Although there are many different models and methodologies, each generally consists of a series of well defined phases and steps.

16.4.1 Software development models

There are several models for software development, each describing approaches to a variety of tasks or activities that take place during this process. There are also many variants, on the different models, with some people breaking down the phases while others are merging them. However, they all share a common objective: to form an overall picture of how software systems are developed and brought into production. In the remainder of this section we briefly examine different software development paradigms ranging from classical software development techniques to iterative development.

16.4.1.1 Waterfall model

The simplest rendition of system development projects is the *waterfall* model. This model usually has five identifiable phases: analysis, design, implementation, testing and maintenance. Further, it assumes that all requirements can be specified *a priori* and once a phase is completed, it cannot be re-entered again. Unfortunately, requirements grow and change throughout the software development process and beyond, calling for considerable feedback and iterative consultation. Therefore, while the waterfall model offers an orderly structure for software development, it is inappropriate for large scale and dynamic environments.

16.4.1.2 Spiral model

The next evolutionary step from the waterfall model is where the various steps are staged for multiple deliveries or handoffs. The ultimate evolution from the waterfall model is the spiral model, taking advantage of the fact that development projects work best when they are both incremental and iterative, and where the development team is able to start small and benefit from enlightened trial and error along the way.

The spiral model emphasises the need to go back and reiterate earlier stages a number of times as the project progresses. It is actually a series of short waterfall cycles, each producing an early prototype representing a part of the entire project. The spiral methodology goes through successive risk analysis and planning, requirements analysis, engineering and evaluation phases. The incremental and iterative nature of this methodology divides the software product into successive design and build activities where sections of the software under development are created and tested separately. The spiral methodology should be planned methodically, with tasks and deliverables identified for each phase in the spiral. This approach will likely find errors in user requirements quickly, since user feedback is solicited for each stage and because code is tested soon after it is written.

16.4.1.3 Iterative methodologies

Iterative development stipulates the construction of initially small but ever larger portions of a software project to help all those involved to uncover important issues early before problems or faulty assumptions can lead to failure [Larman 2003].

Currently, the most popular iterative methodology is the rational unified process (RUP) whose aim is to support the analysis and design of iterative software development. RUP encourages the use of components to assemble a system [Kruchten 2004]. RUP delivers proven best practices and a configurable architecture that enables software developers to select and deploy only the process components needed for each stage of a large scale software development project. A large part of RUP is about developing and maintaining models of the system under development. The Unified Modeling Language (UML) is used as a graphical aid for this purpose. RUP includes a library of best practices for software engineering, covering everything from project management to detailed test guidance. Proven best practices for the RUP are based on the Capability Maturity Model (CMM) [Paulk 1993], which is a framework that describes the elements of an effective software process.

RUP has the principles of object oriented and component based development (see next section) as its foundation, and therefore does not lend itself readily to be aligned to SOA design and development [Zimmermann 2004]. RUP views the architecture of a system in terms of the structure of its major components, which interact via well defined interfaces. These are composed of increasingly smaller components down to a class level of granularity. In contrast, the architecture of an SOA generally comprises fully encapsulated and self describing services that interact with each other and satisfy a generic business objective that can be easily mapped to a business process modelling solution. Nevertheless, several of RUP's milestones can be appropriately adjusted and fitted in the context of service oriented solutions since it provides support for both the bottom up and top down development approaches through activities such as architectural analysis to identify architectural elements such as reusable components [Ganci 2006]. Currently, there are several RUP attempts to extend RUP in a number of places to provide guidance on the development of architectural and design models of a service oriented solution.

16.4.2 Object oriented and component based development

It is always useful to rely on experiences gained from older generation methodologies prior to introducing a new software development methodology. SOA application development has its roots in existing modular software methodologies, which emphasise a software design technique that increases the extent to which software is composed of separate, interchangeable components, called modules. Conceptually, modules represent a separation of concerns, and improve maintainability by enforcing logical boundaries between components. Modules are typically incorporated into the program through interfaces. A module interface expresses the elements that are provided and required by the module.

Two modular development methodologies that can serve as a springboard for SOA development include object oriented development (OOD), component based development (CBD) as well as contemporary business process modelling approaches. These methodologies, although useful within their own scope, cannot be directly applied to service oriented application development. However, they can assist with the service oriented development process as they provide sound practices that can support the identification and definition of appropriate abstractions within an SOA.

16.4.2.1 Object oriented development

Object oriented development is an extension of structured programming that emphasises the benefits of modular and reusable code by concentrating on modelling real-world objects, just as structured programming emphasises the benefits of properly nested structures. Object oriented development allows designers to focus attention on low level first class constructs such as classes and objects, which match business concepts, and provide modelling facilities directly to represent them.

The application of OOD results in the practice of designing rich and complex interfaces on each object, which merely serves to tie the application into a finite set of possible operating modes that are impossible to unravel. The main issue with object oriented design practices is that its level of granularity is centered on the class level, which is at far too low a level of abstraction for service modeling [Zimmermann 2004]. Strong associations such as inheritance create a rather tight coupling (and, consequently, a strong dependency) between the involved objects. In contrast, the service oriented computing paradigm attempts to promote flexibility and agility through the use of loose coupling and relatively coarse grained service interfaces.

16.4.2.2 Component based development

Object oriented development is an enabler of CBD, which offers an improved approach to the design, construction and implementation of software applications, and provides an opportunity for greater reuse than is possible with object oriented development. CBD was devised to address the shortcomings of OOD, such as failure to address large scale development and application integration problems. CBD introduces a software development approach based on first class constructs called components. A component is defined by its external specification, which is used without any knowledge of its internal implementation that could be realised by different programming languages (see Section 1.11). In fact, CBD is a set of technologies, guidelines and techniques about how business systems should be conceived, analysed, architected, designed, developed and evolved. Obviously this approach focuses on its core concept, the component, which like its predecessor the object, leads to a large number of low level interfaces and tight coupling. Essentially, the view that components are merely distributable objects, deployed on some middleware server, carries with it all the difficulties of object modelling and yet multiplies the complexity by increasing the scale of the model, let alone if models are extended across enterprise boundaries.

CBD offers valuable concepts such as the *separation of internal and external perspectives* and the motivation for both components is often expressed in terms of reusability, composability and flexibility, which is also useful for service oriented applications. However, it is quite diverse in nature from a service oriented approach for SOA development. In Section 1.11 we explained that components and Web services present differences along the dimensions of type of communication, type of coupling, type of interface, type of invocation and type of request brokering. However, in so far as development is concerned, they also differ fundamentally in the way that they approach flexibility and reusability. Services are subject to continuous maintenance and improvement in scope and performance so that they can be offered to an ever increasing number of clients. Providers achieve this by monitoring the use and quality of services and improving it. On the other hand, consumers of services have the ability to switch between alternative service implementations offered by diverse providers. The selection of a service is usually done dynamically on the basis of a set of policies. Use of installed components does not allow for the same kind of reuse and dynamic behaviour.

16.4.3 Process modelling methodologies

As we already explained earlier in Chapter 15, process modelling methodologies are useful when designing business processes, as they are used to enable application users and developer groups to adopt a common approach to specification of application requirements. When we examine most of the popular first generation business process methodologies, such as business process re-engineering, the IDEF0 – a standard for functional modelling (http://www.idef.com/idef0.html) – the DMAIC (Define–Measure–Analyze–Improve–Control) methodology (http://www.isixsigma.com/me/dmaic/), and the various methodologies of consulting companies, such as Catalysis, and those of the various vendors, such as ARIS, we find that these approach business process redesign and improvement in the same general way [Harmon 2003b]. They all analyse each new business process as if it were unique. One begins by defining the scope of the process to be analysed, and then proceeds to decompose the process, identifying its major sub-processes, and then the sub-processes of those, identifying their major activities, and so on down to whatever level of granularity the designer chooses. More interesting from a service oriented design point of view are second generation approaches to business modelling which began to emerge a few years ago. These emphasise methodologies that are based on best-in-class business practices and that target the analysis of entire end-to-end supply chain processes. The most notable methodology is the Supply-Chain Operations Reference (SCOR) Framework proposed by the Supply-Chain Council, which we examined in Chapter 15. From an SOA based perspective, the SCOR model is essentially a process reference model in that it integrates the well known concepts of business process re-engineering, benchmarking, and process measurement into a cross-functional framework, defines common supply chain management processes, and helps match them against *best practices* where deemed appropriate.

To summarise the above points, conventional development methodologies such as the ones that we reviewed so far do not address the three key elements of an SOA: services, service assemblies and flows (composition), and components realising services. These methodologies can only address part of the requirements of SOA based applications and fail when they attempt to develop true service oriented solutions while being applied independently of each other. This explains why service oriented design and development requires an interdisciplinary approach that fuses together and appropriately extends elements of object oriented and component design with elements of business modelling.

OOD and CBD can contribute general software architecture principles, such as information hiding, modularisation and separation of concerns. On the other hand, business modelling can contribute conventions that help analyse the structuring of process chains, help define amongst other things standardised business processes and operating procedures, and create a shared understanding of how a business functions so that workflow implementations are successful.

16.5 Elements of SOA based applications

Before we introduce a methodology and the key characteristics of SOA development it is useful to provide an overview of the essential elements involved in an SOA application. These are summarised and illustrated in Figure 16.2.

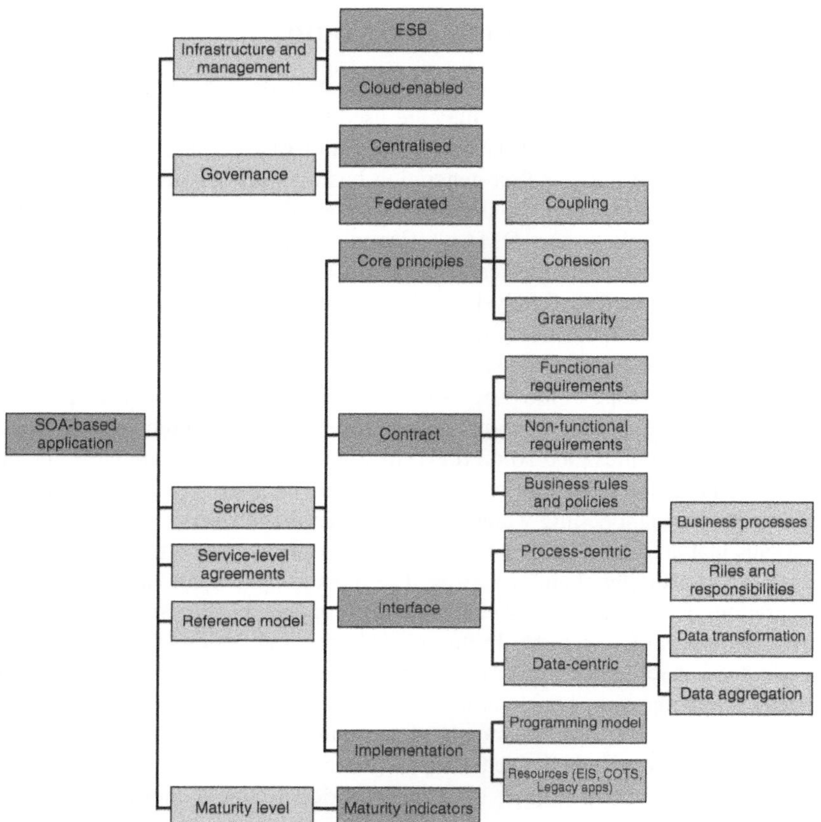

Figure 16.2 Elements of an SOA-based application

As one would expect, SOA applications revolve around services. These are, in effect, orchestrations of multiple simpler services or business processes that can be located virtually anywhere and implemented in a variety of ways. The real challenge is of course to create robust composite SOA applications out of existing IT applications and services that are cross-linked with other services from a variety of sources in a consistent and unobtrusive manner. Service composition and assembly is a factor of paramount importance that greatly determines which elements are present in an SOA application and hence illustrated in Figure 16.2.

Figure 16.2 illustrates that services comprise the usual constituent parts that we have introduced in this book, namely service contract, interface and implementation. They also follow important principles, such as loose coupling, strong cohesion and are offered to clients at the appropriate level of granularity. These principles become the major driving forces for successful SOA design. This important topic is discussed in Section 16.12.

16.5.1 Data-centric versus process-centric SOA applications

One of the most important points in Figure 16.2 is that we concern ourselves with two types of SOA applications: process-centric versus data-centric. So far we have focused on process-centric services and SOAs, but you have to understand that a data-centric SOA represents a critical application breed for many organisations where data is a critical strategic asset. A *data-centric SOA* builds an SOA strategy around authoritative data sources. In data-centric SOAs, providing a consistent, accurate and complete view of the most important data in an organisation matters most. Consequently, managing, in a single place, the uniqueness, integrity and interrelationships of organisational data becomes the most important mission of data driven SOAs. For example, if a system updates the wrong customer record with new contact information, it could affect such operations as advertising, customer relations, privacy protection, security, accounting, billing and regulatory compliance. Customers could be billed inaccurately; products and marketing collateral could be sent to the wrong address; or credit histories could contain the wrong information, causing a company wrongly to extend or deny credit. This is the kind of risk that enterprises simply cannot afford.

Data-centric SOAs usually provide data originating from various repositories or databases as a service, by bundling it together with the software needed to interpret it into a software service. Data provided as a service was at first primarily used in Web 2.0 applications and mashups [McKendrick 2006]. In this book we shall not concern ourselves with data offered as a service any further (although strictly speaking this is considered part of cloud computing, which we cover in Chapter 18).

SOA applications are normally developed under the guidance of an SOA reference model, as we shall see in Section 16.7. The purpose of an SOA reference model is to describe the important concepts and relationships in a specific domain (e.g. healthcare or logistics) and organise SOA functionality at the most appropriate level of detail, independent of the technologies, protocols and products that are used to implement the domain.

16.5.2 SOA operational control and visibility

When we consider SOA applications, *operational control and visibility* becomes an important and complex issue. This is due to the fact that SOA applications integrate multiple discrete services and/or applications that are incorporated into the SOA fabric. In an SOA application the notion of SLA is an instrument that makes it possible to exercise operational control and achieve visibility of composed end-to-end services (see Section 1.9.2). It formally specifies the exact conditions (functional, non-functional, partner behaviour, regulatory requirements, sanctions, etc) under which the services are delivered to a client.

To be commercially viable an SOA application requires the ability to create and enforce SLAs with its internal and external service providers and meet both business level QoS properties, such as on time delivery deadlines and number of active orders, as well system level QoS properties, like process cycle times and process throughput. This has major implications, as it requires that SOA application SLAs are being met in an ongoing, end-to-end manner that spans multiple providers as expected by an end client. Exercising end-to-end control of a service in a manner that satisfies the application SLAs is facilitated by the IT infrastructure that implements and manages the SOA, for instance, the ESB.

The SOA application infrastructure usually provides automated monitoring tools, which detect patterns of events that can adversely impact SLAs, in which case resources within the IT infrastructure can be automatically leveraged to meet business driven SLAs (see Section 8.5.3). As Figure 16.2 illustrates, the SOA application infrastructure can be implemented ESB technology, as we learned in Chapter 8, or cloud computing technology, which is the topic of Chapter 18.

16.5.3 SOA maturity and governance

Organisations that tread the SOA path often find it useful to benchmark their current state of SOA application maturity in order to plan ahead or to compare their products and processes with those of their competitors. A *maturity model* is benchmark for both evaluating and assessing the current maturity state of an SOA and an instrument to help chart SOA plans, and thus puts forth a realistic business and technology view of what it takes for companies successfully to adopt SOA [Moreland 2006].

A maturity model can have distinct levels of SOA maturity, ranging, for instance, from an initial opportunistic SOA pursuit, which is about doing the first SOA projects, to industrialised SOA production, which is about delivering an enterprise that is integrated both internally and with partners, and that can capitalise on new opportunities, and where services can deliver the agility demanded by business. As companies pursue the specific transition paths to SOA appropriate to their needs, they can correlate their paths with an SOA maturity model to see the organisational needs, technology needs and goals as they move up the levels of SOA maturity.

An SOA maturity model includes goals, characterisation of the scope and business benefits of each level of SOA development, e.g. cost reduction or business responsiveness, the important industry standards, key practices, and critical success factors, both technological and organisational. It provides a procedure to create a roadmap for incremental adoption which maximises business benefits at each stage and optimises processes along the way. It also provides the means for developing a value proposition and transformation roadmap to achieve a target state of maturity from a given current maturity state.

Currently, the Open Group Service Integration Maturity Model (OSIMM) provides the most complete SOA maturity model [Open Group 2009a]. This model consists of seven levels of maturity and seven dimensions of consideration within an organisation or scope defined by a project, and acts as a quantitative model to aid in assessment of a current state and designation of a desired future state. SOA maturity models, although an important element of SOAs, will not be covered in this book as they are concerned primarily with organisational, business and ROI issues. The OSIMM report is an excellent, comprehensive source for readers interested in the topic of SOA maturity.

The final element in Figure 16.2 is SOA governance. SOA governance ensures that the services and SOA solutions within an organisation are adhering to the defined policies, guidelines and standards that are defined as a function of the objectives, strategies and regulations applied in the organisation. The goal of the SOA governance is to ensure consistency of the service and solution portfolio and the SOA development lifecycle processes. One of the key objectives of the SOA governance is to support the target SOA maturity level of the organisation.

SOA governance addresses three aspects of managing SOA for the entire or extended enterprise: organisational governance, SOA lifecycle governance and operational governance (see Section 16.19). Organisational governance focuses on business alignment, which ensures the SOA implementation takes into consideration all business level agreements. Lifecycle governance focuses on the entire lifecycle of an SOA application or service, from design to development to test to deployment and maintenance. Finally, operational governance consists largely of policy management, and of enforcement and management of service level agreements.

16.6 Best practices for developing SOA based applications

We can distinguish between several important design and development practices that drive service oriented solutions and their underlying SOA implementations. Important design and development practices that stand out include: reducing costs by reusing existing functionality, minimising disruption, employing an incremental mode of integration, providing increased flexibility, scalability, operational visibility and control, as well as adherence to standards. These are examined briefly below.

- *Reusing existing functionality:* One of the major advantages of SOA is that it promotes the reuse of services or portions of system implementation in order to support a growing and changing set of business requirements. The first step in effective reuse to support SOA is the ability to service enable processes and applications, so they can be loosely coupled for reuse in new and evolved composite applications. It is important that developers have the tools, e.g. adaptors or wrappers, to build application-centric processes and quickly expose them as services. A significant question then arises about which services to build from scratch and which to repurpose to meet changing needs. This depends on the particular circumstances of the business and the scope of the existing services. Reusable services can be identified by finding commonly used services and must be implemented with special consideration for reuse. This is a topic that is addressed in Section 16.11 where we introduce the concept of service analysis. Service reusability in SOA is greatly assisted by the fact that application specific policies such as security (authentication and authorisation), SLAs, QoS and audit information are not included in the service definition but are rather configured and applied outside it using standards such as WS-Policy.
- *Minimising the cost of disruption:* Service oriented solutions and SOA implementations make use of existing, working infrastructure already in place within the organisation. Elements that are part of an enterprise integration solution, such as application servers, integration brokers, databases, messaging products and so on,

can be service enabled and used in the context of an Enterprise Service Bus (see Section 8.5.3) as part of an orchestrated service oriented solution. As SOA implementation matures, an ESB architecture will most likely provide the translation and routing of messages between different services. The adoption of specific *integration logic* functionality that enables orchestration of existing, working technology in the form of services results in minimising the costs associated with disruption of existing technologies in order to enable the creation of an integration solution.

- *Employing an incremental mode of integration:* One of the key benefits of the SOA approach is that integration can be delivered on a gradual, requirements driven basis, but yet still amount to a cohesive whole in the long term. In this way, tactical decisions can be targeted in the knowledge that the solutions provided could be combined later into an enterprise wide system. It should also be understood that the architecture itself could be adopted in an incremental fashion.
- *Providing increased flexibility:* SOA solutions provide the ability quickly and easily to evolve and adapt applications in order to meet changing business requirements and new technologies. Service oriented solutions allow designers to isolate their business processes and services from their applications, which gives them the flexibility to add, upgrade or replace applications without redefining all of their business process or service interfaces.
- *Providing scalability:* SOA solutions may be able to leverage the processing power of multiple application servers – making it potentially possible to process large applications more quickly by spreading the load of processing across many servers, see Section 8.5.7. Web service messages may arrive at high burst rates but, since they are using a queuing mechanism, they can be consumed by an application server at whatever rate it can process them. The only requirements are that, over some period of time (many hours or even days), the service can handle the average traffic load, and that the queue has the capacity to store a sufficient number of transaction messages.
- *Achieving operational visibility and control:* SOA governance is a key critical success factor for achieving sustained benefits of an SOA, helping to ensure the full architectural benefits of reuse. An effective SOA governance establishes an enterprise wide and cross-project scope that is needed to avoid overlapping and inconsistent governance models embedded within individual projects that may lead to confusion and slow downs. Lastly, SOA governance enables compliance by realising more standardised operational procedures, provides the basis for a comprehensive security solution, and enables better visibility into business operations and exception conditions.
- *Complying with standards:* Business development is being driven by the formation and rapid acceptance of key industry open standards. Standardisation leads to commoditisation, which is quite attractive to SOA based application clients as it enables agility through the ability to choose from multiple service providers which all conform to the same standards. Trying to execute a business process without relying on Web service standards and SOA based application integration

techniques would be out of the question. Compliance with standards may include business definitions, standard business processes and protocols, such as the sequencing of messages. This is a topic that we discussed in Section 13.4.

The SOA design and development practices that we have identified in this section are used to provide the basic ingredients that drive the SOA development lifecycle that we present in the remainder of this chapter.

16.7 Reference model for SOA development

When software developers are building a service oriented application, they must rely on an SOA development methodology. The methodology typically focuses on analysing, designing and producing an SOA in such a way that it aligns with business process interactions between trading partners in order to accomplish a common business goal, e.g. requisition and payment of a product, and stated functional and non-functional business requirements, e.g. performance, security, scalability and so forth.

Introducing SOA in an organisation environment moves organisations from a vertically constrained architecture to a horisontally layered approach, which embraces such abstract entities as business domains, e.g. finances, insurance, wholesale, retail, transportation, etc, and business processes that may span enterprises, right down to the level of hardware resources that are used to execute these processes.

In this section we present a layered SOA reference model that interrelates entities in an SOA development effort and helps streamline, discipline and structure the work of software professionals who aim to create successful and widely used SOA based applications.

16.7.1 Layers in the SOA reference model

SOA based development should be viewed as a distributed assembly of service interactions. Adopting a service oriented approach to solutions development necessitates a broader review of its impact on how solutions are designed; what it means to assemble them from disparate services; and how deployed services oriented applications can evolve and be managed. This requires addressing common concerns such as the identification, specification, and realisation of services, their flows and composition into processes, as well as the enterprise scale components needed to realise them and ensure the required QoS. In fact, SOA based development is facilitated when we view the way that SOA based applications operate as comprising a number of layers of abstract functionality in a reference model, as we explained in Section 1.7.4.

The reference model describes the important concepts and relationships in the domain, focusing on what distinguishes the elements of the domain, each with its own category of entities and characterised by its own set of concerns, properties and relationships. Each layer in the reference model helps organise SOA functionality at the most appropriate level of detail independent of the technologies, protocols and products that are used to implement the domain.

16.7.1.1 Navigating the reference model

The SOA reference model illustrated in Figure 16.3 is an elaboration and refinement of the SOA layers in Figure 1.5 into two major categories: the logical and physical view of SOA development. This model is independent of any specific technology implementation and takes a layered approach to SOA development. This figure illustrates that the basic SOA reference model is divided into six major layers of abstraction: domains, business processes, business services, infrastructure services, service realisations, and operational systems and IT resources. The SOA reference model provides the characteristics and definitions for the elements in each layer and identifies relationships between them. It helps in the placement of the main SOA building blocks such as services, service compositions/decompositions, service flows, QoS policies and their underlying physical resources (assets), which collectively support the development SOA based applications, on to each layer.

Starting from the top, each SOA preceding layer relies on its successor layer to accomplish its functional objectives. For instance, the business domain describes the line of business that an enterprise is engaged in. The business process layer provides the entities (namely, business processes) that collectively fulfil the functions of a specific business domain. The business process layer is decomposed into a number of business services, which are implemented in the lower level layers by reusing IT resources and legacy applications. What is important is that the SOA reference model is technology independent. However, as we already explained the implementation of business

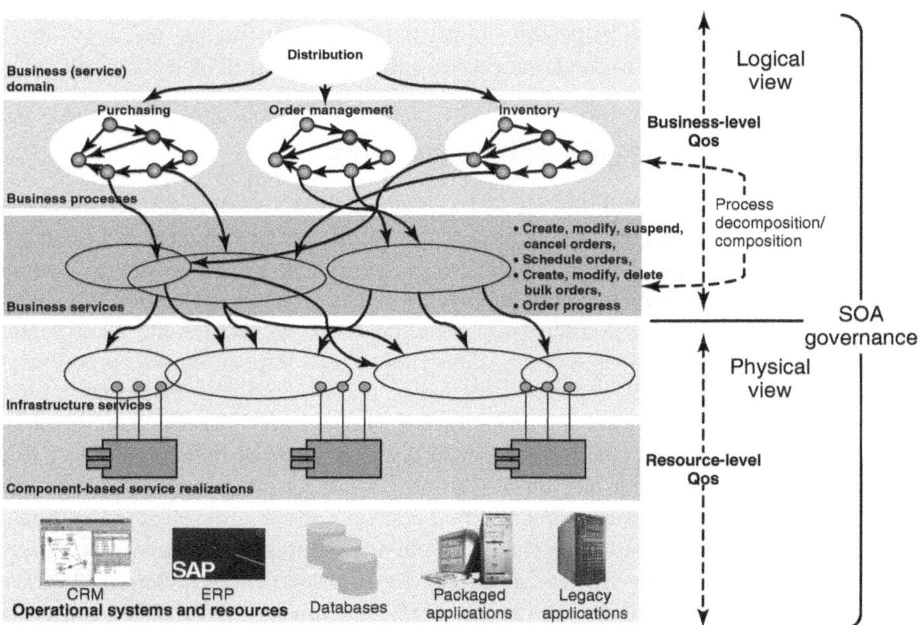

Figure 16.3 SOA reference model and functionality layers

processes and business services by means of Web services and related standards greatly facilitates SOA development.

The sequence employed in the layered SOA development usually focuses on a top down, a bottom up, or a meet-in-the-middle development approach. The characteristics of each approach is examined briefly below.

- The *top down SOA development approach* requires an holistic view of business processes and their interactions in an enterprise and emphasises how business domains are decomposed into a collection of core business processes, how these business processes are decomposed into assemblies of business services, and how these services are implemented in terms of pre-existing enterprise resources.
- In contrast, the *bottom up SOA development approach* emphasises how existing enterprise resources (e.g. databases, enterprise information systems, legacy systems and applications) can be leveraged and exposed as reusable services and building around those services.
- The most common approach for an SOA design and development methodology is, however, to combine top down and bottom up approaches, starting at each end and meeting in the middle (this is explained in Sections 16.11.5 and 16.13). This is commonly known the *meet-in-the-middle SOA development approach.*

Unfortunately in practice many SOA initiatives start from purely technology driven considerations and resources with no regard to business requirements, something that should be discouraged.

16.7.1.2 The logical view of the SOA reference model

The SOA reference model in Figure 16.3 regards SOA development in terms of two views, the logical and physical views, each of which addresses a specific set of engineering concerns.

The logical view of the SOA reference model captures the layers of business domain, business processes and business services, which we shall revisit briefly below for reasons of completeness.

Business domain. SOA development commences by concentrating on the concept of a *business domain,* which is a collection of high level, implementation independent business processes and services, which are further described in terms of their operational properties and non-functional characteristics. An enterprise may comprise one or more business domains, e.g. healthcare, HR, logistics, financials, etc.

Classifying business processes into logical business domains simplifies an SOA by reducing the number of business processes and services that need to be addressed. Such domains can be leveraged from multiple architectural perspectives, such as load balancing, access control, and vertical or horizontal partitioning of business logic. Each business domain is managed by several business analysts and developers, who are responsible for developing the business entities and technical integrations to produce business services that are shared across the lines of business (see Section 16.19).

Business processes. SOA models a business domain as a collection of business processes, which are accessible across the enterprise. Monolithic stove-pipe applications are dissolved in favour of self contained coarse grained business processes, which perform specific business functions. These processes can be invoked using a standard protocol, thus ensuring their availability across the enterprise and beyond. Business processes are important for a service development methodology, as they are associated with operational objectives and business goals, e.g. customer credit check has defined triggering (initiation) conditions for each new process instance, e.g. the arrival of an order and has defined outputs at the completion of a credit check for each specific customer.

Figure 16.3 shows that a service domain, such as distribution, is subdivided into a small number of higher level standard business processes, such as purchasing, order management and inventory. The processes in this figure are the same processes introduced in the SOA based sales management application illustrated in Figure 16.1, and their functionality was explained in Example 16.1.

Business services. Business processes orchestrate the execution of several finer grained business services to fulfill the required business functionality, and are thus the units of decomposition (top down approach) or composition (bottom up approach). Business services are operational services that represent a fine grained (possibly atomic) activity with significance to the business, e.g. creating a customer record, creating an invoice or closing an open customer service ticket. For example, the order management process in Figure 16.3 provides business services for creating, modifying, suspending, cancelling, querying orders, for creating and tracking orders for a product, a service or a resource, and capturing customer selected service details. Business analysts use the business services layer to identify critical business functions that are needed to run the enterprise, while system developers use this layer to identify and expose technical functions and realisations that match business analysts' requirements.

In an SOA the business services layer provides a kind of conceptual bridge between the higher level business oriented layers and the lower level technical implementation layers of the SOA physical view.

16.7.1.3 The physical view of the SOA reference model

In a similar manner to the logical part of the SOA development lifecycle, we may think of the infrastructure services, the component based realisations and the operational systems layers as comprising the *physical view* of the SOA development lifecycle. The physical view of the SOA reference model captures the layers of infrastructure services, component based service realisation, and operational systems and resources. This physical view of SOA development is intended to accelerate service implementation, including its numerous integration and transformation touchpoints, system management, security, networking aspects and messaging infrastructure.

Infrastructure services. An obvious requirement for the SOA reference model is that pre-existing applications should be reused to the extent possible and become addressable as services. This requires a layer of software – infrastructure services in Figure 16.3 – that understand the business service interface specifics at one end, and can accept and deliver standards based messages at the other end using pre-existing applications and systems, performing the necessary mapping in between. These technical services provide the infrastructure providing *integration and transformation* mechanisms for services through the introduction of a reliable set of capabilities, such as intelligent routing, protocol mediation, and transformation, e.g. protocol and legacy transformation, and integration mechanisms, often considered as part of the Enterprise Service Bus (see Chapter 8).

The service infrastructure layer also provides *technical* and *management services.* Technical services are required for enabling the development, orchestration, e.g. a BPEL compositions of WSDL exposed services, delivery, maintenance and provisioning of business services. Management services include capabilities that monitor, manage and maintain QoS, such as security, e.g. using WS-Security standards, performance and availability. They also provide services that monitor and manage the health of SOA applications, giving insights into the health of systems and networks, and into the status and behaviour patterns of applications, making them thus more suitable for mission critical environments (see Chapter 17).

Component based services. At the end of the day, service domains, business processes and services are layered on a backdrop of a collection of operational systems and IT resources available from pre-existing assets such as ERP, databases and CRM systems, as well as other enterprise resources. The component realisation layer provides an implementation façade where service components aggregate functionality harvested from multiple disparate, pre-existing operational systems and resources, e.g. legacy and/or acquired applications, while hiding this complexity from the business service they implement. To achieve this, components make use of infrastructure services such as legacy application transformation services, intelligent routing and protocol transformation and mediation services, security services, transaction services and so on.

Here, bottom up analysis of existing applications and systems is required. This results in component based service implementations that are candidates of reuse and may implement business services. It is important to state that business services are oblivious of service components.

Component implementation is an issue that can seriously impact the quality of available services. Both services and their implementation components must be designed with the appropriate level of granularity. The granularity of components should be the prime concern of the developer responsible for providing component implementations. An implementation component can be of various granularity levels. Fine grained component (and service) implementations provide a small amount of business process usefulness, such as basic data access. Larger granularities are compositions of smaller grained components and possibly other artifacts, where the composition taken as a whole conforms to the enterprise component definition. As we shall see later in this chapter, the coarseness of the service operations to be exposed depends on business usage scenarios and requirements and should be at a relatively high level, reflecting the requirements of business processes.

IT assets. Business operations are designed around a set of services that require IT assets, which typically include best of the breed packaged applications, custom applications and legacy applications and systems, to be service enabled.

Examples of packaged applications are Customer Relationship Management (call centre, sales force automation, campaign management, marketing, etc.), Enterprise Resource Planning (human resources, finance, contract management, etc.) or other industry specific large application suites.

Custom applications are usually developed by organisations, which prefer to create a distinct brand of software systems for their customers and partners that is significantly different than the one offered by the off-the-shelf packaged applications.

Legacy IT systems and applications are undoubtedly part of the service provider implementation of an enterprise and need to be integrated into the SOA infrastructure based on transformation techniques, such adaptation and wrapping (see Section 8.5.6).

The SOA physical view requires the providing of a consistent seamless interface to the service users (both internal and external) so that IT assets can be leveraged and integrated with other relevant services.

16.7.2 QoS considerations in the SOA reference model

SOA development requires early architectural decisions supported by well understood design techniques, structural patterns, and styles that go beyond ensuring the functional requirements highlighted in the previous section. SOA development also deals with non-functional service concerns (see Section 1.9). Non-functional (or QoS) considerations are critical for implementations structured according to SOA principles, due to the loose coupling of services and applications, and their operation across organisational boundaries.

The reference model in Figure 16.3 illustrates that non-functional design concerns are separated into two broad areas, each of which is associated with the logical and physical partitions of the SOA reference model: business level versus resource level QoS. These have significant impact on the overall design and deployment of an SOA and have enormous implications regarding how consumers accept and use business services.

- *Business level QoS* is associated with the logical view of the SOA reference model and concerns itself with SLA associated metrics distilled in key performance indicators (KPIs) that specify business application conditions and ranges. It is also associated with regulatory and legal constraints, or compliance to standards established in specific vertical industries. For instance, business related KPIs in an SLA related to the SOA based sales management application in Figure 16.1 may specify required delivery dates and conditions, shipment deadlines, pricing and payment deadlines and associated penalty conditions, conditions for grouping of orders for simultaneous execution, conditions for interconnect billing and settlement and so on.
- *Resource level QoS* is associated with capacity, performance, security and transactional integrity related issues in connection with operational systems and resources, and its objective is to match the technical capacity of a service to agreed upon SLA stipulations. This is also reflected in key performance indicators associated

with services, which specify upper and lower performance ranges (wherever applicable). Resource level QoS also describes resource utilisation requirements, physical infrastructure and resources that are needed to run a particular service, choice of specific application packages, legacy applications, and commitments to industry specific technical standards.

SOA policies and QoS considerations will be re-examined in Section 16.12.4.

16.8 Guiding principles of SOA application development

In the remainder of this chapter we shall concentrate on an SOA development methodology that focuses on the elements of the SOA shown in Figure 16.2 and the levels of the SOA reference model depicted in Figure 16.3. As already explained, a methodological approach to SOA design and development focuses on business processes, which it considers as reusable elements that are independent of applications and the computing platforms on which they run. This promotes the idea of viewing enterprise solutions as federations of services connected via well specified contracts that define service interfaces.

Two key principles serve as the foundation for service design in SOA based application development: service coupling and cohesion. The purpose of these two principles is to create services that encompass the right amount of functionality to be useful and to encourage code reuse. Service coupling and cohesion are inextricably associated with service granularity.

16.8.1 Service coupling

When developing SOA applications, it is important that the grouping of activities in business processes is as independent as possible from other such groupings in other processes, otherwise failures within the individual services tend to disable the entire SOA application. This is directly related to the degree of interdependence (or coupling) between two business processes. Tight coupled designs can be difficult to maintain, because changes in one system sub-component usually require the other sub-component to adapt immediately. Loosely coupled services are seen as a better alternative; a service failure does not disable the entire system, provided a fail-over service server is in place.

The objective is to minimise coupling for SOA development; that is, to make (self-contained) business processes as independent as possible by not having any knowledge of, or relying on, any other business processes. Low coupling between business processes indicates a well partitioned system that avoids the problems of service redundancy and duplication.

Coupling can be achieved by reducing the number of connections between services in a business process, eliminating unnecessary relationships between them, and by reducing the number of necessary relationships – if possible. Loose coupling can only be achieved when each service is unaware of its counterparts or about its environment in general. The degree of coupling is directly tied to the amount of preconceived information required from a specific service to engage its counterparts in an SOA enabled computation. As coupling is a very broad concept for service design, it can be partitioned along the following dimensions:

1. *Representational coupling:* Business processes should not depend on specific representational or implementation details and assumptions of one another, e.g. business processes do not need to know the scripting language that was used to compose their underlying services. These concerns lead to the exploitation of interoperability and reusability for service design. Representational coupling is useful for supporting:

   (a) *Interchangeable/replaceable services:* Existing services may be swapped in or out with new service implementations – or ones supplied by a different provider offering better performance or pricing – without disrupting the overall business process functionality.

   (b) *Multiple service versions:* Different versions of a service may work best in parts of a business process depending on the application's needs. For example, a purchase order service may provide different levels of detail, e.g. internal or external requisition details such as internal or external accounts, depending on the ordering options.

2. *Identity coupling:* Connection channels between services should be unaware of who is providing the service. It is not desirable to keep track of the targets (recipients) of service messages, especially when they are likely to change or when discovering the best (optinal) service provider is not a trivial matter.

3. *Location coupling:* One of the major benefits provided by SOA development is the decoupling of the client requesting the service and the service itself. SOA applications achieve this by relying on the principle of location transparency, which allows clients not to know (or care) about where a process or service is actually located.

4. *Temporal coupling:* In many cases service implementations rely on synchronous invocations. This may lead to rather tightly coupled implementations, which are sometimes viewed as shortcomings of the SOA itself. When service invocation is based on an event based or asynchronous messaging communication backbone, temporally decoupled SOA application are achieved.

5. *Message exchange pattern coupling:* A sender of a message should rely only on those effects necessary to achieve effective communication. The number of messages exchanged between a sender and addressee in order to accomplish a certain goal should be minimal, given the applied communication model, e.g. one-way, request/response, and solicit/response. For example, a one-way asynchronous

message, where a service endpoint receives a message without having to send an acknowledgement, places the lowest possible demands on the service performing the operation. The service that performs the operation does not assume anything about when the effects of the operation hold, or even about the fact that a notification might be needed back to indicate completion.

Low coupling increases the degree of isolation of one business process from changes that happen to another; which simplifies design understanding and increases the reuse potential.

16.8.2 Service cohesion

Another important principle to achieve robust SOA developments is service cohesion. *Service cohesion* is the degree of the strength of functional relatedness of operations within a service. Service developers should create strong, highly cohesive business processes, business processes whose services and service operations are strongly and genuinely related to one another. A business process with highly related services and related responsibilities, which also has a rather narrow scope, has high design cohesion.

The guidelines by which to increase service cohesion, in order of the lower to the higher type of cohesion, are as follows:

1. *Logical service cohesion:* A logically cohesive service is one whose operations all contribute to a single well defined task of the same general category by performing a set of independent but logically similar functions (alternatives) that are tied together by means of control flows.
2. *Temporal service cohesion:* Temporal service cohesion is when parts of a process or service are grouped by the time when they are processed, i.e. the parts are processed at a particular time in the service execution.
3. *Communicational service cohesion:* A communicationally cohesive service is one whose operations are grouped because they operate on the same input data or messages. Communicationally cohesive business processes are cleanly decoupled from other processes as their activities are hardly related to activities in other processes.
4. *Sequential service cohesion:* Sequential cohesion is when operations of a service are grouped because the output from one operation is the input to another part like in an assembly line
5. *Functional service cohesion:* A functionally cohesive business process should perform one, and only one, problem related task and contain only services necessary for that purpose. At the same time the operations in the services of the business process must also be highly related to one another, i.e. highly cohesive.

Example 16.2: Cohesive services for a sales management service

Figure 16.4 illustrates several examples of different types of cohesive service in the sales management business process using BPMN constructs:

- *Pricing Service:* Is an example of a logically cohesive service where a choice of operations (pricing strategies) is provided under the same pricing, with each of these strategies dealing with a different type of customer. Pricing service is also communicationally cohesive as all of its three operations use same kind of input data, the list of ordered items.
- *Inventory Management Service:* Is an example of a functionally cohesive service where all of its operations contribute to the same task *Inventory Reservation.* It is also sequentially cohesive as its operations are performed in sequence, and output of a preceding operation matches input of its succeeding operation.

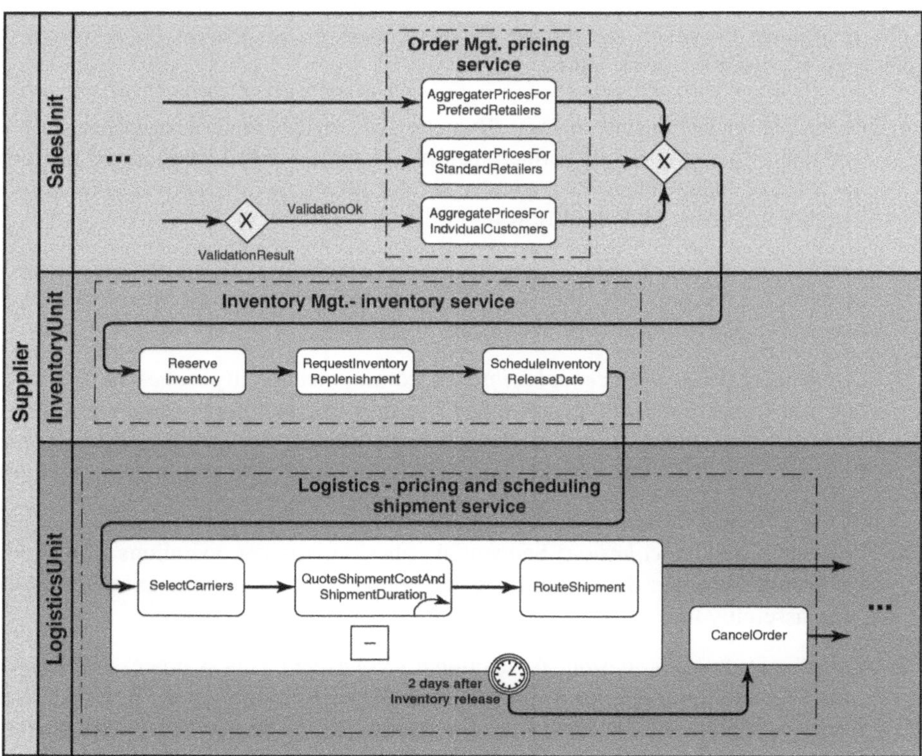

Figure 16.4 Examples of cohesive services in the sales management process

- *Pricing and Scheduling Shipment Service:* Grouping here is also based on functional cohesion. This service is also temporally cohesive as all of its operations may happen in no less than two days after inventory release.

Like low coupling, high cohesion is a service oriented design and development principle to keep in mind during all stages in the methodology. It is an underlying goal continually to consider during all service design aspects. High cohesion increases the clarity and ease of comprehension of the design, simplifies maintenance and future enhancements, achieves service granularity at a fairly reasonable level, and often supports low coupling. Highly related functionality supports increased reuse potential, as a highly cohesive service module can be used for very specific purposes.

16.8.3 Service granularity

Service granularity refers to the scope of functionality exposed by a service. Services may exhibit different levels of granularity. Services may range from fine grained, meaning that they are small in size and functional purpose, to coarse grained, meaning that they are of a larger size and functional purpose and often contain or refer to fine grained services. The granularity level of a service is critical to an SOA production environment as it affects the service capabilities, performance, and consumption rates.

An example of a fine-grained service that addresses a relatively small unit of functionality, or exchanges a small amount of data, is a service that exposes through its interfaces access to low level operations such as `ReviewPurchaseOrder`, `StoreNew-PurchaseOrder`, `SetShippingAddress`, `AddItemtoOrder`, and so forth. This example illustrates that fine grained services are services that provide basic data access or rudimentary operations. These services are of little value to business applications. Services of the most value are coarse-grained services that are appropriately structured to meet specific business needs.

Example 16.3: A submit purchase order coarse grained service

As an example of a coarse grained service, consider the service interface `Submit-PurchaseOrder` in Figure 16.5. This figure illustrates that the service `SubmitPurchaseOrder` provides a single interface and a combined, complete processing through its implementation part for all of its lower level private operations such as `ReviewPurchaseOrder`, `StoreNewPurchaseOrder`, `ApproveOrder`, and `SetShippingAddress`. This coarse grained service can be created from one or more existing systems by defining and exposing interfaces that meet business process requirements. In fact the figure reveals that the service `SubmitPurchaseOrder` contains all of the business logic needed to define a purchase order service and may combine different types of back end systems, *access right* decisions and business rules for its various operations.

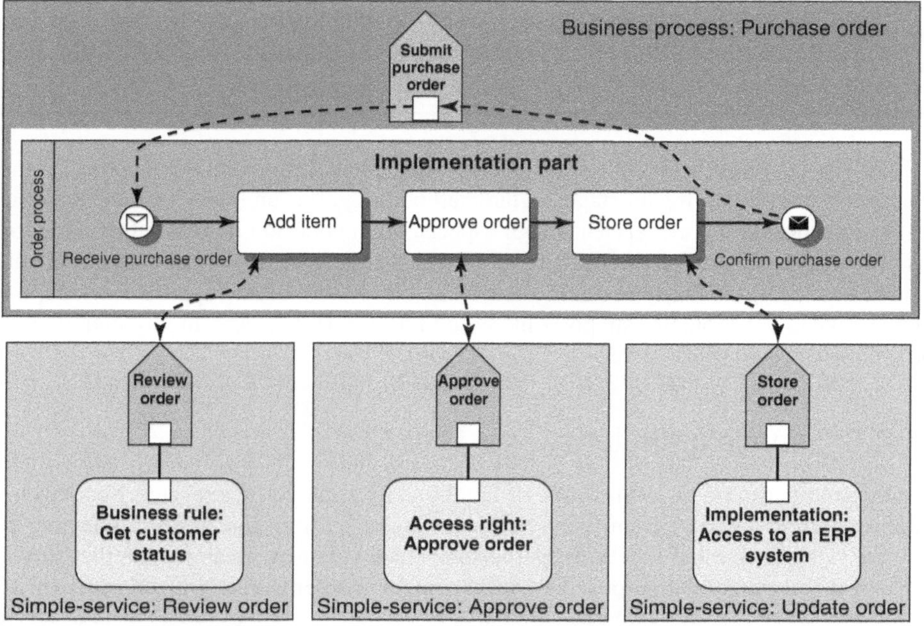

Figure 16.5 Example of a coarse granularity service

Example 16.4: Combining granularity and cohesion for a sales management service

Figure 16.6 is an example of how service granularity and cohesion can be combined to create sound services for an SOA. The `InvoicingService` and `CreditCardChargingService` are each functionally cohesive coarse grained services, `ShippingMgtService` is functionally cohesive and cannot be decomposed any further due to granularity concerns.

When SOA services are constantly deployed across the Internet the frequency of message exchange becomes an important factor. Sending and receiving more information in a single request is more efficient in a network environment than sending many fine grained messages. Fine grained messages result in increased network traffic and make handling errors more difficult. As such, using a small number of coarse grained messages would reduce the number of transmissions in a SOA solution and increase the likelihood of a message arriving and a transaction being completed while the connection was still available.

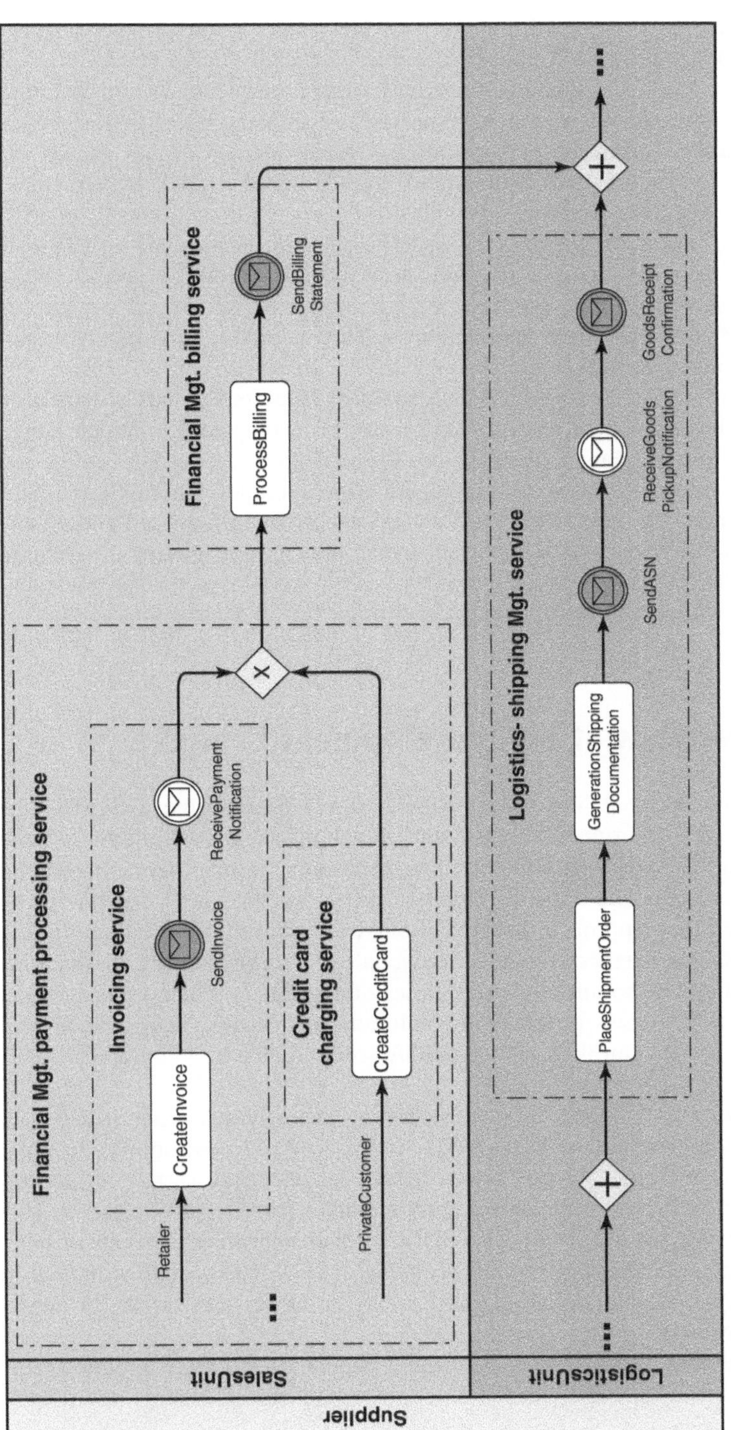

Figure 16.6 Example combining service granularity and cohesion

It can sometimes prove difficult to pick the correct granularity of a service. If the service is too fine grained, it may need to rely constantly on other services – which can lead, in effect, to tight coupling of the interdependent services. By contrast, if a service's functionality is too broad, a company can lose some of the benefits of service reuse and interchangeability. From the perspective of service oriented design and development it is preferable to create higher level, coarse grained interfaces that implement a complete business process. This technique provides the client with access to a specific business service, rather than getting and setting specific data values and sending a large number of messages. Enterprises can use an atomic service to accomplish a specific business task, such as billing or inventory control, or they may compose several services together to create a distributed e-Business application such as customised ordering, customer support, procurement and logistical support.

One approach to specifying the right granularity level for services in a top down fashion is to start with some concrete business process and decompose it into increasingly smaller services until services cannot be decomposed any further (see the SOA reference model in Figure 16.3). The more processes that a company decomposes in this way, the more they can see commonality across their services and thus have a chance at building an appropriate set of reusable services. An important criterion, when considering the formation of service during the process of granularity analysis, is that business analysts must comply with the service coupling and cohesion principles described in the previous section.

16.9 Overview of SOA development lifecycle

In this section we shall introduce an SOA development lifecycle (SDLC), a highly iterative or service oriented design and development methodology for developing, implementing, deploying and maintaining SOA applications that comprise numbers of interacting services. The SOA development lifecycle provides a continuous refinement using a closed loop approach that transitions from phase to phase in the lifecycle, providing end-to-end business process functionality. To this end the methodology facilitates designing SOA solutions as assemblies of services in which each service assembly is a managed, first class aspect of the solution, and, hence, amenable to analysis and change. Developers can then view an SOA solution as a choreographed set of service interactions.

SDLC builds on valuable lessons learned from applying earlier successful development methodologies such as RUP, CBD, SCOR and BPM, while introducing new concepts, patterns and practices of its own. SDLC has also been largely influenced by ITIL (IT Infrastructure Library): a standard approach and a framework of best practice guidance for IT Service Management (itil.org). SDLC applies appealing elements of this approach for IT Service Management (which provides a framework and operational guidelines for identifying, planning, delivering and managing IT services for the business) to SOA design and development.

SDLC provides models, best practices, standards, reference architectures and run time environments that are needed to supply guidance and support through all SOA development, deployment and production phases. It incorporates a broad range of capabilities, technologies, tools and skill sets that include [Brown 2005]:

- Managing the entire service lifecycle – including analysing, identifying, designing, developing, deploying, finding, applying, evolving and maintaining services.
- Establishing a SOA platform and programming model, which includes connecting, deploying and managing services within a specific run time platform.
- Adopting best practices and tools for architecting SOA solutions in repeatable, predictable ways that deal with changing business needs. This includes analysing existing applications to discover potential services, repurposing existing assets and functionality to extend their utility and make those capabilities accessible as services, creating new services, and *wiring* together services by connecting behaviour exposed through their interfaces.
- Delivering accurate, workable service oriented solutions that respect QoS requirements. These solutions may be implemented as best practices, such as tried and tested methods for implementing security, ensuring performance, compliance with business rules and enterprise policies, and designing for interoperability.

Fundamental to the above capabilities is that business goals and requirements should always drive downstream design, development and testing to transform business processes in a business domain into composite applications that automate and integrate enterprises. In this way, application requirements can be traced across the entire SOA lifecycle from business goals, through software designs and code assets, to composite applications.

Central to the SDLC are the SOA reference model functional layers depicted in Figure 16.3. SDLC is organised around a service lifecycle, which includes: the phases of SOA planning, analysis, design, implementation, testing, provisioning, deployment, execution and monitoring. Figure 16.7 gives a detailed view of the SDLC phases along with the main steps in each phase. The SDLC phases are traversed in an iterative and incremental manner where feedback is cycled to and from phases in iterative steps of refinement. The methodology may actually be built using a blend of forward and reverse engineering techniques, or other means to facilitate the needs of SOA applications. With each iteration the SDLC forces the development team to drive the SOA development project's artifacts closer to completion in a predictable and repeatable manner. This approach considers multiple realisation scenarios for business processes and services that take into account both technical and business concerns.

In the following we shall describe a blend of principles and *how-to* guidelines for readers to understand how developers can transition an IT infrastructure into a working SOA solution. We shall present phases that are particular to service oriented design and development at a level of detail that is appropriate to achieve reader understanding and appreciation. Conventional software development methodology activities, such as planning, testing and execution, will be described only briefly as they can be supported by traditional software development techniques such as the RUP. The workings of the SDLC methodology will be exemplified by means of the order management process that we introduced earlier.

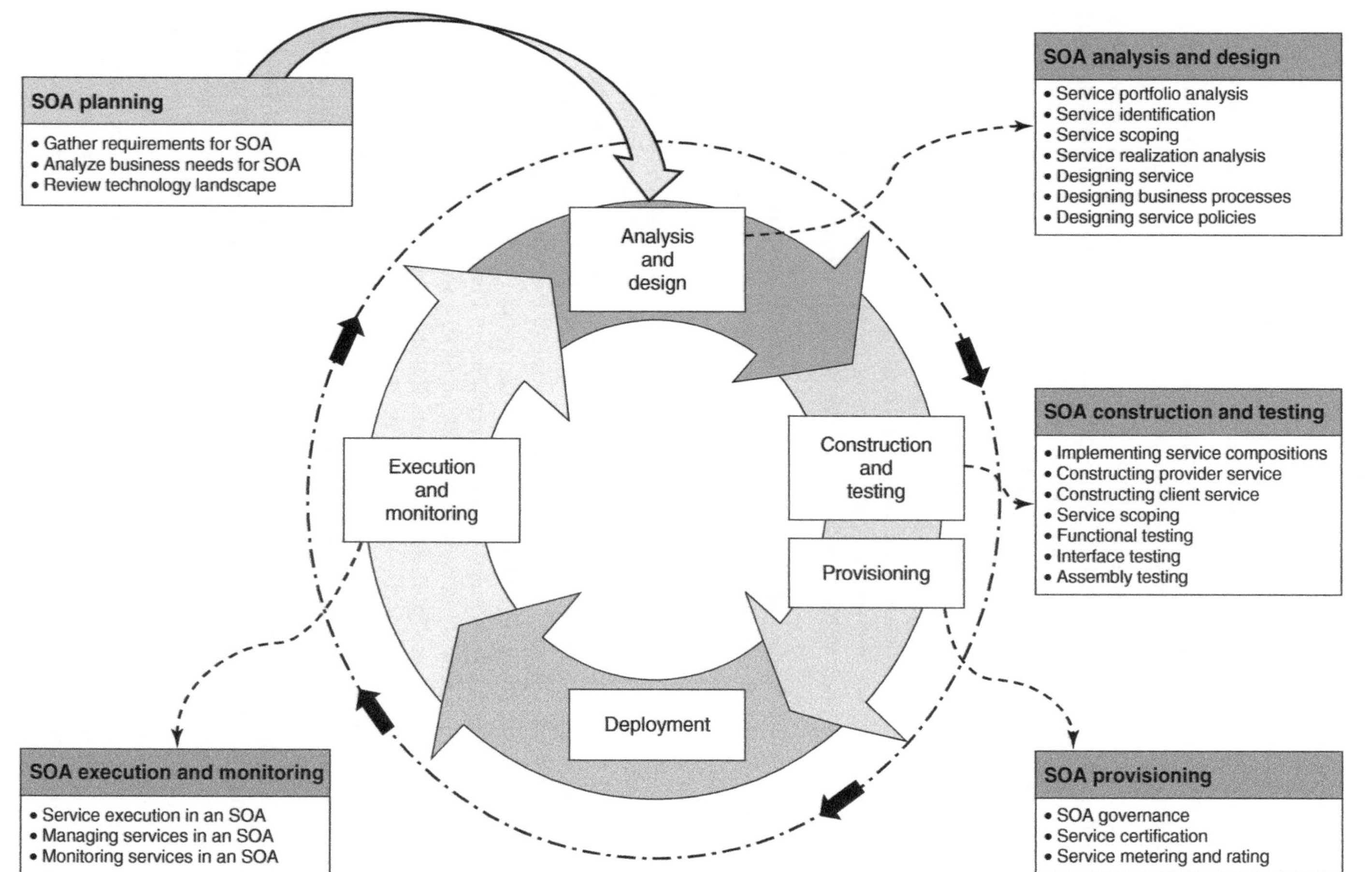

SOA planning
• Gather requirements for SOA
• Analyze business needs for SOA
• Review technology landscape
SOA analysis and design
• Service portfolio analysis
• Service identification
• Service scoping
• Service realization analysis
• Designing service
• Designing business processes
• Designing service policies
Analysis and design
Execution and monitoring
Construction and testing
Provisioning
Deployment
SOA construction and testing
• Implementing service compositions
• Constructing provider service
• Constructing client service
• Service scoping
• Functional testing
• Interface testing
• Assembly testing
SOA execution and monitoring
• Service execution in an SOA
• Managing services in an SOA
• Monitoring services in an SOA
SOA provisioning
• SOA governance
• Service certification
• Service metering and rating

Figure 16.7 An overview of the SDLC and its main phases

16.10 The SOA planning phase

The overview of the SOA development lifecycle in the preceding chapter offers advice on what phases to choose and how to develop and implement an SOA solution. This section focuses on the first phase in the SDLC, namely on how to plan for an SOA project.

The *SOA planning phase* is a preparatory phase that serves to streamline and organise consequent phases in the SDLC methodology. During this phase, the project feasibility, goals, rules and procedures are set and requirements are gathered. More specifically, this phase determines the feasibility, nature and scope of service solutions in the context of an enterprise. A strategic task for any organisation is to achieve an SOA *fit* within its current environment. The key requirement in this phase is therefore to understand the business environment and to make sure that all necessary controls are incorporated into the design of a service oriented solution. Here, an SOA project team creates the rules, processes, metrics and organisational structures needed for effective planning, decision making, steering and controlling the SOA efforts. Typical steps in this phase include:

1. analysing the business needs in measurable goals;
2. reviewing the current technology landscape;
3. conceptualising the requirements of the new SOA environment;
4. conducting a financial analysis of the SOA transition costs and benefits, including a budget and a software development plan of tasks, deliverables and schedule.

SOA planning should not result in a big bang replacement of an existing IT environment. Rather, it should result in a progressive SOA adoption roadmap [Bierberstein 2005]. A well developed view of a future SOA application and business service portfolio, clearly connected to and driven by the enterprise's business strategy, provides the context organisation's need in order to support SOA investments. An enterprise has several options for entry points into an SOA. These options identify how much the SOA model penetrates into the business and defines levels of adoption. The options are as follows [Bierberstein 2005]:

- *Early adoption:* Enterprises that want to reduce risks initially go through a technology validation and a readiness assessment for SOA adoption. This includes the ability to service enable existing legacy systems, evaluation of the non-functional SOA requirements, and the availability of appropriate support infrastructure. It also includes an evaluation of the organisational structure required to support the SOA transition in the enterprise, especially addressing skills gaps and governance structures.
- *Line of business adoption:* At this level, the enterprise will identify a line of business and prioritise processes where the agility and flexibility that SOA offers will increase business value, e.g. logistics and transportation, insurance, etc. This involves a broader initial assessment phase and the identification of key metrics and critical success factors.

- *Enterprise adoption:* This level of adoption involves the creation of a business view of an entire service oriented enterprise, with a complete prioritisation of software projects based on business value followed by an architecture reference model, such as the one depicted in Figure 16.3, and implementation phases.
- *Enterprise and partner network adoption:* At this level, not only the enterprise but also its business partners, suppliers, distributors or customers are involved. This is the level where transformation of existing business models or the deployment of new business models, insourcing and outsourcing decisions are made. SOA has the potential to enable outsourcing by enabling service providers to specialise in certain processes or take granular pieces of a process and concentrate on them, and thus create more significant economies of scale for an enterprises' benefit.

The SOA planning phase shares similar concerns and has many commonalities with conventional software development methodologies. For instance, it has many elements in common with the RUP inception phase. Several RUP aspects including service identification, existing asset analysis to identify opportunities for asset reuse and, software development best practices; and others can be used in the subsequent phases of service analysis described in the remainder of this chapter.

16.11 The SOA analysis phase

The SOA analysis phase in SDLC is based on a thorough business case analysis, whose main purpose is to identify the requirements of an SOA based implementation. This includes reviewing the business goals and objectives of an enterprise that drive the development of business processes. The analysis phase helps focus SOA initiatives by creating a *process map* that identifies business domains and a portfolio of current processes of particular interest to an enterprise. From the process map, business analysts can identify candidate business services that relate to these business processes.

SOA analysis helps centre efforts on business domains within an enterprise that can be mapped to core business processes and helps prioritise domain specific business processes and services where SOA can contribute to improvements and offer business value potential. It aims at identifying, conceptualising, and rationalising business processes as a set of interacting services. In particular, the analysis phase places emphasis on identifying and describing the processes and services in a business problem domain and on discovering potential overlaps and discrepancies between processes under construction, and available system resources that are needed to realise atomic services and business processes. It, therefore, examines the existing services portfolio at the service provider's side to understand which patterns are in place and which need to be introduced and implemented.

The objective of service analysis is to provide an in depth understanding of the functionality, scope, reuse and granularity of candidate business processes and services. Three important factors drive the service analysis phase:

- Viewing the IT capabilities of an organisation as a set of services that are assembled to meet specific business requirements. This provides better insight into how business processes can be realised.

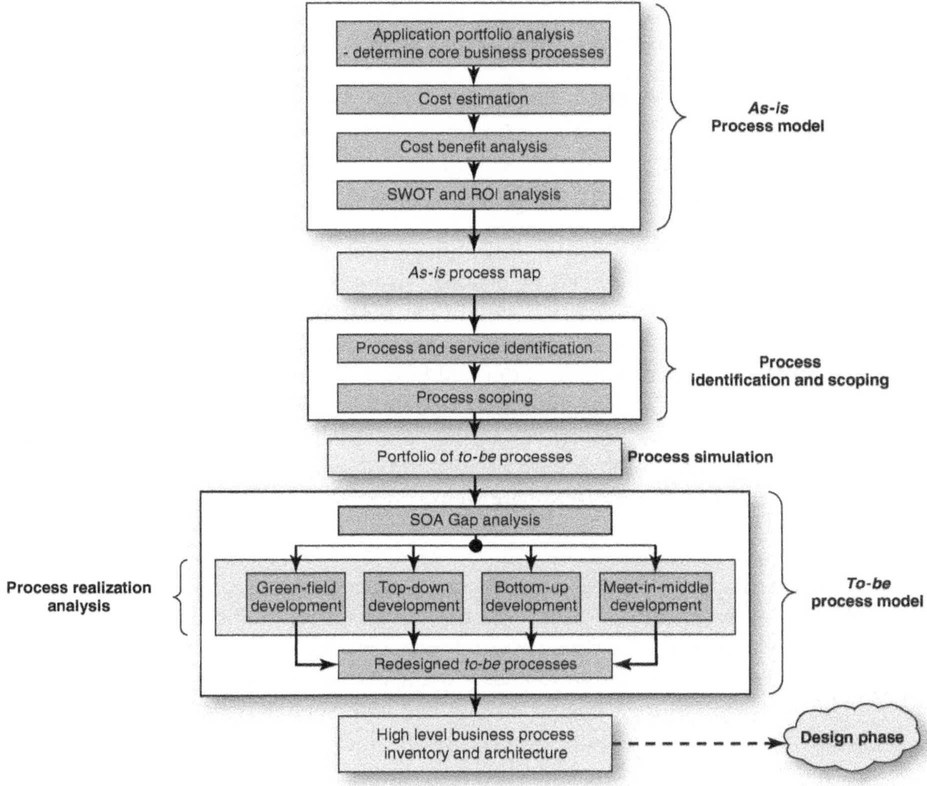

Figure 16.8 Steps in SOA analysis

- Assembling atomic services into processes, and processes into composite applications in turn, as business conditions demand.
- Focusing on organisational asset reuse and management to obtain greater business efficiency.

To achieve its objective, the analysis phase encourages a more radical view of process (re) design and supports the re-engineering of business processes. Its main objective is the reuse (or repurposing) of business process functionality in new composite applications. Figure 16.8 illustrates the main steps in the SOA analysis, which need to be performed in sequence. These are:

1. *as-is* service portfolio analysis;
2. service identification;
3. service scooping;

4. SOA gap analysis;
5. service realisation analysis.

Each of the SOA analysis steps is explained in some detail in the sections that follow.

16.11.1 *As-is* process model analysis

In the SDLC SOA analysis phase the predominant role is that of a business analyst who harvests the functional requirements of business users and provides domain knowledge. Figure 16.8 shows that during the first step in the SOA analysis phase business analysts complete an *as-is* process model. This model allows the various stakeholders to understand the portfolio of available applications and business processes.

The *as-is* process model is the present IT model of an enterprise largely based on pre-SOA technologies. The *as-is* process model can be used as a basis for conducting a thorough re-engineering analysis of the current portfolio of available software resources in the enterprise. This may involve the following steps:

1. *Current business process portfolio analysis:* Portfolio analysis requires that the applications and current (*as-is*) business processes that are candidates for re-engineering be prioritised according to their technical quality and business value. If an application has low business and technical quality it can be retired. If it has low business value but high technical quality it should be carefully reassessed. If the application has high business value and low technical quality it must be redeveloped. Finally, if an application has high business and technical quality it must be modernised.

2. *Cost estimation:* Cost estimation is a function that involves identifying and weighing all processes to be re-engineered to estimate the cost of the re-engineering project.

3. *Cost benefit analysis:* In this step, the cost of re-engineering is compared to the expected maintenance cost savings and value increases.

4. *SWOT analysis:* The preceding steps result in performing a business process strength, weaknesses, opportunities and threats (SWOT) analysis, which may reveal some processes as being significant strengths and others as significant weaknesses. This may have serious consequences for the business model of an organisation because it could allow the processes which are major strengths to become the core processes of the organisation and lead to further process in sourcing activities, while processes with significant weaknesses could become the targets of outsourcing [Jeston 2008].

5. *ROI analysis:* Before an organisation commits to any changes to any *as-is* business processes, it needs to design, simulate and analyse potential changes to its current process portfolio for potential return on investment (ROI). ROI represents the measurable, direct benefits that an SOA project will deliver to an enterprise upon completion of the project. It addresses the key benefits in terms of: operations cost reduction, revenue generation, productivity gain and customer satisfaction.

Three main activities in an enterprise may help determine ROI: the IT conversion process, the SOA consumption process, and the competitive process [Soh 1995], [Marks 2006]. The IT conversion process represents the conversion of funding and labour into creation of SOA technical assets, such as processes and support infrastructure. The SOA consumption process involves determining how customers, suppliers and internal users consume these newly created services, and how they impact the organisation by creating organisational value. The competitive process determines how the organisational value created by the SOA results in competitive advantage and better organisational performance for an organisation and its partners.

The conduct of SWOT and ROI analysis results in discerning a number of candidate business processes that have potential value for an organisation [Marks 2006]. These are evaluated in terms of reuse, business impact and organisational value, and are further analysed during the service identification step to ascertain what kind of business logic should be encapsulated in each of them.

The activities of the *as-is* process analysis step result in a portfolio of reusable *as-is* processes, which are described in an *as-is* process map. This *as-is* process map identifies processes that are part of the conceptual *to-be* process model that an SOA solution is intended to specify and implement. The goal of the *to-be* process model is to produce a conceptual model, which satisfies the current and future goals of an enterprise. The *to-be* model provides improvements and alternatives to the current situation, which is represented by the *as-is* process model. By comparing and contrasting *as-is* and *to-be* models the business analysts can determine if the existing business processes are sound and only need minor modifications, or if re-engineering exercises are required to correct problems or improve process efficiency.

16.11.2 Atomic service and business process identification

Understanding how business processes work, and how functionality differs or can get adjusted between applications, is an important milestone when trying to transform *as-is* services and identify candidate business processes, which compose atomic services. When analysing an application, business analysts must first analyse application functionality and develop a logical model of what an enterprise (or business domain) does in terms of business processes and the services the business requires from them, e.g. what is the shipping and billing address, what is the required delivery time, what is the delivery schedule, etc. The service developer may eventually implement these concepts as a blend of atomic services. The objective of this step is to identify:

- not only business processes of interest to an enterprise, but also potential atomic services that could be aggregated into a highly cohesive business process;
- in addition to the *as-is* process map, further business processes and services that are required to derive the desirable SOA functionality.

By identifying business processes and atomic services that are critical to an enterprise, it is possible to reason about those services that already exist and the services that are missing. This means that in addition to the *as-is* processes retained from the previous step, and which may be candidates for re-engineering, additional services must now be identified. This includes all new business processes and services required to derive the desirable SOA functionality. The overall objective is to create an exhaustive list of services that are potential candidates for exposure in an SOA application and then group these services according to the principles of service granularity, coupling and cohesion into robust and reusable business processes to create a comprehensive *to-be* process model.

Service identification is a top down effort that involves the decomposition of the business domain into its logical functional areas, including the decomposition of its conceptual business processes into sub-processes and eventually atomic services. The emphasis is placed now on the identification of the list of services that will ultimately constitute the *to-be* service portfolio. This undertaking leads to the formation of an exhaustive list of *conceptual to-be* services that are categorised in logical groupings. To achieve this, consolidation, composition and decomposition, reuse, simplification and re-factoring of legacy assets are taken into account.

The key factor in service analysis is being able to recognise functionality that is essentially self-sufficient for the purposes of a candidate *to-be* business process. A business process should be specified with an application or the user of the service in mind. It is important to identify the functionality that should be included in it and the functionality that is best incorporated into other business processes. Overlapping services functionality and capabilities, e.g. different services that share identical business logic and rules, is also identified and common functionality should be factored out. Likewise, related services with conflicting functionality should be analysed and dealt with. Several factors, such as encapsulated functionality, business logic and rules, business activities, can serve to determine the granularity of business services and processes. During this procedure, we must also apply the principles of service coupling and cohesion to achieve the desired effect. For instance, we may identify a sales management process and determine that it must have low communication protocol coupling with a material requirement process that we have also identified.

It is desirable to map business functionality against industry templates to identify a *heat map* of *to-be* business processes that are candidates for SOA tenancy [Bieberstein 2006]. Good candidates for business processes are those that represent commonly required functionality for standard applications, such as sales order management, credit checking and inventory management. Business process reference models, such as, for example, SCOR (see Chapter 15), ACORD (for the insurance sector), enhanced Telecommunications Operations Map (eTOM) for the telecommunications domain and so on, or business protocols such as RosettaNet (see Chapter 14) can greatly simplify this undertaking. Process identification could, for instance, start with comparing the conceptual *to-be* business process portfolio (see Figure 16.8) to standard process definitions. For instance, supply chain applications may use RosettaNet's *Manage Purchase Order* (PIP3A4) as a standard process for processing orders. This process encompasses four complementary services supporting the entire chain of activities from purchase order creation to tracking and tracing, each of which is further decomposed into multiple individual processes.

Service identification results in a portfolio of *to-be* business processes and atomic services that exhibit relatively coarse and fine granularity, respectively. These candidate services need now to be further refined by applying scoping rules to meet business analysis and design criteria.

16.11.3 Business process scoping

A business process should allow a developer to integrate a precise solution as opposed to one that provides features over and above a basic requirement. Defining the scope of business processes helps ensure that a process does not become monolithic and mimic an entire application. Unbundling functionality into separate business processes will prevent business processes from becoming overly complex and difficult to maintain. For example, designing a business process that handles on line purchasing would require the removal of packaging and shipping information, and costs to different business processes. In this example, the three functions are mutually exclusive and should be implemented separately. The functionality included in these business processes is not only discrete and identifiable, but also loosely coupled to other parts of the application.

The *scope of a business process* is defined as an aggregation of aspects that include where the process starts and ends, the typical customers (users) of the process, the inputs and outputs that the customers of the process expect to see, the external entities that the process is expected to interface with, and the different types of events that start an instance of the process. Process scoping is conceptual in nature and comprises a top down exercise beginning with the coarse grained generalised business processes and services that were identified in service analysis. Common contextual relationships of business services are identified and are grouped accordingly. The scope of the process identifies not only the issues directly related to the flow of the process itself, but also key external entities related to the process, such as users of the process, e.g. suppliers or logistics providers. As usual, services that are internal to a process should be tightly linked activities that belong naturally together.

Toolsets enable analysts to model, simulate and analyse complex business processes quickly and effectively. Such toolsets can be used to model *as-is* and *to-be* business processes, allocate resources, and perform *what-if* simulations to optimise and estimate business benefits [Brown 2005]. More specifically, *process simulation* is a useful tool to verify an existing process model, identify bottlenecks, and prepare for process optimisation. It provides the means to specify the costs of activities, resource utilisation, waiting costs and other relevant process aspects. In addition, it provides support for examining different scenarios whereby the load and behaviour patterns of activity in a process can change, while leaving the general flow of the process unaffected. These simulation models can then be transformed into BPMN to jump-start process specification activities.

Figure 16.8 illustrates how business identification and scoping interact. This step results in a set of re-engineered and repurposed high level (abstract) business processes that can be reused and are candidates for service design. The high level abstract business process model shows the services that are part of a process, as well as a limited number of well structured activities that represent the high level process flow. At the end of this step the portfolio of abstract *to-be* processes and services are of sufficient detail so that an initial, albeit crude, BPMN representation (see Chapter 15) of the candidate *to-be* process model can be generated.

16.11.4 SOA gap analysis

The natural step that follows service identification and scoping is that of assessing the gaps between the portfolio of *to-be* services and the IT resources (assets) that are available to implement them, and then putting in place a gap mitigation strategy. *SOA gap analysis* is therefore a technique that purposes a *to-be* business process and services realisation strategy (see the following section) by incrementally adding more implementation details to an abstract service/process. Gap analysis commences with comparing the portfolio of *to-be* service functionality to potentially available software service implementations so these can be assembled within the enclosures of a newly conceived business process. This step is illustrated in Figure 16.8.

SOA gap analysis tries to determine which available software assets, such as legacy systems, COTS, and ERP packages (and possible component implementations of these) can be used to construct *to-be* business processes. In particular, gap analysis ascertains which existing resources and applications (or parts thereof) can become service enabled to provide *to-be* service content.

An SOA gap analysis strategy may be developed in stages and results in a recommendation to do development work, reuse, or purchase services. There might exist software components internal to an organisation that provide a good match to implement candidate service functionality. These may include service implementations previously developed by the enterprise, externally supplied service realisations available on a subscription or pay-per-use basis, and so forth. In this way, portfolios of services possibly accessible on a global scale will complement and sometimes even entirely replace monolithic applications as the new fabric of business processes.

16.11.5 Process realisation analysis

SOA gap analysis results in a realisation plan and strategy that describes at a high level how a service provided interface could be applied to an orchestrated portfolio of existing services and SOA enabled applications. This is illustrated in Figure 16.9. Service content in Figure 16.9 can be provided in several ways: as a separate software component (simple Web service), as an existing resource that can be service enabled, or as an assembly of existing atomic services into a higher order business process. As we already explained, service enabled content may include software components such as legacy systems, custom applications, ERP packages and the like.

Process realisation analysis is an approach that considers diverse business process realisation scenarios which determine how existing asset functionality can be leveraged to realise parts of, or even an entire process in the *to-be* business process portfolio. The process realisation analysis estimates existing and expected operational costs, integration costs, service and process customisation costs, service and process provisioning costs, and architecture costs for each realisation scenario. To determine the quality of a specific asset, quality metrics are used that evaluate its flexibility, extensibility, maintainability and level of cohesion and coupling.

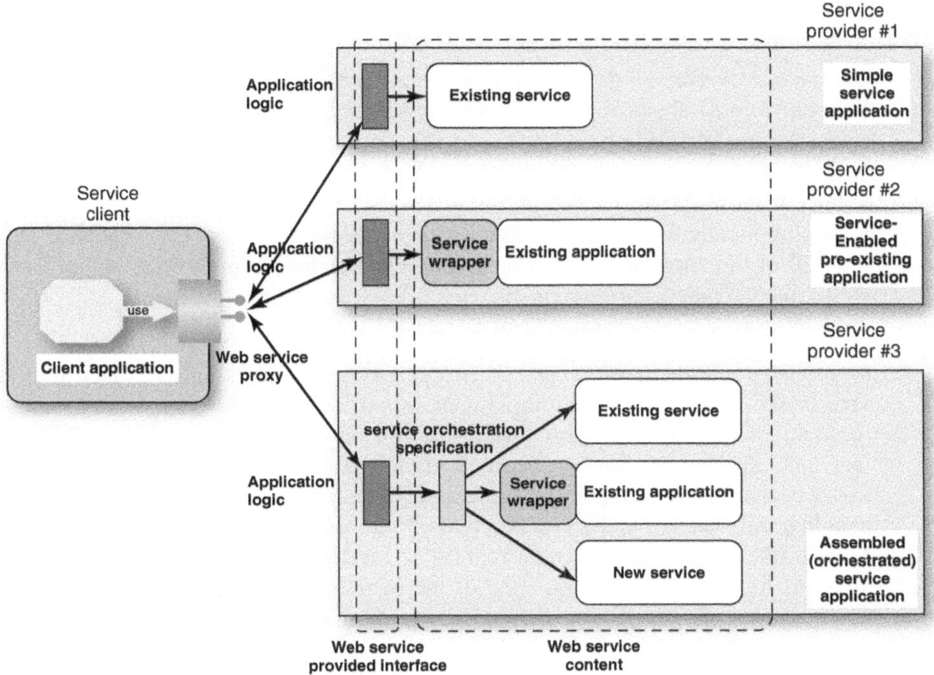

Figure 16.9 Process realisation scenarios

Service providers consider the following four realisation options (which may be mixed in various combinations) to develop new business processes [Brittenham 2001]:

1. *Greenfield development:* This step involves describing how a new interface for an atomic service will be created on the basis of the service implementation. Greenfield development assumes that first a service is implemented and subsequently the service interface is derived from the new service implementation. During this step the programming languages and models that are appropriate for implementing the new service are also determined.

2. *Top down development:* Using this realisation option a new atomic service can be developed that conforms to an existing service interface. This type of service interface is usually part of an industry standard that can be developed by any number of service providers. Processes are usually deployed in a top down fashion from a business level process blueprint. The main benefit of the top down service development is the consistency of the applications and integration mechanisms. It is also rather easy to evolve the service oriented solution across the enterprise as the industry evolves. Main problems with this realisation option are the costs involved

in development as well as the costs of achieving consensus on a high level SOA architecture throughout the enterprise [Graham 2005].

3. *Bottom up development:* SOA implementation strategy rarely starts on a green field and almost always integrates existing systems at the physical part of the SOA reference model in Figure 16.3. Using this option a new atomic service interface is developed for an existing application. The existing application can be coded as a Java, C++ program, Enterprise Java Beans (EJB), etc. or could be a back end legacy application. This option usually involves creating a service interface from the API of the application that implements the service. Bottom up development is well suited for an environment that includes several heterogeneous technologies and platforms or uses rapidly evolving technologies.

4. *Meet-in-the-middle development:* This option is used when an already existing service interface – for which an implementation already exists – is partially mapped on to a new service or process definition. This option involves service realisations that mix services and service enabled implementations. This approach may thus involve creating a wrapper for the existing applications that need to be service enabled and that are to be combined with the already existing service interface. Meet-in-the-middle development realisation strategies offer a middle ground that attempts to take advantage of some of the benefits of the other approaches while extenuating some of the most notable problems and risks.

The above service realisation options result in removing service redundancy and create opportunities for business services. However, one of the issues with the top down, bottom up, and meet-in-the-middle development options is that they are rather ambiguous regarding which business processes an enterprise should start from, and how these can be combined to form business scenarios. To address this problem, service development solutions need to target specific focal points and common practices within the enterprise, such as those that are specified by its corresponding sector reference models.

Example 16.5: Using RosettaNet to guide service developement

Reference models, a typical example of which are SCOR or RosettaNet, address a common large proportion of the basic plumbing for a specific sector, from a process, operational function, integration and data point of view. Such a verticalised development model presents the ideal architecture for supporting service development as they can serve as a starting point for message, service and process specification. This ensures that the software development team is aware of known best practices and standard processes so that it does not reinvent the wheel. The first level of analysis that needs to be done is to determine the subset of industry artifacts that are applicable to the clients of the SOA based application. For example, developers could use RosettaNet's standard processes such as PIP4B2 (*Notify of Shipment Receipt*) and PIP4C1 (*Distribute Inventory Report*) for the part of our case study in which suppliers develop replenishment plans for consignment inventory. Similarly, product receipt and inventory information can be notified using standard processes such as PIP4B2 and PIP4C1, respectively between consignment warehouses and suppliers.

Semantic issues come into play at the level of end-to-end business processes that span multiple organisations, see Chapter 13. To address terminology and semantic mismatch problems, consistent naming schemes of typical business process or objects, such as a purchase order or an invoice, can be used for business processes to achieve cognitive consistency among relevant business communities. Several standard industry models exist which provide detailed descriptions of reusable functional models, process models and data objects to assist with this endeavour. Typical examples include the APQC's Process Classification FrameworkSM (PCF) taxonomy of cross-functional business processes, the TeleManagement Forum's eTOM and Next Generation Operations Support System (NGOSS), or IBM's Information Framework for the banking industry.

The service realisation strategy involves choosing from an increasing diversity of realisation alternatives and requires making the right choice. The different options for service realisation may be mixed in various combinations. Service realisation alternatives that need to be considered in an SOA include:

1. Reusing or repurposing already existing Web services, business processes or business process logic.
2. Developing new Web services or business process logic from scratch.
3. Purchasing/leasing/paying per use for services. This option is covered in Section 16.15.2, which concentrates on service metering and billing.
4. Outsourcing service design and implementation regarding Web services or (parts of) business processes. Once a service is specified, the design of its interfaces or sets of interfaces, and the coding of its actual implementation, may be outsourced.
5. Using wrappers and/or adapters to revamp existing enterprise (COTS) components or existing (ERP/legacy) systems. Revamping software components, including database functionality or legacy software, results in introducing service enabling implementations for these systems in the form of adapters or wrappers.

Process realisation results in an inventory of conceptual business process and corresponding architecture represented by the set of normalised business functions extracted from the analysis of these processes. We illustrate this in Figure 16.8.

The process architecture now includes a model of end-to-end abstract processes that provides a high level overview of all their necessary characteristics, including business rules and policies, that may be modelled using BPMN. The process architecture also describes such information as ownership of the processes, scope of the process, composed services in a process, support processes, outsourced processes, insourced processes provided from external organisations, and process reference models that were used for the description of processes in the architecture. This abstract business process architecture is used as input to the SOA design phase so that atomic services, and business processes and their interfaces, can be specified in detail.

16.12 The SOA design (specification) phase

In the transition from the SOA analysis level to the design level in SDLC, the exhaustive list of abstract processes and services are transformed from abstract entities in the abstract business process architecture into a set of concrete service interfaces. During this step, all service flows and all necessary service functionality are also specified prior to constructing the services. In other words, SOA design in SDLC focuses on the specification of appropriate services, including their interfaces, internal architectures, processes, policies and documentation, to meet agreed SOA application requirements.

SOA design begins with an exhaustive abstract business process inventory and architecture, which resulted from the SOA analysis phase. The SOA design phase has the objective to *fill in the gaps* provided by the analysis picture with the full service functionality and specify concrete services and processes. Service specification is concerned with specifying the model of end-to-end abstract processes that results from the process architecture depicted in Figure 16.8. This includes specifying all necessary service characteristics, including business rules and policies. To achieve this endeavour this phase encompasses the following steps:

- specification of atomic services and service interface design;
- specification of business processes as a composition of services, and their interface design;
- specification of policies for both atomic services and business processes as well as process metrics for expressing non-functional attributes.

During the design phase, business process modelling tools, such as the BPMN tool, can be used to model aspects of business processes during the early design stages, and progressively refine them as the later stages of SOA design unfold. The business process modelling tool should provide capabilities for business analysts and users easily to model processes, define business rules and key performance indicators (KPIs), simulate, test and develop end-to-end process flows and business protocol message exchanges.

The modelling of the business process during the SOA design phase should be introduced with a view to achieving the following objectives:

- To simulate a new process through multiple scenarios before committing to the resources for executing it.
- To align the business processes in the logical layers of the SOA reference model in Figure 16.3 closely with the components and IT resources that are necessary to implement them in the physical layers of the SOA reference model.

Figure 16.10 illustrates the steps in SOA design. More specifically, it points out that SOA design is based on a twin track design approach that provides two production lines, one along the logical view and one along the physical view of the SOA reference model in Figure 16.3. The purpose of logical SOA design is to specify atomic services and

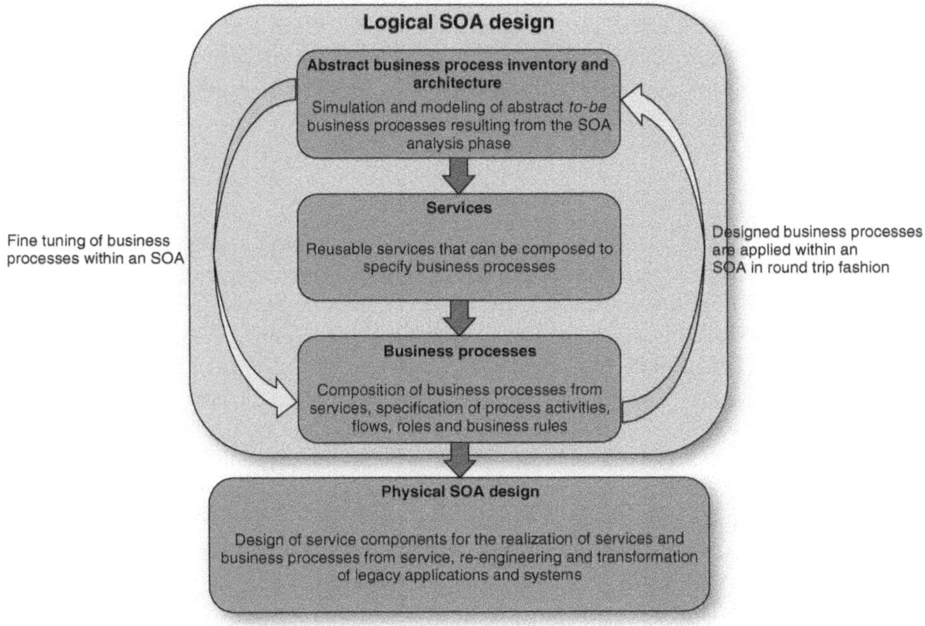

Figure 16.10 Steps in SOA design

assemble (compose) these services into business processes at the right level of granularity. This calls for a business process model that forces developers to determine how services combine and interact jointly to produce higher level services and business processes. The physical SOA design trajectory focuses on how to design component implementations that implement services at an acceptable level of granularity. Physical design is based on techniques for leveraging legacy applications and CBD techniques. CBD falls outside the scope of this book. Readers interested in this topic can find an overview of CBD methodologies and a wealth of ideas in the following sources: [Allen 2001], [Atkinson 2002], [Veryard 2001], [Whitehead 2002].

In the remainder of this chapter we shall mainly focus on logical SOA design issues, and make appropriate references to the physical SOA design issues only when necessary to improve readability and understanding. We shall first begin our coverage to SOA design by describing a broad set of key service design considerations and then concentrate in turn on the three design steps identified above.

16.12.1 Key service design considerations

A number of important key service design considerations exist which influence SOA design decisions and result in an efficient design of service interfaces, if taken seriously. In Section 16.8 we explained that SOA design principles, such as low coupling and high cohesion, and the distinction between coarse and fine granularity (i.e. scope of functionality) can have profound effect on the quality of SOA design, and provide guidance for SOA developers. These concerns form the core elements of design principles for SOA applications. Additional concerns include designing for service reuse, and designing for service composability.

16.12.1.1 Designing for service granularity

The granularity of business services and service implementation components is the prime concern of the developer responsible for providing the service specification. This subject was discussed briefly in Section 16.8.3. However, what is important to realise is that, just like a business service, a component implementation (see Figure 16.3) can be of various granularity levels. This will be explained in this sub-section.

Services analysis provides an initial granularity assessment based on the top down logical analysis of service functionality and scope, which can be used as a starting point for designing concrete service interfaces. There are several heuristics that can be used to identify the right level of granularity for business services (as well as implementation components). These include clearly identifiable business concepts, highly usable and reusable concepts, concepts that have a high degree of cohesion and low degree of coupling, and concepts that relate to service integration and interoperability. Many vertical sectors, e.g. automotive, travel industry and so on, have already started standardising business entities and processes by choosing their own levels of granularity. It is important that developers who implement the service still think about granularity so they can change parts of the implementation with the minimum of disruption to other components, applications and services.

In determining the granularity of components that implement services, developers need to consider parity with granularity of business services and take into account performance. Fine grained services such as Enterprise Java Beans (EJBs) are typically easier to understand and implement for business services. However, if service parity and performance is a consideration, then aligning services with existing EJBs may not turn out to be the optimal solution. In order to reduce the effects of network latency, system I/O and thread/process wait states, it is much better to create a coarse grained component that internally assembles multiple fine grained components and, therefore, uses fewer messages.

Component granularity must take into account legacy system interfaces that are (and must remain) unaware of the new protocol. In determining granularity, developers must consider the possibility of future changes to the underlying legacy implementation [Durvasula 2006]. The objective is to insulate services from changes to the underlying implementation, by designing them at a level of granularity that will allow for future expansion with little impact to the clients.

16.12.1.2 Designing for loose coupling and high cohesion

The objective of SOA design is to build highly cohesive processes and to maintain loose coupling between those processes, based on the principles and along the dimensions of coupling and cohesion covered in Sections 16.8.1 and 16.8.2.

The aim is to minimise service coupling within and across services to limit the effect of changes as the complexities of individual services are encapsulated from its consumers. In addition, loose coupling provides greater flexibility to choose optimised strategies for performance, extensibility and scalability for different services of an SOA development project independently. High cohesion, on the other hand, means well structured services, better performance and reduction of complexity by eliminating complex sequences of interaction between the services.

16.12.1.3 Designing for service reusability

When designing services, it is important to be able to design them for reuse so that they can perform a given function wherever this function is required within an SOA. To design for service reuse one must make services more generic, abstracting away from differences in requirements between one situation and another, and attempting to use the generic service in multiple contexts where it is applicable. Designing a solution that is reusable requires keeping it as simple as possible. There are intuitive techniques that facilitate reuse and that are related to design issues, such as the granularity and loose coupling of services. These include looking for common behaviour that exists in more than one place in the system and trying to generalise behaviour so that it is reusable.

When designing a service based application, it is possible to extract common behaviour and provide it by means of a generic service so that multiple clients can use it directly. It is important, however, when designing services that business logic is kept common and consistent across the SOA solution. Nevertheless there are cases where fine tuning, specialisation, or variation of business logic functionality is required. Consider, for instance, discounting practices that differ depending on the type of customer being handled. In those cases it is customary to produce a generalised solution with customisation points to allow for service variations.

16.12.1.4 Designing for service composability

In order to design useful and reliable services we need to apply sound service design principles that guarantee that services are self-contained, modular, and support service composability. Service should be able jointly to contribute to a common business objective and participate in multiple business processes without compromising the functional and non-functional requirements for the process. The design principles that underlie service composability revolve around the well known service design principles of granularity, coupling and cohesion that we examined earlier.

16.12.2 Specifying atomic services

Figure 16.10 illustrates that the first step in the logical SOA design phase is the specification of atomic services. During this phase, an important design requirement for SOA based applications is to provide a formal interface contract in some service description language (e.g. WSDL). Atomic service design in SDLC results in the definition and the interface signature of the service; the schema of the messages the service exchanges, including its service data; the dependencies the service has on other services; and integrity constraints that are appropriate to service implementation assumptions. Semantics must also be addressed if strongly cohesive services are to be specified. RDF can therefore be used to model semantics when inserted as annotations for the WSDL syntactic types.

A service specification is a set of three specification elements, all equally important. These are [Johnston 2005]:

1. *A structural specification:* This focuses on defining the service types, messages, port types and operations.
2. *A behavioural specification:* This entails understanding the effects and side effects of service operations and the semantics of input and output messages. If, for example, we consider a *cancel order,* and an *update order* atomic service, the behavioural specification for this service might describe the necessary functionality and conditions under which a user can or cannot update or cancel an order they placed, or specify that, after an order has been cancelled, it cannot be updated.
3. *A policy specification:* In addition to service syntax and semantics, QoS considerations must also be addressed. To this end a policy specification mechanism is necessary. Policy specification describes policy assertions and constraints on the service. Policy assertions may cover security, manageability, etc. For instance, a policy specification may require that certain elements of the order need be encrypted, denoting the encryption techniques to be used, certificates to use and so forth. Such non-functional requirements can be specified using appropriate constructs from the WS-Policy specification framework.

Like service analysis, service design is greatly facilitated when reference models, such as SCOR or RosettaNet (see Chapter 14), are available. Service interfaces and functionality can then be derived on their basis.

In the following, we shall briefly examine the course of specifying an interface for an atomic Web service in the WSDL standard. For this purpose we shall use Web service specifications in WSDL for the services described in the running example and in Figures 16.1 and 16.3. The effects of service message exchanges will be also examined. Following this, the service programming style will be determined. Service policy specifications will be introduced after we examine the business process specification.

16.12.2.1 Structural and behavioural service specification

Atomic service interface specification comprises four steps: describing the service interface, specifying operation parameters, designating the messaging and transport protocol, and finally fusing port types, bindings and actual location (a URI) of the Web services. These steps themselves are rather simple and already described in depth in the literature, e.g. in [Siddiqui 2001], where a detailed approach for specifying services is outlined. While performing these steps, the developer should apply the guiding SOA principles that we outlined in Section 16.8 and associated guidelines.

Example 16.6: Designing the interface of a *Receive Purchase Order* service

When designing an atomic service, such as a Receive Purchase Order for a Sales_Management service, the design principles and guidelines guarantee that the service encapsulates the required amount of business logic and that loose coupling is introduced between interacting services. More specifically, they impact key decisions regarding the structural and behavioural characteristics of the service. For example the interface of the service Receive Purchase Order should only contain the following:

- From a structural point of view, only port types (operations) that are logically related or functionally cohesive. For example, the atomic service Receive Purchase Order may capture the operations Receive Purchase Order Request and Acknowledge Purchase Order as they are functionally cohesive.
- From a behavioural point of view, messages that are tightly coupled by using representational coupling and communication protocol coupling. For example, the operation Receive Purchase Order Request may have one input message (PurchaseOrderID) and one output message (PurchaseOrder) sharing the same communication protocol (e.g. SOAP) and representation (atomic XML Schema data types). In addition, from a behavioural point of view, coupling between services should be minimised. For example, the atomic services Receive Purchase Order and Query Order Status are autonomous, having no interdependencies.

Atomic service design guidelines are examined below.

1. *Specifying the service interface:* A WSDL specification outlines operations, messages, types, and protocol information. Listing 16.1 shows an abridged specification for a service interface, and operation parameters for the Receive Purchase Order service that is part of the order management process in Figure 16.1. The WSDL example in Listing 16.1 illustrates that the Web service defines one <portType> named Receive Purchase Order. This <portType> supports three <operation>s, which are named Receive Purchase Order Request, Acknowledge Purchase Order and Confirm Purchase Order.
2. *Specifying operation parameters:* After having defined the operations, designers need to specify the parameters they contain. A typical operation defines a sequence containing an input message followed by an output message. When defining operation parameters (messages) it is important to decide whether simple or complex types will be used. The <operation> Receive Purchase Order Request in Listing 16.1 contains an output message Purchase Order Request Received which includes a single part named PO-body. This part is shown in

```
<portType name="ReceivePurchaseOrder_PortType">
    <!-- name of operation is same as name of message -->
    <operation name="ReceivePurchaseOrderRequest">
        <output message="tns:PORequestReceived"/>
    </operation>

    <operation name="AcknowledgePurchaseOrder">
        <output message="tns:PurchaseOrderAcknowledgment"/>
    </operation>
    <!-- name of operation is same as name of message -->
    <operation name="ConfirmPurchaseOrder">
        <output message="tns:PurchaseOrderConfirmation"/>
    </operation>
</portType>
```

Listing 16.1 WSDL excerpt for *Request Purchase Order.*

Listing 16.2 to be associated with the complex type `PurchaseOrderRequest` that is further specified to the level of XSD types in the service compartment that is enclosed within the `<wsdl:types>` tags. Listing 16.2 indicates that well factored Web services often result in a straightforward `<portType>` element where the service complexity is moved into the service data declaration.

Several graphical Web service development environments and toolkits exist today. These enable developers rapidly to create, view and edit services using WSDL, and manage issues such as correct syntax and validation, inspecting and testing Web services, and accelerating many common XML development tasks encountered when developing service enabled applications.

16.12.2.2 Specifying the service interaction style

In addition to structural and behavioural service specifications, another important concern in designing the service interface is the style of interaction between the service client and provider. The service programming (or interaction) style describes the pattern of the service's operation signatures and specifically how data is passed in and out of the service. It also describes the type of synchronisation of request and response messages.

Determining the service programming style is largely a design issue, as different applications impose different programming style requirements for Web services. Consider, for example, an application that is part of sales management in Figure 16.1 and deals with purchase order requests, purchase order confirmations and delivery information. This application may require that request messages should contain, as input, purchase orders in the form of XML documents, while response messages should contain purchase order receipts or delivery information as output, again in the form of XML documents. Moreover, there is no real urgency for a response message to follow a request

```
<message name="PORequestReceived">
     <part name="PO-body" type="tns:PurchaseOrderRequest"/>
</message>
  ...   ...   ...
<wsdl:types>
     <xsd:complexType name = "PurchaseOrderRequest">
           <xsd:sequence>
                <xsd:element ref = "PurchaseOrder"/>
                <xsd:element ref = "fromRole"/>
                <xsd:element ref = "toRole"/>
                <xsd:element ref = "thisDocumentGenerationDateTime"/>
                <xsd:element ref = "thisDocumentIdentifier"/>
                <xsd:element ref = "GlobalDocumentFunctionCode"/>
           </xsd:sequence>
     </xsd:complexType>

     <xsd:complexType name = "PurchaseOrder">
           <xsd:sequence>
                <xsd:element ref = "deliverTo" minOccurs = "0"/>
                <xsd:element ref = "comment" minOccurs = "0"/>
                <xsd:element ref = "packListRequirements"
                                     minOccurs = "0"/>
                <xsd:element ref = "ProductLineItem"
                                     maxOccurs = "unbounded"/>
                <xsd:element ref = "GlobalShipmentTermsCode"/>
                <xsd:element ref = "RevisionNumber"/>
                <xsd:element ref = "prePaymentCheckNumber"
                                     minOccurs = "0"/>
                <xsd:element ref = "QuoteIdentifier" minOccurs = "0"/>
                <xsd:element ref = "WireTransferIdentifier"
                                     minOccurs = "0"/>
                <xsd:element ref = "AccountDescription" minOccurs = "0"/>
                <xsd:element ref = "generalServicesAdministrationNumber"
                                     minOccurs = "0"/>
                <xsd:element ref = "secondaryBuyerPurchaseOrderIdentifier"
                                     minOccurs = "0"/>
                <xsd:element ref = "GlobalFinanceTermsCode"/>
                <xsd:element ref = "PartnerDescription"
                                     maxOccurs = "unbounded"/>
                <xsd:element ref = "secondaryBuyer" minOccurs = "0"/>
                <xsd:element ref = "GlobalPurchaseOrderTypeCode"/>
           </xsd:sequence>
     </xsd:complexType>
</wsdl:types>
  ... ... ... ...
```

Listing 16.2 Specifying operation parameters for operations in Listing 16.1

immediately, if at all. The purchase order request application uses document oriented or asynchronous Web services. This application uses document style messaging (see Section 4.4.2) where the service is sent an entire document, which it processes, and may or may not return a document as a response.

Now consider another application that provides an order management application with up-to-the-instant credit standings. Before completing a business transaction, a business may require to check a potential customer's credit standing. In this scenario, a request would be sent to the credit check service provider, e.g. a bank, and a response indicating the potential customer's credit rating would be returned. This type of Web service relies on an RPC or synchronous programming style, in contrast to the previous example. In this type of application the client invoking the Web service needs an immediate response or may even require that the Web services interact in a back and forth conversational way. This application uses an RPC style messaging (see Section 4.4.1) where the service is primarily designed to provide access to data, and the operation signatures contain one or more request parameters and provide a response in the form of data values.

Using document based messaging results in loose coupling, since the message constructs the document but does not indicate the steps to process that document. With document based messaging, it is only the receiver that knows the steps to handle an incoming document. Thus, the receiver can add additional steps, delete steps and so on, without impacting the client. In general, there is no reason for the Web service client to know the name of the remote methods.

16.12.3 Specifying business processes

Following the specification of atomic services, the next step in SDLC is to design business processes. Business process design means explicitly modelling, designing, simulating and redesigning processes in an SOA based application. During this step, a detailed process map is developed including all process activities, flows, roles and business rules. The process map provides information about how to compose a process by orchestrating services, or to decompose a process into a number of services. In particular, it gives designers the necessary information to compose (or decompose) processes, and relate to each other's process models that are developed in different parts of an enterprise or by its partners. Industry best practices and patterns must also be taken into account when designing processes, as they can act as blueprints for subsequent concrete process specification and implementations.

Prior to specifying business processes, designers must determine the type of service composition. The choice is between service orchestration and choreography (refer to Section 9.6 for definitions of these two terms). If a choice for orchestration of services is made, then three tasks follow to orchestrate a process:

- deriving the process structure and behaviour (including the process flow logic);
- linking the process to business roles, which reflect responsibilities of the trading partners, e.g. a buyer, a seller, and a shipper in the order management process;
- specifying policies and non-functional characteristics for the business process.

The design and specification of orchestrated services will influence how they will be scripted in a process execution language such as WS-BPEL (see Section 9.7). In the following we shall focus on service orchestration, given that today there are several implementations for WS-BPEL while WS-CDL is still under development.

16.12.3.1 Specifying the business process structure

The following step in SOA design is to describe the business structure and the functions (behaviour) of business processes. The business process structure refers to the logical flow or progression of a business process. A business process reveals how an individual process activity (`<portType>`) is linked with another such activity in order to achieve a business objective. To assemble a higher level service (process) by composing existing atomic Web services, the service developer needs to select potential services that need to be composed, depending on how these services, their operations and their flows fit within the enclosures of a business process and how they relate to one another. Subsequently, the service provider needs to connect the process interface to the interfaces of imported services and plug them together. Business processes can be scripted using WS-BPEL (see Chapter 9) by specifying the interactions between Web services.

Recall from Chapter 9 that WS-BPEL can be applied by means of abstract and executable business processes that share the same expressive power. An abstract process may be used to describe observable message exchange behaviour of each of the parties involved, without revealing their internal implementation. An abstract process in WS-BPEL is a partially specified process that is not intended to be executed, and hides some of the required concrete operational details expressed by its executable counterpart. In this section we shall focus on the specification of abstract WS-BPEL processes that compose existing services.

The abstract description of a process in SDLC encompasses the following tasks:

1. *Identification, grouping, and description of the activities and services that implement together a business process:* The objective of this action is to identify the services that need to be assembled and composed in order to generate a business process and then describe the provided interface of the overall business process. For instance, the registration of a new customer is an activity in a sales order process. The structure of a business process describes how an individual process activity (`<portType>`) is linked with another in order to assemble a higher level service from possibly atomic Web services. During this procedure the service designer needs to:

    (a) Select the services to compose by looking at how these services and their operations fit within the context of a business process and how they relate to one another.

    (b) Connect the provided interface of the business process to the interfaces of imported services and plug them together.

2. *Description of activity dependencies, conditions and synchronisation points:* A process definition can organise activities into varying structures, such as

hierarchical, conditional and activity dependency definitions. In a hierarchical definition, process activities have a hierarchical structure. For instance, the activity of sending an insurance policy for a shipped order can be divided into three sub-activities: *compute the insurance premium, notify insurance,* and *mail insurance premium to customer.* In process definitions that have a conditional activity structure, activities are performed only if certain conditions are met. For instance, it may be company policy to send a second billing notice to a trading partner when an invoice is more than two months overdue. An activity dependency definition may signify synchronisation dependencies between activities and sub-activities in a process. In any process definition, sub-activities can execute only after their parent activity has commenced. This means that sub-activities are implicitly dependent on their parent activity. In other cases there might be an explicit synchronisation dependency between activities: an activity may only be able to start when another specific activity has completed. For instance, a shipment cannot be sent to a customer if the customer has not been sent an invoice.

3. *Description of the implementation of the business process:* This task concentrates on providing a specification in WS-BPEL, which maps the operations and interfaces of imported services to those of other services in order to create the provided interface of the business process.

Listing 16.3 illustrates a snippet of a possible WS-BPEL specification for the purchase order management process, which is part of the sales management application in Figure 16.1. The first step in the process flow is the receipt of a purchase order. The listing shows that three activities are planned in parallel. The final price for the order is calculated, a shipper is selected and the production and shipment of the order is scheduled. When these three concurrent paths are completed, invoice processing can proceed and the invoice is sent to the customer. The WS-BPEL elements in the above listing were explained in Chapter 9.

```
<process  name="purchaseOrderProcess"
  ...
<!- Receive Purchase Order -->
<sequence>
  <receive partnerLink="purchasing" portType="lns:purchaseOrderPT"
    operation="sendPurchaseOrder" variable="PO" createInstance="yes">
  </receive>

 <flow>
   <links>
      <link name="ship-to-invoice" />
      <link name="ship-to-scheduling" />
   </links>
   <!- A parallel flow to handle shipping and invoicing -->
      ...
```

```
    <sequence>
      <invoke partnerLink="shipping" portType="shippingPT"
        operation="requestShipping"
        inputVariable="shippingRequest" outputVariable="shippingInfo">

        <!- Decide on Shipper -->
        <sources> <source linkName="ship-to-invoice" /> </sources>
      </invoke>

      <receive partnerLink="shipping"
        portType="lns:shippingCallbackPT"
        operation="sendSchedule" variable="shippingSchedule">

        <!- Arrange for Logistics -->
        <sources> <source linkName="ship-to-scheduling"/> </sources>
      </receive>
    </sequence>
    <sequence> <!- Price Calculation -->
      <invoke partnerLink="invoicing" portType="computePricePT"
        operation="CalculateInitialPrice" inputVariable="PO">
      </invoke>

      <invoke partnerLink="invoicing" portType="computePricePT"
        operation="sendShippingPrice" inputVariable="shippingInfo">

        <!- Complete Price Calculation -->
        <targets> <target linkName="ship-to-invoice" /> </targets>
      </invoke>
      <receive partnerLink="invoicing" portType="invoiceCallbackPT"
       operation="sendInvoice" variable="Invoice" />
    </sequence>
    <sequence> <!- Scheduling the production and shipment for the order -->
     ...
    </sequence>
  </flow>

  <!- Invoice Processing -->
  <reply partnerLink="Purchasing" portType="purchaseOrderPT"
       operation="sendPurchaseOrder" variable="Invoice"/>
  </reply>
</sequence>
</process>
```

Listing 16.3 WS-BPEL process flow for the PurchaseOrder process

16.12.3.2 Specifying roles and responsibilities

The second step during business process design is to identify responsibilities associated with business process activities and the roles that are responsible for performing them. Each service provider is expected properly to fulfil the business responsibility of implementing a business activity as one or more port types of a service, which perform a specific role. The result of this phase actually constitutes the foundation for implementing business policies, notably role based access control and security policies (see the following section).

Example 16.6: Defining roles for the Purchase Order composite service

Figure 16.11 illustrates the services that are orchestrated together to form composites to make the purchase order management process during SOA design. `<PartnerLinkType>`s are used to represent dependencies between services. Each `<partnerLinkType>` defines up to two *role* names, and lists the port types that each role must support for the interaction to be carried out successfully. In this example, two `<partnerLinkType>`s, `"PurchasingPLT"` and `"SchedulingPLT"`, list a single role because, in the corresponding service interactions, one of the parties provides all the invoked operations. The `"purchasingPLT"` `<partnerLinkType>` represents the connection between the process and the requesting customer, where only the purchase order service needs to offer a service operation (`"sendPurchaseOrder"`). The `"schedulingPLT"` `<partnerLinkType>` on the other hand represents the interaction between the purchase order service and the scheduling service, in which only operations of the latter are invoked. The two other `<partnerLinkType>`s, `"invoicingPLT"` and `"shippingPLT"`, define two roles because both the user of the invoice calculation and the user of the shipping service (the invoice or the shipping schedule) must provide callback operations to enable notifications to be sent. This is `"InvoiceCallbackPT"` and `"ShippingCallbackPT"` port types as illustrated in Listing 16.4.

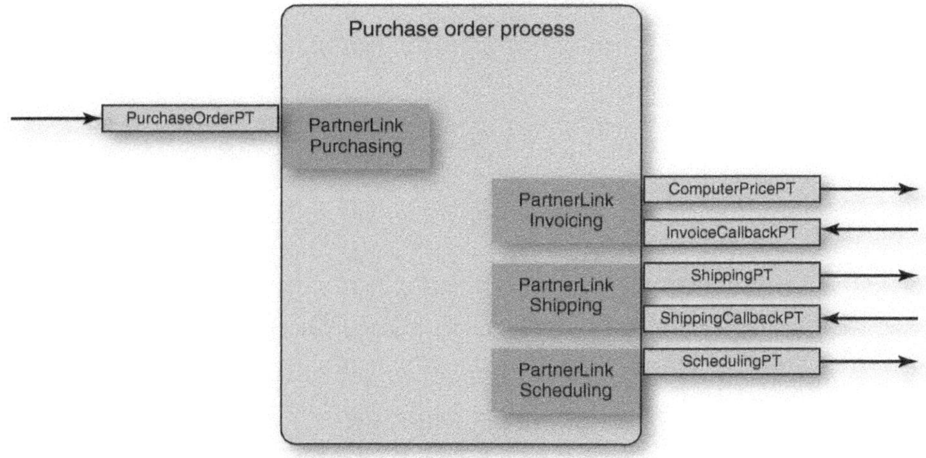

Figure 16.11 Composed services in the order management process

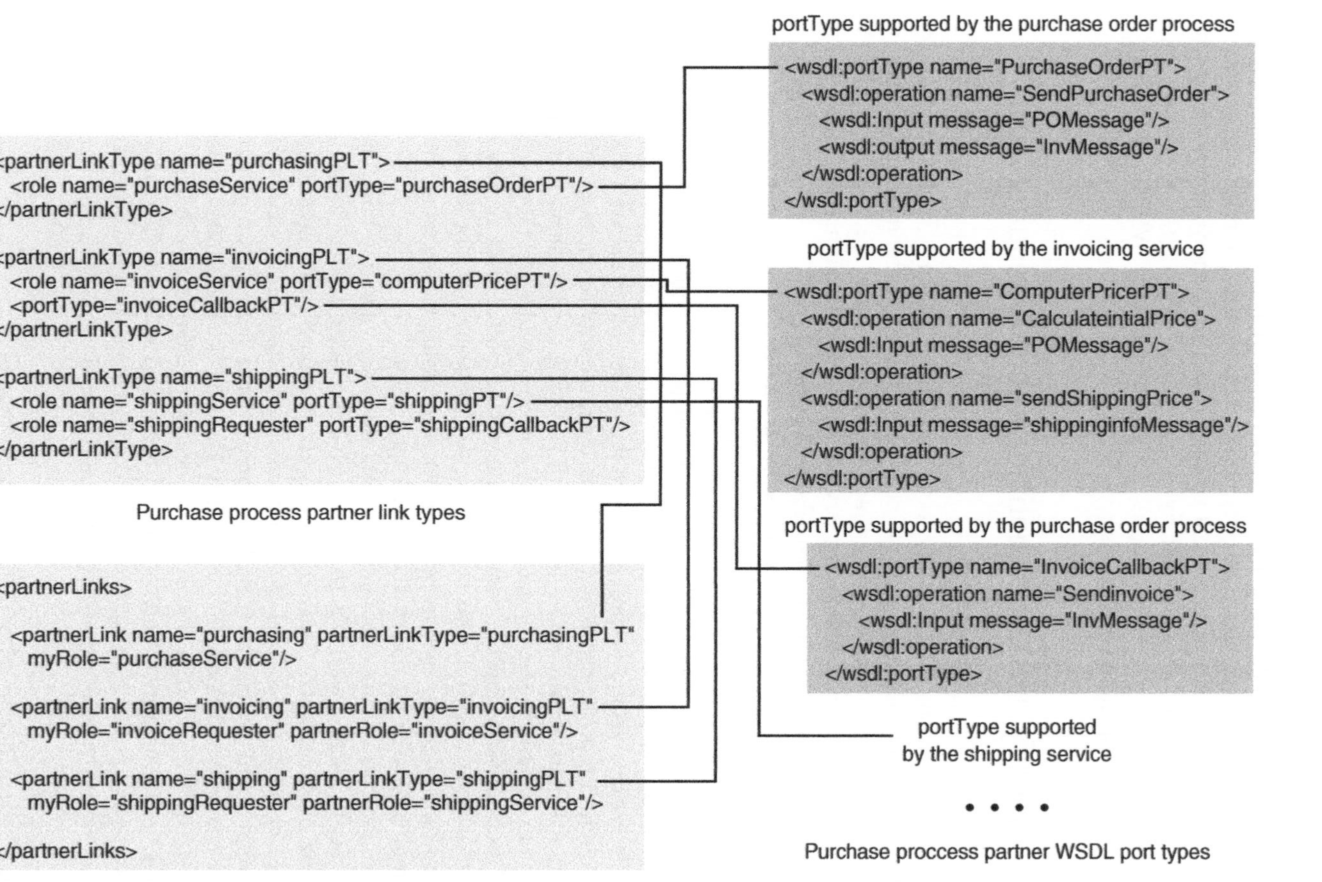

```
<partnerLinkType name="purchasingPLT">
  <role name="purchaseService" portType="purchaseOrderPT"/>
</partnerLinkType>

<partnerLinkType name="invoicingPLT">
  <role name="invoiceService" portType="computerPricePT"/>
  <portType="invoiceCallbackPT"/>
</partnerLinkType>

<partnerLinkType name="shippingPLT">
  <role name="shippingService" portType="shippingPT"/>
  <role name="shippingRequester" portType="shippingCallbackPT"/>
</partnerLinkType>
```

Purchase process partner link types

```
<partnerLinks>

  <partnerLink name="purchasing" partnerLinkType="purchasingPLT"
    myRole="purchaseService"/>

  <partnerLink name="invoicing" partnerLinkType="invoicingPLT"
    myRole="invoiceRequester" partnerRole="invoiceService"/>

  <partnerLink name="shipping" partnerLinkType="shippingPLT"
    myRole="shippingRequester" partnerRole="shippingService"/>

</partnerLinks>
```

Purchase process partner link declarations

portType supported by the purchase order process

```
<wsdl:portType name="PurchaseOrderPT">
  <wsdl:operation name="SendPurchaseOrder">
    <wsdl:Input message="POMessage"/>
    <wsdl:output message="InvMessage"/>
  </wsdl:operation>
</wsdl:portType>
```

portType supported by the invoicing service

```
<wsdl:portType name="ComputerPricerPT">
  <wsdl:operation name="CalculateintialPrice">
    <wsdl:Input message="POMessage"/>
  </wsdl:operation>
  <wsdl:operation name="sendShippingPrice">
    <wsdl:Input message="shippinginfoMessage"/>
  </wsdl:operation>
</wsdl:portType>
```

portType supported by the purchase order process

```
<wsdl:portType name="InvoiceCallbackPT">
  <wsdl:operation name="Sendinvoice">
    <wsdl:Input message="InvMessage"/>
  </wsdl:operation>
</wsdl:portType>
```

portType supported by the shipping service

• • • •

Purchase proccess partner WSDL port types

Listing 16.4 Defining roles in WS-BPEL

Listing 16.4 illustrates the different parties that interact within the purchase order business process (which is specified in Listing 16.3 and described in Figure 16.11) in the course of processing a client's purchase order. This listing specifies how the `"PurchaseOrder"` process is interfaced with the `<portType>`s of associated service definitions in WS-BPEL to create an order management process. This listing shows how each `<partnerLink>` definition is characterized by a `<partnerLinkType>`. Furthermore, it shows how each `<partnerLinkType>` is associated with WSDL `<portType>` definitions and corresponding operations.

16.12.4 Specifying service policies and QoS requirements in an SOA

SOA establishes a set of principles for loose coupling, modularity, reuse and composability that can be only achieved when, in addition to the functional requirements that we already examined in this chapter, policies and QoS requirements are also met. This is an important requirement when composing services from business partners and other service providers outside of an enterprise operational environment.

The support of QoS features in an SOA is defined according to service level agreements that must ensure the correct delivery of services. Recall that an SLA is an agreement between a client and its service provider that sets the expectations between these two parties by recording their common understanding about services and the responsibilities of both parties, see Section 1.9.2. This agreement establishes the parameters for how the service should be provided over the course of its use to a client, and can include policies on performance and response time, security features, or other desirable non-functional characteristics from the point of view of a service client. In an SOA based application to quantify the performance of the service provider and monitor adherence to the SLA, each service (simple or composite) must have QoS metrics, or Key Performance Indicators, associated with it. This is the only way to ensure that, for instance, stipulated service run time qualities, such as performance, scalability, transactional integrity, security and fault tolerance, are met in SOA based applications.

This section lays out important concepts and discusses capturing non-functional SOA requirements in such a way that they can drive architectural decisions, and they can validate the SOA approach. This section concentrates on the two main QoS categories: business level and resource level QoS requirements, introduced in section 16.7.2. It provides examples and a range of typical key performance indicators for each category to enable the reader to understand how to identify key aspects of non-functional SOA design. Both these types of non-functional service design requirements can be defined using WS-Policy assertions, which we examined in Section 12.4. In addition, as SOA security is a quintessential property of service oriented applications, and since it spans both QoS categories, we shall examine it in a dedicated sub-section.

16.12.4.1 Business level SOA QoS requirements

Business level QoS concerns itself with SLA associated metrics, distilled in key performance indicators (KPIs) that specify business rules or conditions, as well as with compliance to regulatory and legal constraints, or standards established in specific vertical industries. We shall examine both these cases in this subsection.

For instance, in the SOA based sales management application in Figure 6.1 inventory starts with the physical flow of parts, from the point of supply, through the factory and shipment through flexible distribution channels. Business level inventory policy may consist of guidelines concerning what to purchase or manufacture, when to take action and at what quantity. It also includes policies regarding inventory management practices, e.g. centralised inventory management versus independently managing inventory at each stocking facility. Such business conditions or rules need to be associated with the appropriate inventory services.

Typical business level KPIs associated with supply chain SOA applications and processes (such as those we examined for the SCOR model, see Section 15.3.1) may include, for example:

- Delivery performance: requested versus actual dates at the line item level.
- Line count fill rate: the amount of order lines shipped on the initial shipment verses the amount of lines ordered.
- Cash-to-cash cycle time: measuring the time it takes to close the loop between fund utilisation (material acquisition) and collection (invoice payment).
- Pay on receipt: measuring the time required to match and reconcile invoices.
- Order accuracy: products delivered versus what was ordered.
- Replenishment: the time it takes to replenish inventory and the accuracy of the replenishments.
- Customer service level/fill rate: items available in stock for delivery per purchase order.
- Performance to promise dates: when distributors place a Purchase Order against a manufacturer, they have certain expectations of when they will receive the items ordered. The original expectation is the `"OnTime Delivery"` KPI. However, the manufacturer may give the distributor a revised estimate as to when they expect to fill the order. The manufacturer's promise is called the `"Performance to Promise Date"` KPI.

In addition, to business level conditions and rules, business level QoS is also intimately associated with compliance. This allows management to ascertain that internal control measures that govern their key business processes in SOA development can be checked, tested, and potentially certified with their underlying services. *Compliance* is about ensuring that business processes, operations and practices are in accordance with a prescribed and/or agreed on set of norms [Sadiq 2007]. This includes, but is not limited to, data acquisition and archival, document management, data security, financial accounting practices, shareholder reporting functions and to know when unusual activities occur. In a broader perspective, compliance can pertain to any explicitly stated rule or regulation that prescribes any aspect of an internal or cross-organisational business process; including for example public policies, customer preferences, partner agreements and jurisdictional provisions.

A *compliance constraint* (requirement) refers to any explicitly stated rule or regulation that prescribes any aspect of an internal or cross-organisational business process.

As business processes form the foundation for all SOA development they are impacted by industry or government regulations. Without explicitly associating compliance constraints with business processes and the independent services that these processes compose, and without SOA audit trails that provide for non-repudiation, organisations face litigation risks and even criminal penalties. Compliance regulations, such as the Health Insurance Portability and Accountability Act (HIPAA, see www.hhs.gov), the recommendations on banking laws and regulations framework Basel II (www.bis.org), and the Sarbanes-Oxley Act (SOX, see www.soxlaw.com) for standards for all U.S. public company boards, management and public accounting firms and others, require all organisations to review their business processes and ensure that they meet the compliance standards set forth in the legislation. For instance, a SOA based application should be able to specify that all financial business processes comply with SOX Section 409 by reporting in real time all events that could affect financial results. In another example, a typical financial reporting control in SOA development might mitigate the risk of misstating revenue due to inadequate physical or electronic security over sales documents. This helps implement a compliance regulation act, such SOX Section-404, which mandates that well defined and documented processes and controls be in place for all aspects of company operations that affect financial information and reports.

16.12.4.2 Resource level SOA QoS requirements

Resource level QoS is typically associated with capacity, performance, scalability, availability, security and transactional integrity related issues in connection with operational systems and resources. Its objective is to match the technical capacity of a service to agreed upon SLA stipulations. Typical examples of quantifiable, timeliness KPIs for resource level QoS include:

- upper and lower performance response time ranges and service availability (measured as total uptime hours/downtime hours per month and displayed as a percentage of availability up to one-tenth of a per cent, e.g. 99.93%);
- SOA performance (throughput, response time, transit delay, latency, etc.);
- MTBF (Mean Time Between Failure);
- MTRS (Mean Time to Restore Service).

Network bandwidth is also associated with SOA performance. The network and processing nodes between service consumer and provider endpoints may severely impact the level of service. This requires that network capability with guaranteed bandwidth and propagation delays must be utilised whenever appropriate.

In the following we shall describe the implications of typical resource level QoS requirements for SOA design.

With resource level QoS, service performance is perceived as a combination of response time and throughput and can be impacted by decisions regarding such factors as service granularity, service binding choices, message passing and data volume, network bandwidth, scalability and security choices [Bieberstein 2006]. The granularity of exposed services needs to be carefully designed. As already explained, fine grained services lead to a lot of interactions and introduce performance overheads. On the other hand, services that are unnecessarily coarse grained lead to very large information exchanges also impacting performance. When using WSDL as a service description medium, services can be invoked using different binding options. To improve SOA performance, binding optimisation policies could be introduced supporting, for instance, multiple service bindings with faster protocols.

Scalability is another important issue for SOA applications and was addressed in the context of the ESB (see Section 8.5.7). Scalable services can be designed effectively only when capacity planning, service provisioning and policy based routing is carefully controlled [Bieberstein 2006]. Capacity planning is determined from existing transaction measurements and is largely relevant to internal use of services within an enterprise. Here we may use KPIs to measure processor usage by workload and application, min/max transactions per second, on line response times and trends, and so on. Capacity planning for SOA must gracefully introduce additional processing power. Service providers that expose their services to clients or partners usually need to define a provisioning mechanism that enables them to evaluate the number and type of additional resources required to deliver services complying with SLA stipulations. Finally, policy based routing allows different SLAs that include agreements, ranging from best effort delivery to guaranteed response time, to be applied per service customer group. In this way, better scalability control can be exercised.

It is interesting to note that resource level QoS also describes resource utilisation requirements, physical infrastructure and resources that are needed to run a particular service, choice of specific application packages, legacy applications, and commitments to industry specific technical standards for SOA applications. For instance, a service provider may declare specific technical features that must be taken into account for a service to operate properly. These include: storage space, data transfer bandwidth, CPU capability, specific computing and/or storage resources, e.g. Blade servers with quad-core Intel Xeon processors. All these decisions can impose constraints on the design and development of SOAs. To service-enable such enterprise assets, adaptation, re-engineering and repurposing mechanisms may be used in conjunction with SOA implementation (see Section 8.5.6).

16.12.4.3 SOA security considerations

Since SOA applications should allow access to sanctioned clients, security is a first order business consideration. Normally, an integrated approach to security is required whereby all technical system aspects, as well as business policies and processes, are taken into consideration.

There are several unique security related characteristics that need to be addressed by a service design methodology. SOA security is applicable to all layers of an SOA model: across business process services, infrastructure and development services. At a high level, we can define the following broad areas in the SOA security model, which correspond to the two security mechanisms that were examined in Chapter 11, namely network level and application level security. In the following we shall focus on application level security issues.

When designing for SOA security, a service provider could, for instance, specify a policy stating that a given service in the SOA development requires Kerberos tokens, digital signatures and encryption. Potential clients use such policy information to determine whether they can use this particular service. In many cases in SOA development an SLA is used to bundle security policies to protect multi-party collaborations. Knowing that a new business process adopts a Web service message level security standard such as WS-Security is not enough information to enable successful composition. The client needs to be aware of the transport security policies that state the type of protection offered in the actual delivery protocols, e.g. use of standards such as SSL, message level security policies that specify end-to-end message protection by using encryption and digital signatures, and security token policies that specify the type of security token used during interactions. Trying to compose (orchestrate) services in an SOA without understanding these technical details will inevitably lead to erroneous results. For example, when designing a purchase order service in the order management process it is necessary to understand what types of tokens and certificates it accepts. For instance, the purchase order service may indicate that it only accepts user name tokens that are signed using an X.509 certificate, which is cryptographically endorsed by a specific third party. If other services communicating with this service as part of a service composition (viz. business process) fail to do so, then the entire composition will break.

In addition to the previous security concerns, SOA development is also concerned with application level security concerns, primarily authentication, authorisation, message integrity and confidentiality. In SOA development there is a clear need to need to authenticate and authorise SOA users who come from outside an enterprise. To deal with the security challenges inherent in securing third parties, an SOA security solution can utilise federated authentication. Recall from Section 11.6.9 that federated authentication is a process whereby multiple parties agree that a designated set of users can be authenticated by a given set of criteria. Federated authentication relies on the use of federated identity techniques to enable cross-boundary single sign-on, dynamic user provisioning and identity attribute sharing. In other cases, the authentication process will result in the SOA security solution creating a Security Assertion Markup Language assertion that expresses the authenticity of the user in a way that will be accepted by the service that the user is invoking, (refer to Section 11.5.4).

Increasingly, authorisation capabilities are emerging as a major security requirement for business collaboration. An enterprise not only needs to know who the requesters accessing its services are, it also needs to control what Web services that requester has access to, what factors affect availability of the Web services to that customer, and what auditing is required to ensure the non-repudiation of transactions with that requester. Client authentication may rely on different authentication policies. For instance, an authentication policy may require that a client authenticates itself by presenting its encoded credentials or may require that XML signatures be generated for Web service requests.

The design of a simple SOA development security scenario regarding the development of an order processing application employing the SOA security mechanisms discussed above can be found in Section 11.6.4.1 and Figure 11.22.

Good sources for designing robust security models that secure SOA enabled business applications are [Steel 2006] and [Buecker 2007]. [Steel 2006] covers the rationale for adopting a security methodology, the process steps of a security methodology, and how to create and use security patterns within that methodology. [Buecker 2007] introduce a reference model to address the requirements, patterns of deployment and usage, and an approach to an integrated security management for SOA. This reference also describes approaches to SOA securities that are discussed in the context of scenarios and observed patterns.

16.12.4.4 Specifying SOA policies

An SOA policy is a declarative specification of service characteristics that is applied to a service and enforced in order to guarantee that the use of that service contributes to the desired SOA project outcome. An SOA policy is comprised of a collection of assertion statements associated with services. Each assertion represents some specific aspect of what a service is supposed to accomplish, how to control its behaviour, or how to achieve its purpose. Some policy assertions specify traditional requirements and capabilities that will ultimately manifest on-the-wire (e.g. authentication scheme, transport protocol selection). Other policy assertions, such as privacy policy or QoS characteristics, have no wire manifestation and yet are critical to proper service selection and usage. In this section we shall express such service assertions using WS-Policy (see Chapter 12).

Recall from Chapter 12 that WS-Policy is an extensible grammar, which defines a Web service policy to be a collection of policy alternatives, where each policy alternative is a collection of policy assertions. Also recall that WS-Policy does not specify how policies are discovered or attached to a Web service. Such mechanisms are defined by WS-PolicyAttachment, which allows for associating policy with arbitrary XML elements, WSDL artifacts and UDDI elements.

Example 16.7: A security policy for the Receive Purchase Order service

In the policy example used in this section we shall concentrate on a service security policy that requires two kinds of certificate to authenticate users. Listing 16.5 illustrates how we can express a security policy using assertions defined in WS-SecurityPolicy for the for the `Receive Purchase Order` service that was defined earlier. The listing specifies a set of policy assertions for authentication using the `<wsp:ExactlyOne>` policy operator that is used to group policy assertions into policy sets. This policy includes two specific security policy assertions that indicate that the `<operation>` of the service `Receive Purchase Order Request` can be authenticated with either Kerberos or X509 authentication tokens.

```
<wsp:Policy
 xmlns:wsp="http://schemas.xmlsoap.org/ws/2004/09/policy"
 xmlns:wsu="http://docs.oasis-open.org/wss/2004/01/.. "
 ... ... ...
 wsu:Id="AuthenticationPolicy">
 <wsp:ExactlyOne>
   <wsse:SecurityToken>
     <wsse:TokenType> wsse:Kerberosv5TGT </wsse:TokenType>
   </wsse:SecurityToken>
   <wsse:SecurityToken>
     <wsse:TokenType> wsse:X509v3 </wsse:TokenType>
   </wsse:SecurityToken>
 </wsp:ExactlyOne>
</wsp:Policy>
```

Listing 16.5 Specifying authentication policies for the operations in Listing 16.3

```
... ... ... ...
  <portType name="ReceivePurchaseOrder_PortType">
 <operation name="ReceivePurchaseOrderRequest">
      <output message="tns:PORequestReceived"/>
 </operation>
    ... ... ...
  </portType>
    ... ... ...
  <binding name="ReceivePO_SoapBinding"
         type="tns:ReceivePurchaseOrder_PortType">
    <wsp:PolicyReference URI="#AuthenticationPolicy"
      wsdl:required="true" />
    <soap:binding style="document"   ...   />
  <operation name="ReceivePurchaseOrderRequest">
     <input>
       <soap:body use="literal"/>
     </input>
     <output>
       <soap:body use="literal"/>
     </output>
  </operation>
  </binding>
```

Listing 16.6 Referencing the policy in Listing 16.5

Notice the use of the `<policyRefence>` element in the binding to associate the `<operation> Receive Purchase Order Request` with the authentication policy.

Listing 16.6 shows how the WSDL definitions of the operation `Receive Purchase Order Request` can reference the security policy defined in Listing 16.5. This listing shows the `<wsp:PolicyReference>` element is used to include the content of the policy expression in the service definition. To understand better the code excerpts in the above listing you need to recall that a `<PortType>`, an `<Operation>` and a `<Binding>` element are related in terms of the same set of messages.

16.13 The SOA construction phase

SOA construction is a phase of the physical part of the SOA reference model that involves implementing services and business processes on the basis of the service and process specifications that were created during the design phase. The construction phase in the SDLC is the phase wherein a specific technology, programming language and platform are used to transform the design specifications and realisation strategies into concrete service executions. As a consequence, the construction phase focuses on the realisation of services and the creation of the hosting environment for SOA based applications and the actual deployment of those applications. This includes implementing the process realisation strategies that were determined during the analysis phase (see Section 16.11.5), leveraging legacy assets, resolving the application's resource dependencies, operational conditions and capacity requirements. This phase may involve greenfield code development; however, in most cases it will consist of modifying existing services or constructing wrappers on top of existing legacy applications. It must noted that SDLC, at this point in time, does not address the actual implementation of services but it provides guidelines and enough information so that an SOA construction phase can concentrate on the development and implementation of services.

The specialised nature of SOA run time platform elements is the primary differentiating factor in the construction phase. Applications built within SOA initiatives require a specialised run time platform. This platform may include application servers, which provide advanced facilities for publishing service interfaces and hosting their implementations; ESB implementations which can transparently apply QoS policies and transformations to service requests and replies; service orchestration engines; and so on.

In the following we shall briefly examine in succession three important elements of SOA construction: harvesting implementations from legacy applications, the SOA programming and implementation model and finally, service construction.

16.13.1 Leveraging legacy applications

Enterprises are still burdened with older generation operational applications that were constructed to run on various obsolescent hardware types, programmed in obsolete languages. Such applications are known as legacy applications [Ulrich 2002]. Legacy applications are critical assets of any modern enterprise as they provide access to mission critical business information and functionality, and thus control the majority of an organisation's business processes.

Typical shortcomings of mission critical legacy applications include, among other things: the impediment that they present to corporate growth; slow response to growing customer demands; and the lack of integration with trading partners' systems. The ever expanding universe of enterprise applications requires connecting dissimilar legacy applications with newer generation applications. Being able to leverage this value in new SOA based solutions would provide an extremely attractive return on existing investments. Therefore a best-of-breed SOA characteristic is to offer connectivity for legacy applications.

It is not possible properly to integrate legacy systems into Web service solutions without extensive, intrusive modifications to those systems. Modifications are needed to reshape legacy systems to provide a natural fit with SOA architectural requirements, and carefully retrofit business logic so that it can be used with new applications. Therefore, legacy applications need to be re-engineered in order to reuse the core business processes entrenched in legacy applications. The legacy application re-engineering procedure involves the disciplined evolution of an existing legacy application to a new *improved* environment by reusing as much of it (requirements, design, specification and implementation) as possible and by adding new capabilities. Through re-engineering, business processes become more modular and granular, exposing sub-modules that can be reused and are represented as services. In its most fundamental form, the legacy application re-engineering includes three basic tenets. These are:

- understanding of an existing application, resulting in one or more logical descriptions of the application;
- restructuring or transformation of those logical descriptions into new, improved logical descriptions;
- development of the new application based on these improved logical descriptions.

These three broad phases comprise a series of six steps, briefly described in the following. The re-engineering and transformation steps below have been considerably simplified. The purpose of these steps is to facilitate the process of legacy application modernisation by modularising legacy processes and business logic separately from presentation logic and data management activities, and representing them as components. These components can then be used to create interfaces for new services, thereby service enabling legacy applications. The legacy application re-engineering and transformation steps are as follows:

- *Understanding existing applications:* Before beginning the modernisation process, the first task is to understand the structure and architecture of the existing application. This task includes gathering statistics about size, complexity, the amount of dead or unused code, and the amount of bad programming for each application [Comella-Dorda 2000], [Seacord 2001]. In addition, in selecting which programs to improve together, selecting the ones that affect common data is a critical step when planning to move through all of the legacy modernisation stages, including re-engineering for reuse and/or migration.
- *Rationalising business logic:* A typical legacy application is composed of a large number of independent programs. These programs work together in a hard wired net of business process flows. Once an application's program code is clean, any programming anomalies have been removed, and non-business logic has been filtered, it is possible to apply pattern matching techniques across all of the application's programs to identify and segregate candidate common business logic.

- *Identifying business rules:* When candidate reusable business logic has been rationalised to a subset of distinct, single occurrences of each service, it is then possible to determine whether each should become part of a process or express a business rule. To achieve this, sophisticated algorithms are used to extract business rules from monolithic legacy applications within which business rules exist in many different guises. The extraction of business rules from legacy code is generally termed business rule recovery. The accuracy with which this task is performed is key to legacy application modernisation.
- *Extracting components:* Extracted business rules can be grouped together, based on their contribution to achieve the intended business functionality. A group of rules is normally processing some common set of data to achieve intended business functions. Candidate business rules and associated business data are then extracted and appropriately represented as a cohesive legacy component. The number of rules that need to be grouped together is a matter of choice, depending on the desired granularity of the legacy component. A callable interface needs to be provided for these components.
- *Wrapping component implementations:* Legacy applications were, for the most part, not implemented in a fashion that lends itself to componentisation. Presentation logic is often intertwined with business logic, which is intertwined with systems and data access logic. During this step, system level and presentation level legacy components are identified and separated from business level legacy components. In this way, candidate components are identified for wrapping. Wrapping provides legacy functionality for new service based solutions in much shorter time than it would take to build a replacement from scratch and recreate those dependencies, see Section 8.5.6. Wrapping requires that the appropriate level of abstraction for components be determined. When it comes to wrapping and legacy componentisation, one should concentrate on identifying coarse grained components, as they have greater reuse value. Smaller components are more likely to be frequently used, but their use saves less effort. This implies that fine grained components are less cost effective.
- *Creating service interfaces:* Component wrappers result in well defined boundaries of functionality and data. However, the modernised legacy application as a whole is still tightly coupled with components hardwired to each other via program-to-program calls. The SOA approach to large scale application coupling requires removing from the individual component wrappers any direct knowledge of any other such components. This can be accomplished by breaking up program-to-program connectivity and replacing it with service enabled APIs that can be used in conjunction with event driven and business process orchestration mechanisms. These APIs are then used to implement the service and process specifications that were the outcome of the design phase.

For a more detailed description of the re-engineering and transformation steps, interested readers are referred to [Comella-Dorda 2000], [Seacord 2001], [Ulrich 2002], [van den Heuvel 2007].

16.13.2 The SOA programming and implementation model

Service component architecture (SCA) provides a programming model for building applications and systems based on a Service Oriented Architecture. It is based on the idea that a business function is provided as a series of services, which are assembled together to create solutions that serve a particular business need. These composite applications can contain both new services created specifically for the application and also business functions from existing systems and applications, reused as part of the composition.

SCA provides a model both for the composition of services and for the creation of service components, including the reuse of existing application functions within SCA compositions. SCA is a set of specifications geared towards developing SOA based applications in which the SCA framework can shield the applications from both the component's internal implementation as well as access methods [Bieberstein 2008]. This section briefly introduces the SCA model. A detailed treatment of the subject is beyond the scope of this book. A good source for materials relating to SCA specifications is [Barber 2009].

SCA encourages an SOA organisation of business application code based on components that implement business functions and logic, e.g. services defined in WSDL and BPEL. SCA also introduces the concept of a module, which groups together service components and provides further specification and encapsulation of functions offered by components through service oriented interfaces, called service references. Finally, SCA defines a standard deployment model for packaging components into a service module. SCA components with their associated dependencies can be defined and packaged together into deployable units. SCA divides up the steps in building a service oriented application into two major parts:

1. The implementation of service components, which provide services and consume other services.
2. The assembly of sets of components to build business applications, through the wiring of service references to services.

SCA emphasises the decoupling of service implementation and of service assembly from the details of infrastructure capabilities and from the details of the access methods used to invoke services. SCA components operate at a business level and use a minimum of middleware APIs.

SCA specifies how to create components, combine them, and expose the component assembly as a service. Based on SCA defined programming models, components can be built with a variety of programming languages, both including conventional object oriented and procedural languages such as Java™, PHP, C++, COBOL, XML-centric languages such as BPEL and XSLT, and also declarative languages such as SQL and XQuery. SCA also supports a range of programming styles, including asynchronous and message oriented styles, in addition to the synchronous call-and-return style. With SCA communication is technology neutral. A component assembly can consist of services using SOAP, Java Message Service, Representational State Transfer (REST) or other communication mechanisms.

The basic artifact in SCA is the composite, which is the unit of deployment and which holds services that can be accessed remotely. A composite contains one or more

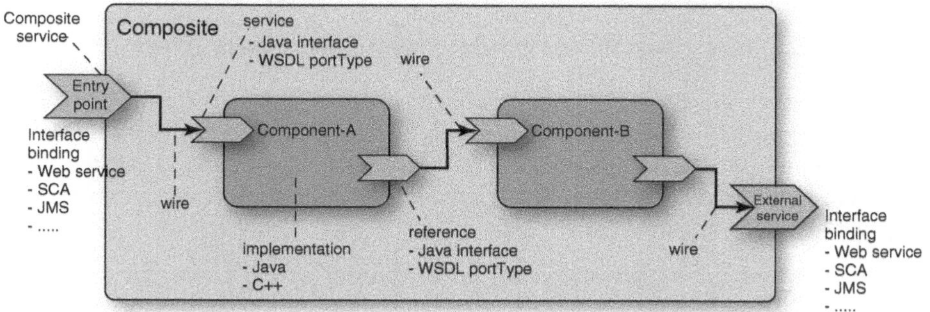

Figure 16.12 Example of a composite application implemented using SCA modules

components, which contain the business function provided by the module. Components offer their function as services, which can either be used by other components within the same module or which can be made available for use outside the module through entry points. Components may also depend on services provided by other components by means of references. References can either be linked to services provided by other components in the same module, or references can be linked to services provided outside the module, which can be provided by other modules. References to services provided outside the module, including services provided by other modules, are defined by external services in the module. Also contained in the module are the linkages between references and services, represented by wires. Figure 16.12 shows the main building blocks of SCA.

An SCA component consists of a configured implementation, where an implementation is the piece of program code implementing business functions. The building blocks of SCA can be combined and assembled together to create composite applications, as shown in Figure 16.12. A composite application can be thought of as a composition of related SCA components, each providing a relatively coarse grained business function. Component implementations can be the result of applying wrapping techniques to component-enable legacy applications as described in the previous sub-section.

16.13.3 Service construction

Service construction is a two pronged activity. It involves constructing services at both the service provider and the service client sides involved in an SOA based application. On the provider side the implementation of a service can be provided by creating a new service, or by transforming existing applications into services, or by composing new services from other (reusable) services and applications. Unlike the previous phases that focus only on the provider, the service construction phase also considers service requesters. On the service client side, although the service requester progresses through similar lifecycle stages as the service provider, different tasks are performed during each construction step. In the following we shall concentrate on the development concepts for atomic services for reasons of brevity and simplicity. Business processes can be created in a similar manner.

16.13.3.1 Constructing an SOA service: the provider perspective

When creating a service there are two possible implementation paths [Wahli 2004]:

1. There is an already existing implementation (service content) for the service, e.g. in Java code. By using this implementation the developer can build the service definition (WSDL document) using SCA or a related technology. Once the WSDL definition has generated the WSDL document, the developer can assemble the service application.
2. A service definition already exists in the form of a WSDL document. By using this WSDL document the designer can build or adapt the implementation (e.g. in Java) code to realise that service. Once the code is implemented, the developer can assemble the service application.

In the following we shall briefly examine how the four service realisation options, which were identified during service analysis in Section 16.11.5, are constructed, starting with greenfield development. There are two ownership possibilities as regards the service realisation options. The service provider could own both the WSDL interface and the service implementation. Alternatively, the service provider could own a WSDL interface whose implementation was constructed and owned by an application service provider.

The greenfield development method considers how a new service is created and comprises two steps [Brittenham 2001]:

1. *Developing a new service content:* This step includes the design and coding of the service content required to implement the service, and the testing to verify that all the interfaces of the service implementation components work correctly. For example, a service provider may construct an artifact, e.g. a Java program, which contains the business logic and code to access the required back end systems in an enterprise to develop the implementation component of a new service.
2. *Defining a new service interface:* Once the new service has been designed and developed, its interface definition in WSDL can be generated from the SCA implementation of the service. The WSDL interface for the service cannot be created unless the artifact, e.g. SCA composite, which represents the implementation and business logic underlying the service, is complete. This is due to the fact that the WSDL interface matches the exact implementation of the service.

Figure 16.13 illustrates the greenfield development approach and distinguishes between the logical and the physical part of the service lifecycle methodology. The WSDL specification in Figure 16.13 corresponds to a service specified during the design phase and is associated with the logical view of the SOA reference model. Likewise, the service implementation in Figure 16.13 is realised by SCA like technologies and is associated with the physical view of the SOA reference model.

The top down approach is commonly used when we have a standard service definition for which there exists no service implementation. The developer then needs to build a service implementation conforming to the service interface. The top down realisation option is divided into two distinct steps:

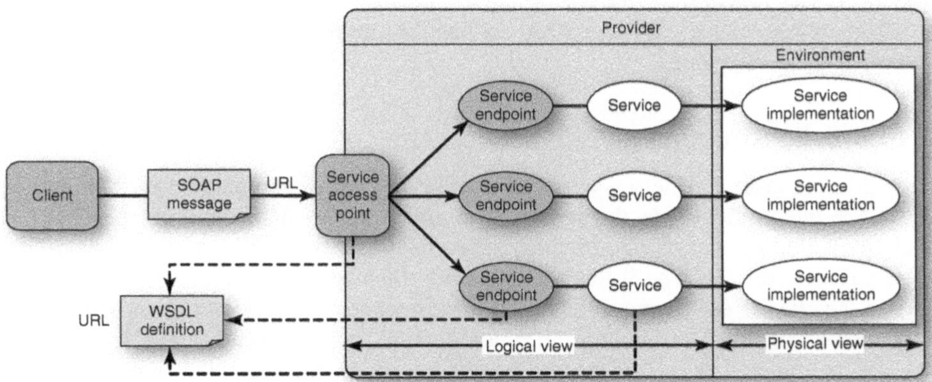

Figure 16.13 The provider perspective on service construction

1. *Generate the service implementation skeleton:* An implementation skeleton for the service is generated using the service interface definition. This skeleton contains all the operations and parameters that must be used so that a compliant implementation of the service interface can be realised.

2. *Develop the new service:* Using the implementation skeleton created in the previous step, a developer must subsequently design and develop the application and business logic that implements the service. This step includes the SCA design and coding required to implement the service, and the testing, verifying that all the interfaces of the service implementation components work correctly.

The bottom up approach is the most common way to build a service. Developers start with the service content, which comes in the form of a business application that is already developed, tested, and running in an enterprise. The bottom up realisation option comprises only one step: developing the service interface. The service interface is derived from the API of the non-service application that represents the service content by creating a wrapper. Therefore, developers start with the service content and generate a WSDL definition document for it, providing all the desired functionality that needs to be externally exposed as a service.

The meet-in-the-middle realisation option is used when a service interface and service content already exist. The prime concern of the meet-in-the-middle development is to map existing application interfaces to those specified in the service WSDL interface definition. We can distinguish two steps for this realisation option:

1. *Generate the service implementation skeleton:* Using the service interface definition that is going to be used to implement the service, an implementation template of the service is generated.

2. *Develop the service wrapper:* Using the implementation skeleton created in the previous step, a wrapper is designed and implemented that will map the service interface into the existing application interface.

All processes follow the same construction trajectory. The developer composes process parts from new services, service enabled applications, or existing services, or from a combination of those elements.

16.13.3.2 Constructing an SOA service: the client perspective

The build time tasks for the service requester are dictated by the method for binding to a service. On the provider side, the construction time tasks are dictated on the basis of how the client is binding to a service provider. The client uses a local service stub or proxy to access a remote service. The WSDL definition of the service is used to generate a stub or proxy at the client's environment. The stub or proxy knows at request time how to invoke the service on the basis of binding information. Binding to a service could happen either statically or dynamically. This results in distinguishing between two types of service clients: static clients versus dynamic clients.

A *static client* is created at construction time by locating the service implementation definition for the single service that will be used by the service client. The service implementation definition contains a reference to the service interface, service binding, and service endpoint that will be used to generate the service proxy code. The service proxy contains a complete implementation of the client application that can be used by the service client to invoke service operations. There are three steps involved in this realisation option:

1. First, the service requester must acquire the service definition either directly from the provider or by looking up the UDDI.
2. Following this step, the designer generates a proxy or stub using the information contained in the WSDL document. This stub is a local representation of the remote service. There are currently several tools available that automatically generate stubs from WSDL definitions.
3. Finally, the service is tested and subsequently deployed in the client run time environment.

A *dynamic client* is used when a service requester wants to use a specific type of service with a known service definition, whose implementation is not known until run time or can change at run time. This means that service operations, the parameters associated with the operations, and the way to bind to the service are already known; however, the endpoint where this service is provided is not known at design time. A typical example of this is when a vertical industry defines a service interface that is implemented by several providers. In that case, a service requester may wish to choose at run time out of a pool of providers a particular provider on the basis of specific quality criteria, such as performance, cost and so forth. The use of a public, private or shared UDDI registry is involved in the process dynamically to provide to the client a range of entry points available at a given time. There are three steps involved in this realisation option:

1. First, the service requester must acquire the service definition document obtaining information about the types, the messages, the port type with the operations and the binding of the WSDL document, using the same mechanisms as in the case of a static client.

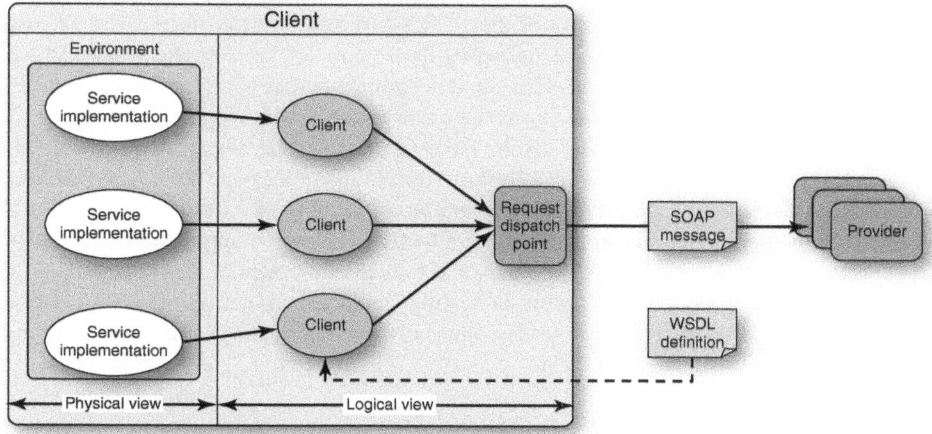

Figure 16.14 The clienzt perspective on service construction

2. Following this step, the designer generates a proxy, using the information contained in the WSDL document. This proxy is a local representation of the remote service and can be used to access any implementation of the service interface. The only difference between the service proxy of a dynamic client and the one generated for a static client is that the static client uses a service proxy that has knowledge of only a single specific service implementation, while the dynamic client uses a generic service proxy that contains the code to locate a service implementation by searching a service registry.
3. Finally, the service is tested and subsequently deployed in the client run time environment.

Figure 16.14 illustrates the construction approach from the perspective of a service client. Notice that, just like the case of the provider in Figure 16.13, the client must also be concerned both with the logical and the physical aspects of proxy services.

16.14 The SOA testing phase

Testing is arguably is a very important phase in any software development project. The goal of testing is to analyse or operate the SOA implementation in a test environment in order to expose any failures that are latent in the code as it is integrated, configured, and run on diverse platforms. *SOA testing* is generally characterised as a validation exercise at the physical level, ascertaining that requirements have been met and that the deliverables are at an acceptable level, and in accordance with existing standards, during the analysis, design and construction phases of the services lifecycle. The result of testing is a *healthy* service oriented application that performs well enough to satisfy the needs of its customers.

Enterprises normally start out with pilots and proof-of-concept implementations to test the performance and availability of their SOA services. Pilot projects offer an excellent opportunity for enterprises to set informal QoS goals for their applications and track against them. For instance, an enterprise can determine whether or not it can provide 99% 24/7 availability for a claims processing service that is used by its worldwide partners. This enterprise can then evaluate the test results from its pilot project and, if it is satisfied with the QoS levels attained, it may decide to roll out the claims processing service to its brokers in multiple phases, with each phase including a larger number of external users. Using the service testing approach, this enterprise can gradually fine tune its applications, set realistic expectations with its community of brokers, and reduce any potential business risks.

Service testing spans various forms of testing, including dynamic testing, functional testing, interface testing, assembly testing and performance testing. These are examined in turn below.

Dynamic testing: The most interesting type of testing for service implementations is *dynamic testing,* which consists of running the implementation and comparing its actual to its expected behaviour before it is deployed. If the actual behaviour differs from the expected behaviour, a defect has been found. In the context of services, dynamic testing is used to perform a variety of types of tests, such as functional tests, performance and stress tests assembly tests and interface tests.

Functional testing: This covers how well services in an SOA execute the functions they are expected to provide – including user commands, data manipulation, searches and integration activities. The objective of functional testing in service oriented environments is to ensure that the business process design has been correctly implemented. Functional testing covers the obvious service interface and operations, as well as the ensuing operations on back end systems, including security functions, database transactions, and how upgrades affect the service oriented system [Culbertson 2001].

Interface testing: The objective of *interface testing* is to ensure that any service in an SOA based application is developed to interface properly with other service functions outside its surrounding process. Interface testing should be performed while testing the function that is affected, e.g. an order management process calling an inventory service.

Assembly testing: This ensures that all services function properly when assembled into business processes. It also verifies that services, which interact and interoperate, function properly when assembled as parts of business processes.

Performance testing: Finally, *performance testing* in service oriented environments focuses on monitoring service on line response times and transaction rates under peak workload conditions. It also involves load testing, which measures the service's ability to handle varied workloads. Performance testing is related to *stress testing,* which looks for errors produced by low resources or competition for resources. It is also related to *volume testing,* which subjects the service to larger and larger amounts of data to determine its point of failure. During performance testing it is important to document all of the testing performed, issues that were encountered, and fixes that were made.

In addition to functional tests, interface and assembly tests, performance and stress tests there are a variety of other tests that may need to be performed during the service test phase. These include network congestion tests, security tests, installation tests, compatibility tests, usability tests and upgrade tests. For instance, security tests have to be conducted to ensure service security requirements such as privacy, message integrity, authentication, authorisation, and non-repudiation.

16.15 The SOA provisioning phase

The provisioning requirements for services impose serious implications for SDLC. Service provisioning is a complex mixture of technical and business aspects for supporting service client and provider activities, and involves choices for service certification, service enrolment, service auditing, metering, billing, and managing operations that control the behaviour of a service during its use. In what follows we provide an overview of the most prominent features of service provisioning.

16.15.1 Service certification

An item of importance is whether one can trust the service QoS. *Service certification* deals with this service aspect and may involve establishing that a service possesses particular properties, most often in conformance with some specification against which the service or business process is certified [Bachmann 2000]. This ensures that application developers work with *known quantities.* To establish that a service possesses some desired property we need to use knowledge to predict the overall properties that an assembled application may attain.

Certification identifies which properties of services are material for predicting or achieving some end system properties, such as performance, safety, scalability and so on, and how to predict the *values* of end system properties from service properties. Measurement techniques must be in place to determine, to a desired level of confidence, the degree to which a service exhibits these properties.

It is foreseeable that an independent trusted group within an organisation, or even a third party, might certify that services and processes are fit for their stated purpose and attest to the truth of this conformance. This has consequences for the development of consumer trust.

16.15.2 Service metering and rating

SOA development should take into account several important aspects relating to the accounting process for service provisioning. This process requires that service providers come up with viable business models that address factors such as service metering, rating and billing, as explained in the following.

Service metering model: Use of a service by a client must be metered if the service provider requires usage based billing. This could typically be done on a periodic basis and requires that a metering and accounting model for the use of the service be established. The metering model can cover diverse payment possibilities, such as a fee-for-use model, a subscription model, and a lease model. The model could allow the establishment of a service contract for each new subscriber, as well as tracking and billing for using the subscribed hosted services. To achieve this, the service metering model could operate on the assumption that services with a high degree of business value are contracted via, for example, SLAs. The service contract lays the foundation for metering the services to be used, by covering all aspects of how they will be offered by the provider and used by the requester.

Service rating/billing model: Software organisations that are used to the traditional up front licence/ongoing maintenance pricing structure for software should come up with annuity based pricing models for the services they provide. The pricing (rating) model could determine subscriber rates based on subscription and usage events. For example, the pricing model could calculate charges for services based on the quality and precision of the service and on individual metering events based on a service rating scheme. The billing model associates rating details with the correct client account. It provides adequate information to allow the retrieval and payment of billing details by the client and the correct disbursement of payments to the service provider's suppliers.

16.16 The SOA deployment phase

Once the provisioning model has been established, the SOA based application services may be deployed and advertised. Deployment means rolling out new processes to all the participants, including other enterprises, applications and other processes. The executable entities (processes and services) must now be deployed on a run time infrastructure that supports SOA based applications, e.g. an application server or an ESB. During this phase, executable business processes, implemented by orchestrating atomic and composite services and conforming to the BPEL specifications, rely on a BPEL run time environment to execute. The service implementations are deployed on an application server, whereas the service definitions are provisioned into a service registry that may also provision the definitions of the executable processes.

The tasks associated with the deployment phase of the SDLC include the publication of the service interface and service implementation definition. It is assumed that services are deployed at the service provider side according to the service realisation options that were examined in Sections 16.11.5 and 16.13.3.

For services that were developed in a greenfield manner, during which an interface for a new service was developed, we may distinguish the following four deployment steps [Brittenham 2001]:

1. *Publish the service interface:* Service providers publish their service definition in a service registry, such as UDDI, so that service requesters can use it to determine how to bind to the service.

2. *Deploy the service:* The run time code for the service, and any deployment metadata that is required to run it, are deployed during this step. Some services will require a deployment environment that provides support for functions such as service billing, service auditing, service security and logging. After a service has been deployed, service requesters can use it.

3. *Create the service implementation definition:* Service providers provide a service content implementation definition based on how and where the service was deployed, e.g. using a SCA component. This will contain all of the operations and parameters that are required by the component implementation of a service and are compliant with the service interface in Step 1. The service implementation definition may contain references to more than one version of the deployed service. This allows the service provider to implement different levels of service to suit the requirements of multiple service requesters.

4. *Publish the service implementation definition:* The service implementation definition contains the definition of the network accessible endpoint or endpoints where the service implementation can be invoked. After the service implementation definition has been published, service clients can discover the service definition and use it to bind to the service.

For services that were developed in a top down manner, during which a service implementation is created for a standard service definition, we may distinguish the following three deployment steps [Brittenham 2001]:

1. *Deploy the service:* The run time code for the service and any deployment metadata that is required to run it are deployed during this step.

2. *Create the service implementation definition:* The service implementation definition is created based on how and where the service was deployed.

3. *Publish the service implementation definition:* The service implementation definition contains the definition of the network accessible endpoint or endpoints where the service can be invoked.

For services that were developed in a bottom up fashion, during which an interface is created for existing service application content, we may distinguish the following four deployment steps [Brittenham 2001a]:

1. *Deploy the service:* This step is the same as Step 2 in greenfield service development.

2. *Create the service implementation definition:* This step is the same as Step 3 in greenfield service development.

3. *Publish the service interface definition:* The service interface definition must be published first and then publication of the service implementation can follow.

4. *Publish the service implementation definition:* This step is the same as Step 4 in greenfield service development.

The deployment steps for the meet-in-the-middle method are similar to those for the bottom up option. The only difference is that the service interface is already published.

16.17 The SOA execution phase

The service execution phase in the SDLC methodology deals with the execution of services. This phase includes the actual binding and run time invocation of the deployed services, as well as managing and monitoring their lifecycle. Execution means ensuring that all participants – people, other organisations, systems and other services, if applicable – carry out a business process. During the execution phase, services are fully deployed and operational. In this stage of the lifecycle, a service client can find the service definition and invoke all defined service operations. The run time functions include static and dynamic binding, service interactions as a function of SOAP serialisation/deserialisation and messaging, and interactions with back end legacy systems (if necessary).

16.18 The SOA management and monitoring phase

Once services and business processes become operational, their progress needs to be managed and monitored to gain a clear view of how services perform within their operational environment, make management decisions, and perform control actions to modify and adjust the behaviour of service enabled applications. Run time management is essential to the successful adoption of an SOA. In an SOA, run time management needs to focus on the delivery of services by providers and the consumption of services by consumers within the boundaries of the metrics stipulated in the SLAs, as well as tracking the relationships between the business processes, the services and their associated IT infrastructure.

Key challenges for SOA management and monitoring include:

- understanding the relationship between services;
- managing services as resources;
- logging and analysis of service execution details;
- ensuring that both functional and non-functional requirements are achieved;
- ensuring compliance with SLAs and regulations;
- determining appropriate control actions to take in response to business situations;
- monitoring the end-to-end service solutions using historical service performance data for continuous service improvement.

SOA service management and monitoring requires that a set of QoS metrics be gathered on the basis of SLAs, given that an SLA is an understanding of expectation of service. In addition, workloads need to be monitored and service weights for request queues might need to be readjusted. This allows a service provider to ensure that the promised performance level is being delivered, and to take appropriate actions to rectify non-compliance with an SLA, such as reprioritising and reallocating resources.

To determine whether an objective has been met, SLA available QoS metrics are evaluated based on measurable data about a service (e.g. response time, throughput, availability and so on), performance during specified times and periodic evaluations, see Chapter 17. SLAs include other observable objectives, which are useful for service monitoring. These include compliance with differentiated service level offerings, i.e. providing differentiated QoS for various types of customer, individualised service level offerings and requests policing, which ensures that the number requests per customer stays within a predefined limit. All these also need to be monitored, assessed and managed. A key aspect of defining measurable objectives is to set warning thresholds and alerts for compliance failures. This results in pre-emptively addressing issues before compliance failures occur. For instance, if the response time of a particular service is degrading then the client could be automatically routed to a back up service.

16.19 SOA governance

Enterprises that progress towards SOA development wish to ensure continuity of their business operations, manage their security exposure, align technology implementation with business requirements, manage liabilities and dependencies and, in general, reduce the cost of operations. One of the key disciplines to assist in addressing these challenges is governance. Governance is a decision and accountability framework, which provides a collection of solutions and policies, plans, procedures and organisational structures to make and control decisions in a way that encourages desirable strategic behaviour. Implementing a governance solution requires well defined enterprise policies.

16.19.1 SOA versus IT governance

IT governance is the most critical area of corporate governance in today's competitive enterprise. *IT governance* is a formalisation of the structured relationships, procedures and policies that ensure the IT functions in an organisation support, and are in line with, its strategic objectives. IT governance aligns IT activities with the goals of the organisation as a whole and includes the decision making rights associated with IT investment, as well as the policies, practices and processes used to measure and control the way IT decisions are prioritised and executed [Holley 2006]. Leadership, organisational structure and processes are used to leverage IT resources and drive alignment, the delivery of value, management of risk, optimisation of resources and performance measurement.

Organisations typically adopt SOA to drive down costs through reuse of developed services and to deliver value. To deliver value, SOAs must exercise control in areas ranging from how a service is built and the process of service deployment, to granular items such as XSD schemas and WSDL creation. However, as the SOA matures and expands enterprise wide, it goes far beyond reuse of a few services across a project or application – often growing into a difficult to manage initiative that dominates reuse across the organisation. The cross-organisational nature of end-to-end business processes that are composed out of variety of service fragments (which may need to be maintained separately by different organisations) makes the management of QoS a factor of paramount importance. This requires that, on the one hand, organisations establish a company wide framework for deciding what services will be created and how they will be managed throughout their lifecycles. On the other hand, organisations must not only enforce QoS but they must also be able to prove and demonstrate QoS levels to service consumers, to gain their trust and create an effective shared service environment. From affecting a few developers on a project, SOA then evolves into an architecture that affects IT staff members both within and across organisations, including architects, business analysts, developers and IT managers.

For these reasons, an efficient service strategy is required that oversees the entire lifecycle of an enterprise's service portfolio and identifies, specifies, creates and deploys enterprise services, and oversees their proper maintenance and growth [Mitra 2005]. Otherwise, an enterprise cannot fully reap the benefits that SOA has to offer. Only when SOA enabled business investments are managed well within an effective governance framework can enterprises harvest significant opportunities to create value.

SOA governance focuses on the creation, communication, enforcement and adaptation of *policies* used to direct and control the creation and implementation of the lifecycle of services in an SOA application. SOA governance is a natural extension of IT governance that focuses on the development, deployment, operations and management of services. As a specialisation of IT governance, SOA governance suggests how an IT governance's decision rights, policies, procedures and measures need to be modified and augmented for successful SOA adoption. It mitigates many of the business risks inherent in SOA adoption by establishing decision rights, guiding the definition of appropriate services, managing assets and measuring effectiveness.

Effective SOA governance requires equal focus on the people, processes, decisions and technology aspects of SOA. According to the Open group, an SOA governance model should cover three main governance aspects [Open Group 2009b]:

1. Processes – including governing and governed processes.
2. Organisational structures – including roles and responsibilities.
3. Enabling technologies – including tools and infrastructure.

16.19.2 SOA governance types

A complete SOA governance solution should address SOA challenges that can be grouped into three broad areas: organisational, lifecycle and operational.

- *Organisational governance* focuses on business alignment, which ensures the SOA implementation takes into consideration all business level agreements.
- *Lifecycle governance* focuses on the entire lifecycle of an SOA application or service, from design to development to test to deployment and maintenance.
- Finally, *operational governance* consists largely of policy management and of enforcement and management of service level agreements (SLAs).

Essentially, SOA governance clearly defines the decision making rights, ownership responsibilities and communication paths that empower people to bring about the necessary organisational changes to share services and ensure SOA success. It helps ensure that the decision making structure is solid, that relationships between services and parties are managed, and that there is compliance with the laws, policies, standards and procedures under which an organisation operates.

SOA governance can be logically divided into design time and run time governance:

- *Design time governance:* Design time SOA governance addresses the concerns of service policy management, service lifecycle management and quality management for services. Typical issues for design time governance considerations include whether the right types of service have been selected, whether all requirements for new services have been identified, whether all security policies have been considered and addressed and so forth. To gain the most reusability across lines of business, departments and projects, it is important to enforce consistency in use of standards, use best practices and reference architectures that are used as both blueprints for new designs and a yardstick by which service design is evaluated. Other design time review issues also include whether the use of a particular service within an application would conform to enterprise specific or government mandated privacy rules, whether service implementation does not compromise QoS requirements as stipulated in SLAs or enterprise specific intellectual property, and so on.
- *Runtime governance:* This is the act of enforcing run time policies after a service has been deployed. It involves message inspection, as well as the monitoring of business services while they execute, and applies to deployment and management of service oriented systems. To achieve its stated objectives and support an enterprise's business objectives on strategic, functional and operational levels, SOA governance provides a well defined structure. It defines the rules, processes, metrics and organisational constructs needed for effective planning, decision making, steering and control of the SOA engagement to meet the business requirements of an enterprise and its customers [Balzer 2004].

An enterprise can address the service governance challenge most effectively by establishing an internal governance body comprising business analysts, line of business decision makers, security specialists, network operations experts, users and others. Such teams can play a crucial role in engineering an SOA environment that functions for the greater benefit of the enterprise. The essential responsibilities of the governance body include strategic alignment, value delivery, risk, resource and performance management [Mitra 2005]. An enterprise's SOA governance body ensures that the enterprise's IT sustains and extends its strategies and objectives by laying down service related policies, and decides about which people in the enterprise are empowered to make those decisions, and can thus monitor, define and authorise the changes to the existing suite of services supported within the enterprise.

Services that flow between enterprises must also have defined owners with established ownership and governance responsibilities. These owners are responsible for gathering requirements, development, deployment and operations management for any mission critical or revenue generating service [Bieberstein 2005]. The service must meet the functional and QoS objectives both within the context of the business unit and the enterprises within which it operates. To this end, SOA governance introduces the notion of *business domain ownership,* where domains are managed sets of services sharing some business context. Typical examples of such business scopes are customer relationship management, customer information and entitlements, order management, financing, taxes and so forth. At least two different governance types are possible. These are central governance versus federated governance and are discussed below.

> *Central governance:* With central governance, the governing body within an enterprise has representation from each business domain, as well as from independent parties that do not have direct responsibility for any of the service domains. There is also representation from the different business units in the organisation and partner organisations, as well as subject matter experts who can talk to the developers who implement key technological components of the service solution. The central governance council reviews any additions or deletions to the list of services, along with changes to existing services, before authorising the implementation of such changes. Central governance suits an entire enterprise.
>
> *Federated governance:* With federated governance each partner organisation (or business unit) has autonomous control over how it provides the services within its own enterprise. A central governance committee can provide guidelines and standards to different teams. This committee has an advisory role, in that it only makes recommendations and does not have to authorise changes to the existing service infrastructure within any business unit. Federated governance suits enterprise chains better.

To facilitate the definition, design and implementation of SOA governance and service lifecycle management, and enable organisations to define and deploy their own focused and customised SOA governance model, the Open Group has proposed an SOA Governance Framework [Open Group 2009b]. This framework consists of a SOA Governance Reference Model, which is utilised as a starting point, and a SOA Governance Vitality Method, which is a definition/improvement feedback process to define a focused and customised SOA Governance regimen.

The SOA Governance Reference Model (SGRM) is a generic baseline SOA governance model that is used to expedite the process in tailoring a SOA governance model for an organisation. All aspects of the SOA Governance Reference Model are reviewed and considered for customisation to the organisation's environment. The SOA Governance Reference Model defines a number of constituent parts, including: SOA governance guiding principles, SOA governing and governed processes, SOA governance process artifacts, SOA governance roles and responsibilities and SOA governance technology.

The SOA Governance Vitality Method (SGVM) is a process that utilises the SOA Governance Reference Model as a baseline and then follows a number of phased activities to customise this baseline model to cater to the organisation's variants. SOA governance is viewed as a continuous improvement loop, whereby progress is measured, and course correction and updates to the SOA governance regimen and SOA governance roadmap

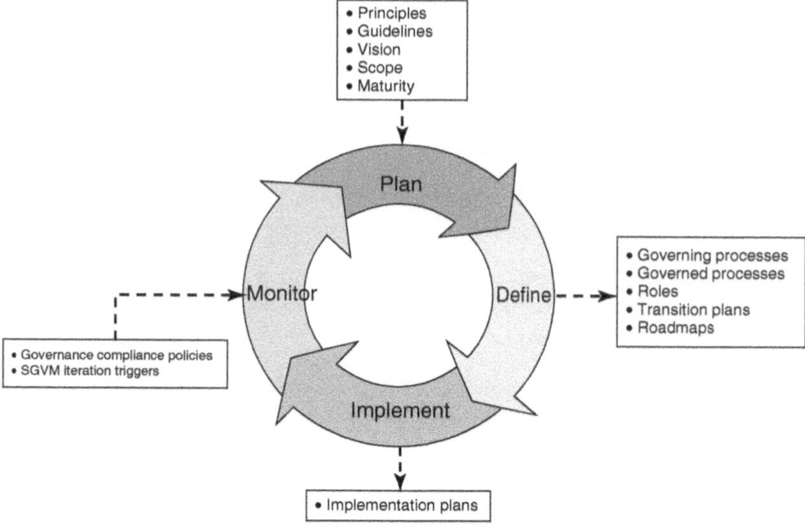

Figure 16.15 SGVM phases and artefacts

are performed when needed. The SOA Governance Vitality Method defines four phases, which are illustrated in Figure 16.15:

- *Plan:* Identify and analyse the core governance areas for improvement. Establish objectives/plan and specific measures for a proposed increment. Previously deployed increments are also evaluated for any necessary improvement.
- *Define:* Define the SOA Governance Model transition plans required to deliver the objectives defined in the Plan phase.
- *Implement:* Implement the transition plans, including deployment of processes, organisation and technology aspects of the SOA Governance Model.
- *Monitor:* Monitor the effectiveness of the currently deployed SOA Governance Regimen and whether it is meeting its intended purpose. This phase may start another iteration of the SGVM.

16.20 Summary of learning objectives

To build an application that conforms to SOA principles, an SOA development lifecycle methodology needs to be established and followed. This methodology allows the design and development of solutions as assemblies of services and is based on an iterative and incremental procedure that comprises eight distinct main phases that revolve around business processes and may be traversed iteratively.

- The planning phase determines the feasibility, nature and scope of SOA solutions.
- Service oriented analysis identifies the requirements of new applications.
- Service design requires modelling and defining well documented interfaces for all major software modules prior to constructing them. It considers both functional and non-functional service characteristics.
- Service construction includes the definition of the service interface description, and the definition of the service implementation description.
- Testing analyses the service implementation in a test environment in order to expose any failures that are latent in the code as services are integrated, configured and run on diverse platforms.
- Service provisioning involves choices for service governance, service certification, service enrolment, service auditing, metering, billing and managing operations.
- Service deployment includes the service implementation definition and the publication of the service interface.
- Finally, during the execution phase Web services are fully deployed and operational, while during the monitoring phase services are monitored to gain a clear view of how they behave within their operational environment and address any deviations in their behaviour.

Review questions

- How does a Web service development methodology compare to traditional methodologies, such as object oriented analysis and design and component based development?
- What are business services and how do they relate to infrastructure services and implementation components?
- Briefly describe the milestones of service oriented design development.
- What is service coupling, service cohesion and service granularity?
- Briefly describe the phases of the Web service development lifecycle.
- What is the purpose of *as-is* process analysis?
- What is service gap analysis?
- What are the major service design concerns?
- What are the steps for specifying Web services and business processes?
- What is the purpose of the service integration model?
- What is the purpose of the service test phase?
- What are the objective and major elements of SOA governance?

Exercises

1. Consider an enterprise that is operating a coordination system for aircraft landing activities. This system comprises interconnected older generation systems for ticket booking, crew management, flight coordination and flight operation, which are implemented on mainframe computers that typically run COBOL/CICS transactions. These four systems are responsible for retrieving passenger details from the ticket booking system, crew information from the crew management system, flight schedule and arrival information from the flight coordination system, and cockpit information from the flight operation system. The application also checks safety of the airport parking spot and the status of the unloaded cargo. In the current implementation, events are tightly coupled and business logic for collaboration between the four systems is hard coded so that the integration functionality cannot adapt to new business requirements. This enterprise wishes to migrate to SOA based integration for its applications and develop modern business processes on an ESB platform. In particular, the enterprise requires that data from the crew management, ticket booking and flight operation be merged and the landing management process be notified of flight arrivals before checking the parking spot. Flight arrival is a typical event that requires detection by the flight operation system. Conduct an *as-is* and *to-be* analysis for this SOA based application and produce a high level view of the service components and their interconnections on the ESB platform.

2. Consider a simple retail inventory process that offers integration with warehouses, suppliers, or third-party fulfilment centres. First the client selects a product from a catalogue by specifying its product number. Then the availability of this product is checked in a local store inventory against the appropriate quantities. If the product is not available, then the order recipient forwards the request to a warehouse by specifying demand information. If the warehouse cannot meet the requirements of the quote, it may then identify another supplier for the customer. In this case, a referral is sent to the customer. Decompose this process into a number of discrete services and design their interfaces according to the service design steps in Section 16.11. Finally, design the process and specify it abstractly in WS-BPEL according to the process design steps in Section 16.12.3.

3. EU-Rent is a fictitious car rental company that has over 1000 branches worldwide (http://www.businessrulesgroup.org/egsbrg.shtml). At each branch vehicles, classified by vehicle group, are available for rental. The company offers a wide variety of current model vehicles on a short term rental basis, including daily, weekly and monthly, at a variety of locations such as airports, residential areas and resorts. Most rentals are by advance reservation; the rental period and the car group are specified at the time of reservation. Assume that EU-Rent implements its vehicle rental processes using older generation technologies and now wishes to implement an SOA solution for added flexibility. Further, assume that EU-Rent has conducted an *as-is,* ROI and SWOT analysis and has come up with a *to-be* process model that contains the following core vehicle rental business processes: vehicle rental reservation, vehicle handover, vehicle return from rental, and payment processing. Conduct business service identification, business scoping, gap analysis, and realisation analysis (including functional and non-functional, e.g. security, requirements) for the four core EU-Rent vehicle rental processes.

4. Consider a loan processing application. This application comprises a loan management service that receives requests from clients and is responsible for managing a request for a new loan application or an extension of a current loan; a new account service that is responsible for opening new loan applications; a loan application service that is responsible for processing new and existing loan applications; and a credit verifier service for verifying customer credibility. Develop a service integration transportation model employing two transportation patterns, service broker interceptor and service bus for the loan processing application. Subsequently, define a service integration process flow for the service integration transportation model.

5. Consider the brokered enterprise topology in Exercise 8.5. This topology, just like any other, impacts SOA governance. Describe the responsibilities of business analysts and service developers in implementing an appropriate SOA governance solution for this ESB topology.

6. Describe an SOA governance model that applies to large enterprises. Explain the role and responsibilities of teams that are involved in implementing this SOA governance model. Common activities within this model include, among other things, determining SOA architecture oversight, establishing SOA policies, implementing SOA governance processes, governing services definition, creation and publishing, and establishing policies and processes for QoS enforcement. Finally, explain how the governance model can be launched in this enterprise. Some useful ideas regarding governance principles and launching the governance model can be found in [Balzer 2004].

PART IX

Service management

CHAPTER 17

SOA and Web service management

Learning objectives

In SOA solutions, service usage patterns, SLA criteria and metrics and failure data should be continuously collected and analysed. Without such information, it is often quite challenging to understand the root cause of performance or stability problems that concern an SOA based application. To tackle these challenges there is a critical need for organisations to manage and monitor business operations to ensure that the Web services supporting a given SOA application are performing in accordance with service level objectives.

This chapter explores traditional distributed management approaches and their underlying architectural concepts and relates them to SOA and Web service management techniques and upcoming standards. After completing this chapter you will understand the following key concepts:

- The necessity for managing distributed computing infrastructures.
- The nature and architectural types of Enterprise Management Systems.
- Conceptual management architectures and standard management frameworks.
- The features of SOA and Web service management.
- Architectural approaches for the management of Web services.
- The Web Services Distributed Management standard.

Chapter preview

This chapter discusses the importance of managing distributed applications. We describe enterprise management frameworks, distributed management concepts and architectures, as well as standard distributed management initiatives. Subsequently, we explain how the initiatives and approaches to distributed systems management have influenced Web service management and introduce standards that seek to unify management infrastructures by providing a vendor, platform, network and protocol neutral framework for enabling management technologies to access and receive notifications of Web service management enabled resources.

17.1 Managing distributed systems

Distributed (or composite) applications are increasingly being used in mission critical roles and the need to monitor, track and measure them has never been greater. Distributed applications spread functionality and components over a variety of resources, including Web servers, application servers, messaging backbones, legacy resources, applications and so on. These elements must work together seamlessly to support the implementation and delivery of business processes necessary for business operations. This requires new management approaches and capabilities.

Although most organisations have traditional monitoring tools to manage individual resources at a high level, many lack an integrated solution automatically to monitor, analyse and resolve problems (failures) at the service, transaction, application and resource levels. Distributed applications are more difficult to monitor and measure than applications running on a centralised computing system within a single system image. Any procedure for linking processing activities on multiple systems to a single business transaction must operate across an especially complex environment. As a result, when users experience application problems, e.g. service brownouts and slowdowns, it is difficult and time consuming to trace and identify the cause of the failure to an individual server, network link or software element, and fix the problems.

Problems arise because there is no generalised method for tracing the flow of transactions from one system image to another. It would be useful for an administrator to know unambiguously when transactions begin and end, both those that are visible to the user as well as the component transactions that invoke local transactions on remote servers. Distributed systems management addresses such issues by monitoring and controlling the activities of a distributed system, making management decisions and performing control actions to modify the behaviour of the system.

17.1.1 Purpose of distributed systems management

Traditional distributed systems and network management has evolved from the need to manage successive layers of new technologies and devices as they have been deployed into distributed computing environments. A *managed* (or *manageable*) *resource* in a distributed environment could be any type of hardware or software component that can be managed and that can maintain embedded management related metadata. A managed resource could be a server, storage unit, database, application server, service, application, or any other entity that needs to be managed.

A bewildering array of standalone utilities has gradually been merged into comprehensive management suites that are integrated through the ability to share events and common data and are controlled through a consistent interface. A distributed application management system controls and monitors an application throughout its lifecycle, from installing and configuring to collecting metrics, and tuning the application to ensure responsive execution. The system's functionality must cover all operational activities – including starting and stopping processes, and rerouting operations – as well as problem detection functions, such as application tracing and message editing.

Distributed application manageability in this context signifies the ability to exercise administrative and supervisory actions and receive information that is relevant to such actions on a variety of distributed resources. Manageability can be distinguished by three functional parts [Murray 2002]:

- *Monitoring:* The ability to capture run time and historical events from a particular component, for reporting and notification.
- *Tracking:* The ability to observe aspects of a single unit of work or thread of execution across multiple resources.
- *Control:* The ability to alter the run time behaviour of a managed resource.

Manageability provides a mechanism to ensure that an application is both active and functioning properly, as well as that of checking an application's performance over time. Any management solution must address four necessary management questions [Mehta 2003]:

1. What resources need to be managed?
2. What are their properties?
3. How is the management information exchanged (operations, notifications and kinds of protocols needed)?
4. What are the relationships among the managed resources?

In distributed systems management, management tool suites and utilities monitor distributed system activities to facilitate management decisions and system behaviour modifications. Such toolsets provide tools, programs and utilities that give systems administrators and network managers insights into system and network health, as well as into application status and behaviour patterns.

Figure 17.1 shows management toolsets that have been developed to support both systems administration functions, e.g. client–server management, configuration management and the like, and network management functions, e.g. LAN/WAN management, and remote access management. Distributed systems management tools can, for instance, provide an analysis of processing activities on multiple systems that link to a single business transaction that is providing meaningful service to an end user.

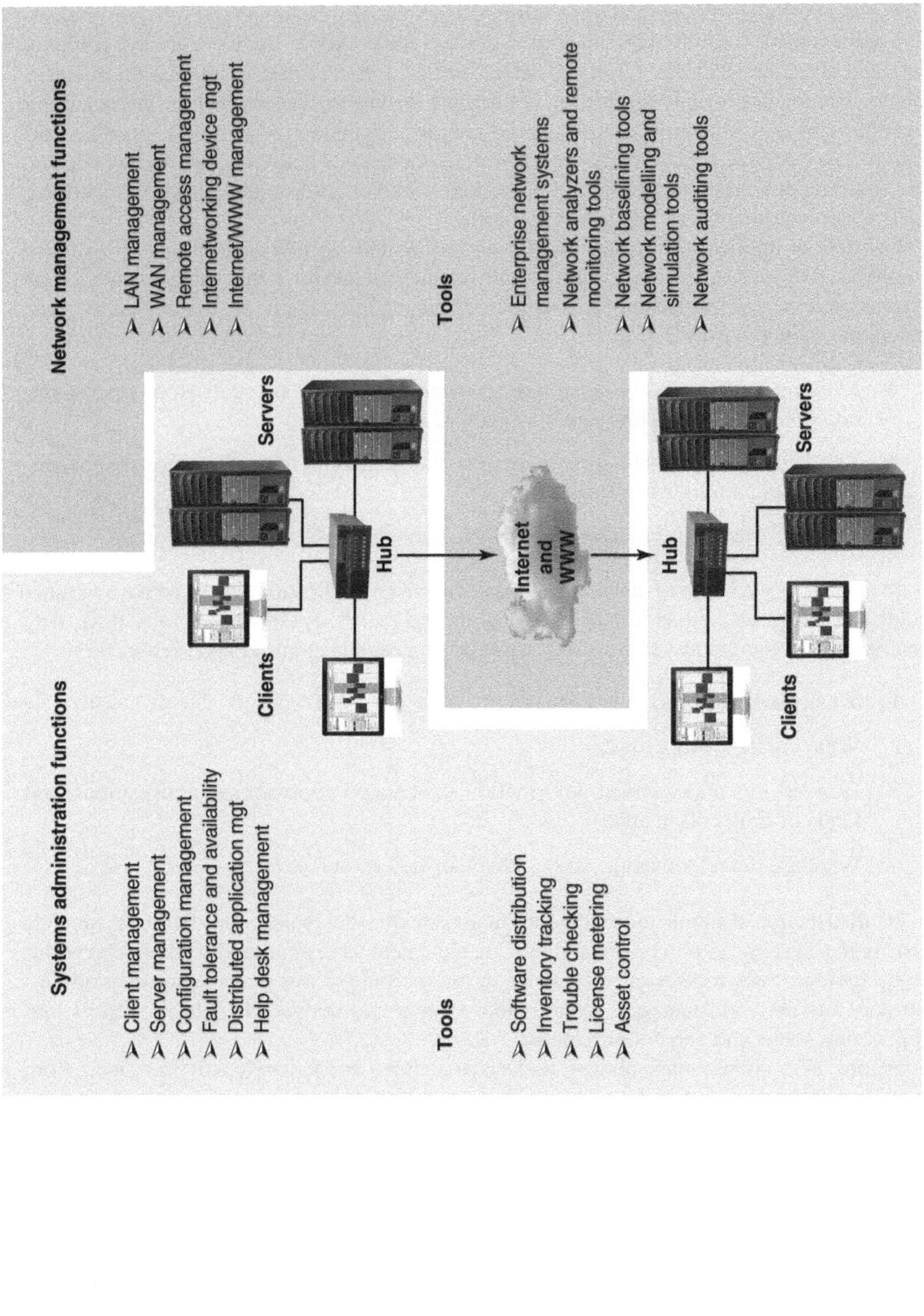

Figure 17.1 Distributed computing infrastructure administration and management

Although toolsets and utilities have existed in traditional distributed computing environments for many years, we have yet to develop equivalent technologies for the complex world of loosely coupled, Web service based applications.

17.1.2 Distributed management for Web services

Businesses orchestrate distributed services nowadays into many different configurations to support multiple business processes. An orchestrated service implementation forms a logical network of services layered over the infrastructure (including software environments, servers, legacy applications and back end systems) and the physical connectivity network. When a Web service network grows, its existence and performance become as relevant to the business's core activities as other critical computing resources. This has changed the enterprise traffic patterns and increased the dependency on mission critical enterprise services and infrastructures. Consequently, any such environment should be managed in order to provide the security, usability and reliability needed in today's business environment.

Traditionally, distributed systems and network management focused on managing successive layers of new technologies and devices as they were deployed into distributed computing environments. However, such techniques concentrate on providing solutions at the systems and network management levels and fail to meet enterprise requirements in a service-centric world, because they lack the business awareness functions required by service management products. Also, many existing system management infrastructures do not support SLA reporting or collect specific service information from Web service applications for troubleshooting purposes.

Distributed management solutions for Web services should offer a clear view of how services perform within their operational environment, to enable management decisions and to perform control actions to modify and adjust the behaviour of SOA based applications that are implemented using Web service technology. Some of the essential components needed for proper management of service-centric architectures are briefly outlined below and depicted in Figure 17.2. These are:

User experience monitoring: Services must be monitored for availability and performance from the application user's perspective so that the management infrastructure and administrators understand when the user experience is failing to meet objectives. Front end processing, e.g. on line purchasing, can be understood by monitoring actual user transactions, while back end processing, e.g. account billing, can be captured by monitoring the back end fulfilment processes for timeliness and completion.

Infrastructure monitoring: Distributed resources must be monitored for availability, performance and utilisation so that developing problems can be quickly detected. This includes not only servers and networks, but also critical software infrastructure. The management infrastructure must know how many instances of a service are running, whether a service is performing adequately and when it has

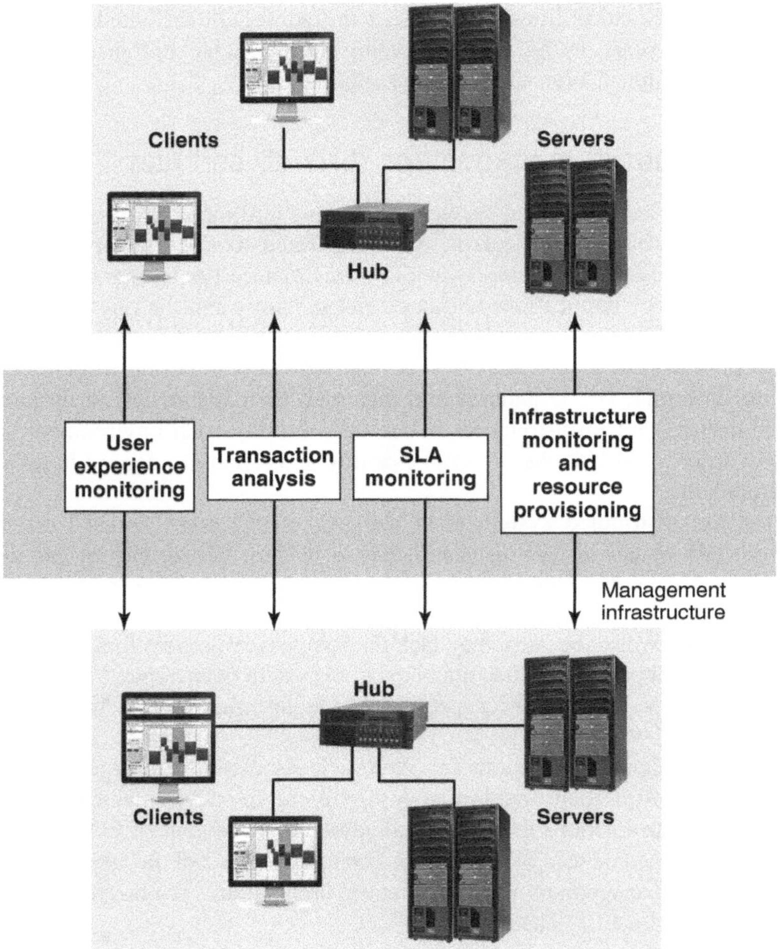

Figure 17.2 Essential components of service-centric management architecture

stopped functioning, and how readily to connect and disconnect services and their clients without breaking applications or infrastructure. For systems administrators to tackle these challenges, they require management capabilities specific to the Web services environment.

Transaction monitoring: The growing complexity of global Web services brings together large numbers of services, suppliers and technologies, all with potentially different performance requirements. Therefore, when user experience degrades, individual transactions must be traced through the system to see which servers and which application components are involved and where the problem lies.

Resource provisioning: When a Web services based application is running, careful monitoring of system activity can help to identify potential problems before they are manifested in overloads or failures. For example, when a particular resource is in danger of being completely consumed then, as long as the operations staff are aware that this situation is arising, they may be able to take corrective action before a failure occurs. For instance, when a server cluster no longer has the capacity to handle the demands being made upon the application, additional servers are provisioned and configured.

SLA monitoring: In the context of Web services, an SLA reflects the most rigorous requirements for the key performance indicators for all services supported by the SLA. The SLA ties together systems and services from multiple groups and multiple vendors, defining the boundaries and operational characteristics of these groups. The enterprise SLA's goal is ultimately to improve the service's quality of experience (QoE) to its internal or external clients. QoE entails a shared foundation for measuring service or product quality, including performance, overall customer satisfaction, pre- and post-sale service, and product and service delivery [Open Group 2004]. To achieve an effective contract, the provider must often establish and monitor several SLAs, whether internally (for business or end users) or externally (for service providers, partners, outsourcers, suppliers and so on). For every tier or peer SLA, one party can be considered a supplier or provider and the other a customer. An SLA can add value in providing the business application to an end customer only when the individual service applications are instrumented adequately so that metrics can be determined. Such metrics ensure conformance, attempt to prevent or warn of non-conformance, and measure non-conformance. Thus, the goal of establishing and managing an end-to-end enterprise SLA is only possible by mapping the requirements and objectives of the amalgamated SLA to measurable parameters at the SLA tiers.

Ensuring quality: service focused management requires measurable key performance indicators (KPIs) for applications and services. Generic KPIs for business applications include service availability, response time, transaction rate, service throughput, service idle time and security. The service provider must know whether the services it has contracted to deliver are meeting its KPI objectives and issue warnings and alarms, if they fail to do so. Service providers must therefore set the service KPIs and their objectives, and be able to measure, analyse, and report on the KPI values achieved against these objectives.

To tackle the above challenges there is a critical need for a Web service measurement and management infrastructure and associated toolset, which exists external to the application services to address the needs like the ones listed above.

To understand better the principles behind the concept of Web service management we shall first introduce the topic of enterprise management systems, and describe standard management frameworks that are currently in wide use for the development of distributed applications, before delving into this intricate concept. Subsequently, we shall describe a conceptual architecture for the management of distributed resources.

17.2 Enterprise management frameworks

Enterprise Management Systems are network management systems capable of managing heterogeneous devices, independent of vendors and protocols, in IP based enterprise networks [Kakadia 2002]. This section provides a brief summary of typical architectures of Enterprise Management Systems and functionality to help the reader better understand the contemporary Web service management solutions.

Most Enterprise Management Systems (EMS) use common functions, such as fault management, configuration management, accounting management, performance management and security management [Kakadia 2002].

- *Fault management* applications include processing all events and determining if a fault is detected. Fault detection requires other functions, including filter events, logging to maintain historical records that detect long term trends, monitoring, notification and reporting by generating alarms.
- *Configuration management* allows the operator to verify and modify the configuration of managed devices.
- *Accounting management* maintains usage based statistics for billing purposes.
- *Performance management* provides utilities to the operator to define and periodically measure performance related variables.
- *Security management* allows network services to be accessed in a secure manner in a distributed network and includes authentication, authorisation, data integrity – to verify the integrity of the cryptographic data checksum that confirms the integrity of unaltered data – and auditing (historical tracking of logs used in post-mortem investigations as a result of security incidents or proactive precautionary measures).

EMS can be organised in a variety of architectures depending on how network managers are organised. To describe how an EMS is deployed, a *network architecture* is employed. Models can be a single central manager, hierarchical managers, distributed peer managers and so on. A network architecture also includes the management protocols that are used to communicate information about the management resource between network managers and agents. The choice of architecture has a direct impact on scalability, availability, performance and security.

Figure 17.3 provides an overview of the main types of Enterprise Management System architectures. In this figure, network management systems (NMS) manage a particular device, often implemented by the device manufacturer.

Centralised architecture. Figure 17.3(a) illustrates a *centralised architecture,* where a single NMS manages all the devices on an enterprise network. The single NMS has limited performance and scalability, in terms of network and computing capabilities. All management applications that carry out one or more fault, configuration, accounting, performance and security functions are performed on the central server. The single network connection is a single point of failure that quickly becomes congested as the number of managed devices increases, and the management server also reaches its limits in terms of polling for events and processing traps. The NMS console in Figure 17.3 is the management console

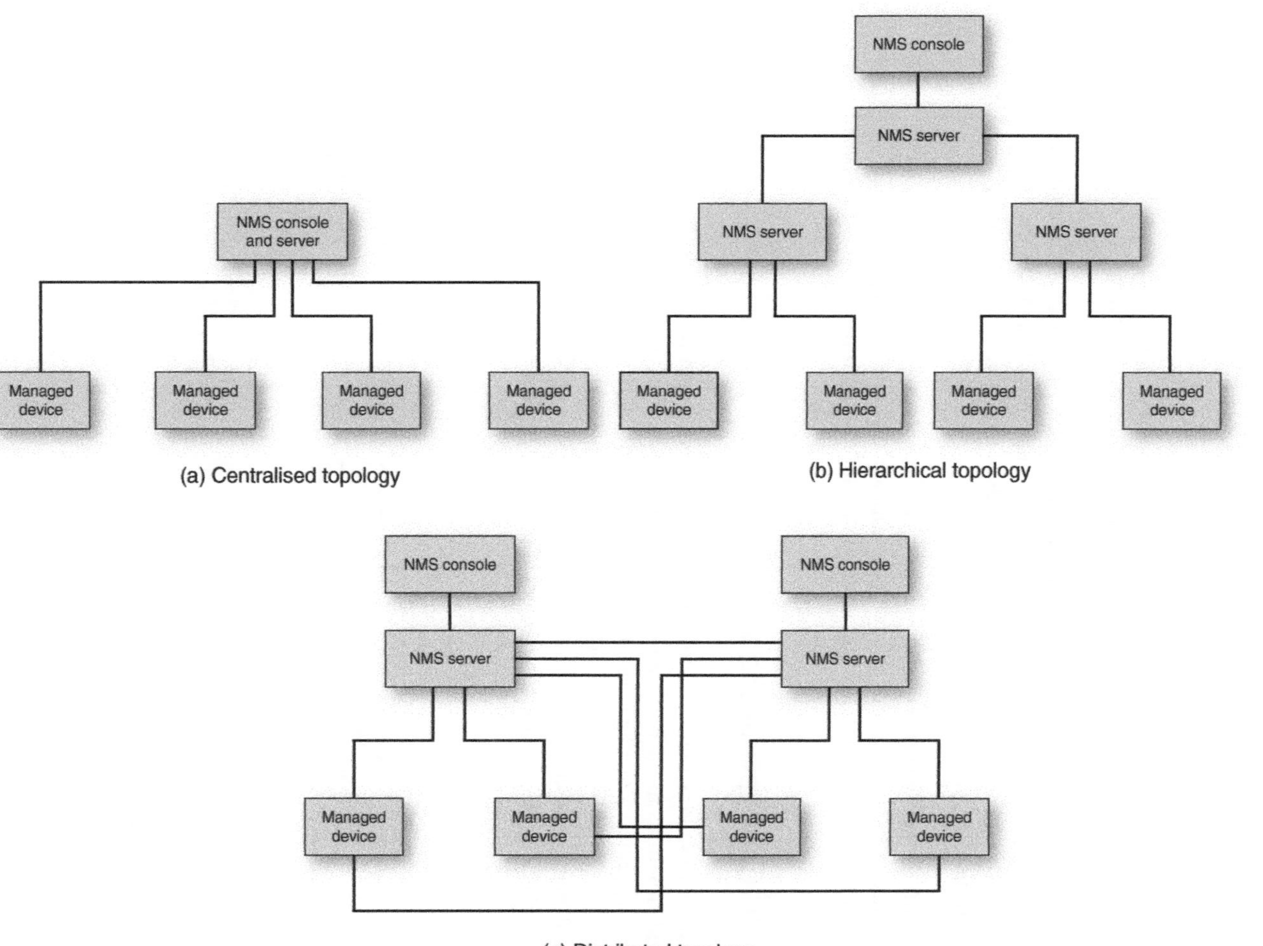

Figure 17.3 Overview of the main types of Enterprise Management System topologies

for the display and manipulation of all distributed network related management information. Management consoles are capable of displaying management information in a human comprehensible manner. The console will typically provide a number of topological views into the distributed network platform and the associated management environment, suitable for different types and levels of operation and administrative staff.

Hierarchical architecture. Figure 17.3(b) illustrates a *hierarchical architecture,* where there are many local management servers managing small local networks and propagating important events to a higher central management system. This model offers better network and server processing performance capabilities. The bulk of the network traffic is localised, because only filtered and correlated events and information are forwarded to the central server. This architecture provides increased availability and avoids the problems of the centralised server architecture.

Distributed architecture. Finally, Figure 17.3(c) depicts a *highly distributed system,* where any management server can communicate with any managed device. This architecture offers high availability and scalability, and also permits specialisation of services.

17.3 Conceptual management architecture

Distributed systems management technologies monitor and respond to managed resource related situations in the environment, basically functioning as a control loop. They collect details regarding a managed resource and act accordingly.

Figure 17.4 shows that we can view the management infrastructure in terms of a conceptual management architecture that fuses together various components. These include managed resources, resource managers and a management console.

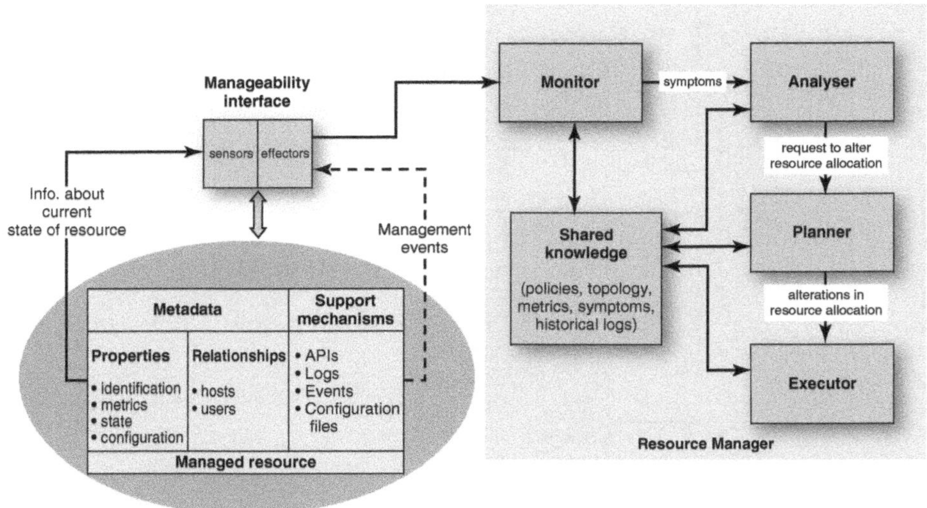

Figure 17.4 Conceptual management architecture

The *management console* displays management information through its management interface, which lets administrators control and supervise managed resources and change their behaviours. Manageable resources are all kinds of hardware and software resources, both physical and logical, such as software applications, business processes, services, hardware devices, networks, servers, etc., whose management capabilities could be exposed as Web services that implement various management interfaces, such as those defined in Web Services Distributed Management (see Section 17.6).

A *management interface* of a resource could be described by a corresponding WSDL definition, resource properties schema, metadata information, and potentially a set of management related policies [Kreger 2005a]. A service provider then exposes this management interface. As the oval in Figure 17.4 shows, the interface also uses metadata about the resource's properties, including:

- *identification,* which denotes an instance of the managed resource;
- *metrics,* which provide information and operations for resource measurements, such as throughput, utilisation, and so on;
- *configuration,* which provides information and operations for the configurable attributes of a managed resource.

Management interfaces also require information about a resource's relationships with its immediate environment, including its users and hosts. Finally, the interface retrieves information about the current state of a managed resource and the management events (notifications) that might occur when the resource undergoes significant state changes.

17.3.1 Management capabilities and functions

The resource manager in Figure 17.4 is a component that implements a control loop, which collects details regarding a managed resource and acts accordingly. The resource manager realises the management capabilities and functions of management solutions. To achieve this, it must have an automated method to:

- collect the details it needs from the system;
- analyse those details to determine if something needs to change;
- create a plan, or sequence of actions, that specifies the necessary changes;
- perform those actions.

These four parts work together to provide the *control loop functionality.*

The manageability interface in Figure 17.4 is divided into sensors and effectors [IBM 2004]. Sensors help managers to access the state of the managed resource, either on demand or through notifications, when state changes occur [IBM 2004]. An example of a sensor is an endpoint that exposes information about the current operational status of a managed resource and transitions in that operational state. Effectors provide the means for a manager to affect the state and behaviour of the managed resource by means of management operations or configuration capabilities. For instance, it may provide an operation to stop the managed resource; that is, change its operational status to *stopped.*

The sensor and effector interfaces support four unique styles of interaction:

- request/response;
- send notification;
- perform operation;
- solicit/response.

A resource manager uses the request/response interaction mode when it needs to retrieve details about a managed resource through its interface. In a similar fashion a managed resource uses the notification interaction mode when it needs to inform its corresponding resource manager of impending events that may affect the status of the resource.

The monitor module in Figure 17.4 collects, aggregates, filters and reports managed resource details, e.g. metrics, collected from a managed resource [IBM 2004]. The collected managed resource metadata can include such information as metrics, topology information, configuration property settings, offered capacity, throughput and so on. The monitor module aggregates, correlates and filters the metadata, and organises it into symptoms that require analysis. For example, the monitor function could collect details about initiating and completing transactions. It then calculates the response time for the transaction measurements. If the response time exceeds a pre-specified threshold, the monitor module could produce a *missed response time* symptom. Such transaction measurements are passed to the resource manager through the *retrieve-state* and *receive-notification* interaction modes of the management interface. A resource manager could subsequently use the monitored data, e.g. during the analysis process, to generate a change request or the execute function to perform system self-optimisation. Selected monitored data could also be presented to a systems administrator on a management console.

The analyser module in Figure 17.4 provides the mechanisms that observe, correlate and analyse complex situations (e.g. employing prediction techniques such as time series forecasting and queuing models) [IBM 2004]. These mechanisms allow the resource manager to learn about the computing environment and help predict future situations where changes may eventually need to be made. For example, the analyser module may determine that some policy is not being met or is violated. In many cases, the analyser module models complex behaviour so that it can employ prediction techniques, such as time series forecasting and queuing models, to allow a resource manager to learn about the environment surrounding a managed resource and help predict future behaviour.

Policies in this environment are coded by system analysts and specify the criteria that a resource manager uses to realise a definite goal, or to accomplish a course of action. For instance, a resource manager involved in workload management uses the specified workload policies to guide its analysis and decisions. These workload policies might include QoS goals for accomplishing the workload. Using the symptom data delivered by the monitor module, the analyser module can understand how the involved systems commit their resources to execute the workload, and how changes in allocation affect performance over time. It then uses the transaction measurements from the monitor component and performance goals from pre-specified workload policies to generate a change request to alter resource allocations. For example, the analyser module could add or delete a resource to optimise performance across these multiple systems.

The plan module provides the mechanisms that construct the actions needed to achieve goals and objectives [IBM 2004]. It achieves this by creating or selecting a procedure to enact a desired alteration in the managed resource on the basis of policy information. The plan module passes the appropriate change plan, which represents a desired set of changes for the managed resource, to the executor module. A plan can take on many forms, ranging from a single command to a complex workflow. For instance, the plan module could use a change request created by the analyser to generate or select a change plan for improving workload management. It might produce a workflow that will add or delete specific resources; or redistribute portions of the workload to different resources.

The executor module provides the mechanisms to schedule and perform the necessary changes to the system [IBM 2004]. These mechanisms control the execution of a plan with considerations for dynamic updates. For instance, an executor module involved in workload management may use the change plan delivered by the plan function to make the necessary modifications to the managed resource.

The four parts of a resource manager that provide the control loop functionality rely on shared knowledge represented in a uniform (standard) way to perform their tasks. Shared management knowledge includes data such as topology information, historical logs, metrics, symptoms and policies, and so on. Shared system knowledge can be divided into three general types: solution topology knowledge, policy knowledge and problem determination [IBM 2004].

- *Solution topology knowledge* captures knowledge about the components and their construction and configuration for a solution or business system. The planner module can use this knowledge for installation and configuration planning.
- *Policy knowledge* is knowledge that needs to be consulted to determine whether or not changes need to be made in the system.
- *Problem determination knowledge* includes monitored data, symptoms and decision trees. The problem determination process also may create knowledge. As the management system responds to actions taken to correct problems, learned knowledge can be accumulated and stored in an appropriate format for use by the resource manager modules.

The conceptual management architecture that we examined in the previous section accomplishes three main functions, repair, adaptation and optimisation as follows:

- *Repair:* The conceptual management architecture can discover, diagnose and react to managed resource disruptions. It can detect system malfunctions and initiate policy based corrective action without disrupting the existing computing environment. Corrective action could involve a product altering its own state or effecting changes in other components in the environment.
- *Adaptation:* The conceptual management architecture can also adapt to changes in the environment, using policy based configuration actions. Such changes could include the deployment of new components or the removal of existing ones,

or changes in the system characteristics and configuration. The conceptual management architecture can monitor and tune resources to meet end user or business needs.

- *Optimisation:* Finally, the tuning actions could mean reallocating resources – such as in response to dynamically changing workloads – to improve overall resource utilisation, or ensure that particular business transactions can be completed in a timely fashion. For instance, optimisation actions could divert excess server capacity to lower priority work when an application does not fully use its assigned computing resources. Optimisation helps provide a high standard of service for both system and application end users.

17.4 Standard distributed management frameworks

Diverse technologies that are currently in wide use and relevant to Web service management are suitable for building application manageability. The two most prominent include the Simple Network Management Protocol (SNMP) and the Common Information Model and Web-Based Enterprise Management (CIM/WBEM). Of these two distributed management frameworks, we shall give a brief overview of SNMP and then focus on CIM/WBEM as it comes closer to Web service management.

17.4.1 Simple Network Management Protocol

SNMP, developed by the Internet Engineering Task Force (ITF), is an application layer protocol that was developed for TCP/IP based networks and facilitates the exchange of management information between network devices [Case 1999]. SNMP's network elements are devices – such as hosts, gateways and terminal servers – with management agents that perform the functions requested by network management stations. The SNMP framework lets network administrators manage network performance, find and solve network problems and plan for network growth. SNMP is today's *de facto* industry standard for network management.

SNMP defines a client–server relationship. The client program (called the network manager) makes virtual connections to a server program (called the SNMP agent) that executes on a remote network entity (often a device, but this could be an application platform also). Agents provide information to the network manager regarding the remote entity's status. An SNMP agent is therefore required on each machine on which an application is running, to monitor that application or component. An SNMP agent is a network management software module that resides in a managed device, which is a network node.

Managed devices collect and store management information and make this information available to network managers using SNMP. Managed devices can be routers and access servers, switches and bridges, hubs, computer hosts or printers. An agent has local knowledge of management information and translates that information into a form compatible with SNMP. A network manager executes applications that monitor and control managed devices and provides services to management applications. Network managers provide the bulk of the processing and memory resources required for network management. One or more network managers must exist on any managed network.

SNMP is used for exchanging messages between network managers and agents by encoding management information in basic encoding rules. The database of management information that is used and controlled by the SNMP agent is referred to as the SNMP Management Information Base (MIB), and is a standard set of statistical and control values. Finally, SNMP uses a management information model defining all managed resources in a pseudo object oriented manner – a manner where all objects are stored virtually in a management information base.

In summary, we should note that SNMP is essentially a protocol. The management information structure of SNMP has its network transport protocol very closely tied to the representation of management information. This prevents SNMP from significantly moving forward because of the backward compatibility coexistence requirements it has to meet [Cole 2002].

17.4.2 The Common Information Model/Web-Based Enterprise Management

CIM, developed by the Distributed Management Task Force (DMTF), describes managed elements across the enterprise, including systems, networks and applications. CIM includes schemas for systems, networks, operating systems, applications and devices. It provides mapping techniques for interchange of CIM data with MIB data from SNMP agents. CIM is implementation independent, allowing different management applications to collect the required data from a variety of sources. One of the main functions CIM offers is the ability to define the associations between components. CIM's object oriented approach makes it easier to track the relationships and interdependencies between managed objects.

The CIM specification details a language and methodology for describing management data. The CIM schema enables applications from developers on different platforms to describe management data in a standard format that can be shared between varieties of management applications. It supplies a set of classes with properties and associations that provide a well understood conceptual framework within which it is possible to organise the available information about the managed environment.

The CIM schema itself is structured into three distinct layers: the core schema, common schemas and extension schemas. The *core schema* is an information model that captures notions that are applicable to all areas of management. *Common schemas* are information models that capture notions that are common to particular management areas, but independent of a particular technology or implementation. The common areas are systems, devices, networks, applications, metrics, databases, the physical environment, event definition and handling, users and security, policy and so forth. Finally, *extension schemas* represent organisational or vendor specific extensions of the common schema. These schemas can be specific to environments, such as operating systems (e.g. UNIX or Microsoft Windows).

The formal definition of the CIM schema is expressed in a managed object file (MOF), which is the standard textual syntax for specifying the description of managed resources. The function of MOF is analogous to MIB for SNMP.

Having a common model such as the one advocated by CIM does not achieve interoperability. A common protocol and a standard encoding scheme are also required. To address these requirements DMTF members developed the WBEM (Web-Based Enterprise Management) to deliver an integrated set of standards based management tools leveraging emerging Web technologies. WBEM is a standard that uses XML, HTTP and SSL to manage systems and networks throughout the enterprise. XML provides the information encoding, HTTP provides transport – thereby creating a platform independent, distributed management infrastructure – and SSL provides for security requirements.

WBEM provides a rich model of manageable entities featuring inheritance and associations, an extensible set of operations that can be performed on these objects, and a protocol to encode the objects and operations for communication over a network. To use a WBEM approach, the developer is required first to model the required managed objects in an object oriented style. Then the developer maps their managed application objects into the CIM, or a derived extension of it.

Existing management standards (such as SNMP and CIM) primarily focus on data collection and not on supporting rich management applications for the adaptive infrastructure required by Web services. Moreover, they are too low level to allow flexible, coordinated interaction patterns involving business processes. Using Java based technologies, which we describe in the next subsection, circumvents some of these problems.

17.5 Web service management

As traditional, centralised management applications transition to highly distributed and dynamic SOAs, they can more flexibly deploy essential management functions. With SOAs, a standard Web services management framework can provide support for discovering, introspecting, securing and invoking managed resources, management functions, and management infrastructure services and toolsets. This section describes the architectural characteristics, structure and responsibilities of the Web services management and support infrastructure.

17.5.1 Features of Web service management

In the previous sections we have talked about enterprise management frameworks, distributed management concepts and architectures, as well as standard distributed management initiatives that are currently in use and relevant to Web services management. In what follows, we shall explain how the initiatives and approaches to distributed systems management have influenced Web services management.

Currently, management vendors offer only instrumentation at SOAP endpoints and intermediaries, or at UDDI servers. Although this provides information about Web services while such applications use them, the view is clearly incomplete and lacks critical information regarding the state and characteristics of Web services. For example, many existing system management infrastructures, e.g. SNMP, CIM and Java Messages Extensions (JMX), do not support SLA reporting or the collection of specific service information from (Web services) applications for troubleshooting purposes. To derive such information, Web services must become measurable and much more manageable. This can only be achieved by a standard approach to managing Web services, which can provide, among other things, end-to-end visibility and control over all parts of a long lived, multi-step transaction spanning multiple applications, human actors and enterprises. Only by watching over business operations can analysts and administrators identify opportunities and diagnose problems as they occur, and can ensure that the Web services supporting a given business task are performing in accordance with service level objectives. Web service management is therefore expected to become a critical component of production quality Web service applications in the near future.

To deliver sound SOA applications, Web services need to be managed in at least two dimensions:

1. The *operational management* dimension where a systems administrator starts and stops Web services and keeps track of how many instances of a Web service are running, in which containers, and on which remote systems.
2. The *tactical* (or *business management*) dimension that provides a number of business activity monitoring and analytical capabilities that enable some human agent to watch over business operations, identifying opportunities and diagnosing problems as they occur so as to ensure that the Web services supporting a given business task are performing in accordance with service level objectives. Tactical Web service management provides end-to-end visibility and control over all parts of a long lived, multi-step information request or transaction/process that spans multiple applications and human actors in one or more enterprises.

Tactical management is directly related to the concept of business process management and monitoring that we addressed in Sections 8.5.3 and 8.5.4 in the context of the Enterprise Service Bus. Therefore, in the remainder of this section we shall concentrate only on the activities and features of operational service management.

Operational Web service management (henceforth referred to simply as Web service management) is defined as the functionality required for discovering the existence, availability, performance, health, patterns of usage, extensibility, as well as the control and configuration, lifecycle support and maintenance of a Web service or business process within the context of SOAs. This definition implies that Web services can be managed using Web service technologies. In particular, it suggests a manageability model that applies to both Web services and business processes in terms of manageability topics (identification, configuration, state, metrics and relationships) and the aspects (properties, operations and events) used to define them [Potts 2003]. In fact, these abstract concepts apply to understanding and describing the manageability information and behaviour of any managed resource, including business processes and Web services.

17.5.2 Functional characteristics of Web service management

A Web service management framework is a set of components and objects that enable SLA management, auditing, monitoring, troubleshooting, dynamic service provisioning and service management for Web service infrastructure and applications. A Web service management framework performs four activities as part of managing end-to-end Web services:

- Measuring end-to-end levels of service for user based units of work, e.g. individual Web services, business processes, application transactions and so on.
- Breaking such units of work down into identifiable, measurable components, e.g. requests for application transactions.
- Attributing end-to-end service levels and resource consumption to such units and their components. This involves tracing and monitoring them through multi-domain, geographical, technological, application and supplier infrastructures.
- Identifying and predicting current problems and future requirements in user terms.

To perform the above activities a Web service management framework must take into consideration a number of interrelated Web service management aspects. The most prominent functions of service management include the following:

Metrics/performance indicators: Key operational metrics of a Web service at the operational level include:

- the number of request messages that the Web service endpoint has received;
- the number of successful requests handled by a Web service endpoint;
- the total elapsed time (in seconds) that the Web service endpoint has taken to process all requests (successfully or not);
- the maximum time duration (in seconds) between all requests received and their completion or failure;
- the last recorded time duration (in seconds) between the last request received and its completion or failure.

This set of basic metrics for a Web service revolves mainly around the concept of response time, and is currently provided by Web service management standard initiatives, such as the Web Services Distributed Management (see Section 17.6). In addition to the above basic Web service metrics, additional useful Web service metrics include connect time, response time, round trip delay, transaction rate and throughput. *Connect time* denotes how long a service takes to start. *Round trip* delay denotes the time taken between making a request and seeing the response. *Transaction rate* is the rate that the system can service requests. It is important to understand how the system or service reacts when presented with transaction rates higher than the value required. Burst rates and sustained rates and their periods should be defined. Finally, *throughput* is the total amount of information that is offered to the system.

Auditing, monitoring and troubleshooting: This item may include the providing of service performance and utilisation statistics, measurement of transaction arrival rates and response time loads (number of bytes per incoming and outgoing transaction), load balancing across servers, measuring the health of services, and trouble shooting. Web services should be audited and these measurements can be used to compare against SLAs. Resources should be monitored for bottlenecks and for user defined thresholds that exceed the prescribed limits. These measurements can be recorded and the historical performance data collected and used for capacity planning. Today, several toolsets found on platforms for developing, deploying and managing service applications provide process monitoring capabilities.

SLA management: This feature may include:

1. QoS criteria (e.g. sustainable network bandwidth with priority messaging service);
2. service reporting (e.g. acceptable system response time);
3. service metering.

Service redeployment/dynamic rerouting and graceful degradation: The Web services management framework should allow the service to be redeployed (moved) around the network for performance, redundancy for availability, or any other reasons. The management framework should support dynamic rerouting for fail-over or load balancing. In case a service fails or is overloaded, it should fail in a controlled and gradual manner, servicing the highest priority tasks for as long as possible.

Service lifecycle and state management: The Web service management framework should provide the following functionality.

- It should expose the current state of a service and permit lifecycle management including the ability to start and stop a service, the ability to configure a deployed Web service, and to support versioning of Web services.
- It must be able to affect the lifecycle state and configuration parameters of a Web service, or a group of related Web services.
- It should have some control over the versions of deployed Web services. Multiple versions of the same Web service can be active simultaneously in the framework controlled by the service management system.
- It must be able to route a client request to an appropriate version of the Web service.

Service change management and notification: The Web service management framework should support the description of versions of Web services and notification of a change or impending change to the service interface or implementation.

Scalability/extensibility/availability: The Web service management framework should be extensible and must permit discovery of supported management functionality in a given instantiation.

Dynamic service (and resource) provisioning: Provisioning occurs at all phases of running a solution, ranging from bringing solutions into production, managing production execution, and removing them from production [Kreger 2005b].

Provisioning moves solutions into production by automatically triggering deployment, installation, configuration and activation of the solution and all of its elements. The Web service management framework should support the provisioning of services and resources to authorised personnel, dynamic allocation/de-allocation of hardware, installation/de-installation of software, changing of workloads *on-demand basis,* while ensuring SLAs, management policies for messaging routing and security, and reliable SOAP messaging delivery.

Security management: Like Web services, manageable service architecture implementations need to be secure, including support for authorisation, confidentiality, integrity, non-repudiation and so on. These issues were discussed in some detail in Chapter 11, which deals with security aspects of Web services.

Service maintenance: The Web service management framework should allow for the management and correlation of new versions of the service.

A Web service management framework that is based on the above service management functionality can provide end-to-end, cross-architecture, business level and process level monitoring and management facilities. These can be used to determine whether an organisation is realising desired benefits from a particular service or composite application. It must be noted that this functionality is only covered partially by current commercial systems.

17.5.3 Service management architectural approaches

A standard Web service management framework provides an abstraction layer that allows discovery of, and interaction with, managed resources, as well as a standard, model agnostic way of describing resource capabilities. The preferred model is an abstraction layer on top of physical resources that presents the *capabilities* of the system, encapsulating the details of the physical resources. The abstraction layer pushes down on to the aggregation of the lower level physical resource sensors and actuators, and enables standardisation of how developers view resource consumption, and how they measure baseline metrics. In this way, there is no need for every new type of resource to have individual software written in order to communicate with each management application, and developers and system administrators need not understand many different control protocols in order to provide efficient systems management. As such, the same Web service technologies that are used to define and execute business processes can now interact directly with resource managers, management infrastructure services and managed resources.

In a Web service environment, all essential communication between service providers and consumers is carried out using standardised SOAP messages. SOAP messages can facilitate Web service management in several ways. First, developers can use SOAP messages to mark the beginning and endpoints of service transactions. Also, because a SOAP message's source and destination are readily identifiable, it is easy to obtain detailed performance measures for applications that span platforms and enterprises by sniffing and altering SOAP messages – which can be intercepted at many points in the network of applications connected via Web services. Service containers facilitate the request/response message flow environment (see Sections 5.4 and 8.5.5). As already explained in Chapter 8, the Web service containers entail the physical manifestation of an abstract service endpoint and provide the service interface implementation.

Currently we may distinguish between service management capabilities injected into the SOAP pipeline by using either a container based and/or intermediary architectural approach. These two approaches are composable, in that we can have management functions incorporated in both containers and intermediaries. They are discussed briefly below.

> *Container based service management* reflects a purely container based style of Web service management. Here, the platform's native Web service container hosts the management capabilities. From an architectural perspective, the container can leverage the infrastructure configuration of the Web service node (the application server), which administrators can cluster and secure for required service levels. The container based management scenario is shown in Figure 17.5.
>
> *Intermediary based management* centres on an intermediary or broker, which acts as the client endpoint and passes the request to the actual service endpoint (see Figure 17.6). This is in contrast to the container based scenario, which directly links the Web service management servers to containers. In Figure 17.6 capabilities are deployed on the intermediary, which acts as a client endpoint. Following monitoring and control, the intermediary passes the request to the service endpoint. Administrators deploy management capabilities on the intermediary, allowing for monitoring and control. The intermediary model is completely decoupled from the Web service nodes, and can be used in any environment. Services from multiple platforms can be routed through the intermediary, which also facilitates central management and configuration. The intermediary model is particularly useful in simplifying administration and technical support without requiring a container

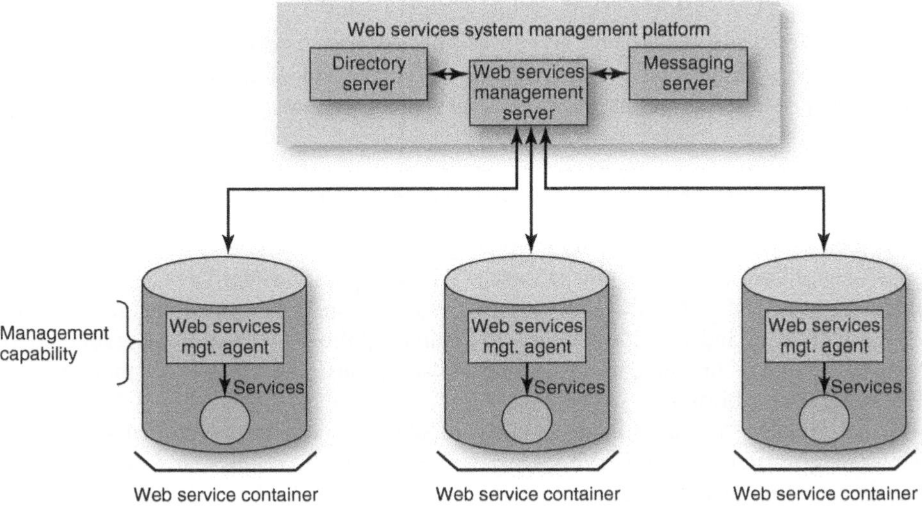

Figure 17.5 Container based management scenario

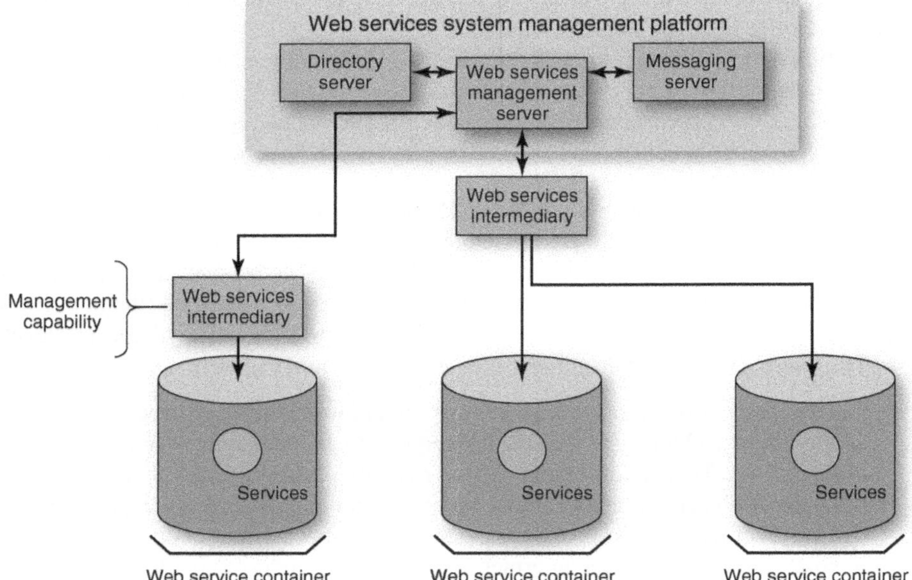

Figure 17.6 Intermediary based management scenario

for each individual Web service node. However, intermediaries do require network address reconfiguration. Also, if there is no infrastructure to cluster the Web service intermediaries, they can constitute single points of failure and thus create problems in environments that require high reliability.

In conclusion, there is no distinctive functional difference between the container based and intermediary based scenarios for Web service management apart from the standalone (intermediary) versus server plug-in (container) configuration.

17.5.4 Management infrastructure services

To manage services, the Web service management framework uses the *manageability capabilities* of various architecture resources. These capabilities define standard schemas, metadata and WSDL interfaces that describe resource specific behaviour that resources use to advertise – and provide access to – manageability information [Kreger 2005b]. Typically, resources implement only applicable selections rather than all of their standard manageability capabilities.

Basic computing resource manageability capabilities include operational status, metrics and relationships. Manageability capabilities are realised through a *manageability information model* that represents resource manageability and related information, such as state, configuration and relationships [Potts 2003]. The service management framework uses this model's information to retrieve manageability information and exert control. Manageability information might, for example, indicate that a SOAP message header contained a digital certificate of the client's identity. The Web service management framework would then extract that information and translate it into the client's identification for later use (such as when counting a particular client's SOAP messages to a particular Web service).

A Web service is manageable if its manageability capabilities are exposed via standard management interfaces, which are similar to a Web service's functional interfaces [Potts 2003]. The management interfaces differ only in that they convey management related semantics and that a Web service management system, rather than a client, uses them.

The Web service management framework uses management infrastructure services to define standard interfaces for commonly available functions in the infrastructure's information [Kreger 2005b]. Management infrastructure services include metering, metric and event mediation, monitoring, system scanning, policy enforcement and management, and model bridges. The standard management interfaces enable higher value utility functions, management of end-to-end processes, or management applications such as availability and performance management, optimisation, capacity planning, billing, configuration management, asset protection, problem determination and business analytics. These mechanisms also offer interfaces and content for management consoles.

Figure 17.7 shows the management interfaces (viz. management channel) exposed by a manageable Web service and accessible by the Web service management framework. This management framework is positioned between Web service clients and providers (viz. the application channel) and offers a centralised management and policy framework. In this figure application channels are developed in accordance with SOA principles and are continuously connected and directed into the management channel. A WSDL document describes the management interfaces and the endpoints to which the Web service management framework can send messages with management related payloads. A management service could be a Web service based on the Web Service Distributed Management model that is described in Section 17.6.

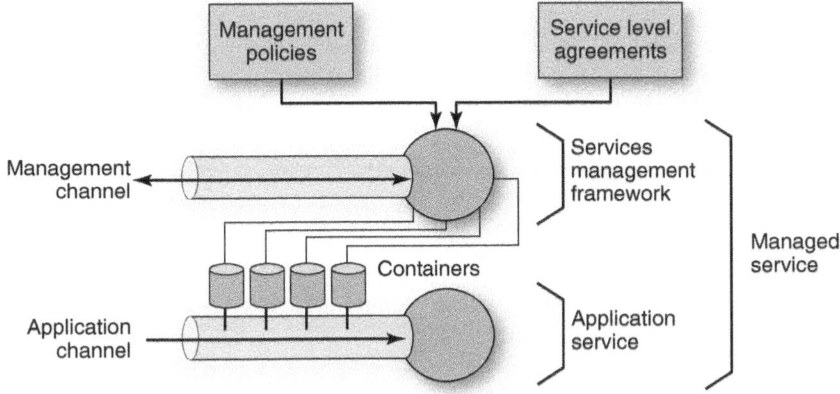

Figure 17.7 Integrating application and management based services

To manage event driven processes, the management service might support an event mechanism for notification push. Because they are in the same memory space, the containers and management service interact via direct message calls. In the memory space, information from the management channel controls the containers. Any information that the containers collect is passed to the management service, which then makes it available on the management channel.

As Figure 17.7 shows, along with distributed monitoring and policy enforcement, the Web service management framework offers a centralised management and policy framework. This framework works in concert with service directories and identity management solutions, both in receiving information (such as service performance statistics, alerts and service interdependency information) and in sending information. Policy, in the form of rule sets, is sent to the service management components. These rules define service management component behaviour – that is, when to raise alerts, how to process transiting message traffic, where to route messages, how to enforce security policies and SLAs, and so on.

17.5.5 Connecting service management and application channels

In addition to traditional application service development facilities, a Web services based SOA requires two key features to manage effectively systems and applications:

- A management framework that is consistent across an increasingly heterogeneous set of participating component systems.
- Support for complex, cross-component management scenarios, such as SLA enforcement and dynamic resource provisioning.

Figure 17.8 shows the conceptual architecture components that combine service management and application channels developed in accordance with SOA principles. This architecture continuously connects to the Web service application channel and directs it into the management channel. The architecture depicted in Figure 17.8 provides the connection points between different functional units. The use of Web services as an implementation platform of an integrated SOA based management and application development solution, among other things, encourages implementers to leverage existing approaches and support multiple binding and marshalling techniques. This means that the management channel enables the use of common management services. Typical management services that are common across both the applications and management channels include:

- SLA and QoS management, including the measurement of performance and availability, as well as alerting services.
- Visibility and control capabilities, including interactive monitoring, administration and reporting.
- Service adaptability, including versioning, routing, differentiated services and message transformation.
- Web services and service security standards based mechanisms.

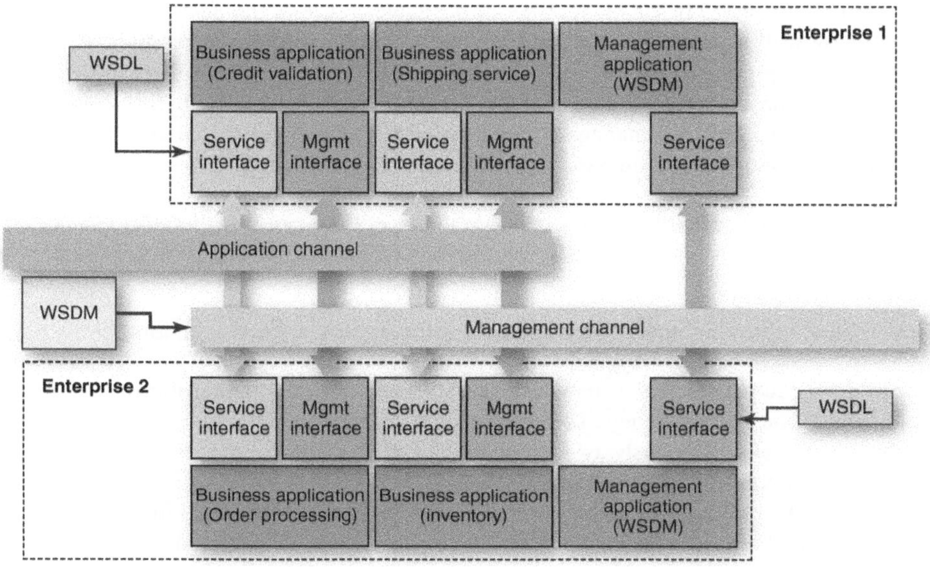

Figure 17.8 Developing and managing Web-services-based applications

In the architecture depicted in Figure 17.8, service management involves a collection of management infrastructure services that communicate with each other – passing data or coordinating some activity – to facilitate the delivery of one or more business services. Rather than prescribe a particular management protocol or instrumentation technology, the architecture can work with SNMP, JMX, WBEM, and other existing and future distributed management technologies and standards.

In Figure 17.8, managed resources include physical and logical hardware and software resources. These resources expose their management capabilities as Web services that implement various management interfaces, such as those defined in the Web Services Distributed Management standard (see the following section).

Resource managers can directly access managed resources as part of a business or management process. As Figure 16.8 shows, a business process integrates basic services such as credit validation, shipping, order processing, and inventory services originating from two collaborating enterprises. The architecture's management applications, such as performance management, capacity planning, asset protection and job control, manage resources through their management interfaces or management infrastructure services [Kreger 2005a].

The management interface of a given resource is described by a WSDL document, resource properties schema, metadata documents, and (potentially) a set of management related policies. Resource managers interact with managed resources and management infrastructure services using the Web service interfaces. In addition, service managers leverage Web service technologies, such as WS-BPEL, to describe and execute management processes that perform a *scripted* management function [Kreger 2005a]. The use of management processes based on Web services enables reuse of the business process infrastructure, as well as invocation of resource services, management infrastructure services and business components.

In large scale enterprises where manageability capabilities and interfaces are standardised, multiple resource managers may be used to manage individual services. The two most common multiple resource manager scenarios are [Potts 2003]:

1. Separation of responsibilities between managers. This means that, for instance, one manager performs performance monitoring while another one takes care of deployment changes.
2. Installations that include management software from various vendors.

In those circumstances, the management interface and the manageability model must enable operational consistency. In addition, the management architecture must ensure consistency of simultaneously executed operations, and that managers do not execute operations that conflict with each other.

Finally, a hierarchical structure of managers may be introduced. In all such cases standards must be used to coordinate and negotiate usage of service manageability. For example, federated coordination may be supported by WS-Coordination.

17.6 The Web Services Distributed Management initiative

While standards such as SNMP or CIM are effective in managing specific resources within the enterprise, they do not address the management requirements of business processes and the services they compose. In fact, until recently there was no distributed management standard available for expressing the relationships that exist between resources, business processes and related services. And there is a significant gap for management standards to provide a means to correlate business and systems development activities. In many cases, a management solution is driven by systems based goals and metrics, which may not be optimally aligned with the overall business goals. In addition, management solutions based on the preceding standards provide a single point of control for resources within the scope of a specific set of management tasks or processes. While this approach may work well, particularly within the confines of a single management system, it can be difficult to integrate different enterprise management systems to provide an overall view of cross-application (end-to-end) business processes. The goal of the OASIS Web Services Distributed Management (WSDM) standard is to address this expressed need.

The WSDM standard specifies how the manageability of a resource is made available to manageability consumers via Web services [Bullard 2006]. WSDM defines a protocol for the interoperability of management information and capabilities via Web services. The focus of the WSDM architecture is the manageable resource. The manageable resource must be represented as a Web service. In other words, management information regarding the resource must be accessible through a Web service endpoint. A simple example of a managed resource could be a server that indicates when its storage capacity is low, or a Web server that reports congestion due to an excessively high number of hits.

To provide access to a resource, a Web service endpoint must be able to be referenced by an endpoint reference as defined in the WS-Addressing standard (see Section 7.1.1). Endpoints that support access to manageable resources are called *manageability endpoints.* A manageability endpoint realises a number of management interfaces. Each management interface represents all or part of a manageability capability. Similarly, a single manageability capability may be represented in one or more interfaces.

The implementation behind manageability endpoints must be capable of retrieving and manipulating the information related to a manageable resource. The WS-Addressing endpoint reference provides the target location to which a manageability consumer directs messages. The manageable resource may also direct notifications of significant events to a manageability consumer, provided the consumer has subscribed to receive notifications. A manageability consumer discovers the Web service endpoint and exchanges messages with the endpoint in order to request information, subscribe to events, or control the managed resource associated with the endpoint. An example of a manageability consumer is a management system, or a business process, or simply any Web service application.

Essentially, a WSDM service is a management interface for a manageable resource present on the Web. WSDM allows management components to become a direct part of a business process. WSDM can, therefore, be used to monitor the end-to-end response time of a BPEL process as well as the time taken by each step. Business analysts can use this information to monitor timely delivery of (telecommunications or financial) services to their customers. In addition, WSDM based notifications can be forwarded to the business analysts when exceptional circumstances occur. In this way, WSDM can be used to monitor a business process and correlate that process with systems level associated events.

The WSDM standard is built upon W3C and other OASIS standards. In that respect, WSDM leverages many of the capabilities provided by the WS-Addressing, WS-BaseNotification, WS-Topics and WS-BrokeredNotification standard families (see Sections 7.1.1, and 7.2.1), such as the ability to expose properties, expose several resources in a collection, and standardise faults and notifications.

To resolve distributed system management problems, WSDM focuses on two distinct standards, Management Using Web Services (MUWS) and Management of Web Services (MOWS), for managing devices as well as Web services using Web services. These are inherently dependent upon a Service Oriented Architecture foundation. In particular:

- The MUWS specification addresses the use of Web service technologies as the foundation of a modern distributed systems management framework. With MOWS, the WSDM addresses the specific requirements for managing Web services themselves.
- The MOWS specification is based on the MUWS specification's concepts and definitions. As with MUWS, MOWS aims to build on existing model frameworks to define the management model of a Web service, rather than reinvent a general managed resource object model scheme.

The following two sections describe the MUWS and MOWS principal components of the WSDM architecture, their general characteristics, their modes of interaction, and the facilities they provide.

17.6.1 Management Using Web Services (MUWS)

MUWS facilitates the management of distributed computing resources using Web services. The purpose of MUWS is to achieve universal management interoperability across the many different varieties of distributed computing resources. In particular, MUWS defines how to describe the manageability capabilities of managed resources using WSDL documents. Expressing capabilities enables more efficient discovery and introspection of resources, since managers typically focus on a particular management task or domain, and therefore need to be able easily and efficiently to determine the relevant capabilities of a managed resource.

MUWS is not creating a new model for representing managed resources. Rather, the requirement is that MUWS must be able to work with multiple, existing, domain specific models. CIM from DTMF is the most prominent, but not the exclusive, model for this work. SNMP information models will also be considered. The objective is to bind a unifying layer on top of these various models to facilitate consistent management in a heterogeneous distributed environment.

MUWS defines a set of foundation manageability capabilities generally expected in distributed computing management systems [Murray 2006a]. Examples of manageability functions that can be performed via MUWS include:

- monitoring QoS;
- enforcing SLAs;
- controlling tasks;
- managing resource lifecycles.

New or domain specific capabilities can extend existing foundational capabilities as appropriate.

In order to discover the Web service endpoint providing access to a particular managed resource, a manageability consumer first obtains an endpoint reference as defined by the WS-Addressing specification, and then obtains any other required descriptions, including, but not limited to, a WSDL document, an XML schema, or a policy document. MUWS uses the same mechanisms for obtaining references and their associated descriptions, as used by regular Web service implementations and their applications. To exchange messages with a manageability endpoint, a manageability consumer needs to understand all of the required descriptions for the endpoint. The manageability consumer sends messages targeted to the managed resource by using information contained in the endpoint reference, e.g. an address and other reference properties in accordance with WS-Addressing conventions.

MUWS defines several standard capabilities whose purpose is to identify and categorise various aspects of distributed management. A *manageability capability* is a set of properties, operations and events, enabling a resource to be managed in a particular way. Each capability has its own distinct semantics. A manageable resource must be capable of supporting one or more capabilities that expose the manageable features of the resource. In MUWS each manageability capability is identified by a standard URI and has a WS-Notification topic used to identify and categorise capability specific notifications. In addition, each capability has metadata defined for its properties and operations. The most prominent MUWS capabilities include:

- The *Operational Status* capability exposes the high level health of a manageable resource from a simple operational perspective. An operational status capability in MUWS defines three very simple status levels (available, partially available, unavailable and unknown) as well as events for status changes for interoperability.
- The *Metrics* capability exposes metric information relevant to the performance and operation of a manageable resource. WSDM defines some metrics for a Web service resource and allows all resources to define any suitable and relevant metrics.
- The *Configuration* capability exposes properties of the manageable resource that can be modified by the manageability consumer, and which change the operation behaviour of the resource. The *Configuration* capability supports configuration management tasks and also supports fault and performance management for the automated correction of faults. Configuration management tasks include gathering and storing the configuration of resources and services, tracking changes made to a configuration and the configuration or provisioning of circuits.
- The *Relationships* capability exposes the relationships in which a resource participates. Facilities exposed by this capability include retrieving relationships, querying a resource for its participation in a specific type of relationship, and notifying on the creation or the deletion of a relationship in which the resource participates. The MUWS Relationship capability ensures that configuration, fault and performance tasks can be accomplished for resources within the context of a distributed processing environment.
- The *Advertisement* capability defines a standard event to be sent when a new managed resource is created or destructed.

Each management capability is associated with a topic on which notifications can be generated. For example, the topic associated with state is *State Capability*. Each topic in WSDM is associated with a message type of management event. A message issued on a topic associated with a manageability capability has a precise format specified by the WSDM Event Format (WEF). The WEF contains an event identifier, information regarding the source of the event, the reporter of the event, a message about what happened to the resource, and the date and time of the event. The WSDM Event Format provides a basis for programmatic processing, correlation, and interpretation of events from different products, platforms and management technologies.

More information and examples of WSDL MUWS specifications can be found in the MUWS primer [Murray 2006a].

17.6.2 Management of Web Services (MOWS)

The Web Services Distributed Management (WSDM) specification for the Management Of Web Services (MOWS) [Murray 2006b] provides a means of managing Web services. MOWS is an extension of MUWS in that MOWS uses and extends the capabilities defined in MUWS. At its simplest level, MOWS uses the same resource properties exposed by MUWS manageability capabilities. Like MUWS activities, MOWS aims to build on existing model frameworks (such as, for instance, DMTF CIM) in its definition of the management model of a Web service, rather than reinventing a general managed resource object model scheme.

The MOWS model requirements are being primarily driven by a set of management tasks that should be supported. These management tasks are numerous and include such varied activities as service metering, auditing, billing, performance profiling, SLA management, problem detection, root cause failure diagnosis, service deployment and lifecycle management.

WSDM MOWS defines the following MUWS capabilities applicable to Web service endpoints [Murray 2006b]:

- *Identity:* The MUWS identity capability defines a unique identity for the Web service.
- *Identification:* The identification capability is used to help establish the Web service endpoint being managed. The identity capability may be used to determine whether two manageability endpoints provide manageability of the same resource or not.
- *Metrics:* The MOWS metrics capability defines a set of basic metrics for a Web service. These include number of requests, number of failed requests, number of successful requests, service time, max response time and last response time.
- *Operational State:* The MOWS operational state capability provides the current operational state of the service. A valid state is `up` which indicates that a service endpoint is capable of receiving new requests. The `up` state has the sub-states of `busy`, which means that the Web service endpoint is capable of accepting new requests during processing of other requests, and `idle`, which means that the Web service endpoint is capable of accepting new requests and is not processing any other requests. Another valid state is `down`, which indicates that a service endpoint is not capable of accepting new requests.
- *Operational Status:* The MUWS operational status capability provides the high level status of the services. A manageability consumer can learn whether a managed Web service is available, unavailable or partially available. For example, the Web service may be unavailable because the Web service is shut down for maintenance. Alternatively, the Web service may be only partially available because an operation lacks access to a necessary resource.
- *Request Processing State:* The MOWS request processing state capability defines a request state diagram and provides a mechanism to define events to be sent when request processing states change.

More details and examples about how to manage manageable resources that are Web services, using the MOWS standard, can be found in [Sedukhin 2005], and [Murray 2006b].

17.7 Summary of learning objectives

Distributed management becomes a clear requirement in SOAs because the growing complexity of global Web services brings together large numbers of services, suppliers and technologies, all with potentially different performance requirements.

Web service management provides visibility into the Web service run time environment to enable: monitoring of availability, accessibility, performance of Web services, SLA compliance tracking, and error detection, resolution, auditing and controlling of the Web service infrastructure.

The OASIS Web Services Distributed Management (WSDM) is a key standard for Web service management. The WSDM standard defines:

- a basic set of manageability capabilities, such as resource identity, metrics, configuration, and relationships, which can be composed to express the capability of the management instrumentation and a standard management of events;
- WSDL interfaces, which allow management events and metrics to be exposed, queried and controlled by a broad range of management tools.

Review questions

- What is distributed computing systems management?
- How does Web service management differ from conventional distributed computing systems management?
- Briefly describe the three main topologies of Enterprise Management Systems.
- What are the main ingredients of a conceptual management architecture?
- Briefly describe the main characteristics of standard distributed management frameworks.
- What is operational and what is tactical service management?
- What are the most prominent functions of service management?
- Briefly describe the container based and the intermediary based architectural approach.

- How are the application and management channels interlinked in a Web service management architecture?
- What is the purpose and main characteristics of the Management Using Web Services specification?
- What are the purpose and main characteristics of the Management of Web Services specification?
- How are the Management Using Web Services and Management of Web Services specifications related?

Exercises

17.1. Consider the example of a company that would like to streamline its manufacturing and fulfilment processes across multiple factories and warehouses, as well as suppliers' facilities. The company has decided to outsource the manufacturing of low margin parts that are not in inventory when orders are placed. Depending on the available-to-promise inventory levels, the company will either fulfil the order from one of its warehouses or place the order directly with one of its established suppliers for outsourced manufacturing. This end-to-end order fulfilment process covers multiple inter- and intra-company independently controlled Web services that rely on other services and processes to complete a task. How can this manufacturer apply service management solutions effectively to manage end-to-end quality objectives in a manner that aligns desired business objectives and guarantees acceptable level of service? Your solution should leverage the content and context of the messages that are exchanged between Web services and combined with system level information in a way that ensures that business tasks are performing in accordance with service level objectives.

17.2. Use the Management EJB (MEJB) component (Chapter JSR77.7, *J2EE Management EJB Component*) technology to develop an application that accesses the attributes of a managed object of the J2EEApplication type through the MEJB.

17.3. Implement an application that illustrates how a J2EE component creates an MEJB session object, how managed objects of a certain type are found, and how the attributes of a managed object can be retrieved and their values determined.

17.4. Implement an application that illustrates how a method with a specific signature can be invoked.

17.5. Define and implement a manageable resource and create a management interface for it. The resource should be an abstract construct that represents purchase orders, and stores such information as purchase order ID, shipping and billing addresses, and dates.

17.6. Consider an implementation which creates a large number of many management services at run time. This application would clearly suffer from bad performance, as management services consume sizeable chunks of the CPU time because of their operation execution times. Eventually the excessive use of management services will dominate consumption of resources over the business functions of the application – a clear case of overusing management service technology. Explain what decisions you need to make to overcome this problem.

PART X

Emerging trends

CHAPTER 18

Cloud Computing

Learning objectives

Cloud Computing as a potential long term IT solution is appearing at a time when enterprise wide system consolidation and cost savings are a high priority. At its core, Cloud Computing is a business service delivery model designed to help organisations procure and consume service based solutions as needed, based on some metering and pricing scheme. It allows organisations to move costs from capital expenditure to operating expenditure while allowing them to become more flexible and service oriented.

This chapter explores the Cloud Computing approach, its enabling technologies and underlying architectural concepts and relates them to SOA and Web services. After completing this chapter you will understand the following key concepts:

- The nature and importance of Cloud Computing.
- The essential characteristics of Cloud Computing.
- Cloud Computing delivery and deployment models.
- Virtualisation techniques for managing systems and resources.
- Architectural approaches for Cloud Computing.
- Security risks and countermeasure recommendations for Cloud Computing.

Chapter preview

This chapter explains how organisations cut down operational costs and increase productivity by relying on the Cloud Computing model that makes use of SOA principles, fast wide area networks and high performance virtualisation for commodity hardware, and delivers software, platform and infrastructure as a service solution. We first provide a standard definition for Cloud Computing and then we delve into its essential characteristics, delivery and delivery models. We explain the concept of multi-tenancy to allow the provider's computing resources to be pooled to serve multiple consumers, describe cloud architectural model security solutions, lifecycle approaches and standards. We conclude by exploring its business advantages, challenges and risks.

18.1 What is Cloud Computing?

Currently enterprises are faced with a continuing demand for business expansion and, as a result, they often need to invest in stand alone servers or software that traditionally demand heavy capital investment but remain frequently under utilised. In addition, as technological innovations take place, existing IT resources become quickly obsolete and must be replaced with the latest in the field, if the enterprise has to operate efficiently; and this, of course, calls for yet more capital investment. IT infrastructures have become too complex and brittle. It is an indicative factor that, today, almost 70% of IT investment concentrates on maintenance, leaving little time to support strategic development projects. With users demanding faster response times and management demanding to reduce IT infrastructure operating costs, enterprises are struggling to maintain sufficient IT capacity to buffer new customer demands.

For companies in search of a cost effective use of computing resources Cloud Computing technology is rapidly becoming a commercially viable service delivery model. Cloud Computing is a new approach that reduces IT complexity by leveraging the efficient pooling of on demand, self-managed virtual infrastructure, consumed as a service. Cloud Computing eliminates the need for large capital outlays to launch new applications, moving the decision out of the investment realm and into the operational. In fact, experts predict that by 2012, 80% of Fortune 1000 enterprises will pay for some Cloud Computing service, while 30% of them will pay for Cloud Computing infrastructure [Dignan 2008].

Cloud Computing is an evolving term that describes a broad movement toward the use of wide area networks, such as the Internet, to enable interaction between information technology service providers of many types and clients. With Cloud Computing practices, service providers can expand their offerings to include the entire traditional IT stack, ranging from foundational hardware and platforms to application components, software services, and entire software applications. This is possible as Cloud Computing separates application and information resources from the underlying infrastructure and the mechanisms used to deliver them.

The foundation of Cloud Computing is the delivery of dynamically scalable, and often virtualised resources, that are provided as a service over the Internet to multiple external clients, while its focus is on the user experience. The essence is to decouple the delivery of computing services from their underlying technology. Beyond the user interface, the technology behind the cloud is opaque to the user, abstracting away from technology in order to make Cloud Computing user friendly.

Cloud Computing is a term without a single consensus, as many service providers and product vendors spar over buzzwords for marketing purposes. The most clear and comprehensive definition of Cloud Computing definition is given by the National Institute of Standards and Technology (NIST). NIST defines Cloud Computing as:

A consumption and on-demand delivery computing paradigm that enables convenient network access to a shared pool of configurable and often virtualized computing resources (e.g. networks, servers, storage, middleware and applications as services) that can be rapidly provisioned and released with minimal management effort or service provider interaction [Mell 2011].

This definition distinguishes cloud characteristics, delivery model and deployment method.

Cloud Computing is particularly appealing for various types and sizes of companies, as it does not only provide flexibility but also numerous business benefits that include almost zero upfront infrastructure investment, just-in-time infrastructure, more efficient resource utilisation, elastic capacity (scale up or down) to respond to application demands, usage based costing, and potential for reduction in application processing time [Varia 2008]. Small sized enterprises in particular can avoid upfront capital expenditure and reduce their operating expenses through the reduction in their on site provisioning and hosting of infrastructure.

According to NIST, the Cloud Computing model is normally composed of five essential characteristics, three service layers, and three deployment methods. In the rest of this section we will look at the attributes of Cloud Computing, the cloud service delivery models and deployment methods, and explore the different types of offering and configuration available today.

Providers of Cloud Computing services can potentially offer platforms for building and delivering new applications using massive and distributed computing resources, global class design, and Web-centric architectures and languages. With Cloud Computing solutions the ability to deliver specialised services in IT can be paired with the ability to deliver those services in an industrialised and pervasive way. The reality of this implication is that users of IT related services can follow a SOA like approach, meaning that they can focus on what the services provide to them, rather than how the services are implemented or hosted.

Given the economics of the cloud and the new business models emerging around the delivery of cloud based services, novel applications could be created and delivered at a lower cost when compared with conventional approaches. However, cloud computing is in its early stages, and many of the technological and business models are, as yet, unproven.

18.1.1 Essential characteristics of Cloud Computing

Cloud Computing can be viewed as a holistic ecosystem of computing components and software applications, not a point product or single vendor solution, and has basic, specific characteristics to meet the needs of diverse organisations. Cloud Computing describes the use of a collection of services, applications, information and infrastructure comprised of pools of computing, network, information and storage resources. These components can be rapidly orchestrated, provisioned, implemented and decommissioned, and scaled up or down thereby providing for an on demand, utility like model of allocation and consumption. Essentially, Cloud Computing separates application and information resources from the underlying infrastructure, and the mechanisms used to deliver them.

The most commonly accepted essential characteristics of Cloud Computing are briefly summarised below.

- *On demand self-service:* Service providers offer clients the ability to provision computing capabilities, such as cloud servers, dedicated servers, cloud storage, hardware load balancers and network storage, on demand, and automatically to build and scale their Cloud Computing infrastructure without requiring human interaction with each provider of services. Self-service cloud offerings usually provide easy to use, intuitive user interfaces that equip users productively to manage service delivery.
- *Ubiquitous network access:* The term ubiquitous network access means that the cloud provider's resources are available over the network and can be accessed through standard mechanisms by both thick and thin clients (e.g. mobile phones, laptops and PDAs). As usual, typical examples of computing resources may include storage, processing, memory, network bandwidth and virtual machines.
- *Location independent resource pooling:* Location independent computing resources are pooled or shared and can be dynamically assigned to clients. This means that the provider's computing resources are pooled and effectively shared between several clients (this concept is known as multi-tenancy as will be explained in Section-18.4). Different physical and virtual resources can be dynamically assigned and reassigned according to consumer demand. There is a sense of location independence, in that the client generally has no control or knowledge over the exact location of the provided resources but may be able to specify location at a higher level of abstraction (e.g. country, region or data centre).
- *Rapid elasticity and provisioning:* Elasticity is an essential characteristic of Cloud Computing. It signifies the ability to scale resources both up and down, as needed by client applications. Capabilities can be rapidly and elastically provisioned, in some cases automatically to scale out quickly and rapidly released to scale in quickly. To the client, the cloud appears to be infinite, and the client can purchase or lease capabilities available for provisioning in any quantity at any time. An elastic infrastructure is critical effectively to supporting the nature of service provisioning and de-provisioning as requested by users, while maintaining high levels of reliability and security. The consolidation provided by virtualisation, coupled with automated provisioning of resources, creates a high level of utilisation and reuse, ultimately yielding a very effective use of capital equipment.
- *Pay-per-use measured service:* With Cloud Computing clients consume resources and pay only for resources that they use. To this effect, Cloud Computing platforms usually employ consumption based billing mechanisms to charge for cloud service use. For this purpose they usually employ a metered, fee-for-service, or advertising based billing model. In a measured service, aspects of the cloud

service (e.g. storage, processing, bandwidth and active user accounts) are controlled and monitored by the cloud provider. Resource usage is monitored, controlled and reported, providing transparency for both the provider and consumer of the utilised service. This is crucial for the process of billing, access control, resource optimisation, capacity planning and other tasks.

In summary, all of the above five essential characteristics are necessary for producing a cloud capable of achieving business value. Business value includes savings on capital equipment and operating costs, reduced support costs and increased agility. In addition to the above essential characteristics, the cloud must exhibit further characteristics that include performance and manageability and capabilities that address the best-in-class requirements of the enterprise – such as providing for privacy and security. These requirements and related issues are discussed in Sections 18.4 and 18.5 where we respectively present architectural approaches for the cloud and discuss security risks and countermeasures.

18.1.2 Cloud service delivery models

Cloud Computing is typically divided into three models of service delivery (commonly referred to as cloud service layers). This is shown in Figure 18.1. The *cloud service delivery layers* illustrated in Figure 18.1 are *Software as a Service* (SaaS), *Platform as a Service* (PaaS), and *Infrastructure as a Service* (IaaS).

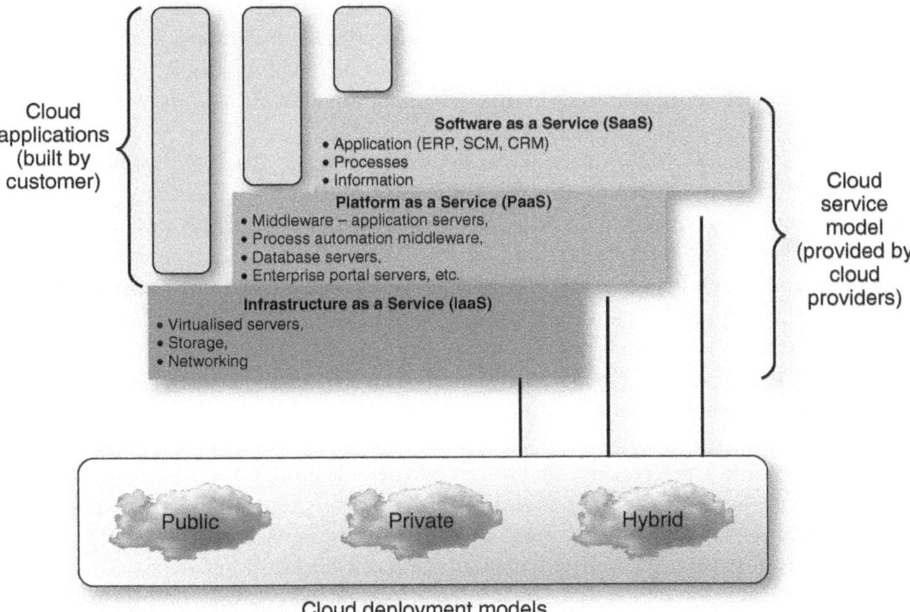

Figure 18.1 The Cloud Computing model

In essence, the three layers of cloud service offerings provide an effective means of resource pooling, dynamically assigning resources to clients and balancing the supply of computing resources to match the demand for volume operations (cloud provisioning and elasticity). The Cloud Computing layers do not simply encapsulate on demand resources at differing operational levels; they also help define a new application development model. Each layer of abstraction provides numerous possibilities for defining services that can be offered on a pay-per-use basis. These three levels support virtualisation and management of differing levels of the computing solution stack, as will be described in the following.

18.1.2.1 Infrastructure as a Service (IaaS)

Infrastructure as a Service is at the lowest layer and is a means of delivering very basic computing capability machines with operating systems and storage as standardised services over the network. Servers, storage systems, switches, routers and other specialised physical resources are pooled (through virtualisation technology, for example) to handle specific types of workload – from batch processing to server/storage augmentation during peak loads.

IaaS offers computational services so that users can, for instance, use CPU cycles without buying computing devices, while storage services provide a way to store data and documents without having continually to grow farms of storage networks and servers. The consumer does not manage or control the underlying cloud infrastructure but has control over operating systems, storage, deployed applications, and can possibly select networking components (e.g. firewalls and load balancers).

The IaaS layer allows the infrastructure provider to abstract away infrastructure specific details, such as the exact hardware an application is using and where the application is running. This layer is an evolution of traditional hosting that does not require any long term commitment and allows users to provision resources on demand. IaaS incorporates the capability to abstract resources, as well as deliver physical and logical connectivity to those resources, and provides a set of APIs, which allow interaction with the infrastructure by clients.

Advances in server virtualisation technologies have made the IaaS layer of the cloud stack very efficient by allowing a higher utilisation of processing and storage resources than were previously practical. In addition, virtual machine concepts have also enabled a useful separation of underlying hardware implementation details from the view of developers, and the ability more rapidly to scale server resources in response to changing demand. The concept of virtualisation and its use in Cloud Computing will be discussed in detail in Section 18.3.

Currently, the most prominent example of IaaS is Amazon Web Services, whose Elastic Compute Cloud (EC2) and Simple Storage Service (S3) products offer bare bones computing and storage services, respectively.

Amazon's EC2 is a Web service that provides resizable computing capacity in the cloud. It presents a true virtual computing environment, allowing clients to use Web service interfaces to launch instances with a variety of operating systems, load them with a client's custom application environment and manage network access permissions. It allows the client to define, manage and startup virtual machines, based on Amazon Machine Images (AMIs), which have network access and can be completely controlled by the client using as many systems as desirable. This service is offered for a fee, based on the uptime of virtual machines and the network bandwidth used. An AMI can be either public or private. All EC2 clients can start up public AMI instances based on this public AMI. In contrast to this, the client who created a private AMI, and any other EC2 users who have been granted access to it by the owner, can only use a private AMI.

Network based, large scale storage on demand is another example of service offerings at this layer of Cloud Computing. A good example of this type of offering is the Amazon Simple Storage Service (Amazon S3). Amazon S3 provides storage for the Internet, designed to make Web scale computing easier for application developers who can purpose for this a Web service interface for the storage and retrieval of data. The data can be of any kind, and can be stored and accessed at any time from anywhere on the Web, for a fee.

18.1.2.2 Platform provider as a Service (PaaS)

Platform provider as a Service or *platform as a service* (PaaS) is interposed between IaaS and SaaS, as shown in Figure 18.1. PaaS refers to an environment where developers build and run an application platform in the cloud, using whatever pre-built components and interfaces that particular platform provides as a service to developers over the Web. In this way, PaaS facilitates development and deployment of applications without the cost and complexity of buying and managing the underlying infrastructure.

At this level the PaaS provider facilitates deployment of cloud applications by entirely managing the cloud software development platform (often an application hosting, middleware environment), providing all of the facilities required to support the complete life cycle of building and delivering Web applications and services entirely available from the Internet. The PaaS consumer does not manage or control the underlying cloud infrastructure, including network, servers, operating systems or storage, but has control over the deployed applications and possibly application hosting environment configurations.

PaaS consists of infrastructure software, and typically includes a database, middleware and development tools for delivering Web applications and services from the Internet. PaaS allows customers to develop new applications using APIs deployed and configurable remotely. Consumers can create applications by, for instance, adding features from Google Maps, Google Calendar and other services and make these features part of their applications. Some PaaS offerings have a specific programming language or API. For example, Google AppEngine is a PaaS offering where developers write in Python or Java. The client's application, however, usually cannot access the infrastructure underneath the platform.

One serious drawback with conventional PaaS offerings is that they are constrained by the capabilities that are available through the PaaS provider and do not allow easy extensibility or customisation options.

Currently, there exist several examples of PaaS, the most well known being Google App Engine and Force.com, which we briefly examine below.

> *Google App Engine.* This lets customers run their Web applications on Google's infrastructure. App Engine applications are relatively easy to build, easy to maintain, and easy to scale under heavy loads and large amounts of data. The Google App Engine environment provides full support for common web technologies,

and includes persistent storage with queries, automatic scaling and load balancing, APIs for authenticating users and sending email using Google Accounts, and a fully featured local development environment that simulates Google App Engine on a client's computing facilities. Google App Engine applications are implemented using the Python programming language. The run time environment includes the full Python language and most of the Python standard library.

Force.com. This provides the platform and building blocks necessary to build business applications. Using the Force.com platform, enterprises and commercial software providers can create and run custom business applications over the Internet, without the need for up front software and hardware expenditures, configuration and maintenance. In addition to supporting the sales, marketing and support applications for which *Salesforce.com* is best known, Force.com makes the core technologies behind Salesforce CRM available for developing enterprise-class applications that serve a wide range of business needs and customer interactions. As the design of Force.com meets all requirements of cloud applications, service providers can deliver trusted, secure, configurable and customisable services that can support multiple devices and are easy to upgrade and integrate with other applications.

18.1.2.3 Software as a Service (SaaS)

Software as a Service is an *on-demand* application delivery model over the Internet built upon the underlying IaaS and PaaS layers. SaaS is essentially software applications that are owned, delivered and managed remotely by one or more software providers. A cloud application can be loosely defined as a collection of work items to solve a certain problem or to achieve desired results using cloud infrastructure. The provider delivers software based on a single set of common code and data definitions that are consumed in a one-to-many model by all contracted customers anytime, on a pay-per-use basis, or on a subscription basis.

SaaS delivers a standardised application running on a cloud infrastructure, that allows for accessibility and sharing from various client devices through a thin client interface such as a Web browser. This layer provides a self-contained operating environment used to deliver the entire user experience, including the content, its presentation, the application(s) and management capabilities. SaaS provides the most integrated functionality built directly into the offering with no option for consumer extensibility.

At this level, SaaS providers offer services through their multi-tenant shared facilities so that clients can focus on their businesses without buying software applications. The SaaS consumer, however, can only access the exposed functions of the application.

SaaS is being adopted in multiple enterprise markets, such as CRM on demand, human capital management (for example, performance management and recruitment), workplace collaboration, procurement, and enterprise integration facilities. Typical examples of the SaaS level are SalesForce.com that offers CRM applications accessible by subscription over the Web and the Amazon Fulfillment Web Service (Amazon FWS).

Currently, Salesforce.com offers enterprise and small business CRM solutions for sales, marketing and customer service. Each of these applications must be able to scale up as quickly and inexpensively as possible to accommodate growing loads and periods of peak capacity, such as when order entry activity picks up during busy shopping periods or when financial software is run to close the books at the end of a billing period. Such utility services offered in these clouds are a distinct product with a specific set of features, which follows a specific roadmap and runs on a dedicated proprietary cloud stack that developers cannot control.

Another typical SaaS example is the *Amazon Fulfillment Web Service*. This SaaS application allows merchants to access Amazon.com's fulfilment capabilities through a simple Web service interface and send order information to Amazon with instructions physically to fulfil customer orders on their behalf.

Finally, an interesting recent development is SalesForce for Google Apps, which allows Google's range of communication and collaboration tools to be integrated into Salesforce's various customer management applications. Customers, who use Salesforce's on line service to manage sales, marketing and customer relations, can now access Google Apps within the Salesforce interface. This means Google's spreadsheet, text editor, calendar, instant messaging, e-mail and other tools are not just available through the same interface but work together with Salesforce.com's tools. For example, Google Gmail e-mails can be sorted and saved in the appropriate components of the Salesforce app as leads or to-do tasks.

Taken together, the three cloud service layers of Cloud Computing have substantial implications for enterprises, as they bring about important operational considerations:

- The cloud shifts ownership of applications and software from the customer to a third party provider, which means that software ceases to be an expensive product but rather becomes a pay-per-use service.
- The cloud creates economies of scale, in that specialised applications and software are no longer limited to large corporations. Instead, small enterprises can also access the same powerful applications as powerful players in the market.

18.1.3 Cloud deployment models

The continuous pressure on IT departments and infrastructure providers to offer computing infrastructure at the lowest possible cost have made them realise that, by effectively leveraging the concepts of resource pooling, virtualisation, dynamic provisioning, utility and commodity computing, they can create cost effective cloud solutions. This has resulted in three major cloud deployment models [Armbrust 2009].

- The first cloud deployment model, where developers leverage applications that are available from, and run on, public facilities, is collectively referred to as the *public cloud* model.
- The second cloud deployment model, where developers develop their own *on-premise* or *internal* cloud solutions, is collectively referred to as the *private cloud* model.
- The third and final cloud deployment model concerns developers who integrate and federate services across both the public and private cloud. This model is collectively referred to as the *hybrid cloud* model.

The characteristics and deployment options of the three deployment models are described in what follows.

18.1.3.1 Public cloud

The *public cloud* is open to a largely unrestricted universe of potential users; it is designed for a market and not for a single enterprise or group of enterprises. With public cloud formations, applications from different customers are likely to be mixed together on the cloud's servers, storage systems and networks. Public clouds are most often hosted away from customer premises and are run by third parties. They provide a way to reduce customer risk and cost by providing a flexible, even temporary extension to enterprise infrastructure. This transfers the cost from a capital expenditure to an operational expense and can quickly be scaled to meet the organisation's needs.

Temporary applications, or applications with burst resource requirements, typically benefit from the public cloud's ability to provide resources when needed and then scale them back when they are no longer needed. Applications delivered over the Internet in the software-as-a-service model, and computing resources such as storage or compute cycles delivered in the infrastructure-as-a-service model, are the most common forms of public Cloud Computing.

Public clouds are made available in a *pay-as-you-go* manner to the general public. While public clouds are similar to private clouds from a technological perspective, they create unique challenges due to their nature as remote, shared entities. These include hosting an enterprise's data in an off-site organisation as well as dependency on external suppliers for business critical infrastructure – with an associated loss of control. In addition, as most public clouds leverage a worldwide network of data centres, it is difficult to document the physical location of data at any particular moment. This use of a shared environment may suffer from potential availability, latency, security, privacy and regulatory problems.

18.1.3.2 Private cloud

A *private cloud* is user-centric and offers access to software as services, which is fully configured, production ready software available to authorised users in a self-service deployment model. A private cloud, also known as a *corporate cloud,* is designed for and access restricted to a single enterprise (or extended enterprise) and is offered in the form of an internal shared resource. Regardless of the user role or private cloud focus – infrastructure, platform or applications – the goal of a private cloud is to offer scalable and available services that are self-provisioned, without the need for staff support beyond creating the images and packaging of services available for use.

A private cloud uses infrastructure and technology such as virtualised servers in a scalable architecture to run applications behind the corporate firewall. In a private cloud, the infrastructure for implementing the cloud is controlled completely by the enterprise internal data centres of a company and is not made available to the general public. The organisation or a third party that owns the private cloud may manage the infrastructure. A private cloud infrastructure may be owned by and/or physically located in the organisation's data centres (on premise) or that of a designated service provider (off premise) with an extension of management and security control planes controlled by the organisation or designated service provider respectively. Network bandwidth and availability issues or potential security exposures that may be associated with public clouds do not burden these types of clouds.

Private clouds can offer the client greater control, security and resilience. The consumers of the service are considered *trusted.* Trusted consumers of a service are those who are considered part of an organisation's legal/contractual umbrella, including employees, contractors and business partners. Untrusted consumers are those that may be authorised to consume some/all services but are not logical extensions of the organisation.

Because integration flexibility and control over quality of service and security are high priority for larger enterprises, and because such enterprises are likely have the financial resources to optimise for costs over time rather than upfront costs, many enterprises will naturally gravitate towards the private variant in their adoption of Cloud Computing. This deployment model is ideal for enterprises that are organised with a shared services IT infrastructure.

18.1.3.3 Hybrid cloud

Hybrid cloud computing refers to the combination of external public cloud computing services and internal resources in a coordinated fashion into a unified solution. Hybrid clouds permit organisations to make choices about when to consolidate, virtualise and automate internal IT resources, and when to purchase third party services to supplement or replace in-house systems that can satisfy business requirements more efficiently and economically than existing in-house solutions.

Hybrid cloud computing implies significant integration or coordination between the internal and external environments. Hybrid cloud architectures are designed to enable enterprises to integrate private and public cloud solutions across a common management and service level reporting space with sufficient security and built in resilience that applications can be placed in multiple locations, such that if one location fails, a second one can take over. The ability to augment a private cloud with the resources of a public cloud can be used to maintain service levels in the face of rapid workload fluctuations.

Hybrid cloud computing can take a number of forms, including *cloud-bursting,* where an application is dynamically extended from a private cloud platform to an external public cloud service, based on the need for additional resources. More ambitious cloud applications may comprise a series of granular services, each of which may run in whole or in part on a private cloud platform, or on a number of external cloud platforms. In this setting the actual execution is determined at run time on the basis of changing technical, financial and business conditions.

Hybrid clouds introduce the complexity of determining how to distribute applications across both a public and private cloud. Therefore implementation of a hybrid model requires additional coordination between the private and public service management systems. Among the issues that need to be considered is the relationship between data and processing resources. If the data volume is small, or the application is stateless, a hybrid cloud can be much more successful than if large amounts of data must be transferred into a public cloud for a small amount of processing.

As already explained in the present section, cloud deployment models serve different purposes. What cloud deployment model to choose may depend on several factors, including the size of an organisation, IT resources, time to market (speed of implementation), security requirements and so on. For instance, SaaS in the public cloud provides organisations with limited resources a way to implement a needed application quickly and with low upfront costs. A private cloud, on the other hand, requires significant initial investment but offers *behind-the-firewall* security assurance.

18.2 SOA meets the Cloud

Modern enterprises are facing today costly data storage and data processing challenges, which stem from the vast amount of information they collect and analyse as a part of their mission. While SOA promises to provide the agility and flexibility organisations need to address these challenges, this promise is not always realised when SOA projects go into production.

SOA based projects that attempt to address rapidly changing challenges on data processing and storage often prove inadequate, and enterprises usually incur lost time and greater costs, trying to scale resources to meet storage and computing demand. SOA based projects must be able to accommodate growing loads and periods of peak capacity, such as when order entry activity picks up during busy shopping periods or when financial software is run to close the books at the end of a billing period. As a result, each SOA application typically has much more capacity than it needs and each organisation has more servers and storage devices than it needs. This is due to an inherent weakness in SOA that does not let it make any assumptions regarding service deployment. It rather leaves it up to the discretion of the service developer to make this deployment choice, which is a daunting task and often leads to failure when trying to contain infrastructure sprawl. To address these serious shortcomings it is sensible to direct our attention to Cloud Computing, as it provides both the economies of scale of a shared infrastructure as well as a flexible delivery model that naturally combines with the service orientation of SOA.

18.2.1 Comparing SOA with Cloud Computing

When we compare SOA with Cloud Computing solutions, we notice that SOA is an architecture pattern while the cloud can be viewed as a target deployment platform for that architecture pattern. In particular, Cloud Computing provides the ability to leverage on demand new computing resources and platforms that SOA applications require but an organisation does not own. In fact, we observe that Cloud Computing and SOA have important overlapping concerns and common considerations. Both Cloud Computing and SOA share concepts of service orientation. Services of many types are available on a common network for use by clients. The most important overlap occurs near the top of the Cloud Computing layers in the area of cloud application services (or SaaS), which are network accessible application components and software services, such as contemporary Web services [Raines 2009].

Cloud Computing and SOA can be certainly pursued independently. However, as the cloud provisioned infrastructure is also designed to scale in the way implied by the

SOA approach to application architecture, cloud processing (dynamic allocation of CPU resources) and cloud storage (Web service API access to storage resources) infrastructure are natural target platforms for SOA application deployment. This combination facilitates service deployment and collaboration with partners over the Web to deliver global SOA solutions to multiple clients across multiple geographic locations.

Modern SOA applications should be based on the premise that services are designed to be location independent, implementation neutral, and distributed (potentially heterogeneous) intermediary based. When the service implementation infrastructure is realized *inside-the-cloud* it allows all these three options. When SOA and Cloud Computing are pursued in tandem the platform and storage service offerings of Cloud Computing can provide a value-added underpinning for SOA development efforts. Using this approach, the service orientation provided by SOA relies on the *cloud* as a natural deployment medium. A cloud enabled SOA puts the service infrastructure on the Web and makes it available on demand.

The cloud SOA merger offers unprecedented control in allocating resources dynamically to meet the changing needs of service based applications, which is only effective when the service level objectives at the application level guide the cloud's infrastructure management layer. In this way, SOA solutions can capitalise on the ability of the cloud to virtualise server storage devices and applications, dynamically move and optimise service workloads across the shared infrastructure, and integrate added resources to scale.

Because Cloud Computing *abstracts* away the details of the infrastructure's hardware and software, it turns the lower levels into a utility whose implementation details are no longer visible to the user. Cloud Computing can therefore advance the focus on composable services and software capabilities that sit on top of the cloud's commodities. As a result, more high value, end user capability can be acquired in the long term by taking advantage of cloud and SOA concepts.

18.2.2 SOA deployment: Cloud Computing versus the ESB

To conclude the above discussion we note that, today, the cloud SOA fusion is a viable and cost effective alternative to keeping on premises middleware infrastructure (such as maintaining expensive Enterprise Service Buses) for each service application developer or service provider in a service system. The cloud enabling SOA applications that comprise standardised services allow us to shift the focus away from the Enterprise Service Bus, see Chapter 8.

The ESB has been, up to now, far too central in many enterprise SOA implementations. Common belief is that all an enterprise needs to do is to develop a collection of Web services, place them on an ESB and that this constitutes a complete SOA solution. In contrast to the traditional monolithic architecture and *one-size-fits-all* philosophy of ESB implementations, users of cloud related services are now able to access and activate significant resources on demand that would be impossible with ESB infrastructures. Entire SOA solutions can, therefore, literally be provisioned and deployed fairly quickly and inexpensively on the cloud. Moreover, these SOA solutions can then be easily resized and scaled up – without needing explicitly to add new integration broker functionality as is the case with the ESB (see Section 8.5.7) – downsized or even decommissioned.

18.3 Virtualisation

As noted earlier in this chapter, virtualisation is an important and common (but not the only) path to Cloud Computing. *Virtualisation* is the technique of managing systems and resources functionally, regardless of their physical layout or location and hiding their physical characteristics from the way in which other systems, applications or end users interact with them. It enables important attributes of a Cloud Computing provider, such as scalability, elasticity and share-ability.

Virtualisation allows servers, storage devices and other hardware resources, which are normally kept separate, to be treated as a pool of resources rather than discrete systems, so that these resources can be allocated on demand to accommodate the peaks and lows of business demand. This includes making a single physical resource (such as a server, an operating system, an application or storage device) appear to function as multiple logical resources, or it can include making multiple physical resources (such as storage devices or servers) appear as a single logical resource. Virtualisation is therefore extremely well suited to an elastic cloud infrastructure, because it provides important advantages in sharing, manageability and isolation, and contributes to significant cost savings.

Virtualisation supports isolation and paves the way for multi-tenancy (another important attribute of Cloud Computing) as it permits multiple users and applications to share physical resources without affecting each other.

In the following we shall describe types of virtualisation, and explain how to manage virtualisation environments.

18.3.1 Types of virtualisation for Cloud Computing

Cloud services are most often, but not always, utilised in conjunction with, and enabled by, virtualisation technologies to provide dynamic integration, provisioning, orchestration, mobility and scalability. Virtualisation helps decrease the server hardware footprint, energy consumption and cost and complexity of managing IT systems and resources, while increasing the flexibility of the overall IT infrastructure. There exist however many different types of virtualisation and a lot of confusion over their definitions.

To facilitate understanding of the importance of virtualisation for Cloud Computing we present in this section key types of virtualisation usually associated with Cloud Computing models and explain their role.

18.3.1.1 Network virtualisation

Network virtualsation is a method of giving multiple groups access to the same physical network capabilities while keeping them logically separate to a degree that they have no visibility into other groups. The idea is that virtualisation disguises the true complexity of an entire network by partitioning it into manageable parts. Network virtualisation achieves this by combining the available resources in a network and by splitting up the available bandwidth into channels, each of which is independent from the others, and each of which can be assigned (or reassigned) to a particular server or device.

18.3.1.2 Server virtualisation

Sever virtualisation (also known as *system virtualisation*) is a method of partitioning a physical server into multiple servers so that each has the appearance and capabilities of running on its own dedicated machine.

Server virtualisation is essentially where the base hardware is virtualised, allowing multiple guest operating environments to run directly on top of the hardware, without requiring a complete host operating system. Consolidation via server virtualisation, as well as advances in the direction of system convergence, promises some relief to help address scalability, performance and manageability requirements. With server virtualisation, typically virtualisation software will run on the base hardware, and the operating systems will be installed on to that virtualisation software. The intention is to spare the user from having to understand and manage complicated details of server resources, while increasing resource sharing and utilisation and maintaining the capacity to expand later.

18.3.1.3 Server clustering

Clustering is a method that allows multiple servers to be treated as a single server. Server clustering is a form of virtualisation that makes several locally attached physical systems appear to the application and end users as a single processing resource. This differs significantly from server virtualisation technologies, which normally achieve the opposite effect, i.e. making a single physical system appear as multiple independent operating environments.

A typical use case for clustering is to group a number of identical physical servers to provide distributed processing power for high volume applications, or as a *Web farm,* which is a collection of Web servers that can all handle load for a Web based application.

18.3.1.4 Storage virtualisation

Storage virtualisation is a method that pools physical storage from multiple network storage devices into what appears to be a common storage pool and isolating servers from physical storage. Storage virtualisation is commonly used in storage area networks (SANs). Often part of a storage area network, virtualised storage appears to be one device to the server operating systems and can be centrally managed and provisioned from a single view.

Virtualised storage allows adding a storage device without server/network reconfiguration, removing and/or changing storage volume definitions and assignments from one storage device to another, aggregating hard disk drives of different speeds and sizes and from different vendors, and dynamically reallocating storage space as workload or seasonal conditions warrant.

18.3.1.5 Application virtualisation

Virtualised applications separate the use of the software application from where the application is housed and maintained, enabling the user to enjoy full application functionality without having actually to have the application on their computing device. A virtualised application is not installed in the traditional sense, although it is still executes as though it were. The application is deceived at run time to believing that it is interfacing directly with the original operating system and computing resources that it manages.

In Cloud Computing nomenclature the term virtualisation typically refers to running multiple operating systems simultaneously on the same computer, which is part of what we called server or system virtualisation in this chapter.

As system virtualisation has become a key technology deployed by most Cloud Computing solutions we shall describe in the following subsection how it is managed to improve overall understanding of this important technology.

18.3.2 System virtualisation and management

A core capability of system virtualisation offerings is the ability to execute multiple operating system instances on shared hardware. Functionally, an application deployed to an operating system hosted in a virtualised environment is generally unaware that the underlying platform has been virtualised. However, any type of platform virtualisation requires efficient management solutions that consistently manage the virtualised environment.

To address the complexity of managing virtualised environments, the Distributed Management Task Force has introduced standards to define a consistent way for managing any virtualised environment. DMTF is the leading industry organisation developing standards for systems management and promoting interoperability of solutions using these standards.

The principal elements of a system virtualisation environment are based on the DMFT Common Information Model (CIM) System Virtualisation [DMFT 2009] and are illustrated in Figure 18.2. This figure shows that the resources that make up the virtualisation

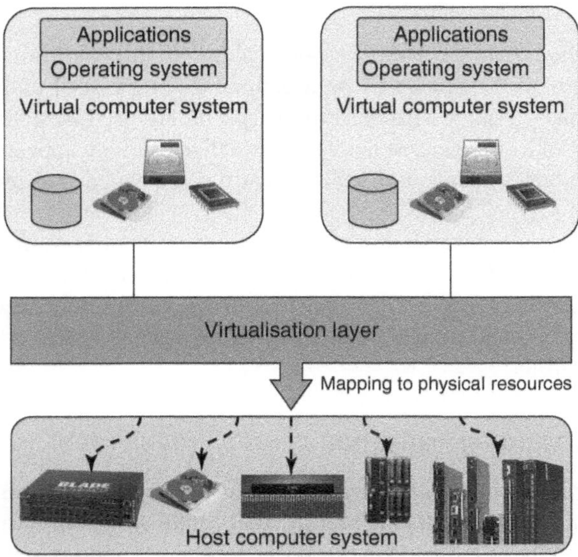

Figure 18.2 Components of the System Virtualisation Environment

environment are typically supplied by one or more host computer systems. A virtualisation layer (usually firmware or software, but possibly hardware) manages the lifecycle of a virtual computer system, which is composed of resources allocated or assigned from the host computer system. The virtualisation layer allows multiple operating system instances to run concurrently within virtual machines on a single computer, dynamically partitioning and sharing the available physical resources such as CPU, storage, memory and I/O devices.

The system virtualisation model that is depicted in Figure 18.2 illustrates how a client can manage the virtualisation layer and the full lifecycle of the hosted virtual computer systems. In system virtualisation, a host computer system provides the resources that compose virtual computer systems and their constituent virtual devices. Resources of the virtual computer system may have different properties or qualities than those of the underlying physical resources. For example, virtual resources may have different capacities or qualities of service for performance or reliability than those of their underlying physical resources.

Virtualisation approaches use either a hosted or a hypervisor architecture.

- A *hosted architecture* installs and runs the virtualisation layer as an application on top of an operating system and supports the broadest range of hardware configurations.
- In contrast, a *hypervisor* (bare metal) *architecture* installs the virtualisation layer directly on a clean system. Since it has direct access to the hardware resources rather than going through an operating system, a hypervisor is more efficient than a hosted architecture and delivers greater scalability, robustness and performance.

18.4 Multi-tenancy

In cloud environments network fabric, storage, virtual servers and applications need to be efficiently shared between multiple clients. This important requirement is addressed by the concept of multi-tenancy. Multi-tenancy constitutes an important attribute of Cloud Computing in addition to virtualisation and the five essential characteristics mentioned earlier in Section 18.1.1. High degrees of multi-tenancy over large numbers of platforms are needed for cloud computing to achieve the envisioned flexibility of on demand provisioning of reliable services and the cost benefits and efficiencies due to economies of scale.

Multi-tenancy is the capability to service multiple organisations (clients) from a shared, common hosting environment by sharing the same physical instance and version of the cloud application. Multi-tenancy in cloud computing is typically done by multiplexing the execution of virtual machines from potentially different users on the same physical server [Ristenpart 2009].

The multi-tenant style of interaction allows one tenant to customise an application's interface and business logic without affecting the functionality or availability of the application for all other tenants. Furthermore, an application should be easily upgraded without breaking other tenant specific customisations. By sharing resources and creating standard offerings, multi-tenancy reduces cost and improves efficiency of composite service operations [Roy-Chowdhury 2007].

A typical user (or tenant) of a multi-tenant system is unaware that the common computing resources, as well as data, applications and services, are being shared across multiple clients. The multi-tenant architecture provides separation of data between clients, enforces security boundaries and provides a mechanism for billing based on resource usage. Tenants can use and customise an application as though they each have a separate instance, yet their data and customisations remain secure and insulated from the activity of all other tenants. The single application instance effectively morphs at run time any particular tenant.

Multi-tenant cloud architectures typically use virtualisation to increase resource utilisation, load balancing, scalability and reliability. Multi-tenancy is achieved by a combination of hardware and virtual network components architected in such a way as to ensure reliability and availability, while also securing the flexibility and isolation of configuration and data customers demand to ensure reliability and availability while also securing the flexibility and isolation of data customers' demand.

Multi-tenancy offers several advantages to both cloud clients and providers. From the client perspective it allows them to operate in virtual isolation from one another, while from the provider perspective it offers tremendous economy of scale. In fact, from the service provider point of view multi-tenancy is a technical solution that can optimise resource utilisation and reduce capital cost.

18.4.1 Approaches to multi-tenancy

Figure 18.3 gives a view of different options for multi-tenancy at the application level and is based on characteristic approaches for enabling multi-tenancy for Cloud Computing applications found in [Osipov 2009] and [Godinez 2010]. These approaches are summarised below to improve overall understanding of the material that follows in this chapter.

1. *Shared middleware approach with single application instance:* Using this approach the application resides on the middleware and all tenants share the operating system, servers and a single instance of the middleware, and the same code for the application. This approach requires that the application be designed to provide the capability to isolate each tenant's data and customisations from the other tenants.
2. *Shared middleware approach with multiple application instances sharing a common address space:* Tenants here use different instances of the application deployed on a single instance of the middleware, operating system and servers, they also share a single address space. This model requires that tenant isolation be maintained at the middleware layer.
3. *Shared middleware with multiple application instances each in a separate address space:* Using this approach tenants use different instances of the application deployed on different instances of middleware, and share the operating system and servers. Since the middleware instance is different, each tenant is allocated its own address space. Therefore, this model requires that tenant isolation be maintained at the operating system layer.
4. The fourth and final approach is based on virtualisation techniques used to run *multiple virtualised tenants running on a single instance of the middleware, operating system and servers.* This model requires that virtualised tenants and tenant isolation be maintained at the middleware layer.

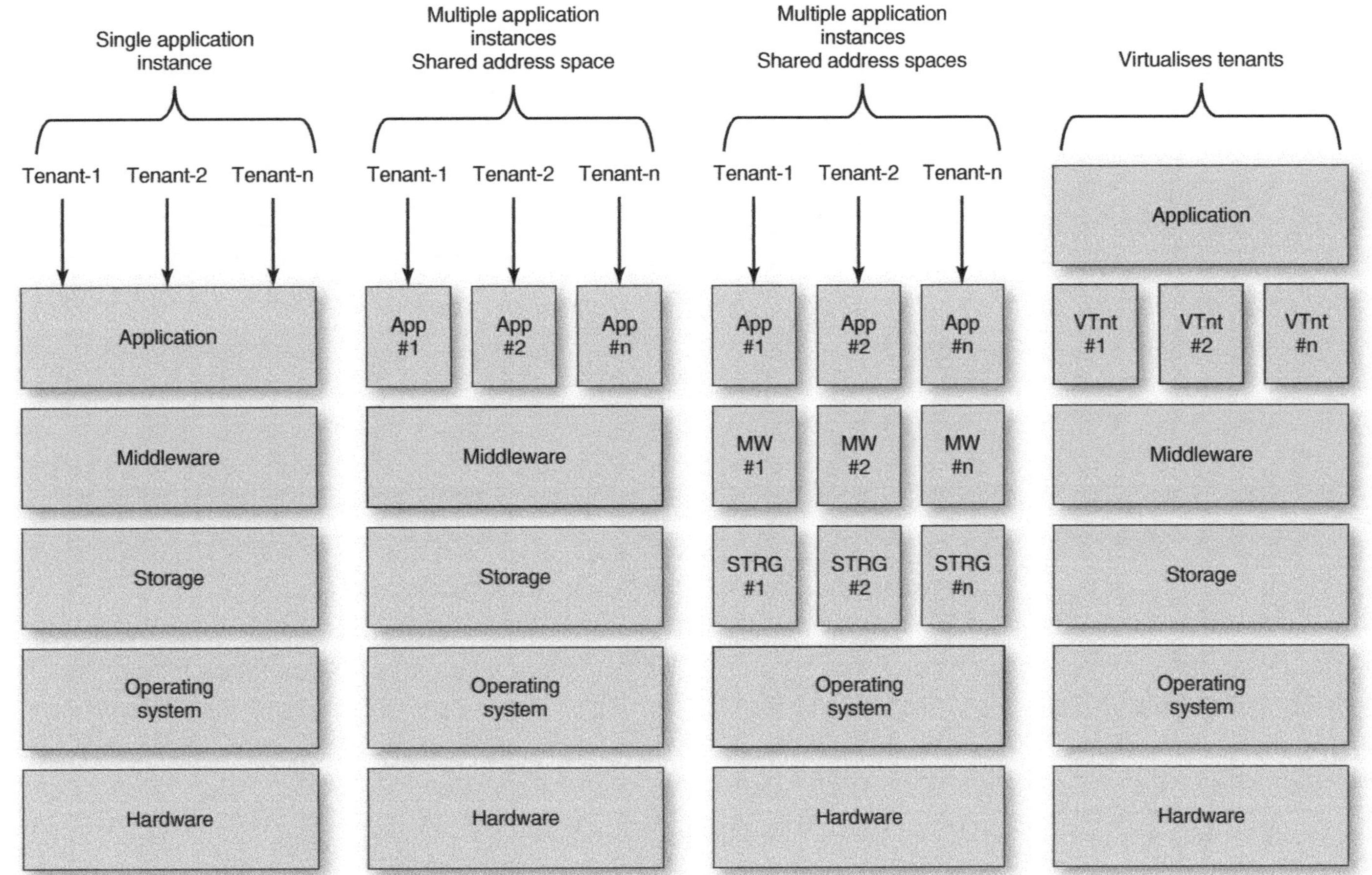

Figure 18.3 Approaches for enabling application level multi-tenancy

18.5 Architecture model for Cloud Computing

A cloud architecture, like any software system architecture, structures the various functional modules in a Cloud Computing environment, indicates how they perform their tasks, and describes how they interact with each other. Figure 18.4 depicts a cloud architecture model inspired by reference architecture models proposed by the Cloud Computing Use Case Discussion Group [Ahronovitz 2010] and the Distributed Management Task Force [DMTF 2009].

This figure illustrates, from a high level architecture point of view, a cloud architecture model that is logically divided into functional components, building blocks, and other key elements such as actors, interfaces, templates, data sources and systems with an indication of interrelationships among these elements.

18.5.1 Operational roles in cloud architecture

Figure 18.4 illustrates that a cloud architecture model is viewed from three different perspectives (or operational roles). Service consumers use the services provided through the cloud, service providers manage the cloud infrastructure and service developers develop the cloud service applications themselves. An organisation may simultaneously play any of these operational roles, or any combination of these three roles. Each role is described in more detail below.

- The *cloud service provider* is responsible for creation and maintenance of the hardware infrastructure that supports Cloud Computing applications. It makes services available to cloud service consumers (clients) at agreed service levels and costs. The services may be of any type or complexity. The provider manages

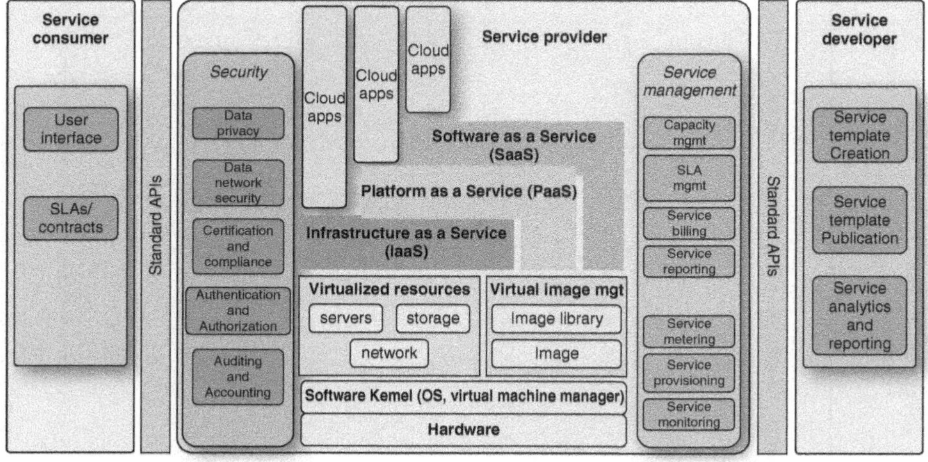

Figure 18.4 Functional roles and modules in a cloud architecture

the technical infrastructure required for providing the services and provides billing and other reports to consumers.

- The *cloud service consumer* (or client) represents an organisation or individuals who contract for services with cloud service providers to use their services. The cloud service consumer could be another cloud that in turn is a provider to other consumers. The consumer is responsible for selecting the appropriate services, arranging payment for the services, and performing the administration necessary to use those services, such as managing user identities.
- The *cloud service developer* designs and implements the components of a service. The developer describes the service in a *service template*. The developer interacts with the cloud service provider to deploy the service components, based on the description in the templates, which the provider may customise before making them available as service offerings to service consumers.

In the following we shall examine the three different operational parts in the cloud architecture that are defined by the three roles that we presented above.

18.5.2 Functional parts in the cloud architecture

The service consumer functional part of the architecture is the part where the eventual end user or enterprise that actually uses the cloud services (SaaS, PaaS or IaaS) resides. Depending on the type of service used and their role, the consumer works with different user interfaces and programming interfaces. User interfaces could be at the application level, while others could provide administrative functions such as starting and stopping virtual machines or managing cloud storage. Consumers writing application code use different programming interfaces, depending on the application they are coding.

Consumers work with SLAs, which define the policy that a cloud service provider allows per consumer and specify how service resources (virtual machines, network conductivity, storage and so on) are to be treated by the cloud service provider on behalf of the consumer. A provider deploys (or modifies) a service instance as specified by an SLA with the consumer. Whenever the consumer deploys services in the cloud service provider infrastructure, the policies that have been agreed upon by the cloud service provider and consumer in an SLA must be imposed before making virtual images operational in the cloud service provider's infrastructure.

In the service provider functional part of the architecture the lowest layer of the stack is the hardware on which the cloud environment is based. Above it sits the software kernel, either the operating system or virtual machine manager that hosts the infrastructure beneath the cloud. The virtualised resources and image modules in this part of the architecture include the basic Cloud Computing services, such as processing power, storage and middleware. The virtual images management module allows the organisation of image repositories and virtual images used in the cloud to facilitate the interaction of the final user with different virtual applications. Virtual image management provides a single, unified view of all system image templates and virtual server images to help manage and deploy computing resources. A virtual image management system manages a library of ready to deploy system templates that meet specific hardware and software requirements. These image templates can be used to create, customise and clone virtual and physical images.

At a higher level, service management involves capacity management, SLA management, service provisioning, metering, monitoring, service billing mechanisms and modules, as well as reporting facilities for administrators. Service management ensures that the capacity of IT resources can be provided to match the demands for cloud services in a timely and cost effective way. Important tasks that are considered in capacity management include: matching the capacity of the cloud services and infrastructure to the current and future identified needs of the business; and to have a scalable plan for IT infrastructure, knowing the usage trend of IT capacity and to avoid incidents that are caused by a lack of capacity; and tuning the IT components to have an efficient operation and better utilisation.

SLA management ensures that the terms of service agreed to by the provider and consumer are adhered to. To support the capacity management process effectively and to ascertain whether the terms of an SLA are being met, a range of metering and monitoring tools are provided. In addition, billing tools as well as tools that offer audit trails concerning regulatory compliance are provided.

Security applies to all aspects of the service provider's operations. Providers who deliver cloud based services need to implement comprehensive security for the cloud. The many levels of security requirements deserve a more detailed treatment and are therefore examined in a dedicated section.

The cloud service provider publishes various relevant parts of a service offering in a service catalogue. More generally, the service catalogue contains information about services through their entire lifecycle. The service catalogue provides the description of the services, the types of service, cost, supported SLAs, and who can view or use the services. It contains service templates (created by developers), service offerings (created by providers), and deployed service instances for customers. The catalogue typically stores several types of policy, such as service level agreements (SLAs), service level objectives (SLOs), deployment constraints, data residency constraints, auditability constraints, security constraints and so on. After a consumer or developer and a provider agree to a set of constraints these constraints will govern how each party (especially the provider) acts.

Finally, the purpose of the service developer functional part of the architecture in Figure 18.4 is to provide the modules that assist in designing, implementing and maintaining templates that describe the technical content and interfaces of a particular cloud service. Templates are created, updated and deleted. They are stored and made available (published) in a service template catalogue. As already noted, service templates are components of the service offering, which is provided by the service provider and are typically the applications that are delivered directly to end users via the SaaS, IaaS and PaaS cloud providers. Templates may be added to an offering, modified while part of an offering, or removed from an offering.

18.5.3 Cloud APIs

In the cloud architecture the architecture parts and their modules communicate with each other over application programming interfaces, usually by means of Web services. To this end Figure 18.4 shows that the cloud architecture model exposes a set of software interfaces or APIs that developers and customers use to manage and interact with cloud services. Provisioning, management, orchestration and monitoring are all performed using these interfaces. A cloud architecture offers at least three broad kinds of APIs:

Cloud functionality interfaces: These are programming interfaces through which developers and consumers interact with providers to request, deploy, reconfigure, administer and use services. These types of interfaces include managing the security related aspects of a cloud as well as managing and modifying instances of deployed services [DMFT 2009]. In addition, they include interfaces for image and infrastructure management. These APIs control details such as firewalls, node management, virtual machine and network management as well as load balancing.

Data functionality interfaces: These are the channels through which data flows in and out of the cloud. These APIs encompass various forms of cloud data sources, documents, web portals, maps, etc, and are used for reading, writing, updating and querying data. For instance, most SaaS providers offer API calls to read (and thereby *export*) data records. Data functionality APIs also include simple APIs for file storage services, document storage services and so on.

Application cloud interfaces: Application cloud APIs provide methods to interface and extend applications on the Web. These APIs provide functionality beyond data access. They are hallmarks of most SaaS providers, easing integration of on premise vendor and home grown applications. Application cloud APIs connect to applications such as CRM, ERP, financial, billing, desktop productivity and social media/network applications, and so on. These applications are delivered as *Software as a Service.*

18.6 Cloud security

The impact of Cloud Computing on security is profound. Cloud Computing poses a lot of challenges as it changes some of the basic expectations and relationships that influence how we assess security and perceive risk [Jansen 2011].

Enabling service providers to migrate to a cloud environment demands the ability to provide secure isolation, while still delivering the management and flexibility benefits of shared resources. Public cloud service providers must securely isolate all customer data, communication and application environments from other tenants. With public clouds, the separation must be so complete and secure that the tenants can have no visibility of each other. Private cloud service providers must deliver the secure separation required by their organisational structure, application requirements or regulatory compliance.

The most significant difference between cloud security and traditional security controls stems from the sharing of infrastructure on a massive scale. Users spanning different corporations and trust levels often interact with the same set of computing resources. The security and availability of general cloud services is dependent upon the security of basic APIs. From authentication and access control to encryption and activity monitoring, these interfaces must be designed to protect against both accidental and malicious attempts to circumvent policy. Furthermore, organisations and third parties often build upon these interfaces to offer value-added services to their customers. This introduces the complexity of a new layered API. It also increases risk, as organisations may be required to relinquish their credentials to third parties in order to enable their agency. Other aspects about Cloud Computing also require a major reassessment of security and risk. For instance, inside the cloud it is difficult to locate physically where data is stored. Security processes that were once visible are now hidden behind layers of abstraction. This lack of visibility can create a number of security and compliance issues.

The above security challenges call for end-to-end cloud security with a heavier emphasis on strong isolation, integrity and resiliency. Therefore, from a security standpoint, not only are the security issues found on Web services, such as the need for end-to-end security (see Section 11.6.2) applicable to Cloud Computing solutions, but Cloud Computing introduces a new breed of security issues and associated mitigations that we discuss in the next two sub-sections.

18.6.1 Cloud security risks

A key issue for Cloud Computing is that aspects of traditional infrastructure security move beyond an organisation's control and into the cloud. This leads to fundamental changes in the number and roles of security stakeholders as enterprises turn over control of security infrastructure and processes to outside contractors. In addition, trust relationships between the various cloud stakeholders (users, corporations, networks, service providers, etc.) need careful consideration as public Cloud Computing evolves to manage sensitive enterprise data.

This section describes security in terms of the various types of resource that need to be protected and identifies the most typical classes of cloud specific risks (excluding legal risks). These cloud specific security risks come in addition to the Web service security risks that we described in Section 11.1.1.

Data isolation failure: Multi-tenancy and shared resources are defining characteristics of Cloud Computing. In multi-tenancy situations, data must be held securely in order to protect it when multiple customers use shared resources. This risk category covers the failure of mechanisms separating storage, memory, routing, and even reputation between different tenants [Catteddu 2009]. Virtualisation, encryption and access control are the most important mechanisms for enabling varying degrees of separation between corporations, communities of interest and users.

Data protection failure: Cloud Computing poses several data protection risks for cloud customers and providers [Catteddu 2009]. In some cases, it may be difficult for the cloud customer effectively to check the data handling practices of the cloud provider and thus be certain that the data is handled in a lawful way. This problem is exacerbated in cases of multiple transfers of data in federated clouds. Some cloud providers just provide information on their data handling practices, while others may also offer certification summaries on their data processing and data security activities and the data control they have in place. For instance, they may offer SAS70 certification, which ensures that a service organisation has been through an in depth audit of their control objectives and control activities.

Lack of granular data security: As the sensitivity of data increases, the granularity of data classification enforcement must increase. In current data centre environments, granularity of role based access control at the level of user groups or business units is acceptable in most cases because the information remains within the control of the enterprise itself. However, it may be necessary to provide specific interfaces for cloud users to have the option of more granular visibility of, and control over, how their security policies and requirements are met by the service providers.

Lack of governance and compliance: Achieving certification (e.g. industry standard or regulatory requirements) may be put at risk by migration to the cloud. A key requirement is, therefore, the creation of management and validation procedures – monitoring and auditing the security state of the information with logging capabilities. With such procedures not only is it important to document access and denials to data, but to ensure that computing resources are configured to meet security specifications and have not been altered. Expanding retention policies for data policy compliance will also become an essential cloud capability. In essence, Cloud Computing infrastructures must be able to verify that data is being managed per the applicable local and international regulations, e.g. Sarbanes-Oxley Act (SOX), Health Insurance Portability and Accountability Act (HIPAA) and industry standards like Payment Card Industry Data Security Standard (PCI-DSS), with appropriate controls, log collection and reporting.

Insecure interfaces and APIs: Cloud Computing providers expose a set of software interfaces or APIs that customers use to manage and interact with cloud services. The security and availability of general cloud services is dependent upon the security of these basic APIs [CSA 2010a]. From authentication and access control to encryption and activity monitoring, these interfaces must be designed to protect against both accidental and malicious attempts to circumvent policy. Furthermore, organisations and third parties often build upon these interfaces to offer value-added services to their customers. This not only introduces the complexity of the new layered API but also increases risk, as organisations may be required to relinquish their credentials to third parties.

Threat of malicious insiders: The threat of malicious attacks from within the cloud is intensified for consumers of cloud services, due to the convergence of IT services and customers under a single management domain combined with a general lack of transparency into provider security procedures [CSA 2010a]. For example, a provider may not reveal how it grants employees access to physical and virtual assets, how it monitors these employees, or how it analyses and reports on policy compliance.

18.6.2 Cloud application security

Cloud security shares all of the Web service security concerns that were mentioned in Chapter 11, while introducing additional ones because of the wide sharing of a collection of distributed services, applications, information and infrastructure, comprised of pools of computing, network, information and storage resources by a variety of users and the dependence on multiple service providers, which are often managed by different entities. The different delivery layers of Cloud Computing have various ways of exposing their underlying infrastructure to the client. This influences the degree of direct control over the management of the computing infrastructure and the distribution of responsibilities for managing its security.

This section considers security issues and their implications for each of the three common cloud application delivery models. The following discussion is based on guidelines for the application security domain as proposed by the Security Guidance for Critical Areas of Focus in Cloud Computing document released in July 2010 by the Cloud Security Alliance (CSA) [CSA 2010b]. The Security Guidance provides broad recommendations for operational security concerns including application security, encryption and key management, and identity and access management for Cloud Computing.

18.6.2.1 IaaS level application security

On an IaaS cloud platform, the cloud vendor provides a set of virtualised components, such as virtual machines, raw storage and other components that can be used to construct and run an application. The IaaS model transfers control, and responsibility for security, from the cloud provider to the client. In this delivery model, access is available to the operating system that supports virtual images, networking and storage. The CSA cloud security reference model identifies the following guidelines and recommendations to address security *pain points* within a cloud IaaS environment:

> *Trusting virtual machine images:* A potentially weak element introduced by Cloud Computing, both public and private, is the vulnerability at the hypervisor (virtual machine monitor) layer and the effect on cloud services that rely on virtualisation (for instance, a typical IaaS delivery model). A typical security concern at the IaaS level is that of securely managing the virtual machine images that encapsulate applications in the cloud. These virtual machine images are provided to vast numbers of clients by IaaS providers or are built by external providers. Virtual machine images must have high integrity because the initial state of every virtual machine in the cloud is determined by some image. The best option is to rely on an enterprise's own image that conforms to the same security policies as internal trusted hosts and apply the same degree of security verification and hardening as that for hosts within the enterprise. An alternative option is to use virtual images from a trusted third party that provides value-added services above the infrastructure components provided by the IaaS provider. A detailed overview of image security risks and challenges in a cloud environment is discussed in [Wei 2009] where the authors propose an image management system that is designed with built in image security functionality, which mitigates several image security risks.
>
> *Hardening hosts:* Hosts running within an IaaS infrastructure are akin to hosts running in the demilitarised zone or DMZ of an enterprise's network (see Section 11.4, which deals with enterprise security topologies). All of the same strong operational procedures, used to harden hosts running in the DMZ in an enterprise, should be applied to virtual images in an IaaS environment. Images should

be hardened and standard images should be used for instantiating virtual machines in a public cloud [Mather 2009]. A good practice for cloud based applications is to build custom operating system and application platform, virtual machine images that have only the capabilities necessary to support the application stack.

Securing inter-host communication: A cloud based application must design in explicit controls to prevent the disclosure of sensitive information between hosts. The application must take on the responsibility for securing the communication in a cloud based application because the hosts are running in a shared infrastructure with other companies. Securing such communication depends on the mode of message exchange. For synchronous communication, such as point-to-point network connections, channel level security is sufficient. For asynchronous communication, such as using a message queue based mechanism, message based security is needed to protect the sensitive information while the data is in transit.

Managing application keys and federated identities: With Cloud Computing the user is actually accessing many applications on a hybrid Cloud Computing environment, which goes beyond the boundary of an enterprise. The cloud environment must enforce the user's access control, i.e. this should happen outside the enterprise data centre, and this creates new challenges for the enterprise when adopting Cloud Computing solutions. Cloud Computing introduces risks for identity, access and key management. To circumvent these risks, cloud service providers should provide and store local identities, access roles, cryptographic keys, delegation specifications and so on. In addition, the cloud environment must support federated identity management facilities, as user information is stored across multiple, distinct identity management systems and a user's authentication process is integrated across multiple organisations. To integrate cloud service into an enterprise's remote access portal with *single-sign-on,* an identity federation open standard such as SAML is highly beneficial. The SAML protocol decouples both the SAML identity provider and the SAML service provider, (see Section 11.5.4). This enables the enterprise to have a centralised identity provider that can support many other service providers in a distributed fashion. The SAML identity provider focuses on identity management, access policy management and security token generation, while SAML service providers receive the remote security token, retrieve credential data, and reinforce user access policies locally.

In particular, IaaS platforms require an application key on all API calls to identify a valid account. The application key must be passed on all of the calls to make use of the services provided by the IaaS provider, such as the calls to connect and communicate between application nodes. Most application security programs have standards and best practices for handling key material, e.g. enterprises can leverage their Public Key Infrastructure (PKI) and have full key lifecycle management, including the ability to issue, sign, revoke and validate X.509 certificates, (see Section 11.3.7.1). These standards and practices will need some modification for IaaS application keys. For instance, by introducing key pairs, enterprises may introduce extensive control over authentication, message integrity and privacy while interacting with an IaaS. When available, *data-at-rest* encryption (as used in WS-Security) should also be used for invoking IaaS management services.

Additional requirements for handling sensitive data: Web applications running on an IaaS public platform must ensure that all data flow over the network is secured in order to prevent leakage of sensitive data during processing. For this purpose all IaaS hosted applications must be designed with standard security countermeasures to safeguard against improper handling of sensitive information. This involves the use of strong network traffic encryption techniques, such as Secure Socket Layer and Transport Layer Security. Specialised filtering and masking mechanisms are also needed for handling operation and exception logging, especially when debugging information is logged because the storage for this information may be shared and managed by an outside party.

18.6.2.2 PaaS level application security

Platform as a Service cloud (public or private) offers an integrated environment to design, test, deploy and support custom applications on top of services provided by IaaS platforms. For example, an IaaS provides a message queue for asynchronous messaging, whereas a PaaS could supply middleware in the form of an Enterprise Service Bus that provides both the asynchronous messaging, as well as services such as message routing. Just like IaaS environments where the network is multi-tenanted, the PaaS environment introduces additional security threats because applications are running across multiple shared platforms. This requires both security on the PaaS platform and security of customer applications deployed on a PaaS platform [Mather 2009].

Multi-tenant security and segregation of data: The multi-tenant nature of the PaaS platform means that different physical and virtual resources are dynamically assigned and reassigned according to consumer demand, and that the application instances and data stores may be shared across multiple enterprises. This allows the PaaS vendor to make more efficient use of resources and helps achieve lower costs. There is, however, a degree of location independence in that the customer generally has no control or knowledge over the exact location of the provided resources. In addition, as the PaaS platform's services are shared, applications cannot make assumptions about trusting messages placed on or taken off the platform middleware. Sufficient security checks need to be adopted to ensure data security and prevent unauthorised access to data of one tenant by users from other tenants. This involves hardening the data store as well as the application to ensure data segregation.

Addressing the risks associated with these security threats require a change in the application's security architecture to include application level controls, such as secure, message level communication and an update to existing secure design, coding and testing guidance. In general, securing the PaaS platform software stack that runs customer applications becomes the responsibility of PaaS providers, who offer a multi-tenant computing model that guarantees a containment and isolation of multi-tenant applications from each other.

Securing message level communication: Developers should expect PaaS providers to offer a set of security features, including user authentication, single-sign-on, authorisation management, and Secure Sockets Layer protocol or Transport Layer Security protocol support made available via specialised PaaS APIs. Securing the messages on the PaaS platform becomes the responsibility of application developers, because controls such as partitioning the platform based on data classification are not available in PaaS environments. For SOAP based messages, standard service security standards, such as WS-Security, can and should be used.

Managing application keys and federated identities: Just as in IaaS platforms, PaaS platforms require an application key on all API calls to the platform itself, and for calls to services within the PaaS environment from the hosted application. The application key must be maintained and secured along with all other credentials required by the application, as already explained in the IaaS case.

Additional requirements for handling of sensitive data: PaaS platforms have the same requirements for application level handling of sensitive information as IaaS platforms.

18.6.2.3 SaaS level application security

Software as a Service provides application capabilities that are made available to customers on demand, over the Internet. It also provides the management of infrastructure and programming environment facilities that support these application capabilities. The application's capabilities provide end user functions as well as becoming part of the programming platform. External applications can exchange data through the APIs the SaaS platform provides.

SaaS platforms inherit the same security concerns and mitigations as we described for the PaaS and IaaS environments. Data exchanged through the SaaS platform's external APIs are subject to existing security policy and standards for any type of external data exchange. This involves the use of strong encryption techniques for data security and fine grained authorisation to control access to data. Dedicated public cloud providers help to build secure SaaS solutions by providing infrastructure services that aid in ensuring perimeter and environment security. This involves the use of firewalls, intrusion detection systems and so on. A self-hosted SaaS deployment, however, requires the vendor to build these services and assess them for security vulnerabilities.

In general, security solutions for end-to-end Web services used in conjunction with access (authentication, authorisation), confidentiality, non-repudiation, and integrity of information that we covered in Chapter 11 apply to SaaS application security.

An additional important consideration for the SaaS deployment model is that it needs to be periodically assessed for conformance to regulatory and industry standards. Access, storage and processing of sensitive data needs to be carefully controlled and is governed under regulations such as ISO-27001, Sarbanes-Oxley Act, Health Insurance Portability and Accountability Act and so on.

18.7 Cloud service lifecycle

Cloud service lifecycle focuses on exposing the actual cloud service functionality, which is one or more aggregated resources exposed as a single unit of management, and managing the lifecycle of a service in a distributed multiple provider environment in a way that satisfies service level agreements with its customers [Breiter 2009].

The DMTF formed the Open Cloud Standards Incubator to aid the industry in addressing challenges that affect the interoperability, portability, and security of Cloud Computing environments [DMTF 2009]. One of the purposes of the Open Cloud Standards Incubator is address the characteristics of the cloud service lifecycle. The DMTF identified the following aspects of the lifecycle of a cloud service:

- description of the cloud service in a template;
- deployment of the cloud service into the cloud;
- offering of the service to its consumers;
- consumer entrance into contracts for the offering;
- provider operation and management of instances of the service;
- decommissioning of the service offering.

In the following we shall briefly explain these aspects of the lifecycle of a cloud service on the basis of the cloud architecture model shown in Figure 18.4 and in terms of Figure 18.5, which describes the various phases in the cloud service lifecycle.

Figure 18.5 provides an overview of the life cycle of cloud services. This figure illustrates that in the first phase, called *description,* all information required to create a certain type of cloud service is captured in a service template. A service template contains all knowledge that is needed to instantiate a cloud service and to manage the resulting cloud service instances. After a developer has created the components of a service, the developer begins the process of making it available to cloud consumers by creating a template that defines the content of, and interface to, the service. This *cloud service template* describes the service in a generic manner completely independently of how the service is exposed to potential service subscribers. For example, it does not include any pricing information or information about data centre specific resources required for hosting instances of the service.

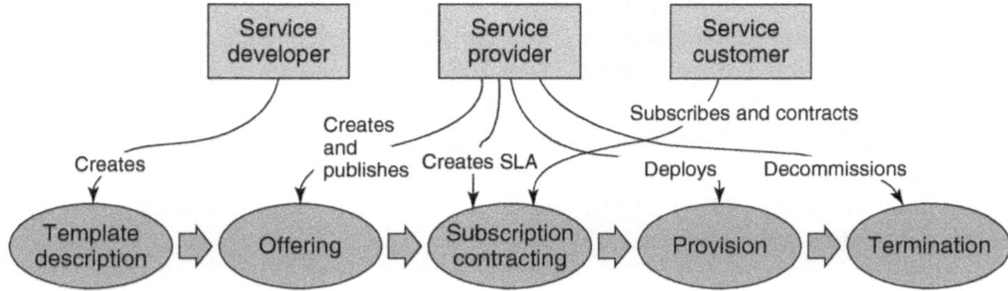

Figure 18.5 Phases in the cloud service lifecycle

In the *offering phase,* a provider who creates a service offering for consumption by one or more consumers, customises the cloud service template. This may include aspects such as the prices associated with the respective offering and specific technical information, such as which machines, Internet Protocol address ranges, and storage requirements for hosting instances of this specific offering. An offering is the unit that a consumer requests by establishing a contract with the provider for that offering.

When a cloud service offering is published in the service catalogue, the *subscription and contracting* phase begins. From the catalogue, a requester can select an offering and then specify the necessary parameters for the cloud service instance, such as capacity, availability, performance and duration. The provider and customer then agree on the SLA terms that stipulate the use of this particular service offering. Subsequently, the provider provisions a service instance in the *service provision* phase that satisfies the constraints defined in the SLA offering, and the consumer uses the instance as defined in the contract. The provision phase incorporates run time monitoring and maintenance functionality where a provider manages a deployed service and all its resources, including monitoring resources and notifying the consumer of critical situations. After the contract is terminated, the provider *decommissions* the offering by reclaiming the service instance and its supporting resources.

18.8 Cloud standards

Standards are critical for the successful adoption and delivery of cloud computing, both within the public sector and more broadly. Several of the existing Web service standards, such as management and security related standards, as well as standards for virtualisation apply in general terms to the cloud. However, for applications that need to be migrated to the cloud, these standards need to be re-evaluated and assessed to address cloud specific outstanding fundamental problems. As an example, DMTF has exhibited proven standards, such as the Open Virtualisation Format (OVF), which provides open packaging and distribution formats for virtual machines, and the Virtualisation Management (VMAN), which includes a set of specifications that address the management lifecycle of a virtual environment, to help promote interoperable Cloud Computing services.

Of particular importance will be the development of standards for Cloud Computing and frameworks for interoperating between clouds, while standard reference architectures for Cloud Computing are expected to be fully embraced. Outstanding fundamental issues that need to be addressed by such standards include security, governance, SLAs, portability/interoperability across clouds, compliance, legacy systems integration, APIs, and virtualised resource management.

Several standards initiatives, such as the Open Cloud Standards Incubator of DMTF and the Open Cloud Consortium (OCC), focus on the development of standards for interoperating between federated clouds.

18.8.1 Interoperability standard initiatives

The DMTF's Open Cloud Standards Incubator focuses on ways to facilitate operations between private clouds within enterprises and other private, public or hybrid clouds, by improving the interoperability between platforms through open cloud resource management standards. The group also aims to develop specifications to enable cloud service portability and provide management consistency across cloud and enterprise platforms. It currently focuses on addressing resource management, packaging formats, and security mechanisms that need interoperability.

The Open Cloud Consortium (opencloudconsortium.org) is a member driven organisation that supports the development of standards for Cloud Computing and frameworks for interoperating between clouds. It also strives to develop benchmarks for Cloud Computing, supports open source reference implementations for Cloud Computing, and manages Cloud Computing test beds.

18.8.2 Security standard initiatives

There are also considerable advances in so far as security standards for Cloud Computing are concerned. Recently, the National Institute of Standards and Technology has created the Cloud Security Alliance (www.cloudsecurityalliance.org) a non-profit organisation to promote the use of best practices for providing security assurance within Cloud Computing. The objectives of CSA are to promote a common level of understanding between the consumers and providers of Cloud Computing regarding the necessary security requirements and attestation of assurance. CSA also aims to promote independent research into best practices for Cloud Computing security, and plans to create consensus lists of issues and guidance for cloud security assurance.

18.8.3 API standard initiatives

Finally, one of the most severe problems when developing, porting and delivering applications across multiple PaaS clouds is the lack of standards for PaaS API design. There is unfortunately also no concerted effort by PaaS providers to develop ubiquitous and consistent APIs across clouds. This lack of accepted API standards has ramifications for both security management and the portability of applications across the cloud. To address these problems, the Open Grid Forum's Open Cloud Computing Interface (OCCI) working group (www.occi-wg.org) is currently developing an API specification for remote management of Cloud Computing infrastructure. This will allow for the development of interoperable tools for common tasks, including deployment, autonomic scaling and monitoring. The scope of the specification will be all high level functionality required for the life cycle management of virtual machines (or workloads) running on virtualisation technologies (or containers) supporting service elasticity.

18.9 Benefits and risks of Cloud Computing

The rise of Cloud Computing could radically change the way companies manage their technology assets and computing needs. At a more basic level of responding to day to day business demands, Cloud Computing is delivering innovative solutions to organisations in numerous fields, from healthcare to telecommunications, to logistics and others, spanning enterprises of all sizes. As Cloud Computing begins to take hold, it has become evident that it represents several tangible benefits due to its unique technological approach. However, at the same time it exhibits several serious risks.

18.9.1 Potential benefits of Cloud Computing

The following list enumerates a handful of tangible benefits of Cloud Computing to customers:

Cost reduction/avoidance: The cloud helps in shifting the IT cost structure from capital expenditure to operating expenditure and as such it offers enterprises the option of scalability without the serious financial commitments required for infrastructure purchase and maintenance. There is little to no upfront capital expenditure with cloud services. Cloud users consume computing and storage services on demand and pay for them as they go, using an operating expenses budget, instead of paying for infrastructure resources upfront using capital expenditure. The ability to pool resources, virtualise them, and then dynamically provision from the resource pool yields a much higher utilisation rate and thus better economics – sometimes from 15% to 90% utilisation [Mayo 2009].

Shifting of resources towards higher value activities: By using the Cloud Computing model for IT services, it is estimated that a substantial reduction of data center infrastructure expenditure can be achieved [Kundra 2011]. Similar efficiency improvements will be seen in software applications and end user support. Cloud computing can allow IT organisations to simplify, as they no longer have to maintain complex, heterogeneous technology environments. Focus will shift from the technology itself to the core competencies and mission of the organisation.

Enhanced service delivery: Cloud Computing enables the dynamic availability of IT applications and infrastructure, regardless of location. More rapid service delivery results from the ability to orchestrate the tasks to create, configure, provision and add computing power in support of IT and business services much more quickly than would be possible with today's computing infrastructure. Enhanced service delivery reinforces efforts for customer retention, faster time to market and horizontal market expansion.

Agility and scalability: Cloud Computing differs from more traditional forms of distributed computing in the way it scales computing and storage resources up and down. Instead of drawing from a fixed set of resources, consumers can add or remove capacity at will, almost instantaneously, and only pay for them as they grow (or shrink). With unconstrained capacity, cloud services offer increased flexibility and scalability for evolving IT needs. Provisioning and implementation are done on demand, allowing for traffic spikes and reducing the time to implement new services.

Efficiency: Reallocating service management operational activities to the cloud offers organisations a unique opportunity to focus efforts on their core competencies and innovation. This allows for business growth and may be even more beneficial than the financial advantages offered by the cloud. More rapid service delivery results from the ability to orchestrate the tasks to create, configure, provision and add computing power in support of IT and business services. Enhanced service delivery reinforces efforts for customer retention, faster time to market and horizontal market expansion.

Resiliency: One big advantage that all types of Cloud Computing offer is that, by its nature, Cloud Computing removes single points of failure. Cloud Computing provides a highly resilient computing environment. The failure of one node of the system has no impact on availability of information and does not result in perceivable downtime. Cloud providers have mirrored solutions that can be utilised in a disaster scenario as well as for load balancing traffic.

18.9.2 Potential risks of Cloud Computing

Despite all the benefits of Cloud Computing, serious perils must be weighed. Once an organisation decides to move to the cloud, it is at the mercy of network failures, policy concerns, interoperability problems, and a multitude of security concerns (including privacy, trust and protection). In addition, there is ambiguity regarding jurisdictional issues, which provokes a host of vexing privacy law concerns. The most characteristic technology related risks are summarised below.

Cloud service outages: Despite employing architectures designed for high service reliability and availability, cloud computing services can and do experience outages and performance slowdowns [Leavit 2009]. At a level of 99.95% reliability, 4.38 hours of downtime are to be expected in a year [Jansen 2011]. Periods of scheduled maintenance are also usually excluded as a source of downtime in SLAs and able to be scheduled by the cloud provider with short notice. The level of reliability of a cloud service and its capabilities for backup and recovery need to be addressed in the organisation's contingency planning to ensure the recovery and restoration of disrupted cloud services and operations, using alternate services, equipment and locations, if required.

Lack of interoperability between computing clouds: The absence of standardisation across cloud platforms creates unnecessary complexity and results in high switching costs and potential vendor lock-in. Each cloud vendor has different application models, many of which are proprietary, vertically integrated stacks that limit platform choice. There is currently little on offer in the way of tools, procedures or standard data formats or service interfaces that could guarantee data, application and service portability. This can make it difficult for the customer to migrate from one provider to another or migrate data and services back to an in-house IT environment. This usually results in a dependency on a particular cloud provider for service provision, especially if data portability, as the most fundamental aspect, is not enabled. Application or resource lock-in is the most obvious form of customer lock-in (although it is not specific to cloud services).

Lack of compatibility with existing applications: Many existing cloud technologies do not provide inherent compatibility with existing applications. Some current computing clouds in the public domain have sacrificed application compatibility in order to provide better scalability and other features. What this can potentially mean is that organisations have to develop entirely new applications specific to that computing cloud, or, at the very least, make very significant modifications to their existing applications before they will run in the computing cloud.

IT policy concerns: One of the key issues in Cloud Computing is the move towards a multi-sourced IT environment, where some services are provided in-house, some from other external partners, and some from a range of infrastructure, application and process suppliers in the form of private, public, community or hybrid clouds. Any preparation for such transitioning requires a thorough review of an organisation's IT strategy in light of its mission needs. It is important for an organisation to assess which fundamental capabilities need to stay in-house as mission critical and which are better suited for the pay-per-use cloud approach. These considerations should be made in conjunction with the imperative to consolidate, simplify and optimise an organisation's IT environment, to reduce costs and free up investment for other mission focused initiatives. If such considerations are not made then the operational efficiency of the cloud solution will be severely hampered.

Security and privacy risks: While outsourcing relieves operational commitment on the part of the organisation, the act of engaging a cloud provider's offerings for public cloud services poses security and privacy risks against which an organisation needs to safeguard itself.

At the heart of cloud infrastructure is this idea of multi-tenancy and decoupling between specific hardware resources and applications. By design, most external cloud vendors typically support multi-tenancy computer environments. Organisations must look for the right balance between the security of an internal, dedicated infrastructure and the improved economics of a shared, external cloud environment. In the jungle of multi-tenant data, organisations need to trust the cloud provider that their information will not be exposed. Regardless of which approach an organisation takes, enterprises that deploy mission critical applications require assurances of reasonable system responsiveness through service level agreements.

Organisations also require protection through data isolation in a multi-tenant environment, fail-over protection to minimise service outages and predictable recharge rates. This means that security and unauthorised access to information in the cloud are significant concerns. The public cloud does offer security. However, it is still not clear to many organisations whether the level of security offered would meet the needs of corporations that are notoriously protective of their data. Convincing corporate security management that data stored with a third party is safe remains a significant challenge, and there is also the question of liability if any data is compromised.

18.10 Summary of learning objectives

Cloud Computing is a computing paradigm and an associated set of business models used to provide on demand access to a shared pool of configurable, scalable computing resources delivered as a service to external customers via the Internet. Examples of cloud services include storage, processing, memory, network bandwidth and virtual machines.

The cloud model promotes availability and is composed of five essential characteristics:

- *Broad network access:* capabilities are available over the network and accessed through standard mechanisms that promote use by heterogeneous thin or thick client platforms.
- *Resource pooling:* to serve multiple clients with different physical and virtual resources assigned and reassigned dynamically according to client demand.
- *On demand self-service:* a consumer can unilaterally provision computing capabilities as needed automatically without requiring human interaction.
- *Rapid elasticity:* capabilities can be rapidly and elastically provisioned from quick scale-out and rapid release to quick scale-in.
- *Measured service:* resource is controlled and optimised by leveraging a metering capability at some level of abstraction appropriate to the type of service utilised.

It also promotes three categories of service models: Cloud Software as a Service (SaaS), Cloud Platform as a Service (PaaS), Cloud Infrastructure as a Service (IaaS); and three types of deployment models: Private Cloud, Public Cloud, and Hybrid Cloud.

Cloud Computing usually relies on virtualisation techniques for managing systems and resources functionally, regardless of their physical layout or location and hiding their physical characteristics from systems, applications or end users.

Review questions

- What is Cloud Computing?
- What are the essential characteristics of Cloud Computing?
- Briefly describe the three Cloud Computing delivery models.
- Briefly describe the three Cloud Computing deployment models.
- How is Cloud Computing related to SOA initiatives?
- What is virtualisation and how does it relate to Cloud Computing?
- Briefly describe the different types of virtualisation. Discuss their merits with respect to Cloud Computing.
- What is multi-tenancy? Why is it important for Cloud Computing?
- What are the main parts of the Cloud Computing architecture?
- Why is security important for Cloud Computing? How does cloud security relate to Web service security?
- Discus the implications of application level security for SaaS, PaaS and IaaS.
- What are the perceived benefits of Cloud Computing? What are the major risks and how can they be circumvented?

References

[Ahmed 2001] K. Ahmed *et al.,* "XML Metadata", Wrox Press, 2001.

[Ahronovitz 2010] Ahronovitz, *et.al.,* "Cloud Computing Use Cases", Cloud Computing Use Cases Discussion Group, white paper, version 4, July 2010, available from: http://cloudusecases.org/

[Aldrich 2002] S. E. Aldrich, "Anatomy of Web Services", Patricia Seybold Group, Inc. 2002, available from: www.psgroup.com.

[Alexander 2004] J. Alexander *et al.,* "Web Services Transfer (WS-Transfer)", September 2004, available from: http://www.w3.org/Submission/2006/SUBM-WS-Transfer-20060315/.

[Allen 2001] P. Allen, *Realizing e-Business with Components,* Addison-Wesley, 2001.

[Armbrust 2009] M. Armbrust *et al.,* "Above the Clouds: A Berkeley View of Cloud Computing", Technical report, UC Berkeley Reliable Adaptive Distributed Systems Laboratory, February 2009, available from: http://radlab.cs.berkeley.edu.

[Anagol-Subbaro 2005] A. Anagol-Subbaro, *J2EE Web Services on BEA WebLogic,* Prentice Hall, 2005.

[Anderson 2007] T. Anderson "Understanding web services specifications, Part 5: WS-Policy", IBM Developer Works, February 2007, available from: http://www.ibm.com/developerworks/webservices/tutorials/ws-understand-web-services5

[Alves 2007] A. Alves *et al.* (eds.), "Web Services Business Process Execution Language version 2.0", April 2007, available from: http://docs.oasis-open.org/wsbpel/2.0/OS/wsbpel-v2.0-OS.pdf.

[Antoniou 2008] G. Antoniou, F. van Harmelen, *A Semantic Web Primer,* 2nd edition, MIT Press, 2008.

[Arkin 2002] A. Arkin, "Business Process Modelling Language (BPML) specification", BPMI, June 2002, available from: http://www.bpmi.org/index.esp.

[Atkinson 2002] C. Atkinson *et al., Component-based Product Line Engineering with UML,* Addison-Wesley, 2002.

[Austin 2004] D. Austin *et al.* (eds.), "Web Services Choreography Requirements", W3C Working Draft, March 2004, available from: http://www.w3.org/TR/ws-chor-reqs/.

[Bachmann 2000] F. Bachmann *et al.,* "Technical Concepts of Component-Based Software Engineering", Technical Report, Carnegie-Mellon University, CMU/SEI-2000-TR-008 ESC-TR-2000-007, 2nd edition, May 2000. http://www-128.ibm.com/developerworks/library/specification/ws-fed/.

[Ballinger 2006] K. Ballinger *et al.,* "Web Services Metadata Exchange (WS-MetadataExchange), Version 1.1", August 2006, available from: http://msdn.microsoft.com/library/en-us/dnglobspec/html/ws-metadataexchange.pdf.

[Balzer 2004] Y. Balzer, "Improve your SOA project plans", IBM developerWorks, July 2004, available from:
http://www-106.ibm.com/developerworks/library/ws-improvesoa/.

[Barber 2009] G. Barber (editor) "Service Component Architecture Specifications", April 2009, available from:
http://www.osoa.org/display/Main/Service+Component+Architecture+Specifications.

[Barreto 2007] C. Barreto *et al.* (eds),"Web Services Business Process Execution Language Version 2.0 Primer", May 2007, available from:
http://docs.oasis-open.org/wsbpel/2.0/Primer/wsbpel-v2.0-Primer.pdf.

[Bass 2003] L. Bass, P. Clements, R. Kazman, *Software Architecture in Practice,* 2nd edition, Addison-Wesley, 2003.

[Bean 2003] J. Bean, *XML for Data Architects: Designing for Re-use and Integration,* Morgan Kaufmann, 2003.

[Bean 2010] J. Bean, *SOA and Web services Interface Design,* Morgan Kaufmann, 2010.

[Beckett 2004] D. Beckett (ed.), "RDF/XML Syntax Specification (Revised)", W3C Recommendation, February 2004, available from:
http://www.w3.org/TR/rdf-syntax-grammar/.

[Bieberstein 2005] N. Bieberstein *et al.,* "Impact of Service-Oriented Architecture on Enterprise Systems, Organizational Structures, and Individuals", IBM Systems Journal, vol. 44, no. 4, pp. 691–708, 2005.

[Bieberstein 2006] N. Bieberstein *et al.,* "Service-Oriented Architecture (SOA) Compass", IBM Press, 2006.

[Bieberstein 2008] N. Bieberstein *et al.,* ,"Executing SOA", IBM Press, 2008.

[Bloomberg 2004] J. Bloomberg, "Events vs. Services", ZapThink White Paper, October 2004, available from:
www.zapthink.com.

[Bosworth 2004] A. Bosworth *et al.,* "Web Services Addressing (WS-Addressing)", August 2004, available from:
http://msdn.microsoft.com/ws/2004/08/ws-addressing/.

[BRCommunity 2005] "A Brief History of the Business Rule Approach", Business Rule Community 2005, available from:
http://www.BRCommunity.com.

[Breiter 2009] G. Breiter, M. Behrendt "Life cycle and characteristics of services in the world of cloud computing", IBM Journal of Research & Development, vol. 53 no. 4, August 2009.

[Brickley 2004] D. Brickley, R. V. Guha (eds.), "RDF Vocabulary Description Language 1.0: RDF Schema", W3C Recommendation, February 2004, available from:
http://www.w3.org/TR/rdf-schema/.

[Brittenham 2001] P. Brittenham, "Web Services Development Concepts (WSDC 1.0)", IBM developerWorks, May 2001, available from:
http://www-106.ibm.com/developersworks/library/.

[Brown 2005] A. Brown *et al.,* "SOA Development Using the IBM Rational Software Development Platform: A Practical Guide", Rational Software, September 2005.

[Buecker 2007] A. Buecker *et. al.,* "Understanding SOA Security Design and Implementation", IBM Redbooks, 2nd edition, November 2007, available from:
ibm.com/redbooks.

[Bullard 2006] V. Bullard, B. Murray, K. Wilson (eds.), "An Introduction to WSDM", OASIS Committee Draft, February 2006, available from:
http://docs.oasis-open.org/wsdm/wsdm-1.0-intro-primer-cd-01.pdf

[Candadai 2004] A. Candadai, "A Dynamic Implementation Framework for SOA-based Applications", *Web Logic Developers Journal: WLDJ,* September/October 2004.

[Cantor 2004] S. Cantor *et al.* (eds.), "Assertions and Protocols for the OASIS Security Assertion Markup Language (SAML) V2.0", OASIS, Committee Draft 03, December 2004, available from: http://www.oasis-open.org/committees/documents.php?wg_abbrev=security.

[Cappelli 2007] W. Cappelli "Managing Applications in the Age of SOA and Web Services", Gartner IT Infrastructure, Operations & Management Summit, June 2007.

[Carzaniga 2000] A. Carzaniga, D. S. Rosenblum, A. L. Wolf, "Content-based Addressing and Routing: A General Model and its Application", Technical Report CU-CS-902-00, Department of Computer Science, University of Colorado, January 2000.

[Carzaniga 2001] A. Carzaniga, D. S. Rosenblum, A. L. Wolf, "Design and Evaluation of a Wide-Area Event Notification Service", ACM Transactions on Computer Systems, vol. 19, no. 3, pp. 332–83, August 2001.

[Case 1999] J. D. Case *et al.,* "Introduction to Version 3 of the Internet-standard Network Management Framework", Internet Engineering Task Force (IETF), RFC 2570, April 1999, available from:
www.rfc-editor.org/rfc/rfc2570.txt.

[Catteddu 2009] D. Catteddu, G. Hogben (eds), "Cloud Computing: Benefits, risks and recommendations for information security", European Network and Information Security Agency report, Nov. 2009, available from:
http://www.enisa.europa.eu/.

[Cauldwell 2001] P. Cauldwell *et al., XML Web Services,* Wrox Press, 2001.

[Channabasavaiah 2003] K. Channabasavaiah, K. Holley, E. M. Tuggle, Jr., "Migrating to a Service-Oriented Architecture", IBM developerWorks, December 2003, available from:
http://www-106.ibm.com/developerworks/library/ws-migratesoa/.

[Chappell 2004] D. A. Chappell, *Enterprise Service Bus,* O'Reilley, 2004.

[Chappell 2005] D. Chappell, "ESB Myth Busters: Clarity of definition for a growing phenomenon", *Web Services Journal,* pp. 22–6, February 2005.

[Chappell 2006] D. Chappell, L. Liu "Web Services Brokered Notification 1.3 (WS-BrokeredNotification)" OASIS Standard,October 2006, available from:
http://docs.oasis-open.org/wsn/wsn-ws_brokered_notification-1.3-spec-os.pdf.

[Clark 2001] J. Clark *et al.* (eds.), "ebXML Business Process Specification Schema: Version 1.01", OASIS, May 2001, available from:
www.ebxml.org/specs/ebBPSS.pdf.

[Clement 2004] T. Clement *et al.,* "Universal Description, Discovery and Integration specification UDDI Version 3.0.2", UDDI Spec Technical Committee Draft, September 2004, available from: http://uddi.org/pubs/uddi_v3.htm.

[Colan 2004] M. Colan, "Service-Oriented Architecture expands the vision of Web services, Part 2", IBM developerWorks, April 2004, available from:
http://www-106.ibm.com/developerworks/library/ws-soaintro2/.

[Cole 2002] G. Cole, "SNMP vs. WBEM – The Future of Systems Management", available from:
http://www.wbem.co.uk.

[Colgrave 2003a] J. Colgrave, "A new approach to UDDI and WSDL: Introduction to the new OASIS UDDI WSDL", IBM developerWorks, August 2003, available from:
http://www-106.ibm.com/developersworks/library/.

[Colgrave 2003b] J. Colgrave, "A new approach to UDDI and WSDL, Part 2: Queries supported by the new OASIS UDDI WSDL Technical Note", IBM developerWorks, September 2003, available from: http://www-106.ibm.com/developersworks/library/.

[Colgrave 2004] J. Colgrave, K. Januszewski, "Using WSDL in a UDDI Registry, Version 2.0.2 – Technical Note Using WSDL in a UDDI Registry, Version 2.0.2", OASIS, June 2004, avaialble from: http://www.oasis-open.org/committees/uddi-spec/doc/tn/uddi-spec-tc-tn-wsdl-v202-20040631.htm.

[Comella-Dorda 2000] S. Comella-Dorda *et al.*, "A Survey of Legacy System Modernization Approaches", Technical Note CMU/SEI-2000-TN-003, Software Engineering Institute, Carnegie-Mellon University, April 2000, available from:
http://www.sei.cmu.edu/publications/pubWeb.html.

[Coulouris 2001] G. Coulouris, J. Dollimore, T. Kindberg, *Distributed Systems: Concepts and Design,* 3rd edition, Addison-Wesley, 2001.

[CSA 2010a] Cloud Security Alliance (CSA), "Top Threats to Cloud Computing V1.0", March 2010 available from:
http://www.cloudsecurityalliance.org/.

[CSA 2010b] Cloud Security Alliance (CSA), "Guidance for Application Security V2.1" July 2010, available from:
http://www.cloudsecurityalliance.org/.

[Culbertson 2001] R. Culbertson, C. Brown, G. Cobb, *Rapid Testing,* Prentice Hall, 2001.

[DAML] Darpa Agent Markup Language, available from:
http://www.daml.org.

[Davis 2009] M. Davis *et al.*, "Web Services Reliable Messaging (WS-ReliableMessaging) Version 1.2", OASIS Standard, February 2009, available from:
http://docs.oasis-open.org/ws-rx/wsrm/v1.2/wsrm.pdf.

[Dignan 2008] L. Dignan "Cloud computing: A look at the myths", ZDNet, April 2008, available from:
http://www.zdnet.com/blog/btl/cloud-computing-a-look-at-the-myths/8409.

[DMTF 2009] Distributed Management Task Force "Interoperable Clouds", White Paper CIM Version 1.0, document DSP-IS010, November 2009, available from:
http://www.dmtf.org.

[Duftler 2002] M. Duftler, R. Khalaf, "Business Process with BPEL4WS: Learning BPEL4WS, Part 3", IBM developmentworks, October 2002, available from:
http://www-106.ibm.com/developerworks/Webservices/library/.

[Durvasula 2006] S. Durvasula *et al.*,"SOA Practitioners' Guide Part 3: Introduction to Services Lifecycle", SOA Blueprint, September 2006, available from:
www.soablueprint.com.

[Eastlake 2002] D. Eastlake, J. Reagle (eds.), "XML Encryption Syntax and Processing", W3C Recommendation, December 2002, available from:
http://www.w3.org/TR/xmlenc-core/

[Eastlake 2008] D. Eastlake, *et al.* (eds.), "XML-Signature Syntax and Processing", W3C Recommendation, June 2008, available from:
http://www.w3.org/TR/xmldsig-core/.

[Elmagarmid 1992] A. Elmagarmid (ed.), *Database Transaction Models for Advanced Applications,* Morgan Kaufmann, 1992.

[Endrei 2004] M. Endrei *et al.*, "Patterns: Service-Oriented Architecture and Web Services", IBM Redbooks SG24-6303-00, April 2004, available from:
http://publib-b.boulder.ibm.com/Redbooks.nsf/redbooks/.

[Eswaran 1976] K. Eswaran *et al.*, "The Notion of Consistency and Predicate Locks in Database Systems", *Communications of the ACM,* vol. 19, no. 11, pp. 624–33, November 1976.

[Feingold 2007] M. Feingold, R. Jeyaraman (eds), "Web Service Coordination: (WS-Coordination)", Version 1.1, OASIS Standard, July 2007, available from:
http://docs.oasis-open.org/ws-tx/wstx-wscoor-1.1-spec.pdf.

[Ford 1997] W. Ford, M. S. Baum, *Secure Electronic Commerce: Building the infrastructure for digital signatures and encryption,* Prentice Hall, 1997.

[Freund 2009] T. Freund, M. Little (eds), "Web Services Business Activity (WS-BusinessActivity) Version 1.2", OASIS standard, February 2009, available from:
http://docs.oasis-open.org/ws-tx/wstx-wsba-1.2-spec.pdf

[Galbraith 2002] B. Galbraith *et al., Professional Web Services Security,* Wrox Press, 2002.

[Ganci 2006] J. Ganci *et al., Patterns: SOA Foundation Service Creation Scenario,* IBM Redbooks, September 2006.

[Garcia-Molina 1987] H. Garcia-Molina, K. Salem, Proceedings of the ACM SIG on Management of Data, 1987 Annual Conference, San Francisco, May 1987, ACM Press, pp. 249–59.

[Garcia-Molina 2002] H. Garcia-Molina, J. D. Ullman, J. Widom, *Database Systems,* Prentice Hall, 2002.

[Gardner 2002] J. Gardner, Z. Rendon, *XSLT and XPath,* Prentice Hall, 2002.

[Godinez 2010] M. Godinez, *et. al., The Art of Enterprise Information Architecture: A Systems-Based Approach for Unlocking Business Insight,* IBM Press, Pearson Education Inc., April 2010.

[Goldfarb 2001] C. Goldfarb, P. Prescod, *The XML Handbook,* 3rd edition, Prentice Hall 2001.

[Goodner 2009] M. Goodner, A, Nadalin (eds), "Web Services Federation Language (WS-Federation) Version 1.2", OASIS Standard, May 2009, available from:
http://docs.oasis-open.org/wsfed/federation/v1.2/ws-federation.pdf

[Graham 2004] S. Graham *et al., Building Web Services with Java,* SAMS Publishing, 2004.

[Graham 2005] S. Graham *et al., Building Web Services with Java,* 2nd edition, SAMS Publishing, 2005.

[Graham 2006] S. Graham, D. hull, B. Murray (eds.), "Publish-Subscribe Notification for Web Services", March 2004, available from:
http://docs.oasis-open.org/committees/dowload.php/6661/WSNpubsub-1-0.pdf.

[Gray 1993] J. Gray, A. Reuter, *Transaction Processing: Concepts and Techniques,* Morgan Kaufmann, 1993.

[Gruber 1993] T. R.Gruber, "Toward Principles for the Design of Ontologies used for Knowledge Sharing", KSL-93-04. Knowledge Systems Laboratory, Stanford University, 1993.

[Gudgin 2003] M. Gudgin *et al.* (eds.), "SOAP 1.2 Part 1: Messaging Framework", Martin Gudgin, W3C Recommendation, June 2003, available from:
http://www.w3.org/TR/2003/REC-soap12-part1-20030624/.

[Hall-Gailey 2004] J. Hall-Gailey, *Understanding Web Services Specifications and the WSE,* Microsoft Press, 2004.

[Hallam-Baker 2004] P. Hallam-Baker *et al.* (eds.), "Web Services Security X.509 Certificate Token Profile", OASIS Standard 200401, March 2004, available from:
http://docs.oasis-open.org/wss/2004/01/oasis-200401-wss-x509-token-profile-1.0.

[Handfield 2002] R. B. Handfield, E. L. Nichols, *Supply Chain Redesign,* Prentice Hall, 2002.

[Harmon 2003a] P. Harmon, "Analyzing Activities", *Business Process Trends,* vol. 1, no. 4, pp. 1–12, April 2003.

[Harmon 2003b] P. Harmon, "Second Generation Business Process Methodologies", *Business Process Trends,* vol. 1, no. 5, pp. 1–13, May 2003.

[Holley 2006] K. Holley, J. Palistrant, S. Graham, "Effective SOA Governance", IBM OnDemand Business, March 2006, available from:
http://www-306.ibm.com/software/solutions/soa/gov/lifecycle/.

[IBM 2004] IBM Corporation, "An architectural blueprint for autonomic computing", IBM Autonomic Computing White Paper, October 2004, available from:
http://www-03.ibm.com/autonomic/pdfs/ACBP2_2004-10-04.pdf.

[Irani 2002] R. Irani, "An Introduction to ebxml", in *Web Services Business Strategies and Architectures,* P. Fletcher, M. Waterhouse (eds.), ExpertPress, 2002.

[Jaenicke 2004] C. Jaenicke, "Canonical Message Formats: Avoiding the Pitfalls", WebLogic Journal, September/October 2004.

[Jansen 2011] W. Jansen, T, Grance, "Guidelines on Security and Privacy in Public Cloud Computing", NIST Special Publication 800-144,January 2011, available from:
http://csrc.nist.gov/publications/drafts/800-144/Draft-SP-800-144_cloud-computing.pdf.

[Jeston 2008] J. Jeston, J. Nelis, "Business Process Management: Practical Guidelines to Successful Implementations", 2nd edition, Butterworth–Heinemann, 2008.

[Jin 2002] L. J. Jin, V. Machiraju, A. Sahai, "Analysis on Service Level Agreement of Web Services", Technical Report HPL-2002-180, Software Technology Laboratory, HP Laboratories Palo Alto, June 2002, available from:
www.hpl.hp.com/techreports/2002/HPL-2002-180.pdf.

[Johnston 2005] S. Johnston "Modelling Service-oriented Solutions", IBM Developer Works, July 2005, available at
http://www-128.ibm.com/developerworks/rational/library/johnston/.

[Kakadia 2002] D. Kakadia *et al.*, "Enterprise Management Systems: Architectures and Standards", Sun Microsystems, April 2002, available from:
http://www.sun.com/blueprints/0402/ems1.pdf.

[Kaufman 1995] C. Kaufman, R. Perlman, M. Speciner, "Network Security, Private Communication in a Public World", Prentice Hall, 1995.

[Kavantzas 2004] N. Kavantzas *et al.*, "Web Services Choreography Description Language 1.0", Editor's Draft, April 2004, available from:
http://lists.w3.org/Archives/Public/www-archive/2004Apr/att-0004/cdl_v1-editors-apr03-2004-pdf.pdf.

[Keen 2004] M. Keen *et al.*, "Patterns: Implementing an SOA Using an Enterprise Service Bus", IBM Redbooks SG24-6346-00, July 2004, available from:
http://publib-b.boulder.ibm.com/Redbooks.nsf/redbooks/.

[Kifer 2005] M. Kifer, A. Bernstein, P. M. Lewis, *Database Systems: An Application-Oriented Approach,* 2nd edition, Addison-Wesley, 2005.

[Kreger 2005a] H. Kreger, "A Little Wisdom about WSDM", IBM developerWorks, available from:
http://www-128.ibm.com/developerworks/library/ws-wisdom.

[Kreger 2005b] H. Kreger *et al.*, "Management Using Web Services: A Proposed Architecture and Roadmap", IBM, HP, and Computer Associates, June 2005, available from:
www-128.ibm.com/developerworks/library/specification/ws-mroadmap.

[Kruchten 2004] P. Kruchten, *Rational Unified Process – An Introduction,* 3rd edition, Addison-Wesley, 2004.

[Kundra 2011] V. Kundra "Federal Cloud Computing Strategy", US Chief Information Officers Council, CIO.GOV, February 2011, available from:
http://www.cio.gov/documents/Vivek-Kundra-Federal-Cloud-Computing-Strategy-02142011.pdf.

[Kurose 2003] J. F. Kurose, K. W. Ross, *Computer Networking: A Top-Down Approach Featuring the Internet,* 2nd edition, Addison-Wesley, 2003.

[Lai 2004] R. Lai, *J2EE Platform Web Services,* Prentice Hall, 2004.

[Larman 2003] C. Larman, V. R. Basili, "Iterative and Incremental Development: A Brief History," *IEEE Computer,* vol. 36, no. 6, June 2003.

[Leavitt 2009] N. Leavitt, "Is Cloud Computing Really Ready for Prime Time?", IEEE Computer, January 2009.

[Leymann 2000] F. Leymann, D. Roller, *Production Workflow,* Prentice Hall, 2000.

[Little 2009] M. Little, A. Wilkinson (eds), "Web Services Atomic Transaction (WS-AtomicTransaction) Version 1.2", OASIS standard, February 2009, available from:
http://docs.oasis-open.org/ws-tx/wstx-wsat-1.2-spec.pdf

[Little 2004] M. Little, J. Maron, G. Pavlik, *Java Transaction Processing,* Prentice Hall, 2004.

[Malan 2002] R. Malan, D. Bredemeyer, "Software Architecture: Central Concerns, Key Decisions", 2002, available from:
http://www.ruthmalan.com/.

[Mani 2002] A. Mani, A. Nagarajan, "Understanding quality of service for Web services", IBM developerWorks, January 2002, available from: http://www-106.ibm.com/developerworks/library/ws-quality.html.

[Manola 2004] F. Manola, E. Miller (eds.), "RDF Primer", W3C Recommendation, February 2004, available from: http://www.w3.org/TR/rdf-primer/.

[Marks 2006] E. A. Marks, M. Bell, *Service-oriented Architecture: A Planning and Implementation Guide for Business and Technology,* John Wiley & Sons, 2006.

[Masud 2003] S. Masud, "RosettaNet Based Web Services", IBM developerWorks, July 2003, available from: http://www-128.ibm.com/developerworks/webservices/library/ws-rose1/.

[Mather 2009] T. Mather, S. Kumaraswamy, S. Latif *Cloud Security and Privacy: An Enterprise Perspective on Risks and Compliance,* O' Reilly Media Inc., 2009.

[Mayo 2009] R. Mayo, C. Perng "Cloud Computing Payback: An explanation of where the ROI comes from", IBM Research white paper, Nov. 2009, available from: ftp://service.software.ibm.com/common/ssi/sa/wh/n/diw03009usen/DIW03009USEN.pdf

[McGoveran 2004] D. McGoveran, "An Introduction to BPM and BPMS", *Business Integration Journal,* April 2004.

[McGuiness 2004] D. McGuiness, F. van Harmelen, "OWL Web Ontology Language Overview", W3C Recommendation, February 2004, available from: http://www.w3.org/TR/owl-features.

[McIntosh 2007] M. McIntosh *et al.,* "Basic Security Profile Version 1.0", Web Services Interoperability Organization, March 2007, available from: http://www.ws-i.org/Profiles/BasicSecurityProfile-1.0.html

[McKendrick 2006] J. Service Oriented Joe McKendrick "Mashup vs. SOA app: what's the difference?", ZDNet, June 2006, available from: http://www.zdnet.com/blog/service-oriented/mashup-vs-soa-app-whats-the-difference/647.

[Mehta 2003] T. Mehta, "Adaptive Web Services Management Solutions", *Enterprise Networks and Servers,* vol. 17, no. 5, May 2003, available from: http://www.enterprisenetworksandservers.com/monthly/toc.php?4.

[Mell 2011] P. Mell, T. Grance "Recommendations of the National Institute of Standards and Technology (Draft)", NIST Special Publication 800-145,January 2011, available from: http://csrc.nist.gov/publications/drafts/800-145/Draft-SP-800-145_cloud-definition.pdf.

[Mitra 2005] T. Mitra, "A Case for SOA Governance", IBM developerWorks, August 2005, available from: http://www-106.ibm.com/developerworks/webservices/library/ws-soa-govern/index.html.

[Mitra 2007] N. Mitra, Y. Lafon (ed.), "SOAP Version 1.2 Part 0: Primer 2", W3C Recommendation, April 2007 available from: http://www.w3.org/TR/soap12-part0/.

[Monson-Haefel 2001] R. Monson-Haefel, D. A. Chappell, *Java Message Service,* O'Reilley, 2001.

[Monson-Haefel 2004] R. Monson-Haefel, *J2EE Web Services,* Addison-Wesley, 2004.

[Monzillo 2002] R. Monzillo, "Security", in *Designing Enterprise Applications with the J2EE Platform,* 2nd edition, I. Singh, B. Stearns, M. Johnson (eds.), Addison-Wesley 2002.

[Moreland 2006] B. Moreland, M. Ashar, "The Path to SOA", ebizQ, septemebr 2006, available from: http://www.ebizq.net/topics/soa_security/features/7193.html.

[Moses 2005] T. Moses (ed), "eXtensible Access Control Markup Language (XACML) Version 2.0", OASIS Standard, February 2005, available from: http://docs.oasis-open.org/xacml/2.0/access_control-xacml-2.0-core-spec-os.pdf

[Moss 1985] E. Moss, *Nested Transactions: An Approach to Reliable Distributed Computing,* MIT Press, 1985.

[Moss 1997] J. Moss, "Understanding TCP/IP", PC Network Advisor, no. 87, September 1997.

[Murray 2002] J. Murray, "Designing Manageable Applications", Web Developer's Journal, October 2002, available from:
http://www.webdevelopersjournal.com/articles/design_man_app/.

[Murray 2006a] B. Murray, K. Wilson, M. Ellison (eds), "Web Services Distributed Management: MUWS Primer", OASIS Committee Draft, February 2006, available from:
http://docs.oasis-open.org/wsdm/wsdm-1.0-muws-primer-cd-01.pdf.

[Murray 2006b] B. Murray, K. Wilson, M. Ellison (eds), "Web Services Distributed Management: MOWS Primer", OASIS Committee Draft, February 2006, available from:
http://docs.oasis-open.org/wsdm/wsdm-1.0-mows-primer-cd-01.pdf.

[Mysore 2003] S. Mysore, "Securing Web Services – Concepts, Standards, and Requirements", Sun Microsystems, October 2003, available from:
sun.com/software.

[Nadalin 2006] A. Nadalin *et al.* (eds.), "Web Services Security: SOAP Message Security 1.1" OASIS Standard Specification, February 2006, available from:
http://www.oasis-open.org/committees/download.php/16790/wss-v1.1-spec-os-SOAPMessag-eSecurity.pdf

[Nadalin 2009a] A. Nadalin *et al.* (eds.), "WS-SecurityPolicy v1.3", OASIS Standard, February 2009, available from:
http://docs.oasis-open.org/ws-sx/ws-securitypolicy/v1.3/ws-securitypolicy.pdf.

[Nadalin 2009b] A. Nadalin *et al.,* "Web Services Secure Conversation Language (WS-SecureConversation) v1.4", OASIS Standard February 2009, available from:
http://docs.oasis-open.org/ws-sx/ws-secureconversation/v1.4/ws- secureconversation.pdf.

[Nadalin 2009c] A. Nadalin *et al.,* "WS-Trust v1.4", OASIS Standard, February 2009, available from:
http://docs.oasis-open.org/ws-sx/ws-trust/v1.4/ws-trust.pdf

[Natis 2007] Y. V. Natis, M. Pezzini, "Twelve Common SOA Mistakes and How to Avoid Them", Gartner Research ID number: G00152446, October 2007, available from:
http://www.gartner.com/DisplayDocument?id=537409.

[Niblett 2005] P. Niblett, S. Graham, "Events and Service-Oriented Architecture: The OASIS Web Services Notification Specifications", *IBM Systems Journal,* vol. 44, no. 4, pp. 869–86, 2005.

[OASIS 2004] OASIS: Organization for the Advancement of Structured Integration Standards, "Introduction to UDDI: Important Features and Functional Concepts", October 2004, available from:
http://xml.coverpages.org/UDDI-TechnicalWhitePaperOct28.pdf.

[OMG 2008] Object Management Group "Business Process Model and Notation (BPMN)" Version 1.1, OMG document 2008-01-17, January 2008, available from:
http://www.omg.org/spec/BPMN/1.1.

[O'Neill 2003] M. O'Neill *et al.,* "Web Services Security", McGraw-Hill Osborne, 2003.

[Open Group 2004] "SLA Management Handbook: Enterprise Perspective", version 2, volume 4, issue 0.8, November 2004, available from:
www.opengroup.org/pubs/catalog/go45.htm.

[Open Group 2009a] Open Group "The Open Group Service Integration Maturity Model (OSIMM)", Technical Standard, Document Number: C092, August 2009, available from:
https://www2.opengroup.org/ogsys/jsp/publications/PublicationDetails.jsp?catalogno=c092.

[Open Group 2009b] Open Group "SOA Governance Framework" version 2.4, April 2009, available from:
http://www.opengroup.org/projects/soa-governance/.

[Osipov 2009] C. Osipov, *et. al.*, "Develop and Deploy Multi-Tenant Web-delivered Solutions using IBM Middleware: Part 2: Approaches for enabling Multi-tenancy", IBM developerWorks, May 2009.

[Papazoglou 2003] M. P. Papazoglou, G. Georgakapoulos, "Introduction to the Special Issue about Service-Oriented Computing", *Communications of the ACM,* vol. 46, no. 10, pp. 24–8, October 2003.

[Papazoglou 2005] M. P. Papazoglou, "Extending the Service Oriented Architecture", *Business Integration Journal,* February 2005.

[Papazoglou 2006] M. P. Papazoglou, P. M. A. Ribbers, *e-Business: Organizational and Technical Foundations,* John Wiley & Sons, 2006.

[Papazoglou 2011] M. P. Papazoglou, V. Andrikopoulos, S. Benbernou "Managing Evolving Services", IEEE Software, vol. 28, issue 3, May/June 2011.

[Patil 2003] S. Patil, E. Newcomer, "ebXML and Web Services", *IEEE Internet Computing,* May 2003.

[Paulk 1993] M. Paulk *et al.,* "Capability Maturity Model for Software", version 1.1, Software Engineering Institute, Pittsburgh, Technical Report SE-93 TR-024, 1993.

[Pilz 2003] G. Pilz, "A New World of Web Services Security", *Web Services Journal,* March 2003.

[Potts 2003] M. Potts, I. Sedukhin, H. Kreger, "Web Services Manageability – Concepts (WS-Manageability)", IBM, Computer Associates International, Inc., Talking Blocks, Inc, September 2003, available from:
www3.ca.com/Files/SupportingPieces/web_service_manageability_concepts.pdf.

[Proctor 2003] S. Proctor, "A Brief Introduction to XACML", March 2003, available from:
http://www.oasis-open.org/committees/download.php/2713/Brief_Introduction_to_XACML.html.

[Ragouzis 2008] N. Ragouzis *et al.,* "Security Assertion Markup Language (SAML) V2.0 Technical Overview", OASIS-SSTC, March 2008, available from:
http://docs.oasis-open.org/security/saml/Post2.0/sstc-saml-tech-overview-2.0.html /.

[Raines 2009] "Cloud Computing and SOA", The MITRE Corporation, October 2009, available from:
http:www.mitre.org/work/tech_papers/tech_papers_09/09_0743/

[Richardson 2007] L. Richardson, S. Ruby, *RESTful Web Services,* O'Reilley, 2007.

[Ristenpart 2009] T. Ristenpart *et al.,* "Hey, You, Get Off of My Cloud: Exploring Information Leakage in Third-Party Compute Clouds", 16th ACM Conference on Computer and Communications Security, Chicago, November 2009.

[Robinson 2004] R. Robinson, "Understand Enterprise Service Bus Scenarios and Solutions in Service-Oriented Architecture", IBM developerWorks, June 2004, available from:
http://www-106.ibm.com/developerworks/library/ws-esbscen/.

[Rodriguez 2001] A. Rodriguez, "TCP/IP Tutorial and Technical Overview", IBM Redbooks, August 2001, available from:
ibm.com/redbooks/.

[Rosenberg 2004] J. Rosenberg, D. Remy, "Securing Web Services with WS-Security", SAMS Publishing, 2004.

[Rosenblum 1997] D. S. Rosenblum, A. L. Wolf, "A design framework for Internet-scale event observation and notification", Proceedings of the Sixth European Software Engineering Conference, Lecture Notes in Computer Science 1301, Springer, 1997.

[RosettaNet 2003] "RosettaNet and Web Services", 2003, available from:
http://www.rosettanet.org/RosettaNet/Doc/0/IP0QL046K55KFBSJ60M9TQCPB3/RosettaNet+Web+ServicesFINAL+.pdf.

[RosettaNet 2004] RosettaNet Implementation Guide, "Cluster 3: Order Management Segment A: Quote and Order Entry PIPs 3A4, 3A7, 3A8, 3A9", April 2004, available from:
www.rosettanet.org/usersguides/.

[Ross 2003] R.G. Ross "Principles of the Business Rule Approach", Addison-Wesley, 2003.

[Roy-Chowdhury 2007] A. Roy-Chowdhury, G. Goldszmidt, and S. Osipov, "Building SOA Composite Business Services: Supporting Multi-Tenancy for Composite Business Services", IBM developerWorks, May 2007.

[Sadiq 2007] S. Sadiq, G. Governatori, K. Naimiri "Modeling Control Objectives for Business Process Compliance", 10th International Conference on Business Process Management, Brisbane Australia, 2007.

[Schlosser 1999] M. Schlosser, "IBM Application Framework for e-Business: Security", November 1999, available from:
http://www-4.ibm.com/software/developer/library/security/index.html.

[Schmelzer 2002] R. Schmelzer *et al., XML and Web Services,* SAMS Publishing, 2002.

[Scribner 2000] K. Scribner, M. C. Stiver, *Understanding SOAP,* SAMS Publishing, 2000.

[Scribner 2002] K. Scribner, M. C. Stiver, *Applied SOAP,* SAMS Publishing, 2002.

[SCOR-v10] Supply Chain Council "Supply Chain Operations Reference Model SCOR Overview Version 9.0", 2010, available from:
www.supply-chain.org.

[Seacord 2001] R. C. Seacord *et al.,* "Legacy System Modernization Strategies", Technical Report, CMU/SEI-2001-TR-025, ESC-TR-2001-025, Software Engineering Institute, Carnegie-Mellon University, July 2001, available from:
http://www.sei.cmu.edu/publications/pubWeb.html.

[Sedukhin 2005] I. Sedukhin, "Web Services Distributed Management: Management of Web Services (WSDM-MOWS) 1.0", OASIS-Standard, March 2005, available from:
http://docs.oasis-open.org/wsdm/2004/12/wsdm-mows-1.0.pdf.

[Seely 2002] S. Seely, "Understanding WS-Security", Microsoft Corporation, October 2002, available from:
http://msdn.microsoft.com/library/default.asp?url=/library/en-us/dnwssecur/html/understw.asp.

[Sharma 2001] P. Sharma, B. Stearns, T. Ng, *J2EE Connector Architecture and Enterprise Application Integration,* Addison-Wesley, 2001.

[Shaw 1996] M. Shaw, D. Garlan, *Software Architecture: Perspectives on an Emerging Discipline,* Prentice Hall, 1996.

[Siddiqui 2001] B. Siddiqui, "Deploying Web services with WSDL", available from:
http://www-106.ibm.com/developerworks/library/ws-intwsdl/.

[Siddiqui 2003a] B. Siddiqui, "Web Services Security, Part 2", O'Reilly XML.com, April 2003, available from:
http://Webservices.xml.com/lpt/a/ws/2003/04/01/security.html.

[Siddiqui 2003b] B. Siddiqui, "Web Services Security, Part 3", O'Reilly XML.com, May 2003, available from:
http://Webservices.xml.com/lpt/a/ws/2003/05/13/security.html.

[Siddiqui 2003c] B. Siddiqui, "Web Services Security, Part 4", O'Reilly XML.com, July 2003, available from:
http://Webservices.xml.com/lpt/a/ws/2003/07/22/security.html.

[Singh 2004] J. Singh *et al., Designing Web Services with the J2EE 1.4 Platform,* Addison-Wesley, 2004.

[Skonnard 2002] A. Skonnard, M. Gudgin, *Essential XML Quick Reference,* Addison-Wesley, 2002.

[Skonnard 2003] A. Skonnard, "Understanding WS-Policy", Web Services Policy Framework (WS-Policy), Version 1.01, June 2003, available from:
http://www.ibm.com/developerworks/library/ws-polfram/.

[Soh 1995] C. Soh, M. L. Markus, "How IT Creates Business Value: A Theory Synthesis", Proceedings of 16th International Conference on Information Systems, Amsterdam, December 1995.

[Soni 1995] D. Soni, R. Nord, C. Hofmeister, "Software Architectures in Industrial Applications", in Proceedings of the 17th International Conference on Software Engineering, IEEE CS Press, pp. 196–207, September 1995.

[Steel 2006] C. Steel, R. Nagappan, R. Lai, *Core Security Patterns: Best Practices and Strategies for J2EE™, Web Services, and Identity Management,* Prentice Hall, 2006.

[Tennison 2001] J. Tennison, *XSLT and XPath,* M & T Books, 2001.

[Thompson 2008] R. Thompson "Web Services for Remote Portlets Specification v2.0", OASIS Standard, April 2008, available from:
http://docs.oasis-open.org/wsrp/v2/wsrp-2.0-spec-os-01.html

[Ullman 1988] J. Ullman, *Principles of Database and Knowledge Based Systems,* Computer Science Press, 1998.

[Ulrich 2002] W. Ulrich, *Legacy Systems – Transformation Strategies,* Prentice Hall, 2002.

[UMM 2003] United Nations center for trade Facilitation and Electronic Business "UN/CEFACT Modeling Methodology (UMM) User Guide", CEFACT/TMG/N093, September 2003, available from:
www.utmg.org.

[Valentine 2002] C. Valentine, L. Dykes, E. Tittel, *XML Schemas,* Sybex, 2002.

[Vambenepe 2006] W. Vambenepe (ed.), "Web Services Topics (WS-Topics) v. 1.3", OASIS Working Draft 01, October 2006, available from:
http://docs.oasis-open.org/wsn/wsn-ws_topics-1.3-spec-os.pdf.

[van den Heuvel 2007] W. J. van den Heuvel "Aligning Modern Business Processes and Legacy Systems: A Component-Based Perspective", MIT Press, March 2007.

[Varia 2008] J. Varia "Cloud Architectures", Amazon Web Services, available from:
jineshvaria.s3.amazonaws.com/public/cloudarchitectures-varia.pdf.

[Vedamuthu 2007a] A.S. Vedamuthu *et al.,* "Web Services Policy Framework (WS-Policy) Version 1.5", September 2007, available from:
http://www.w3.org/TR/ws-policy/.

[Vedamuthu 2007b] A.S. Vedamuthu *et al.,* "Web Services Policy 1.5 Attachment", September 2007, available from:
http://www.w3.org/TR/ws-policy-attach/.

[Veloso 2002] "The Automotive Supply Chain", Asian Development Bank, Economics and Research Department, Working paper no. 3, January 2002, available from:
www.adb.org/Documents/ERD/Working_Papers/wp003.pdf.

[VeriSign 2003a] VeriSign Inc., "VeriSign Digital Trust Services", April 2003, available from:
www.verisign.com.

[VeriSign 2003b] VeriSign Inc., "Managed PKI: Securing Your Business Applications", White Paper, May 2003, available from:
www.verisign.com.

[Veryard 2001] R. Veryard, *The Component-Based Business: Plug and Play,* Springer, 2001.

[Vinovski 2004] S. Vinoski, "More Web Services Notifications", *IEEE Internet,* May/June 2004.

[vonHalle 2002] B. von Halle, *Business Rules Applied,* John Wiley & Sons, 2002.

[Wahli 2004] U. Wahli *et al.,* "WebSphere Version 5.1 Application Developer 5.1.1 Web Services Handbook", IBM Redbooks, February 2004, available from:
ibm.com/redbooks.

[Walmsley 2002] P. Walmsley, *Definitive XML Schema,* Prentice Hall, 2002.

[Webber 2001] J. Webber *et al.,* "Making Web Services Work", *Application Development Advisor,* pp. 68–71, November/December 2001.

[Webber 2003a] J. Webber, M. Little, "Introducing WS-Coordination", *Web Services Journal,* vol. 3, no. 5, pp. 12–16, May 2003.

[Webber 2003b] J. Webber, M. Little, "Introducing WS-CAF: More than just Transactions", *Web Services Journal,* vol. 3, no. 12, pp. 52–5, December 2003.

[Webber 2004] D. R. Webber *et al.,* "The Benefits of ebXML for e-Business", International Conference of XML (XML'04), August 2004.

[Weerawarana 2005] S. Weerawarana *et al., Web Services Platform Architecture,* Prentice Hall, 2005.

[Wei 2009] J. Wei, et al, "Managing Security of Virtual Machine Images in a Cloud Environment", 16th ACM Conference on Computer and Communications Security, November 2009, Chicago, Illinois, USA.

[Weske 2007] M. Weske "Business Process Management: Concepts, Languages, Architectures", Springer-Verlag, 2007.

[WfMC 1999] Workflow Management Coalition, "Terminology & Glossary", Document Number WFMC-TC-1011, February 1999.

[WfMC 2008] Workflow Management Coalition, "Workflow Standard Process Definition Interface – XML Process Definition Language", Document Number WFMC-TC-1025, October 2008, available from:
http://www.wfmc.org/xpdl-developers-center.html.

[Whitehead 2002] K. Whitehead, *Component-based Development,* Addison-Wesley, 2002.

[WS-Roadmap 2002] "Security in a Web Services World: A Proposed Architecture and Roadmap", IBM developerWorks, April 2002, available from:
http://www-128.ibm.com/developerworks/library/specification/ws-secmap.

[Yu 2008] Q. Yu , X. Liu , A. Bouguettaya , B. Medjahed, "Deploying and Managing Web Services: Issues, Solutions, and Directions", The VLDB Journal, vol. 17, 2008.

[Zimmermann 2003] O. Zimmermann *et al., Perspectives on Web Services,* Springer, 2003.

[Zimmermann 2004] O. Zimmermann, P. Krogdahl, C. Gee, "Elements of Service-oriented Analysis and Design", IBM developerWorks, June 2004, available from:
http://www-106.ibm.com/developerworks/library/ws-soad1/.

Index